New York
2012

ART FAIR

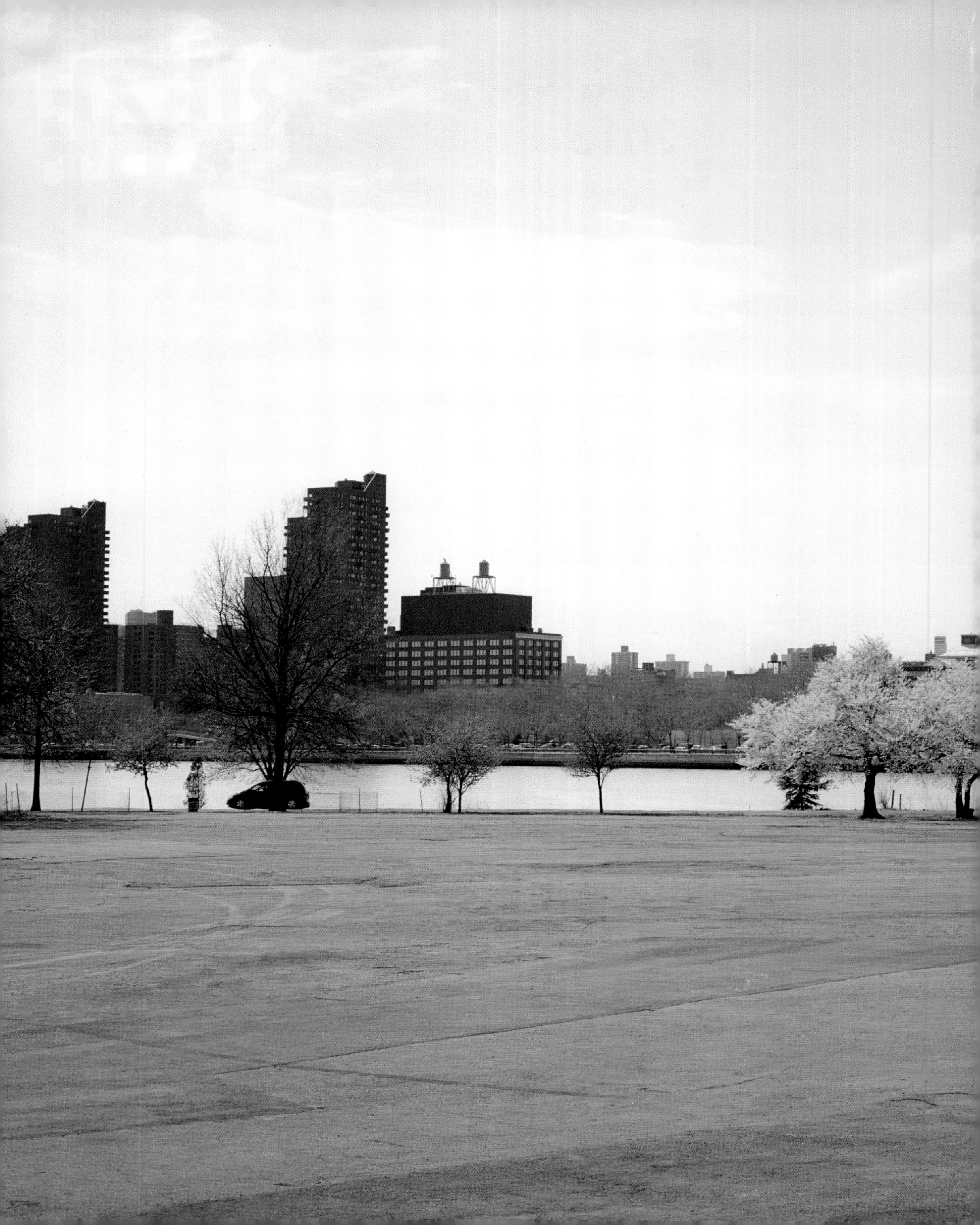

FRIEZE ART FAIR

New York
2012

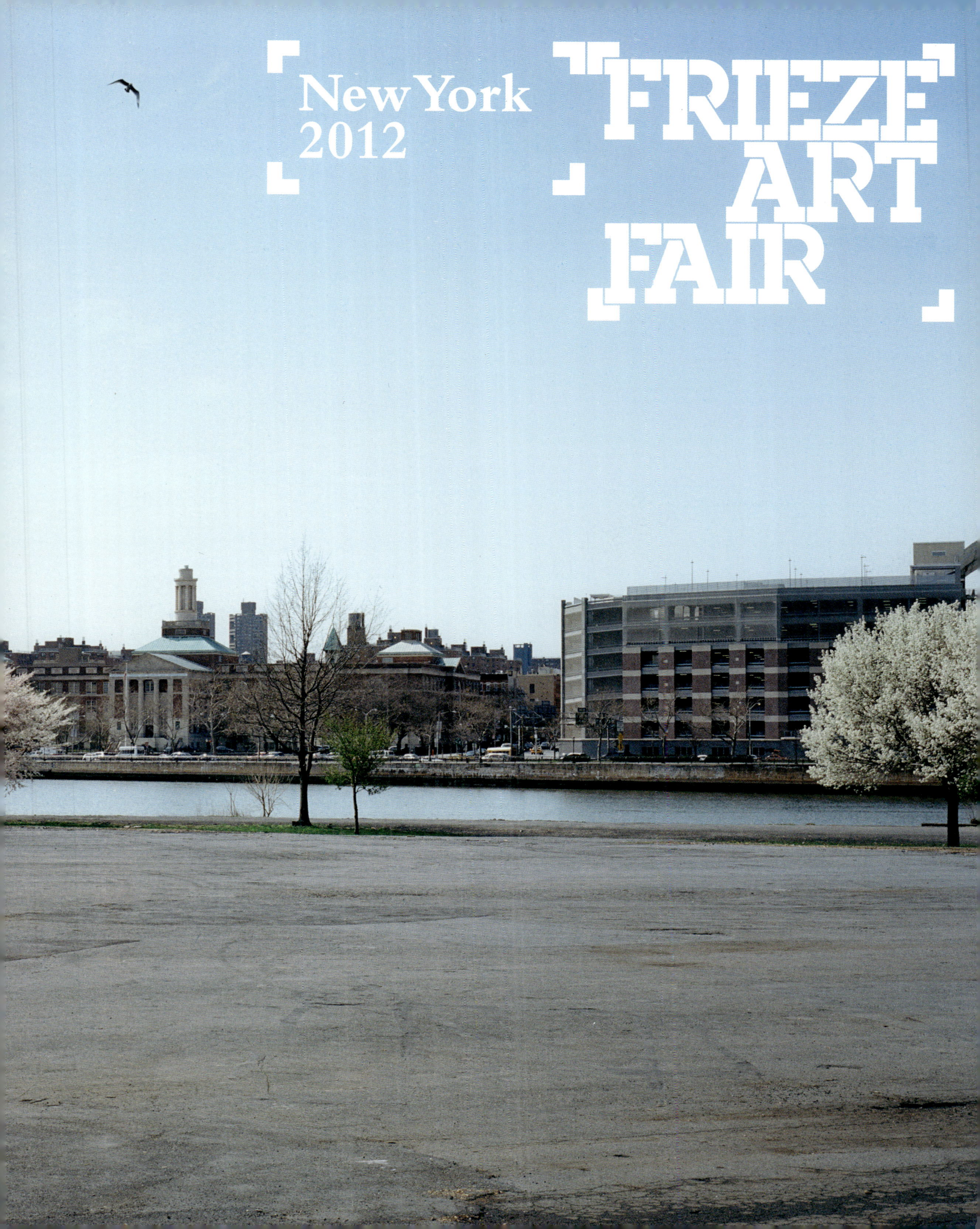

Frieze Art Fair wishes to acknowledge the generous support of the following companies and organizations:

Main Sponsor
Deutsche Bank

Media Partners

FINANCIAL TIMES

NEW YORK

Sponsors and partners

MULBERRY

BMW

LALIQUE-ART.COM

NET-A-PORTER.COM

CHAMPAGNE POMMERY REIMS-FRANCE

outset.

Contents

Participating galleries

303 Gallery
Miguel Abreu Gallery
Air de Paris
The Approach
art: concept
Alfonso Artiaco
Laura Bartlett Gallery
Galerie Guido W. Baudach
Boers-Li Gallery
Marianne Boesky Gallery
Tanya Bonakdar Gallery
Bortolami
The Breeder
Broadway 1602
Gavin Brown's enterprise
Galerie Buchholz
Cabinet
Galerie Gisela Capitain
carlier | gebauer
Cheim & Read
Mehdi Chouakri
James Cohan Gallery
Sadie Coles HQ
Contemporary Fine Arts
Galleria Continua
Galleria Raffaella Cortese
Corvi-Mora
Galerie Chantal Crousel

Massimo De Carlo
Elizabeth Dee
Galerie Eigen + Art
galerie frank elbaz
Foksal Gallery Foundation
Galeria Fortes Vilaça
Marc Foxx
Carl Freedman Gallery
Stephen Friedman Gallery
Frith Street Gallery
Gagosian Gallery
Annet Gelink Gallery
A Gentil Carioca
Greene Naftali
greengrassi
Jack Hanley Gallery
Harris Lieberman
Hauser & Wirth
Herald St
Xavier Hufkens
Gallery Hyundai
Taka Ishii Gallery
Alison Jacques Gallery
Galerie Martin Janda
Catriona Jeffries
Casey Kaplan
kaufmann repetto
Sean Kelly Gallery
Kerlin Gallery
Anton Kern Gallery
Galerie Peter Kilchmann
Tina Kim Gallery
Nicole Klagsbrun Gallery
Johann König
David Kordansky Gallery
Tomio Koyama Gallery
Andrew Kreps Gallery
Galerie Krinzinger
Kukje Gallery
kurimanzutto
Yvon Lambert
Simon Lee Gallery
Lehmann Maupin
Galerie Lelong

Lisson Gallery
Long March Space
Maccarone
Giò Marconi
Metro Pictures
Galerie Meyer Kainer
Meyer Riegger
Massimo Minini
Victoria Miro
Mitchell-Innes & Nash
Stuart Shave/Modern Art
The Modern Institute
Taro Nasu
Galerie Neu
Galleria Franco Noero
David Nolan Gallery
Maureen Paley
Galerie Perrotin
Friedrich Petzel Gallery
Galerie Francesca Pia
Galerija Gregor Podnar
Galerie Praz-Delavallade
Galerie Eva Presenhuber
Rampa
Almine Rech Gallery
Regen Projects
Regina Gallery
Anthony Reynolds Gallery
Galerie Thaddaeus Ropac
Andrea Rosen Gallery
Salon 94
Esther Schipper
Galerie Rüdiger Schöttle
Sfeir-Semler
Sies + Höke
Sikkema Jenkins & Co.

Sommer Contemporary Art
Sprüth Magers Berlin London
STANDARD (Oslo)
Stevenson
Timothy Taylor Gallery
Team Gallery
Richard Telles
The Third Line
Triple Canopy
Vermelho
Susanne Vielmetter Los Angeles Projects
Vilma Gold
Galleri Nicolai Wallner
Wallspace
Galerie Barbara Weiss
Michael Werner
White Columns
White Cube
Wilkinson
Zeno X Gallery
David Zwirner

Focus

Altman Siegel
Johan Berggren Gallery
Galerie Isabella Bortolozzi
Canada
Experimenter
James Fuentes
gb agency
François Ghebaly Gallery
Alexander Gray Associates
Galerie Karin Guenther
Hollybush Gardens
Hotel
Karma International
Kimmerich
Tanya Leighton Gallery
Leto Gallery
Limoncello
Kate MacGarry
Mary Mary
Galerie Mezzanin
Andreiana Mihail Gallery
NoguerasBlanchard
Overduin and Kite
Galeria Plan B
Simon Preston
Rodeo
Micky Schubert
Seventeen
Reena Spaulings Fine Art
Diana Stigter
T293
Galerie Jocelyn Wolff
Alex Zachary Peter Currie

Frame

47 Canal
Ambach & Rice
BaliceHertling
BolteLang
Bureau
Shane Campbell Gallery
Crystal
Figge von Rosen Galerie
Galerie Cinzia Friedlaender
Lüttgenmeijer
Marcelle Alix
Meessen De Clercq
MISAKO & ROSEN
mother's tankstation
Night Gallery
Take Ninagawa
Redling Fine Art
Renwick Gallery
Tang Contemporary Art
Steve Turner Contemporary

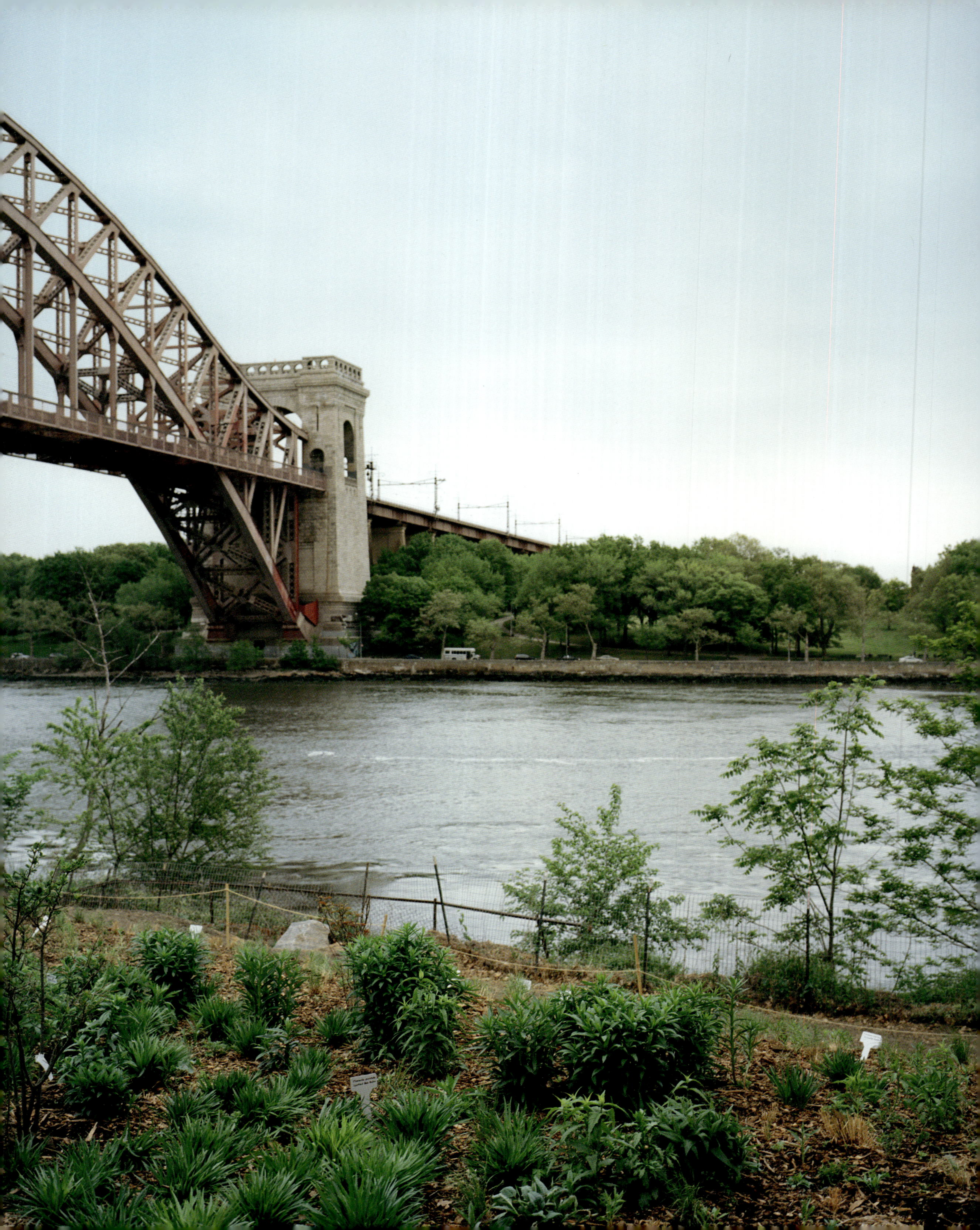

Foreword

It gives us great pleasure to welcome you to the inaugural Frieze New York. The city has always been our second home—Frieze has had a presence here since the first US editor of *frieze* magazine came onboard in 1992, and Amanda has lived in New York since 2000. Our friends in the art world have asked us for years to consider bringing the fair to New York, and it was when we discovered Randall's Island that we felt it was possible. The easy access by car, ferry, and bus, as well as its location on the river, made an ideal site for the fair.

The island has a special history too. Robert Moses planned the redevelopment of Manhattan from his offices here, and it is a location where many movies have been shot, including the final scene of *The French Connection* (1971), which takes place under the dramatic ramps of the Robert F. Kennedy Bridge. And in 2008, Usain Bolt beat the 100 m record at the island's Icahn Stadium. Today it is best known for its sports facilities, including over 60 sports fields, 20 tennis courts, and a golf range, while beautiful parkland is also being developed. We are honored that the fair is the first major art event to take place on Randall's Island.

We were delighted by the gallery response to the fair. Many exhibitors from the London event have joined us in New York, but around a third of the exhibitors are new to Frieze Art Fair. While there is a strong American representation, including 12 galleries from L.A., it remains truly international, with around 70% of the participating galleries traveling from the world's six other continents.

Architecture is always an important part of Frieze Art Fair, and Florian Idenberg and Jing Liu of SO-IL, Brooklyn, have managed to morph the architecture of the pre-fabricated tent into a snake-like shape, relaxing and opening up the usual grid structure of a fair.

This year Frieze Projects, in New York, has been curated by Cecilia Alemani, and sponsored by Mulberry, with additional support from Outset. Responding to the fair's location, the program includes eight artworks, by John Ahearn, Uri Aran, Ulla von Brandenburg, Latifa Echakhch, Joel Kyack, Rick Moody, Virginia Overton, and Tim Rollins and K.O.S..

Frieze Talks are themed around the topic of "The Atlas," and are opened with a keynote lecture by renowned art historian Georges Didi-Huberman. The program also includes, amongst others, panel discussions chaired by Nicolai Ouroussoff, Okwui Enwezor, Joseph Grima and Sofia Hernández; and presentations by artists Allan Sekula and Zoe Leonard.

On the riverfront, the Sculpture Park, which has open public access, includes a number of outdoor works selected by curator Tom Eccles; while Frieze Sounds, presented with BMW, releases three audio commissions by Martin Creed, Rick Moody, and Frances Stark, accessible online. Inside the fair, Frieze Education are produce a young person's guide to Frieze New York in collaboration with 826NYC.

Frieze Art Fair extends a special thanks to Randall's Island Park Alliance, NYC & Company, and the City of New York.

We are delighted to continue our relationship with Deutsche Bank as our main sponsor, and the *Financial Times* as a media sponsor, alongside a new relationship with *New York* magazine.
We hope that you enjoy this first edition of Frieze New York, look forward to welcoming you in London for Frieze London and Frieze Masters this October, and seeing you in New York again next year.

Amanda Sharp and Matthew Slotover
Directors, Frieze Art Fair

Sponsor's foreword

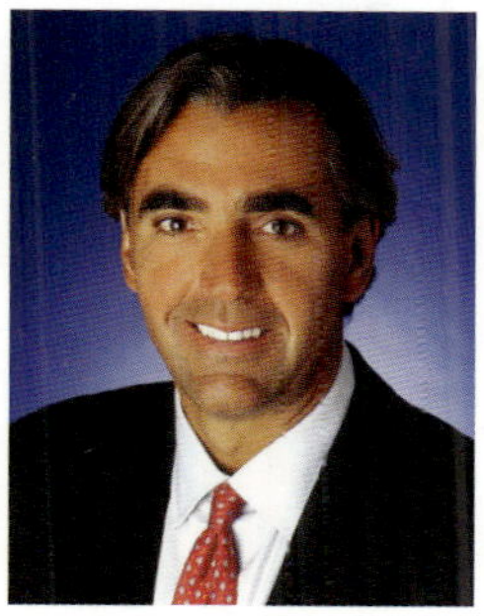

In continuing our tradition of commitment to the arts, 2012 will mark the first year that Deutsche Bank will be the main sponsor of three Frieze fairs on both sides of the Atlantic. We are especially delighted to be associated with the inaugural New York presentation. Our association with Frieze began in 2004 in London and over the years, our relationship with the founders of Frieze, Amanda Sharp and Matthew Slotover, has grown based on a shared understanding of the important role contemporary art plays in today's globalized culture. The expansion of this vision to New York City seemed only natural for both Deutsche Bank and Frieze. As Frieze dramatically galvanized the London art scene, we expect New York will similarly be enriched. We are especially excited that Randall's Island will serve as the venue, introducing a new geography, as well as new artists, to collectors from around the world. Deutsche Bank's history in the arts is anchored in the belief that artists play a defining role in both reflecting the times we live in as well as creating places of vibrancy and vitality that enhance our communities.

I hope you will thoroughly enjoy Frieze New York and the experience of connecting with some of the world's brightest talent in an unparalleled natural setting.

Sincerely,

Seth Waugh
CEO Deutsche Bank Americas

Main Sponsor
Deutsche Bank

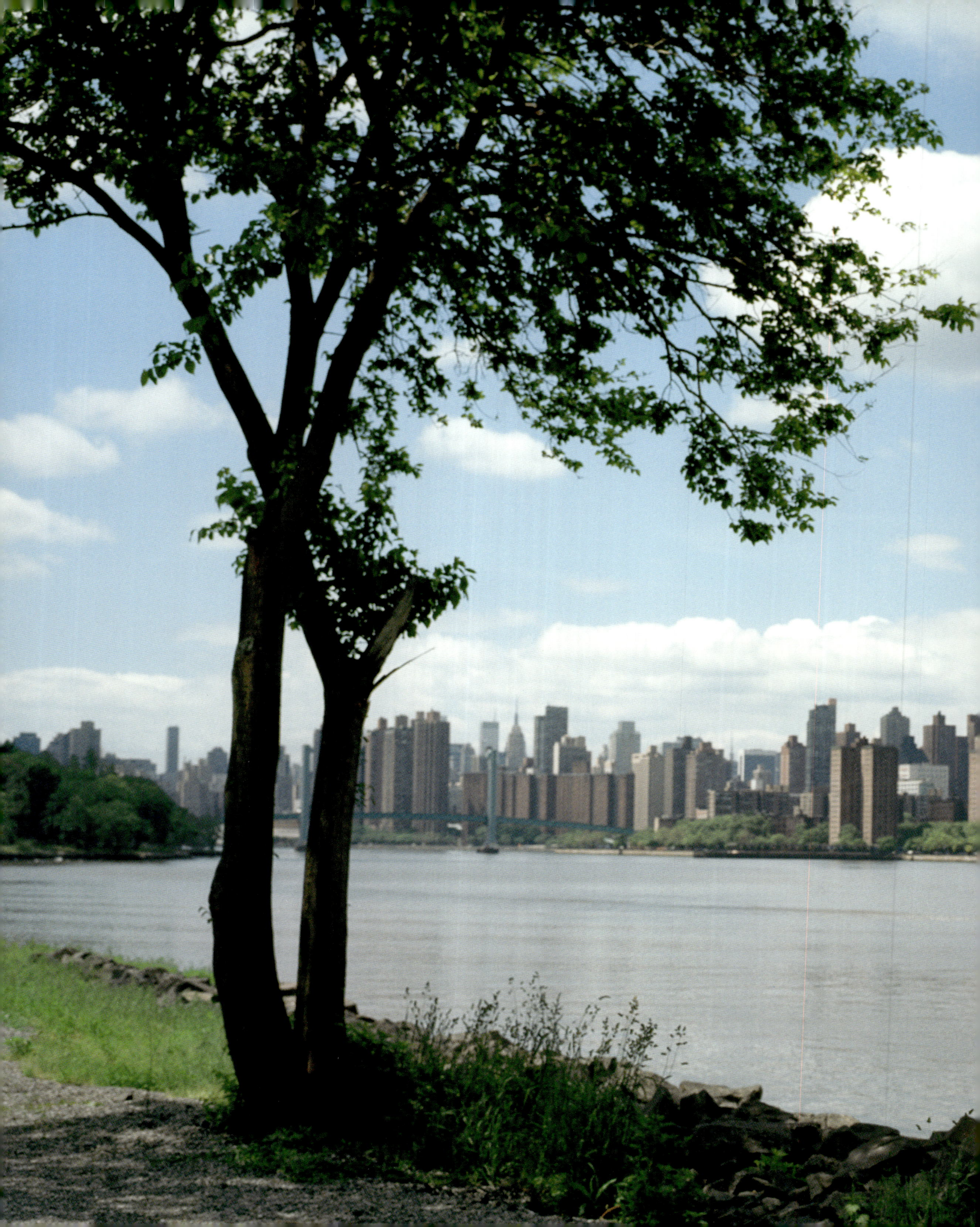

Frieze Projects

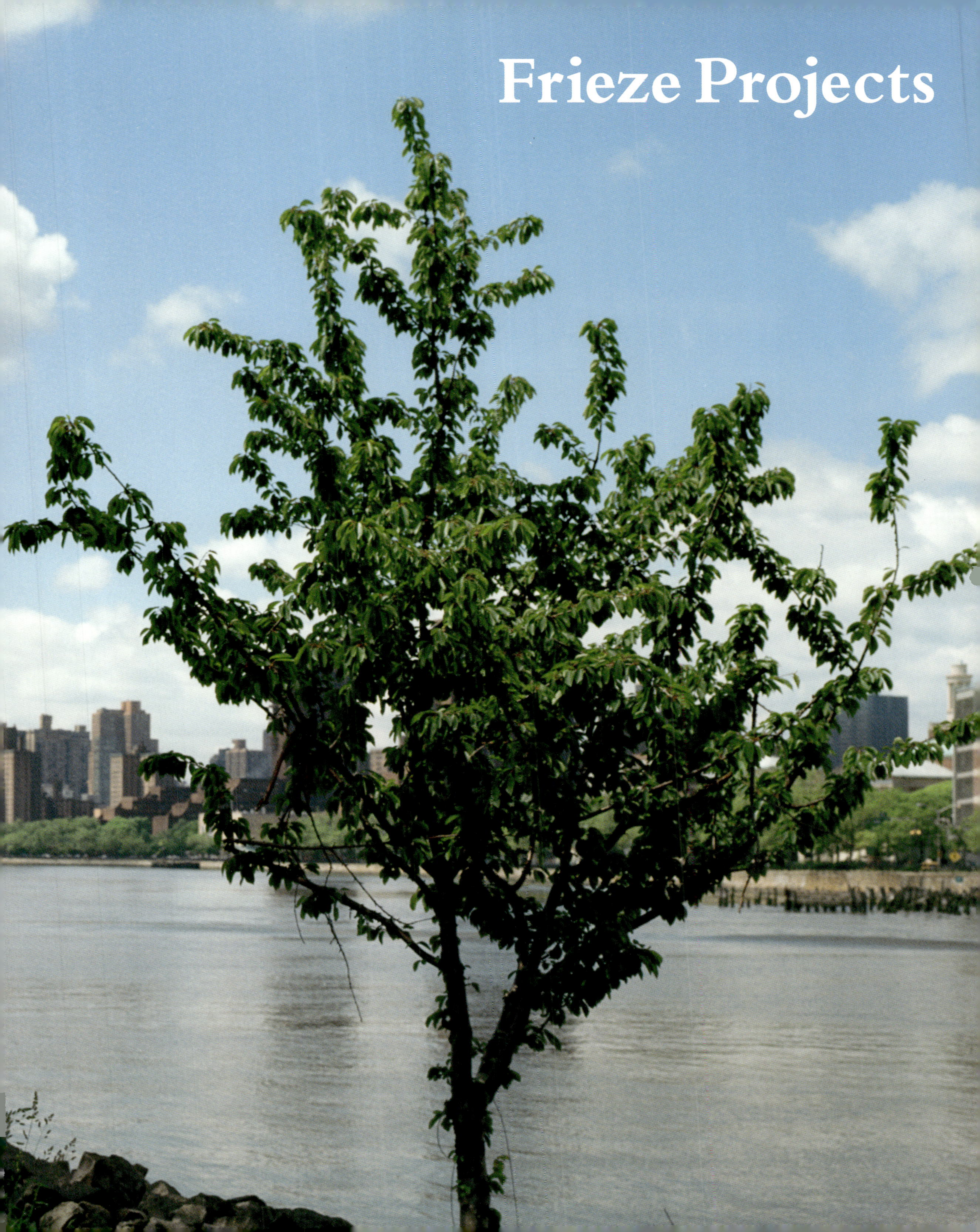

John Ahearn
Uri Aran
Ulla von Brandenburg
Latifa Echakhch
Joel Kyack
Rick Moody
Virginia Overton
Tim Rollins and K.O.S.

Introduction

Randall's Island is one of the most fascinating places in New York. Since the 18th century, it has functioned as a site where the city of New York would confine its outsiders—hospitals and asylums "for the poor, the insane, and the inebriated ones" appear very early on the historical maps of the island. Even today, the skyline of the island is dominated by the daunting presence of the Manhattan Psychiatric Center; a colossal, Kafkaesque building that resides on the island like a relic from the gloomy past. In the 1930s, Robert Moses, the city's infamous Park Commissioner, managed to transform Randall's Island into what it still is now: one of the most important transportation junctions between Manhattan, Queens and the Bronx. Moses built the Triborough Bridge and many recreational facilities, including the 22,000 seat Downing Stadium, which in 1936, hosted the track and field trials for the Berlin Olympics, and where Jimi Hendrix played in 1970. In the last 20 years, through the effort of the Randall's Island Sports Foundation, the island has become, above all, a sports destination. The Downing Stadium was transformed into the Icahn Stadium in 2005, an advanced sports structure where on May 31, 2008, Jamaican sprinter Usain Bolt set a new world record in the 100 m with a time of 9.72 seconds. John McEnroe opened his famous tennis academy on the northern portion of the island, while the rest hosts soccer, football and baseball fields, a golf driving range, and a cute little mini golf course. People may also know Randall's Island because of *The French Connection* (1971), the classic police drama that ends with a memorable car chase shot there.

Lesser known may be the fact that Randall's Island is where all of New York's discarded Christmas trees end up, piled into an enormous mountain. Ever wondered where all the trees go after the holidays? Right there, on Randall's Island. And in the summer—during the electronic music festival called "Electric Zoo"—you can find more than 85,000 kids dancing to techno music, some of them dressed in rabbit costumes. Randall's Island might be used to its fare share of eccentricity, and so it is somehow suitable that the Frieze Art Fair has set up camp on this strip of land.

The artists taking part in Frieze Projects have all come up with proposals for art works that respond to the unique geography of the island, referencing its history, questioning its geographical location, or evoking its social complexities at the cross-section of three deeply different areas—East Harlem, South Bronx, and Queens. The projects on view at Frieze New York are scattered around the island and function as temporary landmarks, enticing the viewer to explore this extraordinary location, as the majority of the projects are sited outdoors, in the lush park surrounding the fair. Frieze Projects in New York are sponsored by Mulberry, with additional support from Outset.

For the first time in the ten-year history of Frieze Projects, a fiction writer has been commissioned to compose what we could call "a site-specific short story." American novelist Rick Moody has sketched the coordinates of Randall's Island on a deliberately undependable GPS device, thus tracing the boundaries of a fictional site.

Literary associations also abound in the works of the visual artists invited as part of Frieze Projects. After all, one cannot hold back memories of imaginary islands, hidden treasures and other fantasy landscapes when visiting Randall's Island.

Uri Aran appropriates one of the most iconic landmarks on the island, an abandoned ticket shack by the pier, and transforms it into a fictional examination room in which actors will play the roles of doctors and patients. Inspired by the many hospitals and shelters that were built on the island throughout the years, the artist comments on the stereotypical role of the doctor in our society and continues to explore the ways in which media and contemporary culture depict authority figures and power relationships.

Some of the projects recreate the atmosphere of a funfair or an amusement park. Located in a peaceful lawn to the left

John Ahearn
Uri Aran
Ulla von Brandenburg
Latifa Echakhch
Joel Kyack
Rick Moody
Virginia Overton
Tim Rollins and K.O.S.

Introduction

Randall's Island is one of the most fascinating places in New York. Since the 18th century, it has functioned as a site where the city of New York would confine its outsiders—hospitals and asylums "for the poor, the insane, and the inebriated ones" appear very early on the historical maps of the island. Even today, the skyline of the island is dominated by the daunting presence of the Manhattan Psychiatric Center; a colossal, Kafkaesque building that resides on the island like a relic from the gloomy past. In the 1930s, Robert Moses, the city's infamous Park Commissioner, managed to transform Randall's Island into what it still is now: one of the most important transportation junctions between Manhattan, Queens and the Bronx. Moses built the Triborough Bridge and many recreational facilities, including the 22,000 seat Downing Stadium, which in 1936, hosted the track and field trials for the Berlin Olympics, and where Jimi Hendrix played in 1970. In the last 20 years, through the effort of the Randall's Island Sports Foundation, the island has become, above all, a sports destination. The Downing Stadium was transformed into the Icahn Stadium in 2005, an advanced sports structure where on May 31, 2008, Jamaican sprinter Usain Bolt set a new world record in the 100 m with a time of 9.72 seconds. John McEnroe opened his famous tennis academy on the northern portion of the island, while the rest hosts soccer, football and baseball fields, a golf driving range, and a cute little mini golf course. People may also know Randall's Island because of *The French Connection* (1971), the classic police drama that ends with a memorable car chase shot there.

Lesser known may be the fact that Randall's Island is where all of New York's discarded Christmas trees end up, piled into an enormous mountain. Ever wondered where all the trees go after the holidays? Right there, on Randall's Island. And in the summer—during the electronic music festival called "Electric Zoo"—you can find more than 85,000 kids dancing to techno music, some of them dressed in rabbit costumes. Randall's Island might be used to its fare share of eccentricity, and so it is somehow suitable that the Frieze Art Fair has set up camp on this strip of land.

The artists taking part in Frieze Projects have all come up with proposals for art works that respond to the unique geography of the island, referencing its history, questioning its geographical location, or evoking its social complexities at the cross-section of three deeply different areas—East Harlem, South Bronx, and Queens. The projects on view at Frieze New York are scattered around the island and function as temporary landmarks, enticing the viewer to explore this extraordinary location, as the majority of the projects are sited outdoors, in the lush park surrounding the fair. Frieze Projects in New York are sponsored by Mulberry, with additional support from Outset.

For the first time in the ten-year history of Frieze Projects, a fiction writer has been commissioned to compose what we could call "a site-specific short story." American novelist Rick Moody has sketched the coordinates of Randall's Island on a deliberately undependable GPS device, thus tracing the boundaries of a fictional site.

Literary associations also abound in the works of the visual artists invited as part of Frieze Projects. After all, one cannot hold back memories of imaginary islands, hidden treasures and other fantasy landscapes when visiting Randall's Island.

Uri Aran appropriates one of the most iconic landmarks on the island, an abandoned ticket shack by the pier, and transforms it into a fictional examination room in which actors will play the roles of doctors and patients. Inspired by the many hospitals and shelters that were built on the island throughout the years, the artist comments on the stereotypical role of the doctor in our society and continues to explore the ways in which media and contemporary culture depict authority figures and power relationships.

Some of the projects recreate the atmosphere of a funfair or an amusement park. Located in a peaceful lawn to the left of the pier by the East River, Ulla von Brandenburg's striped tent evokes an old vintage circus structure. Inside the tent the viewers will see a shadow play, which alternates figures and music. Borrowing from traditions of *Commedia dell'Arte*, burlesque performance, and 19th century Parisian shadow plays, von Brandenburg continues her exploration of the language of theater, examining the strategy of artifice and the always-fascinating power of fiction.

To the other end of the pier, Los Angeles-based artist Joel Kyack has installed a country fair game trailer shaped like a giant human body. Unfolding simultaneously as an installation, a performance space, and a large-scale mobile sculpture, the trailer houses two games, one taking place inside the trailer's "mouth," and the other in its splayed "rib cage." Visitors can play free of charge and win original art works, which are also part of the installation.

Other works establish a dialogue with the surrounding natural environment. Randall's Island, after all, also has an untouched park with blooming trees and wide expanses of grass. Latifa Echakhch turns a patch of lush, green grass on the north entrance of the fair, into an enchanting mirage by mysteriously installing hundreds of tumbleweeds in the incongruous location. Typically seen rolling in the desert or on empty highways in the American southwest, tumbleweed has long become an icon of classic Western movies and the popular imagination. Here at Randall's Island it becomes a constructed illusion that invites us to re-examine a familiar object that is unexpectedly made present to us in an idiosyncratic context.

The bucolic aspect of the island is the backdrop for Virginia Overton's installation. Among a cluster of the trees on the island's waterfront, the artist wedges panels of acrylic mirror, transforming a minimal, seemingly cold material into a sensual, weightless combination of nature and artificiality.

Some of the projects are conceived as participatory platforms, which engage with the fair's visitors and different local communities. Working on a 40-foot table under a canopy of large leafy oak trees, the collaborative team, Tim Rollins and K.O.S., will be conducting their first open youth workshop. The participants will join forces to create a choral painting inspired by Shakespeare's *A Midsummer Night's Dream,* painted on sheet music from a 1828–42 composition by Felix Mendelssohn, written to accompany a production of the play.

Inside the fair, John Ahearn presents a reconstruction of his 1979 legendary exhibition "South Bronx Hall of Fame," a show of sculptural casts originally installed at Fashion Moda, a pioneering South Bronx alternative space founded by Stefan Eins in 1978, and open until 1993. The presentation at Frieze New York includes a series of sculptures originally displayed at Fashion Moda, and realized in collaboration with Rigoberto Torres, as well as a casting station where Ahearn and Torres will be making a new series of commissioned portraits, live, for the whole duration of the fair.

Frieze Talks also takes as inspiration the distinctive location of the fair at the cross section of different geographical, social, and cultural neighborhoods. This year's program is organized thematically. Focusing on the notion of "The Atlas," and investigating various ways of mapping, describing, and exploring the world from geo-political maps to fictional sites, from geographical explorations to mental states, Frieze Talks present different ways in which art and artists have tried to represent and organize the world. The series includes: panel discussions on museums expansions, recent episodes of land occupations, geographically-specific collections, and the rise of new ethics; a lecture by French philosopher Georges Didi-Huberman on André Malraux and his *Le Musée Imaginaire*; a reading by writer Rick Moody; a presentation by Allan Sekula and a conversation between Zoe Leonard and Rhea Anastas. Meanwhile, Frieze Sounds—a new platform for sound works—presented with BMW, features three specially commissioned audio works by Martin Creed, Rick Moody, and Frances Stark. The works are accessible at friezenewyork.com and are available to download and listen to when you are in transit to the fair.

Cecilia Alemani
Curator, Frieze Projects

John Ahearn

For Frieze Projects John Ahearn restages his exhibition "South Bronx Hall of Fame," reconstructing a piece of New York art history from the Seventies.

John Ahearn (b.1951) is an American artist based in New York. He has worked collaboratively with Rigoberto Torres since the late 1970s. Recent exhibitions include "Automatic for the People," at Aljira, a Center for Contemporary Art, Newark (2010), and "Inhotim," at Alexander and Bonin, New York (2007). The exhibition "South Bronx Hall of Fame" originally took place at Fashion Moda, South Bronx, New York, in 1979.

Cecilia Alemani What was the genesis of the "South Bronx Hall of Fame" show at Fashion Moda, New York (1979)?

John Ahearn I had just moved from a basement space to the underground actress Patti Astor's Lower Eastside apartment. I was writing a screenplay for an art monster movie. Then I spied a book of Patty's called *Makeup for Television and Movies*. It had a section on life-casting to make monster face parts. I wanted to learn the technique right away.

Alemani How did you transition from monster making into portrait making?

Ahearn All my first life-casting experiments were on my friends, such as Tom Otterness, Robin Winters, Coleen Fitzgibbon, and Kiki Smith. In January of 1979, a fellow Colab artist Robert Cooney invited me to share a performance with him that he called *Corporate Casting*. He performed as if he was part of a corporation, and I cast him live for an audience. I discovered that I liked working in front of people. My twin brother Charlie said "why don't you go and do that at Stefan's place in the Bronx?"

Alemani So you went up to Fashion Moda?

Ahearn I went up to Fashion Moda to do a cast of Stefan. There I met Hector, Stefan's assistant from the neighborhood. I asked Hector to place his hands over Stefan's eyes when I was making the mould. In my mind Stefan was all about alien intelligence and supernatural science fiction—I was trying to represent Stefan as a space alien, and Hector was supposed to represent reality. So Stefan was a "blind visionary." We made the cast in the front window and a crowd of people gathered and they all wanted to know one thing—how do I get one of these? How do I get one done? And I'm like "you have to wait, we're going to be doing this tomorrow right here on the same spot."

We had kids passing by, going to and from school. You can see in the Kristof Kohlhofer photograph that there were a lot of kids hanging around, and they were "looking" more than gawking at what was happening. Some people thought there had been an accident because someone was lying down and covered up. The kids that were there in that photograph arrived early and stayed until it was all over.

Big City
1979
Acrylic on plaster
14 × 3 × 8"
(35.5 × 33 × 20.5 cm)
Courtesy of Alexander and Bonin

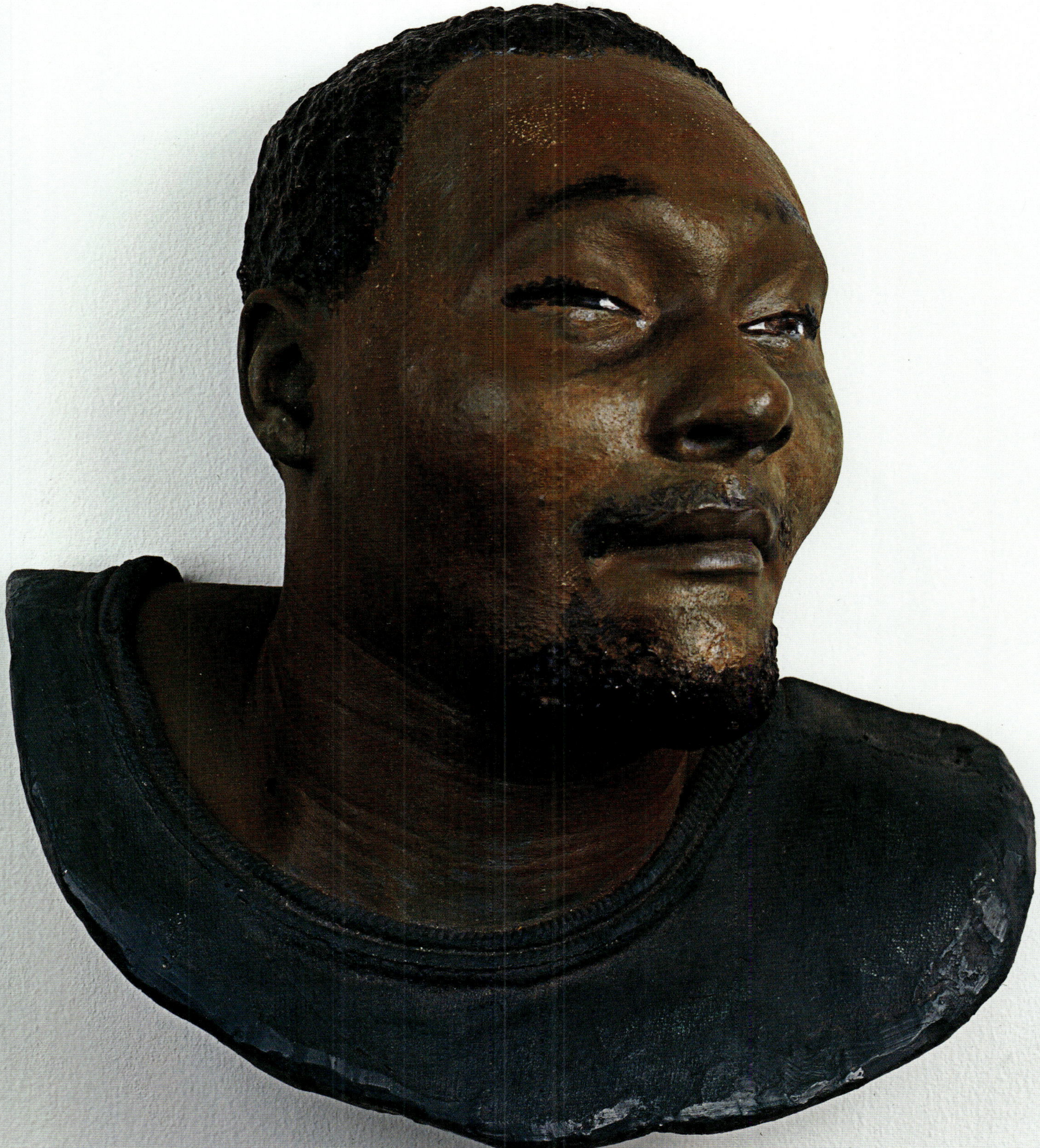

Robert with Tounge Out
1979
Acrylic on cast plaster
Dimensions variable
Courtesy of Alexander and Bonin

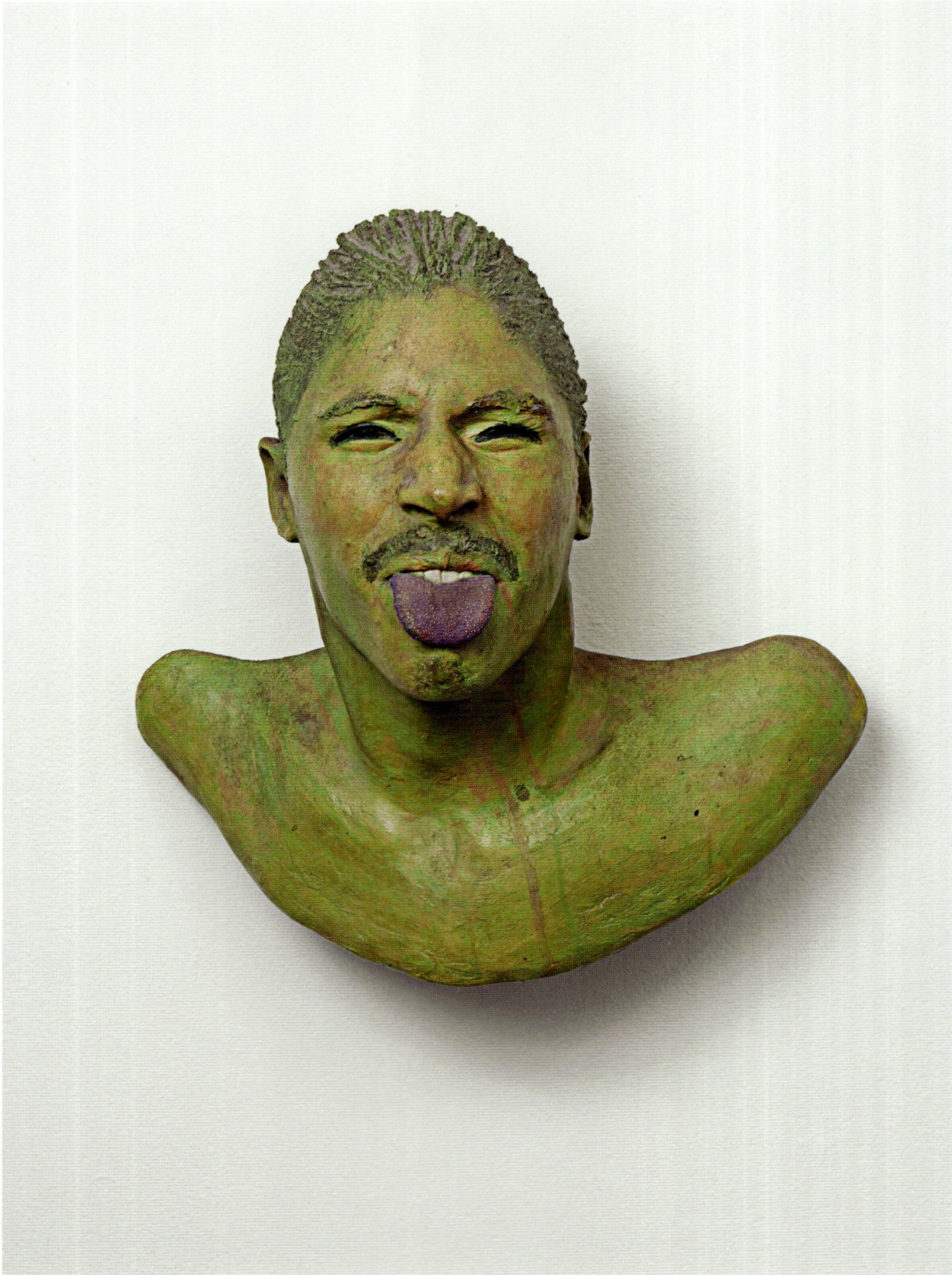

Alemani What was Fashion Moda like in the late 70s?

Ahearn It was real mix of South Bronx neighborhood street culture and young downtown artists. Joe Lewis, who was part of the downtown Colab group co-directed Fashion Moda with Stefan. William Scott, a bright 15 year old kid who lived near Fashion Moda, became the junior director. Stefan intentionally never put in security gates or shutters on the storefront. Unlike all other places on the block, it was left pretty vulnerable (open) with a Plexiglas frontage and nothing else.

Alemani When did you decide to move to the Bronx?

Ahearn For the whole of 1979, I was carrying everything back and forth between uptown and downtown. After meeting and casting Rigoberto Torres, I realized that he and I shared interests in crucial ways: He was a Puerto Rican kid still in High School, who had been inspired by working in his uncle's Bronx statuary factory, and he saw the life-casting as an extension of that work. Being a twin, I was unconsciously seeking a partner to help me understand people.

Alemani Did your casting technique improve or change after you met Rigoberto?

Ahearn We developed teamwork styles of casting. Rigoberto has a perfect sense of people's character. He opened my eyes and continually taught me about being alive and living with people.

Alemani Let's go back to Frieze Projects. You will show the majority of the original

"We made the cast in the front window and a crowd of people gathered and they all wanted to know one thing—how do I get one of these? How do I get one done?"

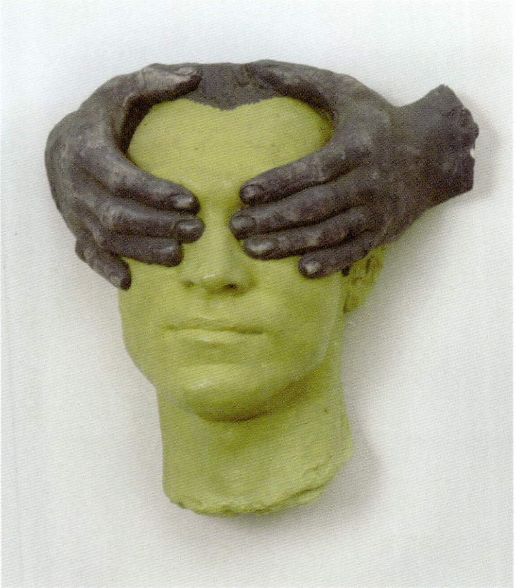

Stephan with Hector
1979
Acrylic on plaster
12 × 12 × 6"
(30.5 × 30.5 × 15 cm)
Courtesy of Alexander and Bonin

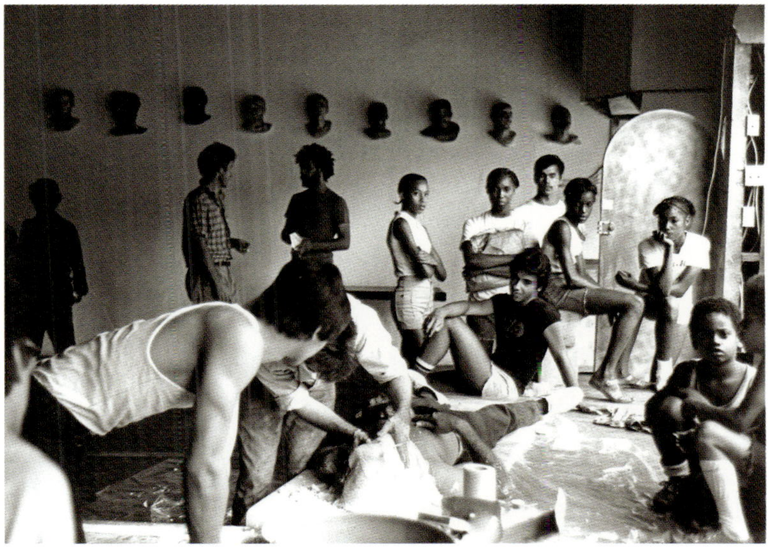

Left:
Rigoberto Torres (left, in white undershirt) and John Ahearn (center) during the casting of *Carlos*, with Fashion Moda co-directors, Stefan Eins and Joe Lewis (standing background, left to right). Photograph: Christof Kohlhofer

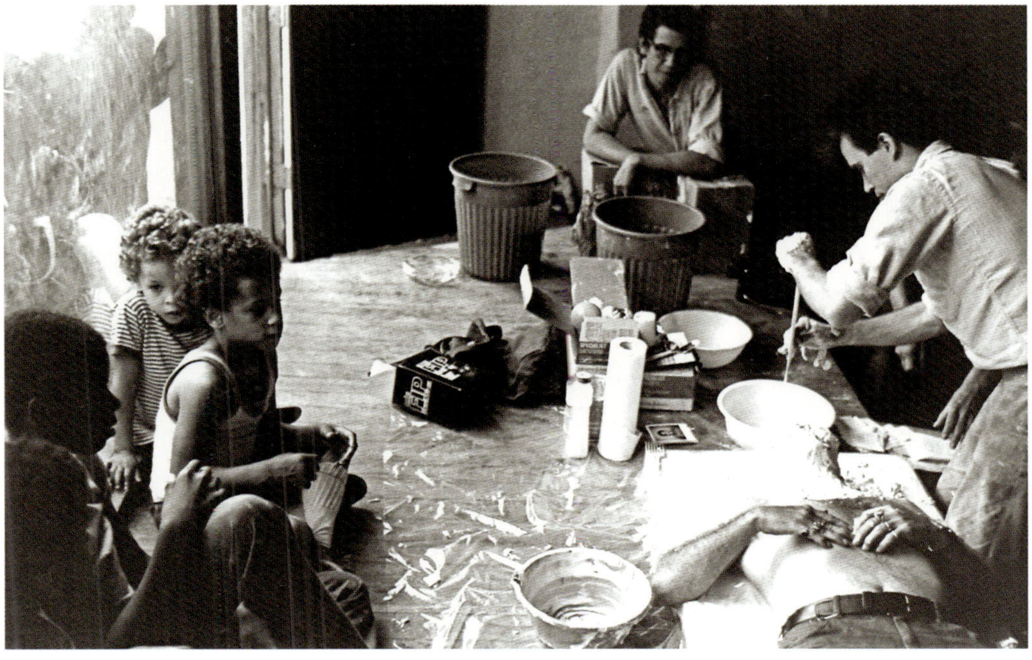

Below:
Tom Otterness (background, center) watching Ahearn cast Carlos Fashion Moda, July 1979. Photograph: Christof Kohlhofer

casts from "South Bronx Hall of Fame" at Fashion Moda. How did you think people will react to your project?

Ahearn There's a thin line in our culture between priceless treasure and worthless trash. There was very early interest from art world with this work. In January 1981, Kasper Koenig sent me a letter from Cologne about the pieces made at Fashion Moda—he was going to have an important survey show in Cologne called "Westkunst." From time to time, people with art world positions have seen value in this work. So I see my Frieze Project as a sign from the art world that they're reconsidering the value of it. These original Fashion Moda portraits are personal things that Rigoberto and I love very much. What you're offering to us is an opportunity to be considered in the context of contemporary art, a commercial art world context. And we appreciate that. And what we'd like most from this is that it is fruitful and fun.

Uri Aran

Negotiating the roles of power and responsibility, Uri Aran adopts a unique location on Randall's Island to stage a dynamic new performance work.

Untitled (Shany)
2011
Computer drawing and inkjet on paper
11¼ × 14¾"
(4.5 × 6.5 cm)
Courtesy of Gavin Brown's enterprise and mother's tankstation

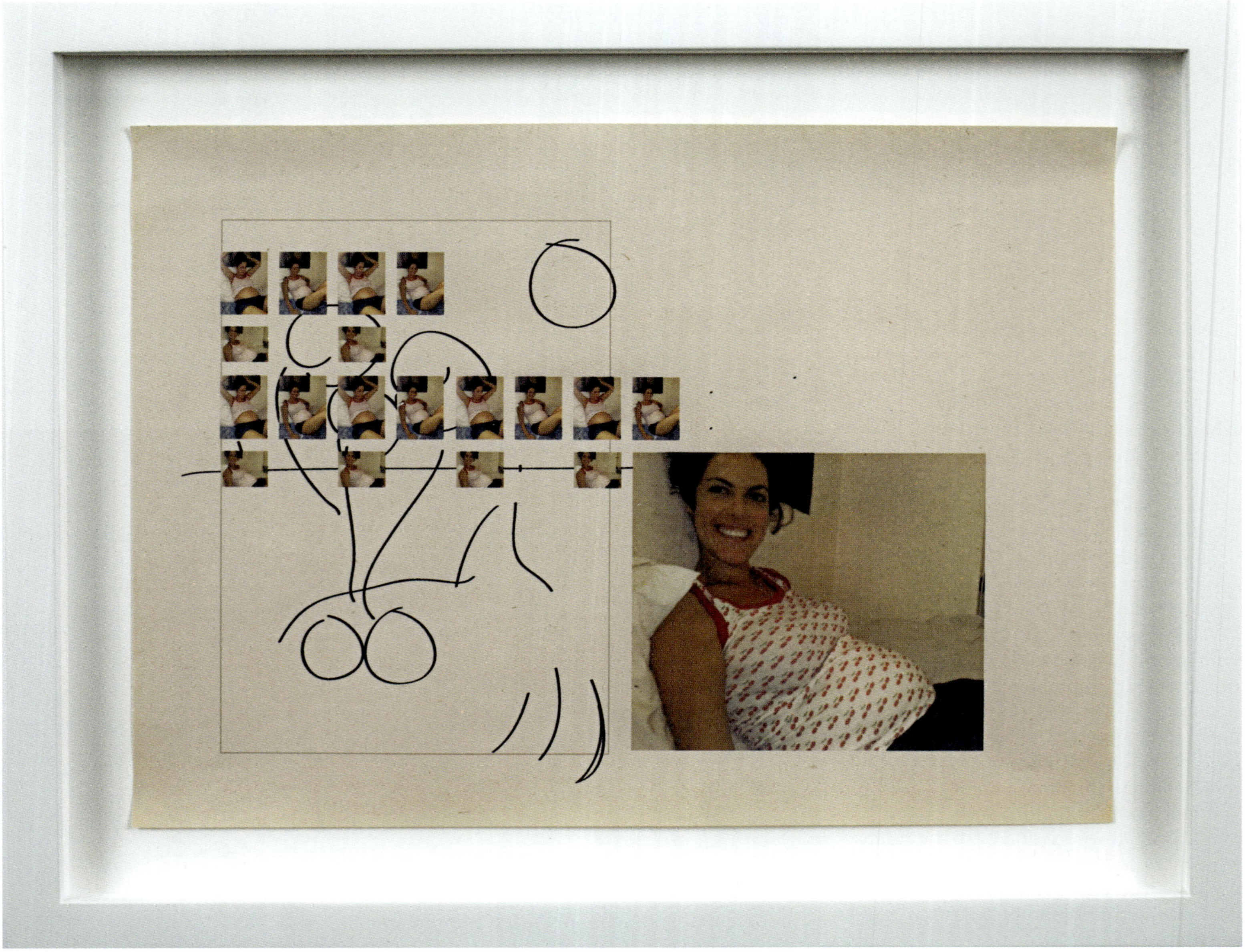

Uri Aran (b. 1977) is an Israeli-born artist based in New York. His sculptural practice was the subject of the solo exhibitions "Doctor, Dog, Sandwich," at mother's tankstation, Dublin (2010), and "Geraniums," Rivington Arms, New York (2008). In early 2012, he participated in the two-person show "Tommy Hartung & Uri Aran," at White Flags Projects, St. Louis. His first solo show at Gavin Brown's enterprise, New York, "by foot, by car, by bus," took place in early 2012.

Untitled (Brave Horse)
2011
Mixed media
Dimension Variable
Courtesy of Gavin Brown's enterprise and mother's tankstation

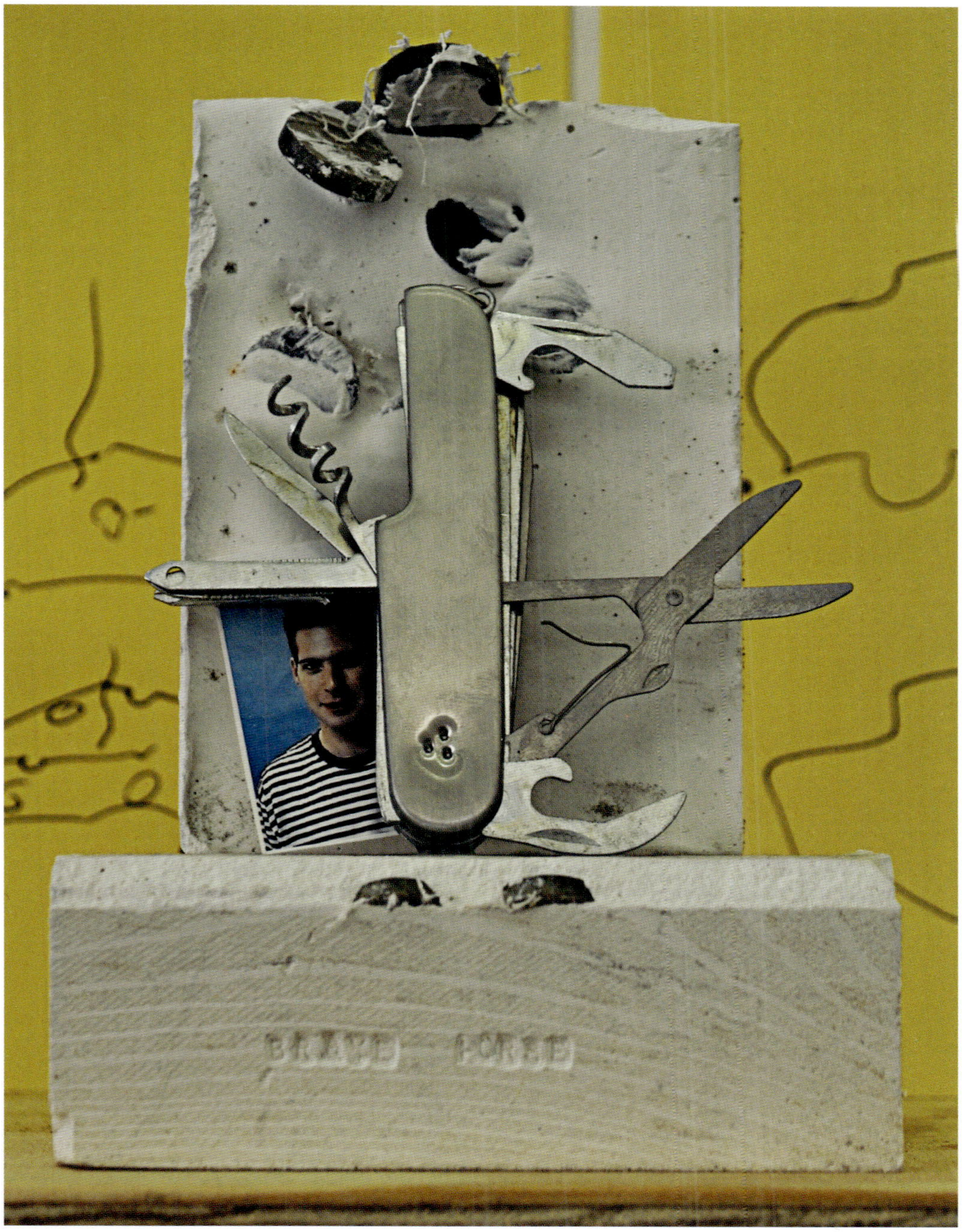

Cecilia Alemani What are you planning for Frieze Projects and how did you come up with the idea?

Uri Aran Medical services and structures are integral to the history of Randall's Island, but my project doesn't necessarily speak to these ideas directly. Those facts were really just a starting point from which to explore aspects of public and private experience and to manipulate certain tropes that interest me. I was immediately attracted to the island's old ticket shack—it looks like a little theater and it almost invites some kind of spectacle. The structure feels childish—it's not infantile, but it does have something to do with a kind of conditioning, education and language, and even a kind of moral authority. I am always working with these concepts and they connect with the idea of a hospital, which made me think about the role of the doctor.

Alemani So the project will have a performative element?

Aran It has two components—a live performance inside the shack and a feed of what is taking place, which is broadcast inside the fair. A number of times during the day the public will be able to view the performance through the windows of the shack. There will be three different sets of actors of different ages and genders taking the roles of patient and doctor, and in each pairing a physical examination will take place.

Alemani What will the shack look like?

Aran I'm not going to try to transform the shack into a fully functioning clinic. There will be very identifiable "doctor" things, like a stethoscope and a blood pressure

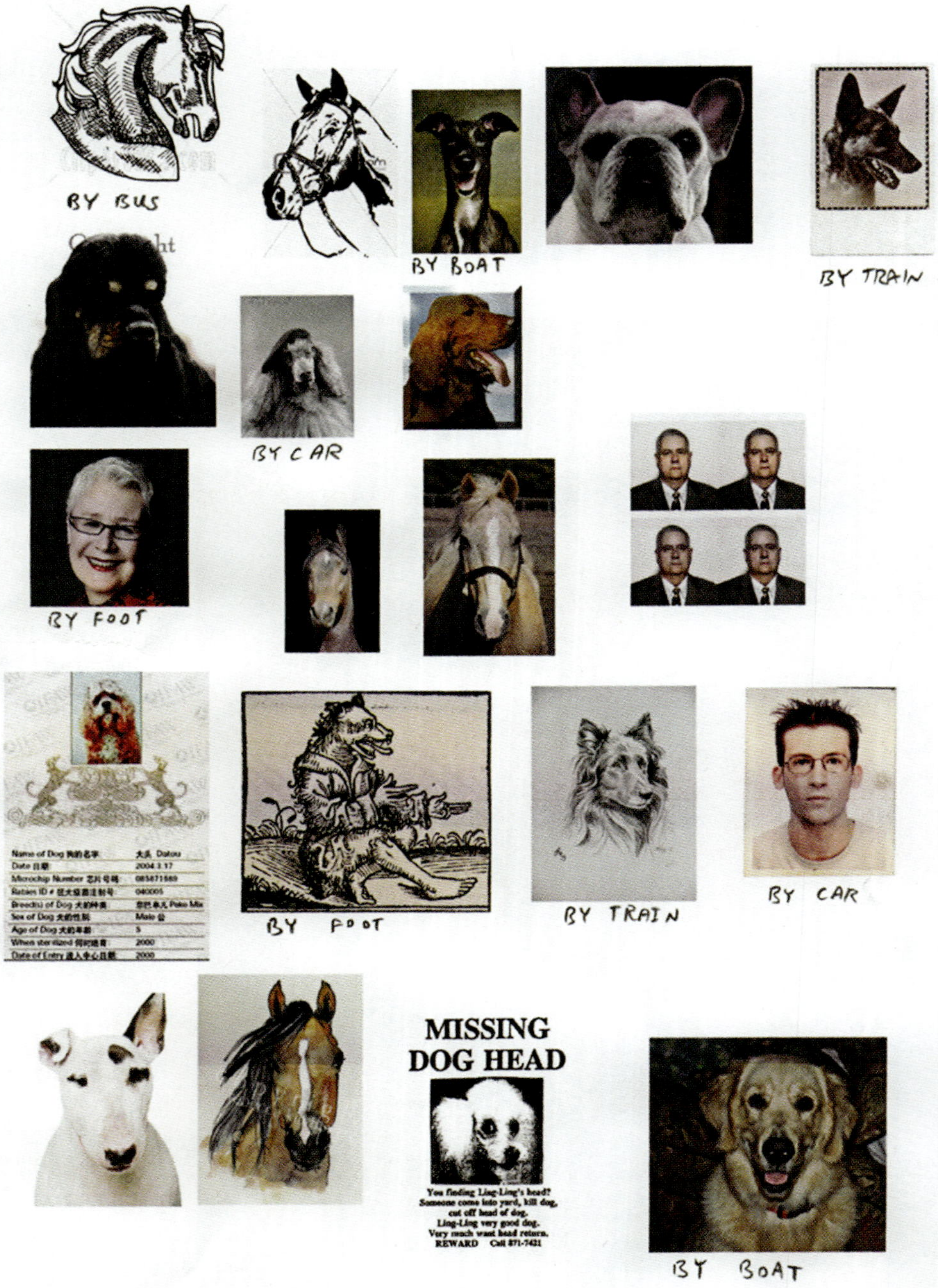
BY BUS
BY BOAT
BY TRAIN
BY CAR
BY FOOT
Name of Dog
Date
Microchip Number
Breed(s) of Dog
Sex of Dog
Male
Age of Dog
Date of Entry
BY FOOT
BY TRAIN
BY CAR
MISSING
DOG HEAD
You finding Ling-Ling's head?
Someone come into yard, kill dog,
cut off head of dog.
Ling-Ling very good dog.
Very much want head return.
REWARD Call 871-7421
BY BOAT

"Visiting the doctor is usually something you do in private—it's usually the patient and the doctor, or the patient, the nurse, and the doctor. In this case, it's going to be the patient, the doctor, and everybody else..."

cuff. There will be some tools but no machines. I'm not trying to imitate a real doctor's clinic, but I do want to quote one. Quotations, for me, are more interesting in general than recreations.

Alemani Are you interested in that because of TV? When you talk about it, I'm reminded of TV series like *ER* (1994–2009). It's very American.

Aran I see the role of the doctor as internationally symbolic.

Alemani Do you think that representations of doctors are always connoted as positive? Or is it a stereotype?

Aran Well, I think there's both something real and obviously invented about it. Being a doctor is in some way a sacrifice. They're helping others and the notion of giving has the disposition of being good. There are many different paradigms, or different equations, that relate giving to goodness, therefore a doctor is good.

The relationship between private and public activity are also at the core of this piece. Visiting the doctor is usually something we do in private—it's usually the patient and the doctor, or the patient, the nurse, and the doctor. In this case, it's going to be the patient, the doctor, and everybody else...

Alemani Right, and because you are going to record the live performance and it's going to be transmitted inside the fair, there is also a mediation of images. How do you think the footage inside the fair will be received?

Aran While the examination is taking place, I, or someone else, will be capturing the interactions on video. The viewers watching the live event are seeing this all as it happens, and at the same time they're looking at the artwork being made. Inside the fair, the footage can be viewed on screen, but this will be more similar to TV. You don't see the camera or any of the behind-the-scenes bits, just the documentation of what is normally a private event, only it will be in slowed down slightly.

Alemani Why will the video be slowed down?

Aran First of all it will slow down the process of consumption; it's a form of estrangement. I'm only slowing it down marginally to distinguish it from the live event. The project will be somewhere between live and recorded, so in that sense I'm talking about manipulation. I'm physically manipulating something, and directly talking about the idea of manipulation.

Alemani Did you watch a lot of TV when you were a kid? Do you watch a lot of TV now?

Aran I have always been interested in TV in relation to popular culture. I really register the vernacular. Maybe because English is not my first language but most of the TV I see is in English, and I think a lot about the discord between what I see and what I hear.

Alemani What are the relationships between the sculptural element of the work, the video component, and the live component?

Aran This is the first time I've done something live so it's an introduction to a new kind of environment, or production method, but I do still see it primarily in a sculptural way. I'm very interested in sequencing, and in the viewing experience as a timeline, so I think it makes a lot of sense for me to work live or in video.

Left:
Untitled (By)
2010
Digital Print with unique pencil additions
32 × 24"
(81.5 × 61 cm)
Courtesy of Gavin Brown's enterprise and mother's tankstation

Below:
Untitled
2012
Mixed media
Dimension variable
Courtesy of Gavin Brown's enterprise and mother's tankstation

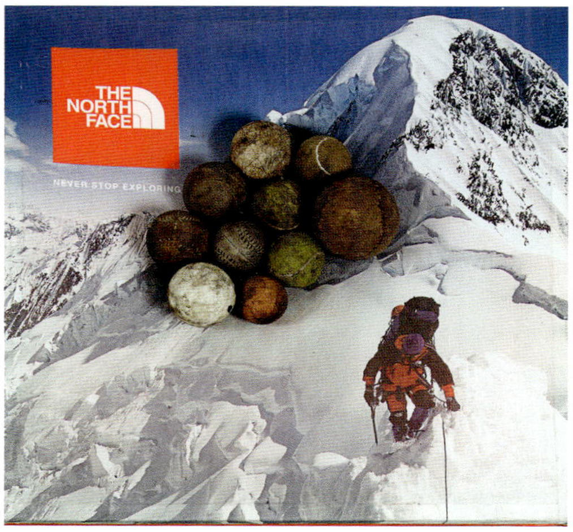

Ulla von Brandenburg

Films and installations enclose complex relationships for Ulla von Brandenburg. Her new work for Frieze Projects provides a site for her take on shadow theater.

Forêt orange (Orange Forest)
2011
Dimensions variable
Installation view at Le Magasin, Grenoble
Courtesy of art: concept, Pilar Corrias, and Produzentengalerie

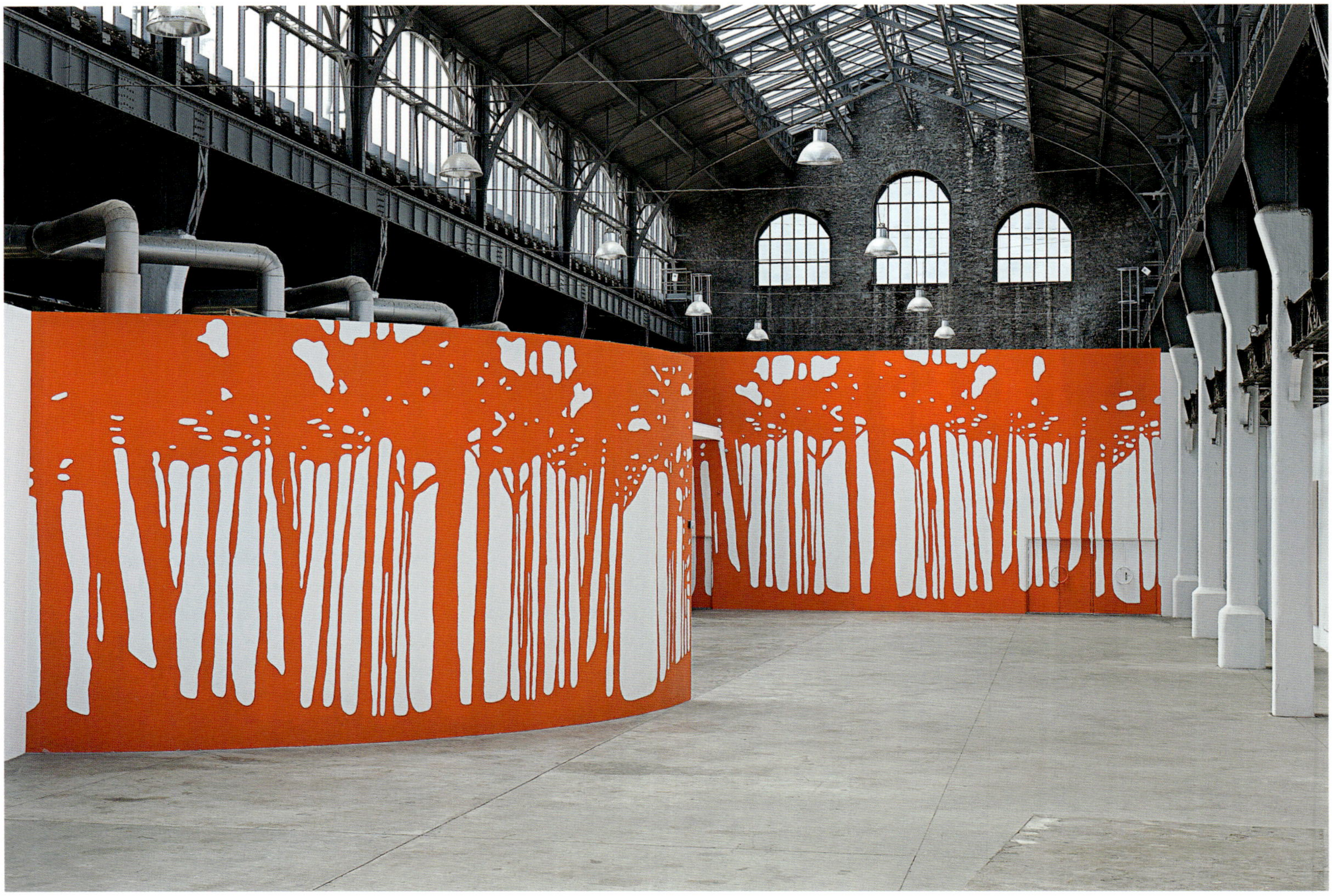

Ulla von Brandenburg (b. 1974) is a Paris based artist born in Germany. Her films and installations have been the subject of numerous solo exhibitions, including: "Le Chevalier Inexistant" (The Nonexistent Night), at Rosascape, Paris (2012), and "Mirrorsong," at Pilar Corrias, London (2012). She participated in the 11th Biennale de Lyon, and "Making Worlds," at the 53rd Venice Biennale (2009).

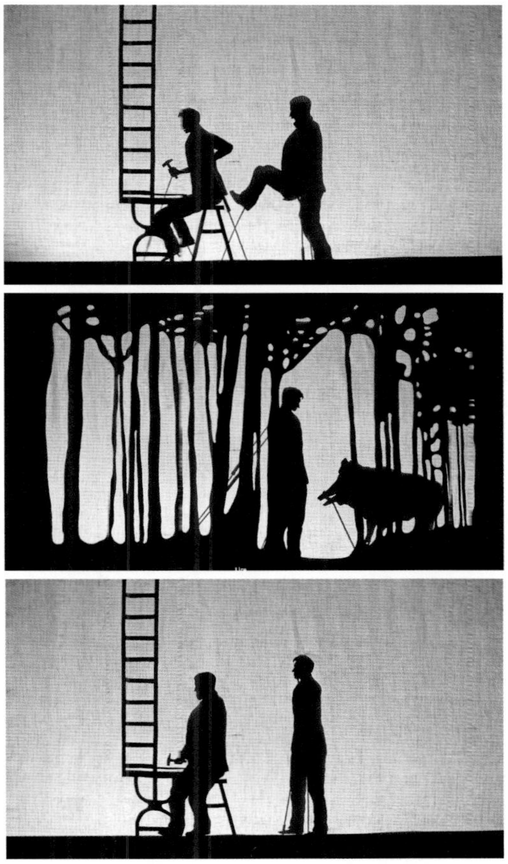

Right:
Two men and the wild boar
2011
HD video
4 min. 30 sec.
Courtesy of art: concept, Pilar Corrias, and Produzentengalerie

Below:
Chorspiel
2010
HD video, sound
10 min. 35 sec.
Courtesy of art: concept, Pilar Corrias, and Produzentengalerie

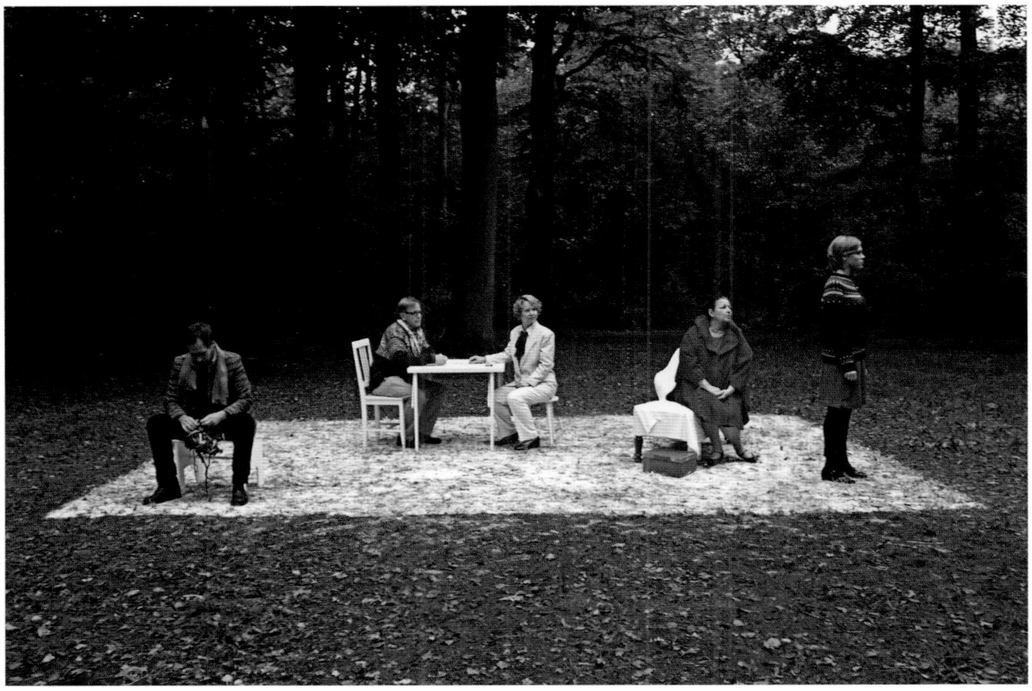

Cecilia Alemani What will visitors find on Randall's Island?

Ulla von Brandenburg They will find a tent that is reminiscent of a circus tent, or a tent where marionette plays or puppet theater might take place. The tent on Randall's Island is striped, which is, of course, the link to the circus, and puppet theater. You will enter the tent and sit down—on the screen you will see a shadow play. Actually, the shadow play is a projection, but the scale is one-to-one, and when you watch it you won't immediately think it's a projection. It could be live, because there could be real people behind the screen.

Alemani Is there a narrative?

Von Brandenburg Yes, but like all of my films it's more about the psychological and sociological drama and the relationship between the people you see: I often use fictive family structure from an analytical point of view. I'm much more interested in psychological structures over real narrative.

Alemani Have you ever worked with shadow theater before?

Von Brandenburg Yes, I did with an artist friend, Julia Horstmann. We did many shadow play performances, but we used actual cut-outs and read stories. We were invited to several institutions in different countries including Sweden and England. The texts we read had meaning to the country we were in, so in England, we choose Virginia Woolf, and in Sweden, Selma Lagerlof.

Alemani And in those instances did you build a structure to show the shadow play, or did you use an existing theater?

"Who is the object and who is the subject? In the end, we are all playing roles."

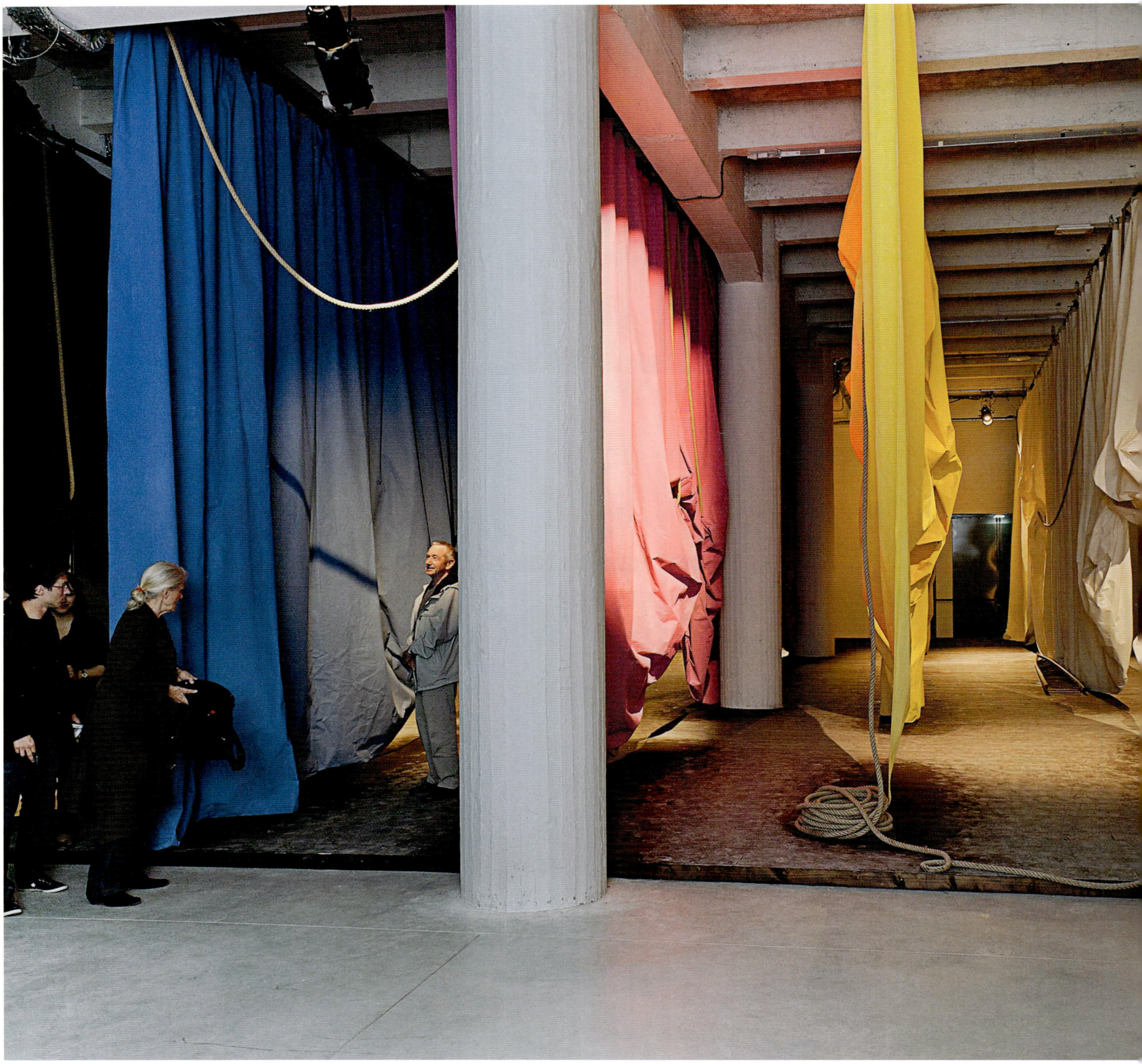

Kulissen (Sceneries)
2011
Mixed media
Dimensions variable
Installation view at the 11th Lyon Biennale
Courtesy of art: concept, Pilar Corrias, and Produzentengalerie

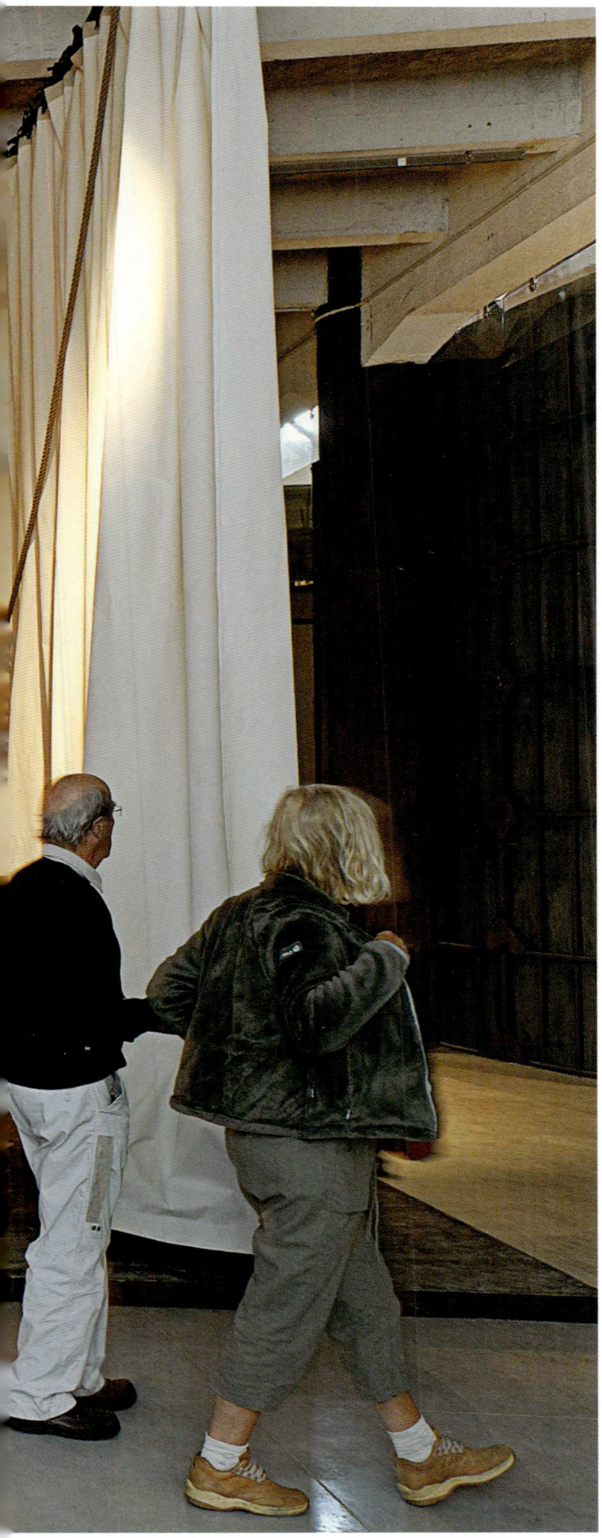

Von Brandenburg No, we used a bed sheet. The aim was to stay very, very minimal, and very much like, let's say, street theater, or what you would do if you made a theater in your own home.

Alemani When you did those shadow plays, were they for all kind of audiences, or were they for kids?

Von Brandenburg The shadow plays I did with Julia Horstmann were always for an arty audience. But I also made one shadow play film for a project by Gareth Moore, who invited artists to make films for children. I thought that was a very nice idea because I had to conceive the piece in a different way. But for Frieze Projects, because I don't think that many kids are buying art yet, it is more for adults, of course.

Alemani What role does music play in your films? Do you compose your own music?

Von Brandenburg I have made tableau vivant with film, and captured still scenes with actors for the length of one roll of 16mm film—2 minutes 30 seconds. Soon after making these works I was invited to do a performance; I wanted to do something like tableau vivant, but there was the problem of duration. How long should it be? I didn't want to make an exhausting tableau vivant that existed until the actors started fainting. So I thought, ah, let's do it to music, because music has a beginning and an end, and then I have a duration. It's my story, I make the music with the artist Laurent Montaron, and it's my voice the actors use to sing. It's my set too.

Alemani What did you study?

Von Brandenburg I started studying scenography, but I found it really boring because you have to do the things that other people tell you to do. If you do set design it's always the director who makes the decisions. But because my scenography course was taught in an art school, I met so many artists, and I began to think that art was so much more interesting. At first, when I studied art, I was interested in Minimalism and abstraction; but theater gradually became more and more important in my work. Over the last five years, it has become astonishingly visible.

Alemani When you say theater, what do you refer to?

Von Brandenburg The mechanisms of theater—the curtain that separates the audience and the actors, for example. Who is the object and who is the subject? In the end, we are all playing roles.

Alemani What about the physical elements that refer to the theater? You mentioned curtains. Your piece for the 11th Lyon Biennale, *Kulissen* (Sceneries), 2011, was inspired by them.

Von Brandenburg In Lyon, I wanted the visitors to enter the space and feel as if they were in a stage-like location, but in reverse. Meaning, the curtains were painted on the side you couldn't see, as if you were entering from the back of a stage. As you passed the curtains which were different colors, you physically travel from dark to the light, from black to white. And behind the last curtain, the white one, there should be an audience, but there is of course no audience. You are, in a way, an actor in the play. The artwork does not exist without visitors, without those who witness it. The visitor decides if he or she wants to remain a spectator, or if they are going to become actors in their own play.

Latifa Echakhch

The displacement of objects contradicts perception in the installations of Latifa Echakhch—for Frieze Projects she brings home the iconography of the American West.

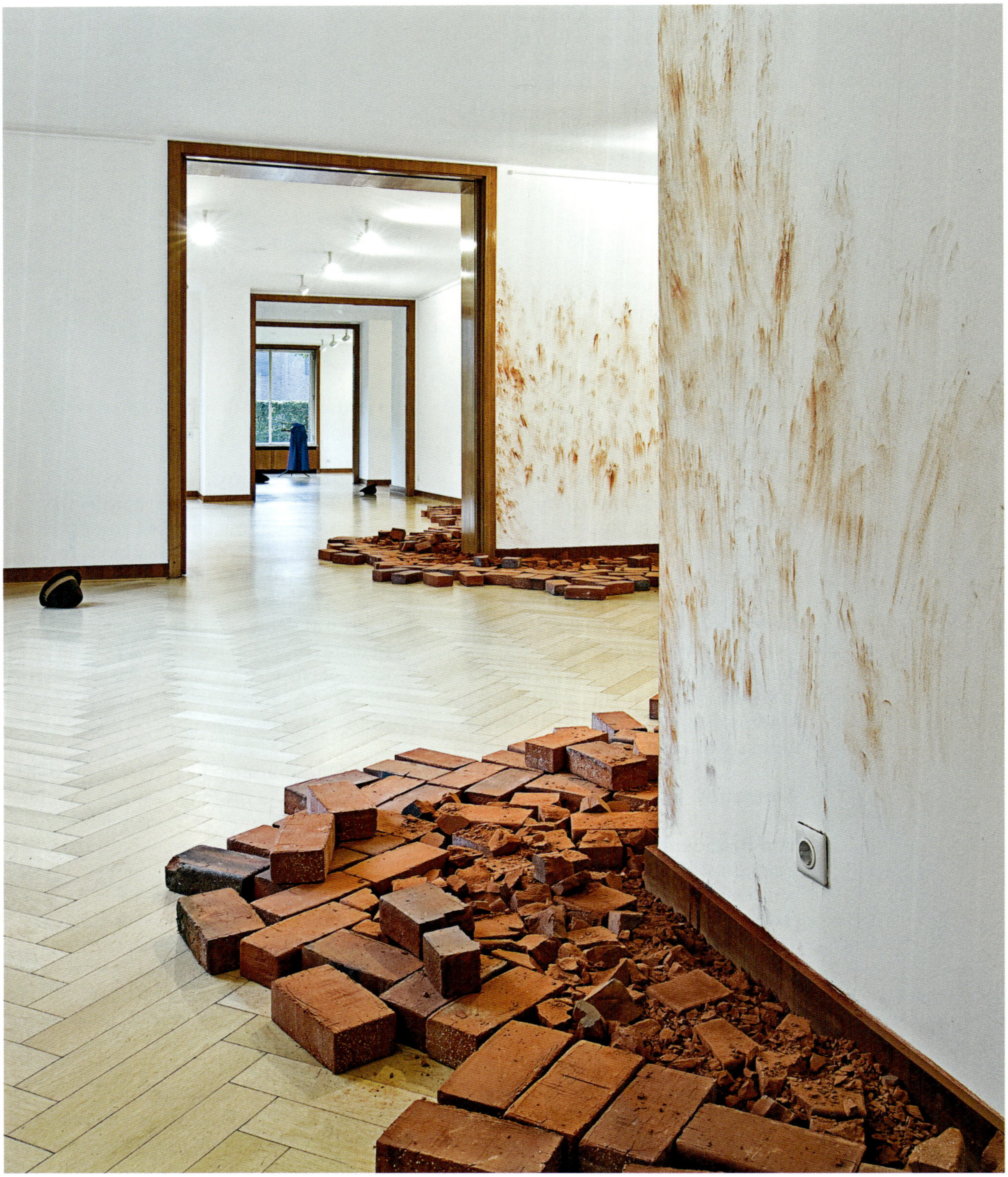

Tkaf
2011
Bricks and sanguine pigment
Dariable dimension
Installation view at Museum Haus Esters, Krefeld
Courtesy kaufmann repetto

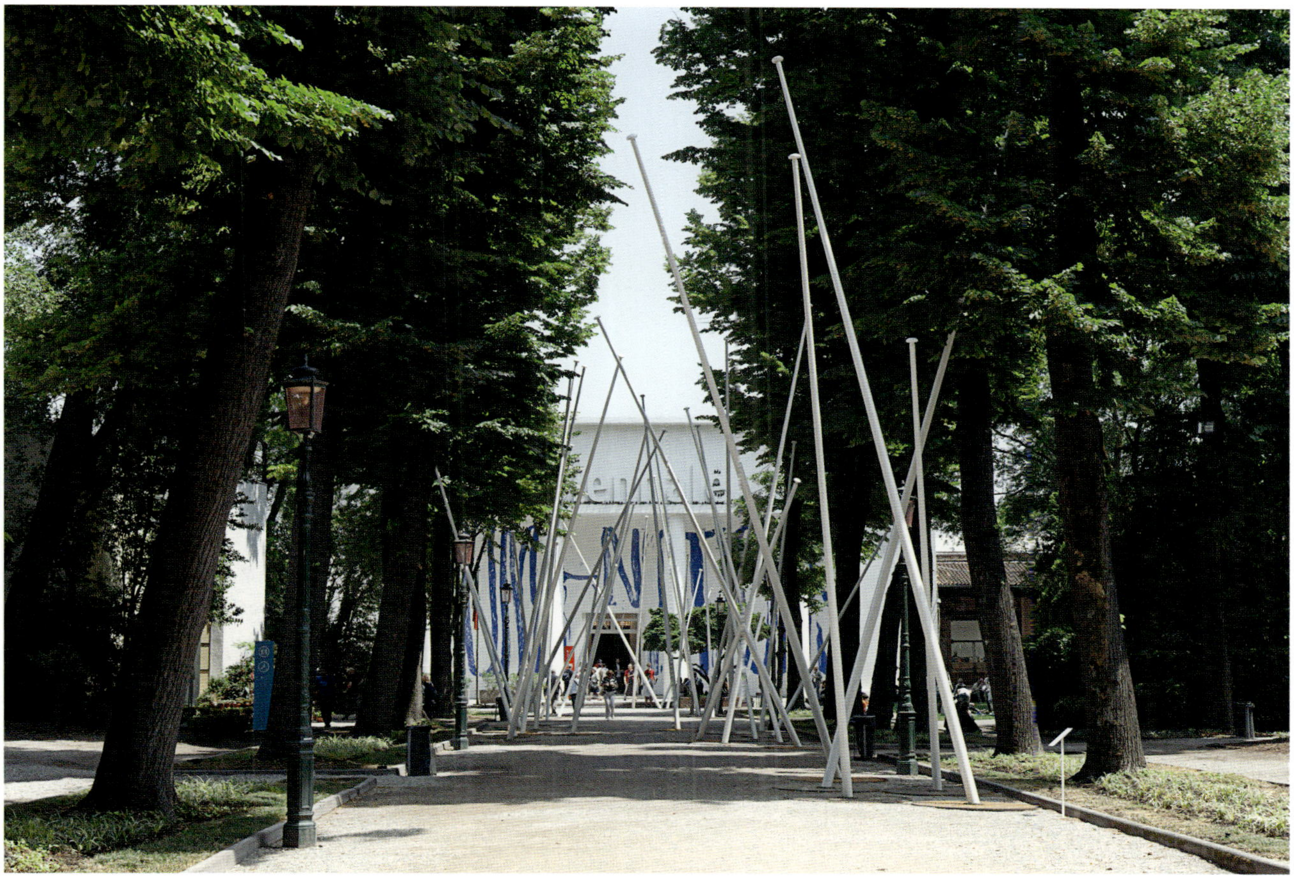

Fantasia
2011
Fibreglass flag poles and steel bases
Dimensions variable
Max. height 10 m., min. height 6 m
Installation view at the 54th Venice Biennale
Courtesy kaufmann repetto

Latifa Echakhch (b. 1974) is a Moroccan artist based in Martigny, Switzerland. Her installations and sculptural interventions frequently populate galleries and public spaces in Europe and the Unites States. Recently the solo exhibitions "From threshold to threshold," at Museum Haus Esters, Kunstmuseen, Krefeld (2011), and "Le rappel des oiseaux" (The Call of the Birds), at the Galleria d'Arte Moderna e Contemporanea, Bergamo (2010), celebrated her work

Cecilia Alemani For Frieze New York, you will install hundreds of tumbleweeds on the lush green grass at Randall's Island. How did you come up with the idea?

Latifa Echakhch The idea of using tumbleweeds comes from the Western movies I've watched I have always been fascinated by these poor pieces of dry vegetation, which enter scenes only to accentuate moments of suspense, or underline the eeriness of deserted ghost towns and dry cities. I only learnt recently that it is completely natural for the plant to be carried away by the wind—leaving the ground to sow seeds as it tumbles along. They are an iconic part of the American landscape, and they are what I thought of when I was invited to do an outdoor project for Frieze New York.

Alemani Every time I think of this project I imagine it as a mirage, an uncanny vision in the middle of nowhere. How do you think people will react to the installation?

Echakhch I do not know how people will react, but when anybody sees tumbleweed, they know exactly what the plant implies; its meaning is logged in our collective memory.

Alemani There is something slightly romantic about appropriating one of the most iconic symbols of Americana and translating it in such incongruous context. Do you often play on similar contrasts?

Echakhch The island, with its gigantic psychiatric hospital—almost entirely abandoned—is such a specific context. The majority of the land is used for sport events or farming; it has a quiet promenade, but it's not far from the crowed city. I imagine the island once all of the visitors have gone, when it is empty. I am interested in the fact that visitors will come from the city to discover something semi-rural, a place that looks like somewhere much further away than it actually is, and find something that accentuates that feeling.

“There is no mystery, no idea of genius, or extraordinary ability in the objects’ making.”

Les sanglots longs
(The Long Sobs)
2009
Installation
view, Kunsthalle
Fridericianum, Kassel
Courtesy kaufmann
repetto

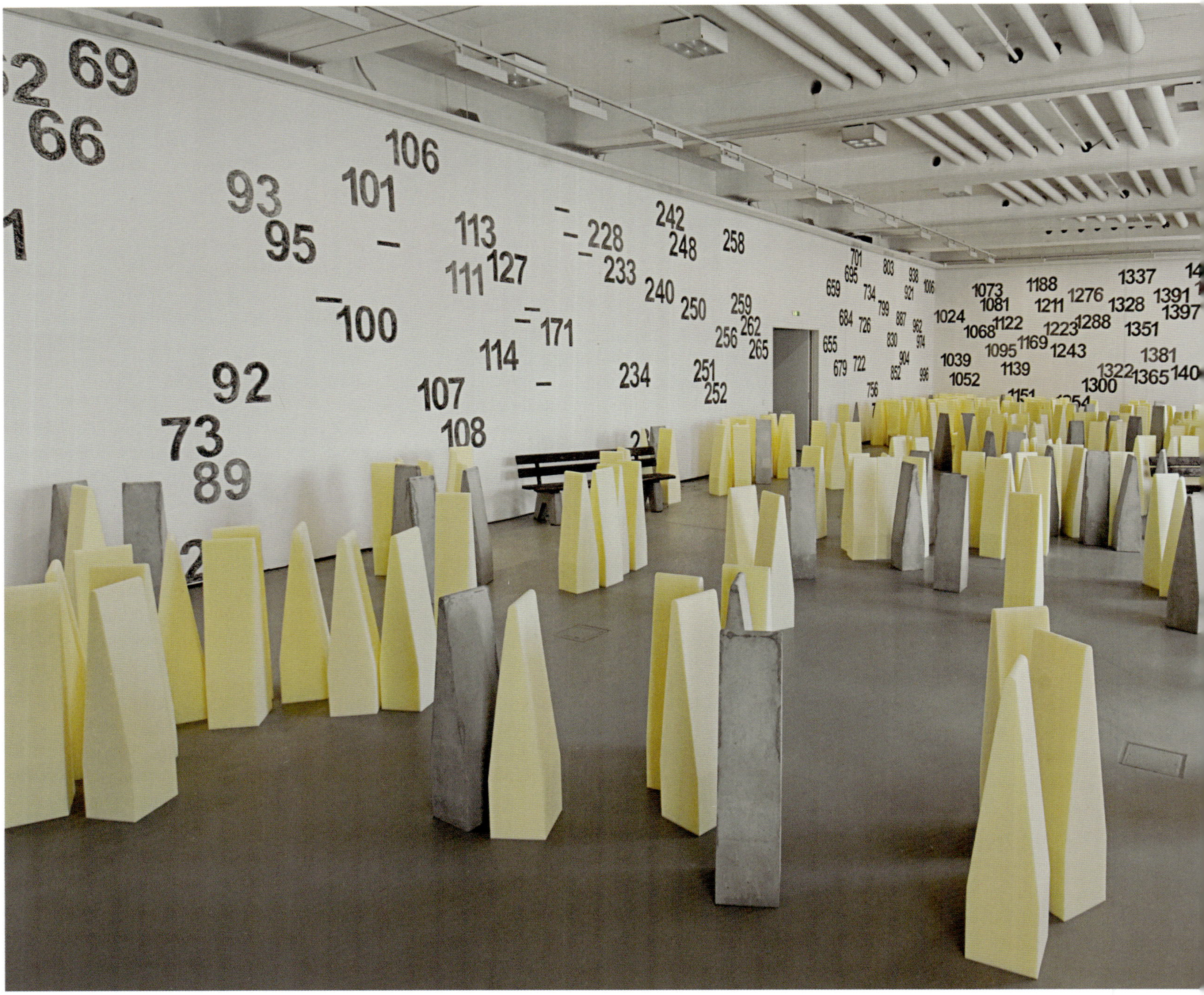

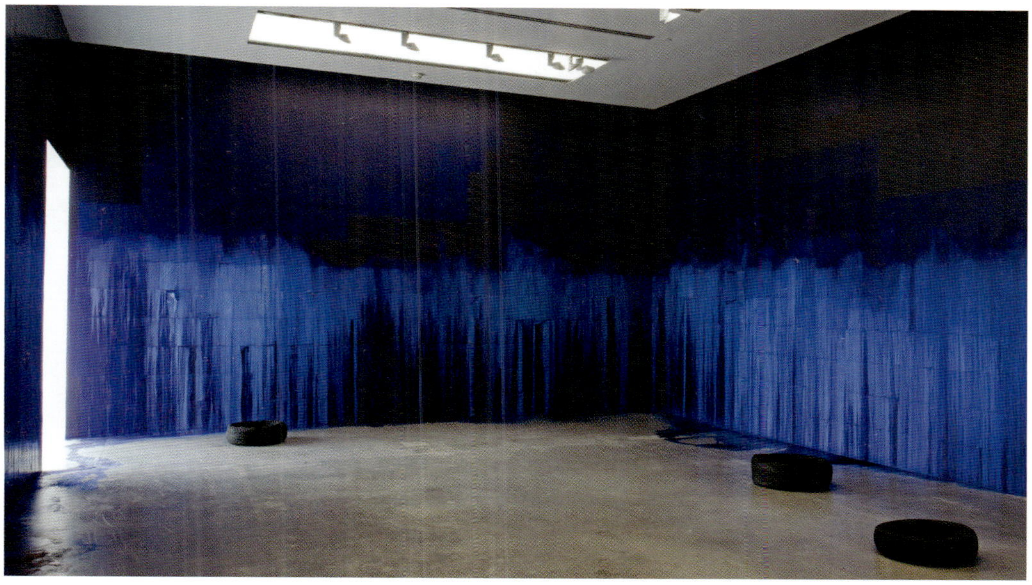

A chaque stencil une révolution (For Each Stencil a Revolution)
2007
A4 carbon paper, glue, and methylated alcohol
Dimensions variable
Installation view, Tate Modern, London
Courtesy kaufmann repetto

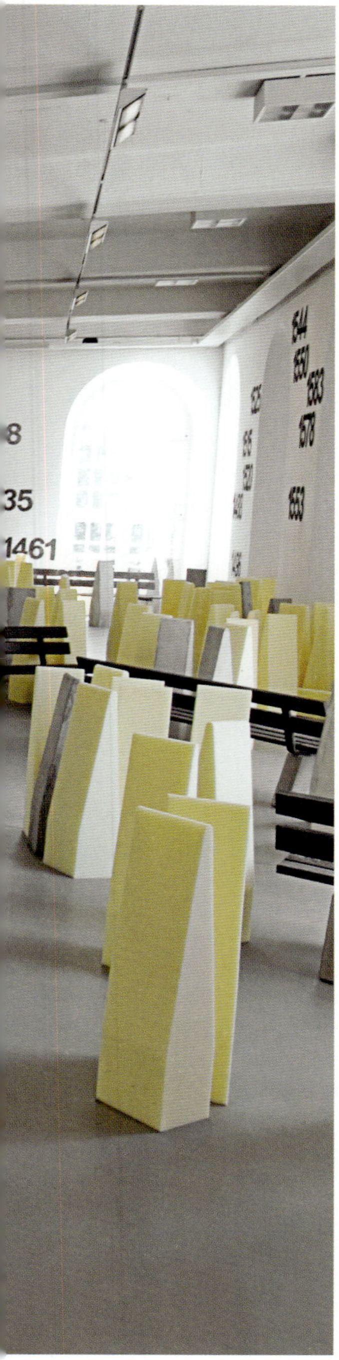

Alemani In other works, you have invited the viewer to re-examine a familiar object that is unexpectedly presented to us in an idiosyncratic context. Can you talk about this strategy of displacement?

Echakhch This idea of strangeness is a central point in my interest in art, and I often accentuate it by using objects that you can recognize easily, placing them in situations or environments where you wouldn't normally expect to find them. There is no mystery, no idea of genius, or extraordinary ability in the objects' making. Doing this leaves only a few gaps for aesthetic fascination, so one can go directly to questioning the object itself and the context in which it is found.

Alemani This is not your first public work. For "ILLUMInations" at the 54th Venice Biennale in 2011, you presented an installation of several flagpoles in the Giardini in front of the Italian Pavilion. How does your work change when presented outdoors, in a public space?

Echakhch There aren't that many differences, but conservation, sun damage, and risk of wind all come into play. On the island, the fragility of the installation is the opposite of the *Fantasia* (2011) installation in the Giardini in Venice. Maybe the fact that the work is outdoors accentuates the idea of landscape. In an indoor exhibition, it's about the building of a landscape, as a viewer you can almost forget the objects and become completely absorbed as you walk through the installation itself, and then be surprised again when you step back and see the installation as a whole.

Alemani Your work often seems to exist between physical sculptural presence and its dissolution: I am thinking of a work like *Erratum* (2004–9), in which you smashed several Moroccan tea glasses against the gallery wall. Can you talk about this polarity?

Echakhch The difference is between the gesture and its meaning. First, the sculptural installation is aesthetic—contemplative—and it's mostly about color, materiality, and space. One can also recompose the temporality of the gesture; the how, the why, and what is behind its intention.

Alemani Your work seems to hover between a very poetic approach and a deep political involvement. How do you reconcile these two elements in your work?

Echakhch Poetry is a system of feelings, but also an end in itself. It can be so easy to construct but also so difficult to find, because there is nothing more fragile than the poetry around us. In the same way, I consider the political in an art work as a layer of understanding that could easily be ignored, like it often is in society. But because there is so much around us, in history and in other objects or images, it has to carry a kind of necessity. I just organize, in different ways, how one edits, perceives, and considers these two layers in the installations I make; from there the viewer is free to take it as far as they want.

Joel Kyack

Joel Kyack brings the country fair to Frieze New York, with a performative, participatory installation that invites visitors to try their luck and win a prize—an art work.

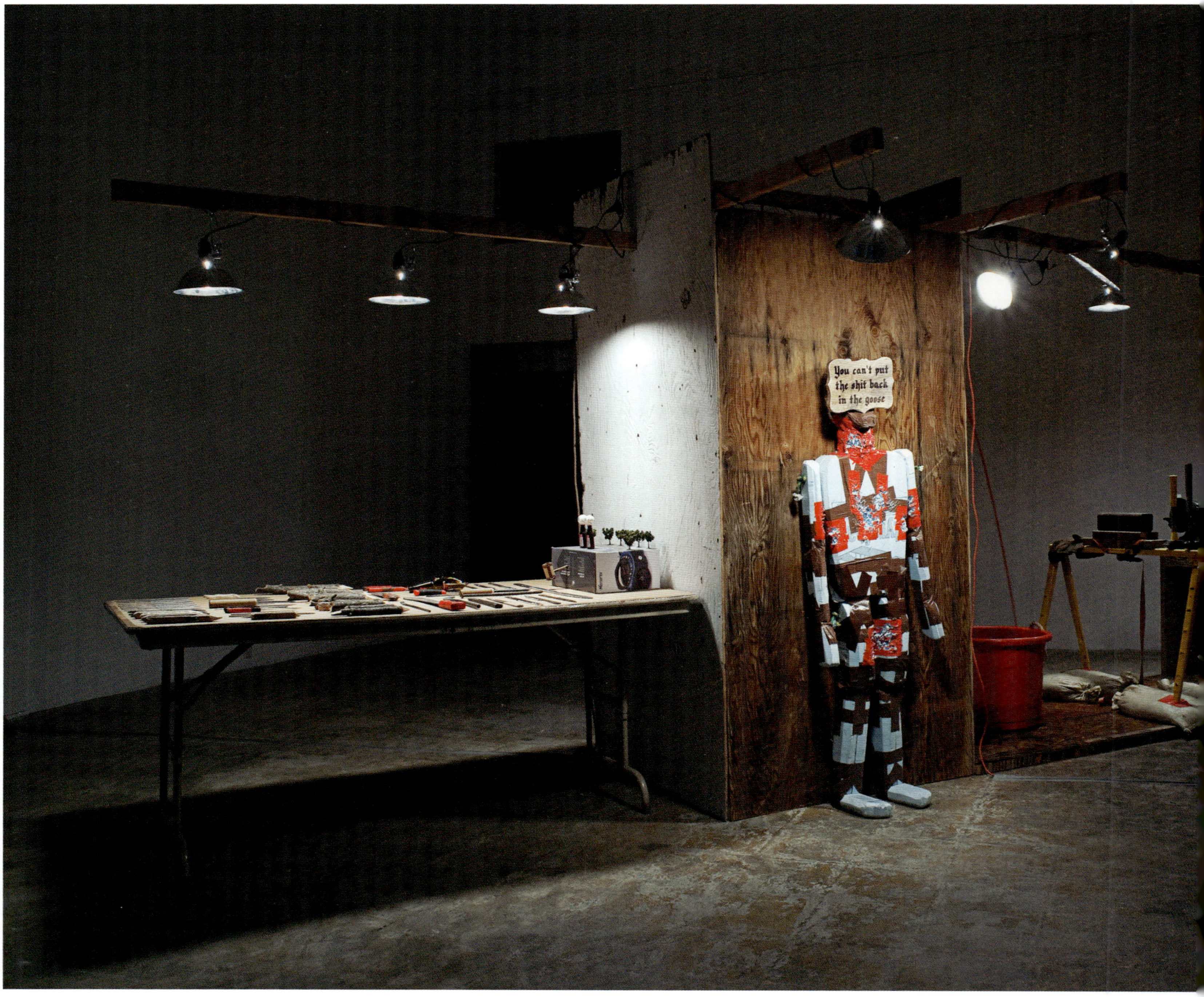

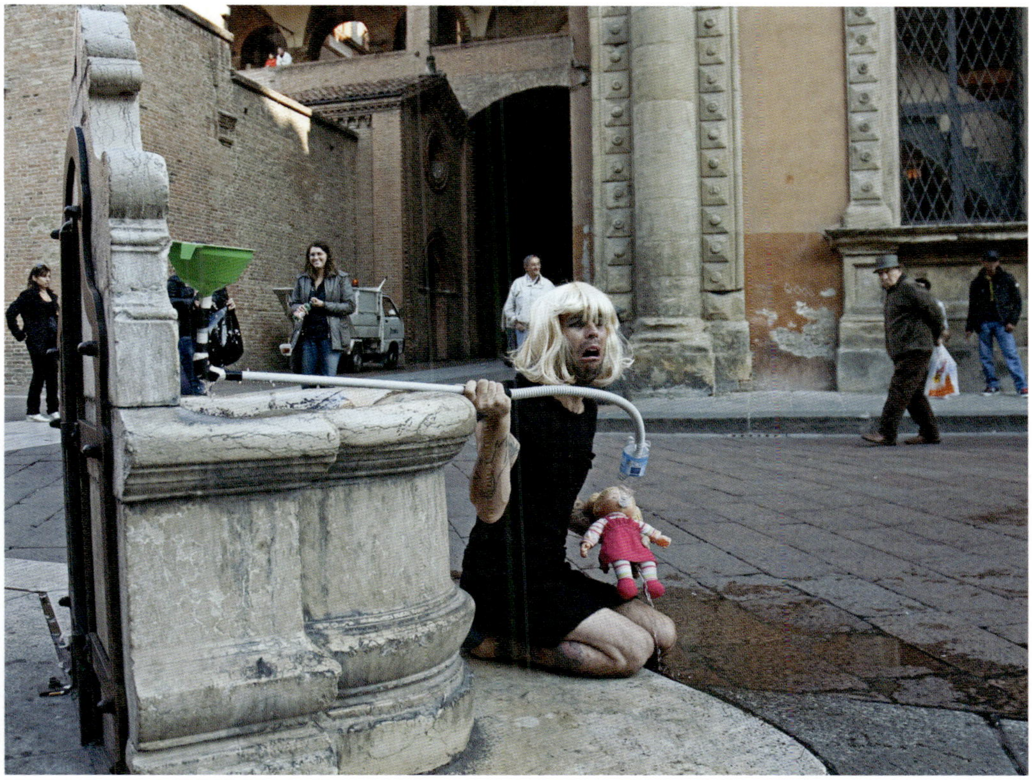

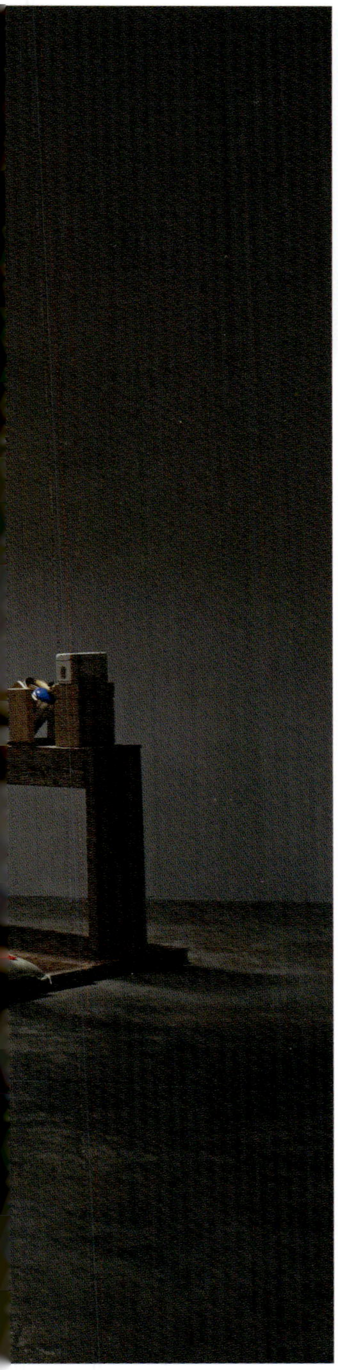

Left:
Crossing the Line
2010
Performance at
Fontana di Nettuno,
Bologna
Mixed media
Dimensions variable
Courtesy of Brand
New Gallery

Opposite:
The Knife Shop
2009
Mixed media
276 × 96 × 60"
(701 × 244 × 152.5 cm)
Courtesy of François
Ghebaly

Joel Kyack is an American sculptor and performance artist based in Los Angeles. In 2011 he had the solo shows "Escape to Shit Mountain," at François Ghebaly Gallery, Los Angeles; "River / Stream / In-Between," at Kate Werble Gallery, New York; and in 2010 he mounted the exhibition "Superclogger," at the Hammer Museum, Los Angeles. He has a forthcoming solo show at Brand New Gallery, Milan, in 2012.

Cecilia Alemani Your commission for Frieze Projects is a country fair style game trailer. Can you talk about the genesis of this work and how it relates to your personal history?

Joel Kyack *Most games are lost, not won* (2012), inserts a different model of "fair" into the art fair setting. The game booth at a country fair is already wonderfully interdisciplinary—sculpture, painting, installation, and performance. I have long been drawn to doing something with one because I already enjoy the combination of those media. I realized quickly that the invitation from Frieze Projects was the perfect opportunity to make this piece, and I began thinking about the work functioning in an art fair context as an experiential counterpoint, a leveler. The booth is free, and any attendee of the fair can participate, with occasional luck being disproportionately rewarded with works of art as prizes. It distorts the mechanics of the art fair booth by introducing the element of chance into acquisition. It's a place where money, reputation, and connection provide no advantage. When I was growing up, my family was involved in the country fair that came to our town every year. We ran a three-game booth trailer, and my father was one of the organizers of the event. I felt it was a complex stage to construct and perform on, so I'm here exploring those possibilities.

Alemani What kind of dynamics do you want to create between you, the trailer, and the viewer?

Kyack I guess my ideal would be something of a cross between an authentic country-fair game experience and an art performance/installation. This is an environment where the odds are stacked against the viewer, yet I want him or her to

"If they win, they leave with art, as they would in the art fair if they decided to acquire something."

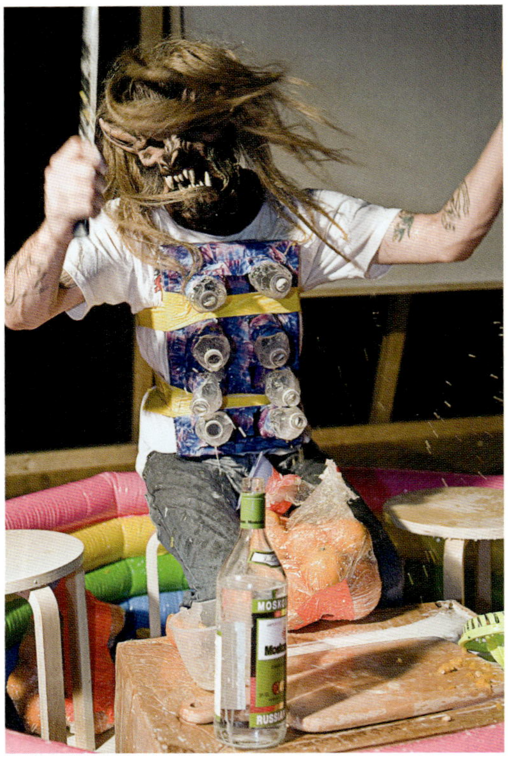

Growing Pains Leave Stains
2011
Performance
Kaleidoscope ARENA, Macro Testaccio, Rome, mixed media
Courtesy of Kaleidoscope

still feel compelled to play. That will be the responsibility of the installation and performer to create that space. If they win, they leave with art, as they would in the art fair if they decided to acquire something. But winning art in a game of chance is a very different experience from buying it. I want the dynamic to reflect this obvious difference.

Alemani It seems that themes of chance and failure are integral parts of this project. Do these concepts play an important role in your work?

Kyack Yes. If chance and failure are, as I see it, fundamental to all experience, then they become places of connection, spaces of use, they reference some elemental part in us all. I like to use that. They're both a bit scary, or rather exciting, perhaps, and that's good too.

Alemani This is not your first public art work. In 2010, you realized one of your most well-known art works, *Superclogger*, in Los Angeles. Can you talk about that with particular regard to how the piece interacted with the audience in the public sphere?

Kyack *Superclogger* interacted with an unsuspecting audience on their turf—in their vehicles, gridlocked on the congested freeway. The piece consisted of a series of four puppet plays that took place in the back of a capped pickup truck. A sign directed motorists to tune in to a particular radio station to hear the soundtracks to the play. It became a performance *en route*, where the work came to the viewer even though the viewer was actually "nowhere." They watched something visual happening outside of their car, while they listened to the audio inside, on their car radio. The same ompartmentalization of experience will happen with *Most games are lost, not won* as well —the installation inside the booth and the performance of the "carnies," the gaze of the non-participant viewer from outside the booth, and the exchange that happens at its lip when a viewer becomes a player.

Alemani Throughout your work there is a recurrent theme connected to the tradition of Americana. How do you relate with the history of your own country and how to you integrate it in your work?

Kyack I relate to it with requisite ambivalence and good boots. I integrate it the same way.

Alemani Often your sculptures depict grotesque human bodies, partly mutilated and almost decaying. Do you feel any affinity with the tradition of the American grotesque, as seen in the work of Mike Kelley and Paul McCarthy?

Kyack Without a doubt, especially McCarthy. His raw energy in performance and object making, and I find his embrace of the *base* is very intense. The first piece of contemporary art that really shook me was an image I saw when I was 18 from the performance *Death Ship* (1981). For me, then, he was opening a space to communicate our most basic guarantees—our lives will end, things will change and fall apart. Making this sort of work is a celebration of those guarantees.

Alemani In previous performances, you pushed your own body to the extreme of

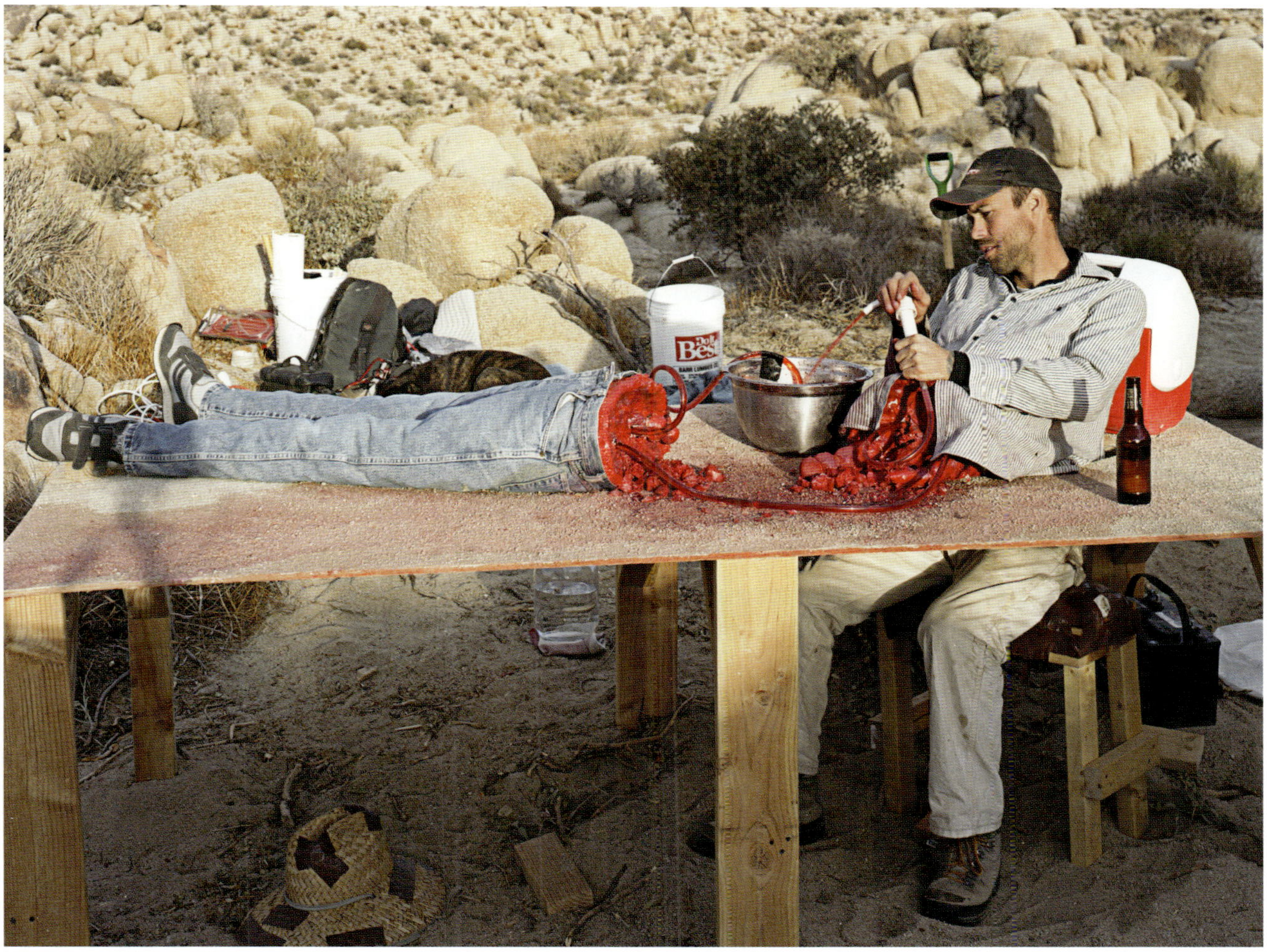

Left:
Incident at Stoney Lake
Mixed media
72 × 79 × 60"
(183 × 201 × 152.5 cm)
Courtesy of François Ghebaly

Below:
Superclogger
2010
Performance on various highways, Los Angeles
Mixed media
Dimensions variable
Courtesy of François Ghebaly, LA><ART, and The Hammer Museum

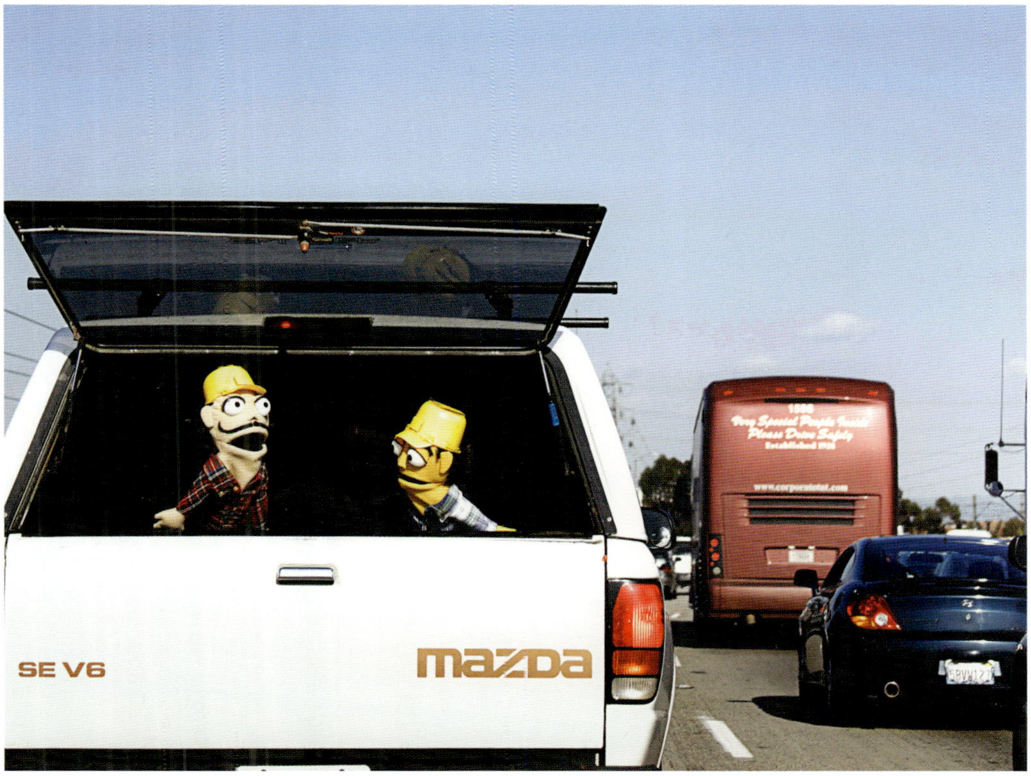

physical and mental exhaustion. How do you translate this aspect into sculptures or installations?

Kyack I try to employ an energetic style of object making or performance that is defined by an overall lack of refinement in construction and material selection. I'm interested in materials of thrift and convenience, and I want to see a hand in their manipulation. I want the viewer to feel as though the work was finished five minutes before they arrived, that they're seeing it in its raw workings, just discovered, no edges yet smoothed. Objects need to retain a visceral sense if they are to set themselves apart from other objects, mass-produced ones. An object that values itself is already dead.

Rick Moody

Novelist and writer Rick Moody is the first non-artist to contribute to Frieze Projects—Curator Cecilia Alemani finds out what we have in store.

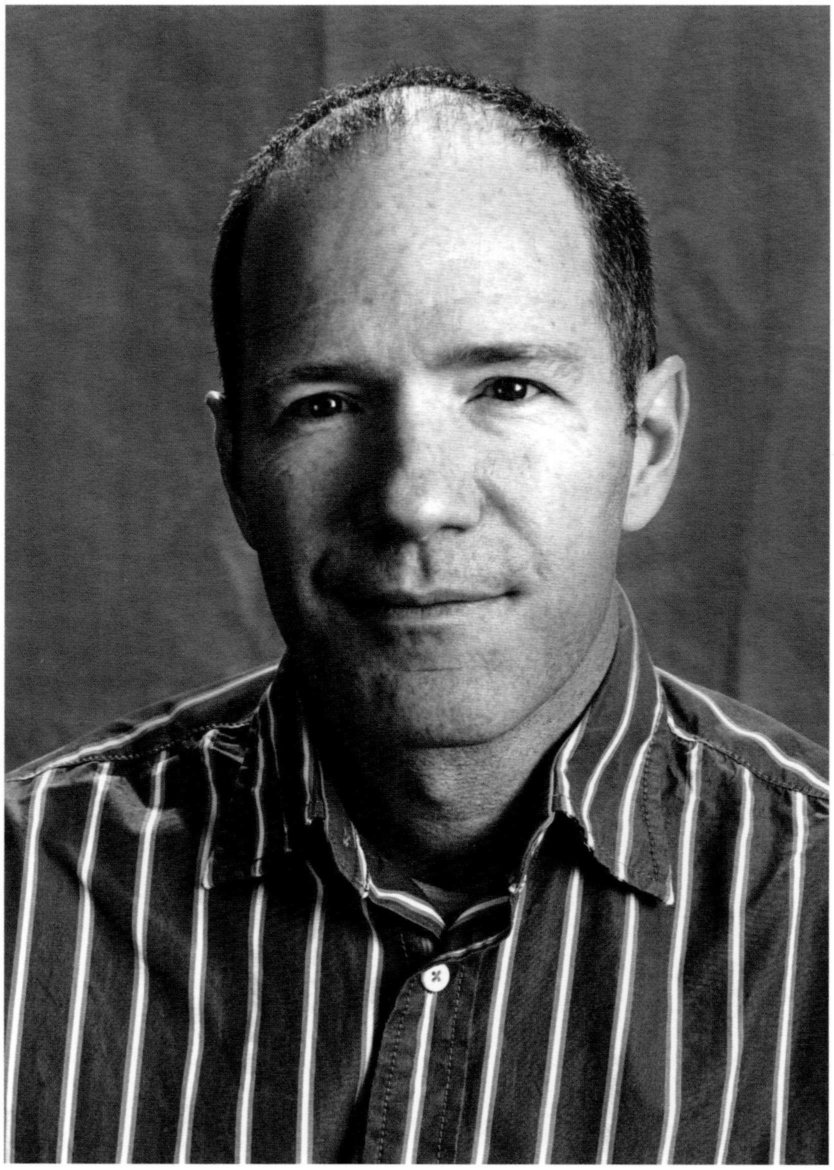

Photograph: ©Don J. Usner

Cecilia Alemani Can you describe your project for Frieze New York?

Rick Moody I'm working on a prototype for an "undependable global positioning device," one which will definitely get the user lost, and will, in the process, force the user to concentrate on the poetical parts of being lost, and on the sense of place, on the here and now, rather than on the intermediary states, the sites through which one must negligently pass, in order to reach a destination. This device is anti-destination. It is in favor of being lost. The prototype will have three phases: 1) a purely textual (literary) phase; 2) an audio phase, in which the text is read by a simulated human voice; and 3) a "real" physical prototype of the "undependable" GPS device. The last phase and much of the conceptual thinking are being coordinated with a really great digital artist acquaintance of mine, Greg Cole. He is the brains of the operation. I am the poetical, and thus wholly undependable, portion.

Alemani Where do you live? Do you go around New York often?

Moody Brooklyn. Yes, I go around New York. And New York goes around in me.

Alemani How does New York City inspire your writings (if it does)?

Moody New York City inspires me in so many ways that it would be impossible to enumerate them all. Sometimes its inspiration is in specific places (as in my novel *The Diviners (2005)*, some of which takes place in Brooklyn and Manhattan), but more often it is the sense of what urban culture is, which for me is derived from having lived here for almost 30 years now. Of the cities I have seen, I know New York best, and I love and revere it, its velocity, its skepticism, its profound enthusiasms, its pluralities, its mystery, its grunge, its impatience. New York is many cities, many places, many peoples, most of them disinclined to put up with bullshit and timidity. These aspects of city life have informed much that I do.

Alemani Alongside your literary production, you have also been writing lyrics and playing music. What kind of role does music play in your creative thinking? What music do you listen to? Does music influence your writing?

Moody Music makes me a better listener to the sounds of the world, and being a better listener makes me a better writer, because writing, after all, is a variety of soundmaking—the type of soundmaking called utterance. So, music is very central to what I do, and always has been. I listen to all kinds of music, but I especially prize experimental "new" music, jazz, and the furthest fringes of rock and roll. Right now, as this very moment: Ravi Shankar.

Alemani What is your favorite depiction of New York in fiction?

Moody *The Recognitions* (1955), by William Gaddis.

Alemani There is an amusing part of your website called "Rick Moody, Life Coach," in which you answer letters from anyone who has life problems. How did you come up with this idea, and what do you get out of it?

Moody I came up with it because my mother always told me I should have another plan in case all this creative stuff went south. It still could all go south, you never know. So I just decided to hang out a shingle as a "Life Coach," because you don't need as many degrees to be a life coach. Also I think fucking up one's own life in many ways is good training for a career as a life coach, and I have assuredly done so now and again. Also: Life Coachery is for people who listen well. I try to listen well.

Rick Moody (b. 1961) is an American writer and novelist based in New York. In 2010, Little, Brown and Company, published *The Four Fingers of Death*. Other novels include: *The Diviners* (2005), *Purple America* (1996), *The Ice Storm* (1994), and *Garden State* (1992). His non-fiction title *The Black Veil: A Memoir with Digressions* (2002) recounts a telling self-portrait.

Virginia Overton

Virginia Overton's sculptural installations mix the absurd with unconventional beauty in works that are simultaneously familiar yet rendered in strange arrangements and compositions.

Virginia Overton (b. 1971) is an American sculptor based in New York. In early 2012 she had solo exhibitions at The Power Station, Dallas, and The Kitchen, New York. Recent group shows include "Shake and Bake," at Praz-Delavallade, Paris (2012), and "Impossible Vacation," at White Flag Projects, St. Louis (2011). She has a forthcoming solo show at Mitchell-Innes & Nash, New York, in 2012.

Cecilia Alemani Can you talk about the project you are planning to exhibit at Frieze New York?

Virginia Overton I'm planning on wedging sheets of acrylic mirror into the "Ys" of a cluster of trees in the grounds of Randall's Island.

Alemani How does the site of Randall's Island inspire you?

Overton It's nice to have the chance to make outdoor sculpture. And Randall's Island is unique in that it's part of New York, but it's a place that no one ever goes to—kind of a no man's land. So it feels like both part of the city and an undiscovered spot. It would be a great place to make a movie.

Alemani When is the first time you used acrylic mirrors in your work?

Overton I used them seven or eight years ago in a temporary outdoor sculpture in Tennessee. The pieces of acrylic mirror were so expensive that I kept them stored in a barn down there, and when I eventually brought my truck up to New York, I loaded them up and brought them too. I've been reusing them ever since.

Alemani Is there a relationship with Robert Smithson and his *Non-Sites* project?

Overton Not directly. The mirrored Plexiglas, by way of its materiality, reflects the space around it, and so as I install it at Randall's Island, it will reflect the Island's natural space, but it will just as easily reflect an indoor space if I move it inside. The things that I make are coming from a point of exercising the materials that I have at hand; seeing how I can use the material, seeing what the material will do … trying new configurations.

Alemani You usually use very simple, almost industrial materials in your work,

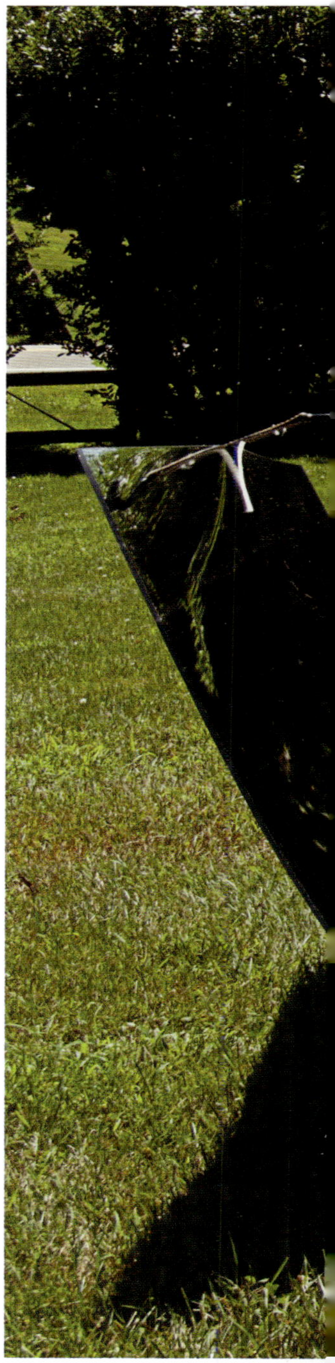

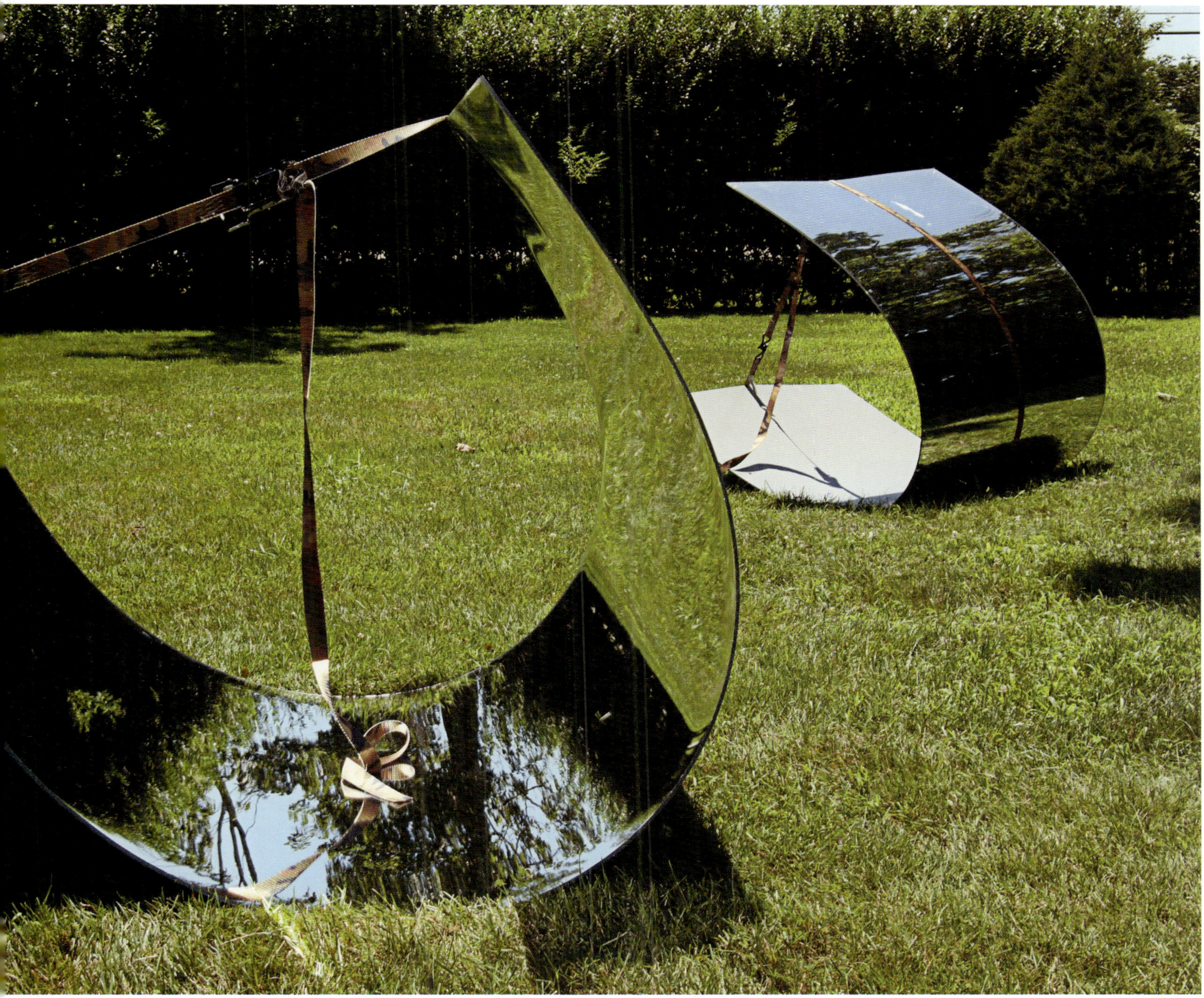

Untitled (Convex)
(foreground) and
Untitled (Concave)
(background)
2011
Acrylic mirror and
ratchet straps
Dimensions variable
Courtesy of Martos
Gallery

“I gather impressions and thoughts of the place, space, and time in which the work will exist. So, in that way, it is site-specific, but it’s also time-specific.”

Untitled (color)
2011
Lightbox construction, acrylic, and inkjet print on paper
35⅝ × 23⅝ × 6¼"
(90.5 × 60 × 16 cm)
Courtesy Mitchell-Innes & Nash

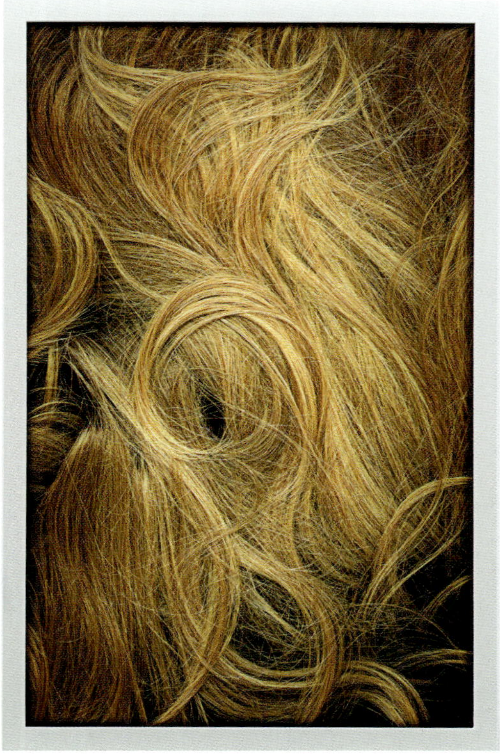

such as wooden beams, construction materials, and plaster. Can you tell me about how you choose these elements and what do they mean for you?

Overton They are what I like, and they are easy to come by. I can even find them on the side of the road. This makes them really cost effective. But it also means that I can be thinking about my work even when I’m at the hardware store getting some part sto fix my bathroom sink.

Alemani Something that I always found really exciting about your work is the sense of scale. Often it seems that your work is trying to compete with the existing architecture or environment. I’m thinking, for instance, of the big triangle you did for Mitchell-Innes & Nash (*Untitled (Triangle)*, 2010). Can you talk about the relationship between your work and the surrounding architecture?

Overton It’s not really about competition, it’s more about fitting. I want the work to make sense in the space that is available to me/it. That can mean that a single piece takes on a crazy scale, like the triangle piece you mentioned, or it can mean that a fluorescent light fixture gets a simple covering to change its function in the room.

Alemani Have you often worked outdoors? How is that different from a more classical gallery environment?

Overton I’ve worked outdoors a little, but it’s usually just for myself, or a very limited audience. The outdoors is varied and organic. Classical galleries are homogeneous and systematic.

Alemani Having worked with you on other occasions, it seems that you have a very intuitive approach to your projects. Can you describe your process of working? Do you usually plan the project fully before you start? Are your ideas very site-specific?

Overton I rarely plan out a project fully in advance. It’s more like just gathering impressions and thoughts of the place, space, and time in which the work will exist. So, in that way, it is site-specific, but it’s also time-specific.

Alemani Despite the seemingly masculine look of your work, there is always something slightly sensual that runs as a *fil rouge* throughout it. I am thinking of works such as the lightbox containing a close-up of your blond hair (*Untitled (Color)*, 2011), or the use of reflective mirrors. How do you negotiate and reconcile these two extremes?

Overton They don’t really feel like they need to be reconciled. They just exist like any two things that may seem opposite. Though, I think in this case, they aren’t that different at all.

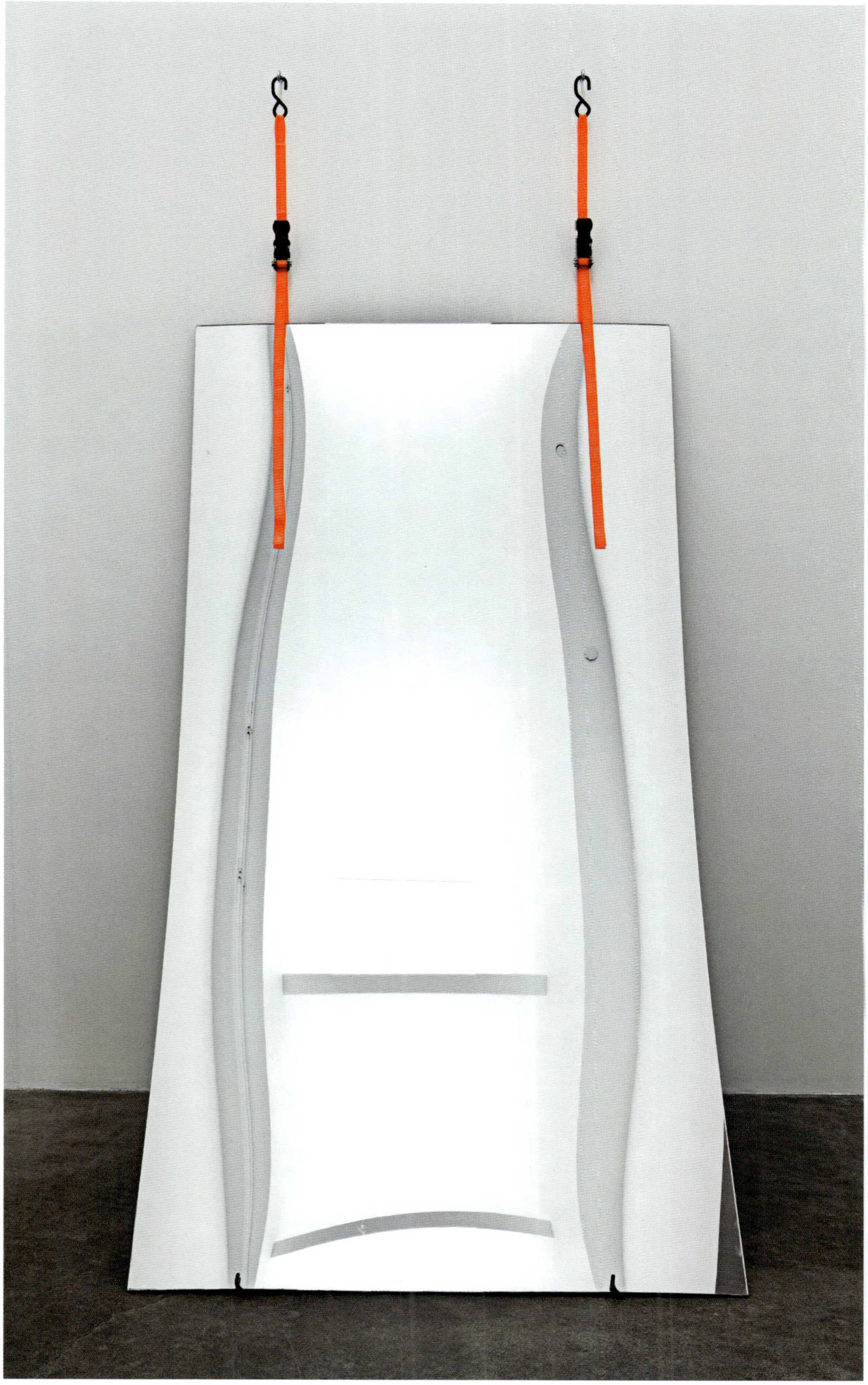

Left:
Untitled (Echo)
2011
Acrylic mirror and ratchet straps
Dimensions variable
Courtesy of Mitchell-Innes & Nash

Below:
Untitled (truck with mirror)
2010
Digital print
Courtesy Mitchell-Innes & Nash

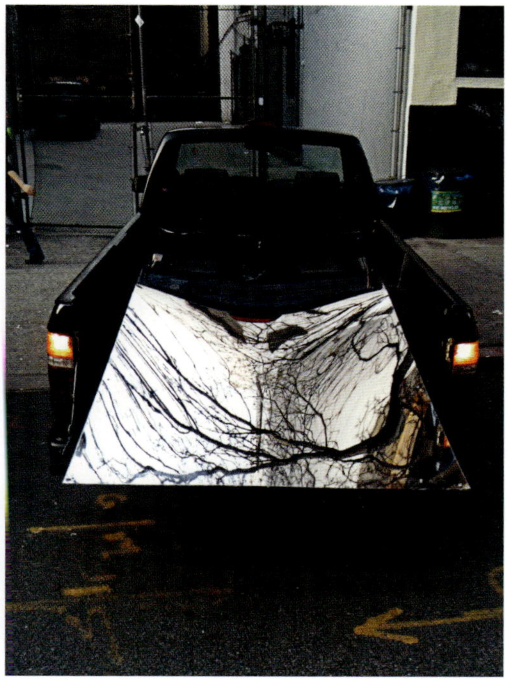

Tim Rollins and K.O.S.

Tim Rollins' collaboration with Kids of Survival (K.O.S.) is an ongoing relationship spanning three decades—and a new venture is planned for Frieze New York.

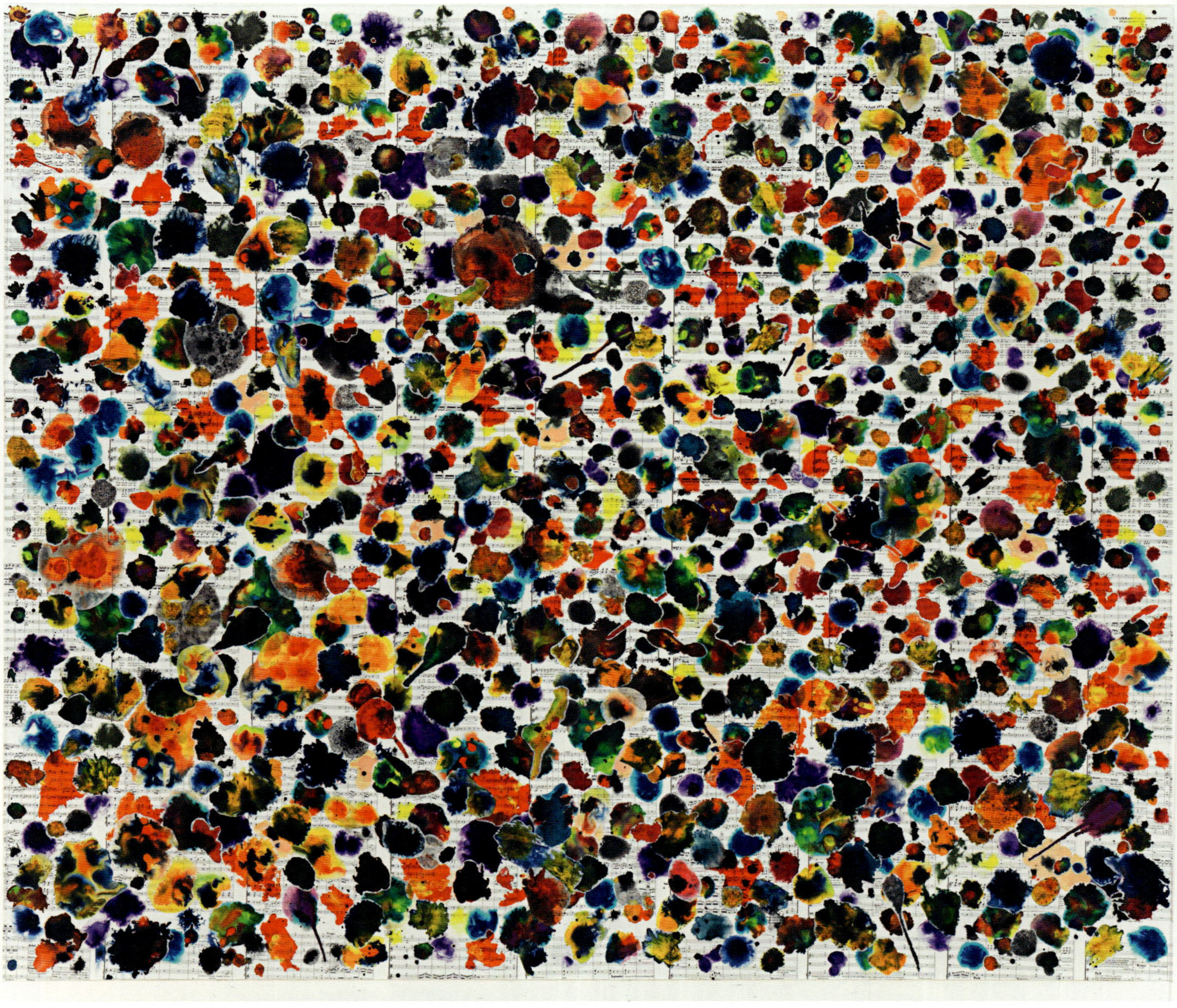

“We are building a beloved community through the collective creation of art. I think our most important political contribution has been to create a new model for education throughout the world.”

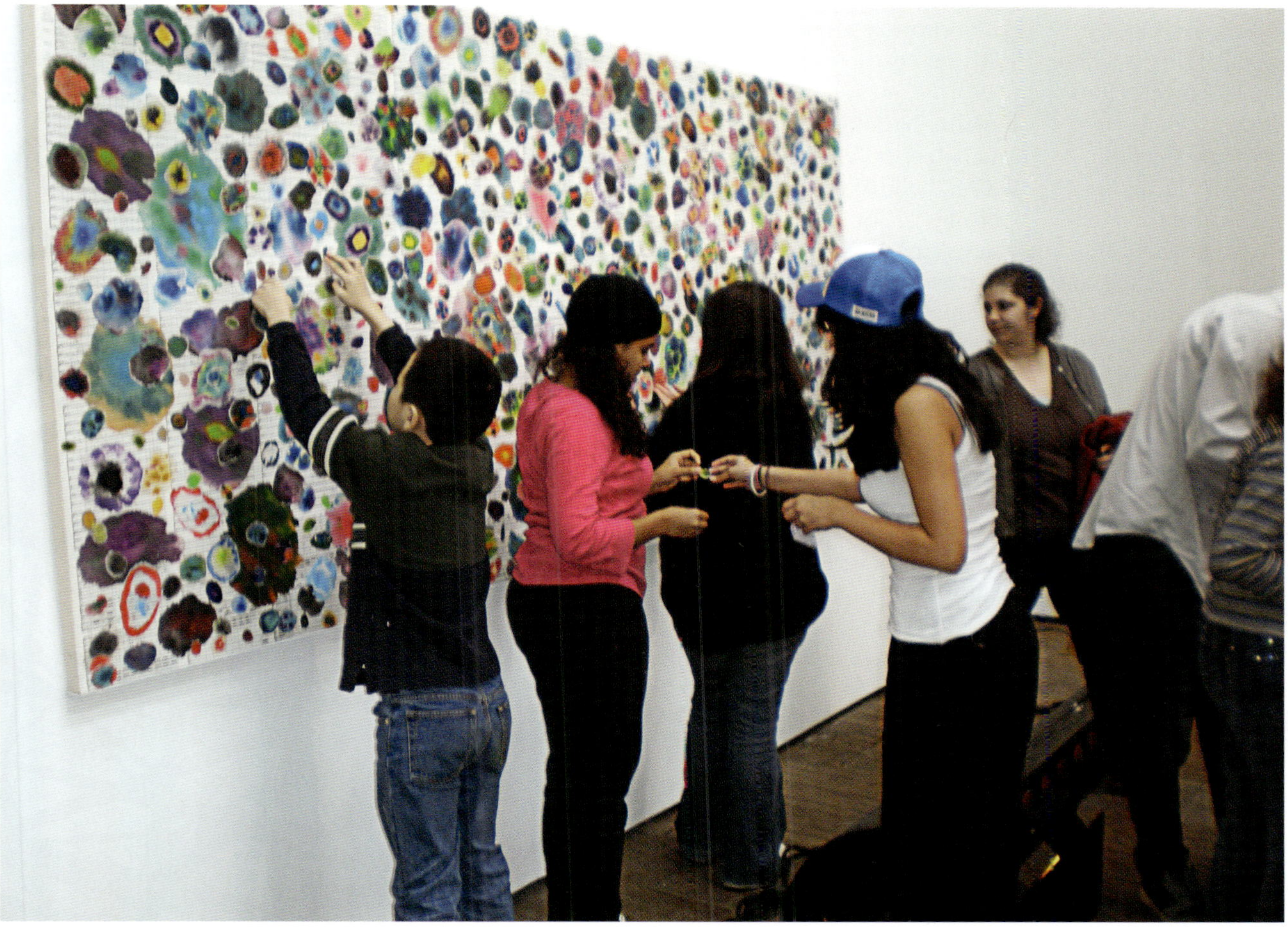

A Midsummer Night's Dream (after Shakespeare and Mendelssohn)
2008
watercolor, acrylic and india ink, abaca and mulberry paper, collage, mustard seed, offset music score on paper on canvas
60 × 156"
(152.4 × 396.24 cm)
In collaboration with neighborhood youth from the Henry Street Settlement House
Courtesy of Lehmann Maupin Gallery

Left:
A Midsummer Night's Dream (after Shakespeare and Mendelssohn)
2011
Watercolor, india and acrylic inks, Thai mulberry paper, collage, mustard seed, and offset lithography on music score pages on canvas
60 × 72"
(152.5 × 183 cm)
Courtesy of Lehmann Maupin Gallery

Tim Rollins and K.O.S. (b. 1955) is an American artist who has been working collaborativley with K.O.S. in New York, since 1984. In early 2012, an exhibition of their work was held at Kunstmuseum Basel, and a forthcoming exhibition will take place at Talbot Rice Gallery, Edinburgh. In 2011, solo shows took place at Galleria d'Arte Moderna e Contemporanea, Bergamo, and Lehmann Maupin, New York.

Cecilia Alemani Your commission for Frieze Projects is the first open workshop for children and youth that you'll organize in the public realm. How do you prepare for a project like this?

Tim Rollins The key is to partner with organizations or individuals familiar with youth, schools, or programs that have experience in these sort of collaborations and would be enthusiastic and appreciative collaborators. In this case, K.O.S. hopes to work with RIK (Randall's Island Kids, who serve kids from the East Harlem and South Bronx neighborhoods of New York City). But, of course, any young person who wants to jump in will be welcome.

Alemani The title of your project is *A Midsummer Night's Dream (after Shakespeare and Mendelssohn)*. Why did you choose such literary and musical references?

Rollins We believe that the central character of Shakespeare's rather twisted comedy is Puck. Puck is a creature who loves to create transformations just for the sheer, impish joy of it. He is the paradigm of the artist and a role model especially for kids, who like to conjure up things in material. In the case of the workshop, I ask the kids to invent their own magic flowers—elements in watercolor on Mulberry paper—hundreds of them. These bizarre but beautiful blossoms should look like they possess a nectar that, when squeezed on the eyelids of some sleeping someone, will make them fall madly in love with the first living creature they see upon awakening. We use Mendelssohn's *Midsummer Night's Dream* music because we like the idea that he began the composition when he was only 16 years old. That's inspiring for young folk.

Alemani How do you think the live/performative element will impact the viewer experience?

Rollins Conducting the K.O.S. project for 30 years now, I still find it surprising that many just can't figure out how we make the paintings we do. They are very curious about the process, and so here is an opportunity to see our team in action working live and in person.

Alemani Music always plays a crucial role in your work. Can you talk about it?

Rollins I doubt Studio K.O.S. would have existed without the influence of Leonard Bernstein's Young People's Orchestra, without someone like John Cage, who we knew well and was close to our hearts, without someone like the Rev. James Cleveland and all the black gospel mass choirs he organized all across the US, without the emergence of hip hop in our South Bronx neighborhood in the early 1980s. Without jazz. More than the music itself is the improvisational and group process that produces the sounds. We're like a choir, but we sing with our paintings.

Alemani Can you speak about the relationship between music and drawing in your work?

Rollins The music inspires and directs the drawing. We are not trying to replicate the sounds and rhythms of the music. We want to make the feeling of the music visual.

Alemani Since the very beginning of your practice, your work has been based on collaboration. How has the very concept of collaboration shifted—if it has—from the 1980s, when you started working, to now?

Rollins No, the collaboration has become much deeper. You see, several members of K.O.S. began with the studio when they were 11, 12, or 13 years old, in the '80s. They remain vitally involved with the team as adults. We've become a very strong family, while still recruiting new members as young as ten. The conceptualization, research, development and realization of the art work are far more shared now, which is thrilling.

Alemani Your work has always had a great deal of political content. Can you talk about your interest in history and how your work speaks of current events?

Rollins Actually very few of our series display overt socio-political protest imagery (our "ANIMAL FARM" works being the obvious and hilarious exceptions). Our work is political by the very nature of its making. It's made WITH people … not "the people" as an ideological construct. We work as a collection of individuals—usually youth from distressed neighborhoods. We are building a beloved community through the collective creation of art. I think our most important political contribution has been to create a new model for education throughout the world. For our folk, art becomes a means to a higher, broader knowledge.

Alemani Do you see your work as a form of pedagogy for the public and/or for your collaborators?

Rollins All I can say is that with the success of K.O.S., folk can no longer claim that "it can't be done." The cynics need to take a walk at this point.

Alemani What is the most important lesson you have learned as an artist?

Rollins Art is Love.

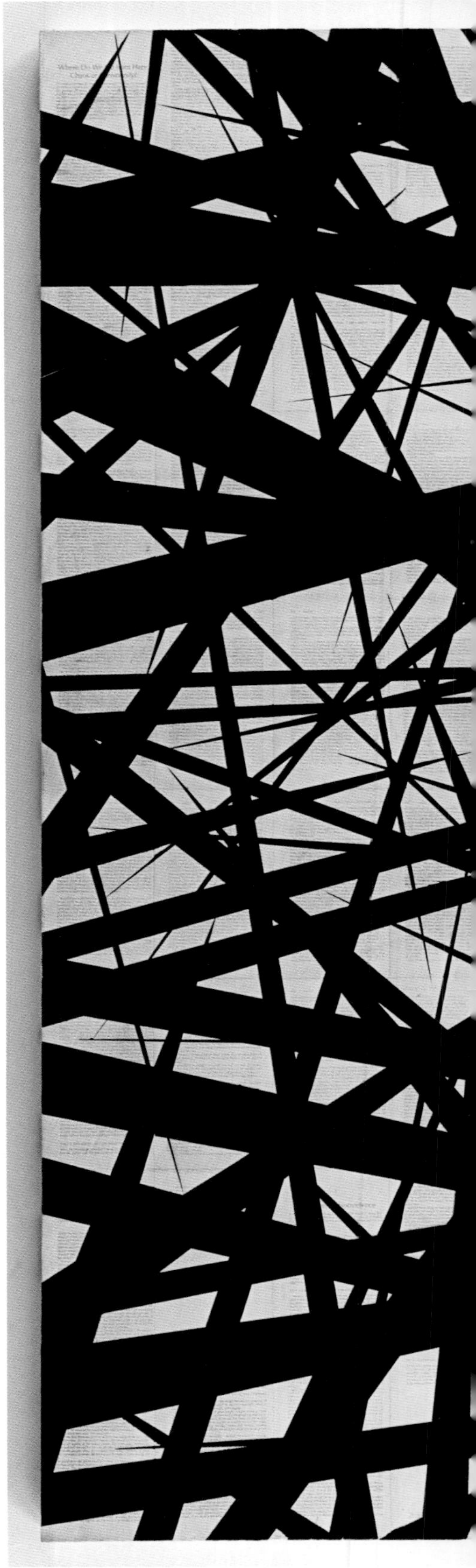

Where Do We Go
From Here
2008
Matte acrylic and book
pages on canvas
72 × 96"
(183 × 244 cm)
Courtesy of Lehmann
Maupin Gallery

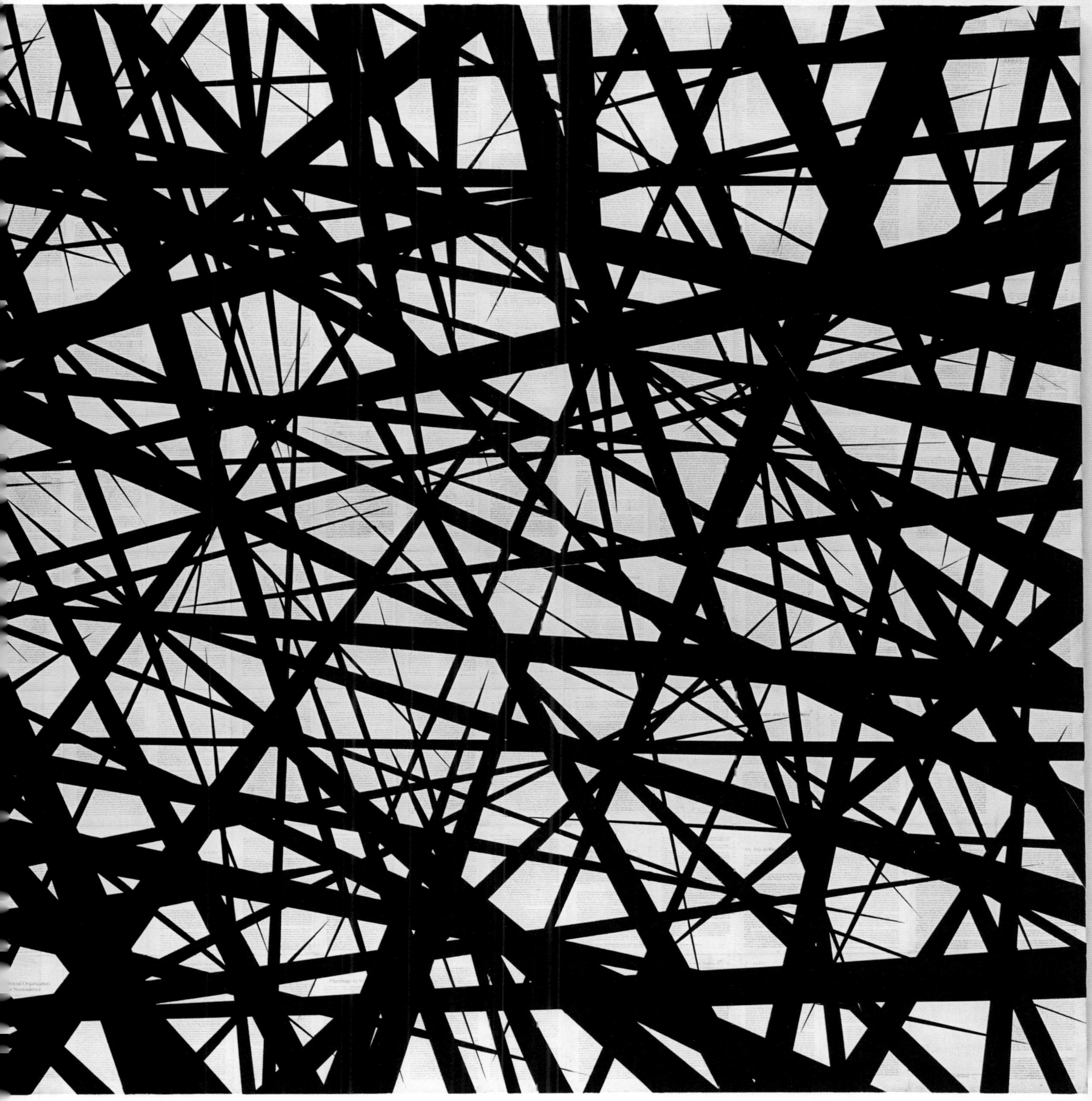

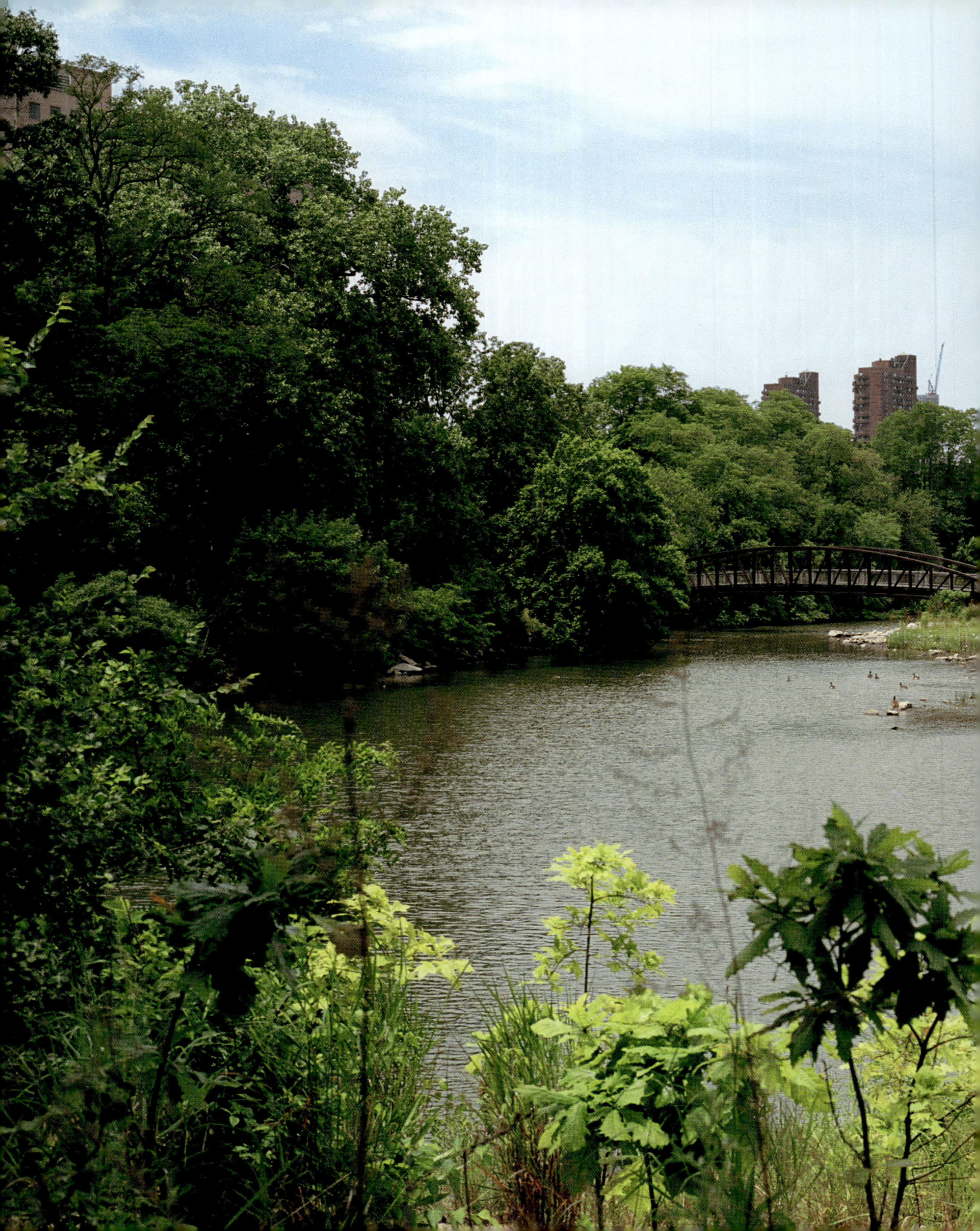

Artists

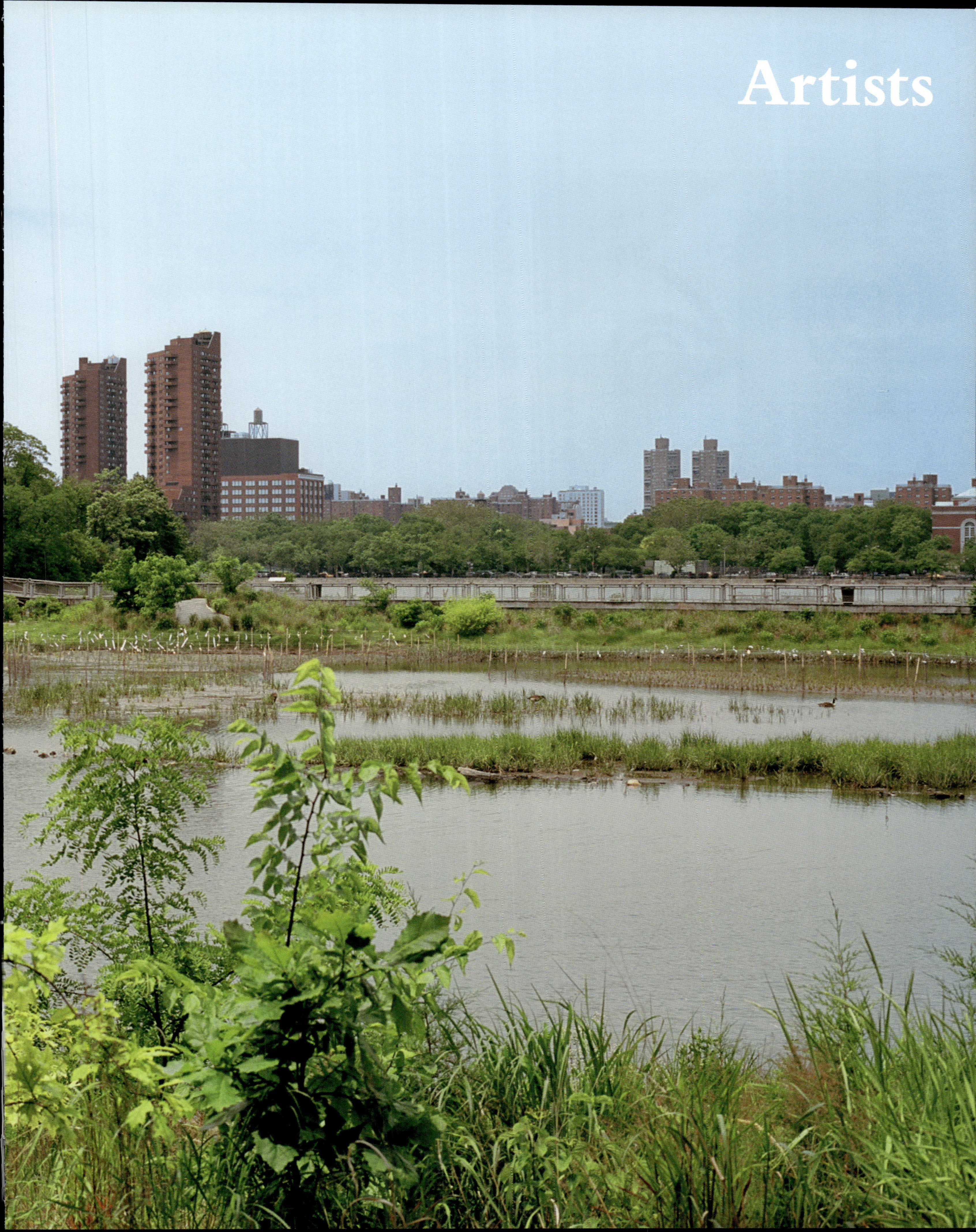

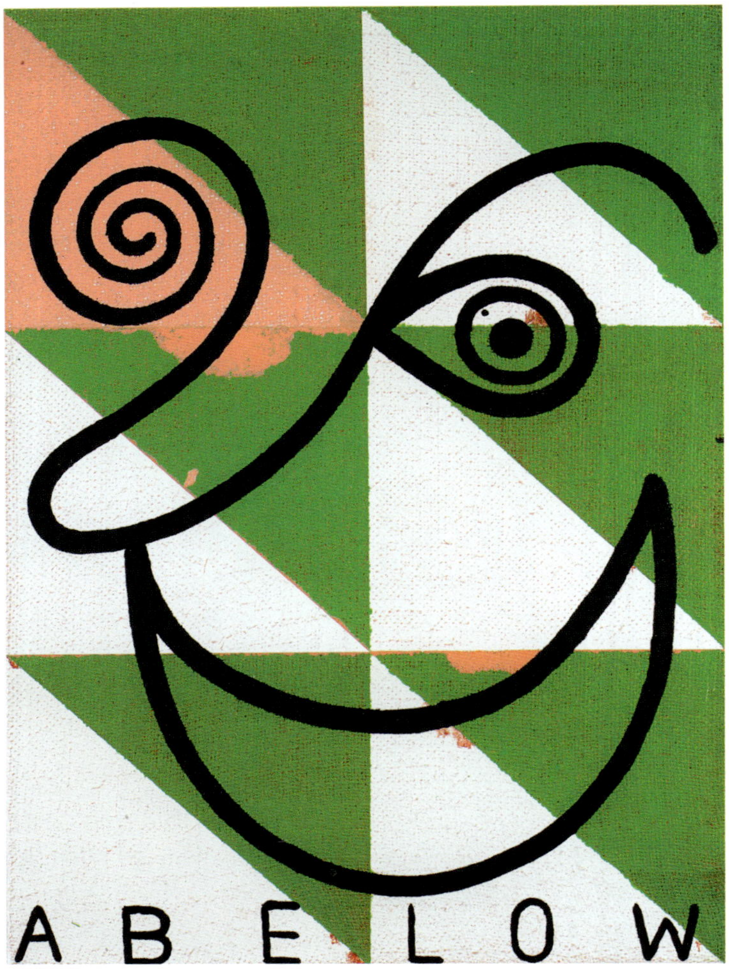

1

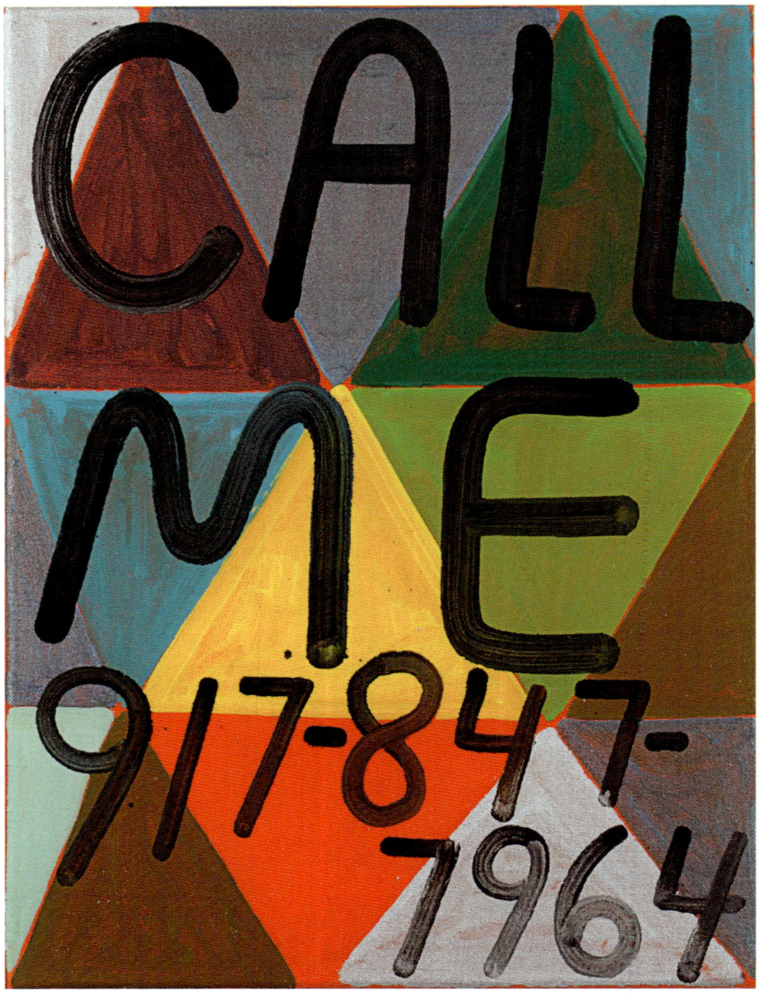

2

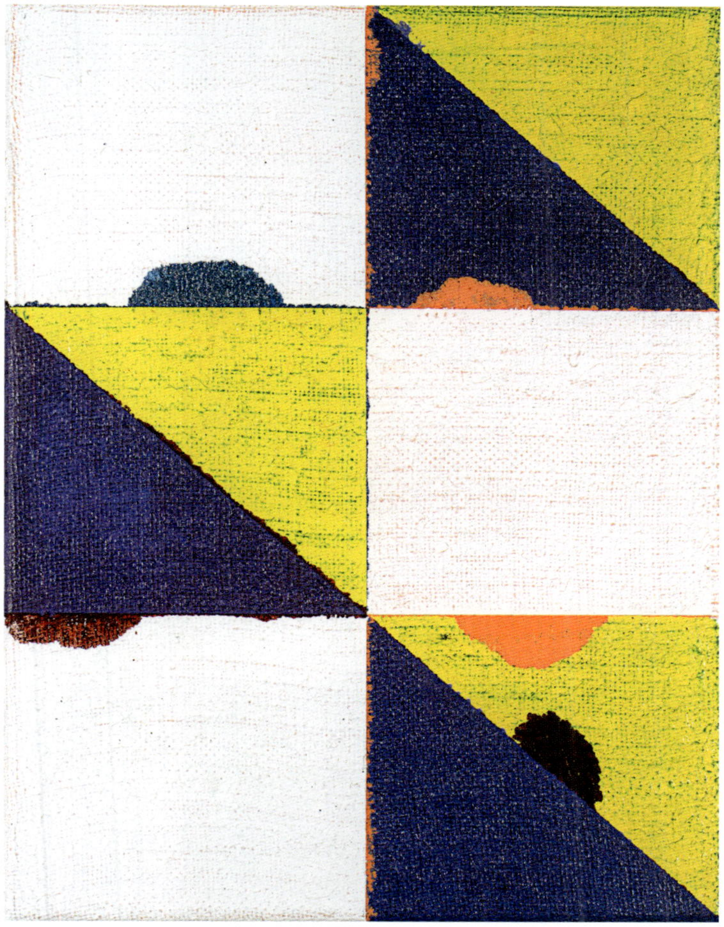

3

Shown by
James Fuentes F24

Biography
Born 1976
Lives in New York

Abelow has exhibited in the United States, Europe, and Canada since the early 2000s. In 2011 he had solo shows at James Fuentes LLC, New York, and Tomorrow Gallery, Toronto. He also hosted a series of curatorial projects in Ross Bleckner's Chelsea studio under the title "ART BLOG ART BLOG" (2011). In 2012 he will have a solo show at the aptly titled gallery, Sorry We're Closed, in Brussels.

1
Self-Portrait
2011
Oil on burlap
24 × 18"
(61 × 45.5 cm)
Courtesy of
James Fuentes

2
Call Me Abstract
2007
Oil on linen
18 × 14"
(45.5 × 35.5 cm)
Courtesy of
James Fuentes

3
Untitled (Abstraction "NZ")
2011
Oil on burlap
18 × 14"
(45.5 × 35.5 cm)
Courtesy of
James Fuentes

Focus
Joshua Abelow

Joshua Abelow's paintings, drawings, and deadpan poetry circle around the symbolic baggage of being an artist. His paintings range from geometric abstractions in pre-selected color combinations to self-deprecating, *faux*-primitive self-portraits with dogs sprouting from his head. Others bluntly repeat phrases, such as "HARDER FASTER" and "HANG ME." Abelow's freely drawn pencil drawings—which recall both men's-room graffiti and Picasso's gleeful sketches of satyrs—mock the stereotype of the artist as macho virtuoso, as in *OH! ABELOW* (2010), in which a woman seems to swoon on hearing his name, or *PAINTER* (2010), which depicts a naked, beer-bellied, cigarette-puffing figure wielding giant paintbrushes as his penis sags on the ground underneath some kind of hairy beast. KMJ

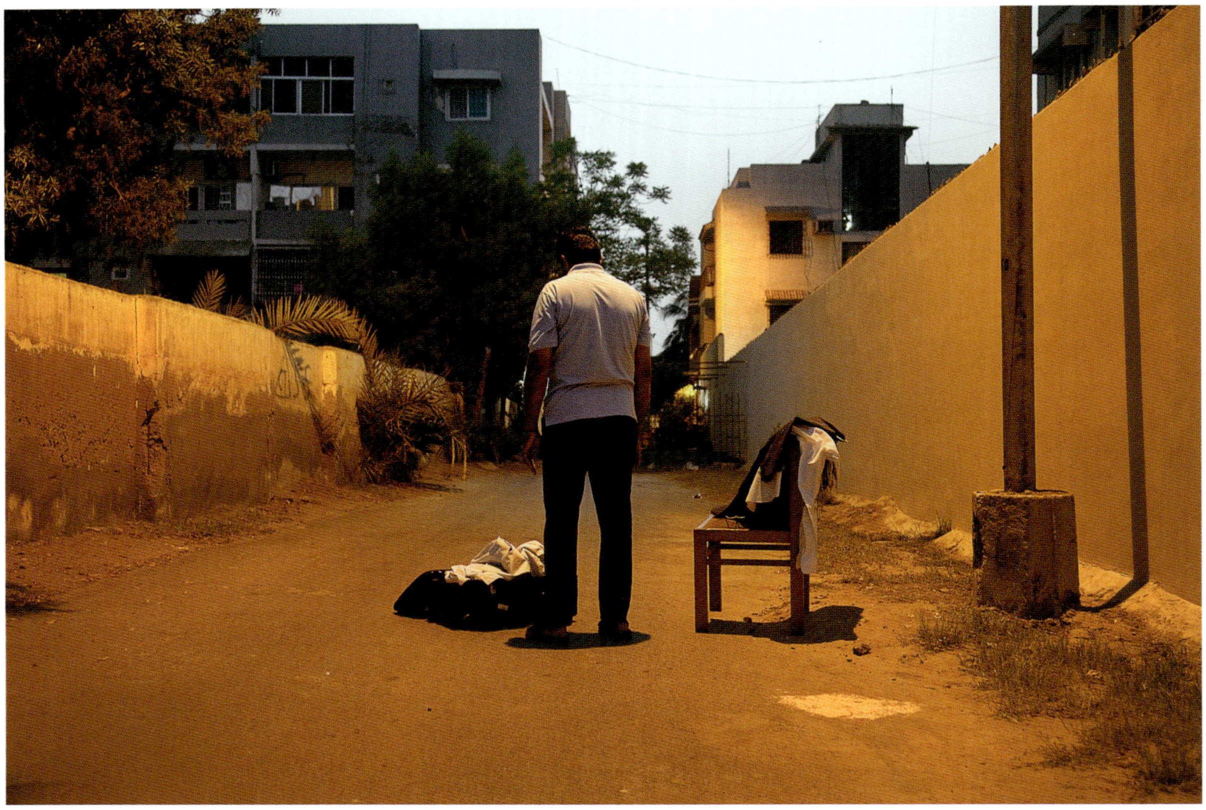

1

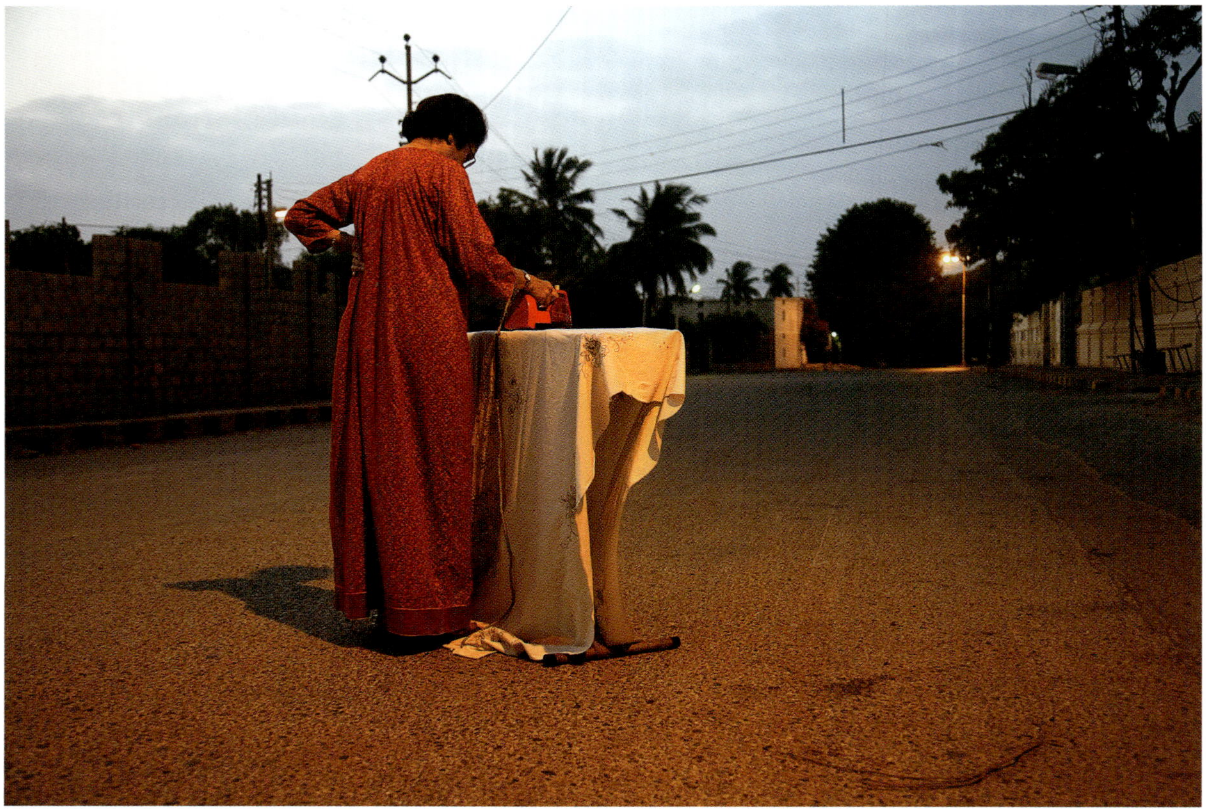

2

Shown by
Experimenter F23

Biography
Born 1971
Lives in Berlin and New Delhi

Pakistan-born Abidi's socio-political work has travelled across continents in the exhibitions "Section Yellow" at Project88, Colaba, Mumbai (2010), and The Baltic Centre for Contemporary Art, Gateshead (2011–12); and "Karachi" at V.M. Art Gallery, Karachi, and Green Cardamom, London (2009). In 2012, she participated in the group exhibition "Making Normative Orders—Demonstrations of Power, Doubt and Protest" at Frankfurter Kunstverein, Frankfurt. Abidi was resident on the DAAD artist-in-Berlin Program (2011–12).

Focus
Bani Abidi

If all the world's a stage, then Bani Abidi finds political potential in its re-staging. Her videos, drawings, and installations isolate mundane moments to highlight the physical and mental spaces that we as individuals willingly occupy between the state and the public. In her videos, orchestrated performances and situations are recorded and presented as deadpan documentary: for example, in *Yellow Lines* (2010), which places the bureaucracy, security checks, and interminable waiting of an immigration office in the barren wasteland of an empty lot. Similarly, in the "Security Barriers Type A–L" (2008) series of digital drawings—which illustrate the range of physical devices used to block and guide people on the streets of Karachi—Abidi explores the unexpected points where life and authority intersect. CFW

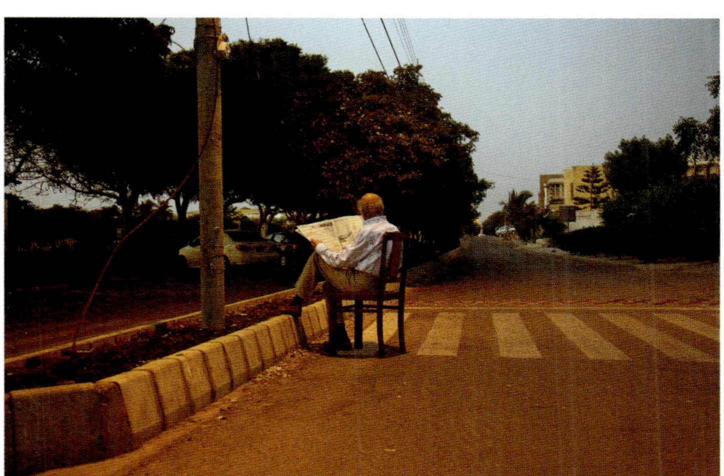

3

1
Ashish Sharma - Karachi Series - 1
2009
Duratrans lightbox
20 × 30"
(51 × 76 cm)
Courtesy of Experimenter

2
Pari Wania - Karachi Series - 1
2009
Duratrans lightbox
20 × 30"
(51 × 76 cm)
Courtesy of Experimenter

3
Jerry Fernandez - Karachi Series - 1
2009
Duratrans lightbox
20 × 30"
(51 × 76cm)
Courtesy of Experimenter

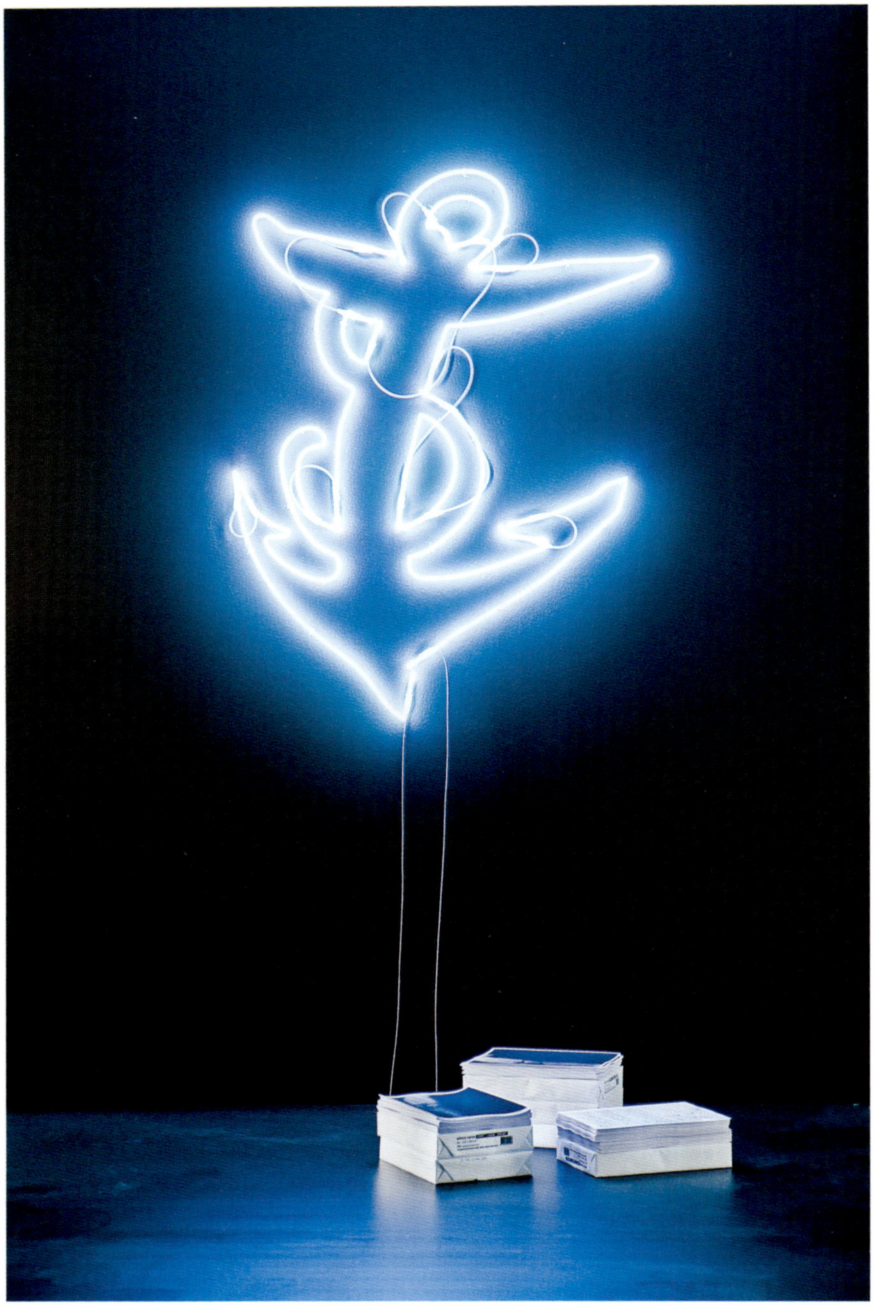

1

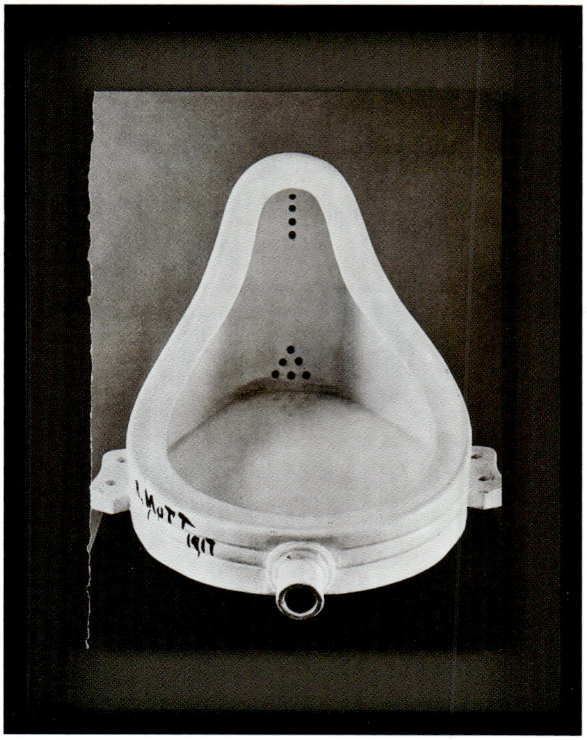

2

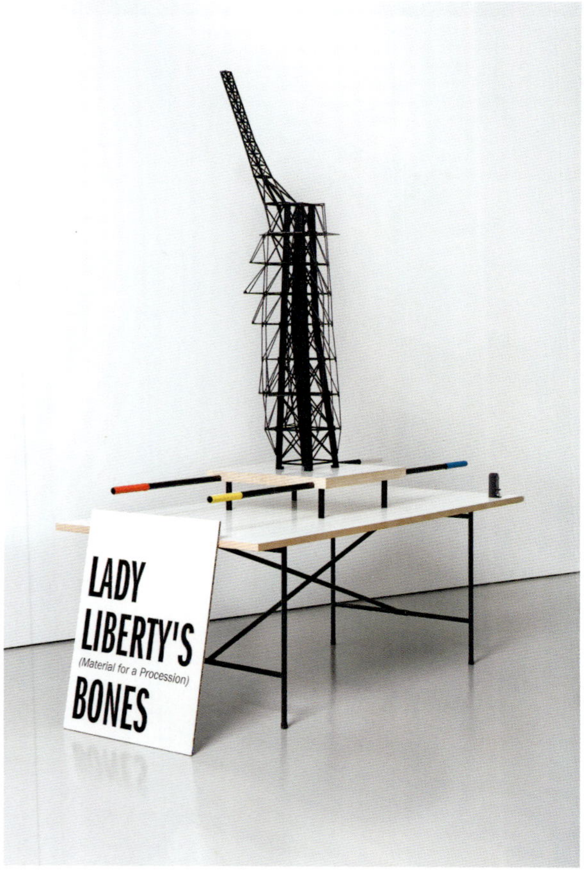

3

Shown by
Mehdi Chouakri C24
Xavier Hufkens B23

Biography
Born 1970
Lives in Berlin

French artist Afif's complex installation-based practice has occupied numerous European galleries in recent years. In early 2012 the solo show "Anthologie de l'humour noir" (Anthology of Black Humor), which originated at Centre Pompidou, Paris, in 2010, took place at MMK Zollamt, Frankfurt. Other recent solo shows include "The Fairytale Recordings" (2011) at Schinkel Pavillon, Berlin; "A lecture, a recording & few witnesses" (2010) at OPA, Guadalajara; and "Varieté" (2009) at Mehdi Chouakri, Berlin. In 2009 he was the recipient of the Marcel Duchamp Prize, Paris.

1
Untitled (More, More, 2006 / Neon, pile of photocopies / 110 × 50 cm)
2009
Mixed media
51⅞ × 39⅜"
(132 × 100 cm)
Courtesy of Mehdi Chouakri

2
Fountain Archive 0084
2010
Magazine page
13⅛ × 10½ × 1⅜"
(33.5 × 27 × 3.5cm)
Courtesy of Mehdi Chouakri

3
Lady Liberty's Bones (Material for procession)
2009
Mixed media
71¼ × 74⅞ × 23⅝"
(181 × 190 × 60 cm)
Courtesy of Mehdi Chouakri

Saâdane Afif

Exploring authorship and collaboration, Saâdane Afif often commissions others to write songs or texts in response to his exhibitions—they then adorn the gallery walls in text form, and are the basis of unique events. His sculptural performance *Lady Liberty's Bones (Material for procession)* (2009) featured a scale model of Gustave Eiffel's armature for the Statue of Liberty that is carried on a funeral-like procession, symbolically mourning liberty's death. His "Fountain Archive" (2010–ongoing) draws together images of Marcel Duchamp's *Fountain* (1917), torn from books and magazines. Framing each page, he highlights ideas of originality and authorship, as Duchamp's *Fountain* is reported to exist in many versions. Linking geographical, social, and historical references, Afif weaves together narratives that exclaim their relevance in the present. QL

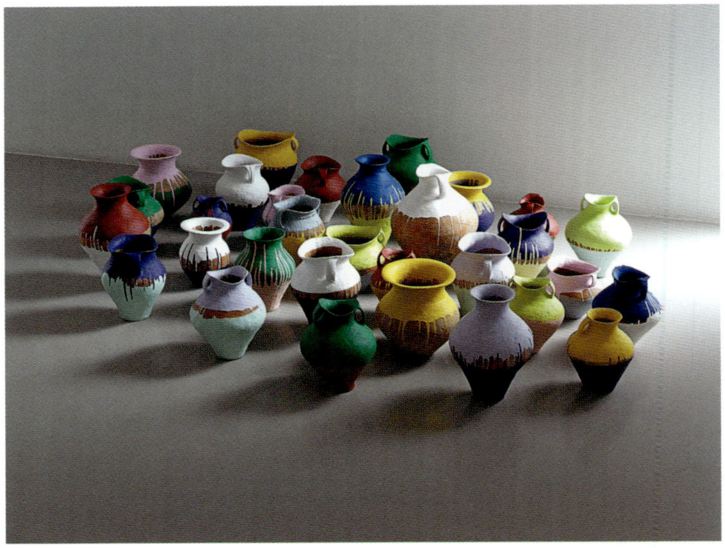

2

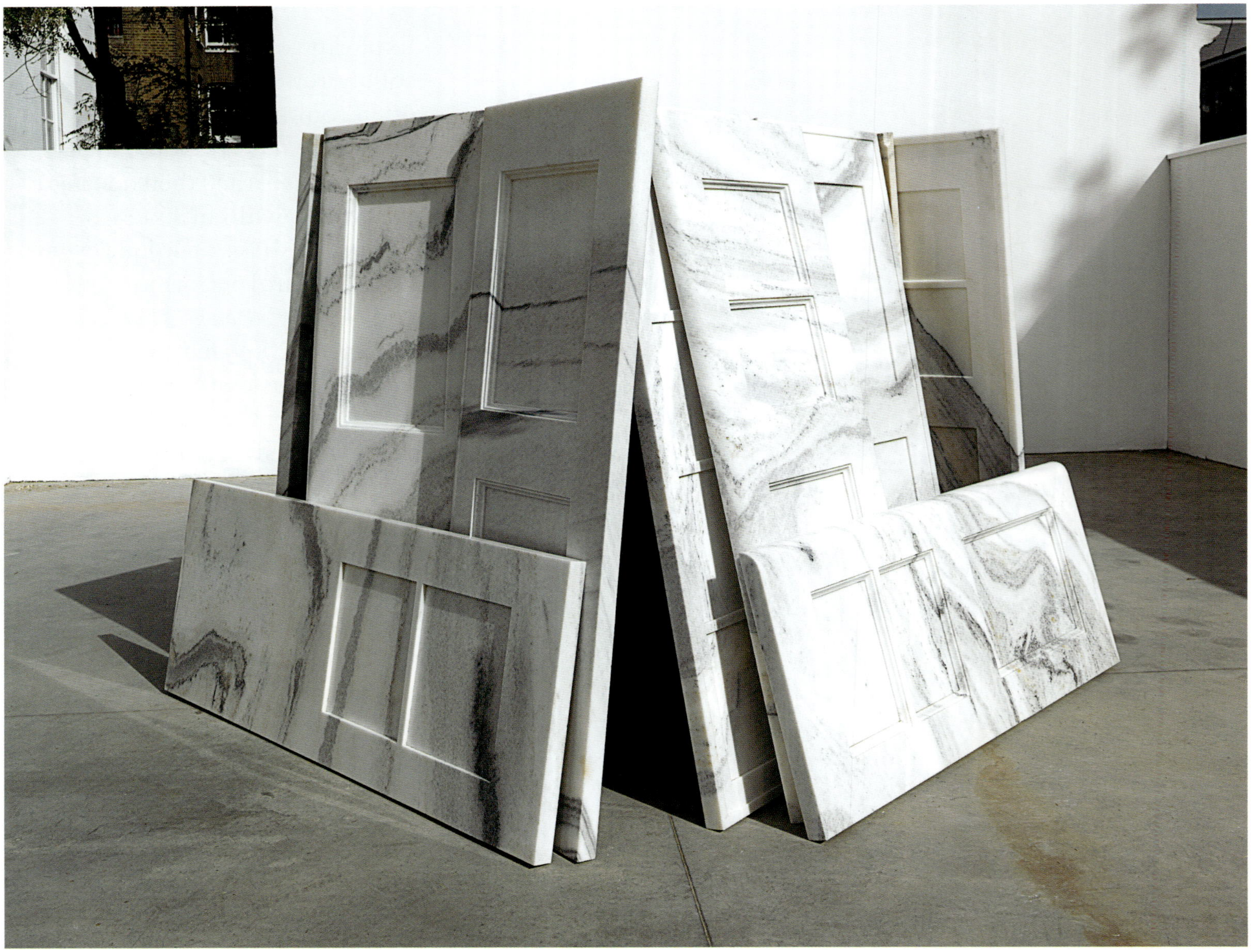

1

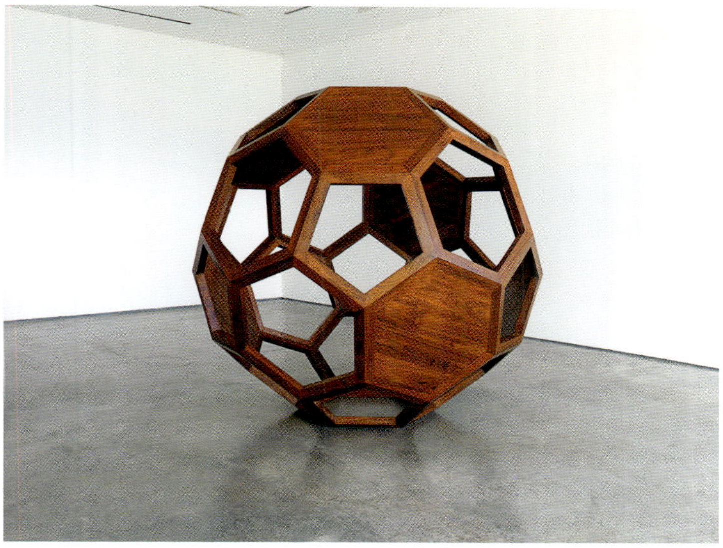

3

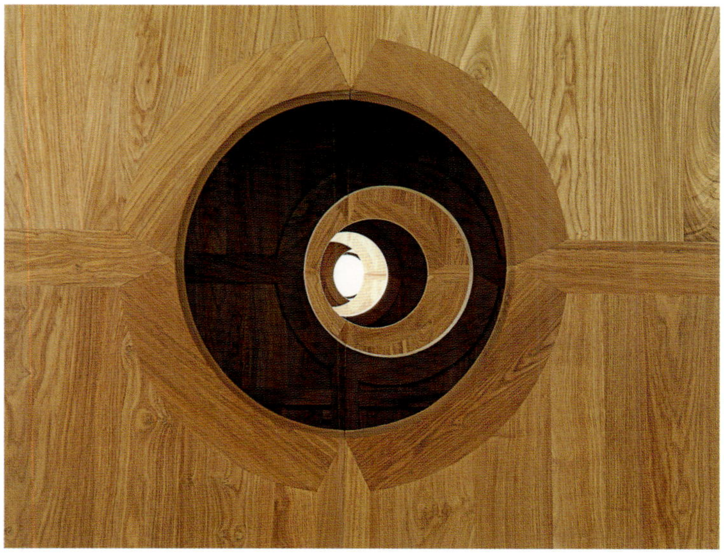

4

Shown by
Lisson Gallery C5
Gallery Hyundai C20

Biography
Born 1957
Lives in Beijing

Chinese artist Ai Weiwei's political and often provocational work has gained him attention inside and outside the art world. In 2011, the exhibition "Ai Weiwei: Absent" (2011) took place at Taipei Fine Arts Museum and marked his inability to travel for political reasons, while the multi-venue exhibition "Circle of Animals/ Zodiac Heads" (2010–ongoing) takes 12 bronze sculptures across the globe. He had self-titled solo shows at Louisiana Museum of Modern Art, Humlebæk (2011), and installed an expansive work for "The Unilever Series: Ai Weiwei" (2010), at Tate Modern, London.

1
Marble Doors
2006
Marble
Dimensions variable
Courtesy of Lisson Gallery

2
Colored Vases
2010
31 Han Dynasty vases and industrial paint
Dimensions variable
Courtesy of Lisson Gallery

3
Divina Proportione
2010
Huali wood
Diameter 66½" (169 cm)
Courtesy of Lisson Gallery

4
Moon Chest (detail)
2008
Huali wood
125⅞ × 62⅞ × 31½" (320 × 160 × 80cm)
Courtesy of Lisson Gallery

Ai Weiwei

Designer, thinker, performer, activist, and artist Ai Weiwei came to worldwide attention last year, when he was detained for nearly three months by the Chinese authorities, but for some time he has been acting out a subtle critique of cultural standards and the political potential of art. From larger gestures, as artistic consultant on the Beijing Olympics' "Bird's Nest" stadium, to the installation of millions of hand-painted porcelain *Sunflower Seeds* (2010) in Tate Modern's Turbine Hall, he also excels at the potential of the small, intimate gesture. His *Colored Vases* (2011) defaced a series of ancient Chinese ceramic pots from AD 220, dipping them in crude, bright colors, defiantly showing how the past can be remade or erased. CFW

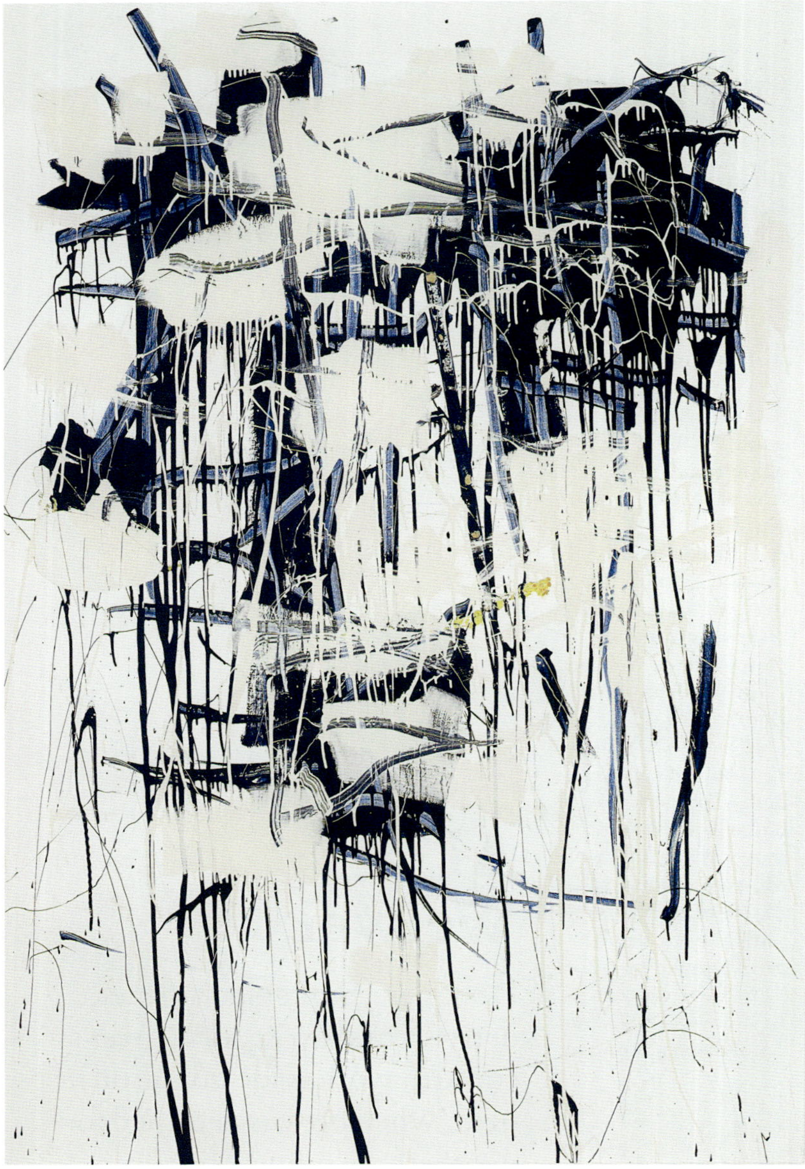

1

2

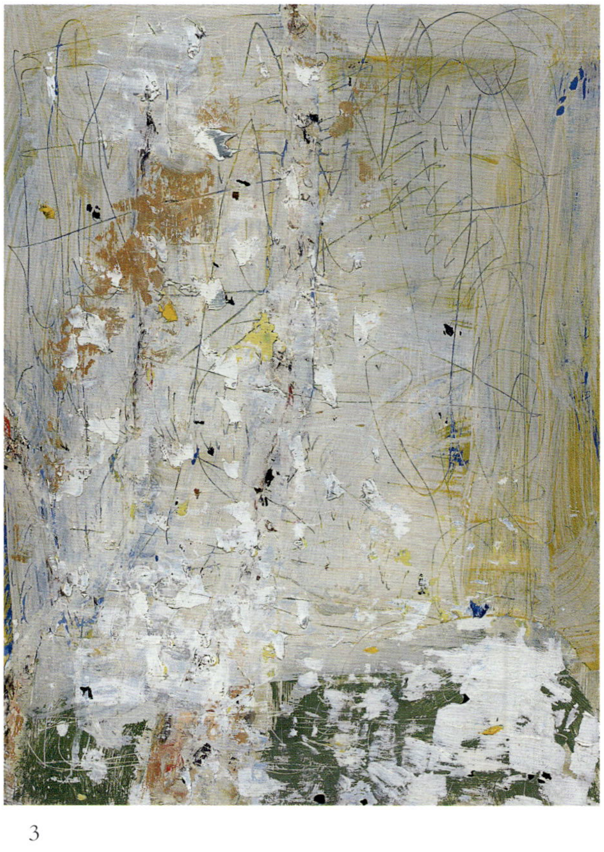

3

Shown by
Bortolami A9
Corvi-Mora A16
MISAKO
& ROSEN R19

Biography
Born 1975
Lives in New York

Aldrich's recent solo shows at SFMoMA, San Francisco (2011), and the aptly titled "Richard Aldrich and the 19th Century French Painting" at the Contemporary Art Museum St. Louis (2011), defined his work among some of the best painters emerging from the United States. As the aforementioned title suggests, his forays in Europe have also proved significant, with exhibitions at Corvi-Mora, London (2011), and Dépendance, Brussels (2009).

1
Lancelot Du Lac
2011
Oil, enamel, and wood on cut linen
84 × 58"
(213.5 × 147.5 cm)
Courtesy of Bortolami

2
Future Painting 1
2008
Gessoed muslin on artist stretcher
20¼ × 13 × 2"
(51.5 × 33 × 5 cm)
Courtesy of Bortolami

3
Untitled
2011
Oil and wax on panel
19⅞ × 14¾"
(50.5 × 37.5 cm)
Courtesy of Bortolami

4
Untitled
2010
Oil, wax, pencil, and collage on linen
84 × 58"
(213.5 × 147.5 cm)
Courtesy of Bortolami

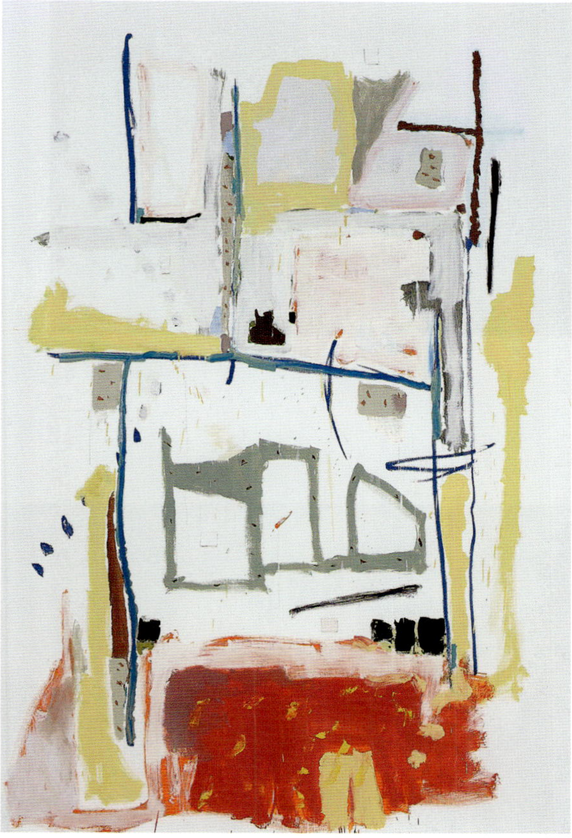

4

Richard Aldrich

Richard Aldrich's works—which are, for the most part, abstract paintings in oil and wax, though they also include text and cut pieces, portraits, and collage—evoke, as Natalie Haddad has noted, "the genres of 20th-century painting like distant memories." More recently, each of the "Slide Paintings" (2010) comprises a bare canvas inlaid with a single back-lit slide, which displays one of the artist's previous performances or one of his now destroyed paintings and installations. As was suggested by the title of his 2008 exhibition, "Narrative with Five Characters" (which also included four sculptures), Aldrich's works may be best viewed as part of a continuing conversation—between themselves, their precedents, and the artist's own obsessions. ST

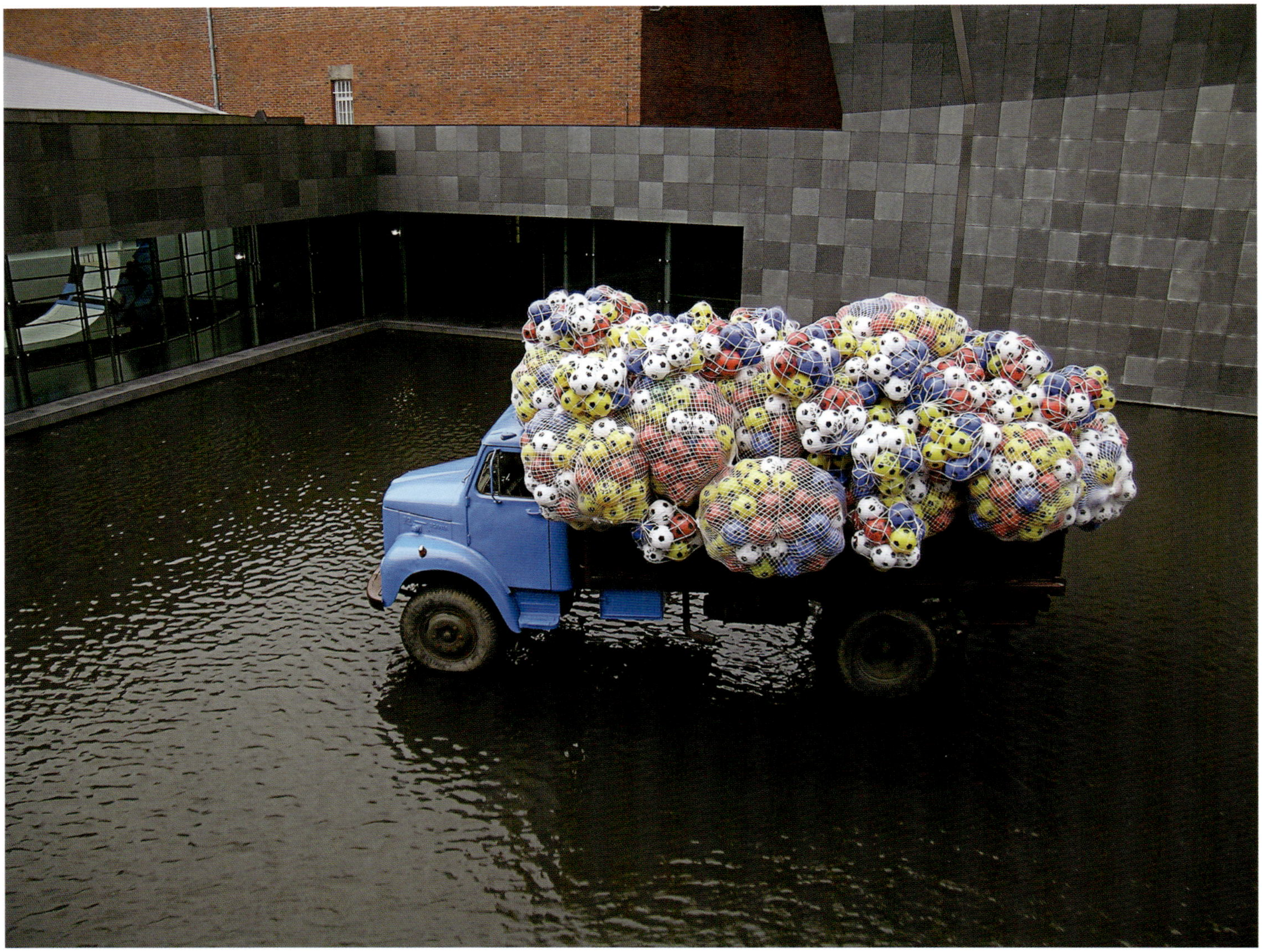

1

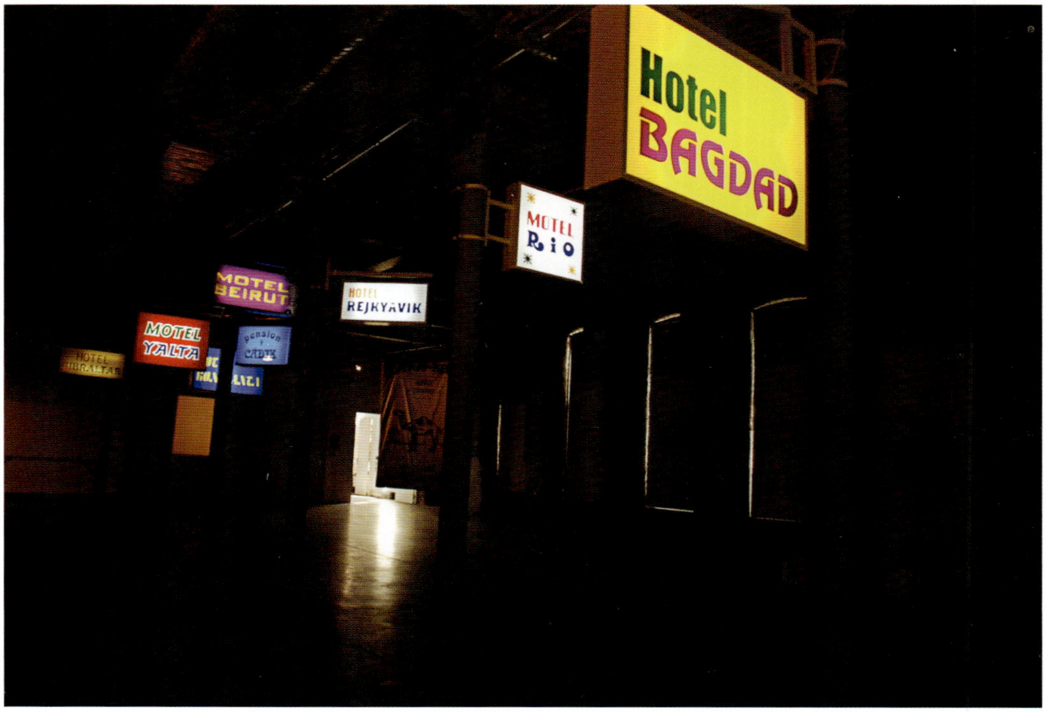
Hotel
BAGDAD
MOTEL
Rio
HOTEL
REJKYAVIK
MOTEL
BEIRUT
MOTEL
YALTA
pension

2

Shown by
Rampa B31

Biography
Born 1957
Died 2007

The late Turkish artist Alptekin's career began in academia. In the early 1990s his focus turned to artistic production and he began making installations, videos, and collages. In 2011 the retrospective exhibition "I am not a studio artist" was held at SALT Beyoğlu, Istanbul. He represented Turkey at the 52nd Venice Biennale (2007), and participated in the Istanbul Biennial (1995, 2005 and 2009), and São Paulo Biennial (1995).

1
Hüseyin Bahri Alptekin / Michael Morris
Truque (Truck)
1995
Turkish licensed blue truck with counterfeit soccer balls
Dimensions variable
Courtesy of the estate of Hüseyin Bahri Alptekin, M.D. Morris, and Rampa

2
H-Fact: Hospitality / Hostility
2003–7
Hotel signs
Dimensions variable
Courtesy of the estate of Huseyin Bahri Alptekin, and Rampa

3
Contemplation
1999
Print on dibond
44⅞ × 33"
(114 × 84 cm)
Courtesy of the estate of Hüseyin Bahri Alptekin, and Rampa

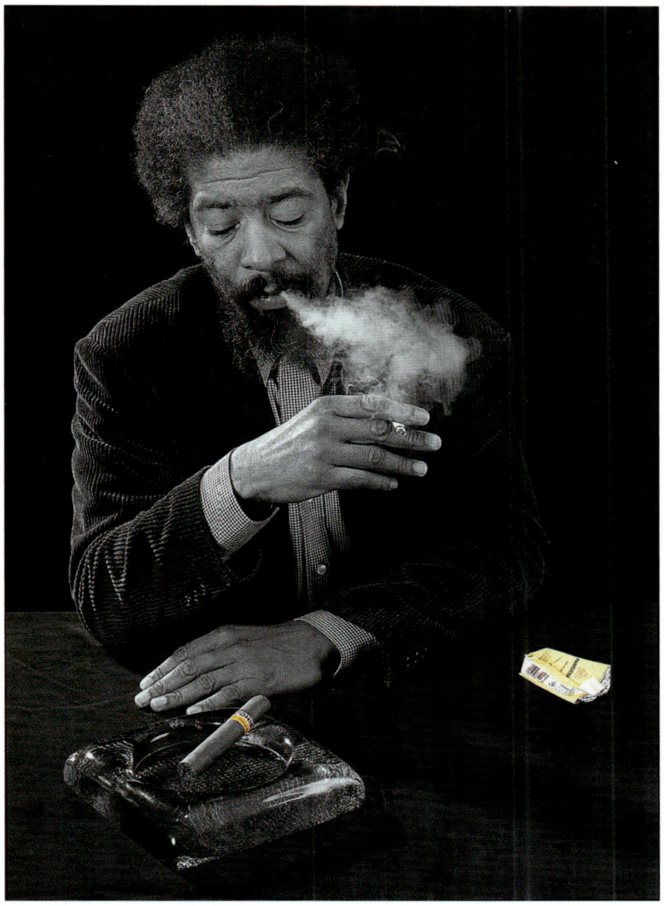

3

Hüseyin Bahri Alptekin

Boredom and displacement were some of the themes that Hüseyin Bahri Alptekin pursued throughout his diverse practice. *Capacity* (2003), a cluster of photographs of hotels named after places where they are not, suggests a longing for better times, for previous lives. When reconstructed as *H-fact: Hospitality/Hostility* (2003–7)—clustering wall- and ceiling-mounted illuminated signs for Motel Beirut or Pension Cadiz, with cheerful typefaces and jazzy colors—their insistence on elsewhere turns sinister. Alptekin often worked collaboratively, with M.D. Morris on *Heterotopia* (1992), for instance, where their collection of cheap goods from markets is organized into a wall display that evidences global economies of banal excess. SOR

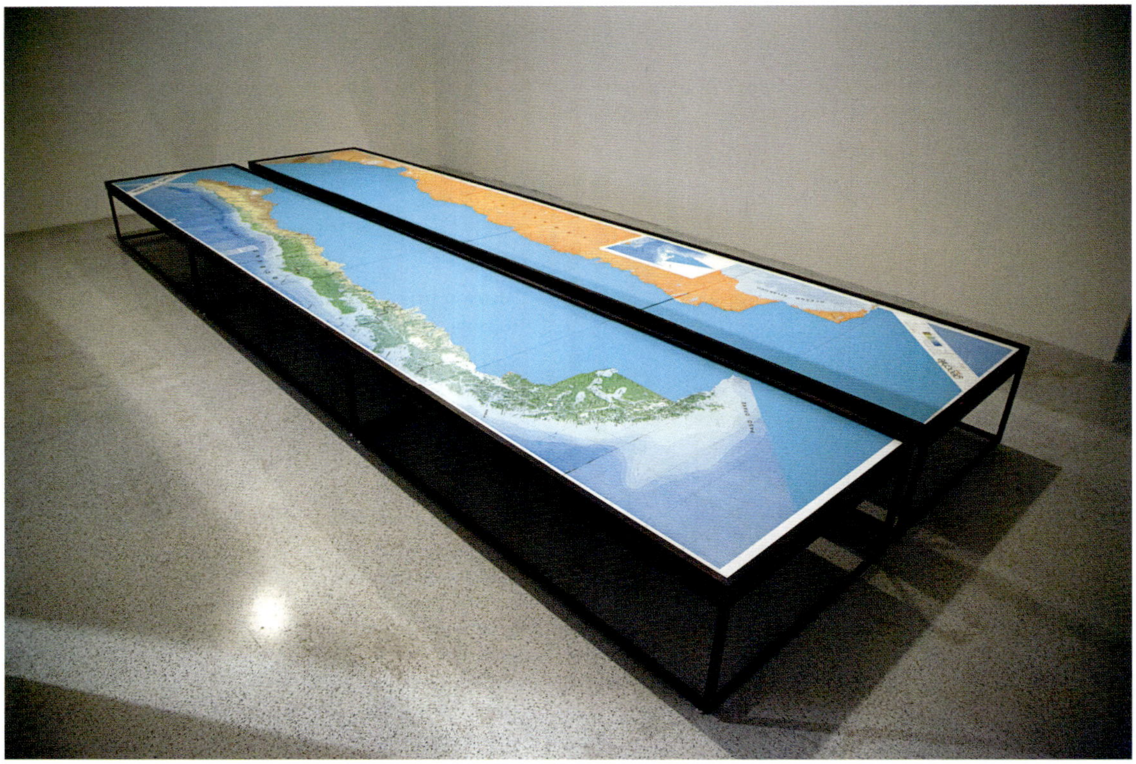

1

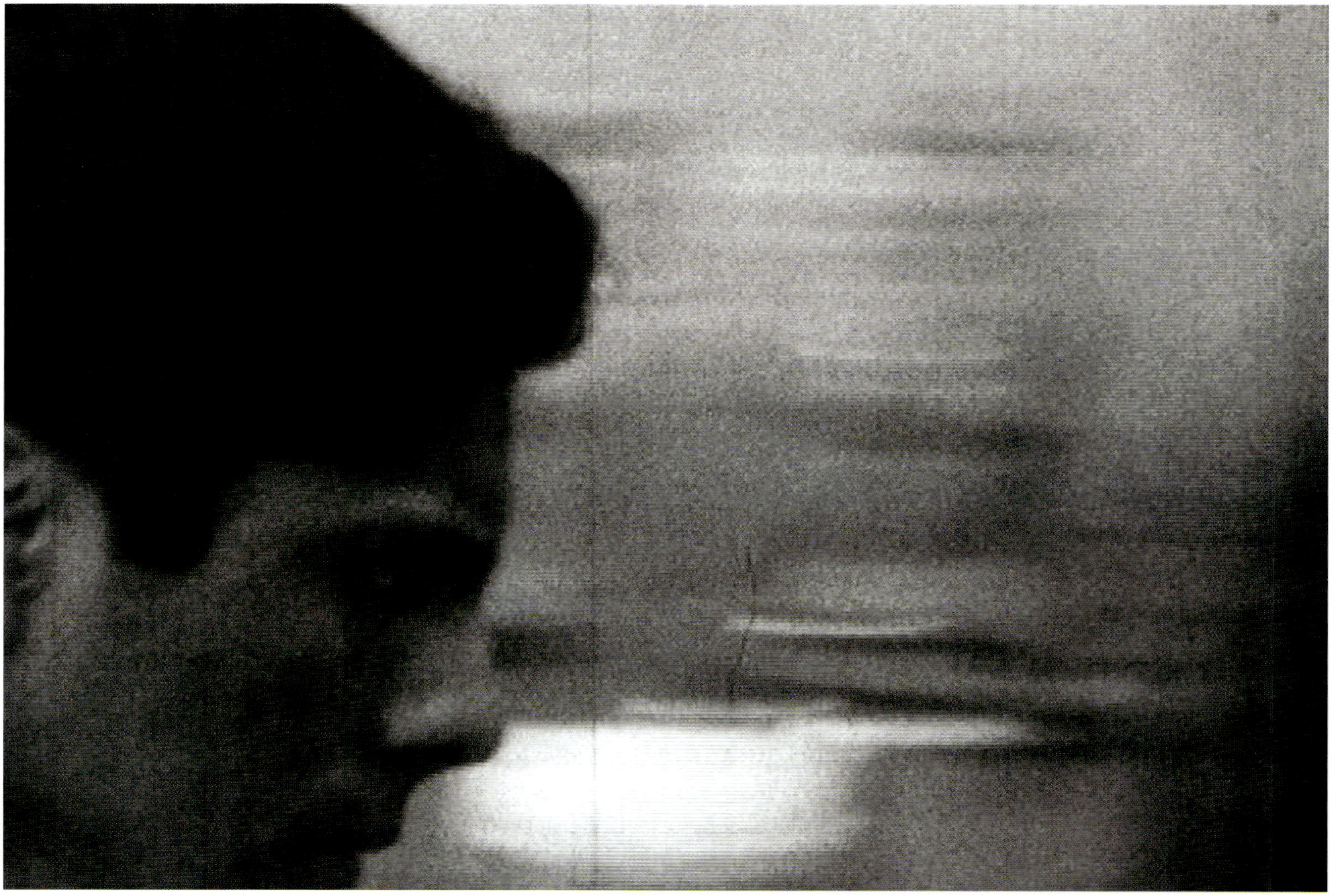

2

Jonathas de Andrade

Shown by
Vermelho B26

Biography
Born 1982
Lives in Recife

Brazil-born De Andrade's concept-driven, image-based work has been included in numerous group and survey shows in recent years. In 2010 he had a solo show at Centro Cultural São Paulo. The solo exhibition "Tropical Hangover" took place at Instituto Cultural Banco Real, Recife, in 2009, before travelling to Galeria Vermelho, São Paulo, in 2010. He is included in the survey show "The Ungovernables" (2012) at New Museum, New York, and participated in "Untitled, 12th Istanbul Biennial" (2011) and "29th São Paulo Biennale" (2010).

1
Litoral Pacífico Sulamericano (South American Pacific Coast)
2011
Collage on wood
15¾ × 33½ × 196⅞"
(40 × 85 × 500 cm)
Courtesy of Vermelho

2
4000 disparos
(4000 Shots)
2010
Super 8 transferred to DVD
Loop (60 min.)
Courtesy of Vermelho

Working across photography, film, and installations, Jonathas de Andrade explores cultural amnesia and the legacy of the Modernist project. Often making use of archival research and found artifacts, he weaves fictions that throw fresh light on geopolitical fact. In his recent work *Pacífico* (2010), a large map of the type once used in South American geography classes, and an accompanying animation, tell the story of a massive earthquake that sets Chile adrift in the ocean, restoring the coastline that the now landlocked nation of Bolivia lost in the Pacific War (1879–84). The pedagogical feel of this work underlines De Andrade's interest in the ideological construction of truth and the dubious reliability of state-sanctioned information. TM

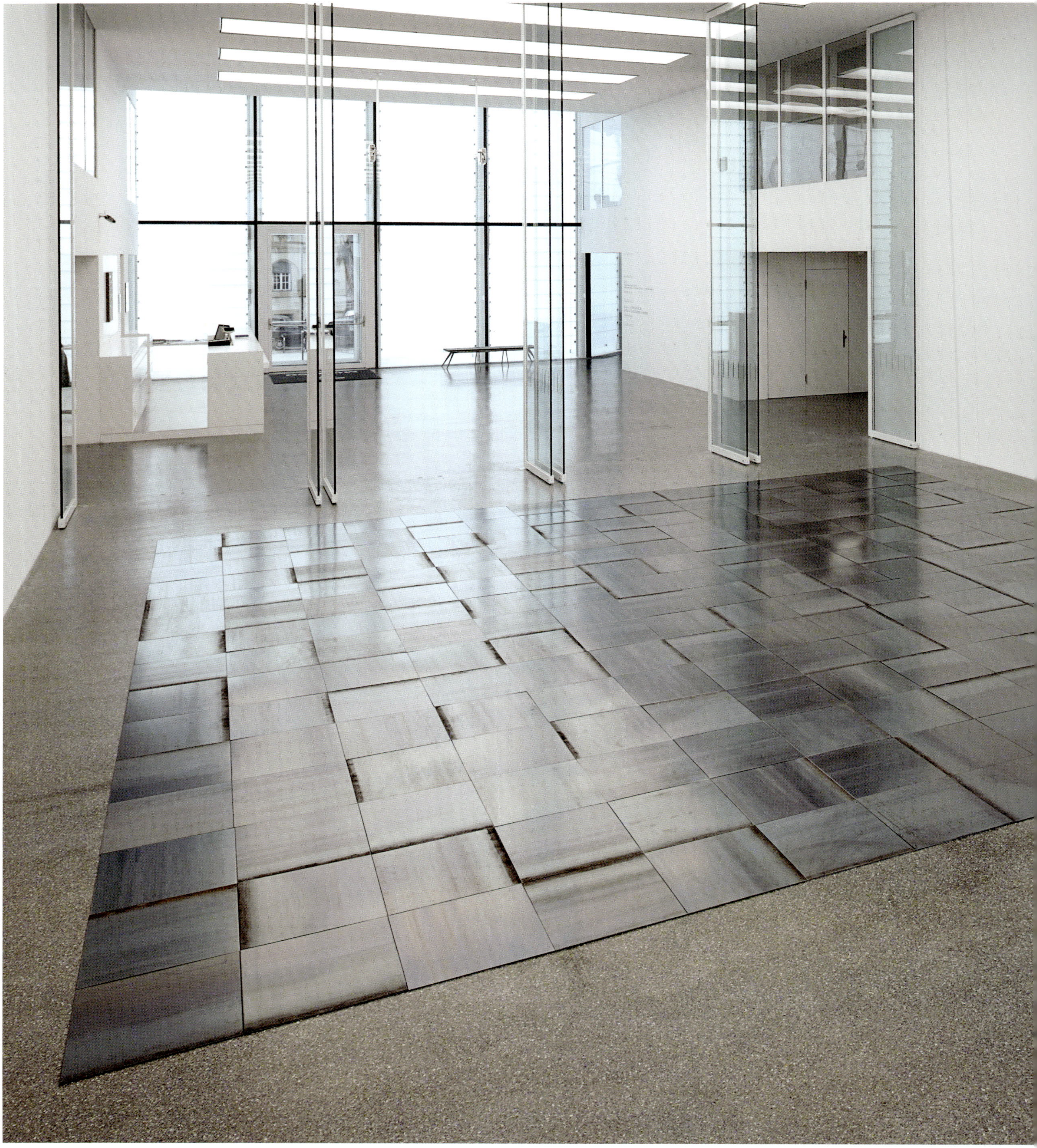

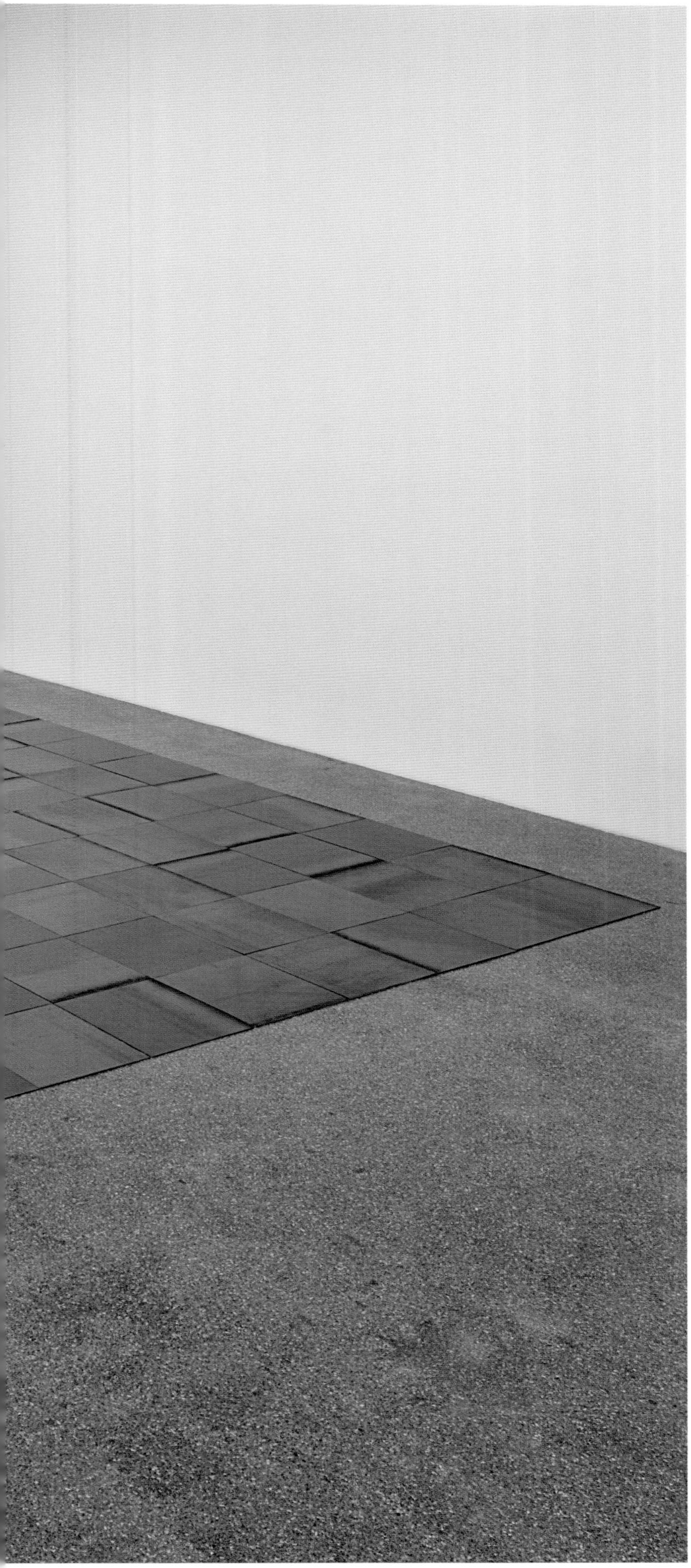

Shown by
Alfonso Artiaco C31
Sadie Coles HQ C15
Yvon Lambert C34

Biography
Born 1935
Lives in New York

Andre's career spans six decades, and retrospectives of his Minimalist sculpture have taken place across the globe, including those held at the Solomon R. Guggenheim Museum, New York, (1970); the Stedelijk Van Abbemuseum, Eindhoven (1987); the Museum of Modern Art, Oxford (1996); and more recently Kunsthalle Basel (2005). His work is in numerous collections, including those of Tate Modern, London, and MoMA, New York. In 2013 a comprehensive retrospective of his work will be held at the Dia Art Foundation, New York.

15 × 15 Napoli Square
2010
Hot rolled steel,
225 units square
¼" × 24' 6" × 24' 6"
(0.5 × 750 × 750 cm)
Courtesy of Alfonso Artiaco / Museion, Bolzano

Carl Andre

The Minimalist sculptor and Concrete poet Carl Andre has defined a "place" as "an area within an environment that has been altered in such a way to make the general environment more conspicuous." This is a definition we might usefully apply to his sculptures, from large public works such as *Lament for the Children* (1977) to his more intimate arrangements of bricks, wooden blocks, or metal tiles displayed on gallery floors, such as *144 Lead Square* (1969). Concerned with material, structure, and site, Andre's sculptures arose, as the artist has said, from a desire to "make something to be in the world," and to sharpen us to that most mysterious and everyday dimension, space. TM

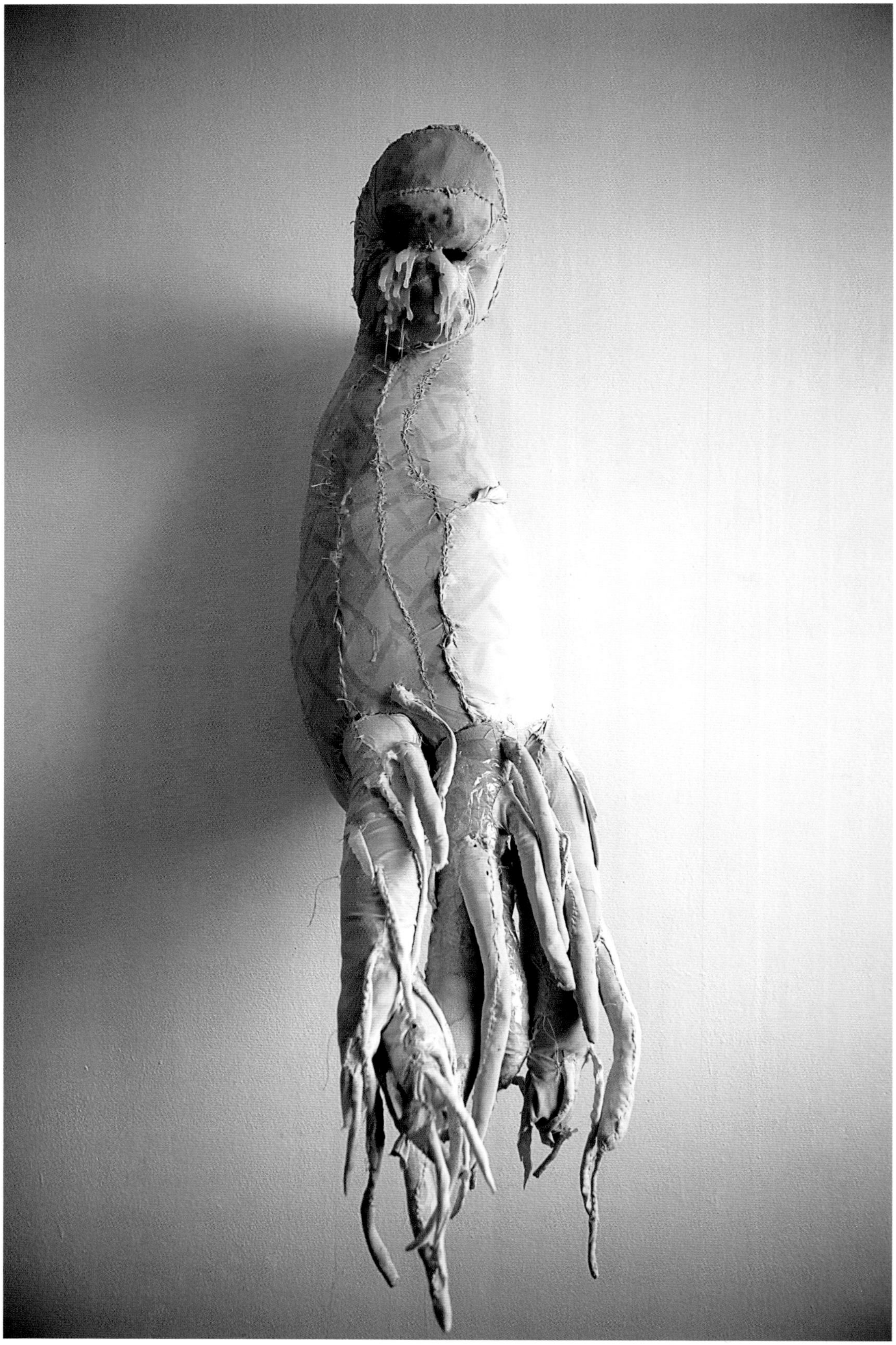

1

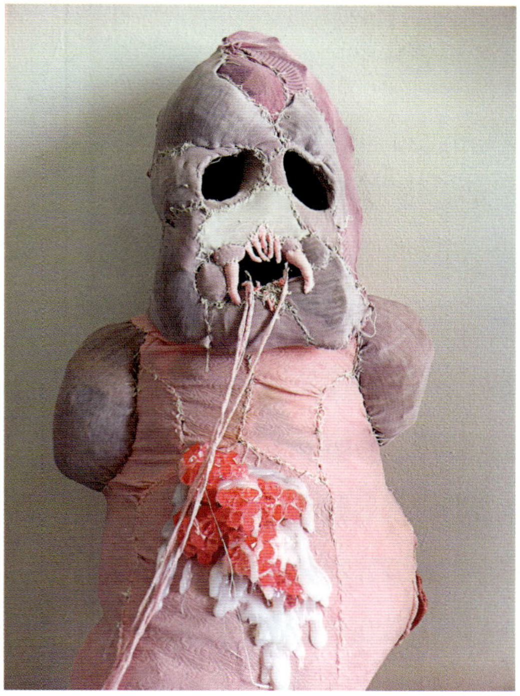

2

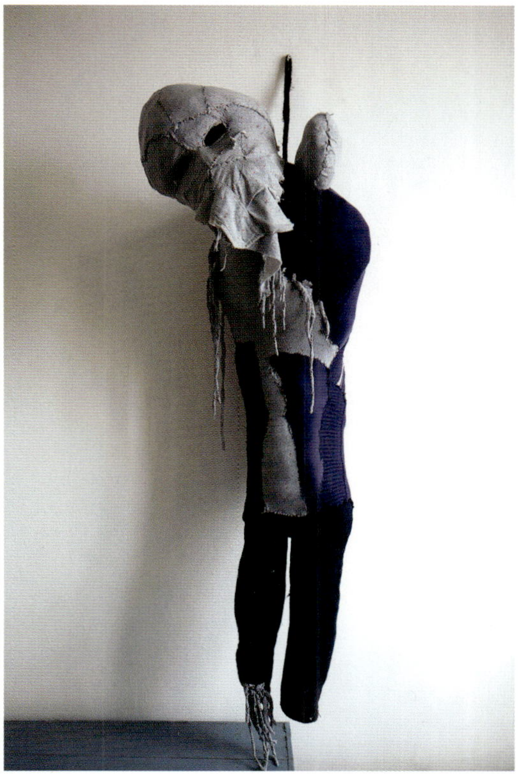

3

Evgeny Antufiev

At the center of Asia lies the remote and inaccessible Siberian Republic of Tuva, where Evgeny Antufiev was born. Folkloric and shamanic traditions still endure there, untouched by recent political history, and provide Antufiev with an earthy vocabulary of mythic forms and symbols. Animal skulls and skeletons have long fascinated the artist; his 2010 exhibit "Bones" consisted chiefly of his extensive collection arranged on shelves. For Antufiev and for the Tuvan people, bones are links to ancestral spirits. The exhibition "Shining" (2011) was made in collaboration with a Tuvan wolf hunter. The hunter's photographs, tools, and drawings were shown beside Antufiev's sewn effigy of a wolf, umbilical cords still attached, poignantly, to her young. JG

Shown by
Regina Gallery B33

Biography
Born 1986
Lives in Tuva and Moscow

Tuva-born Antufiev's intricate work was included in the New Museum, New York, survey of Eastern European and former Soviet art, "Ostalgia" (2011). The same year he also exhibited at Gallery White, Moscow, with Ivan Oyuon, and in 2010 he had the solo exhibitions "Bones" at White Gallery, Moscow; "Objets Protecteurs" at L'Aleatoire, Paris; and "Wings of Horror" at Navicula Artis Gallery, St. Petersburg.

1
Untitled
2010
Textiles, glue, adhesive tape
75⅜ × 15¾ × 23⅝"
(115 × 40 × 60 cm)
Courtesy of Regina Gallery

2
Untitled
2011
Textiles, wire, polyethylene, glue, plastic crystals, paper
69⅞ × 21⅝ × 26"
(175 × 55 × 66 cm)
Courtesy of Regina Gallery

3
Untitled
2010
Textiles, glue, plastic, synthetic winterizer
63 × 15¾ × 19⅝"
(160 × 40 × 50 cm)
Courtesy of Regina Gallery

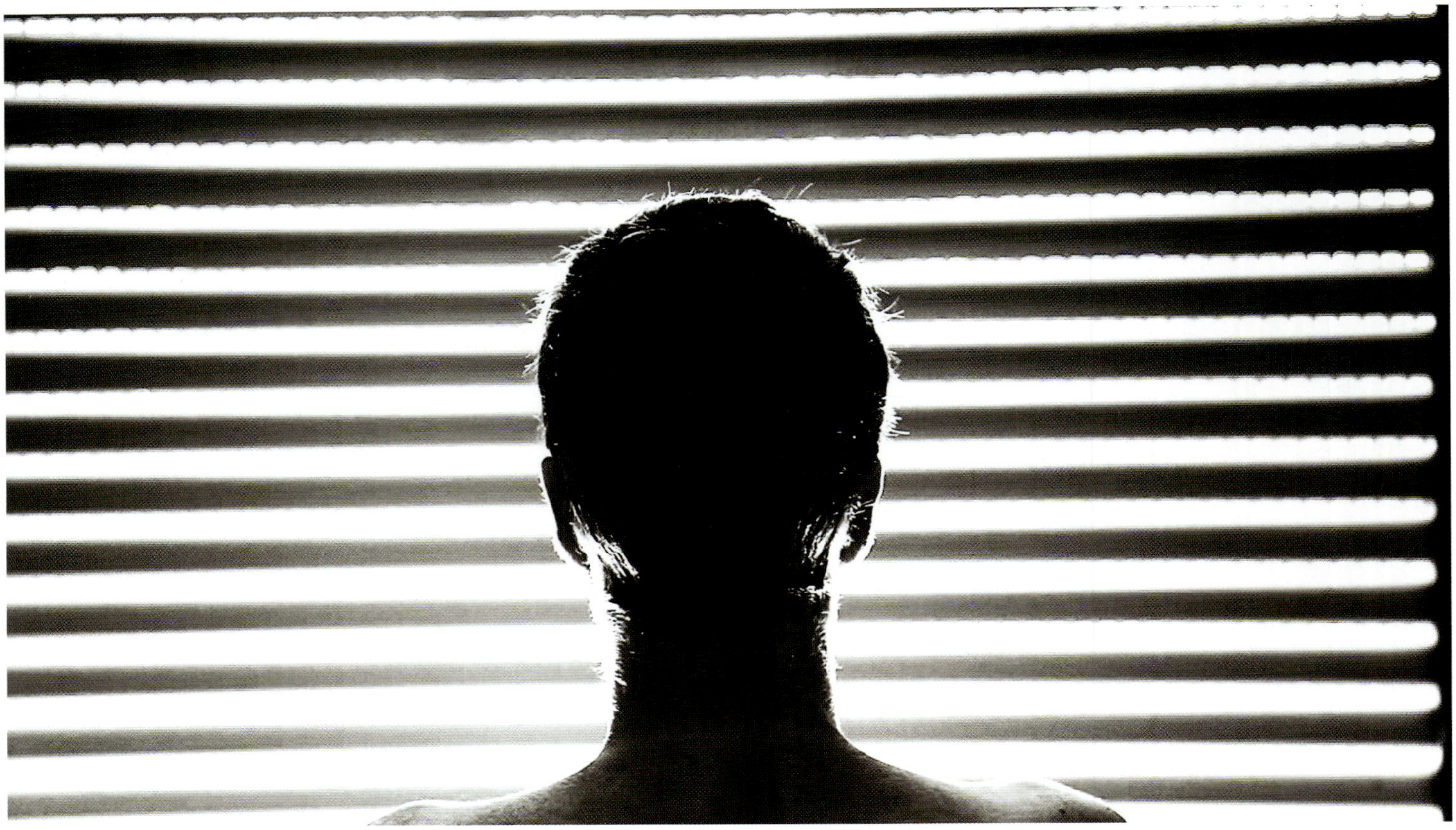

1

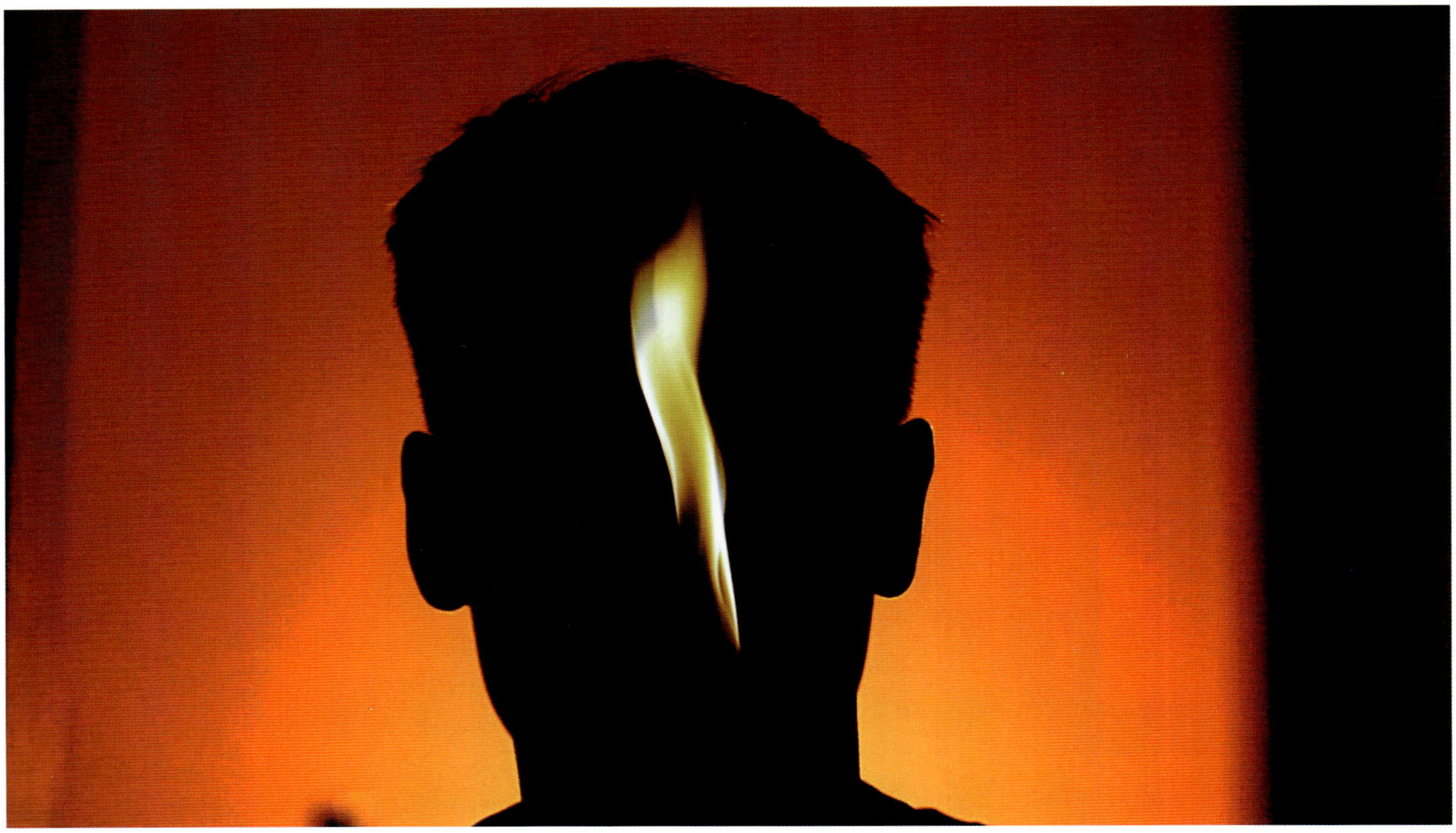

2

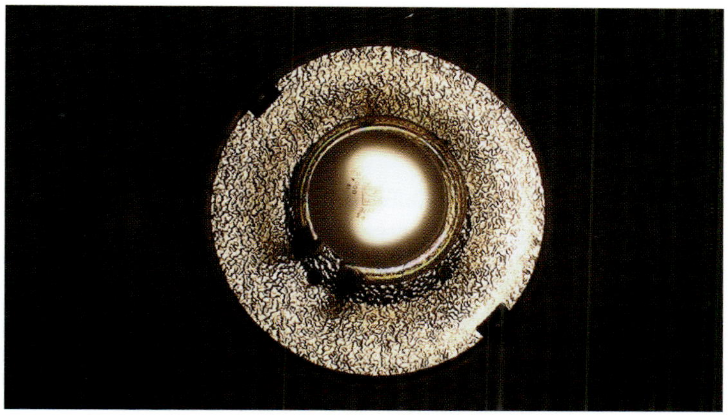

4

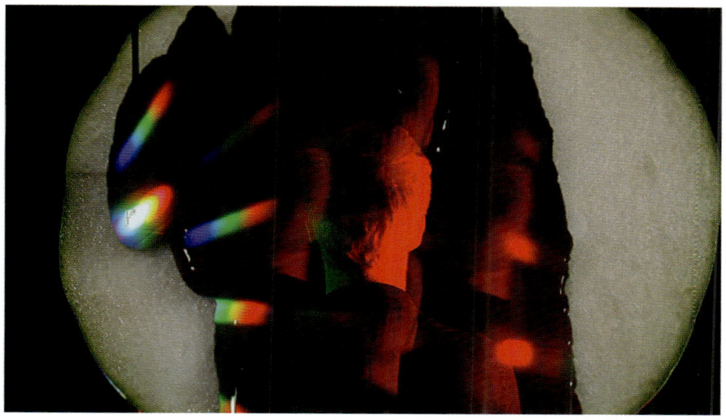

3

Shown by
Galerie Isabella Bortolozzi F18
Cabinet C7

Biography
Born 1982
Lives in London

Atkins' HD videos have been shown in solo and group exhibitions in Europe and the United States in recent years. In 2011, he held solo exhibitions in London, at Cabinet Gallery and Tate Britain, as part of the Art Now series, as well as contributing to a significant group exhibition at SculptureCenter, New York, and a collaborative project for Performa 11, New York. In 2012 Chisenhale Gallery, London, will hold a solo exhibition of his work.

1
A Tumor (In English)
2011
HD video
12 min. 30 sec.
Courtesy of Cabinet

2
Death Mask III
2011
HD video
34 min. 46 sec.
Courtesy of Cabinet

3
Death Mask II: The Scent
2010
HD video
8 min. 19 sec.
Courtesy of Cabinet

4
Cut To
2009
HD video
8 min.
Courtesy of Cabinet

Ed Atkins

The recurring image of the back of a head in Ed Atkins' work doubles our own viewing posture, one of many uneasy stand-ins running through his surreal, cut-up videos, writings, and installations. The body looms large in his high-definition videos, which revel in their electronic immateriality, dropping us in the middle of half-heard conversations punctuated with color-filled screens with empty subtitle boxes, as if we're missing some vital piece of information. His recent work *A Tumor (In English)* (2011) is a video, whose narrator asks, "Would you mind checking the mole on my shoulder?" The tumor is both a physical growth and an idea growing in our own heads. Atkins anxiously asks which, in our information age, has more weight. CFW

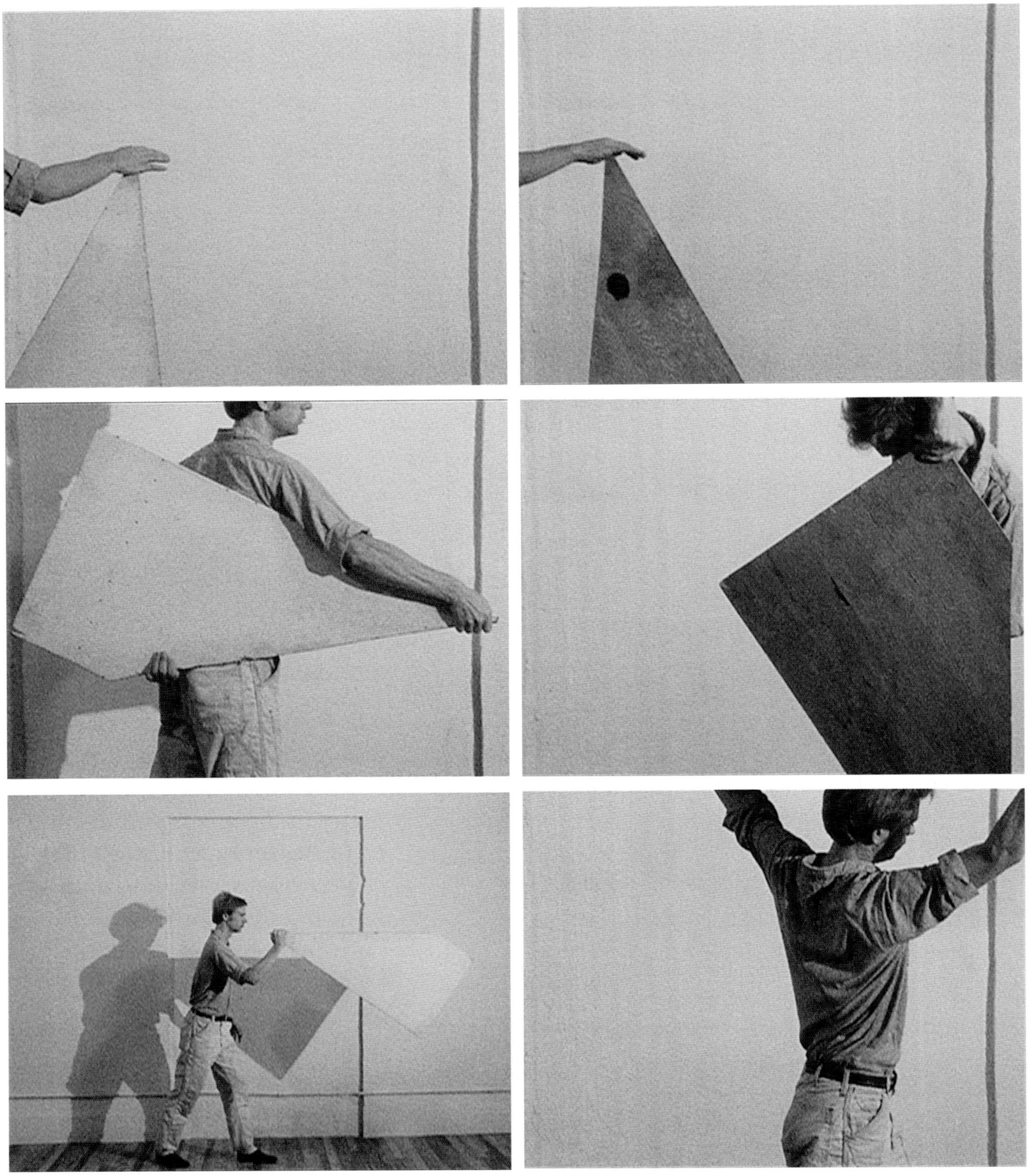

1

Charles Atlas

Over the last 40 years film-and video-maker Charles Atlas has directed upwards of 80 moving-image works in close collaboration with choreographers and musicians. In films made throughout the 1970s with the Merce Cunningham Dance Company, it is not so much that dance is staged for or documented by the camera as that dancers and camera alike are choreographed in concise, interrelated systems of movement. Films made in the 1980s, such as *Hail the New Puritan* (1986)—many of them made with collaborators such as Michael Clark, Leigh Bowery, and The Fall—tap subterranean flamboyancy and cultural transgression, while *Joints 4tet for Ensemble* (1971–2010) remodels Super 8mm footage of Cunningham's flexing body in a multi-channel installation that is at once humanist epitaph and abstract hymn. SOR

Shown by
Vilma Gold A22

Biography
Born 1949
Lives in New York

Atlas' practice has spanned film and video, dance, and performance—from his early collaborations with choreographer Merce Cunningham to the recent performance with New Humans at South London Gallery (2011). In 2012 a retrospective exhibition of his work will be held at De Hallen Haarlem; other recent shows include "Joints Array" (2011) at New Museum, New York; and collaboration with choreographer Michael Clark at Tate Modern, London (2010).

1
Charles Atlas, Nevada
1974
Super 8mm transferred to 16mm and video, silent
2 min. 53 sec.
Courtesy of Vilma Gold

2
Charles Atlas, Mayonnaise Number 1
1973-2010
16mm transferred to DV, silent
11 min. 10 sec.
Courtesy of Vilma Gold

3
Charles Atlas, Teach
1992-8
Video, color, sound
7 min. 47 sec.
Courtesy of Vilma Gold

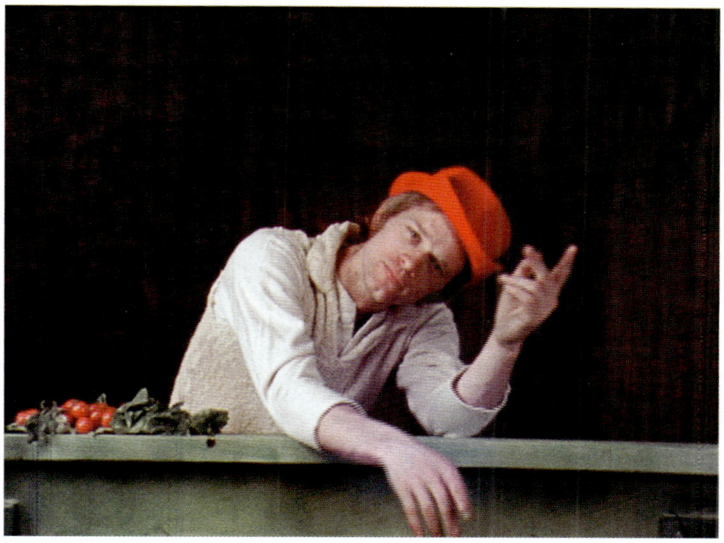

2

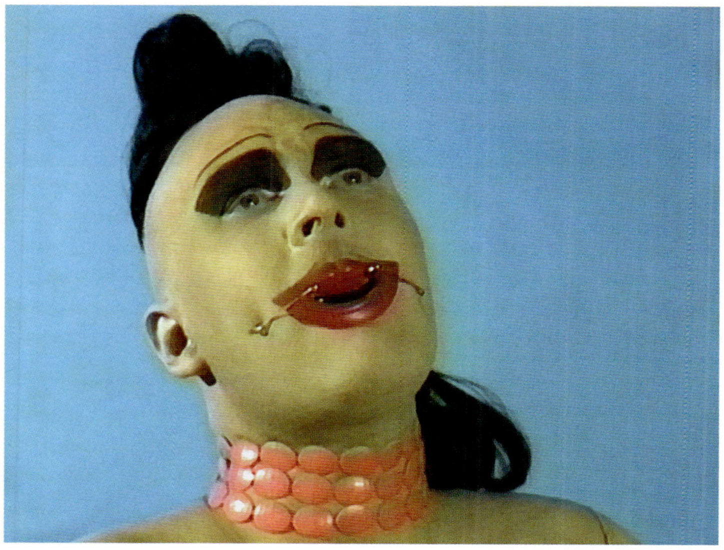

3

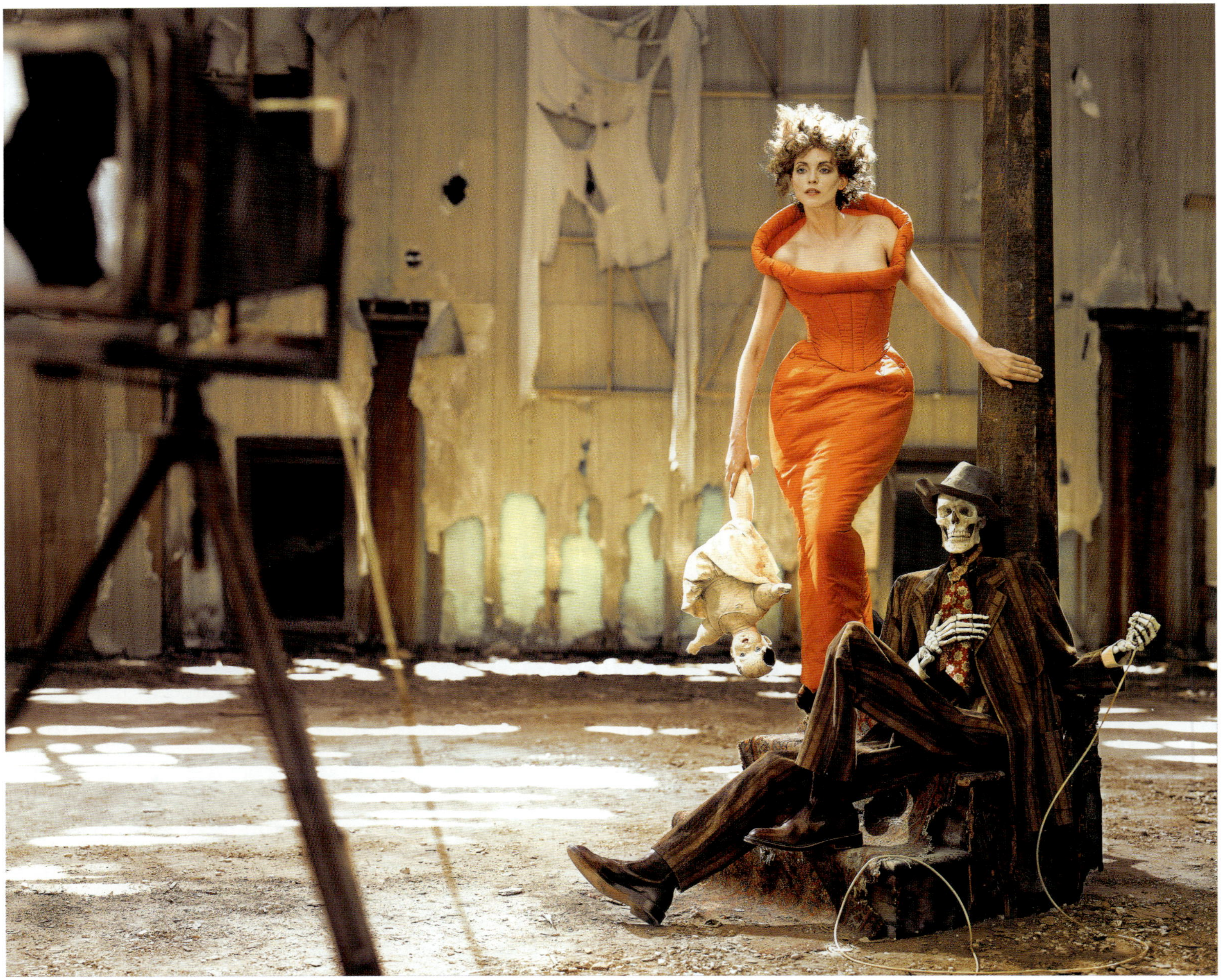

Shown by
Gagosian Gallery D4

Biography
Born 1923
Died 2004

American photographer Avedon had numerous exhibitions during his lifetime, amongst others, the retrospectives "Richard Avedon: Evidence 1944–1994" (1994) at the Whitney Museum of American Art, New York, and "Portraits" (2002) at The Metropolitan Museum of Art, New York. In 2011, the posthumous exhibitions "Avedon/Paris" at Gagosian Gallery, Geneva; "Richard Avedon: Writers" at Gagosian Gallery, Paris; and "Avedon: Artists" at Gagosian Gallery, New York, celebrated his work. His photographs are part of numerous public collections, including the Museum of Modern Art, New York, and the National Portrait Gallery, London. In spring 2012, Gagosian Gallery, West 21st St., New York, will have a major show of his work.

The Comforts Portfolio: A Fable in 24 Episodes, Montauk, New York, August 1995
1998
Iris prints
21¼ × 17"
(54 × 43.2 cm)

Courtesy of Gagosian Gallery

Richard Avedon

Renowned for his black and white portraits and distinctive fashion photography, Richard Avedon's career spanned nearly 60 years. Capturing hundreds of famous figures and anonymous citizens alike, in series including "The Family," his *Rolling Stone* commission documenting the 1976 presidential elections, and "In the American West," a portfolio capturing the people of rural America, he exposed a reality unfamiliar to the genre of portrait photography. Avedon was also the first-ever staff photographer for *The New Yorker*. His series "In Memory of the Late Mr. and Mrs. Comfort" originally appeared in 1995 and features model Nadja Auermann alongside a skeleton in a variety of gothic scenarios—a comment on the luxury, materialism, and life cycle of the fashion industry. SC

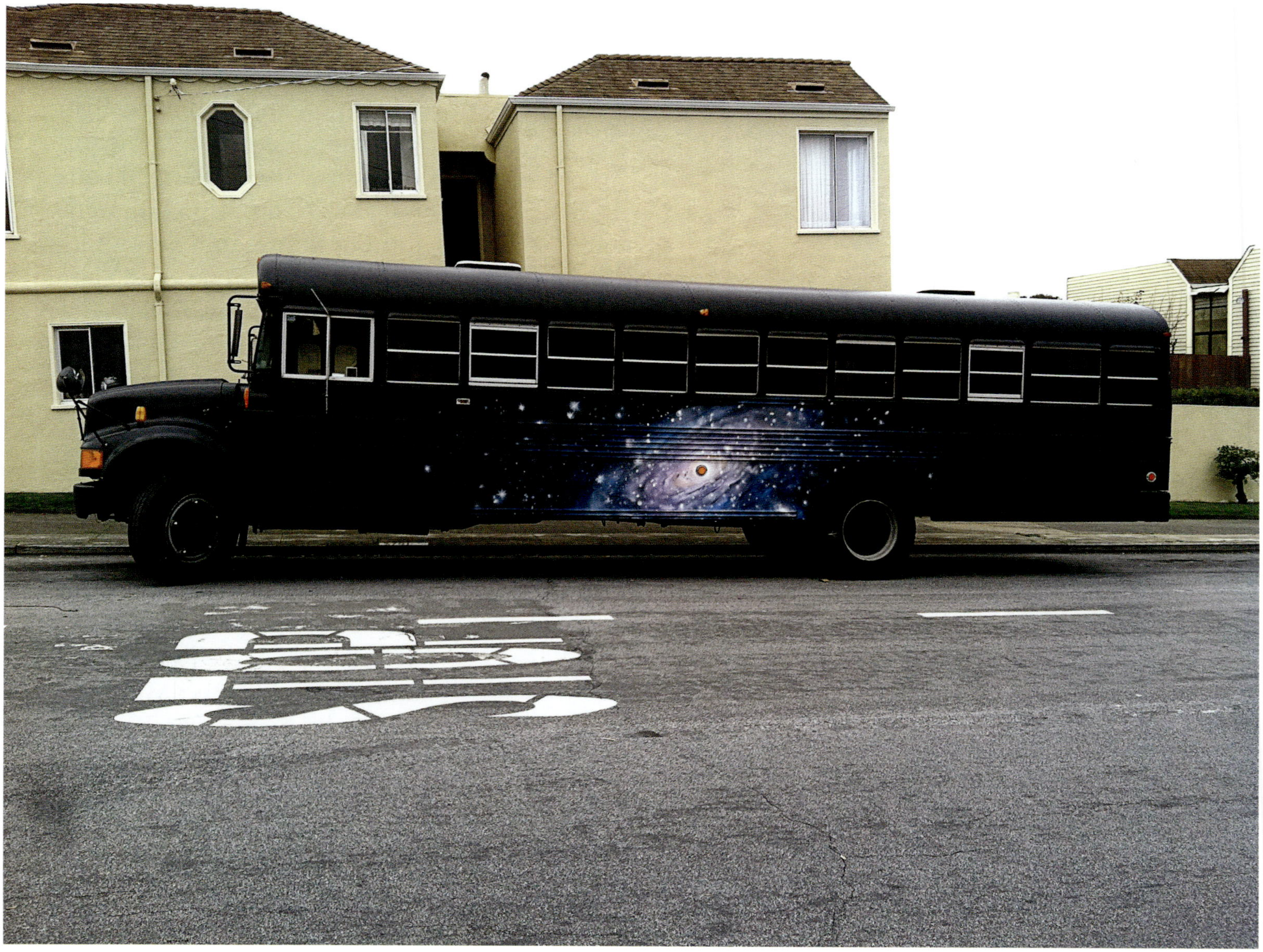

Focus
Lutz Bacher

Shown by
Cabinet C7
Alex Zachary
Peter Currie F2

Biography
Lives in Berkeley

American artist Bacher has exhibited extensively since the 1970s. In early 2012, Alex Zachary Peter Currie, New York, held a self-titled solo exhibition of her work. She is also included in the Whitney Biennial 2012, at the Whitney Museum of American Art, New York. Other recent solo shows were held at Cabinet Gallery, London (2011); "Do You Love Me?" (2009) at Kunstverein München, Munich; and "My Secret Life" (2009) at MoMA PS1, Long Island City.

Untitled
2011
Digital inkjet print
44 × 58½"
(111.5 × 148.5 cm)
Courtesy of Alex Zachary Peter Currie

For around four decades Lutz Bacher has been producing videos, installations, and performances that often build on appropriated images and the details—banal and painful—of her own life. *Closed Circuit* (1997–2000), for example, is a documentary edited down from several months of footage from a surveillance camera mounted above late gallerist Pat Hearn's desk. The titles of her 2009 trilogy of exhibitions—"Spill," "Do You Love Me?" and "My Secret Life"—give a sense of how Bacher's confessional work circles around issues of authorship and cultural overload. Blending the absurd with existential angst, her often damaged and distressed pieces depend on the sometimes twinned processes of illumination and imminent obliteration—of the image, the artist, or the text. ST

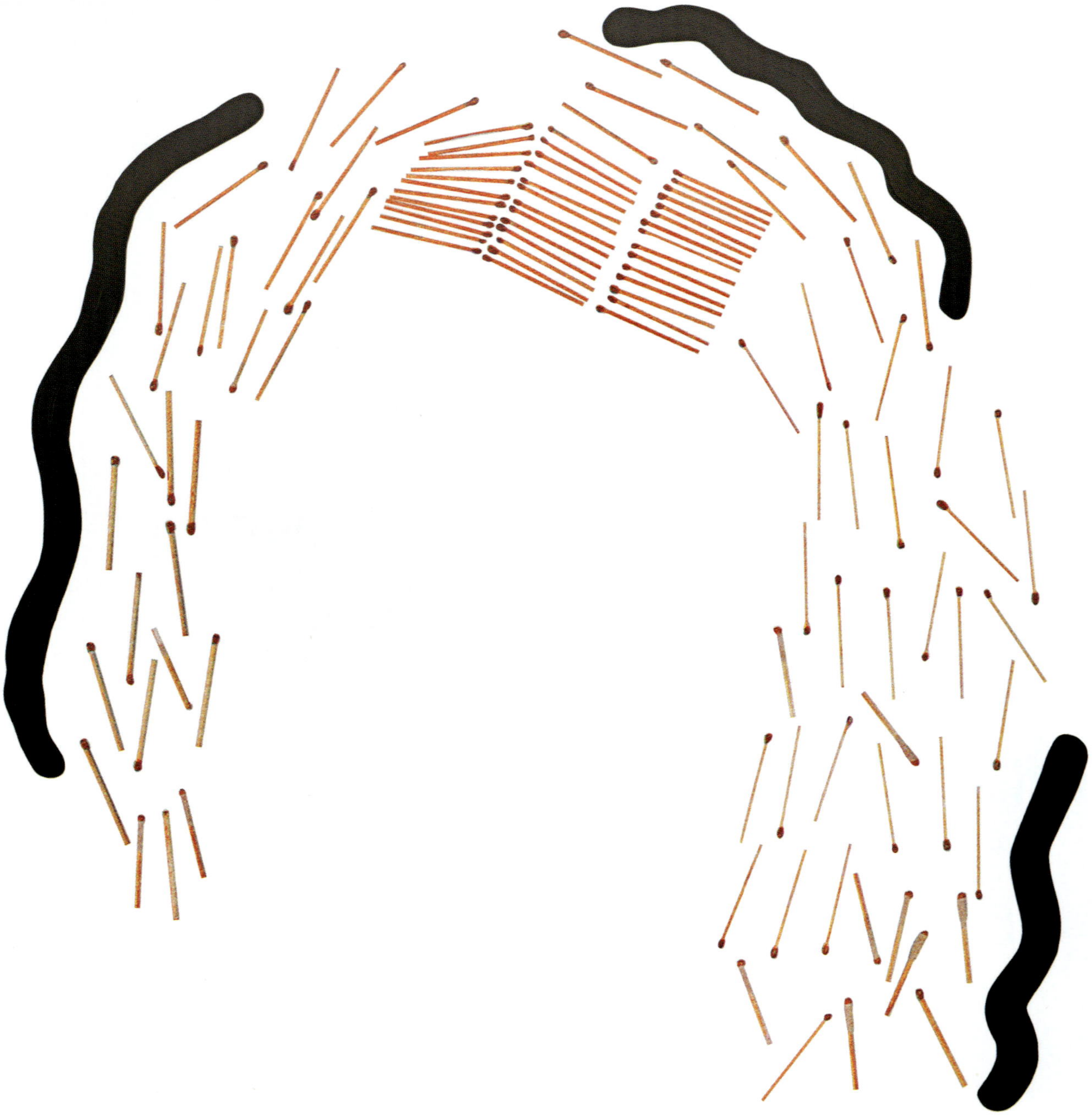

CRISS CROSS

Shown by
Sprüth Magers
Berlin London B37

Biography
Born 1931
Lives in Santa Monica

Seminal artist Baldessari has exhibited his work internationally since the late 1950s. His Conceptual practice has been the subject of numerous retrospective exhibitions, including the recent "John Baldessari: Pure Beauty" (2009) at Tate Modern, London, and "John Baldessari: A Different Kind of Order (Works 1962–1984)" (2005) at Museum Moderner Kunst, Stiftung Ludwig Wien, Vienna. In 2011 he had the solo show "Double Feature" at Sprüth Magers Berlin and participated in the multi-venue Los Angeles survey "Pacific Standard Time."

Double Feature: Criss Cross
2011
Varnished inkjet print on canvas with acrylic and oil paint
84 × 75½"
(213.5 × 192 cm)
Courtesy of Sprüth Magers Berlin London

John Baldessari

John Baldessari foregrounds and redacts imagery to often comic ends, displacing subjectivity through appropriation and collage to invoke universal comedies. Early proto-Conceptual works adopt the blunt methods of slapstick, as in *The Artist Hitting Various Objects with a Golf Club* (1972–3), or display lyrical wit through the re-categorization of images and language. In recent paintings the humor is more formal: the rhythm of the blanked-out faces in *Mystery Street* (2011), for instance, produces a graphic ding-dong within an otherwise lyrical, decorative portrait. Rather than indulging in fanciful inventions, though, Baldessari's method is to push the logical to its extreme until it becomes ridiculous. SOR

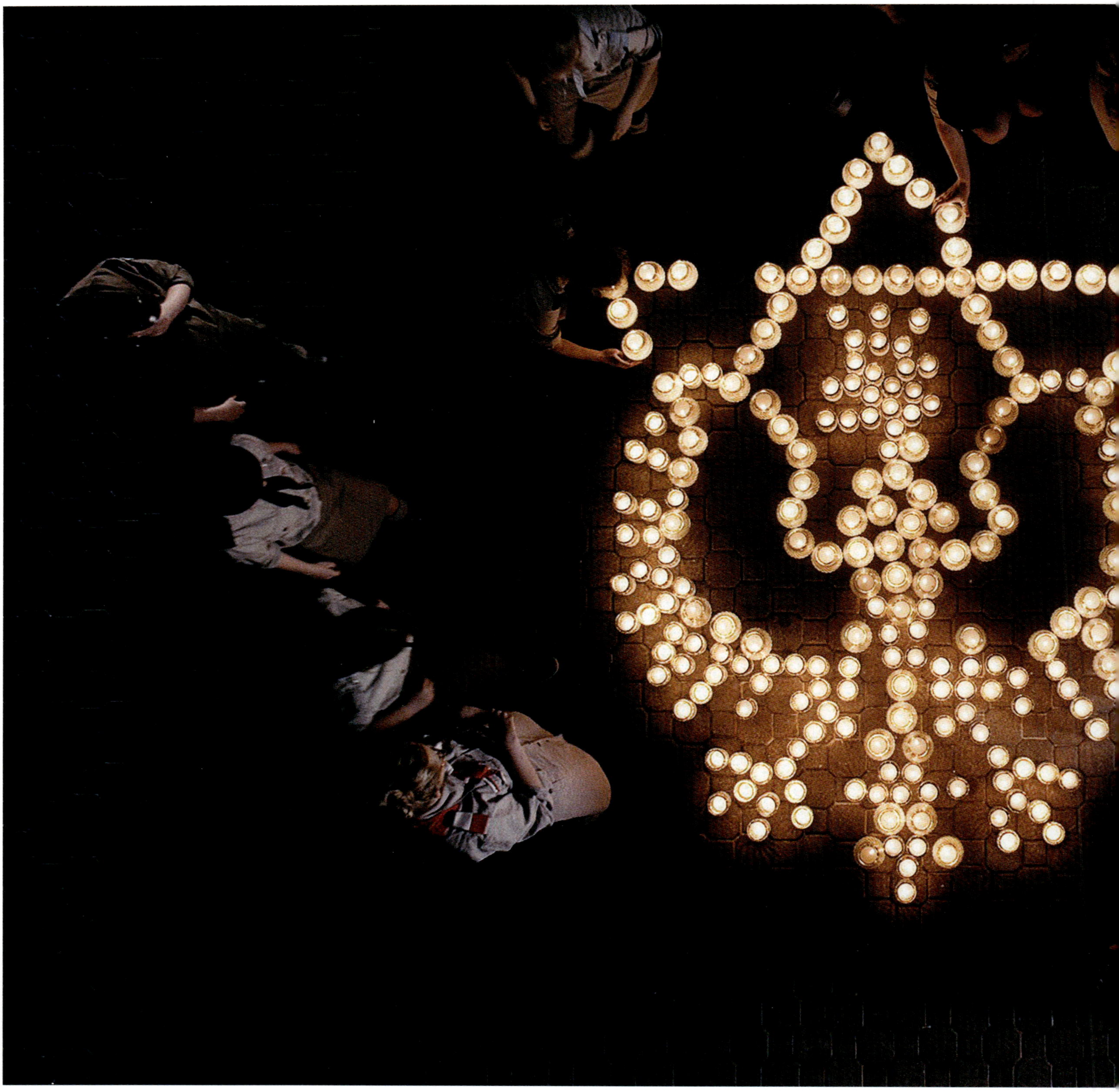

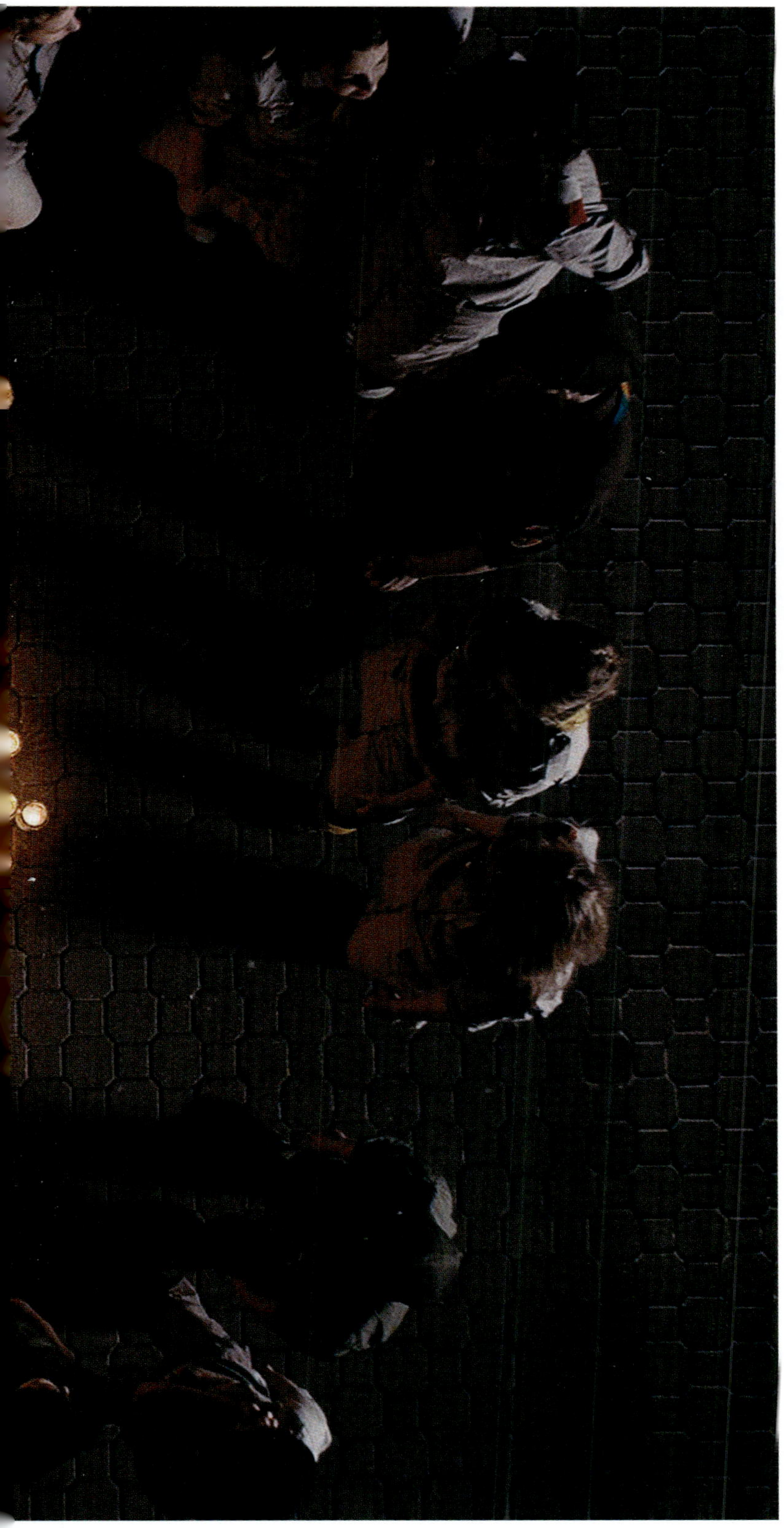

Shown by
Galleria Raffaella Cortese C17
Annet Gelink Gallery A10
Sommer Contemporary Art C37

Biography
Born 1970
Lives in Berlin and Tel Aviv

Israel-born Bartana represented Poland at the 56th Venice Biennale with the exhibition "...And Europe Will Be Stunned" (2011). The similarly titled solo show "And Europe Will be Stunned" (2010) at Modern Museum, Malmö, included five recent video works. In 2009 she had a solo show at Museum of Modern Art, Warsaw, and in 2008 she had a solo show at MoMA PS1, Long Island City. In 2010 she received the 4th Artes Mundi Award, Cardiff, and was awarded the Principal Prize at the Oberhausen Short Film Festival.

Zamach
2011
RED transferred to HD
35 min.
Courtesy of Annet Gelink Gallery

Yael Bartana

Yael Bartana's three videos (2007–11) were the first art works ever by a non-Polish artist to be shown in the Polish Pavilion at last year's 56th Venice Biennale. Remembering, forgetting, territorializing, and moving on, or back, are central operations within the narrative of the three films, which together build through insinuation, lacunae, and direct address, an impression of the complexity and turbulence of Jewish politics and histories in Poland. By presenting accounts of a real kibbutz and a fictional Jewish Renaissance movement in Poland, and by drawing on Leni Riefenstahl's propagandist aesthetics and using the voice of political commentator and literary critic Sławomir Sierakowski, Bartana performs both archeology on and the architectural construction of difficult and insistent mythologies. SOR

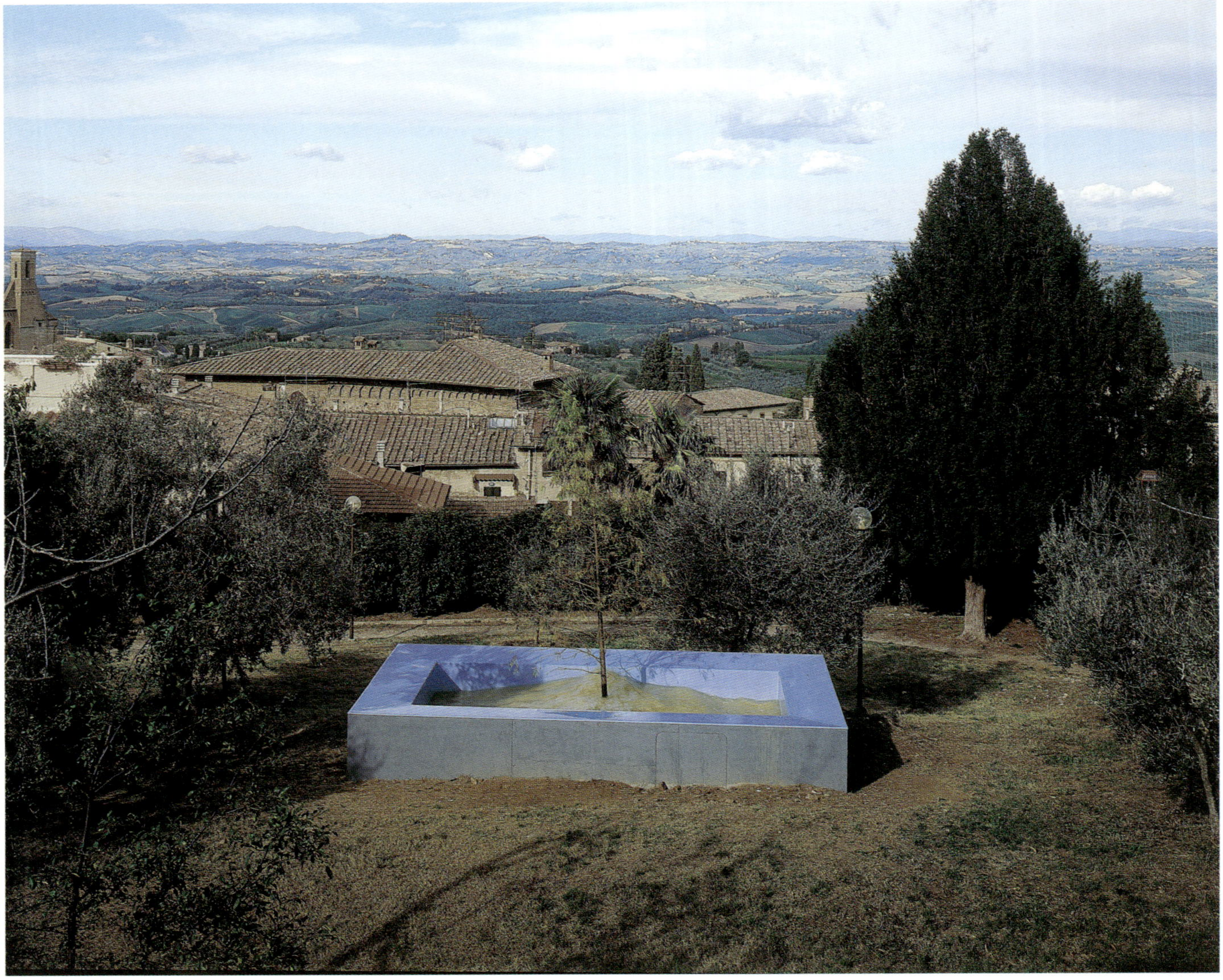

1

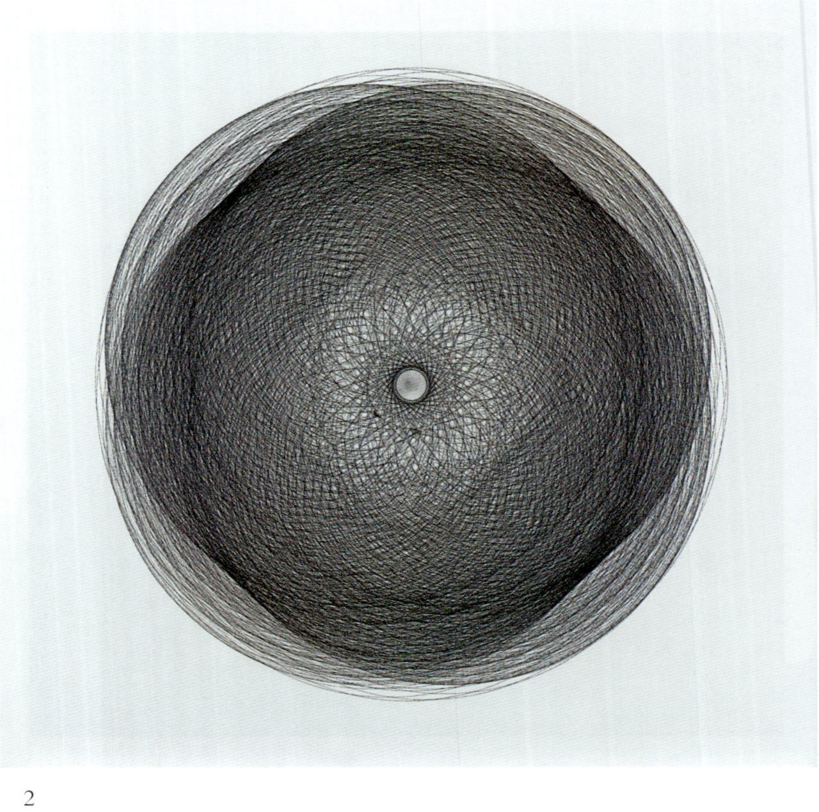

2

Massimo Bartolini

Massimo Bartolini intends his sculptures, site-specific installations, performances, photographs, and drawings to "bring the body to the level of the imagination." His experiential environments include *Flowerbed (Moenchengladbach)* (2007), in which 12 men and women formed a human frame around a square of soil, and the installation series "Testa" (Head, 1997–ongoing), consisting of shadowless white "limbo" rooms with rounded corners, where spectators enter one at a time to observe an object or listen to a puzzling sound. For *Three Quarter Tone Pieces* (2009), Bartolini concealed a motion-activated ventilator within a cabinet, a wardrobe, and a chest, enabling the furniture to emit 30-second bursts of organ music, composed of notes one quarter tone apart. SL

Shown by
Massimo De Carlo B1
Frith Street Gallery C42

Biography
Born 1962
Lives in Cecina

Since the mid-1990s, Italian artist Bartolini has exhibited extensively in Europe. The solo shows "Serce na dłoni" (A Warm Heart, 2011) at the Centre of Contemporary Art, Torun, and "Dews" (2010), at ICA Sofia, profiled his multifarious practice. Recent group shows include "Yokohama 2011: International Triennale of Contemporary Art" (2011) and "The World Belongs to You" (2011) at the Palazzo Grassi, Venice. In summer 2012 he will participate in dOCUMENTA (13), Kassel.

1
Untitled (Wave and Tree)
2004
Mixed media
25 3⁄8 × 137 3⁄4 × 41 3⁄4"
(645 × 350 × 106 cm)
Courtesy of Frith Street Gallery

2
Until it Breaks
2008
Ink on paper
59 × 62 3⁄4"
(150 × 159.5 cm)
Courtesy of Frith Street Gallery

3
Revolutionary Monk
2006
Painted wood, engine, and bronze
17 3⁄4 × 17 3⁄4 × 63"
(45 × 45 × 160 cm)
Courtesy of Frith Street Gallery

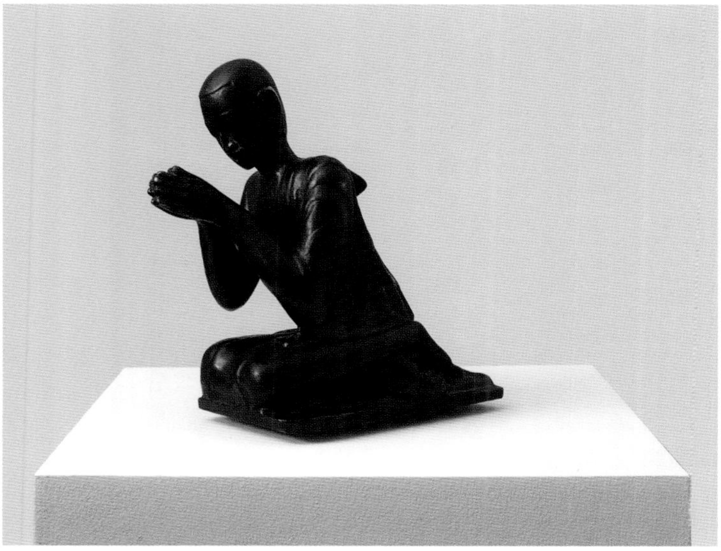

3

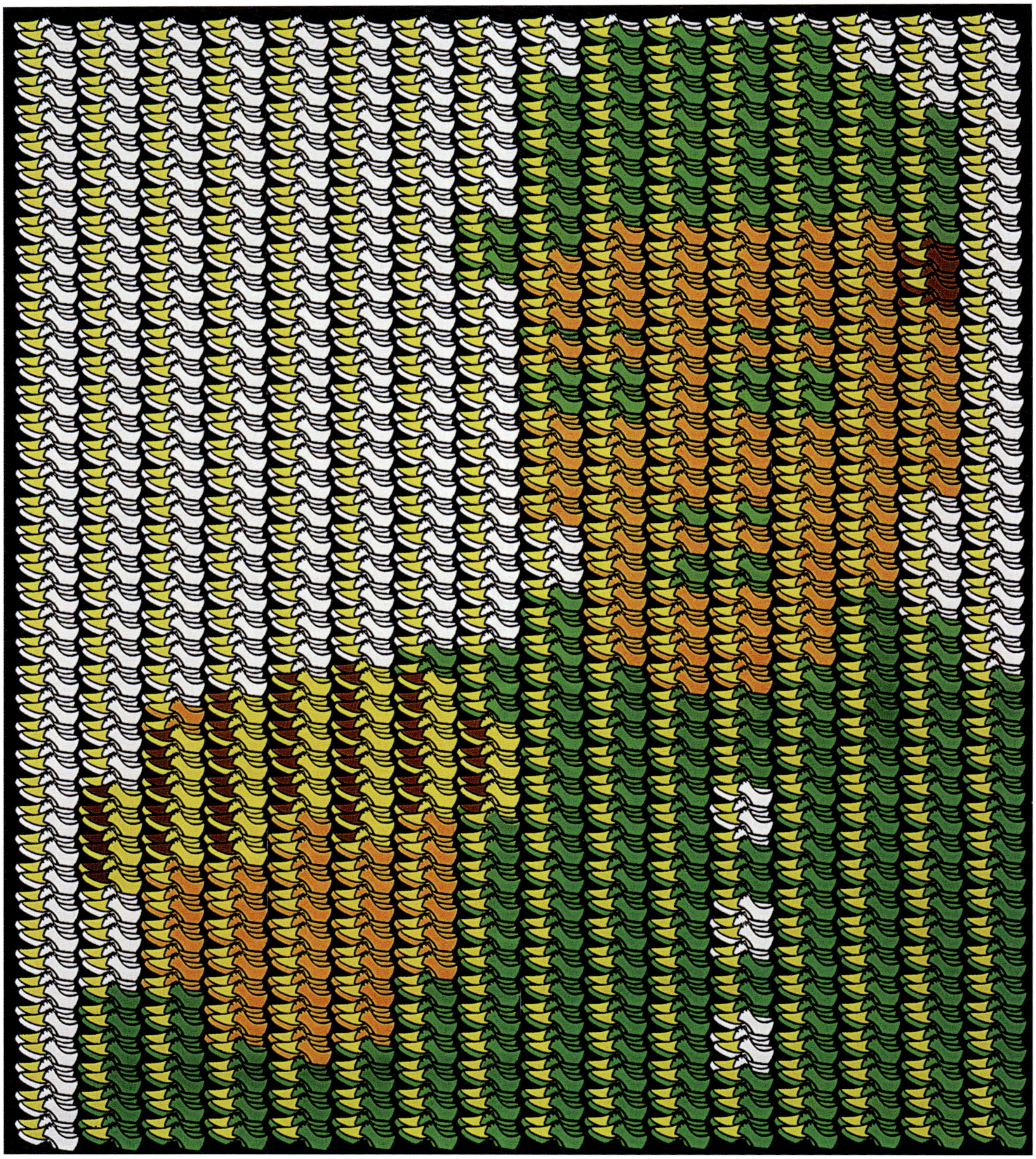

Shown by
Air de Paris C11
Gavin Brown's enterprise B18
Galerie Mezzanin F29
Galerie Francesca Pia F7
Galerie Barbara Weiss A27

Biography
Born 1937
Lives in Frankfurt am Main

German-born Bayrle has been exhibiting internationally for several decades in Europe and the United States. In 2009, his paintings, prints, and sculptures were the subject of a retrospective at the Museu d'Art Contemporani, Barcelona, entitled "I've a Feeling We're Not in Kansas Anymore." His numerous exhibitions include the solo shows "Gummibaum and Materials" (2010) at Base Progetti per l'Arte, Florence, and "Looping" (2008) at Museum Ludwig, Cologne. In 2012 he will participate in dOCUMENTA (13), Kassel.

Butteresser
1968–2002
Silkscreen print on plastic on canvas
98⅜ × 120"
(250 × 305 cm)
Courtesy of Galerie Barbara Weiss

Thomas Bayrle

A pioneering figure of West German Pop art, for more than 40 years Thomas Bayrle has made works that flicker between macro and micro systems, returning time and again to the frictionless flows of information, automobiles, and global capital. While his work takes many different forms—including paintings, collages, sculptures, and computer animations (which he produced as early as the 1970s)—his defining innovation is what he calls the "super-form," in which an image is composed of hundreds of smaller images. For example, *Telefonbau–Normalzeit (Gelb)* (Telephone AT&T (Yellow), 1970) comprises a face formed from a morphed grid of phones. As Bayrle, who for four decades was also an influential teacher in Frankfurt, has himself noted, "The world is not a fixed image." ST

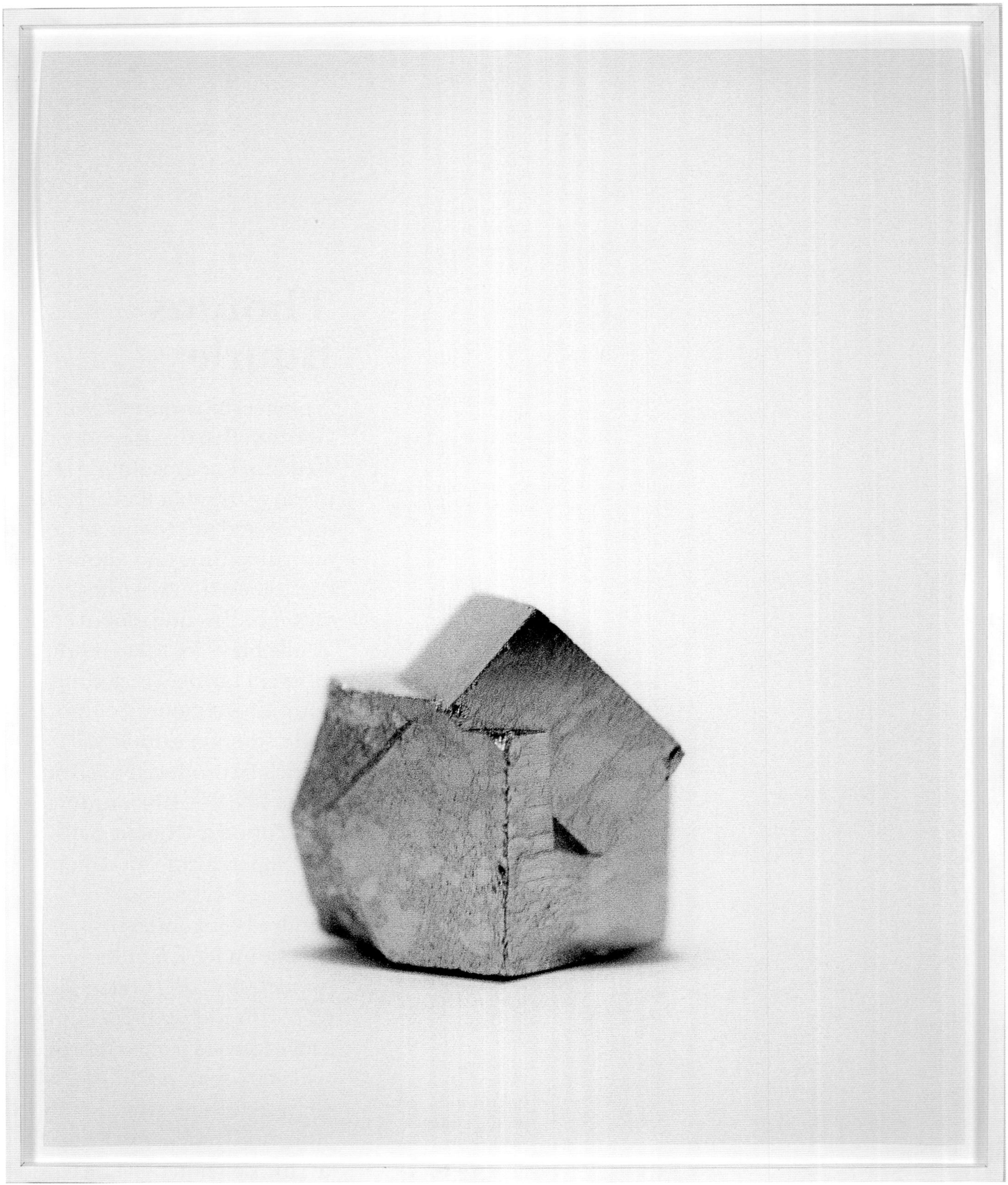

1

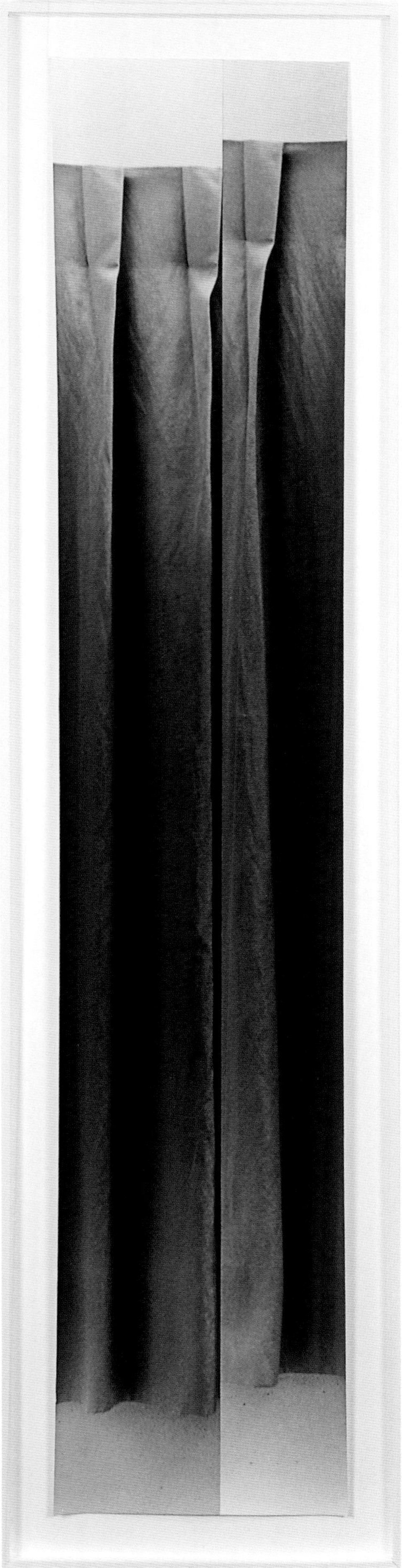

2

Shown by
Laura Bartlett Gallery
C26

Biography
Born 1975
Lives in St. Leonard's on Sea

British artist Beasley's sculptural and graphic works have been the subject of numerous exhibitions in recent years. In 2012 she will have solo shows in London, at Tate Britain as part of the "Art Now" series, at Laura Bartlett Gallery, and at Spike Island, Bristol. She participated in the survey show "British Art Show 7: In the Days of the Comet" at Nottingham Contemporary, which toured to London, Glasgow, and Plymouth. In 2011 she also contributed to the group show "Structure and Material" at Longside Gallery, Wakefield.

1
Untitled KORREKTUR 6 (ENE)
2010
Inkjet on Hahnemühle photo rag 310gsm paper using archival inks, pale yellow acrylic glass
51⅛ × 42⅞"
(130 × 109 cm)
Courtesy of Laura Bartlett Gallery

2
You're (I)
2010
Seamed, matt, gelatin silver prints
55⅜ × 19⅜"
(196.5 × 49 cm)
Courtesy of Laura Bartlett Gallery

Becky Beasley

Literary references and texts frequently provide a starting point, or an underlying narrative, for Becky Beasley's expertly crafted objects and images, which typically play out in series as if articulating an unfolding idea. The Austrian author Thomas Bernhard provided the inspiration for one body of work comprising a series of photographs and objects, including *Brocken I–VIII* (2009), eight hinged plank-like wooden works based on the variously configured arm measurements of the artist's father. They articulate a recurring interest in the idea of something being both object and support for something else. In her project *The Outside* (2011–ongoing), Beasley is exploring the relationship between sculpture and photography, using the Turin apartment of Italian designer Carlo Mollino as her point of departure. AB

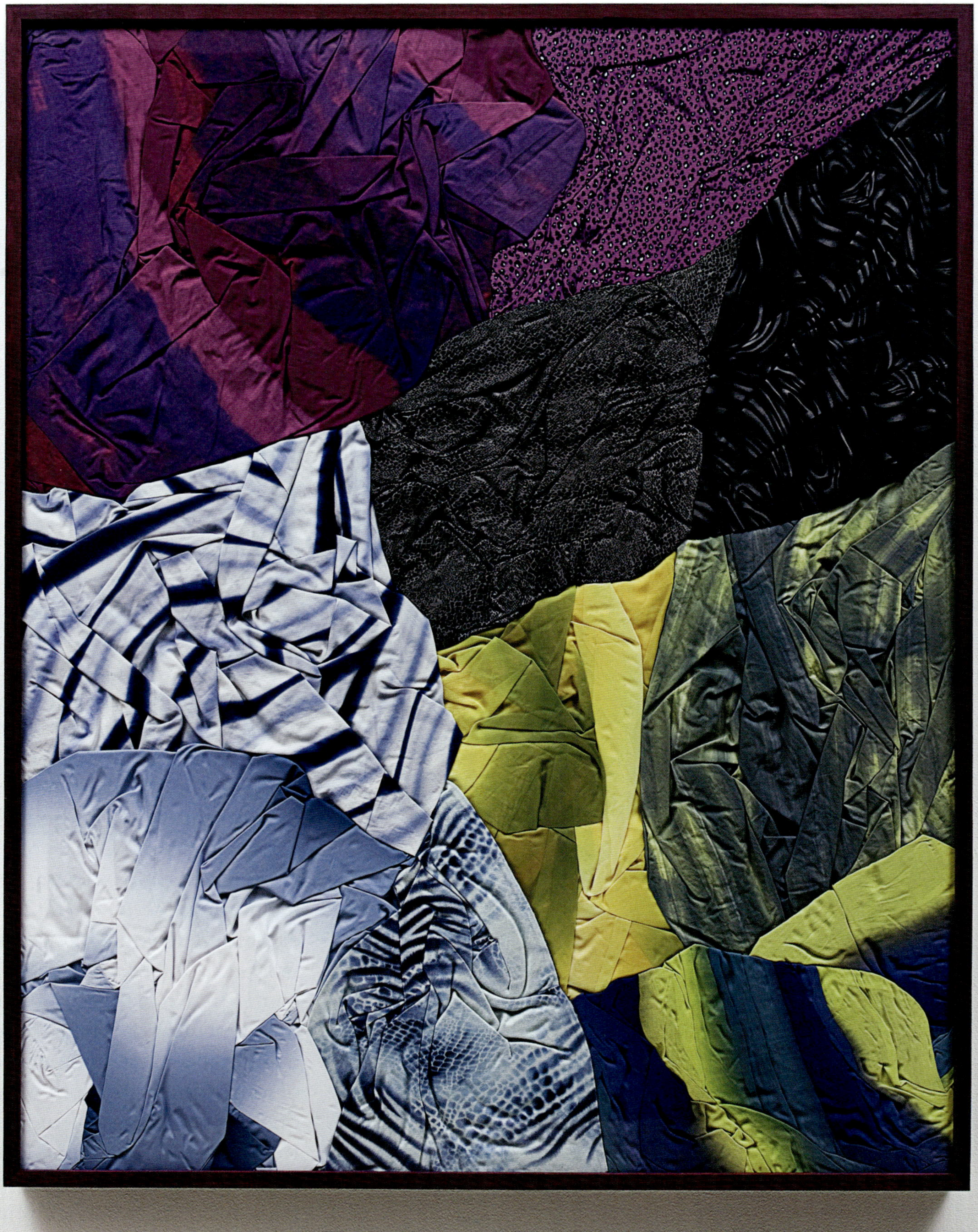

Shown by
Laura Bartlett Gallery
C26
STANDARD (Oslo)
E41

Biography
Born 1975
Lives in Berlin

Denmark-born Beier has exhibited collaboratively with Marie Lund and more recently in solo exhibitions at Laura Bartlett Gallery, London (2012); in "Bleeding Clothes, Drowning Coins" (2011) at STANDARD (Oslo); and in "Nina Beier" (2011) at Kunsthal Charlottenborg, Copenhagen. In 2011 she also participated in the group shows "Modify, as Needed" at Museum of Contemporary Art, Miami; "What Happened to the Other Dollar?" at Proyectos Monclova, Mexico City; and "Museum of Speech" at Extra City, Antwerp.

Portrait Mode [Oslo #6]
2011
Found garments in wooden frame
57⅞ × 47⅝ × 2⅜"
(147 × 121 × 6 cm)
Courtesy of STANDARD (Oslo)

Nina Beier

The sculptural work of Nina Beier highlights what is omitted as much as what is shown. From assortments of crumpled fabrics held within frames in her "Portrait Mode" series (2011) to ladders, chairs, and radiators acting as supports for blown-up stock images in "The Demonstrators" series (2011), the object's use-function is displaced for phenomenological presence. Her sculptural installation *Shelving for Unlocked Matter and Open Problems* (2010)—shown as part of the survey exhibition "Based in Berlin" in 2011, at Berlin's Hamburger Bahnhof—positions a variety of sawn-off small-scale Modernist sculptures and ornaments as load bearers for a stacked and interlocking glass shelving unit, reconditioned sculpture and shelf acting as both plinth and display. PT

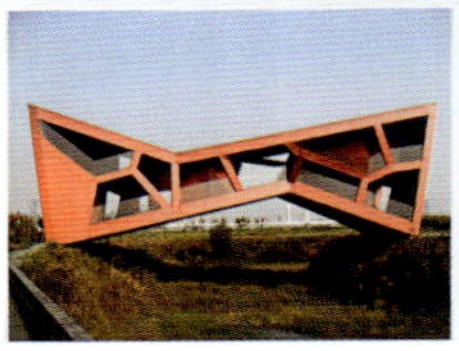
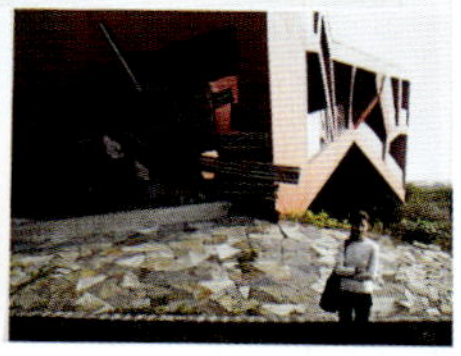

1

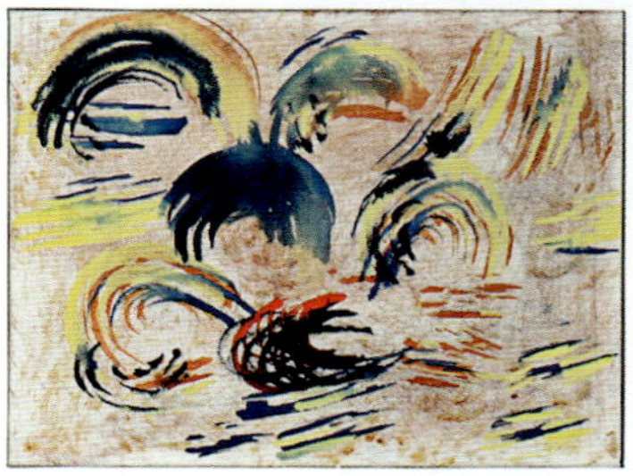

2

Will Benedict

Several of Will Benedict's recent works mimic the reverse of an unwritten postcard (albeit an outsized one). Comprised of framed white foamcore—each with a vertical line running down its center as if to separate the space for the address from the actual message—compositions such as *Tea House*, *Arab Institute*, or *Elevator* (all 2008) flaunt photographic images in their top right corner, like surrogate stamps. For the most part these dispatches lack an addressee, or even so much as a "wish you were here"—although there are notable exceptions, such as *Berlusconi* (2011), where scrawled handwriting cryptically bids the former Italian prime minister "Buona Fortuna con l'Indigestione" ("good luck with the indigestion"). MA

Shown by
Galerie Meyer Kainer
B27

Biography
Born 1978
Lives in Vienna

American artist Benedict graduated from the Staatliche Hochschule für Bildende Künste Städelschule, Frankfurt am Main, in 2006. In 2012 he will have a solo exhibition, "Bonjour Tourist," at Gio' Marconi, Milan; other recent exhibitions include "Village Gossip meets the Newspaper Photo-roman" (2011) at Eternithaus, Berlin, and Galerie Christian Andersen, Copenhagen. In 2011 he also participated in group shows at Portikus, Frankfurt; Renwick Gallery, New York; and Office Baroque, Antwerp.

1
Tea House
2008
Mixed media
24⅜ × 33"
(59.5 × 84 cm)
Courtesy of Galerie Meyer Kainer

2
Camera 1
2008
Mixed media
42½ × 61"
(108 × 155 cm)
Courtesy of Galerie Meyer Kainer

3
Afterwork Dustbowl (Butoh)
2011
Mixed media
42½ × 61"
(108 × 155 cm)
Courtesy of Galerie Meyer Kainer

4
Flag Anxiety
2011
Mixed media
42½ × 61"
(108 × 155 cm)
Courtesy of Galerie Meyer Kainer

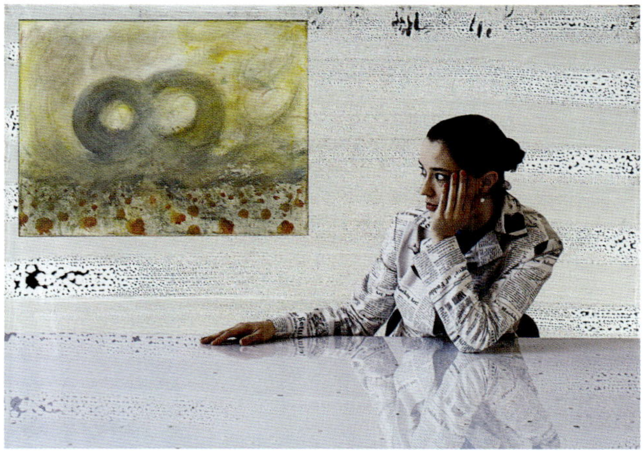

3

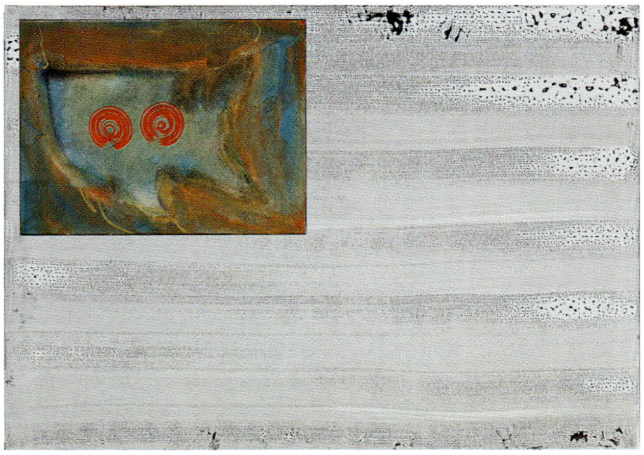

4

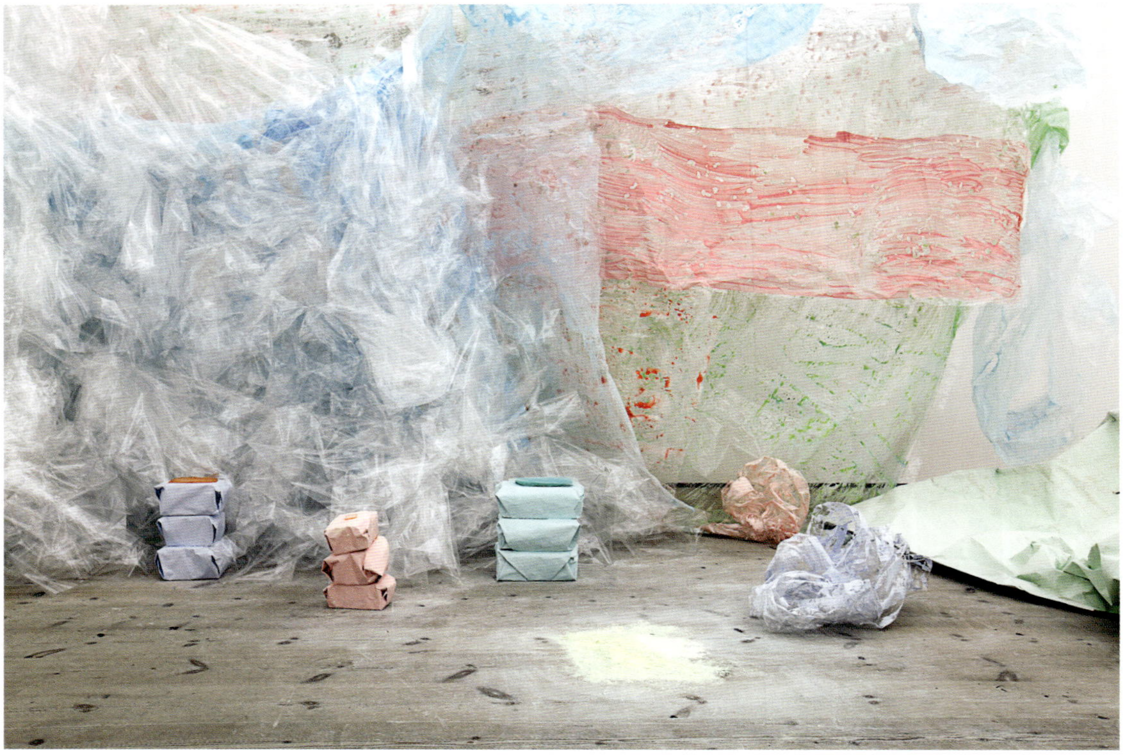

1

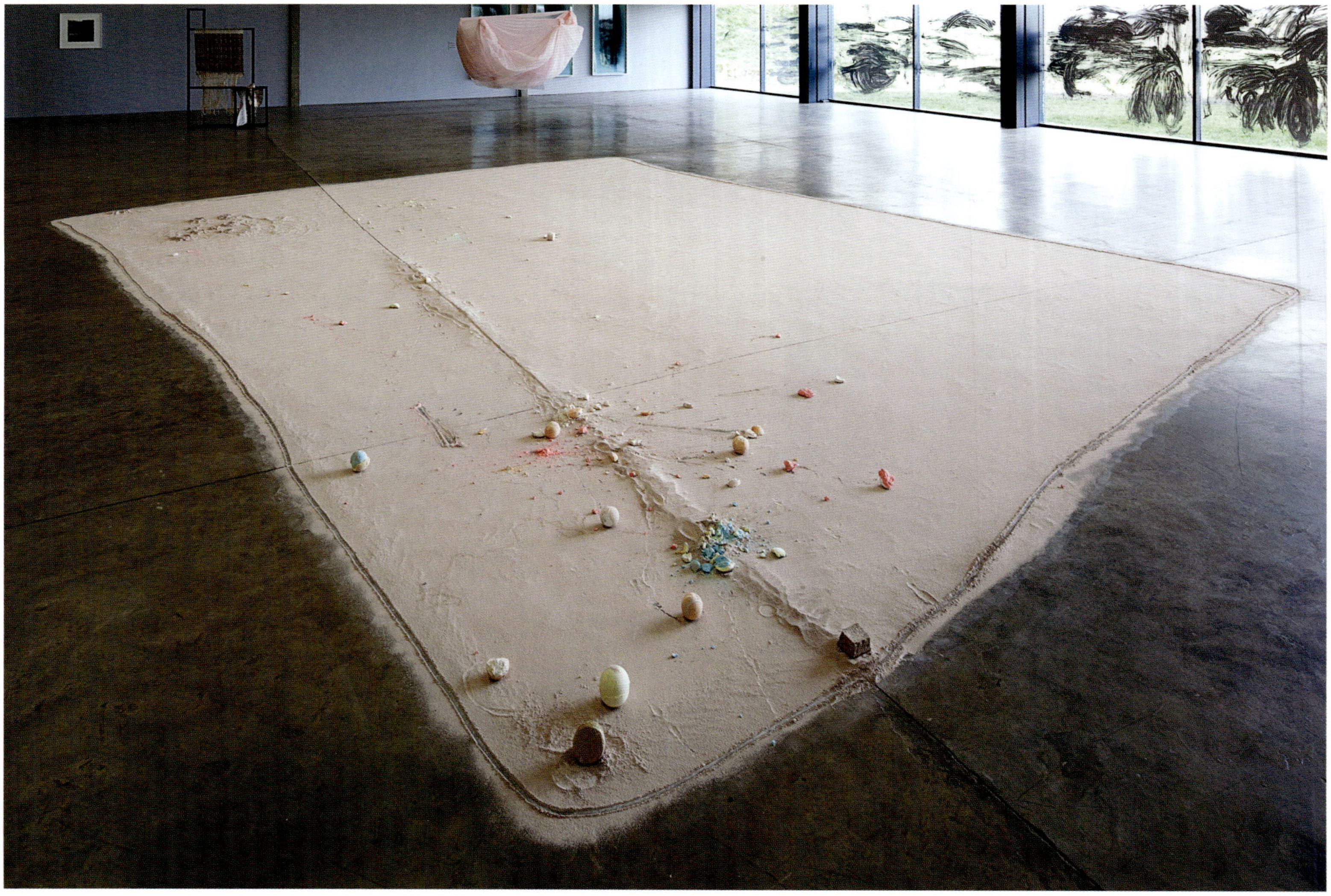

2

Shown by
Galerie Gisela Capitain B19
Stuart Shave/Modern Art C43

Biography
Born 1972
Lives in Glasgow

In recent years Turner Prize 2011 nominee Black has exhibited extensively in Europe. She held the solo exhibitions "Karla Black: Scotland + Venice" (2011) in Venice, and "Ten Sculptures" (2010) at Kunsthalle Nuremberg. Her sculptural works were also shown in solo shows at Inverleith House, Edinburgh (2009); Modern Art Oxford (2009); Kunstverein Hamburg (2009); and Migros Museum, Zurich (2009). In 2010 she was also included in the national survey exhibition "British Art Show 7: In the Days of the Comet."

1
Doesn't Care in Words
(detail)
2011
Mixed media
Dimensions variable
Courtesy of Galerie Gisela Capitain

2
Persuader Face
2011
Bath bombs, powder, eyeshadow, bronzing powder, face powder, lipstick, bath cream
3¾ × 292⅛ × 220"
(9.5 × 742 × 559 cm)
Courtesy of Galerie Gisela Capitain

3
Not A Person In The World
2010
Cellophane, sellotape, ribbon, paint, plaster powder, powder paint
Dimensions variable
Courtesy of Capitain Petzel, Berlin

Karla Black

Karla Black describes making her process-based sculptural pieces as "a material experience that has been prioritized over language." Black transforms familiar household goods and more conventional art materials into colorful abstract compositions, such as *Left Right Left Right* (2010), a vast *mille-feuille* of materials including compost, top soil, sand, hairspray, and spray paint that command the exhibition space. Her Turner Prize 2011 installation comprised two new complementary works: the ephemeral, freestanding construction *Doesn't Care In Words* (made from cellophane, paint, Sellotape, sugar paper, chalk, powder paint, plaster powder, wood, Styrofoam, bath bombs, Vaseline, moisturizing cream, spray deodorant, and brown paper) and the luminous, cloud-like arrangement *More of the Day* (composed using polythene, powder paint, plaster powder and thread). SL

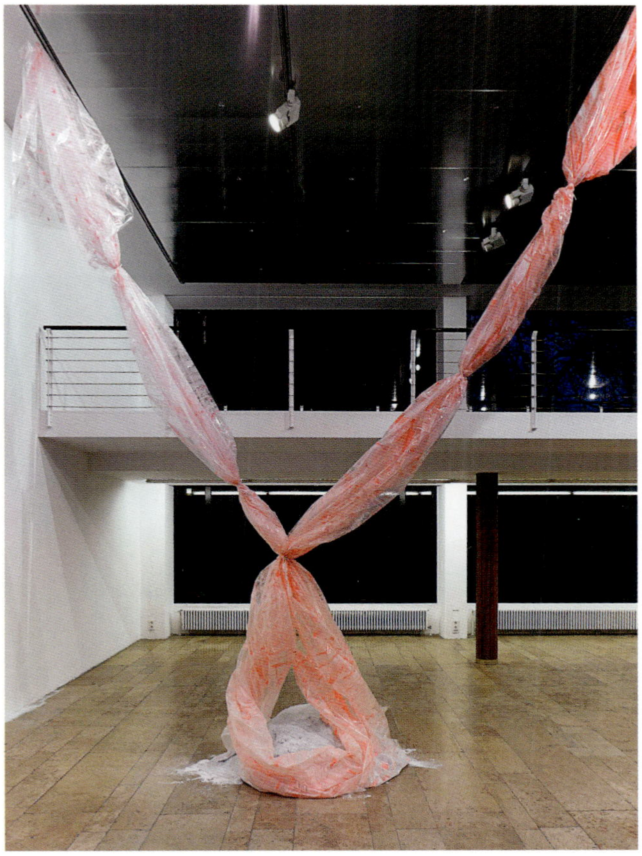

3

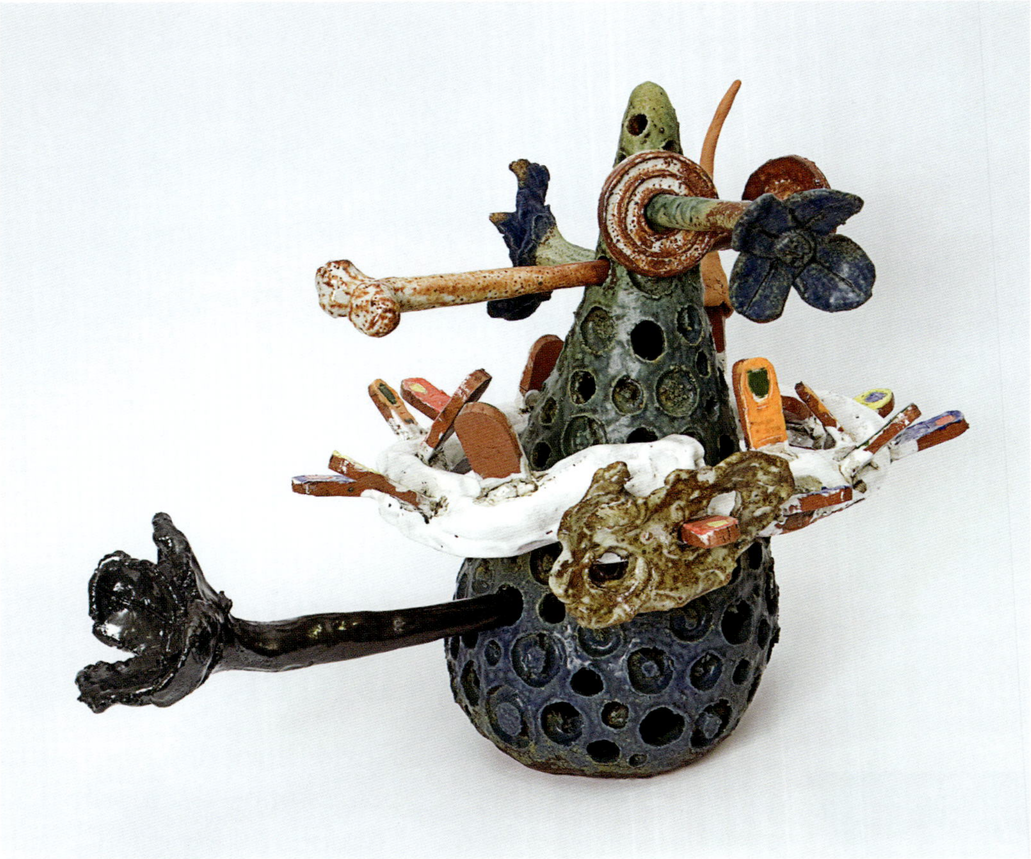

1

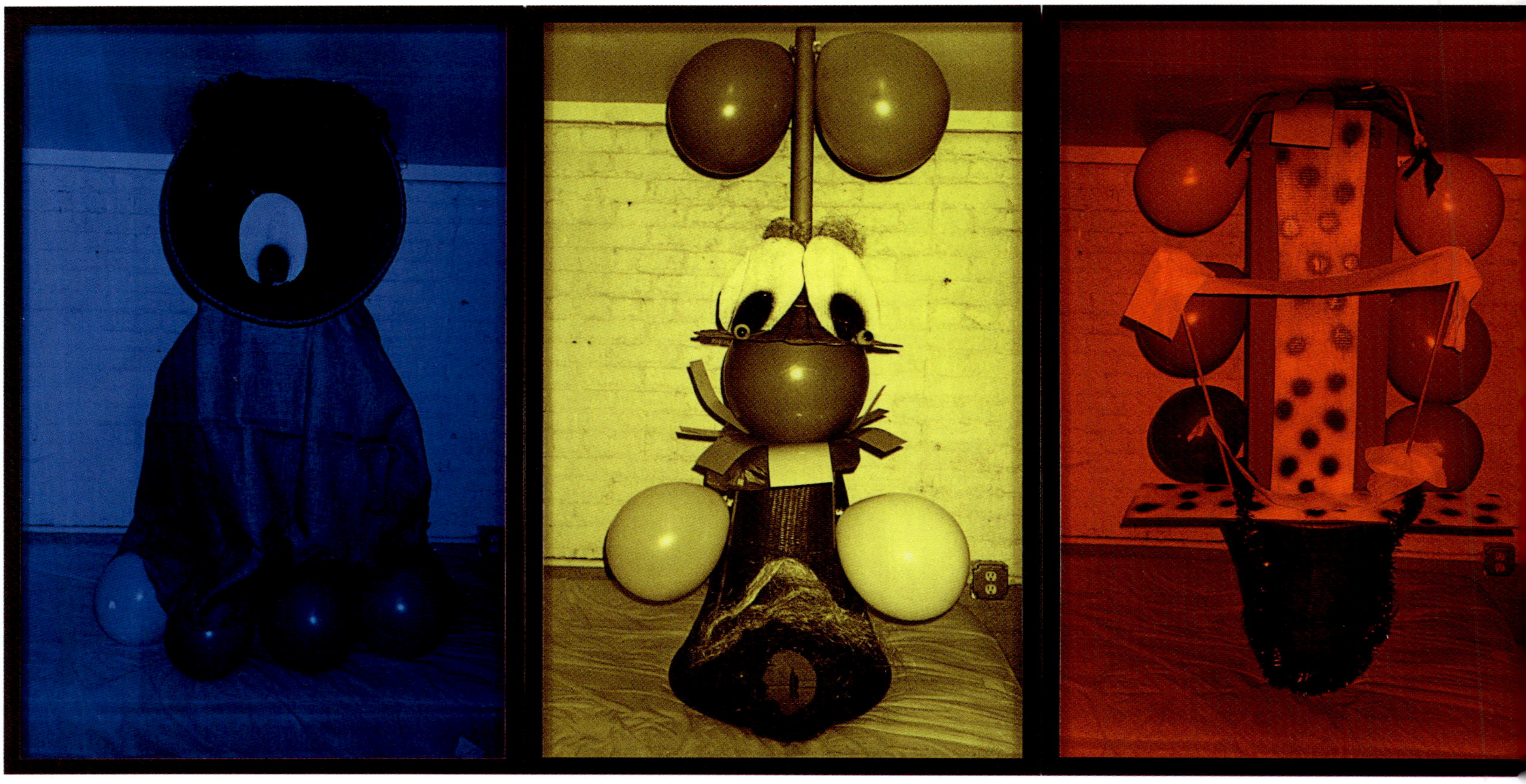

2

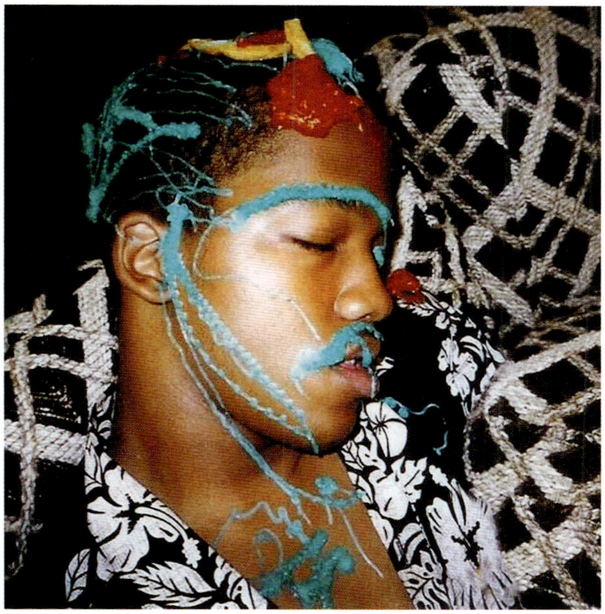

3

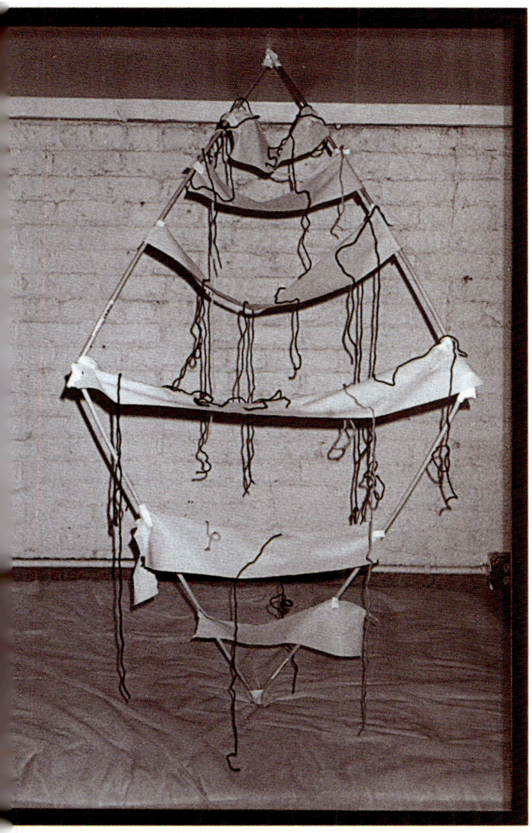

Shown by
Nicole Klagsbrun
Gallery A21

Biography
Born 1969
Lives in Barcelona

American artist Bluechel's sculptures have populated numerous galleries in recent years. Solo shows include "Find Hortense" (2011) at Galerie Joseph Tang, Paris, and "Another with Suspensions" (2011) at Nicole Klagsbrun, New York. Recent group shows include "Paul Clay" (2011) at Salon 94, New York; "Eat Me!" (2010) at Postmasters Gallery, New York; and "On from Here" (2009) at Guild & Greyshkul, New York. Prior to graduating with an MFA from Yale University, he participated in the survey show "Greater New York 2005" at MoMA PS1, Long Island City.

1
Dizzying Hyperactive Ritual
2011
Glazed ceramic
16⅜ × 21 × 15"
(42 × 53.5 × 38 cm)
Courtesy of Nicole Klagsbrun Gallery

2
Untitled
2004
Black and white photographs with gel filters
19¼ × 52" each
(49 × 132 cm each)
Courtesy of Nicole Klagsbrun Gallery

3
Untitled (detail)
2011
C-type print
8 × 10"
(20 × 25.5 cm)
Courtesy of Nicole Klagsbrun Gallery

Sean Bluechel

Happily landed with babbling titles such as *Comets Remind Me of My Friend's Backyard* (2011), *Inspired Mystic Condemned to Solitude* (2011), or *Dizzying Hyperactive Ritual* (2011), Sean Bluechel's ceramic pieces are an irresistible profusion of the childlike and the esoteric. Looking like some forgotten Niki de Saint Phalle public art works, mangled with priapic junk shop pottery curios or implausibly glazed confectionery, they have been exhibited in clusters of four or five on simple wooden trestle tables, all the better to unpretentiously display their creepy–charming energy. Also comprising photography and drawing—and with a career that has embraced creating decorative shrouds for cadavers—Bluechel's art grins with depraved amusement. MA

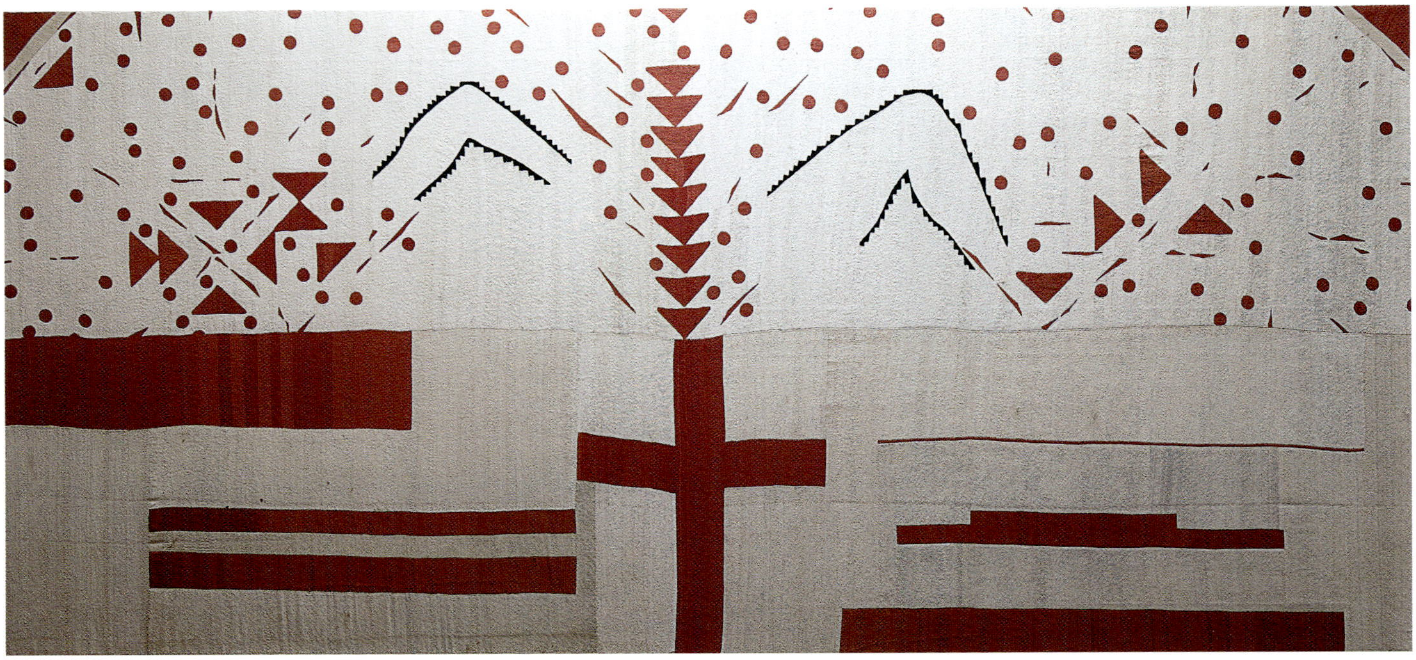
1

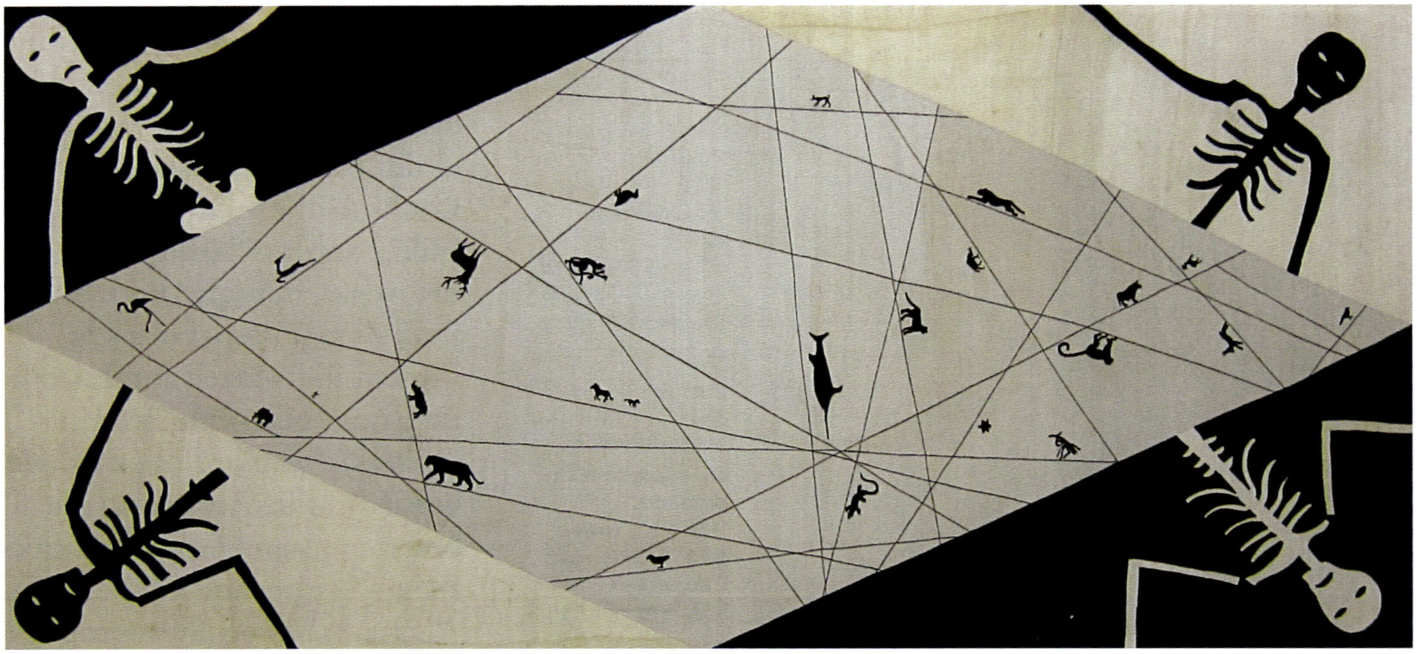
2

Alighiero Boetti

Shown by
Massimo Minini B22
Simon Lee Gallery A5
Sprüth Magers Berlin London B37

Biography
Born 1940
Died 1994

Italian artist Boetti's practice spanned nearly four decades. His contributions to Arte Povera, and contemporary art more generally, mark him out as one of the 20th century's most important Italian artists. There have been several posthumous exhibitions of his work, including "Mettere al mondo il mondo" (Bringing the World into the World, 1998) at Museum für Moderne Kunst, Frankfurt am Main, and "Boetti; the Maverick Spirit of Arte Povera" (1999), at Whitechapel Gallery, London. In early 2012 Tate Modern, London, also staged an exhibition of his work.

Alighiero e Boetti's art is sited within a broad field of significance built as much on chance as on design and can be mapped with methods that become the matter of the art work itself. In 1969 he used the Italian postal service to send wrongly addressed letters to friends; he translates a system of information conduits into a set of stamps and signatures. In an obverse operation, his embroidered maps that constitute the "Mappa" (Map) series—made from the early 1970s onwards, first working in collaboration with traditional artisans in Afghanistan, then relocating to Pakistan following the Russian invasion of 1979—imply the magical compression performed by symbols, in this case national flags, which nonetheless carry immense and unstable meanings. SOR

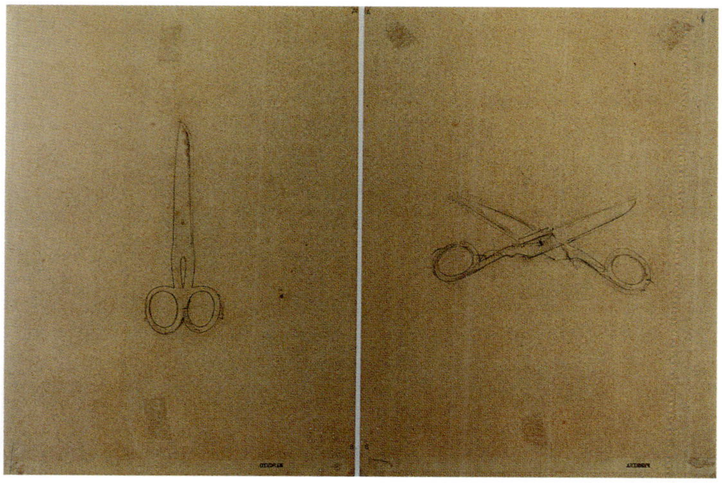

3

1
Alighiero Boetti and Mimmo Paladino
Senza titolo (Untitled)
1989–91
Embroidery on canvas
48⅞ × 107½"
(124 × 273 cm)
Courtesy of Galleria Massimo Minini

2
Alighiero Boetti and Mimmo Paladino
Senza titolo (Untitled)
1989–91
Embroidery on canvas
50 × 109"
(127 × 277 cm)
Courtesy of Galleria Massimo Minini

3
Maschio-Femmina
(Masculine-Feminine)
1970s
Frottage on paper
19⅝ × 29⅛"
(50 × 74 cm)
Courtesy of Galleria Massimo Minini

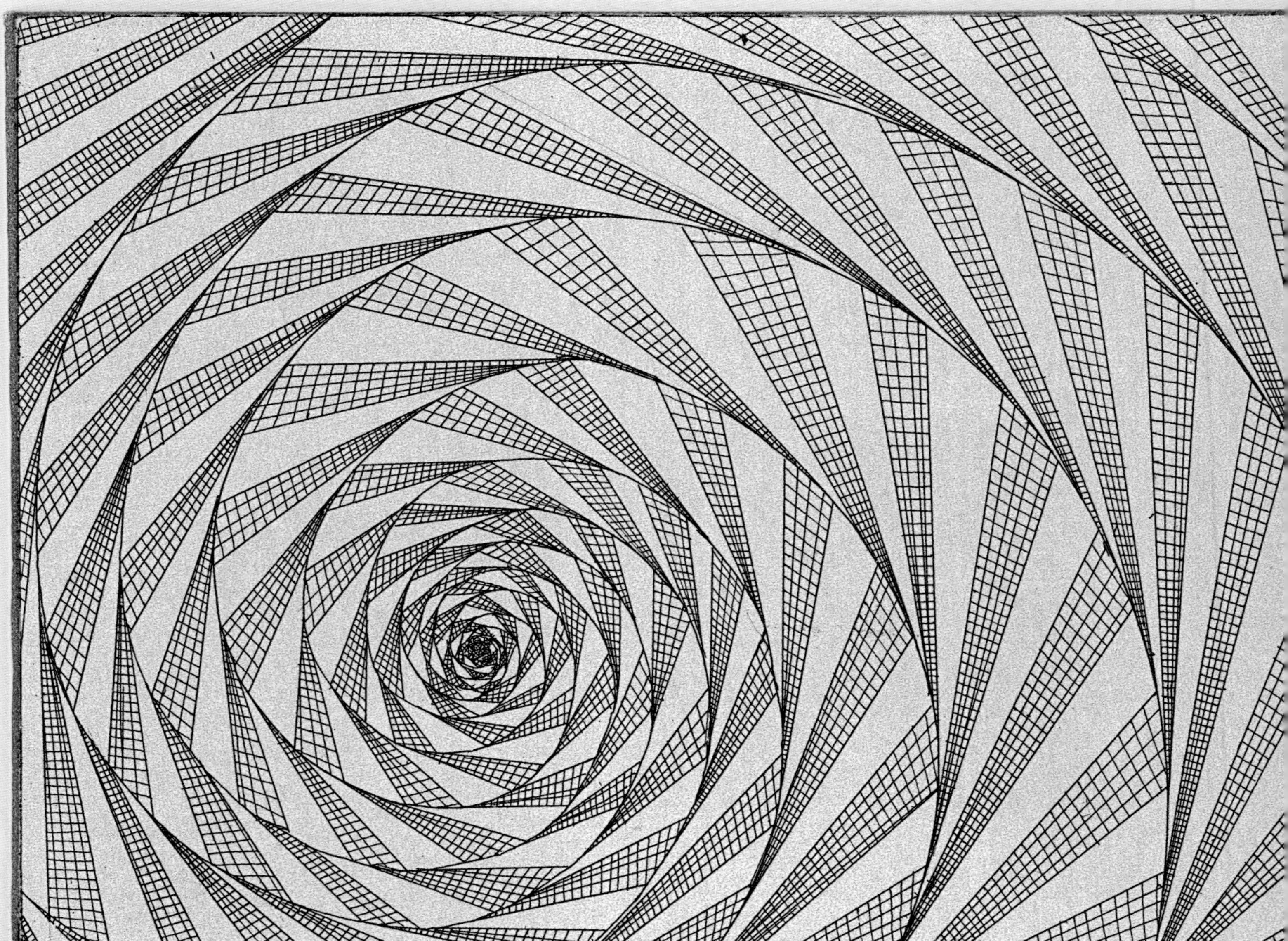

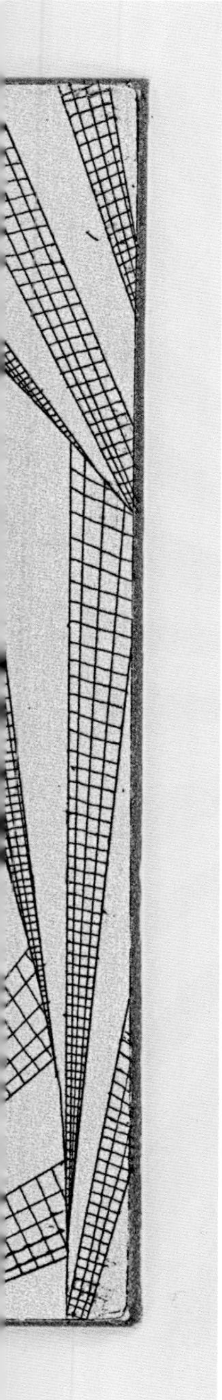

Shown by
greengrassi A11

Biography
Born 1970
Lives in Berlin

American artist Bornstein's drawings, etchings, and films were the subject of a recent solo show at DAAD Galerie, Berlin (2012). Other recent solo shows were held at Stedelijk Museum, Amsterdam (2011), and greengrassi, London (2011). In 2009 she had solo shows at Gavin Brown's enterprise, New York, and Färgfabriken Center for Contemporary Art, Stockholm. Recent group shows include "The Air We Breathe" (2011) at SF MoMA, San Francisco; "You Don't Love Me Anymore" (2011) at Westfälischer Kunstverein; and "At Home, Not at Home" (2010) at CCS Bard College, Annandale-on-Hudson.

Another View of Infinite Space
2010
Etching
4 × 5⅞"
(10 × 15 cm)
Courtesy of greengrassi

Jennifer Bornstein

The technique of copperplate etching has been, as Jennifer Bornstein once said, largely "abandoned" by contemporary art. Around 2003, Bornstein, who had hitherto worked mainly with photography, film, and sculpture, began to make etchings of people around her: students, friends, even actors and other artists. She saw the process as performative: a means of thinking aloud that, in its directness, allowed her to convey more lucidly the relations between herself and her subjects. She still makes sculptural installations, as well as 16mm films such as *Frauenkörperbewegungsbilder (Woman's Movement Moving Pictures,* 2010), which refers to performances by Yvonne Rainer, but it is her etchings that predominate. JG

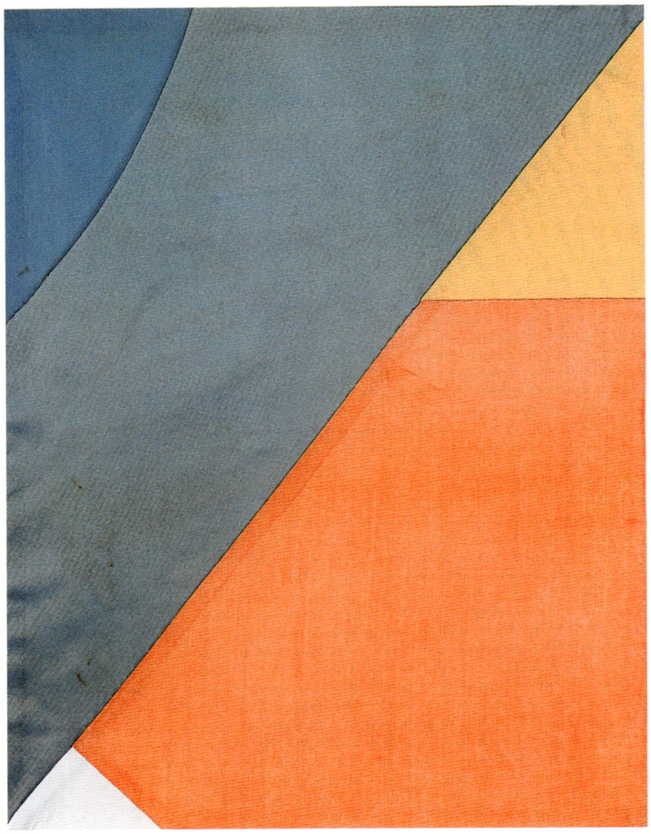

1

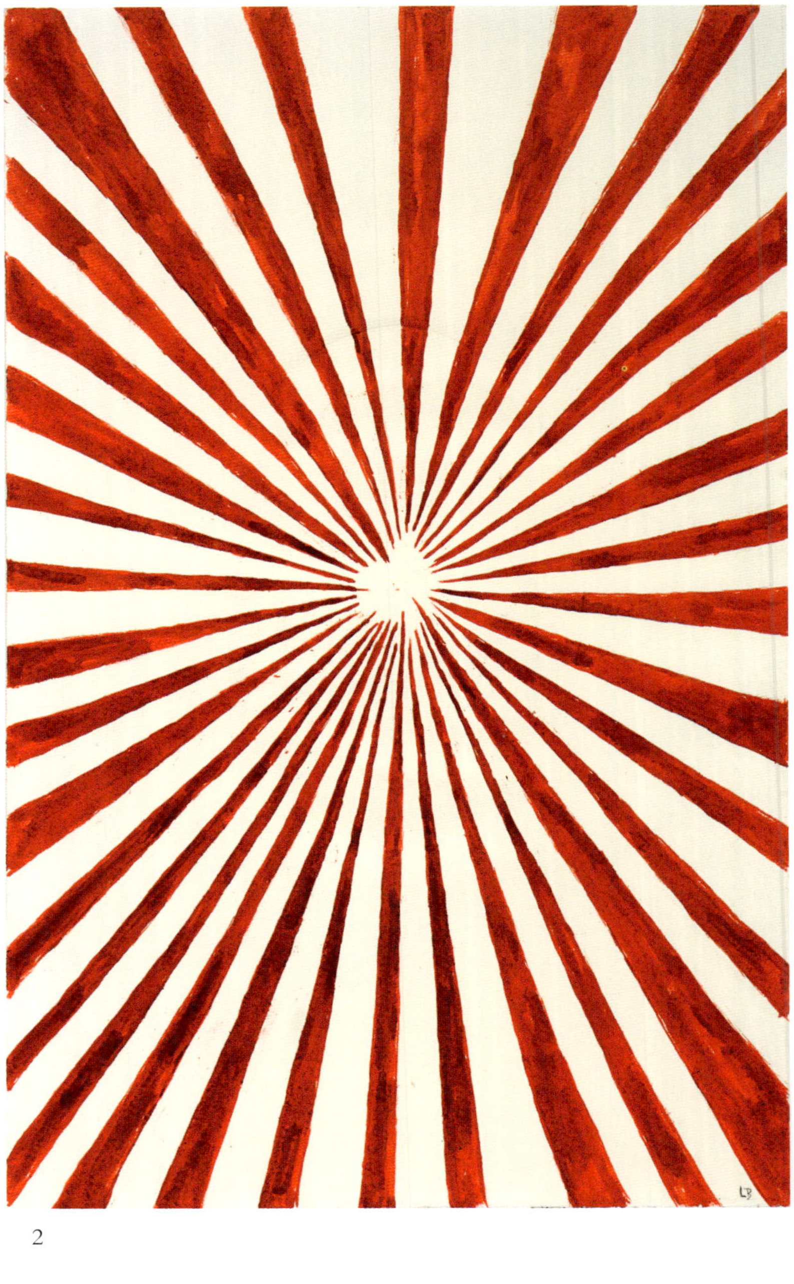

2

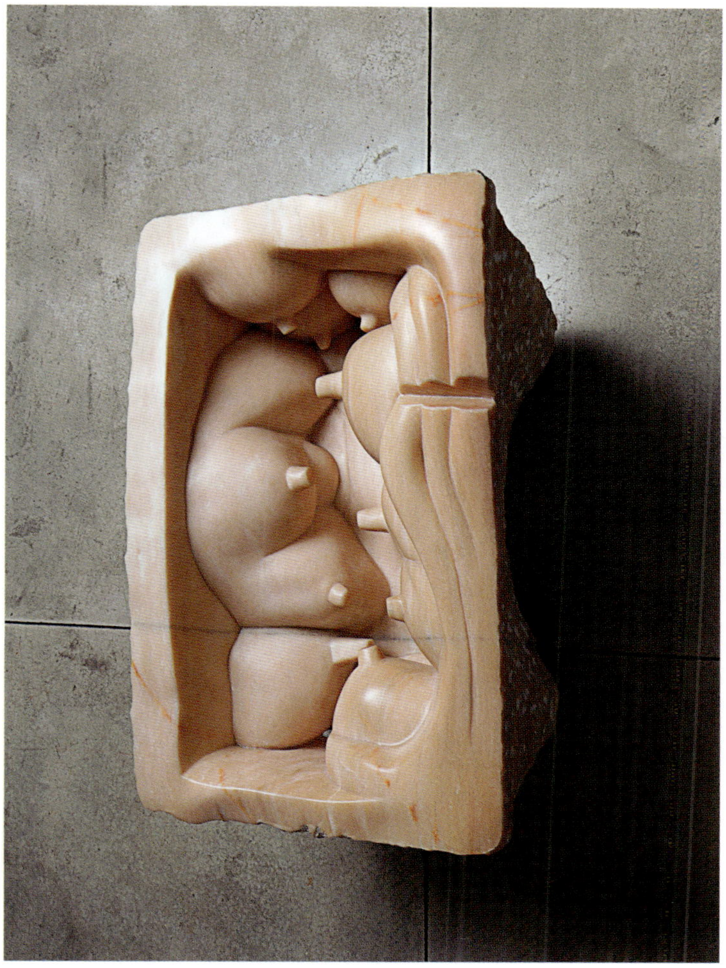

3

Shown by
Cheim & Read C36
Hauser & Wirth B6
Kukje Gallery B36
Xavier Hufkens B23

Biography
Born 1911
Died 2010

In 2012 and 2013 numerous posthumous exhibitions will survey Bourgeois' celebrated work. These include "Louise Bourgeois: The Return of the Repressed" (2012) at Freud Museum, London; "Louise Bourgeois" (2012) at the National Gallery of Canada, Art Gallery of Alberta; "Louise Bourgeois: Passage Dangereux" (2012) at Hamburger Kunsthalle; and "Louise Bourgeois: Conscious and Unconscious" at Qatar Museums Authority QMA Gallery, Doha. An exhibition at Foundation Beyeler, Basel, in late 2010 marked the artist's 100th birthday.

1
UNTITLED
2005
Fabric
18⅛ × 14⅛"
(46 × 36 cm)
© Louise Bourgeois Trust. Courtesy of Cheim & Read

2
UNTITLED
(double sided)
2006
Recto: watercolor on embossed paper. Verso: watercolor and colored pencil on paper
30 × 20"
(76 × 51 cm)
© Louise Bourgeois Trust. Courtesy of Cheim & Read

3
NATURE STUDY NO. 5
1995
Pink marble and steel
20 × 36½ × 23"
(51 × 92.5 × 58.5 cm)
© Louise Bourgeois Trust. Courtesy of Cheim & Read

Louise Bourgeois

Among the last projects that Louise Bourgeois worked on before her death in 2010 was *Do Not Abandon Me*, a collaboration with Tracey Emin. Bourgeois painted male and female torsos on paper, then passed the images to Emin, who later said: "I carried the images around the world with me from Australia to France, but I was too scared to touch them." The two artists shared an interest in and skill with fabric, and the completed works are of a piece with others that engaged Bourgeois in her last decade, such as the abstract fabric drawings composed from clothes collected over many years. Such works recall her parents' tapestry workshop, one of several primal scenes that informed her art. BD

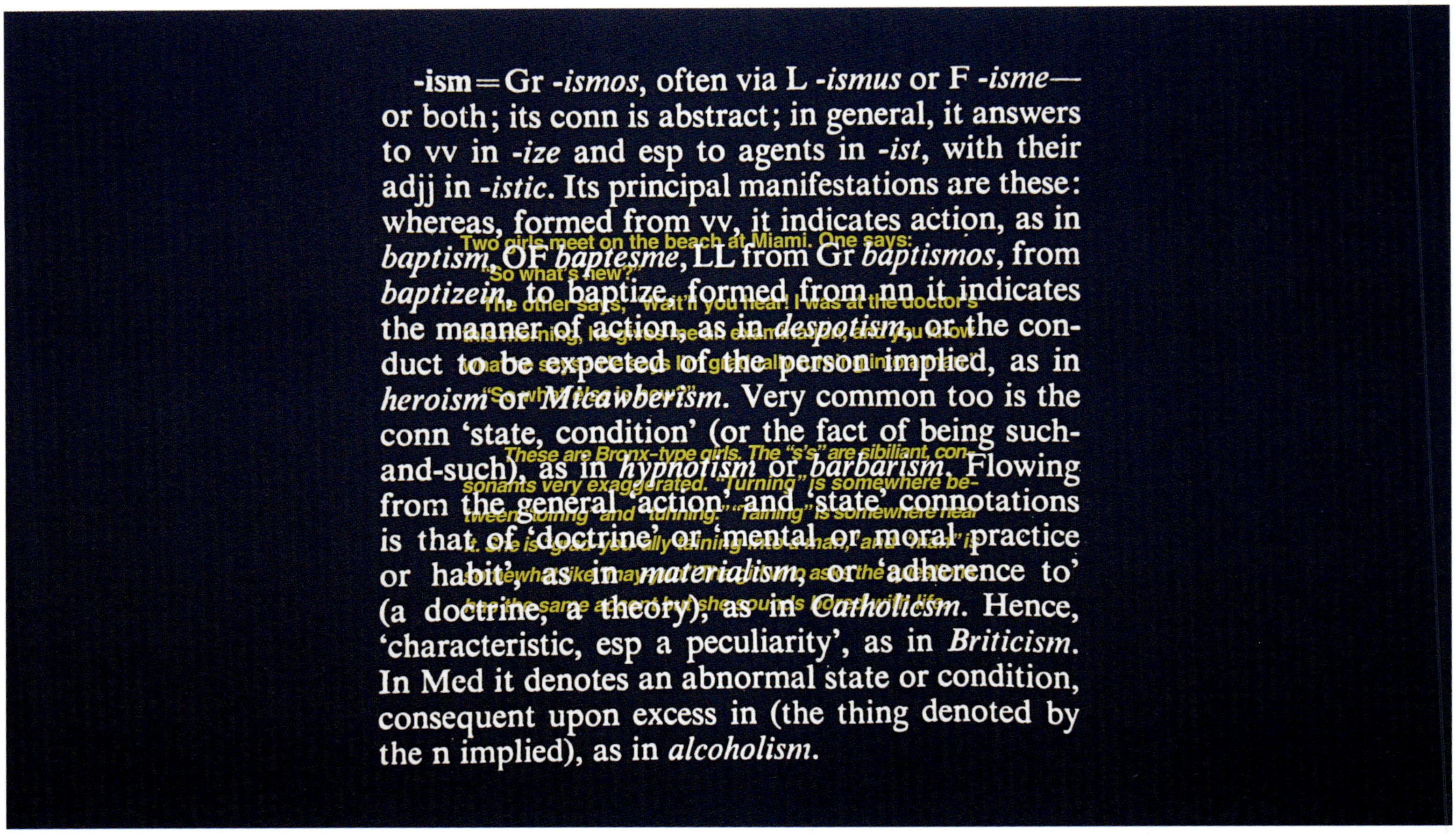
-ism = Gr -ismos, often via L -ismus or F -isme—or both; its conn is abstract; in general, it answers to vv in -ize and esp to agents in -ist, with their adjj in -istic. Its principal manifestations are these: whereas, formed from vv, it indicates action, as in baptism, OF baptesme, LL from Gr baptismos, from baptizein, to baptize, formed from nn it indicates the manner of action, as in despotism, or the conduct to be expected of the person implied, as in heroism or Micawberism. Very common too is the conn 'state, condition' (or the fact of being such-and-such), as in hypnotism or barbarism. Flowing from the general 'action' and 'state' connotations is that of 'doctrine' or 'mental or moral practice or habit', as in materialism, or 'adherence to' (a doctrine, a theory), as in Catholicism. Hence, 'characteristic, esp a peculiarity', as in Briticism. In Med it denotes an abnormal state or condition, consequent upon excess in (the thing denoted by the n implied), as in alcoholism.
Two girls meet on the beach at Miami. One says:
"So what's new?"
These are Bronx-type girls. The "s's" are sibiliant, con-
sonants very exaggerated. "Turning" is somewhere be-

1

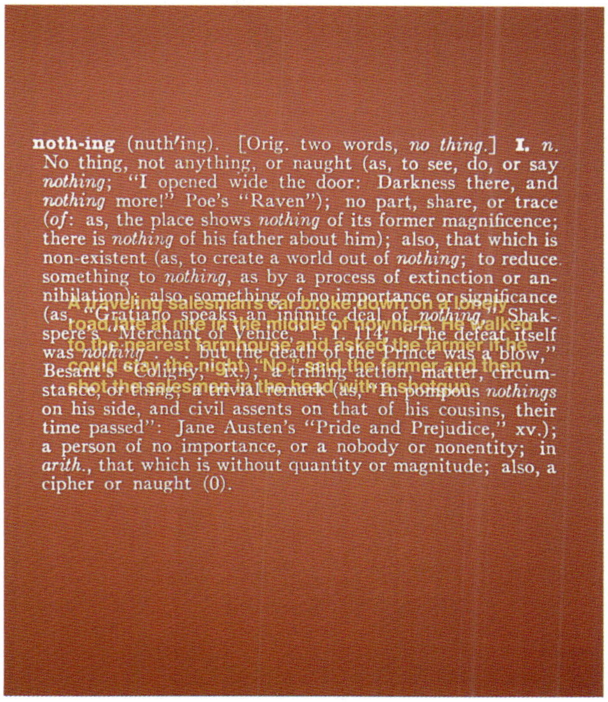

2

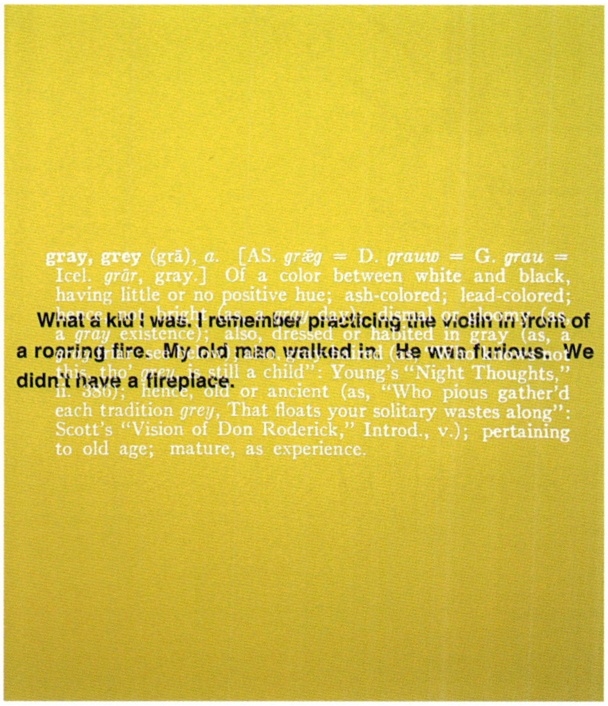

3

Shown by
Yvon Lambert C34

Biography
Born 1975
Lives in Mexico City and London

Mexico-born Brüggemann's recent exhibition "Untitled (Joke & Definition Paintings)" (2011–12) included a new series of paintings of the same name. His text-based works have been shown internationally in the solo shows "The World Trapped in the Self (Windows for Mirrors)" (2011) at Mies van der Rohe Pavilion, Barcelona; "Stefan Brüggemann" (2011) at Galeria de Arte Mexico; and "No Time, No Return, No Title" (2010) at Villa du Parc, Centre d'Art Contemporain, Annemasse.

1
Untitled (Joke and Definition Paintings)
2011
Archival inkjet print on canvas
98⅞ × 56⅝"
(246 × 144 cm)
Courtesy of Yvon Lambert, Paris

2, 3
Untitled (Joke and Definition Paintings)
2011
Archival inkjet print on canvas
52¾ × 60¾"
(134 × 154 cm)
Courtesy of Yvon Lambert, Paris

Stefan Brüggemann

Stefan Brüggemann first gained attention with "Show Titles" (2000–ongoing), a database of hypothetical exhibition titles available for use free of charge as long as Brüggemann was credited. His text-based practice now takes multiple and disparate forms. The individual works—such as a neon sign reading "THIS WORK SHOULD BE TURNED OFF WHEN I DIE" (2011) or the wall text declaring "ALL MY IDEAS ARE IMPORTED, ALL MY PRODUCTS ARE EXPLOITED (ALL MY EXPLANATIONS ARE RUBBISH)" (2003)—refer to tropes of the art world, market, and politics. Brüggemann is interested in the complexities of negation and authorship; a recent collaboration with Pierre Bismuth featured a neon Brüggemann sign reading "(NO CONTENT)," over which Bismuth had graffitied "SHALLOW" (*Shallow,* 2010). KK

SCULPTURE
for
EAST GERMANY

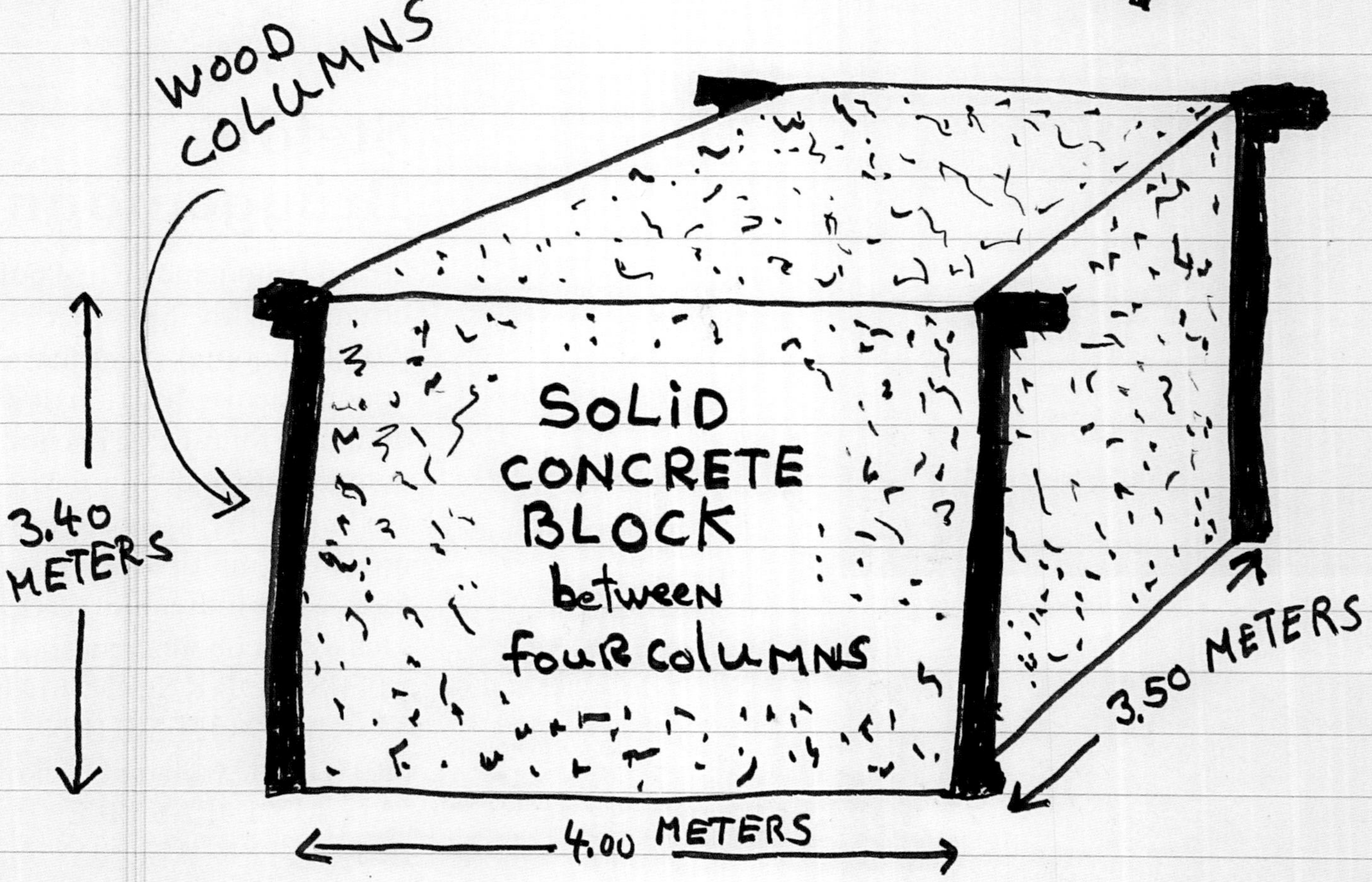

CHRIS BURDEN

April 93

Shown by
Galerie Krinzinger
B24

Biography
Born 1946
Lives in Topanga

Seminal American performance artist and sculptor Burden has exhibited internationally since the 1970s. His work has been the subject of numerous exhibitions and retrospectives. Most recently the solo show "The Heart: Open or Closed" (2010) was held at Gagosian Gallery, Rome. In 2008 the public sculpture *What My Dad Gave Me* (2008) stood outside the Rockefeller Center, New York; the solo exhibition "Yin Yang" (2007) took place at Gagosian Gallery, Beverly Hills; and in 2006 two major public works were exhibited at South London Gallery.

Sculpture for East Germany
1993
Ink on paper
11 × 8½"
(28 × 21.5 cm)
Courtesy of Galerie Krinzinger

Chris Burden

From his series of groundbreaking performance works in the early 1970s, such as *Shoot* (1971), to his later installations and public sculptures, such as *Urban Light* (2008), a grid of 202 antique street lamps installed outside the Los Angeles County Museum of Art, Chris Burden has continually dealt with the limits of risk, endurance, and spectatorship. For the last 25 years, these works have often taken the form of scientific experiments or propositions, such as *When Robots Rule* (1999), an automated assembly line that produced wind-up model airplanes, or *Ghost Ship* (2005), a crew-less, self-navigating vessel. Burden's practice is now as varied and ambitious as ever, busy proving that, in his words, "things you didn't think were possible can be." ST

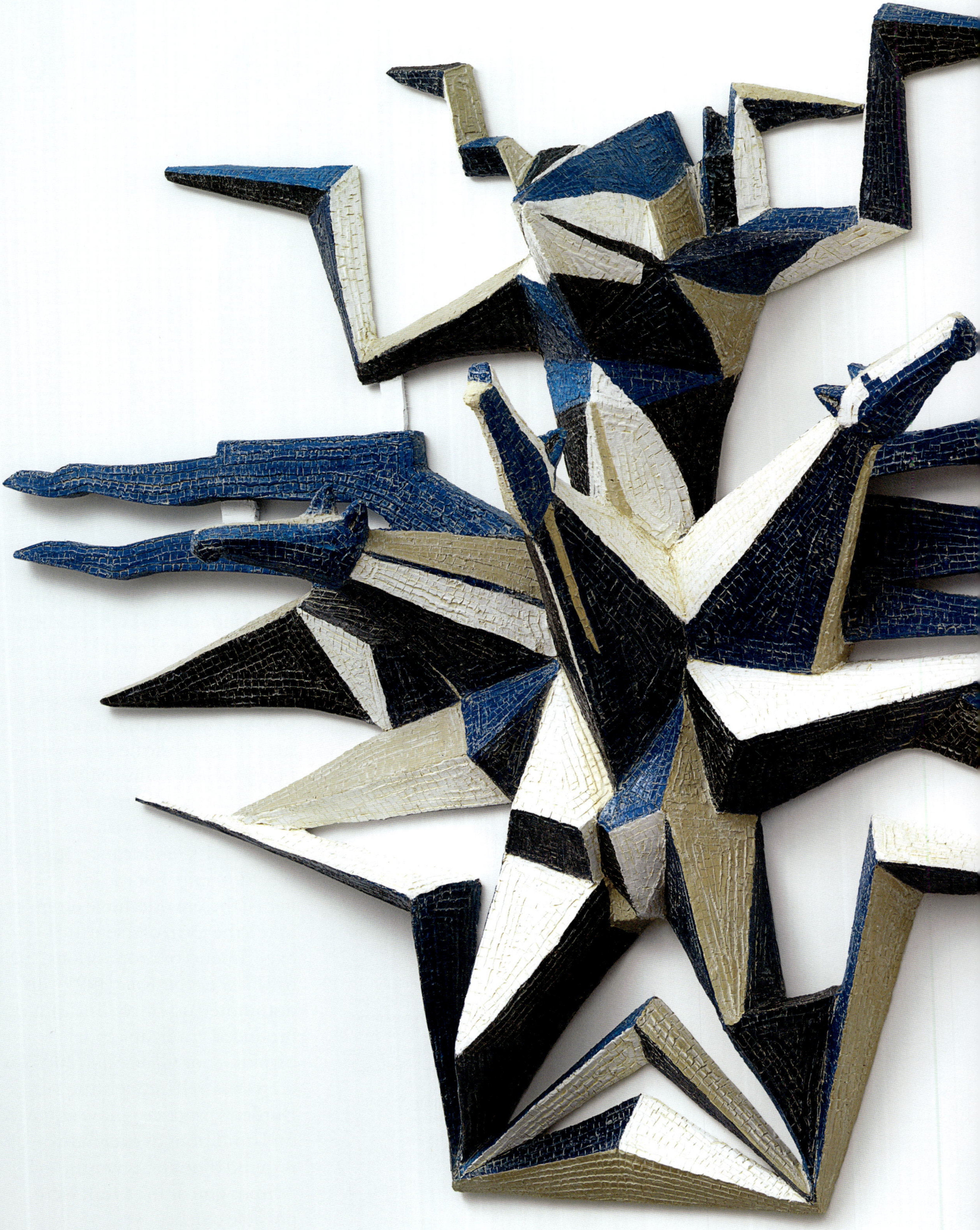

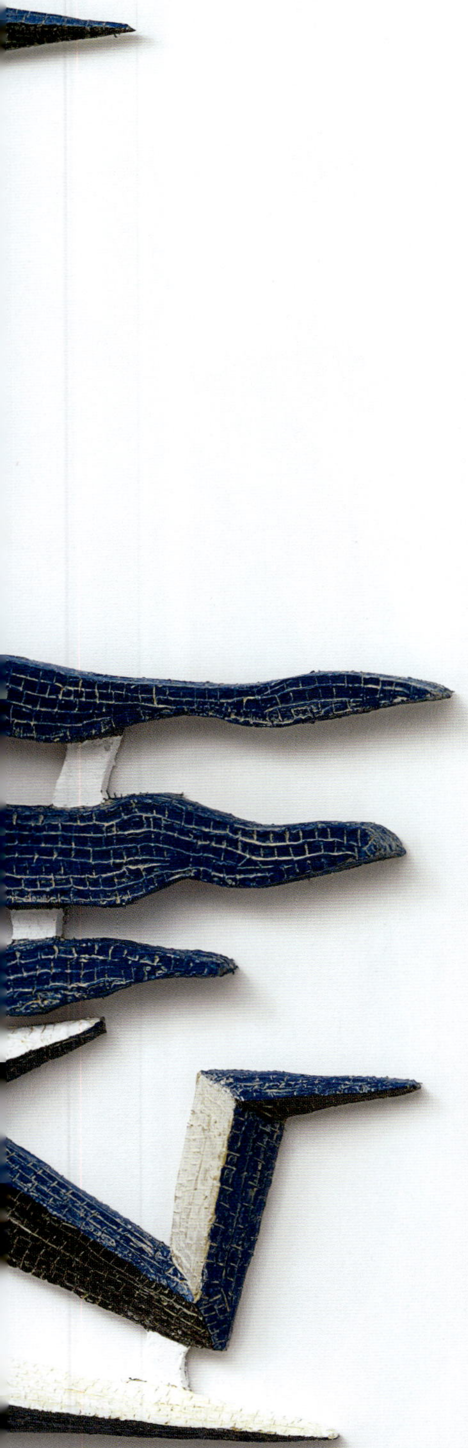

Shown by
303 Gallery B39
David Kordansky C1
Galerie Eva
Presenhuber B29

Biography
Born 1977
Lives in Martigny

Swiss artist Carron has exhibited extensively in Europe in the last decade. A recent solo show took place at 303 Gallery, New York (2012). In 2010 he had two solo exhibitions in Paris, at Praz-Delavallade and "Pergola: Monsieur" at Palais de Tokyo. Recent group shows include "Echoes—La musique faite image" (Echoes—The music-made image, 2011) Centre Culturel Suisse, Paris, and "L'Ecal, un pied à Paris" (The Ecal, a walk in Paris, 2011) Cité Internationale des Arts, Paris. In 2013 he will have a solo exhibition at Kunsthalle Bern.

imperia I
2011
Styrofoam, fiberglass, acrylic resin, acrylic paint, wood, and steel
70⅞ × 59 × 16⅛"
(180 × 150 × 41 cm)
Courtesy of Galerie Eva Presenhuber

Valentin Carron

Subtly deflating the construction of regional identity, many of Valentin Carron's works have alluded to his alpine place of birth, the canton of Valais in Switzerland, where traditions are less ancient and authentic than they seem, many having been invented at the time of a national exposition . For *Château-Synthèse* (2000), Carron produced wine artificially without grapes; he has also created *ersatz* artifacts ranging from reproductions of 18th century French cannons to a replica of a statue of a Roman warrior. Substituting materials yields ironic slippages in tone and meaning in works such as *Clair Matin II* (Clear Morning II, 2009), a copy of a Swiss-chalet-style pergola crafted in black Styrofoam instead of wood, which hangs menacingly over viewers' heads like a grating over a dungeon. KMJ

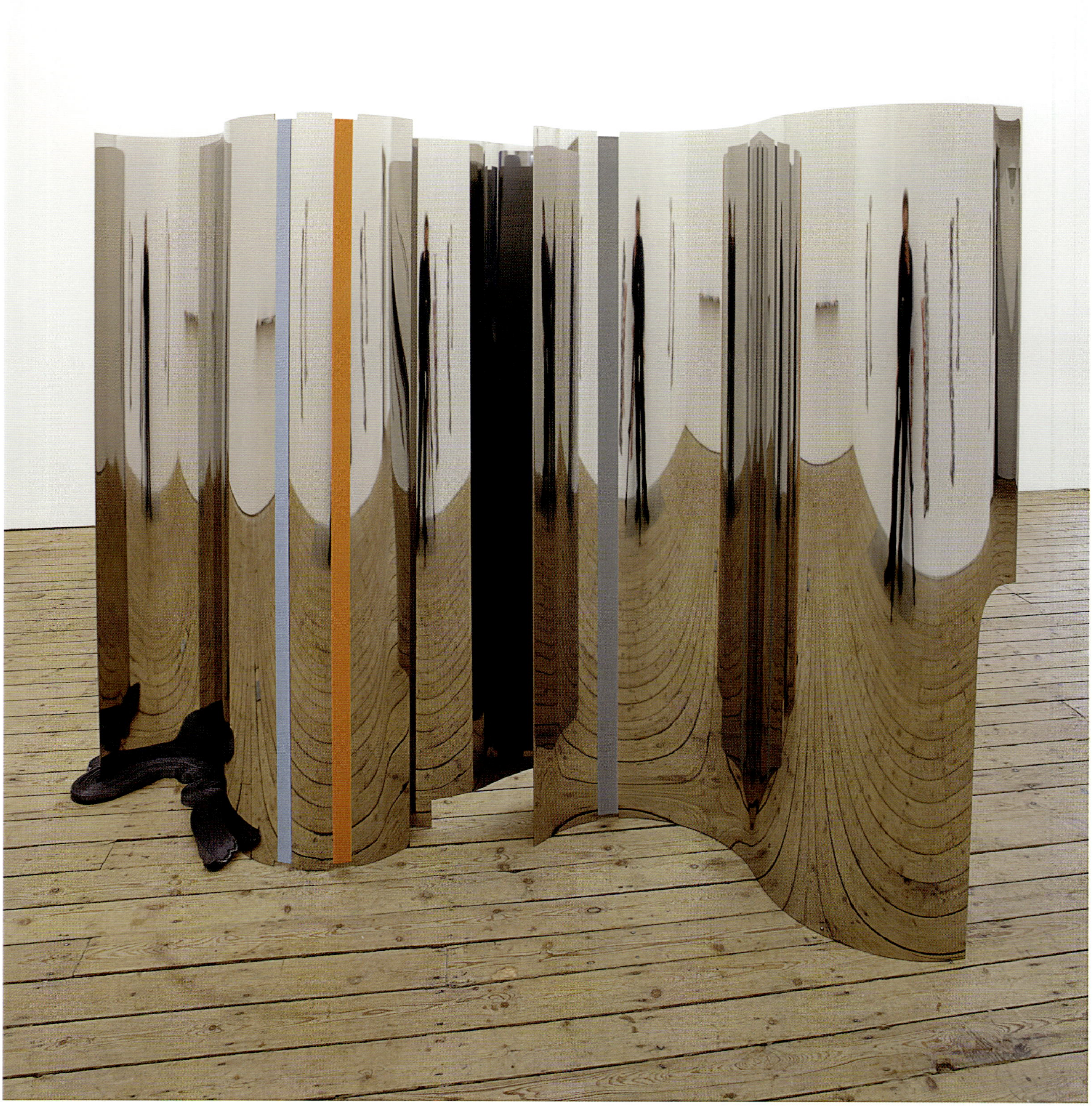

1

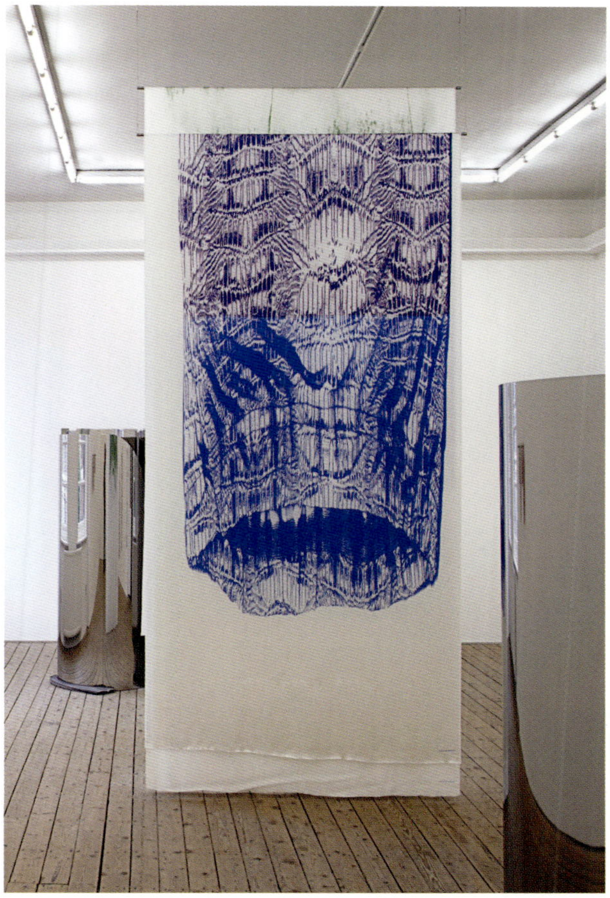

2

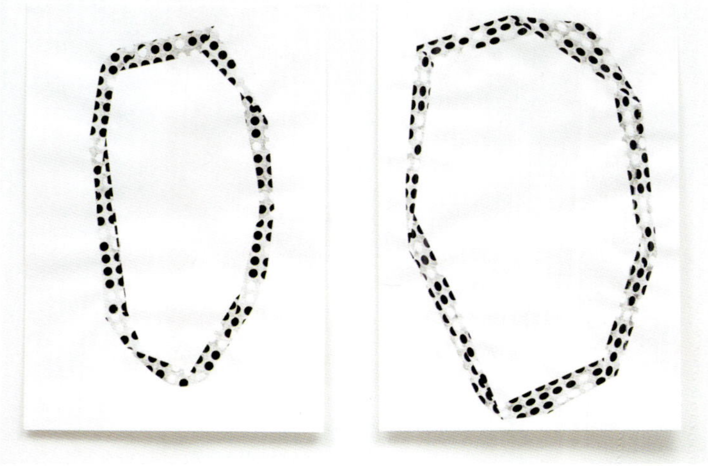

3

Shown by
The Approach B11

Biography
Born 1977
Lives in London

British artist Channer received a BA from Goldsmiths College, London, in 2006, and an MA in sculpture from the Royal College of Art, London, in 2008. In recent years she has exhibited extensively in the United Kingdom and Europe. Recent solo exhibitions include: "Out Of Body" (2012) at South London Gallery; "Body-Conscious" (2011) at The Approach, London; and "Other-Directed" (2011) at BolteLang, Zurich. Upcoming shows will take place at Lisa Cooley, New York (2012), and she will have a major solo show at The Hepworth Wakefield, UK, in 2013.

1
Slip
2011
Mirror polished stainless steel, elastics, hi-tech lamé, accordion pleats
70⅞× 11⅞ × 23⅝"
(180 × 30 × 60 cm)
Courtesy of The Approach

2
Tight Skin
2011
Digital prints on heavy silk satin, chrome bar, cables
131½ × 55⅛ × 4"
(334 × 140 × 10 cm)
Courtesy of The Approach

3
See-Thru
2009
Gouache, pencil, and cigarette ash on and in paper
33⅛ × 23½"
(84 × 59.5 cm)
Courtesy of The Approach

Alice Channer

Borrowing, from the language and techniques of *haute couture* as much as from Minimalism, Alice Channer's sculptures often give the impression of being tailored to fit a specific space. Swooping lines of fabric hang from the ceiling, while bracelet- or scarf-like hoops punctuate the floors and walls—an approach that the artist has described as "dressing a room." Her refined formal vocabulary nods to the crisp glamor of mid-century Dior as well as to the mass-produced patterns of high-street fashion (such as the hanging silk piece *Tight Skin*, 2011), fixating on the way that "the new" is marketed. Channer's art works—as the title of a 2011 exhibition put it—remain acutely "Body Conscious." ST

1

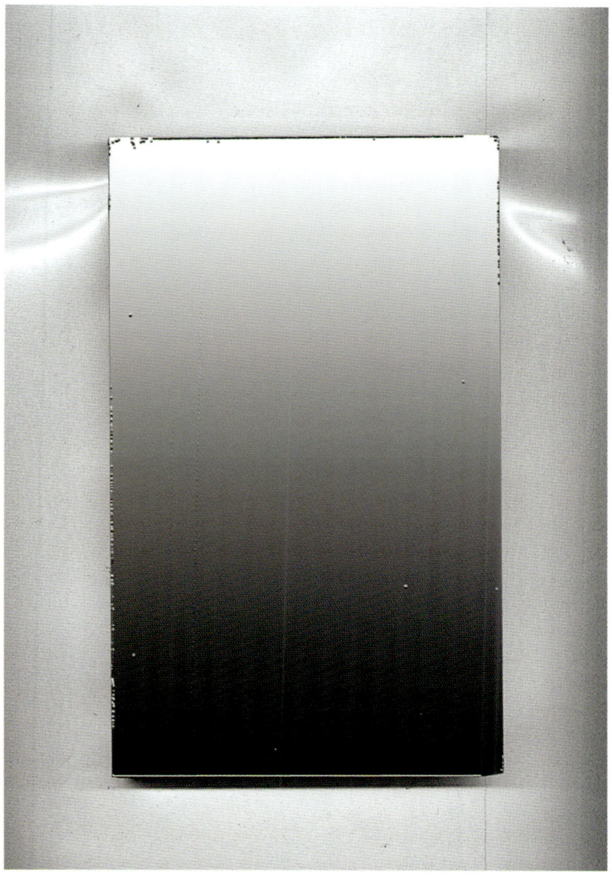

2

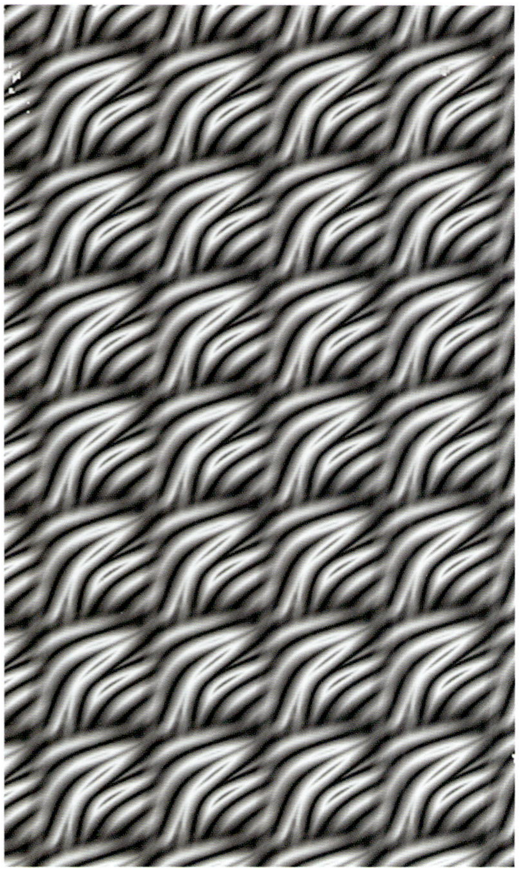

3

Shown by
Micky Schubert F8

Biography
Born 1974
Lives in Berlin

Romanian artist Chirulescu's paintings, prints, and photographs have been the subject of numerous solo exhibitions in recent years. In 2011 she had self-titled shows at White Cube Bermondsey, London; Kunstverein Nürnberg; and "Werke aus der Sammlung Martin" (Work from the Collection Martin), at Neues Museum, Nurenberg. In 2010 Kunsthalle Basel staged an extensive exhibition of her work. She has also participated in a number of group shows, including "Ein Psycho-geographischer Plan" (A Psycho-geographical Map, 2011) at Max Mayer, Dusseldorf, and "Fade into You" (2010) at Herald St, London.

1
Untitled (Big Print 7)
2009
Digital print
56 × 40⅜"
(142× 102.5 cm)
Courtesy of Micky Schubert

2
Untitled
2011
C-type print on canvas
18½ × 13⅛"
(47 × 33.5 cm)
Courtesy of Micky Schubert

3
Untitled
2011
C-type print on canvas
18½ × 12¼"
(47 × 31 cm)
Courtesy of Micky Schubert

Focus
Marieta Chirulescu

Marieta Chirulescu's faded inkjet prints, paintings, and photographs are like spectral invocations of mid-20th-century abstraction, summoning memories of Color Field painting as well as more sinister histories. These geometric arrangements are often monochrome or in a washed-out grayscale, delineated by scoured lines, creases, and scratches, and produced by repeatedly scanning images, allowing digital decay and technological malfunctions to guide the composition. Chirulescu's source material ranges from glitchy screengrabs to photographs taken by her father during Nicolae Ceaușescu's dictatorship in Romania, though all are rendered indecipherable. Her mostly untitled works seem to retain some record—but of what is unclear. As curator Adam Szymczyk has noted, they feel like "reflections of the mechanical unconscious." ST

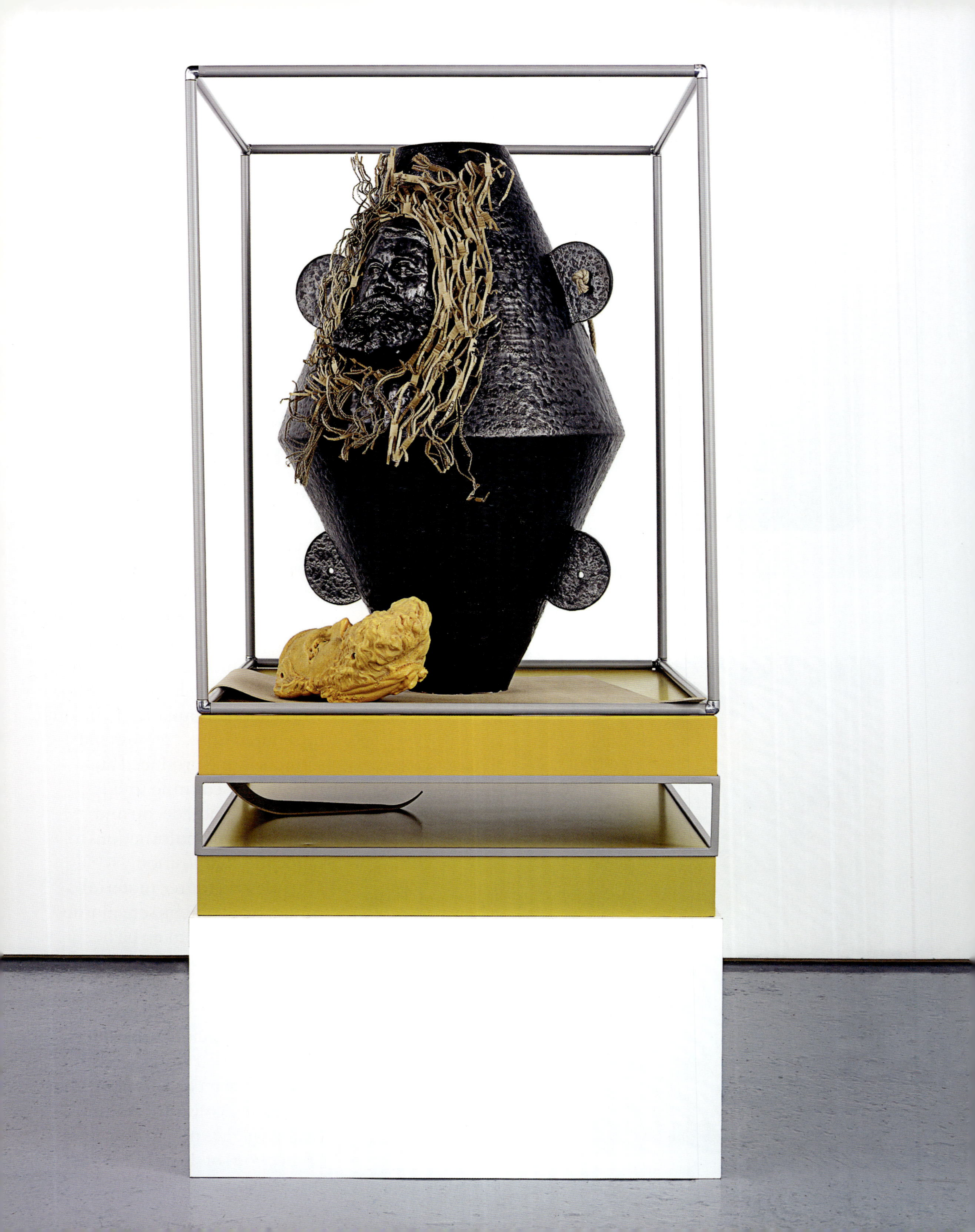

Shown by
Sadie Coles HQ C15
Massimo De Carlo B1
Kimmerich F26
David Kordansky Gallery C1
Galerie Rüdiger Schöttle D3

Biography
Born 1969
Lives in London

Claydon's multifarious practice was recently exhibited in the solo show "Culpable Earth" (2012) at Firstsite, Colchester. Other recent solo exhibitions include "Twickenham Gardens" (2011) at Kimmerich Gallery, New York, and his first solo show in France "Mon Plaisir... Votre Travail..." (My Pleasure... Your Work..., 2011) La Salle de Bains, Lyon. In 2010 the exhibitions "Trom Bell To The Bow Draps" at Hotel, London, and "Golden Times" at Hause der Kunst, Munich, also boasted his sculptural work.

The Commencement of The Thingly (An Arrested Equivalence)
2011
Ceramic, cast foam, gum rubber, rope, cardboard, powder-coated steel, melamine-coated MDF
67 × 32¼ × 32¼"
(170 × 82 × 82 cm)
Courtesy of Sadie Coles HQ

Steven Claydon

Smurfs and Nietzschean moustaches, hessian-covered plinths, and sleek Modernist exhibition architecture, sports equipment, and Neanderthals—Steven Claydon's sculptures and installations offer visions of a world that is somehow archaic, futurist, and familiar. Fiction and location are key issues for him. For example, the artifacts presented in a 2007 exhibition purported to be from New Valkonia, a fictional East European nation (the name is adapted from a T-shirt the artist found in a Warsaw market), while Claydon's 2010 exhibition "Trom Bell to The Bow Draps" was named for a non-existent area of east London mentioned in a novel by Céline. Investigating the different claims of myth, philosophy, and supposed provenance, Claydon focuses on—to paraphrase the title of a 2010 work—the concealment and the showing forth of objects. ST

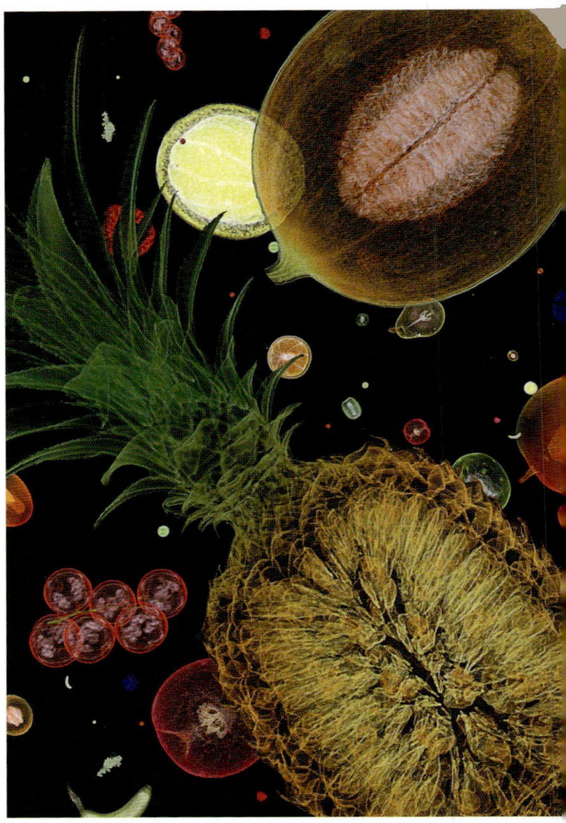

2

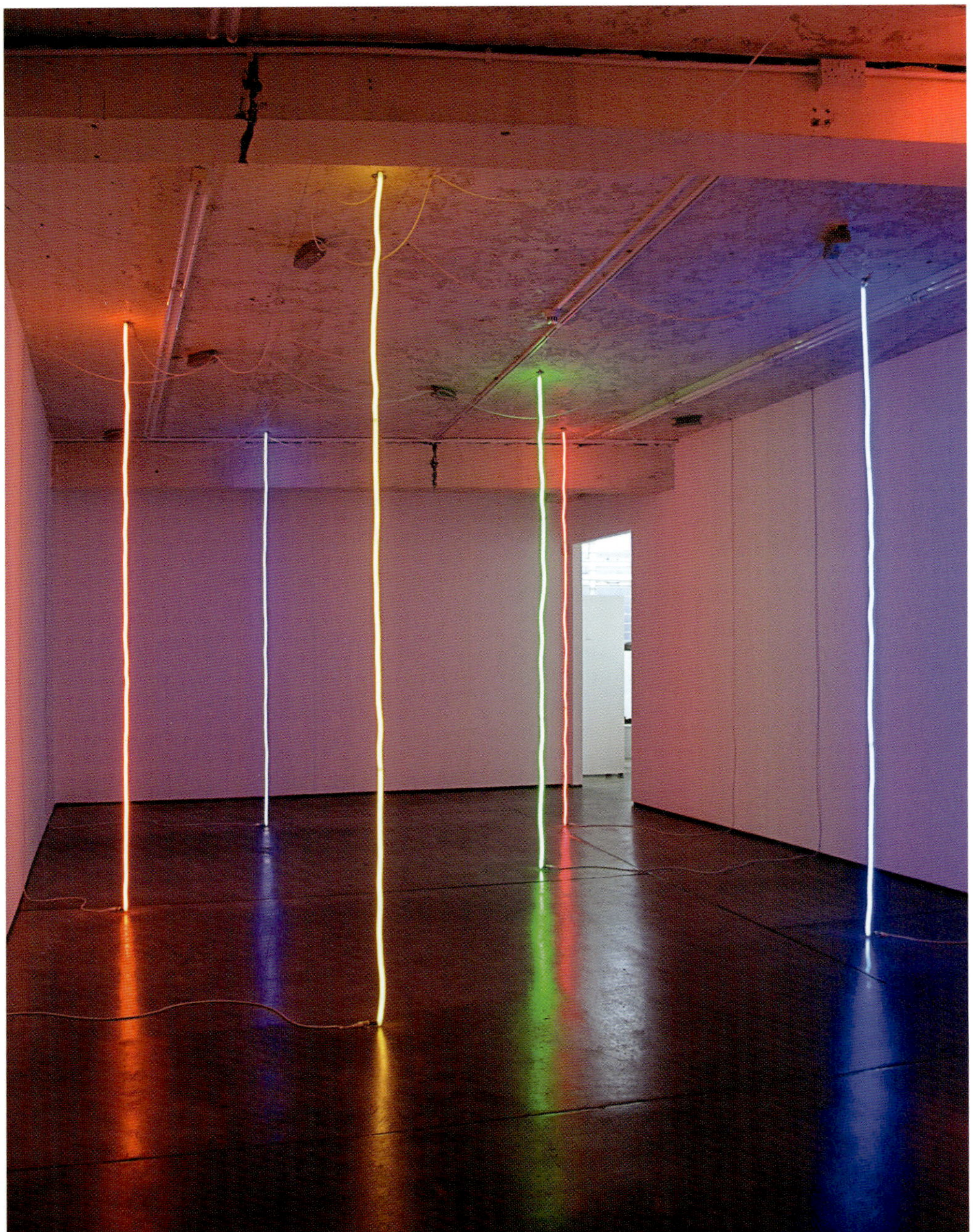

1

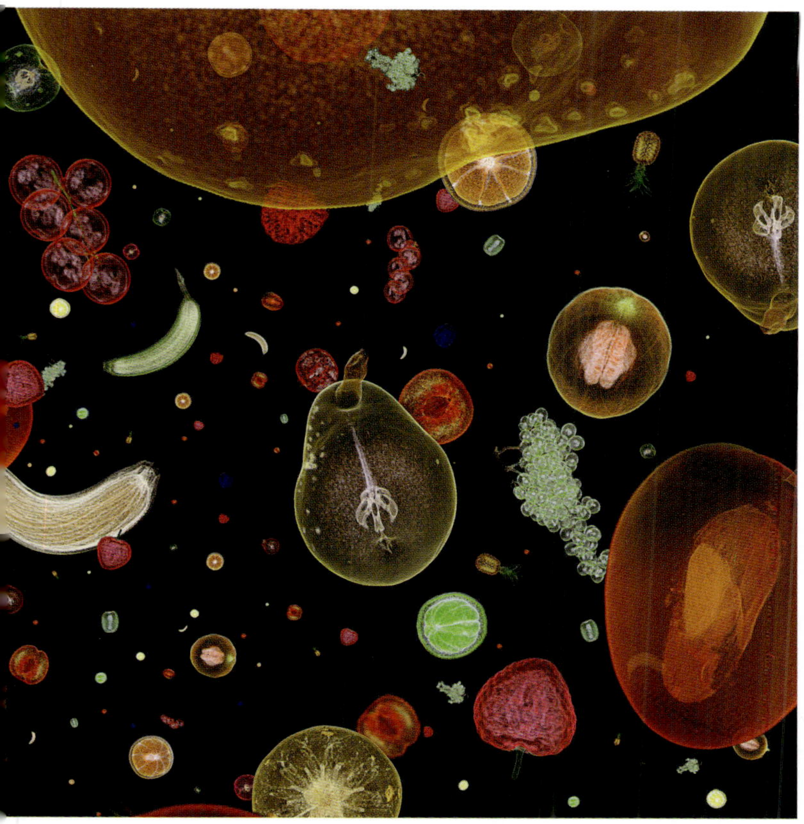

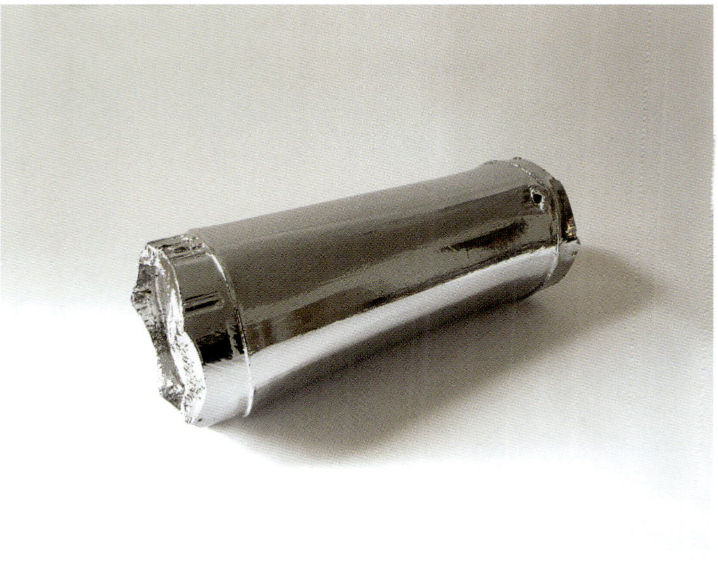

Shown by
Herald St A30

Biography
Born 1972
Lives in New York

American sculptor Coffin's work has been the subject of several solo exhibitions such as at the Barbican, London (2009). Other solo shows include and "Untitled (Sculpture Silhouettes)" (2009) at City Hall, New York. Recent group shows include the "Yokohama Trienale" (2011), Yokohama Museum of Art; "New York Minute" (2010), at Garage Center for Contemporary Culture, Moscow, and Museo D'arte Contemporanea Roma, Rome (2009). In 2013 he will have a significant solo show at the Smithsonian Hirshhorn Museum and Sculpture Garden, Washington, D.C..

1
Untitled (Lines)
2011
Neon
Dimensions variable
Courtesy of Herald St

2
Untitled
2011
HD Video
Dimensions variable
Courtesy of Herald St

3
Untitled (Time Capsule)
2011
Chrome-plated bamboo
5 × 17"
(15 × 43 cm)
Courtesy of Herald St

Peter Coffin

"I am for an art that is political-erotical-mystical, that does something other than sit on its ass," Peter Coffin once professed. His work attempts a kind of fast-and-loose end-of-the-rainbow fusion between New Age wisdom, the popular imagination, and theoretical physics. His installations have involved prop-like sculptures as well as *son et lumière* environments and scenographic pranks, with a clear delight for the sometimes ludicrous complexity of the natural world, and for early cinema, as well as the spirit of scientific discovery. His *oeuvre* is not for those entirely immune to wonder or the magical. For the untitled Barbican Curve Gallery commission in 2009, he combined a heady multiscreen video of Japanese formal gardens with dozens of uncanny 3D objects made by precisely scanning and then distorting everyday objects—a beer can, a trumpet, a bunch of flowers—according to different mathematical formula. MA

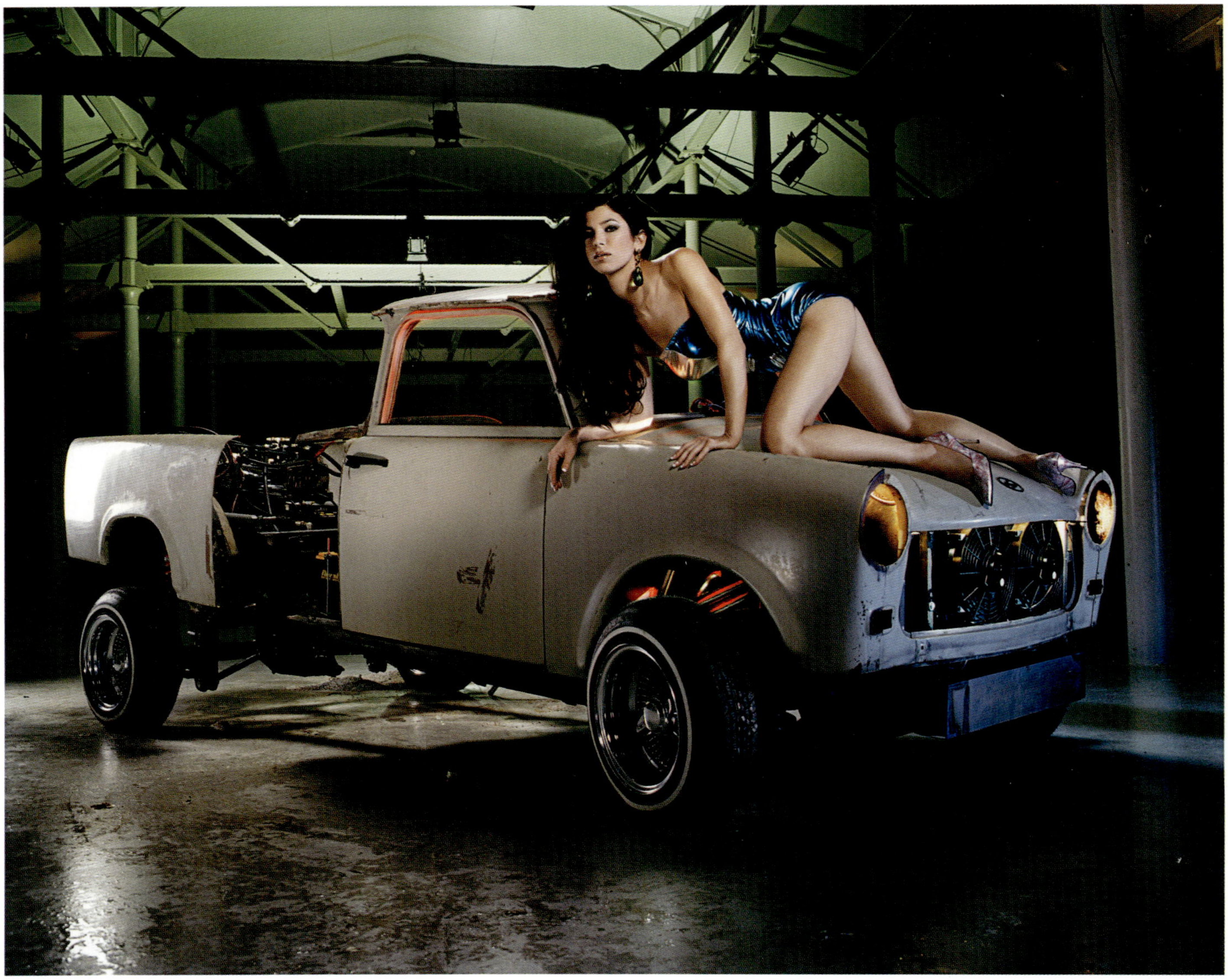

1

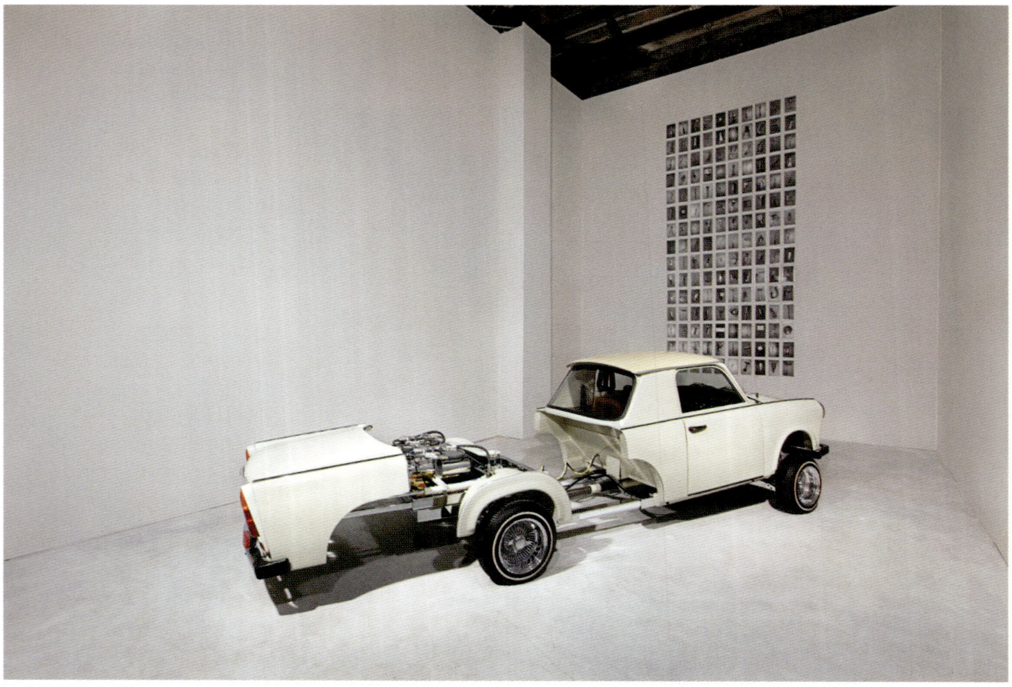

2

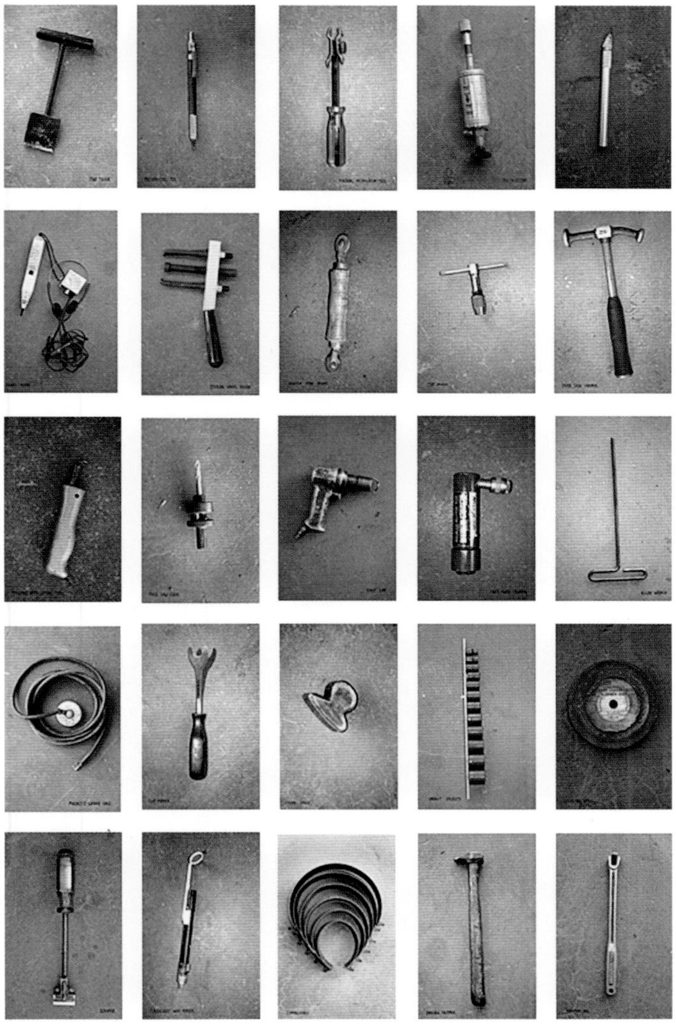

3

Shown by
Salon 94 C38

Biography
Born 1973
Lives in Detroit

Cohen's enduring automotive projects have attracted attention beyond the reaches of the art world. In 2011 the solo exhibition "Trabantimino" took place at Salon 94, New York. She participated in the group exhibition "Autobody" (2011), curated by Neville Wakefield at Ballroom Marfa. Other recent solo shows include "Zwickau Routine" (2010) at Joseph Gross Gallery, Univerisity of Arizona, and "The Builder and the Bikini Model" (2008) at El Paso Museum of Art.

1
Bodywork (Hood)
2006
C-type print
50 × 60¼"
(127 × 153 cm)
Courtesy of Salon 94

2
Trabantimino
2002–10
Mixed media sculpture
112 × 66 × 56"
(284.5 × 167.5 × 142 cm)
Courtesy of Salon 94

3
MTCO-Measure Twice Cut Once (Group 1)
2007
Set of 25 archival inkjet prints
9¾ × 6 × 1"
(25 × 15 × 2.5 cm)
Courtesy of Salon 94

Liz Cohen

Liz Cohen's investigations into the automobile industry are underpinned by a dual transformation: her turning an East German Trabant car into a Chevrolet de Camino, (*Trabantimono*, 2007) and her own physical metamorphosis from mechanic to pin-up girl. Cohen tackles gender stereotypes head-on, questioning the implicit roles of the male mechanic and female sex object by assuming each position, as well as being both observer and observed. Alongside the heft of the vehicle itself, large-scale photographs from the "Bodywork" series (2006) depict the bikini-clad artist both carrying out the car's transformation and posing in more recognizable pin-up fashion, confronting the viewer with all the tools of her trade. AB

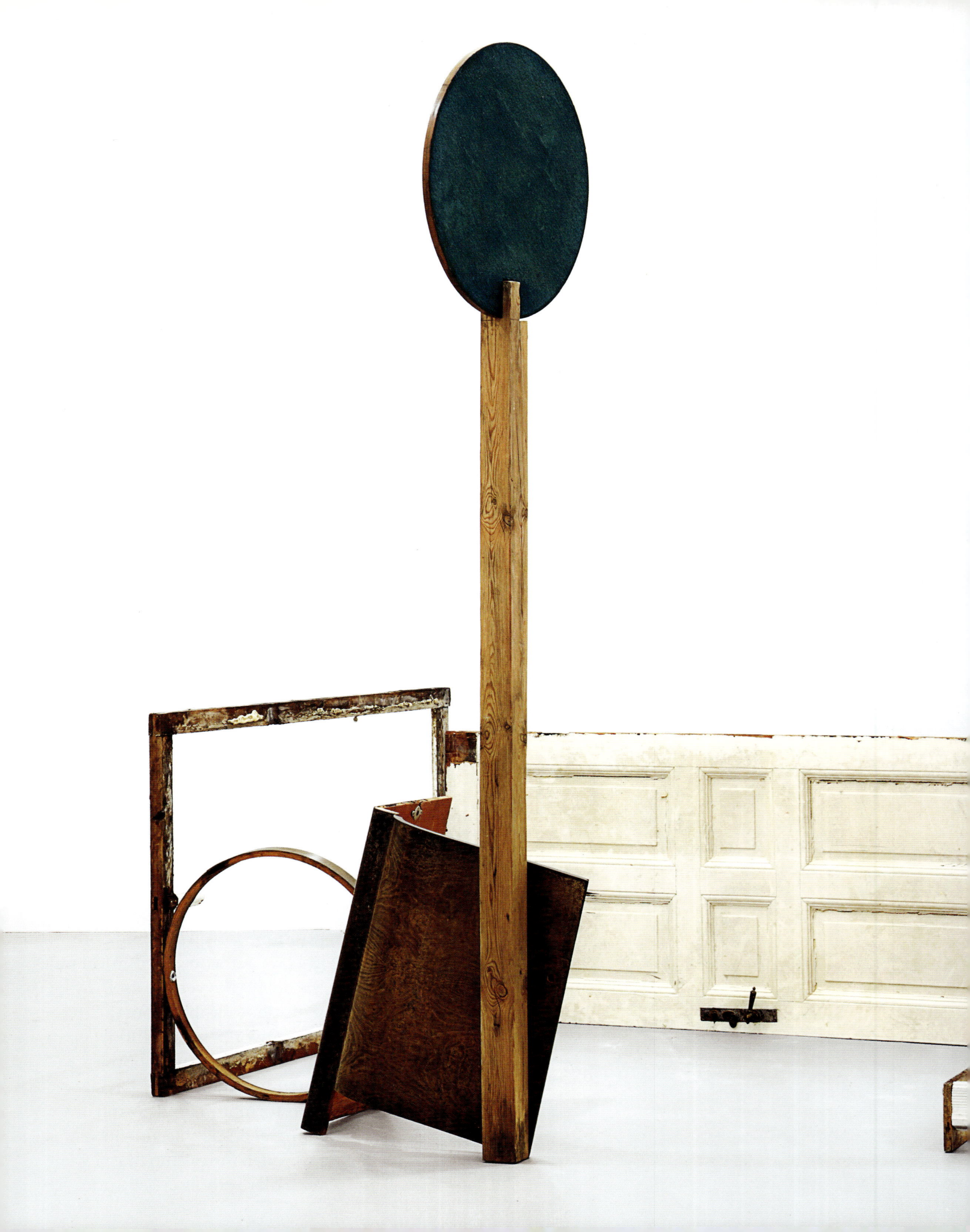

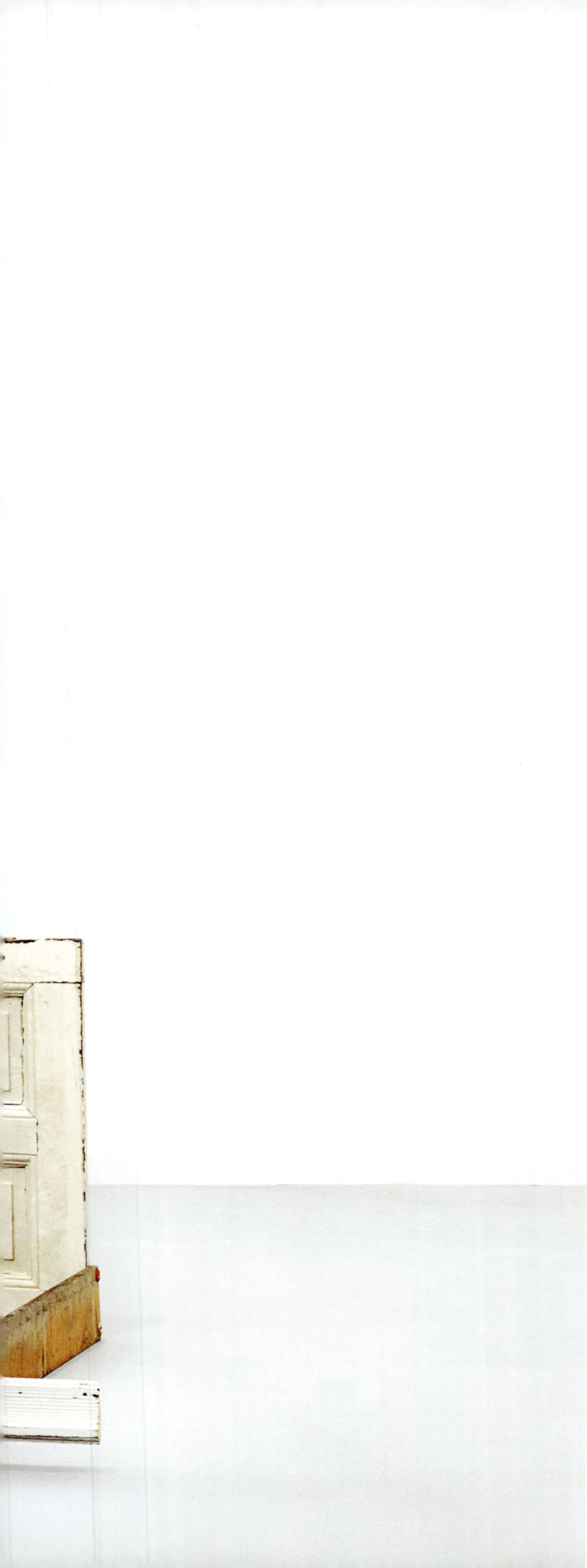

Shown by
Galerie Chantal Crousel B28
kurimanzutto B16

Biography
Born 1968
Lives in Berlin and Mexico City

Mexican writer and Conceptual artist Cruzvillegas has exhibited internationally since the early 1990s. In 2011 the solo exhibition "Autoconstrucción: The Optimistic Failure of a Simultaneous Promise" took place at Modern Art Oxford. The film *Autoconstrucción* (2009) was also shown at New Museum, New York, in 2011. Other recent solo shows were held at kurimanzutto, Mexico City (2010), and Galerie Chantal Crousel, Paris (2010). In 2010 Cruzvillegas was resident on the DAAD artist-in-Berlin program.

Morgenlatte nach einem Hausarrest während der Reichskristallnacht (Palo matutino después de un arresto domiciliario durante la noche de los vidrios rotos) (Morning Shag After House Arrest During the Night of Broken Glass)
2011
Found diverse wooden elements, stainless steel, acrylic paint, felt, and beer bottle caps
110¼ × 98⅜ × 98⅜"
(280 × 250 × 255 cm)
Courtesy of kurimanzutto

Abraham Cruzvillegas

Abraham Cruzvillegas' improvised sculptures relate, in material terms, his upbringing in a rocky area of Mexico City, where ingenuity and cooperation created a community in adverse conditions. *A.C. Mobile* (2008), a portable sound system made in collaboration with a project that provides bicycle repair work for people suffering from mental illness in Glasgow, elaborates Cruzvillegas' engagement with public space and the subjectivities of musical taste. Returning to Mexico City, and leaving the formal gallery altogether, for *La Galería de Comercio* (2010) Cruzvillegas facilitates community interaction with a series of evening events for locals; but, like a sculpture, this is intended to generate encounter rather than produce pedagogy or social change. SOR

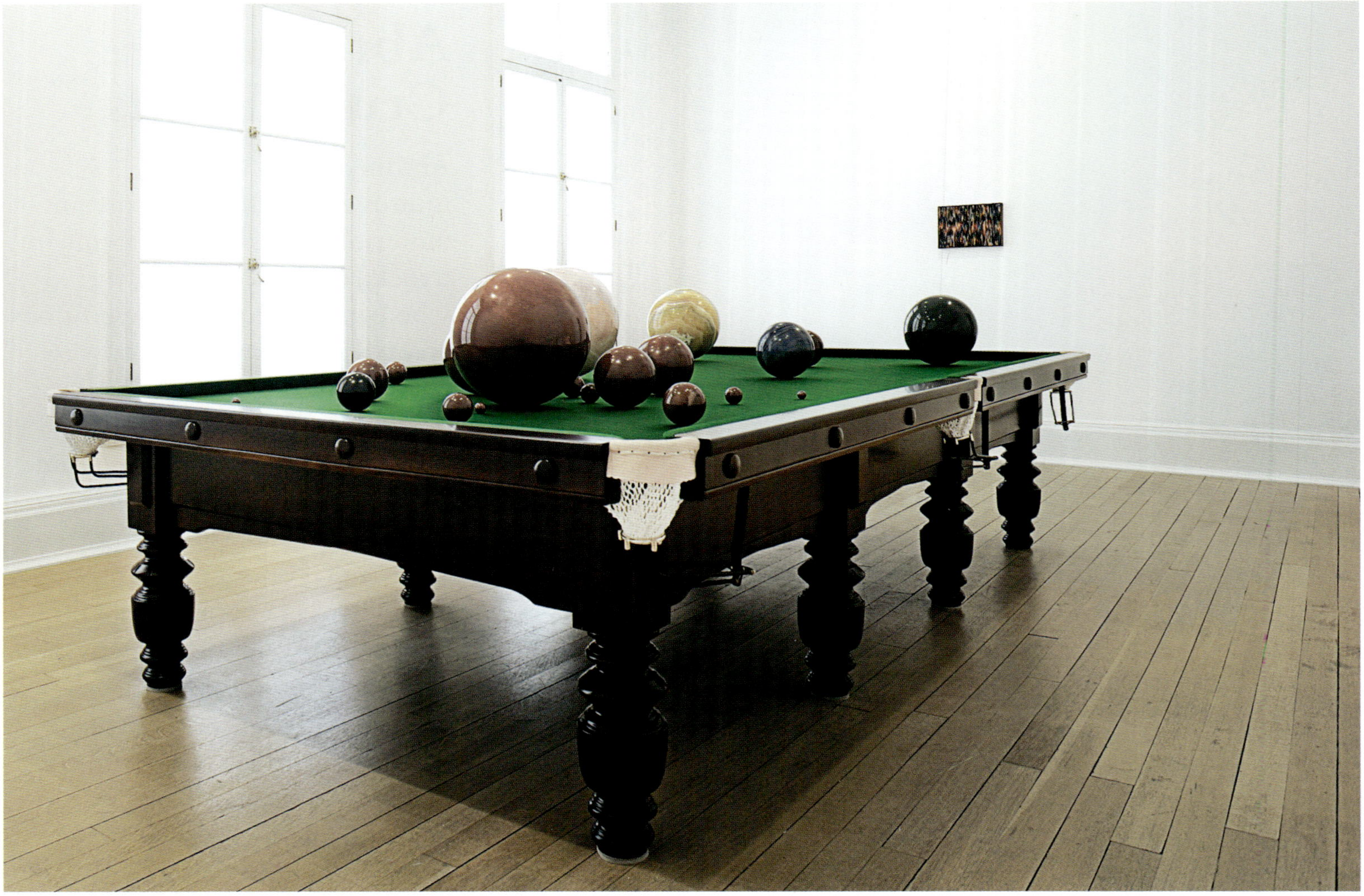

1

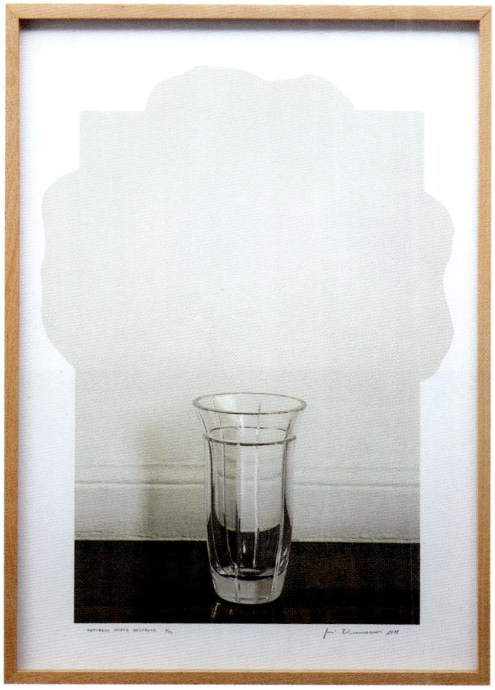

2

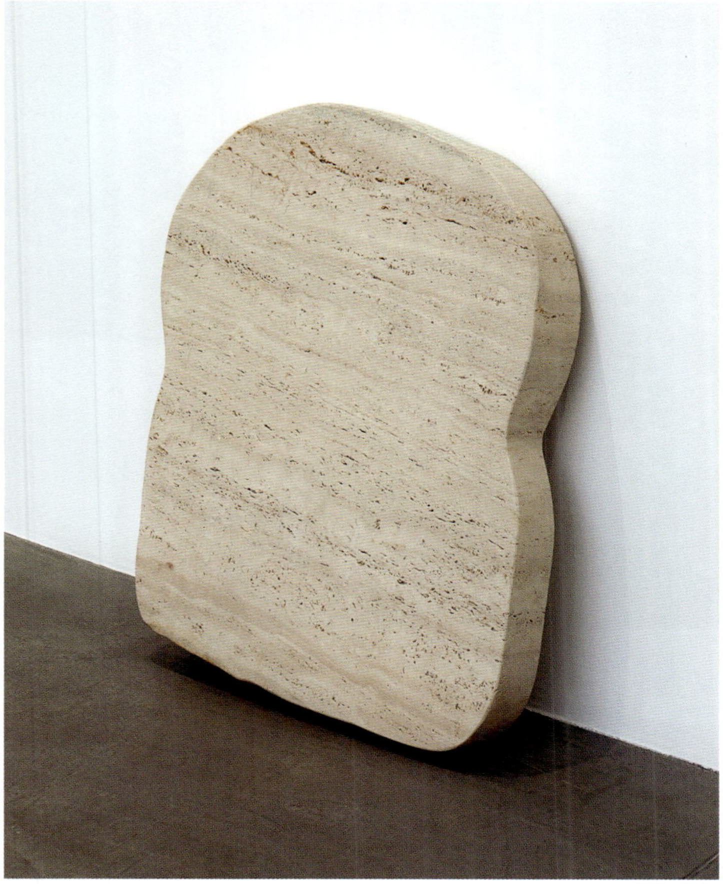

3

Shown by
Galeria Fortes Vilaça
C48

Biography
Born 1968
Lives in Rio de Janeiro

Brazilian artist Damaceno's recent two-person exhibition "Conversa (Conversation)" (2011) at Galeria Fotes Vilaça, São Paulo, drew affinities between his co-exhibitor's practice and his own. In 2010 solo shows were held at Distrito 4, Madrid, and Thomas Dane Gallery, London. He also participated in Prospect 1, New Orleans (2008), and "Think with the Senses, Feel with the Mind: Art in the Present Tense" (2007) at the 52nd Venice Biennale.

1
Integrated Circuit
2010
Mixed media
47⅝ × 151½ × 80¾"
(121 × 385 × 205 cm)
Courtesy of Thomas Dane Gallery

2
Natureza Morta Abstrata (Abstract Still Life)
2011
Silkscreen
19⅝ × 27½"
(50 × 70 cm)
Courtesy of Galeria Fortes Vilaça

3
Fatia (Slice)
2011
Marble
33½ × 27½ × 4"
(85 × 70 × 10 cm)
Courtesy of Galeria Fortes Vilaça

Jose Damasceno

From floor-to-ceiling columns made from shoe-sole shapes snipped out of telephone directories (*Durante o caminho vertical* (During the Vertical Path), 2001) to a "drawing" of exhibition visitors made with clusters of tens of thousands of pencils jammed directly into a wall (*Observation Plan*, 2004) or a snooker table with extraordinarily proportioned semi-precious stone balls (*Integrated Circuit*, 2010), José Damasceno's art radiates playful wisdom. Reveling in transformations, he exalts poor materials that might otherwise be taken for granted, yet in a countermove uses opulent ones to evoke unremarkable objects. *Fatia* (Slice, 2011), for example, is a slab of marble hewn to resemble an outsized slice of bread. MA

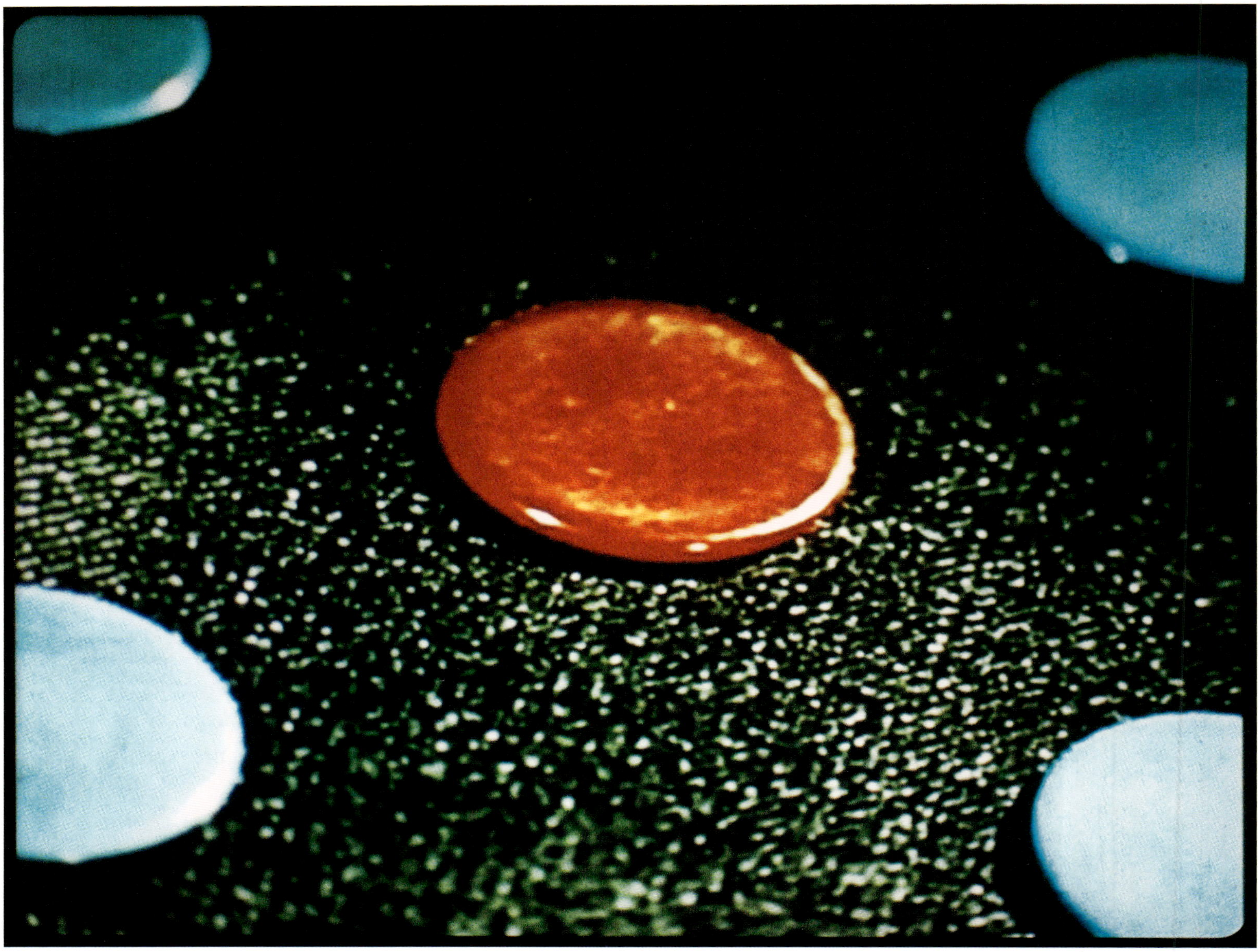

Philippe Decrauzat

The stark and visually striking lines and shapes that move through the paintings and installations of Philippe Decrauzat have attitude—sometimes a slouching relaxedness, sometimes a sterner, confrontational sneer. It might be the liberated dreams of Op art, but there's also a knowing restraint in drawing from the touchstones of Conceptualism and Minimalism, or more an awareness of what these movements inevitably contributed to a contemporary advertising vocabulary. His recent exhibition "On the Retina" placed large green slashes and crosses on the wall overseeing the concrete cast fragments of hoops and bars of *Methode d'objectification critique (dispersion)* (Method of Critical Objectification, 2011) littering the floor. In another room the crosses expanded to become *On Cover* (2011), a dense, disorienting pattern covering the entire wall, moving skillfully and critically between the sensory and the conceptual. CFW

Shown by
Mehdi Chouakri C24
Elizabeth Dee D1
Galerie Francesca Pia A15
Galerie Praz-Delavallade A18

Biography
Born 1974
Lives in Lausanne

Swiss artist Decrauzat has exhibited his paintings and installations extensively in Europe since the mid-1990s. In 2011 he had the solo shows "NYSTAGMUS" at Centre d'édition contemporaine, Geneva; "Philippe Decrauzat—On the Retina" at House of Art, České Budejovice; and "Anisotropy" at Le Plateau, FRAC Ile de France, Paris. He was awarded the Prix Gustave Buchet 2010 by the Musée cantonal des Beaux-Arts de Lausanne. He will have a solo show at Elizabeth Dee Gallery, New York, in 2012.

And to end
2011
16mm film, color
1 min. 12 sec.
Courtesy of Elizabeth Dee

Shown by
Galerie Karin Guenther F20

Biography
Born 1960
Lives in Tounae

Belgian artist Dekyndt has exhibited extensively in Europe and the United States since the mid-1990s. Her videos and installations have been the subject of numerous European solo shows in the last decade, including: "The Painter's Enemy Sources" (2011), at Sollertis Gallery, Toulouse; "Subliminal Rooms" (2011) at Galerie VidalCuglietta, Brussels; and "La femme de Loth" at Synagogue de Delme. Recent solo shows include "Found in Translation" (2011) at Casino Luxembourg, Luxemburg, and "We Make Version" (2011) at Westfälischer Kunstverein, Munster.

3 Juin 2011
(3 June 2011)
2011
Ink on paper
8¼ × 11¾"
(21 × 29.5 cm)
Courtesy of Galerie Karin Guenther

Focus
Edith Dekyndt

Since 1999, Edith Dekyndt has developed her work under the umbrella title "Universal Research of Subjectivity." Fascinated by everyday physics and how the most modest of actions can transform our perceptions of the world, her projects have included an attempt to render Belgium invisible from space by encouraging its inhabitants to switch off their house lights, a menacing black helium balloon that floats through the exhibition space like the security system in the cult TV show *The Prisoner* (1967–8), and—perhaps most tellingly—*One Second of Silence* (2008), a video of a transparent flag raised by Dekyndt at various locations in the USA, through which one could glimpse the blue, borderless sky. TM

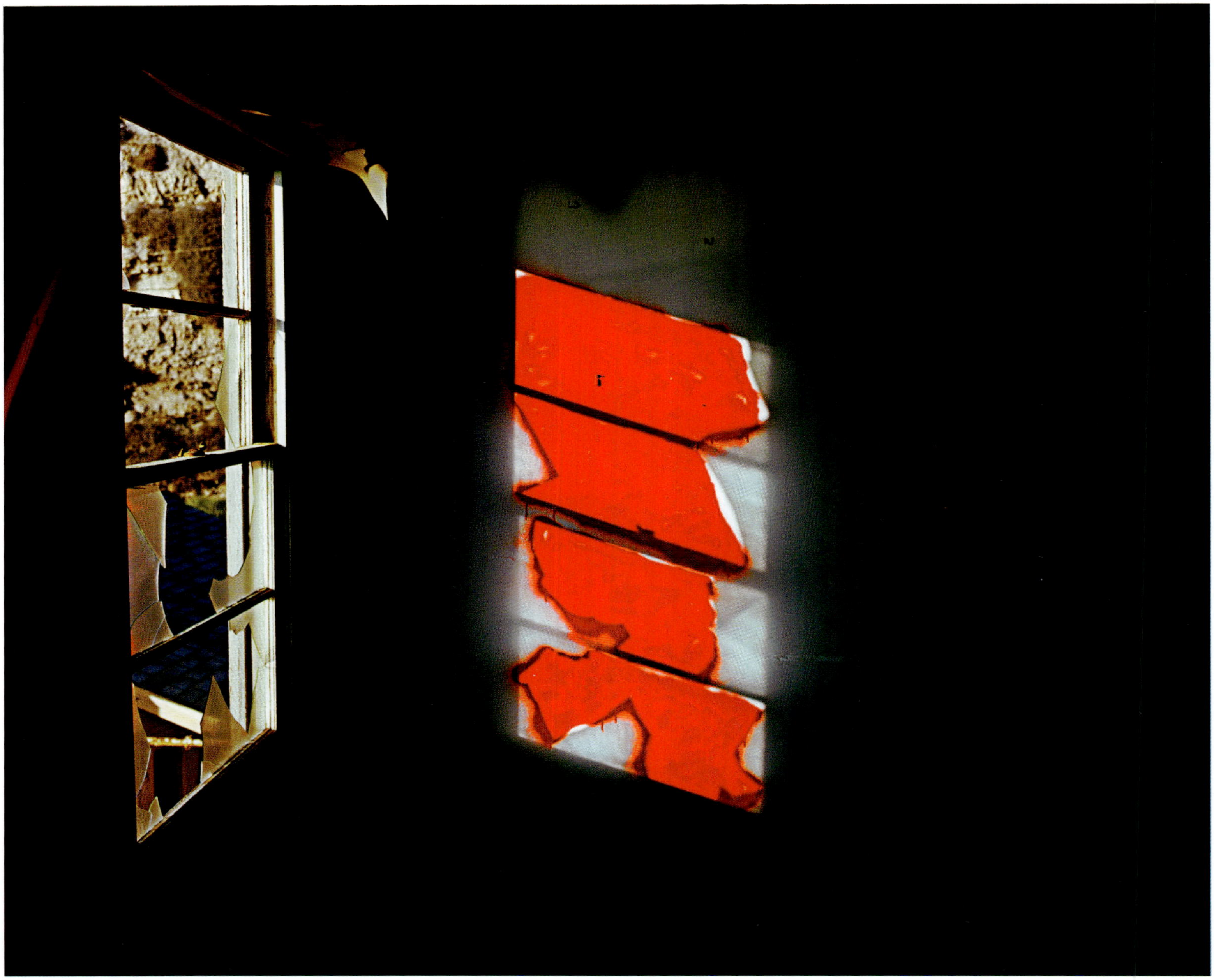

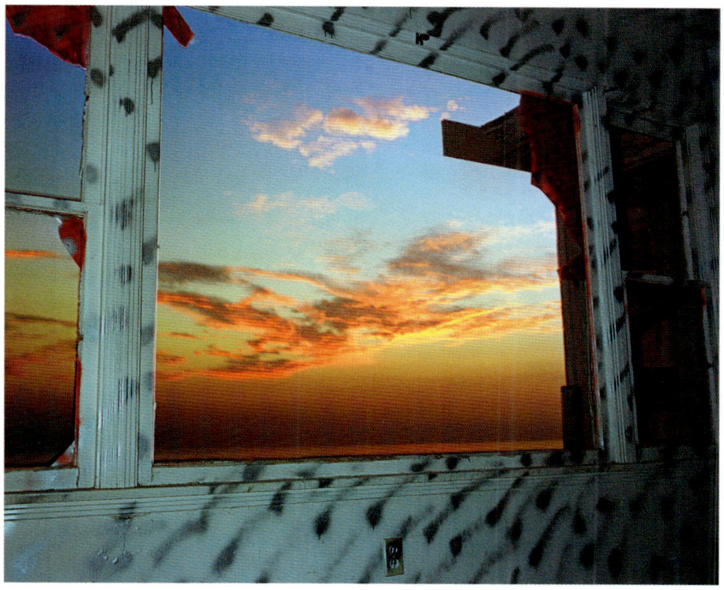

2

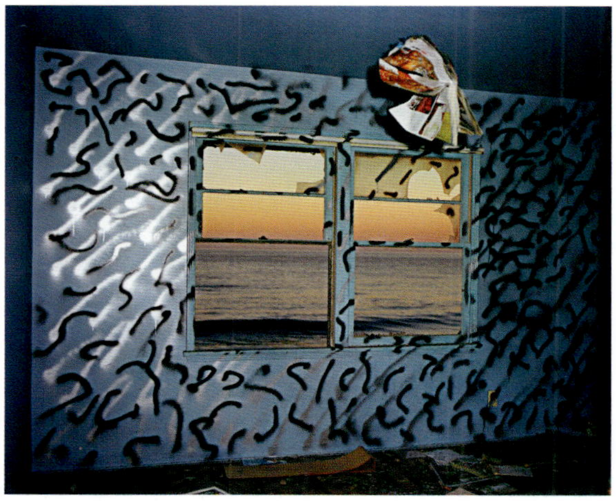

3

Shown by
Laura Bartlett Gallery
C26
Wallspace D7

Biography
Born 1949
Lives in Riverside

American photographer Divola has exhibited extensively in the United States and Europe since the 1970s. His architectural photographs have been the subject of numerous solo exhibitions, most recently "Notes on the Observer" (2012), at Gallery Luisotti, Santa Monica; "Vandalism Series, 1973–75" (2011), at LA><ART, Los Angeles; and "Trees for the Forest" (2011), at Wallspace Gallery, New York. Recent group shows include "Under the Big Black Sun"(2011) at the MOCA, Los Angeles and "View From Here" (2010), at the San Francisco Museum of Modern Art.

1
Zuma #5
1977–2006
Archival pigment print on rag paper
21 × 26"
(53.3 × 66 cm)
Courtesy of Wallspace

2
Zuma #30
1977–2006
Archival pigment print on rag paper
21 × 26"
(53.5 × 66 cm)
Courtesy of Wallspace

3
Zuma #70
1977–2006
Archival pigment print on rag paper
21 × 26"
(53.5 × 66 cm)
Courtesy of Wallspace

John Divola

John Divola's photographs attest a forensic eye for situations in flux. In the 1970s he photographed the interiors of abandoned houses for the series "Vandalism" (1974–5), the houses cleared under the Los Angeles International Airport flight path ("LAX NAZ," 1975–6), and the destruction of a beachfront property in "Zuma" (1977–2006). Adding his own patterned graffiti to the interiors in both the "Vandalism" and the "Zuma" series, these works show a performative engagement with architecture that elides photographic with painting and sculptural concerns. The photograph as image, as process, is again evident in his series "Dogs Chasing My Car in the Desert" (1996–2001), comprising shots taken by the artist from a moving vehicle and captured using high-speed film. PT

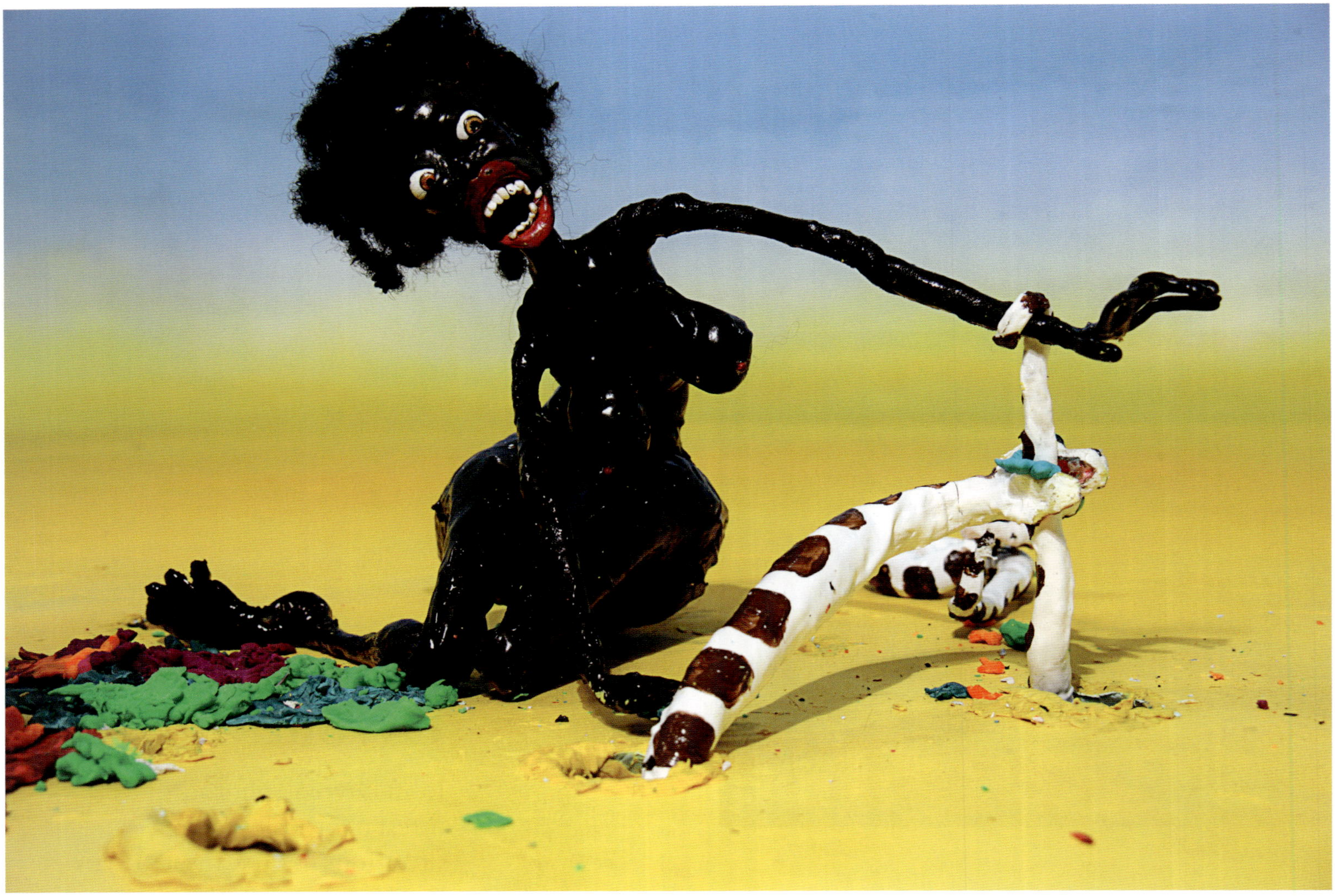

1

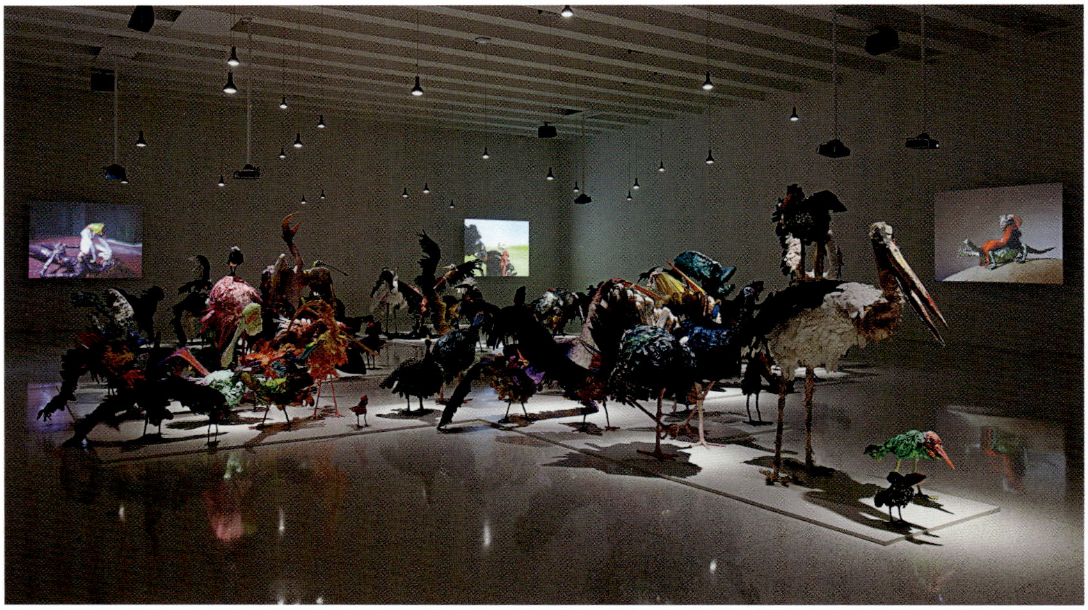

2

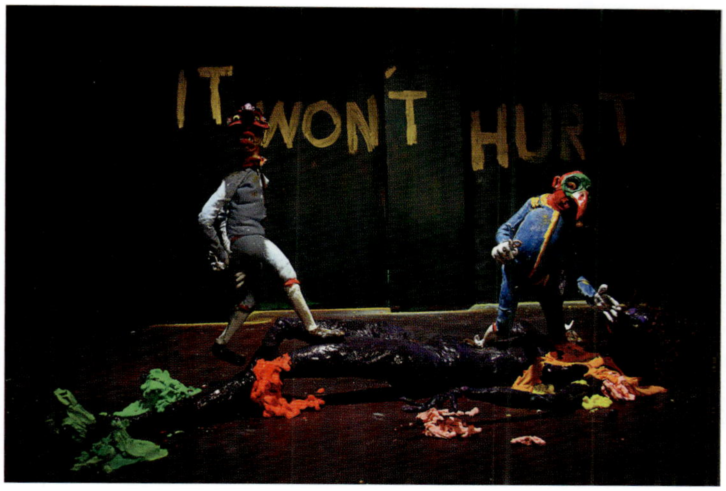

3

Shown by
Giò Marconi A3

Biography
Born 1978
Lives in Berlin

Swedish-born Djurberg's animations and sculptural installations explored new avenues in 2011 with the solo exhibitions "A World of Glass" at Camden Art Centre, London, and "The Parade" at the Walker Art Center, Minneapolis. Other exhibitions in 2011 include "I found myself alone" at Mumbai Art Room; "Human Behaviour" at the Wexner Center for the Arts, Columbus; and "Snakes Knows It's Yoga" at the Museum Boijmans Van Beuningen, Rotterdam, and Kunstforeningen GL STRAND, Copenhagen. In 2012 the New Museum, New York, will hold a solo show of her work.

1
Deceiving Looks
2011
Clay animation, digital video, music by Hans Berg
6 min. 8 sec.
Courtesy of Giò Marconi

2
The Parade
2011
Mixed media
Dimensions variable
Courtesy of Walker Art Center

3
I Wasn't Made to Play the Son
2011
Clay animation, digital video, music by Hans Berg
6 min. 27 sec.
Courtesy of Giò Marconi

Nathalie Djurberg

Nathalie Djurberg's films lure you in with their *faux*-naive claymation aesthetic, only to confront you with fables and fairytales that dance around the darkest sides of human existence, in films such as *The Necessity of Loss* (2006) and *It's the Mother* (2008). Nothing is off-limits in Djurberg's modeling clay world, with her characters engaging in sex and sadism, bestiality and murder, all to the tune of Hans Berg's jovial soundtracks.
In 2009 she was awarded the Silver Lion at the 53rd Venice Biennale for her sprawling installation *Experiment*, which combined three films depicting, among other things, young girls dismembering themselves set among a leering sculpture garden of brightly colored flora and fauna that were at once beautiful and terrifying—an erotic duality crucial to all of Djurberg's work. AB

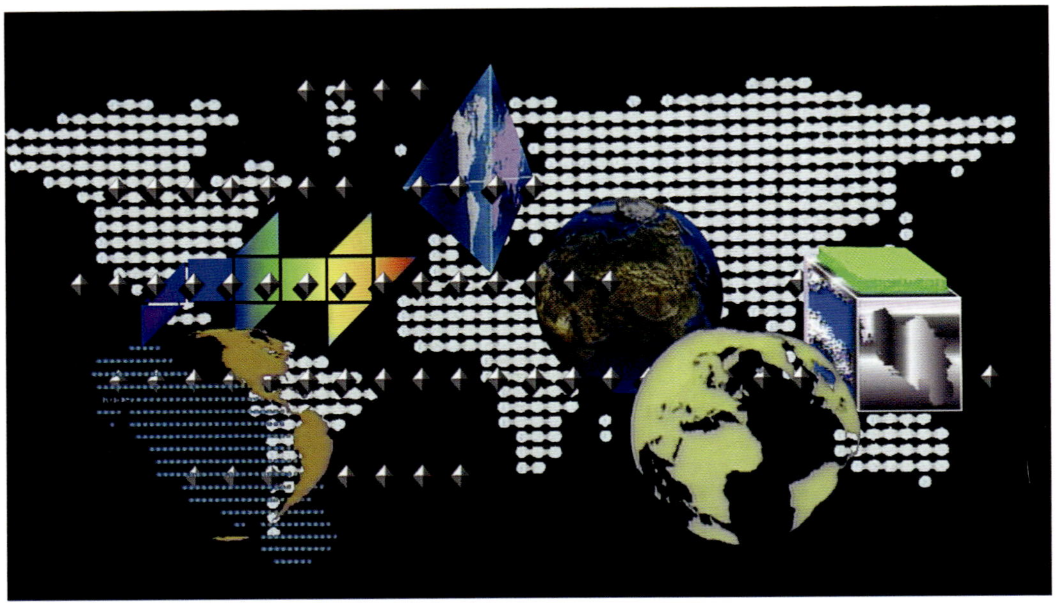

1

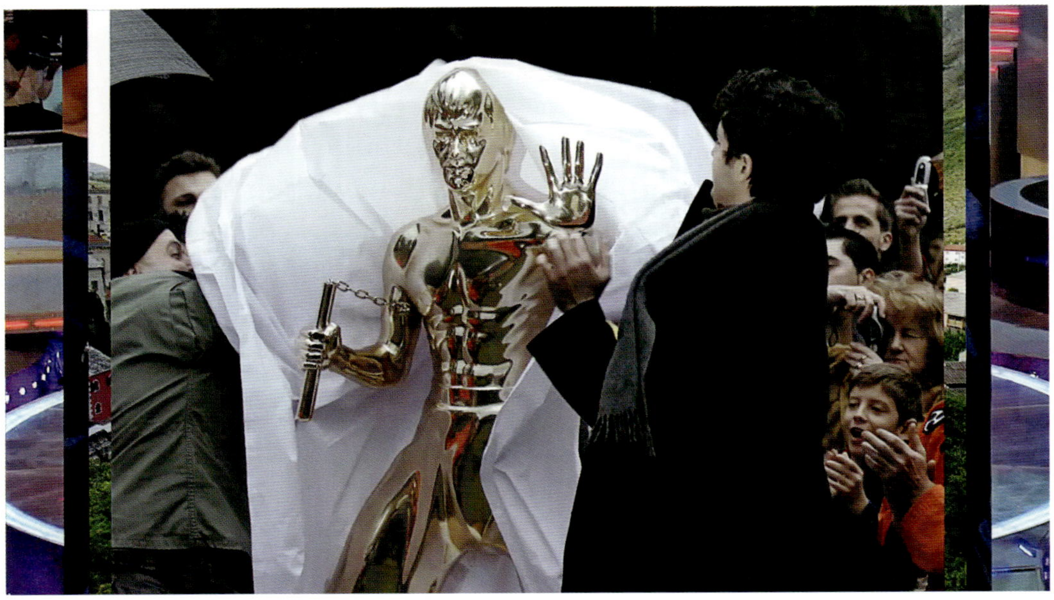

2

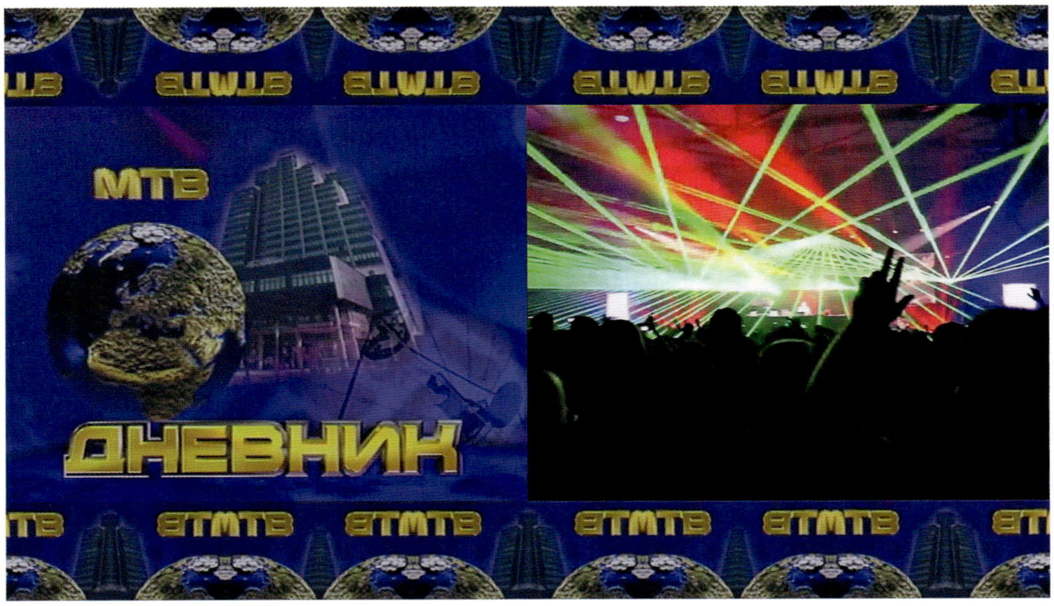

3

Shown by
Tanya Leighton Gallery F16

Biography
Born 1981
Lives in Berlin

In 2012 Domanović's multifaceted practice has been the subject of solo exhibitions at Villa du Parc, Annemass; SPACE, London; Kunsthalle, Basel and Küenstlerhaus Bethanien, Berlin. She has participated in numerous significant group shows, including: the 4th Marrakech Biennale (2012); "In Practice" (2012), at SculptureCenter, New York; "based in Berlin" (2011), at n.b.k., Berlin; and "Imagine Being Here Now" (2011), The 6th Momentum Biennial, Moss. She is a co-founder of the online curatorial platform VVORK (www.vvork.com).

1, 3
19:30
2010–11
HD video
11 min.
Courtesy of Tanya Leighton Gallery

2
Turbo Sculpture
2009–12
HD video
18 min.
Courtesy of Tanya Leighton Gallery

Focus
Aleksandra Domanović

Information flows, web chains, associative flights of fancy and amalgamation, contextual dissonance: such are the obsessions of Aleksandra Domanović's intelligent, quixotic practice, which maps in vividly colored video and multimedia the way images are sublimated or subverted as they move from one cultural or political ground to the next. The video *Turbo Sculpture* (2009–12), for example, examines the spate of monuments to Hollywood characters and celebrities punctuating the landscape of the former Yugoslavia, while *19:30* (2010–11) offers a mixtape of Yugoslav evening news idents, remixed with the help of techno DJs to their music. Both works examine ideas of audience, collectivity, and coexistence, while poignantly tracing the end of the socialist era and the beginning of the next. QL

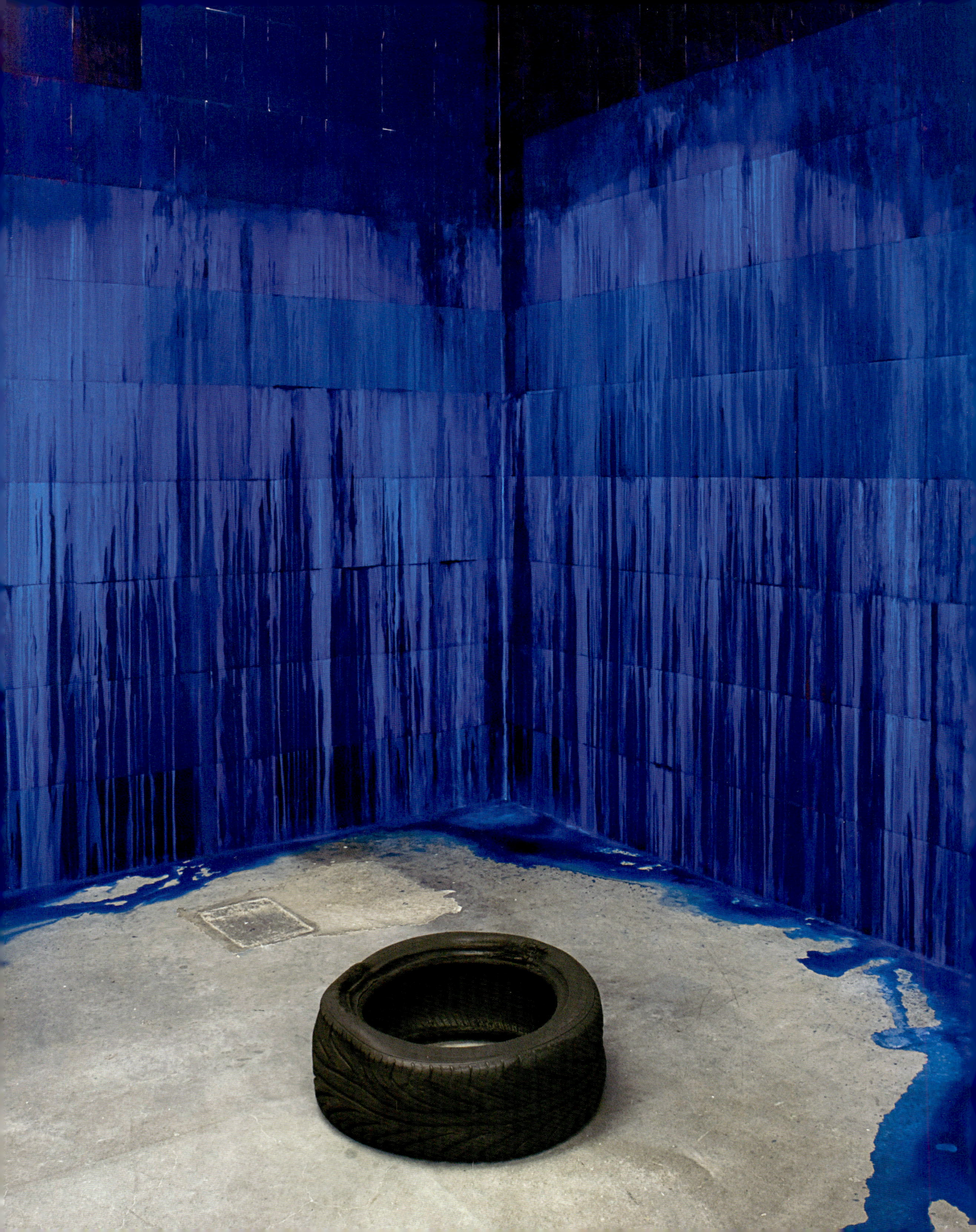

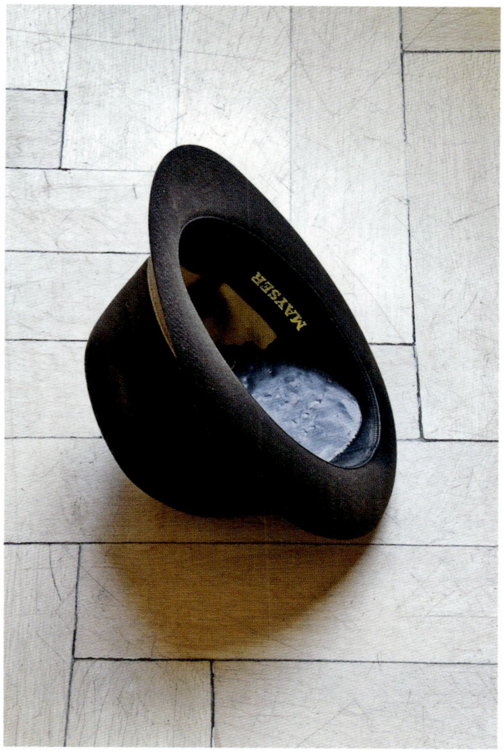

2

Shown by
kaufmann repetto A23

Biography
Born 1974
Lives in Martigny

Morocco-born Echakhch held recent solo exhibitions at Museum Haus Esters, Krefeld (2011); GAMeC, Bergamo (2011), FRAC Champagne-Ardenne, Reims (2011), and MACBA, Barcelona (2011). Other exhibitions include "Movement and Complication" at the Swiss Institute, New York (2009), and "Speaker's Corner" (2008) at Tate Modern's Level Two Gallery, London. Her installations were also included in "ILLUMInation" at the 54th Venice Biennale (2011), and Biennale de Lyon (2009).

1
A Chaque Stencil une Révolution (For Each Stencil a Revolution)
2007
A4 Carbon paper, glue, methylated alcohol
Dimensions variable
Courtesy of kaufmann repetto

2
Chapeau d'encre (Ink Hat)
2011
Hats, polyester glass, Indian ink
Dimensions variable
Courtesy of kaufmann repetto

Latifa Echakhch

Latifa Echakhch's subtle deployment of everyday objects in her sculptures and installations takes place in an ambiguous hinterland between the personal and political. Though born in Morocco, she does not speak Arabic or recall anything of that country, so her use, say, of the Moroccan tea glasses and carpets is more a matter of delicate recontextualization than avowed nostalgia. The obvious postcolonial element in her work is part of a wider exploration of the public and political through frail ephemera: in *A Chaque Stencil une Révolution* (For Each Stencil a Revolution, 2007), for example, blue carbon paper of the sort used to produce protest literature during the Parisian student riots of May 1968. BD

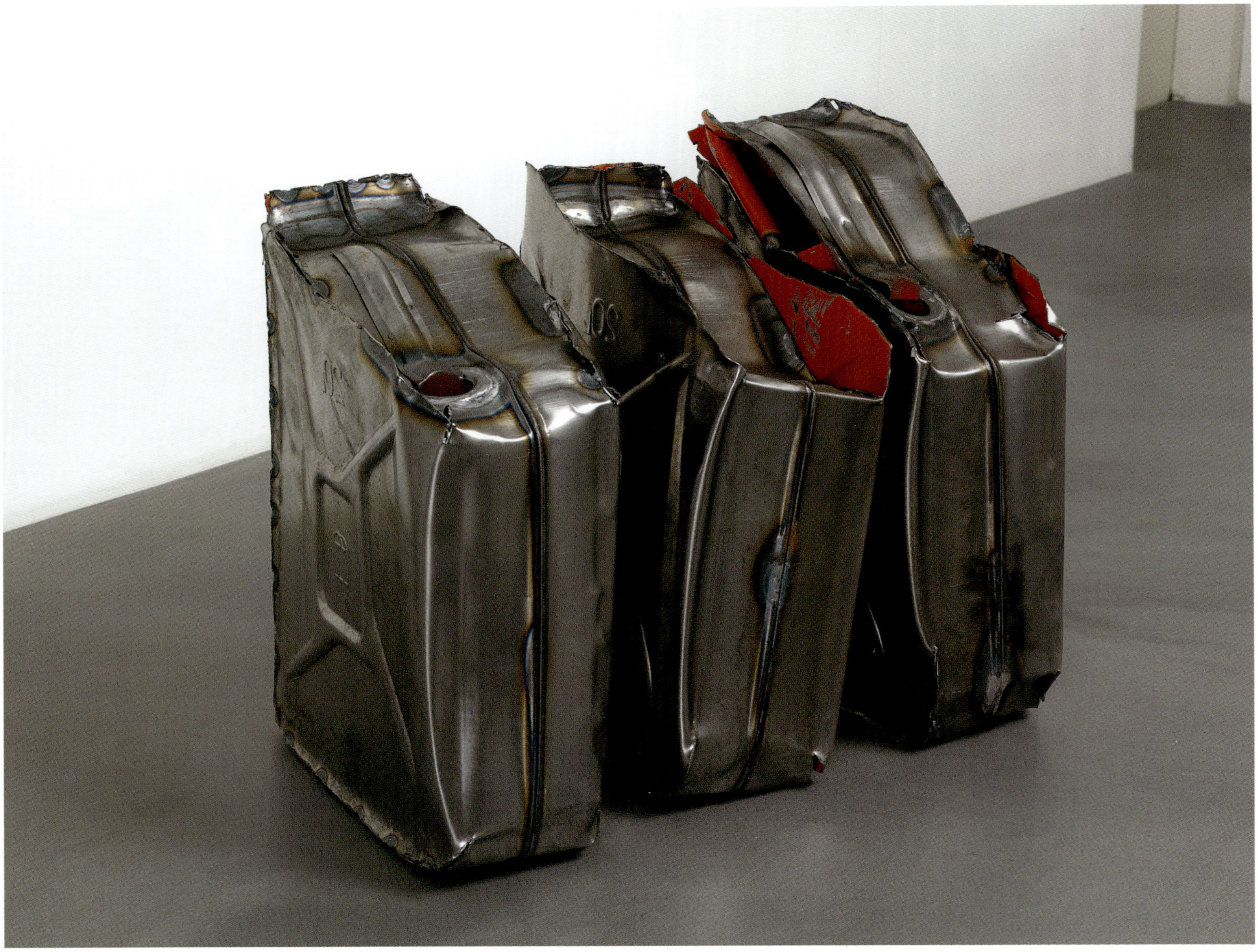

1

Shown by
Simon Lee Gallery A5
Eva Presenhuber B29
Reena Spaulings Fine Art F17
STANDARD (Oslo) B41

Biography
Born 1973
Lives in Oslo

Norwegian artist and writer Faldbakken's sculptures, drawings and collages have been exhibited internationally since the late-1990s. They were the subject of the recent solo exhibition "Oslo, Texas" at The Power Station, Dallas, in late-2011. In 2010 he had multiple solo shows across Europe, including "You Think You Go But You Gon't" at Objectif, Antwerp; "The Hills" at Standard (Oslo); and "Known to Few, Unknown to Fewer" at Simon Lee Gallery, London. His work is included in numerous public collections, including The Dmitris Daskalopoulos Collection, Athens, and Moderna Museet, Stockholm.

2

3

1
Untitled (Everted Jerry Cans 3, 4 & 5)
2011
Everted Jerry cans
Dimensions variable
Courtesy of Simon Lee Gallery

2
Untitled (Garbage Bag #06)
2010
Marker pencil on plastic bag (framed)
53 × 34¾ × 1¾"
(134.5 × 88 × 4.5 cm)
Courtesy of Simon Lee Gallery

3
Untitled (Canvas # 35)
2011
Acrylic molotow tagger pen on Belgian linen unprimed canvas
59 × 59"
(150 × 150 cm)
Courtesy of Simon Lee Gallery

Matias Faldbakken

Matias Faldbakken is habitually described as a radical, a subversive, a nihilist. It is not hard to see how people might get that impression: works made from, among other materials, black trash bags, spray paint, or insulation tape evoke protest and vandalism via the antagonistic aesthetic strategies of punk. However, Faldbakken, who has also written three novels and a play, is mainly interested in exposing the emptiness of so-called subversive art forms. A burnt-out Mercedes is tidily strapped to a trolley and titled, sardonically, *Abstracted Car* (2009). Cool, spare paintings done in white marker pen on beige linen, including *Untitled* (2011), are ambivalent not only about meaning but also about the avant-garde traditions from which they emerge. JG

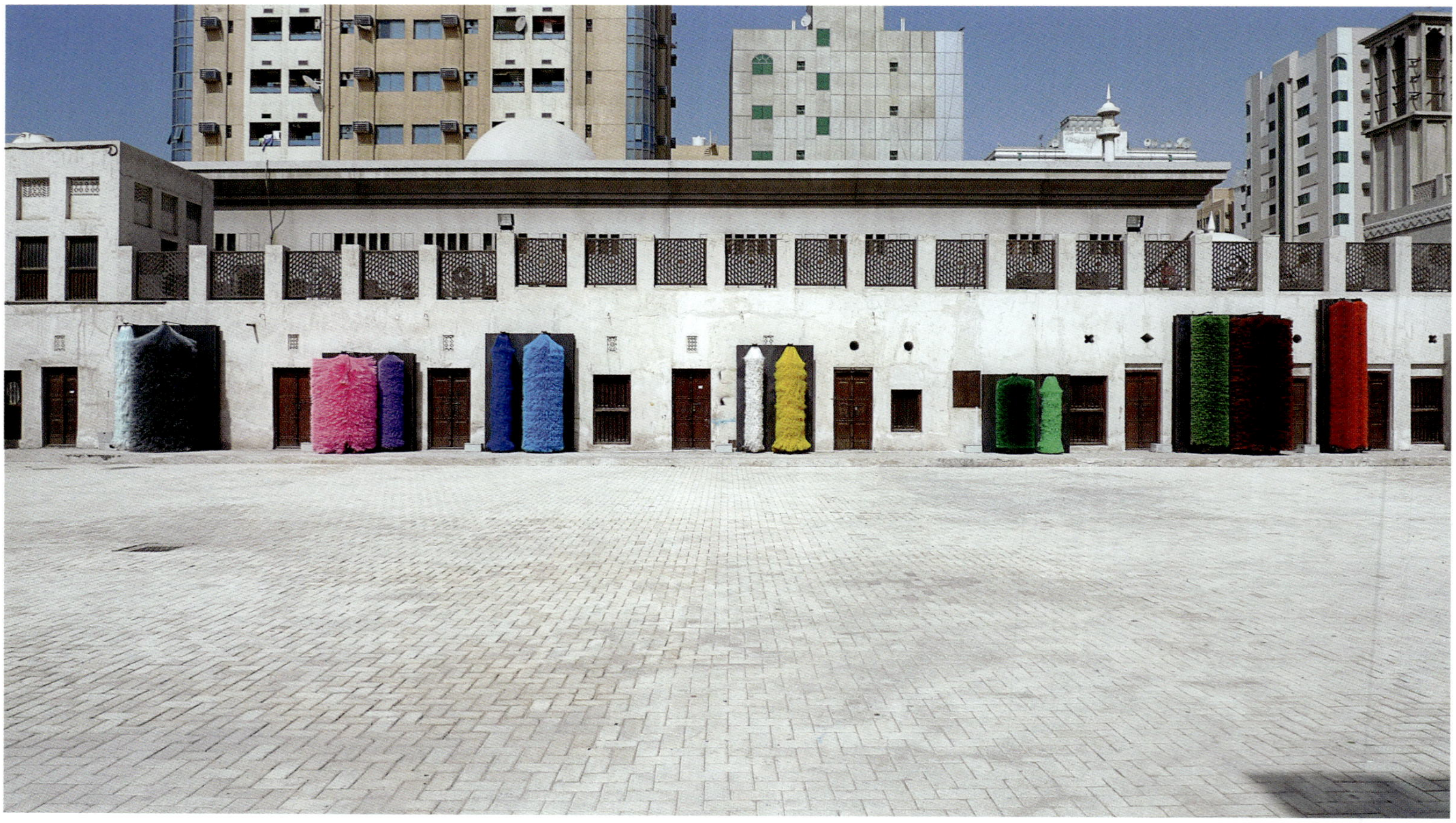

1

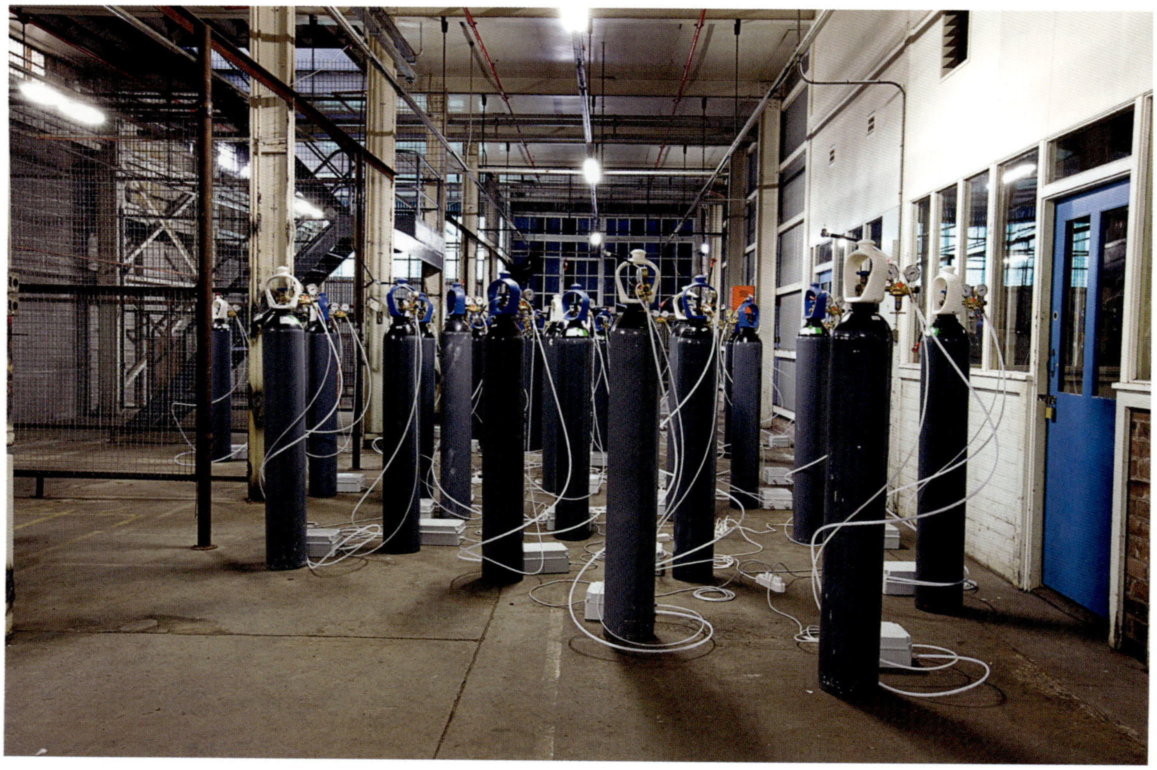

2

Lara Favaretto

Whether in performance or kinetic sculpture, Lara Favaretto explores the space of spectacle and the carnivalesque. In *Confetti Canyon* (2005) she showered a crowd with confetti, shot from cannon-like devices. In *Project for Some Hallucinations* (2007) Favaretto invited the Queen of England to Frieze Art Fair, London. Both works turned on spectacle, collective expectation, and anticipation. Impossibility is another recurring theme in Favaretto's work, as is the attempt to breach the limit of that impossibility. *Project for a Utopia* (2001–ongoing) is a proposal to float a hot air balloon in the shape of a donkey across the borders of Europe. Traveling on board the donkey—politicians, thinkers, and celebrities debating the notion of "dignity." KK

Shown by
Galleria Franco Noero
C50

Biography
Born 1973
Lives in Turin

Favaretto's contribution to Untitled (12th International Istanbul Biennial, 2011), saw suitcases populating the gallery. In 2012 she will contribute to dOCUMENTA (13), Kassel, and hold a solo exhibition at MoMA PS1, Long Island City. Other recent exhibitions include "Painlessly Consumed" (2010) at Galleria Franco Noero, Turin, and "Absolutely no Donations" (2009) at Tramway, Glasgow. In 2009 she contributed to "Making Worlds" at the 53rd Venice Biennale and "Provisions For The Future" at the 9th Sharjah Biennial.

1
Installation view at "Provisions for the Future," 9th Sharjah Biennial
2009
Site-specific installation
Dimensions variable
Courtesy of Galleria Franco Noero

2
Plotone (Platoon)
2005
35 compressed air-tanks, 35 pressure regulators, 35 timers, 35 electrovalves, 35 whistles, plastic cables
Dimensions variable
Courtesy of Galleria Franco Noero

3
Momentary Monument
2009
Black peat, vegetal earth, volcanic sand, aquatic algae, musk, iron, wood, cellulose, fresh water, metal
Dimensions variable
Courtesy of Galleria Franco Noero

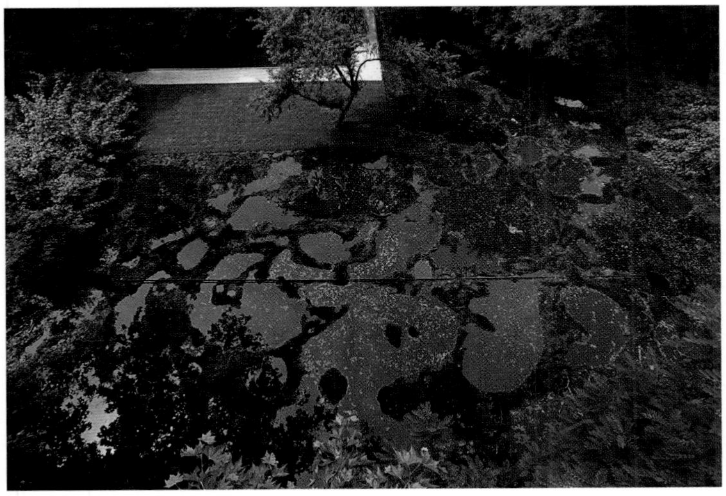

3

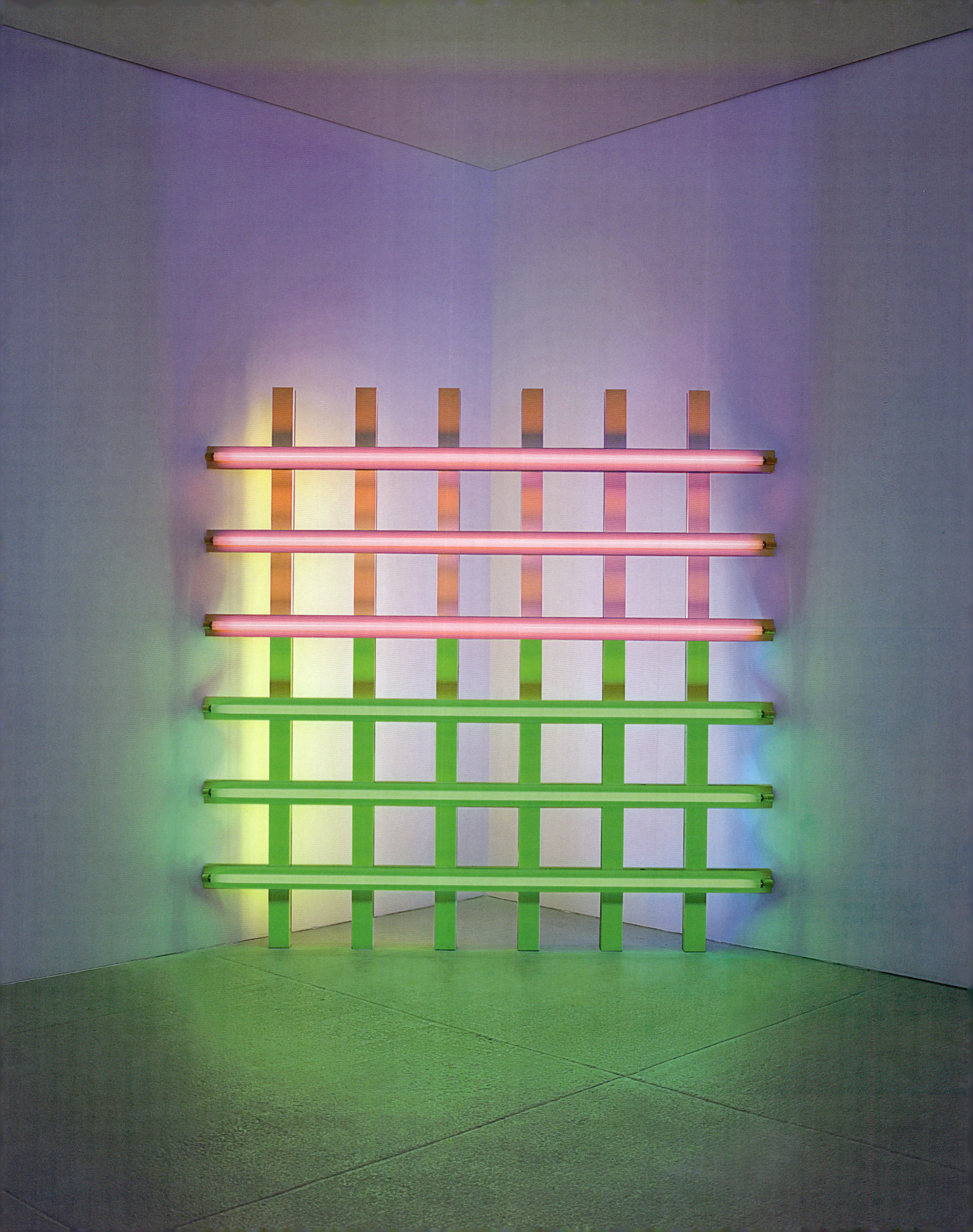

Shown by
David Zwirner C46

Biography
Born 1933
Died 1996

Over the course of his career, Flavin exhibited extensively at international venues. New York's Dia Art Foundation's posthumous exhibition "Dan Flavin: A Retrospective" (2004–07) toured prestigious institutions in Europe and the United States, including the National Gallery of Art, Washington, D.C. (2005); Hayward Gallery, London (2006); and Pinakothek der Moderne, Munich (2007). In spring 2012 the first retrospective of his drawings will be held at The Morgan Library and Museum, New York.

1
untitled (for you, Leo, in long respect and affection) 1
1977
pink, green, yellow, and blue fluorescent light
96 × 96" square across a corner
(244 × 244 cm)
© 2012 Stephen Flavin/Artists Rights Society (ARS), New York. Courtesy of David Zwirner

2
untitled (to dear, durable Sol from Stephen, Sonja, and Dan) one
1969
daylight and cool white fluorescent light
96 × 96" square across a corner
(244 × 244 cm)
© 2012 Stephen Flavin/Artists Rights Society (ARS), New York. Courtesy of David Zwirner

Dan Flavin

By describing his works as "situational," Dan Flavin was among the first generation to consider the architectural, institutional, and social context of sculpture as a fundamental component. His barrier works—room-filling rectilinear constructions of colored neon tubes—did indeed impose upon visitors' movement around the space, not just physically but also psychologically. For Flavin light was a material as tangible and plastic as the metals and resins of his Minimalist peers, and yet titles such as *untitled (to Helga and Carlo, with respect and affection)* (1974) seem to hint at our emotional responses to light, and the romantic and spiritual legacy of luminescence, which is here rendered, deadpan, into sensory information. SOR

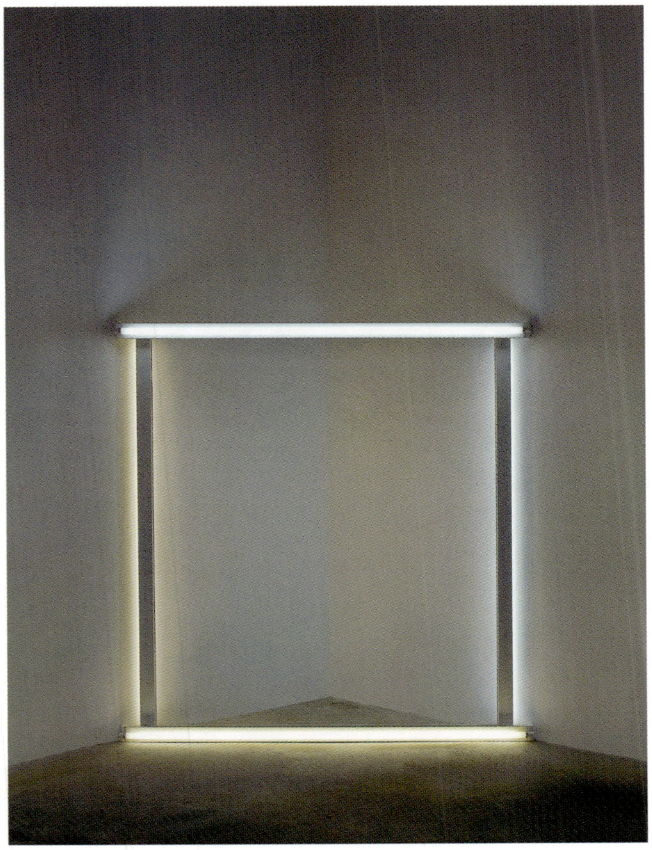

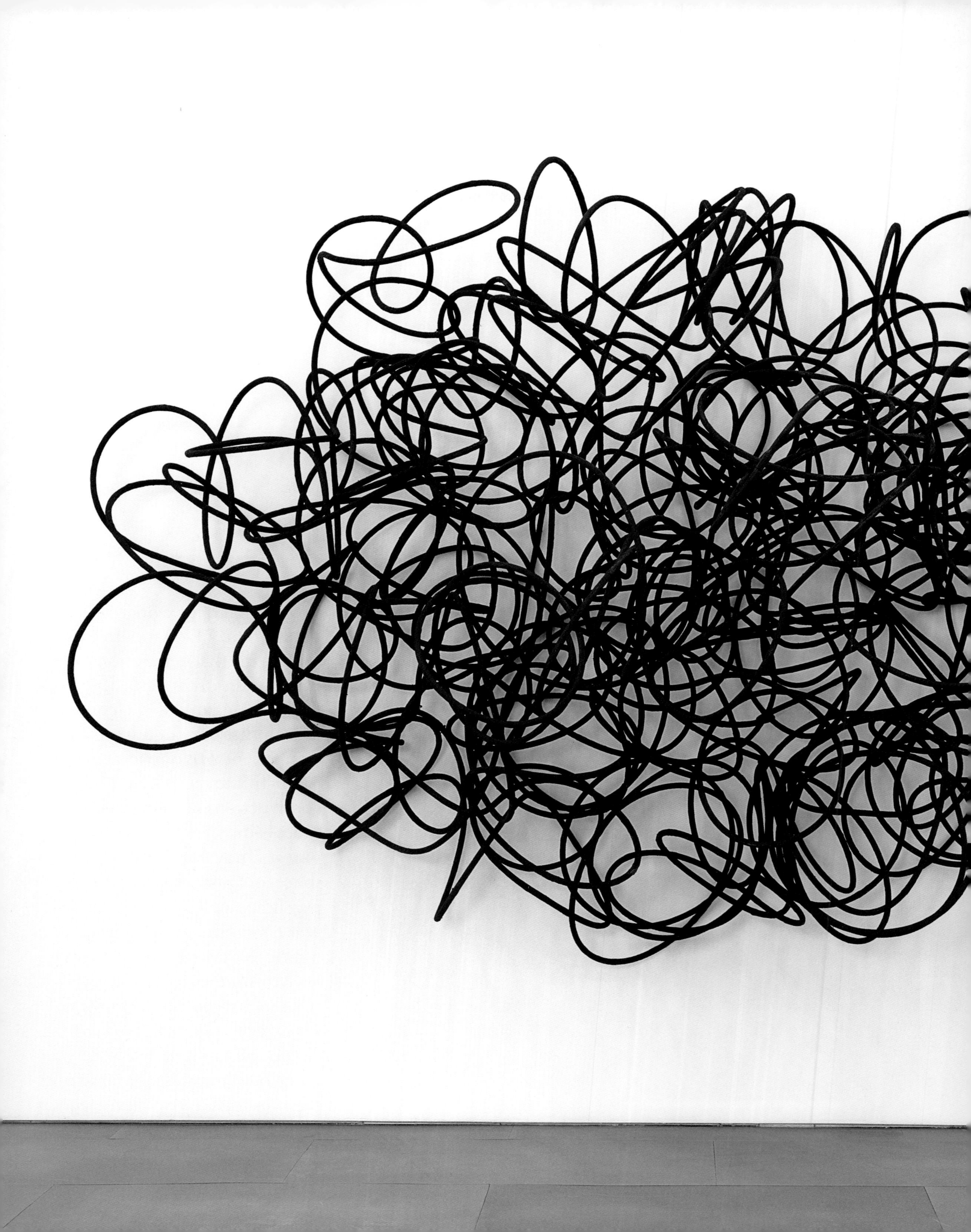

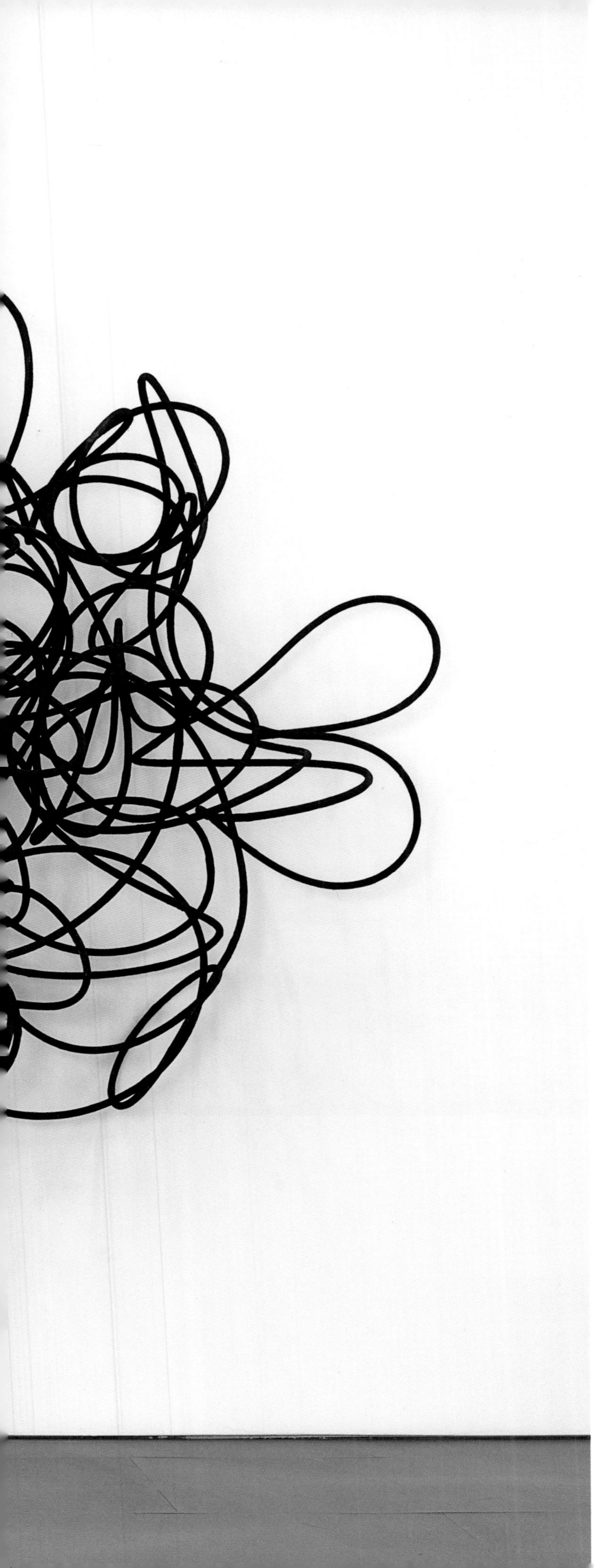

Michel François

Shown by
Bortolami A9
carlier | gebauer C23
Xavier Hufkens B23

Biography
Born 1956
Lives in Brussels

Belgian artist François's sculptures and installations were the subject of his first comprehensive solo show "Retrospective" at SMAK, Gent, and the Institut d'art contemporain, Villeurbanne/Rhône-Alpes, in 2009. In 2010 self-titled solo shows took place at carlier gebauer, Berlin, and Bortolami Gallery, New York. He represented Belgium at the 48th Venice Biennale (1999) and participated in Documenta IX (1992).

Scribble
2010
Aluminum, plaster, indian ink
98⅜ × 157½ × 56"
(250 × 400 × 142 cm)
Courtesy of carlier | gebauer

Michel François' *Pièce détachée* (Spare Part, 2010) is emblematic of his practice, in that it appears to adhere to formalist traditions, and yet the steel rods are held in place by magnets, implying a contingency and reconfigurability that would undermine any monolithic claims. Conversely, *Scribble* (2010) makes fast in aluminum what is generally throwaway. Throughout his practice, François diverts a material's usage or associative meaning into a complex system of poetics and observations. Complex installations of many interrelated elements, such as *Instant Gratification*... (2006), extend the work along allegorical lines, whereas *Crash* (2010), a photograph of two car ends buckled into one another on impact, generates meaning within social space, where materiality has very real implications. SOR

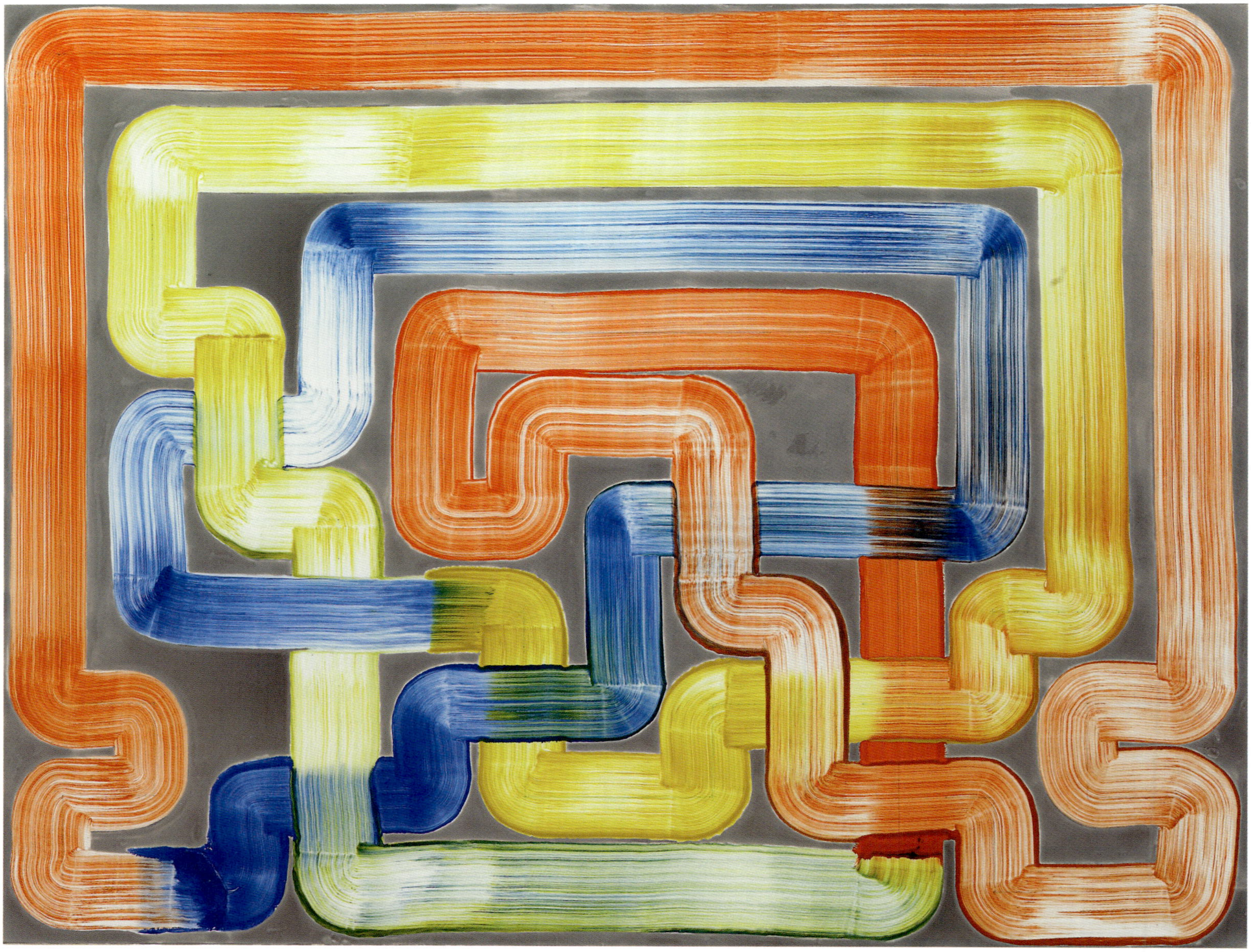

1

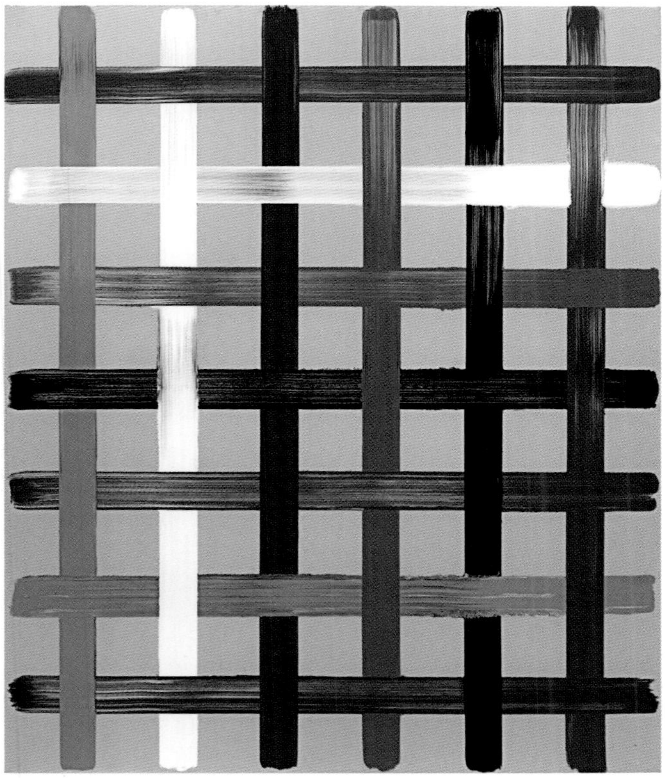

2

Shown by
Simon Lee Gallery A5
Galerie Perrotin C41

Biography
Born 1949
Lives in Paris
and Berlin

For over three decades France-born Frize has exhibited his abstract paintings in Europe and latterly in the United States. In 2011 he was awarded the Fred-Thieler-Preis for painting—the awards exhibition took place at Berlinische Galerie, Berlin, the same year. The solo exhibitions "Ad Nauseam" (2011) at Galerie Perrotin, and the retrospective "And How and Where and Who" (2010) at the Morsbroich Museum, Leverkusen, explored the vast scope of his practice in recent years.

1
Perma
2006
Acrylic and resin
on canvas
52 × 68½"
(132 × 174 cm)
Courtesy of Galerie
Perrotin

2
Armen
2001
Acrylic and resin
on canvas
59⅞ × 51⅝"
(152 × 131 cm)
Courtesy of Galerie
Perrotin

Bernard Frize

Bernard Frize has, over the years, employed many strategies to make his paintings more or less arbitrary: he has collaged the dried skins from paint tins (*Suite Segond*, 1980), he has painted wearing a blindfold, and he has used circular brushstrokes to pattern canvas (*Tuli*, 2011). Recently a performative style of factory production has predominated: in concert with his assistants, he will drag multicolored lines of paint into patterns and knots—complex forms that would be impossible to make on one's own. The surprise is that these rational, predetermined systems—as in the large *Paravent* (2010) or *Oplontis 1987–2010* (2010)—result in pictures that are sensuous, joyful, and uniquely human. JG

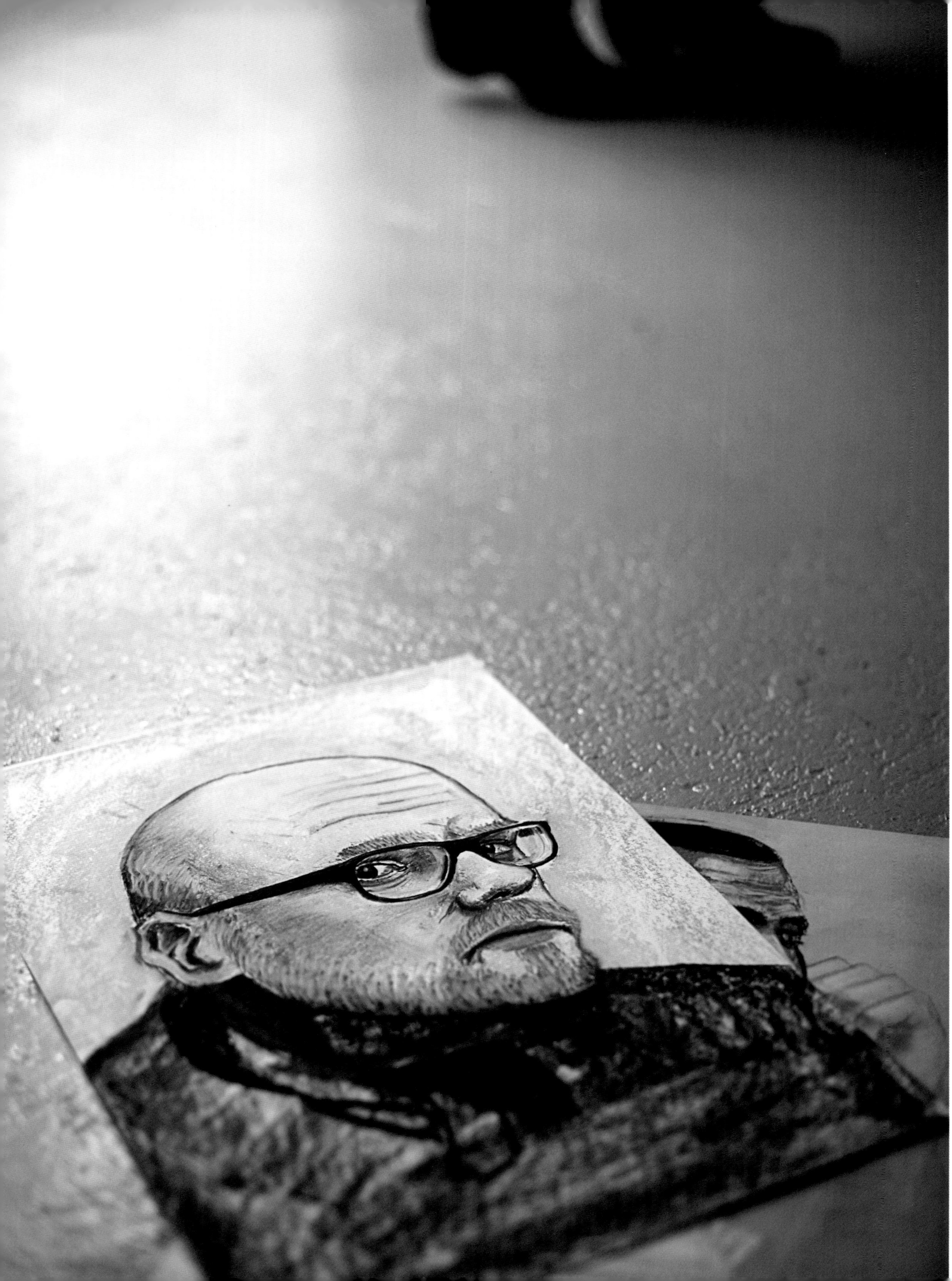

Shown by
gb agency F33
Annet Gelink
Gallery A10
Lisson Gallery C5
TARO NASU C25

Biography
Born 1976
Lives in London

Gander's multi-faceted work has been shown extensively in solo and group exhibitions over the last decade. Recent exhibitions include "Icarus Falling—An Exhibition Lost" (2011) at Maison Hermès, 8th Floor, Le Forum, Tokyo; "New Collisions in Culturefield" (2011) at Johnen Galerie, Berlin; and the Artangel commission "Locked Room Scenario" (2011) at Londonewcastle Depot, London. He was included in the group exhibitions "ILLUMInations" (2011) at the 54th Venice Biennale, and "Manifesta 8" (2010), Murica.

1
True simplicity (A study for "Who said this was true multiplicity anyway")
2011
Gelatin silver print
13⅞ × 10⅞"
(35.5 × 27.5 cm)
Courtesy of
TARO NASU

2
Who said this was true multiplicity anyway
2011
30 portraits of the 30 artists previously shown at the Hermès exhibition space, drawn by a courtroom visualization artist, to represent the artists in the year 2038.
Dimensions variable
Courtesy of
TARO NASU

Ryan Gander

The neon letters "M SSAGE" hung lifeless — broken and forlorn — in a gallery window. Prurient passers-by lured by the sign were disappointed by its title—*The Medium* (2010)—referring not to saucy "massages" but to Marshall McLuhan's famous aphorism. Messages in Ryan Gander's diverse works are invariably circuitous or, as here, incomplete. The artist likes to tease his audience: *Locked Room Scenario* (2011) was an elaborate installation (commissioned by Artangel, London) in which visitors were denied access to the advertised exhibit and instead engaged by orchestrated occurrences around the building. "You have my word," promised the title of a 2011 exhibit at a Japanese Shinto shrine; a buried time capsule, *Like the Air that We Breathe* (2011), meant that Gander's "word" was all we had. JG

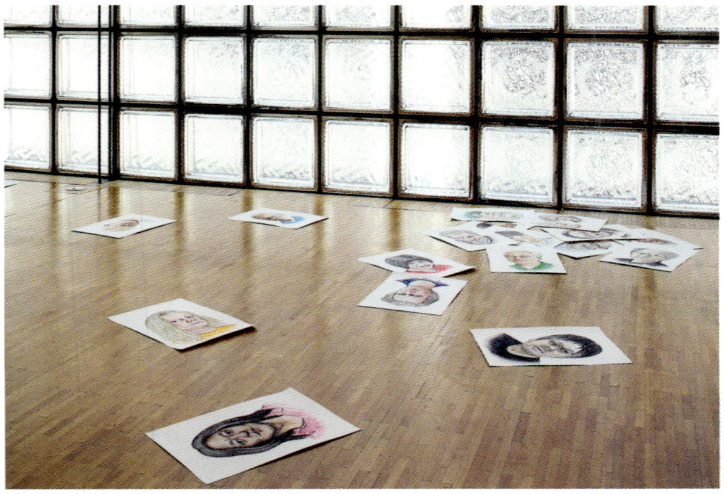

2

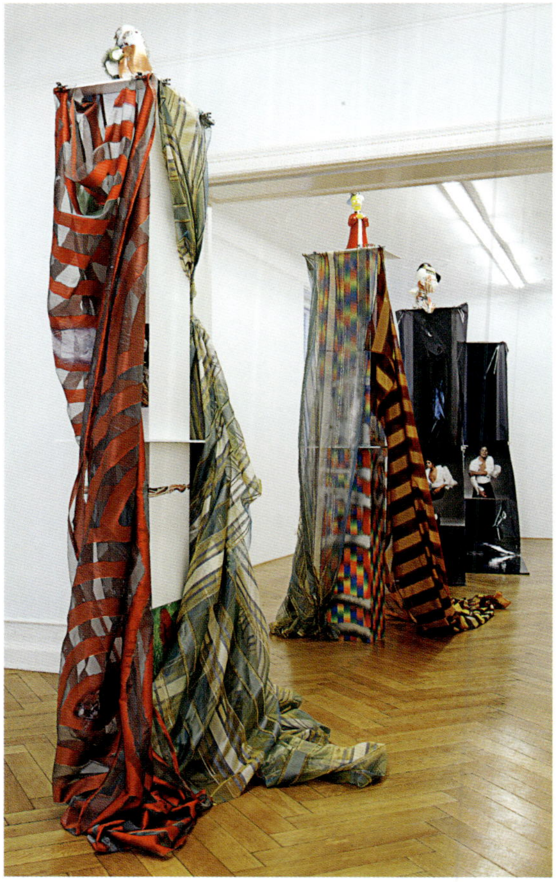

2

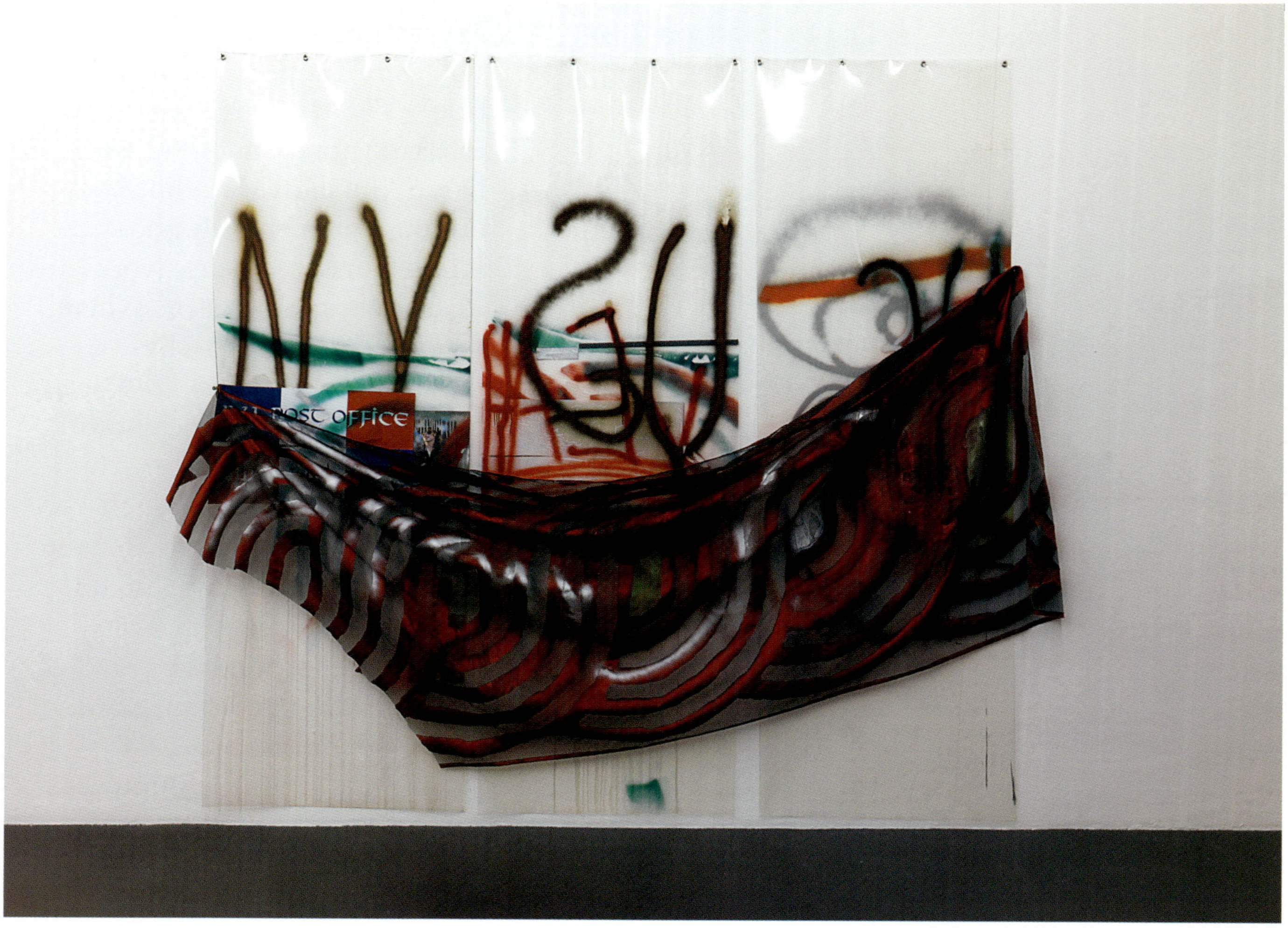

1

Isa Genzken

The German artist Isa Genzken's love letters to New York, like her seminal sculptural works, are akin to those of an ardent maximalist. See her oversize 2006 tome-like publication *I Love New York, Crazy City* (2006), or *Rose II* (2007), her 28-foot-tall sculptural rose rising from the New Museum's Bowery façade in 2010; likewise her sculpture, which often offers this same high-rise, loud-mouthed ethos in cool, minimalist forms. Whether clad in bright epoxy resin or plaster, Genzken's columns, objects, and installations emit a psychedelic punch that is classical and yet speculative in the mix-tape of materials and the fervent look forward—which may explain today's young artists crafting *oeuvres* that look strikingly like hers. Well, imitation is the sincerest form of flattery. QL

Shown by
Galerie Buchholz B35
Galerie Chantal Crousel B28
Hauser & Wirth B6
David Zwirner C46

Biography
Born 1948
Lives in Berlin

German-born Genzken's major retrospective "Open Sesame! (Sesam Öffne Dich!)," shown jointly at the Whitechapel Art Gallery, London, and Museum Ludwig, Cologne, in 2009, looked back at three decades of the artist's practice. Her public sculpture *Rose II* (2007) currently adorns the façade of the New Museum, New York, and her outdoor contribution to Skulptur Projekte Münster (2007) confirm the public nature of her work.

1
Wind (D)
2009
Wood, fabric, ceramics, colour prints on paper, tape, spray paint, CDs, and metal clips
124 × 74⅞ × 43⅜"
(315 × 190 × 110 cm)
Courtesy of Galerie Buchholz

2
Dedicated to Jasper Johns
2009
Plastic foil, spray paint, fabric, color prints, and stickers
120⅛ × 133⅞"
(305 × 340 cm)
Courtesy of Galerie Buchholz

3
Hallelujah II (New Museum)
2012
Wooden boxes, acrylic on canvas, plastic, glass, dried branches, and feather
140¼ × 47¼ × 47¼"
(356 × 120 × 120 cm)
Courtesy of Galerie Buchholz

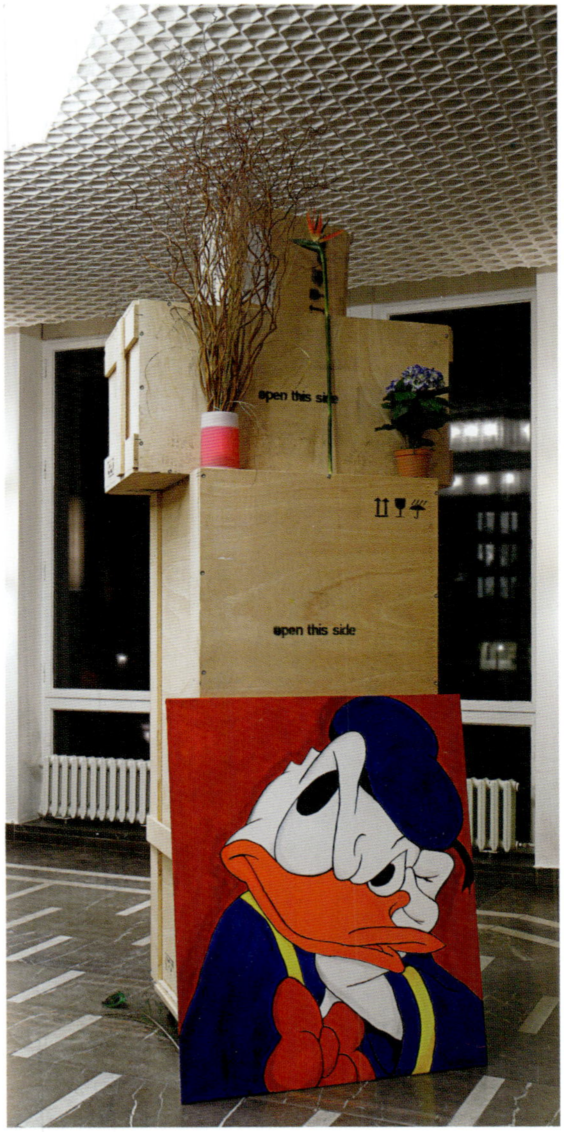

3

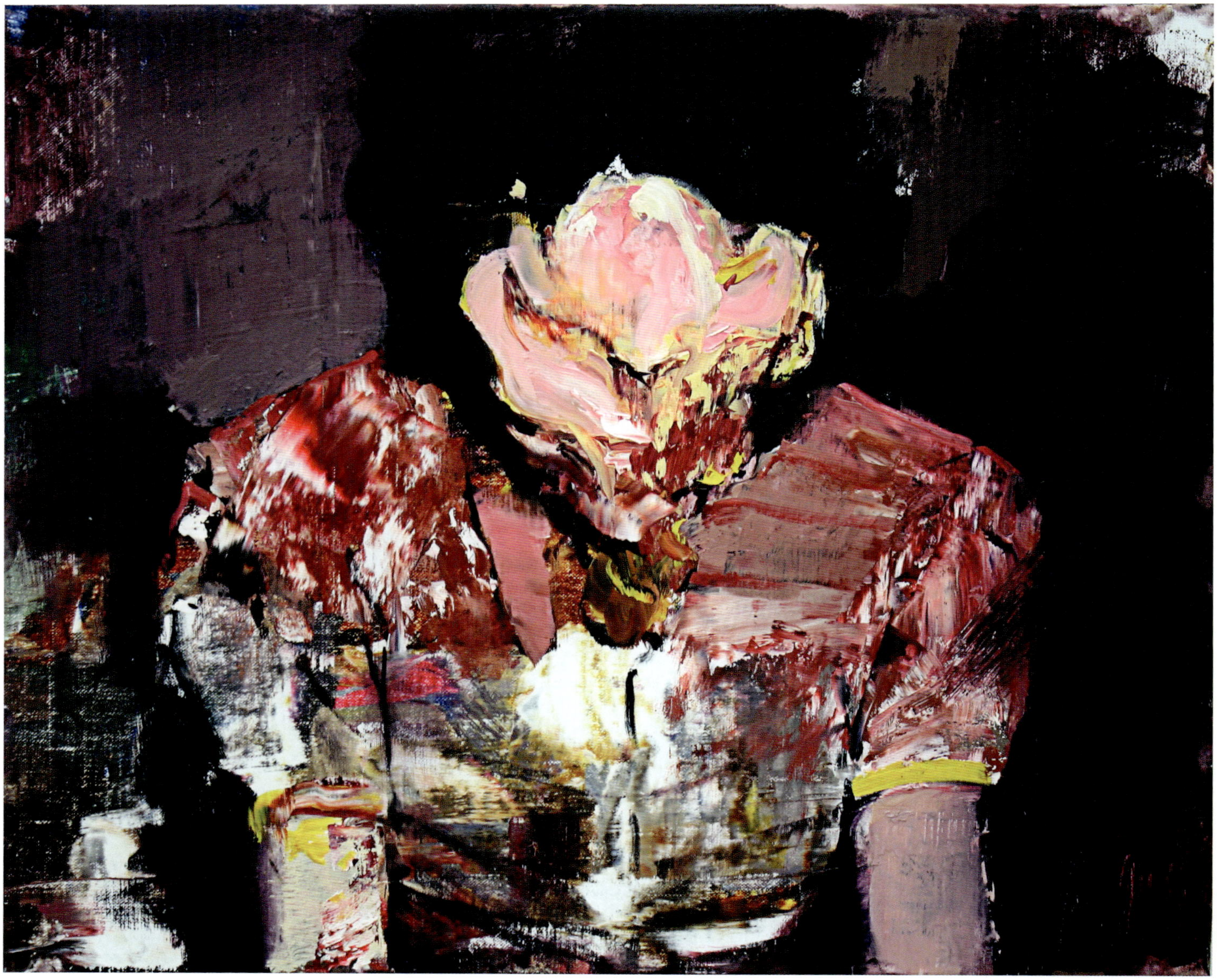
1

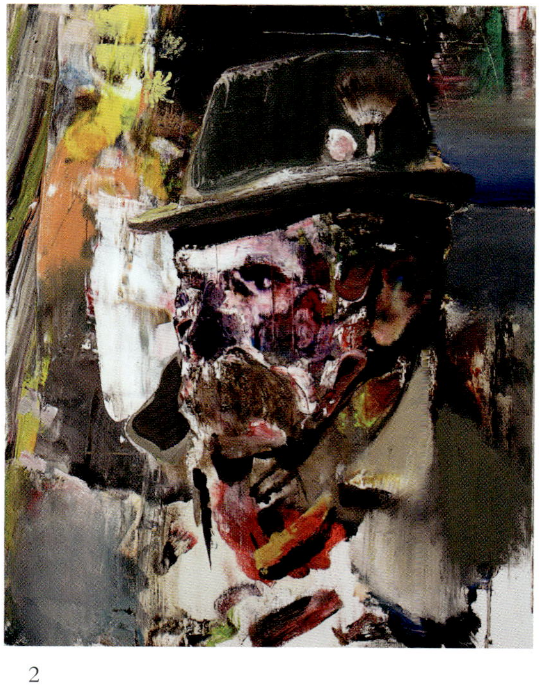
2

Shown by
Galeria Plan BF7

Biography
Born 1977
Lives in Cluj and Berlin

Romanian painter Ghenie's dark and menacing paintings have been exhibited extensively in Europe in recent years. In 2012 his first institutional show in the United States will be held at the Museum for Contemporary Art, Denver. In 2010 he had a solo show at SMAK, Gent, and also participated in the group show "The Crystal Hypothesis" (2010) at GAMeC, Bergamo. Other recent group shows include "Expanded Painting 3—Staging the Grey" at the Prague Biennale 4 (2009); and the Liverpool Biennial (2008). In fall 2012 he will participate in "Six Lines of Flight: Shifting Geographies in Contemporary Art" at the San Francisco Museum of Modern Art.

1
Pie Fight Study
2012
Oil on canvas
15¾ × 19⅝"
(40 × 50 cm)
Courtesy of Galeria Plan B

2
Dr. Josef
2011
Oil on canvas
23⅝ × 19⅝"
(60 × 50 cm)
Courtesy of Galeria Plan B

3
Study for Self Portrait, detail
2011
Collage on canvas
11⅞ × 15¾"
(30 × 40 cm)
Courtesy of Galeria Plan B

Focus
Adrian Ghenie

Adrian Ghenie's paintings possess a claustrophobic, cinematic tenor, and are often populated by historical figures who appear as if ghosts, or corpses. Comedy and terror can operate side by side—witness the series "The Pie Fight Studies" (2008–9), which look more like depictions of horrific injuries. Ghenie often captures dimly lit interiors that appear to be domestic basements or clandestine bunkers—in *The Collector* (2008) Hermann Goering sits amid his looted art collection. While a scuffed portrait of Nicolae Ceaușescu brings to mind the traumas of life under the Romanian Communist regime and its official iconography, the representations of other figures address a kind of rupture in the status of art itself—through a work entitled *Duchamp's Funeral* (2009), for example. MA

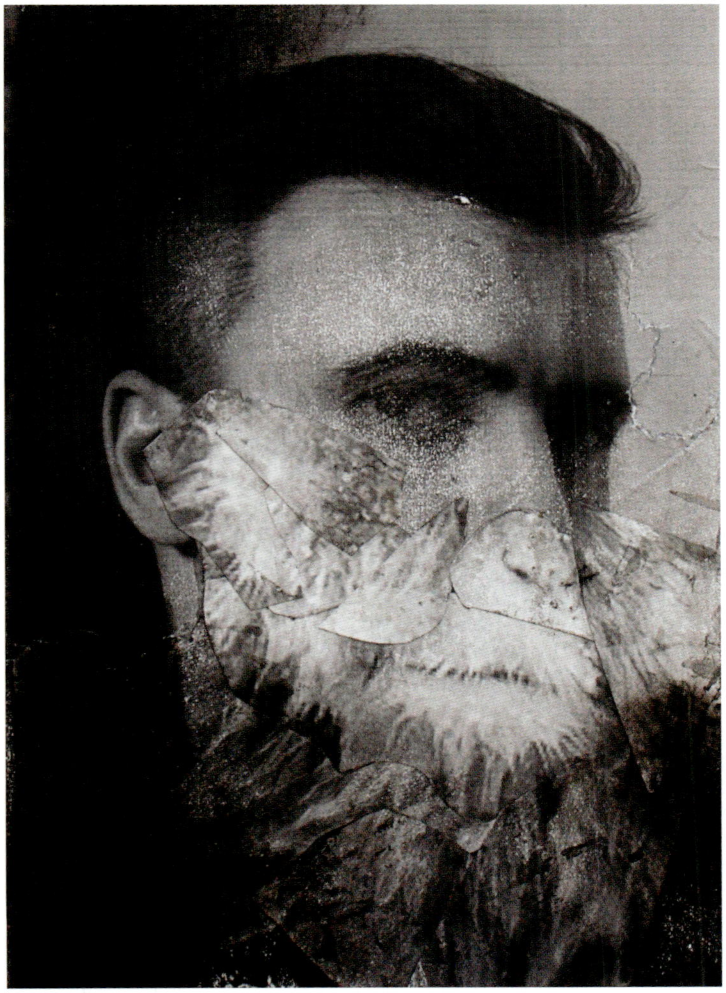

3

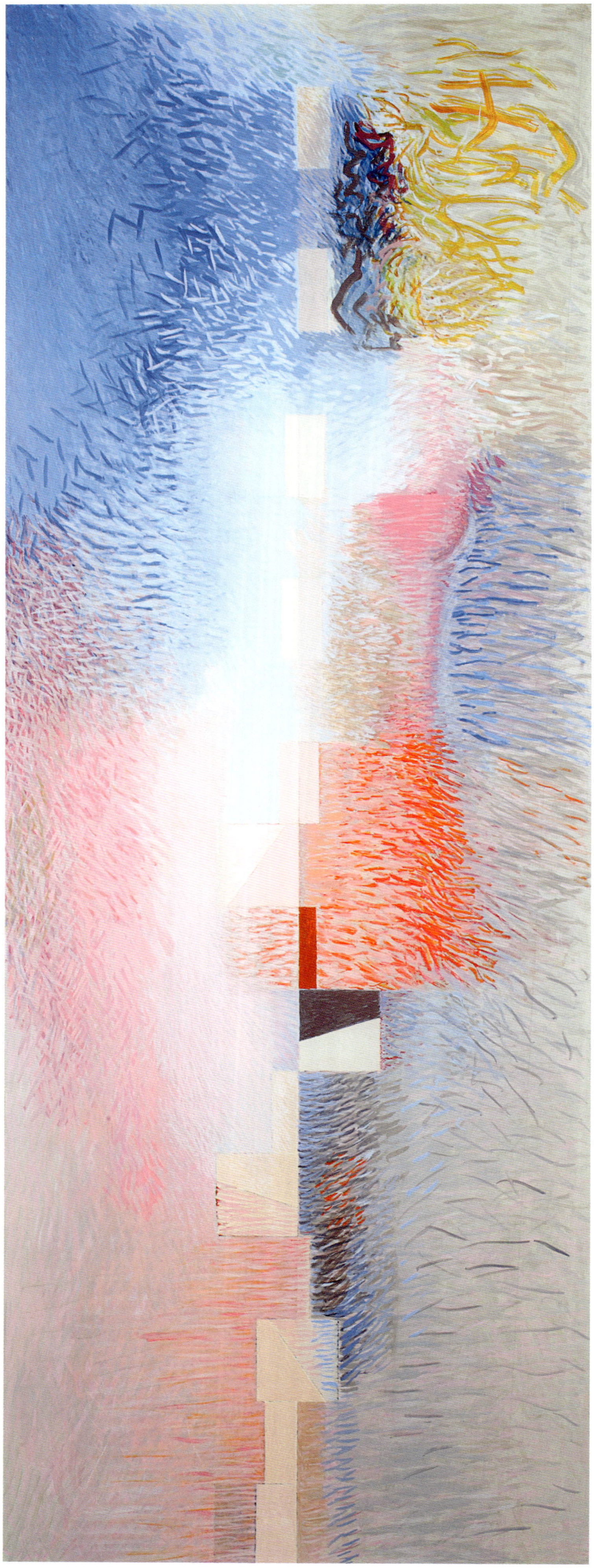

Focus

Jeremy Gilbert-Rolfe

Shown by
Alexander Gray Associates F21

Biography
Born 1945
Lives in Los Angeles

Britain-born Gilbert-Rolfe has exhibited his abstract paintings since the early-1970s. In 2011 he had a self-titled solo show at Alexander Gray Associates, New York. He had solo exhibitions at Anne Mosseri-Marlio Galerie, Zurich (2010), and again at Alexander Gray Associates, New York (2008). His work is part of numerous public collections, including the Lincoln Center, New York, and the Museum of Contemporary Art, Los Angeles.

The Sun Comes Out
2011
Oil on linen
66½ × 25 × 1½"
(168 × 63.5 × 3 cm)
Courtesy of Alexander Gray Associates

Lush and dynamic, Jeremy Gilbert-Rolfe's abstractions rigorously probe the possibilities of painting while eschewing any hint of narrative or representation. He has said his work is often about "beauty rather than brutality, attractiveness rather than argument." His complex formal manoeuvers—in which sensuous color defines space and painting is privileged over drawing—explore the relationship between beauty and meaning. Grids of shifting color combinations structure recent works, such as *Pynchon* (2008), whose horizontal rows of warm and cool vertical strips suggest shuffling rhythms. *More* (2010) is a pixel-like checkerboard, shadowy in one area and exploding into luminosity elsewhere, pulsing with contrasting matte and shiny surfaces, marks and brushstrokes—a tour de force of lucid visual intrigue. KMJ

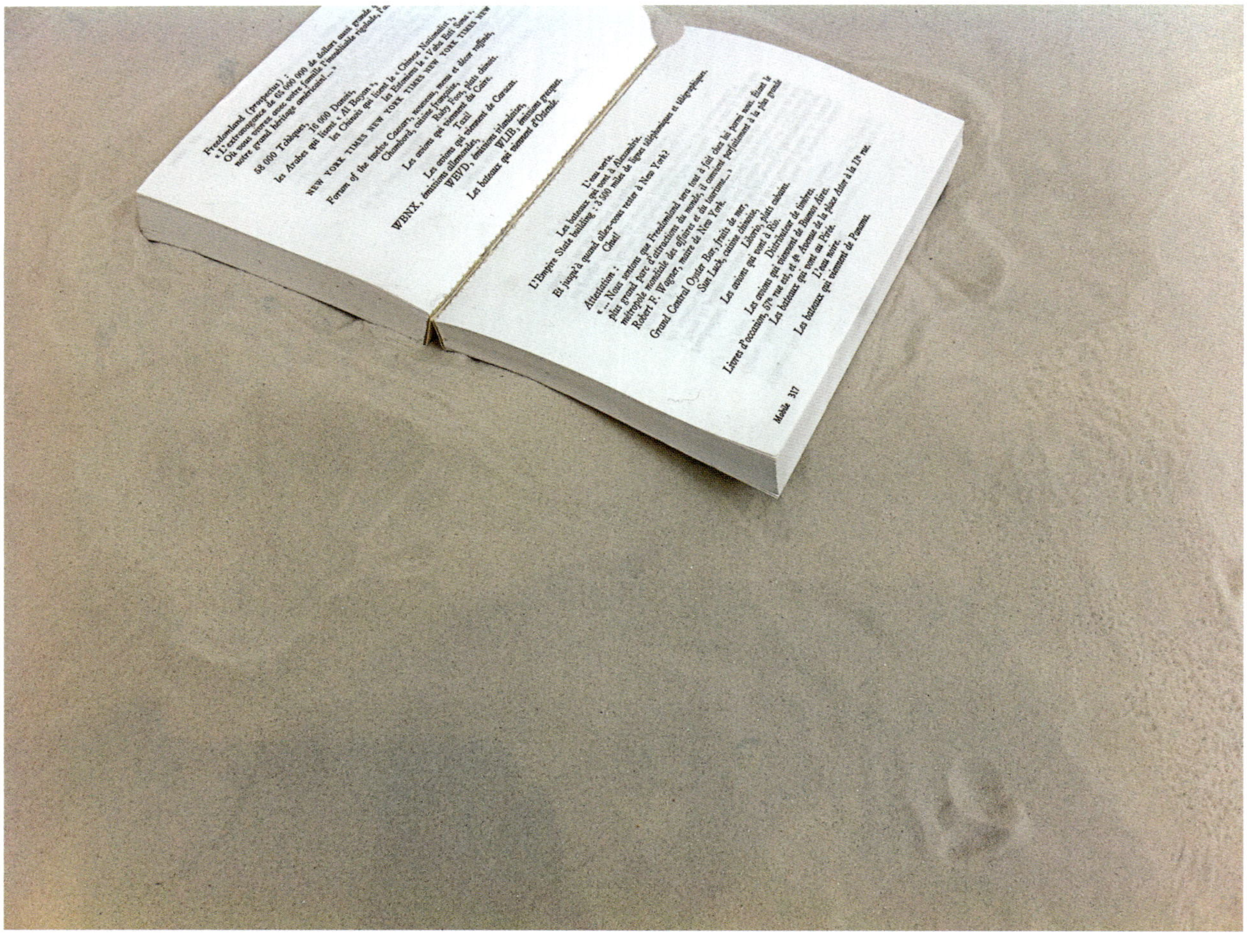
Freedomland (prospectus) :
« L'extravagance de 65 000 000 de dollars aussi grande
Où vous vivrez avec votre famille l'inoubliable rigolade,
notre grand héritage américain ! ... »
58 000 Tchèques, 16 000 Danois,
les Arabes qui lisent « Al Bayan », les Estoniens le « Vaba Esti Sona »,
les Chinois qui lisent le « Chinese Nationalist »,
NEW YORK TIMES NEW YORK TIMES NEW YORK TIMES NEW
Forum of the twelve Caesars, nouveaux, menu et décor raffinés,
Chambord, cuisine française,
Ruby Foo's, plats chinois.
Les avions qui viennent du Caire.
Taxi!
Les avions qui viennent de Caracas.
WBNX, émissions allemandes, émissions irlandaises,
WEVD, émissions allemandes,
WLIB, émissions grecques.
Les bateaux qui viennent d'Ostende.
L'eau verte.
Les bateaux qui vont à Alexandrie.
L'Empire State building : 3 500 miles de lignes téléphoniques et télégraphiques.
Et jusqu'à quand allez-vous rester à New York?
Chut!
Attestation :
« ... Nous sentons que Freedomland sera tout à fait chez lui parmi nous. Étant le
plus grand parc d'attractions du monde, il convient parfaitement à la plus grande
métropole mondiale des affaires et du tourisme... »
Robert F. Wagner, maire de New York.
Grand Central Oyster Bar, fruits de mer,
Sun Luck, cuisine chinoise,
Liborio, plats cubains.
Les avions qui vont à Rio.
Distributeur de timbres.
Les avions qui viennent de Buenos Aires.
Livres d'occasion, 57e rue est, et 4e Avenue de la place Astor à la 11e rue.
Les bateaux qui vont au Pirée.
L'eau noire.
Les bateaux qui viennent de Panama.
Mobile 317

1

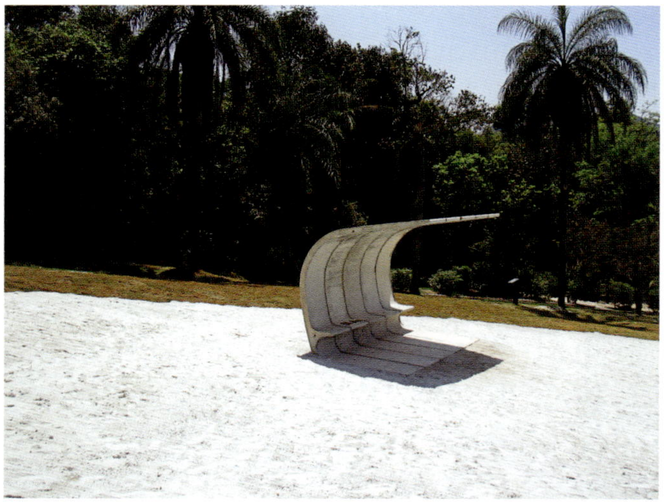

2

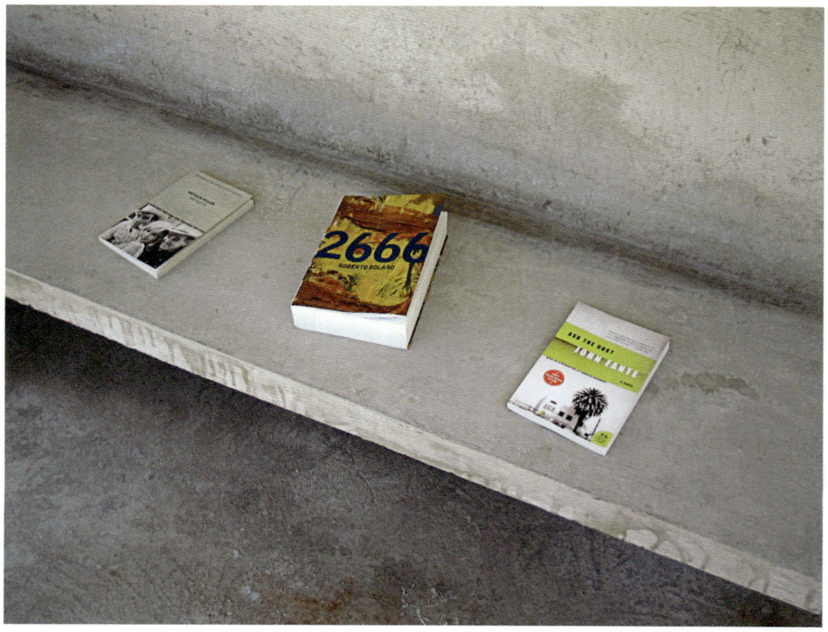
2666
ROBERTO BOLAÑO
ASK THE DUST
JOHN FANTE

3

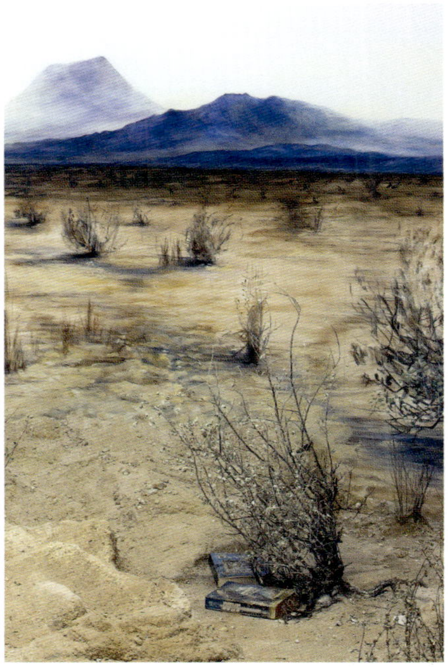

4

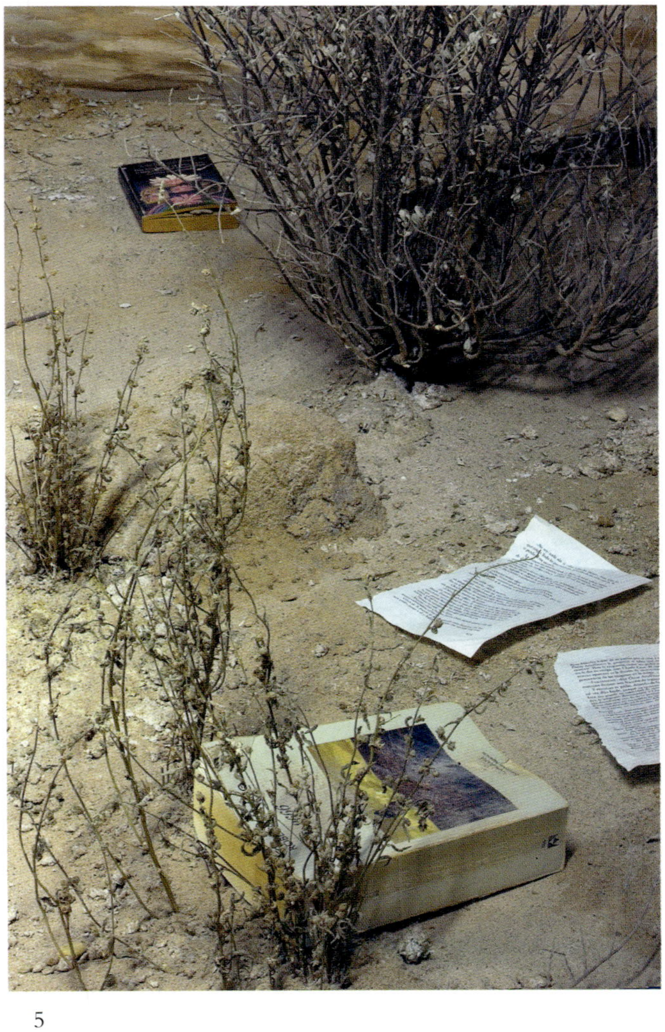

5

Shown by
303 Gallery B39
Corvi-Mora A16
Esther Schipper B2

Biography
Born 1965
Lives in Paris

France-born Gonzalez-Foerster received the Marcel Duchamp Award, Paris, in 2002. Since the mid-1980s she has exhibited prolifically in Europe. Her performance "T.1912" (2011) filled New York's Solomon R. Guggenheim Museum in 2011. Other recent solo shows include "Expodrome" at the Musée de Art Moderne de la ville Paris (2007); "Chronotopes & Dioramas" (2009) at the Dia Art Foundation, New York; and "TH.2058—The Unilever Series: Dominique Gonzalez-Foerster" (2008) at Tate Modern, London.

1
Untitled
2011
Book, sand
Dimensions variable
Courtesy of Esther Schipper

2
Desert Park
2010
Mixed media
Dimensions variable
Courtesy of Instituto Inhotim

3
Desert Park
2010
Mixed media
Dimensions variable
Courtesy of Instituto Inhotim

4
Desertic
2009
Mixed media
Dimensions variable
Courtesy of Esther Schipper

5
Desertic
2009
Mixed media
Dimensions variable
Courtesy of Esther Schipper

Dominique Gonzalez-Foerster

Writing by other means might be a subtle way to characterize Dominique Gonzalez-Foerster's intensely literary, atmospheric artistic practice, which employs books as both material and muse. The cerebral, cinematic spaces the French artist creates often invoke a hushed reaction from spectators—the hush of the library, perhaps. See the Rainer Werner Fassbinder inspired bedroom installation *R.W.F.* (1993), or the selection of books distributed throughout the geographical dioramas at the Hispanic Society, New York, according to thematic and stylistic links with their new "locations" (*chronotopes & dioramas,* 2009). More recently, at Kunsthalle Zurich, Gonzalez-Foerster curated *Human Valley* (2011–12) with Tristian Bera, a changing domestic interior featuring bed, bookshelves, and vitrines. The Kunsthalle installed a guard because museum-goers were stealing books—a fact the artist might enjoy. QL

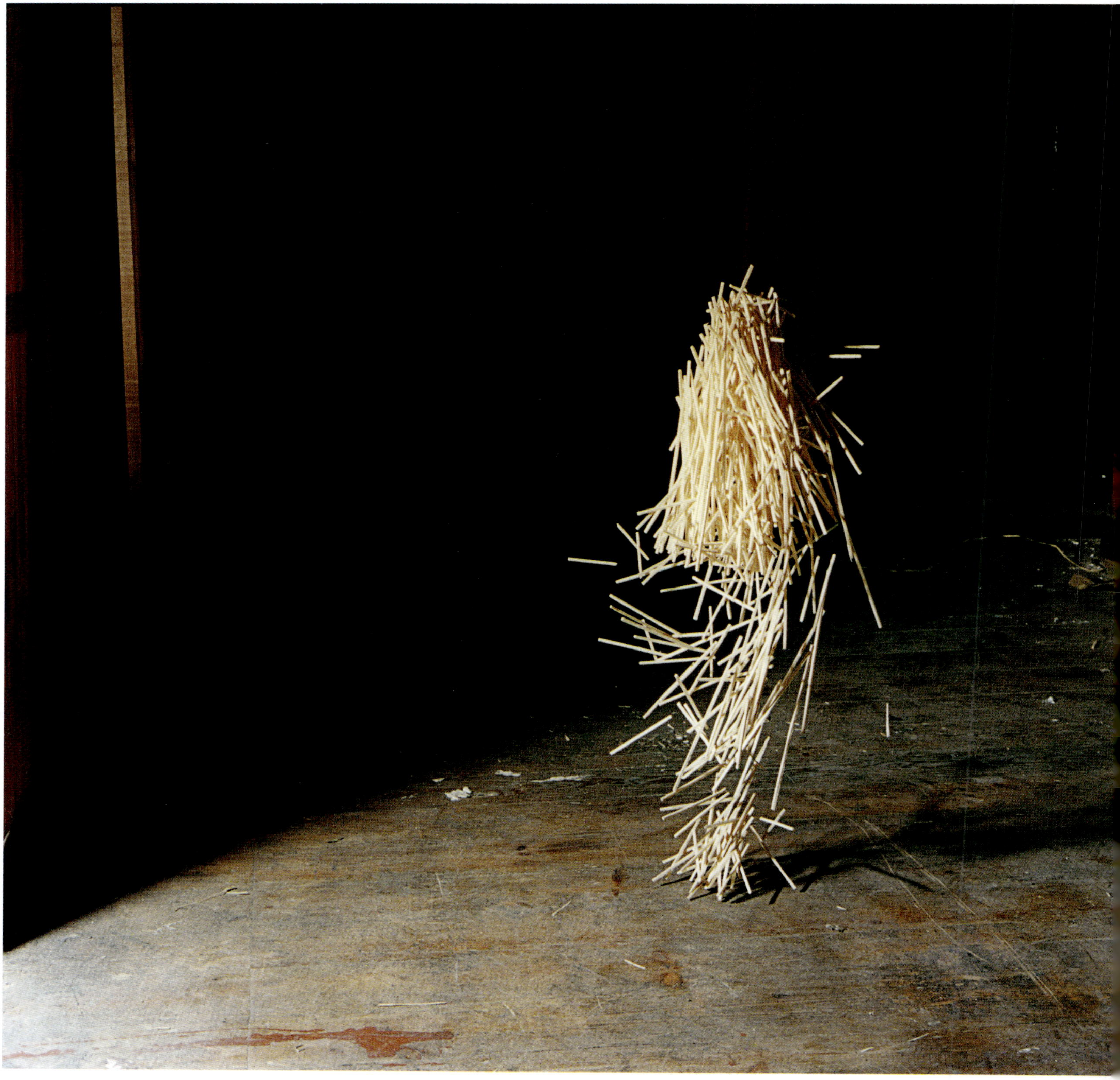

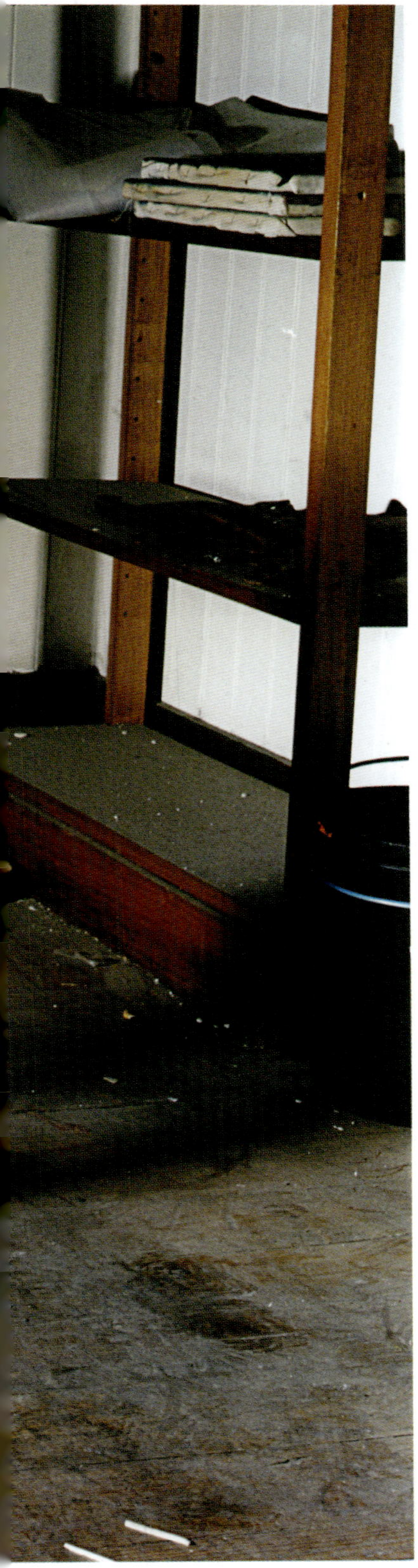

Shown by
Sies + Höke B15

Biography
Born 1979 + 1977
Live in Lisbon

Portuguese artists Gusmão and Paiva have collaborated since 2001. Their films, installations, and sculptures have been exhibited extensively in Europe for the last decade. In 2011 they had multiple solo shows, including "Tem gwef tem gwef dr rr rr" at the Kunsthalle Düsseldorf, Dusseldorf, and "Alien Theory" at Le Plateau, Paris. In 2009 their exhibition "Experiments and Observations on Different Kinds of Air" was the official Portuguese Representation at the 53rd Venice Biennale. In early 2012 they had a solo show at Kunstnernes Hus, Oslo. In May they will open a significant solo show at Kunsthaus Glarus, Switzerland, which will then travel to Fri Art/Centre d'art Friborg, Switzerland in the fall.

Body of Straw
2011
Chromogenic color print
36⅝ × 52"
(93 × 132 cm)
Courtesy of
Sies + Höke

João Maria Gusmão and Pedro Paiva

Broadly speaking, João Maria Gusmão and Pedro Paiva's works adopt one of two different modes. The first resembles an antiquated scientific investigation, the kind of poetic exercise undertaken by curious gentleman–scholars in the 18th century: falling water is "sculpted" (*About the Density of Water*, 2010) while a camera obscura is assembled for *Camera inside Camera* (2010). Their second mode is more like a shoestring illusion, a magic trick that doesn't try hard to hide its method: fruit seems to levitate; rocks roll unaided through a desert—we glimpse the wires, but the effect remains arresting and somehow incomprehensible. Slow-motion fables of the occult and metaphysical, Gusmão and Paiva's films consider the construction of wonder and belief. ST

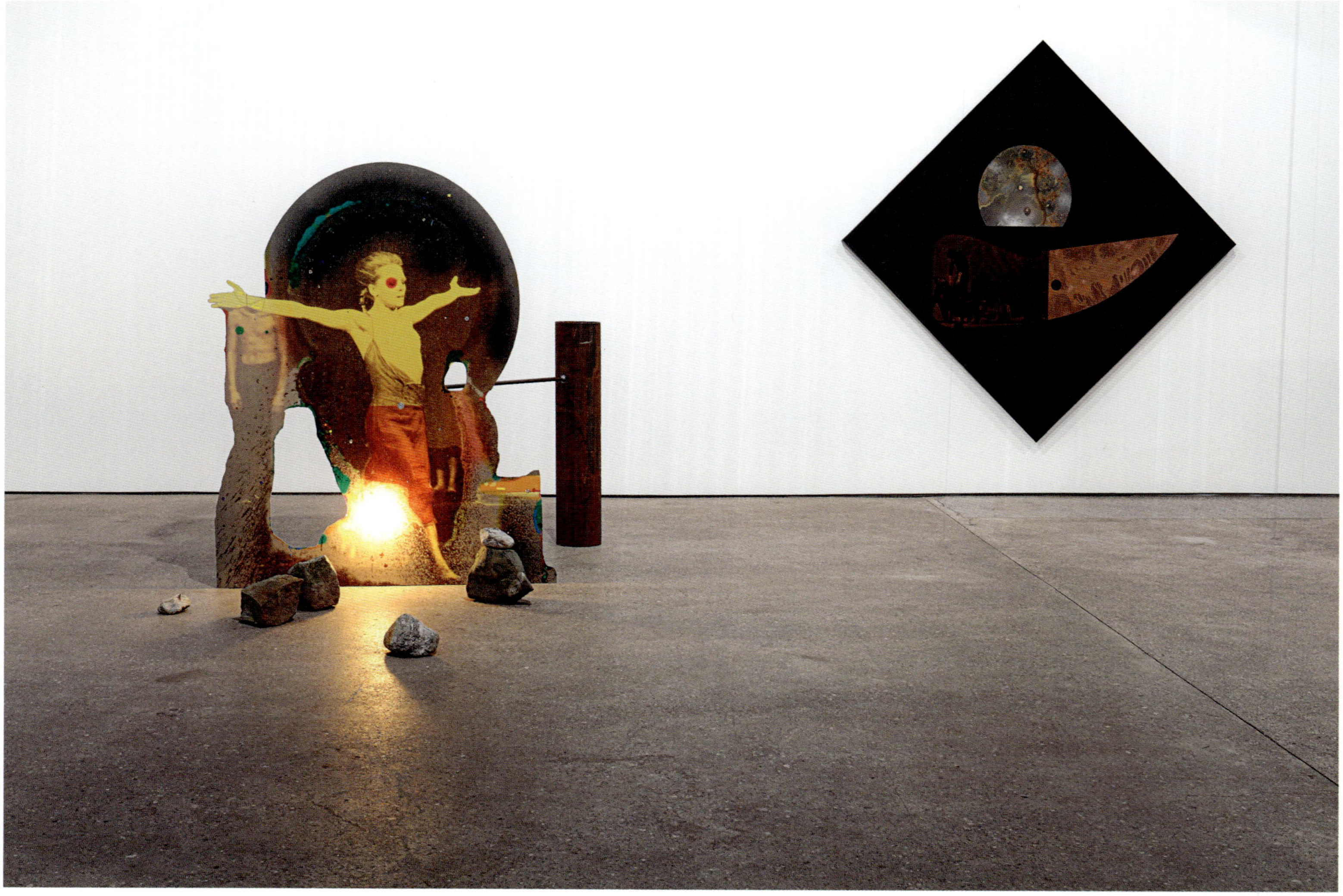

1

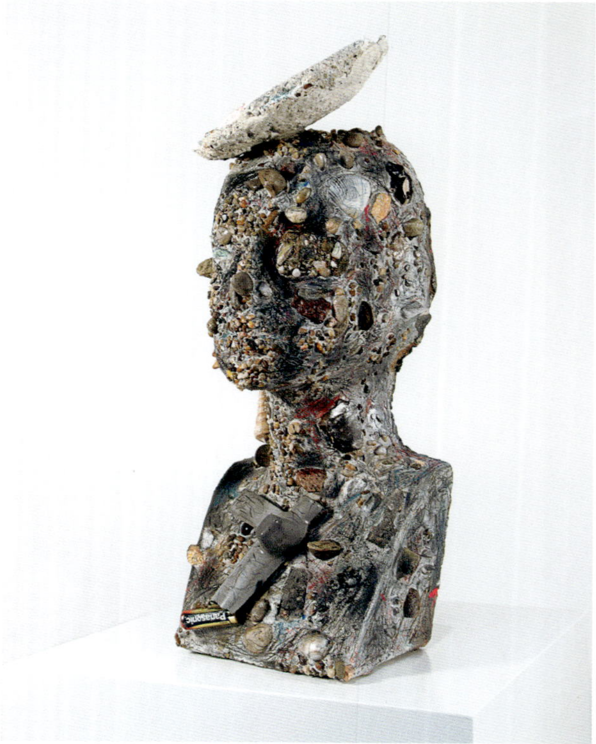

2

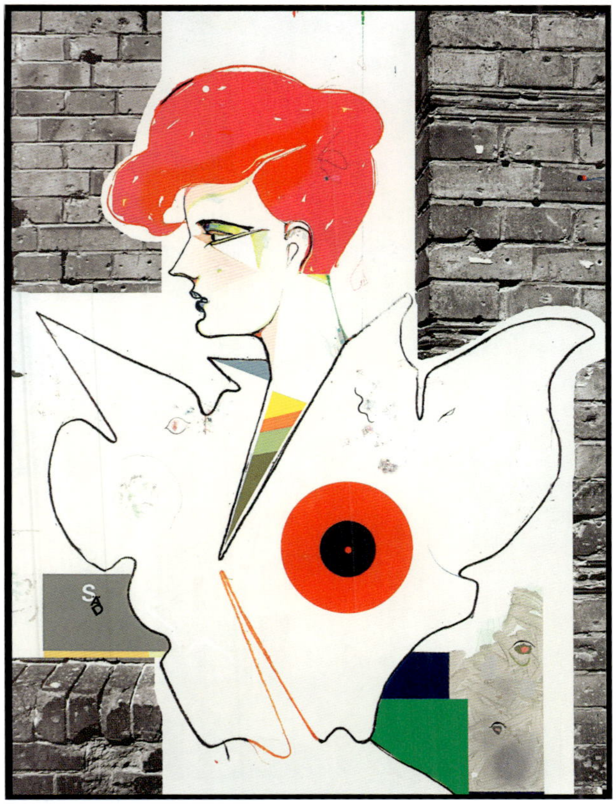

3

Lothar Hempel

Lothar Hempel insinuates meaning through the orchestration of cut-outs and theatrical flats, narrative props and half played-out scenes. Expectation is left hanging, illusions are truncated at their edges, and cultural forms are marooned from their sense-giving contexts. De-skilling may be a mark of practical contingency, but these collations of eclectic materials and reproductions of mass-media imagery imply a sort of seediness that comes not so much from necessity as from a taste for the emotionally contingent. The souped-up portrait and masthead of *Sight and Sound* (2011), for example, set on a concrete podium and embellished with bells, suggest a peculiar mixture of passing whim, impatience with realism, and perhaps even the meaningless invention born of boredom. SOR

Shown by
art: concept A2
Anton Kern Gallery C2
Giò Marconi A3
Stuart Shave/Modern Art C43

Biography
Born 1966
Lives in Berlin

In 2007, Hempel's mid-career retrospective "Alphabet City" at Le Magasin, Centre National d'Art Contemporain, Grenoble, defined the unique position his figurative paintings and sculptures occupy within the gallery. Recent solo exhibitions include "Suedehead" (2011) at Anton Kern Gallery, New York, and "Silberblick/Squint" (2010) at Stuart Shave/Modern Art, London. In 2012, La Conservera, Ceuti (Murcia) host his first comprehensive solo show in Spain.

1
Acid and Iron
2011
Photograph on metal, steel, paint, stones, light bulb and MDF
77⅞ × 78¾ × 100"
(195 × 200 × 264 cm)
Courtesy of Anton Kern Gallery

2
Youth
2011
Cement and various objects
18 × 8 × 7"
(45.5 × 20.5 × 18 cm)
Courtesy of Anton Kern Gallery

3
Blush
2011
Acrylic, oil, color pencil and pigment ink on aluminum
48 × 36½"
(122 × 92.5 cm)
Courtesy of Anton Kern Gallery

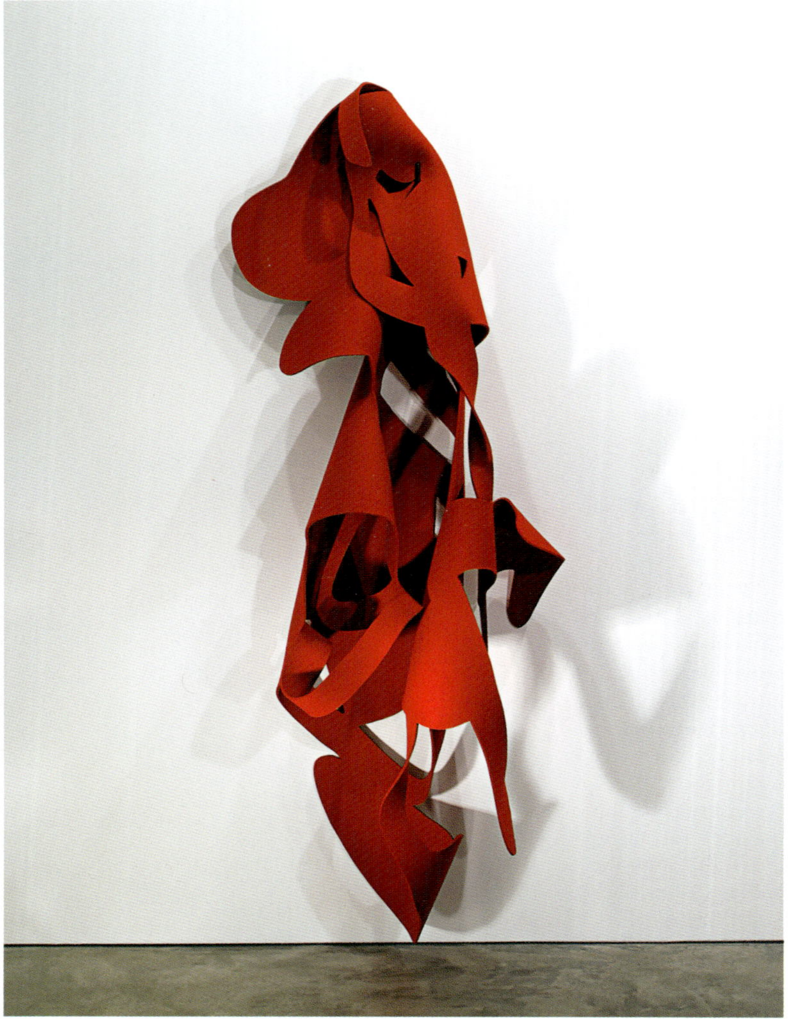

1

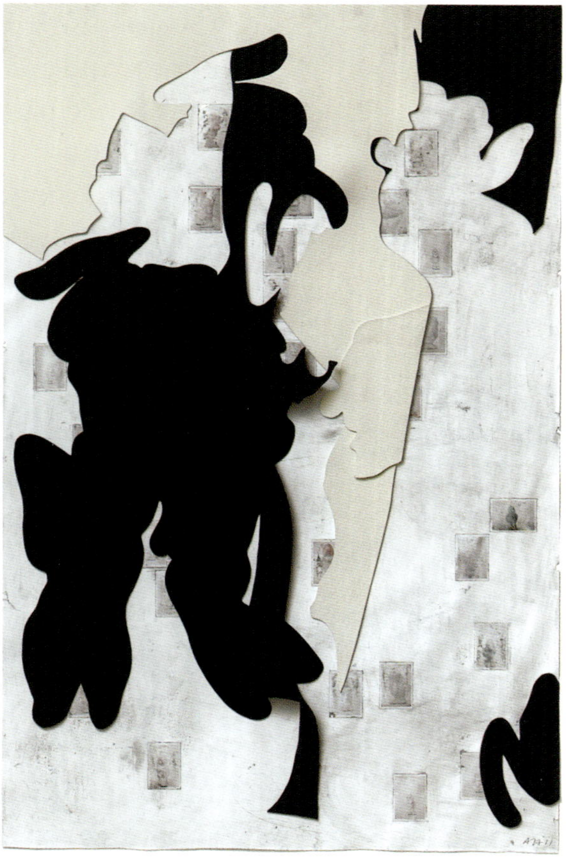

2

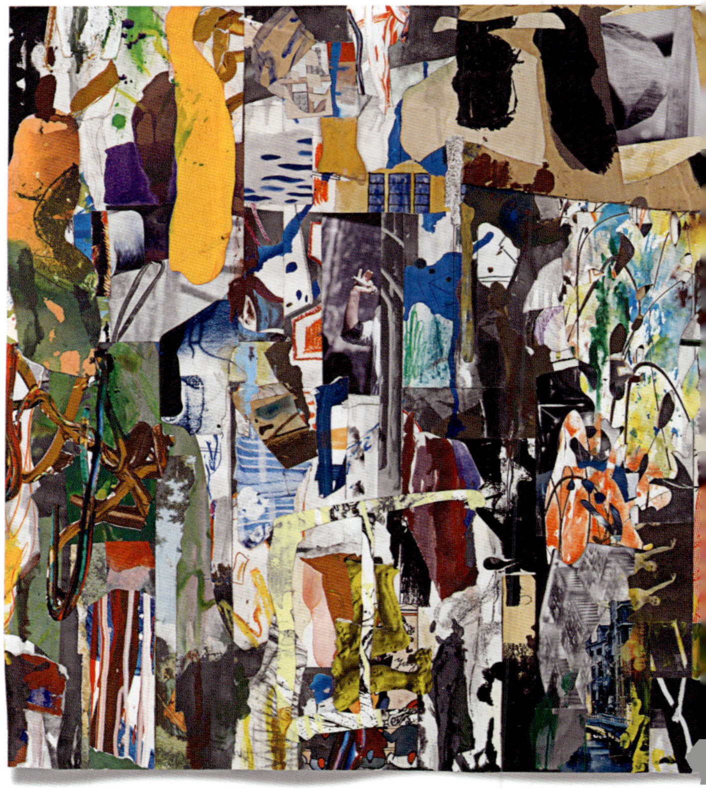

3

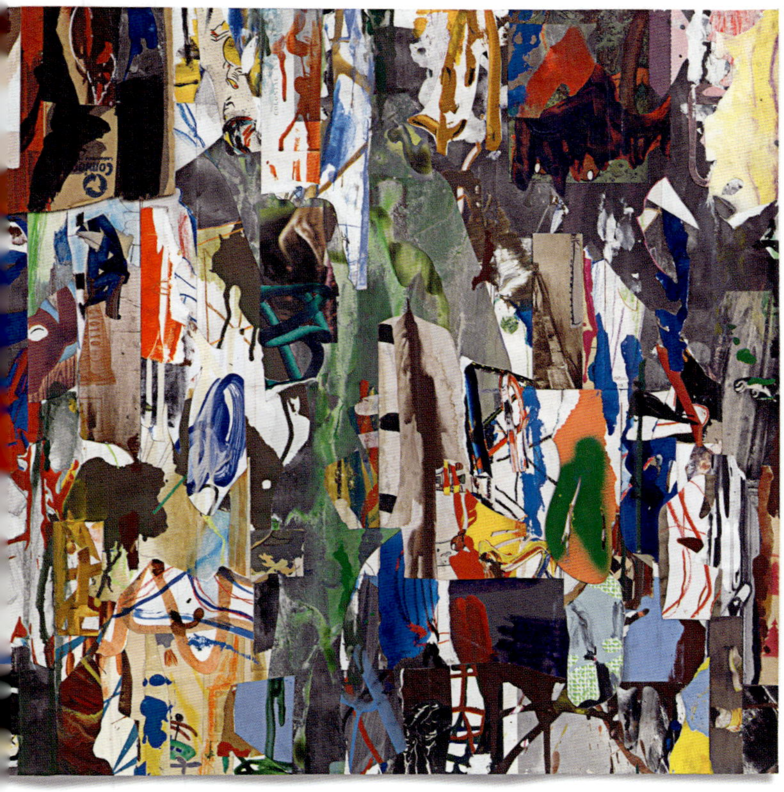

Shown by
Galleria Franco Noero
C50
Sikkema Jenkins & Co.
C44

Biography
Born 1959
Lives in Berlin

Venezuela-born Herrera's recent show at the American Society, New York, (2011) saw him work with audio and video in a two-screen installation. He contributed to the 11th Biennale de Lyon, France, also in 2011, and was part of the "Keeping it Real" (2011) series of exhibitions at the Whitechapel Gallery, London. His paintings and collages were also shown that year at Sikkema Jenkins & Co., New York.

1
Felt #12 / Red
2008
Wool felt
104 × 69⅝"
(264 × 177 cm)
Courtesy of Sikkema Jenkins & Co.

2
Rapt #3
2011
Mixed media on paper, wool felt
96½ × 65"
(245 × 165 cm)
Courtesy of Sikkema Jenkins & Co.

3
Santiago
2010
Mixed media on paper
32⅛ × 51⅝"
(81.5 × 131 cm)
Courtesy of Sikkema Jenkins & Co.

Arturo Herrera

Arturo Herrera's work is often tinged with Surrealism, whether collaged illustrations, photographs, wall drawings, works on paper, or tactile "paintings" cut from red, blue, brown, or black felt. His wall painting *Party for Tom* (2000) featured a shape resembling the paw of an animal, reaching through the ceiling at MoMA P.S.1. Herrera's cut-and-paste collages combine fragments from cartoons, advertisements, and coloring books, often to disconcerting effect, as in *Untitled* (1997–8), in which the torso and webbed feet of Donald Duck marry with a "head" made from a Häagen-Dazs chocolate lolly. His first moving image work, *Les Noces* (The Wedding, 2007), featured a randomized assortment of 80 bold monochromatic drawings, changing in response to the tone of Igor Stravinsky's 1923 ballet suite of the same title. SL

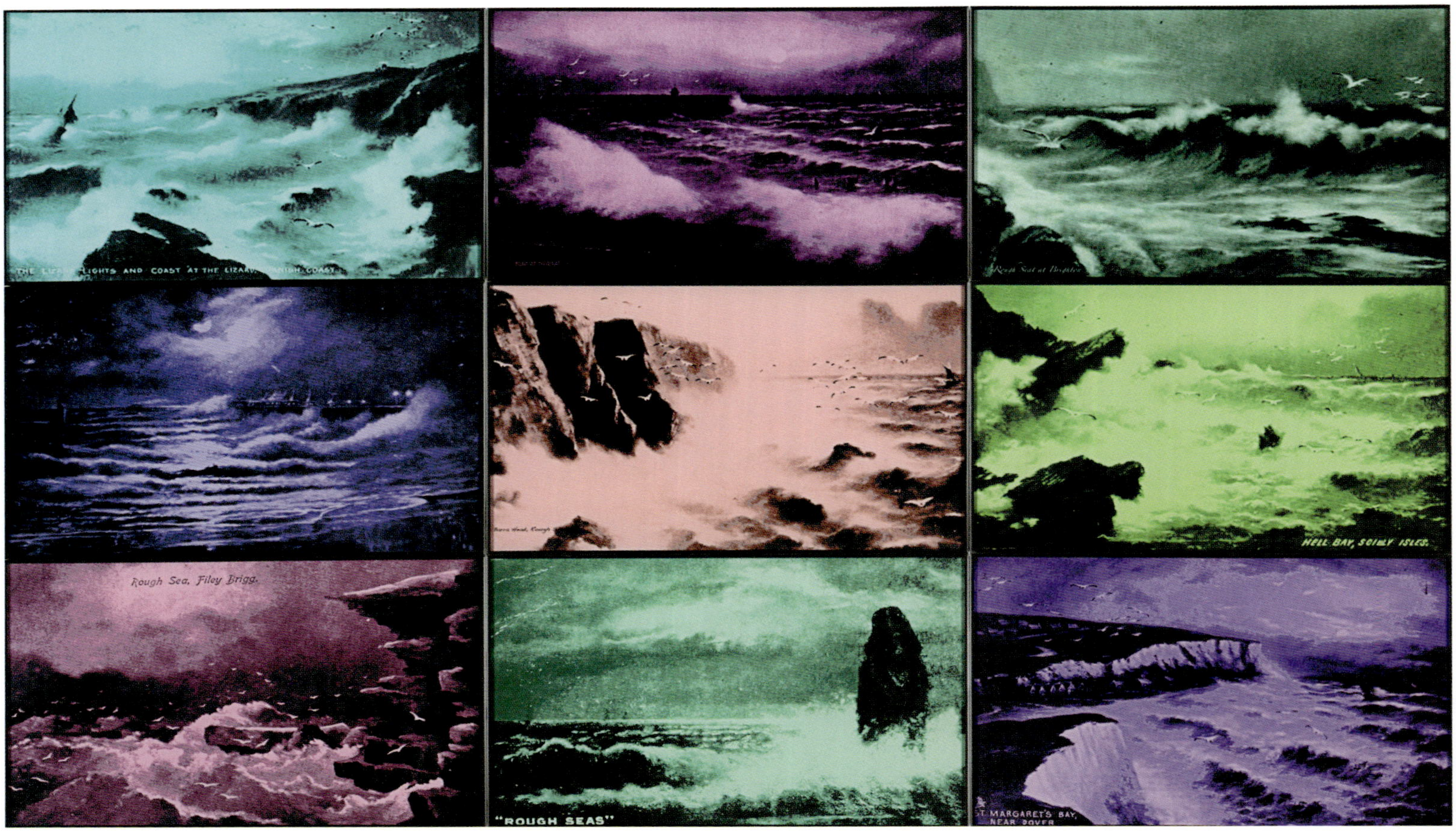
Rough Sea, Filey Brigg.
"ROUGH SEAS"
HELL BAY, SCILLY ISLES.
ST. MARGARET'S BAY,
NEAR DOVER

1

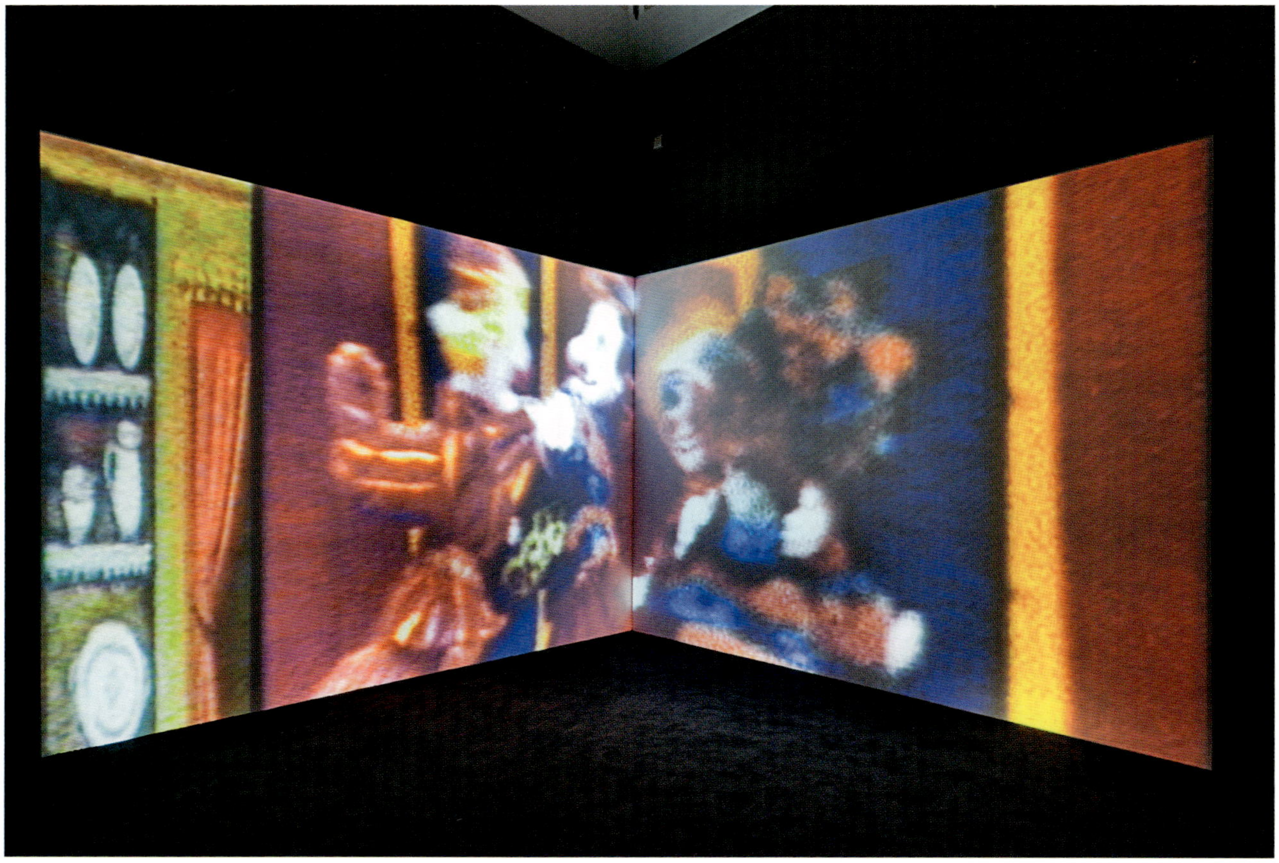

2

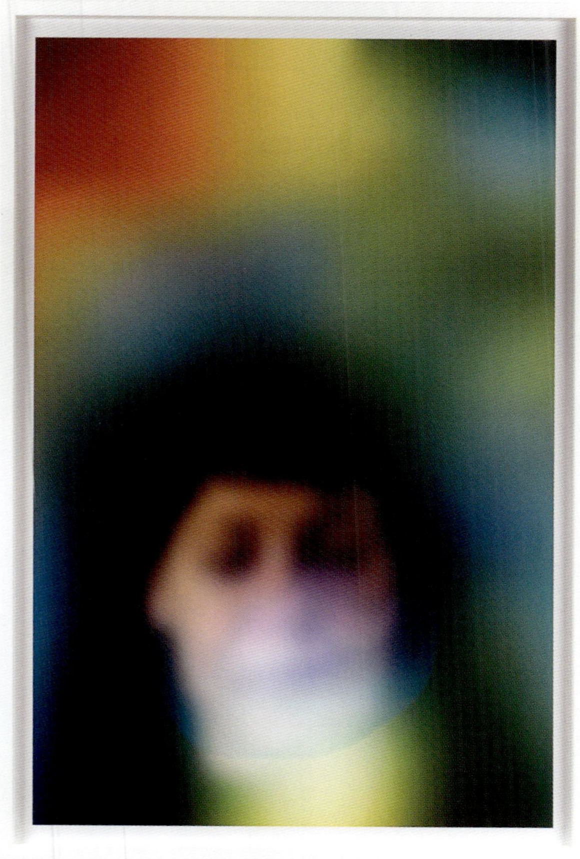

3

Shown by
Timothy Taylor Gallery C8

Biography
Born 1940
Lives in London

American-born artist Hiller has exhibited her videos and installations since the 1970s. Her influential practice was profiled in the recent self-titled retrospective at Tate Britain, London (2011), and at the Kunsthalle Nuernberg, Nuremberg, in late 2011. She was included in the 4th Moscow Biennale (2011) and survey exhibition "September 11" (2011) at MoMA P.S.1., Long Island City. Hiller will participate in dOCUMENTA (13) (2012) in Kassel.

1
Watercolours
2010
Nine archival color dry prints
20 × 30" each
(51 × 76 cm each)
60 × 90" overall
(152.5 × 228.5 cm overall)
Courtesy of Timothy Taylor Gallery

2
An Entertainment
1990
Four synchronized video projections, quadraphonic sound
26 min.
Courtesy of Timothy Taylor Gallery

3
Homage to Marcel Duchamp: Aura (Dark Haired Woman)
2011
Digital C-type archival color print on dibond
48½ × 33½"
(123 × 85 cm)
Courtesy of Timothy Taylor Gallery

Susan Hiller

Since the late 1960s Susan Hiller has essayed a mode of affective, even romantic, Conceptualism that has frequently entailed investigations of psychic or paranormal phenomena. *Sisters of Menon* (1972–9) involved experiments in automatic writing, a practice that has resurfaced in her recent *Homage to Gertrude Stein* (2010). For *Dream Mapping* (1974) she invited people to sleep inside "fairy rings" in an English field and then compare dreams; her video installation *Psi Girls* (1999) collected cinematic instances of female telepathy and telekinesis. Recent works based on found photographs, such as the series "Homage to Yves Klein" and "Homage to Marcel Duchamp" (both 2008), are explicit about a persistent theme: the occult and irrational aspects of the 20th-century avant-gardes. BD

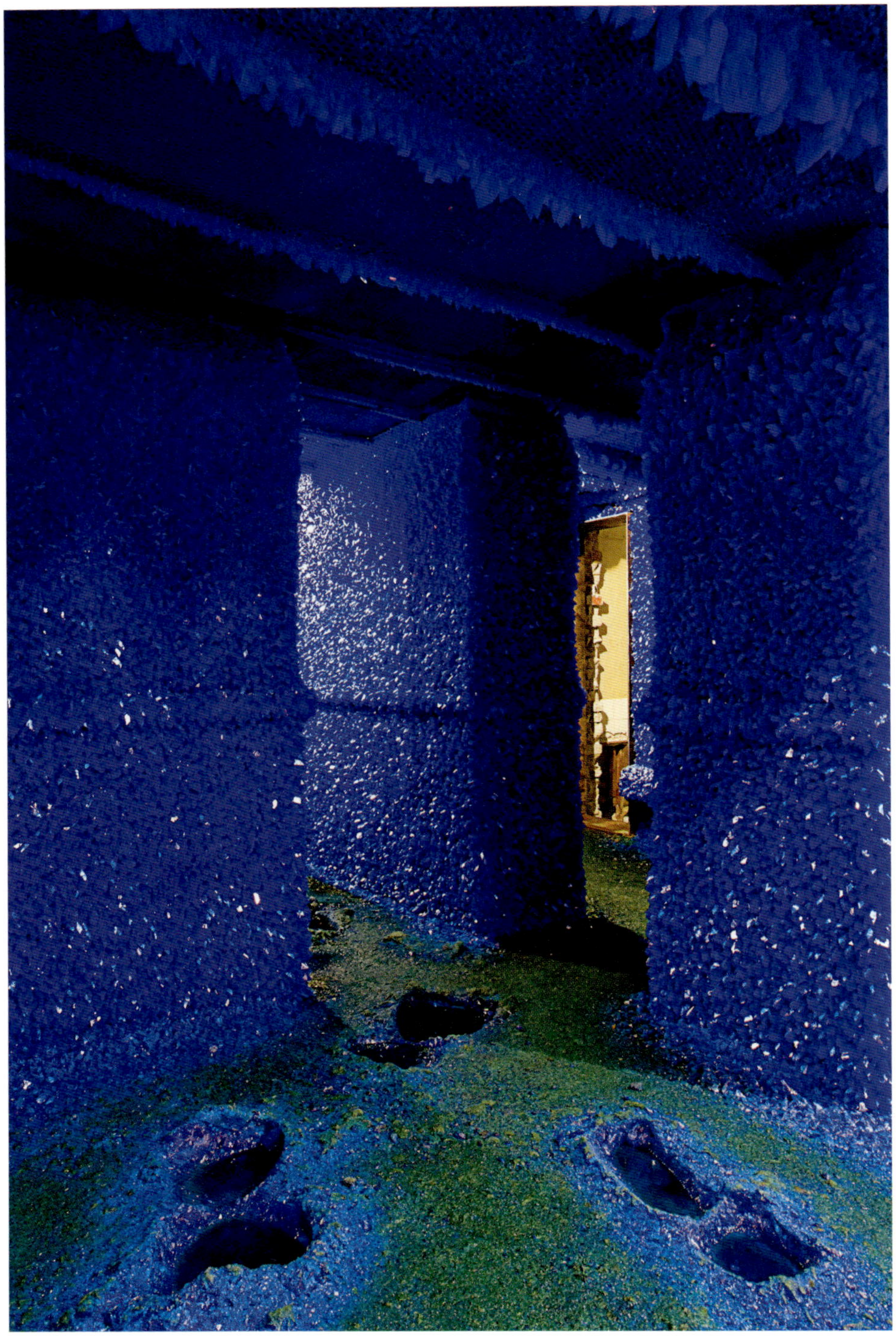

1

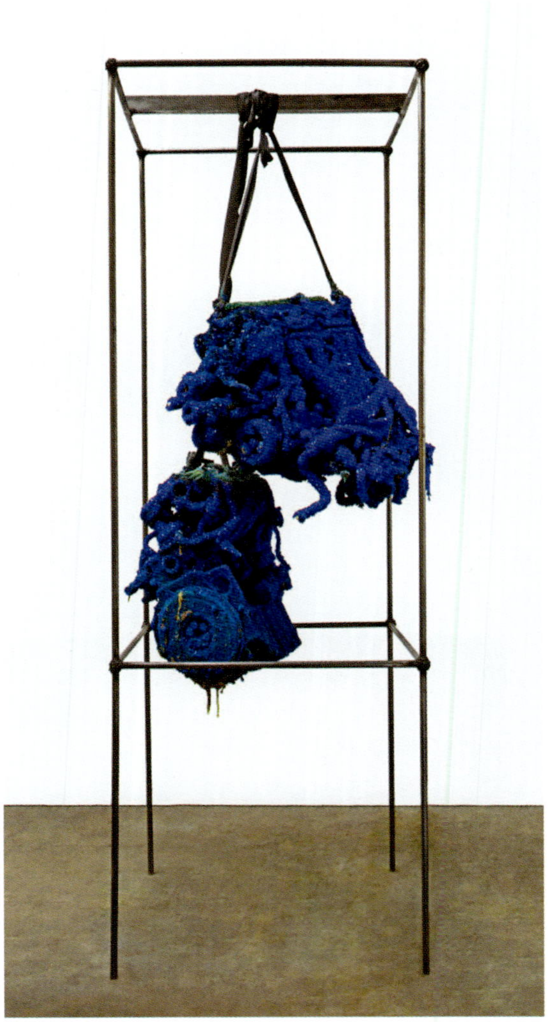

2

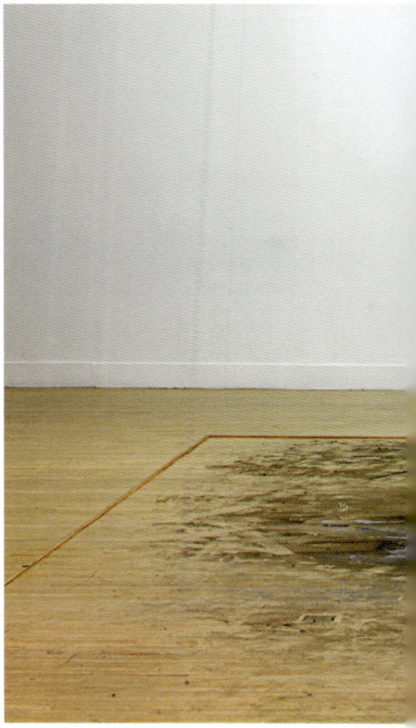

3

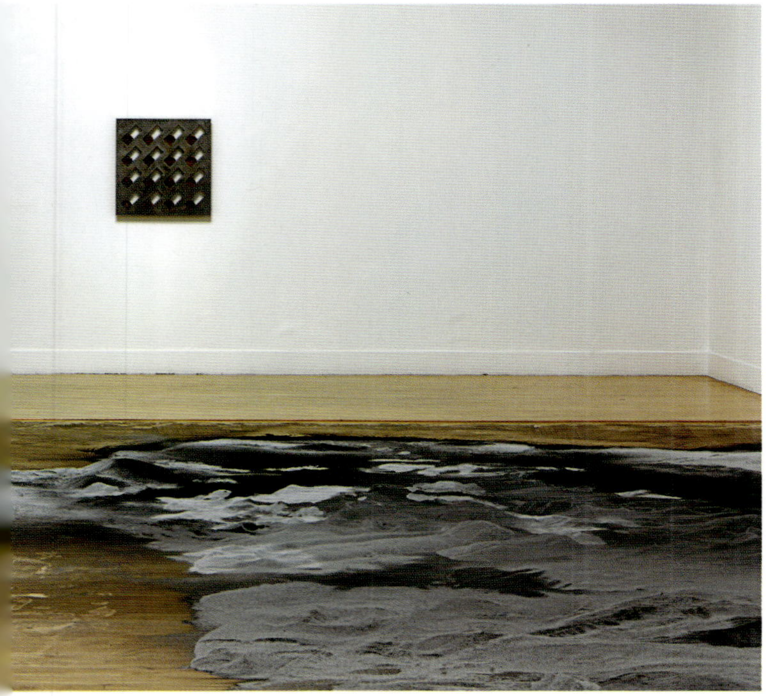

Shown by
Corvi-Mora A16
Marc Foxx C32
Annet Gelink Gallery A10

Biography
Born 1975
Lives in London

Nominated for the Turner Prize in 2009, Hiorns has exhibited his sculptural installations and performances internationally for over a decade. In 2011 he was included in the survey exhibition "British Art Show 7: In the Days of the Comet", which travelled from Nottingham Contemporary to venues in London, Glasgow, and Plymouth. He had recent self-titled solo exhibitions at the Art Institute of Chicago (2010) and Aspen Art Museum (2010). His Jerwood/Artangel commission *Seizure* (2008) was visited by hundreds of people daily in 2008 and 2009.

1
Seizure
2008
Copper sulphate
Site-specific installation, London
Courtesy of Marc Foxx

2
Untitled
2012
Engines, copper sulphate, steel
106¼ × 35½ × 35½"
(270 × 90 × 90 cm)
Courtesy of Marc Foxx

3
Top: *Untitled*
Bottom: *Untitled*
Installed at the Tate Britain for Turner Prize 2009
Top: Steel and brain matter
Bottom: Atomized passenger aircraft engine
Dimensions variable
Courtesy of Marc Foxx
Photo courtesy Tate Photography

Roger Hiorns

Merely in terms of its range of sculptural materials, Roger Hiorns' work mines for secret affinities between the elemental, the modern, and the everyday. Consider this partial inventory of substances: steel, copper sulphate, brain matter, semen, glass, steroids, and Dettol disinfectant. But if Hiorns remains best known for the crystallized apartment of *Seizure* (2008), a grotto where domestic Modernism turned rich and strange, it is the less spectacular imbrications of matter that continue to impress. His *Untitled* (2005–10) mounts an austere theatrical encounter between a metal bench, a small fire, and a frail human body. Meanwhile, *Untitled (Alliance)* (2010) is the latest of his sculptures to infiltrate aircraft engines with eloquent substances—in this case, pulverized antidepressants. BD

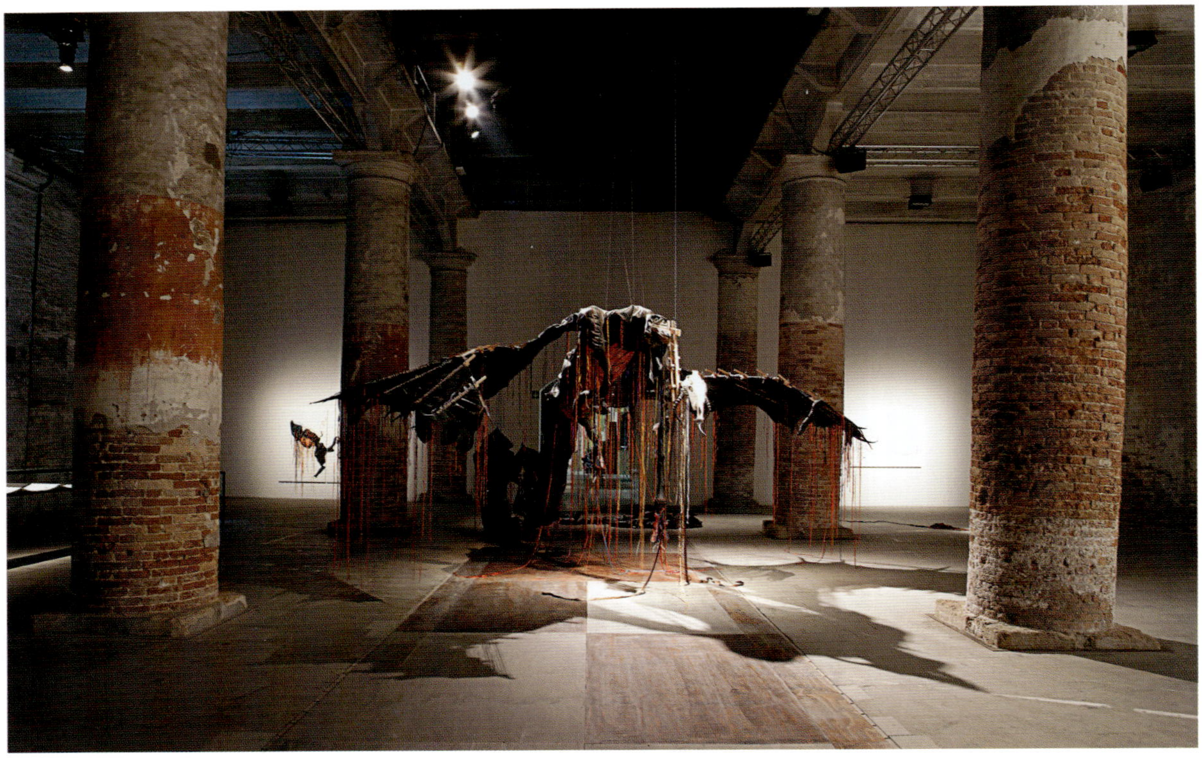

1

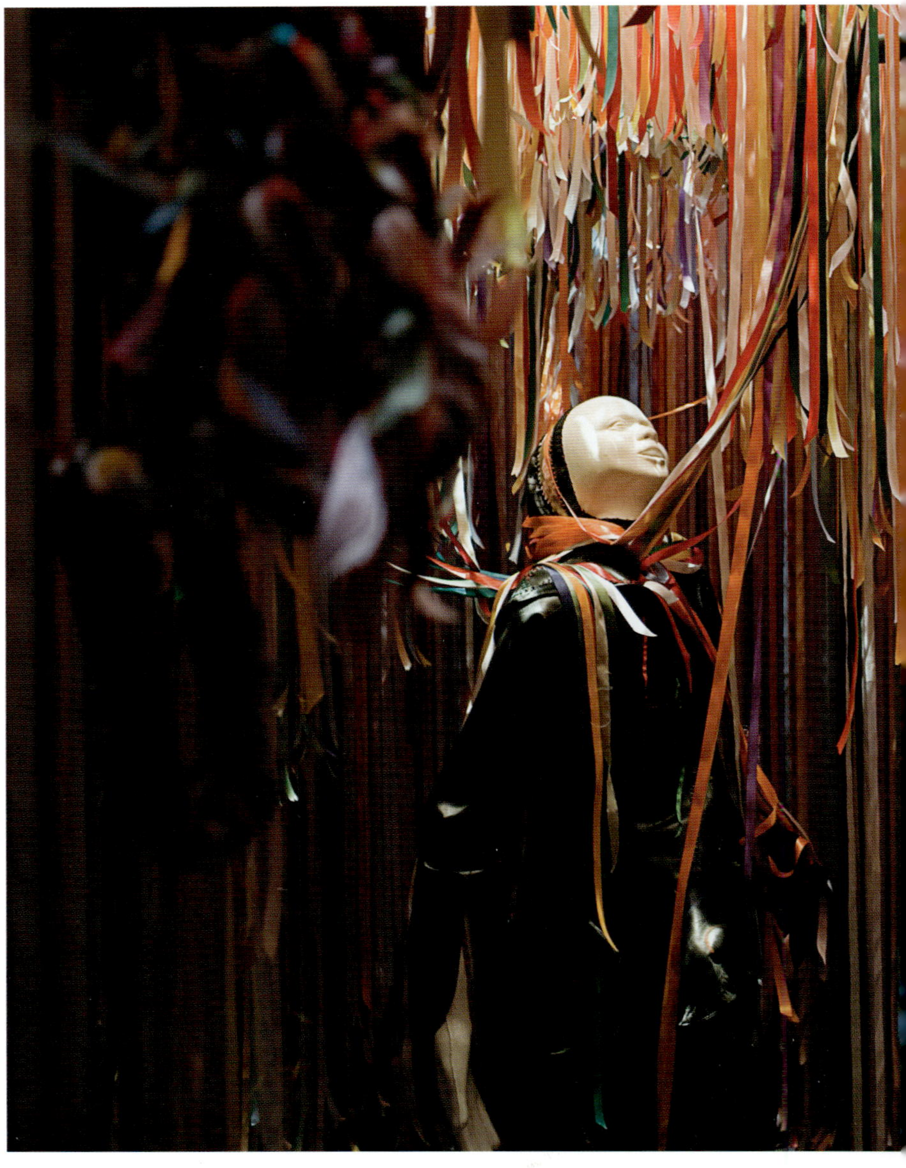

2

Shown by
Stevenson B32

Biography
Born 1975
Lives in Johannesburg

In recent years, South African artist Hlobo has received a number of awards and accolades for his sculptural work, most recently being named the "2010-11 Rolex Visual Arts Protégé" and winning the "Future Generation Art Prize 2010". In 2011 the solo show "Nicholas Hlobo: Sculpture, Installation, Performance, Drawing" was held at the National Museum of Art, Architecture and Design, Oslo. He has participated in numerous significant group shows, including "ILLUMInations" (2011) at the 54th Venice Biennale, and 18th Biennale of Sydney (2012).

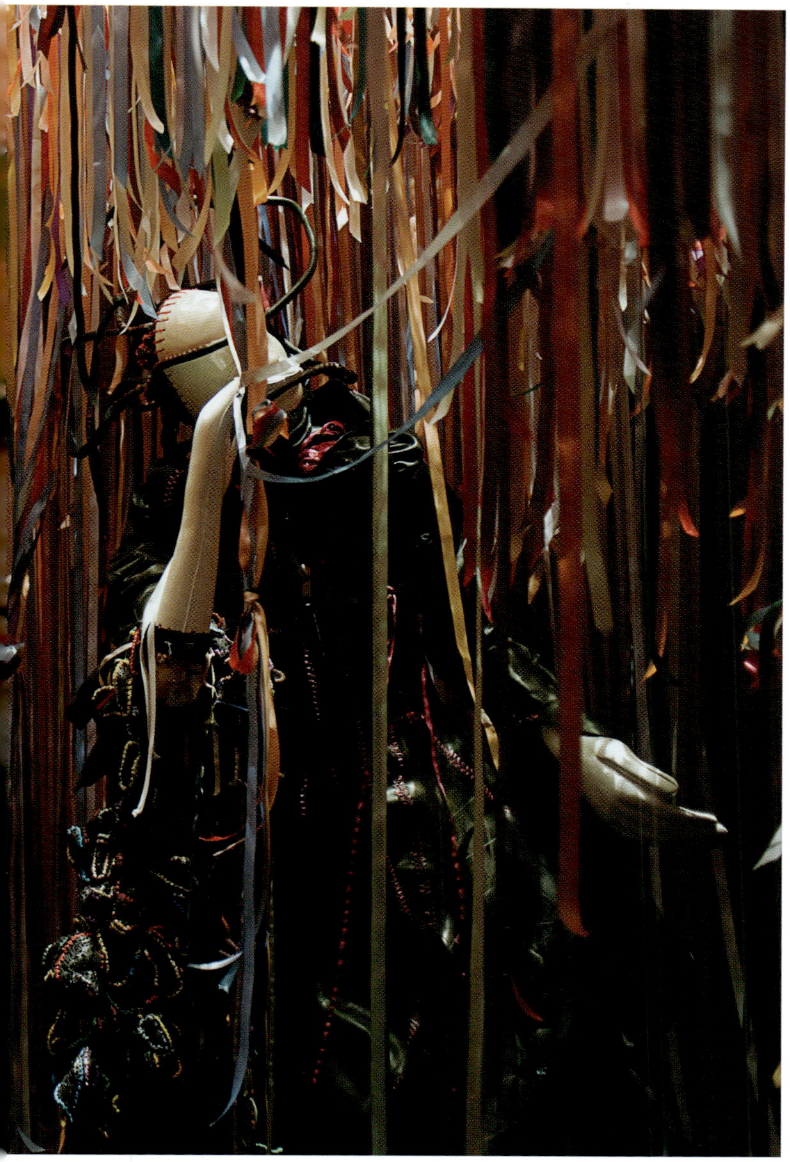

1
Impundulo Zonke Ziyandilandela
(All the Lightning Birds Are After Me)
2011
Rubber, ribbon, and mixed media with sound installation
88½ × 1230⅜ × 181⅛" (225 × 3125 × 460 cm)
Courtesy of Stevenson

2
Ndize
(Seeker)
2010
44 kilometers of ribbon, steel mesh, rubber, leather
259⅞ × 330¾ × 120⅞" (660 × 840 × 307 cm)
Courtesy of Stevenson

Nicholas Hlobo

Nicholas Hlobo employs craft-based techniques to create highly personal works informed by his Xhosa heritage and sexuality. Delicately sewn works in ribbon on paper contrast with his foreboding large-scale sculptural installations made of rubber. Installed in the Arsenale for the 54th Venice Biennale, his *Impundulu Zonke Ziyandilandela* (All the Lightning Birds Are After Me, 2011) showed a monstrous hybrid creature fashioned from used inner-tube tires, suspended from the ceiling and dripping with suspended ribbons. Like his installation *Ndize* (Seeker, 2010) as part of "Touched," the 2010 Liverpool Biennial—an environment of suspended colorful ribbons populated by eerily Frankenstein-like mannequins—Hlobo's works are charged with elements of the otherworldly and a quiet, surreal eroticism. PT

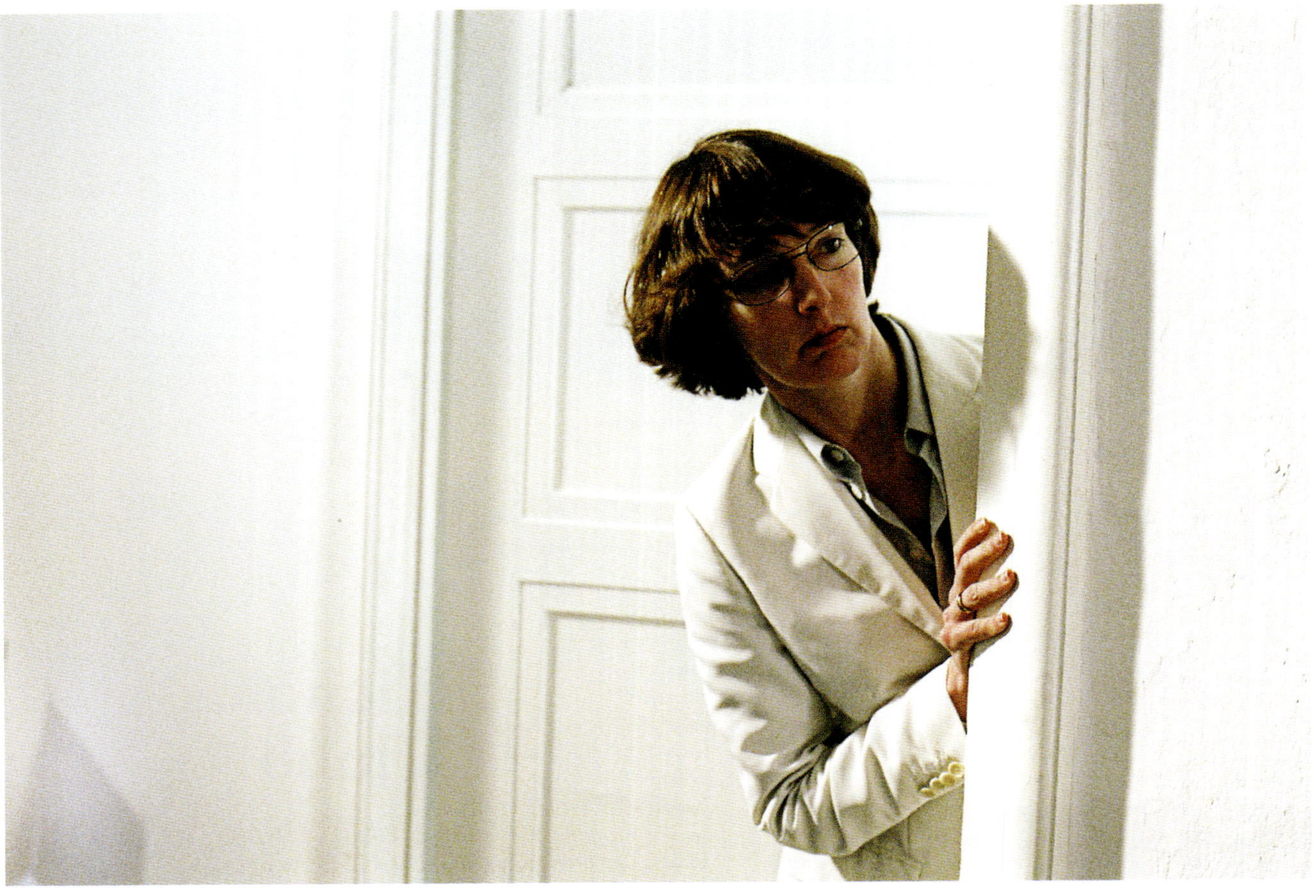

1

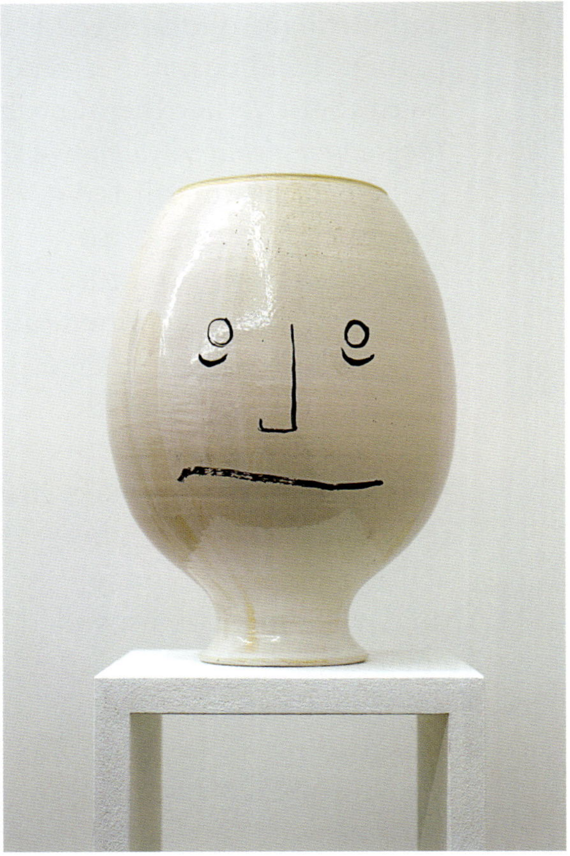

2

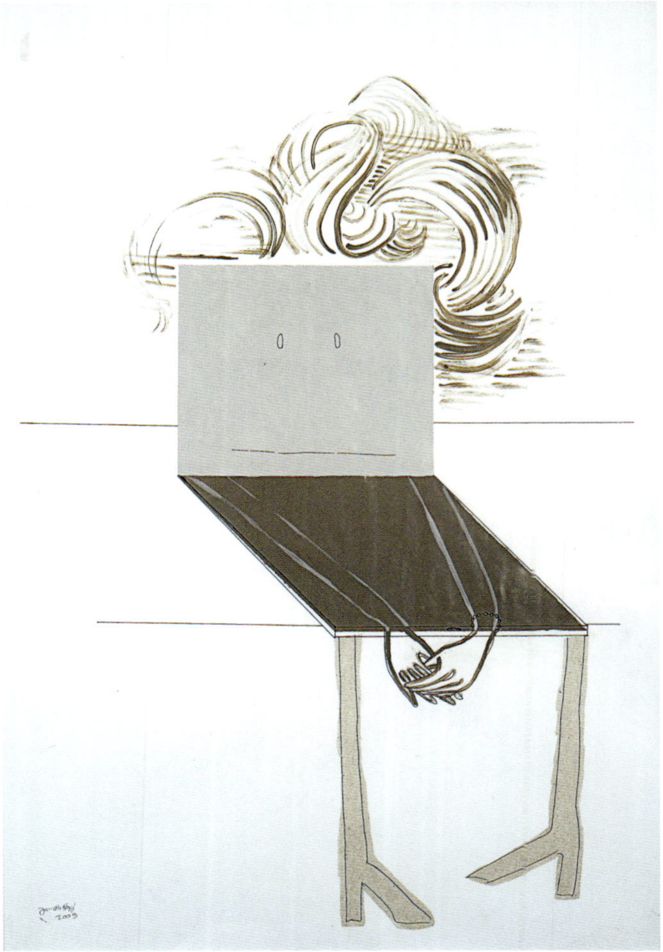

3

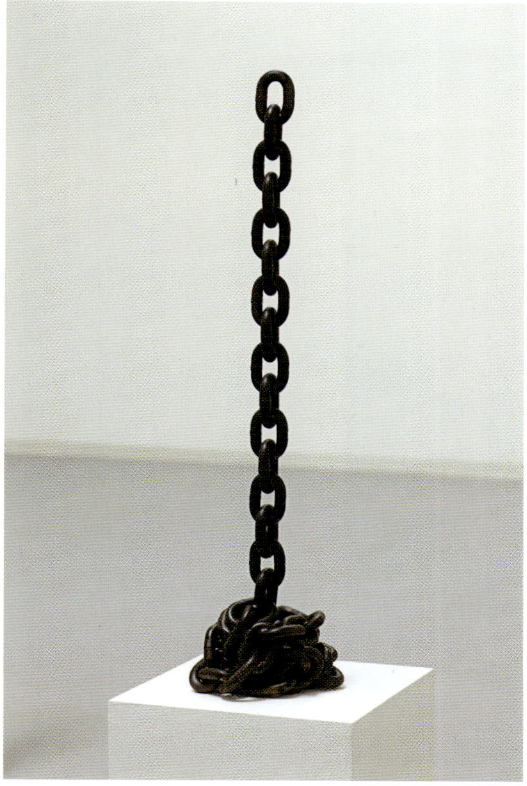

4

Shown by
Hotel F31
kaufmann repetto A20
Alex Zachary Peter
Currie F2

Biography
Born 1969
Lives in Berlin

Hopf's sculptures, videos and installations have been exhibited internationally since the mid-1990s. In 2011 her work was the subject of the solo exhibition "Spoken from a Balcony" at Alex Zachary, New York. The same year the solo show "contrat entre les hommes et l'ordinateur" (contract between people and computers, 2011) took place at after the butcher, Berlin. In 2012 she will participate in dOCUMENTA (13), Kassel, and have a solo show at Hotel, London. She is Professor of Fine Art, at the Städelschule, Staatliche Hochschule für Bildende Kunst, Frankfurt am Main.

1
Judith Hopf and Henrik Olesen
Untitled
2007
Courtesy of Hotel

2
Erschöpfte Vase
(Exhausted Vase)
2009
Ceramic and laquer
11⅞ × 7⅞ × 7⅞"
(30 × 20 × 20 cm)
Courtesy of Hotel

3
Wartender Laptop 1
(Waiting Laptop 1)
2009
Lacquer, ink, collage on paper
40½ × 30¾"
(103 × 78 cm)
Courtesy of Galerie Andreas Huber

4
Ending
2011
Iron
27½ × 7⅞ × 7⅞"
(70 × 20 × 20 cm)
Courtesy of Hotel

Focus
Judith Hopf

Absurdity seeps into the everyday in Judith Hopf's videos, installations, sculptures, and collaborations—unsettling social and political conventions, and exposing the conditions of artistic production. In her video *Hey Produktion* (Hey Production, 2001) she is resting on a park bench when passers-by launch into an awkwardly stylized ballet. *Hospital Bone Dance* (2006), a deadpan collaboration with Deborah Schamoni, shows a communication breakdown between a patient and doctor in a hospital where skeletons and mummies cavort in the hallways. Using modest materials, Hopf's installations such as *Bambus* (Bamboo, 2006), a fragile forest of stacked drinking glasses, and *Cabine* (Cabin, 2006), funhouse mirrors placed at the corners of entryways, heighten viewers' awareness of their bodies as they navigate through uncertain spaces. KJ

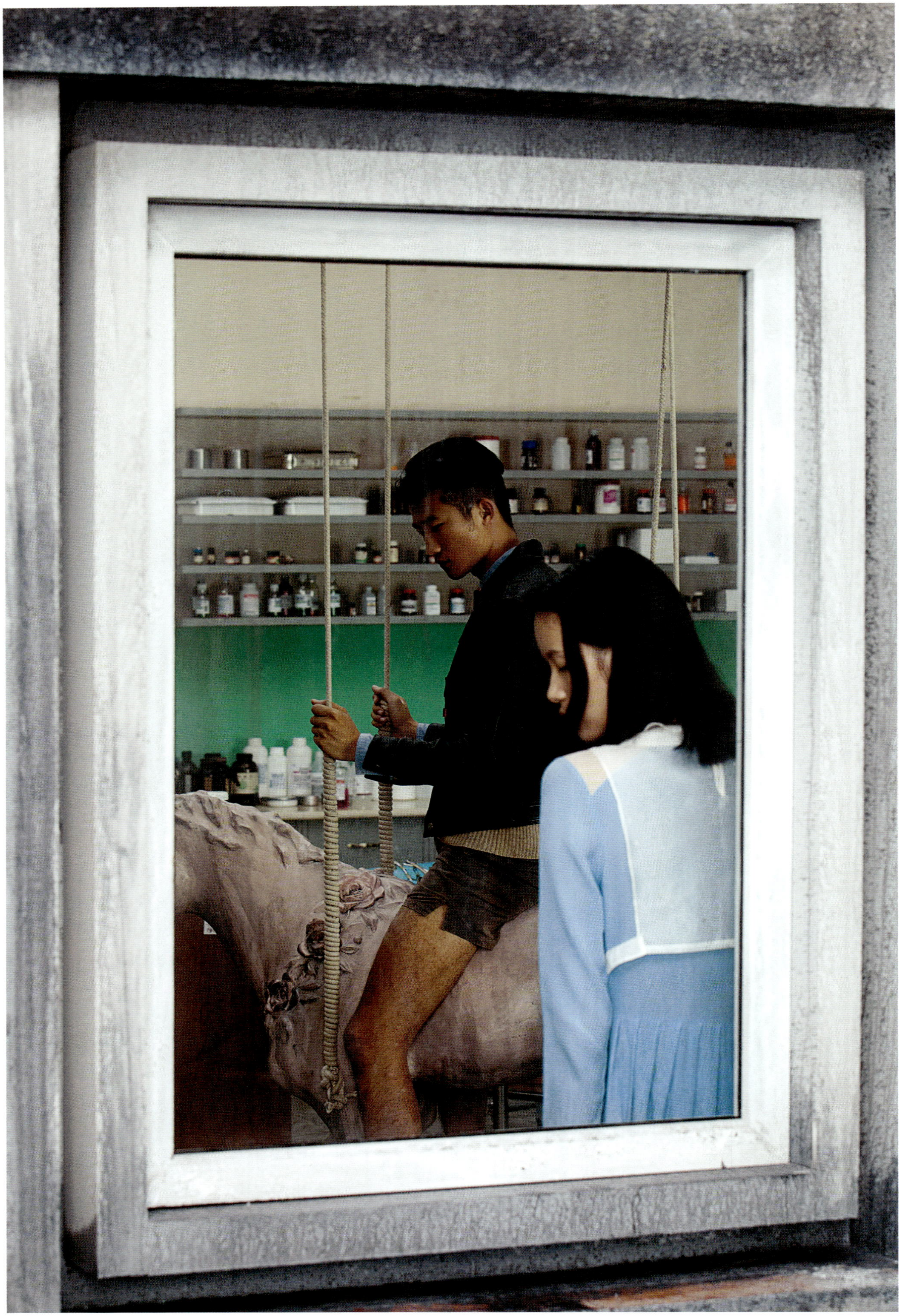

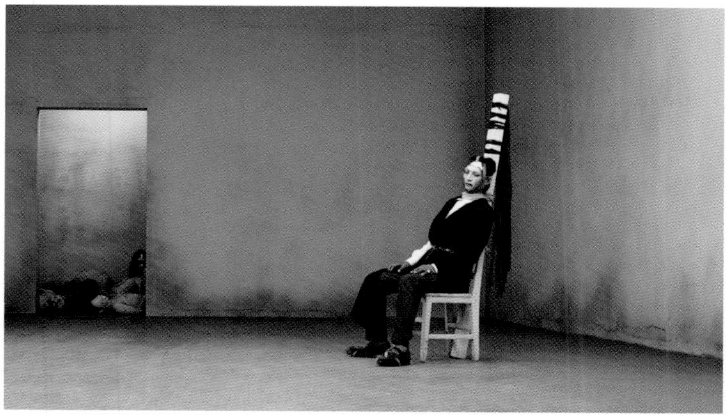

2

Shown by
Long March Space C13

Biography
Born 1982
Lives in Beijing
and London

China-born Huang received an MFA from Goldsmiths College, London, in 2007, and a BA from Birmingham Institute of Art and Design in 2004. In recent years there have been numerous solo exhibitions of his work, including "Blithe Tragedy" (2010) at Space Station, Beijing; "Ran Huang" (2010) at George Polke, London; and "Fake Action Truth" (2010) at Prussian Projekte, Nottingham. In summer 2012 he will participate in the Echigo-Tsumari Triennial.

1
Invitation to The Outrage
2011
Super 16mm film and Arri Alexa Digital
19 min. 51 sec.
Courtesy of Long March Space

2
Blithe Tragedy
2010
Transferred to Betacam, Blu-Ray, and DVD
14 min. 56 sec.
Courtesy of Long March Space

Ran Huang

Ran Huang encircles an aesthetic between the sublime and the morbid. Beauty and violence mingle openly in his highly constructed and cinematic films, photographs, sculptures, and multimedia installations. His works that share the name *Something as beautiful as desirable, as transcendent, as evil* (2010 and 2011) move from a slideshow passively portraying the explosion of the *Challenger* space shuttle in 1986 to a diptych portrait done in the style of a 19th-century anatomical engraving: one image depicts an expressionless man, the second his face covered with festering welts and growths. For Huang, desire and disgust spring from the same ornate fountain. CFW

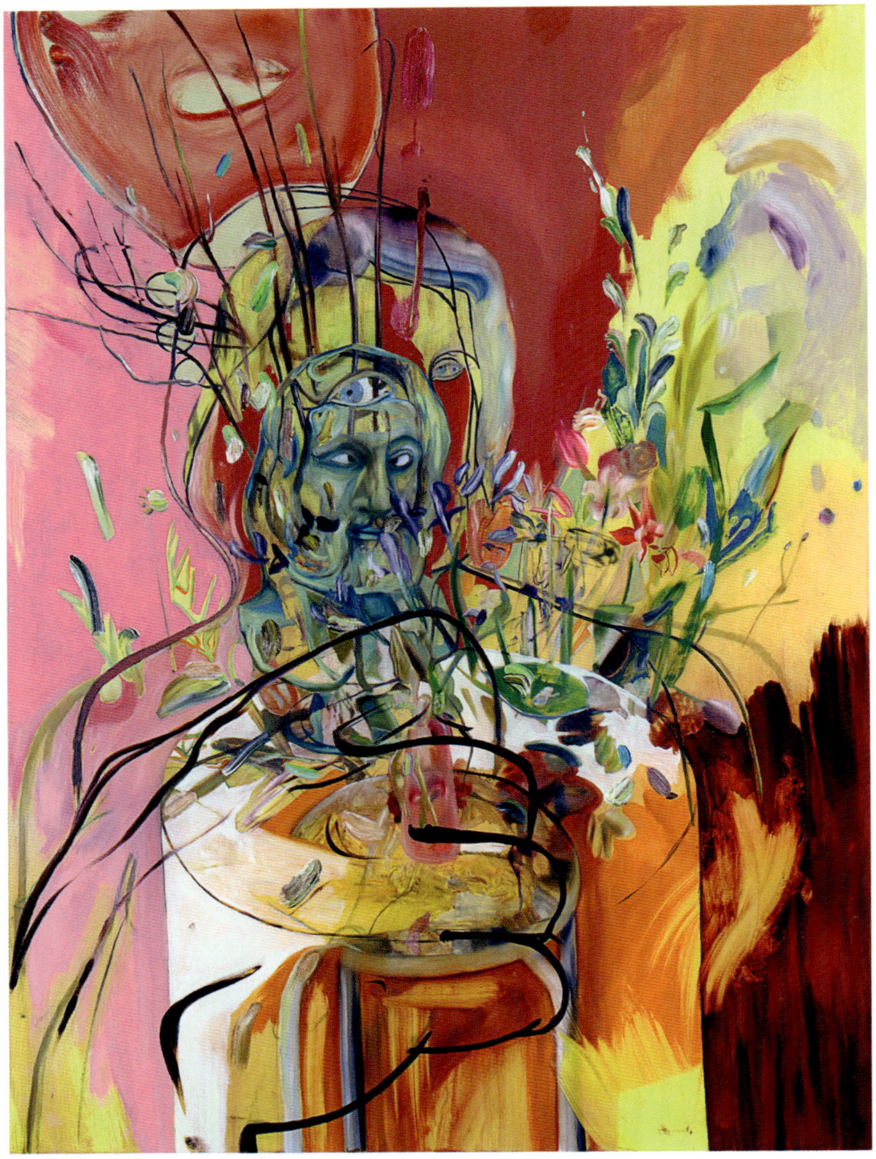

1

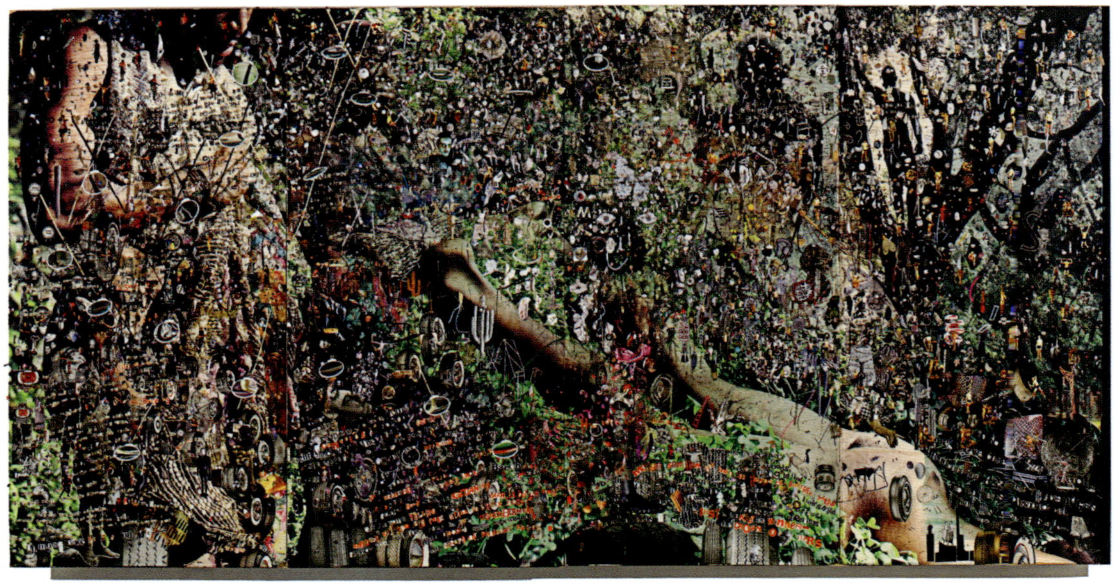

2

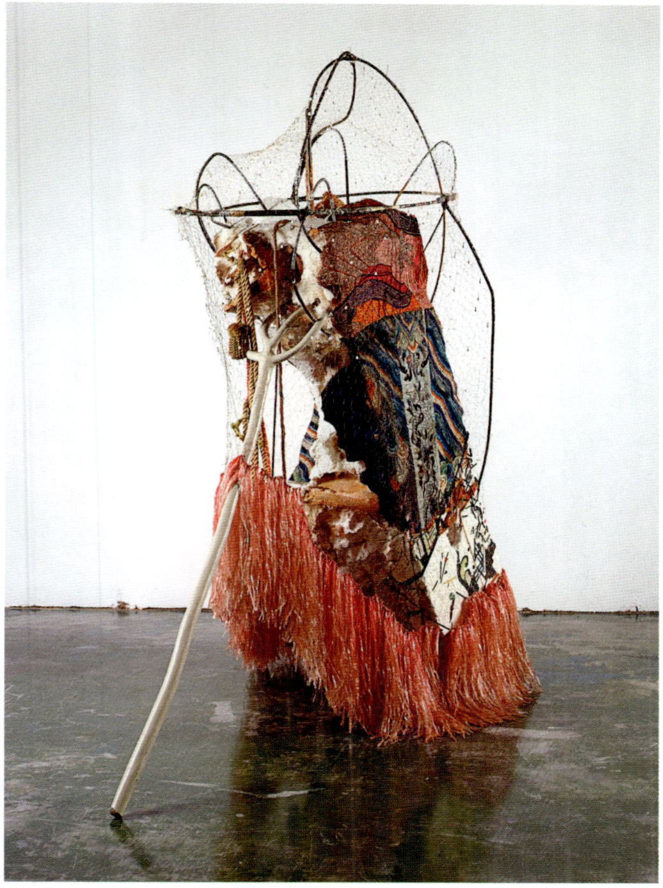

3

Elliott Hundley

Elliott Hundley's paintings come off the wall like fictional characters sneaking into real life. The pell-mell tumble of materials—from the traditional painter's pigments and charcoal to the bricoleur's cardboard and string, to decorative shells and fabric—becomes a conurbation through which narratives pass and where ancient archetypes lodge. *Agave* (2010) bristles with references to Greek mythology—the excesses and indulgences of Bacchus are directly translated into a surface abundant with fragmentary meanings. Collaged photographs of figures in specific but unknowable guises offer glimpses of mediated realities, but these are inevitably subsumed by a plethora of pictorial symbolism that recedes to the babble of human histories. SOR

Shown by
Regen Projects B17
Andrea Rosen Gallery C28

Biography
Born 1975
Lives in Los Angeles

American artist Hundley received an MFA from the University of California, Los Angeles, in 2005 and a BA from Rhode Island School of Design, Providence, in 1997. In 2011 his work was the subject of the solo exhibition "The Bacchae" at the Wexner Center for the Arts, Columbus—the exhibition toured to Nasher Sculpture Center, Dallas, in early 2012. Also in 2011, the solo show "Semele" took place at Regen Projects, Los Angeles.

1
Euripides after De Chirico Obscured by Flowers No.V
2011
Oil on linen
72 × 54 × 2"
(183 × 137 × 5 cm)
Courtesy of Regen Projects and Andrea Rosen Gallery

2
Pentheus
2010
Mixed media
96 × 192½ × 19½"
(244 × 489 × 49.5 cm)
Courtesy of Regen Projects and Andrea Rosen Gallery

3
With her own hands
2010
Expanded Styrofoam, bamboo, wood, wire, found embroidered robes, plastic, rope, pins, feathers, rice paper, glass, shells, photograph, metal, found hay fork
67 × 65 × 39"
(170 × 165 × 99 cm)
Courtesy of Andrea Rosen Gallery

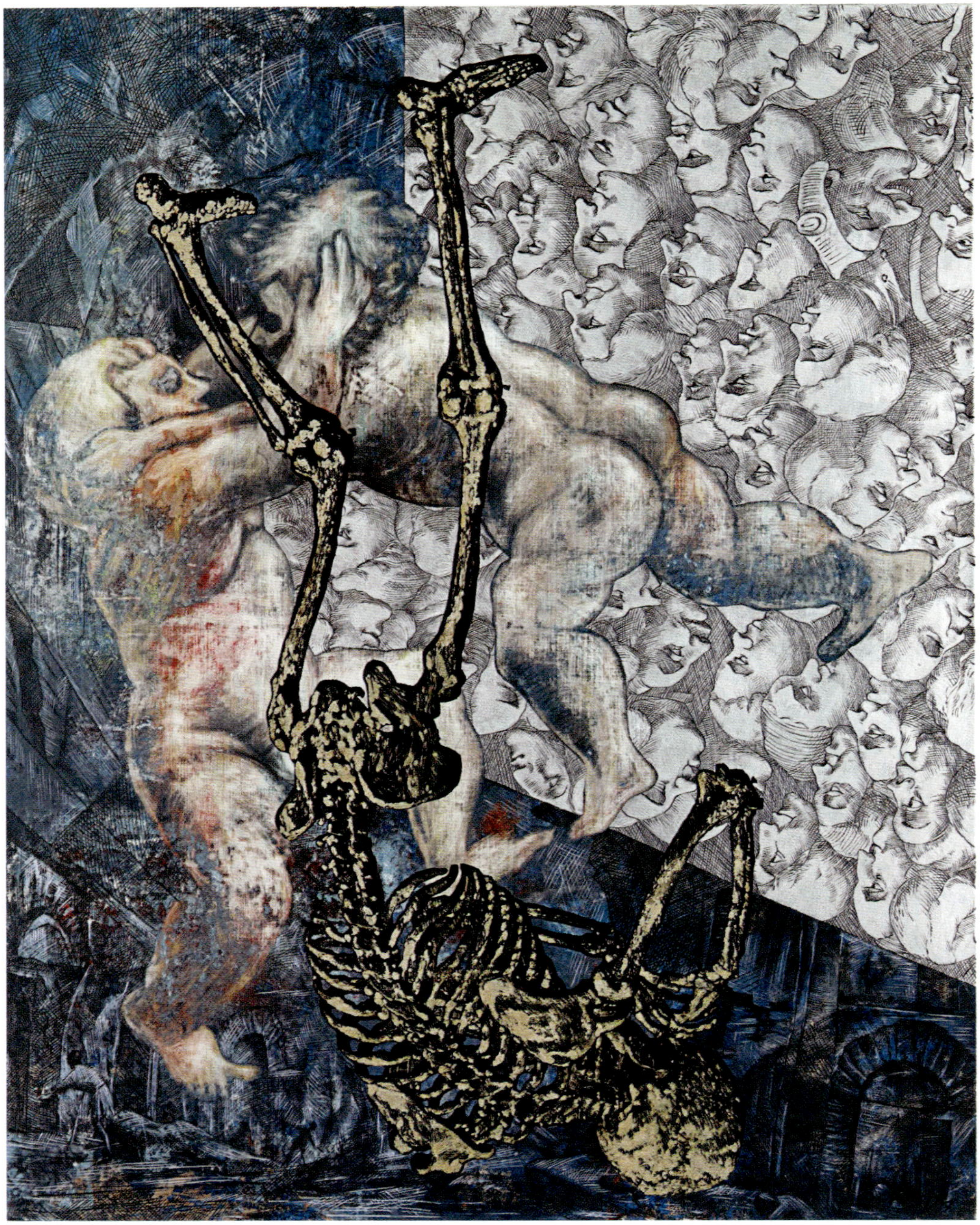

Jörg Immendorff

Shown by
Michael Werner B5

Biography
Born 1945
Died 2007

Immendorff studied art at the Düsseldorf Academy in the 1960s under Joseph Beuys. Before his death in 2007 the German painter held significant solo shows, including "Immendorff. Male Lago—unsichtbarer Beitrag" (Immendorff. Male Lago—Invisible Contribution, 2005) at the Neue Nationalgalerie, Berlin. For five decades his work has been exhibited internationally, and is now included in renowned public collections such as Tate Modern, London, and MoMA, New York.

Untitled
2007
Oil on canvas
78¾ × 63"
(200 × 160 cm)
Courtesy of
Michael Werner

Often large, complex in composition, and teeming with people, Jörg Immendorff's paintings thrum with personal and political histories. His "Café Deutschland" series of the 1970s and '80s is set in a fictional venue on the border between east and west, where Cold War politics is played out through a burlesque show of fearsome grotesques, satires of historic signification, and performed inquiries into national identity. Since the Berlin Wall came down, Immendorff's imagery has remained urgent, his ideas grandiose, and his language guttural. Throughout the untitled paintings that comprised the final show before his death in 2007, the body is equivocally rendered as art-historical imagery, subjective form, and graphic motif, clashing the perpetuity of iconography with the experience of a transitory body. SOR

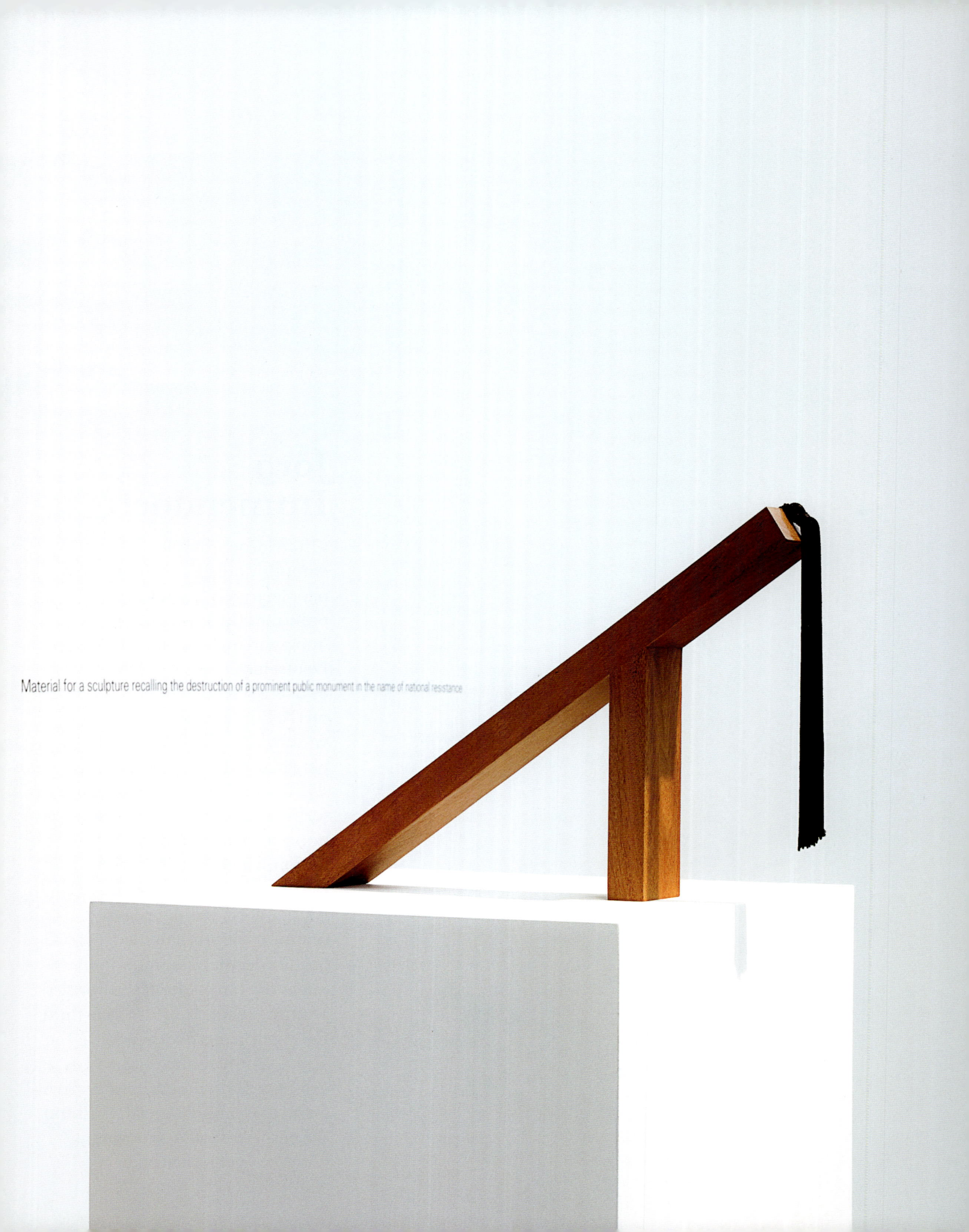

Material for a sculpture recalling the destruction of a prominent public monument in the name of national resistance

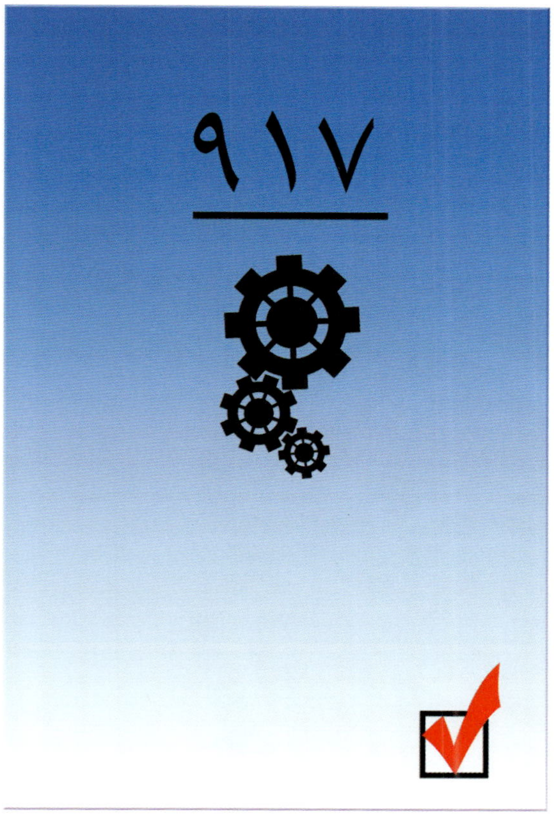

2

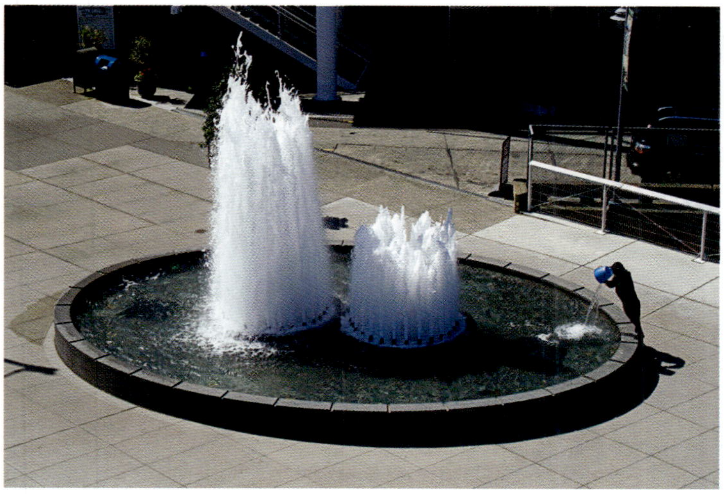

3

Shown by
Rodeo F25

Biography
Born 1979
Lives in New York

Egypt-born Issa has exhibited extensively in recent years. Her concept-driven practice was the subject of the recent solo shows "Material" at Rodeo, Istanbul (2011); "Subjective Projections" (2010) at Bielefelder Kunstverein, Bielefeld; and "Making Places" (2008) at Townhouse Gallery of Contemporary Art, Cairo. In late 2011 she participated in numerous group shows, including "Seeing is Believing" at KW Institute of Contemporary Art, Berlin, and "Short Stories" at SculptureCenter, Long Island City. Her videos were included in the 9th Sharjah Biennial (2009).

1
Material for a sculpture recalling the destruction of a prominent public monument in the name of national resistance
2010
Mixed media
56 × 19¼"
(142 × 49 cm)
Courtesy of Rodeo

2
Material II (Colors, Lines, Numbers, Symbols, Shapes, and Images)
2010
Archival inkjet prints
27 × 18⅞"
(68.5 × 48 cm)
Courtesy of Rodeo

3
Making Places, Bucket
2007
C-type print
27½ × 18⅜"
(70 × 46.5 cm)
Courtesy of Rodeo

Focus
Iman Issa

The city—its imaging, mapping, and memorializing—foregrounds Iman Issa's inquisitive practice. Early architectural works in her native Egypt have recently evolved into an exploration of the jingoistic language engulfing monument-making. And, befitting the artist's purchase on minimalist forms and allusive politics, the titling of these works is more explicit than the objects themselves. *Material for a sculpture recalling the destruction of a prominent public monument in the name of national resistance* (2010), for example, features an inclined slice of dark wood, a black tassel hanging from it; *Material for a sculpture acting as a testament to both a nation's pioneering development and continuing decline* (2011) comprises two speakers, one droning a deep bass, the other a clapping crowd. The questions posed—what is development, what decline?—are well put. QL

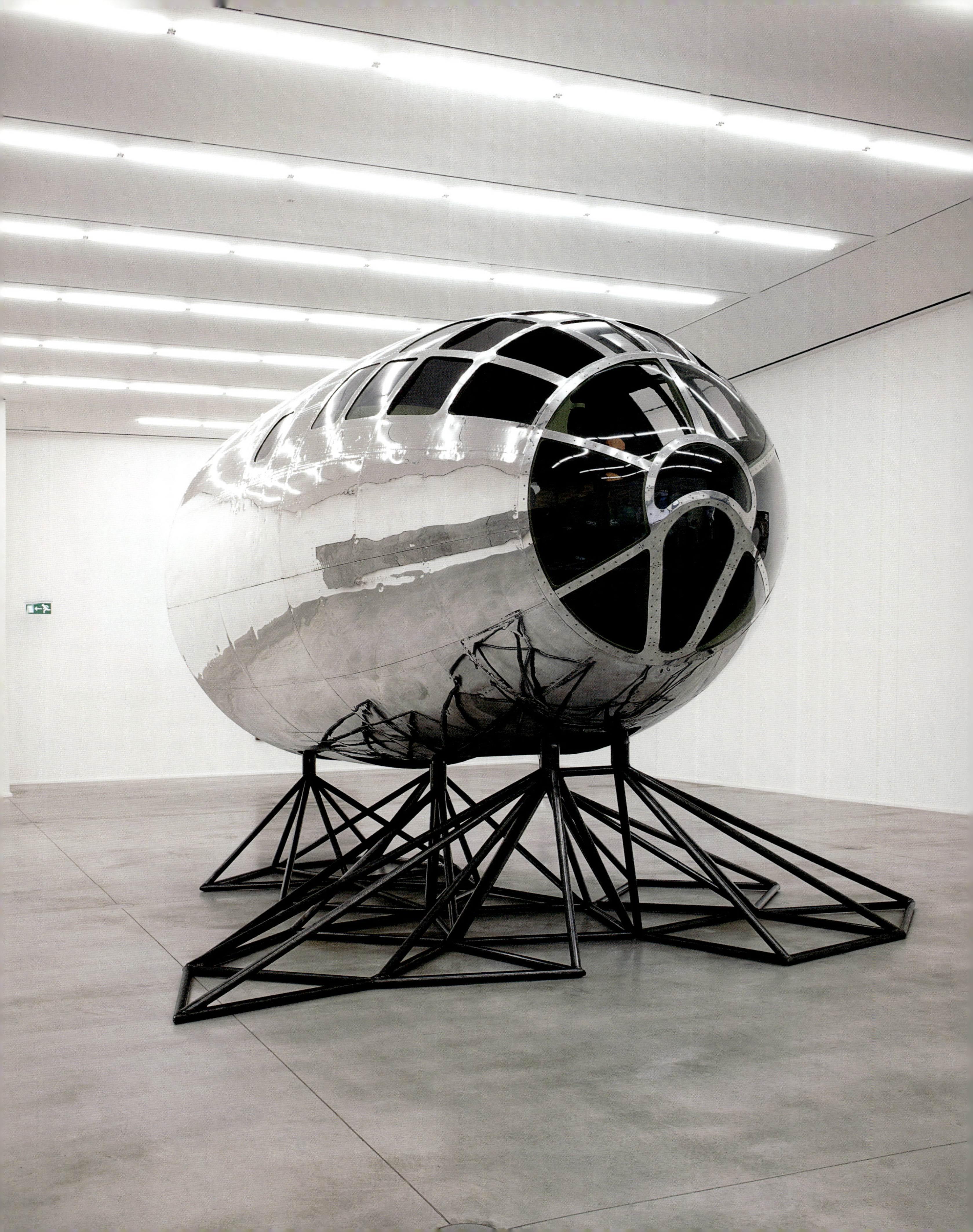

Shown by
Hauser & Wirth B6

Biography
Born 1974
Lives in New York

American artist Jackson has exhibited extensively in the United States and Europe in the last decade. In 2012 "In Search of..." opened at the Gemeentemuseum, The Hague, as the third leg of a touring museum show also at MAMbo, Bologna, and at Kunstmuseum Luzern, Lucerne, in 2011. The same year "Everything Leads to Another" took place at Hauser & Wirth, London. Recent group shows include "The Collectors Show" (2011) at Van Abbemuseum, Eindhoven; "Singular Visions" (2011) at the Whitney Museum of American Art, New York; and "The Spectacular of Vernacular" (2011) at the Walker Art Center, Minneapolis.

1
Axis Mundi
2011
Repurposed cockpit of a B-29 aircraft, aluminum, red oak, glass, steel, plastic, lead, bronze, iron, obsidian, leather, silver, stainless steel, concrete
146⅞ × 189 × 232¼"
(373 × 480 × 590 cm)
Courtesy of Hauser & Wirth

2
August 6, 1945
2010
Scorched wood, found and painted wood, gypsum plaster, resin, lead, stainless steel
84 × 65⅜ × 8¾"
213.5 × 166 × 22 cm
Courtesy of Hauser & Wirth

Matthew Day Jackson

For *Axis Mundi* (2011) Matthew Day Jackson acquired a cockpit from a B-29 Superfortress—the type of plane used to drop the atomic bomb on Hiroshima—which was supported by struts based on Buckminster Fuller's Dymaxion map and hosted a Victorian-style gentleman's library. In *Chariot (The Day after the End of Days)* (2005–6), meanwhile, he grappled with the pioneering myths of the American Old West and the romanticization of the environmental movement by piecing together a covered wagon from discarded timber, industrial plywood, and a repurposed hay cart. "I'm interested in moments in history when beauty and terror were inseparable," the artist explains. His recurrently monumental works turn a critical eye on the American psyche and towards the thresholds of humanity's pursuit of knowledge and technology. MA

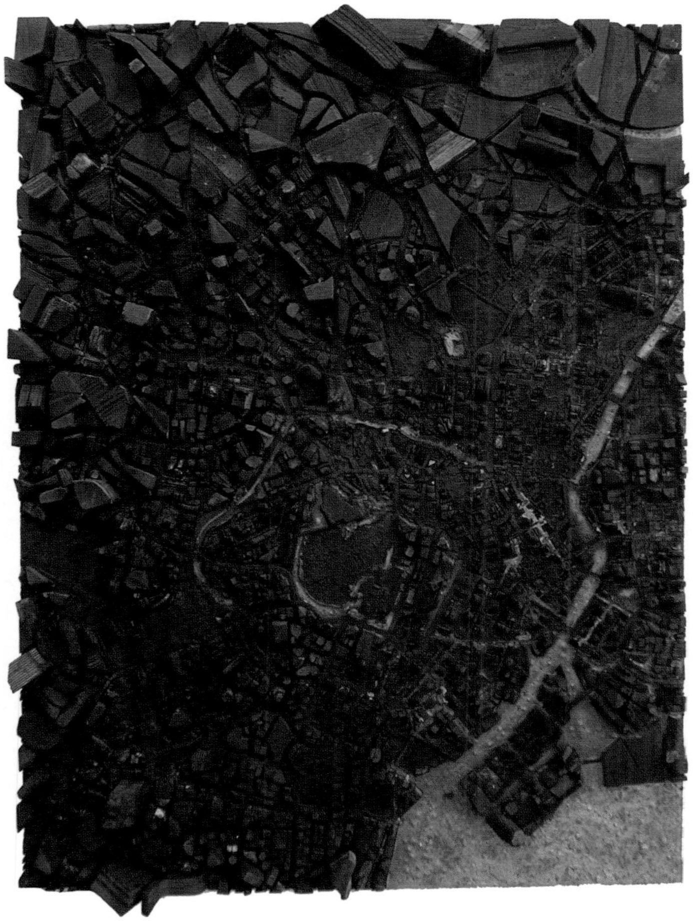

2

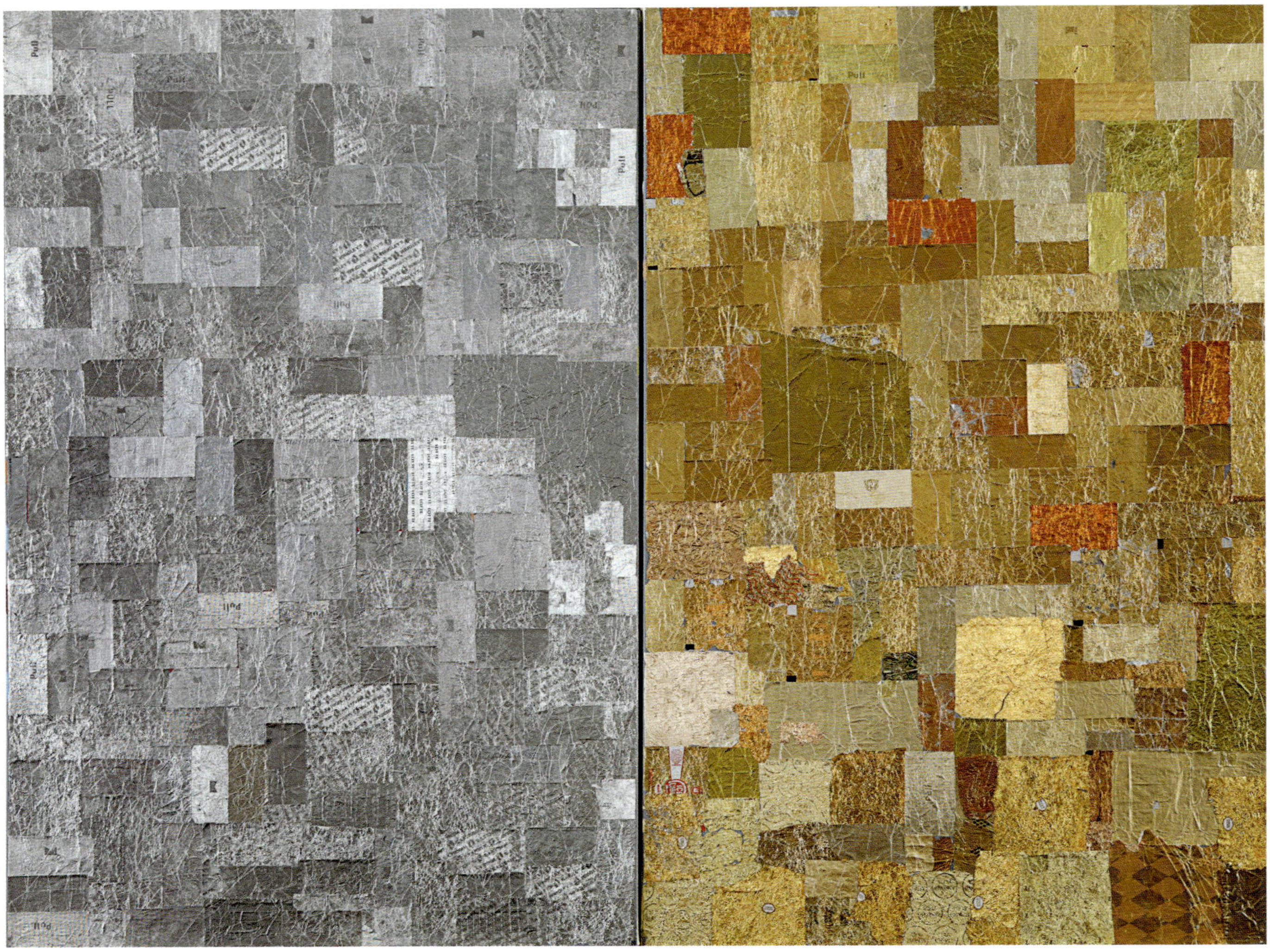

1

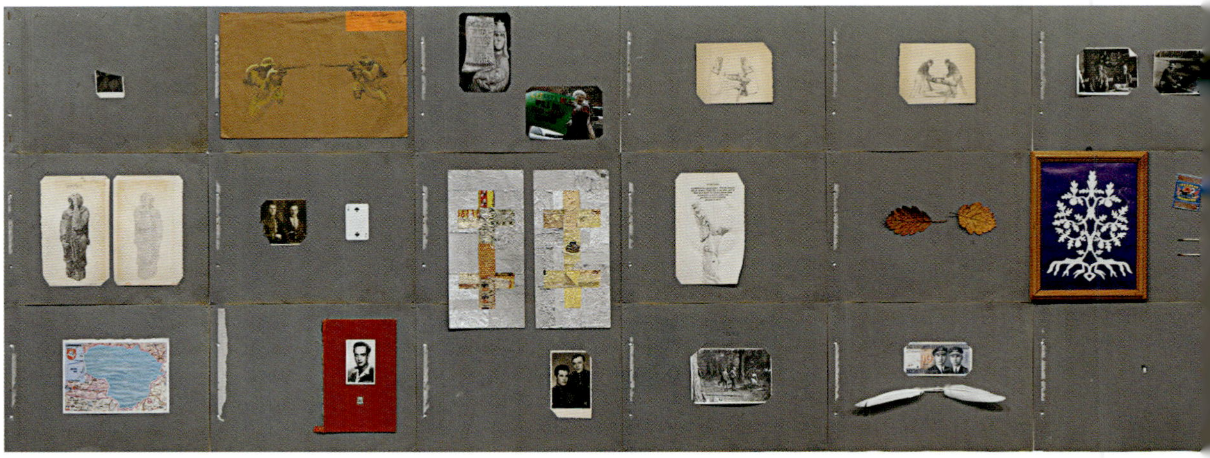

2

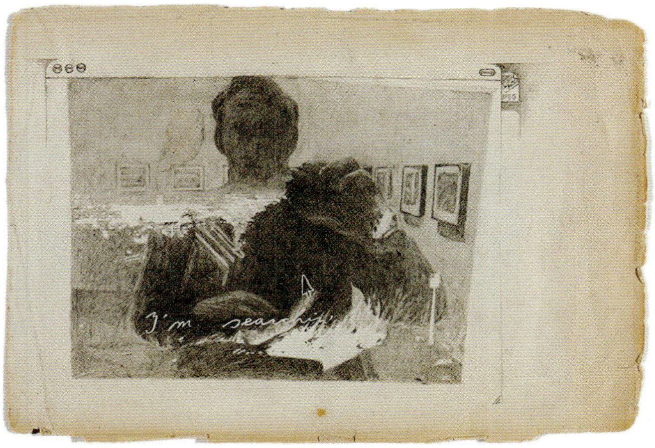

3

Shown by
Corvi-Mora A16

Biography
Born 1975
Lives in San Francisco

American artist Jacobsen's drawings, watercolours, and collages were the subject of a solo show at Corvi-Mora, London in 2011. Other recent solo shows include "Searchin' vs, Buildin'" (2011) at LA><ART, Los Angeles, and "The Exhibition Formerly Known as Passengers" (2010) at the CCA Wattis Institute, California College of Arts, San Francisco. He was nominated for the "2010 SECA Art Award" at the San Francisco Museum of Modern Art. In Europe he participated in a group show at Galerie Krinzinger, Vienna (2010).

1
Street of Dreams
2010
Foil on canvas
24 × 36¼" each
(61 × 92 cm each)
Courtesy of
Corvi-Mora

2
Skye Blue Friendship
2009
Mixed media
Dimensions variable
Courtesy of
Corvi-Mora

3
I'm Searchin'
2010
Graphite on paper
5¾ × 8⅜"
(14.5 × 21.5 cm)
Courtesy of
Corvi-Mora

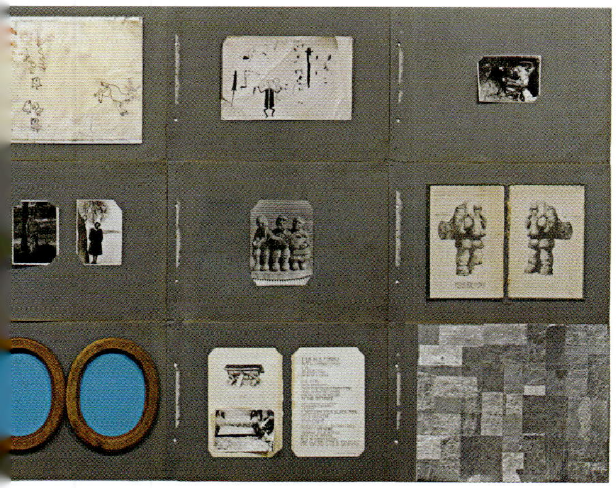

Colter Jacobsen

Colter Jacobsen's works on paper often hinge on a mnemonic or perceptual disparity. He has called these diptychs "memory drawings," working from found photographs, the first is a precise copy, while the second is drawn from memory after a given interval has elapsed. In these works, Jacobsen figures copying as an imperfect attempt to remember or preserve objects. Other works, such as *Refraction* (2010)—in which a pencil dipped in water seems to bend—consider that small gap between what seems to be and what is known. More recently, copied from profile pictures found online (such as the "Facelessbook" series of 2010), Jacobsen's works have begun to consider the way in which the digital circulation of images affects how memories are formed and how they fade. ST

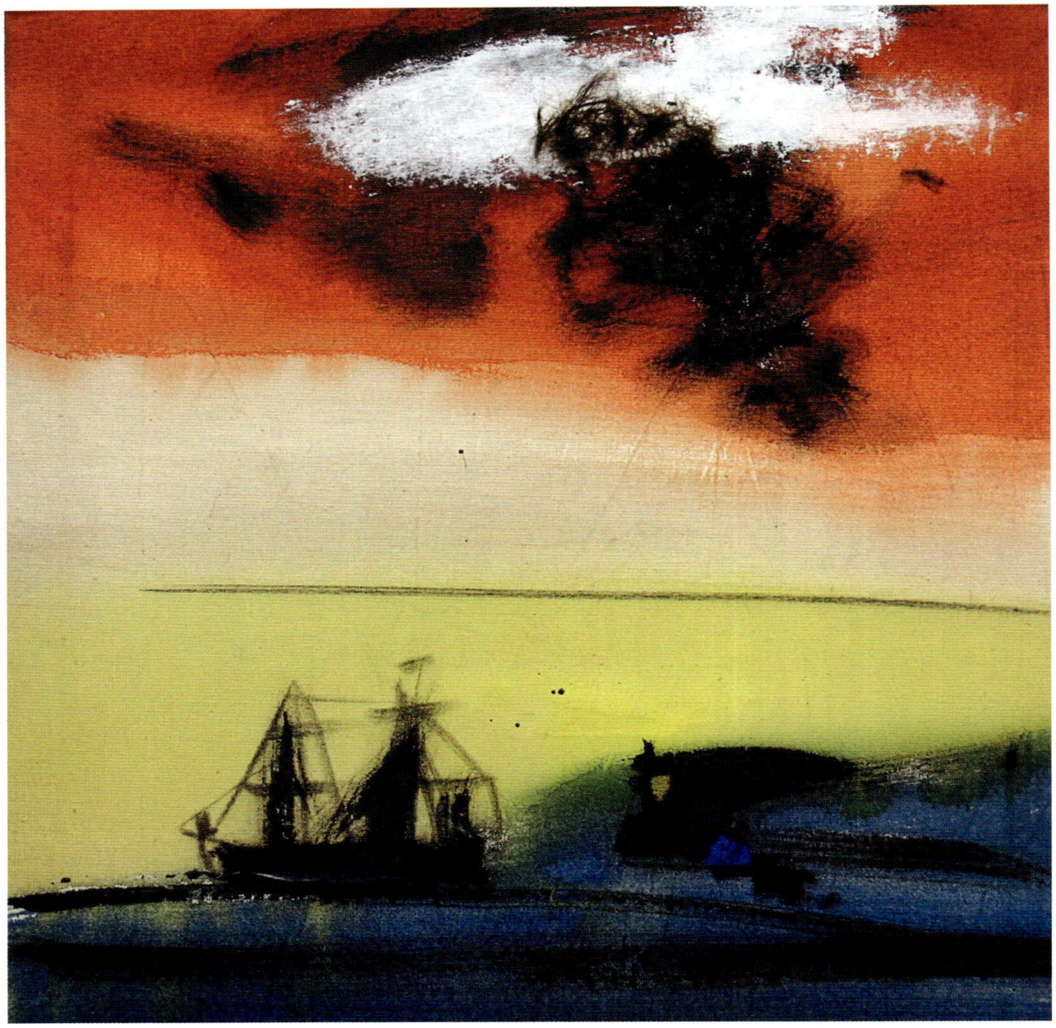
1

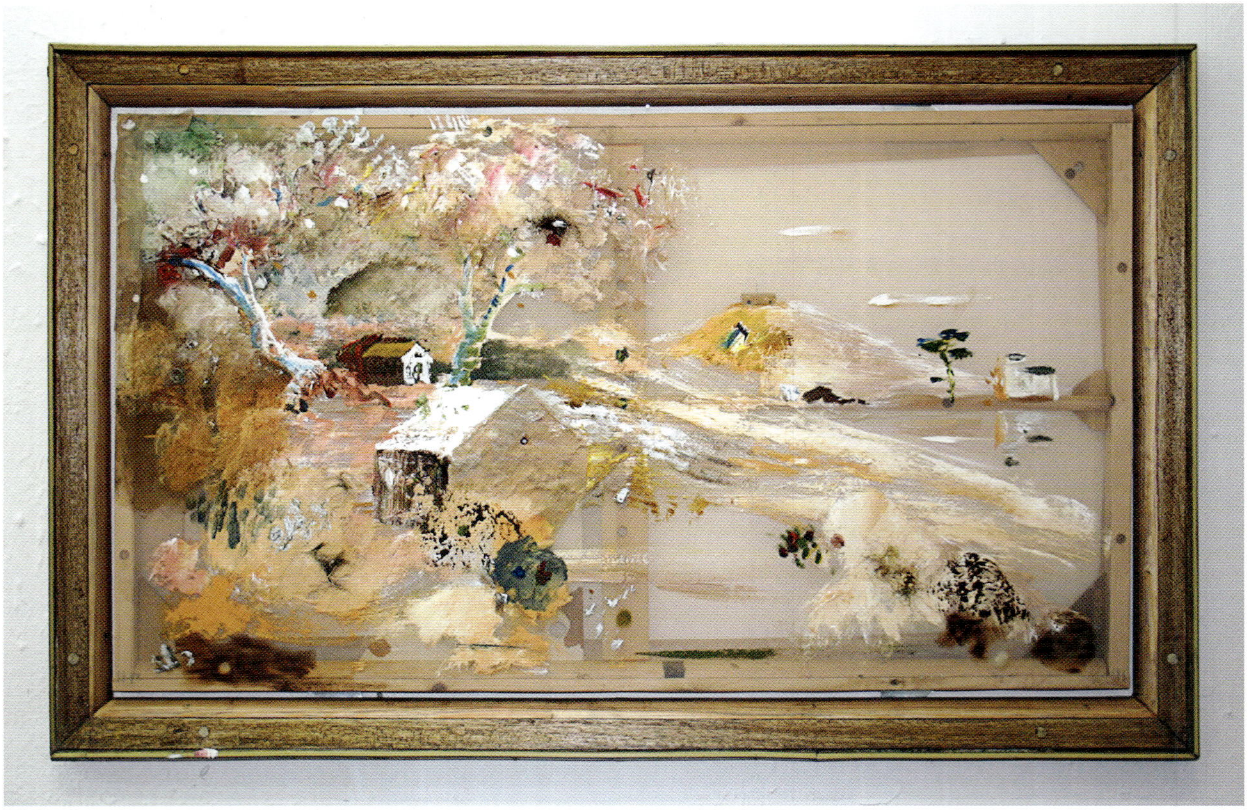
2

Merlin James

Shown by
Kerlin Gallery A19
Sikkema Jenkins & Co. C45

Biography
Born 1960
Lives in Glasgow

Wales-born painter James represented his home country at the Venice Biennale in 2007. His paintings have been exhibited internationally since the early 1990s. In early 2012 a self-titled solo show took place at Douglas Hyde Gallery, Dublin, and included works spanning his career. Other recent solo exhibitions took place at Sikkema Jenkins & Co., New York (2011) and "Frame Paintings" (2010) at Mummery & Schnelle, London. In 2010 he was included in the group show "Self-Consciousness" at Veneklasen Werner, Berlin.

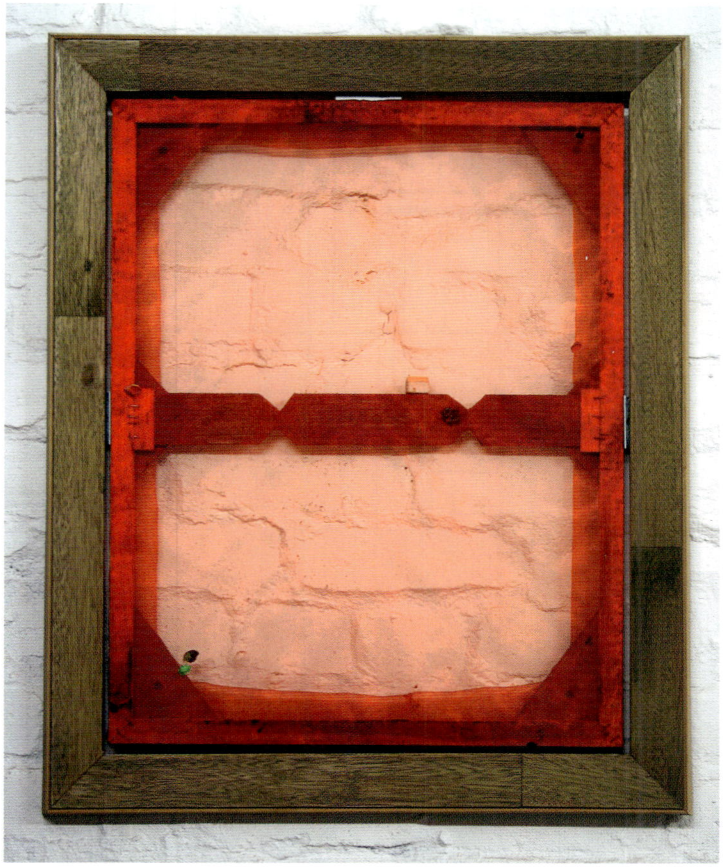

3

1
Crossed
2010
Acrylic on canvas
26½ × 28"
(67.5 × 71 cm)
Courtesy of Kerlin Gallery

2
buildings, water
2011
Mixed media
25½ × 39⅜"
(65 × 100 cm)
Courtesy of Kerlin Gallery

3
Little White House
2010
Mixed media
26½ × 28"
(67.5 × 71 cm)
Courtesy of Kerlin Gallery

Merlin James' paintings reference the history of the medium but remain rooted in the present, investing in the endless possibilities of reinvention. His works, which often gestate over several years, explore architectural spaces and their representation on the flat surface of the painter's canvas. His landscapes divide the picture plane in swathes of flat tonal color—at times erasing the subject matter completely. In *Big Landscape Painting* (2011) several daubs on brown gauze hint at a forest or clouds; the rest can only be imagined. Meanwhile James' recent series of paintings on translucent polyester, including *Crossed* (2011) and *Brownsville* (2011), are composed of small modest patches of acrylic—the work's most prominent feature in each case being the frame that supports it. CFW

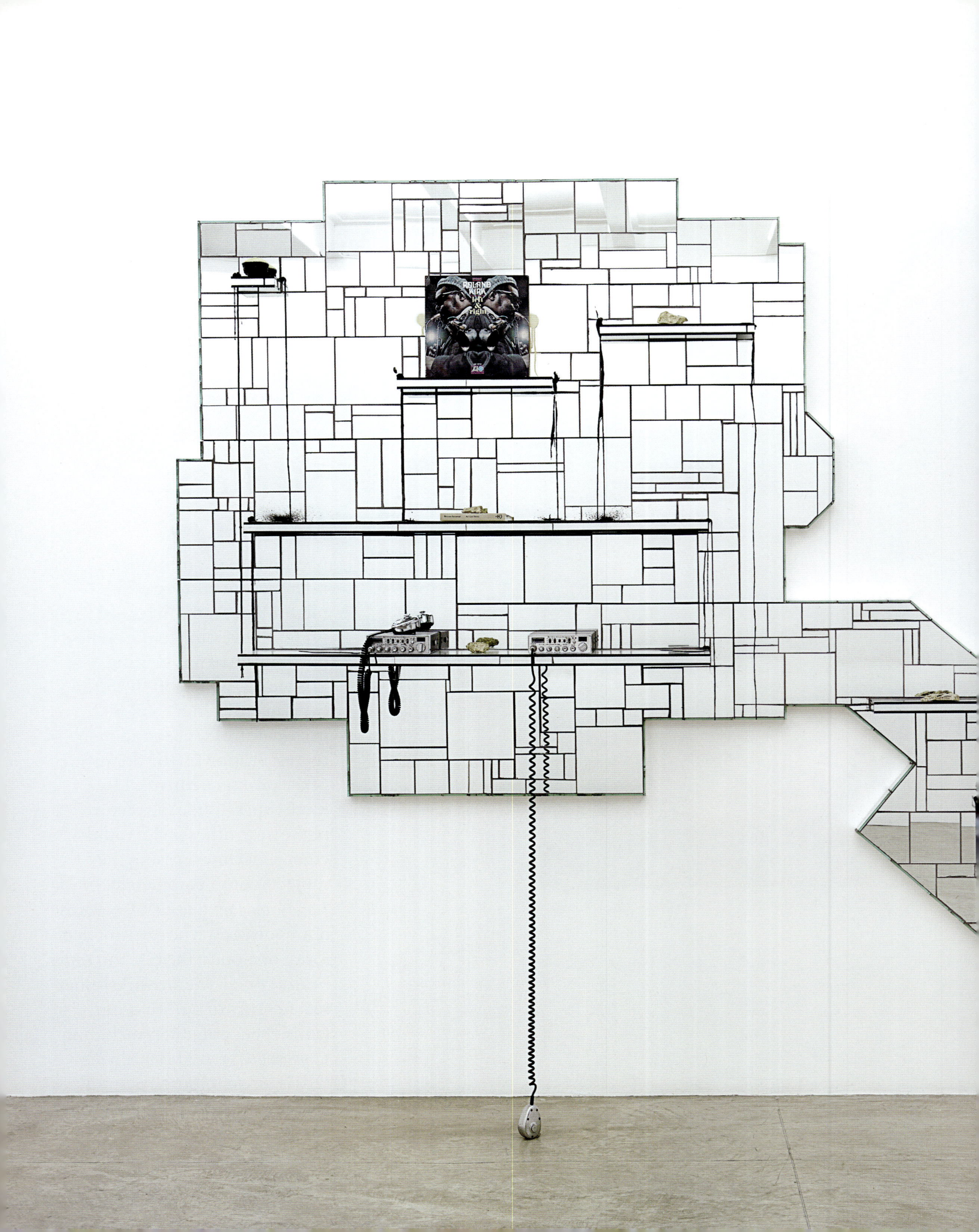
ROLAND
KIRK
left
&
right

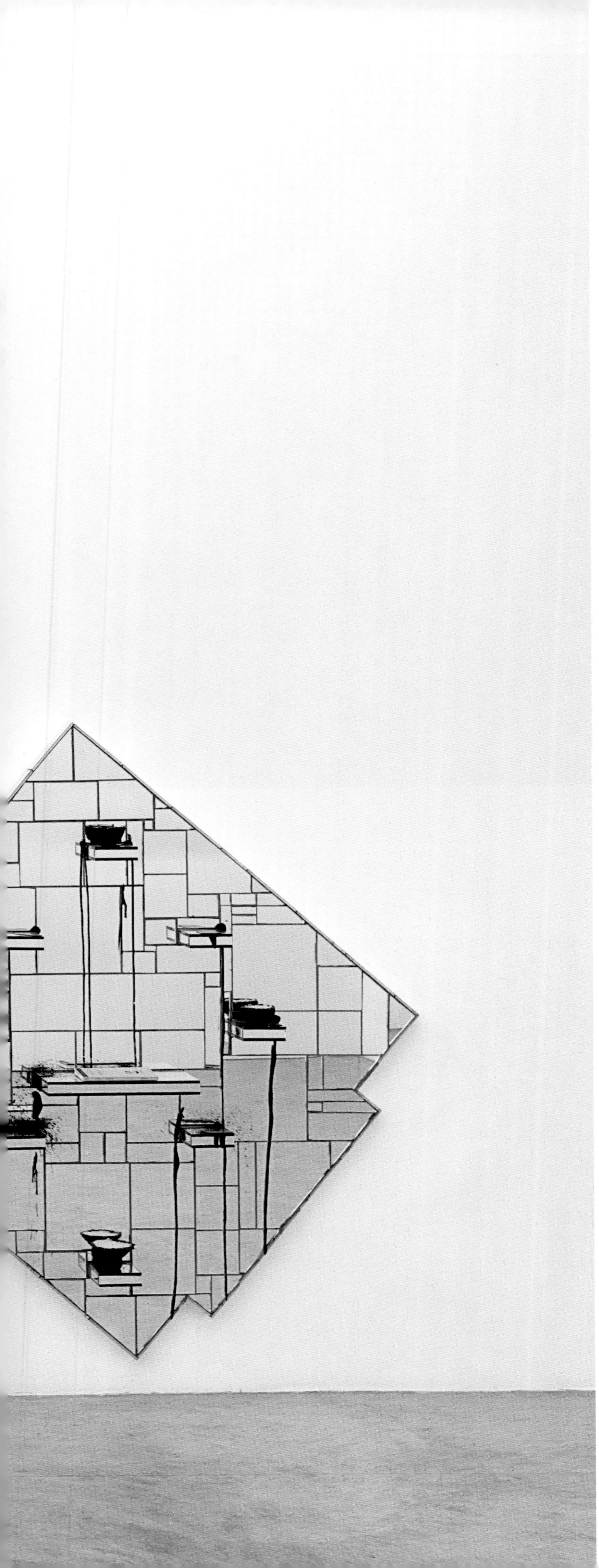

Shown by
Galerie Guido W. Baudach C30
Massimo De Carlo B1
Hauser & Wirth B6
David Kordansky Gallery C1

Biography
Born 1977
Lives in New York

In the last ten years, American artist Johnson has exhibited extensively in the United States and Europe. His sculptures and paintings were the subject of his recent solo show "Rumble" (2010) at Hauser & Wirth, New York. Other solo shows include "Message to Our Folks" (2012) at the MCA Museum of Contemporary Art, Chicago; "25 days after October" (2011) at Carlson/ Massimo De Carlo, London; and "Smoke and Mirrors" (2009) at SculptureCenter, Long Island City. His work was included in "ILLUMInations" at the 54th Venice Biennale.

Left + Right
2010
Mixed media
106¼ × 150 × 15"
(270 × 358 × 38 cm)
Courtesy of Massimo De Carlo

Rashid Johnson

Rashid Johnson's heady works look back, to the history of the African-American intelligentsia and to the 1960s-era political moment that resulted, but also far, far forward—to some speculative cultural space that has not yet arrived. See his powerful black bookcase-like armatures and wall pieces—invoking shades of both Suprematism and Louise Nevelson—made from black soap, tar, and shea butter, and set with records by Al Green, busts, and gold vases (*I Who Have Nothing*, 2008), or the altar-like *Souls of Black Folk* (2010), in which a portrait of Miles Davis sits, like a high priestess, above stacked volumes of W.E.B. Du Bois' eponymous treatise. Formally gorgeous and politically potent, Johnson's works function as time capsules of both the relic-strewn past and the incandescent future. QL

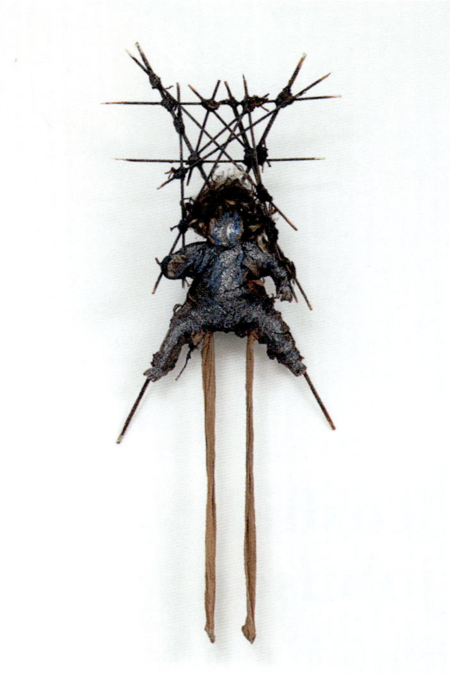

1

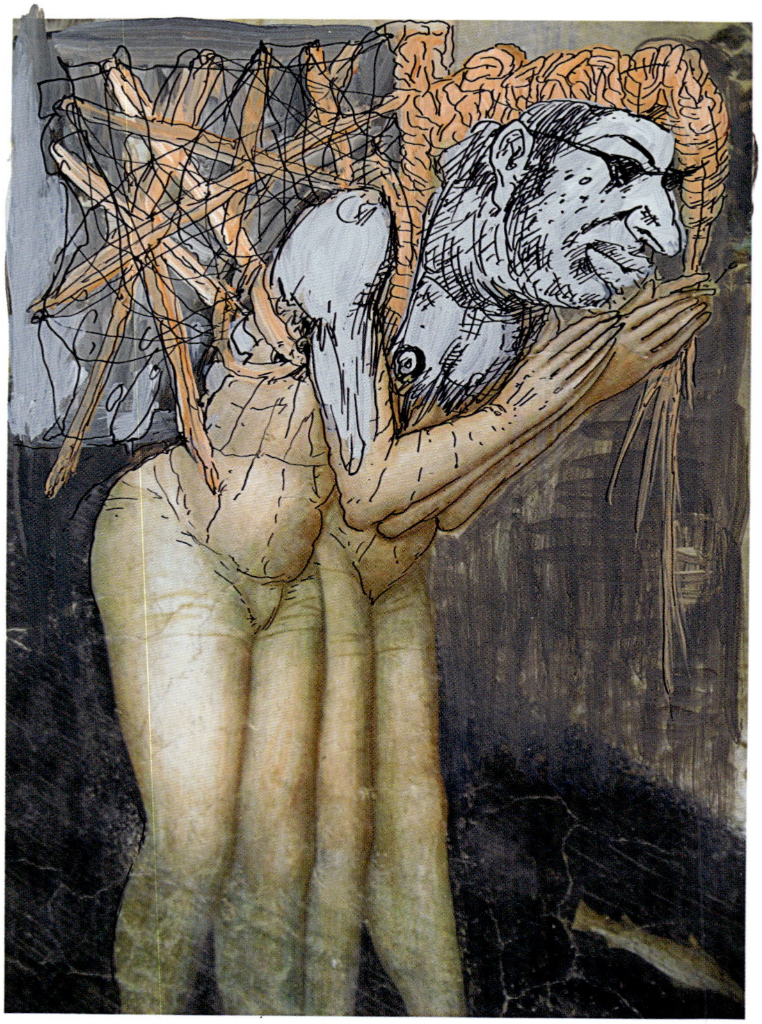

2

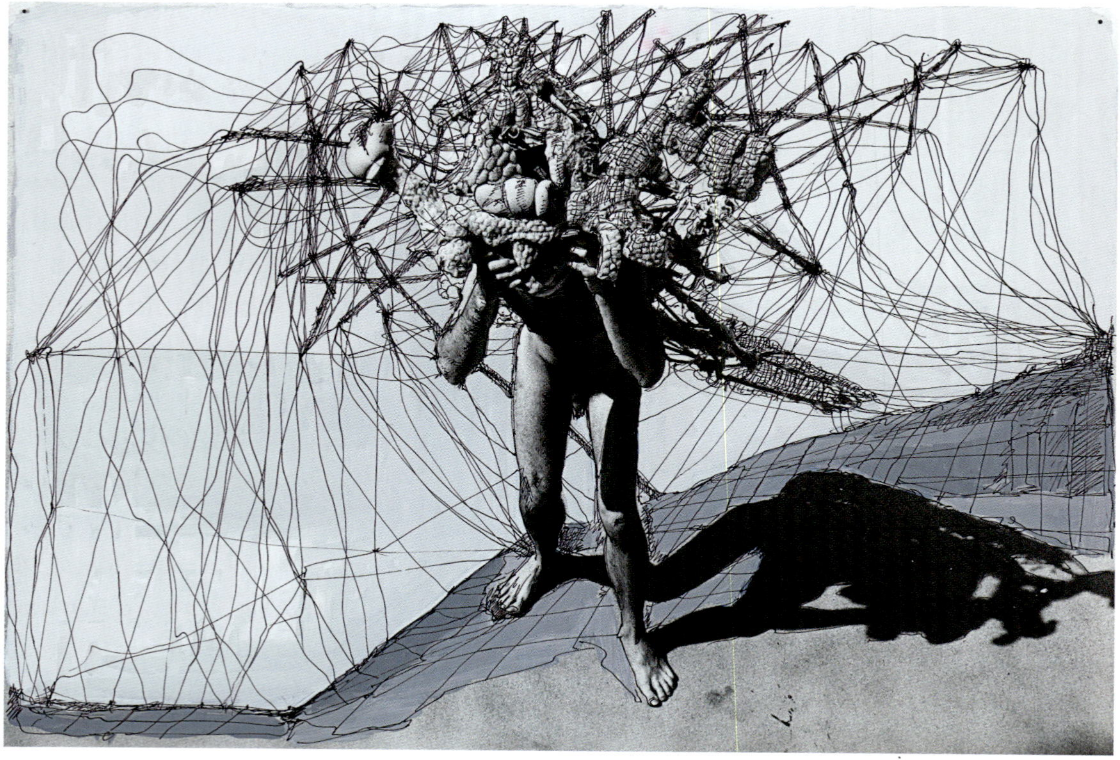

3

Shown by
Zeno X Gallery B3

Biography
Born 1944
Lives in New York

American performance artist Jones has been connecting with society since the 1960s. Practicing in Los Angeles before moving to New York in the 1980s, he has performed and exhibited internationally for five decades. His solo exhibition "Semper Fi" at Zeno X Gallery, Antwerp, took place in fall 2011. Other recent solo shows include "Venice High" (2010) at Pierogi, Brooklyn; and "Kim Jones: A Retrospective" at Henry Art Gallery, Seattle (2008), and Luckman Fine Arts Complex, Los Angeles (2007).

1
Doll - blue face
2003-11
Mixed media
47 × 20 × 9⅞"
(119.5 × 51 × 25 cm)
Courtesy of
Zeno X Gallery

2
Untitled
2010
Acrylic and ink
on photograph
10 × 8"
(25 × 20 cm)
Courtesy of
Zeno X Gallery

3
Untitled
1974
Acrylic and ink
on photograph
16 × 24"
(40.5 × 61 cm)
Courtesy of
Zeno X Gallery

4
Untitled
1974
Acrylic and ink
on photograph
16⅛ × 24"
(41 × 61 cm)
Courtesy of
Zeno X Gallery

Kim Jones

In his early performances in the 1970s, the artist Kim Jones inhabited Los Angeles city streets, subways, and gallery spaces in the guise of "Mudman"—an itinerant earth-encrusted, stick-plumed, stocking-masked quasi-shaman whose primordial appearance and unsettling, somewhat beleaguered, manner was at odds with the frictionless fantasies of modern city life. Since then, his often untitled sculptures, drawings and photographic works, have consistently revisited themes of degradation, contagion, and decay, charting the topology of the battlefield (Jones is a Vietnam veteran) and of the inner life. The recycling of motifs and materials is a key component of his work and points to a determination to transform the dull weight of traumatic experience into something that may take flight. TM

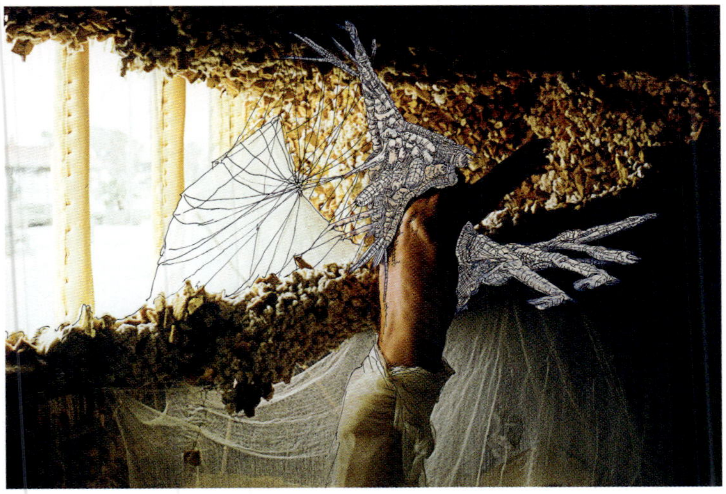

4

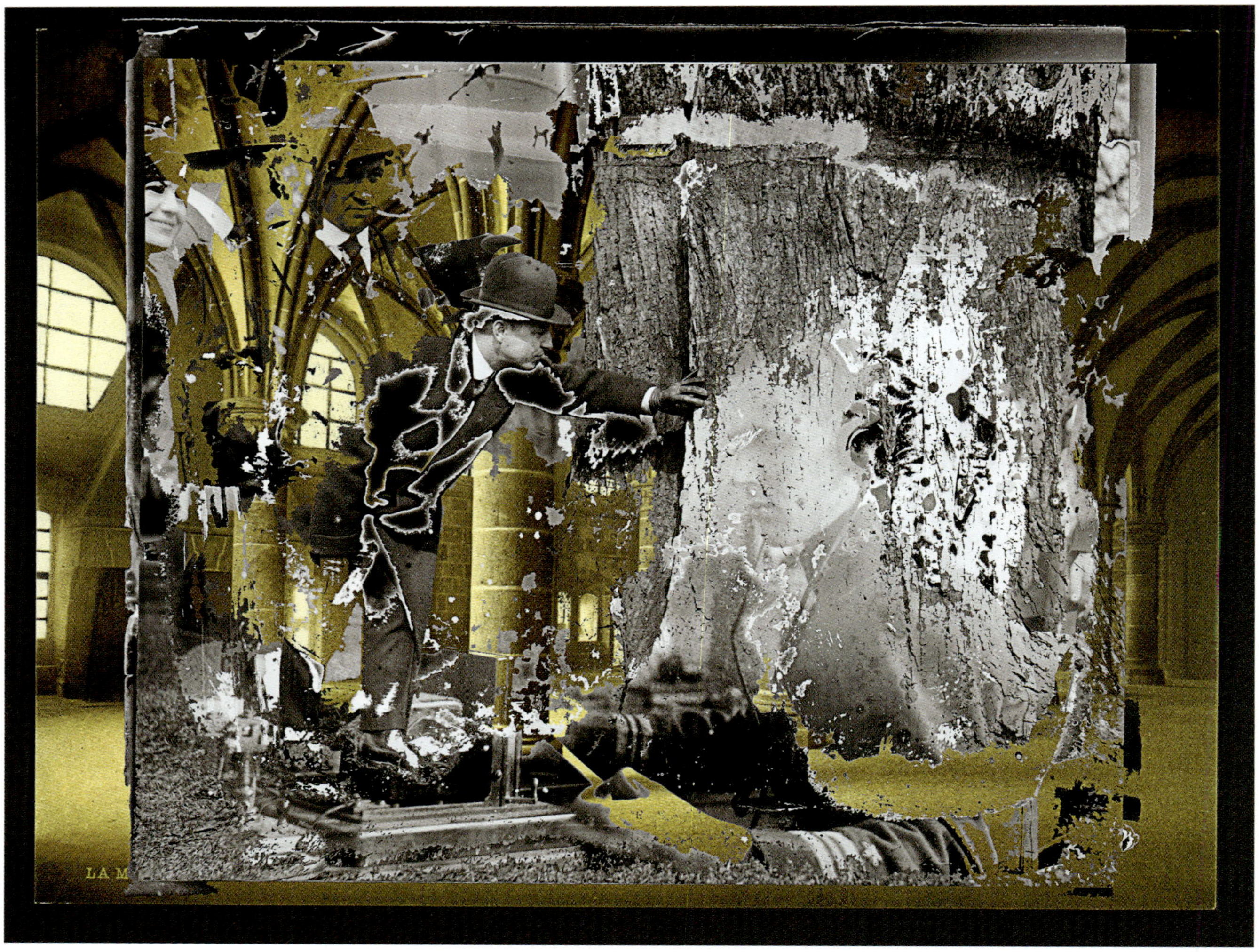

1

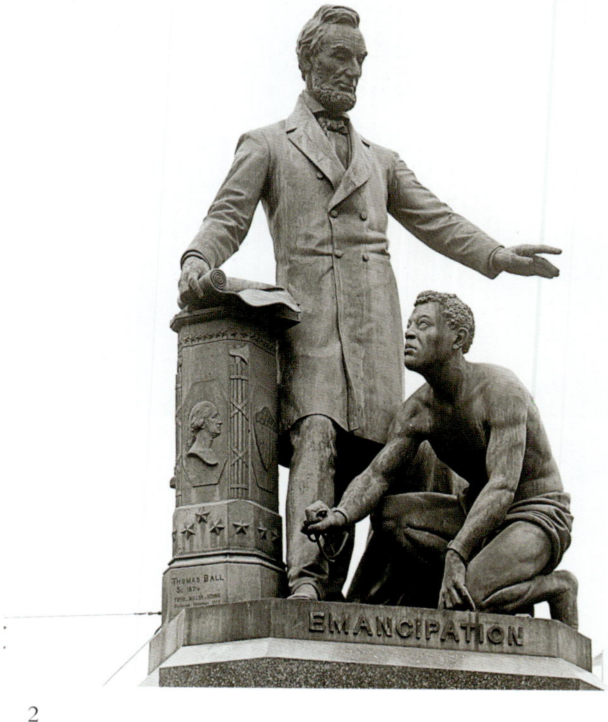

2

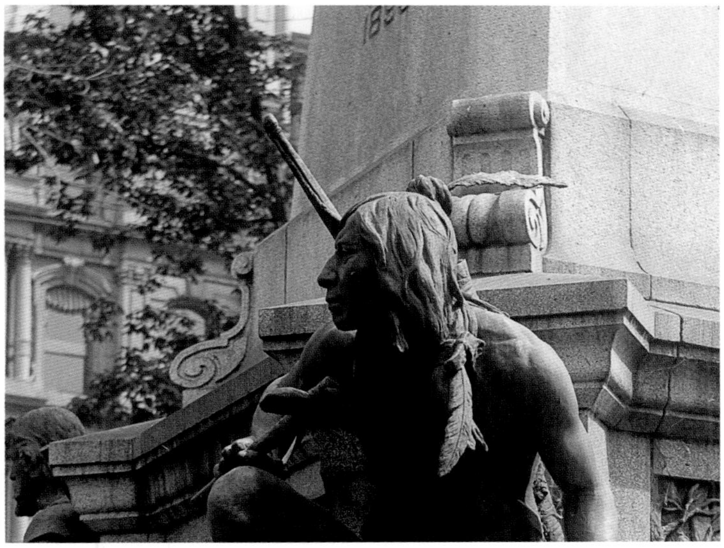

3

Shown by
Galleria Raffaella Cortese C17
David Kordansky Gallery C1

Biography
Born 1962
Lives in Los Angeles

American artist Jones's videos and documentaries have come to prominence in recent years. In 2011 his videos, photographs, and collages were the subject of solo shows at The Modern Institute, Glasgow, and David Kordansky Gallery, Los Angeles. Other recent solo shows include "Alternative Version" at Galleria Raffaella Cortese, (2010), Milan, and "Killed" (2009) at the Wexner Center, Columbus. His book on filmmaker Fred Halsted "Halsted Plays Himself" was published by Semiotext(e) in 2011.

1
National Photo #3
2010
Archival pigment print
24⅜ × 31½"
(62 × 80 cm)
Courtesy of Galleria Raffaella Cortese

2, 3
Monument
2011
Sequence of digital files, black and white, silent
7 min. 52 sec.
Courtesy of Galleria Raffaella Cortese

William E. Jones

The documentaries and short films of Los Angeles-based artist and filmmaker William E. Jones draw on the history and aesthetic of independent filmmaking to analyze the social and political economies of desire, from earlier works, such as *The Fall of Communism as Seen in Gay Pornography* (1998), in which he re-edited clips from porn films rented from his local video store, to his documentary on the Southern Californian subculture of Latino Morrissey fans *Is It Really So Strange?* (2004). More recent works on paper, including a series of photographs taken in his home town of Canton, Ohio, and the short film *Industry* (2011), mirror the decline of industry through the degradation of carefully manipulated archival imagery. PT

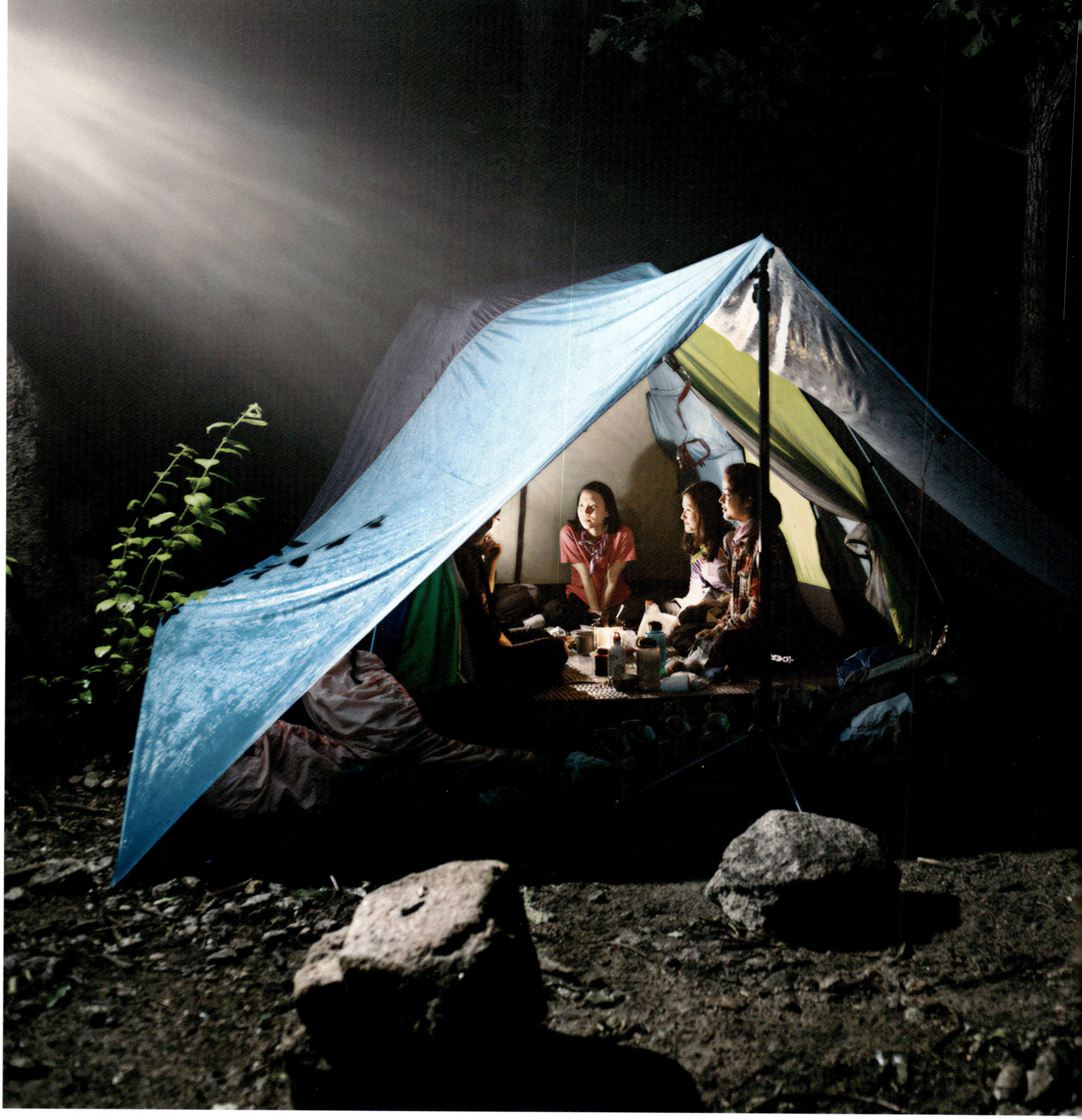

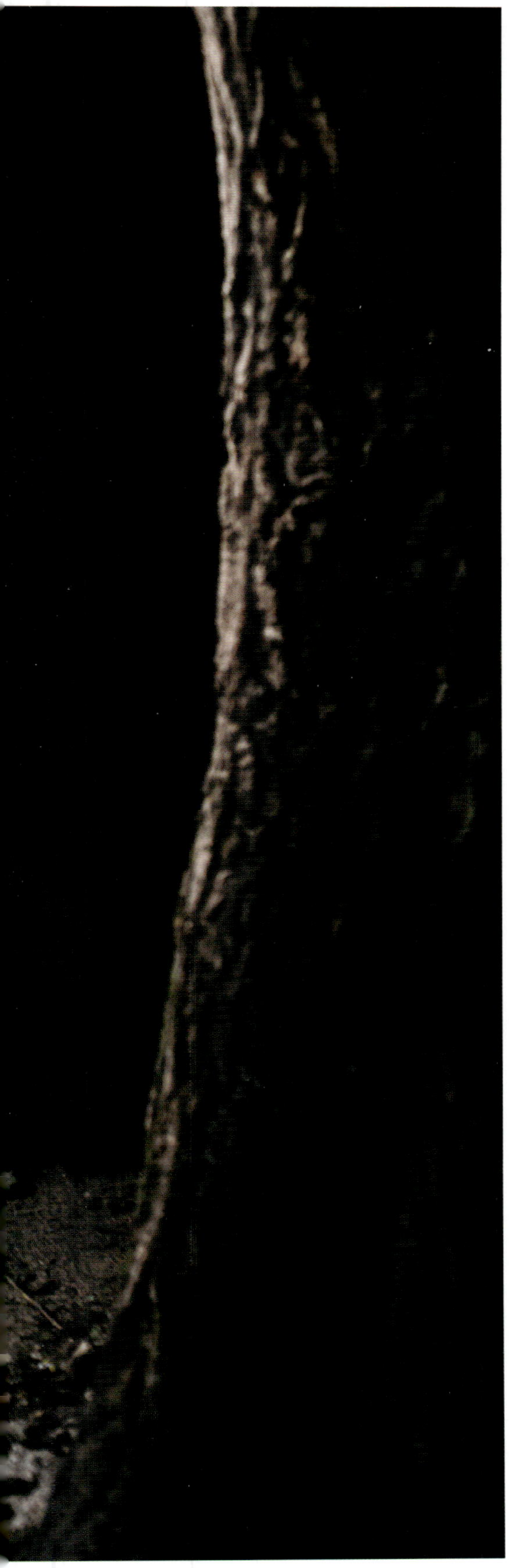

Shown by
Tina Kim Gallery B36
Kukje Gallery B36

Biography
Born 1969
Lives in Seoul

Korean photographer Jung has exhibited extensively in Europe and Asia in the last decade. In 2011 he had a solo exhibition at SCAD, Hong Kong, and in 2010 the solo exhibitions "Innerscape" at Galerie Emmanuel Perrotin, Paris; "Cinemagician" at Galerie Gebr. Lehmann, Berlin; and "An Ordinary Paradise" at Espacio Third Hermes, Singapore. His work is part of numerous public collections, including the Museum of Modern Art, New York, and the Essl Museum, Vienna.

Adolescence #20
2010
Inkjet print on custom paper
42½ × 32¾"
(108 × 83cm)
Courtesy of Tina Kim Gallery

Yeondoo Jung

Photographer and filmmaker Yeondoo Jung focuses on the cracks between illusion and reality. His intricate studio sets give away their own game, the sun in a landscape revealing itself as a lamp or the moon over the sea as a disco ball. Past photographic projects staged realizations of participants' fantasies, or used children's drawings as the basis for studio sets in the series "Wonderland" (2004). His *CineMagician* (2009) performance cast Korea's most popular magician as the artist himself, directing stage hands to construct live replicas of the landscapes he's drawn. Jung is an illusionist who delights in revealing that, yes, he does have something up his sleeve: another sleeve, and within that another, *ad infinitum*. CFW

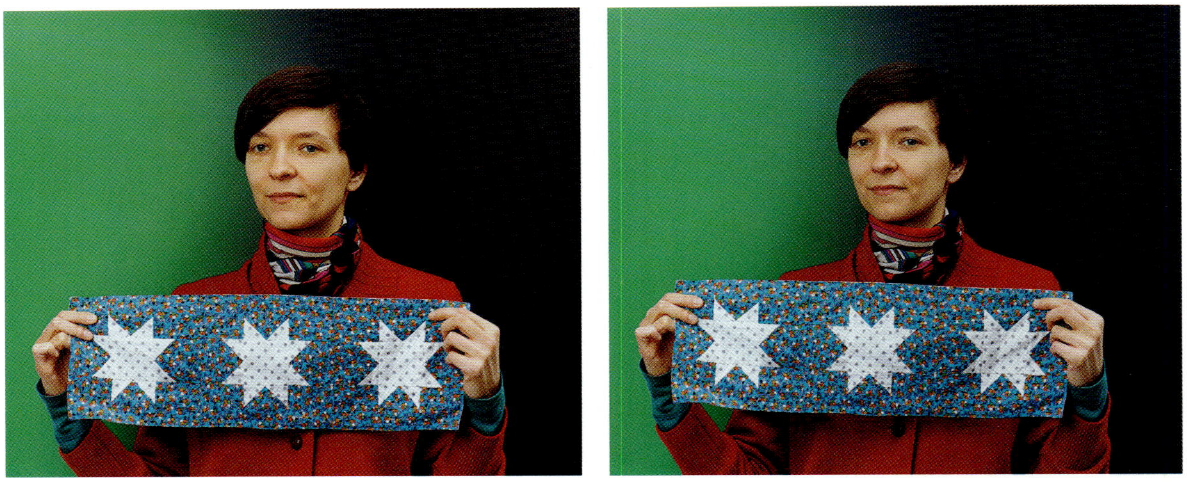

1

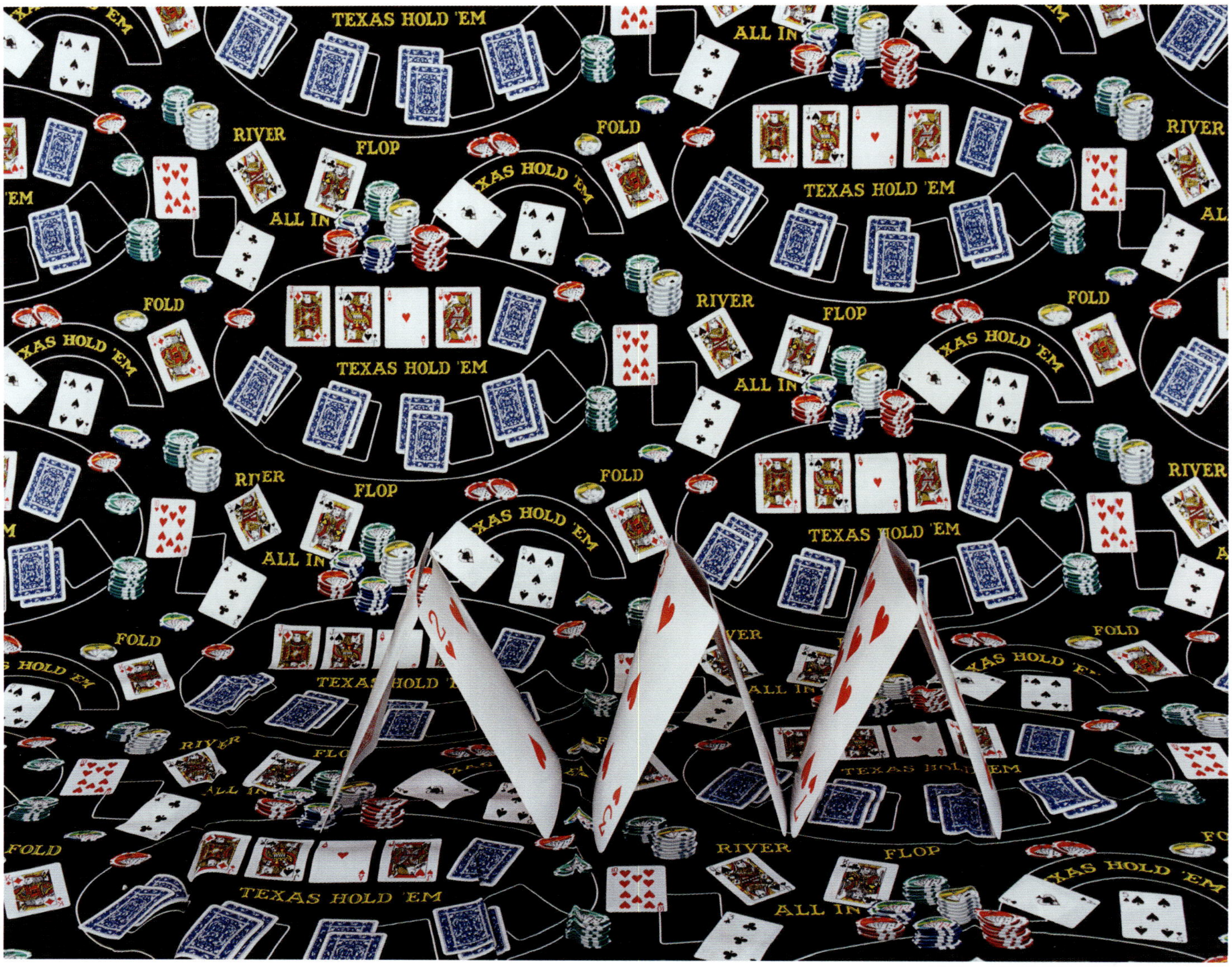

2

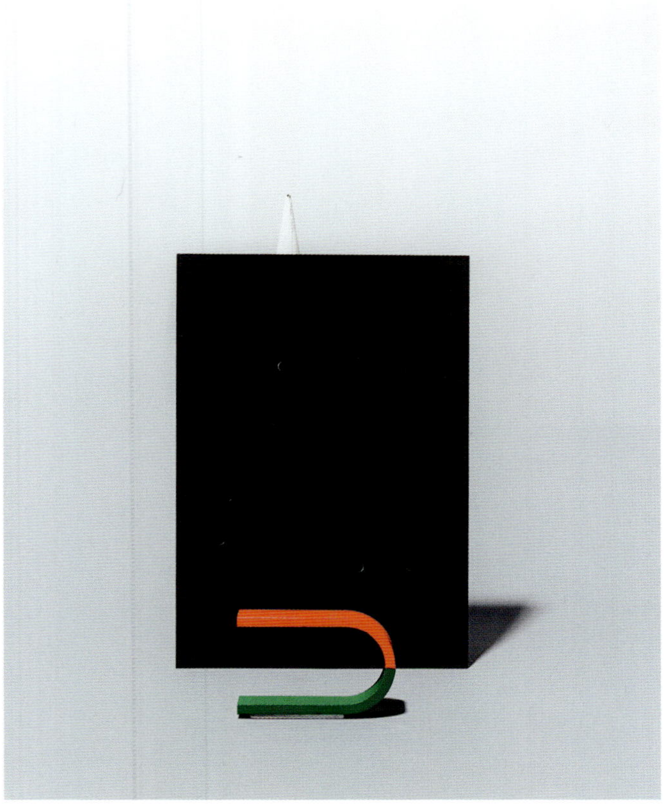

3

Shown by
Marc Foxx C32
Herald St A30
Taka Ishii Gallery B13
Johann König A14
Andrew Kreps Gallery B14
Giò Marconi A3

Biography
Born 1975
Lives in Berlin

German photographer Kelm has shown here unique works in Europe and the United States to audiences that extend beyond the art world. Recent solo shows include "Cards and Plates" (2010) at Gio Marconi, Milan, and "Today" (2010) at Andrew Kreps Gallery, New York; as well as shows at Herald St, London (2009); Kunsthalle Zürich, Zurich (2009); and KW Institute for Contemporary Art, Berlin (2009). Kelm participated in the group show "ILLUMInations" (2011) at the 54th Venice Biennale.

1
Untitled (Cards)
2010
C-type print
26⅝ × 32¾"
(67.5 × 83 cm)
Edition of 5 + 2 AP
Courtesy of Andrew Kreps Gallery

2
Anna # 2
2011
C-type print, framed, two parts
16½ × 20½"
(41.9 × 52.1 cm)
23¾ × 27½"
(60.3 × 69.9 cm)
(framed)
Edition of 5 + 2 AP
Courtesy of Andrew Kreps Gallery

3
Horseshoe Magnet
2011
C-type print
19⅝ × 17⅜"
(50 × 44 cm)
Edition of 5 + 2 AP 2
Courtesy of Andrew Kreps Gallery

Annette Kelm

Annette Kelm draws from the language of studio photography, using its conventions to create precise, claustrophobic, images of artifice. She creates meaning through arrangement and placement, through objects that are culturally significant and emerge from specific geo-political contexts. In *Untitled (Tribal)* (2010), Kelm arranges a ceramic vase, a single-stemmed flower, a United States Postal Service box, and a DayGlo tribal backdrop in a classical composition. Elsewhere, as in *Frying Pan* (2007), she creates associations that deliberately misfire, introducing objects without universal significance and narratives that are highly subjective, discreet cosmologies of her own fashioning. KK

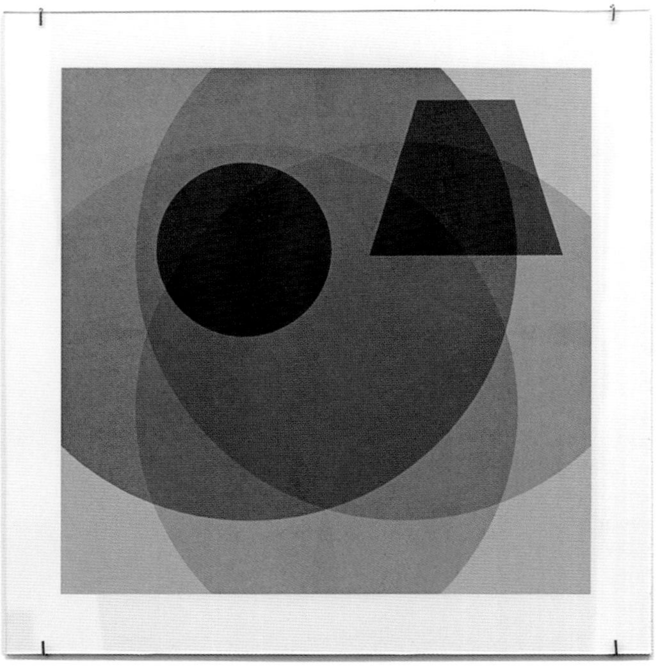
1

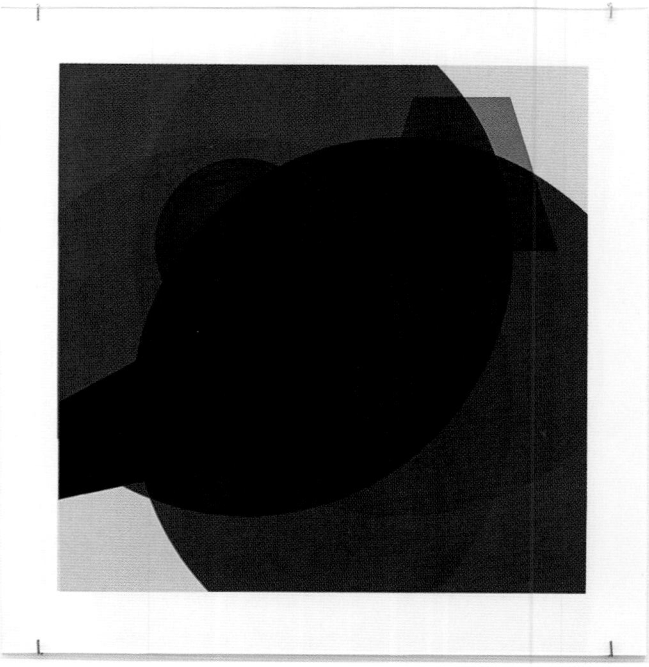
2

3

Janice Kerbel

Things spoken of but not seen in Janice Kerbel's work: an imaginary baseball game, heard only in commentary (*Ballgame*, 2009); a meticulously devised but never enacted robbery (*Bank Job*, 1999); flowers, plants, and trees, outlined starkly on architect's plans (*Home Climate Gardens*, 2004); outlandish female circus performers, advertised on large posters in excitable fonts (*Remarkable*, 2007). Kerbel forces her viewers to reflect on the linguistic and diagrammatic systems that exist to frame her sometimes fantastical, sometimes quite banal, subjects. Her recent play *Kill the Workers!* (2011) was performed entirely by synchronized stage lighting. The lights themselves were assigned roles, silently unfolding their coded narrative in colored patterns that resembled Constructivist paintings on the gallery floor. JG

Shown by
greengrassi A11
Galerie Karin Guenther F20
Catriona Jeffries A17

Biography
Born 1969
Lives in London

Canada-born Kerbel's *Kill the Workers!* (2011) was recently the subject of solo exhibitions at Chisenhale, London (2011); Badischer Kunstverein, Karlsrue (2011); and Walter Phillips Gallery, Banff (2012). In 2012 she will have a solo exhibition at Presentation House Gallery, Vancouver. Her concept-driven work has featured in Tate Britain's "Art Now" series (2010), and "Ballgame (Innings 1–3)" at greengrassi, London (2009).

1, 2, 3
Cue: Selections from Act 1
2011
Silkscreen on paper
22 × 22"
(56 × 56 cm)
Courtesy of
Catriona Jeffries

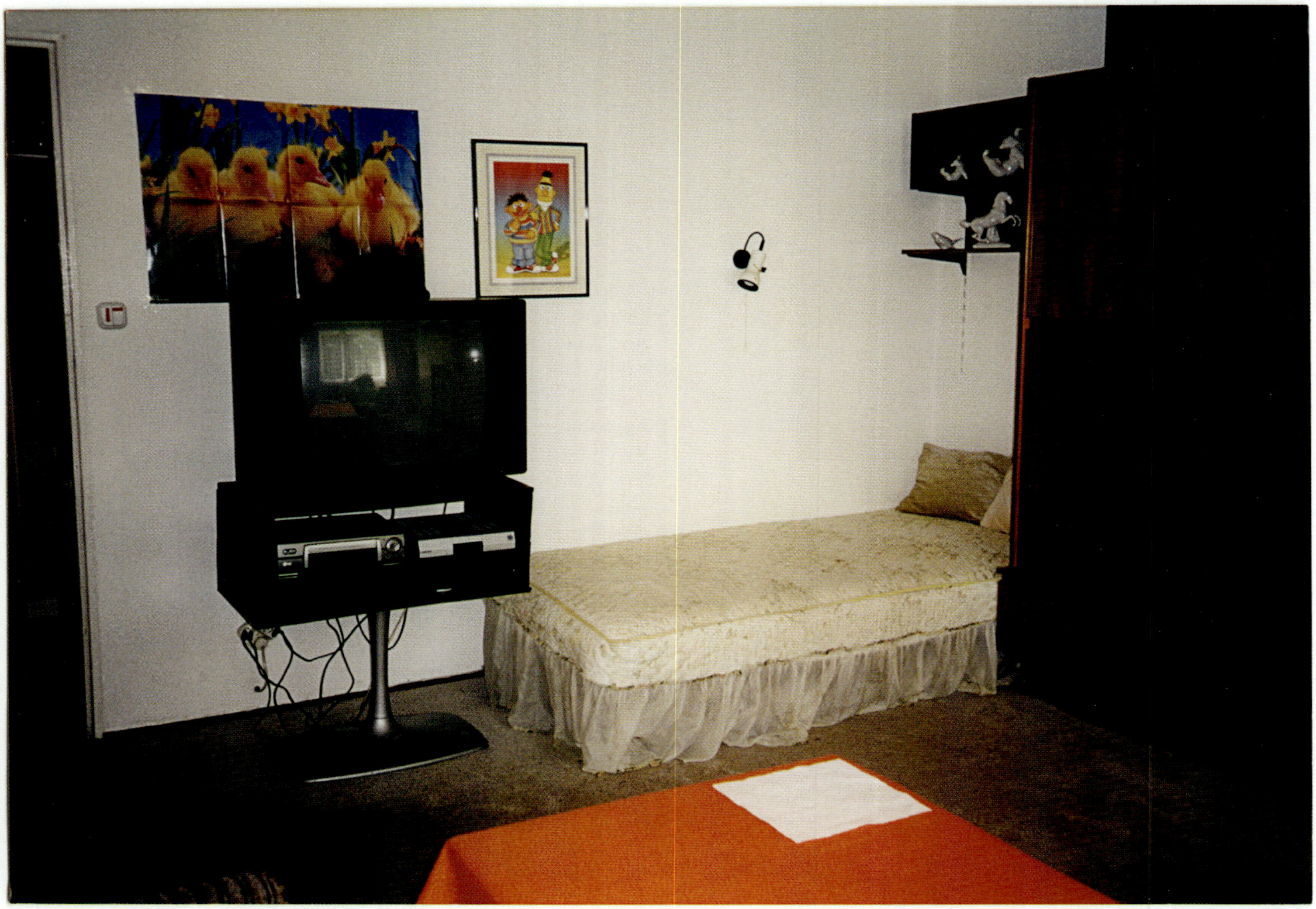

Yuki Kimura

Shown by
Taka Ishii Gallery B13

Biography
Born 1971
Lives in Kyoto

Japan-born Kimura's photographs have been the subject of solo exhibitions at the Contemporary Art Museum St. Louis (2011); "Untitled" (2010) at the Izu Photo Museum, Japan; and "Year 1940 was a leap year starting on Monday" (2009) at Taka Ishii Gallery, Tokyo. Her work is included in significant Japanese collections, including The National Museum of Art, Osaka, and the Museum of Contemporary Art Tokyo.

untitled
2011
Lambda print
41¾ × 61"
(106 × 155 cm)
Courtesy of Taka Ishii Gallery

Yuki Kimura bases her photo collages and installations on various personal archives. Affective image groupings are drawn together across time and space, less by the artist's hand than by the gravitational pull of a shared sensibility. In *7 24 & 138-11* (2010), a sepia-toned scene of travelers boarding a plane is eerily mirrored in a photograph from a more distant era. Such temporal displacements are extended into the present tense through transparent acrylic "shadows" hovering beneath photographs, or stones and plants pressing close to their surfaces, creating an illusionary spatial continuity. *Year 1940 was a leap year starting on Monday* (2009) thematizes the notion of "skipped time" that Kimura herself cultivates—as she puts it, constant déjà vu. SNS

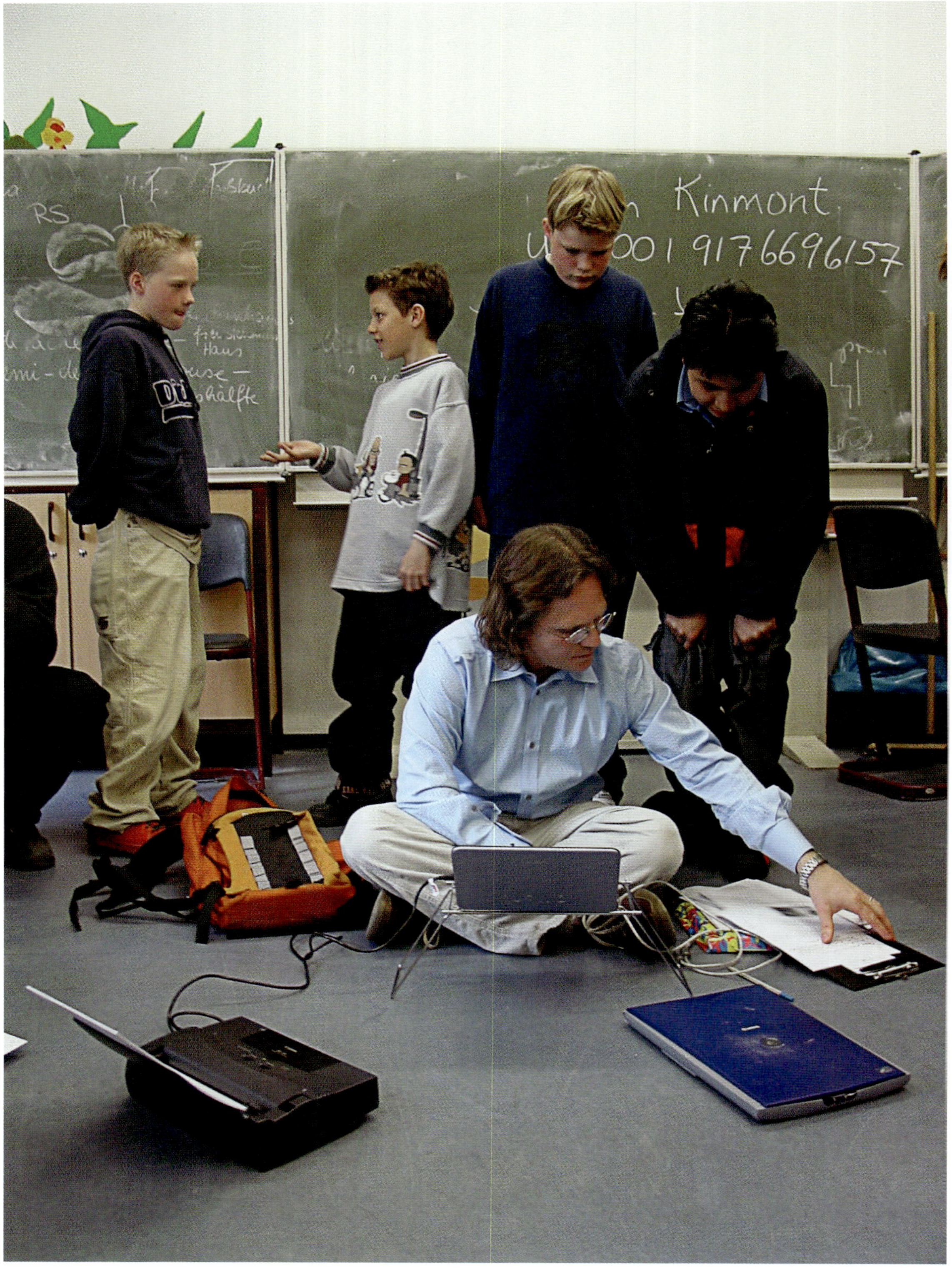
Kinmont
001 917 6696157

Ben Kinmont

Shown by
Air de Paris C11

Biography
Born 1963
Lives in Sebastopol

Kinmont's "Prospectus" was held in early 2012 at Kunstverein, Amsterdam ("Prospectus Amsterdam"), and Kadist Art Foundation, Paris ("Prospectus Paris"). In 2011 the series was hosted at The Fales Library, New York University (in collaboration with Kunstverein NY), and in spring 2012, the show will take place at San Francisco Museum of Modern Art, and Kadist San Francisco.

Moveable type no Documenta (detail)
2002
Conversation and printing with Jutta Krug's class IIIb, Reformschule, Kassel, Germany, 11 April 2002
Dimensions variable
Courtesy of Air de Paris

Whether washing dishes in people's homes or stopping in the midst of running errands to ask strangers whether conversation can be sculpture, Ben Kinmont initiates interactions in which art works facilitate a vital exchange between artist and viewer. Art and life are intimately intertwined in the archive he maintains on his projects, where even money he made selling rare books to feed his family has been poignantly documented. In *For you for me for painting* (1993), he gave paintings to strangers and collectors in return for their signature. And in *Waffles for an Opening* (1991), Kinmont shared breakfast in his home with an array of strangers, then co-signed paper plates with the participants, practicing a radical openness and availability. KMJ

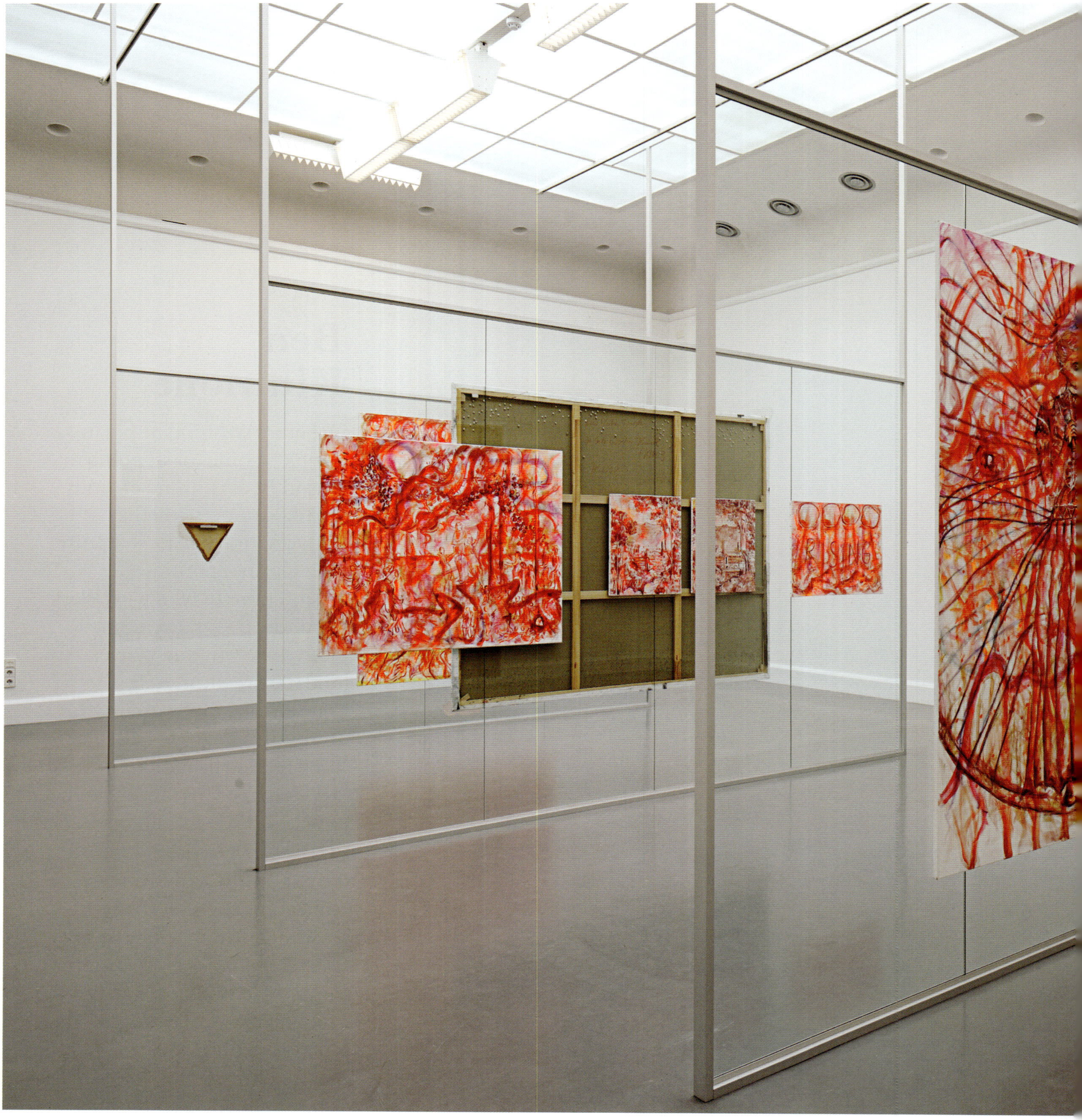
RISING

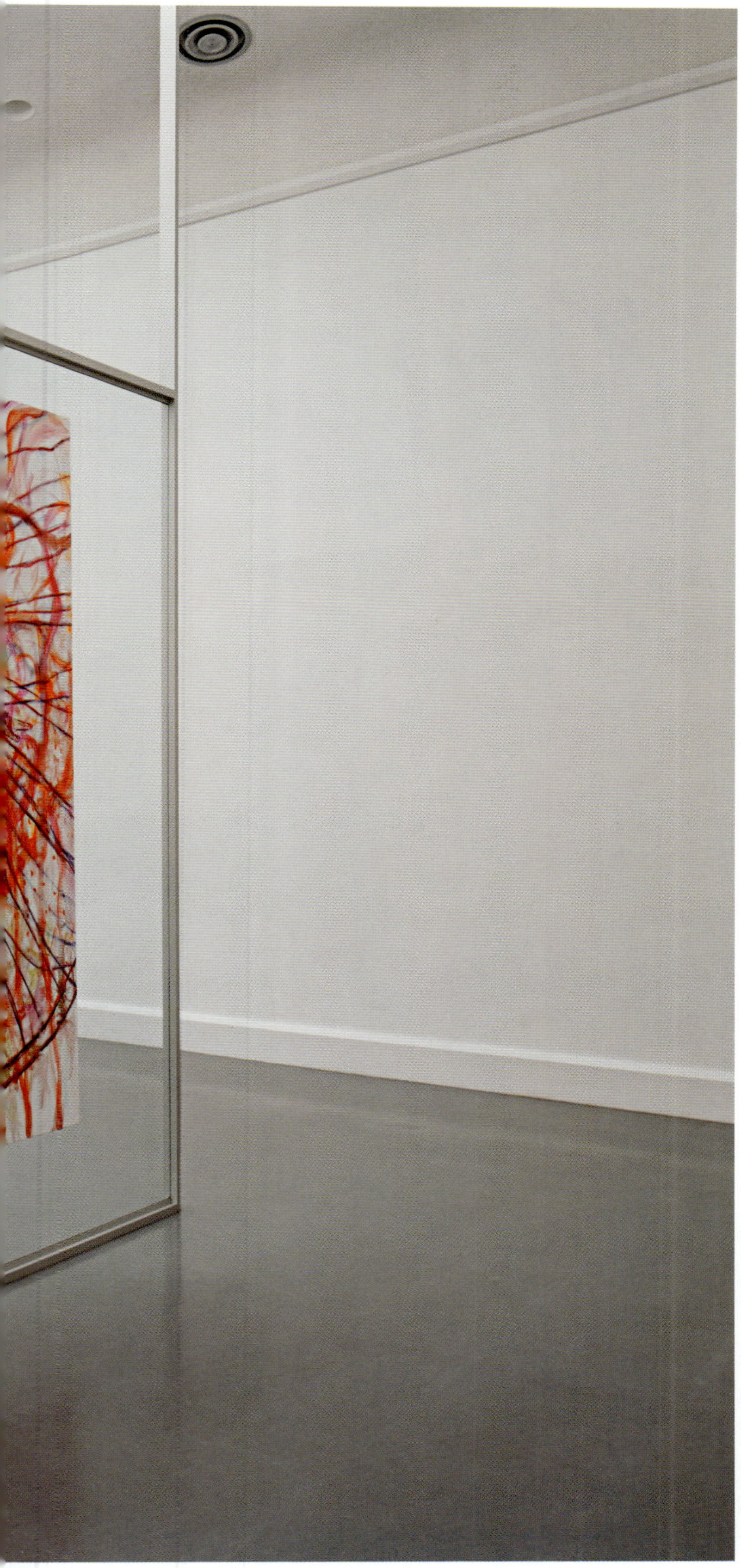

Shown by
Bortolami A9
Galerie Buchholz B35
Galerie Francesca Pia A15
Reena Spaulings Fine Art F17
Susanne Vielmetter Los Angeles Projects C21

Biography
Born 1958
Lives in New York and Berlin

Germany-born Koether's paintings and performances have been the subject of numerous group and solo shows in Europe and America. Most recently, the solo exhibition "The Thirst" (2011) took place at the Moderne Museet, Stockholm. In 2010 she had the solo show "Berliner Schlussel" at Galerie Buchholz, Berlin; and in 2009 participated in "Lux Interior" at Reena Spaulings Fine Art, New York, and "Trio" at Van Abbe Museum, Eindhoven. Her work is included in the Whitney Biennial 2012 and she will also have a solo show at Bortolami, New York, in spring 2012.

Installation view
2009–10
Painting, installation
Dimensions variable
Courtesy of Reena Spaulings Fine Art

Focus
Jutta Koether

Jutta Koether's paintings often exist within complex conceptual frameworks—displayed on or alongside physical interventions in the gallery. Her work embodies performative aspects of the painting process, and performance or live events are often encompassed in her exhibitions. The 2011 solo show "The Thirst" saw paintings suspended on wires and mounted on clear Plexiglas, dividing the halls of the Moderne Museet, Stockholm, into a network of intimate spaces. Washes of pale color regularly emblazon the surfaces of Koether's paintings—figures weave through layered gestural brushstrokes; the painting *Souveraine* (2008) sees an effigy-like gowned figure emanating from a burst of brushwork akin to that of the 1960s Abstract Expressionists. Koether invests weighty ideas in her paintings and installations that embed them in the social contexts they depend upon. SC

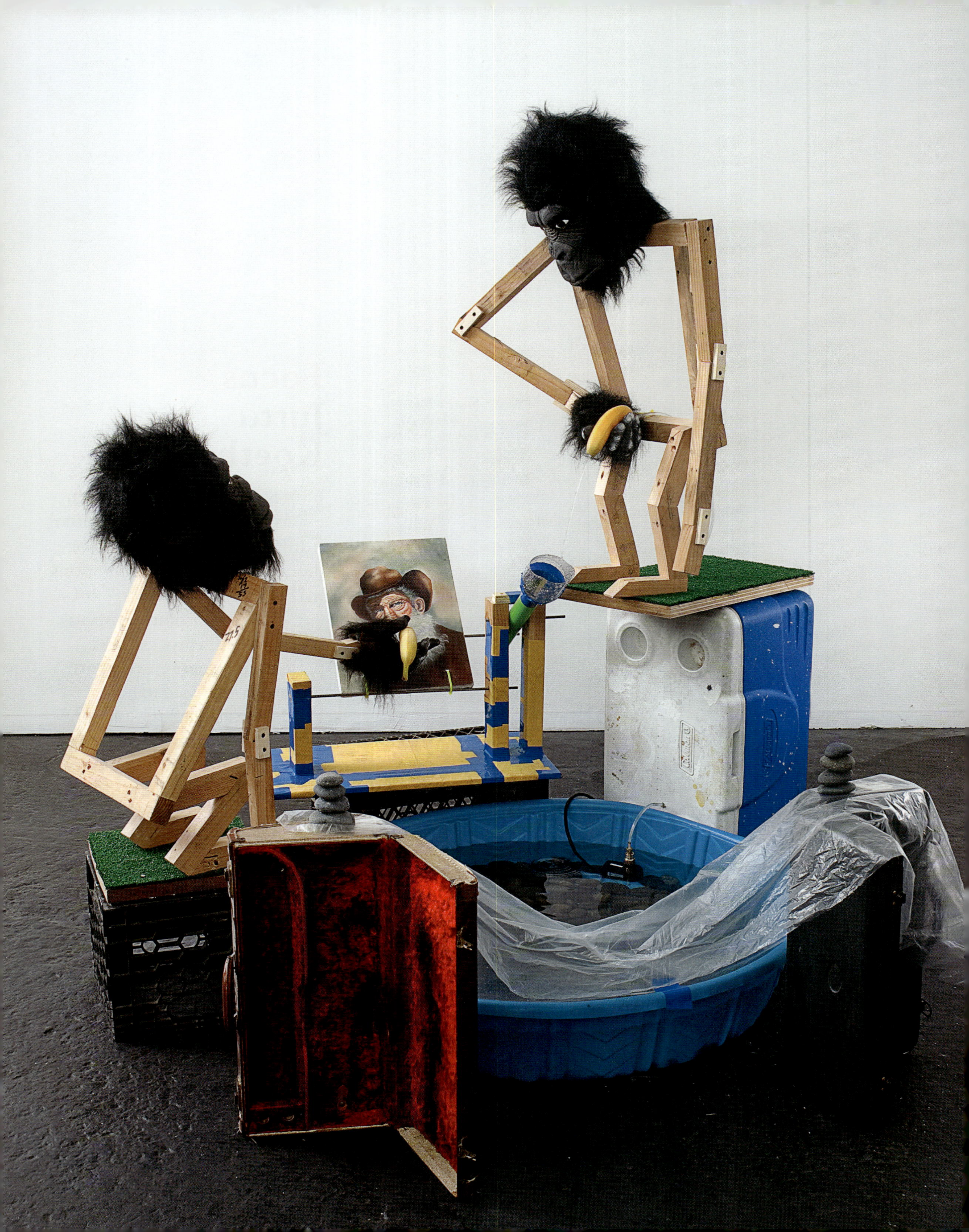

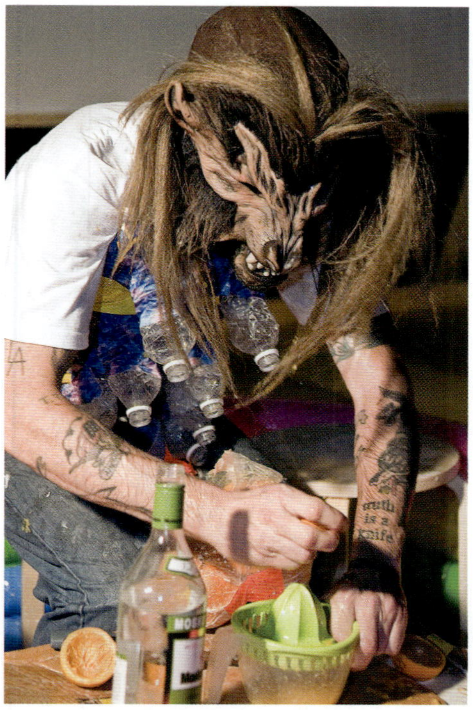

2

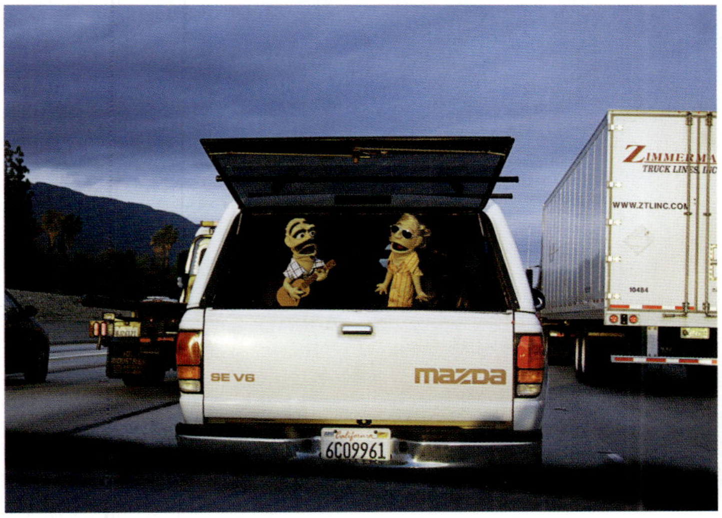

3

Shown by
François Ghebaly
Gallery F32

Biography
Born 1972
Lives in Los Angeles

American interdisciplinary artist Kyack received an MFA from the University of Southern California, Los Angeles, in 2008, and a BFA from Rhode Island School of Design in 1995. In 2011 he had the solo shows "Escape to Shit Mountain" at François Ghebaly Gallery, Los Angeles, and "River/Stream/In-Between" at Kate Werble Gallery, New York. The solo project "Superclogger" (2010) took place in collaboration with Hammer Museum, Los Angeles, and LA><ART, Los Angeles. In 2012 he will have a solo show at Brand New Gallery, Milan

1
Incident at Stoney Lake
2011
Mixed media
76 × 76 × 68⅞"
(193 × 193 × 175 cm)
Courtesy of François Ghebaly Gallery

2
Growing Pains Leave Stains
2011
Performance
Dimensions variable
Courtesy of François Ghebaly Gallery

3
Superclogger
2010
Photo of the performance in Los Angeles traffic
Dimensions variable
Courtesy of François Ghebaly Gallery

Focus
Joel Kyack

Wielding materials ranging from gorilla masks to Astroturf, Joel Kyack explores a goofy, DIY existentialism, and an anarchic, insecure, nature-obsessed masculinity. His deadpan works include: *Dam* (2006), a futile attempt to stop a rushing creek with a piece of plywood; *5'56"* (2011), a cluster of makeshift plastic-bottle hourglasses containing Los Angeles beach sand; and *Pine Woods Municipal Band Tryouts* (2011), a diptych in which a jutting tree stump and the denim-clad butt of a man planting a sapling play a trumpet duet. *Superclogger* (2010), an itinerant performance Kyack presented in a Mazda truck with Michael Hayden, featuring puppet plays with sound sent over an FM radio transmitter, prodded LA commuters stuck in smoggy traffic into meditating on chaos and failure. KK

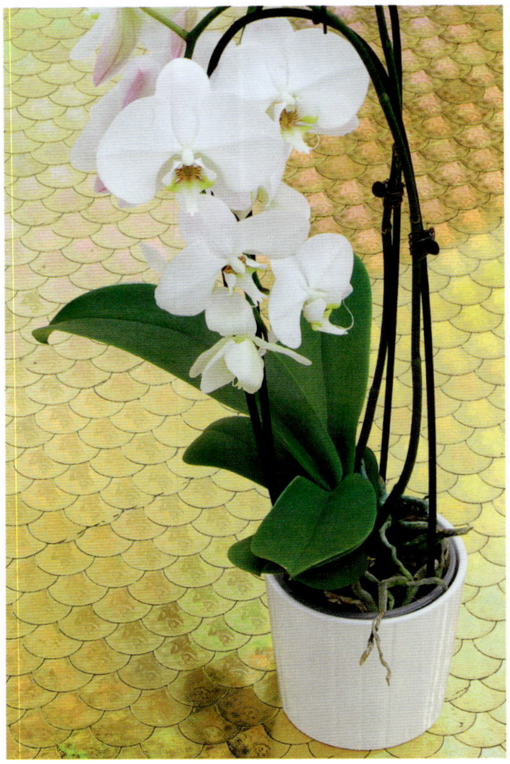

2

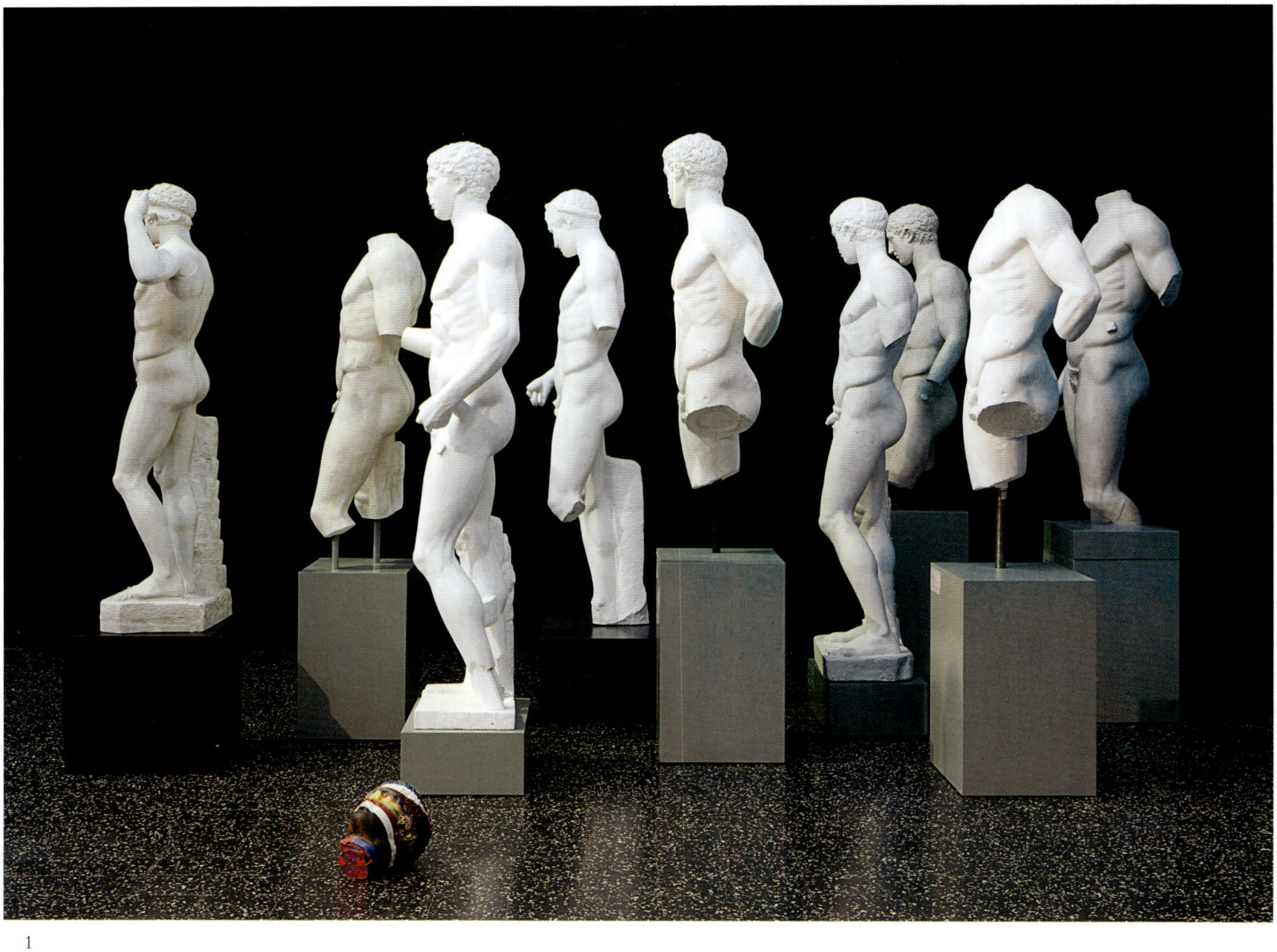

1

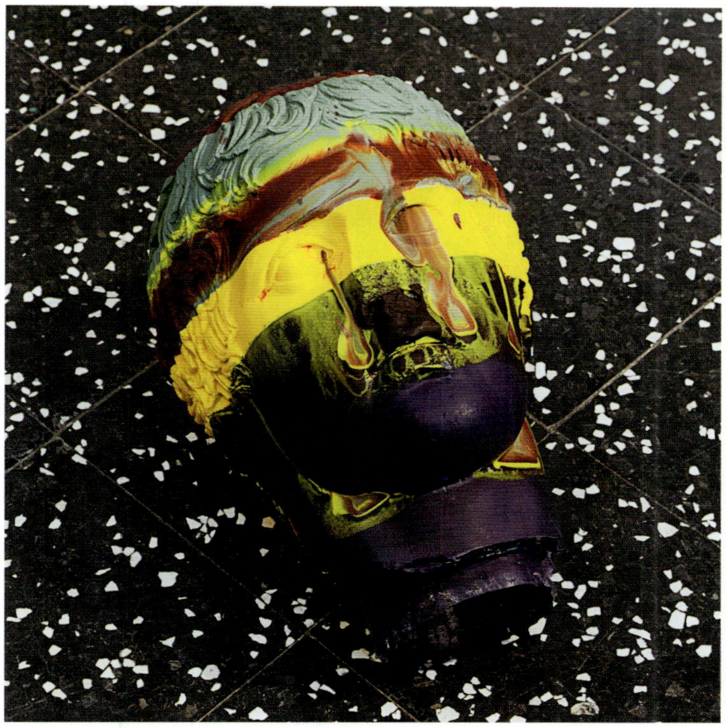

3

Shown by
Tanya Leighton
Gallery F16
Seventeen F11

Biography
Born 1981
Lives in Berlin

Austria-born artist Laric has exhibited his multifarious work prolifically in recent years. In spring 2012 he had a solo show at Tanya Leighton Gallery, Berlin. His concept-driven practice was the subject of the solo exhibitions "Diamond Grill" (2011) at Seventeen, London, and "Versions" at Skulpturhalle Basel. His project "Frieze Stock Footage" (2011) was part of Frieze Projects at Frieze Art Fair 2011.

1
Herakles (Skulpturhalle Basel)
2011
Polyurethane
9⅜ × 17¾ × 9⅞"
(24 × 45 × 25 cm)
Courtesy of Seventeen

2
Doritaenopsis Aung San Suu Kyi
2011
Custom-bred orchid, ceramic
22 × 11⅞ × 8¼"
(56 × 30 × 21 cm)
Courtesy of Seventeen

3
Herakles
2011
Polyurethane
9⅜ × 17¾ × 9⅞"
(24 × 45 × 25 cm)
Courtesy of Seventeen

Focus
Oliver Laric

Oliver Laric explores the hierarchies and dissemination of cultural production. For his exhibition "Diamond Grill" (2011), he commissioned a manufacturer in Shenzhen, China, to produce guilloche hologram stickers bearing images of works such as Rodin's *The Thinker* (1902) or the Ise shrine, a Japanese Shinto monument that has been ritually destroyed and rebuilt every 20 years since AD 690, which were then overlaid on a series of wall-mounted sheets. For his ongoing series of videos "Versions" (2009–) the artist uses an array of images sourced online alongside their copies and manipulated versions to question the historical primacy of the original. *Contra* Walter Benjamin, Laric argues that the bootlegged image continually reinscribes the aura of the original in each of its hybrid varieties. PT

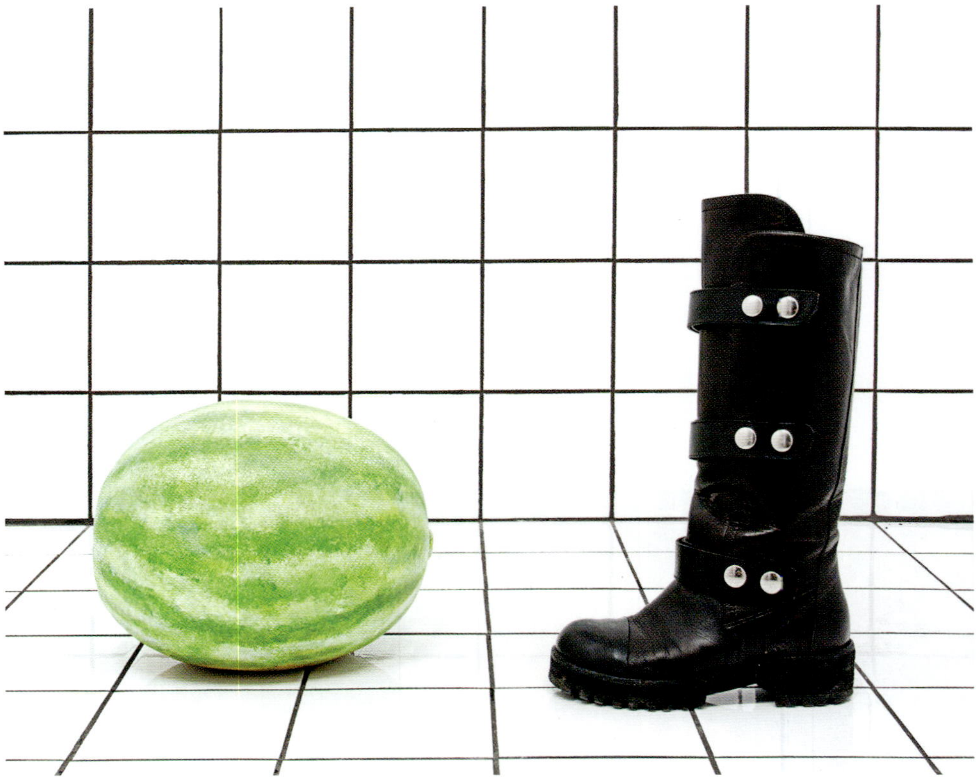

2

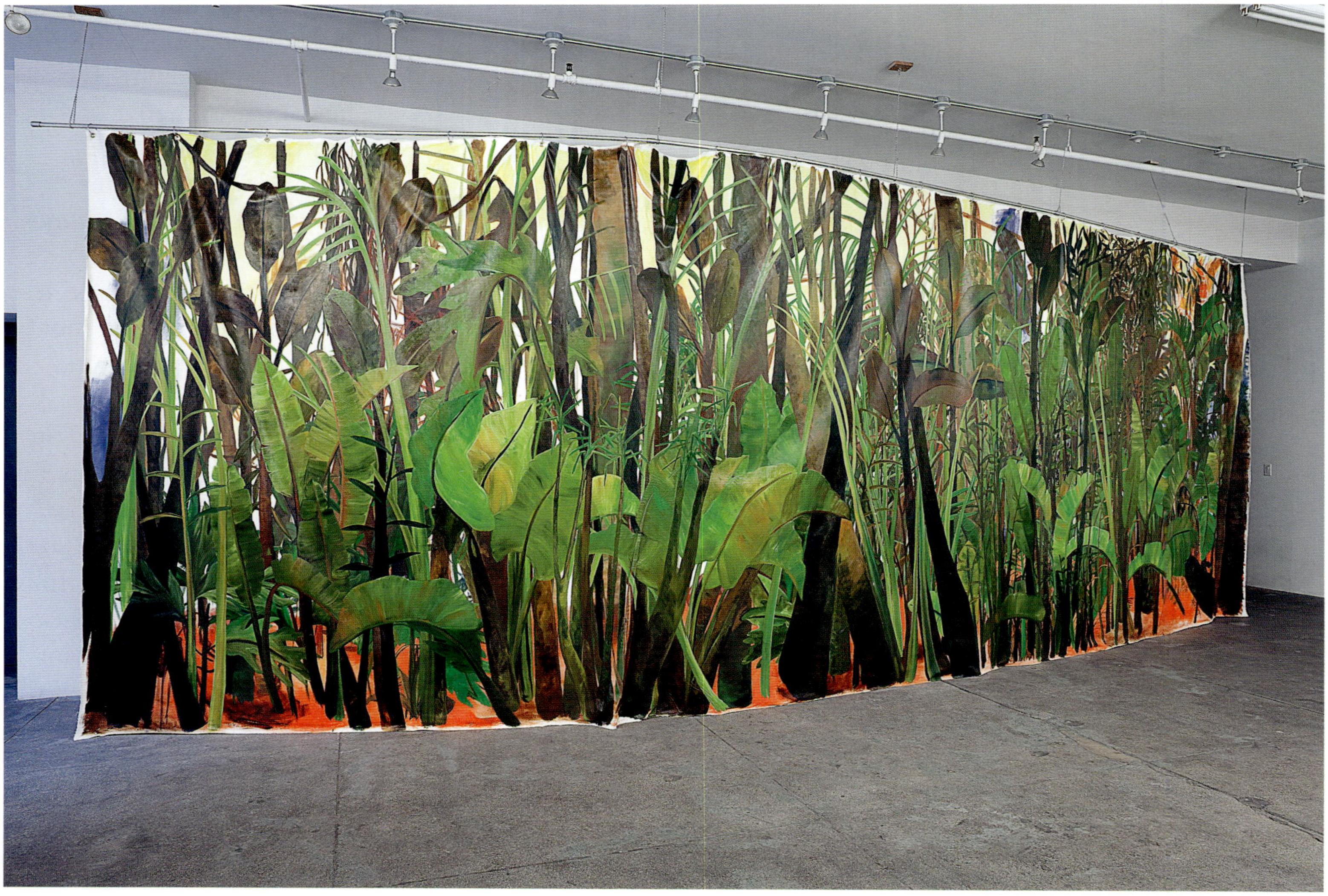

1

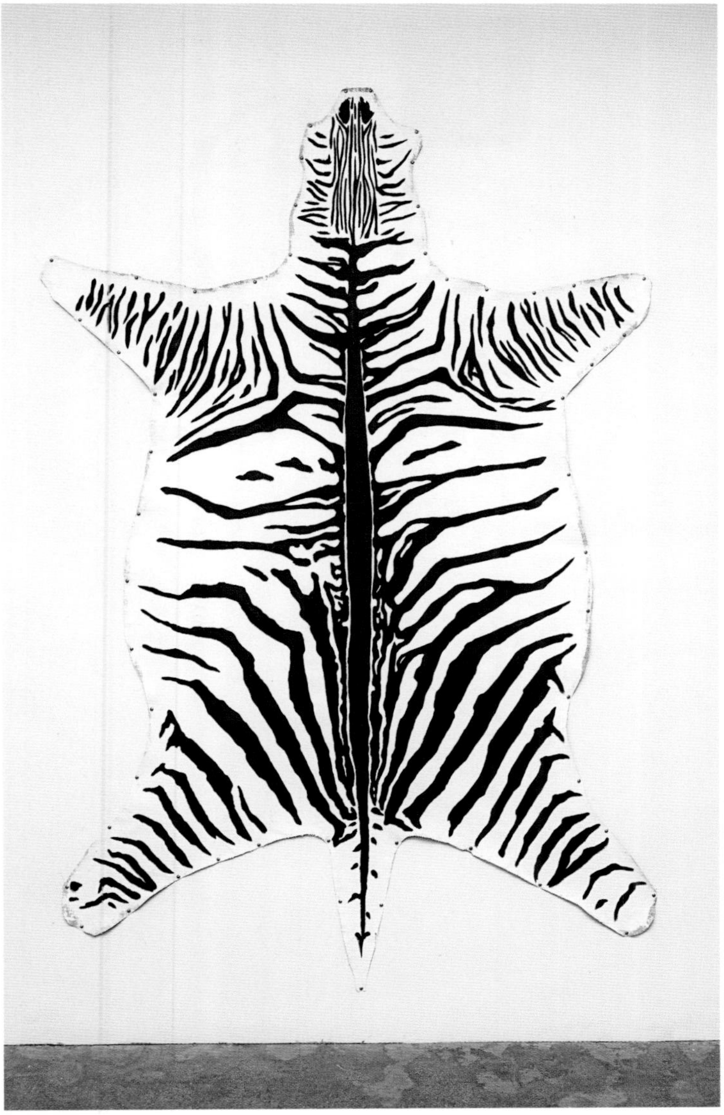
3

Shown by
Jack Hanley Gallery
A1

Biography
Born 1980
Lives in New York

American painter Lee's work was exhibited in the solo show "Waiting for ####" at Jack Hanley Gallery, New York, in 2011. She will be included in a group exhibition at Mitchell-Innes & Nash in 2012. Recently, she collaborated with artist Michele Abeles on work for the group show "Historia Mysteria" (2011) at Renwick Gallery, New York. She also organized the exhibitions "How Do You Do" (2010) at Noma Gallery, San Francisco, and "Today and Everyday" (2009) at X Initiative, New York.

1
Jungle Curtain (is it wrong to be excited about 2012?)
2011
Oil on muslin
120 × 324"
(305 × 823 cm)
Courtesy of the artist

2
Watermelon Boot (anticipation or something)
2011
color photograph
19 × 24"
(48.5 × 61 cm)
Courtesy of the artist

3
Zebra (huh/what)
2011
Oil on linen
108 × 72"
(274.5 × 183 cm)
Courtesy of the artist

Margaret Lee

Margaret Lee's practice is grounded in the idea of kinship between artists, in terms of product and process. This can be acted out in the space of the gallery—as in her collaborative, three-person exhibition "White Room," with Michele Abeles and Darren Bader, at New York's White Columns—or within the boundaries of a photograph—as in *Darren's Chair* (2011), with Ajay Kurian, or *Buddies* (2010), with Gregory Edwards. The nomadic quality of Lee's work, its lack of distinct signature, is one of the indications of the genuine porousness of her process. That interest is the basis of both her curatorial and artistic practice, a concerted move away from the idea of singular authorship. KK

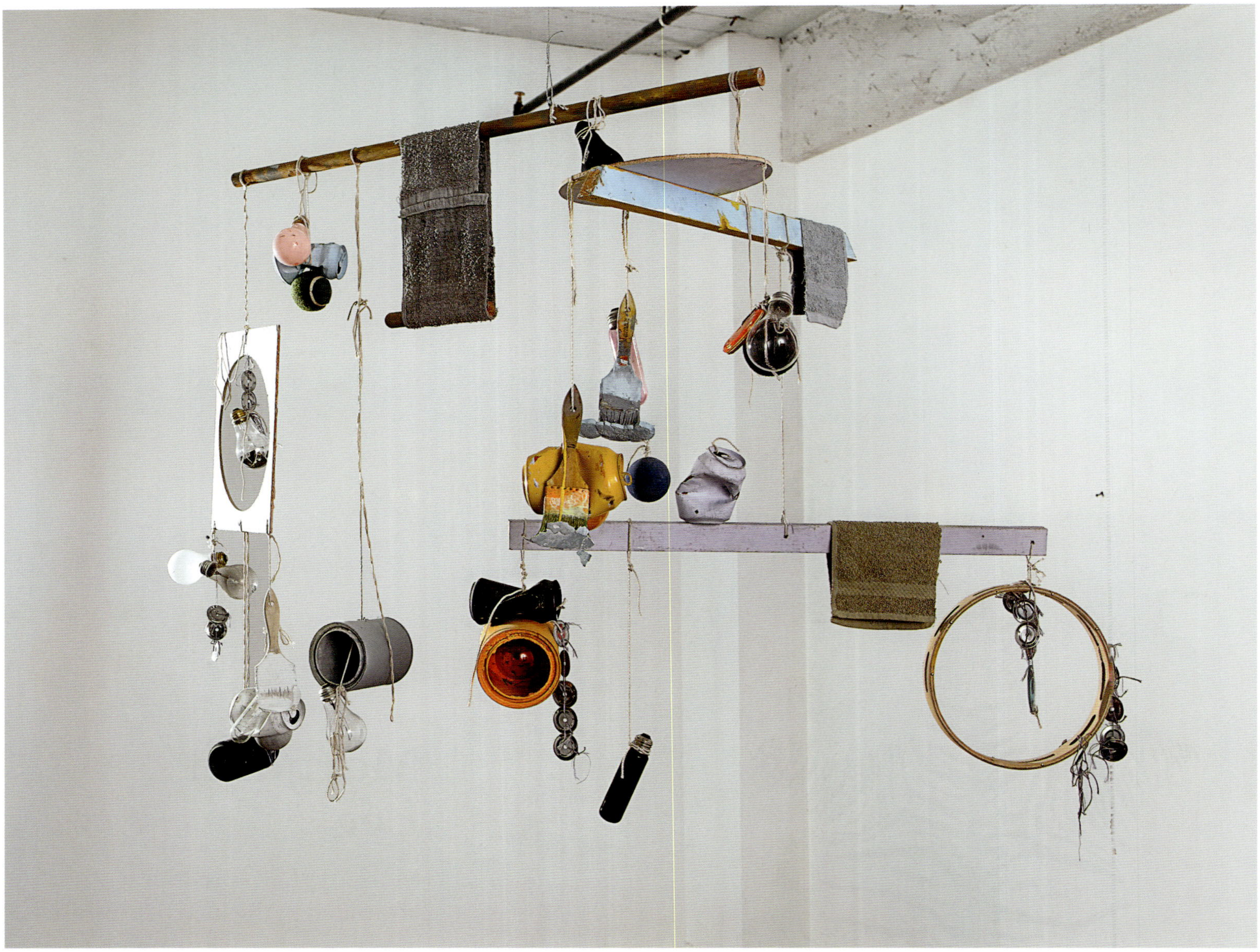

1

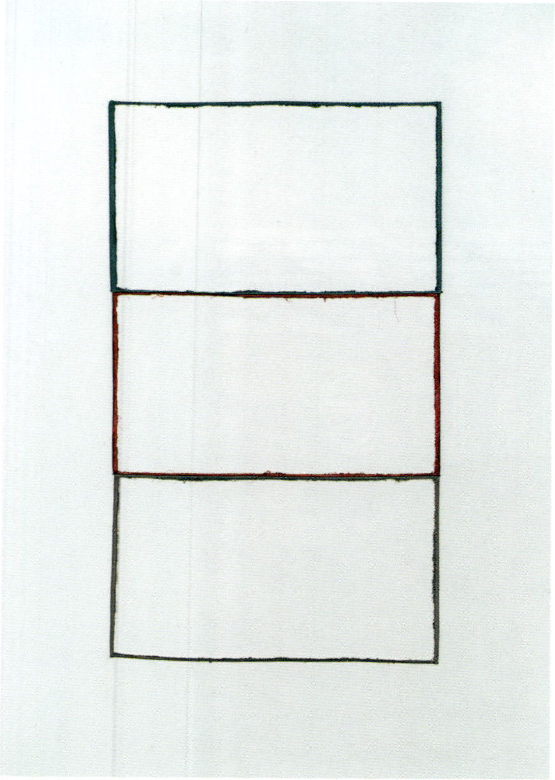

2

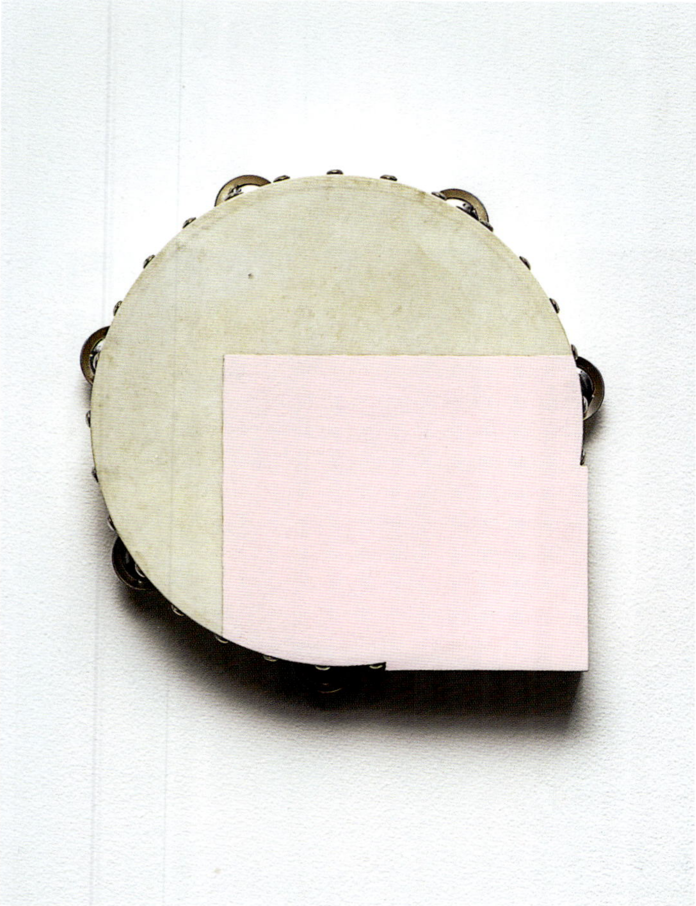

3

Shown by
Maccarone D5
Stuart Shave/Modern Art C43

Biography
Born 1974
Lives in New York

Britain-born sculptor Lee has exhibited prolifically in the United States in the last decade. His delicate and often figurative works were included in the recent group show "Absentee Landlord" (2012), curated by John Waters, at the Walker Art Center, Minneapolis. Recent solo shows include "Moon River" (2011) at Stuart Shave/ Modern Art, London; "Lavender" (2010), at Maccarone, New York; and "Arm's Length" (2009) at Peres Projects, Los Angeles.

1
Clean Up
2011
Mixed media
Dimensions variable
Courtesy of Maccarone

2
Untitled (triple negative, blue, red, pink)
2007
Cut hand-dyed cotton towel
72 × 42"
(183 × 106.5 cm)
Courtesy of Maccarone

3
Untitled (pink corner tambourine)
2010
Oil on tambourine, bass wood
11½ × 11 × 1¾"
(29 × 28 × 4.5 cm)
Courtesy of Maccarone

Paul Lee

There is a sense of a silenced rhythm, cautiously revealed in the sculptures and installations of Paul Lee. Geometric shapes emerge from mute stones and still tambourines, hesitantly breaking into a restrained abstract enunciation. A jaunty white rhomboid extends from the musical instrument of *Untitled (tambourine)* (2011), while the angle revealed within the black mass of *Untitled (cut rock)* (2011) is gentle pink and light blue. The writhing post-Minimalism of Eva Hesse and Richard Tuttle may be looking over his shoulder, but he makes light and colorful work of their lineage. As, for example, in his untitled series of works threading together the empty, slightly frayed outlines of dyed towels that become frames, ladders, tracks, and serene horizons, he carefully sets the contours of a quiet poetry. CFW

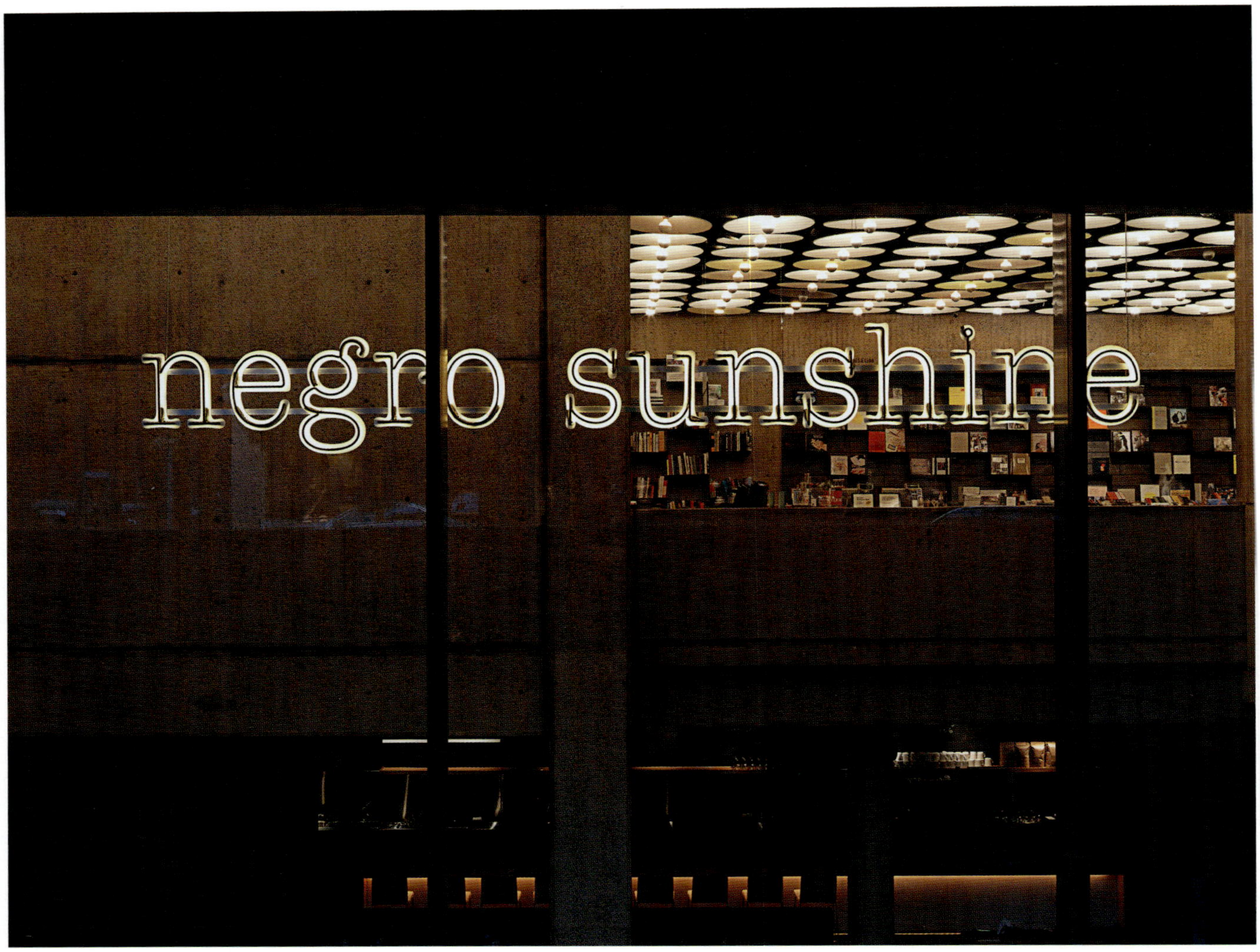
negro sunshine

1

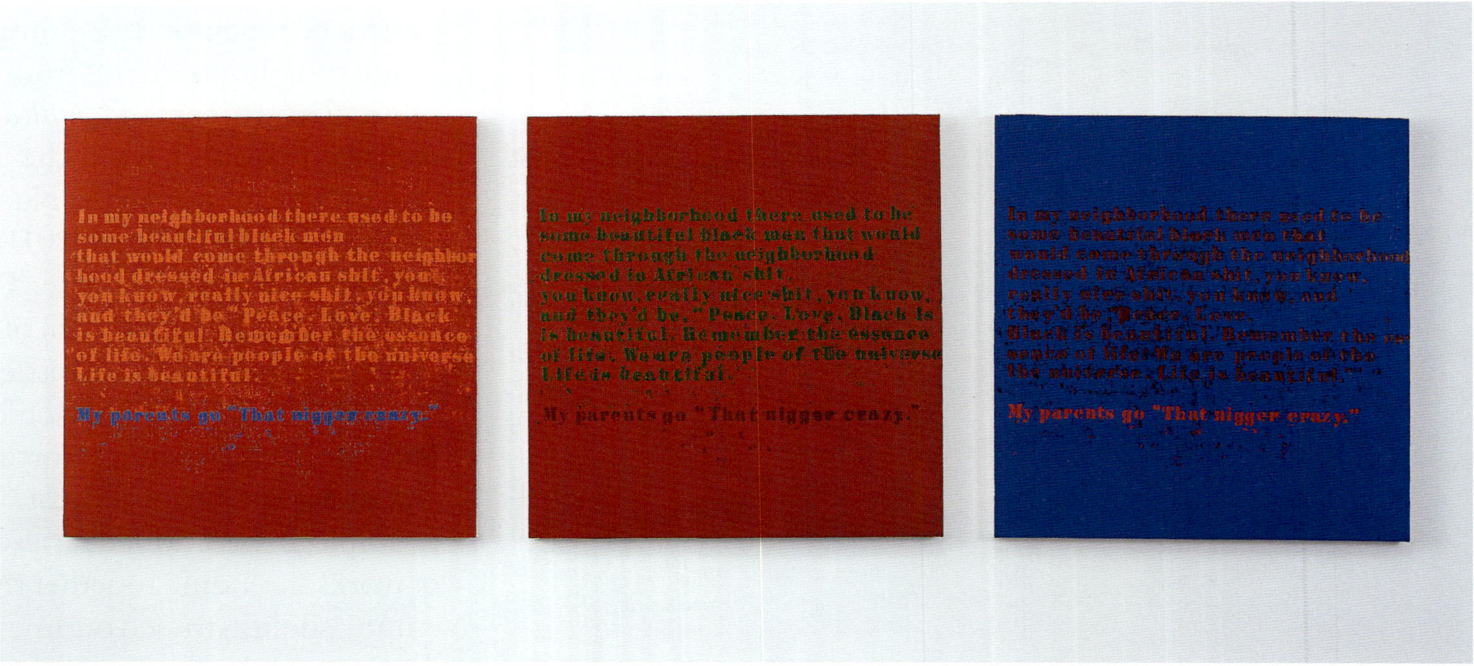
In my neighborhood there used to be
some beautiful black men
that would come through the neighbor
hood dressed in African shit, you
you know, really nice shit, you know,
and they'd be "Peace, Love, Black
is beautiful. Remember the essence
of life. We are people of the universe.
Life is beautiful."
My parents go "That nigger crazy."
In my neighborhood there used to be
some beautiful black men that would
come through the neighborhood
dressed in African shit,
you know, really nice shit, you know,
and they'd be, "Peace, Love, Black is
is beautiful. Remember the essence
of life. We are people of the universe
Life is beautiful."
My parents go "That nigger crazy."
In my neighborhood there used to be
some beautiful black men that
would come through the neighborhood
dressed in African shit, you know,
really nice shit, you know, and
they'd be "Peace, Love,
Black is beautiful. Remember the
of life. We are people of the
the universe. Life is beautiful."
My parents go "That nigger crazy."

2

3

Shown by
Regen Projects B17

Biography
Born 1960
Lives in New York

Since the 1990s, Ligon has been at the forefront of socially-engaged American art. His mid-career retrospective "America" (2011) at the Whitney Museum of American Art, New York, surveyed the breadth of his practice, and travelled to Los Angeles County Museum of Art, Los Angeles (2011), and the Modern Art Museum of Fort Worth (2012). He held solo shows at The Power Plant, Toronto (2010), and "Off Book" (2009) at Regen Projects and Regen Projects II, Los Angeles. His work is included in numerous museum collections, including the Solomon R. Guggenheim Museum, New York; Tate Modern, London; and the Museum of Modern Art, New York.

1
Warm Broad Glow II
2011
Neon, paint, and powder-coated aluminum
29 × 242"
(73.5 × 614.5 cm)
Courtesy of Regen Projects

2
Beautiful Black Men #4, #5 & #6
2004
Oilstick and acrylic on canvas
32 × 32" each
(81.5 × 81.5 cm each)
Courtesy of Regen Projects

3
Stranger #53
2011
Oil, acrylic, and coaldust on canvas
72 × 60"
(183 × 152.5 cm)
Courtesy of Regen Projects

Glenn Ligon

Glenn Ligon is widely celebrated for a body of work that has shaped the discourse on race, sexuality, and identity politics. He is known for appropriating text from sources as disparate as Zora Neale Hurston and Richard Pryor, working and reworking the words in paintings such as *Untitled (I do not always feel colored)* (1990). Elsewhere, he refers to the photographs of Robert Mapplethorpe (*Notes on the Margin of the Black Book,* 1991–3) and the films of Thomas Edison (*The Death of Tom,* 2008). Ligon both celebrates and critiques key works in the 20th century canon, and is a master not only at decontextualizing his chosen cultural fragments but also at creating new and urgent contexts. KK

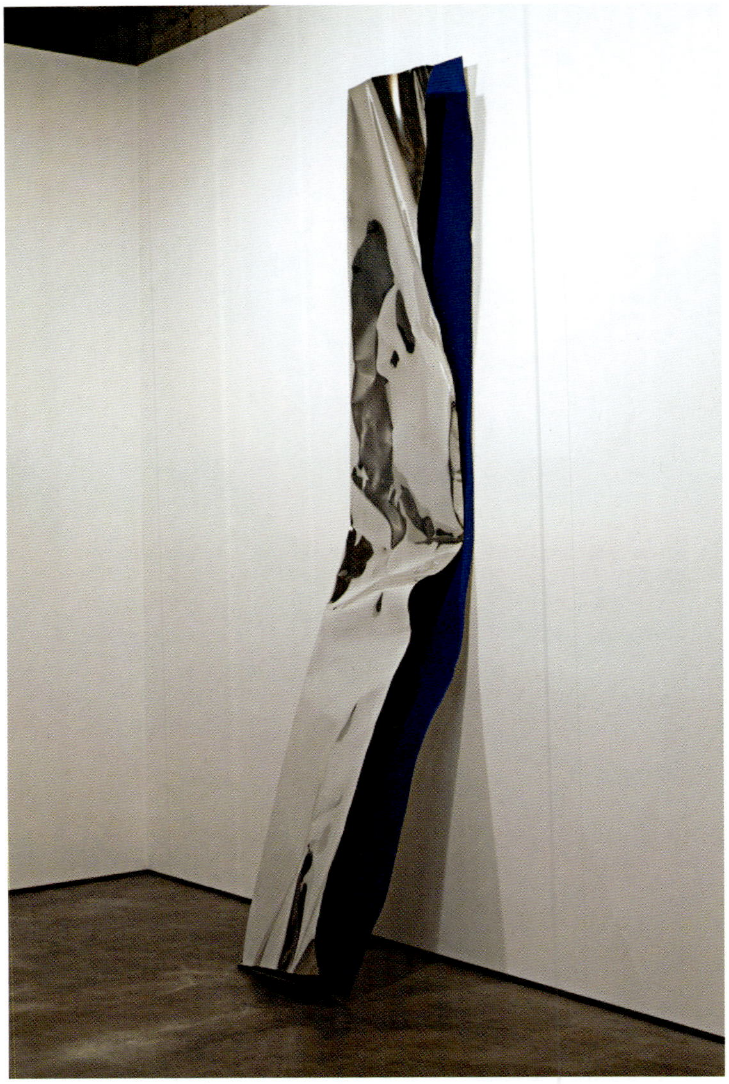

2

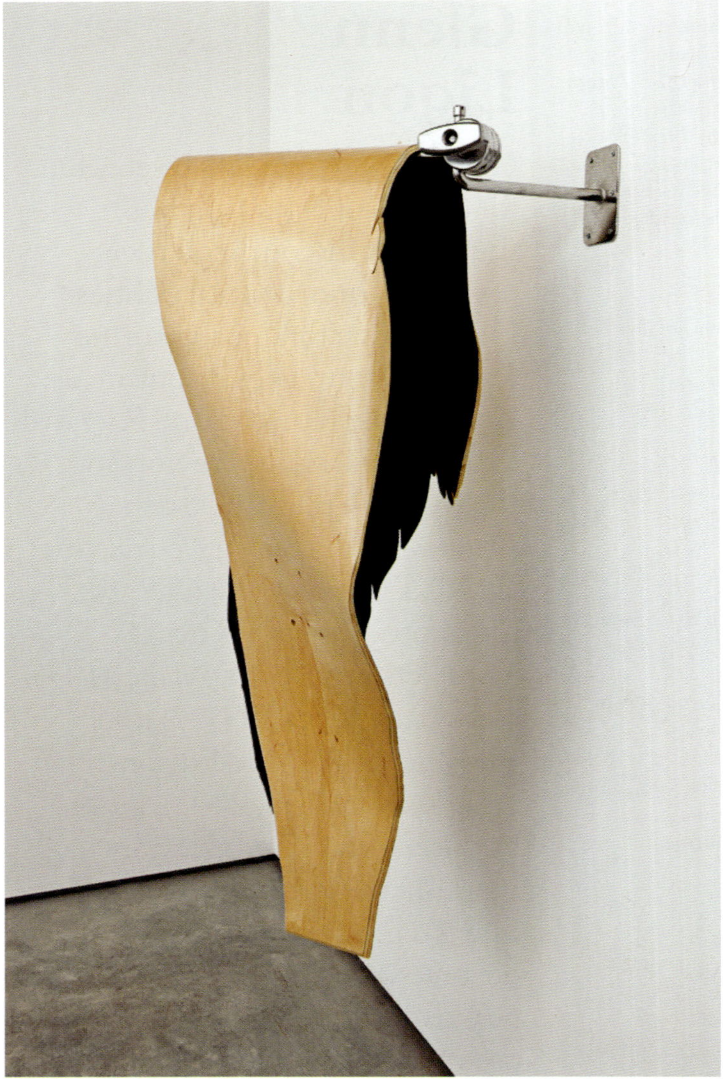

1

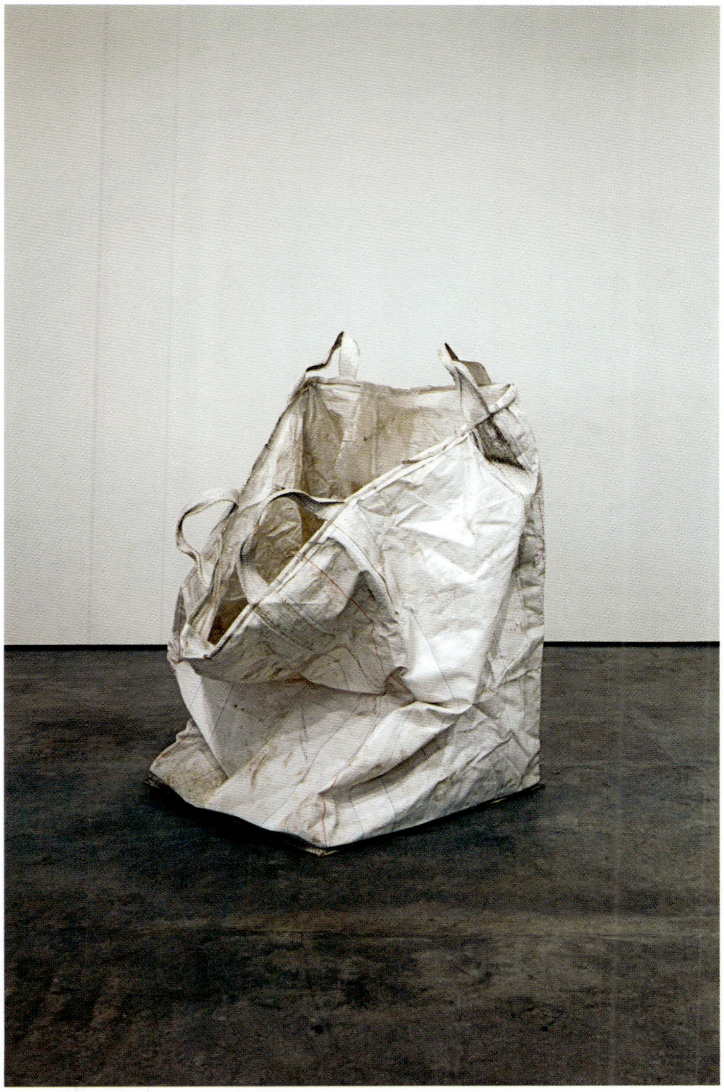

3

Shown by
Simon Preston F22

Biography
Born 1970
Lives in New York

Lopez's sculptural work was the subject of the solo exhibitions "Vertical Neck" (2011) and "The Violent Bear It Away" (2009) at Simon Preston, New York. Other solo shows include "The Year We Made Contact" (2008) at LA><ART, Los Angeles; Wenk Row (2005) at Gallery Paule Anglim, San Francisco; and "Adventures in the Skin Trade" (2001) at Deitch Projects, New York, and Fondazione Nicola Trussardi, Milan. She teaches at the School of Visual Arts, New York.

1
Your Board
2009
Maple plywood, grip tape, and steel
22 × 14 × 48"
(60 × 35.5 × 122 cm)
Courtesy of
Simon Preston

2
Blue Angel
2011
Aluminum and automotive paint
120 × 24 × 12"
(309 × 61 × 30.5 cm)
Courtesy of
Simon Preston

3
Tote
2011
Cement bag and dirt
42 × 42 × 60"
(106.5 × 106.5 × 152.5 cm)
Courtesy of
Simon Preston

Focus
Michelle Lopez

Hardness versus softness, sleekness and speed versus decay and failure—Michelle Lopez's work thrives on fluid contrasts. She has wrapped an automobile in a tender leather "skin" for *Boy* (1999) and then created a violently flattened version for *Woadsonner (Edit)* (2009); she has deflated iconic elements of *Star Wars*, in works such as *C3PO* (2008), a sad-sack gilded-bronze robot shaped like a used condom. The dented 10-foot-tall mirrored-aluminum panels in the "Blue Angels" series (2011) lean against gallery walls like blasé or exhausted ghosts of military jets, John McCracken's fetishistic monoliths, or John Chamberlain's aggressive assemblages. Androgyny is a persistent undercurrent, as in the wittily folded-over plywood pieces in the "Your Board" series (2011), which echo wilted flowers, oversized skateboards, and skinny, slouching skate kids. KK

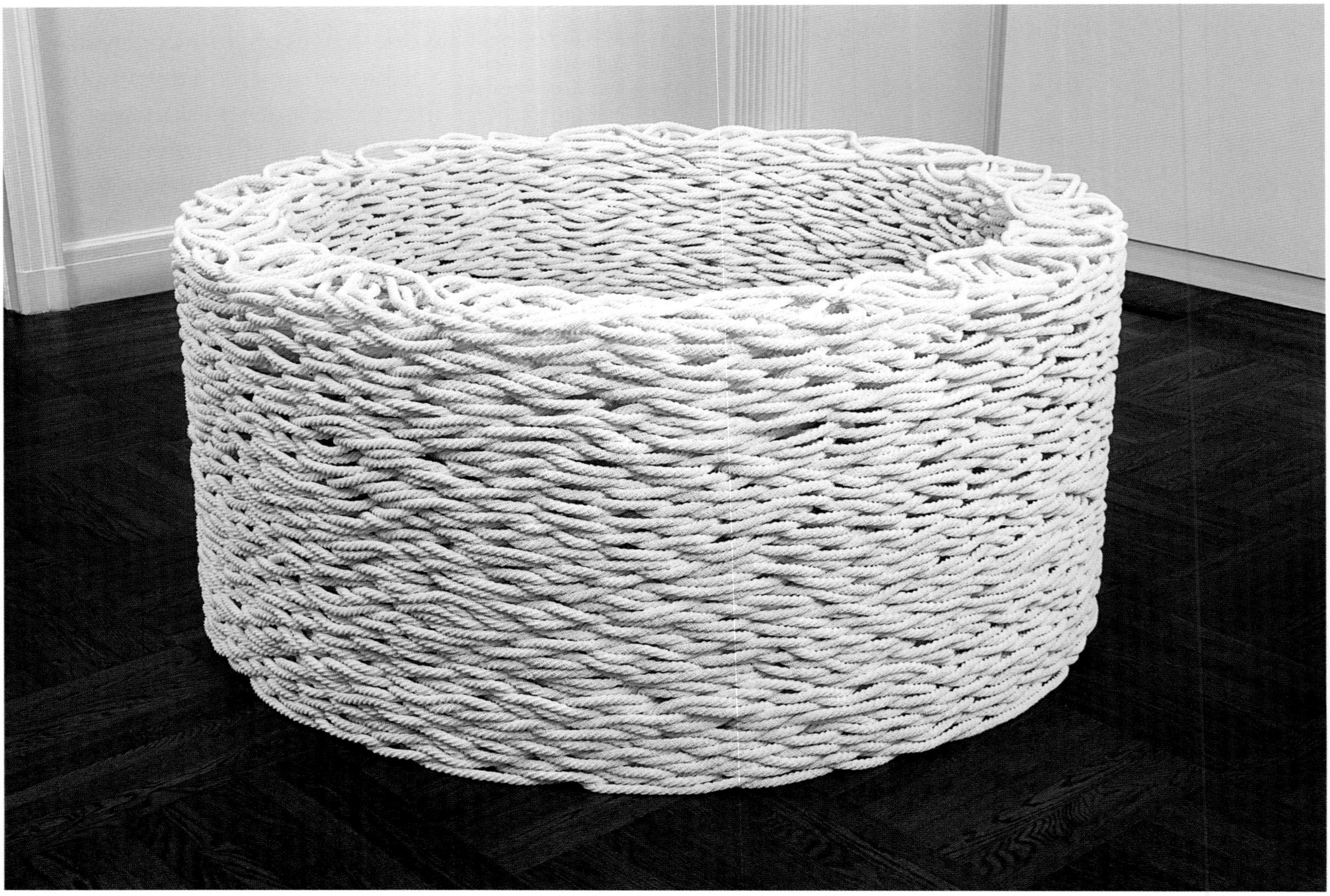

1

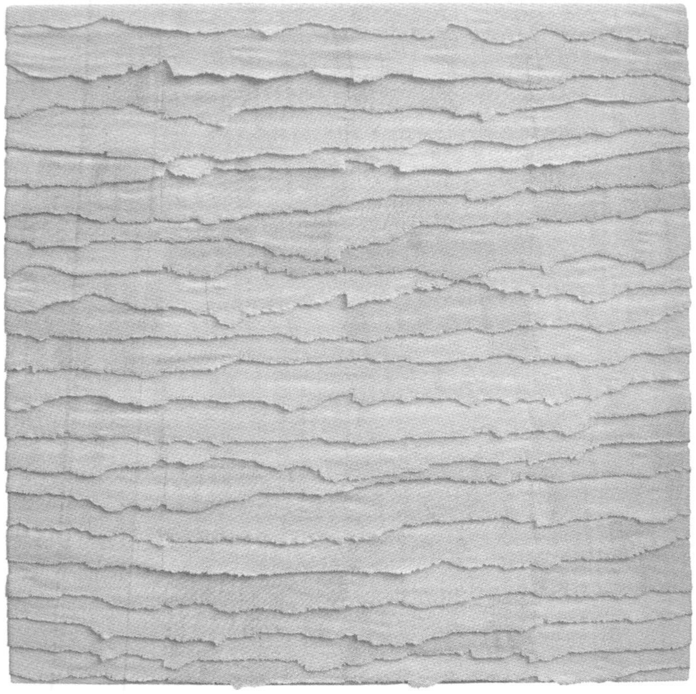

2

Shown by
Galerie Thaddaeus Ropac C12
White Cube E38

Biography
Born 1969
Lives in Los Angeles

Lou's intricate sculptures were displayed in a solo show at White Cube, London, in 2012. In 2011, she had the solo exhibition "Let the Light In" at SCAD Museum of Art, Savannah, and L&M Arts, Los Angeles. "American Idol" (2010) took place at Galerie Thaddaeus Ropac, Paris. She also participated in the group shows "Memories of the Future"(2011) at La Maison Rouge, Paris; "Strange Beauty: Baroque Sensibilities in Contemporary Art" (2011) at I.D.E.A Space Colorado College, Colorado Springs; and "January White Sale" (2011) at Loretta Howard Gallery, New York.

1
Continuous Mile
2006–8
Cotton and white glass beads
31½ × 55⅛"
(80 × 140 cm)
Courtesy of White Cube

2
The Waves
2011–12
Glass beads, cotton on stretcher frame
44⅛ × 44½ × 1⅜"
(112 × 113 × 3.5 cm)
Courtesy of White Cube

Liza Lou

Liza Lou's autobiographical film *Born Again* (2004), in which she relates a childhood scarred by evangelism and abuse, provides an unequivocal lens through which to regard her sculptures. While the bead-encrusted *Security Fence* (2005) can be considered in the context of the South African city of Durban, where it was made, and of the 20 Zulu women who helped to make it, it also bears a personal story where the glister of spiritual promise masks a steely reality. For *Gather (One Million)* (2008–10), a 150-square-foot field of tufts of beads, Lou and her assistants again undertook an absurd process of production, laying luxury bare as a time-consuming, labor-sucking phenomenon, not so far removed from the constraining economics of Africa's free-trade zones. SOR

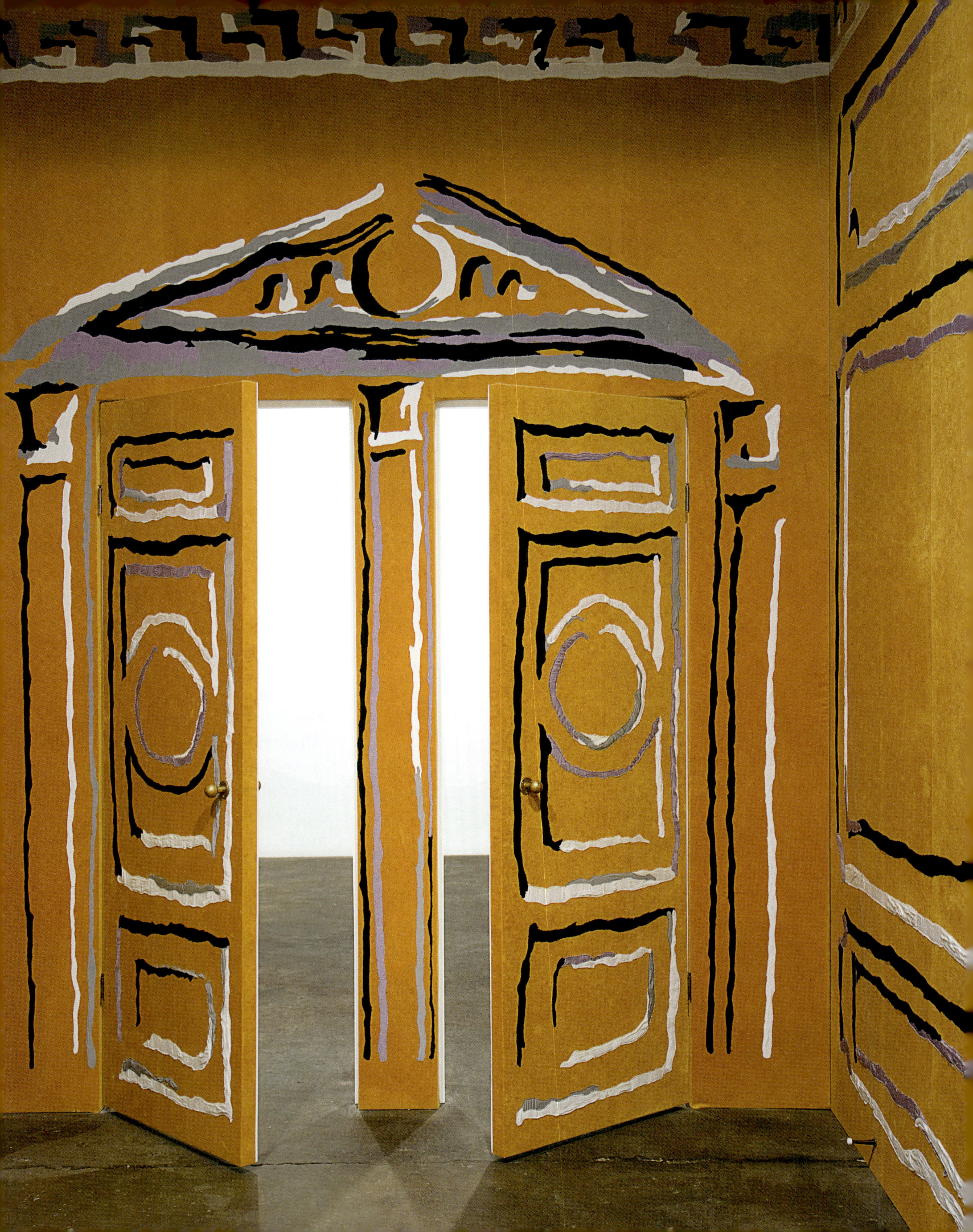

Shown by
303 Gallery B39
Galerie Neu C49

Biography
Born 1980
Lives in New York

Mauss's second solo show at 303 Gallery was held in early 2012. He is included in the Whitney Biennial 2012 and recently had solo exhibitions at Midway Contemporary Art, Minneapolis, in 2011, and FRAC Champagne-Ardenne, Reims, the same year. Mauss also co-curated the recent White Columns "Annual" (2011) with Ken Okiishi, and is currently a guest-professor in the Department of Painting and Drawing at the Hochschule für Bildende Künste, Hamburg.

Concern, crush, desire
2011
Cotton appliqué on velvet, brass doorknobs, and door stoppers
131 × 94 × 115"
(332.5 × 239 × 292 cm)
Courtesy of 303 Gallery and the Nicoletta Fiorucci Collection

Nick Mauss

Much of the writing about Nick Mauss' art agrees that it is evocative of the past, though there is little consensus about which period exactly. This has to do with the way in which his work—from delicate paintings to scratchy pieces in layered silver leaf and skeletal pavilions (such as *Occasion*, 2009)—gestures towards both anachronism and the ineffable feeling of something only half-remembered. Claude Debussy makes an appearance, as does Arthur Rimbaud, whose poem *Une Saison en enfer* (A Season in Hell, 1873) Mauss collaborated on with the artist Ken Okiishi in 2007. As Mauss has said, "I work to put the formation of my sensibility and a trail of influences in the foreground." ST

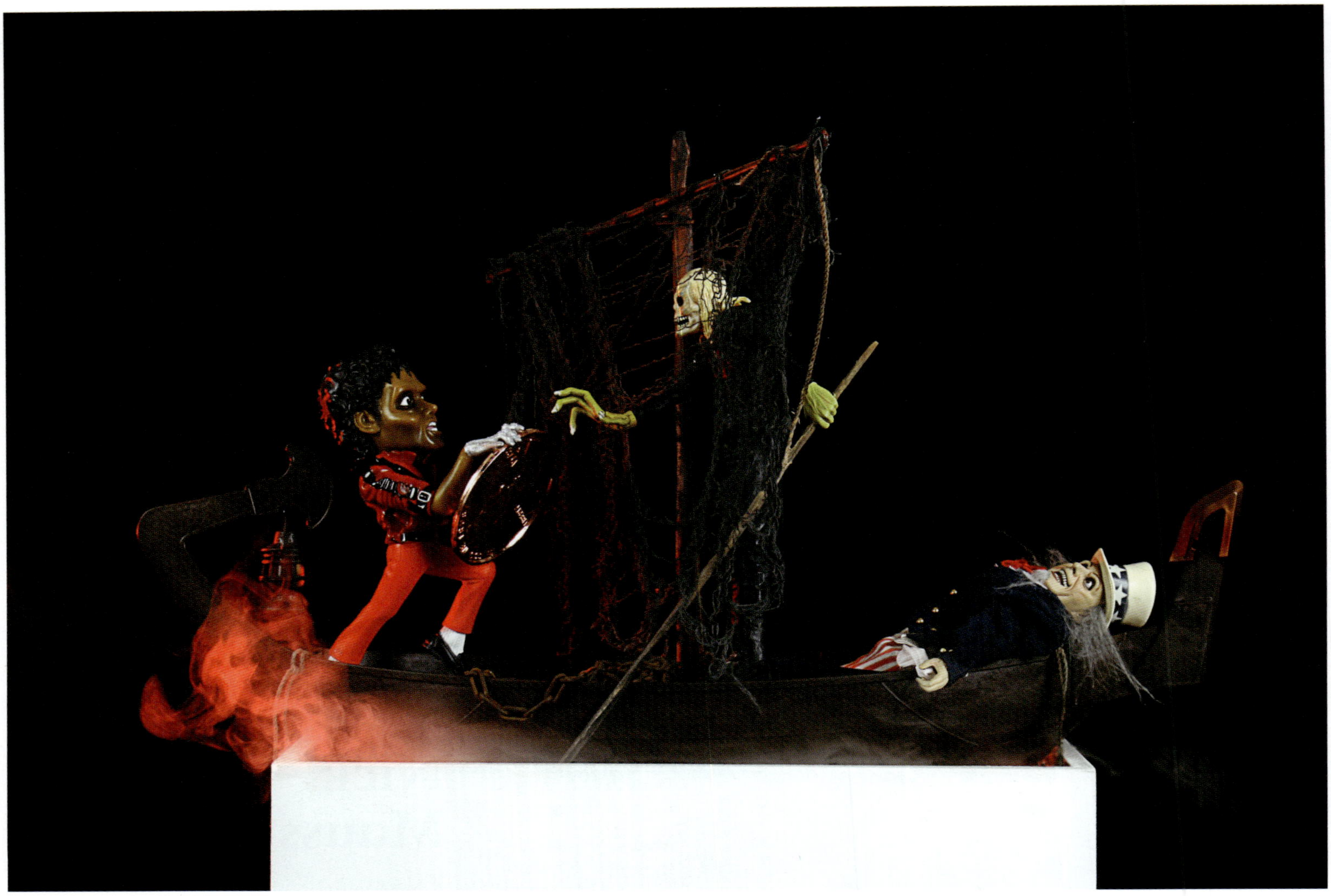

1

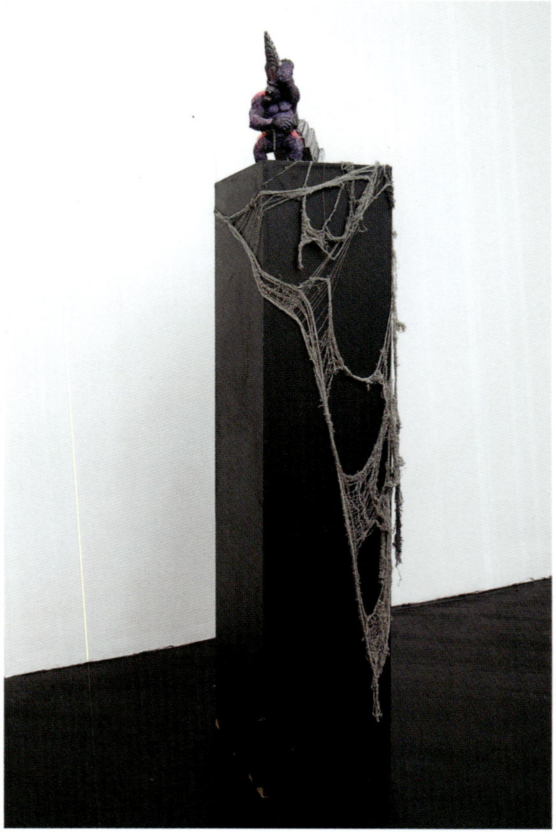

2

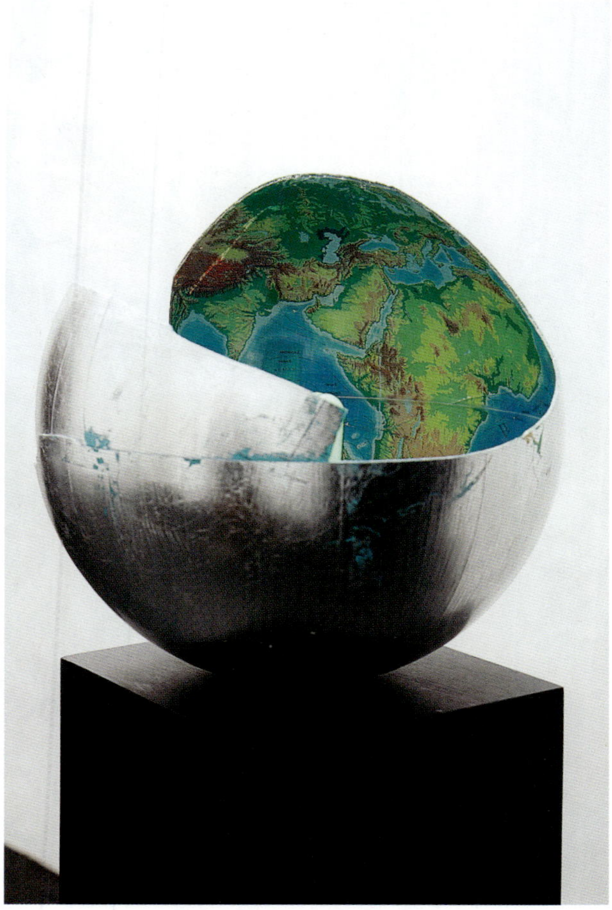

3

Focus

Danny McDonald

In Danny McDonald's 2010 exhibition "Icons of the Invert´s Universe," a cast of unusual comic characters populated numerous plinths around the gallery. Using sculpture and humor in tandem, McDonald mirrors human quirks in miniature form. *Tea-Bagging on Uranus* (2010), sees a plush albino monkey trapped inside a bell jar, astride a white dome-like form, he points toward some awkward form of space travel. Meanwhile his contribution to the Whitney Biennial 2010, *The Crossing: Passengers Must Pay Toll in Order to Disembark (Michael Jackson, Charon, and Uncle Sam)* (2010), sees Jackson, not Uncle Sam, paying to cross the Styx river. Here, we experience the dubious pleasure of omniscient superiority—we know where this is going, and it's nowhere good. SNS

Shown by
Galerie Isabella Bortolozzi F18

Biography
Born 1971
Lives in New York

American artist McDonald's sculptures have been included in the exhibitions "Fetishes of Crisis" (2010) at CACP Musée d'Art Contemporain, Bordeaux; "Take me to your leader: the great escape into space" (2010) at the National Museum of Art, Oslo; and "Icons of the Invert's Universe" (2010) at Isabella Bortolozzi, Berlin. He was also included in the Whitney Biennial 2010 at the Whitney Museum of American Art, New York.

1
The Crossing: Passengers Must Pay Toll in Order to Disembark (Michael Jackson, Charon, and Uncle Sam)
2009
Modified action figures and models, plastic, fabric, foil
60 × 22 × 7½"
(152.5 × 56 × 19 cm)
Courtesy of Galerie Isabella Bortolozzi

2
Queen Kong (With Chrysler Building)
2010
Mixed media
72⅞ × 13 × 16⅛"
(185 × 33 × 41 cm)
Courtesy of Galerie Isabella Bortolozzi

3
Do You Believe In The Future: Part III
2010
Mixed media
60⅝ × 12½ × 12½"
(154 × 32 × 32 cm)
Courtesy of Galerie Isabella Bortolozzi

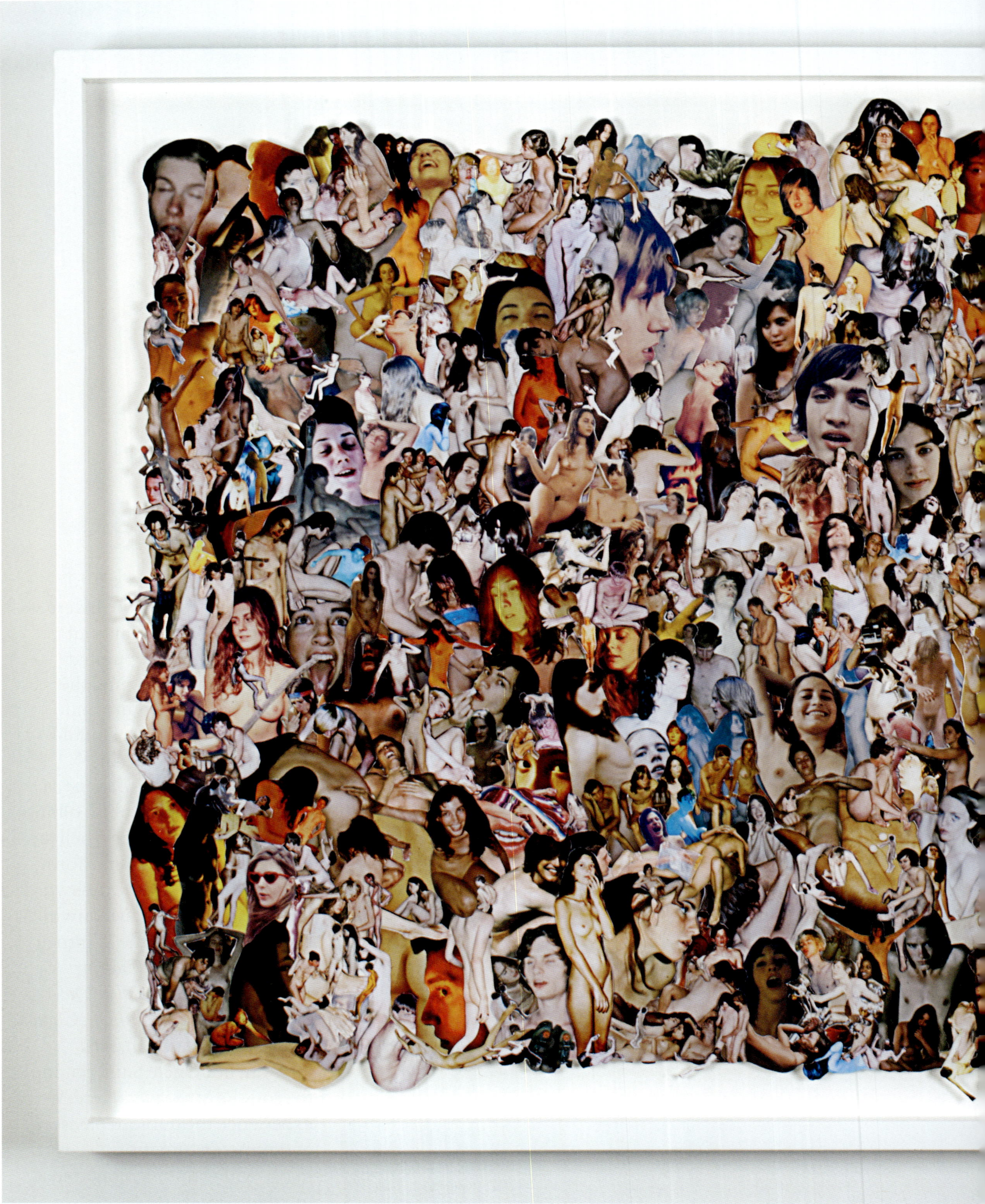

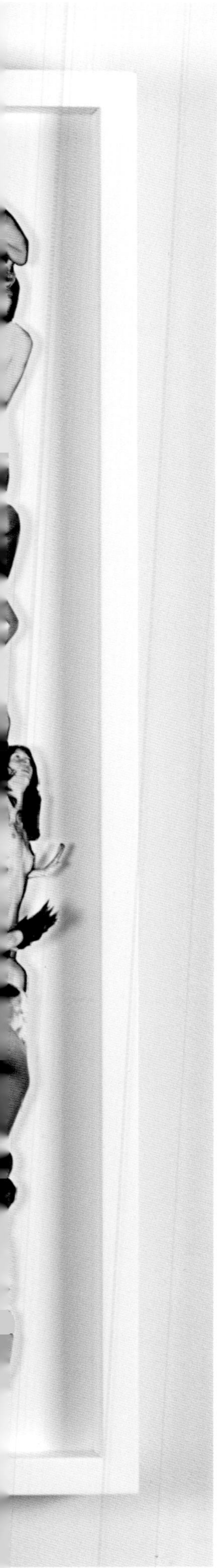

Shown by
The Breeder C22
Alison Jacques Gallery A25
Team Gallery C4

Biography
Born 1977
Lives in New York

In the last decade American photographer McGinley has exhibited his work to an expansive international audience. He had recent solo shows in Amsterdam, Athens, and San Francisco. In 2009 he had a solo exhibition at Alison Jacques Gallery, London. In spring 2012, Team Gallery, New York, will show his work in both of its New York spaces. His work is part of a number of public collections, including the Solomon R. Guggenheim Museum, New York, and The Whitney Museum of American Art, New York.

Whirling Swirl
2011
Collage
25 × 25"
(63.5 × 63.5 cm)
Courtesy of
Team Gallery

Ryan McGinley

Ryan McGinley's photographs are both intimate and epic, capturing his youthful subjects in their East Village haunts and frolicking in the caves and fields of a rainbow-hued American landscape. His images steer clear of weary stereotypes of disaffected youth, instead embracing its carefree exuberance in images such as *Amanda (Haystacks)* (2011), which depicts a naked girl falling ecstatically into flame-like piles of hay. His most recent portraits forgo the fantasy-filled landscapes for the simplicity of the studio in a series of over 150 black and white silver gelatin prints of friends and models. In his honest portraits, McGinley, like David Armstrong and Peter Hujar before him, looks beyond surfaces to capture the life of the person from within. AB

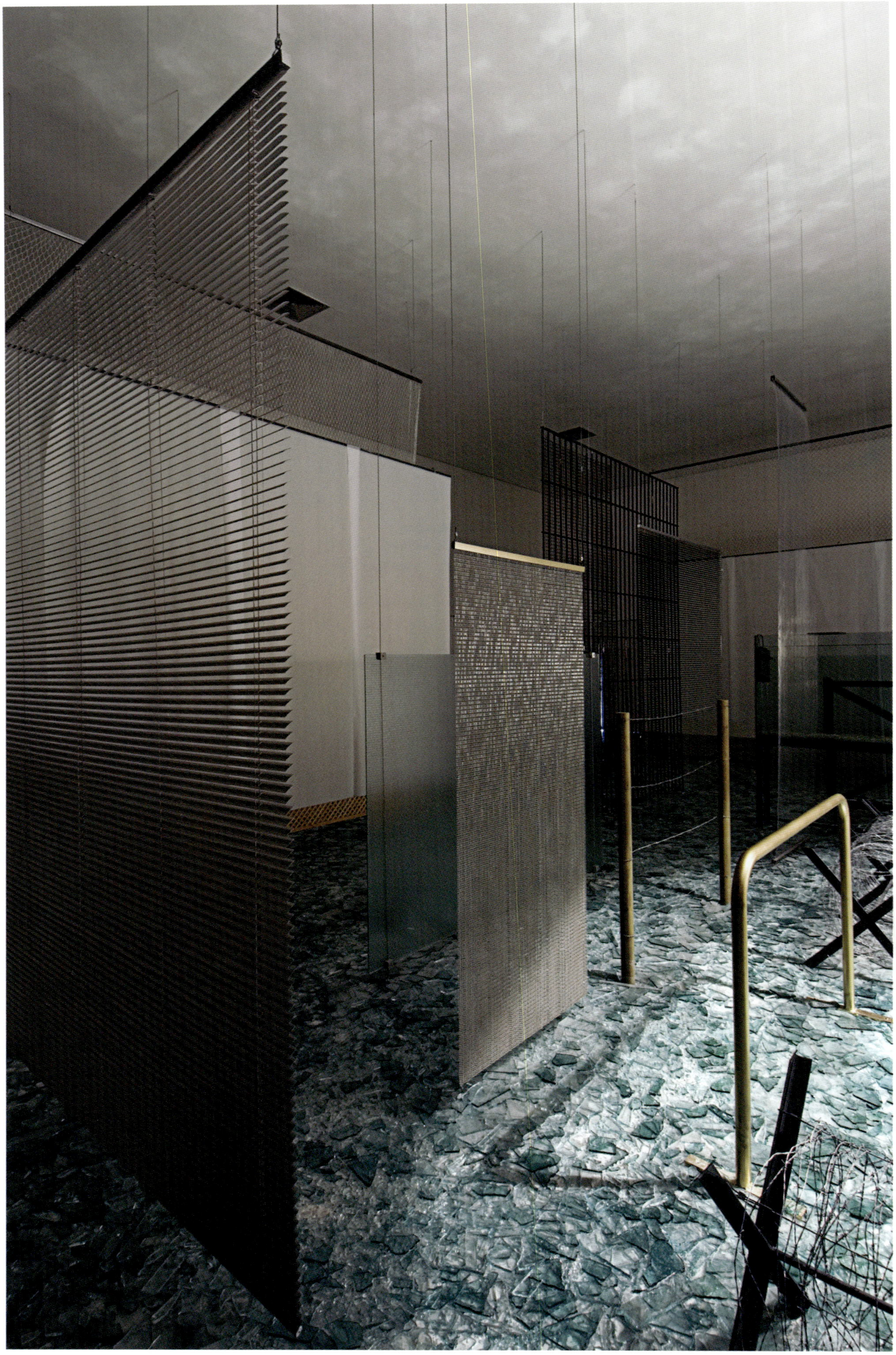

1

Cildo Meireles

"In some way you become political when you don't have a chance to be poetic. I think human beings would much prefer to be poetic," Cildo Meireles has said, conjuring the authoritarian regimes of his youth. Nevertheless, his luminous works limning space and scale have managed both. For *Insertions into Ideological Circuits* (1970–76) the Brazilian artist stamped political messages on banknotes and Coke bottles, whose constant circulation ensured the inscriptions went far. This breadth soon manifested itself in immersive installations: from his famous red rooms to *Mission/Missions (How to Build Cathedrals)* (1987), featuring a ceiling crafted from bones, a floor of coins, and a column of Communion wafers connecting them, to *Babel* (2001), a soaring, babbling tower of radios. QL

Shown by
Galerie Lelong B12

Biography
Born 1948
Lives in Rio de Janeiro

Brazilian artist Meireles's sculptures and installations have been shown internationally since the late-1960s. The self-titled retrospective at Tate Modern, London (2008), travelled to Museu d'Art Contemporani de Barcelona (2009); and Museo Universitario Arte Contemporáneo, Mexico City (2009). In 2013 the solo show "Cildo Meireles" will take place at Fundação Serralves, Porto, before traveling to Museo Nacional Centro de Arte Reina Sofía, Madrid He participated in the survey show "A Terrible Beauty is Born" (2011) at the 11th Biennale de Lyon.

1
Atraves (detail)
1983-9
Courtesy of Galerie Lelong

2
Atraves
1983-9
Fishing nets, voile, reinforced glass, livestock nets, architecture paper, Venetian blinds, garden fencing, wooded gates, prison bars, wooden trellis, iron fencing, mosquito nets, metal city barrier fencing, aquarium, tennis nets, metal stakes, barbed wire
236¼ × 590½ × 590½"
(600 × 1500 × 1500 cm)
Courtesy of Galerie Lelong

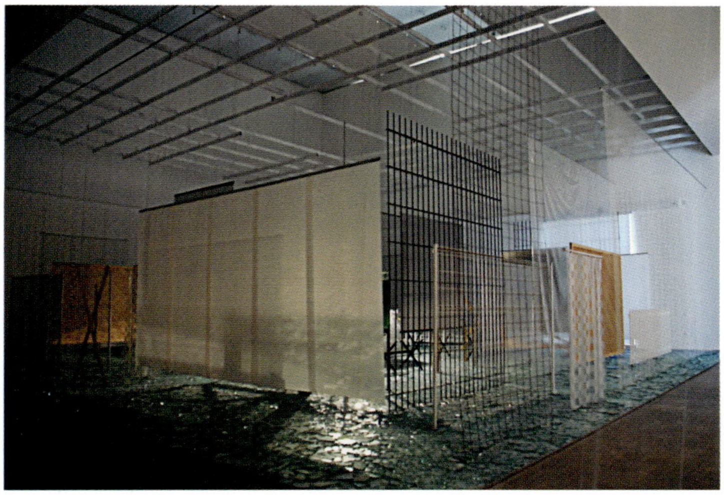

2

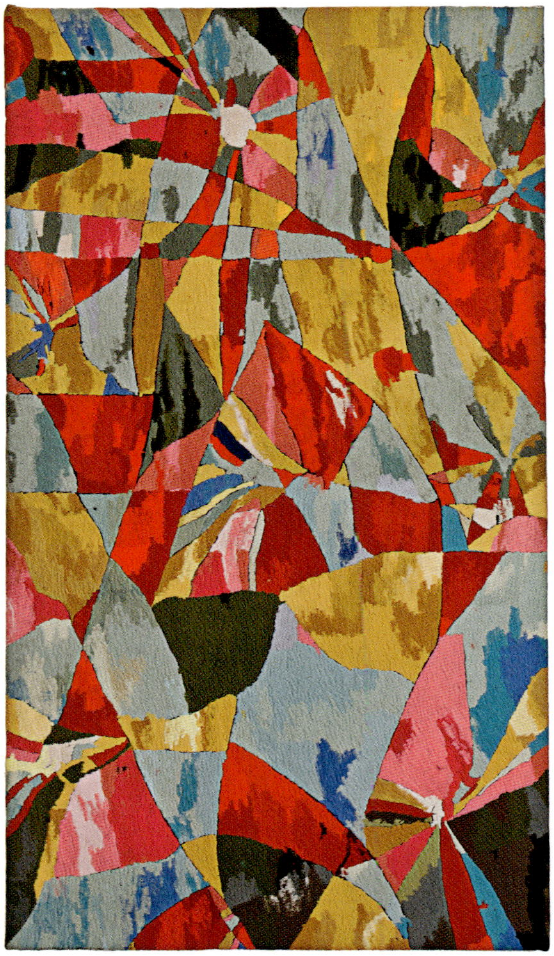

2

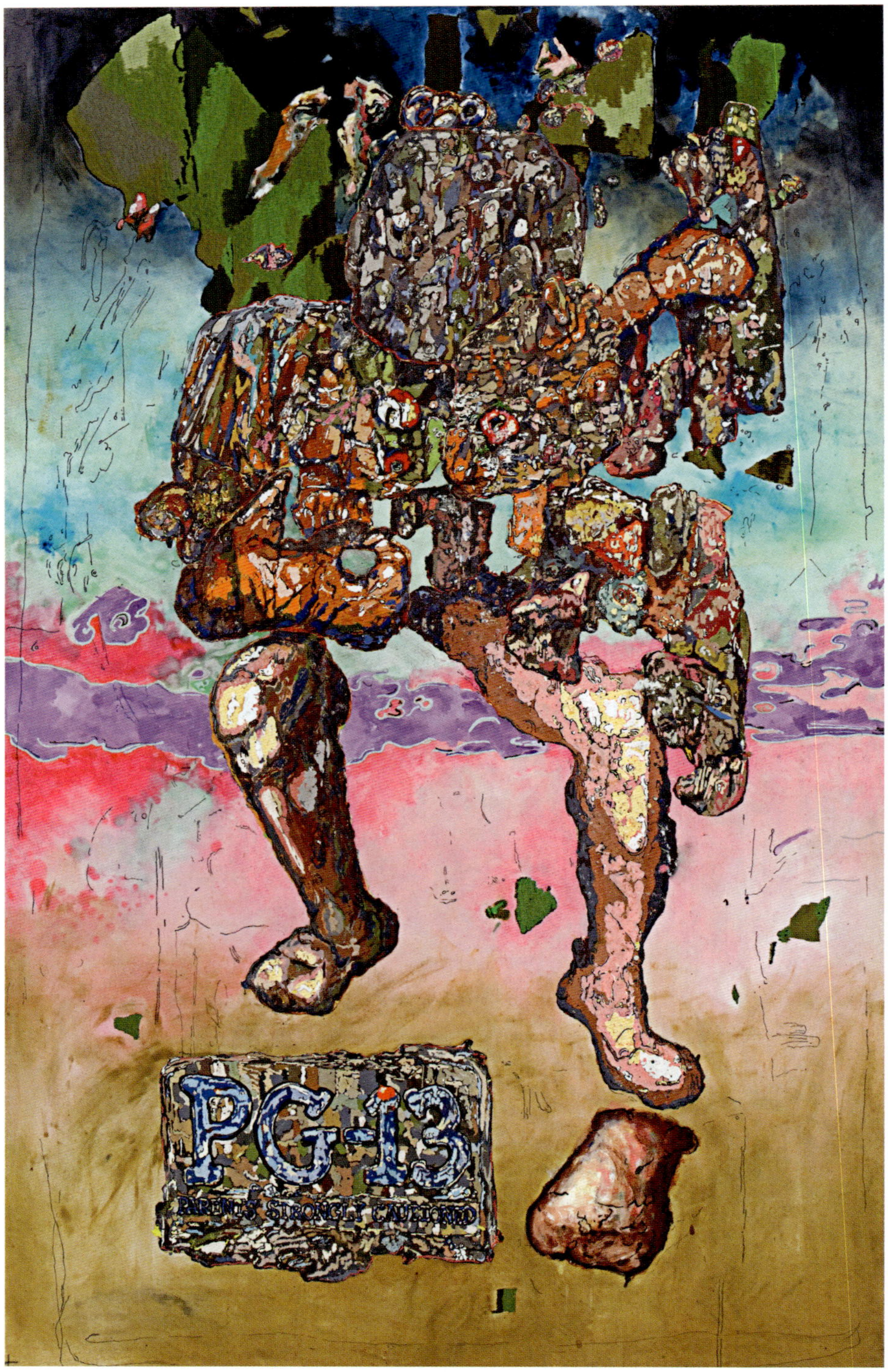

1

Shown by
Kimmerich F26
Richard Telles A20

Biography
Born 1966
Lives in Los Angeles

In recent years American painter Morley has exhibited extensively in the United States. Solo shows were held at Kimmerich, New York (2012, 2011), and Richard Telles Fine Art, Los Angeles (2011). His canvases were included in the group shows "Painting Expanded" (2011) at Tanya Bonakdar Gallery, New York; "The Artist's Museum" (2010) at The Museum of Contemporary Art, Los Angeles, and "Imagination Becomes Reality: Conclusion" (2007) at ZKM, Karlsruhe.

1
Tehachepi (sic)
2011
Oil, thread, acrylic on canvas
80 × 51"
(203 × 129.5 cm)
Courtesy of Kimmerich and Richard Telles

2
Untitled
2010
Thread on canvas
67 × 38½"
(170 × 98 cm)
Courtesy of Kimmerich and Richard Telles

3
From Don, George, and Diane
2010
Oil, wax, and KY Jelly on polyester over wood panel
33 × 27"
(84 × 68.5 cm)
Courtesy of Kimmerich and Richard Telles

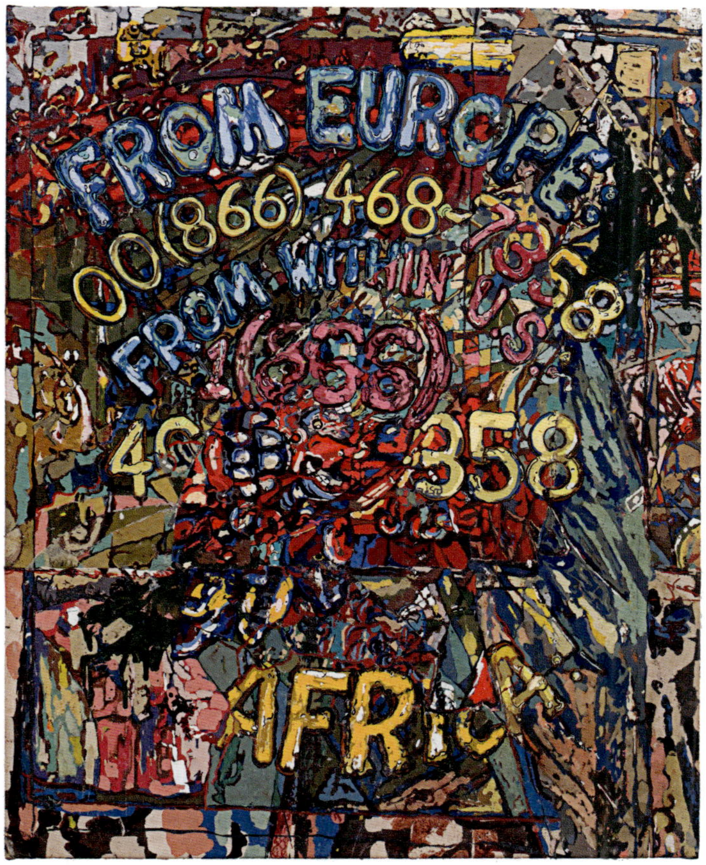

3

Focus
Ivan Morley

Ivan Morley's canvases reveal an organized chaos of references and media, where art-historical tropes butt up against pop-cultural images across painted surfaces perverted by other materials—as in *Tehachepi (sic)* (2011), which collides oil, wax, KY Jelly, thread, and various dyes on linen. His paintings do away with labels such as "abstract" or "figurative," finding a space somewhere in between where he can start to digest the white noise of an accelerated image economy. Our enjoyment of Morley's dense, painterly surfaces, which revel in visual pleasure, is often short-lived, punctured by artfully transcribed telephone numbers and addresses in works such as *From Don, George, and Diane* (2010), which yoke these works to the mundane realities of the world we live in. AB

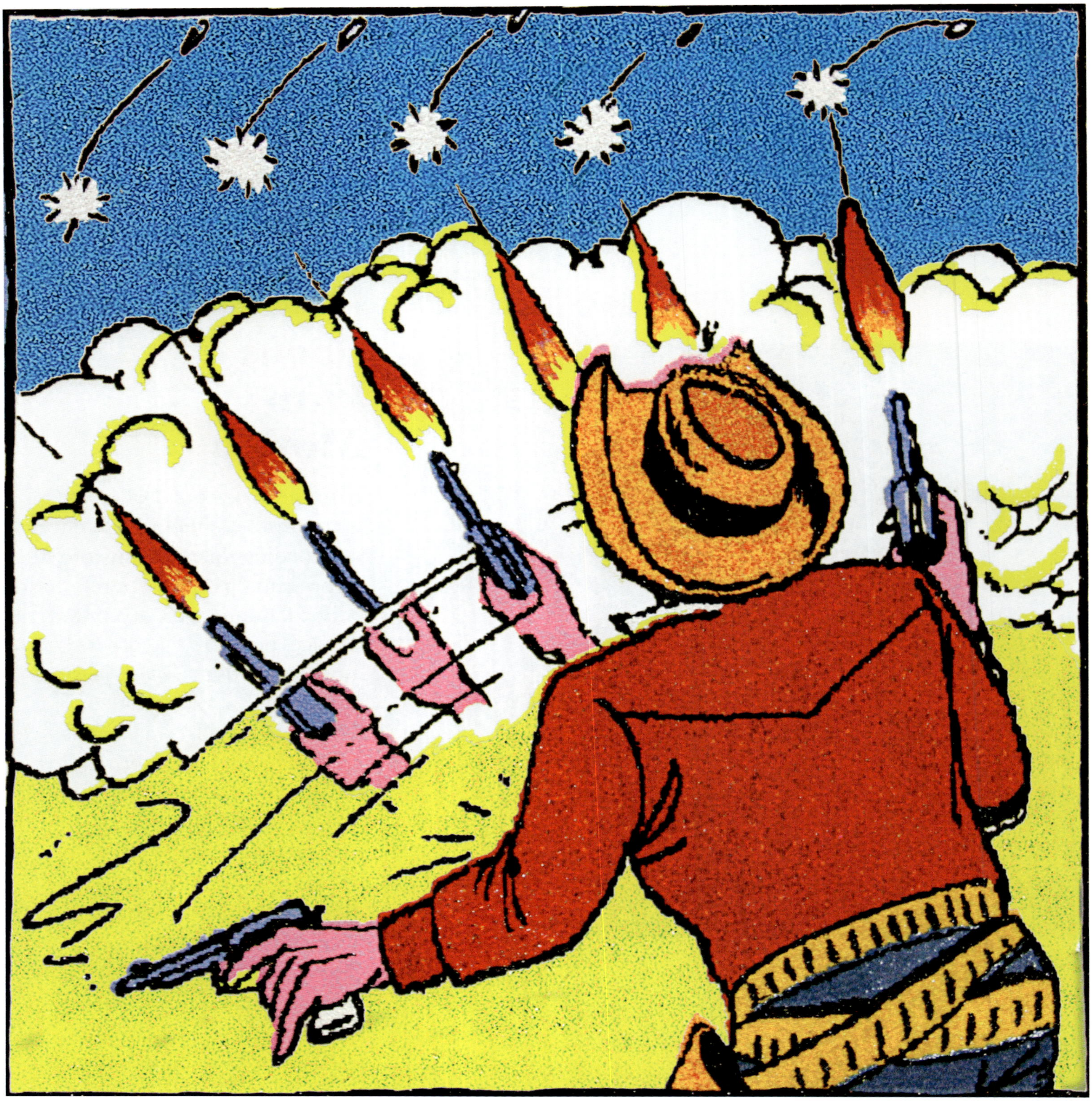

Farhad Moshiri

Shown by
Galerie Perrotin C41
Galerie Thaddaeus Ropac C12
The Third Line C19

Biography
Lives in Tehran

Moshiri has exhibited his prevocational socio-political works across Europe, the United States, and the Middle East since the early 1990s. In recent years he has had solo exhibitions at The Third Line, Dubai (2011); Galerie Thaddaeus Ropac, Salzburg (2010); and "Silly you, Silly me" (2009) at the Galerie Emmanuel Perrotin, Paris. Recent group shows include "How I Learned to Stop Fearing and Love Exotic Art" (2011) at JAMM Art, Kuwait, and "The World Belongs to You" (2011) at the François Pinault Collection, Palazzo Grassi, Venice.

SHOOT 'EM UP
2011
Embroidery and acrylic on canvas on board
68⅞ × 69"
(175 × 175.5 cm)
Courtesy of The Third Line

Iranian artist Farhad Moshiri works with dangerous or seductive materials—whether it's Swarovski crystals, cake icing or razor-sharp knives—using their texture to create works that deliver politically and culturally loaded messages. In *Trench Landscape* (2007), the outline of soldiers bearing flags and rifles is plotted out with pink crystals on an innocuous oil-painted landscape. Employing direct juxtapositions of traditional and contemporary influences, Moshiri depicts antiquated vessels embellished with slang and popular sayings, such as *Only Love* (2007). But elsewhere, the import of Moshiri's works can be deliberately ambiguous, as in the monumental *Shukran* (2011), an installation of 800 knives stabbed into the gallery wall, forming the Arabic word for "Thank You." KK

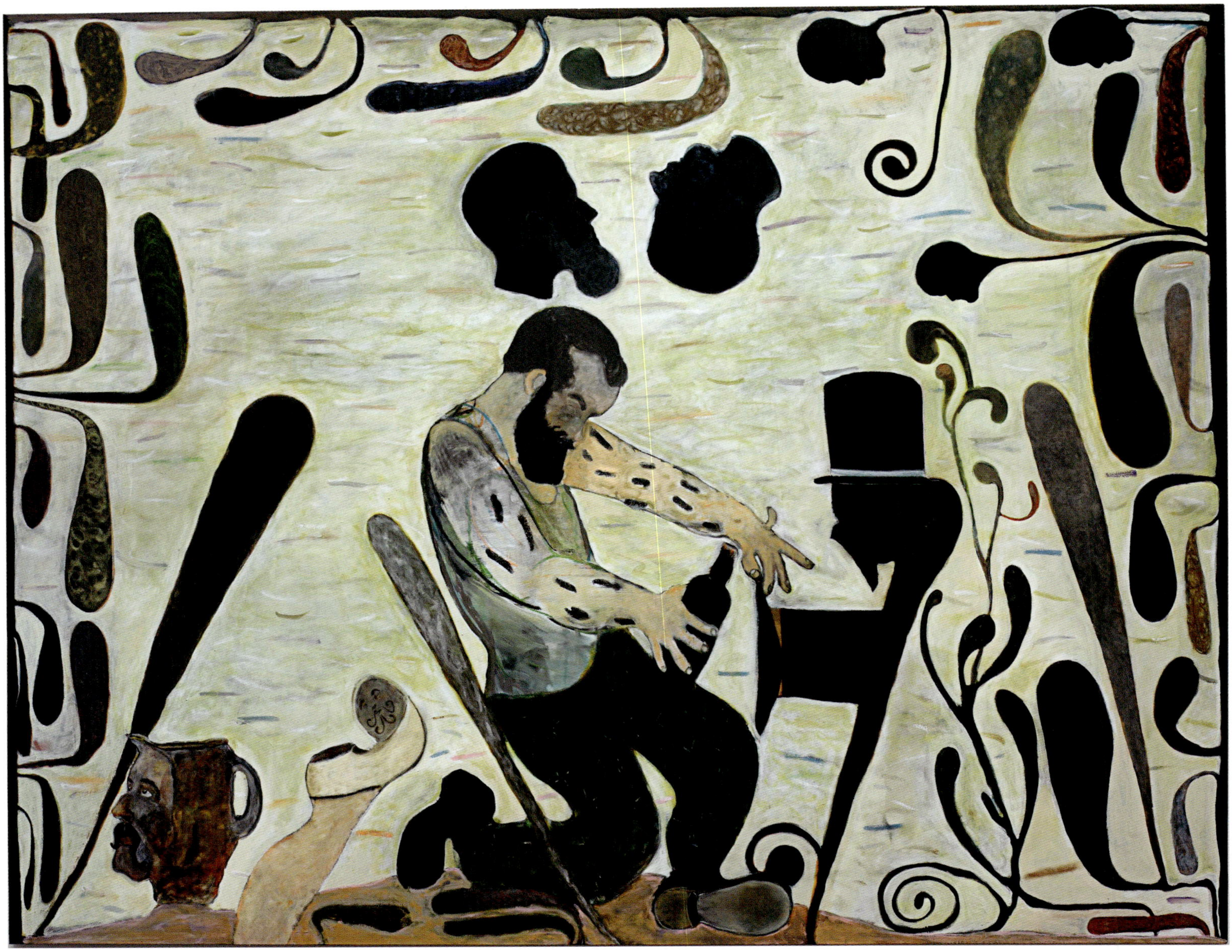

1

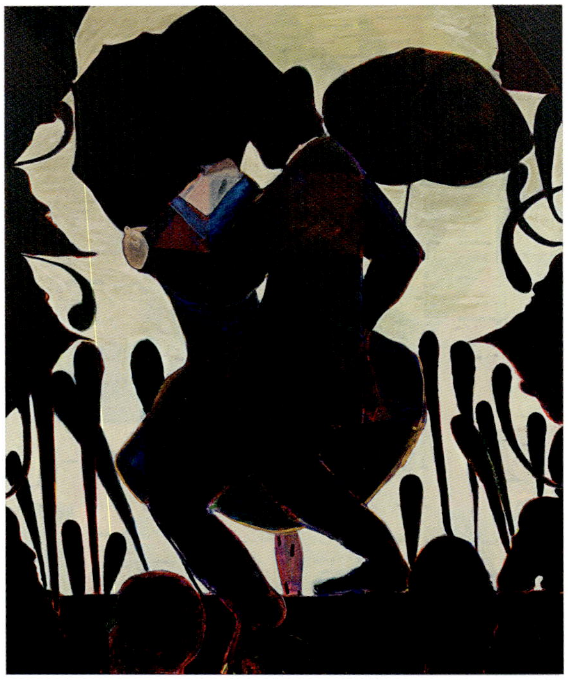

2

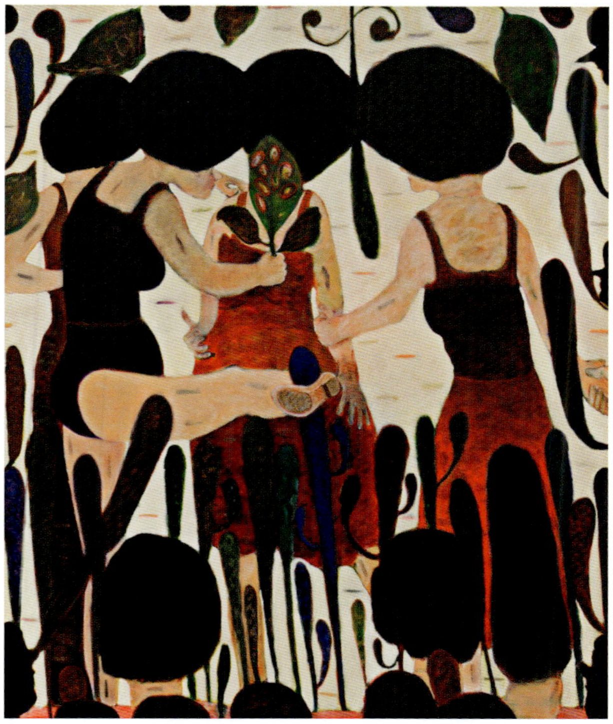

3

Shown by
Galerie Eigen + Art
C33
Alison Jacques Gallery
A25

Biography
Born 1980
Lives in London

British painter Mosley trained at the University of Huddersfield and the Royal College of Art, London. Recent solo shows include the self-titled exhibition at Alison Jacques Gallery, London (2011); "Painting Seánce" (2010) at Grand Arts, Kansas City; and again at Alison Jacques Gallery, London (2010). He was included in the group shows "Labor" (2011) at Galerie Eigen + Art, Berlin; "Make Believe" (2011) at Galleri Magnus Karlsson, Stockholm; and "Newspeak: British Art Now" (2010) at The Saatchi Gallery, London.

1
Waking Édouard
2010
Oil on canvas
82⅝ × 108¼"
(210 × 275 cm)
Courtesy of Alison Jacques Gallery

2
Cave Inn
2011
Oil on linen
84¼ × 70⅞"
(214 × 180 cm)
Courtesy of Alison Jacques Gallery

3
Northern Ritual
2011
Oil on linen
90½ × 75¾"
(230 × 195 cm)
Courtesy of Alison Jacques Gallery

Ryan Mosley

Skulls, cacti, top hats, umbrellas, booze: the world that Ryan Mosley describes in his paintings seems at once cacophonously unhinged and weirdly coherent, even familiar. That may be because many of Mosley's subjects—such as the well-dressed couple canoodling in *Cave Inn* (2011) or the barkeep in *A Bar in France* (2011)—are half-borrowed from famous painters such as George Seurat and Édouard Manet. Elsewhere, carnivalesque notes of James Ensor or William Hogarth add to the fray. Mosley's scenes often take place on theater stages, with lumpen, silhouetted heads gazing up at the action. For him, history barrels into the present to re-perform itself in bits, creating powerfully odd new narratives that are nevertheless dogged by hazy visions of the past. JG

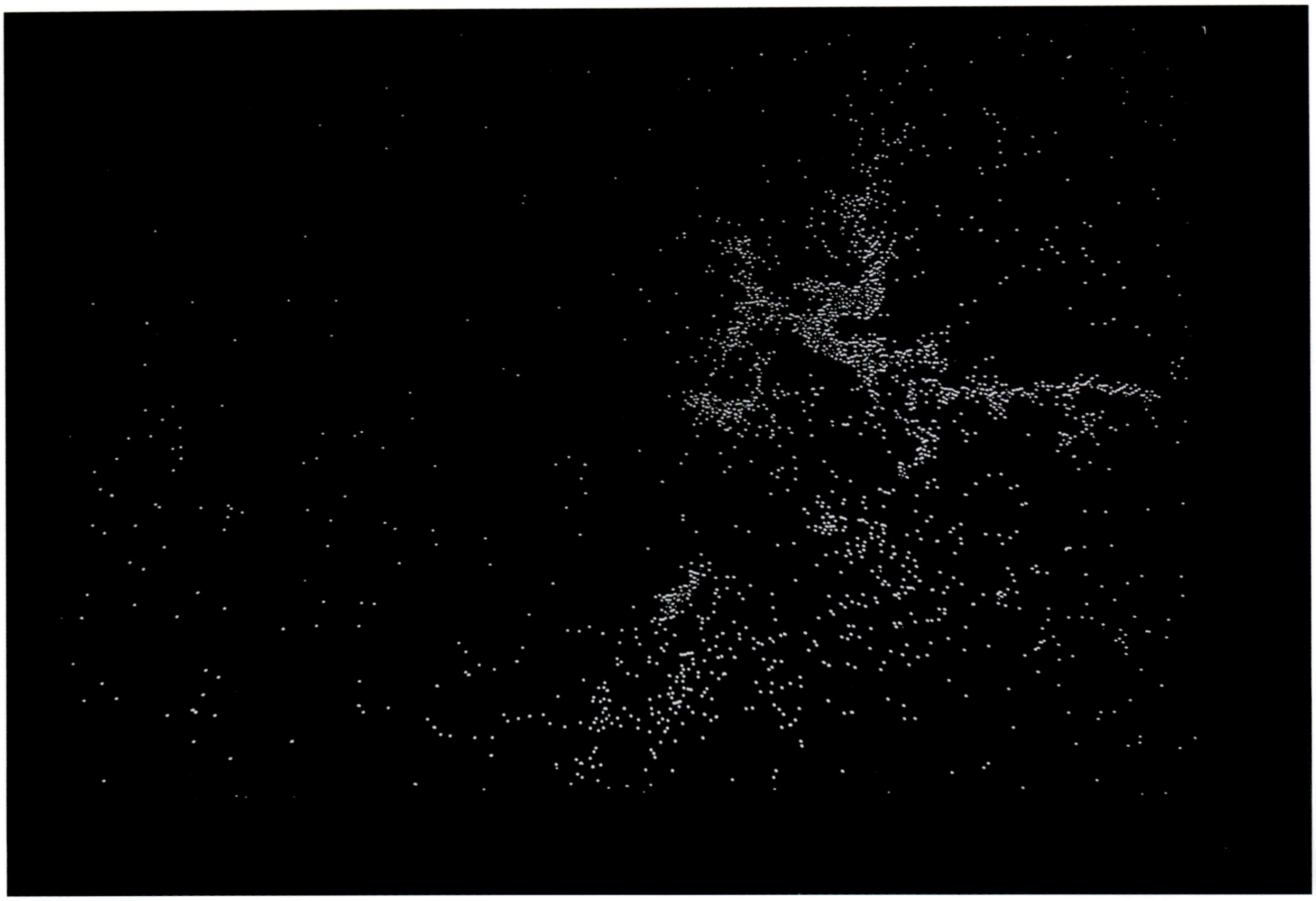

1

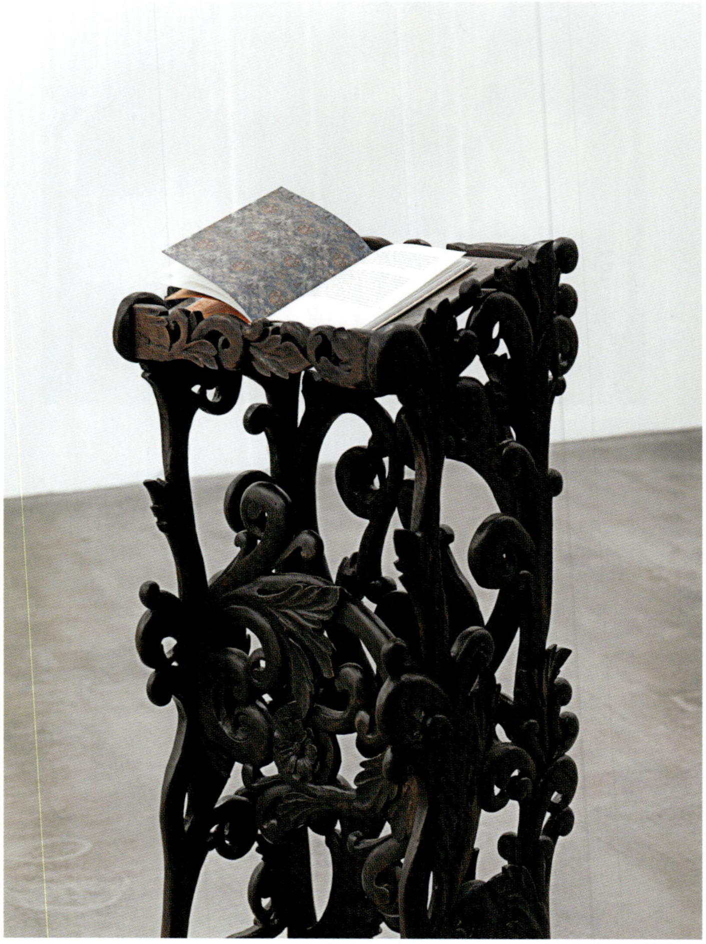

2

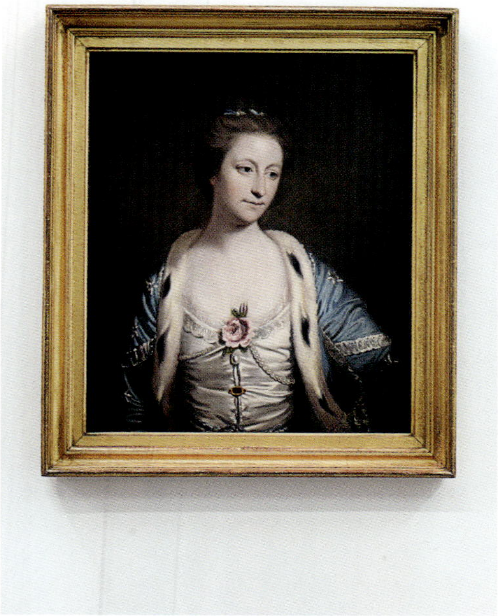

3

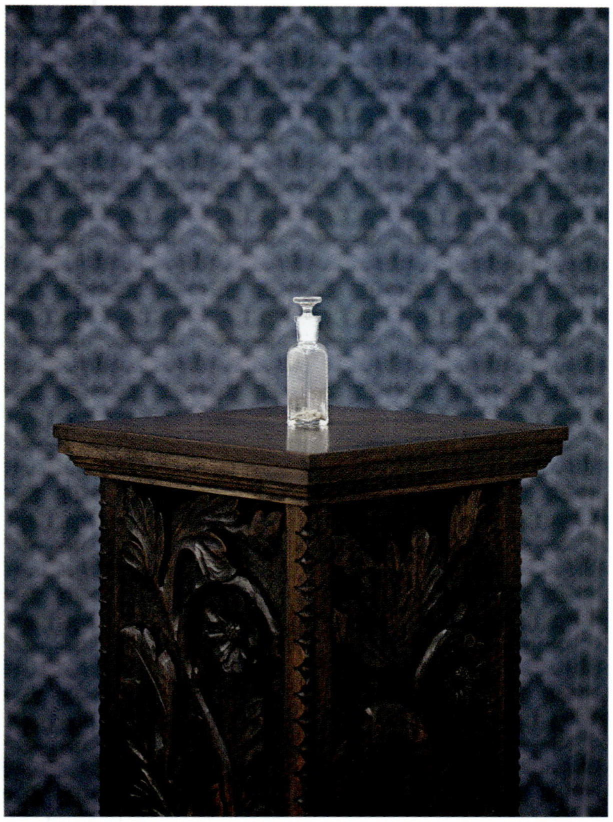

4

Shown by
Meyer Riegger B21

Biography
Born 1977
Lives in Rotterdam

Dutch artist Moti's films and installations have been the subject of numerous solo exhibitions in Europe and the United States. His ambitious 35mm work was included in his solo show "Eigengrau (The Inner Self In Outer Space)" at Meyer Riegger, Berlin, in 2011. The same year he had solo exhibitions at Musée d'Art Moderne Grand-Duc Jean, Luxembourg, and "Open Stores" at the Staatsgalerie Stuttgart.

1, 2, 3, 4
From Dust to Dust
2010
Mixed media installation
Dimensions variable
Courtesy of Meyer Riegger B21

Melvin Moti

The forgotten past, no longer in public view, is often the subject matter of Melvin Moti's films and installations. Part-researcher, part-historian, he endeavours to bring to light unique particularities of generations past by twinning them with contemporary contexts. The installation *From Dust to Dust* (2011) draws together a film depicting close-up dust particles, alongside antiquated painting and other archival materials that are all symbolically linked by Moti's conceptual fascination with the microscopic material. *Eigengrau (The Inner Self In Outer Space)* (2011) examines items from London's Victoria and Albert Museum, and their modes of display. Here the decontextualization of historical artefacts is underlined in a 35mm film depicting objects from the museum collection orbiting in space—the renovation of historical facts gives new life to the narratives that form Moti's practice. SC

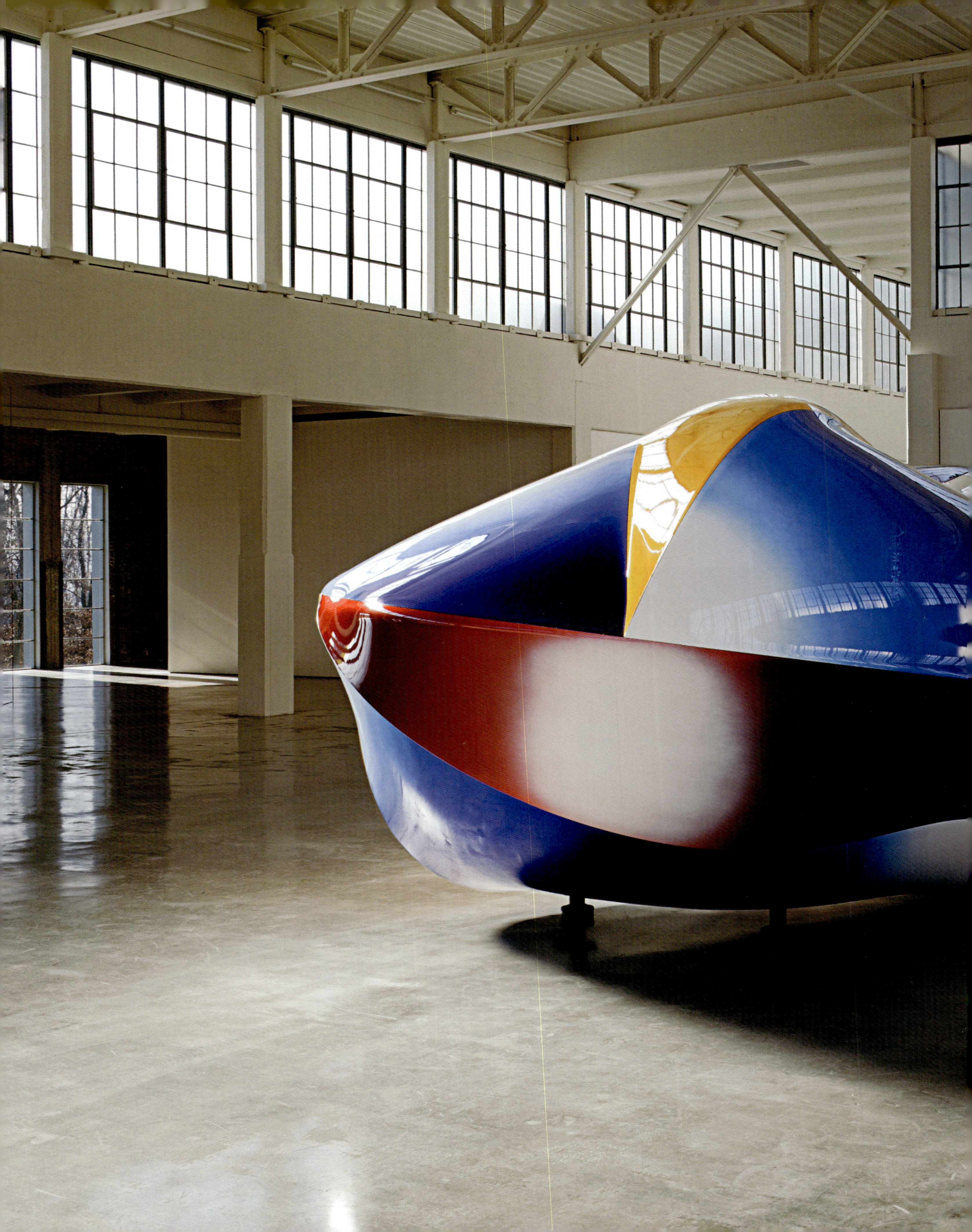

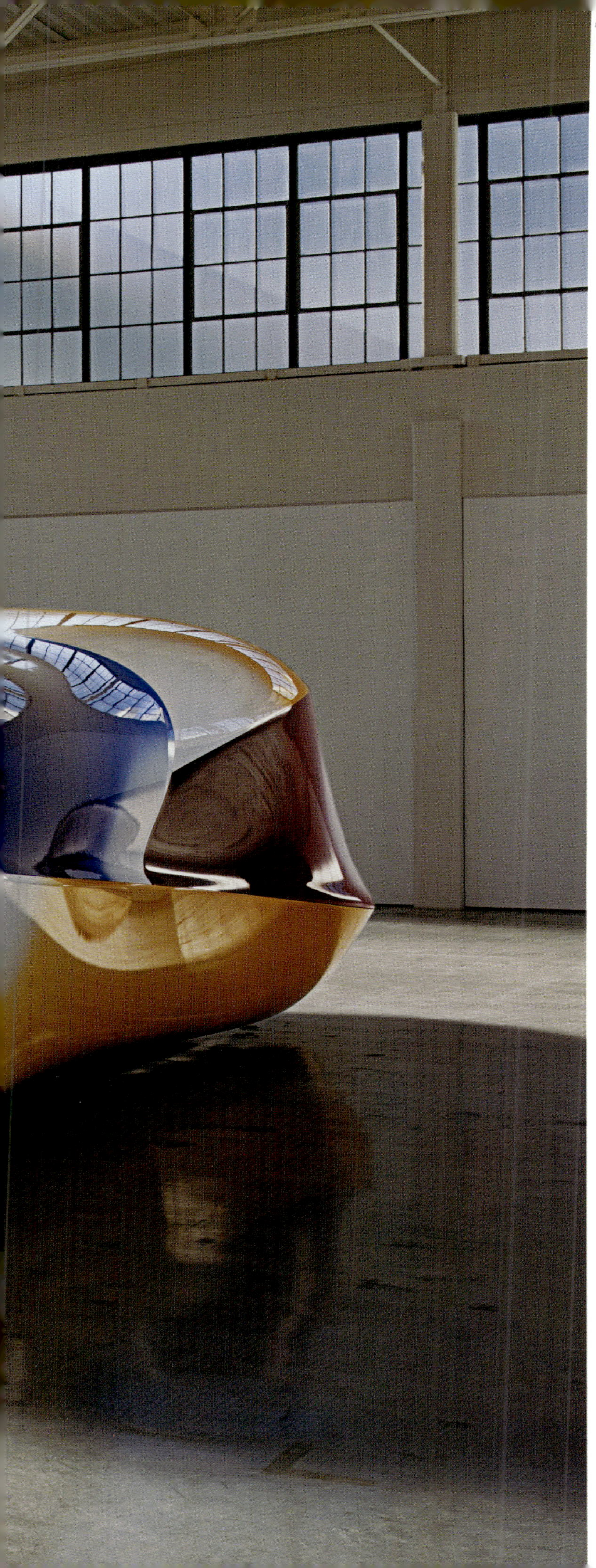

Shown by
carlier gebauer C23
Galerie Chantal Crousel B28

Biography
Born 1955
Lives in Paris

Since the early 1990s, Moulène's sculptures have been exhibited prolifically in Europe. In late 2011 through 2012 his first comprehensive solo show in the United States "Opus + One" will take place at Dia:Beacon. In the last two years he has had solo shows at Carré d'Art, Nimes, and MAMVP, Paris, among others. He participated in the Sharjah Biennial (2010) and Taipei Biennial (2004).

Body
Guyancourt, octobre 2011
2011
Aluminum structure, basalt fiber, pigment, resin
98⅜ × 334⅝ × 137¾"
(250 × 850 × 350 cm)
Produced by Renault Automobiles
Courtesy of Galerie Chantal Crousel

Jean-Luc Moulène

Employing the conventions of commercial photography, Jean-Luc Moulène often shoots his subjects on monochrome backgrounds to isolate them from their context for our scrutiny or delectation. Objects are rendered as half-abstracted or half-anthropomorphized forms, so that stacked bowls or clothed human subjects, such as the man adjusting supermarket shelves in *Chef—Paris, 11 Avril 1998* (2003), become enigmatic ciphers of everyday life. Photographs often cluster on expanses of wall to create irregular tempos; at others an unreal environment is constructed, as in *La Vigie* (2010), where photographs of plants growing through concrete are hung alongside living plants in the gallery, bathed in blue light, implying a research process that remains ultimately opaque. SOR

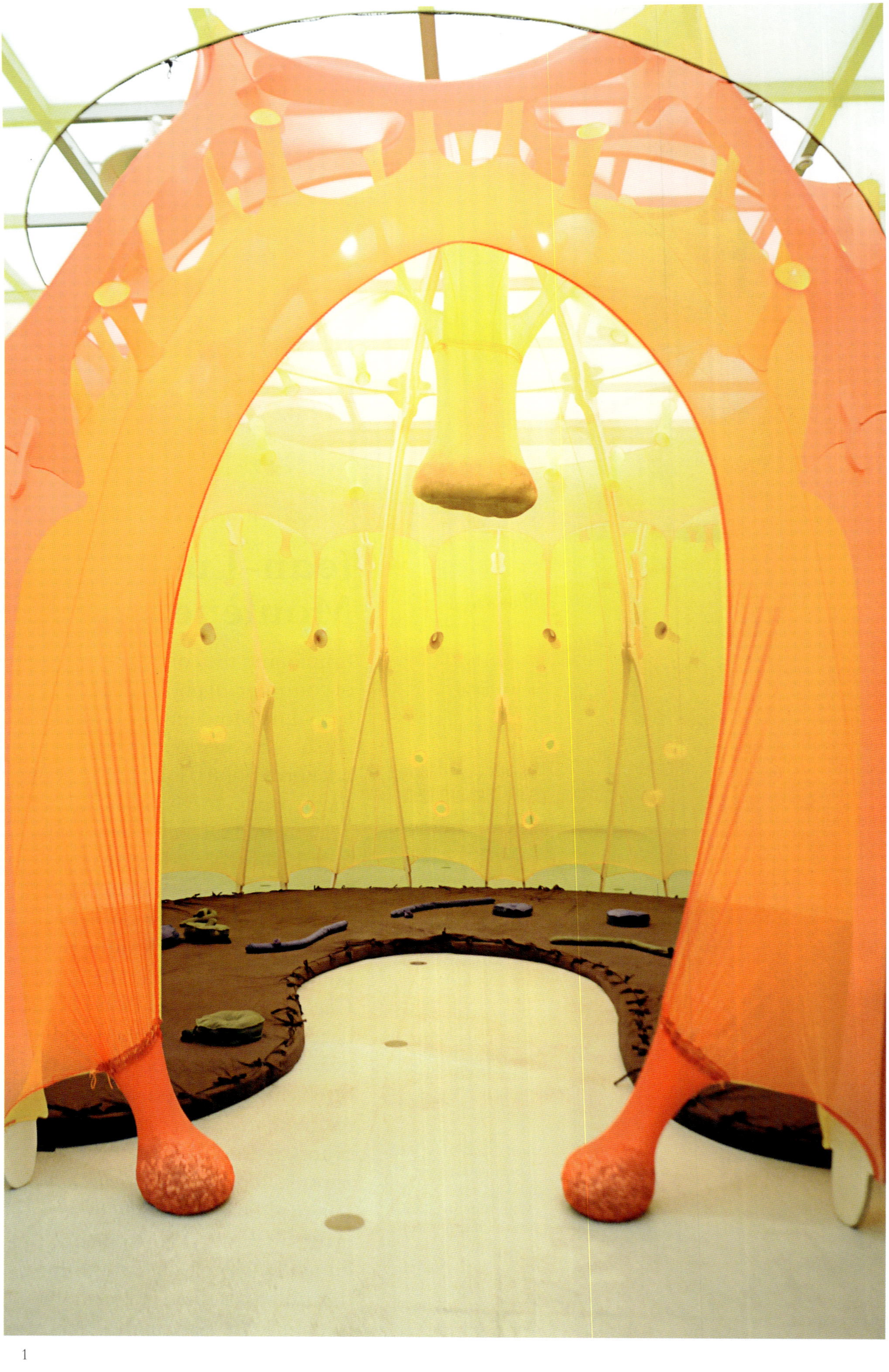

1

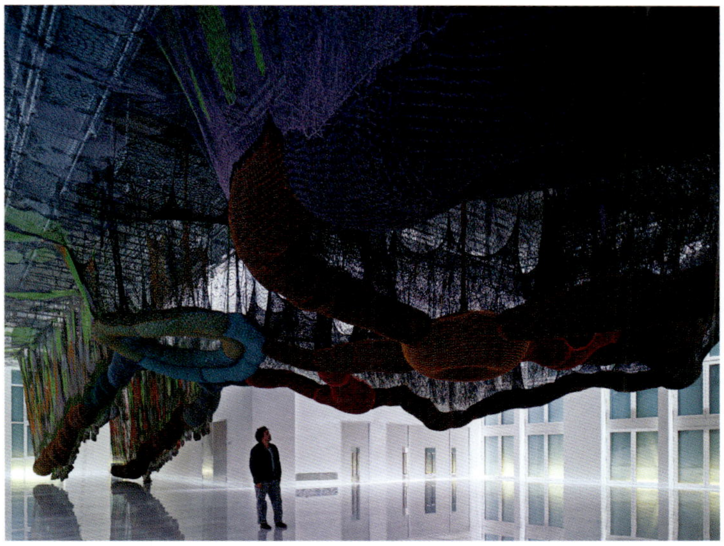

2

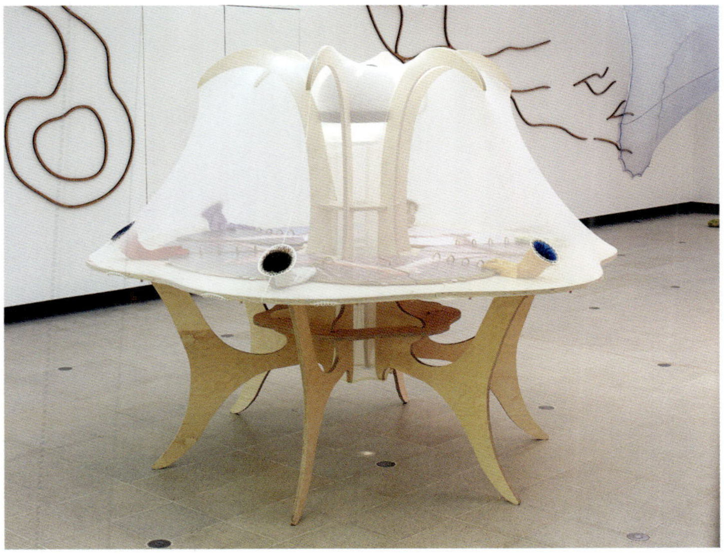

3

Shown by
Tanya Bonakdar Gallery C6
Galeria Fortes Vilaça C48
Tomio Koyama Gallery B8

Biography
Born 1964
Lives in Rio de Janeiro

Since the mid-1990s, Neto has produced a widely exhibited and influential body of sculpture and installation. Recent solo exhibitions include the retrospective "La Lengua de Ernesto Neto" (2011) at Museo de Arte Contemporáneo de Monterrey, Mexico; Los Molinos Exhibition Hall, Faena Art District, Buenos Aires (2011); "Dancing Allowed" (2010) Contemporary Arts Center, Cincinnati, OH (2011); and Hayward Gallery, London (2010). In 2012 he will have solo exhibitions at the Nasher Sculpture Center, Dallas, and Tanya Bonakdar Gallery, New York.

1
The Edges of the World
2010
Mixed media
Dimensions variable
Courtesy of Tanya Bonakdar Gallery

2
Crazy Hyperculture in the Vertigo of the World
2011
Mixed media
Dimensions variable
Courtesy of Tanya Bonakdar Gallery

3
The library mind table
2010
Plywood, MDF, paper-backed book cloth, inkjet on paper, laser etching on paper, polyamide tulle, velvet, acrylic lampshade, glass beads
65½ × 86⅝ × 86⅝"
(174 × 220 × 220 cm)
Courtesy of Tanya Bonakdar Gallery

Ernesto Neto

Through minimal means, Ernesto Neto orchestrates sensory experiences within immersive installations that invoke subtle moments of category readjustment. Stockings are rescued from mundane practicality to be employed as a flexible technology and dynamic surface, referencing at once their petrochemical source and the bodies that wear them. Neto uses smart fabrics that, like viewers, articulate themselves in relation to their surroundings, often loading them with rice and spices, for their olfactory and associational qualities. While installations like *Pantheon* (2006) are pendulous—the perpetual state of suspension evoking a freeze-frame that overcomes gravity—shelter-like structures, such as *Wisdom of the Parts* (2008), speak more of containment, prompting thoughts on the individuality of the viewer and the ambivalent state of commonality and socialization. SOR

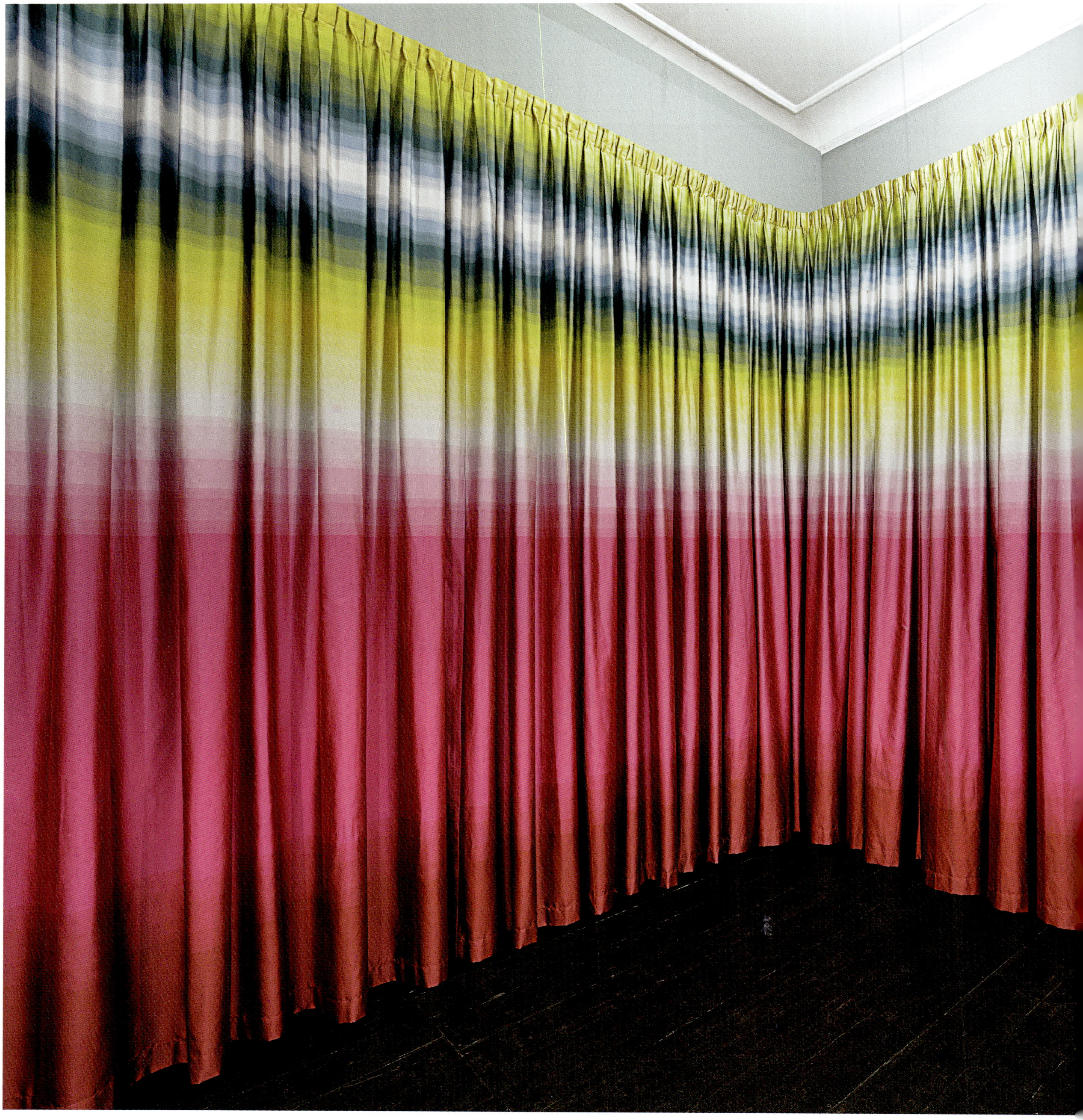

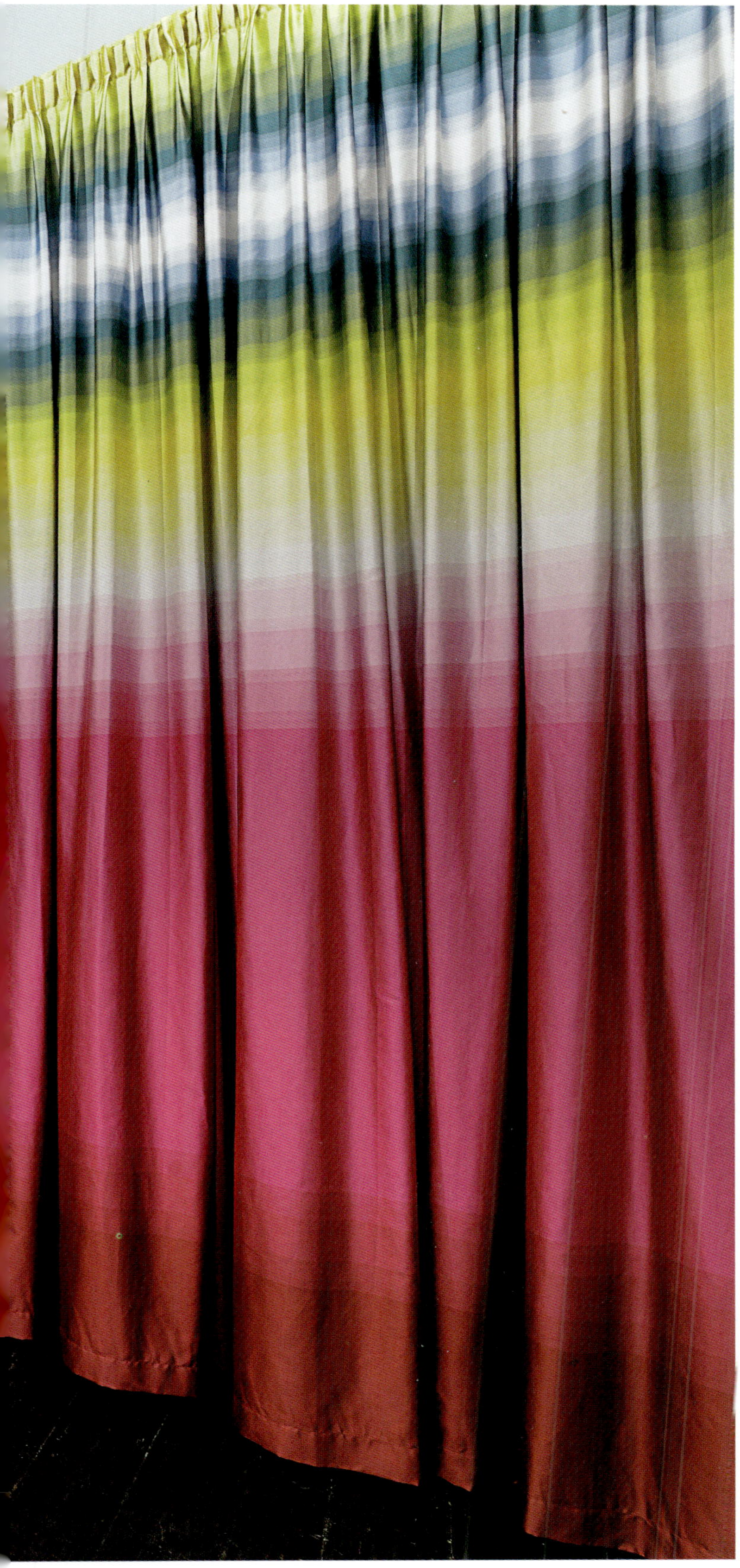

Shown by
Galerie Eigen + Art
C53

Biography
Born 1962
Lives in Berlin

German sound and installation artist Nicolai has been exhibiting his work since the early 1990s. Most recently the solo show "Escalier du Chant (Stair Song)" (2011) at Pinakothek der Moderne, Munich included a vast sound installation for the galleries sweeping staircase. The same year he had a solo show at Galerie EIGEN + ART, Berlin. He participated in the 3rd Thessaloniki Biennale (2011) and in 2012 Kunsthalle Münster, Munster, will hold a solo exhibition of his work.

Warum Frauen gerne Stoffe tragen, die sich gut anfühlen (Why women like to buy textiles that feel nice)
2010
Curtain satinet of cotton and silk, machine woven
Dimensions variable
Courtesy of Galerie Eigen + Art

Olaf Nicolai

In 1937, under the pseudonym Elias Smith, the Austrian sociologist Paul Lazarsfeld—among whose works, before fleeing the Nazis for the US, was a study of unemployment among textile workers—published a survey about consumer behavior that gives its name to one of Olaf Nicolai's most resonant works. *Why women like to buy textiles that feel nice* (2010) ravels together a host of historical references—to Lazarsfeld's sociology of communication, to the Modernist faith in the transformative powers of design and decor—in an installation comprised of a single, sinuous and multicolored curtain. It's of a piece with the artist's continued interest in the ways design and architecture attempt to suborn the ephemeral and atmospheric. BD

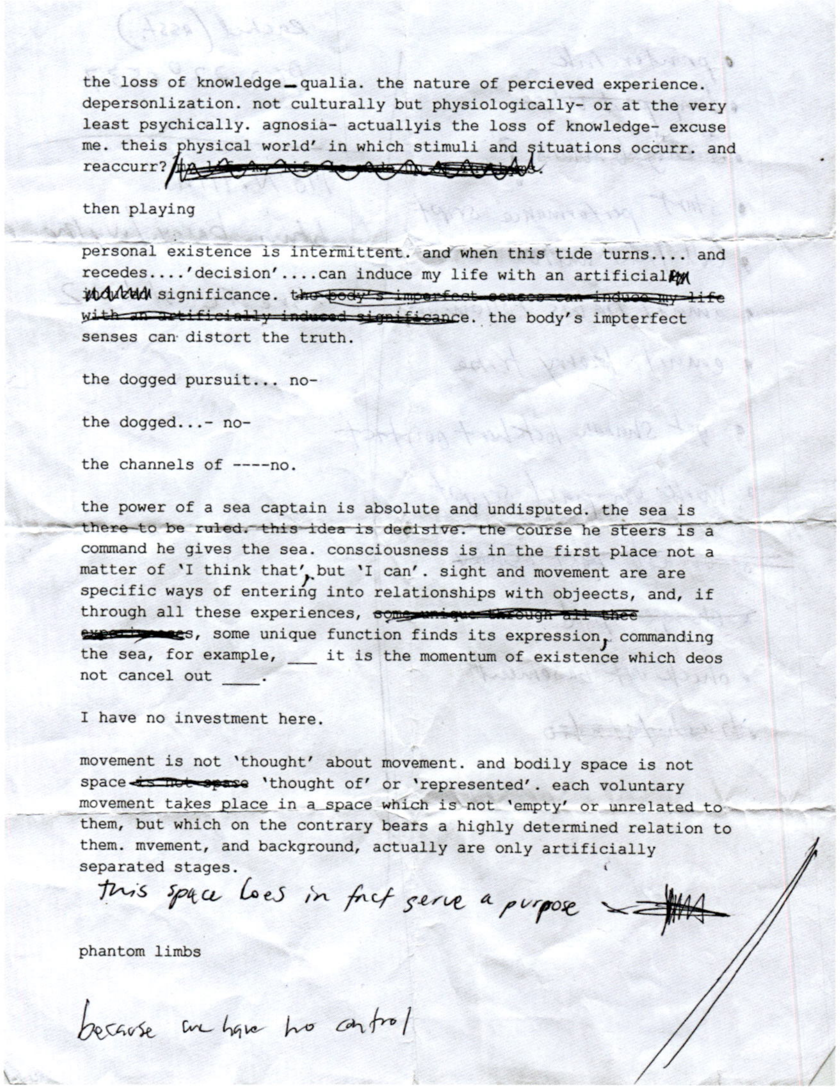

the loss of knowledge- qualia. the nature of percieved experience. depersonlization. not culturally but physiologically- or at the very least psychically. agnosia- actuallyis the loss of knowledge- excuse me. theis physical world' in which stimuli and situations occurr. and reaccurr? [illegible].

then playing

personal existence is intermittent. and when this tide turns.... and recedes....'decision'....can induce my life with an artificial induced significance. ~~the body's imperfect senses can induce my life with an artificially induced significance~~. the body's impterfect senses can distort the truth.

the dogged pursuit... no-

the dogged...- no-

the channels of ----no.

the power of a sea captain is absolute and undisputed. the sea is ~~there to be ruled. this idea is decisive.~~ the course he steers is a command he gives the sea. consciousness is in the first place not a matter of 'I think that', but 'I can'. sight and movement are are specific ways of entering into relationships with objeects, and, if through all these experiences, ~~some unique through all thee experiences~~, some unique function finds its expression, commanding the sea, for example, ___ it is the momentum of existence which deos not cancel out ____.

I have no investment here.

movement is not 'thought' about movement. and bodily space is not space ~~is not space~~ 'thought of' or 'represented'. each voluntary movement takes place in a space which is not 'empty' or unrelated to them, but which on the contrary bears a highly determined relation to them. mvement, and background, actually are only artificially separated stages.

this space does in fact serve a purpose

phantom limbs

because we have no control

2

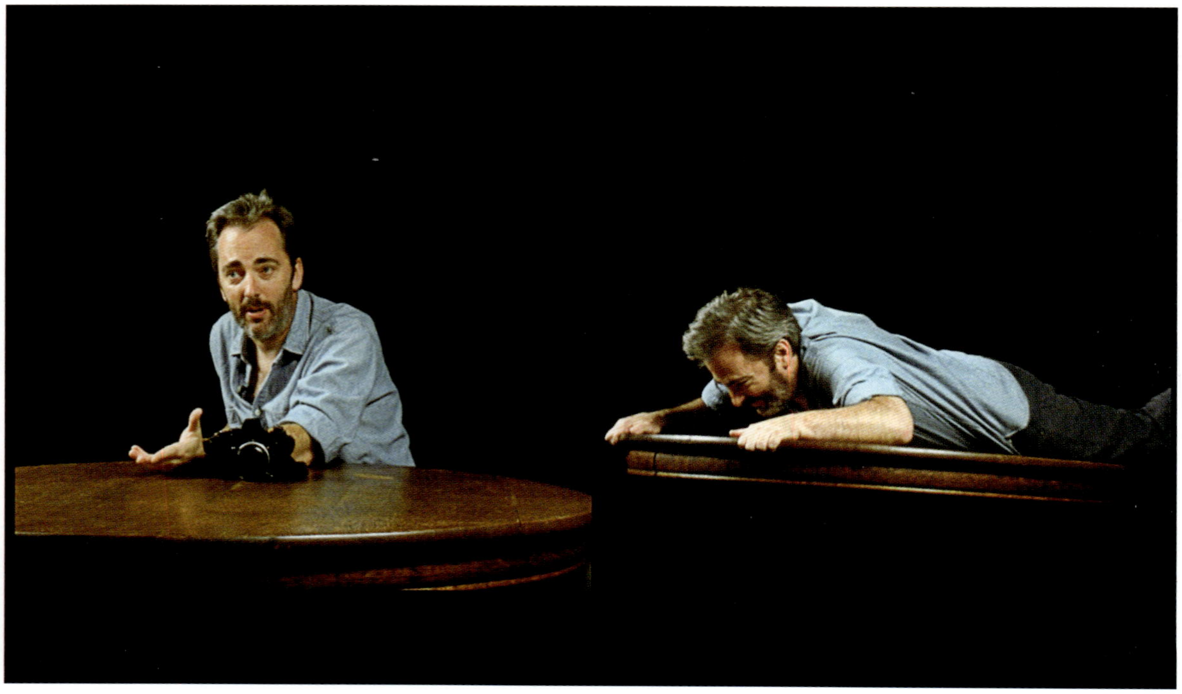

1

Boru O'Brien O'Connell

American artist Boru O'Brien O'Connell has a unique ability to capture the untranslatable in his photographs, films, and installations. His recent two-channel video-installation, *Is it the Wood?* (2011)—a seductive transfer from 16mm—depicted a man's unusual encounter with a wooden tabletop. Meanwhile, his pin-sharp photographs, and video installation, in the exhibition "More Information Has Been Transmitted Via The Telegraph" (2011), captured the site of a trial in Dayton, Tennessee, where a schoolteacher was accused of teaching Darwin's theory of evolution. In a reenactment played out on three monitors, the artist tries to replicate the actions of actors, as they recount the tale. Here, the artist examines the relationship between history, memory, and erasure, unravelling its complexity. SC

Shown by
Triple Canopy A13

Biography
Born 1979
Lives in New York

O'Brien O'Connell received an MFA from Bard College, Annandale-on-Hudson, in 2011. His photographs have appeared in a number of exhibitions, most recently at LaMontagne Gallery, Boston, in the solo exhibition "More Information Has Been Transmitted Via The Telegraph" (2011). In late 2011 he also participated in the group show "Grey Goo" at Night Gallery, Los Angeles. He is a regular contributor to *Bidoun* magazine, and created the interactive video work *State Changes* (2011) for a special issue of Triple canopy in 2011.

1
Is it the Wood?
2011
Two-channel video projection, transferred from 16mm film
Dimensions variable
Courtesy of Triple Canopy

2
Untitled
2012
Ink on paper
8½ × 11"
(21.5 × 28 cm)
Courtesy of Triple Canopy

3
Rhea County Courthouse Structural Framing, from Various Positions
2010
Selenium toned fiber silver gelatin print
18½ × 23½"
(47 × 28 cm)
Courtesy of Triple Canopy

3

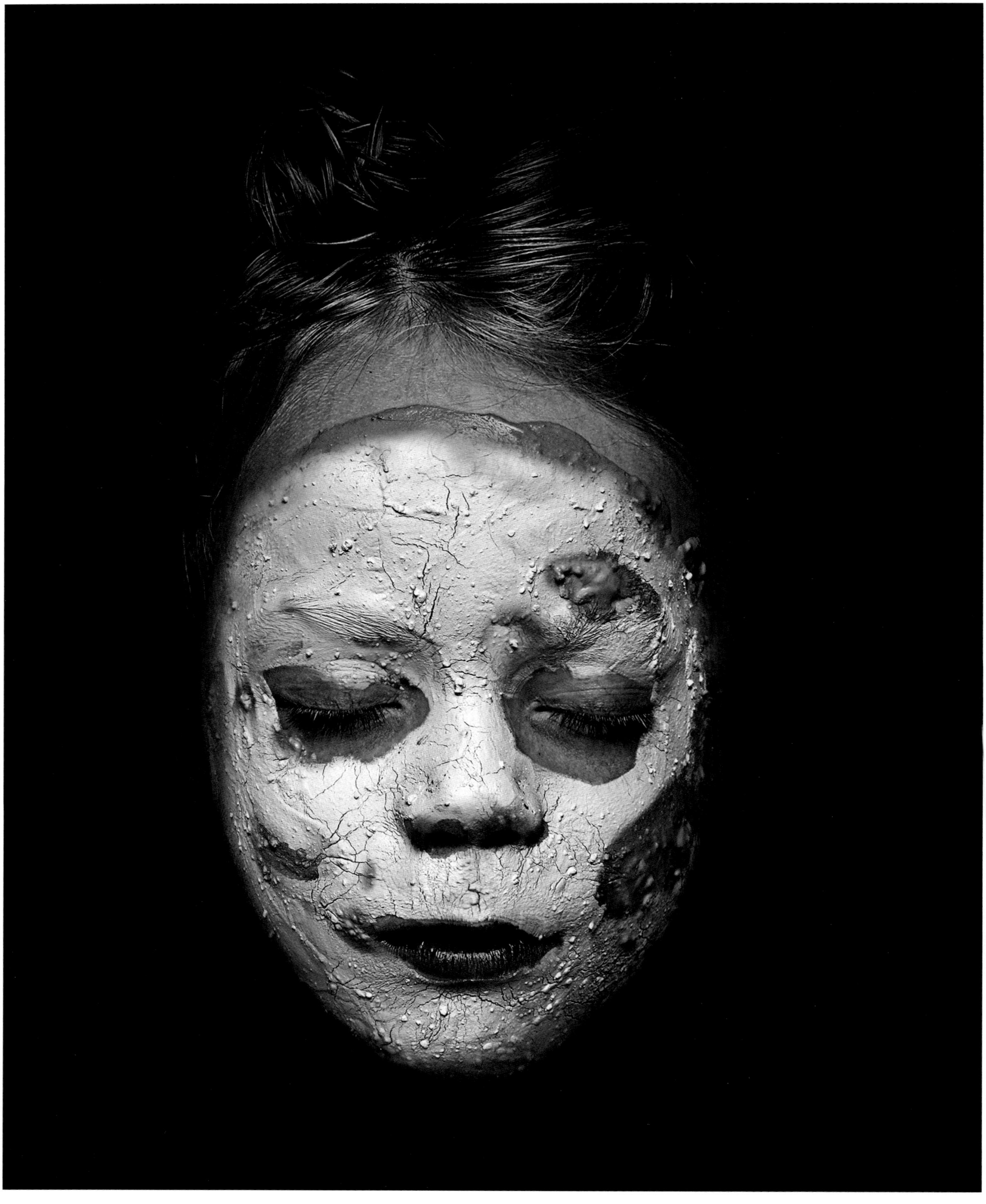

Hans Op de Beeck

Shown by
Marianne Boesky Gallery A26
Galleria Continua C40
Xavier Hufkens B23
Galerie Krinzinger B24

Biography
Born 1969
Lives in Brussels

In the last decade Op de Beeck has exhibited extensively in Europe and the United States. His recent film *Sea of Tranquility* (2010) was shown at Le Grand Café, Centre d'rte Contemporain Saint-Nazaire before travelling to ARGOS, Brussels; Kunstmuseum Thun; and Centro de Arte, Burgos in 2011. The solo exhibitions "Silent Movie" at Marianne Boesky Gallery, New York, and "Black Box" at The Hirshhorn Museum and Sculpture Garden, Washington D.C. took place in 2010.

Faces
2012
HD video
Courtesy of Marianne Boesky

The forms and landscapes in Hans Op de Beeck's film-like *mise-en-scènes* appear emptied out, as if left behind in the wake of an unseen apocalypse. Depicted in an array of media, including sculpture, installation, photography, painting, drawing, and text, the verisimilitude of Op de Beeck's scenarios is always willfully undermined, shifting between an image of reality and reality itself. *Secret Garden* (2010) is a tragicomic installation comprising a lily pond and tree rendered in concrete—an alienating environment that pokes fun at humankind's attempt to give order to nature. In his black and white film *Staging Silence* (2009), immersiveness gives way to miniaturization as a series of doll's-house-like sets are built by various disembodied pairs of hands. AB

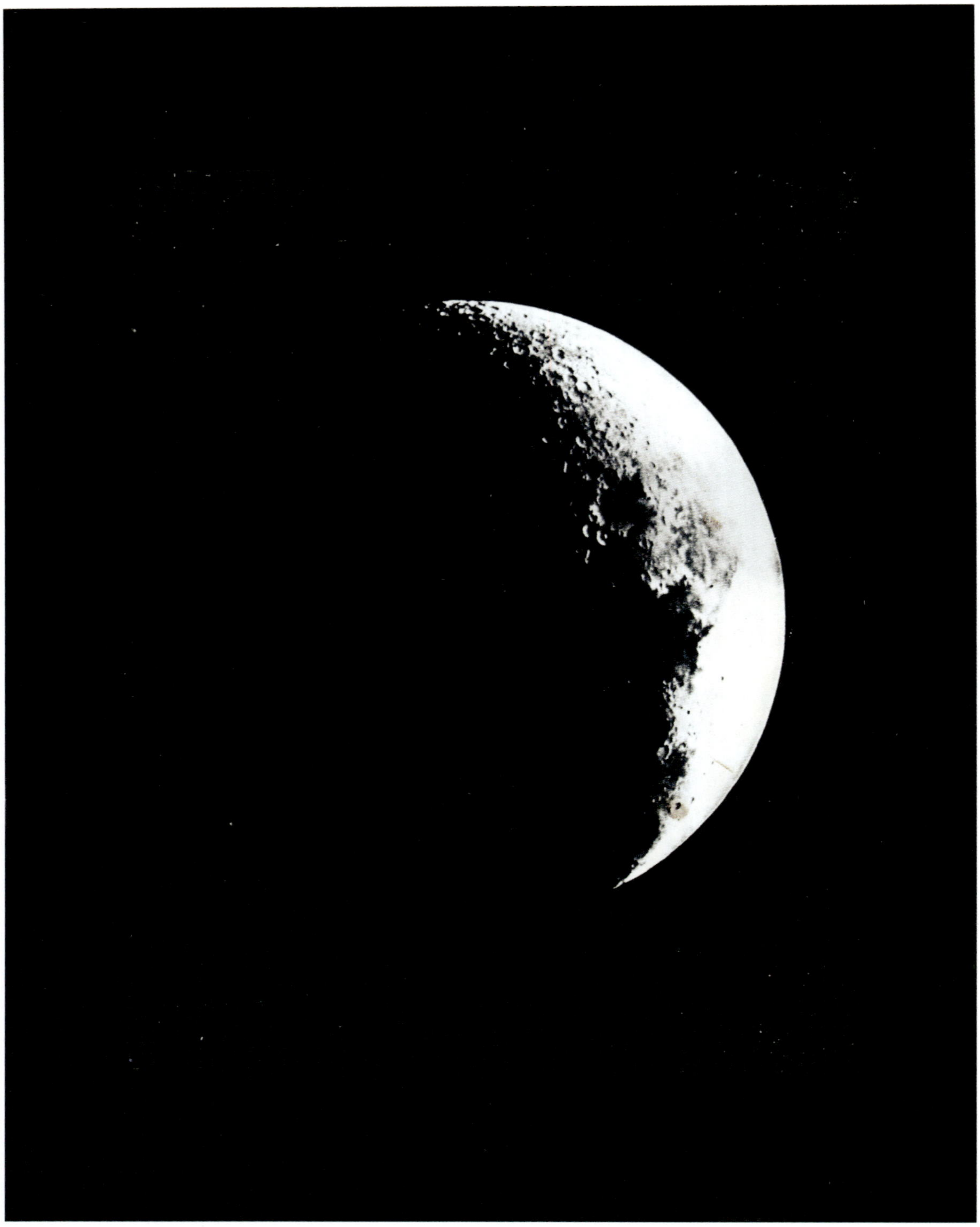

1

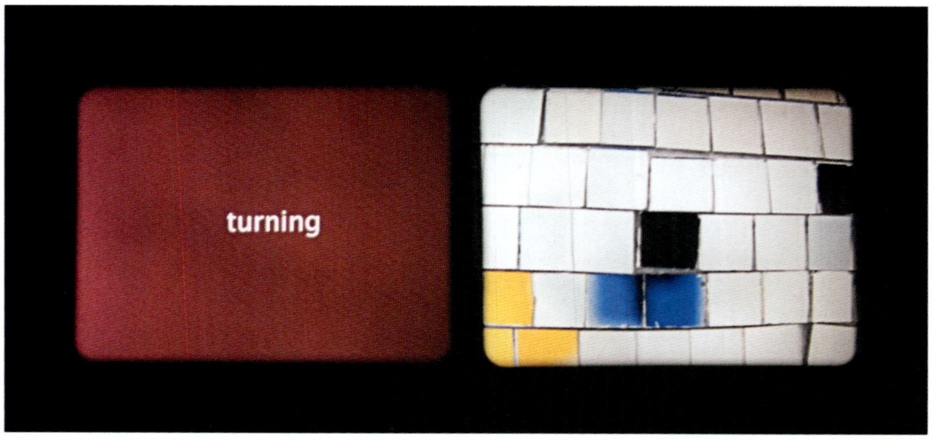

2

Lisa Oppenheim

Lisa Oppenheim's work constitutes an alternative history of photography. Key episodes include the first photographs of the moon, taken in 1851, which Oppenheim re-worked by developing the original negatives in the light of the moon itself (*Lunagrams*, 2010). The cancellation of Polaroid film in 2008 is memorialized in several works that capture instant film as it develops in the "Polaroids" (2008) series; while *Time* magazine's catalog of "100 Photographs that Changed the World" is abstracted by mapping the positions of the stars where the 100 images were taken, in a series of the same name (2007). Making ample use of usable archives of film negatives, Oppenheim composes her history in multiple temporalities by layering, repetition, and erasure. SNS

Shown by
Harris Lieberman B9

Biography
Born 1975
Lives in New York

American artist Oppenheim's films and photographs recall the age of celluloid, and analogue film and photography techniques. Her work has been the subject of numerous solo shows in recent years. In 2012 she will have a solo shows at Harris Lieberman, New York, and 21er Haus, Vienna. Recent solo exhibitions include "Blood to Ghosts" (2010) at Galerie Martin Klosterfelde, Berlin, and a self-titled show at Galerie Juliette Jongma, Amsterdam (2010).

1
Lunagram #1
2010
Unique silver toned photogram
19⅝ × 15¾"
(50 × 40 cm)
Courtesy of Harris Lieberman

2
Cathay (Film Still)
2010
Synchronized double 16mm film projection
7 min. 30 sec.
Courtesy of Harris Lieberman

3
Burning of the Imperial Refinery, Oil City, PA 1846, II
2011
Unique photogram
19⅝ × 15¾"
(50 × 40 cm)
Courtesy of Harris Lieberman

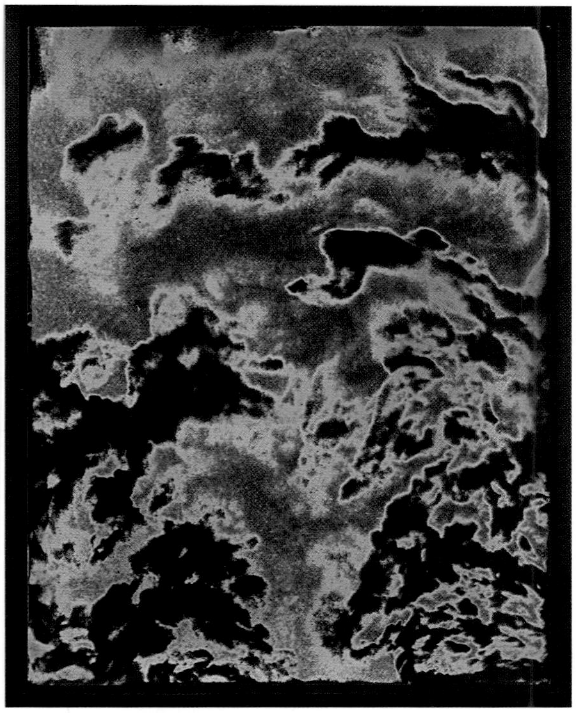

3

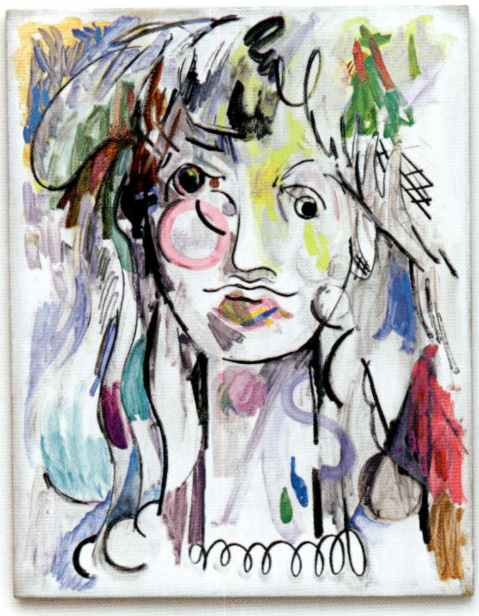

1

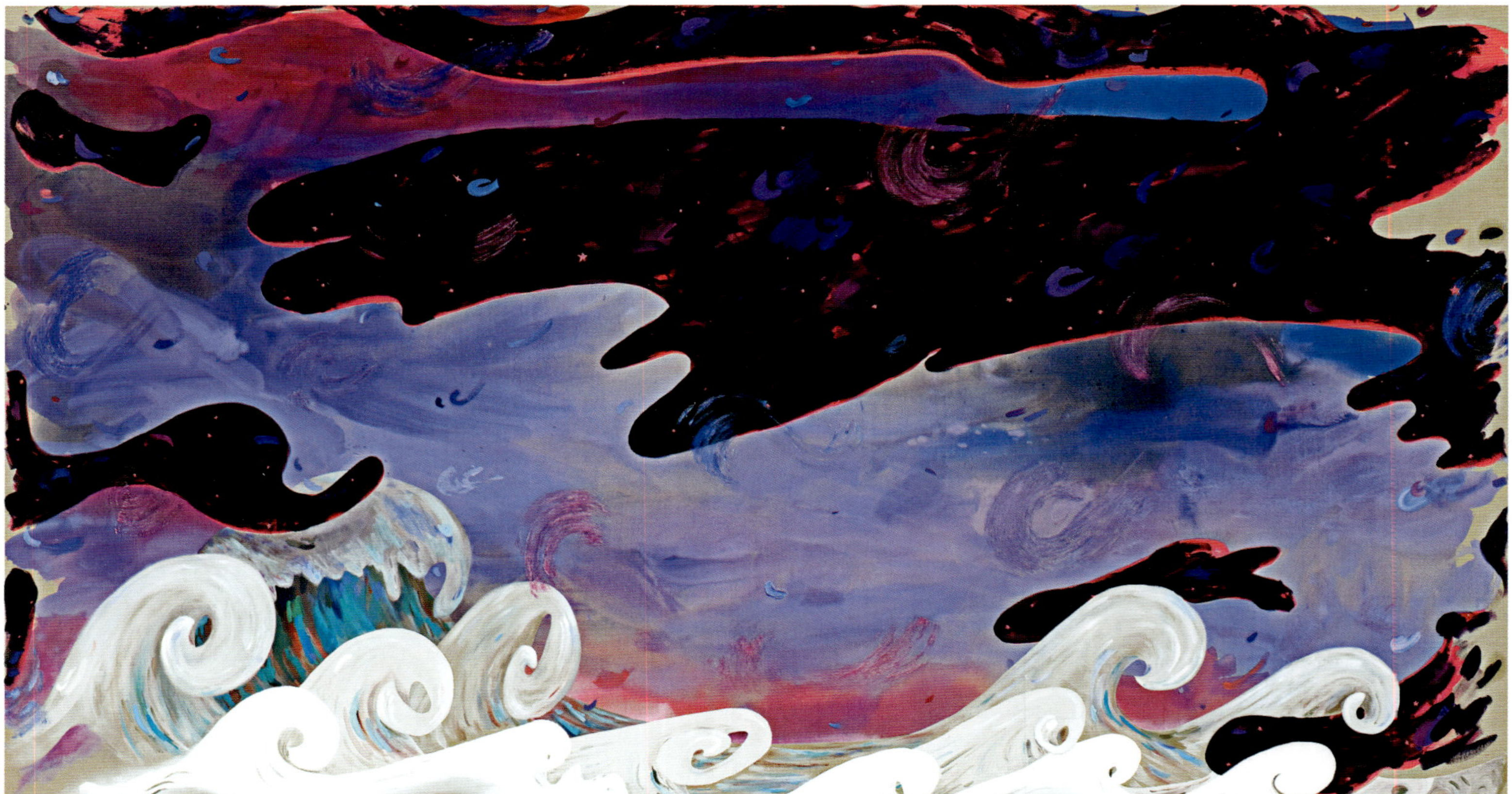

2

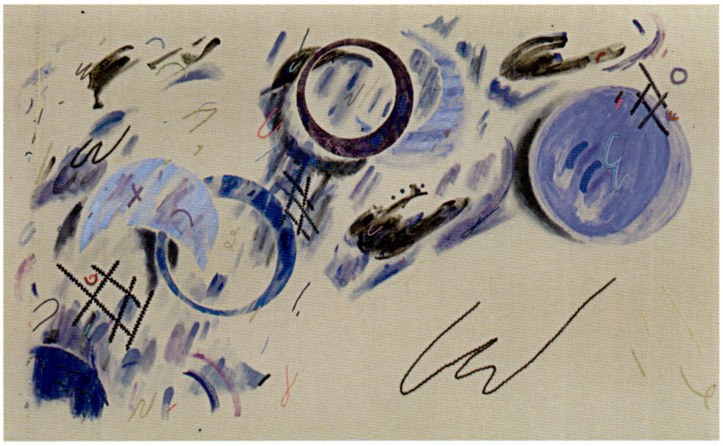

3

Shown by
Gavin Brown's enterprise B18
Galerie Gisela Capitain B19
Sadie Coles HQ C15

Biography
Born 1970
Lives in Los Angeles

American painter Owens has carved out a reputation both sides of the Atlantic as one of the best contemporary painters working today. Her recent solo shows at Kunstmuseum Bonn, in 2011, (her first solo museum show in Germany), and Crown Point Press, San Francisco (2011), have proven her ability to engage the viewer in unique dialogues and mysterious narratives. While recent group exhibitions at MOCA, Los Angeles (2011) and The Walker Art Center, Minneapolis, (2011) have confirmed her place in the wider field of contemporary art.

1
Untitled
2011
Oil and charcoal on canvas
22 × 28" each
(56 × 71 cm each)
Courtesy of Gavin Brown's enterprise

2
Untitled
2009
Acrylic, oil, and graphite on linen
89¾ × 167¾"
(228 × 426 cm)
Courtesy of Gavin Brown's enterprise

3
Untitled
2011
Oil, acrylic, and flashe on linen
81 × 135"
(205.5 × 343 cm)
Courtesy of Gavin Brown's enterprise

Laura Owens

Exuberant, inventive, and nonhierarchical, the paintings of Laura Owens combine influences ranging from the high art territories of Color Field Painting and Abstract Expressionism, to motifs and approaches drawn from folk art, the decorative arts, and children's book illustration. Her dreamy tableaux include a view of a pink sun sinking over a mountain-ringed lake (*Untitled*, 2000) and a depiction of a timid deer amid a landscape of vast oriental blooms (*Untitled*, 2006). In 2010, Owens began making a series of works, "clock paintings," which feature battery-operated clock elements as parts of abstract or figurative compositions, such as the multi-part *Untitled* (2010–11), in which a Picasso-esque monochrome portrait of a woman, whose face consists only of a moving hour and minute hands. SL

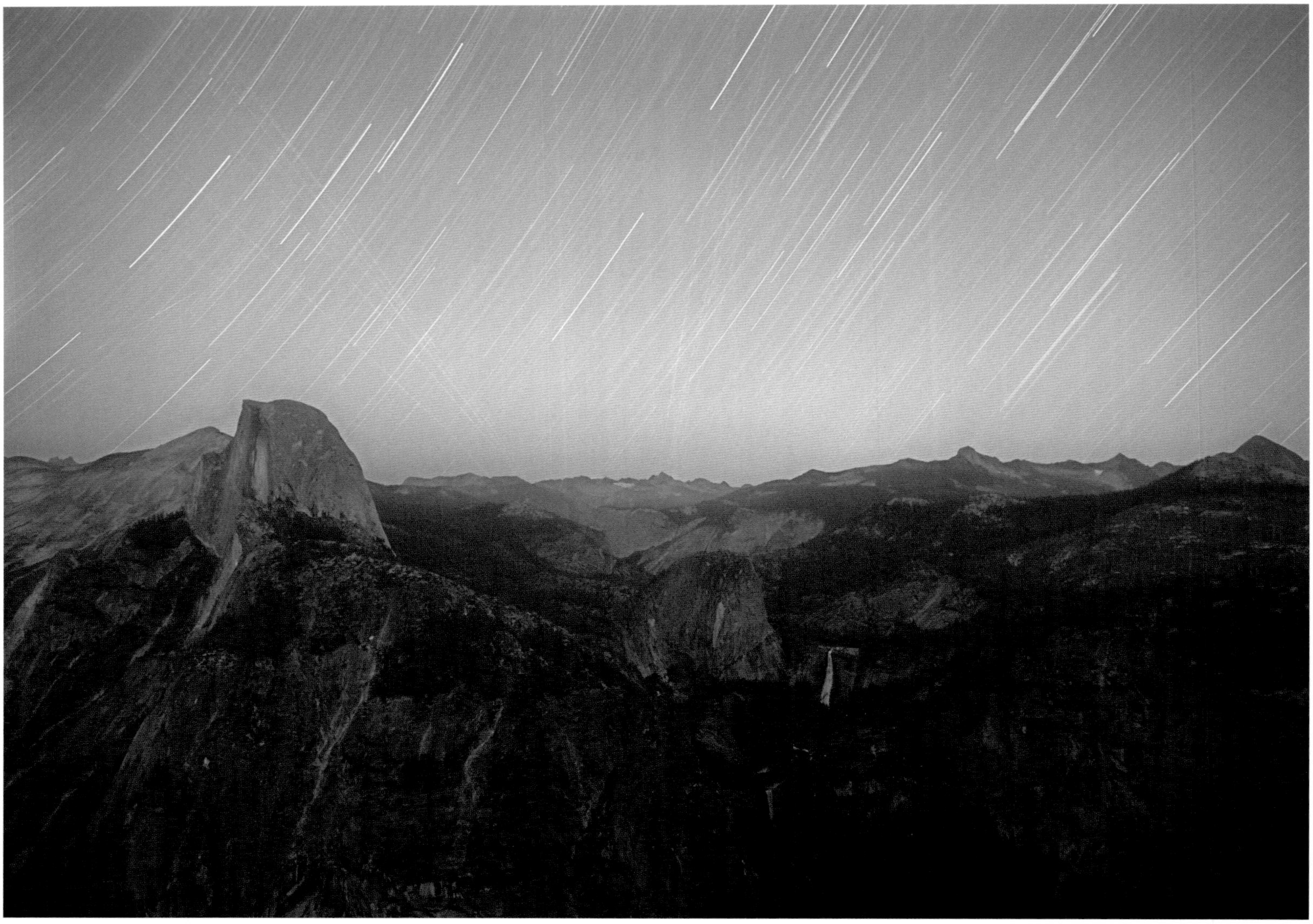

1

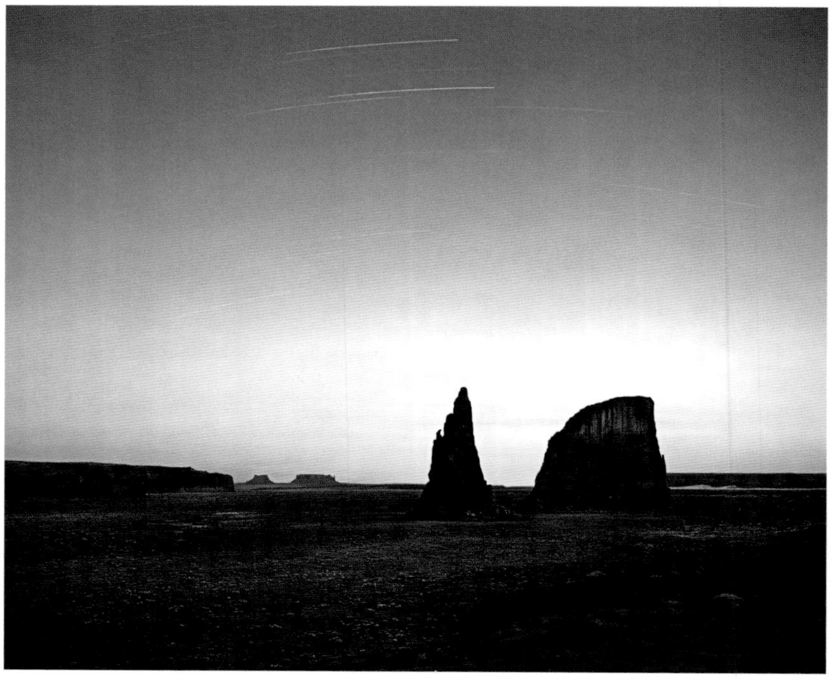

2

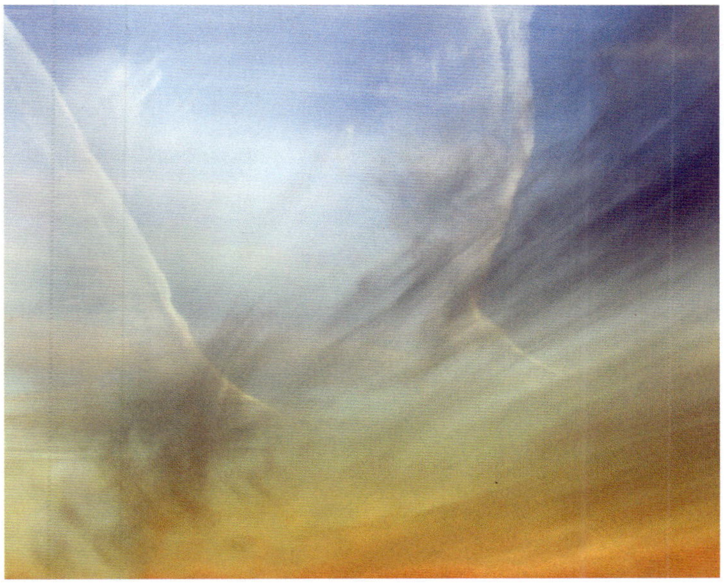

3

Shown by
Altman Siegel F5
Metro Pictures C16

Biography
Born 1974
Lives in New York

American photographer and writer Paglen's politically charged and deceptively aesthetic works have been the subject of numerous exhibitions in the last decade. In 2011 he had the solo shows "Unhuman", at Altman Siegel, San Francisco; "Hidden Landscape" at Aksioma Project Space, Lublijana; and a solo show "The Other Night Sky", at Kunsthall Oslo, Norway. In summer 2012 the group show "Image Counter Image" will take place at Haus der Kunst, Munich.

1
KEYHOLE IMPROVED CRYSTAL from Glacier Point (Optical Reconnaissance Satellite; USA 224)
2011
C-type print
30 × 43"
(76 × 109cm)
Courtesy of Altman Siegel

2
Dead Satellite with Nuclear Reactor, Eastern Arizona (Cosmos 469)
2011
C-type print
48 × 60"
(122 × 152.5 cm)
Courtesy of Altman Siegel

3
Untitled (Reaper Drone)
2010
C-type print
48 × 60"
(122 × 152.5 cm)
Courtesy of Altman Siegel

Focus
Trevor Paglen

Trevor Paglen has been variously described as an experimental geographer, an artist, and an investigative reporter. For almost ten years he has been exploring the clandestine activities of US military, aerospace, and intelligence operations, documenting the all-pervasive apparatus of the "war on terror." With the aid of high-end optical systems, Paglen photographs top-secret government sites in the middle of the desert or classified spacecraft in the Earth's orbit. But his titles, such as *Reaper Drone (Indian Springs, NV Distance—2 miles)* (2010), make claims that the images themselves—blurred long-distance shots, or luminous abstractions of satellite-streaked skies—cannot fully verify. Paglen's work lifts the lid on hidden worlds, in which truth and belief are dependent on visibility. ST

1

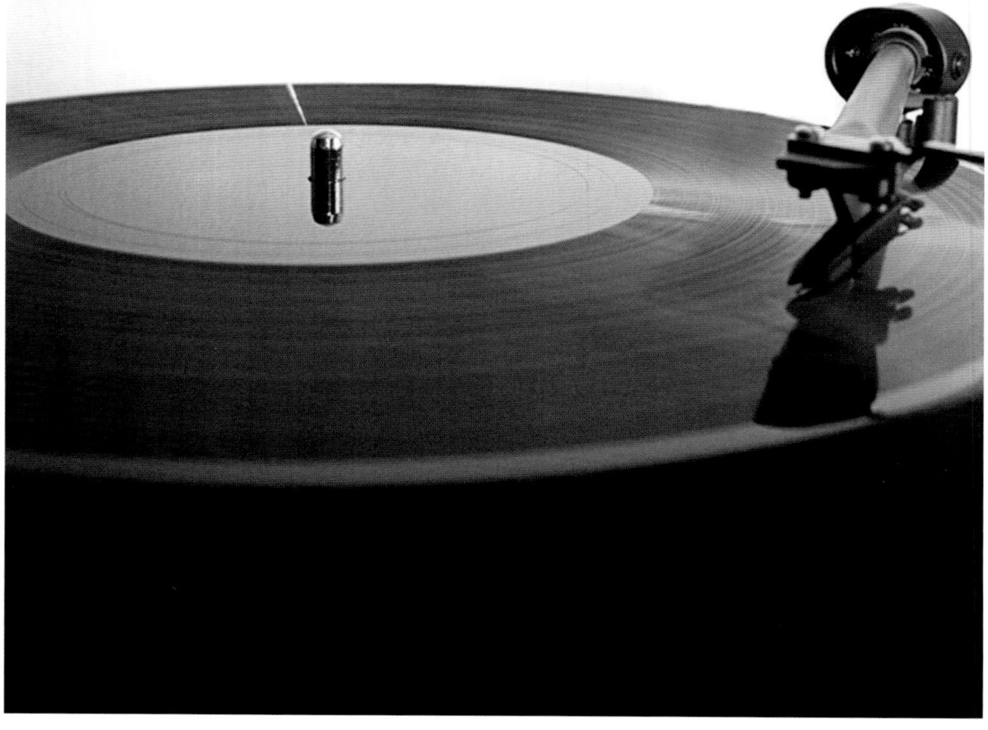
2

Katie Paterson

Is the world getting smaller or bigger? Despite advances in communication technology, Katie Paterson suggests the latter—or at least that the universe's vast proportions are technologically insurmountable. For *Vatnajökull (the sound of)* (2007–8), gallery visitors dialed a phone number to hear a glacier melting, live. The best representational efforts of the crackly phone line were no match for the scale of the glacier's slowness and geographical distance. Just as futile is her project *History of Darkness* (2010–ongoing), where she records the absence of light, in prints and a slide archive, sampled from the farthest reaches of the universe. Darkness—traditionally analogous to ignorance—admits profound insights into the imaginative and pictorial limits of our world. JG

Shown by
James Cohan Gallery
B30

Biography
Born 1981
Lives in London and Berlin

Scotland-born artist Katie Paterson's concept-driven work has been the subject of numerous exhibitions in recent years. In 2012 she will have solo shows at Haunch of Venison, London, and the Modern Art Museum of Fort Worth. Other recent solo exhibitions include a self-titled show at PKM, Seoul (2011) and "Continuum" (2011) at James Cohan Gallery, New York. Paterson participated in the group exhibitions "Cage Mix" (2010) at BALTIC, Gateshead; the Whitstable Biennale (2010); and PERFORMA 09 (2009) New York.

1
Inside this desert lies the tiniest grain of sand
2010
Black and white photograph on resin-coated paper
39 × 48½ × 1⅞"
(99 × 123 × 5 cm)
Courtesy of James Cohan Gallery

2
As the World Turns
2010
Modified Project Debut record player
37 × 2 × 19⅝"
(94 × 5 × 50 cm)
Courtesy of James Cohan Gallery

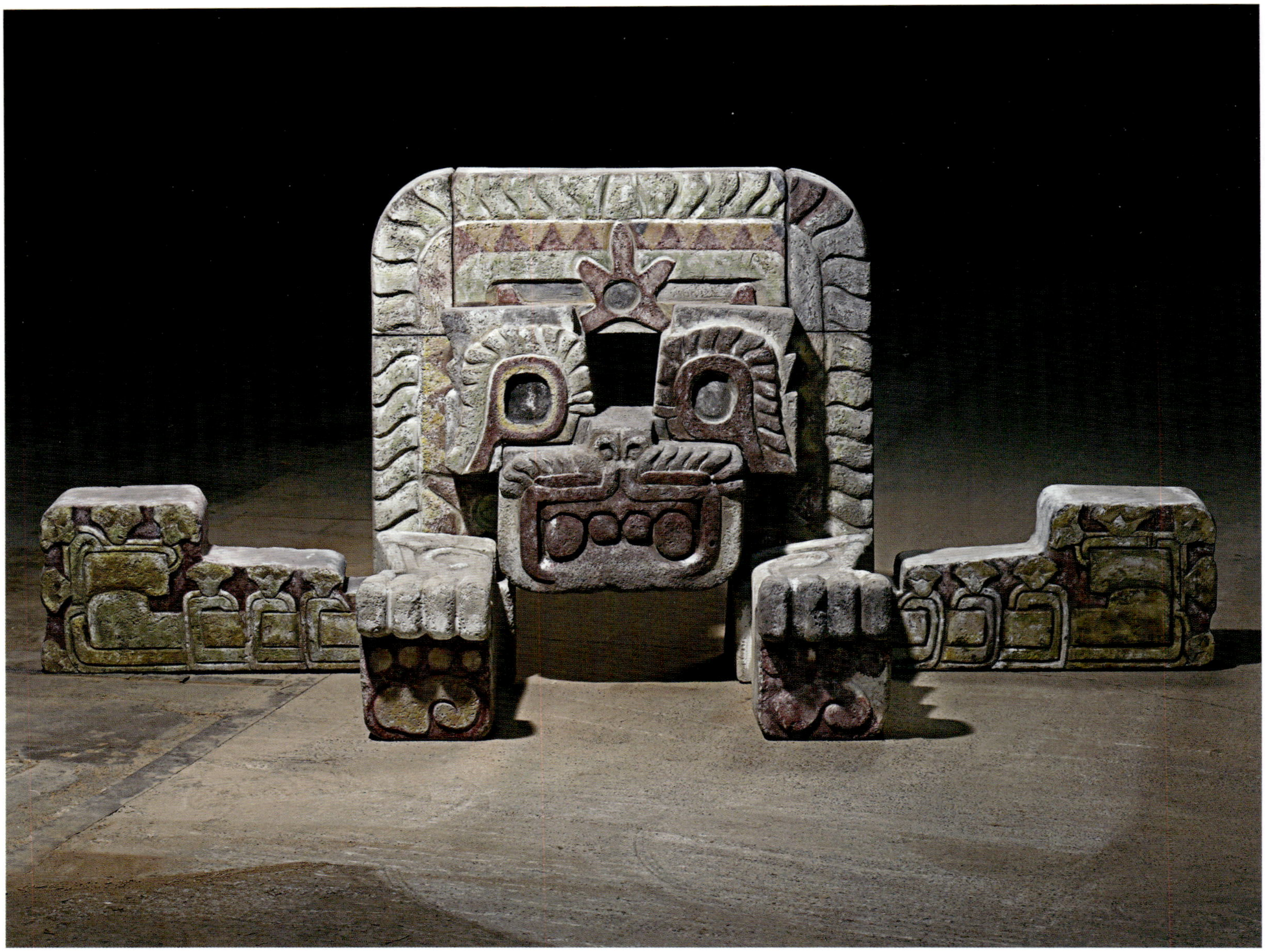

1

Mai-Thu Perret

For over a decade, Mai-Thu Perret has made multifarious art works—large sculptures, costumes, neon signs, ceramic wall pieces and texts, to name but a few of her chosen media—on behalf of an imaginary Utopian feminist commune in the New Mexico desert. Titled *The New Frontier* (1999–ongoing), the project's conceptual framework allows Perret to evade the anxieties of exclusive authorship ("Why me?" she asks) while exploring new media, new influences, and new collaborations. She has recently moved away from the conceit, although she admits it still informs her thinking. Sculptures such as the neon pyramid *Flow My Tears II* (2011) are subtly gendered, referring in this case to auras experienced by migraine sufferers—a predominantly female demographic. JG

Shown by
David Kordansky Gallery C1
Galerie Francesca Pia A15
Galerie Praz-Delavallade A18
Timothy Taylor Gallery C8
Galerie Barbara Weiss A27

Biography
Born 1976
Lives in Geneva

Swiss artist Perret's 2011 exhibition "The Adding Machine" was recently shown at Aargauer Kunsthaus, Aarau and Le Magasin, Grenoble. She also won the Zurich Art Prize that year; the exhibition "I dream of the code of the west" (2011) at Haus Konstructiv, Zurich celebrated this success. Flag (2010) flew outside the Swiss Institute, New York, in 2010, and the 2009 exhibition "2013" at The Aspen Art Museum, as well as solo shows in Paris and Zurich, confirmed her influence on both sides of the Atlantic.

1
The Adding Machine
2011
Polyurethane foam, acrylic paint
38⅜ × 92¾ × 29⅜"
(97.5 × 235.5 × 74.5 cm)
Courtesy of Galerie Francesca Pia

2
Flow my Tears I
2011
Mannequin with a glass head and Schiaparelli "skeleton" replica dress realised by Naoyuki Yoneto
68⅞ × 27½ × 27½"
(175 × 70 × 70 cm)
Courtesy of Galerie Francesca Pia

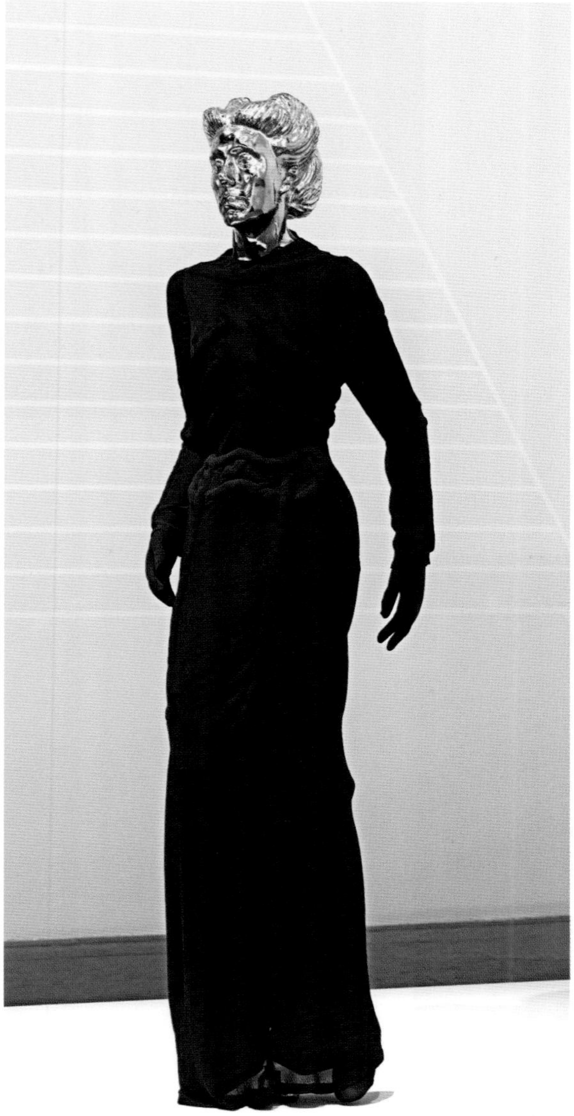

2

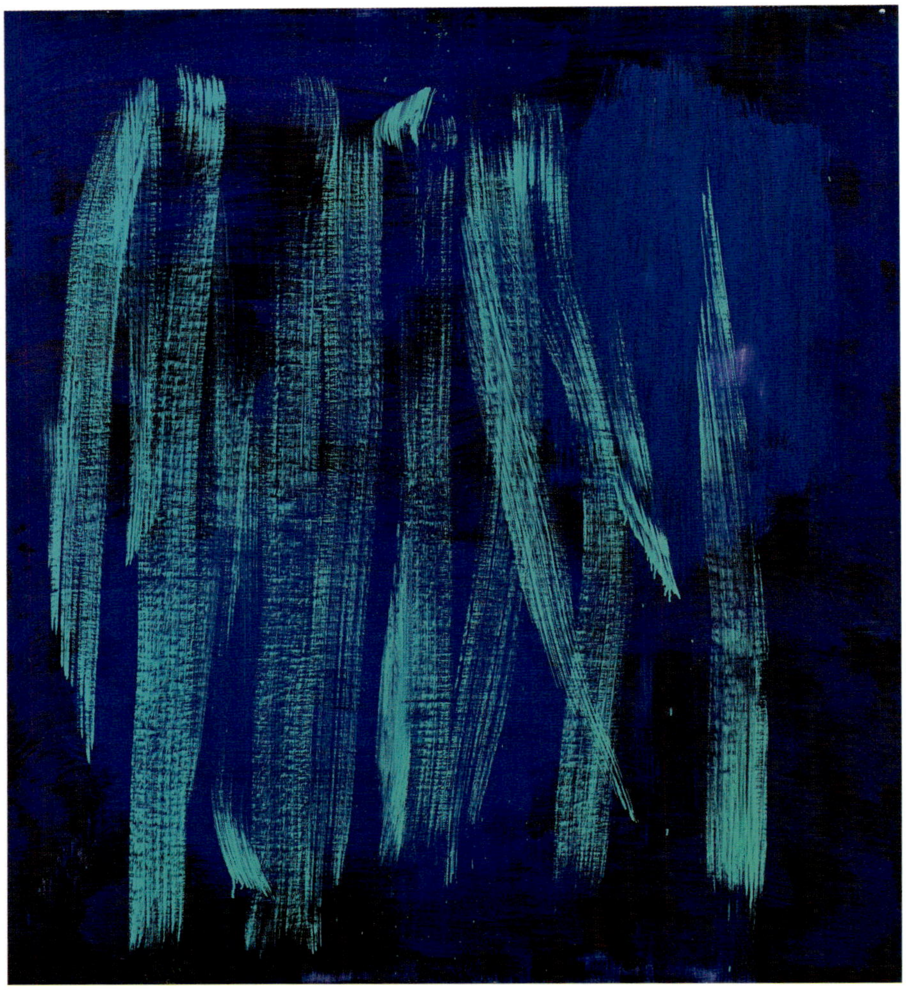

1

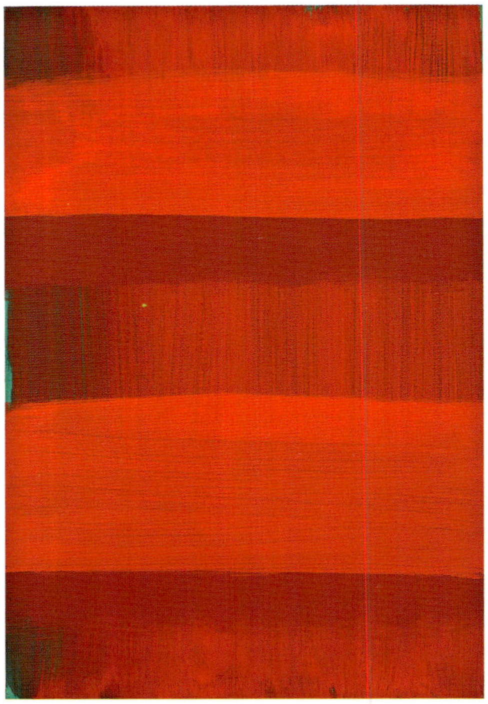

2

3

Shown by
Shane Campbell Gallery R17
David Kordansky Gallery C1

Biography
Born 1969
Lives in Los Angeles

American painter Pestoni received his MFA from UCLA in 1996, and BA from University of California, Berkley, in 1992. In 2012, he will have solo shows at David Kordansky Gallery, Los Angeles, and Shane Campbell Gallery, Chicago. His paintings were also the subject of a solo show at Lisa Cooley, New York (2011). He was included in the group shows "Stirrings" (2011) at Nieuw Dakota, Amsterdam; "Six Pack" (2011) at Richard Telles Fine Art, Los Angeles; and "The Pursuer" (2010) at Greene Naftali, New York.

1
Blue Sweep
2011
Oil on canvas
73 × 67"
(185.5 × 170 cm)
Courtesy of David Kordansky Gallery

2
Raised Widths
2011
Oil on canvas
44 × 30½"
(112 × 77.5 cm)
Courtesy of David Kordansky Gallery

3
Rug Burn
2011
Oil on canvas
55 × 48"
(139.5 × 122 cm)
Courtesy of David Kordansky Gallery

4
Blue None
2011
Oil on canvas
59 × 48"
(150 × 122 cm)
Courtesy of David Kordansky Gallery

Jon Pestoni

At first glance, Jon Pestoni's abstract paintings place primary emphasis on materiality—on brushwork and layering. There is an element of the grid in the paintings, which loosely operate according to horizontal and vertical axes, the logic of right angles, as in *Horizontal Hold (1)* (2009) and *Smoke* (2010). But the use of strong colors, varying brushwork, and amorphous forms make Pestoni's canvases leap off the grid and into bold life. As he moves between heavy paint application and delicate washes of color, Pestoni also builds temporality into his canvases by way of their distinct layering. The paintings make constant reference to the durational nature of their gestation, and the slow resolution of the image. KK

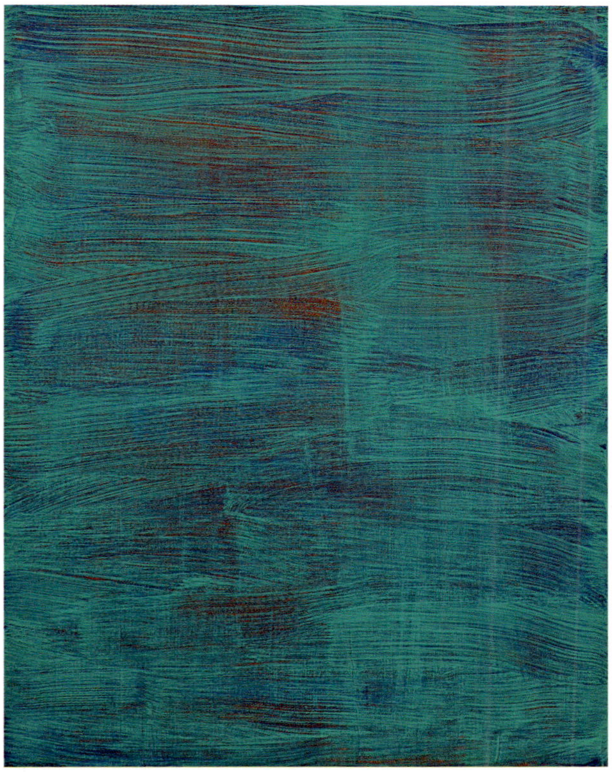

4

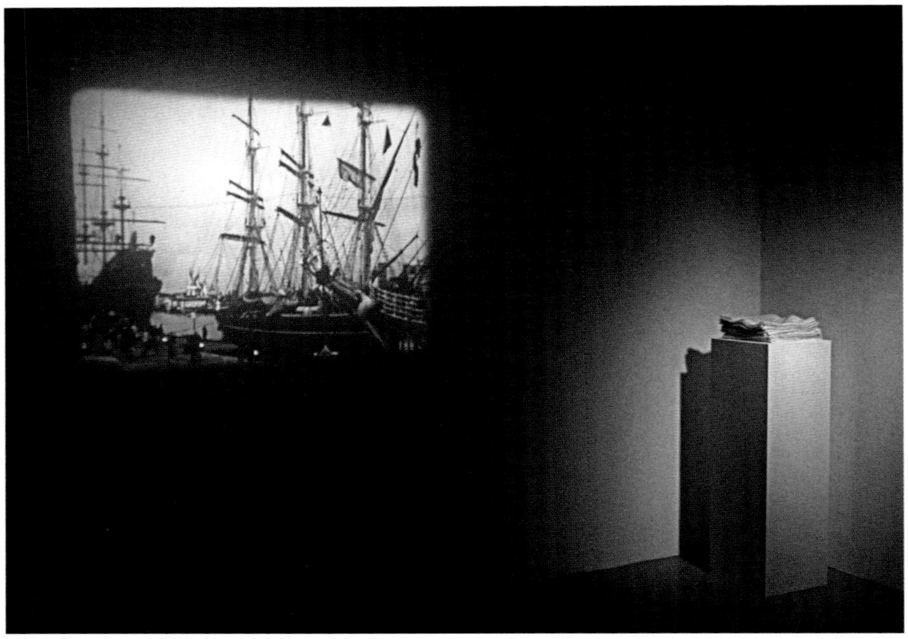

1

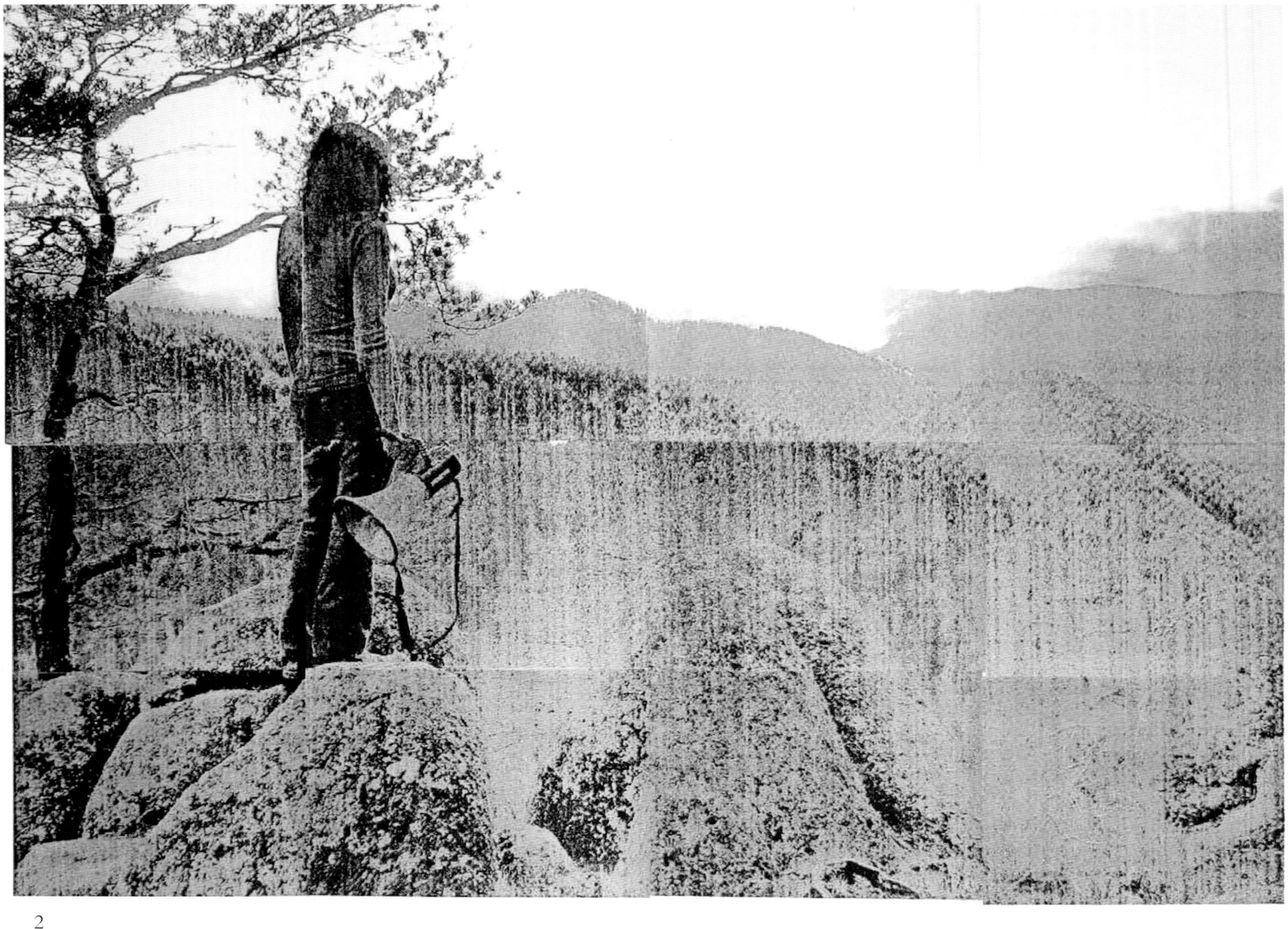

2

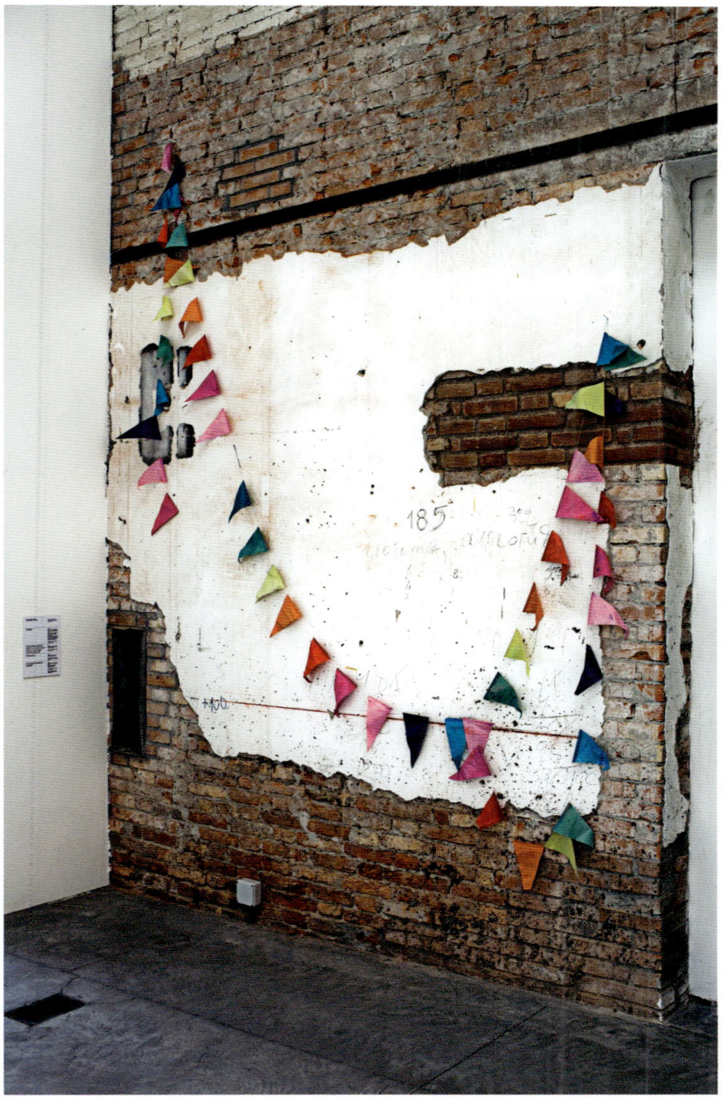

3

Shown by
Marc Foxx C32
Diana Stigter F14

Biography
Born 1978
Lives in London

Argentina-born Pica's installations and sculptures explore method and reason. Her often socially-engaged works were the subject of a self-titled solo show at Kunsthalle Sankt Gallen in early 2012. In 2012 she also completed an off-site project with Chisenhale Gallery, London and a solo show will follow in summer 2012. Other recent solo exhibitions include "Endymion's Journey" (2011) Marc Foxx Gallery, Los Angeles; and "Babble, etc..." at Malmo Konsthall (2010) and Galerie Diana Stigter, Amsterdam (2010).

1
To everyone that waves
2008
16 mm, black and white
3 min. 36 sec.
Courtesy of Diana Stigter

2
Sorry for the metaphor
2005
Images composed of A3 photocopies
Dimensions variable
Courtesy of Diana Stigter

3
Strangers
2008
Mixed media
Dimensions variable
Courtesy of Diana Stigter

Focus
Amalia Pica

Some of That Colour (2009), an art work consisting of dye-soaked bunting and a sheet of paper onto which it has evidently dripped, might be a sly subtitle for Amalia Pica's colorful practice, which exploits the space between memory and reality to create affecting objects, slide shows, and installations. She employs color to evoke nostalgia and false memory in *Hora catedra* (School Period, 2002) by blasting the façade of the House of Tucumán (the building where Argentinean independence was declared) with patriotic yellow floodlights, inducing a questionable memory that it was once yellow, though it has always been white. But the particular is not the point—the expression of abstract longing (for the past, for communication, for the rites of memory) might be. QL

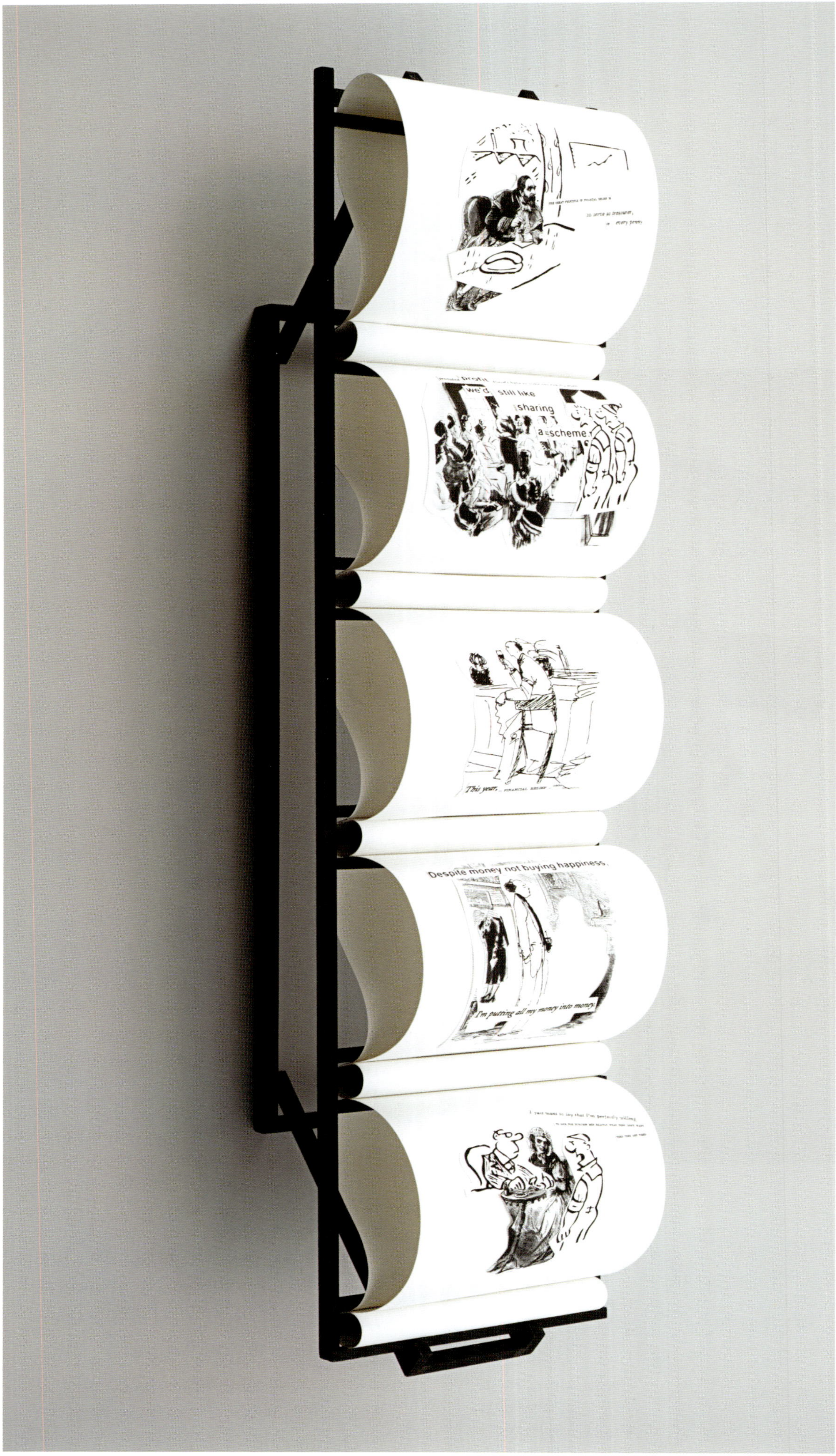

we'd still like
sharing
a scheme
This year,
FINANCIAL RELIEF
Despite money not buying happiness,
I'm putting all my money into money.

Focus
Falke Pisano

Falke Pisano's series of interrelated writings, lecture-performances, objects, and images entitled "Figures of Speech" (2005–10) traced correspondences from text to performance to object and back once more to text. This self-reflexive process was mapped in a 2010 publication of the same title, co-edited by the artist and designer Will Holder. More recently, Pisano's installation *The Body in Crisis (Distance, Repetition and Representation)* (2011) added corporeal concerns to her consideration of the relationship between objects and language, through an abstract sculpture composed of interconnected black screens and black curtained frames, placed in close proximity to a video work representing the human body in acute and specific social and political conjunctures, such as the battlefields of World War I. SL

Shown by
BaliceHertling R12
Hollybush Gardens F9

Biography
Born 1978
Lives in Berlin

Dutch artist Pisano's significant contribution to the 53rd Venice Biennale (2009), signalled a development in the artists practice, and provided a precursor to solo shows at Extra City, Antwerp, in 2010 and the forthcoming solo show at Cologne Kunstverine in 2013. Her work was also recently shown in the group show "Gift Maurice van Valen" (2011) at Stedelijk Museum, Amsterdam.

Repetition and Dispersion / 4 jokes become 5 jokes (economy)
2011
Digital print and black ink on wood and paper
43¼ × 11¾ × 5⅞"
(110 × 30 × 15 cm)
Courtesy of Hollybush Gardens

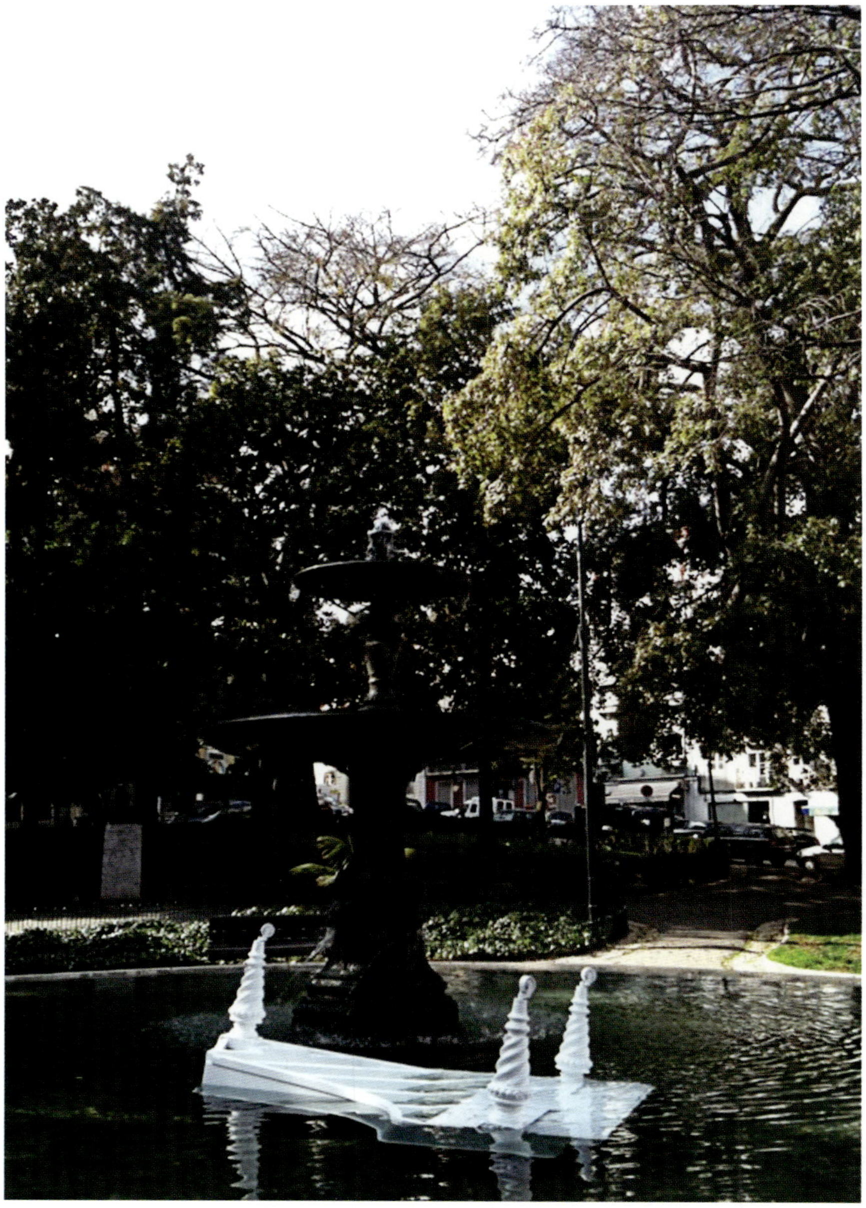

2

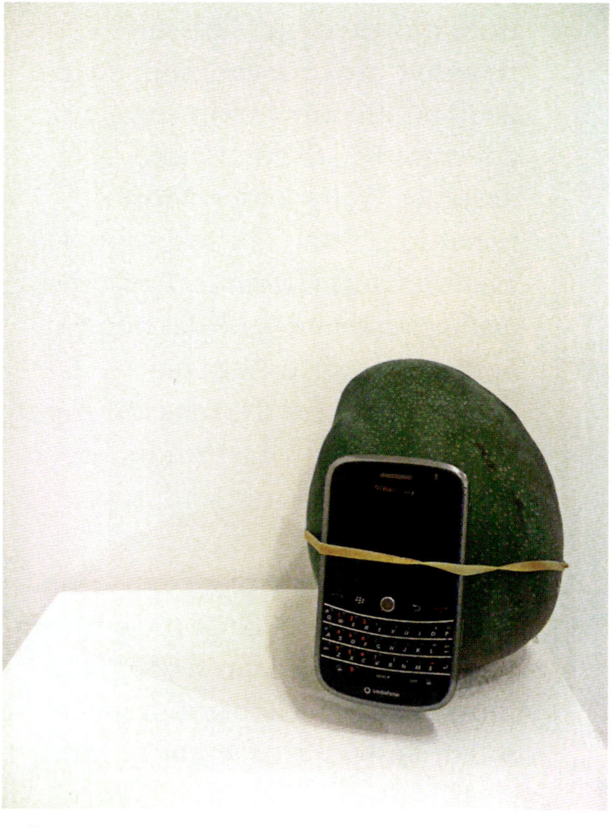

1

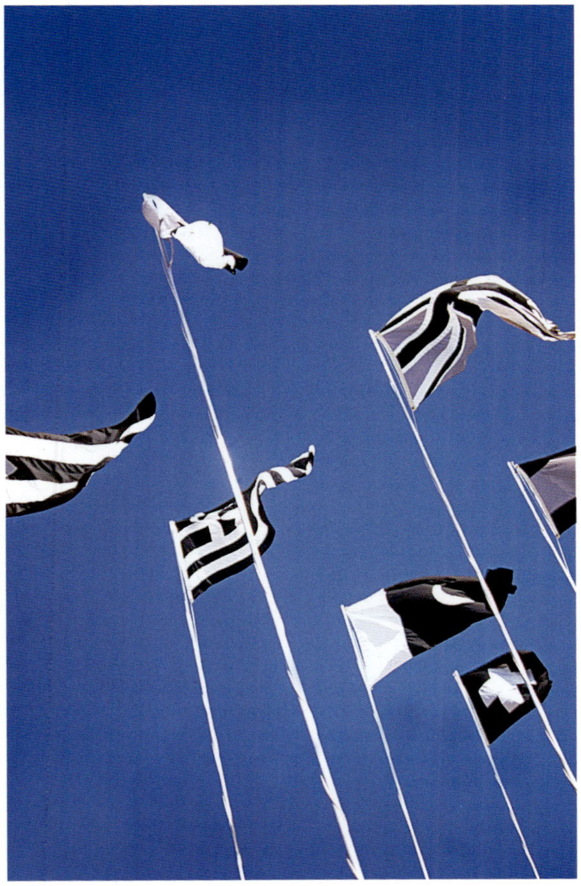

3

Shown by
NoguerasBlanchard
F27

Biography
Born 1978
Lives in Barcelona and Havana

Cuban artist Prieto's sculptural works were the subject of numerous solo exhibitions in 2011. These include "Constructivist and deconstructivist meadow as viewed from a home sofa with your feet on the table" at Spirito Due, Complesso Monumentalle Santo Spirito, Rome. He also exhibited at ARTIUM, Vitoria-Gasteiz; "Amarrado a la pata de la mesa (Tied up to the Table Leg)" at CA2M, Madrid; "Left/Right" at Museo de Arte Contemporánea de Vigo; and "Landscape with the fall of Icarus" at Kunsthalle Lissabon Lisbon.

1
Miren el tamaño de este mango (Look at the Size of this Mango)
2011
Mango and blackberry smartphone
Dimensions variable
Courtesy of NoguerasBlanchard

2
Paisaje con la caída de Ícaro (Landscape with the Fall of Icarus)
2011
Piano in public fountain
Dimensions variable
Courtesy of NoguerasBlanchard

3
Apolitico (Apolitical)
2001
Flags from every country recognized by the UN in gray-scale
Dimensions variable
Courtesy of NoguerasBlanchard

Focus
Wilfredo Prieto

In his objects and installations, Wilfredo Prieto plays with the transubstantiative powers of the white cube gallery, examining and subverting the ideological and conceptual frameworks that can transform familiar objects into art. His works often play with a surreal visual humor, imparted through their titles, where a puddle of water on the gallery floor becomes *Holy Water* (2010) and a single used match becomes *Dying Star* (2010). *Veneno y antidote (Poison and Antidote)* (2011) consists of two small and apparently innocuous unlabeled medical bottles filled with clear liquids, one being poison, the other containing its antidote—objects left awaiting activation, though here possible only in the mind. AB

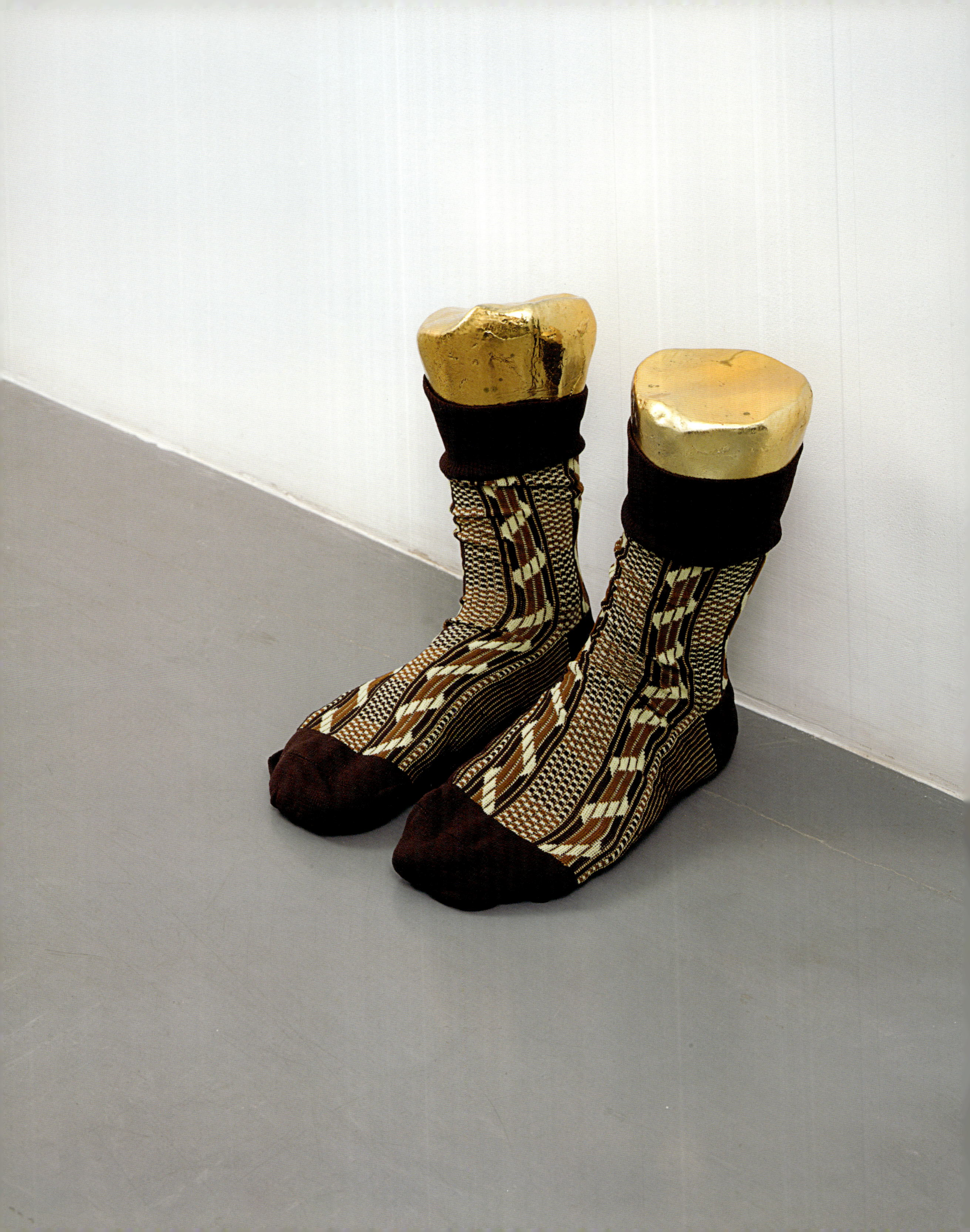

Shown by
Boers-Li Gallery C18

Biography
Born 1977
Lives in Beijing

Chinese painter and installation artist Qui has exhibited his work in Asia and Europe since the early-2000s. His often installation-based practice was the subject of the 2011 solo exhibition "Point of No Return" at Boers-Li Gallery, Beijing. Other recent solo shows include "Invisible journeys" (2009) at Doosan Art Center, Seoul, and "Pagoda of the Discarded" at Art & Public, Geneva. He participated in numerous group shows in 2011, including "Negotiations—The Second Today's Documents" at Today Art Museum, Beijing, and "Trailer" at Boers-Li Gallery, Beijing.

Untitled
2010
Bronze, gold, and socks
Dimensions variable
Courtesy of Boers-Li Gallery

Qiu Xiaofei

Qiu Xiaofei's paintings and installations are rooted in his own memories, but his images of these scenes retain a disquieting sense that the white noise of media imagery and false reminiscences have also become irreversibly entwined. His potentially fictitious photo album runs from the mundane, as in *Watching TV* (2006), where almost a dozen people crowd in a room around a small television, to the surreal, as in the sculpture *Holiday Dreams* (2009), where a meat grinder on a table overflows with a disturbing pink mass. Through openly forming his own self-made history, Qiu questions who we think we're looking at, as well as the stories we tell about ourselves. CFW

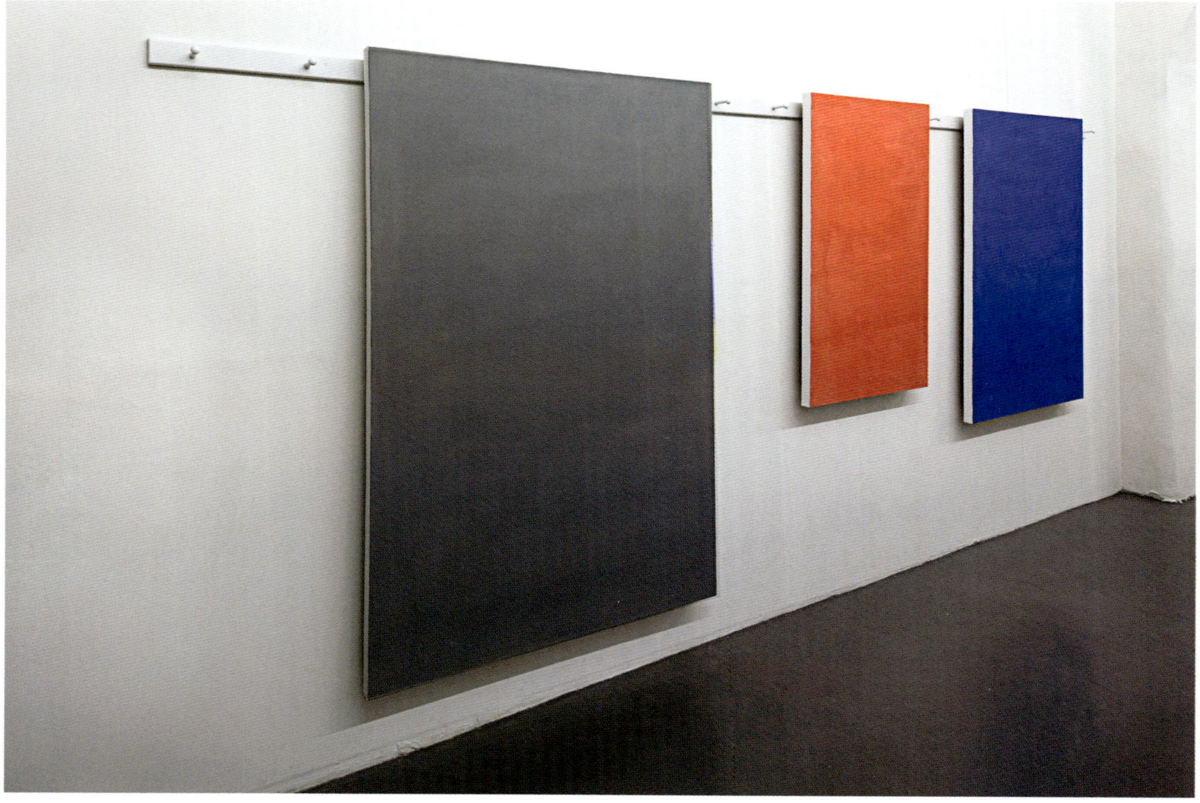

1

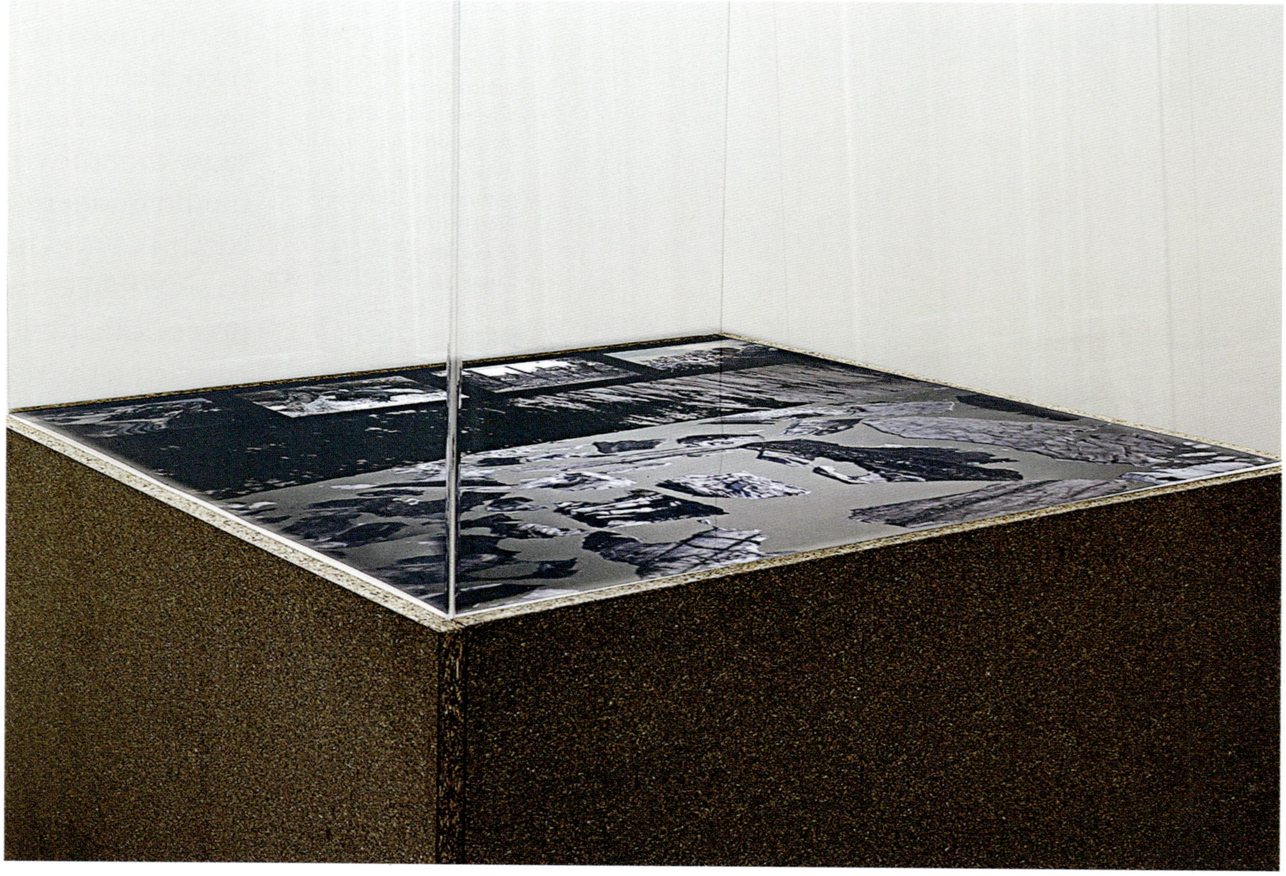

2

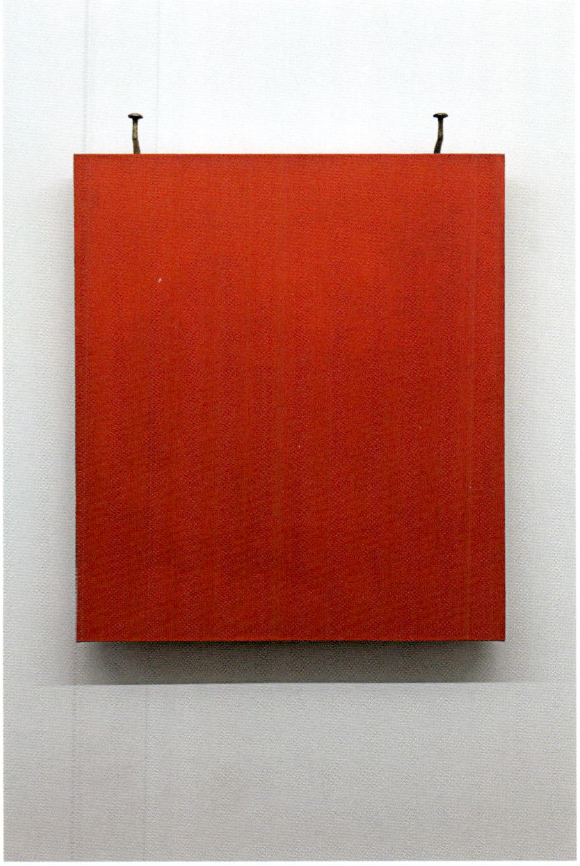

3

Shown by
Tanya Leighton
Gallery F16
T293 F6

Biography
Born 1982
Lives in Berlin

British artist Rees graduated from the Staatliche Hochschule für Bildende Künste Städelschule, Frankfurt am Main, in 2009. In recent years he has exhibited extensively in Europe, including the solo shows "Cryogenic Blue" (2011) at T293, Rome; "Philanthropy" (2011) at Jonathan Viner, London; "Ventricles" (2011) at Galerie Andreas Huber, Vienna; and "Green Room: Dan Rees" (2011) at Museum der Weltkulturen (2011). In the United States, he has participated in the group show "Keep Floors and Passages Clear" (2011) at White Columns, New York, and had a solo show at Wallspace, New York in late 2010.

1
Shaker Peg Painting (Triptych)
2011
Oil on linen, wooden peg rails
70⅞ × 169 × 4"
(180 × 429.5 × 10 cm)
Courtesy of T293

2
Cryogenic Blue III
(detail)
2011
Photographic print on film, transparent plexiglass lid, opaline slab, chipboard, neon tube lights, electrical cables
61 × 31¼ × 29½"
(155 × 79.5 × 75 cm)
Courtesy of T293

3
Untitled (Red)
2011
Oil on linen, brass hooks
33⅞ × 27⅜ × 3⅜"
(86 × 69.5 × 8.5 cm)
Courtesy of T293

Focus Dan Rees

In his *Variable Peace up to 21* (2006–ongoing), Dan Rees discusses art with artists including Jonathan Monk and Simon Starling over a game of table tennis. The irreverence and humor of these filmed interactions characterize much of Rees' playful relationship to art history and ideas, as well as to the work of other artists, from whom he often borrows forms or conceptual frameworks. In *80 Girlfriends in 2007* (2007), Rees took Ed Ruscha's *Five 1955 Girlfriends* (1969) and ran with it, replacing Ruscha's modest five companions with 80 female acquaintances. Rees' most recent body of work comprises seemingly half-finished abstract paintings displayed on Shaker-style coat pegs, drawing painting into the realm of production. AB

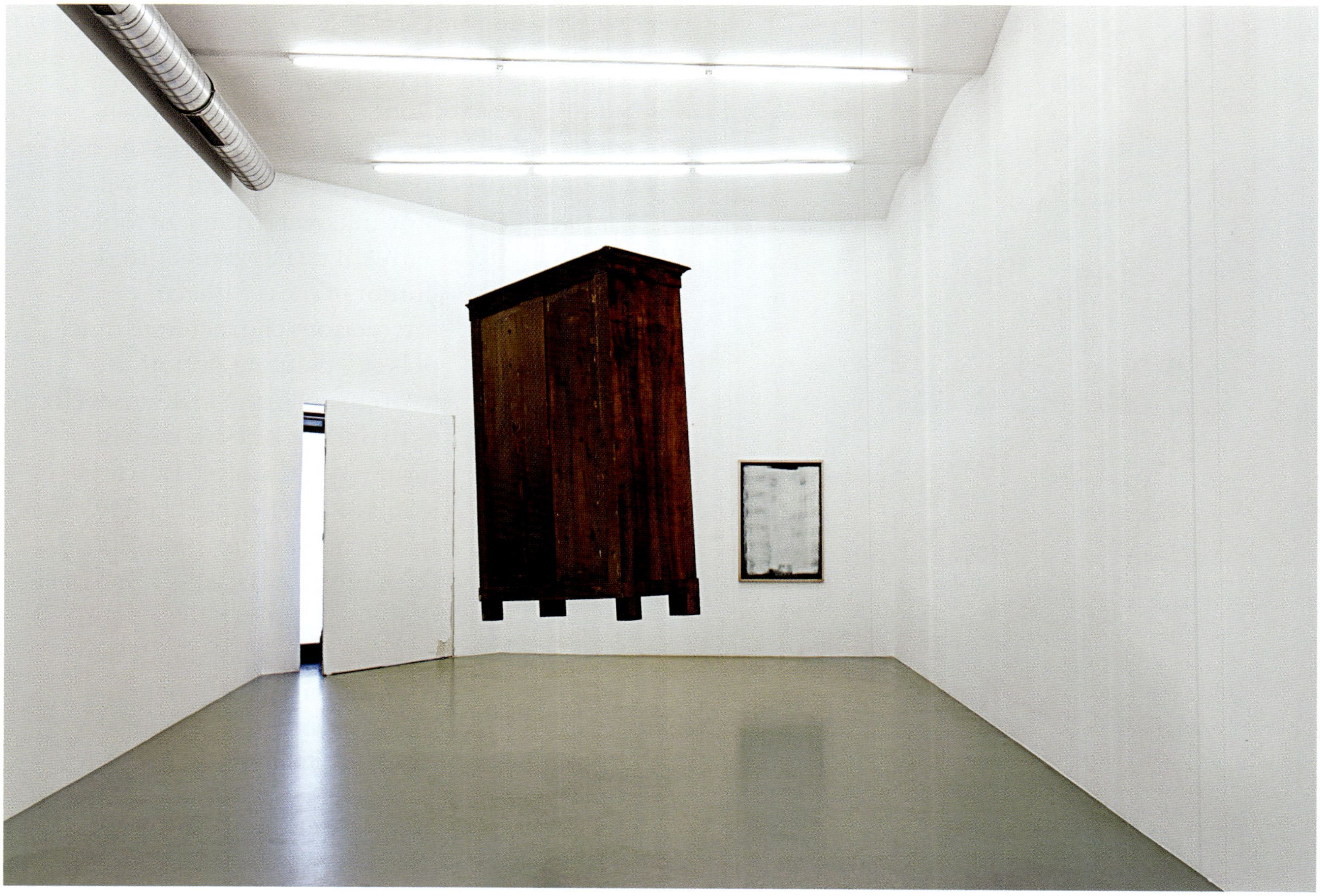

1

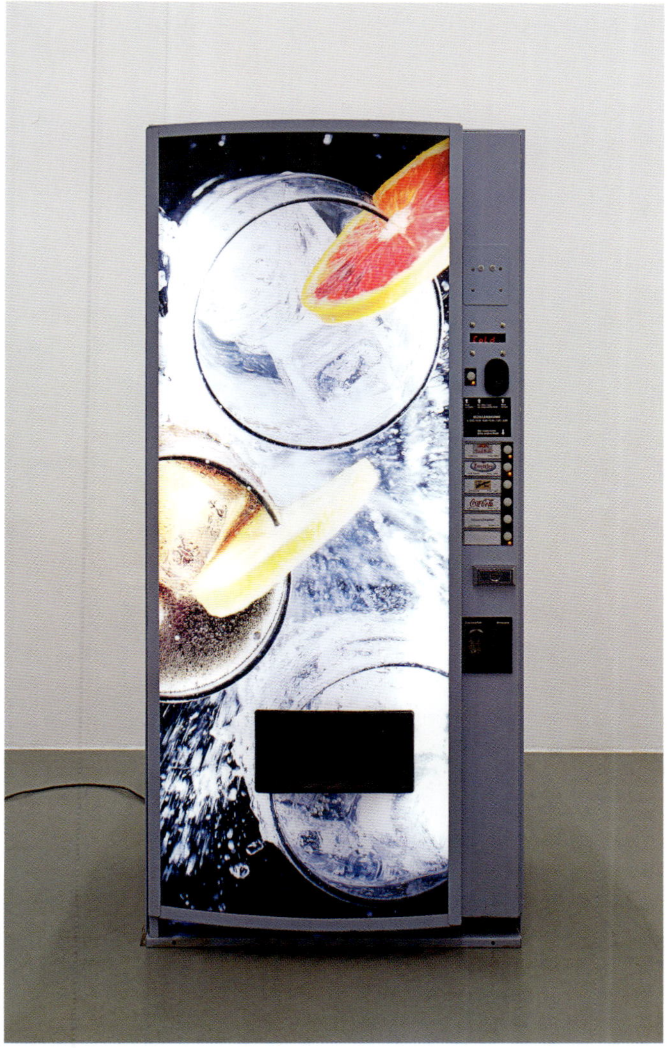

2

Shown by
Galerie Mezzanin F29

Biography
Born 1975
Lives in Berlin

South Africa-born Reuter's conceptual practice has gained a significant European profile in recent years. His sculptural works were the subject of the recent solo show at Neue Alte Brücke, Frankfurt (2012). His installation for the exhibition "A Plot" at De Vleeshal, Middelburg, made a confident mark on the gallery. Other recent solo exhibitions include a self-titled show at Galerie Mezzanin, Vienna (2011); "Here is a Picture" at Gallery Croy/Nielsen, Berlin; and Francesca Minini, Milan (2010).

1
The Agreement, Vienna
2011
Armoire
72 × 33⅜ × 28⅜"
(183 × 85 × 72 cm)
Courtesy of
Galerie Mezzanin

2
Shuteye
2011
Soda vending machine, DMX controller, switch pack
72 × 33⅜ × 28⅜"
(183 × 85 × 72 cm)
Courtesy of Galerie Mezzanin

Focus
Mandla Reuter

The challenge Mandla Reuter's work presents to the viewer is often ambitious and yet understated. With *Untitled* (2009) he blocked the entrance to the Boros Collection, Berlin, with a large stone boulder; the modest *BG* (2007) consisted of a bunch of keys for all the rooms in the Berlinische Galerie, hung on a hook for all to see. Often his work consists of making visitors more aware of the space they are in, as with the set of three large rectangular mirrors he installed to reflect the interior of the Schinkel Pavillon in Berlin in 2009, or the incongruous i-beam he installed in the Gothic interior of De Vleeshal in Middelburg, a work he titled *The Building* (2011). SL

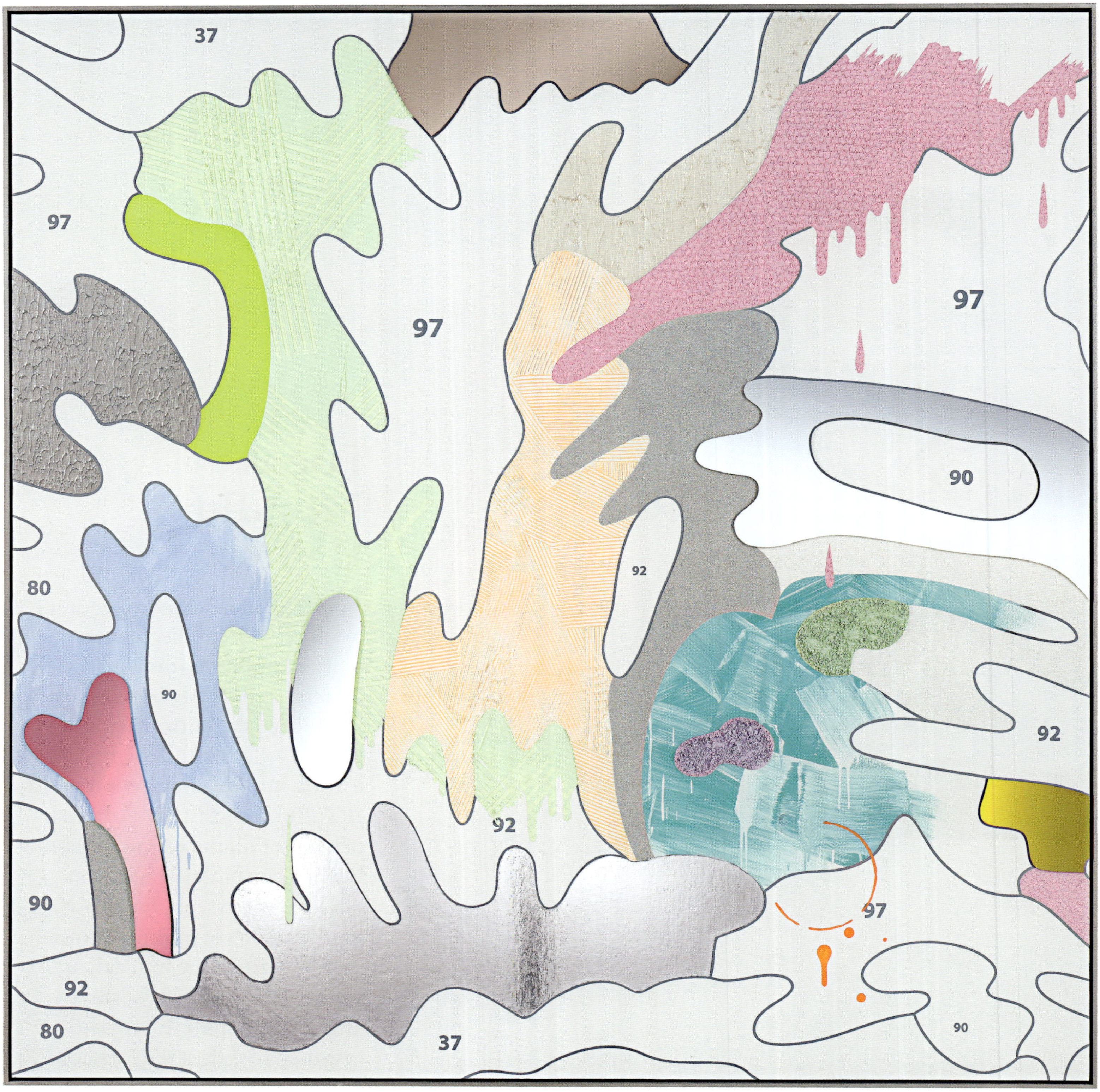
37
97
97
97
90
92
80
90
92
92
97
90
92
80
37
90

Anselm Reyle

Shown by
Contemporary Fine Arts C39
Gagosian Gallery D4
The Modern Institute C29
Almine Rech Gallery B7

Biography
Born 1970
Lives in Berlin

German artist Reyle has exhibited in Europe and the United States since the late 1990s. In spring 2012, he had a two-person show alongside Franz West at the Schinkel Pavillon, Berlin. In 2011 solo shows included self-titled exhibitions at Arken Museum of Modern Art, Ishøj; Des Moines Art Center, Iowa; and "Little Cody" at Contemporary Fine Arts, Berlin. His work is part of the Daimler Art Collection, Berlin, and Fondation Pinault, Venice, among others.

Untitled
2011
Mixed media on canvas, wooden frame
89½ × 88 ⅔ × 2½"
(227.5 × 225 × 6.5 cm)
Courtesy of Contemporary Fine Arts

The recent sculptures and paintings by Berlin-based Anselm Reyle reference postmodernism and 1980s pop culture. His recent paintings echo Warhol's "Paint by Numbers" series, rendering horses, dogs and dolphins in bright compartmentalized color, while other abstract untitled works mimic painterly splats and drips on incomplete canvases, laying bare their numbered surfaces. Reyle's work is immersive, garish, and seductive, and he absorbs the viewer with his saturated palate. A recent untitled series of re-upholstered lounge furniture mixes multiple fabrics and textures, isolating them as objects to be looked at rather than sat on. His manipulation of aesthetics is acute, and his methods are uncanny—Reyle appeals to our deep-seated desire for all things glossy, bright and psychedelic. SC

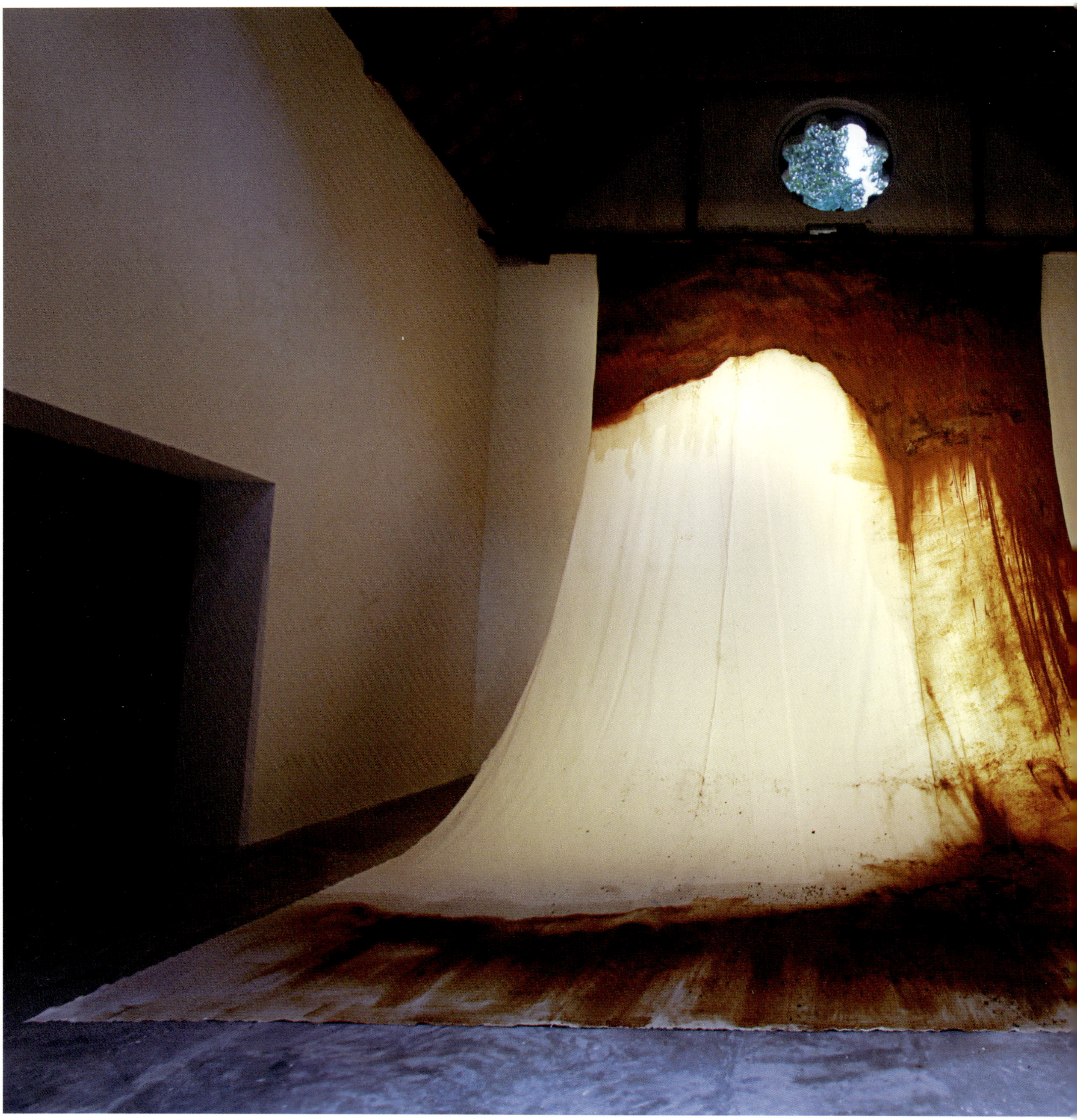

Shown by
A Gentil Carioca C27

Biography
Born 1980
Live in São Paulo

Over the past decade Brazilian artist Rocha Pitta's unique paintings and installations have featured in numerous exhibitions in South America and Europe. In 2012 he will have the solo show "Nostalia pos pangeaat" at Andersen Contemporary, Copenhagen. Previous solo shows include a self-titled exhibition at Galeria Millan, São Paulo (2011), and "Notas de um desabamento" at Parque Lage, Rio de Janeiro (2010). Recent group shows include "The Garden of Forking Paths" at Migros Museum für Gegenwartskunst, Zurich (2011).

Project for a Stormy Weather Painting #5
2010
Iron powder on canvas
511¾ × 275⅝"
(1300 × 700 cm)
Courtesy of A Gentil Carioca

Thiago Rocha Pitta

Thiago Rocha Pitta's work with natural materials—water, fire, salt, air—often suggests the zeal of an inventor: his *Fountain* (2003) is in fact an inverted spring, creating a whirlpool where there should be a jet. Yet his art is equal parts science, mystery, and romance: a love of the ocean inspired the film *Heritage* (2007), which follows out to sea a rowing boat planted with two small trees. *Projects for Temporal Paints* (2005) is among a series of paintings created as if by nature: ink is placed in a gutter, large expanses of canvas are strung alongside, and when it rains the colors pour onto the cloth, creating cloudy fields reminiscent of the works of Turner. MF

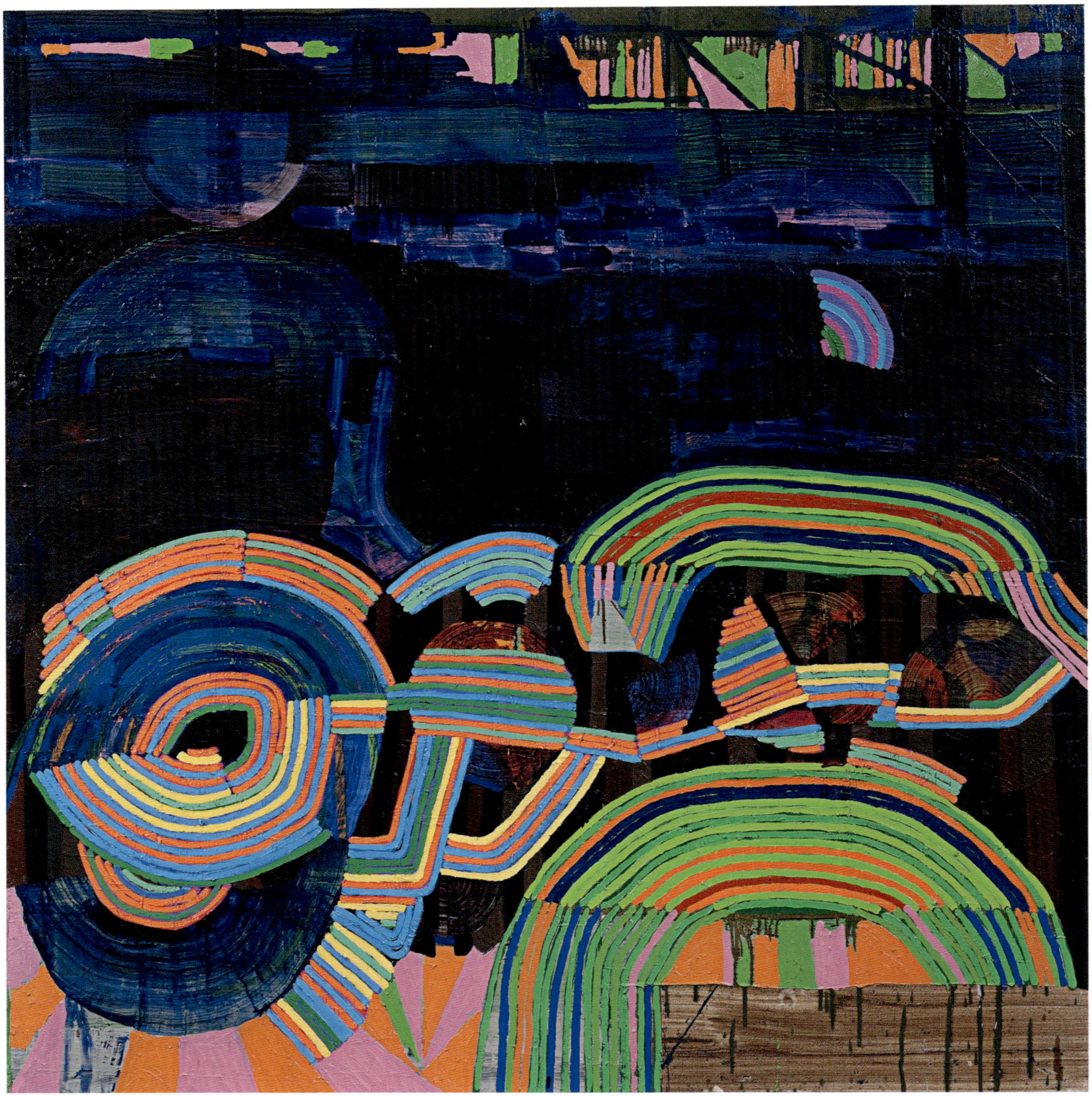

1

Steve Roden

Familiar to many as a sound artist, in 2010, Steve Roden's mid-career survey at The Armory Center for the Arts, Pasadena, pointed up connections across his works on paper, painting, sculpture, film, video, and sound. Beginning with found "scores"—sheet music, old letters or photographs, a Jacques Cousteau book, a Buckminster Fuller sketch, cloud formations, earthquake tremors—Roden invents or adopts associative systems, linking text, numbers, lines, colors, and musical notes. Allowing for some room within the given constraints, the coherence of the initial referent carries through into the final product but can hardly be said to have been "translated" directly. For *bowrain* (2010), notes Roden, "I used the Fuller drawing to generate the score that generated the plan that generated the activity." SNS

Shown by
Susanne Vielmetter Los Angeles Projects C21

Biography
Born 1964
Lives in Pasadena

Multi-disciplinary artist Roden exhibited his paintings and sculptures in the solo show "stone's throw" (2011) at Susanne Vielmetter Los Angeles Projects, and his show "Steve Roden: In Between, A 20-Year Survey" (2010) at the Armory Center for the Arts, Pasadena, encompassed his audio, video and text works. In 2010 he had the solo shows "when words become forms" at Pomona College Museum of Art, Claremont, and "proximities", at the Chinati Foundation, Marfa.

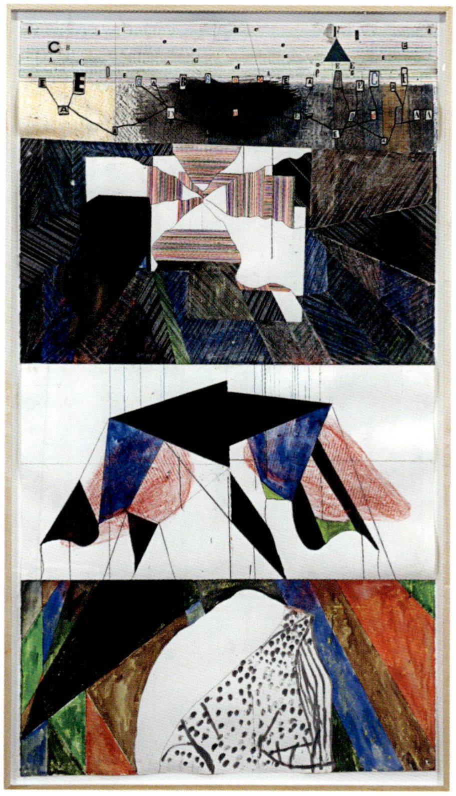

2

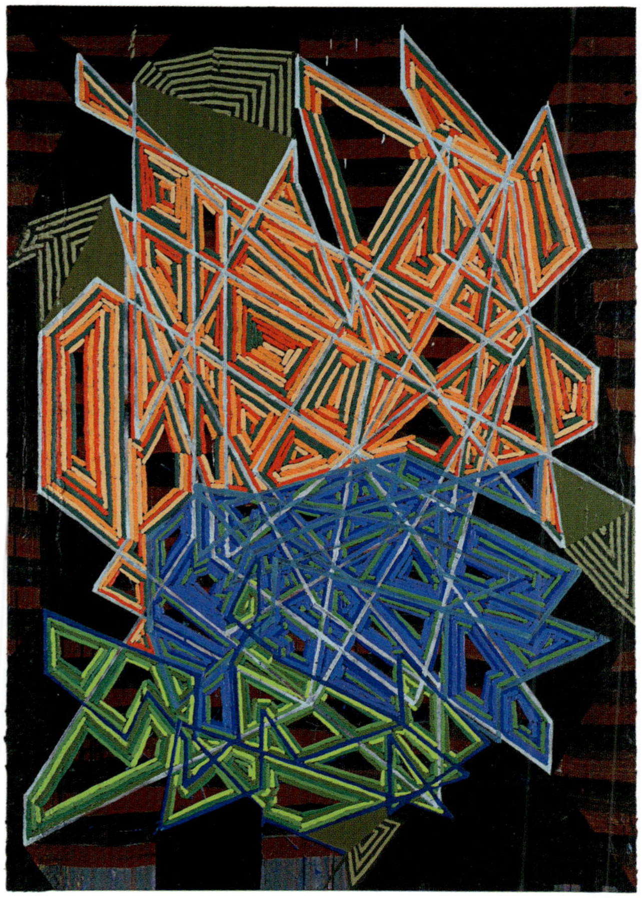

3

1
multiple eyes / multipleviews
2011
Oil and acrylic on linen
59⅞ × 59⅞"
(152 × 152 cm)
Courtesy of Susanne Vielmetter Los Angeles Projects

2
from stone to sound (fingers, birds and foldings)
2010
Sumi ink, watercolor, collage, pencil, cardboard and frottage on paper
81⅛ × 44⅞"
(206 × 114 cm)
Courtesy of Susanne Vielmetter Los Angeles Projects

3
untitled (36/2)
2009
Oil and acrylic on linen
81⅞ × 59⅞"
(208 × 152 cm)
Courtesy of Susanne Vielmetter Los Angeles Projects

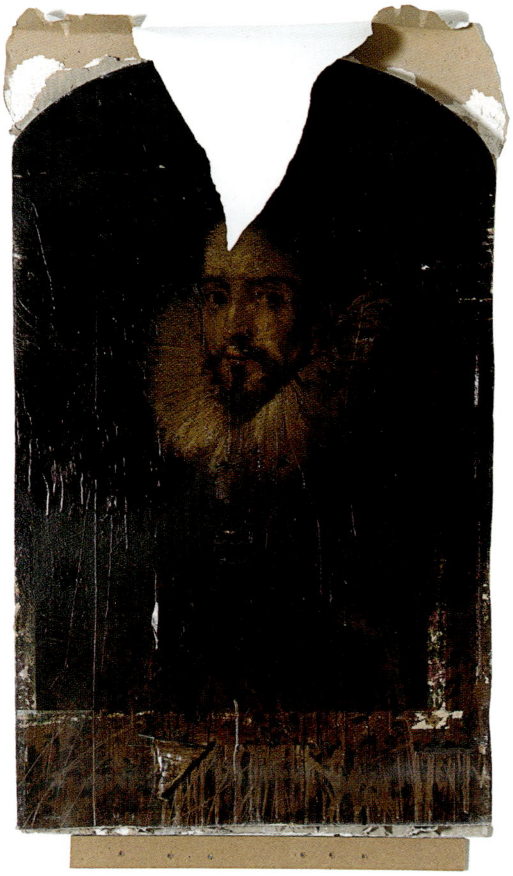

1

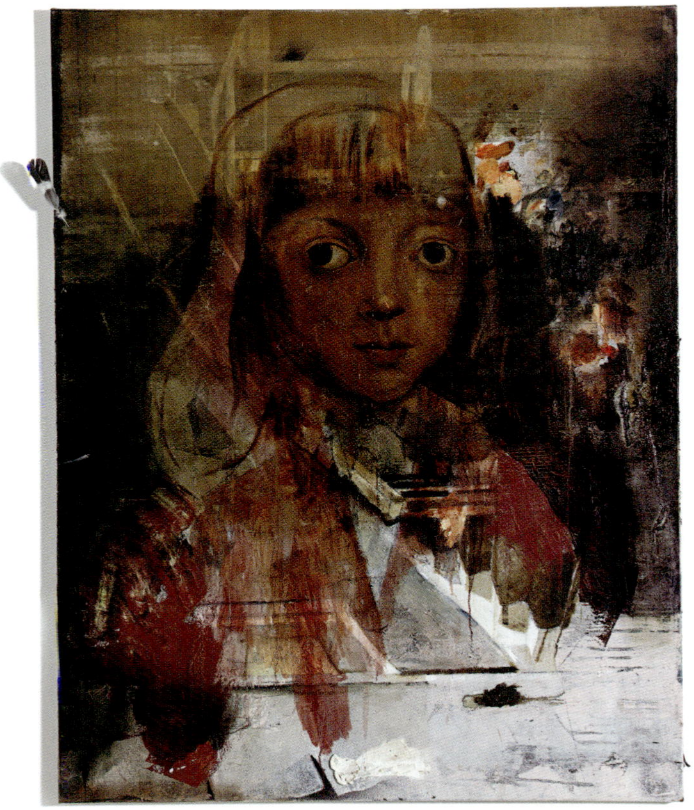

2

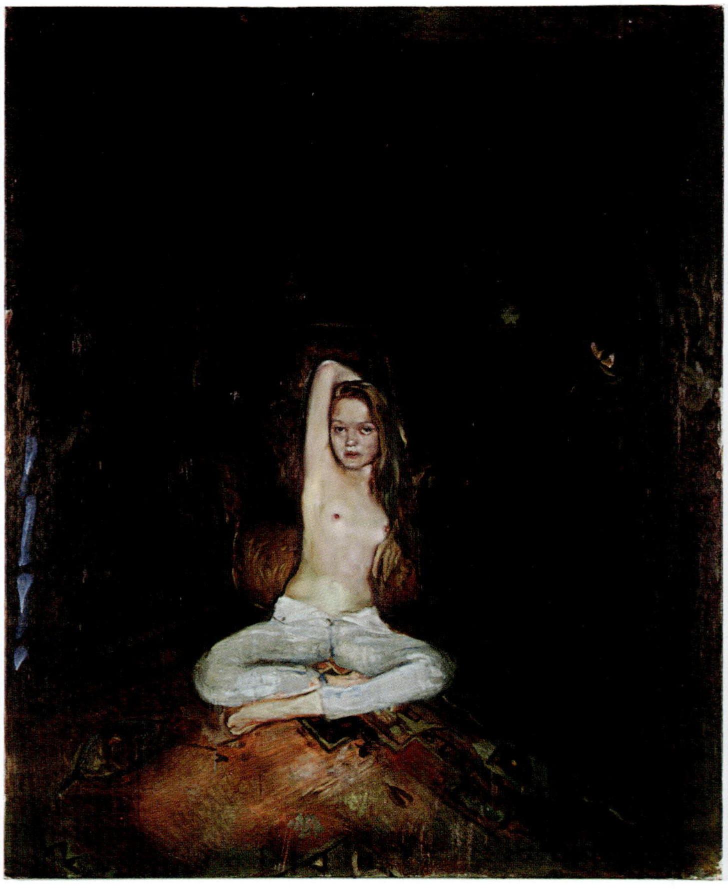

3

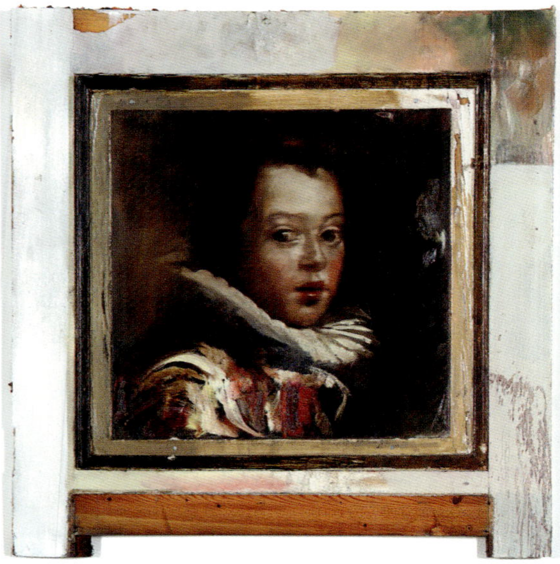

4

Shown by
Almine Rech Gallery
B7

Biography
Born 1981
Lives in Mullem

Belgian painter Ronsse has exhibited extensively in Europe in recent years. In 2011 he had the solo show "Towerplace" at Almine Rech Gallery, Brussels, as well as the group shows "Splendid isolation" at Freestate, Ostend, and "Flemish Masters, That's Life" at Andrea Rosen Gallery, New York. In 2012 he will participate in the Shanghai Biennale.

1
Mouth Breather 2
2011
Oil on Gyproc
58¼ × 31⅞ × 2¾"
(148 × 81 × 7 cm)
Courtesy of Almine Rech Gallery

2
Observer
2011
Oil on canvas
56⅝ × 71⅝"
(144 × 182 cm)
Courtesy of Almine Rech Gallery

3
Jeans
2011
Oil on canvas
74 × 61⅜"
(188 × 156 cm)
Courtesy of Almine Rech Gallery

4
What I throw out of the keyhole is my business (part 2)
2011
Oil on wood
33⅜ × 33⅜"
(85 × 85 cm)
Courtesy of Almine Rech Gallery

Matthieu Ronsse

An air of desolation pervades Matthieu Ronsse's paintings and installations. His work orbits around his practice as a painter—an especially skillful painter, who learns from old masters by paying homage to their work. *Cockfighter* (2010) repeats a figure from Giorgione's *Portrait of a Warrior with his Equerry* (c.1509), but with carelessly unfinished edges and thick varnish defacing Ronsse's delicate brushwork. His 2011 exhibition "towerplace" combined similarly abused portraits with monochromes, paintings from photographs of teenage pin-ups, and faces cut into triangular shards (*C.R.*, 2011). Debris including split paint, crumpled canvases, and rags was strewn across the floor. Despite his apparent authorial deference, Ronsse remains centre stage, especially when he performs with his band or rebuilds his workspaces inside the gallery (*ASYL*, 2007). JG

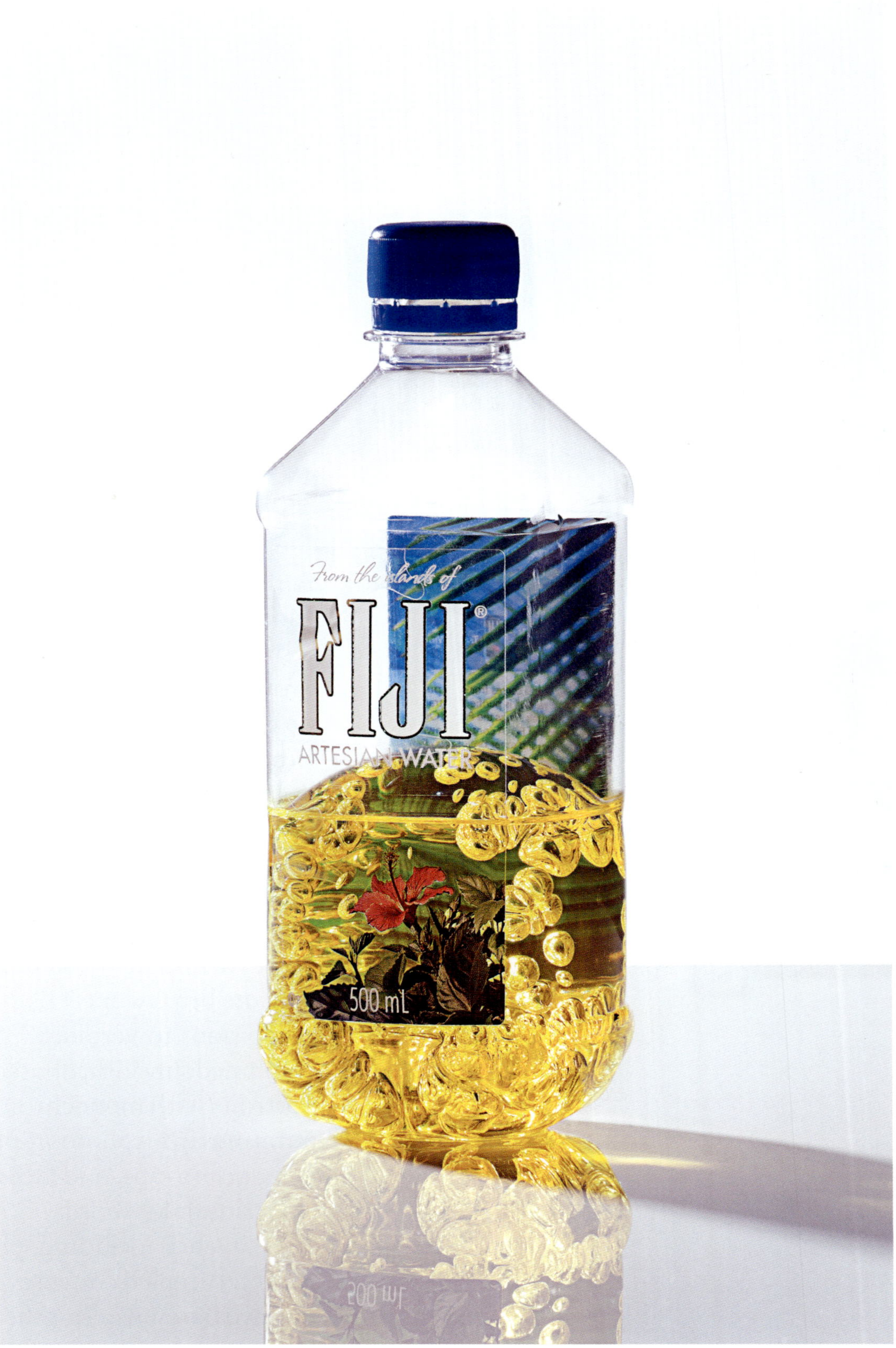

1

Shown by
Miguel Abreu Gallery
C14
Karma International
F10

Biography
Born 1979
Lives in Amsterdam and New York

Swiss artist Rosenkranz's sculptures and installations have featured in multiple solo and group exhibitions in Europe and the United States in recent years. She is currently a resident at the Rijksakademie van beeldende kunsten, Amsterdam. Recent solo shows include "This is not my Color" (2011) at the Swiss Institute, New York; "Untouched by Man" at the Kunstverein Braunschweig; and "No Core" (2010) at the Centre d'Art Contemporain Genève, Geneva. In 2012 she will participate in the Liverpool Biennial, "When Attitude Became Form Become Attitudes" at the CCA Wattis Institute for Contemporary Arts, San Francisco, and have a solo show at Miguel Abreu Gallery, New York.

2

1
Firm Being (Content Water)
2011
Pet-bottle, casting resin with pigments
7 × 2⅓ × 2⅜"
(18 × 6 × 6 cm)
Courtesy of Karma International

2
"Because they tried to bore holes in my greatest and most beautiful work" (IKB_191_3)
2011
Plexiglas, double-sided foil, pigment, inkjet prints (Canon IPF 9000), Ilford photo paper, bubbles, framed
78¾ × 55⅛"
(200 × 140 cm)
Courtesy of Karma International

Focus
Pamela Rosenkranz

The artificiality of the fitness and beauty industries recurs as a central concern in the sculptures, works on paper, videos, and installations of Pamela Rosenkranz. In her "Firm Being" (2009) series of various branded mineral water bottles, filled with flesh-colored silicon ranging from "solar beige" to "fresh ebony," she referred to consumption—while to create her gym-pumped modern-day versions of Yves Klein's *Anthropometries of the Blue Period* (1960–62), acrylic in colors matched to those of mass-produced foundation make-up are applied to the clothed and gloved bodies of assistants, who press themselves against either sheets of bent Plexiglas, Spandex, or emergency foil blankets, as in the work *Express Nothing (Pink Health)* (2011). SL

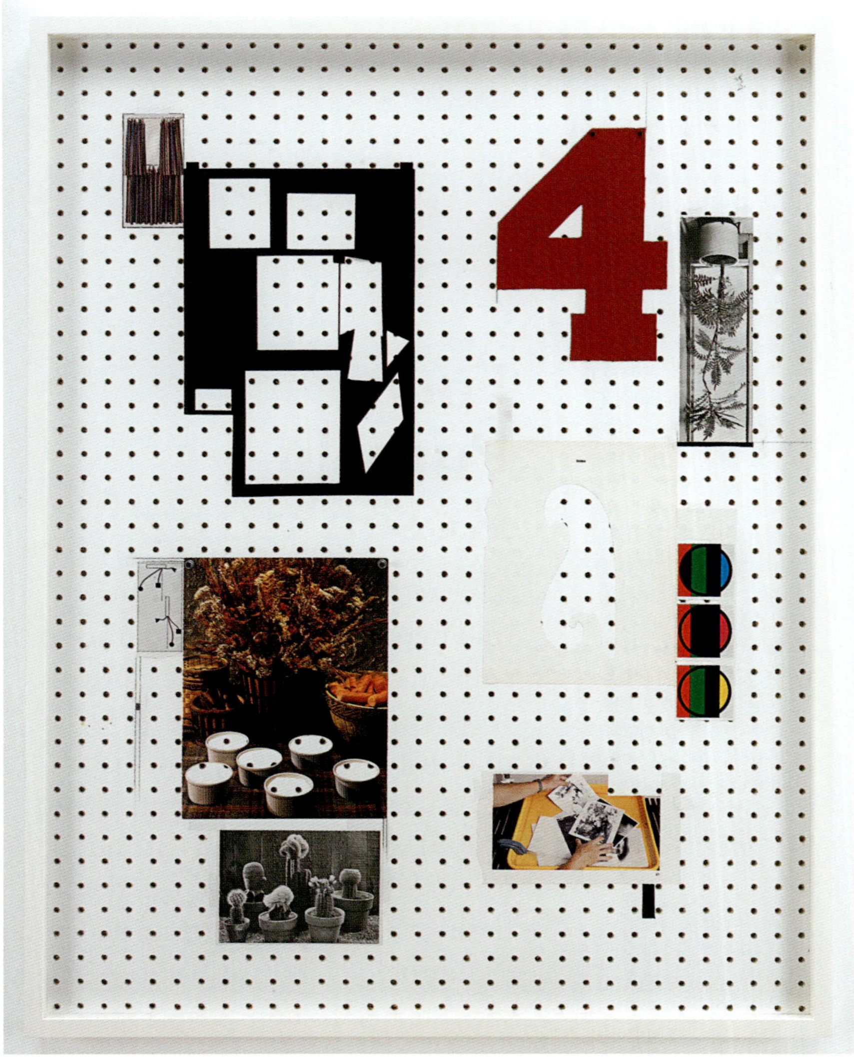

1

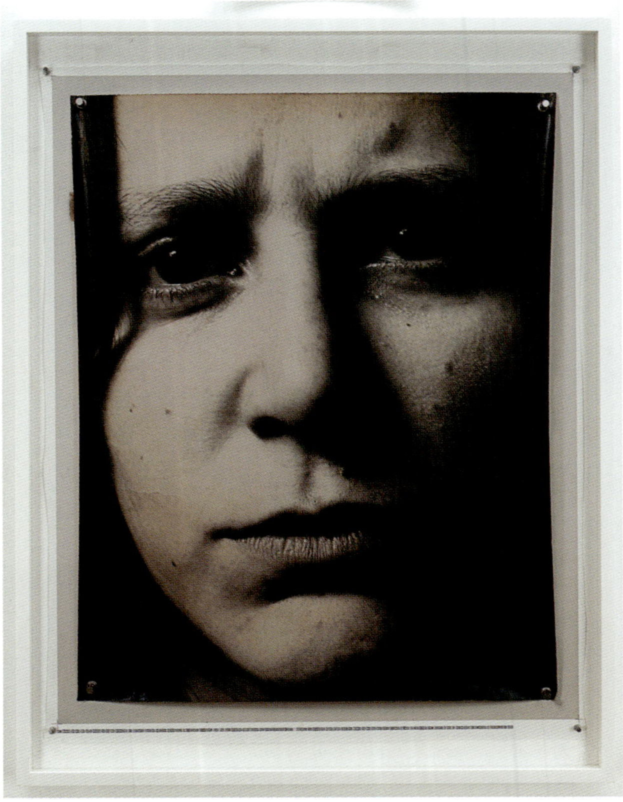

2

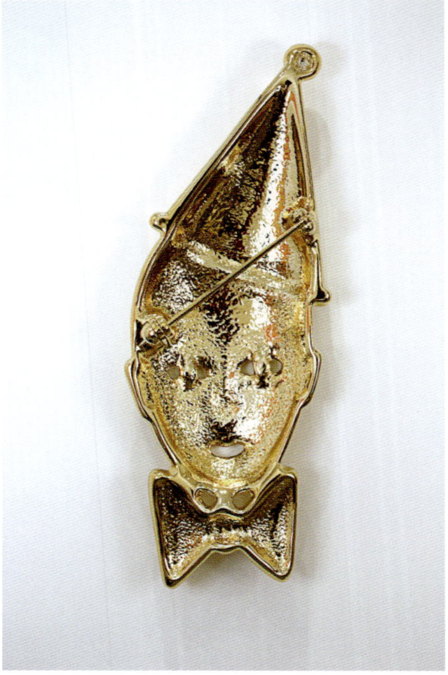

3

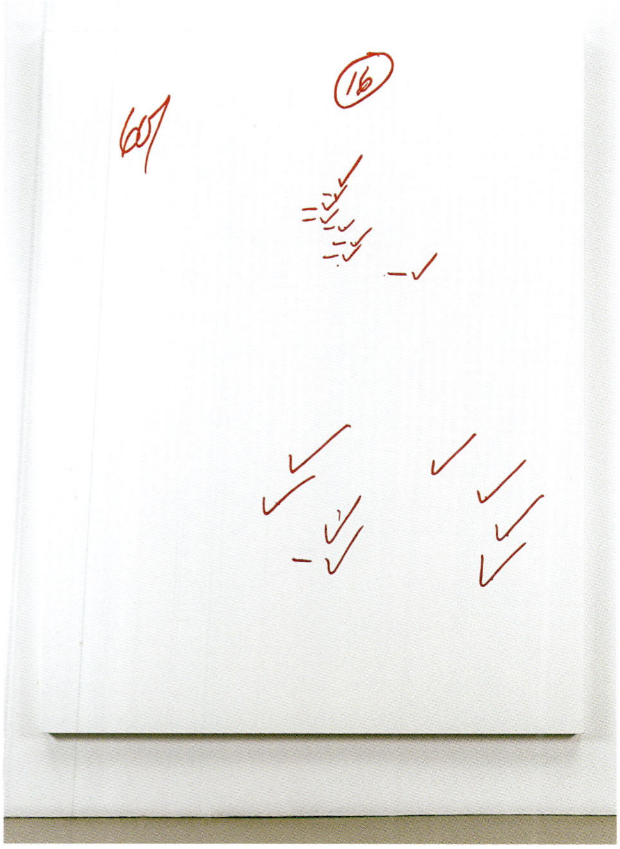

4

Amanda Ross-Ho

Amanda Ross-Ho is "the lens" between "disparate [...] action and [...] articulated work," she tells us, annotating the press release for her 2010 show "A Stack of Black Pants." It is this process of editing—deleting but, more importantly, keeping—from among the clutter of everyday images and objects that perhaps best describes her approach to making and presenting work. Drawing on the vast palette of media and imagery that surrounds us, Ross-Ho assembles tableaux from personal objects, found images, and mundane materials: *Periphery Composition with Basket of Dead Brushes* (2010) shows a piece of canvas pinned to the wall, bearing a found picture of a cat, a black acrylic rectangle, a gold chain, and some scrawled Xs—a basket of used paintbrushes placed at the foot. PT

Shown by
The Approach B11
Shane Campbell Gallery R17
Mitchell-Innes & Nash B20

Biography
Born 1975
Lives in Los Angeles

Ross-Ho's exhibition "Time Waits For No One" (2011) at the Approach, London, was her first in the UK. The American artist's work was also on show in "Untitled Nothing Factory" (2011) at the University of Texas. Her image assemblages were included in the "New Photography" series at The Museum of Modern Art, New York, in 2011, and the Whitney Biennial 2008. In late 2012 she will have a solo show at the Museum of Contemporary Art, Los Angeles.

1
Untitled Still Life (4/Blocking)
2011
Mixed media
41 × 32"
(104 × 81.5 cm)
Courtesy of Mitchell-Innes & Nash

2
Portrait (Hers) Test Print
2011
Mixed media
41 × 32"
(104 × 81.5 cm)
Courtesy of Mitchell-Innes & Nash

3
Double Feature #220
Mixed media
43 × 17 × 8"
(109 × 43 × 20.5 cm)
Courtesy of Mitchell-Innes & Nash

4
Correction #59 (Check Minus Check)
1981–2011
Various red acrylic paints and gesso on canvas
96 × 72"
(244 × 183 cm)
Courtesy of Mitchell-Innes & Nash

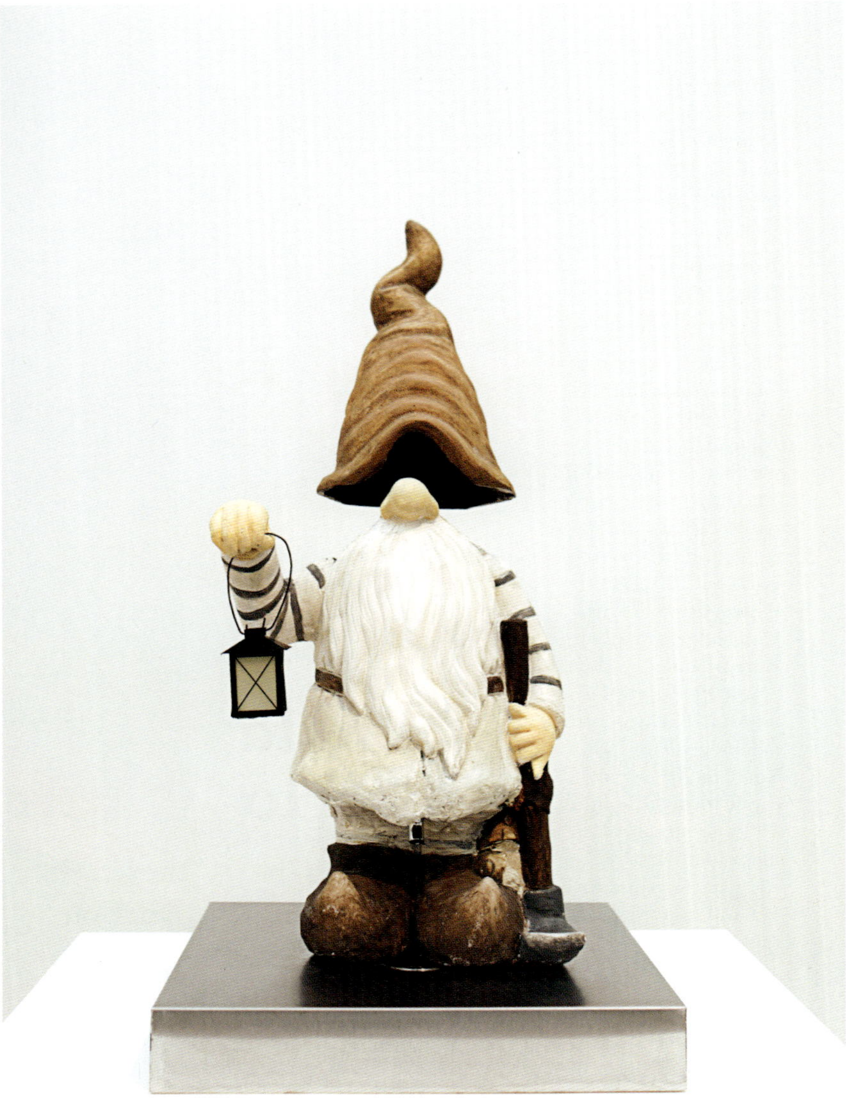

1

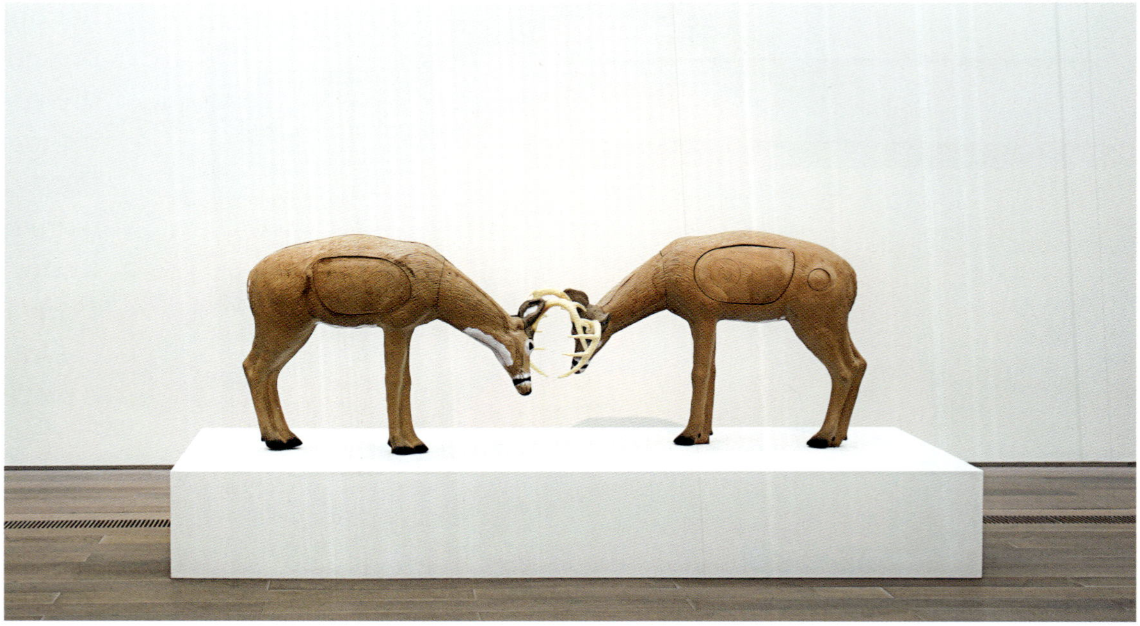

2

Shown by
The Breeder C22
Stephen Friedman Gallery B10

Biography
Born 1970
Lives in New York

Rubell studied Fine Art at Harvard University and attended the Culinary Institute of America, after which she wrote about food for ten years. This, to some extent, explains her interest in foodstuffs and interactive artworks. Her exhibition "Mannequins" at the Dallas Museum, in late 2011, saw female mannequins turned into giant nutcrackers. That year she also showed at Stephen Friedman Gallery, London.

1
Pissing Gnome (Headless)
2011
Resin, refrigerator, stainless steel, wood, paint
76 × 35½ × 35½"
(193 × 90 × 90 cm)
Courtesy of Stephen Friedman Gallery

2
Fighting Bucks
2011
Rubber, glue, pins, wood, paint
50 × 120 × 32"
(127 × 305 × 81.5 cm)
Courtesy of Stephen Friedman Gallery

3
Engagement (with Prince William sculpted by Daniel Druett)
2011
Wax and resin mannequin, wool suit, leather shoes and watch
Dimensions variable
Courtesy of Stephen Friedman Gallery

Jennifer Rubell

Studies in abundance and collective acts of creative destruction, Jennifer Rubell's happenings are part potlatch, part orgiastic feast. Here viewers (or should that be consumers?) are invited to chow down on "food installations" that reference key works from art history—in her *Creation* (2009), for example, a mountainous ton of ribs were drizzled in honey in a nod to Joseph Beuys' 1977 action "Honey is Flowing in All Directions." Meanwhile, her sculptural work *Engagement (with Prince William sculpted by Daniel Druett)* (2011) offers viewers the opportunities to hop up on a plinth with a wax replica of the English Prince, slipping their ring finger into a replica engagement ring. Rubell's practice invites participation, offering moments of fantasy that register her works as lived experience. TM

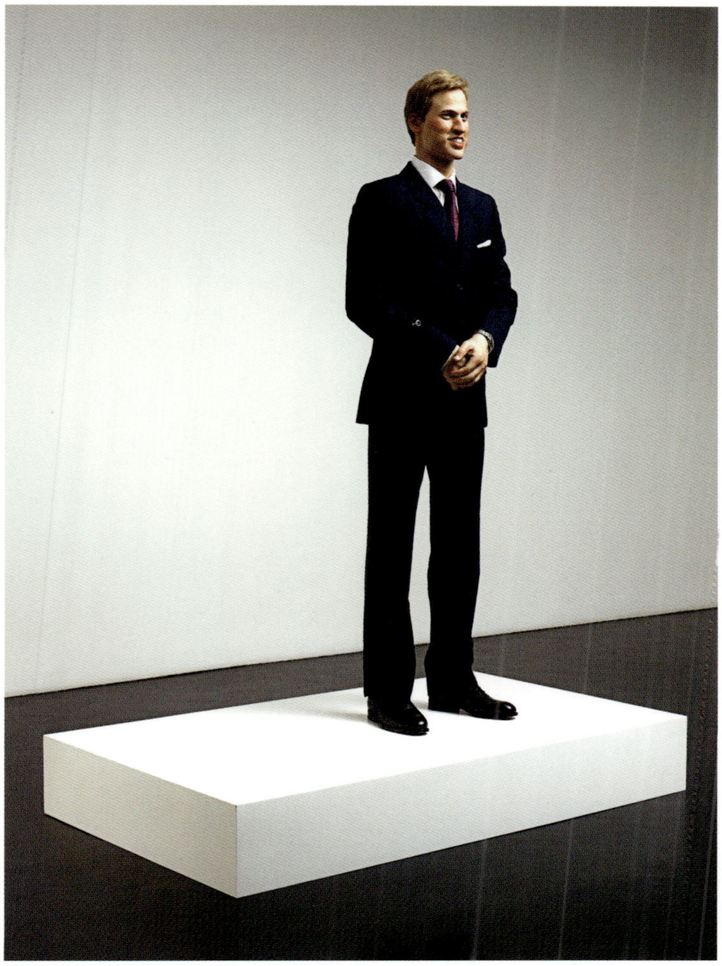

3

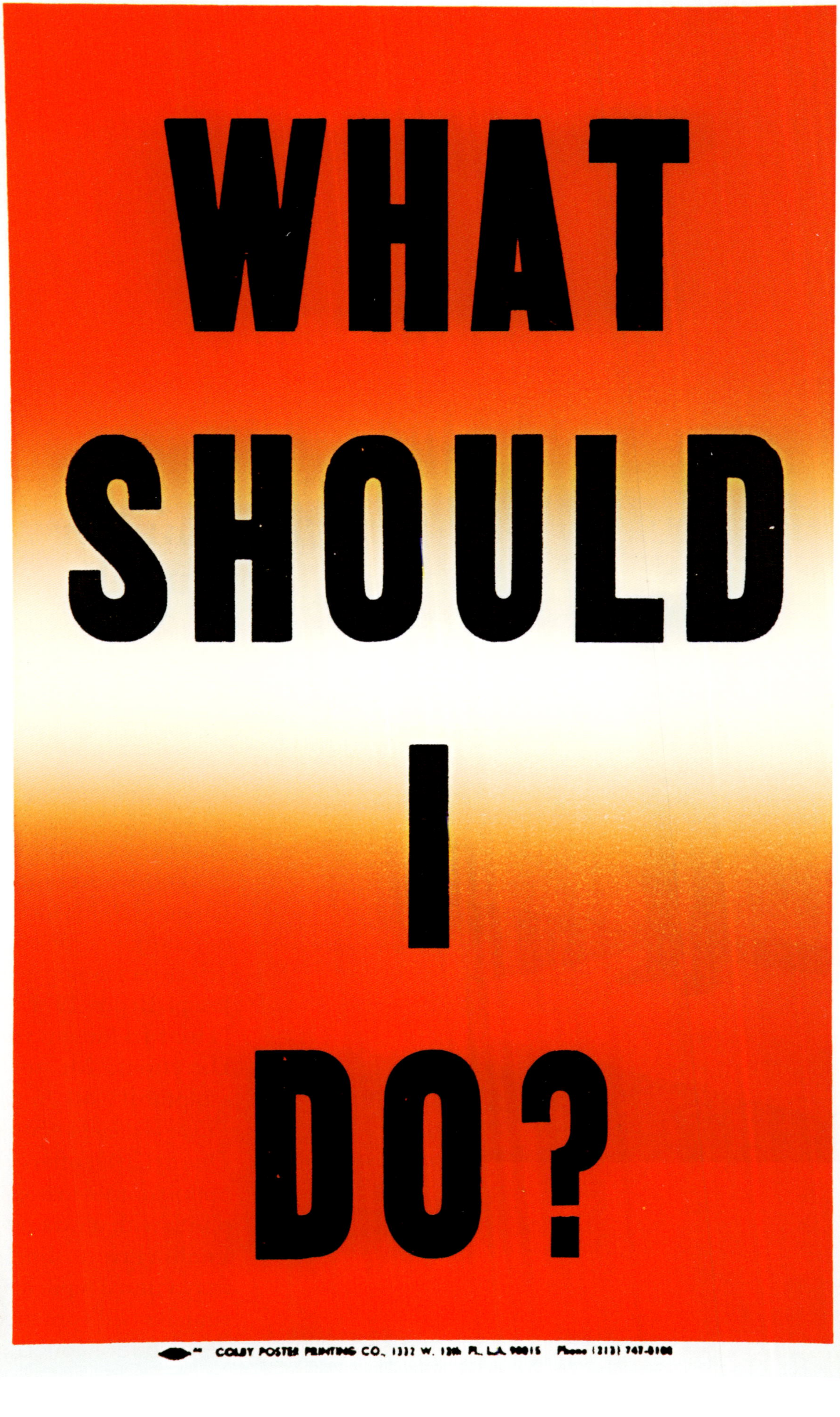
WHAT
SHOULD
I
DO?
COLBY POSTER PRINTING CO., 1332 W. 12th PL. L.A. 90015

Shown by
Air de Paris C11
greengrassi A11
Greene Naftali C44
Galerie Karin Guenther F20
Galerie Martin Janda A28

Biography
Born 1944
Lives in Santa Monica and New York

American artist Ruppersberg has exhibited his graphic, conceptual works since the 1960s. His extensive retrospective "One of Many—Origins and Variants" (2005) at Kunsthalle Düsseldorf, Dusseldorf, toured to Scotland, Spain and France through 2007. Recent solo exhibitions include a self-titled solo show at Greene Naftali, New York (2010), and "You and me or the art of give and take" (2009) at the Santa Monica Museum of Art. His work is included in multiple public collections, including the Los Angeles County Museum and the Museum of Modern Art, New York.

Preview
1988 (detail)
Series of ten lithographs,
22⅛ × 13⅞"
(56 × 35 cm)
Courtesy of Greene Naftali

Allen Ruppersberg

The elevation of the ephemeral to the monumental is a key operation for Allen Ruppersberg, from *The Travel Piece* (1969)—a table and chair with newspapers laid out, corresponding to a bus journey through several US states—to *Big Trouble* (2010), where drawings of statues have been cut out from cartoon strips, enlarged and installed in the gallery as two-dimensional, but life-size, statues. Missing or absent people paradoxically inhabit the work: installations of posters and playbills advertise events long over and far away, while the series "Studies for Bookmarks" (1992) re-presents newspaper obituaries as pencil drawings. Language, Ruppersberg suggests, is better at demonstrating than at describing our worldly battle against the passage of time. SOR

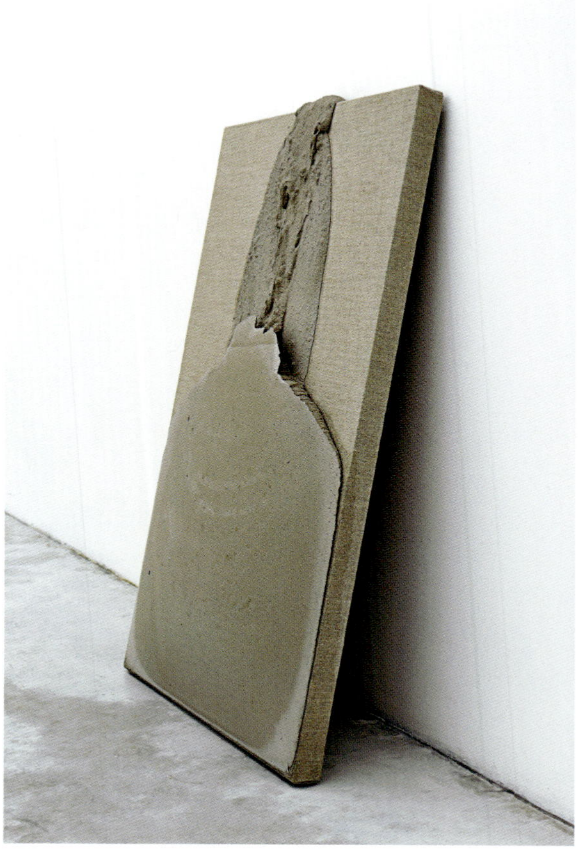

2

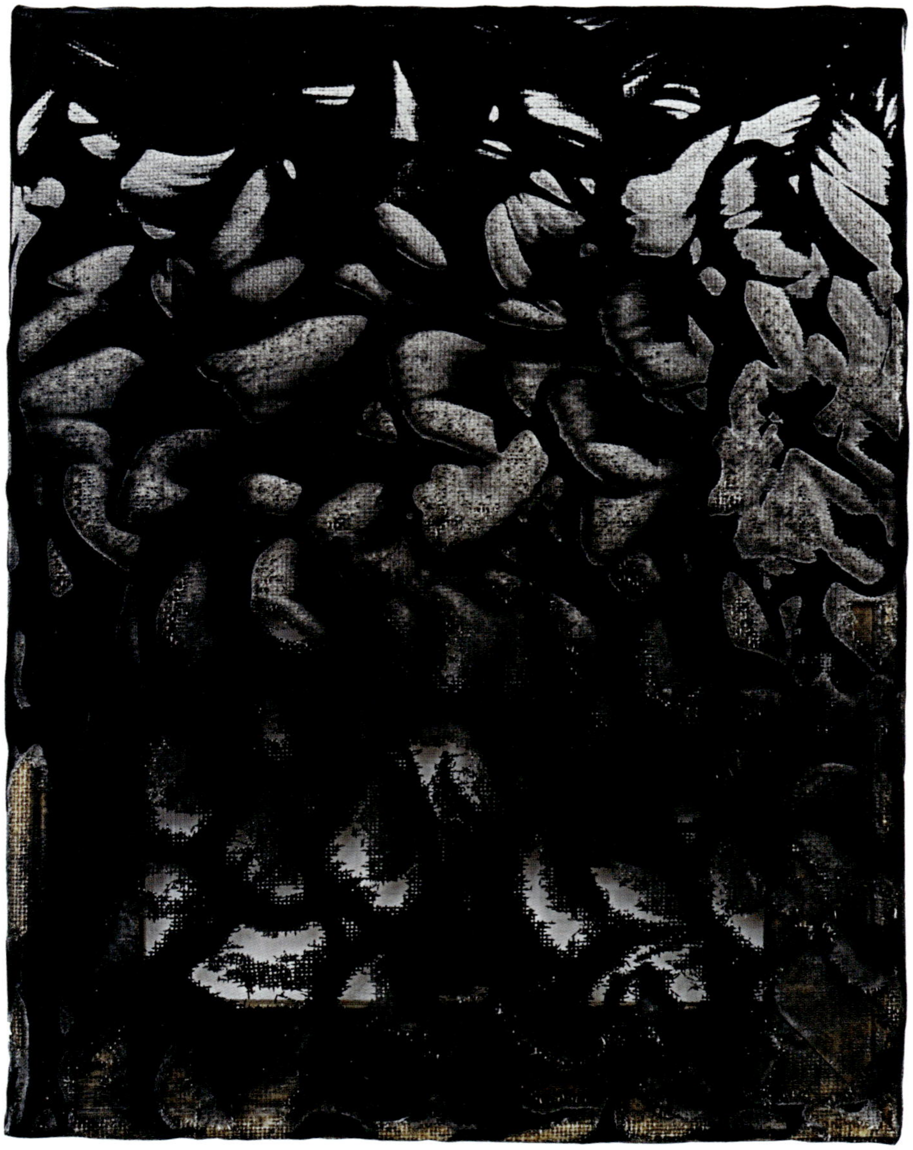

1

Shown by
Tanya Bonakdar
Gallery C6
Galerie Praz-
Delavallade A18

Biography
Born 1980
Lives in Los Angeles

Saban's sculptural paintings were recently installed in the exhibition "Dig" at Praz-Delavallade, Paris, France, in 2011. Her works were also included in the group exhibitions "American Exuberance" (2011) at Rubell Family Collection, and "Painting Expanded" (2011) at Tanya Bonakdar, New York. The Grunwald Center for the Graphic Arts recent donation of works to the Hammer Museum, Los Angeles, included work by Saban which was also on show in 2011.

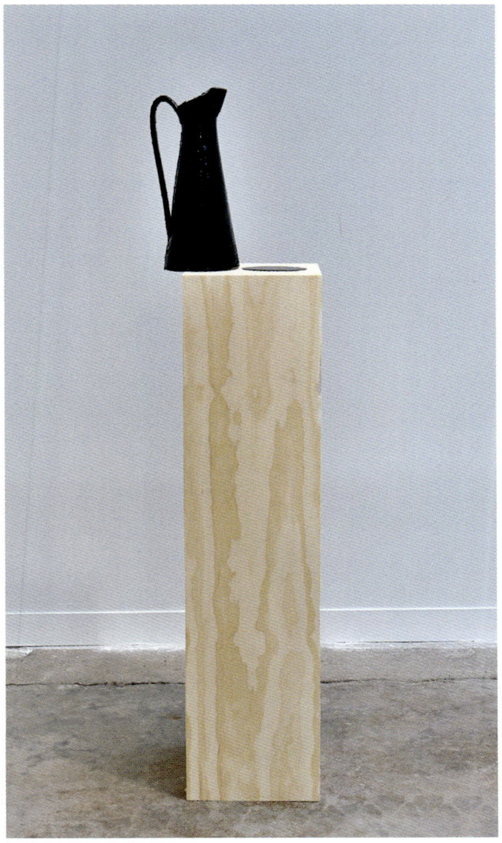

3

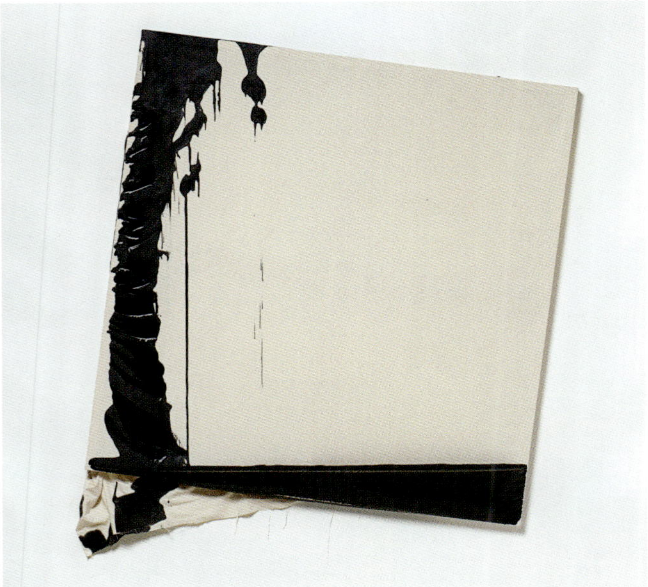

4

1
Fade Out (from Black) #2
2011
Laser-carved acrylic on canvas
9⅞ × 7⅞ × ¾"
(25 × 20 × 2 cm)
Courtesy of Galerie Praz-Delavallade

2
Decant (from Floor) #1
2011
Concrete on canvas
34⅝ × 22 × 2⅜"
(88 × 56 × 6 cm)
Courtesy of Galerie Praz-Delavallade

3
Pitcher with Spill
2011
Acrylic paint on pedestal
64 × 16⅛ × 11⅞"
(162.5 × 41 × 30 cm)
Courtesy of Galerie Praz-Delavallade

4
Decant (Black): Cascade
2011
Encaustic paint on canvas
57 × 57"
(145 × 145 cm)
Courtesy of Galerie Praz-Delavallade

Analia Saban

"I like to see the material for what it is and not for what we intend it to be," Analia Saban says of painting. A canvas becomes mere fabric, unraveled into a gigantic ball of thread; acrylic paint stays liquid, hardens into sculptural casts, or is peeled off in plastic leaves. In the 2010 series "Acrylic in Canvas" and "Information Leaks," paint is poured inside a vertical canvas and seeps out through holes pricked in the surface or pools at the base, the wet works sealed hygienically within oversized plastic bags. The medium's constitutive elements interact alchemically, but the process of their merging is arrested at its most in-between moments. SNS

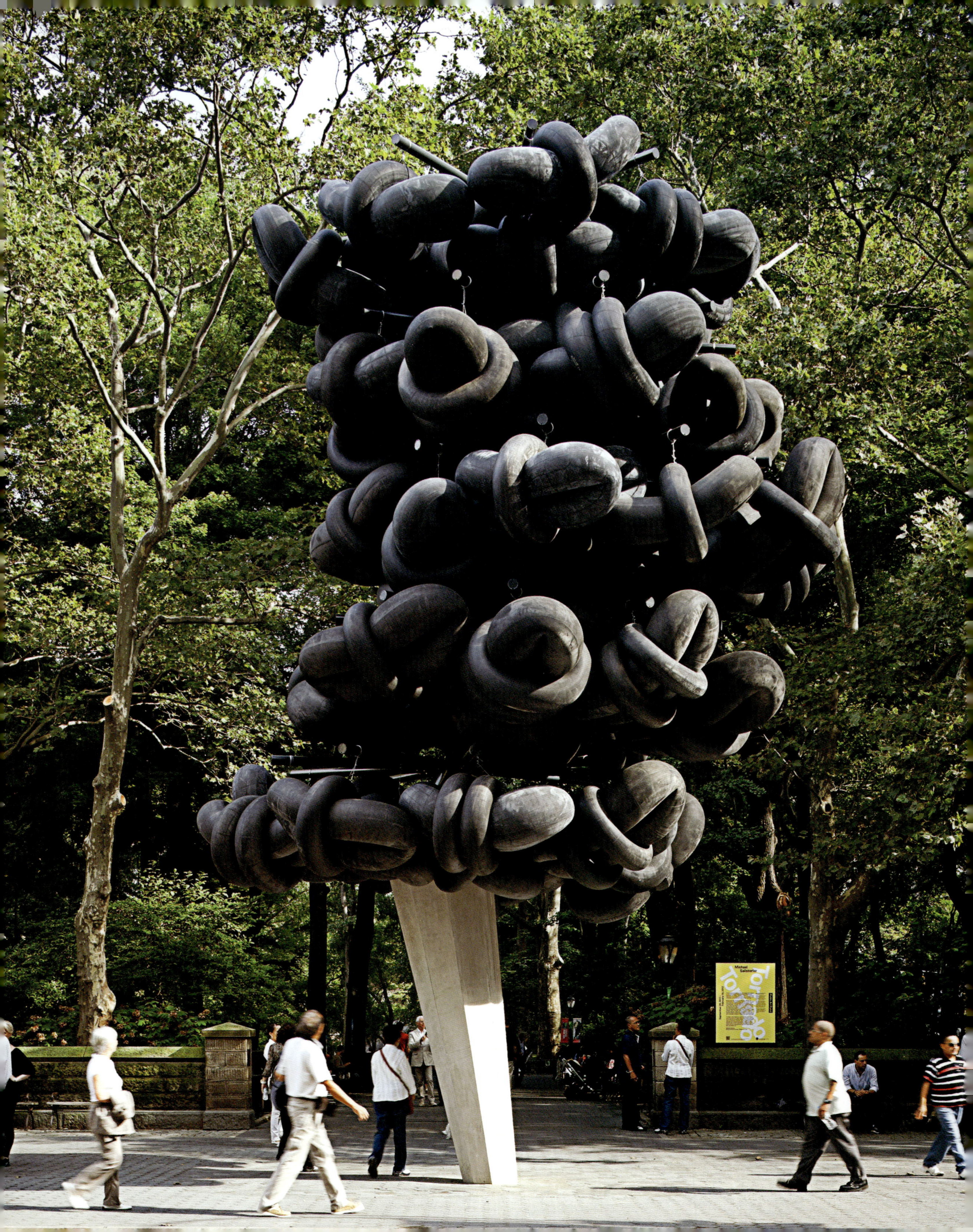
Michael
Tornado

Michael Sailstorfer

Shown by
Galeria Fortes Vilaça C48
Johann König A14
Galerie Perrotin C41

Biography
Born 1979
Lives in Berlin

German artist Sailstorfer's society-conscious sculptures and installations have been exhibited in galleries in Europe the United States, and further afield. In early 2012 he had an exhibition at Johann König, Berlin, that included works made by his father, in the 1980s. In 2011 he had a self-titled solo show at Kunsthalle Nürnberg, Nuremberg, and "If you should die in a car crash" at the Zeppelin Museum Friedrichshafen. His first public work in the United States, *Tornado*, went on show in Central Park, New York, in 2011.

Tornado
2011
Public sculpture
34 × 17'
(518 × 1036.5 cm)
Courtesy of Public Art Fund and Johann König, Berlin

Michael Sailstorfer's sculptures and installations are often bombastic interventions in the public realm, but, on occasion, they manifest as quieter works, such as *Trockenfisch* (Dried Fish, 2010)—an abstracted pale green form reminiscent of a fish on a line—and act as intimate material gestures. His recent public sculpture *Tornado* (2011), situated in Central Park, New York, saw 100 rubber tire tubes twisted together to form the bushels of a tree-like "tornado." His works have a humorous quirk, aiding an immediate impact that opens the door on the embedded subtleties of his practice. In a project initiated in 2009, entitled *Pulheim gräbt* (Pulheim Dig, 2009–10), he used his exhibition budget to buy 28 gold nuggets—he then buried them in a city square, announcing their presence to a shovel-equipped audience. SC

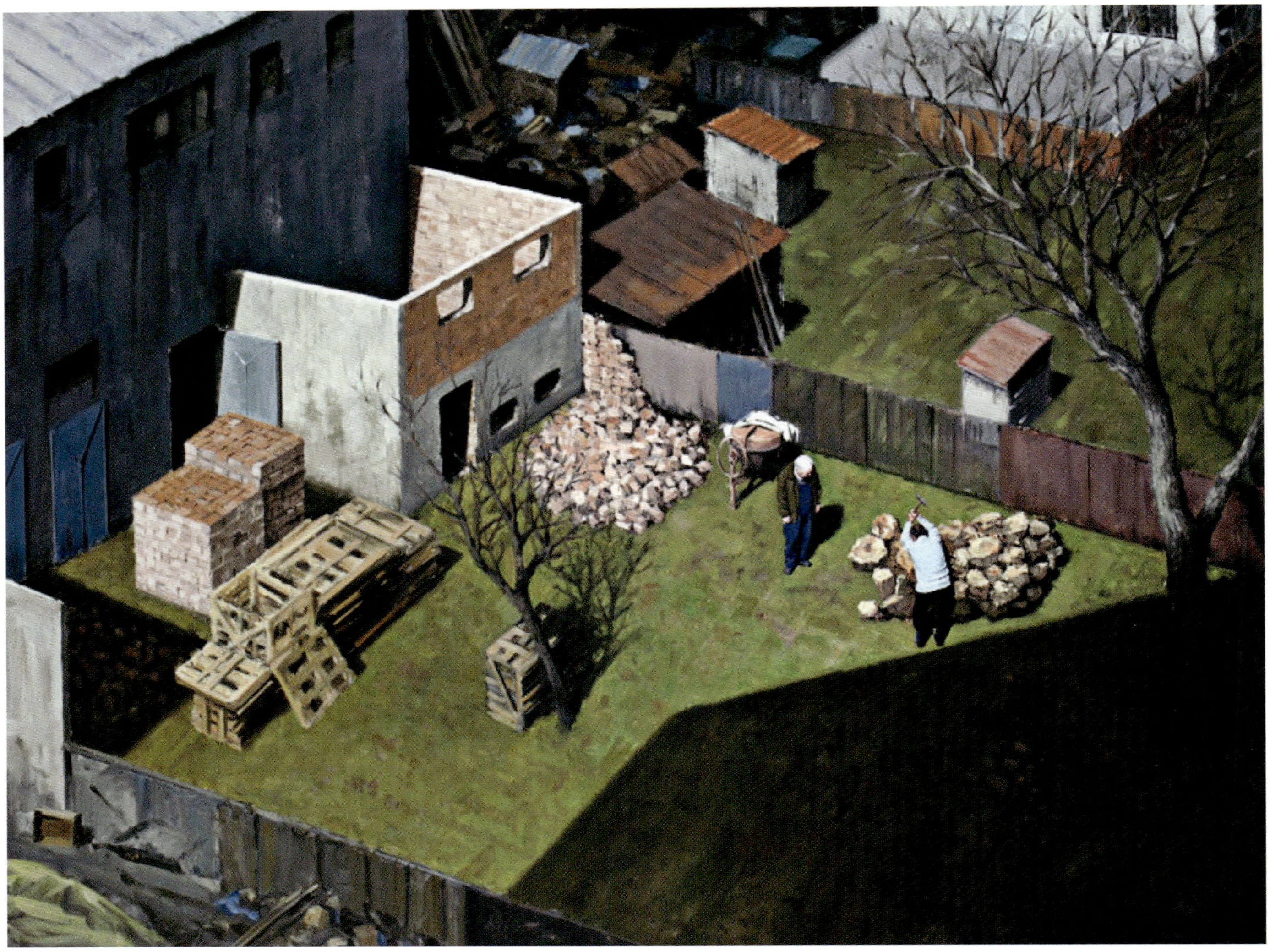

1

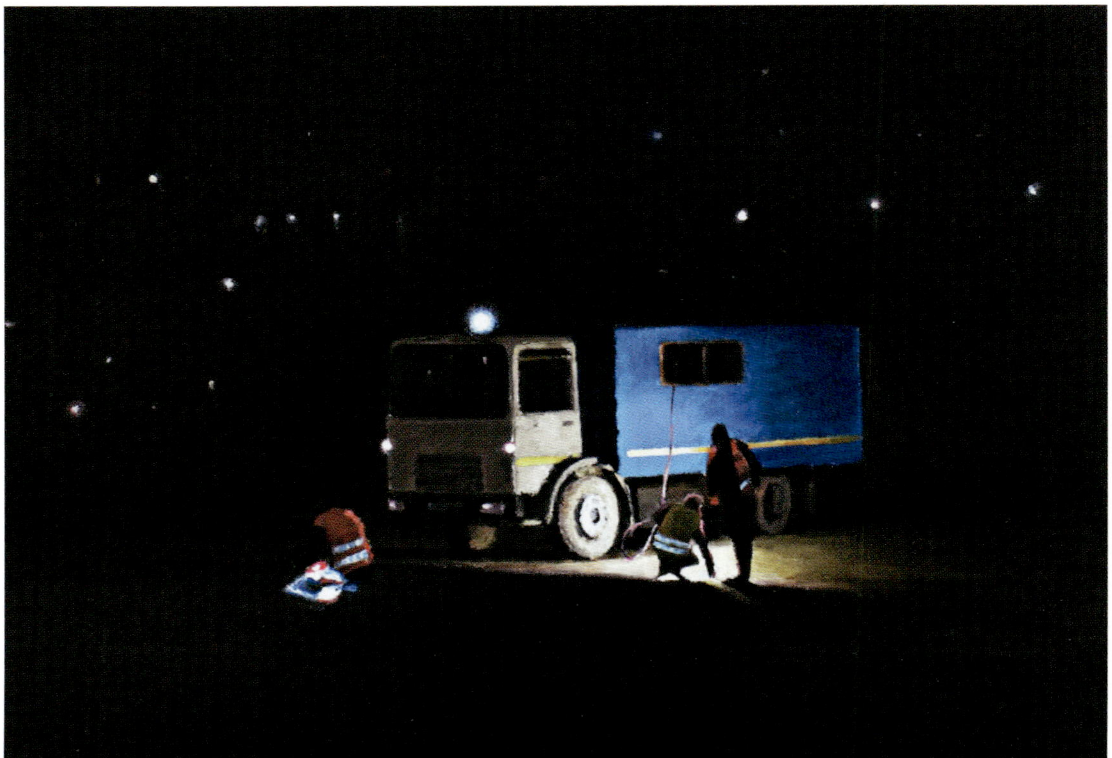

2

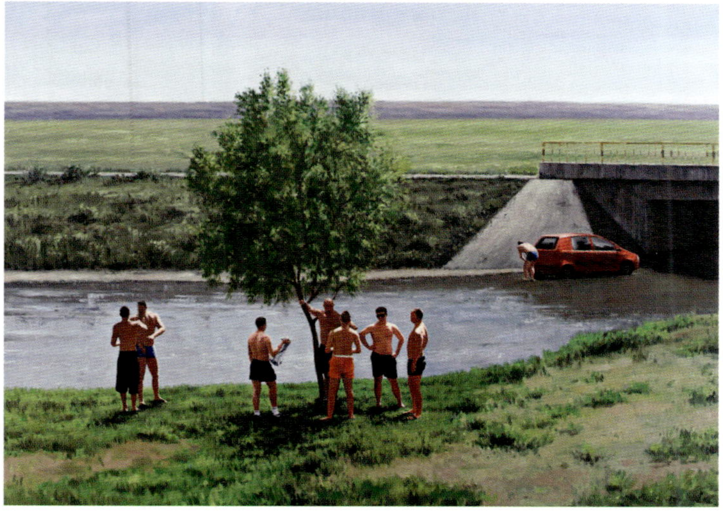

3

Shown by
David Nolan Gallery
A29
Galeria Plan B F7

Biography
Born 1978
Lives in Cluj

Romanian painter Savu's detailed and unnerving paintings have been exhibited in Europe and the United States since the mid-2000s. His canvases, which recall Cold War-era Romania, were the subject of the solo show "Close to Nature" at David Nolan Gallery, New York, in late-2011. The same year, the solo exhibition "Under the Radar" took place at Pitzhanger Manor, PM Gallery and House, London. Other recent solo shows include "Unimportant Stories" (2011) at Nicodim Gallery, Los Angeles, and "Essay on Limits" (2011) at Galerie Hussenot, Paris.

1
The Brick Factory
2011
Oil on canvas
55½ × 74⅞"
(141 × 190 cm)
Courtesy of David Nolan Gallery

2
Intervention Team
2011
Oil on canvas
13¾ × 19⅝"
(35 × 50 cm)
Courtesy of David Nolan Gallery

3
The Bathers
2010
Oil on canvas
74⅞ × 106¼"
(190 × 270 cm)
Courtesy of David Nolan Gallery

Șerban Savu

Șerban Savu's painted landscapes are not so much romantic vistas of natural beauty as places of hard-won subsistence, or boredom at best. In earlier paintings, such as *Early Days of Summer* (2008), figures bathe in lakes or trek across land not quite illuminated by sun or joy. In recent works, such as *Iara Valley* (2011), the halcyon is almost entirely eclipsed by industrial hardware, as dumper trucks, dams, and car parks predominate. Although Social Realism is no longer an imposed genre in Romania since the deposition of Nicolae Ceaușescu, Savu employs its tropes to articulate everyday realities of a citizenry no longer suppressed but slow to shrug off the effects of history. SOR

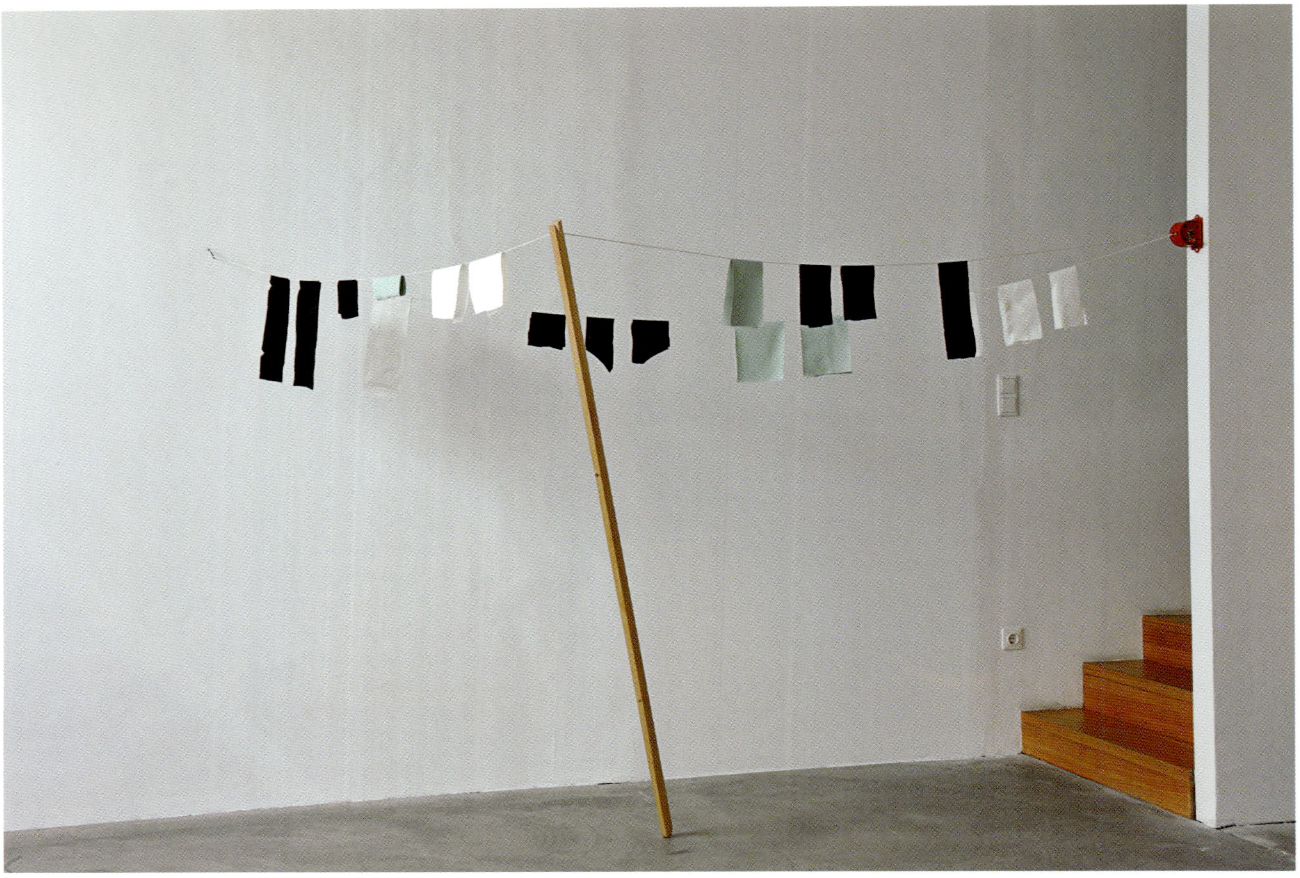

1

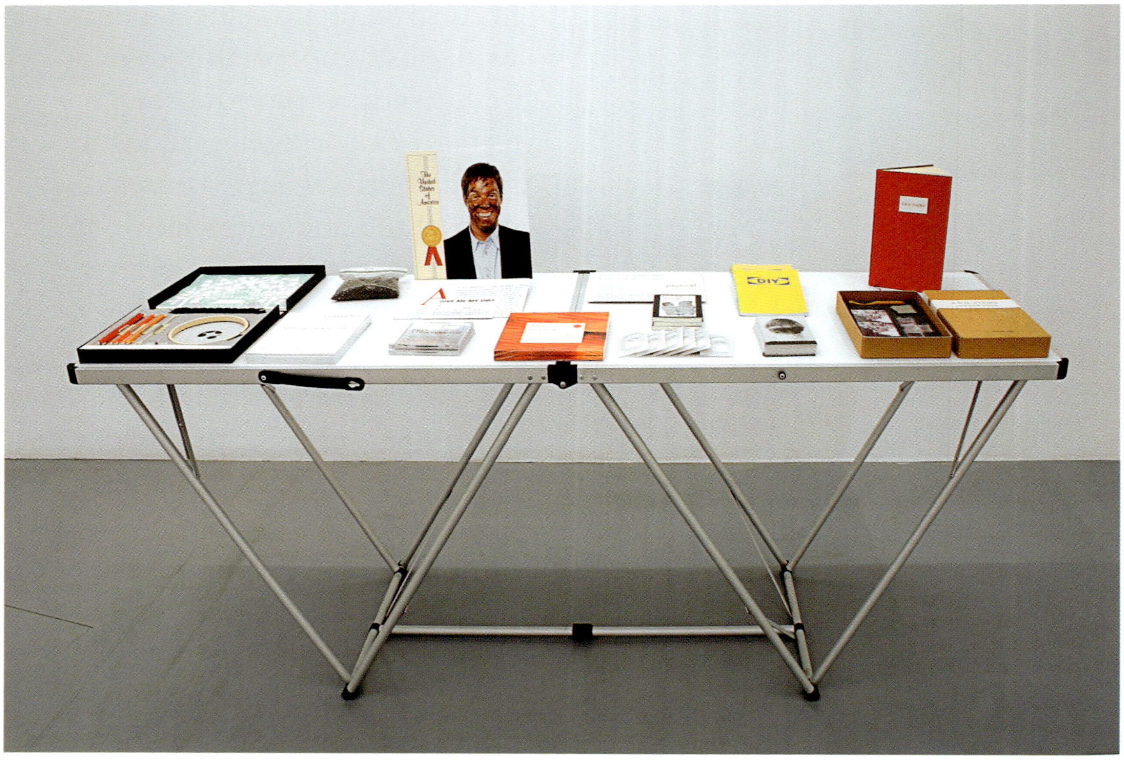

2

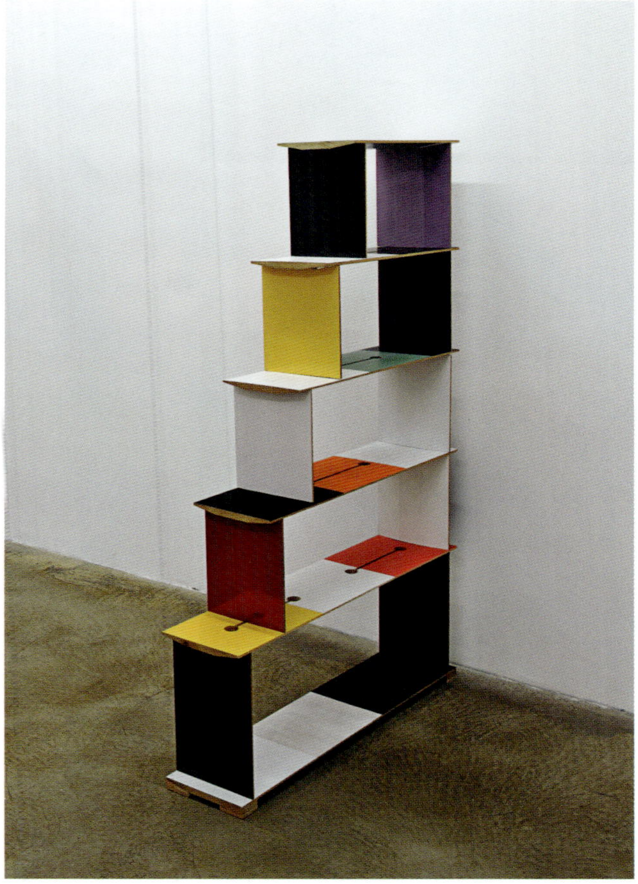

3

Shown by
Galerie Martin Janda
A28

Biography
Born 1961
Lives in New York

American artist Scanlan's solo exhibition "Möbel" took place at Galerie Martin Janda, Vienna, in 2011. He participated in the group shows "In Deed: Certificates of Authenticity in Art" (2011) at De Vleeshal, Middelburg, and "Avant Garde: Specters of the Nineties" (2011) at the Marres Center for Contemporary Culture, Maastricht. In 2012 the solo show "Object Lessons" will be held at Kunstmuseum aan Zee, Ostend, and he will participate in the group exhibition "Foreigners Everywhere" at the Jüdisches Museum, Vienna.

1
Möbel (wite trash)
2011
(Furniture (wite trash))
Enamel-painted metal, string, fabric, galvanised steel, wood
78¾ × 137¾ × 29½"
(200 × 350 × 75 cm)
Courtesy of Galerie Martin Janda

2
Traveling Salesman
2007
Mixed media
41 × 71⅝ × 24½"
(104 × 182 × 62 cm)
Courtesy of Galerie Martin Janda

3
Möbel (color chart)
(Furniture (color chart))
2011
Wood, glue, and enamel paint
63 × 40 × 9⅞"
(160 × 101.5 × 25 cm)
Courtesy of Galerie Martin Janda

Joe Scanlan

From his unique sculptures that masquerade as mass-produced objects to producing work for a fictional artist, Joe Scanlan insistently tests the complex relationship between art, commerce, and consumption. Many of his earliest works—such as *Nesting Bookcase* (1989) and *Bathroom Floor (Improved)* (1993), which were developed as practical solutions to domestic problems—challenge the autonomy of the art object when displayed in the gallery or museum. For over ten years Scanlan has also produced a coherent body of work under the guise of emerging African American artist Donelle Woolford. Taken as far as the hiring of various female actors to play the role of the artist at public events, Scanlan's invented persona destabilizes the notion of authorship within systems of economic value. AB

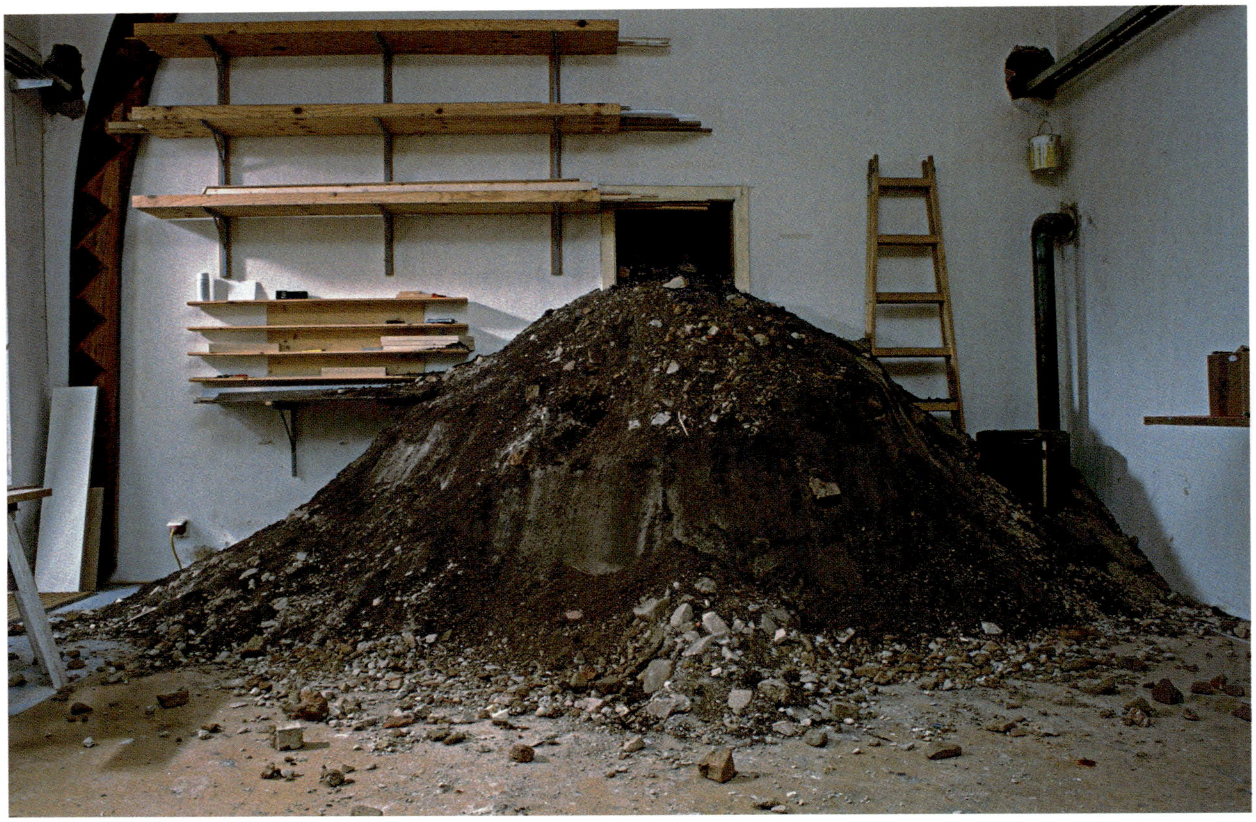

1

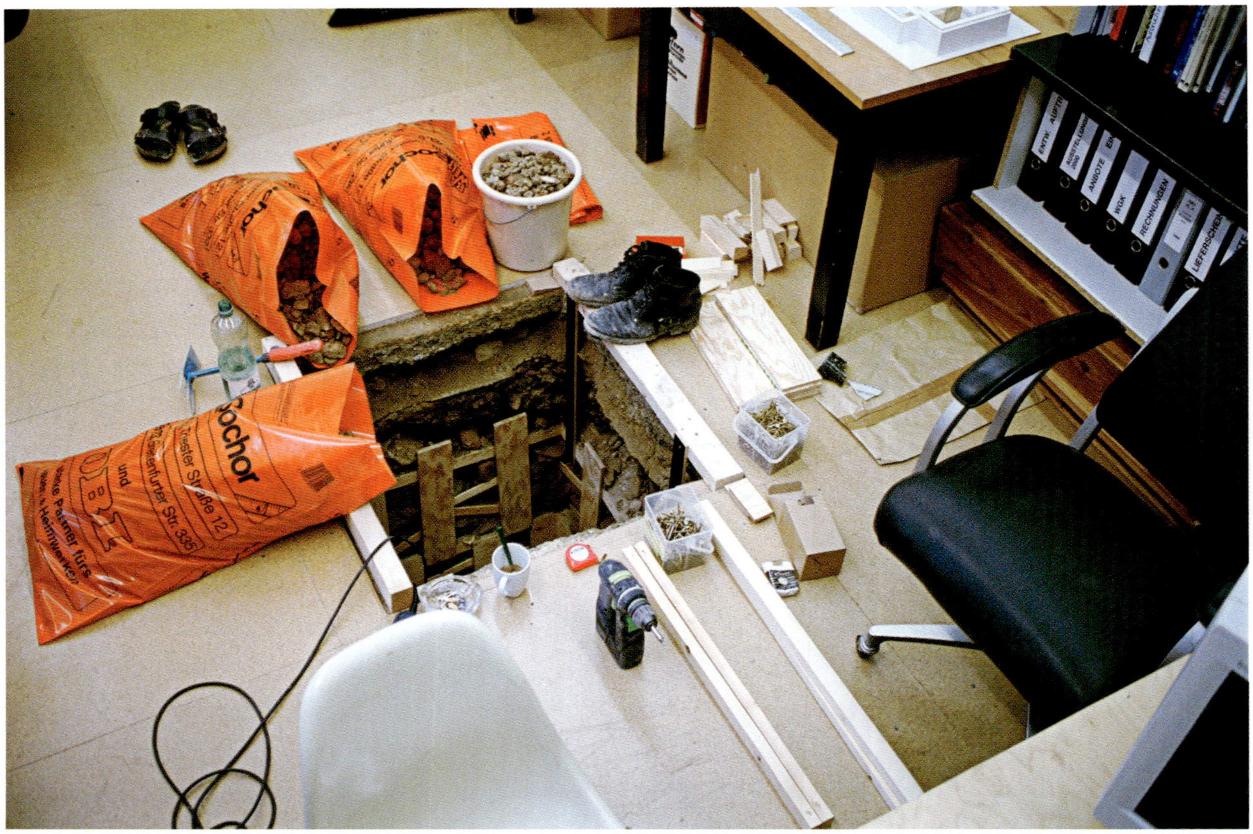

2

Shown by
Simon Preston F22
Galerie Jocelyn Wolff F1

Biography
Born 1970
Lives in Vienna

Austrian artist Schabus has been isolating fragments of daily life in his sculptures and installations since the early 1990s. In 2011 he had a self-titled solo show at Galerie Jocelyn Wolff, Paris; "Die Rocky Horror Hansi Show (The Rocky Horror Picture Show)" at Clubblumen, Vienna; and "Nichts geht mehr (No more)" at the Institut d'Art contemporain, Villeurbanne/Rhône-Alpes. In 2010, he participated in the 6th Berlin Biennale, with a work that would later be shown as part of Nuit Blanche, Paris, in 2010.

1
Schacht von Babel
2003
Digital chromogenic prints mounted, framed
14 × 21⅝"
(35.5 × 55 cm)
Courtesy of Galerie Jocelyn Wolff

2
Schacht von Babel
2003
Digital chromogenic prints mounted, framed
14 × 21⅝"
(35.5 × 55 cm)
Courtesy of Galerie Jocelyn Wolff

Focus
Hans Schabus

Physical and psychological spaces, whether subterranean or celestial, form an endless labyrinth in Hans Schabus' work—with his studio often at its heart. He performs in films and videos, he has said, as "a sort of 'traveling salesman' of my space of possibilities." *Western* (2002) found him wending his way through the Viennese sewer system in a wooden sailboat; the zither music from *The Third Man* on the soundtrack recalls a city parceled into parallel worlds. Recent displacements have included *Klub Europa* (2010), for which he relocated a dilapidated resin stegosaurus and wooly mammoth from an abandoned East German amusement park, and *The Home Is Inviolable* (2010), a poignant, politically resonant display in a gentrifying neighborhood of worn carpets from Berlin apartments. KJ

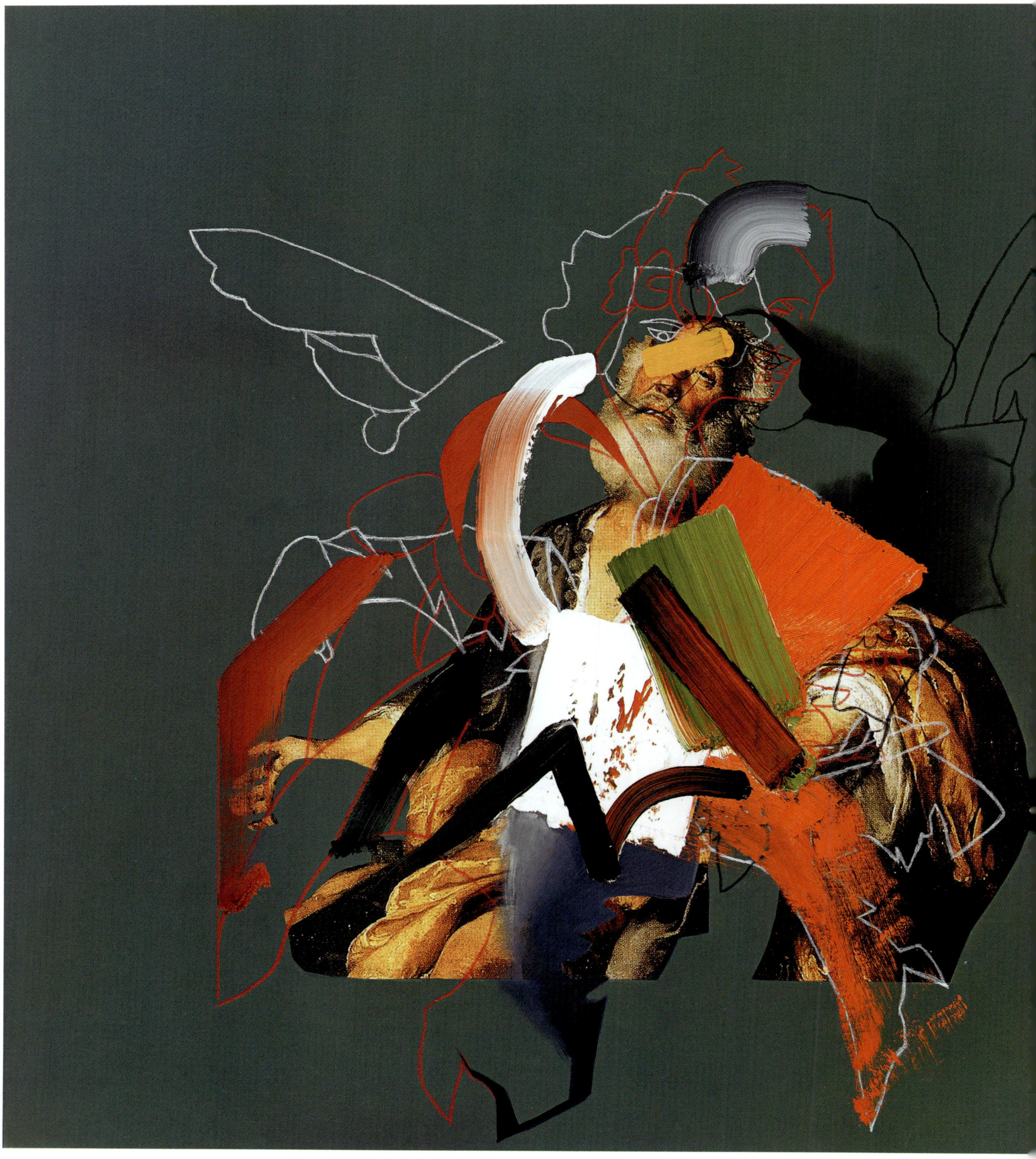

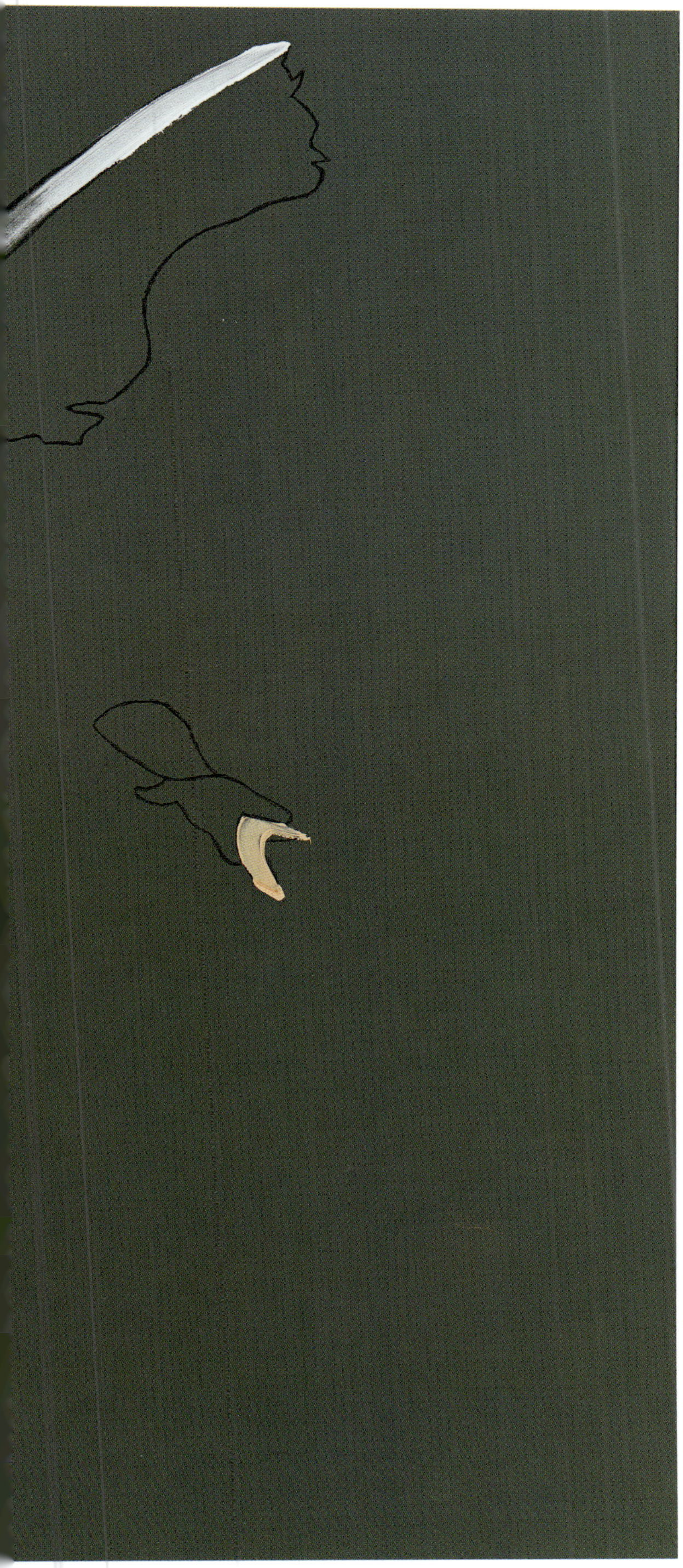

Shown by
Miguel Abreu Gallery
C14

Biography
Born 1970
Lives in New York

Schoolwerth's historically informed paintings have been exhibited in the United States and Europe since the mid-1990s. His series "Portraits of Paintings" was recently shown at Miguel Abreu Gallery, New York (2010), and Galerie Nathalie Obadia, Paris (2010). He has participated in numerous group shows, most recently "New York to London and Back: The Medium of Contingency" (2011) at Thomas Dane Gallery, London.

Portrait of "The Healing of Tobit" (after Strozzi)
2011
Acrylic, oil, giclée print ink, and chalk on canvas
38 × 53"
(96.5 × 134.5 cm)
Courtesy of Miguel Abreu Gallery

Pieter Schoolwerth

Since 2009, Pieter Schoolwerth's series of works "Portraits of Paintings" has seen the New York-based artist rework old master still lifes and landscapes into studies on the technique and form of the history of painting. Distilling art-historical references and compositional styles into biomorphic swathes of figuration, his earlier paintings in this series showed contorted, Bacon-esque faces and Cubist forms overlaying classical backdrops. *Portrait of "The Healing of Tobit" (after Strozzi)* (2011), one of his later studies, edits out the background landscapes entirely: a densely layered mix of figure and form emerging from the monochromatic ground of the canvas—intense bursts of thickly applied paint as well as daubed outlines giving the impression of a quickly applied sketch but gesturing toward the composite image formation of the digital age. PT

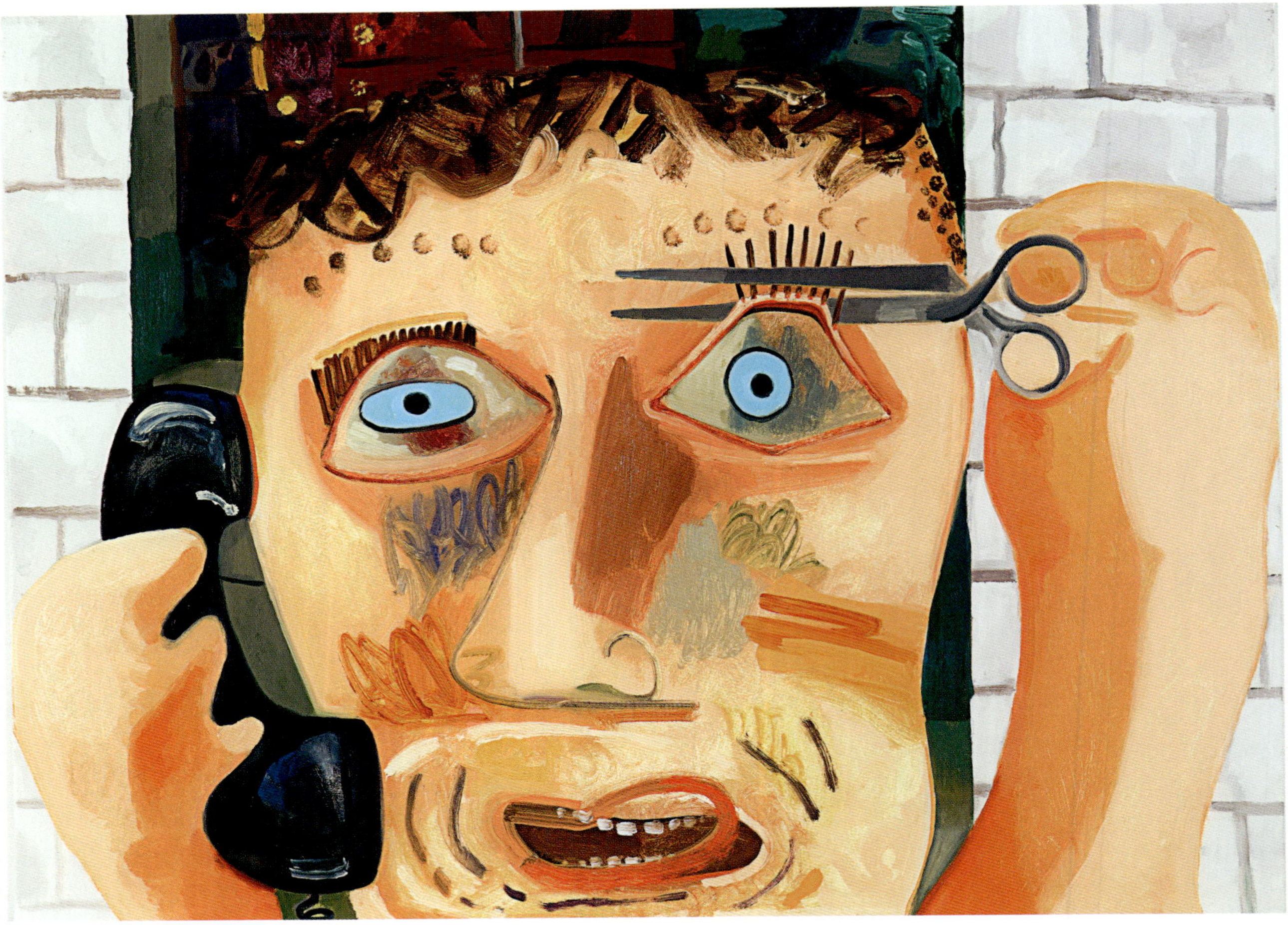

1

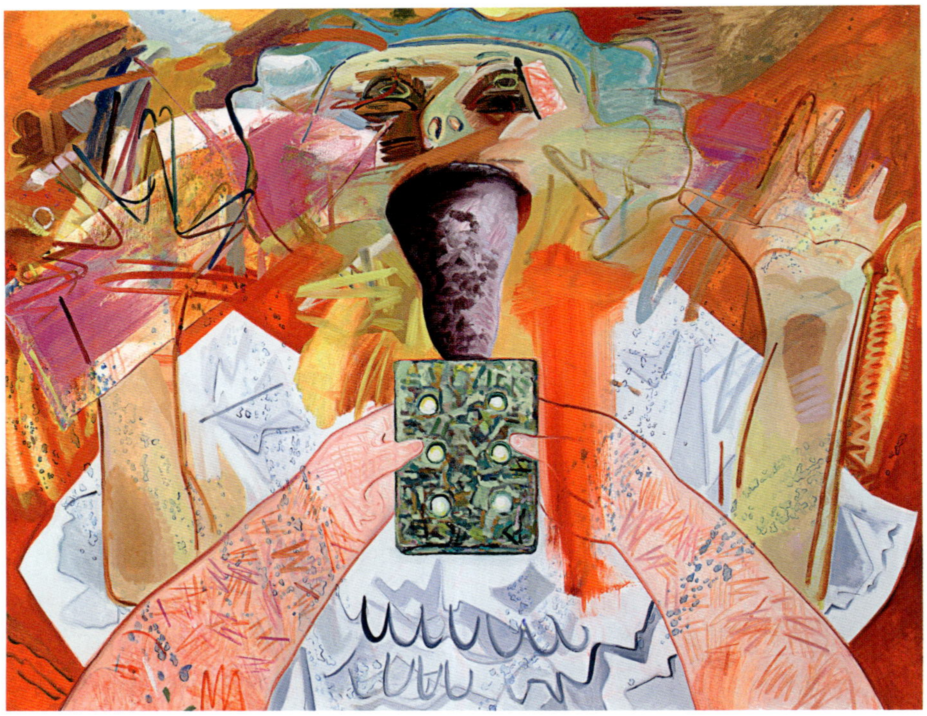

2

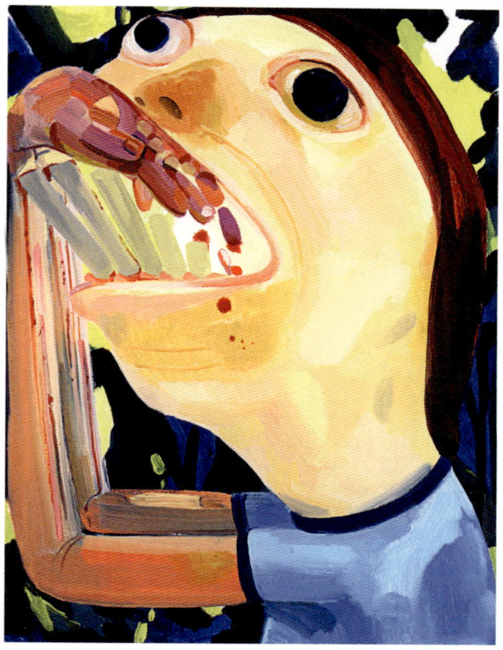

3

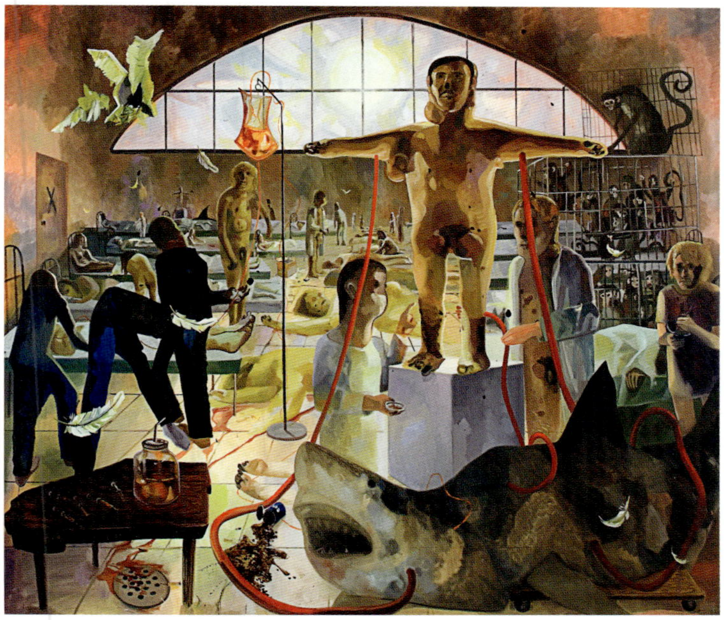

4

Shown by
Contemporary Fine Arts C39
Friedrich Petzel Gallery B4

Biography
Born 1976
Lives in Brooklyn

Schutz's mid-career retrospective "If The Face had Wheels" was shown at the Neuberger Museum of Art, Purchase, and the Miami Art Museum in 2011. Not only celebrated for her painting, the artist recently exhibited monoprints at The Arnold and Marie Schwartz Gallery Met, New York (2012). In spring 2012 Friedrich Petzel Gallery, New York, will host an exhibition of new paintings, and in the fall MCA Denver will exhibit new works on paper.

1
Talk Talk
2010
Oil on canvas
28½ × 40"
(72.5 × 101.5 cm)
Courtesy of Friedrich Petzel Gallery

2
Licking a Brick
2011
Oil on canvas
64 × 84"
(162.5 × 213.5 cm)
Courtesy of Friedrich Petzel Gallery

3
Devourer
2004
Oil on canvas
28 × 22"
(71 × 56 cm)
Courtesy of Friedrich Petzel Gallery

4
How We Cured the Plague
2007
Oil on canvas
120 × 144"
(305 × 366 cm)
Courtesy of Friedrich Petzel Gallery

Dana Schutz

"They could eat themselves and then remake themselves to be any form they wanted to be." Thus Dana Schutz, describing her "Self-Eaters" (2004): a series of paintings of figures engaged in ecstatic autophagy, including a cannibal who performs the ultimately self-reflexive act of devouring his own face. Schutz's comic grotesques have included a woman stripping a wooden floor with her teeth, a portrait of herself as an elephant, and the autopsied corpse of Michael Jackson. (This last was produced four years before the pop star died: "The idea that he could even have an inside was really weird.") But it is as much the crazed and lurid surface of her paintings that renders them, as she puts it, "scuzzy and contagious." BD

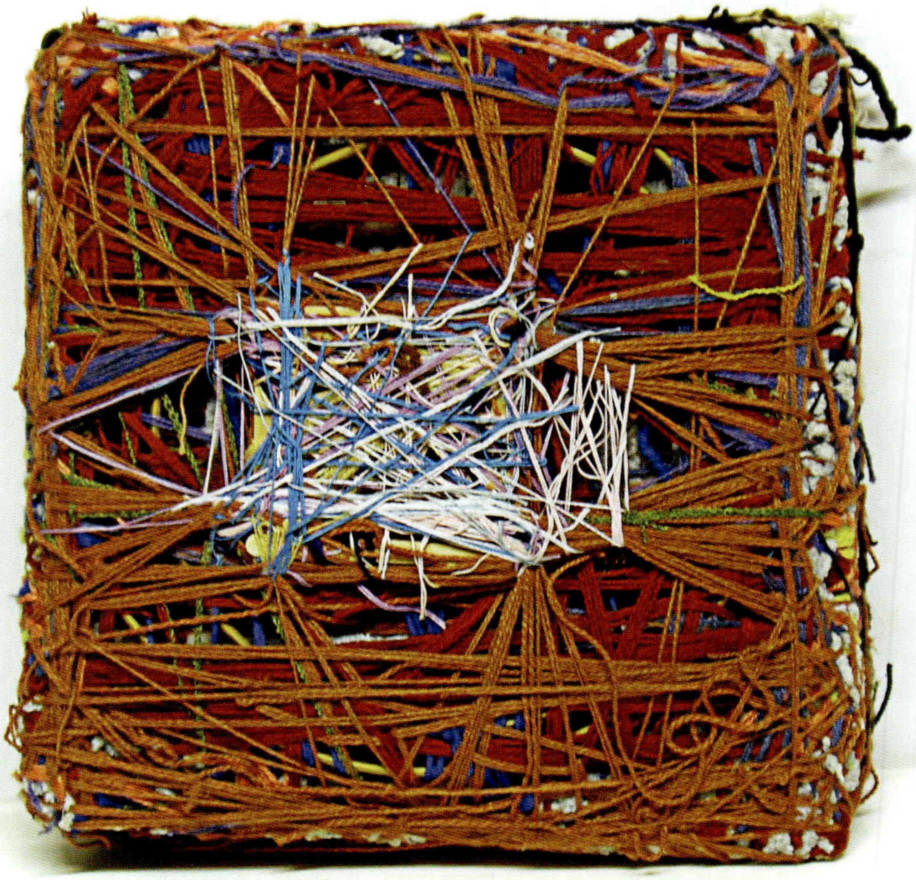

1

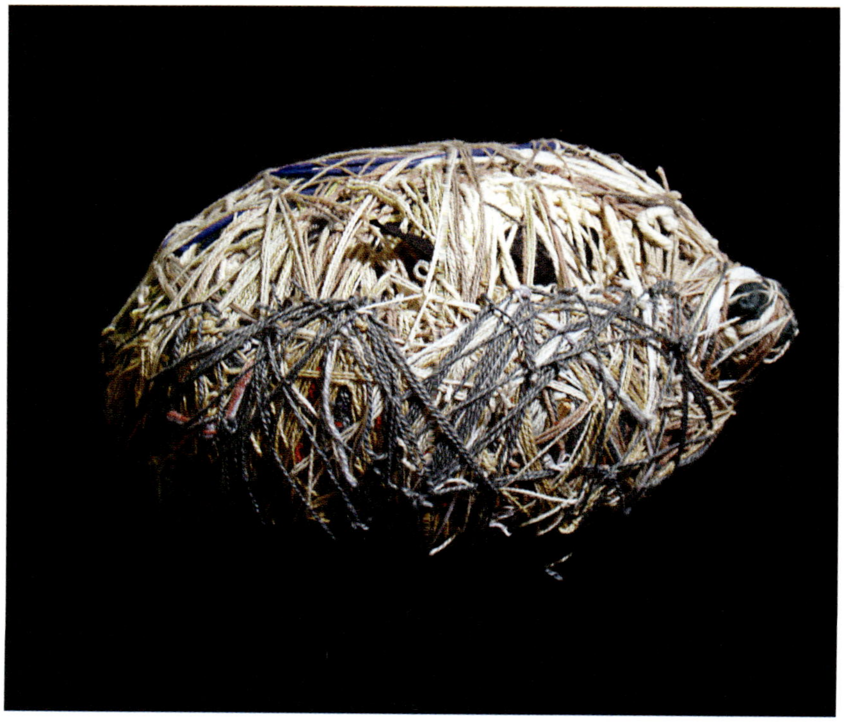

2

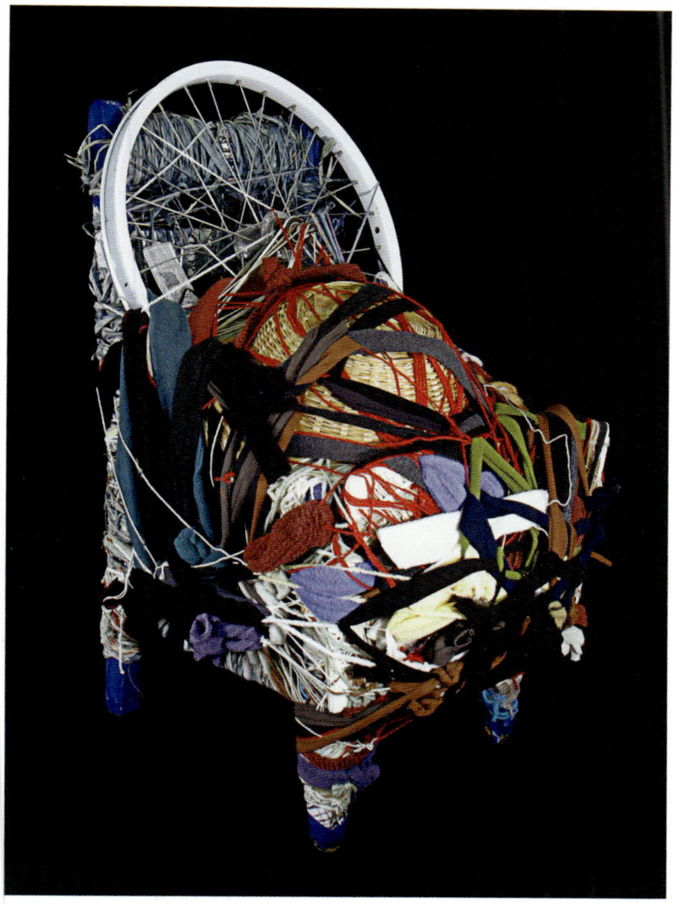

3

Shown by
White Columns A12

Biography
Born 1943
Died 2005

Born with Down syndrome, Scott had an exceptional career as an artist in the eighteen years before her death in 2005. Her sculptures have been the subject of numerous exhibitions, including posthumous shows at White Columns, New York (2010), and "The Perfect Man Show," also at White Columns (2007), curated by artist Rita Ackermann. Her work is also part of the public collections at the Museum of American Folk Art, New York, and L'Aracine Musee D'Art Brut, Paris.

1
Untitled
No date
Mixed media
14½ × 14½"
(36.6 × 36.5 cm)
Courtesy of Creative Growth Art Center, Oakland, CA

2
Untitled
No date
Mixed media
18 × 15 × 11"
(45.5 × 38 × 28 cm)
Courtesy of Creative Growth Art Center, Oakland, CA

3
Untitled
No date
Mixed media
30 × 18 × 12"
(76 × 45.5 × 30.5 cm)
Courtesy of Creative Growth Art Center, Oakland, CA

Judith Scott

The bound sculptures of American-artist Judith Scott, weave colored strings and other fibrous material around objects, often rendering them anonymous in their new bulbous forms. These cocoon-like untitled works were created over weeks and months at her studio in The Creative Growth Art Center, Oakland. Scott was profoundly deaf, mute, and suffered from Down syndrome. In the two-decades before her death at age 61, she was recognized for her unique talents by both mainstream and Outsider Art galleries alike. The simplicity of her approach, her use of color, tone, and texture, define her works as renegade to any defined art movement, yet she continues to be an influence on contemporary generations, marking out her own place in art history. SC

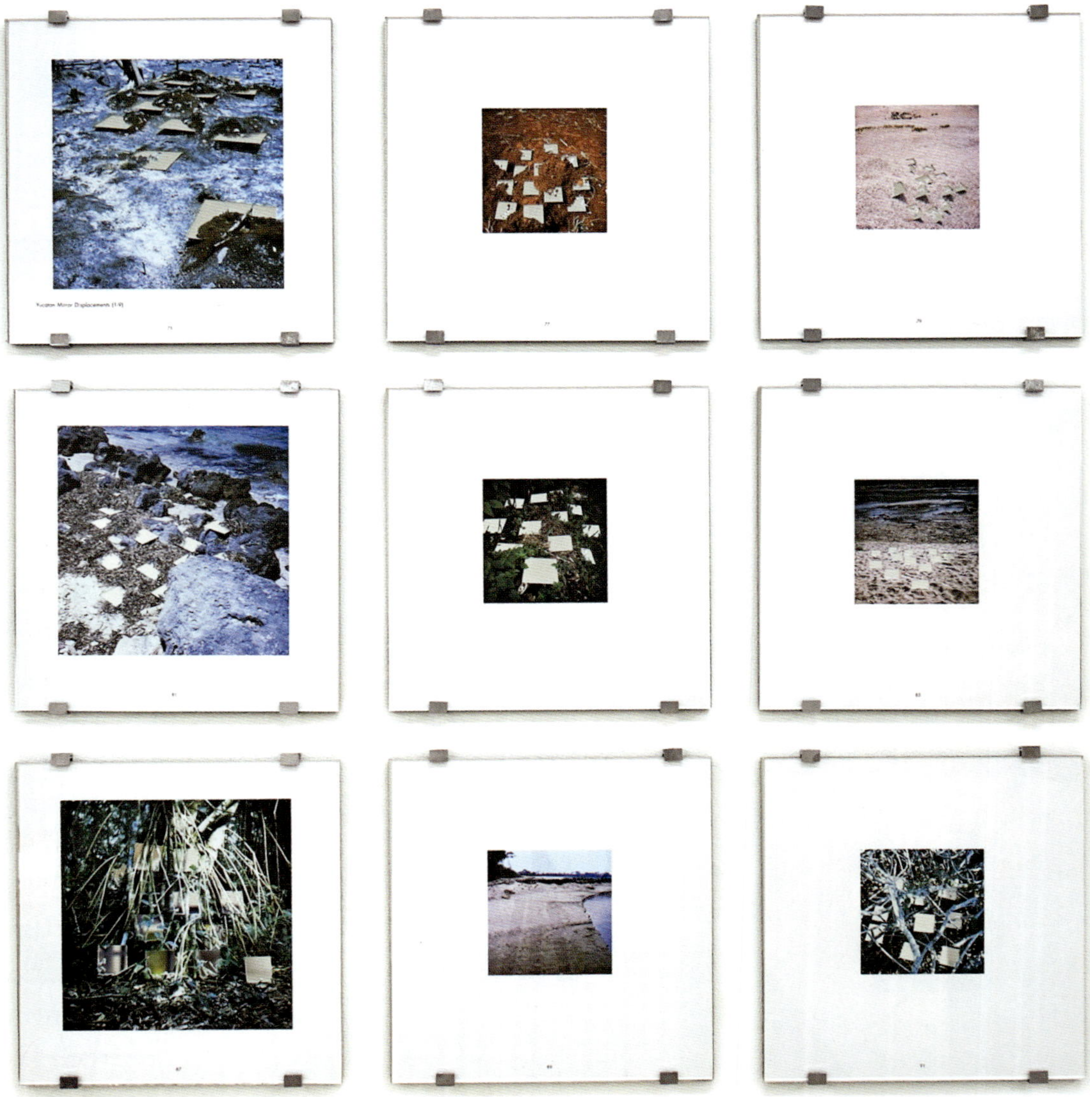
Yucatan Mirror Displacements (1-9)

Focus
Yann Sérandour

Shown by
gb agency F33

Biography
Born 1974
Lives in Rennes

French artist Sérandour has exhibited in Europe and the United States in recent years. In 2011 his solo show "Cloudy with a Chance of a Ray of Sunlight" took place at gb agency, Paris. He participated in "Incidents of Mirror Travels in Yucatan and Other Places" (2011) at Museo Tamayo Arte Contemporaneo, Bosque de Chapultepec; "Studies for an Exhibition" (2011) at The David Roberts Art Foundation, London; and "The Way Beyond Art: Wide White Space" (2011) at CCA Wattis Institute for Contemporary Arts, San Francisco.

Yucatan Mirror Displacements (1-9)
2008
Pages torn from a book, mirrors, glasses and hanging devices
Dimensions variable
Courtesy of gb agency

Conceptual artist Yann Sérandour's installations often consist of disparate objects, photographs, and historical artifacts. He makes reference to 1960s land art in *Yucatan Mirror Displacements (1–9)* (2008), a series of pages torn from a book containing Robert Smithson's work of the same name. Cutting out Smithson's mirrors from each page, Sérandour fills the void with real mirror, its surface shining through the pages perforated surface. His gestures are often simple, yet he weaves together complex narratives, performing the role of historian, storyteller and artist. He fills the gaps between events from our recent past and those of the present, inventing new narratives to connect disparate and sometimes forgotten events that have significant relevance today. SC

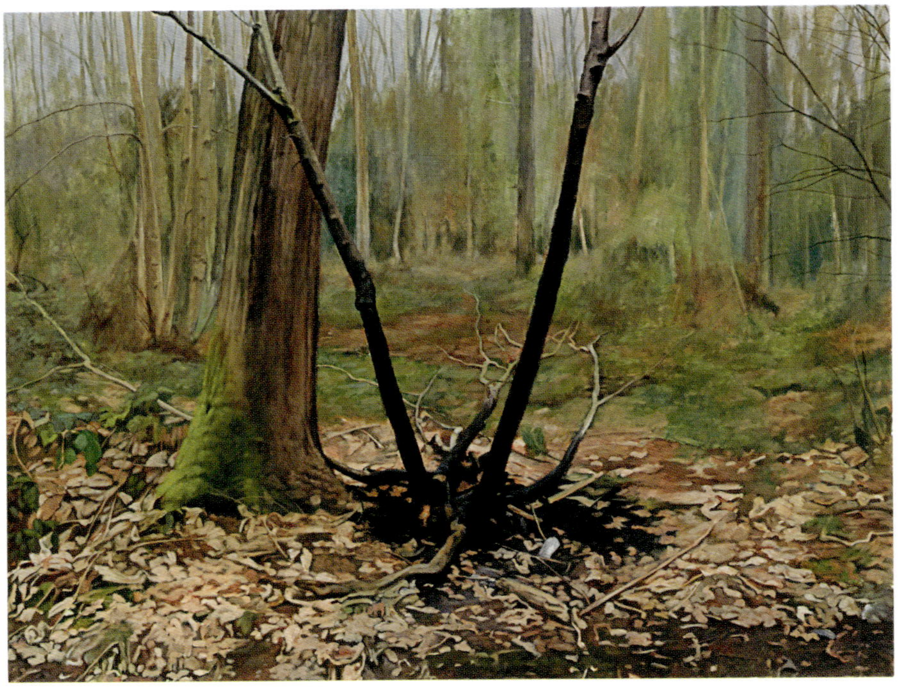

1

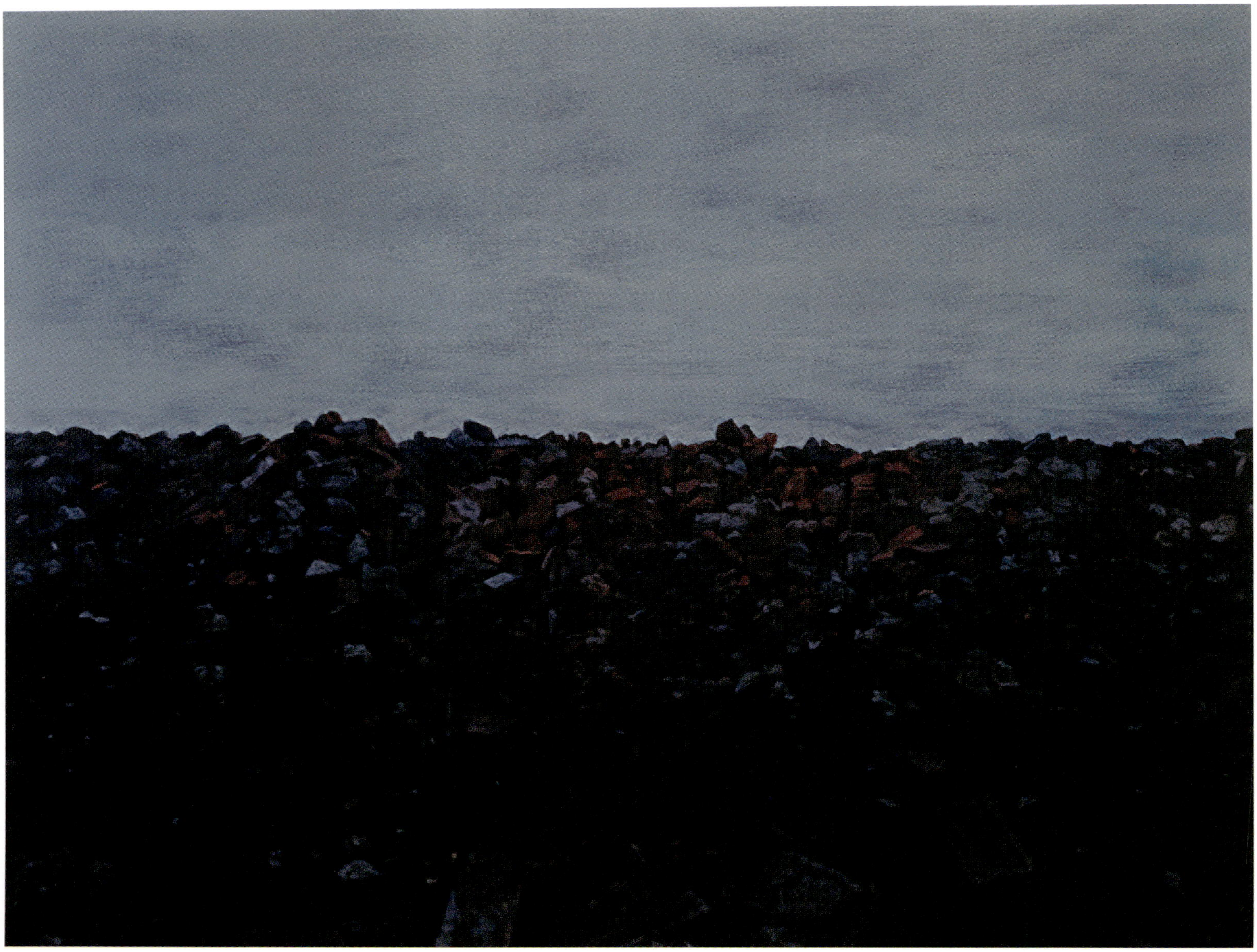

2

Shown by
Wilkinson D2

Biography
Born 1966
Lives in Devon

Shaw's intricately detailed paintings saw him nominated for the Turner Prize 2011. His consistent focus, on painting scenes from his home town, has resulted in numerous solo shows in Europe and the United States. Including most recently, the exhibitions "I woz ere" (2011) at The Herbert, Coventry; and "The Sly and Unseen Day" (2011), BALTIC, Gateshead which then travelled to the South London Gallery. In 2013 he will have exhibitions at Douglas Hyde Gallery, Dublin, and Wilkinson Gallery, London.

1
The Devil Made Me Do It
2011
Humbrol enamel on board
22 × 29¼"
(56 × 74 cm)
Private collection

2
The Same Old Crap
2011
Humbrol enamel on board
21¼ × 29¼"
(54 × 74 cm)
Private collection

George Shaw

Rendered in the enamel model aircraft pigments beloved of bedroom hobbyists, George Shaw's paintings revisit, time and again, the postwar Coventry social housing estate where the artist grew up. This is a place of damp pavements and greying net curtains, loomed over by the dull-eyed pub depicted in *The Age of Bullshit* (2010). But while a painting such as *The Assumption* (2011), with its unremitting phalanx of iron railings, may seem gloomy, even stifling, suggesting both a longing to escape and the impossibility of returning home, Shaw's work also has a (very English) visionary aspect, as though the raptures of William Blake or Samuel Palmer were being channeled through the transcendental melancholy of the poet Philip Larkin. Above all, these are works about time—creeping minutes, and speeding decades. TM

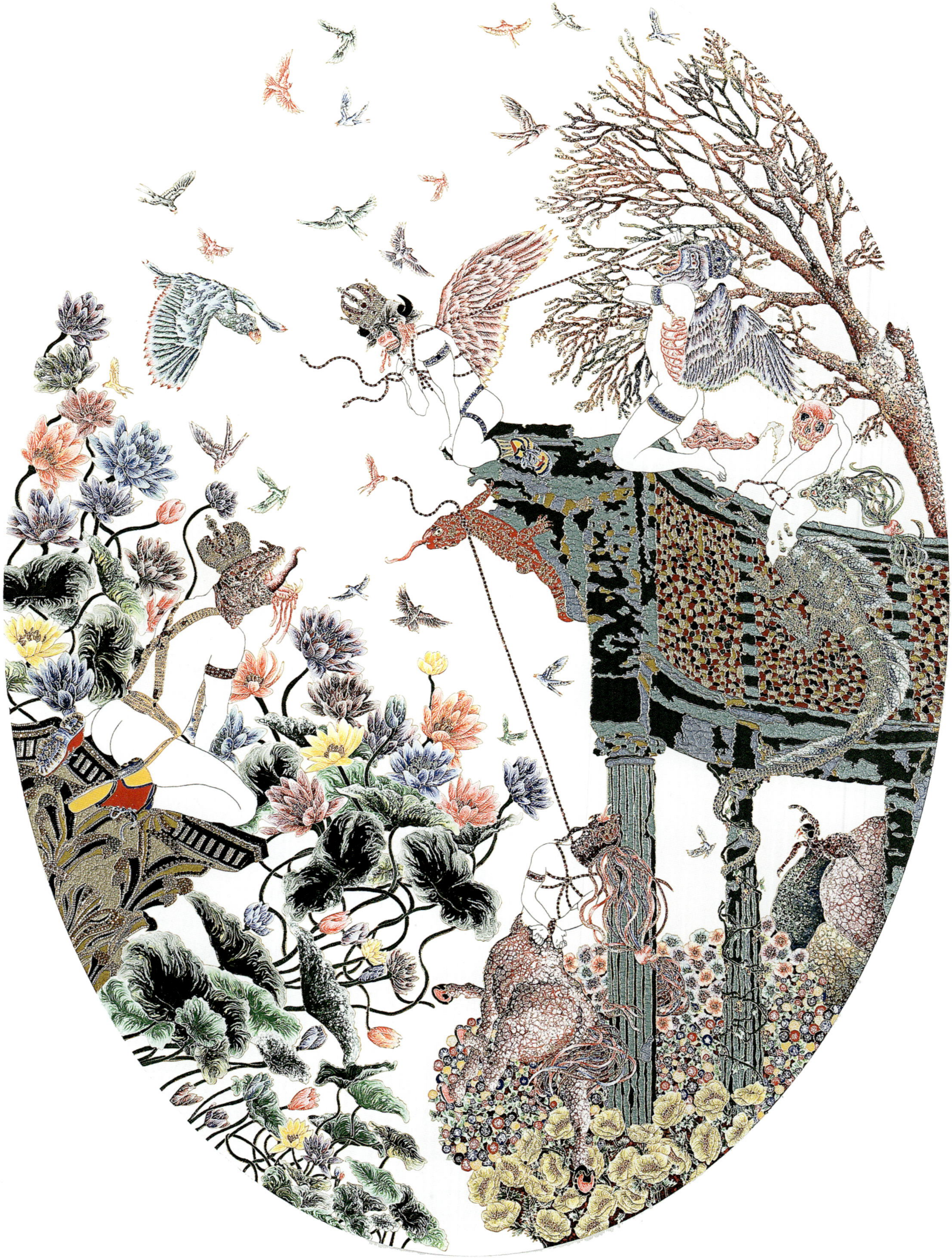

Raqib Shaw

Shown by
Galerie Thaddaeus Ropac C12
White Cube B38

Biography
Born 1974
Lives in London

Calcutta-born Shaw's intricate works were the subject of a recent solo show at White Cube, London (2011). His exhibition "The Absence of God" (2011) was staged at Karlsplatz Project Space, Kunsthalle Wien, Vienna. In 2008 the Metropolitan Museum of Art, New York, staged the self-titled solo show "Raqib Shaw." He was also included the recent group show "Painting Between the Lines" (2011) at the CCA Wattis Institute for Contemporary Arts, San Francisco, and the 17th Biennale of Sydney (2010).

The Stupor of the Lotus Easters
2008
Acrylic, enamel, glitter, and rhinestones on paper
50 × 36½"
(127 × 92.5 cm)
Courtesy of Galerie Thaddaeus Ropac

Persian miniatures, medieval bestiaries, oriental and occidental mythologies, erotica and *fin-de-siècle* opulence all entangle amorously in Raqib Shaw's tumbling imagery. Paintings on board, often bejeweled with rhinestones, glitter, and enamels, unabashedly adopt traditional decorative techniques and assume the guise of artisanal paneling. But then symbols of man's conflicting, grandiose, and mortal sense of self—skulls, gods, and beasties—intermingle with contemporary signifiers of kitsch and camp, so that what might be easily assimilated is necessarily re-categorized. *The Garden of Earthly Delights III* (2003), for example, has obvious Western canonical references, and a methodical, virtuoso approach to representation; but Shaw disturbs its apparent conservatism with details of phallo-rich debauchery and psychodramas roiling with untoward desire. SOR

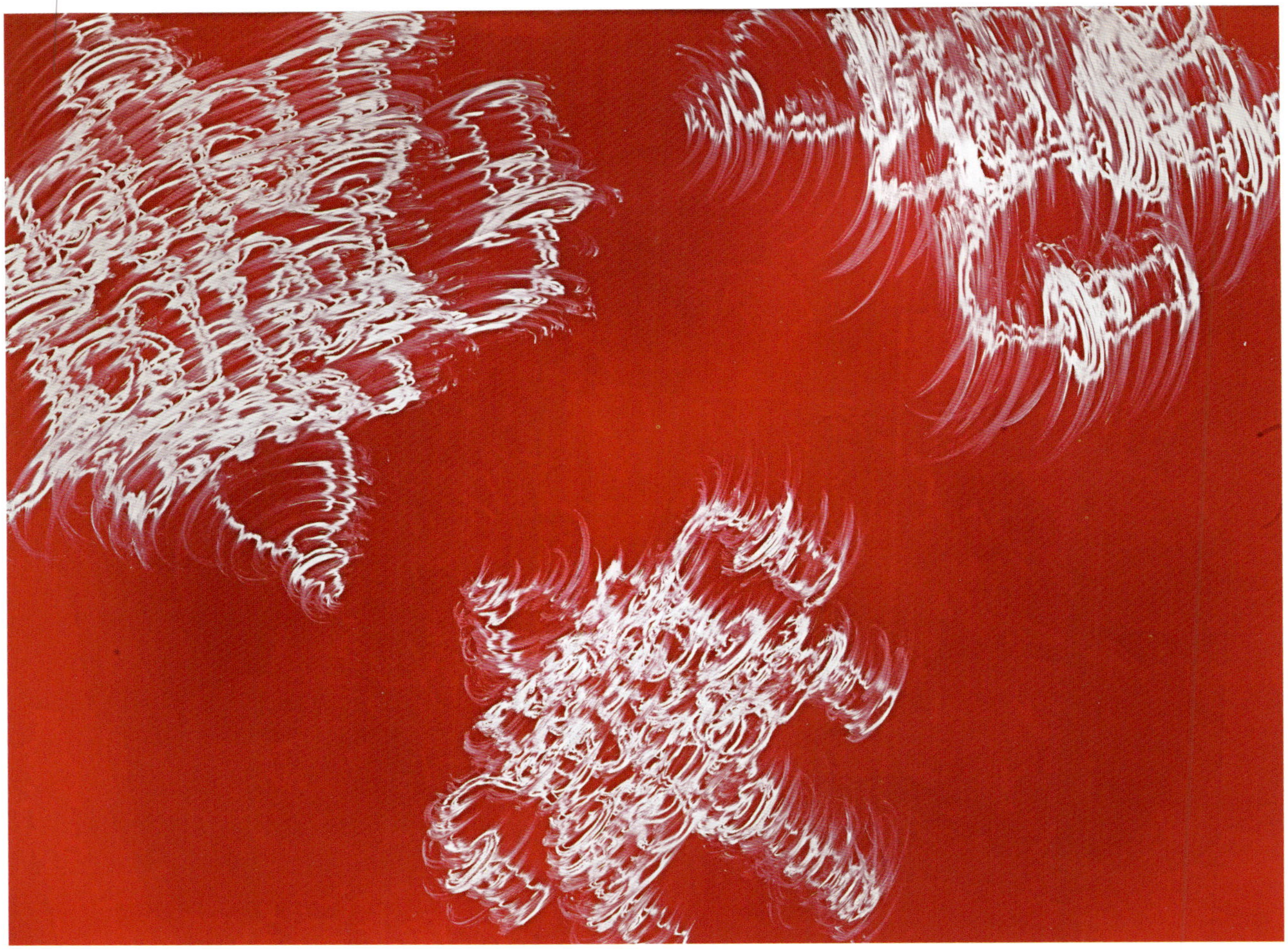

1

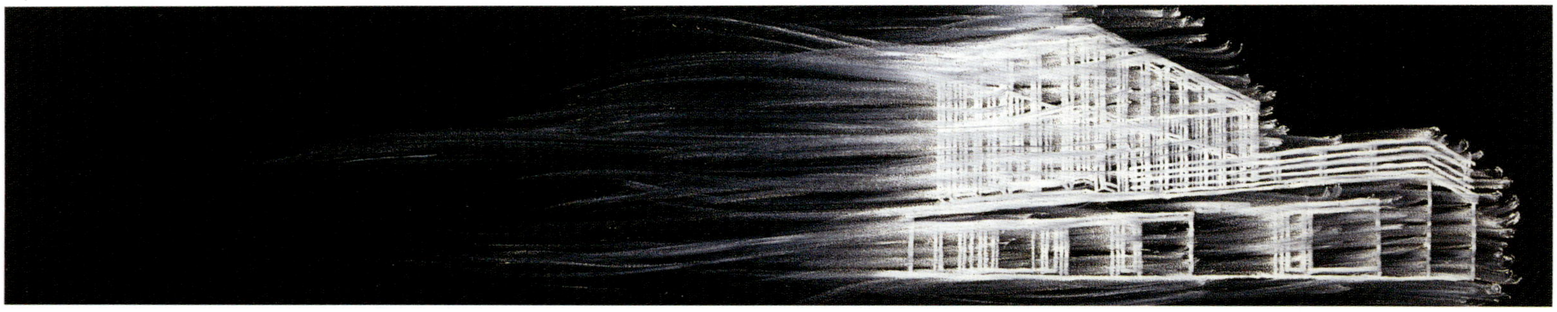

2

Shown by
Simon Lee Gallery A5
Metro Pictures C16

Biography
Born 1964
Lives in New York

American artist Simmons's socially engaged works are part of numerous public collections, including the Hirshhorn Museum and Sculpture Garden, Washington D.C., and the Museum of Modern Art, New York. His paintings, drawings and installations have been exhibited internationally since the early-1990s, most recently in the solo show "Shine" (2011) at Simon Lee Gallery, London. Other recent solo shows include "Black Marquee" (2010) at Anthony Meier Fine Arts, San Francisco and "Midnight Matinee" (2010) at Metro Pictures, New York.

1
Marnie's Nightmare
2006
Pigment and oil stick on wall
Dimensions variable
Courtesy of Metro Pictures

2
Glass Pavilion Drag
2006
Pigment, oil paint, and cold wax on canvas
18¼ × 92"
46.5 × 233.5 cm
Courtesy of Metro Pictures

Gary Simmons

Gary Simmons is perhaps best known for his "erasure" drawings—blurred and partially obliterated chalked images derived from film, architecture, and (African American) history, presented on colored panels that recall both the schoolroom and Modernist monochrome canvases. While his practice draws on the gestural qualities of Abstract Expressionism, it is also intimately engaged with memory. Often employing the iconography of popular cinematic fantasy to explore very real world concerns—*The Conquest of the Planet of the Apes* (1972), for example, has served as a lens on the 1965 Watts riots—this is work that summons the ghosts of events that the powerful might prefer to forget. TM

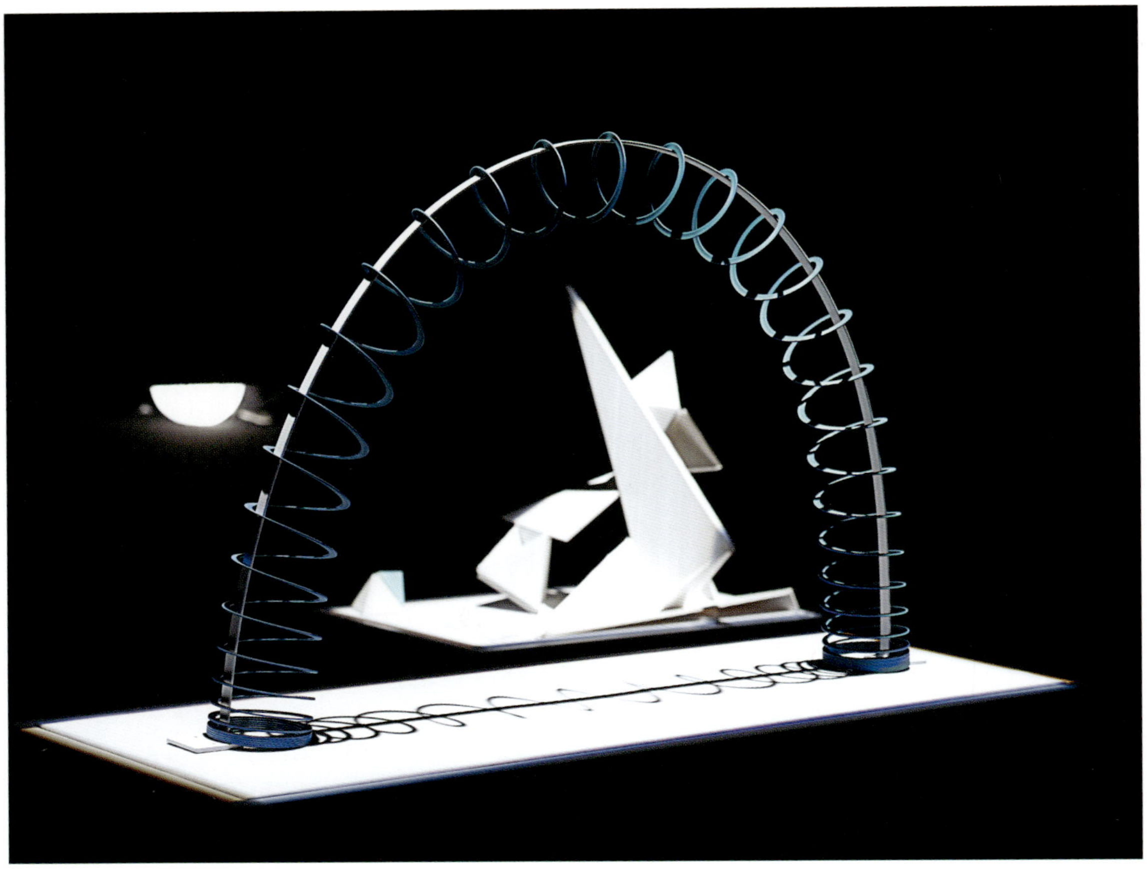

1

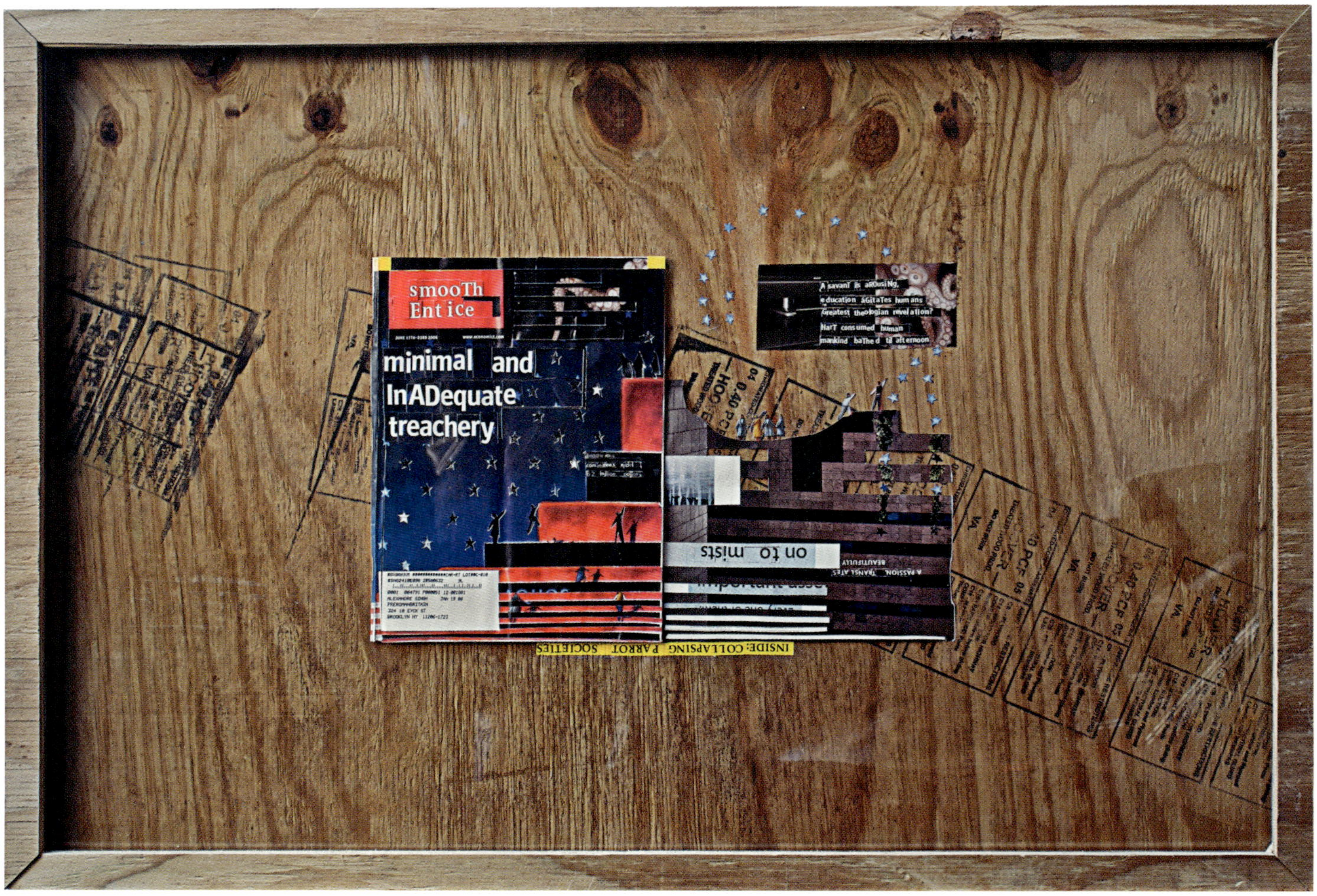
smooTh
Ent ice
minimal and
InADequate
treachery
A savanT is aROusiNg,
education aGitaTes humans
Greatest theologian revelation?
HarT consumed human
mankind baThed alternoon
on to mists
INSIDE: COLLAPSING PARROT SOCIETIES

2

Alexandre Singh

The performances, lectures, and installations of Alexandre Singh throw up constellations of disparate references and imagery that land in an elaborate medley of fact and fiction. Notable figures from the worlds of literature and science—Manzoni, Yves Klein, Goethe, and Newton—are summoned to cross-pollinate in nebulous systems of collaged imagery and outlandish narratives that belie the regimented, quasi-scientific presentation of their display. The latest version of his ongoing "Assembly Instructions" series, *The Pledge* (2011), presents pseudo portraits of real people—a museum director, a playwright, and a neurobiologist—based on interviews with them. The diagrammatic display of a medley of black and white images acts as a system of classification for a series of plausible and not so plausible fictions. PT

Shown by
art: concept A2
Sprüth Magers Berlin London B37

Biography
Born 1980
Lives in New York

France-born artist and writer Singh's work has been included in numerous international exhibitions in recent years. In 2011 the exhibition "Assembly Instructions: The Pledge" was held at art: concept, Paris and Monitor Gallery, Rome,—the show will travel to The Drawing Center, New York, in summer 2012. The solo exhibition "La critique de l'école des objets" (The School for Objects Criticized), Palais de Tokyo, Paris, also took place in 2011.

1
La Critique de l'Ecole des Objets (Critique of the School for Objects) (detail)
2010
Mixed media
Dimensions variable
Courtesy of art: concept

2
The Economist (Smooth Entice)
2007
Collage of cuts from *The Economist* on pressure-treated lumber
24 × 36 × 1⅝"
(61 × 91.5 × 4 cm)
Courtesy of art: concept

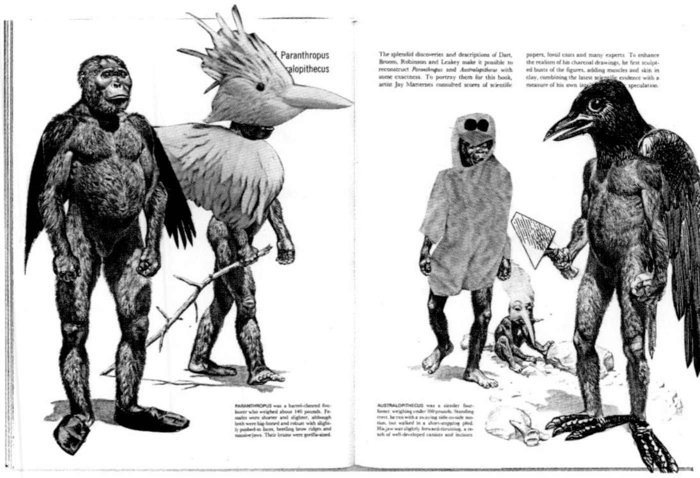

3

3
Assembly Instruction (The Pledge: Alfredo Arias) detail
2011
Framed inkjet ultrachrome archival prints
15¾ × 19⅝"
(40 × 50 cm)
Courtesy of art: concept

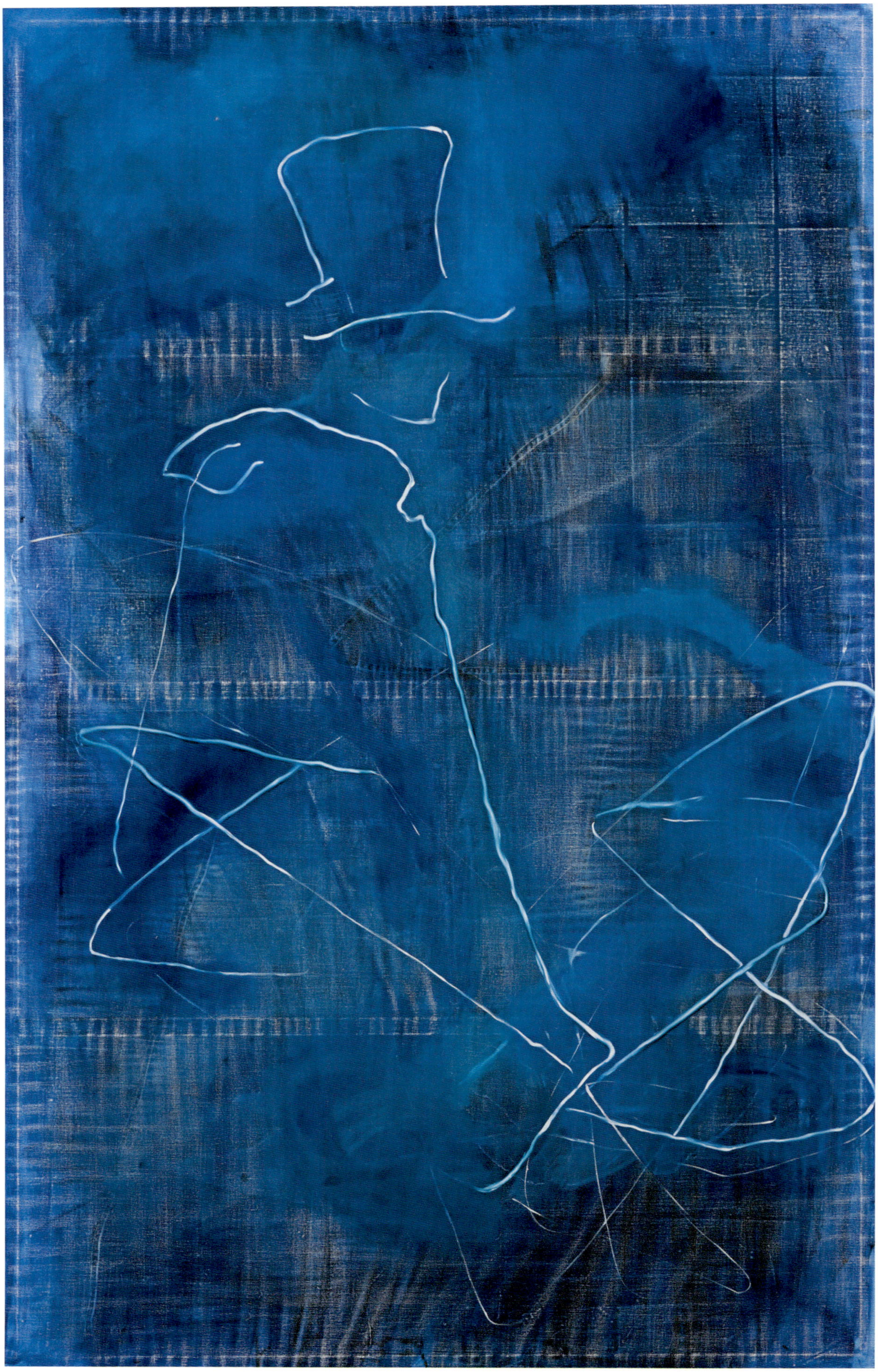

Shown by
Tomio Koyama Gallery B8

Biography
Lives in Miami

Argentinan artist and curator Singh has exhibited extensively in the United States since the early-2000s. His paintings, drawings, and sculptural work all featured in the recent solo exhibition "Table for one." (2011) Tomio Koyama Gallery, Tokyo. In 2010 he had the solo shows "Pathological Liar/Stalker" Fredric Snitzer Gallery, Miami and "Bulletproof" Mendes Wood Gallery, São Paulo. Recent group shows include "Summer Time Blues" (2011) Fredric Snitzer Gallery, Miami and "Selections from the De La Cruz Collection for Art Basel Miami Beach 2010" (2010) De La Cruz Collection, Miami.

The New Yorker
2011
Oil on linen
120⅛ × 76¾ × 1¾"
(305 × 195 × 4.5 cm)
Courtesy of Tomio Koyama Gallery

Diego Singh

Blue, denim-like canvases, some bleached of color, form a recent series of paintings by Diego Singh. His abstract oil on linen works suggest the simultaneous application and removal of paint, and the inherent uncertain nature of abstract painting. Works such as *The New Yorker* (2011) suggest figurative forms—immediately identifiable, yet rendered abstracted in a painterly battle on the linen's surface. Other works, including *False Bottom* (2011), feature meditative gestures, modest applications of paint contained within the painting's edges, while *A New Logo for The New Yorker* (2011), propose Singh's alternative take on identity and authenticity, suggesting new and undefined avenues of experimentation. SC

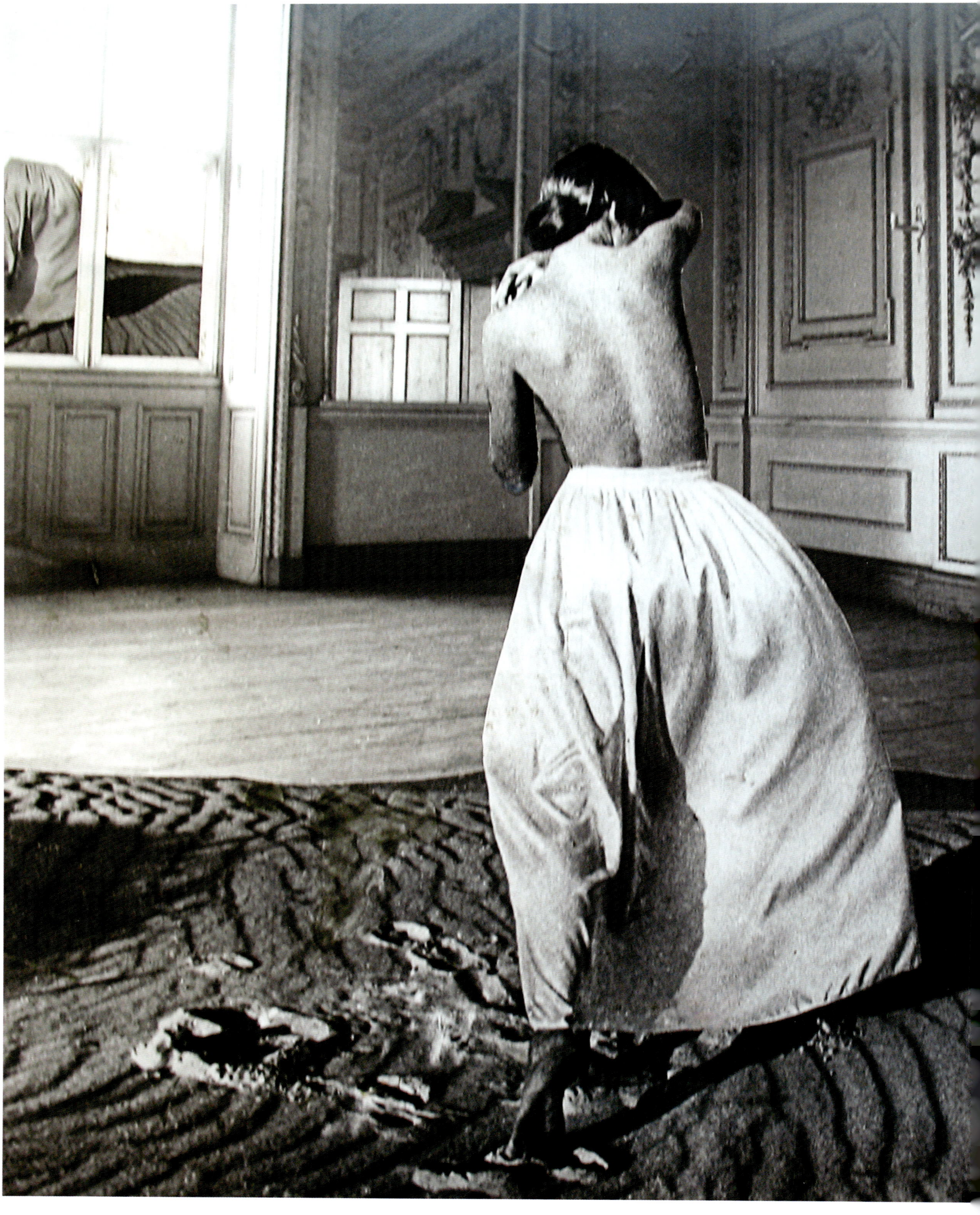

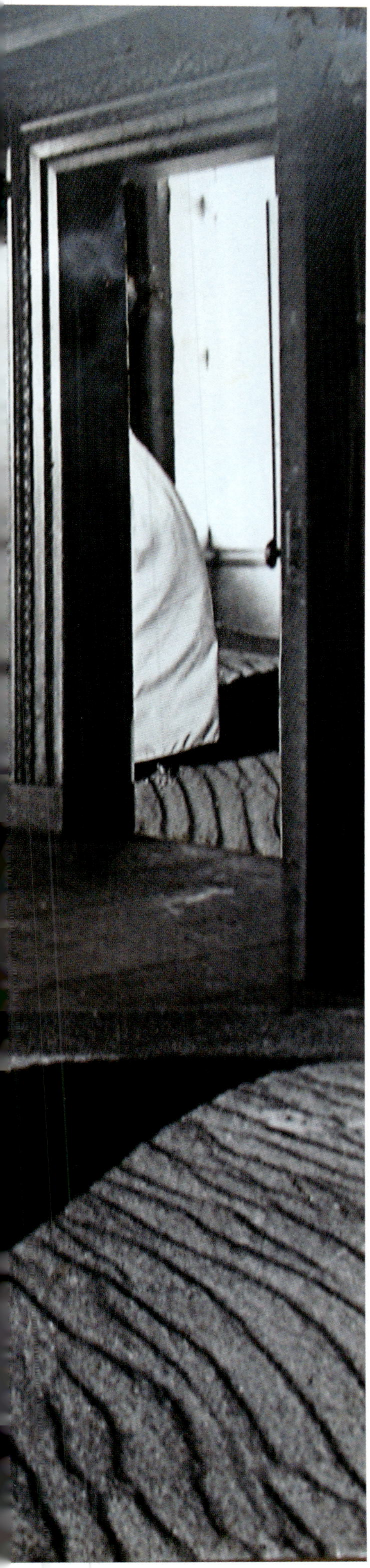

Penny Slinger

Shown by
Broadway 1602 C9

Biography
Born 1947
Lives in Boulder Creek

American artist Slinger has questioned social-norms with her sculptures and collages for over four decades. On graduating from Chelsea College of Art, London, in 1969, she participated in the group show "Young and Fantastic" (1969) at the Institute of Contemporary Arts, London. She also exhibited in "Surrealism & Company In This Decade" (1978) at Camden Arts Centre, London and "Metamorphosis" (1978) at the University of Cambridge.

Who Turns Her Back
1977
Collage mounted on board
15 × 17"
(40.5 × 45.5 cm)
Courtesy of Broadway 1602

In the late 1960s, Penny Slinger began exploring themes of female sexuality, alchemy, and rebirth in hauntingly surreal photo-collages, many featuring photographs of her own naked body. Potent imagery fuels works such as *I Hear What You Say* (1973), an ear wearing a demure pearl earring that fills up a woman's mouth like an oyster in a shell, stifling her speech. Slinger has also created sculptural assemblages that were feminist gothic visions: a wedding cake topped with a sleeping bride's head—its base complete with a sculpted vagina (*The Sugar Bride (Have your cake and eat it)*, 1973). More recently, she has used paint, pastel, and printmaking, as well as photography, in hallucinatory Photoshopped works that draw on sources that include Tantra and Caribbean culture. KMJ

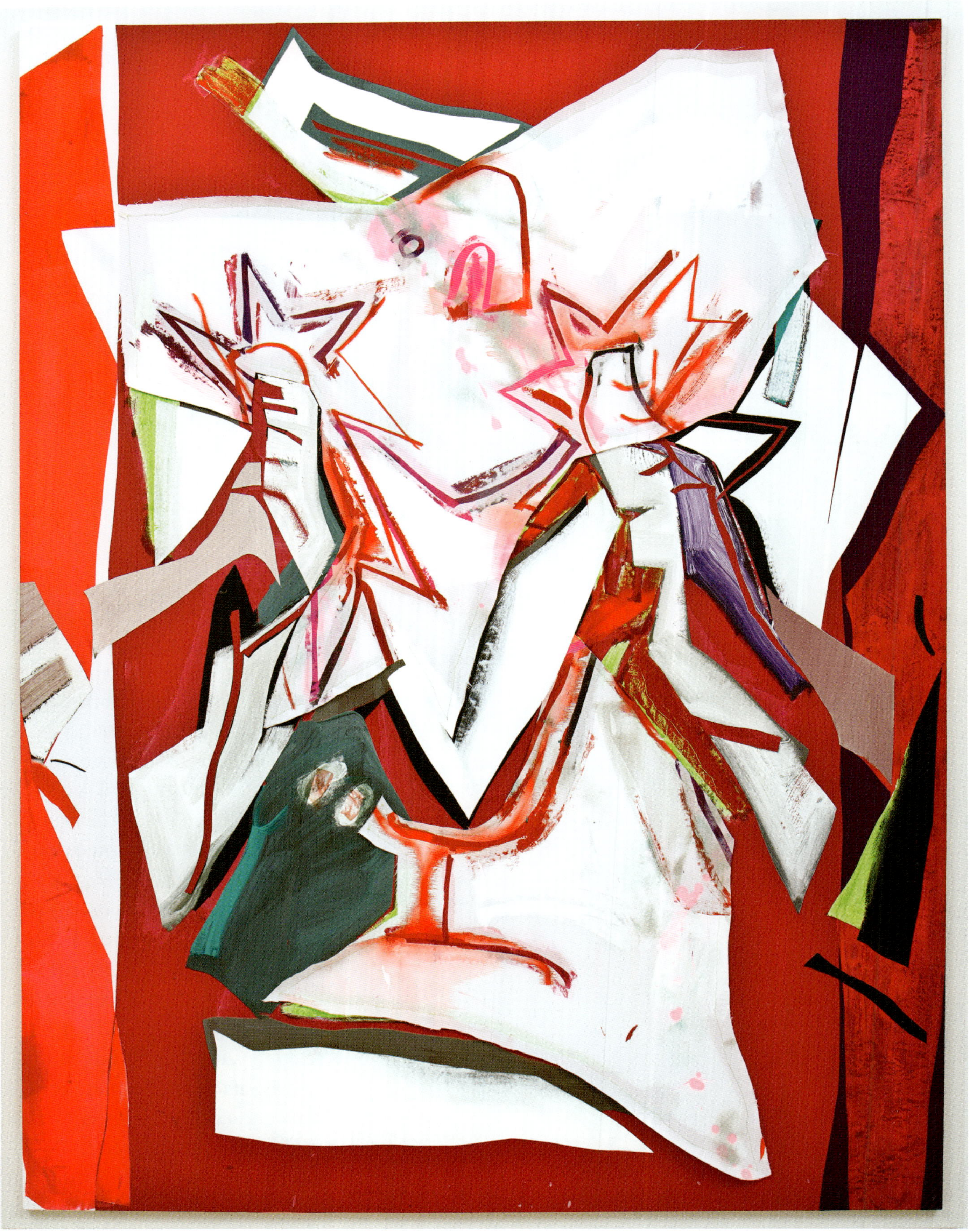

1

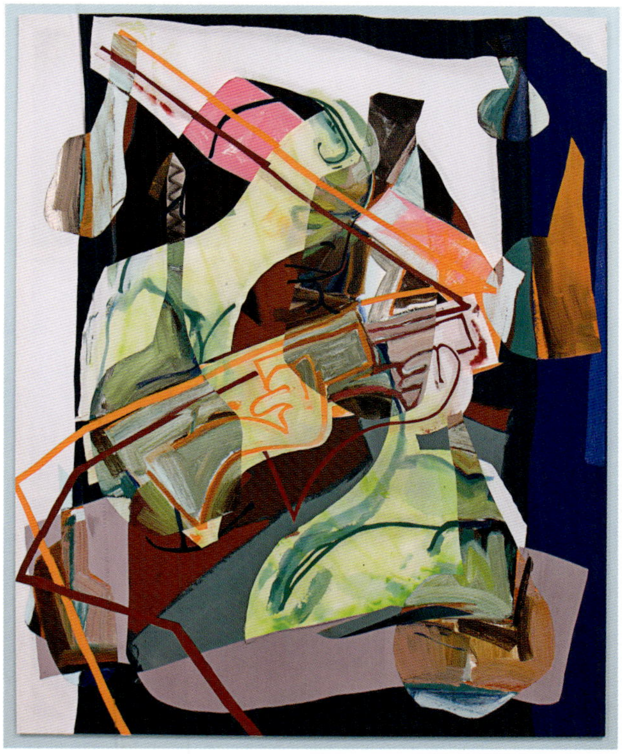

2

Shown by
Richard Telles A20

Biography
Born 1981
Lives in Los Angeles

Canada-born Sluggett has most recently shown his paintings in a solo show at Richard Telles Fine Art, Los Angeles (2012). In 2011 he graduated with an MFA from UCLA, Los Angeles, and held a solo exhibition at UCLA's New Wight Gallery, Los Angeles, the same year. Other solo shows include "Impressionablism" (2010), TrépanierBaer, Calgary.

1
Kick Smile
2012
Fabric dye, tempera, acrylic and oil on fabric, artist-made frame
97 × 75"
(246.5 × 190.5 cm)
Courtesy of Richard Telles

2
Sad Baby Swipe,
2012
Fabric dye, tempera, acrylic and oil on fabric, artist-made frame
96 × 79"
(243 × 201 cm)
Courtesy of Richard Telles

Ryan Sluggett

Ryan Sluggett's paintings flaunt both figuration and abstraction in equal measure; color and human-like contours fill his large canvases. An outline of a man peering through binoculars in *Downward Binoculars* (2012) is painted on a ground of loose, abstract forms in a visually intriguing riddle. Sluggett's paintings also boast a heritage—hopscotching through the recent past, he has picked up the defining features of movements from Cubism to Abstract Expressionism, mixing them together in heady compositions. The recent *Sad Baby Swipe* (2012) weaves outlines of cartoon-like hands with purple and blue shapes, while dashes of orange differentiate the works layers. His fresh approach invests new life in pure and understood forms. KK

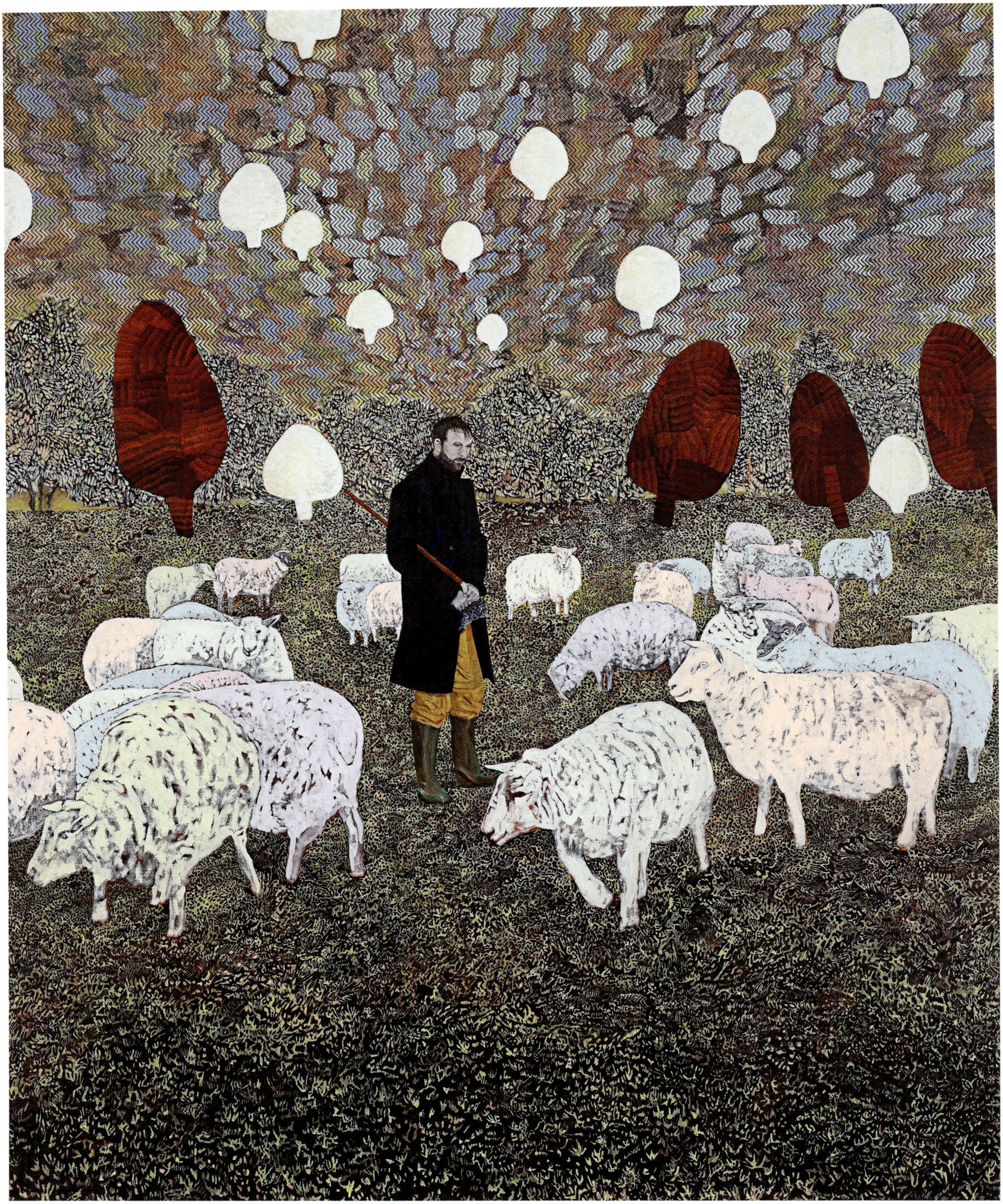

1

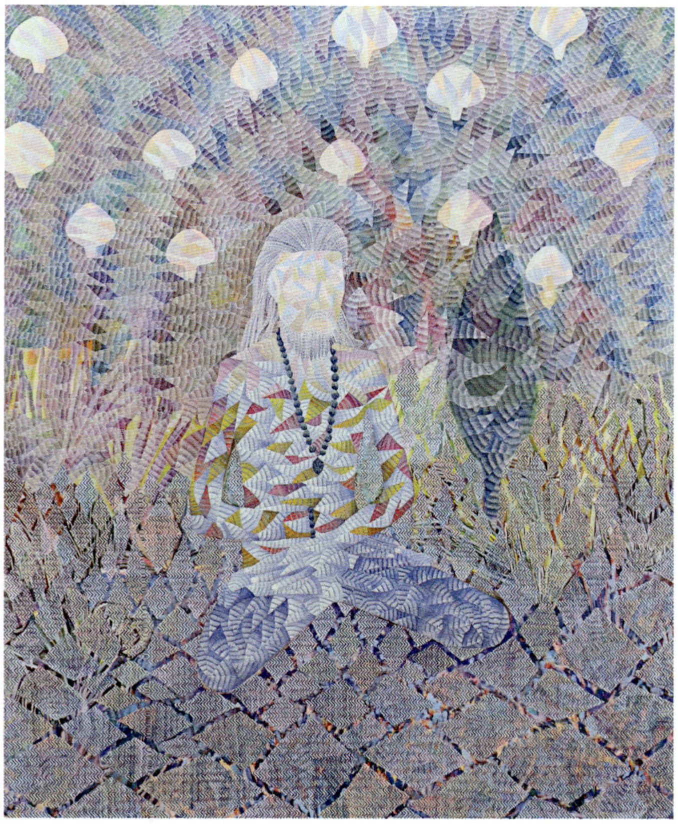

2

Shown by
Carl Freedman
Gallery C35

Biography
Born 1981
Lives in London

Britain-born Smith has exhibited in group shows at Galerie VidalCuglietta, Brussels, and Weltraum, Munich, in 2011. Closer to home, his work has been show in the "Newspeak" (2010) series of exhibitions at the Saatchi Gallery, London, which signalled a new wave of British art. He has also shown regularly at Carl Freedman Gallery, London, since 2007.

1
My Soul Hath Them In Remembrance and Is Humbled In Me
2011
Oil and gold leaf on herringbone linen
70⅞ × 59"
(180 × 150 cm)
Courtesy of Carl Freedman Gallery

2
Bowerbird
2011
Oil on herringbone linen
70⅞ × 59"
(180 × 150 cm)
Courtesy of Carl Freedman Gallery

David Brian Smith

The motif of shepherd and flock is held in particularly high esteem by David Brian Smith, who hails from a farming family in Shropshire, England. Yet the allusion to pastoral and spiritual traditions allows the image's symbolism to exceed the merely autobiographical. Working on herringbone linen "because of its association to rural heritage, to flat caps and tweed jackets," Smith's brushwork and palette exhibit a stylistic affinity with the early canvases of Peter Doig, recalling their hallucinatory qualities. Borrowing its title from the Old Testament's Book of Lamentations, *My Soul Hath Them in Remembrance and is Humbled in Me* (2011) seems to offer a suspended theological thought as the shepherd figure watches his pastel-colored sheep. MA

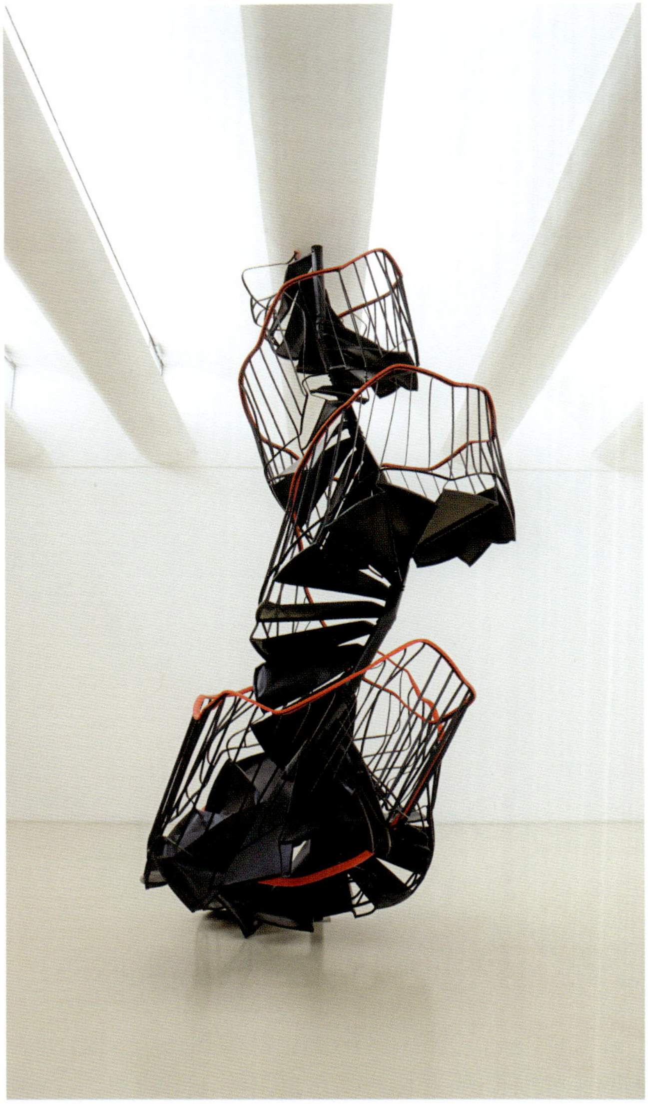

1

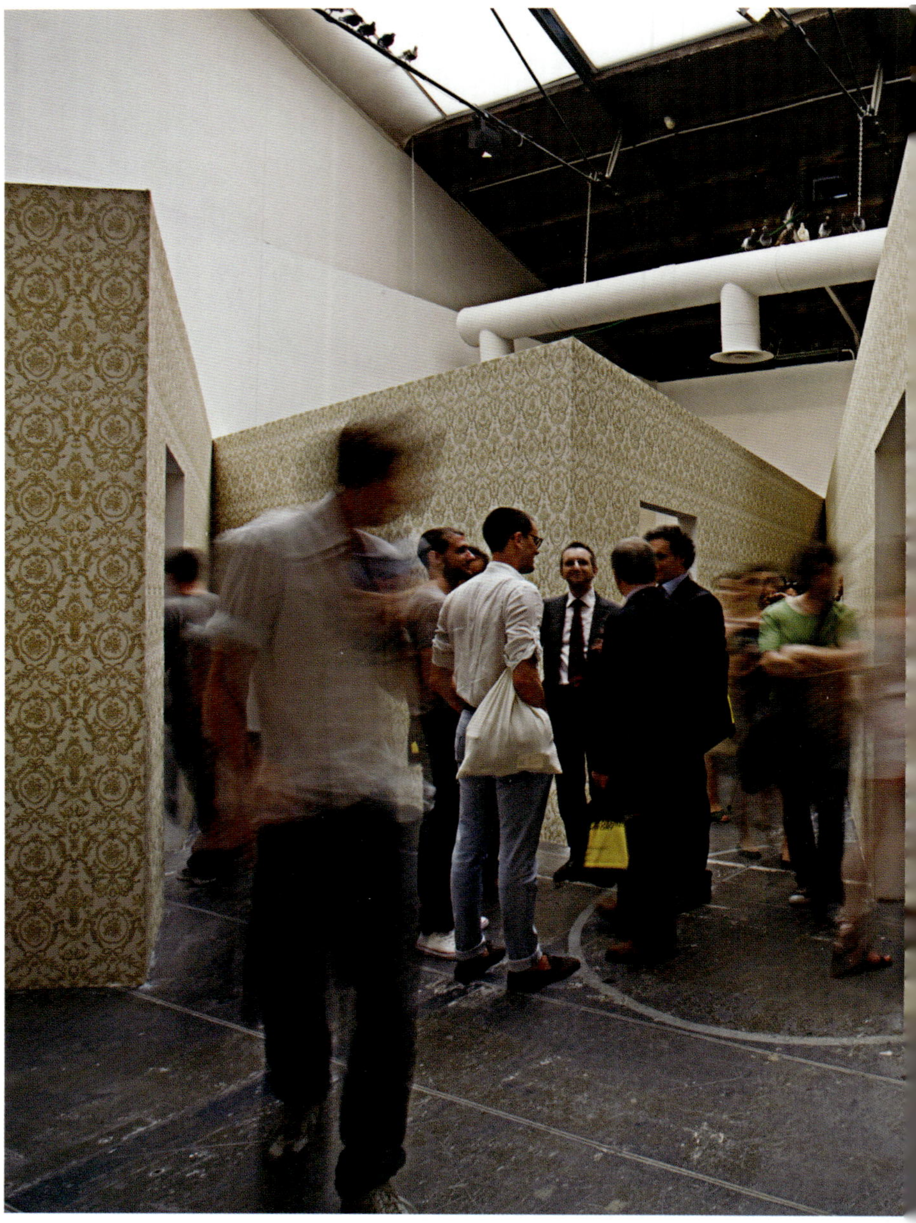

2

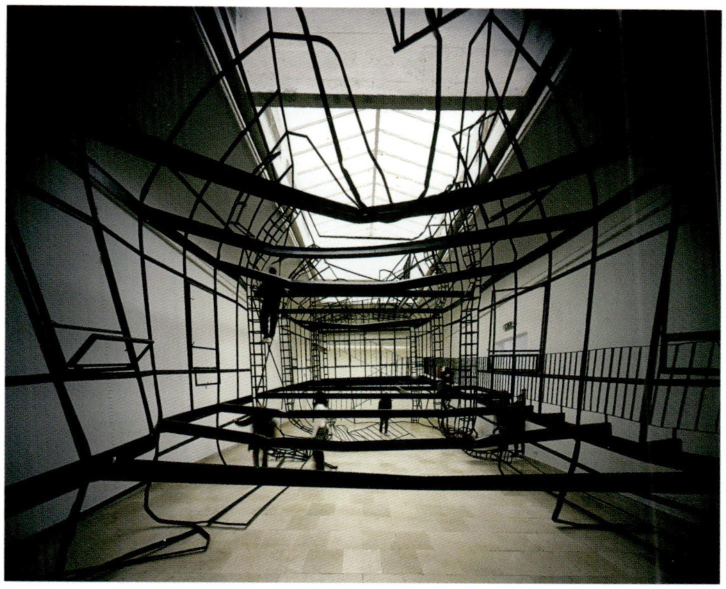

3

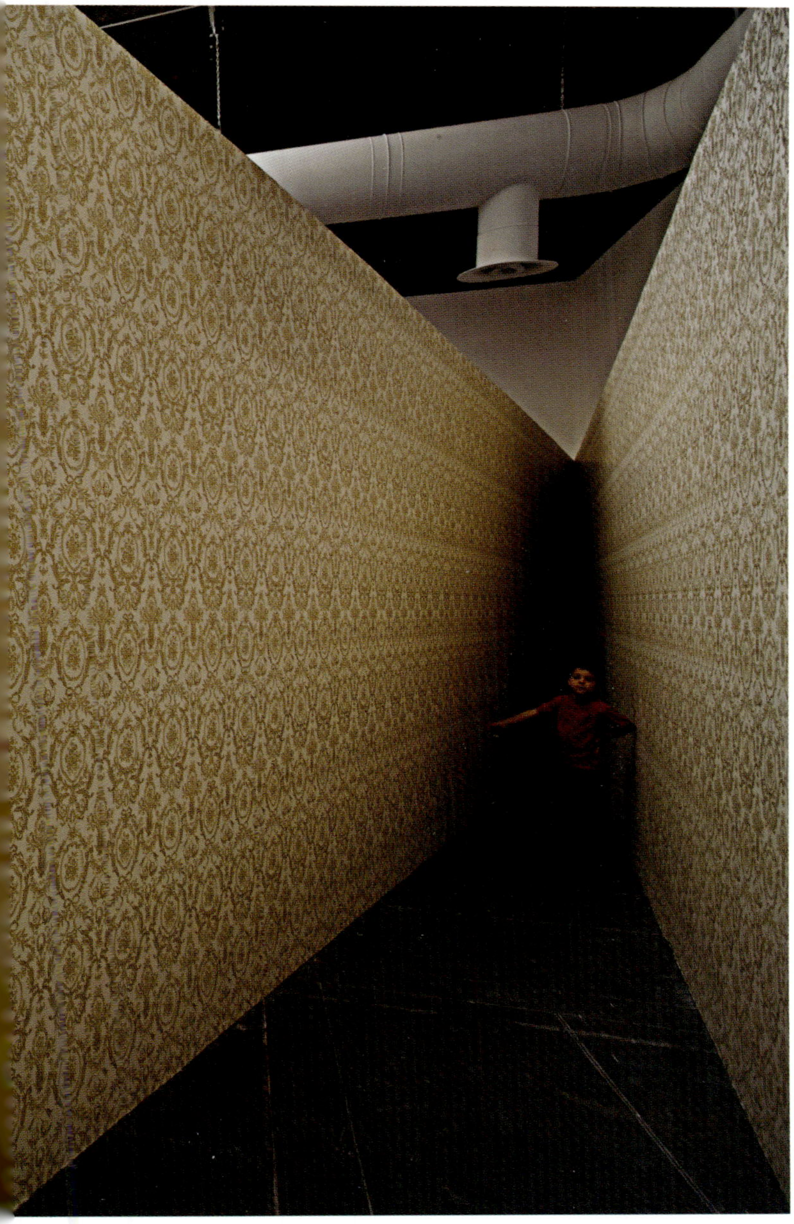

Shown by
Galerie Gisela Capitain B19
Foksal Gallery Foundation B40
Hauser & Wirth B6
kurimanzutto B16
The Modern Institute C29

Biography
Born 1972
Lives in Warsaw

Sosnowska's sculptural installations for "ILLUMInations" at the 54th Venice Biennale (2011), and the Polish Pavilion at the 52nd Venice Biennale (2007) highlighted the expansive nature of her practice. Other recent exhibitions include the solo shows "El Jardín" (2011), at kurimanzutto, Mexico City and Fire Escape commission for the Museo Tamayo Arte Contemporaneo, Mexico City (2011). Forthcoming solo exhibitions will be held at the Contemporary Art Gallery, Vancouver in 2012, and Aspen Art Museum in 2013.

1
Untitled
2010
Metal, PVC handrail
98⅜ × 222½"
(250 × 565 cm)
Courtesy of Foksal Gallery Foundation

2
Antechamber
Installation view, "ILLUMInations," 54th Venice Biennale
2011
Mixed media
Dimensions variable
Courtesy of Foksal Gallery Foundation

3
1:1
Installation view, Polish Pavilion
52nd Venice Biennale
2007
Painted steel
Dimensions variable
Courtesy of Foksal Gallery Foundation

Monika Sosnowska

Engendering perceptual confusion and insecurity, Monika Sosnowska's large-scale sculptures and installations have been termed "environments of controlled response." In the past, she has created plywood labyrinths, tilted rooms, and corridors that shrink or else slant impossibly upwards to the ceiling. Sosnowska's works are often monumental in scale, such as *1:1* (2007)—the crushed skeleton of a housing block—or the star-shaped, wallpapered "para-pavilion" commissioned as part of "ILLUMInations" at the 54th Venice Biennale in 2011. However, the title of an earlier work, *Little Alice* (2001), suggests that Lewis Carroll might be as much of an influence on these spatial distortions as the politicized spaces of Soviet architecture. As Kirsty Bell has noted, Sosnowska engages with the architecture of illusion and disillusion. ST

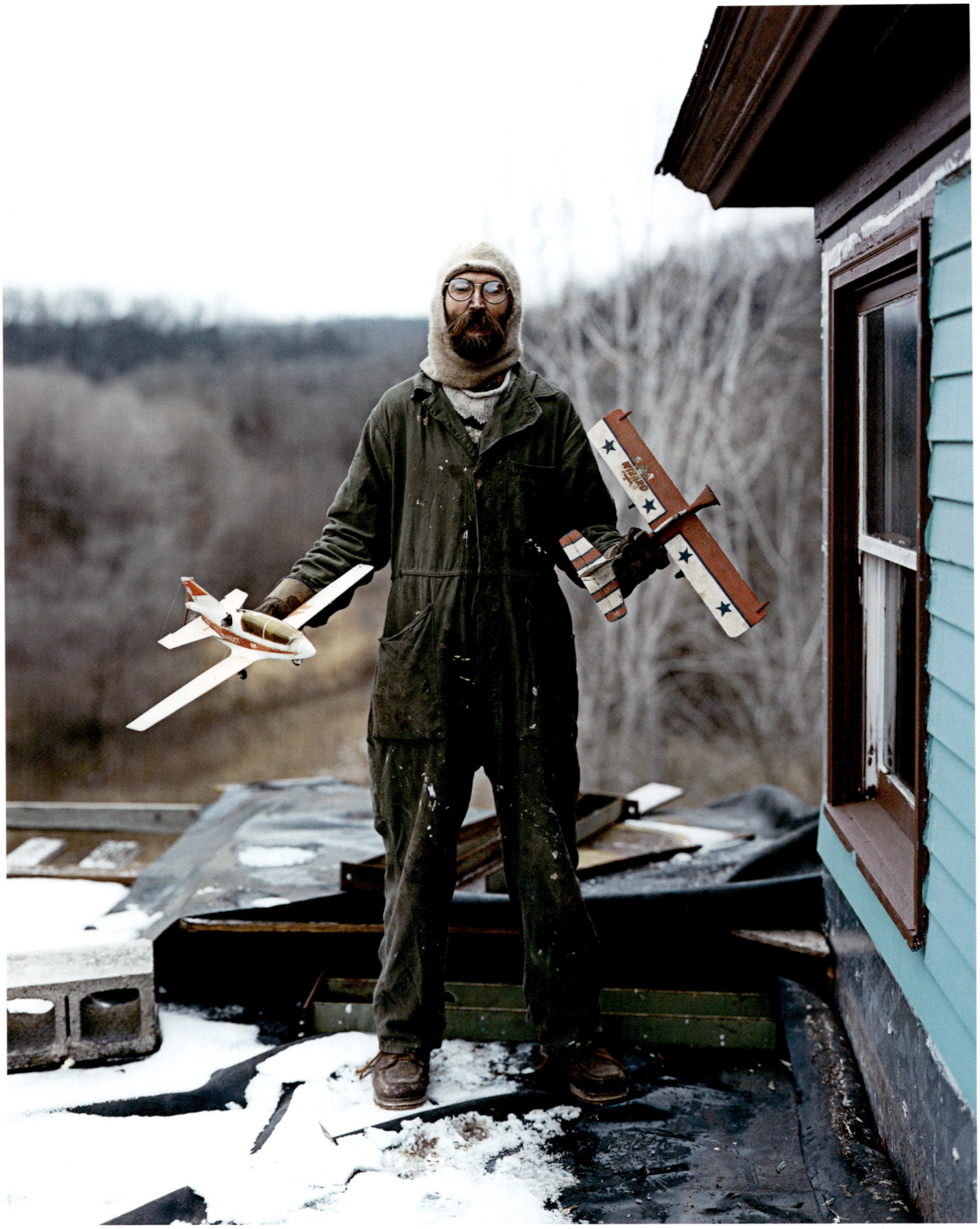

1

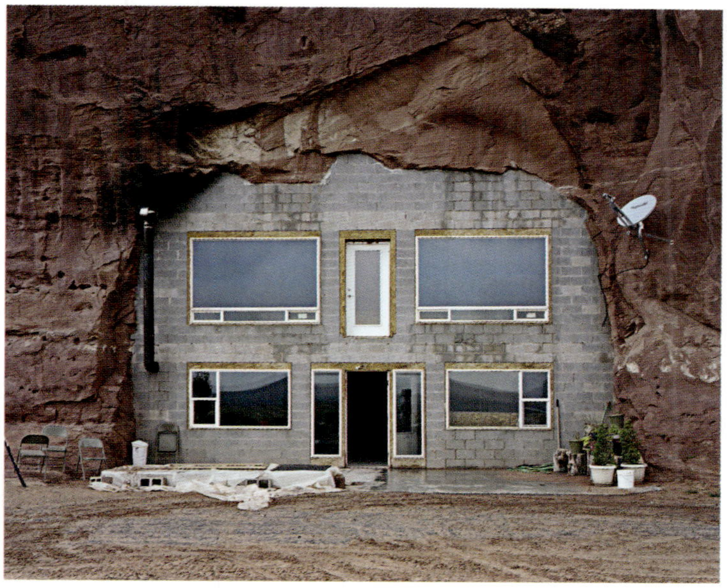

2

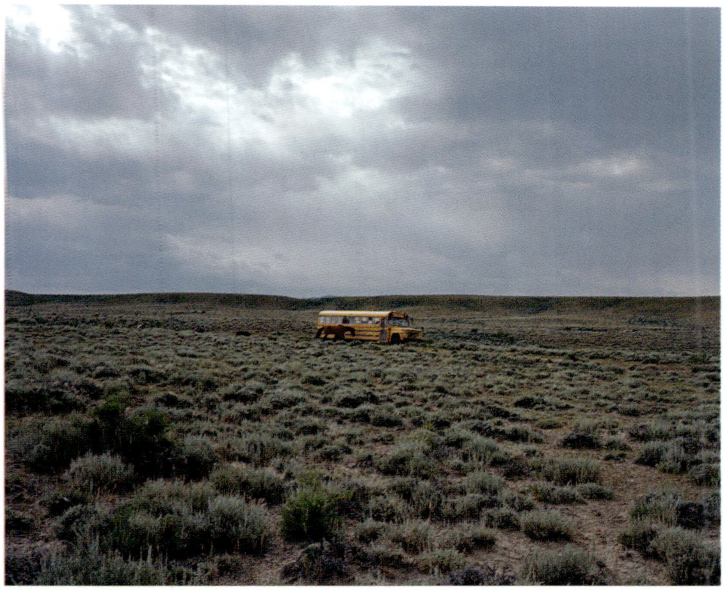

3

Shown by
Sean Kelly Gallery
B25

Biography
Born 1969
Lives in Minneapolis

American artist Soth's unique photographs were the subject of the recent exhibition "Broken Manual" (2012) at Sean Kelly Gallery, New York. In 2010 at the Walker Art Center, Minneapolis staged the first survey of his work with the exhibition "From Here to There: Alec Soth's America"—the show later toured to Everson Museum of Art, Syracuse (2011). European solo shows were held at Fotomuseum Winterthur (2008) and the Jeu de Paume, Paris (2008).

1
Charles Vasa, Minnesota
2002
C-type print
50 × 40"
(127 × 101.5 cm)
Courtesy of Sean Kelly Gallery

2
2008_08zl0238
2008
Archival pigment print
35⅛ × 43"
(89 × 109 cm)
Courtesy of Sean Kelly Gallery

3
2008_08zl0047
2008
Archival pigment print
35⅛ × 43"
(89 × 109 cm)
Courtesy of Sean Kelly Gallery

Alec Soth

Alec Soth knows that, as a photographer, he reveals complex truths about himself just by deciding where next to point his camera. For his series (and subsequent book) "Sleeping by the Mississippi" (1999–2002), Soth followed the course of the giant river that runs through his home town of Minneapolis. With a large-format camera, he composed unhurried portraits of the people and places he encountered along the way. His compassionate eye is far from objective, despite his interest in socio-documentary realism. His recent book *Broken Manual* (2006–10), which includes images of rural recluses such as *2008_08zl0238* (2008), is a tribute—maybe even a how-to guide—to life "off the grid." JG

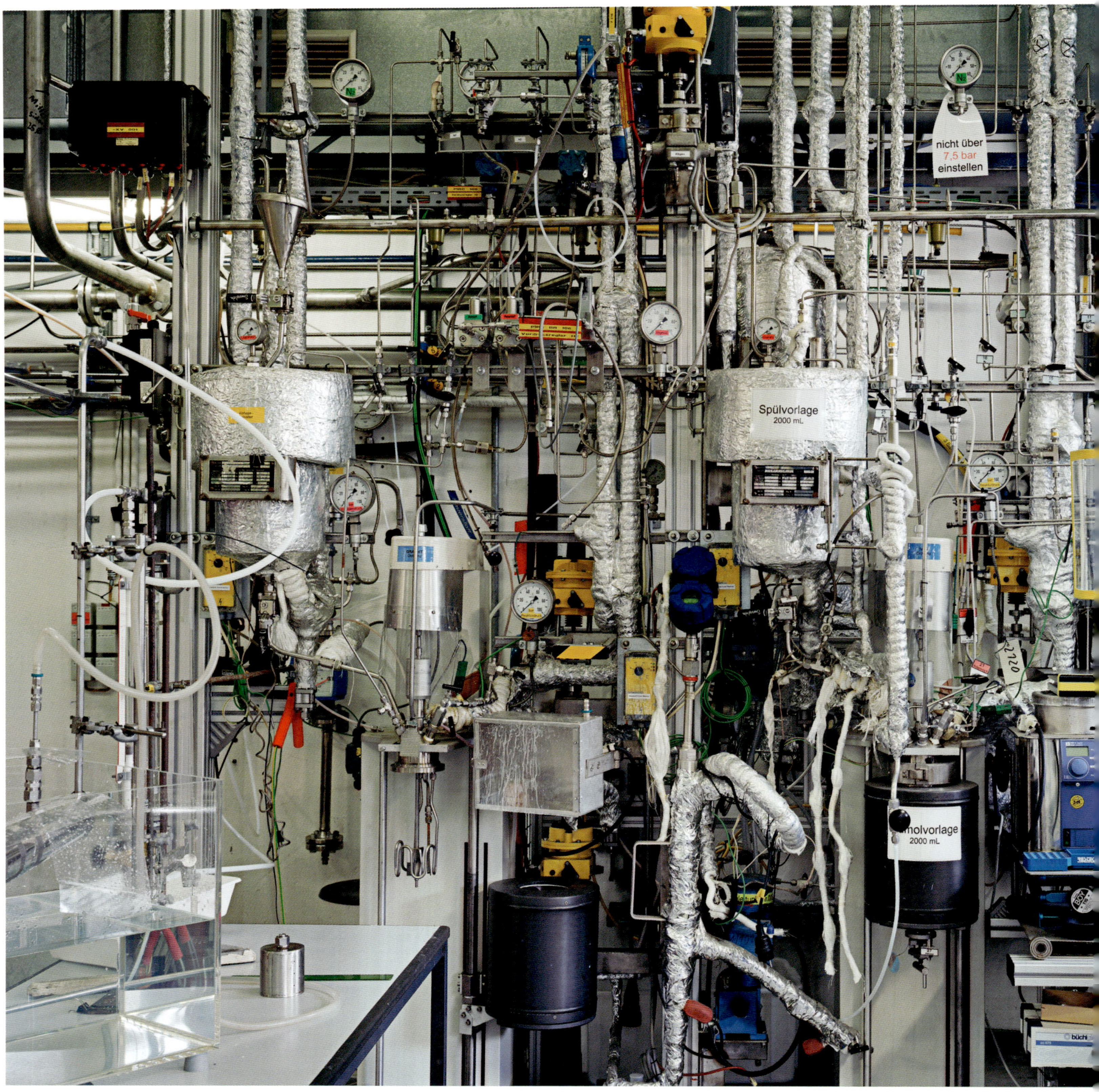
nicht über
7,5 bar
einstellen
Spülvorlage
2000 mL

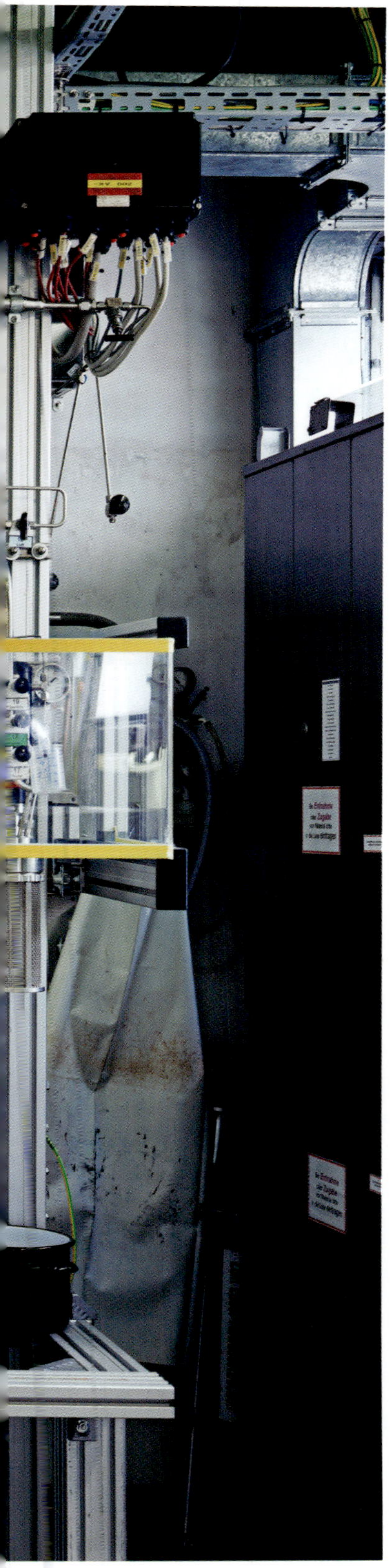

Shown by
Gallery Hyundai C20
Galerie Rüdiger Schöttle D3

Biography
Born 1954
Lives in Berlin

For three decades German photographer Struth has exhibited his detailed large-scale works in Europe and the United States. In 2010 the retrospective "Photography 1978–2010" opened at Kunsthaus Zürich, Zurich, before traveling to Kunstsammlung Nordrhein-Westfalen; Whitechapel Gallery, London; and Museu Serralves, Porto in 2011. Solo exhibitions were also held at Gallery Hyundai, Seoul; Galerie Max Hetzler, Berlin; and Marian Goodman Gallery, New York in 2010.

Lab Reactors Gladbeck
2009
C-type print
51⅜ × 67½"
(130.5 × 171.5 cm)
(framed)
Courtesy of Galerie Rüdiger Schöttle

Thomas Struth

Thomas Struth's monumental color photographs range in subject matter from tourists enraptured by art in cavernous museums to intimate family portraits, from the technological sublime of the Kennedy Space Center to the steaming vigor of tropical jungles. There is something disorienting about these works' clarity, and their superabundance of pictorial information—as the artist has said, "I wanted to make photographs in which everything was so complex and detailed that you could look at them forever and never see everything." But if Struth's photographs aim, in their jeweled intricacy, toward the inexhaustible, it is surely because this is the nature of the world beyond his lens. TM

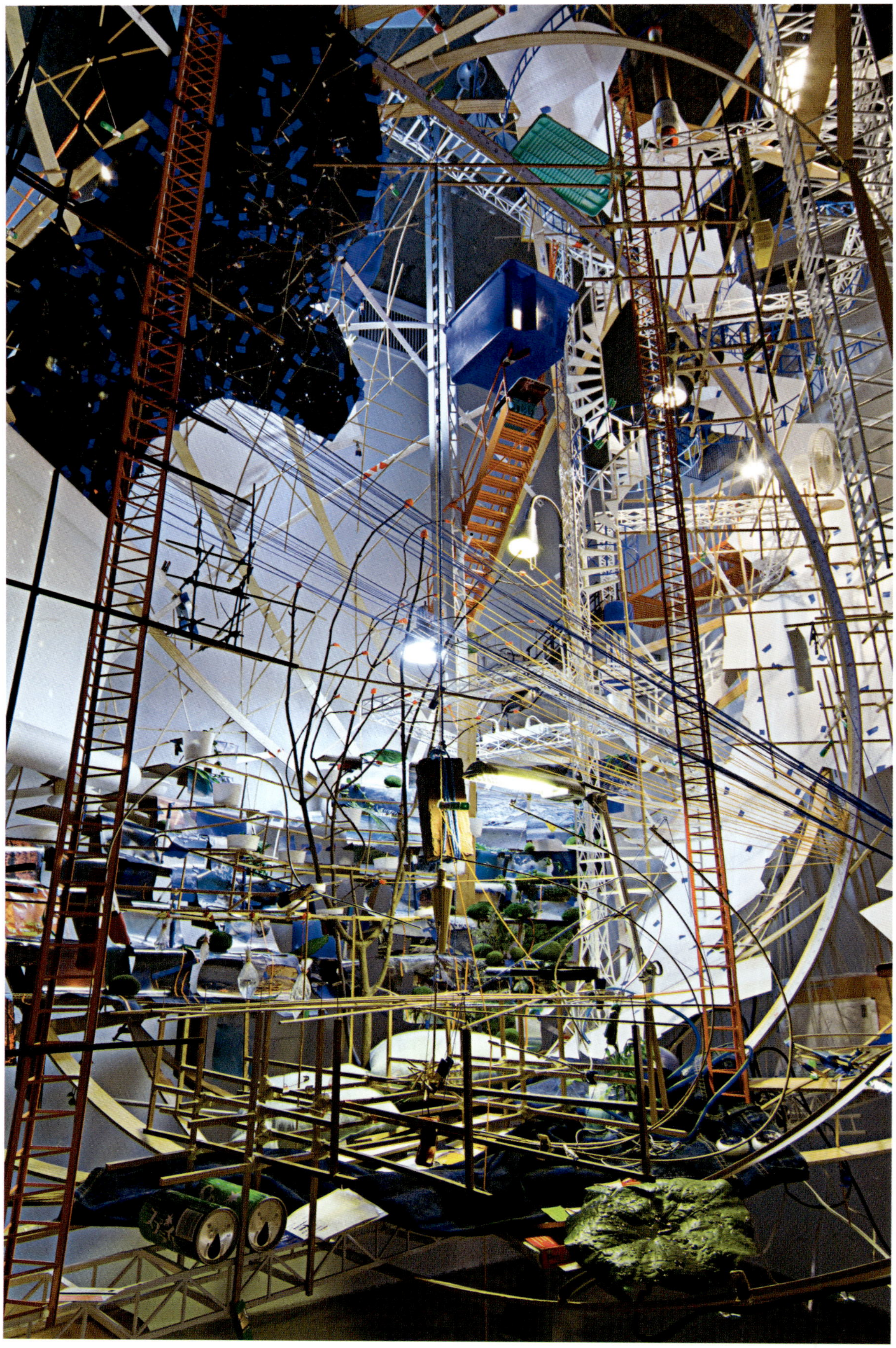

Shown by
Tanya Bonakdar Gallery C6
Victoria Miro C47

Biography
Born 1969
Lives in New York

Sze's commission for the High Line, New York, "Still Life with Landscape" (Model for a Habitat), is on view until June 2012. Recent solo exhibitions include the self-titled "Sarah Sze" (2012) at Mudam Luxembourg and "Infinite Line" (2011) at the Asia Society, New York. Her installations are on permanent display at Estuaire, Nantes. In 2012 she will have solo shows at Victoria Miro, London; High Museum of Art, Atlanta; and the Fabric Workshop and Museum, Philadelphia, in 2013.

360 (Portable Planetarium)
2010
Mixed media, wood, paper, string, jeans, and rocks
162 × 135 × 185"
(411.5 × 345.5 × 470 cm)
Courtesy of Victoria Miro

Sarah Sze

Fashioned from everyday objects and detritus—everything from bus tickets, cotton buds, and empty bottles to ladders and pot plants—Sarah Sze's sprawling sculptural constructions infiltrate and consume the spaces they inhabit. That her installations resemble miniature worlds is reflected in their titles, such as *Tilting Planet* (2009), which among other configurations includes an orrery-like arrangement of Styrofoam cups, or *360 (Portable Planetarium)* (2010), a spherical collision of objects, images, and light representing the Earth and its ecological crisis. Her recent *Still Life with Landscape (Model for a Habitat)* (2011) for the High Line public park in New York is both a sculptural object and a habitat for the park's butterflies, birds, and insects. AB

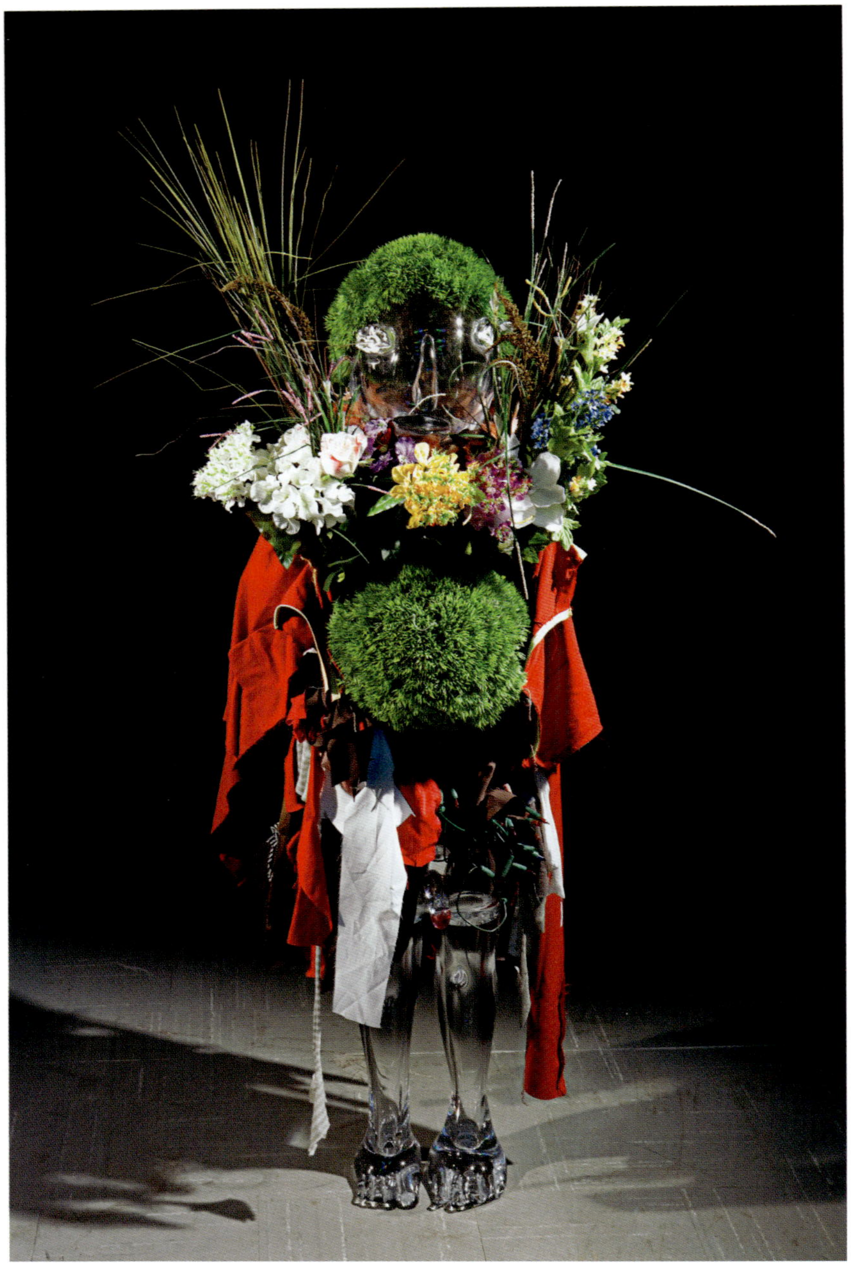

1

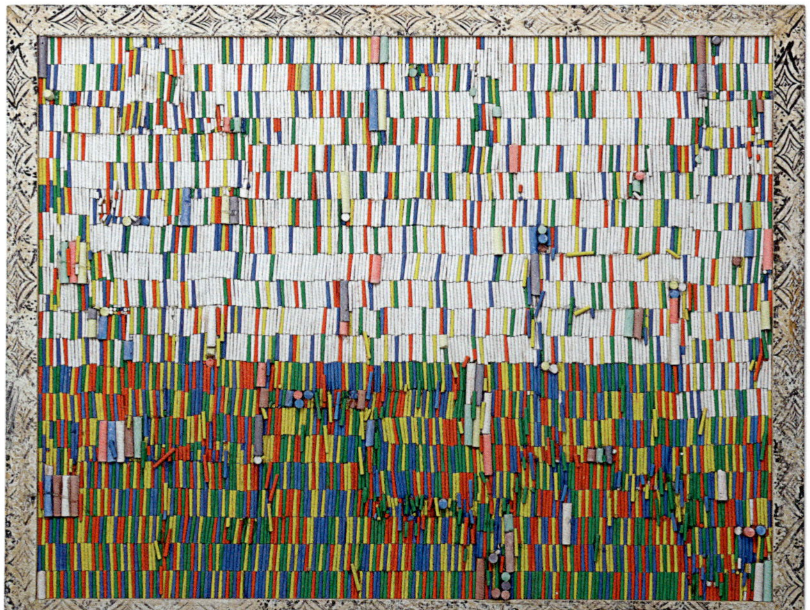

2

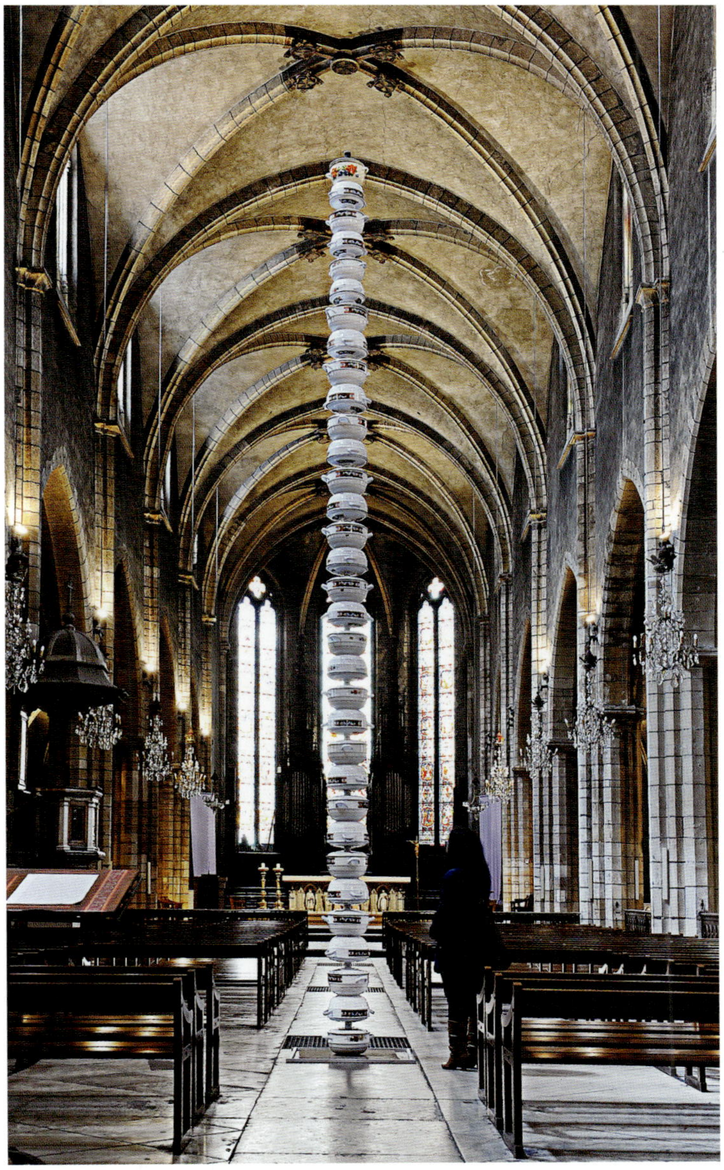

3

Shown by
Galleria Continua C40

Biography
Born 1967
Lives in Ghent

Cameroon-born Tayou has exhibited his sculptural works internationally since the mid-1990s. In late 2011 the solo exhibition "Black Forest" took place at the Museum of Modern Art, Luxembourg. The same year he also had solo shows at Maison Revure Noire, Paris; Musée d'art contemporain de Lyon; and Musée du Louvre, Paris. He has participated in numerous survey exhibitions, including "Fare mondi/Making Worlds" (2009) at the 53rd Venice Biennale, and "Altermodern: Tate Triennial 2009" at Tate Britain, London.

1
Fashion Street
2010
Mixed media
53⅛ × 19⅝ × 15¾"
(135 × 50 × 40 cm)
Courtesy of Galleria Continua

2
Chalk F
2008
Wood, chalks
65 × 83½ × 2¾"
(165 × 212 × 7 cm)
Courtesy of Galleria Continua

3
Colonne Pascale
2010
22 enamel pots
209⅜ × 23⅝ × 23⅝"
(532 × 60 × 60 cm)
Courtesy of Galleria Continua

Pascale Marthine Tayou

The photos, performances, drawings, and installations of Pascale Marthine Tayou have the presence of contemporary totems and the potency of modern talismans. In *Poupées Pascale* (Pascale's Dolls, 2010), a crystal idol stands on a tree stump, bound with plastic zip ties to be gagged with an array of pink, yellow, and green feathers. *Home Sweet Home* (2011) is an itinerant abode made from a jumble of birdhouses and shredded paper, propped up high on logs—an aerial island populated with microphones and African figurines. Tayou playfully moves between nomadic identities with an uncertain magic, fashioned out of plastic bags and pots. CFW

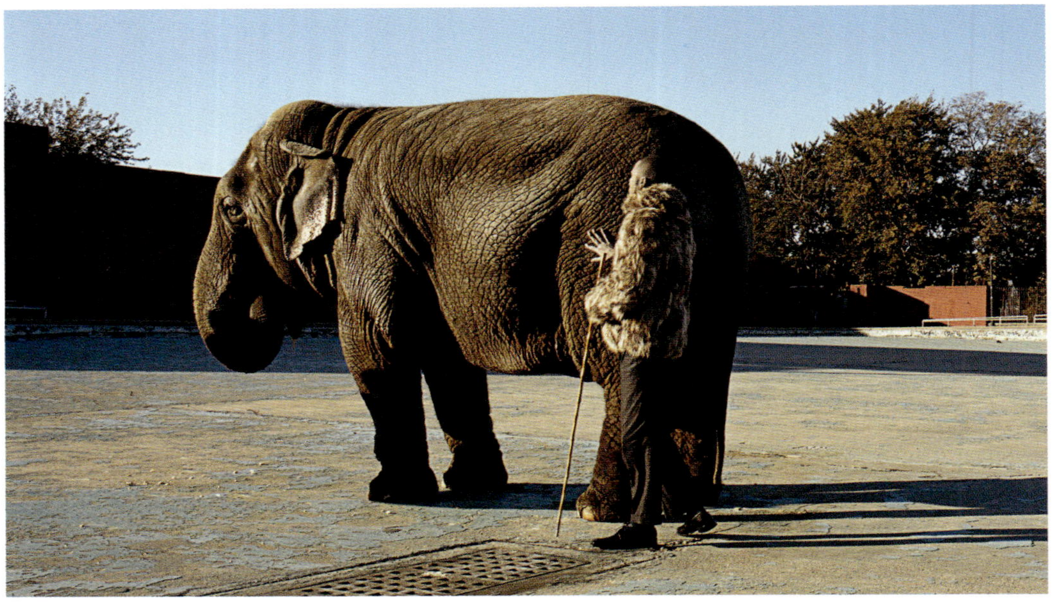

1

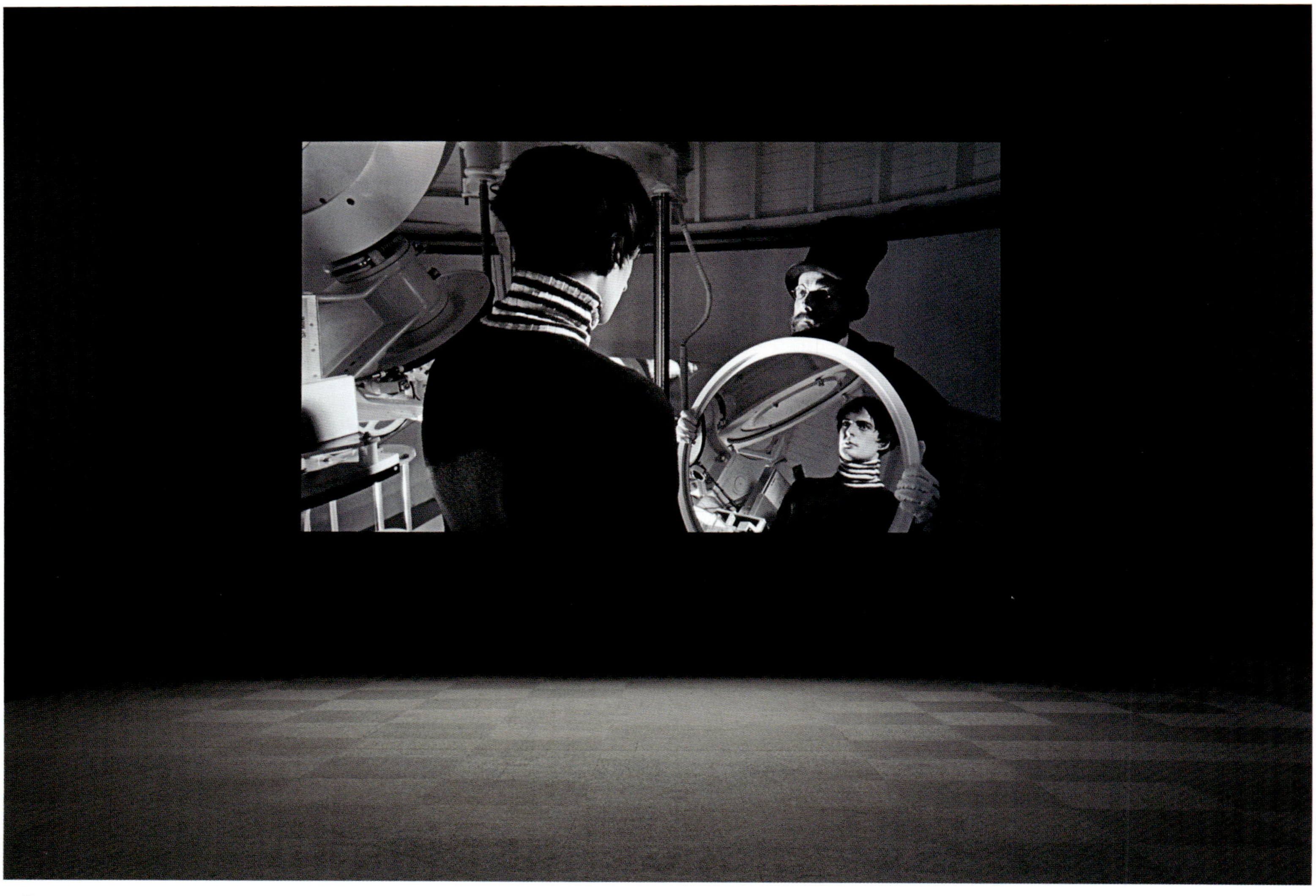

2

Shown by
Figge von Rosen
Galerie R8
Galerie Peter
Kilchmann A24

Biography
Born 1969
Lives in New York
and Berlin

Venazuela-born Téllez's video installations were shown in the exhibition "Rotations" at Galerie Peter Kilchmann, Zurich, in early 2012. Other recent solo exhibitions include "Letter on the Blind for the Use of Those Who See" (2011) at the Museum of Contemporary Art, Cleveland, and the two-venue "Larger than Life" (2010–11) at Museo de Arte Contemporáneo de Vigo, and Fundação Calouste Gulbenkian, Lisbon. In 2011 Téllez was also included in the 11th Biennale de Lyon.

1
The Elephant and the Blind Men [Nathan]
2008
C-type print mounted on aluminum
37¾ × 65¾"
(96 × 167 cm)
Courtesy of Galerie Peter Kilchmann

2
Caligari und der Schlafwandler
(Caligari and the Sleepwalker)
2008
Video installation
27 min. 07 sec.
Courtesy of Galerie Peter Kilchmann

3
Snow White Doesn't Live Here Anymore
2010
Mixed media
Dimensions variable
Courtesy of Galerie Peter Kilchmann

Javier Téllez

"Cinema is the wound and stain, no doubt, but the stain in motion!" So has said the New York-based Venezuelan artist Javier Téllez, riffing on Jean-Luc Godard's injunction about film being truth "24 frames a second." This conflation of wound and stain is invoked in Téllez's lucid, parable-like films featuring the mentally or physically ill. Take *Letter on the Blind for the Use of Those Who See* (2007), which stages a moving encounter of six blind people touching an elephant in an empty swimming pool. Or consider *O Rinoceronte de Dürer* (Dürer's Rhinoceros, 2010), in which the titular embalmed animal is wheeled through a Portuguese hospital to the patients'—and the audience's—amazement. In this shared moment the pathology of difference is, fleetingly, erased. QL

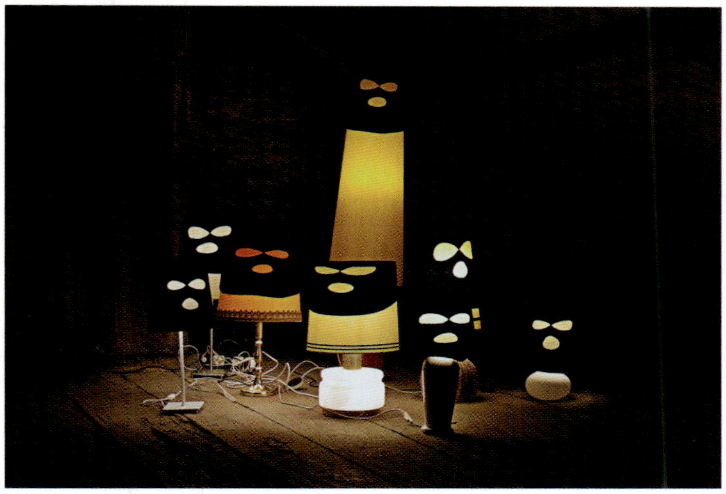

3

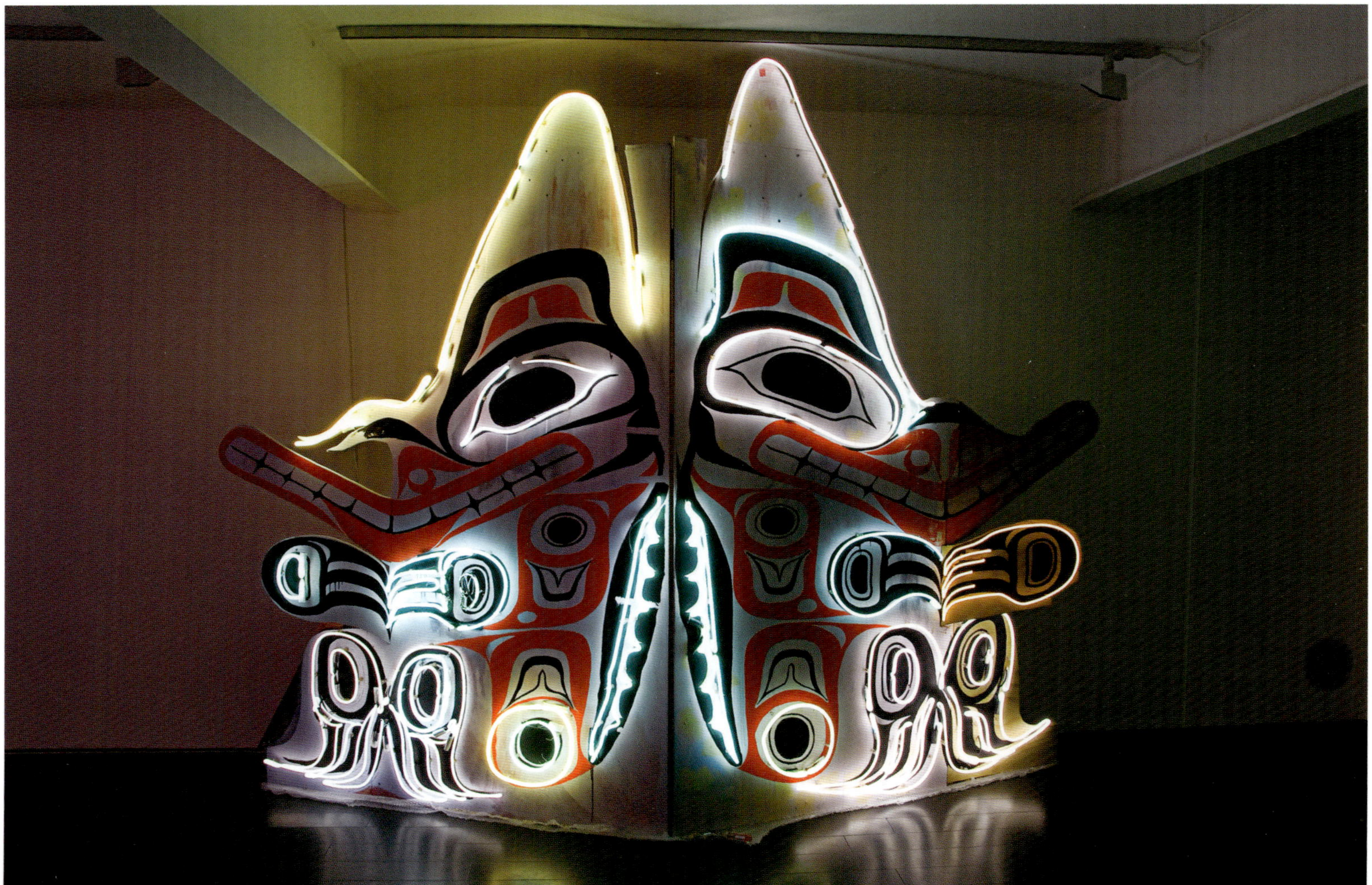

Blair Thurman

Shown by
galerie frank elbaz D6

Biography
Born 1961
Lives in New York

American artist Thurman has exhibited his installations in Europe and the United States extensively in the last two decades. Recent exhibitions include a self-titled solo show at Triple V, Paris (2011); "Aus Unseren Kellern" (From Our Cellars, 2011) at Klemens Gasser & Tanja Grunert, Inc., New York; and "American exuberance" (2011) at the Rubell Family Collection, Miami. Galerie frank elbaz, Paris, will hold a solo show of his work in 2012.

Honey Badgers
2009
Plywood, acrylic, neon
145⅝ × 107⅞ × 35⅜"
(370 × 274 × 90 cm)
Courtesy of galerie frank elbaz

Blair Thurman's paintings, sculptures, and neon works are like enigmatically sneering advertising logos or malicious highway signs, lurking in the corner, beckoning to lead you astray. Punctured candy-colored fields and dizzying targets line the walls to play fast and loose with puns on the bold punches of Pop abstraction. The painting *Pop-Sirkle (CCKSCKR Hat II)* (2011) is an oblong, enlarged distortion of a red, white, and blue peppermint lollypop, dirtied and green-tinged at parts to take on the feeling of a menacing vortex. Thurman's curled canvases, angular wooden wall pieces, and rolled-up cloth spirals act as the dark, silent icons realized by America's Technicolor dreaming. CFW

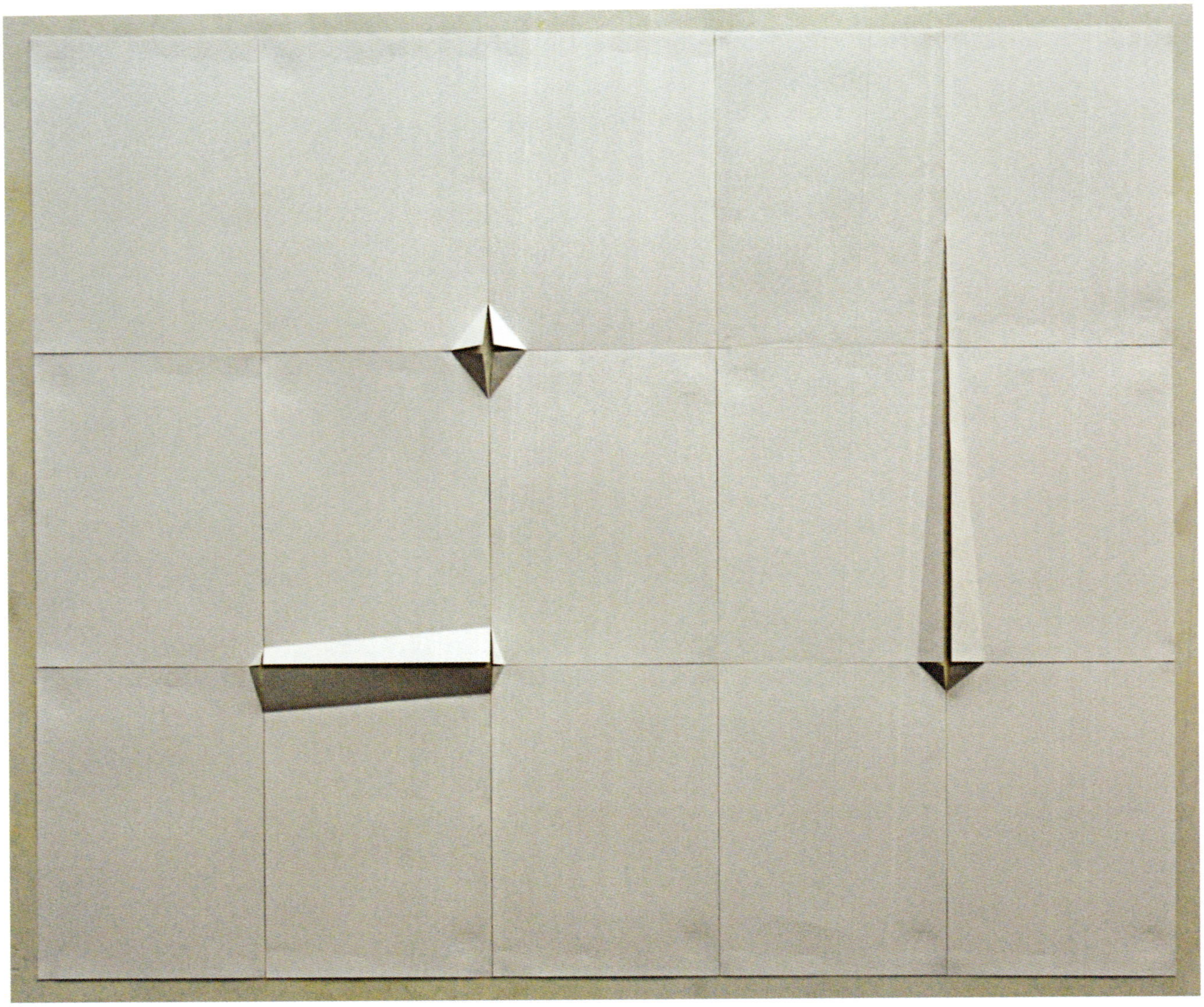

1

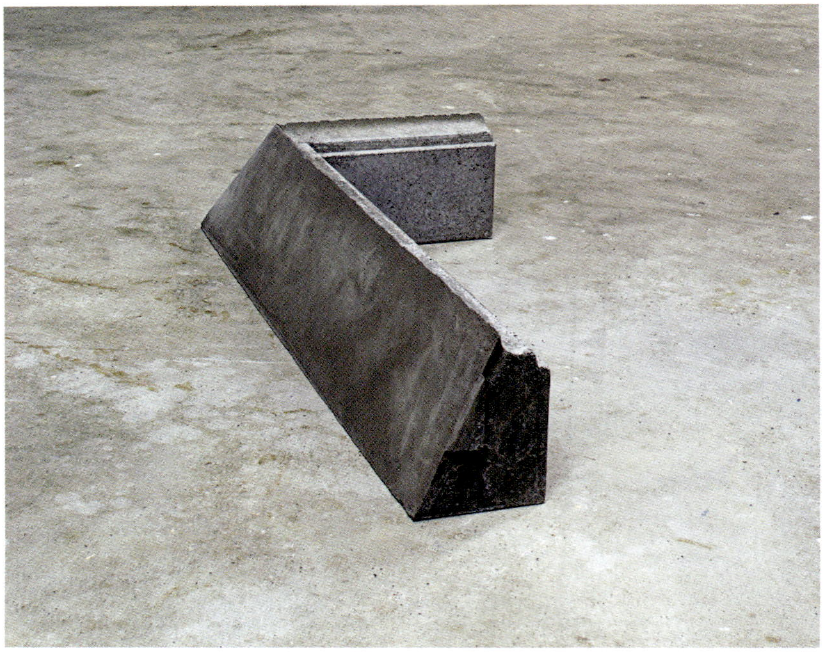

2

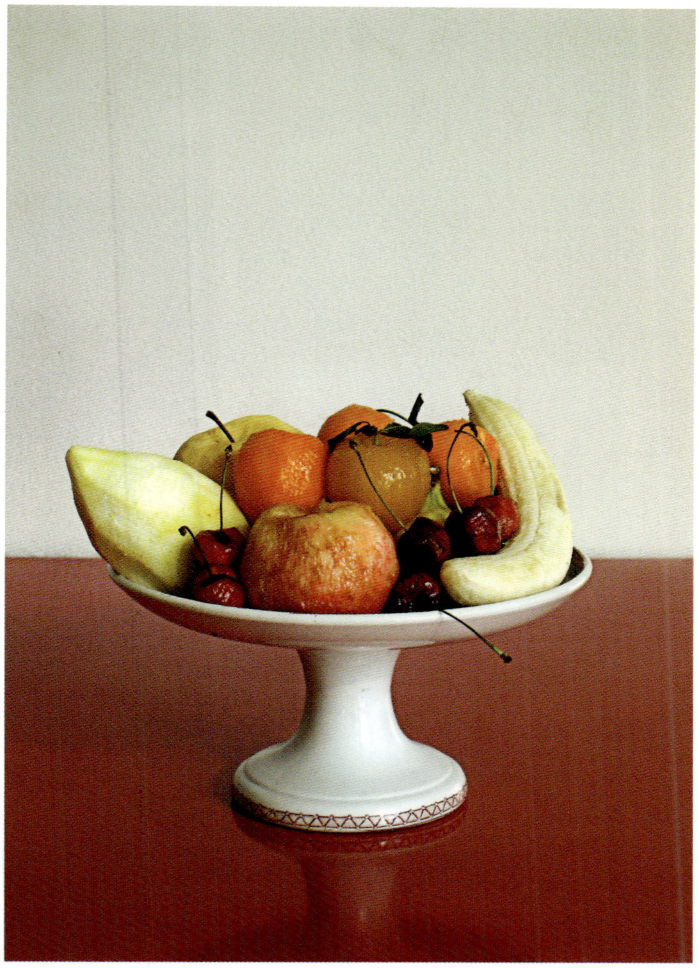

3

Shown by
Limoncello F19

Biography
Born 1979
Lives in London

Italy-born Tolone will complete his MFA at The Slade School of Fine Art, London, in 2012. In early 2012 Limoncello staged his first solo show at the gallery, and he has participated in numerous group shows, including "Mr. Rossi" (2011) at Limoncello, London, and "Ariane De Rothschild Prize" (2011) at Palazzo Reale, Milan. In 2010 he contributed to shows at Apexart, New York, and Fondazione Sandretto Re Rebaudengo, Turin, among others.

1
Flatland
2009
Paper
39 × 47¼ × 1⅛"
(99 × 120 × 3 cm)
Courtesy of Limoncello

2
Step's Shadow
2010
Concrete
11¼ × 6⅝ × 34¼"
(28.5 × 17 × 87 cm)
Courtesy of Limoncello

3
Emmanuelle
2009
C-type print
14½ × 10¼"
(37 × 26 cm)
Courtesy of Limoncello

Focus
Santo Tolone

For Santo Tolone, a simple act of subtraction can yield dramatic shifts in form and content. In *Salami* (2009), peppercorns arrayed to reflect their arrangement in a piece of meat become an elegant constellation. For the photograph *Emmanuelle* (2009), Tolone peeled the fruit in a compote—an otherwise classical still life—suggesting a moist, passive eroticism. The public realm offers fodder for other transformations: in *Fontana Angelica* (2010), he re-created the plumbing for a fountain designed by Piero Portaluppi, drawing on the architect's open-ended ideas about restoration but reversing his emphasis on surfaces; he has also etched images of public sculpture on brass, highlighting their pure geometric forms by altering their scale and lifting them from their original context. KMJ

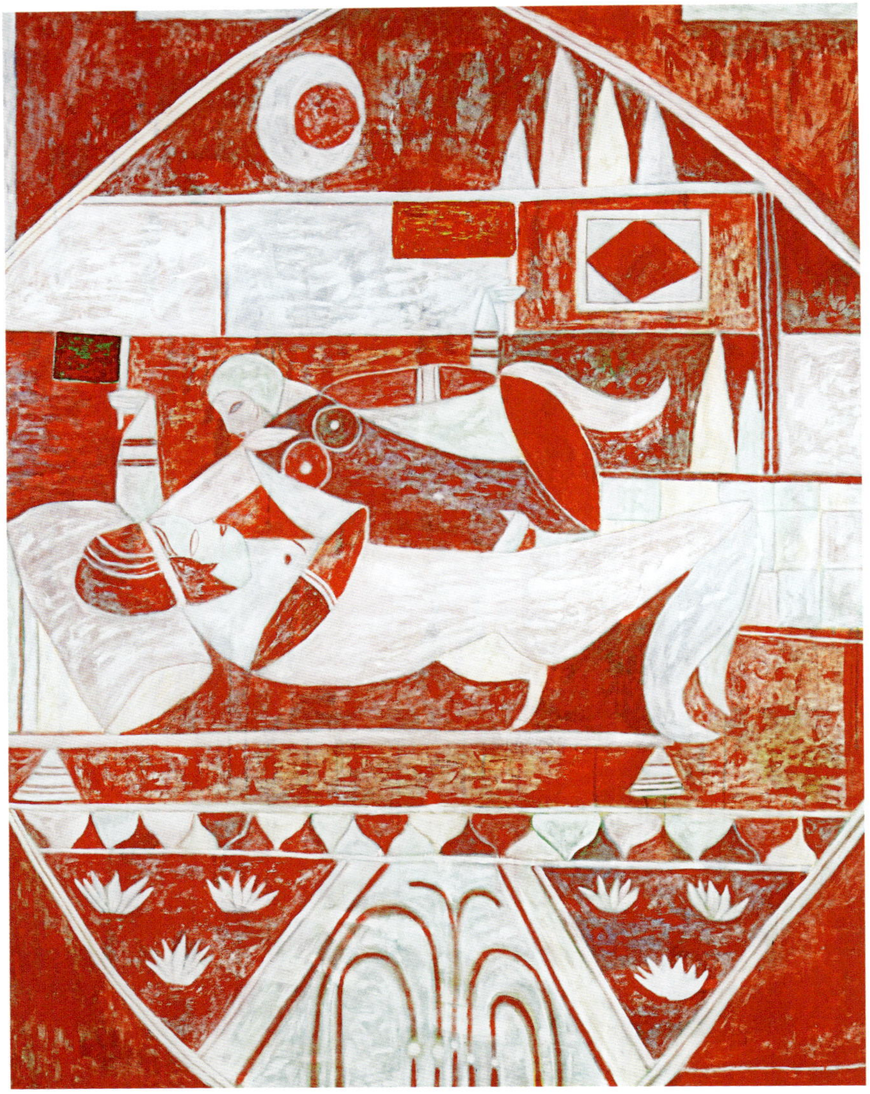

1

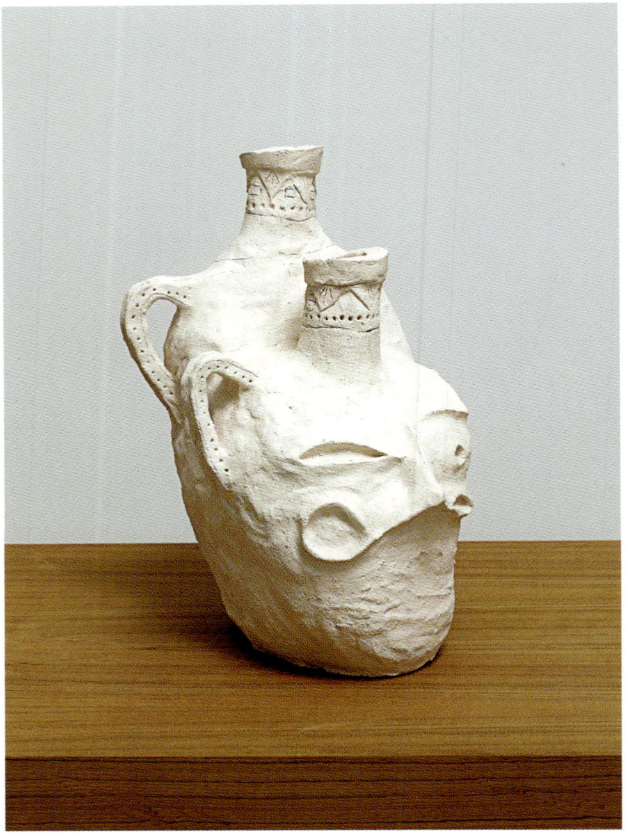

3

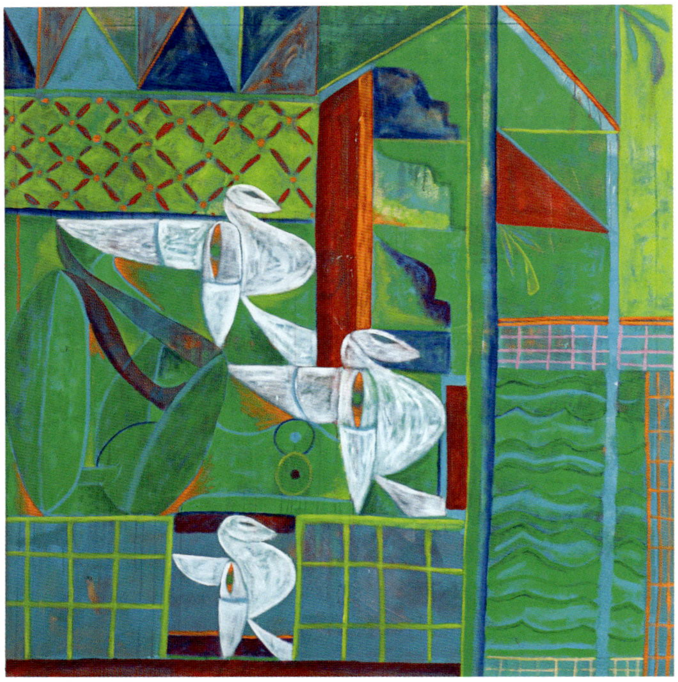

2

Shown by
Galleri Nicolai Wallner A7

Biography
Born 1983
Lives in Copenhagen

In early 2012 Tovborg held the solo exhibition "Giverny" at Brand New Gallery, Milan. Other recent solo exhibitions include "Tre" (2011) at the Museet for Religiøs Kunst, Lemvig, and "New Eternity" (2010) at Galleri Nicolai Wallner, Copenhagen. He also participated in the two-person show "Sacra Conversazione" (2012) at Galleri Nicolai Wallner, Copenhagen, with Jeppe Hein and the group show "Folklore—Old New Forms" (2011) at Kunsthallen 44 Moen, Askeby.

1
Tourist (II)
2011
Acrylic on canvas
74⅞ × 59"
(190 × 150 cm)
Courtesy of Galleri Nicolai Wallner

2
Tourist (VII)
2011
Acrylic on canvas
66¾ × 66¾"
(169.5 × 169.5 cm)
Courtesy of Galleri Nicolai Wallner

3
The Communicator (IV)
2010
Ceramics
17⅜ × 15 × 10¼"
(44 × 38 × 26 cm)
Courtesy of Galleri Nicolai Wallner

4
The Communicator (Violet)
2011
Acrylic, pastel crayon, and handmade paper on canvas
118⅛ × 78¾"
(300 × 200 cm)
Courtesy of Galleri Nicolai Wallner

Alexander Tovborg

It's hard to tell, from his art alone, whether Alexander Tovborg is religious, but he works with the intensity and devotion of a believer. Indeed, religious art's iconography and conventions provide much of the reference material for Tovborg's luminous paintings and sculptures. Recent paintings, such as *Triptykon (Brown)* (2010–11), have adopted the Christian structure of the triptych, despite including in that instance an abstracted rabbi kneeling in prayer. In the series "Turist" (Tourist, 2011), Tovborg sews a patchwork of global styles that abuts Indian erotic imagery with decoration and mythical animals. Even in the otherworldly landscape *But You Are a Wankster* (2010), there is a sense that aesthetic choices can subtly amount to a private moral code. JG

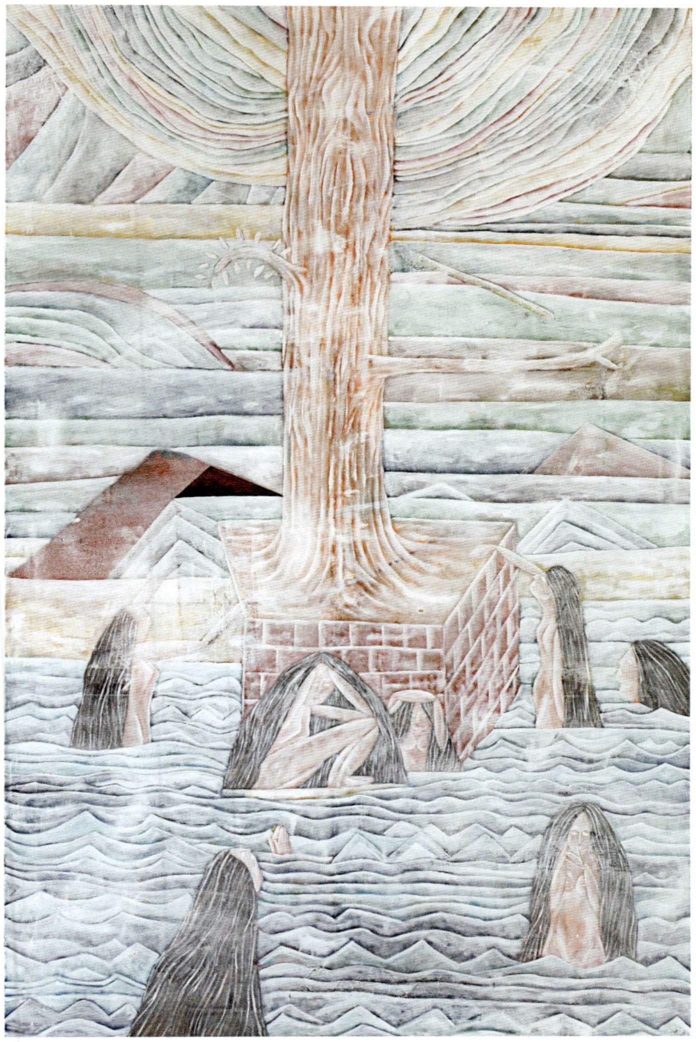

4

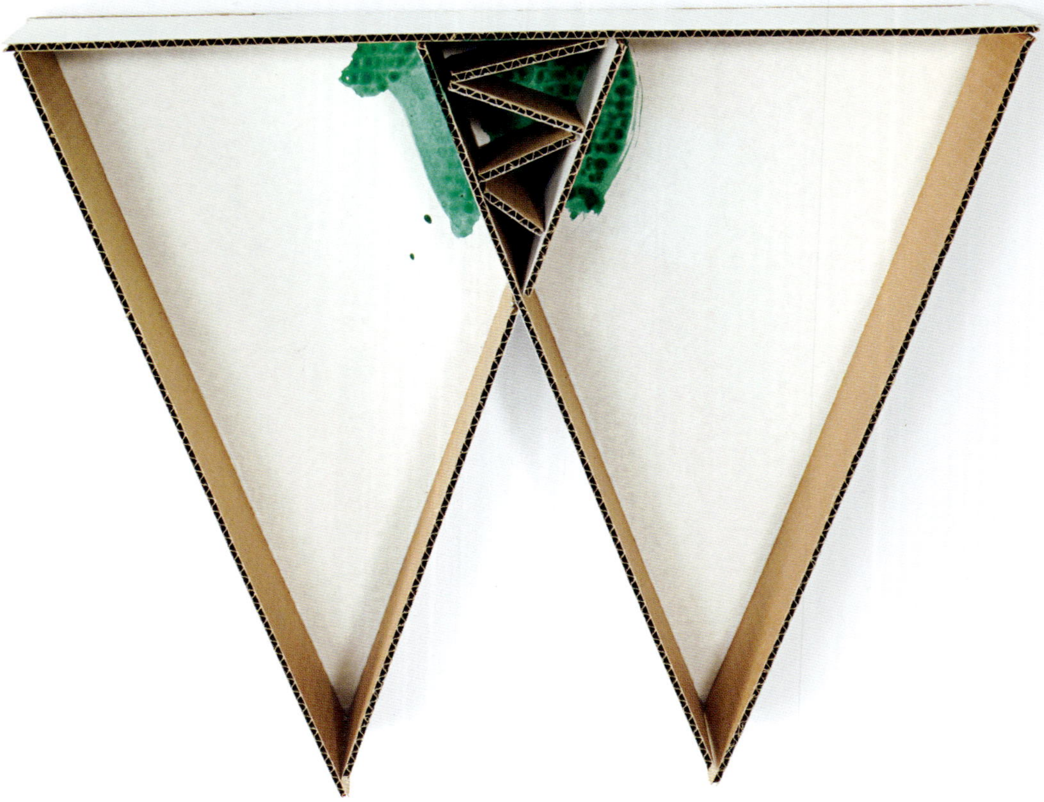

1

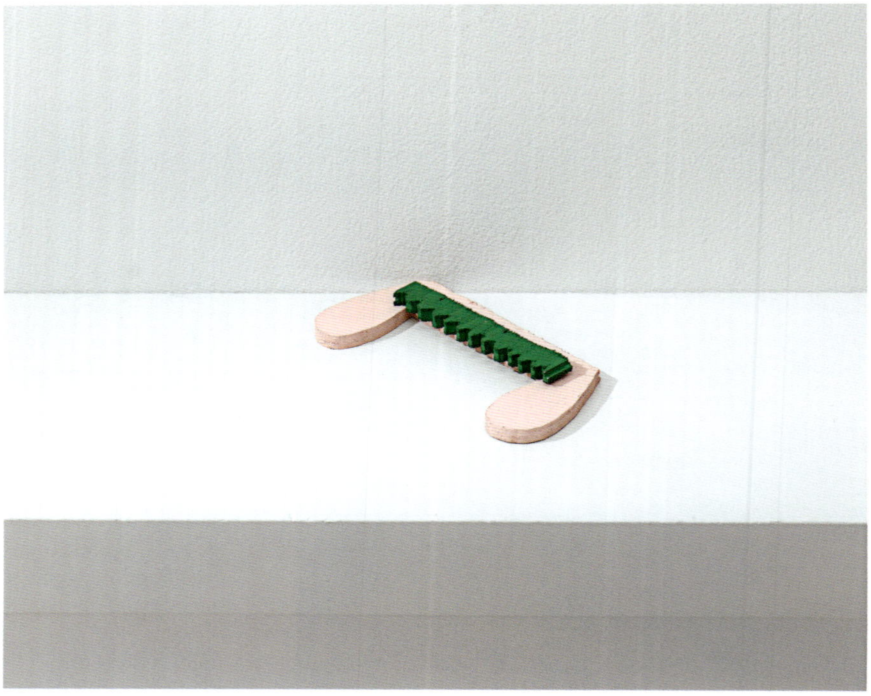

2

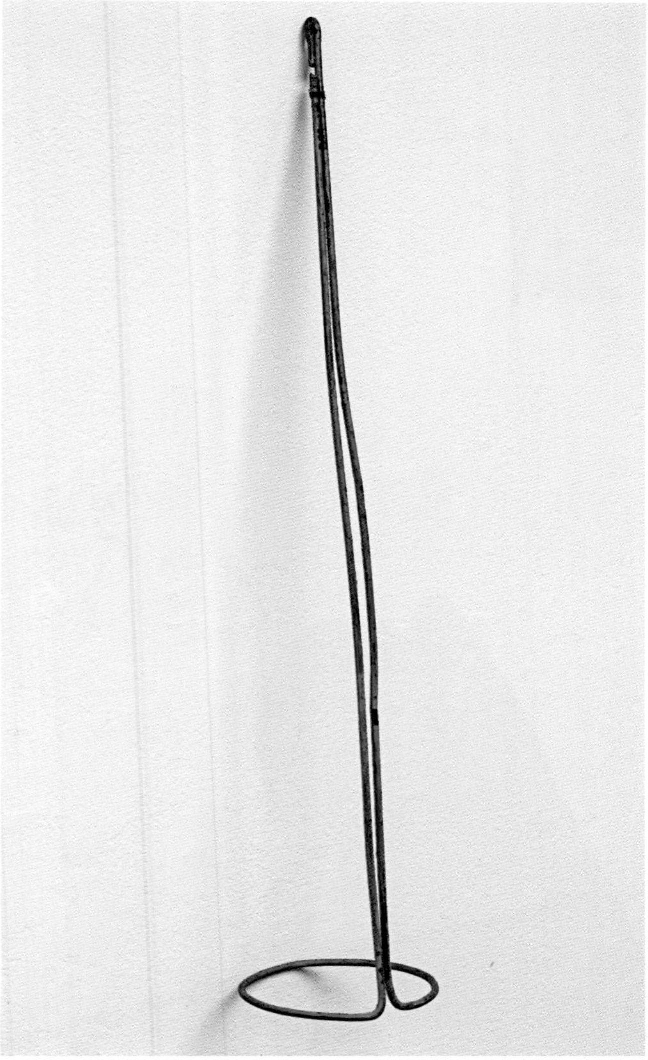

3

Shown by
Tomio Koyama
Gallery B8
Stuart Shave/Modern Art C43
Galleri Nicolai Wallner A7

Biography
Born 1941
Lives in New York

American artist Tuttle's work has been the subject of solo shows for the past five decades. Recent exhibitions include "Triumphs" (2011) at Dublin City Gallery and "The Use of Time" (2008) at Kunsthaus Zug. The extensive touring retrospective "The Art of Richard Tuttle" (2005–07) began at the San Francisco Museum of Modern Art, before traveling to the Whitney Museum of American Art, New York; Des Moines Art Center; Dallas Museum of Art; the Museum of Contemporary Art, Chicago; and the Museum of Contemporary Art, Los Angeles.

1
Boys Let's Be Bad Boys (5)
1998
Corrugated cardboard and glue
16¼ × 20 × 3¼"
(41.5 × 51 × 8.5 cm)
Courtesy of Stuart Shave/Modern Art and The Pace Gallery

2
Wealth
1973–76
Acrylic on plywood
⅝ × 5½ × 2½"
(1.5 × 14 × 6.5 cm)
Courtesy of Stuart Shave/Modern Art and The Pace Gallery

3
Enrich
1973–76
Paint on coat hanger wire
16 × 3¼ × 3½"
(40.5 × 8.5 × 9 cm)
Courtesy of Stuart Shave/Modern Art and The Pace Gallery

Richard Tuttle

Since his first solo show, in New York in 1965, Richard Tuttle's approach to art has been understated, offbeat, and charmingly philosophical. A critic once described his practice as paradoxically both "sophisticated and infantile," and accordingly his work at the interface of painting, drawing, and sculpture manipulates the most basic ingredients of art-making—line, form, material, color, shape, texture—in mercurial and poetic ways while addressing both seeing and being. Although he is usually thought of as a maker of intimately scaled works, the artist's *Replace the Abstract Picture Plane I* (1996) was a physically imposing arabesque—a network of orange-colored batons covered with verdant green cotton twill—that threaded through the Kunsthaus Zug in Switzerland. MA

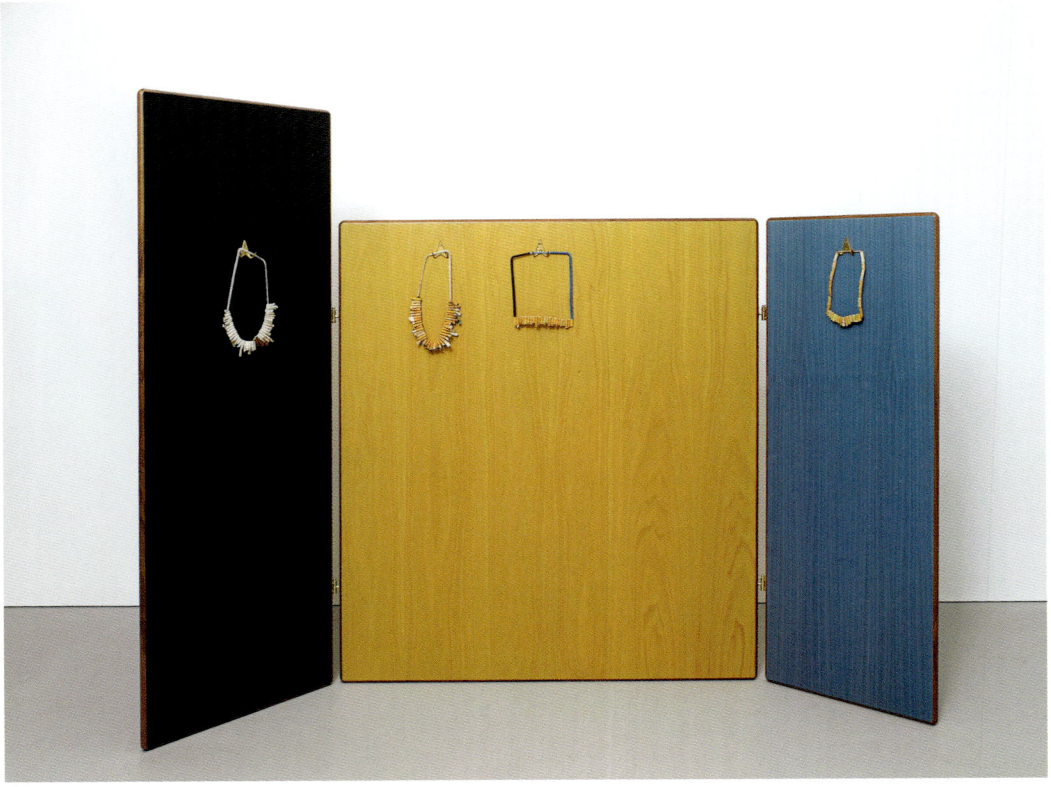

1

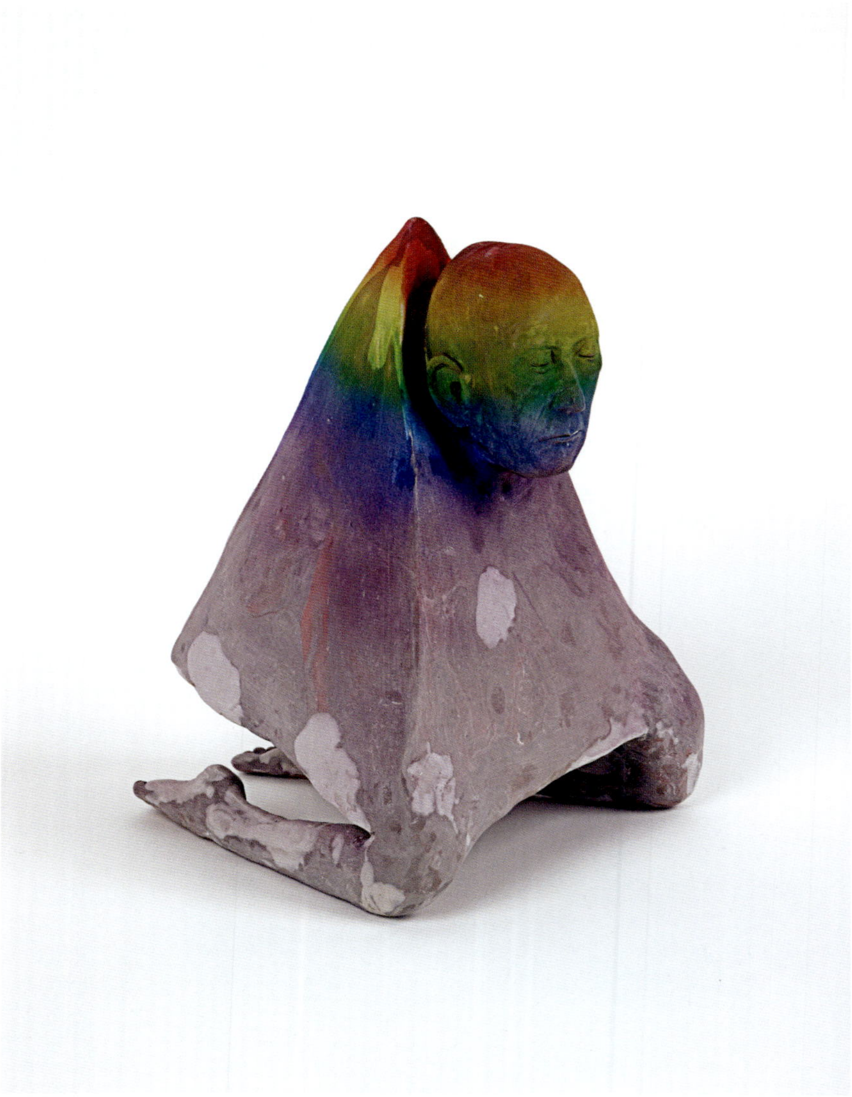

2

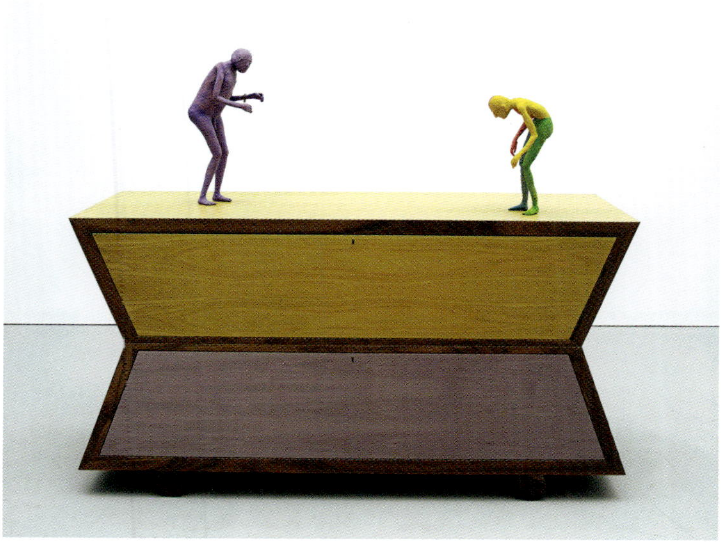

3

Shown by
Kate MacGarry F13
Salon 94 C38

Biography
Born 1976
Lives in London

New Zealand-born sculptor Upritchard has been populating galleries with her unique figurative work since the early-2000s. Her solo exhibition "Echo" (2011) at Kate MacGarry, London, evoked a quasi-domestic environment. In 2010 she had the solo show "In die Höhle (In the Cave)" at Secession, Vienna, and in 2009, she represented New Zealand at the 53rd Venice Biennale. In 2012 she will have self-titled solo shows at Nottingham Contemporary; the Center for Contemporary Art, Cincinnati; and Salon 94, New York.

1
Paravent / Wall
2011
Veneer and Italian oak, brass fittings, cigarette and straw necklaces
70 × 1 × 97⅝"
(178 × 2.5 × 248 cm)
Courtesy of Kate MacGarry

2
Triangle Loos
2010
Modeling material, foil, wire, paint
101/4 × 8⅞ × 9¼"
(26 × 22.5 × 23.5 cm)
Courtesy of Kate MacGarry

3
Echo Cabinet
2011
Veneer and Italian oak, brass fittings, modeling material, wire, paint
39⅛ × 74⅞ × 25½"
(99.5 × 190 × 65 cm)
Courtesy of Kate MacGarry

Focus
Francis Upritchard

From a mummy moaning on the floor and a *faux* sloth splayed out in a vitrine to sculptures of the shrunken heads of British settlers captured by native New Zealanders, Francis Upritchard's work often suggests absurd, unsettlingly reimagined cultural and natural artifacts. Unmoored on plinths and found furniture or trapped under blown glass, her recent polychrome figurines form atomized communities of comical, wistful, and otherworldly humans and beasts. Some pray or zone out, such as *Brother of Clan of Rob* (2009), an ascetic-looking hippie with a rainbow-colored face and a sickly gray body that shades into ruddiness at the extremities—echoing ancient religious statuary, goofy plastic fantasy miniatures, and the failed countercultural dreams of the 1960s and '70s. KJ

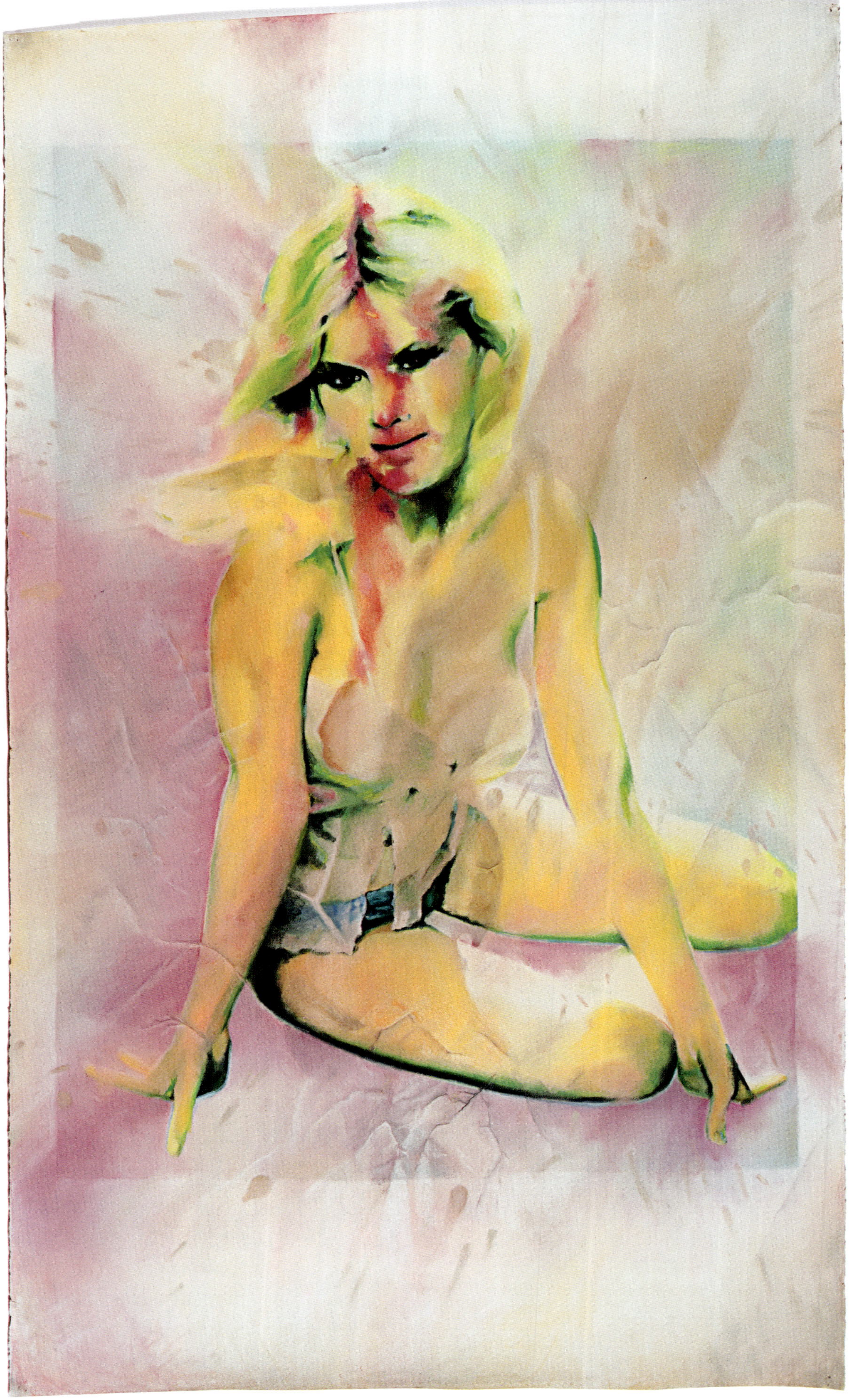

1

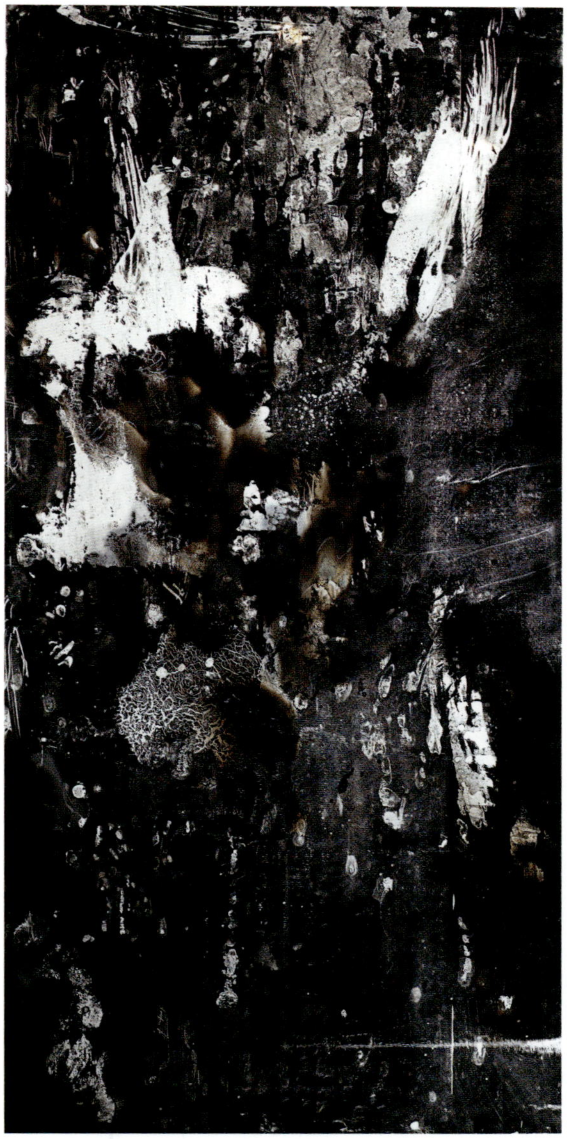

2

Shown by
Overduin and Kite F4

Biography
Born 1972
Lives in Los Angeles

American artist Upson received her MFA and BFA from the California Institute of the Arts, Valencia, in 2007, and 2004, respectively. She has exhibited in several significant solo shows in recent years, including exhibitions at Overduin and Kite, Los Angeles (2011); Maccarone, New York (2009); and Hammer Projects, Hammer Museum, Los Angeles (2007). Recent group shows include "American Exuberance" (2011) at the Rubell Family Collection, Miami, and "George Herms: Xenophilia (Love of the Unknown)" (2011) at MoCA Pacific Design Center, Los Angeles.

1
Mirrored
2011
Pastel on paper
74 × 45"
(188 × 114.5 cm)
Courtesy of Overduin and Kite

2
Untitled
2011
Smoke on aluminum panel
96 × 48"
(244 × 122 cm)
Courtesy of Overduin and Kite

Focus
Kaari Upson

Kaari Upson's main body of work began with a burnt-out house. Exploring the aftermath of a house fire near her family's San Bernardino home in 2003, the artist came across roomfuls of journals, photographs, and junk. The absent owner was a man whom Upson christened Larry, a self-styled playboy, representative of now-faded West Coast aspirations. Upson began to research Larry's life, using his story as a starting point for a more freewheeling narrative in which elements of her own life came to be meshed with his. Producing related works that range from dubious relics to inspired effigies and reconstructions, this ongoing project effaces the line between artist and subject. As Upson has said of Larry, "I am more him than he is." ST

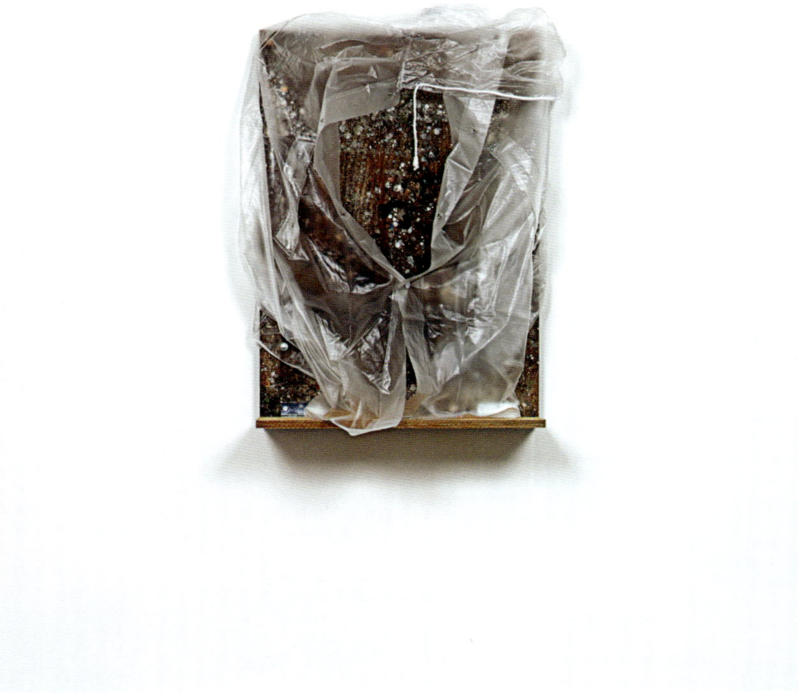

1

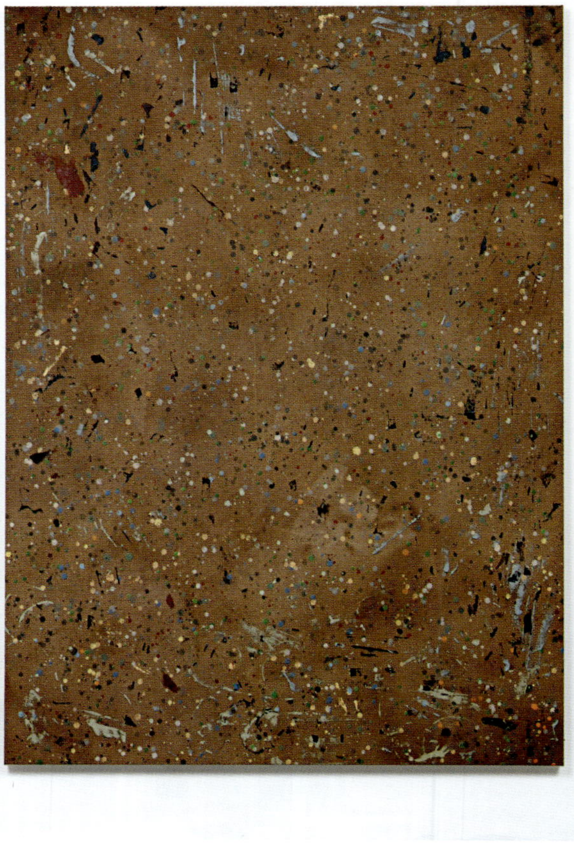

2

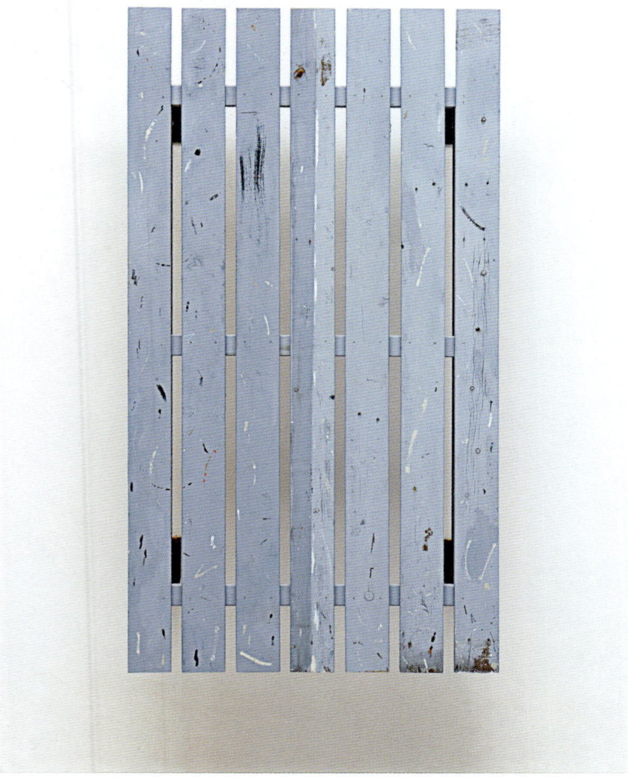

3

Focus
Fredrik Værslev

The process of painting is, for Fredrik Værslev, a conversation. His series of "Shelf" and "Swap" paintings (2010) were made with a range of artist collaborators, while his series of untitled "Terrazzo Paintings" (2010–ongoing) are made in direct dialogue with the subject matter itself. His interest in terrazzo marble lies in its composition, a technique he reinterprets via the process of painting, sanding, and layering to reproduce thousands of minuscule individual marks on the canvas surface. More recently, these works have been laid outdoors for six months, staining and altering the canvases further. In his experiments, Værslev finds a place for painting that shifts between decoration, architecture, and collaborative performance. CFW

Shown by
Johan Berggren
Gallery F15
STANDARD
(Oslo) B41

Biography
Born 1979
Lives in Drøbak

Norwegian painter Værslev has exhibited his sculptural paintings extensively since graduating from the Malmö Art Academy in 2010. A former student of Staatliche Hochschule für Bildende Künste, Städelschule, Frankfurt, he has undertaken solo shows at Tomorrow/Yesterday, Toronto (2011); CIRCUS, Berlin (2011); and STANDARD (Oslo). In 2012 he will have solo exhibitions at Indipendenza Studio, Rome, and Johan Berggren Gallery, Malmo.

1
Shelf Paintings (Dew Problems) #08
2011
Mixed media
30 × 21¼ × 1⅛"
(76 × 54 × 3 cm)
Courtesy of Johan Berggren Gallery

2
Untitled
2011
Spray paint, house paint, corrosion protective spray and, white spirit on canvas
76¾ × 57 × 1⅛"
(195 × 145 × 3 cm)
Courtesy of Johan Berggren Gallery

3
Untitled
2011
House paint, enamel paint, rust, and nails on pressure-impregnated spruce
55 × 30⅞ × 11⅞"
(139.5 × 78.5 × 30 cm)
Courtesy of Johan Berggren Gallery

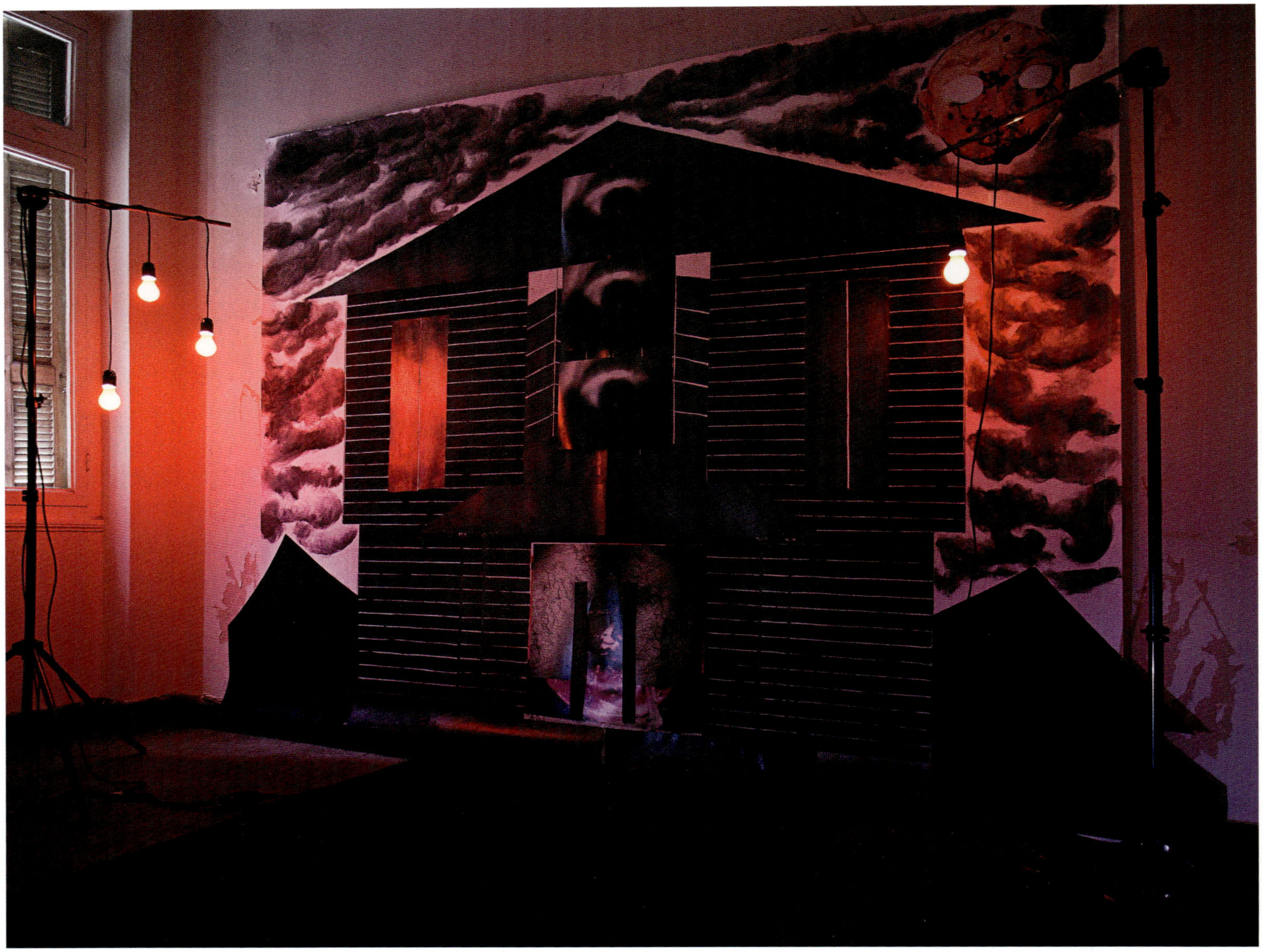

1

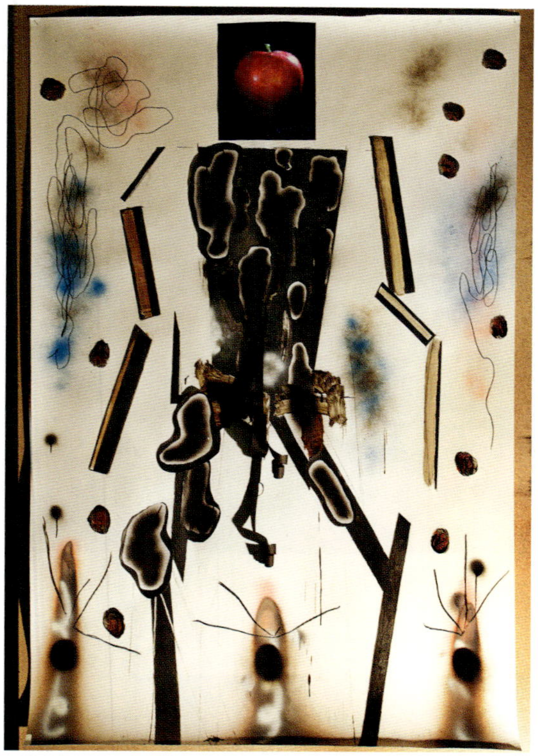

2

Shown by
The Breeder C22

Biography
Born 1977
Lives in Athens and Vienna

Greek artist Varelas's large-scale, collaged paintings and sculptures are the subject of a solo exhibition at the Contemporary Arts Center, Cincinnati, in 2012. In 2011 he had a solo show at Kunsthalle Athena, Athens, and participated in a project for ReMap3, Athens. Other recent solo shows took place at Autocenter, Berlin (2010), and The Breeder, Athens (2009). He participated in the survey shows "Prospect.1 New Orleans" (2008) and "Destroy Athens", the 1st Athens Biennial.

1
The Haus
2011
Mixed media on paper
94⅞ × 118⅛"
(241 × 300 cm)
Courtesy of The Breeder

2
Apple Head
2011
Mixed media on paper
94⅜ × 59"
(240 × 150 cm)
Courtesy of The Breeder

Jannis Varelas

Jannis Varelas' figures are priapic, grungy, messed-up creatures. They might be the bastard offspring of a Surrealists' exquisite corpses, and they may have a splash of Blue Meanie, Ubu Roi, or shamanistic DNA thrown in too; but whatever their provenance, they are collaged and drawn aberrations of the human form. A pair of candles may stand for knees (*Clair, Maid Costume, f/orange*, 2011), or a head might be replaced with an apple (*Apple Head*, 2011), and yet the quadrupedal arrangement, the uprightness, the discordant mess of bits, just about hanging together by geometry alone and implying an equivalently noisy interiority, constitute distinctly human, transgressive individuals with no taste for niceties. SOR

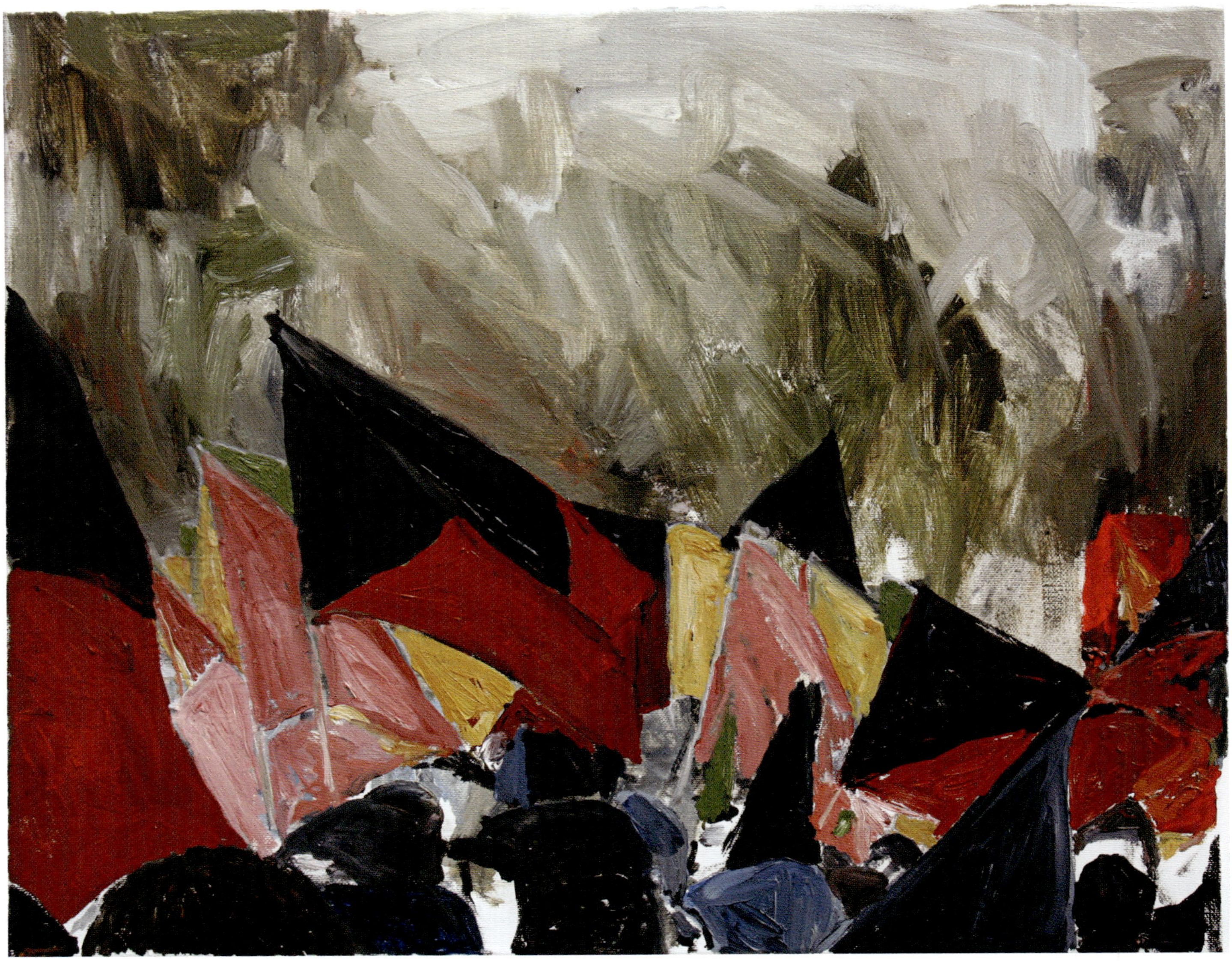

1

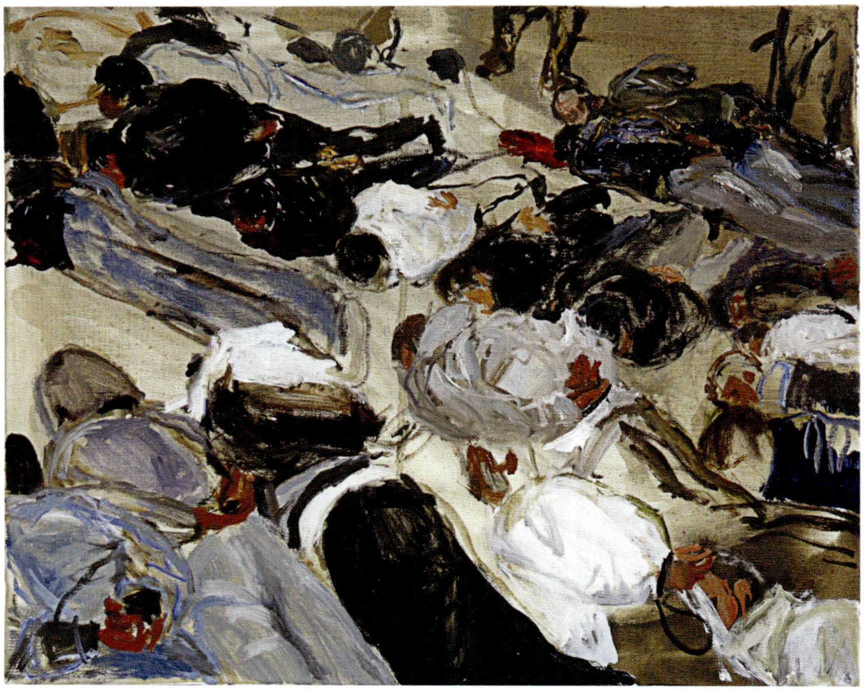

2

Shown by
Andreiana Mihail
Gallery F28

Biography
Born 1968 / 1974
Live in Bucharest

Romanian artists Vatamanu and Tudor have worked together since 2000. In 2009 the solo exhibitions "All Power to the Imagination!" at Secession, Vienna, and "Surplus Value" at BAK, Utrecht, highlighted the significance of their practice. They were included in the Romanian Pavilion exhibition at the 52nd Venice Beinnale (2007); 5th Berlin Biennial (2008); and more recently "Untitled (12th Istanbul Biennale)" (2011). They are currently resident on the DAAD Artist-in-Berlin, Program

1
"Appointment with History, 28 March 2009, London"
2011
Oil on canvas
15¾ × 19⅝"
(40 × 50 cm)
Courtesy of Andreiana Mihail Gallery

2
"Appointment with History, Syria, 2011"
2011
Oil on canvas
15¾ × 19⅝"
(40 × 50 cm)
Courtesy of Andreiana Mihail Gallery

3
"Appointment with History, Madrid Puerta del Sol, May 2011"
2011
Oil on canvas
15¾ × 19⅝"
(40 × 50 cm)
Courtesy of Andreiana Mihail Gallery

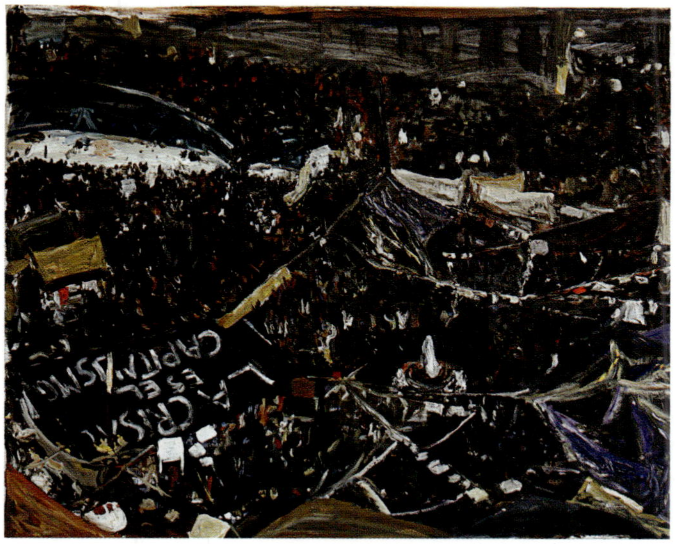

3

Focus
Mona Vatamanu & Florin Tudor

Working together since 2000, the Romanian artists Mona Vatamanu and Florin Tudor explore the revolutionary tendency—through symbols of solidarity and collectivity, and historical and personal memory—of the past century and the current one. Rejecting the ideological polarities of the Cold War, their pointed, poetic works in various media often elucidate Communist Romania and its dead-cold rush into modernity; see the 2003 video *Vacaresti*, which films the former site of an 18th century monastery demolished by Nicolae Ceaușescu for an unrealized building project. But their astute gaze also roves elsewhere. *Întâlnire cu istoria* (Appointment with History, 2007–9), originally mounted at the 2008 Berlin Biennial, offered realist paintings depicting anti-globalization demonstrations in Basel and celebratory crowds on Berlin's Alexanderplatz in that year of years, 1989. QL

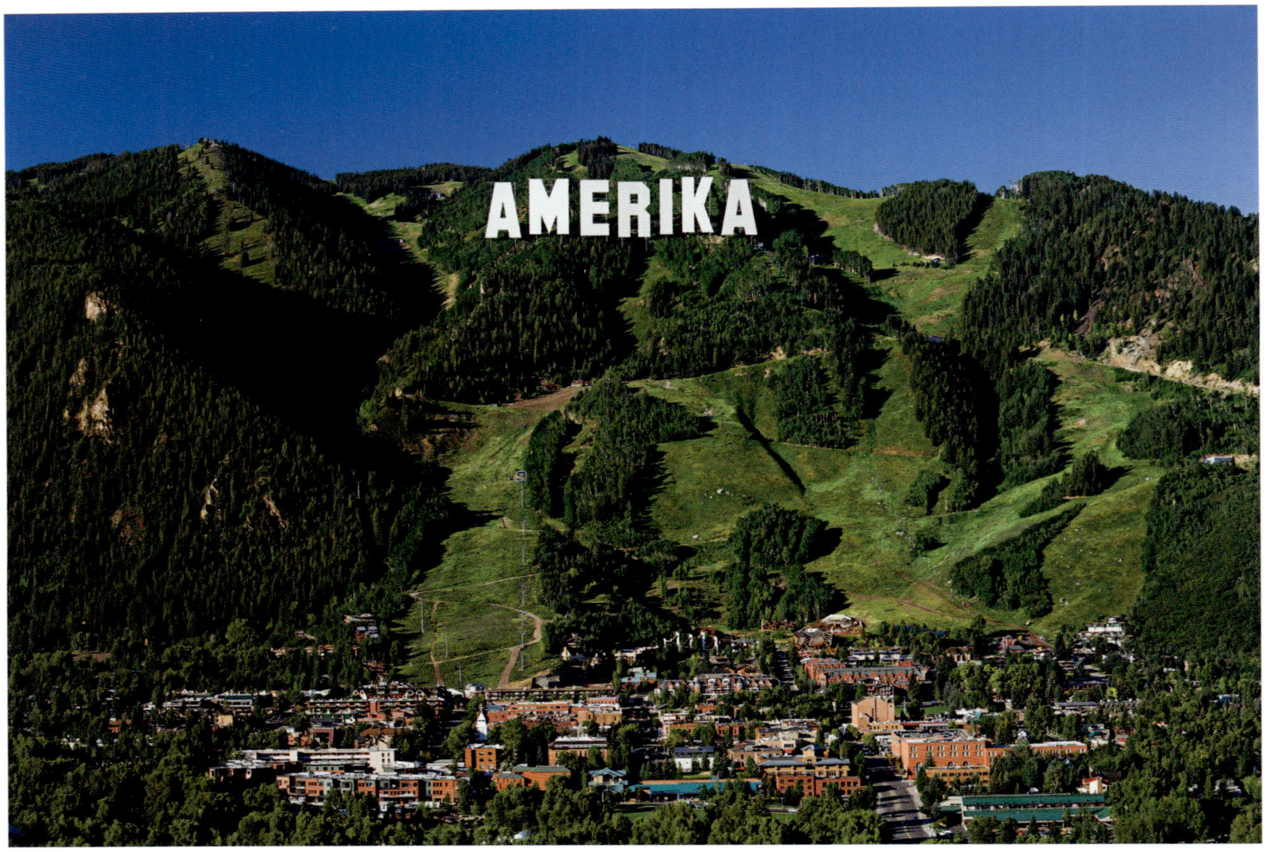

1

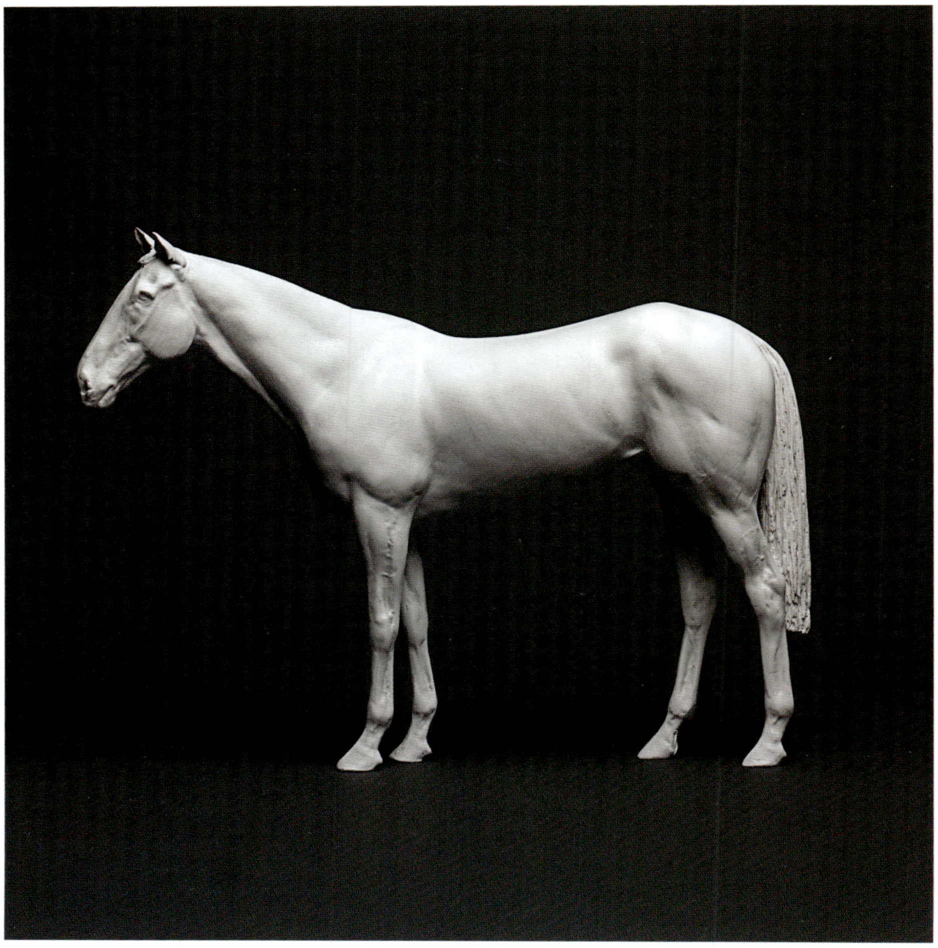

2

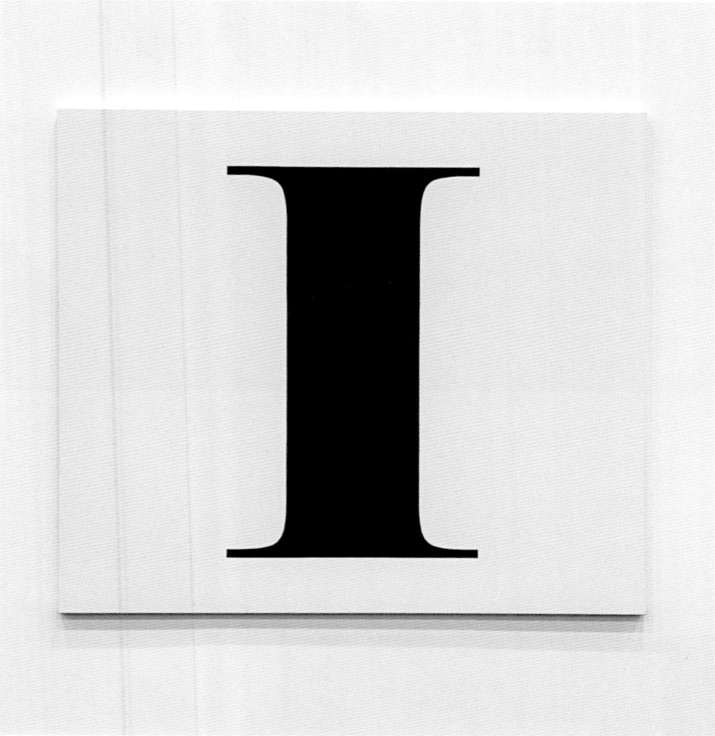

3

Shown by
carlier | gebauer C23
Galerie Krinzinger B24
Anthony Reynolds Gallery C3

Biography
Born 1959
Lives in London

British artist Wallinger's conceptual practice has been the focus of exhibitions since the early 1980s. His socio-political "State Britain" (2007), filled the Duveen Galleries of Tate Britain, London, with a recreation of a protester's peace camp, the original of which was removed from its site outside UK parliament. In 2011, the solo exhibition "MARK" took place at Museum De Pont, Tilburg. In 2010, he had solo shows at Kunstnernes Hus, Oslo, and Sinema Amnesia, Çanakkale. Wallinger won the 2007 Turner Prize, Tate Britain, London.

1
Amerika
2010
Site-specific installation, Aspen Colorado
Courtesy of Anthony Reynolds Gallery

2
The White Horse
2011
Polyester resin and chalk powder
7½ × 10½ × 2½"
(19 × 27 × 6.5 cm)
Edition of 30 + 5AP
Courtesy of Anthony Reynolds Gallery

3
Self-Portrait (Elephant)
2008
Acrylic on canvas
70⅞ × 84"
(180 × 213.5 cm)
Courtesy of Anthony Reynolds Gallery

Mark Wallinger

By re-presenting us with images of authority and value, Wallinger releases broad webs of association that plumb the depths of sociopolitical and historical phenomena. His giant horse proposed for Ebbsfleet, Kent, invokes deliberations on nationalism and class; the human cast on a plinth *Ecce Homo* (1999) introduces an earthbound Christ; the artist in a bear costume at the Neue Nationalgalerie, Berlin, unravels the politics of a divided city (*Sleeper*, 2005); and ranks of chairs, all marker-penned with "Mark" and connected by string to a single elevated point, become a congregation of disembodied self-portraits in thrall to an absent god in *According to Mark* (2011). Wallinger's eclectic formal range articulates contentious or ambivalent ideas with a clarity that aims to confuse assumptions. SOR

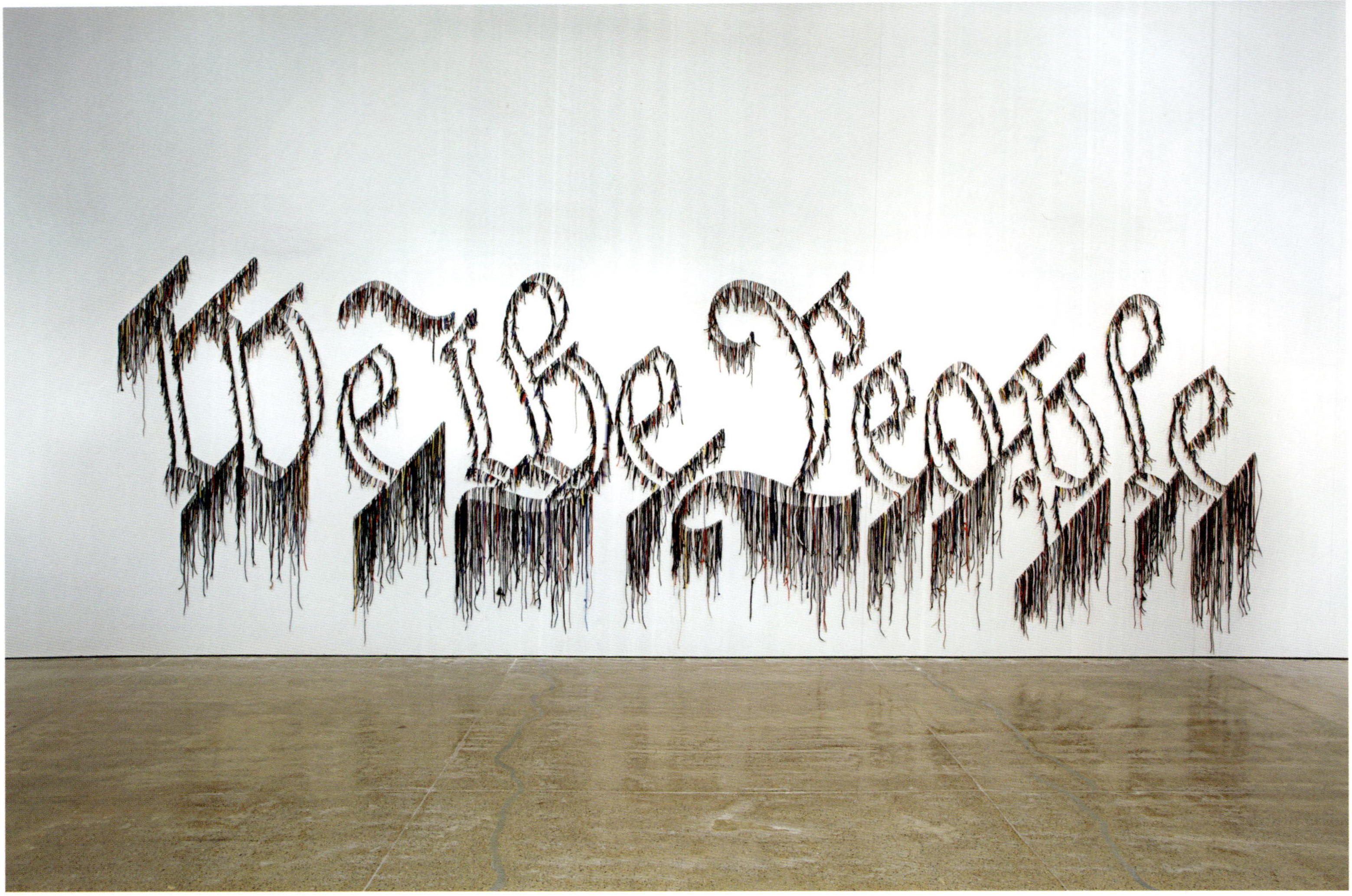

1

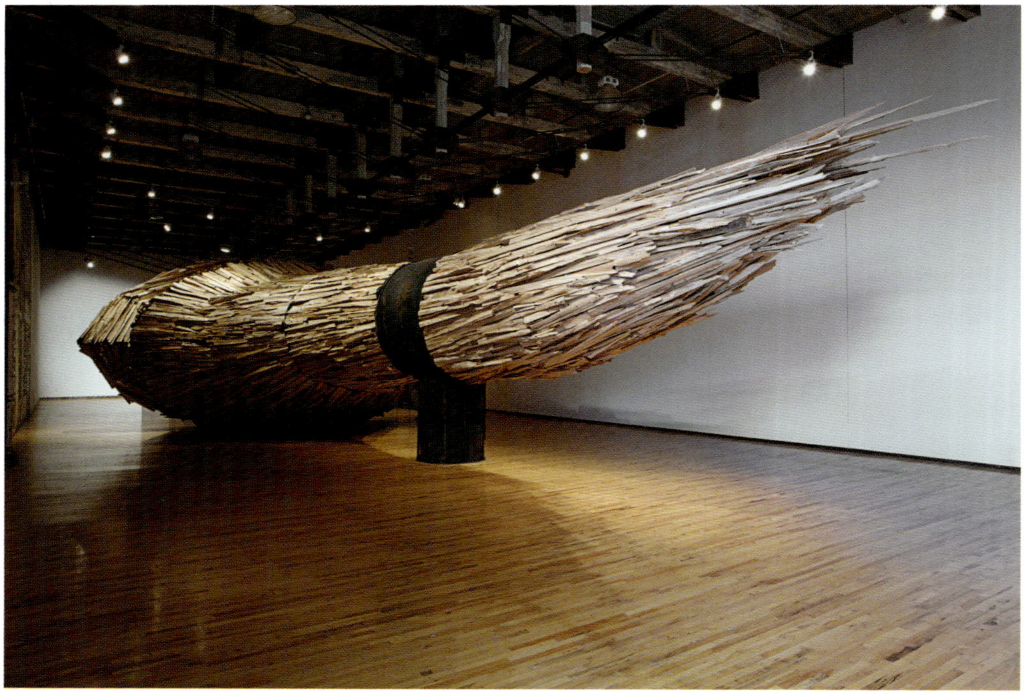

2

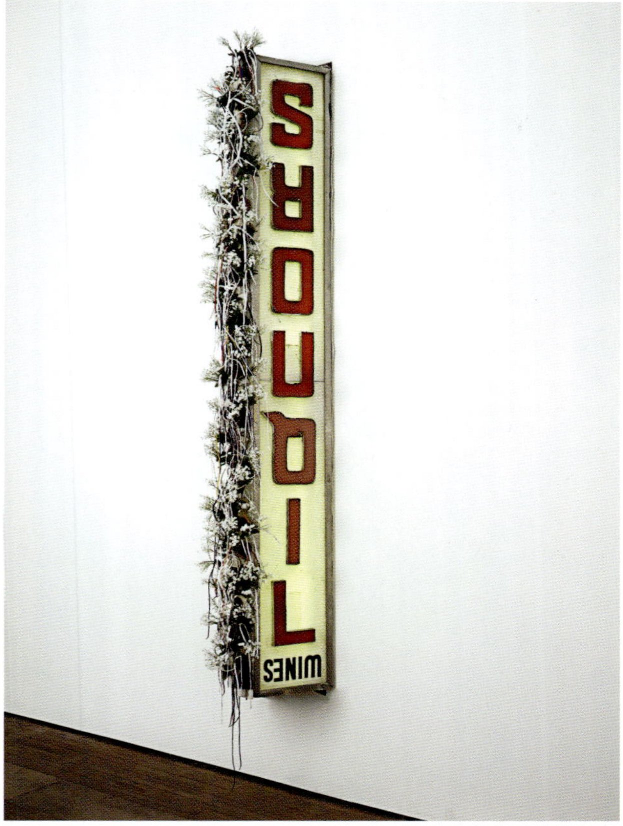

3

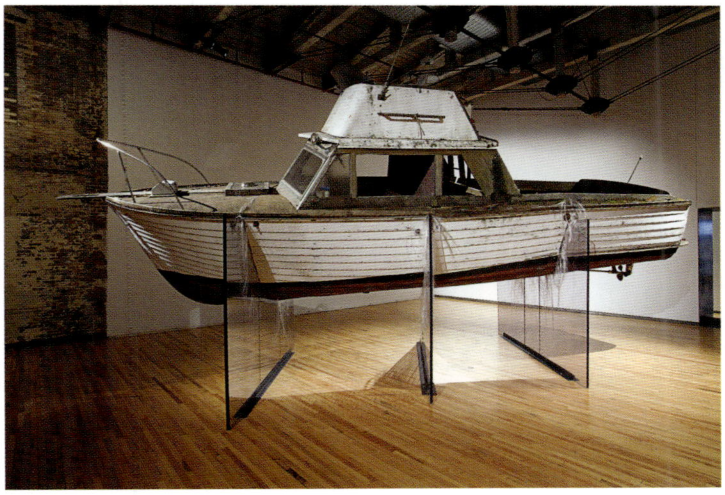

4

Shown by
Galleria Continua C40
Lehmann Maupin C10

Biography
Born 1963
Lives in New York

Jamaican-born artist Nari Ward's bold sculptural works have been the subject of numerous solo exhibitions and included in international survey shows in the last three decades. His exhibition "We the People" (2011), at the Fabric Workshop and Museum, Philadelphia, coincided with a residency at the Museum. In 2011, he also had solo shows at Galleria Continua, San Gimignano, and "Sub Mirage Lignum" MASS MoCA, North Adams. He recently had his second solo exhibition at Lehmann Maupin, New York, in Spring 2012.

1
We the People
2011
Shoelaces
Dimensions variable
Courtesy of Lehmann Maupin

2, 4
Nu Colossus
2011
Mixed media
720 × 336 × 168"
(1829 × 853.5 × 426.5 cm)
Courtesy of Lehmann Maupin

3
Loisaidas LiquorsouL
2011
Mixed media
144 × 30 × 24"
(366 × 76 × 61 cm)
Courtesy of Lehmann Maupin

Nari Ward

The recent sculptural installations of Jamaican-born, Harlem-based artist Nari Ward focus on ideas of collectivity, community, poverty and consumption. An ambulance fills with belches of smoke (*Sick Smoke*, 2010) and walking canes prop up a drooping telescope (*Ambulascope*, 2010) in works that center on healthcare. While hundreds of hand dyed shoelaces wedged into the gallery wall spell out "We the People" (*We the People,* 2011) in a wall text mimicking the original copy of the United States Constitution—a work of symbolic collectivity. Alive to the fragility and fortitude of the powerless in the face of systemic injustices, Ward's work speaks of an America that is too often ignored. TM

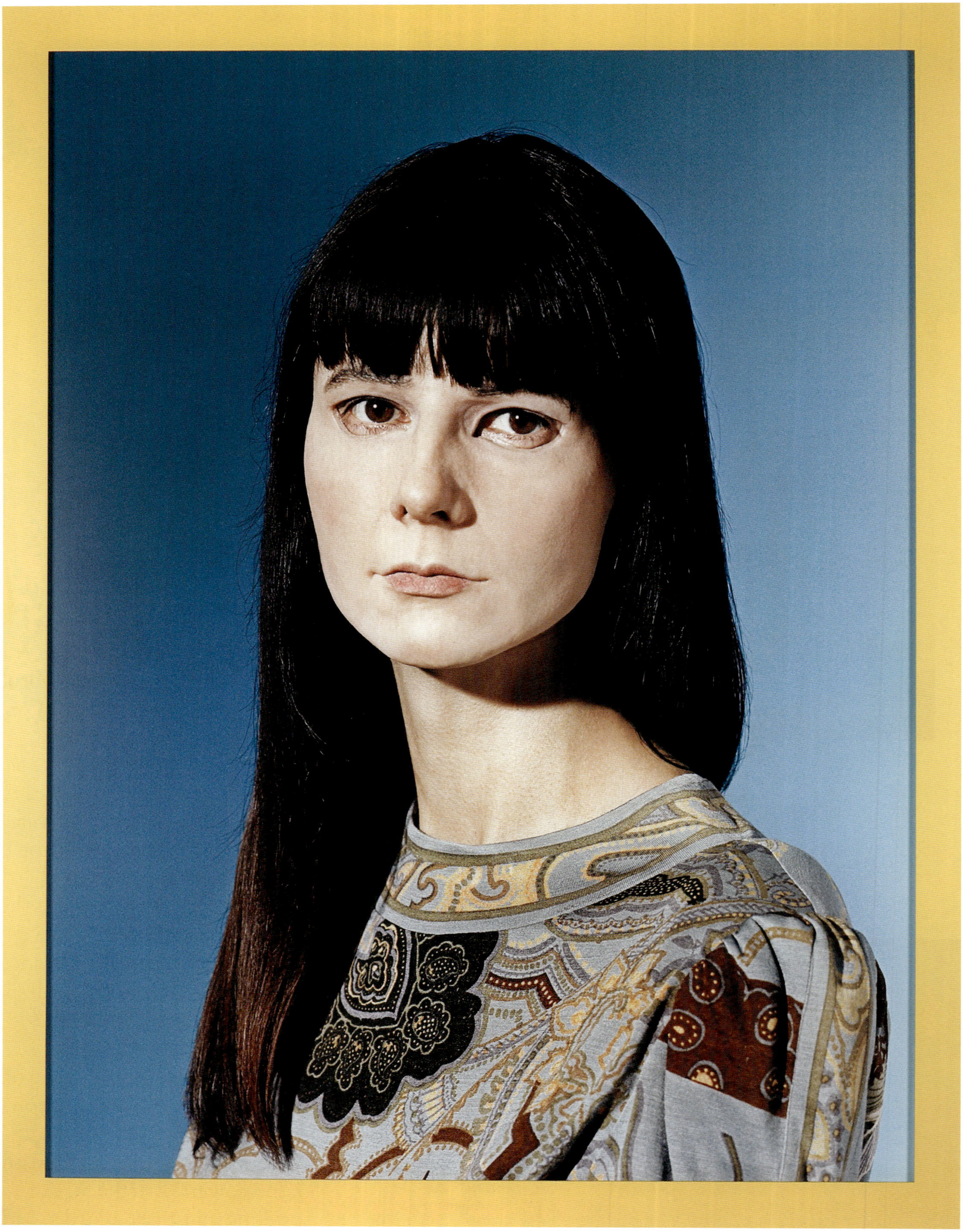

1

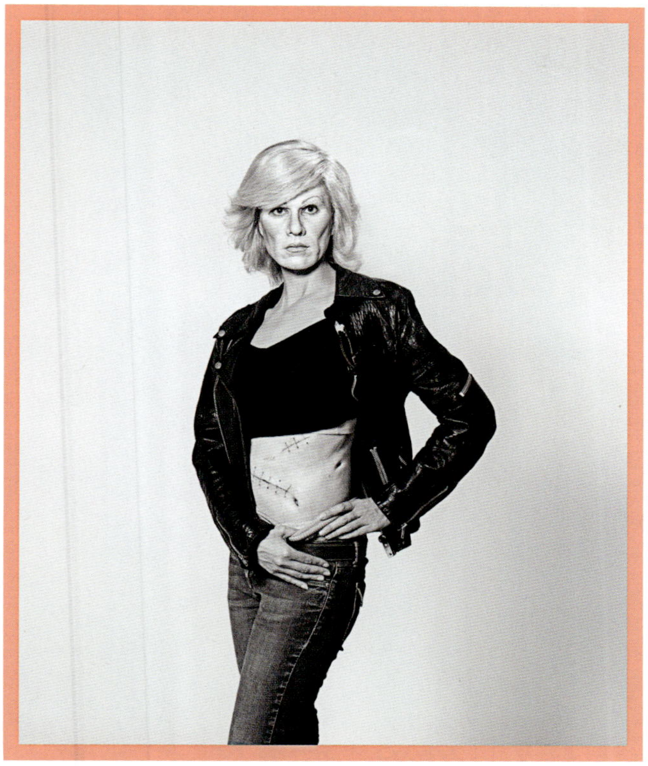

2

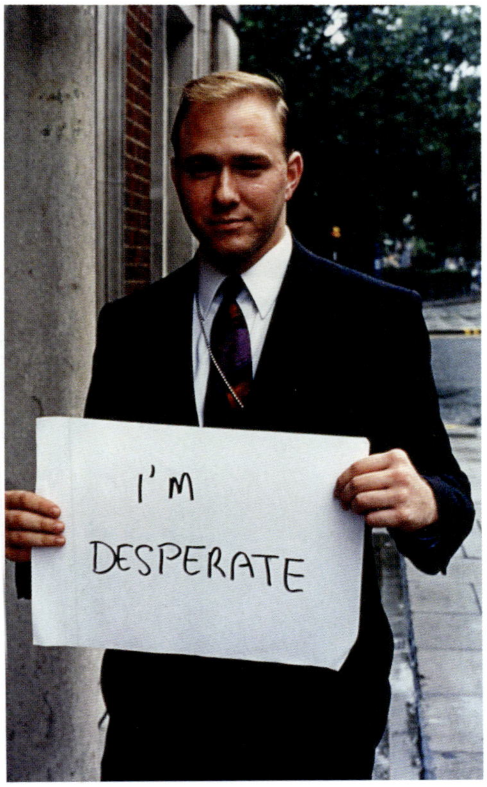

3

Shown by
Tanya Bonakdar
Gallery C6
Maureen Paley 334
Regen Projects B17

Biography
Born 1963
Lives in London

British artist Wearing has exhibited internationally since the early 1990s. In 2011, the Turner Prize-winning artist had the solo shows "People" at Tanya Bonakdar Gallery, New York, and "Confessions/Portraits, Vidéos," at Musée Rodin, Paris. She will have a solo show at Whitechapel Gallery, London, in 2012, which will then travel to Kunstsammlung Nordrhein-Westfalen, Dusseldorf, and Pinakothek der Moderne, Munich.

1
Self Portrait of Me Now in Mask
2011
C-type print
48⅞ × 38⅝"
(124 × 98 cm)
Courtesy of Maureen Paley

2
Me as Warhol in Drag with Scar
2011
Bromide print
61⅜ × 52⅜"
(156 × 133 cm)
Courtesy of Maureen Paley

3
Signs that say what you want them to say and not signs that say what someone else wants you to say, I'M DESPERATE
1992–93
C-type print
48 × 36¼"
(122 × 92 cm)
Courtesy of Maureen Paley

Gillian Wearing

"Confess all on video. Don't worry, you will be in disguise. Intrigued? Call Gillian." The text of the advertisement that Gillian Wearing placed in *Time Out London* in 1994—it later became the title of the work concerned, after masked respondents had unburdened themselves to her camera—reads like a *précis* of much of her video work. In contrast to the shameless choreography of emotional truth in current reality television, Wearing's subjects are not so much performing themselves as oscillating uncomfortably between their sham and authentic selves. The same ambiguity troubles the nine confessional participants in *Secrets and Lies* (2009) and the seven people Method-coached into over-sharing vignettes in the feature film *Self Made* (2010). BD

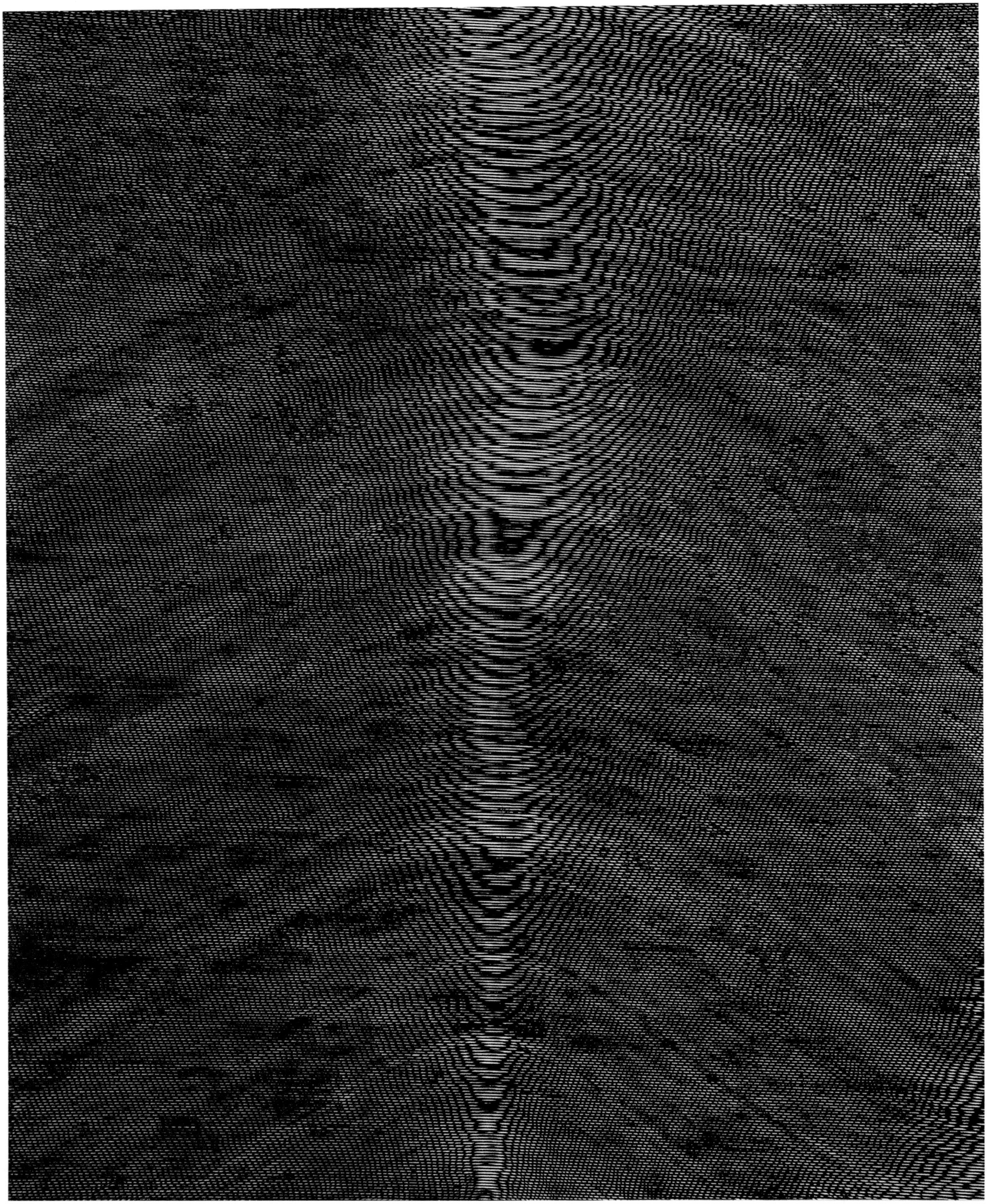

Garth Weiser

Shown by
Altman Siegel F5
Casey Kaplan A6

Biography
Born 1979
Lives in New York

In 2010, Weiser's exhibition at White Flag Projects, St. Louis, saw a dramatic shift in scale for the painter. His canvases were exhibited at Casey Kaplan, New York (2011), and included in the Prague Biennial in 2010. He also held solo exhibitions at Norma Mangione, Turin, and Altman Siegel Gallery, San Francisco, in 2011.

Gilgo
2011
Oil on canvas
100 × 82"
(254 × 208.5 cm)
Courtesy of Casey Kaplan

In Garth Weiser's recent paintings, low-key conversation between canvas and color is interrupted by gestural static. The surfaces of *Tahitian Moon* and *Nautilus* (both 2011) whirr like TV test patterns, their flat grounds activated through Weiser's use of masking tape and three-dimensional fabric paint laid over them. Earlier works such as *TV Keith* (2008) or the series "Nudes" (2009) show dead-flat grounds of bright, solid hues interrupted by parasitic emblems: circular color spectrums, large black dots, and lonely logos inspired by corporate design are assertive and pushy. What appears digital is painstakingly hand-crafted, as Weiser lays down his hard-edged graphics, or coaxes out the elusive color range of an oil slick from his paintings' surfaces. SNS

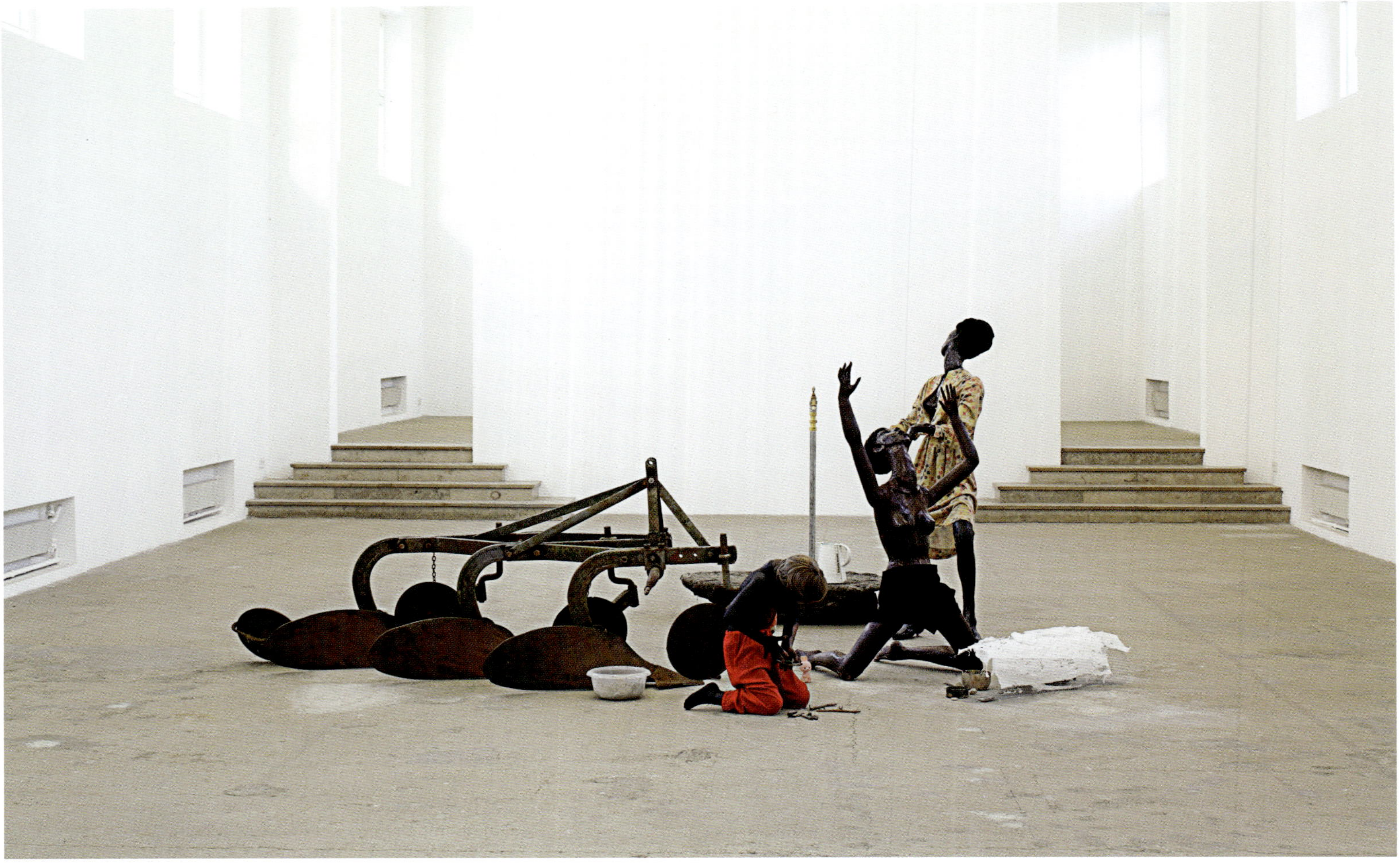

1

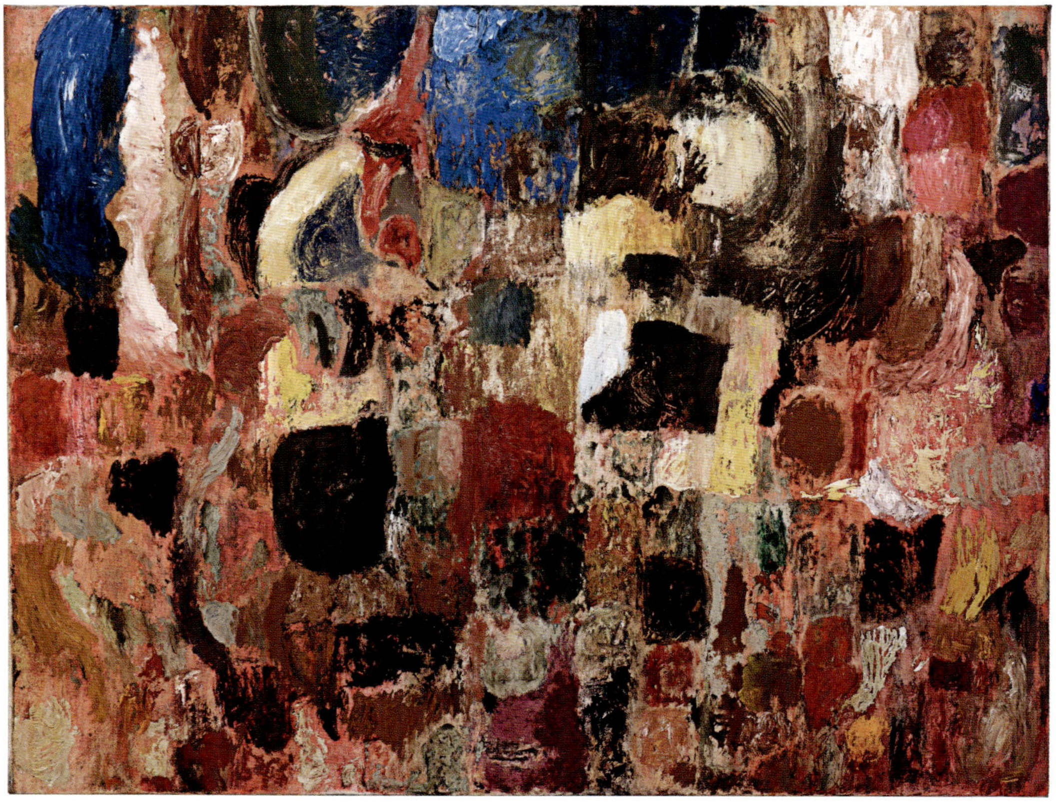

2

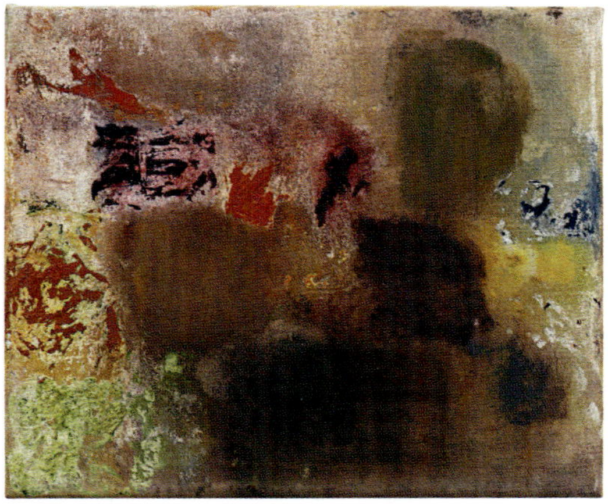

3

Shown by
The Modern Institute
C29

Biography
Born 1967
Lives in Glasgow

Glasgow-born Wilkes' sculptural installations and paintings have been the subject of solo exhibitions across Europe since the early 1990s. Early 2012 saw the exhibition "I Give You All My Money" at The Renaissance Society at the University of Chicago. In 2011 Gesellschaft Fur Aktuelle Kunst, Bremen, and Kunstverein, Munich held exhibitions of her work, and in the United States, Carnegie Museum of Art, Pittsburgh, and Aspen Art Museum, Aspen did the same.

1
No title
2011
Mixed media
Dimensions variable
Courtesy of The Modern Institute

2
Untitled
2011
Oil on canvas
78 × 53⅞"
(183 × 137 cm)
Courtesy of The Modern Institute

3
Untitled
2011
Oil on canvas
18⅛ × 15"
46 × 38 cm
Courtesy of Susan and Larry Marx

Cathy Wilkes

Having come to attention in the early 1990s, Glasgow-based Cathy Wilkes is now best known for her sculptural compositions comprising domestic objects—ladders, tables, TVs, ovens, toilets, strollers—which in recent years have frequently been populated by enigmatic female shop mannequins. Addressing personal experience as well as the problematic ways in which women and the female body are ideologically positioned by commodity culture, installations such as *We Are Pro Choice* (2007) can be encountered as psychological events held in suspense. Wilkes' broodingly delicate abstract paintings have been deployed as if brutal masks stuck on the faces of female mannequins, and latterly the focus of her 2011 exhibition at Aspen Art Museum. MA

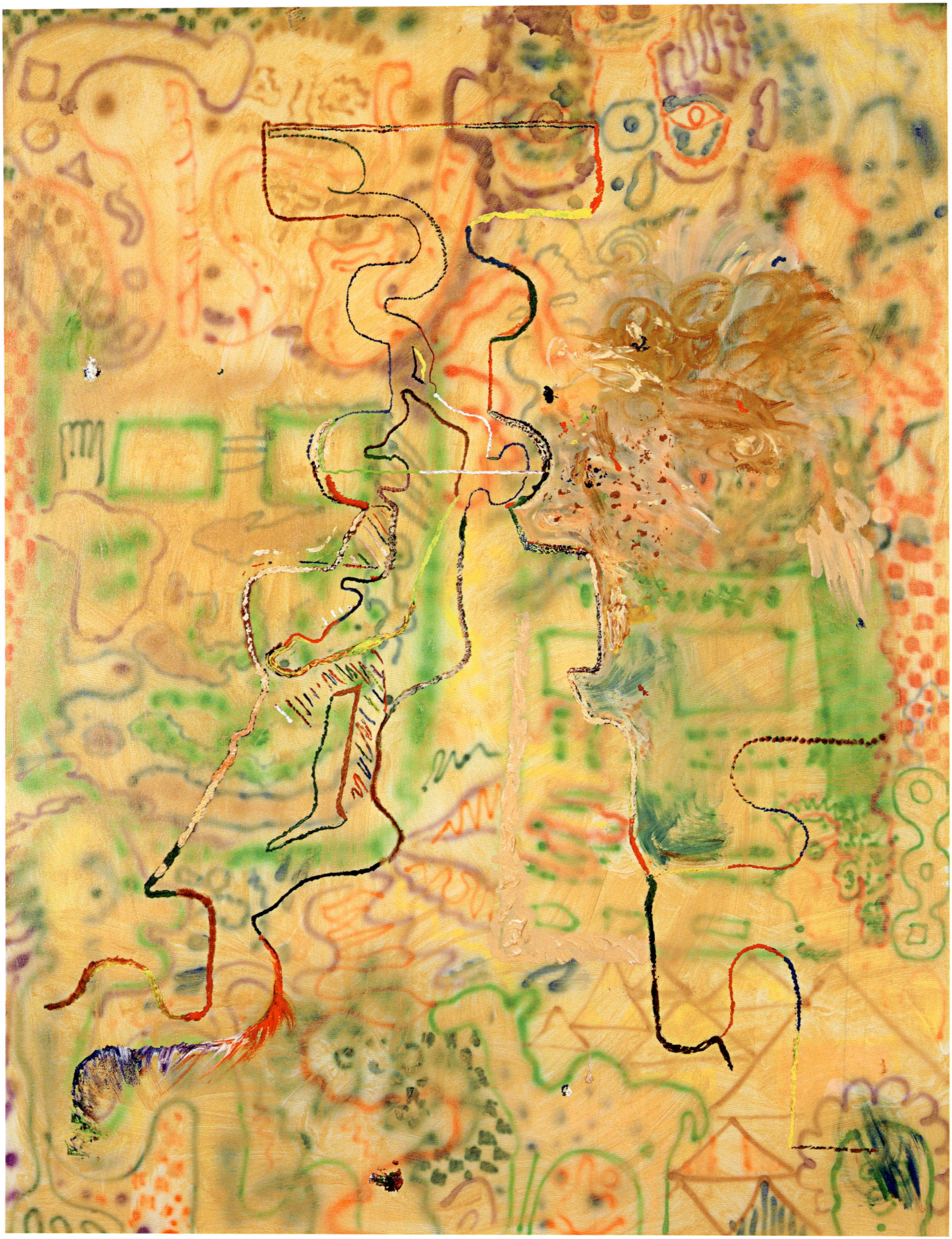

1

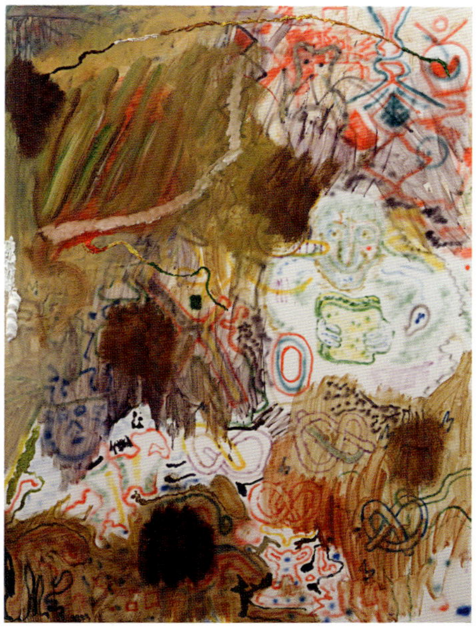

2

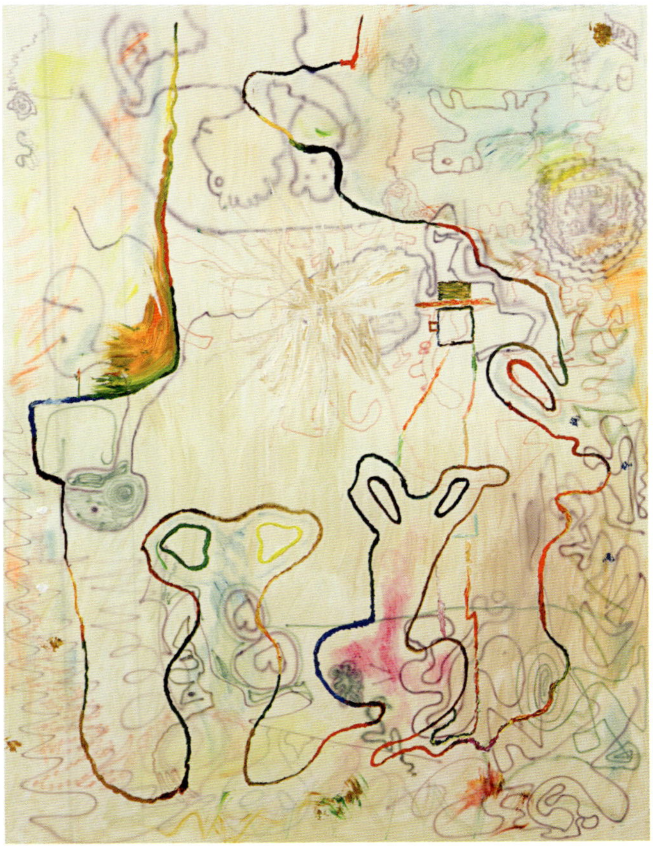

3

Shown by
Canada F30

Biography
Born 1978
Lives in Brooklyn

American painter Williams's large-scale abstract canvases contain subtle humorous narratives. A series of new works were the subject of the exhibition "Montgomery's Tubercles" (2011), at The Journal Gallery, Brooklyn. The same year he also had the exhibition "Straightforward as a Noodle" at CANADA, New York. Other solo shows include "Puzzle Painting" (2010), at LTD Gallery, Los Angeles, and "Uncle Big" (2009), at CANADA, New York.

1
Freddy
2011
Airbrush and oil on canvas
68⅛ × 52"
(173 × 132 cm)
Courtesy of Canada

2
Everything Bagel
2011
Airbrush and oil on canvas
36¾ × 20½"
(68 × 52 cm)
Courtesy of Canada

3
The Man Who Sees Everything (Vilhelm Lundstrom)
2011
Airbrush and oil on canvas
72 × 56¼"
(183 × 143 cm)
Courtesy of Canada

Focus
Michael Williams

Michael Williams' paintings may feature any of the following: a cat traversing a ping-pong table (*Peanut*, 2009), a lobster and an oyster working at a desktop computer (*Surf 'n Turf 2*, 2009)—or, more recently, disembodied heads and other body party in his "Noodle" series (2011). These scenes are humorous and have the strange lucidity of a hallucinogenic trip, located where Pointillism meets pixilation. The work makes reference to Post-Impressionism and Magic Realism, and shares an affinity with an artist like Fred Tomaselli, but Williams' accumulation of detail is looser, more casual and deliberately shambolic; the brushwork itself is eccentric and inconsistent, tipping from thin washes to thick excess. KK

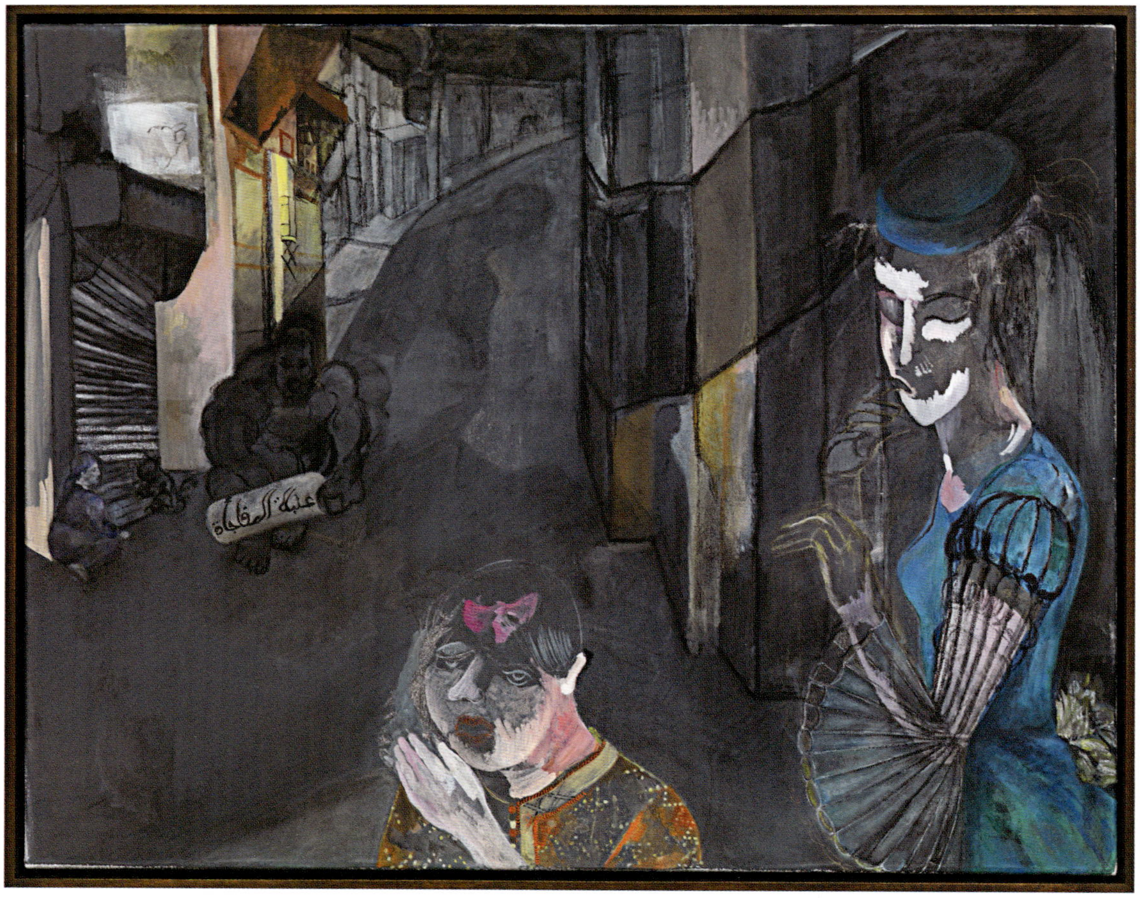

1

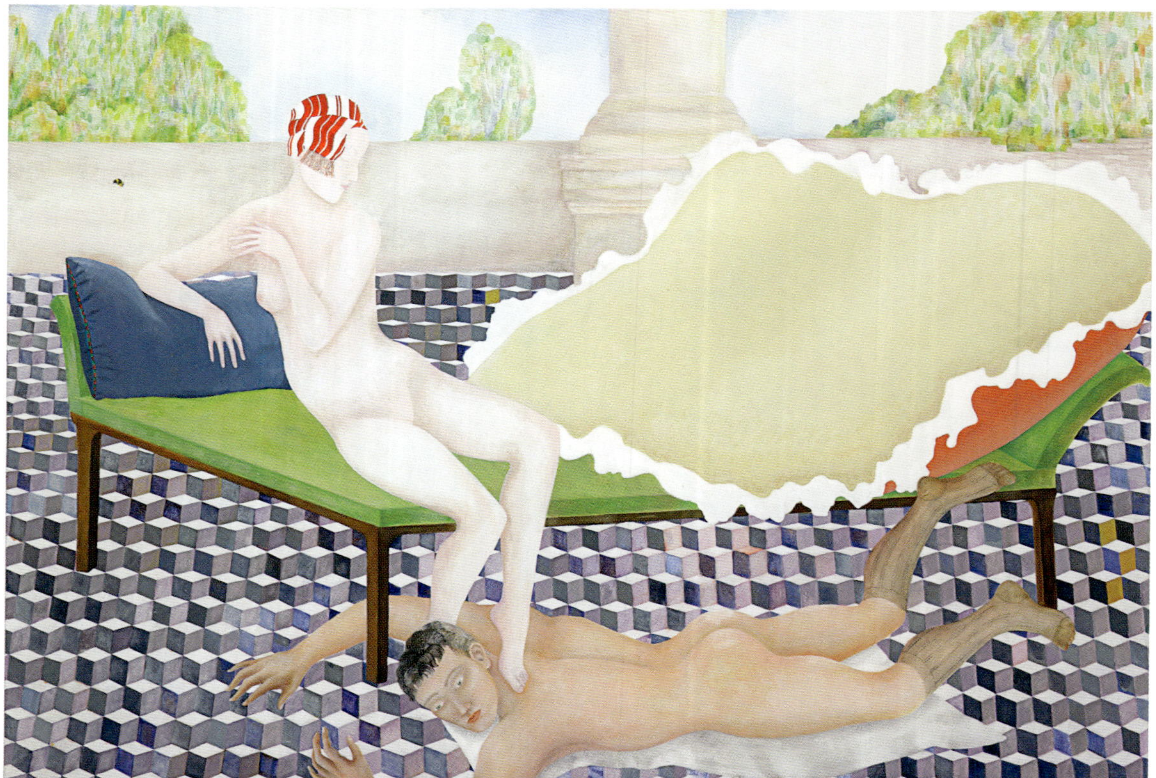

2

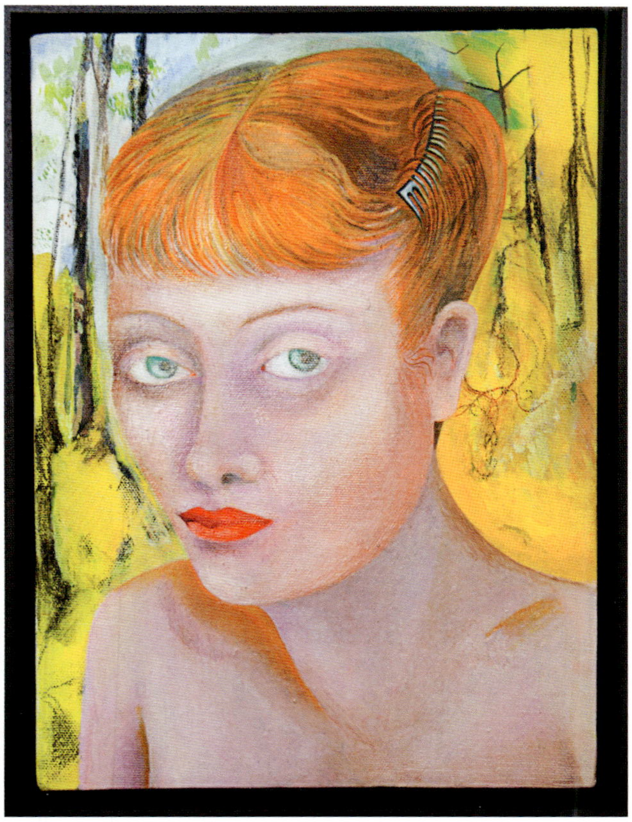

3

Shown by
Galerie Buchholz B35
Greene Naftali C44
Galerie Neu C49

Biography
Born 1968
Lives in Marrakech

German painter Wulff recently held the solo exhibitions "Wanwizzi" (2010), at Greene Naftali Gallery, New York, and "Allô allô mein Hitlir, you na3se" (2010), at Galerie Buchholz, Cologne. She was also included in the group show "Germany Is Your America" (2011) at Broadway 1602, New York. In 2012 the San Francisco Museum of Modern Art will hold a solo exhibition of her delicate, figurative works.

1
Untitled
2011
Oil on canvas
20⅜ × 31½"
(62 × 80 cm)
Courtesy of Galerie Neu

2
Die Verbindung
2008
Oil on canvas
48 × 68⅞"
(122 × 175 cm)
Courtesy of Galerie Neu

3
Untitled
2011
Oil and charcoal on canvas
12 × 9"
(30.5 × 23 cm)
Courtesy of Galerie Neu

Katharina Wulff

Katharina Wulff's small-scale paintings nod to Surrealist and Symbolist traditions but feel distinctly contemporary. Rich in atmospherics and mystery, they feature women in poses of inarticulate discontent. Sometimes these women are paired with men, who are at once ineffectual and potentially menacing. In *Untitled* (2010), a female figure in a blue party dress stands in front of a naked man, whose limbs have been truncated and whose head is blackened; he, in turn, stands before a wall of dismembered heads and masks. There is both humor and unease in Wulff's paintings, this twining of contradictory emotions is rarely explicit but is occasionally brought to the fore, as in a small drawing (*Untitled,* 2010) that depicts the gaping jaw of a snake. KK

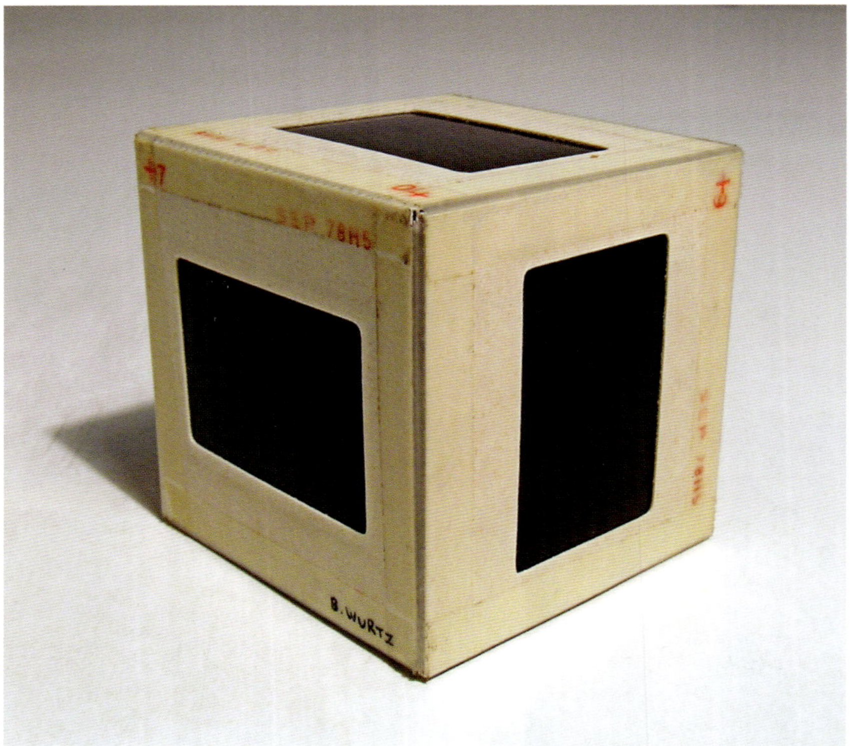
B.WURTZ

B. Wurtz

Shown by
Galerija Gregor Podnar A4

Biography
Born 1948
Lives in New York

American sculptor Wurtz has been exhibiting his delicate, considered works since the 1970s. His solo show at Metro Pictures, New York in summer 2011 surveyed his work from 1970–2011. In 2010 he had a solo show at the Apartment, Vancouver. Recent group shows include "Pandora's Box" (2011) at the Museum of Contemporary Art, Chicago; at "Bridgehampton Biennia" (2011) Martos Gallery, New York; and "Underemployed" (2011) at Zürcher Studio, New York.

Slide Cube (from series)
1979
35 mm slides
2 × 2 × 2"
(5 × 5 × 5 cm)
Courtesy of Galerija Gregor Podnar

For more than 40 years, B. Wurtz has been creating delicate assemblages from found objects. But he has said that, rather than making sculptures or installations, "It would be more accurate to say that I rearrange objects that already exist." Wurtz' homespun way with the throwaway—such as plastic bags, coat-hangers, buttons, and shoelaces—is obvious in early works such as *Unpleasant Private Thoughts* and *Secret Words* (1973), while his "Pan Paintings" (1990–91) were created by doing no more than painting the underside of disposable baking dishes. Wurtz describes his practice as representative of "my feeling that looking at the universe begins with really seeing the everyday objects right in front of one's nose." ST

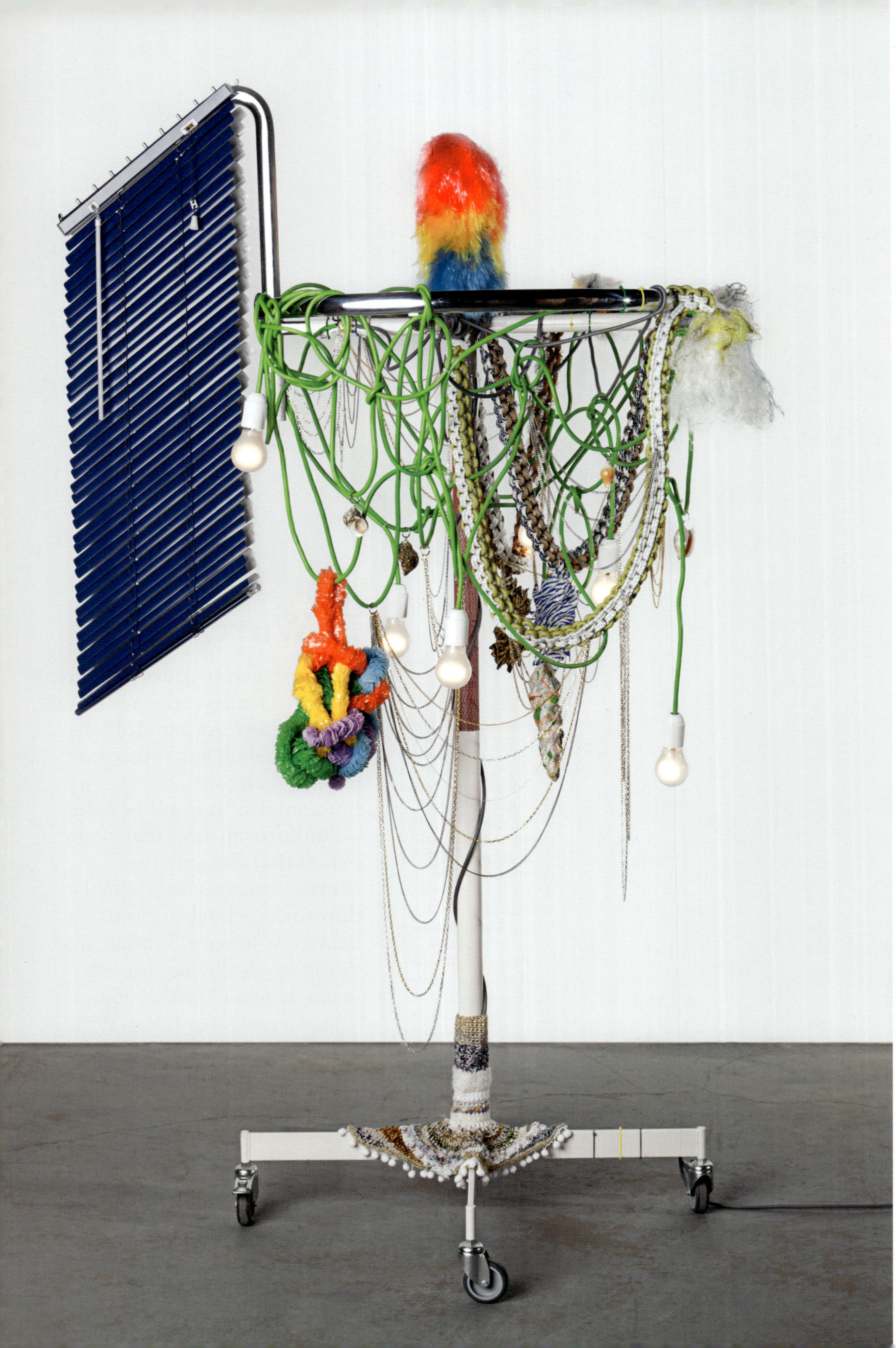

Shown by
Galerie Chantal Crousel B28
Greene Naftali C44
Kukje Gallery B36

Biography
Born 1971
Lives in Berlin

Yang's sculptural installations have gained her significant attention in recent years. Her materials, which include window blinds and other domestic objects, evoke the familiar, yet immerse the viewer in surreal environments. In 2011, she had the solo exhibitions "The Art and Technique of Folding the Land" at Aspen Art Museum, and "Escaping Things and Words" with artist Rivane Neuenschwander at Kunsthalle Lingen. In 2009 she represented South Korea with the exhibition "Condensation" at the 53rd Venice Biennale.

Nosy Clown—Copper Carbonate
2011
Mixed media
82¾ × 49¼ × 43¼"
(210 × 125 × 110 cm)
Courtesy of Kukje Gallery

Haegue Yang

For Haegue Yang an art work is at once a formal proposition, a politicized object that inhabits a busy market place, and the personal product of an emotionally motivated individual. Her installations and videos are of an amphibious nature, in that they can operate in the public realm of encounter and the private domain of associative thoughts and sentiments. A recent series, "Warrior Believer Lover" (2010), comprising 33 upright clothes racks embellished with colorful schmutter and given titles like *Medicine Man–Hairy Noble*, becomes an anthropology of human internal workings, laying out the bizarre atmospherics produced by the deluge of banal and prized objects we keep about us in day-to-day life. SOR

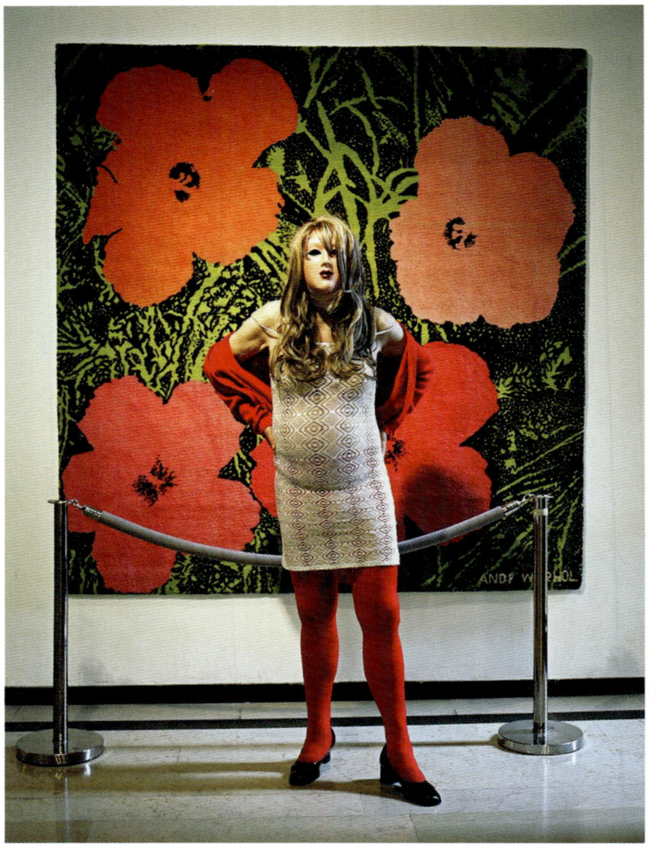

2

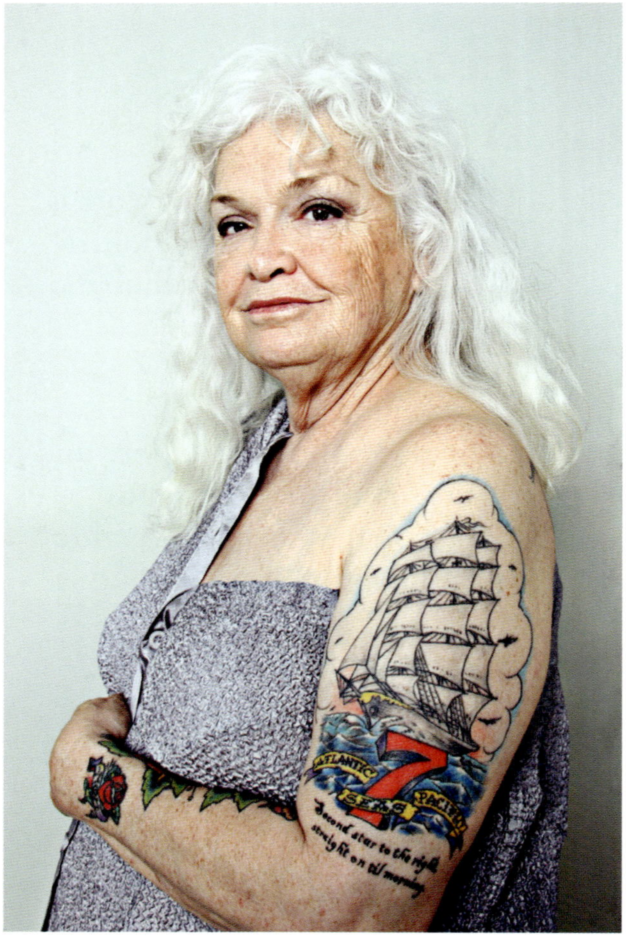

1

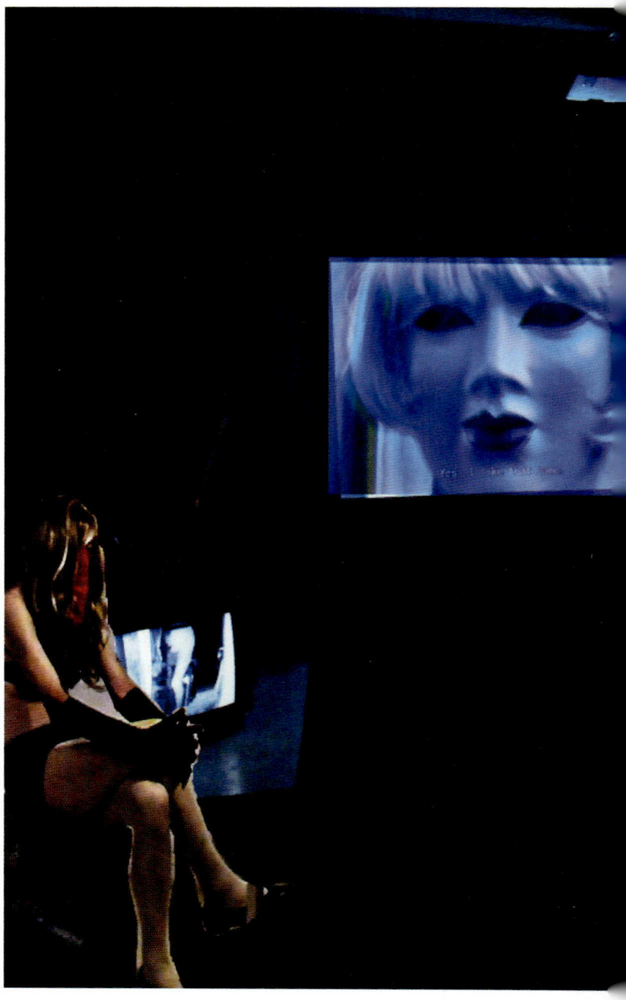

3

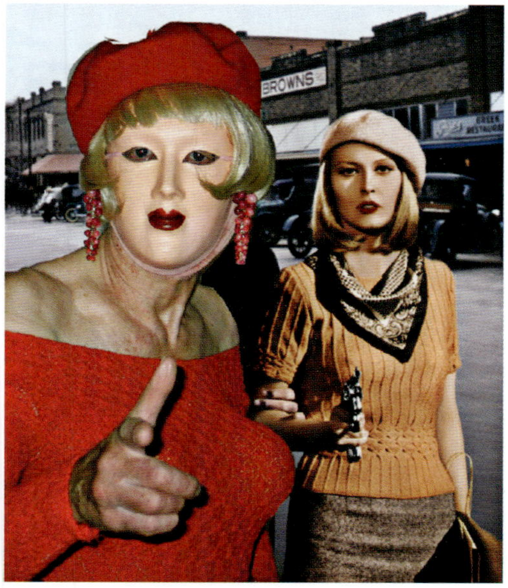

4

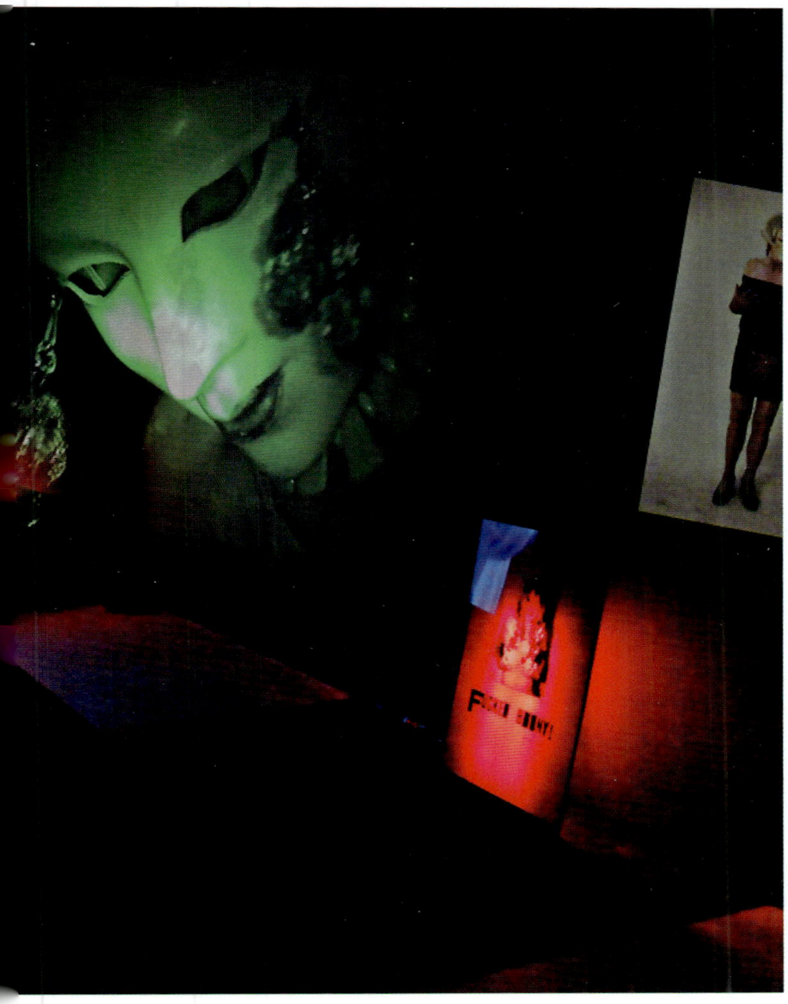

Shown by
Sommer
Contemporary Art
C37

Biography
Born 1972
Lives in Brooklyn

Israel-born Yefman has engaged in a personal dialogue with audiences through her videos and photographs in recent years. In spring 2012, she had a solo show at Sommer Contemporary Art, Tel Aviv and in 2011 "Marath a Bouke (Your Father's Wife) project #4" at Derek Eller Gallery, New York. Other solo shows include "Short Stories: Time Kills" (2011), SculptureCenter, Long Island City, and "Let it Bleed" (2010), at Participant Inc., New York.

1
Shanghai Kate
2009
C-type print
92⅞ × 21⅝"
(76 × 55 cm)
Courtesy of Sommer Contemporary Art

2
Martha B with Andy W Flowers
2011
Lambda C-type print
39¾ × 29⅞"
(101 × 76 cm)
Courtesy of Sommer Contemporary Art

3
Marath a Bouke, Project #4
2011
Mixed media
Dimensions variable
Courtesy of Sommer Contemporary Art

4
Martha & Bonny
2002
Lambda C-type print
16⅞ × 13'
(43 × 33 cm)
Courtesy of Sommer Contemporary Art

Rona Yefman

In the video *Pippi Longstocking, The Strongest Girl in the World* (2006), a perky, pig-tailed protagonist tries to pull apart the Israeli West Bank Barier while women on the street cheer her on. There's no way Pippi will succeed, but perhaps that doesn't matter. "I seek extreme situations and people that embody possibilities of freedom," says Yefman, suggesting that possibility is a worthwhile mode in which to live a life. The series "My Brother and I" (1996–2009) documents her youth with her brother Gil, as he transitioned to a woman and then back to a man. If Gil's body becomes a site of radical, changing possibility lived on individual terms, Yefman's larger documentary archive provides a crucial means for thinking on a larger scale. SNS

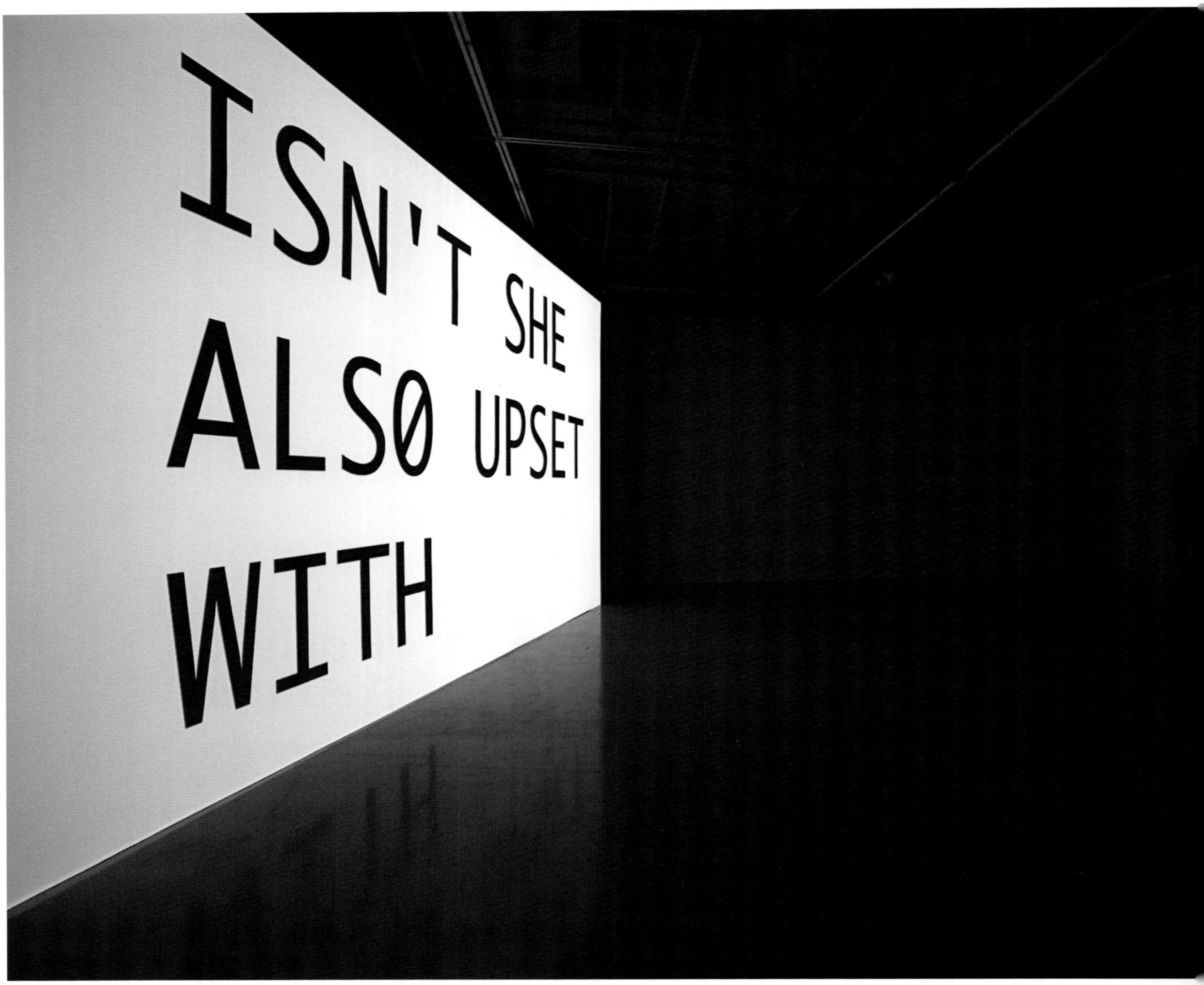
ISN'T SHE
ALSØ UPSET
WITH

1

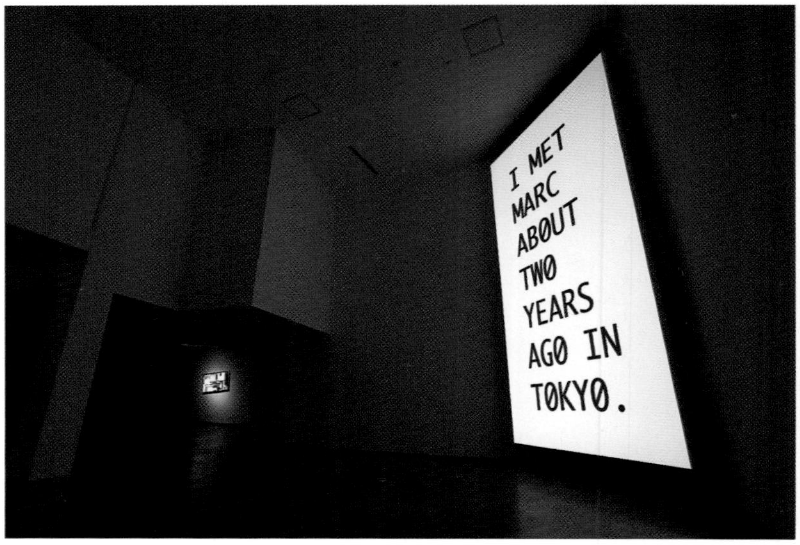
I MET
MARC
ABØUT
TWØ
YEARS
AGØ IN
TØKYØ.

2

Young-Hae Chang Heavy Industries

Young-Hae Chang Heavy Industries' text-based works are rendered in Monaco font, uniformly resonating on flat-screen monitors and in projections—expanding from the Internet, where they often originate, in flashing textual narratives. *HE WAS ACTING CRAZY AND BEGGING ME TO STAY WITH HIM* (2010) sees a text-based work playing out on a computer screen in the corner of a bedroom, the scene itself captured on a flat-screen which hangs on the gallery wall at a 45-degree angle. Other works such as *THE BULLET IS STILL IN MY LEFT WRIST* (2010) are projected large-scale in dark galleries. Their white glow and flashing text flicker in a sensory overload reminiscent of corporate advertising void of branding or capitalist message. SC

Shown by
GALLERY HYUNDAI C20

Biography
Lives in Seoul

Young-Hae Chang Heavy Industries is a collaboration between web artists Young-Hae Chang and Marc Voge. In 2011 their solo exhibition "THERE ARE NO PROBLEM IN ART" at Audain Gallery, Vancouver, featured large-scale narrative text works. "Down in Fukuoka with the Belarusian Blues" at GALLERY HYUNDAI, Seoul, took place in 2010. Recent group shows include "TBA:11" (2011) at Portland Institute for Contemporary Art and "Bienal do Mercosul" (2011), Porto Alegre.

1
THE BULLET IS STILL IN MY LEFT WRIST
2010
HD QuickTime movie, original track, and music soundtrack
2 min. 26 sec.
Courtesy of GALLERY HYUNDAI

2
WEDNESDAY NIGHT HE GOT DRUNK
2010
HD QuickTime movie, original text, and music soundtrack
7 min. 11 sec.
Courtesy of GALLERY HYUNDAI

3
DOWN IN FUKUOKA WITH THE BELARUSIAN BLUES
2010
HD QuickTime movie, original text
6 min. 4 sec.
Courtesy of GALLERY HYUNDAI

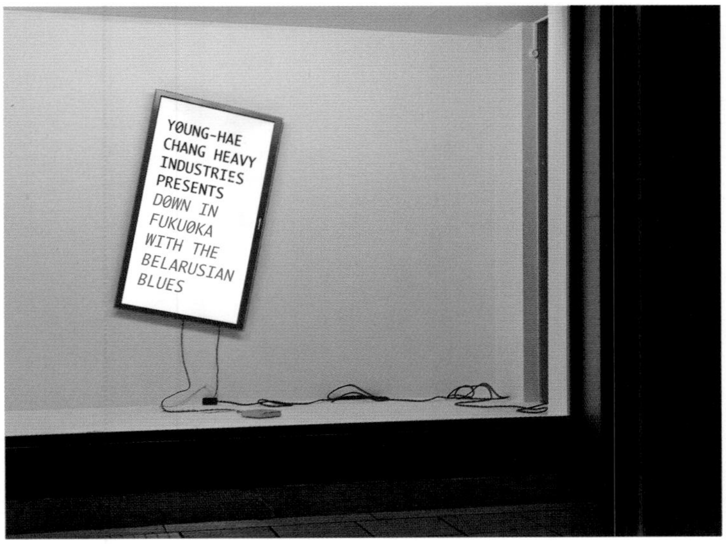

3

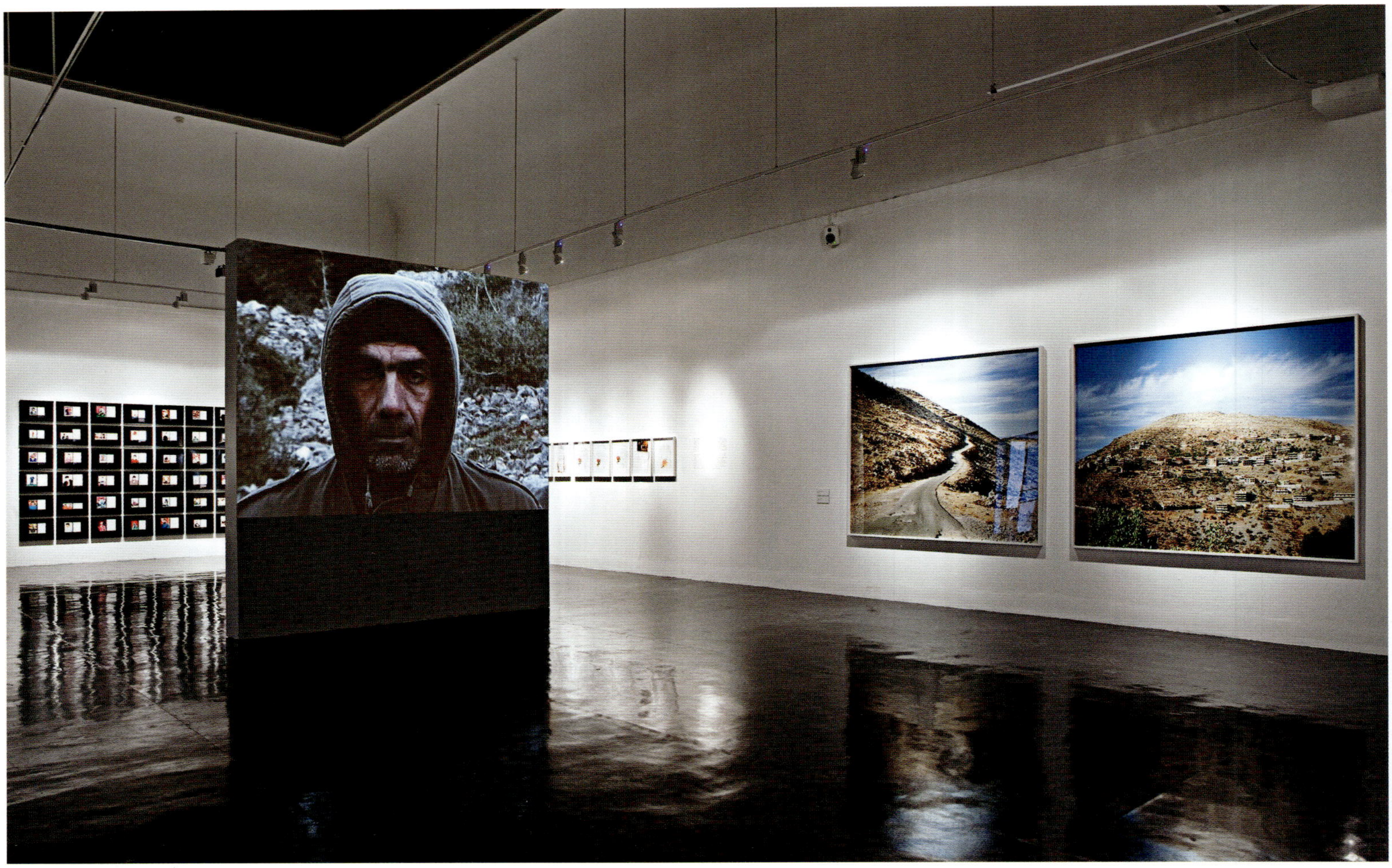

1

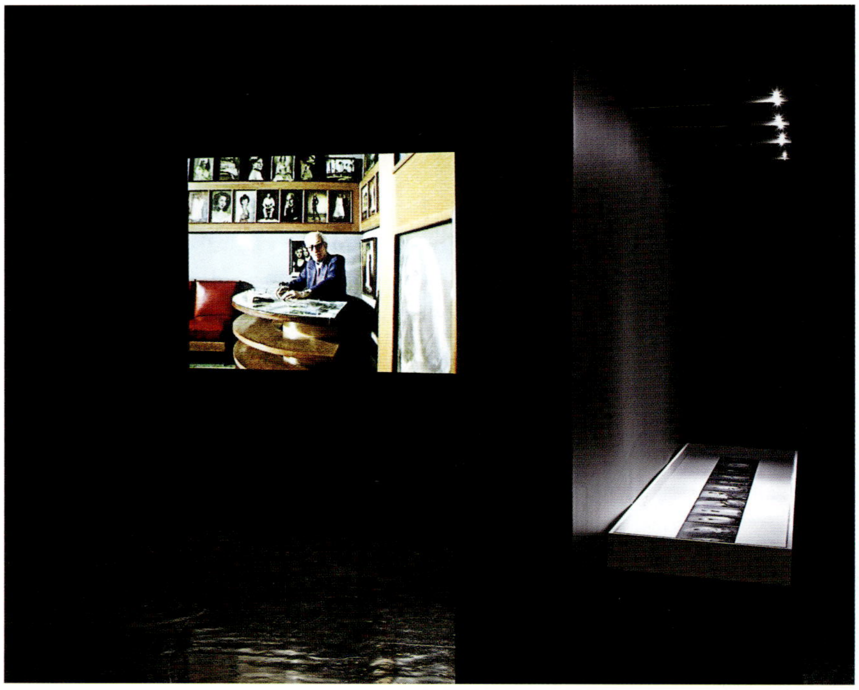

2

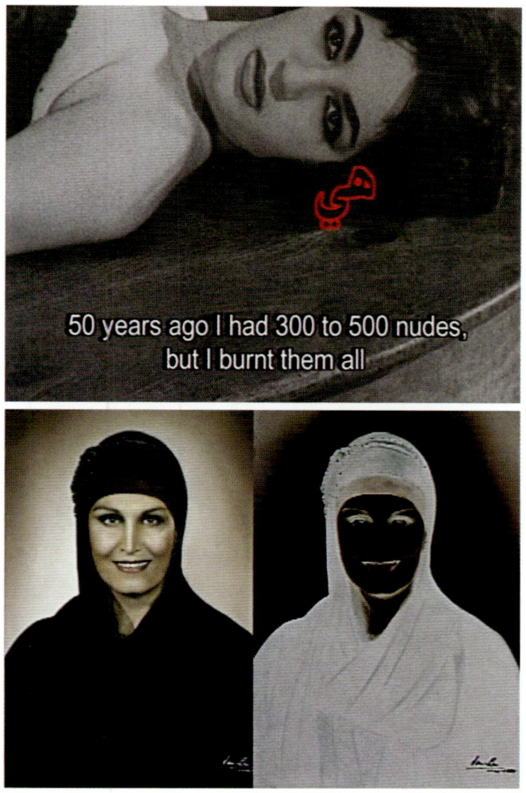

3

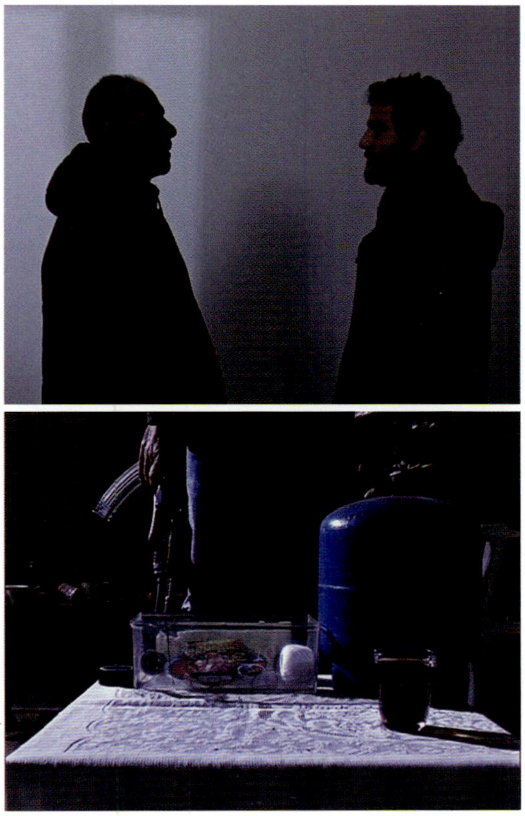

4

Shown by
Sfeir-Semler A8

Biography
Born 1966
Lives in Beirut

Zaatari's politically charged works were the subject of the recent solo exhibitions "Composition for Two Wings" (2011), at Kunsternes Hus, Oslo; "The Uneasy Subject" (2011), at Museo del Arte Contemporáneo de Castilla y León, Spain; and "This Day" (2011) at Moderna Galerija Ljubljana. He participated in Untitled (12th Istanbul Biennial, 2011) and was recipient of DAAD Artist-in-Berlin Program residency the same year. His work is part of many significant collections including the Museum of Modern Art, New York, Centre Georges Pompidou, Paris, and Tate Modern, London.

1
Composition for Two Wings
2011
Exhibition view, Kunsternes Hus, Oslo
Courtesy of Sfeir-Semler

2
Composition for Two Wings
2011
Exhibition view, Kunsternes Hus, Oslo
Courtesy of Sfeir-Semler

3
Her and Him Van Leo
2001
Video
32 min
Courtesy of Sfeir-Semler

4
Nature Morte
2008
Video
11 min
Courtesy of Sfeir-Semler

Akram Zaatari

Operating in a fluid role that shifts between artist, documentary maker, researcher, and film maker, Akram Zaatari's videos, photographs, and installations often focus on the underlying narratives of Lebanon's people, documenting the social and sexual politics of private and public life in a country at war. In 1997, he co-founded the Arab Image Foundation in Beirut, an archive dedicated to the preservation and study of Arab photography. His recent "Body Builders" series (2011) consists of photographs printed from damaged negatives taken in 1948, while the video *Tomorrow Everything Will Be Alright* (2010) captures an online discussion between two former lovers as it is typed up on an outmoded typewriter. Zaatari traverses history and technology to reframe the past, giving new meaning to our contemporary concerns. ST

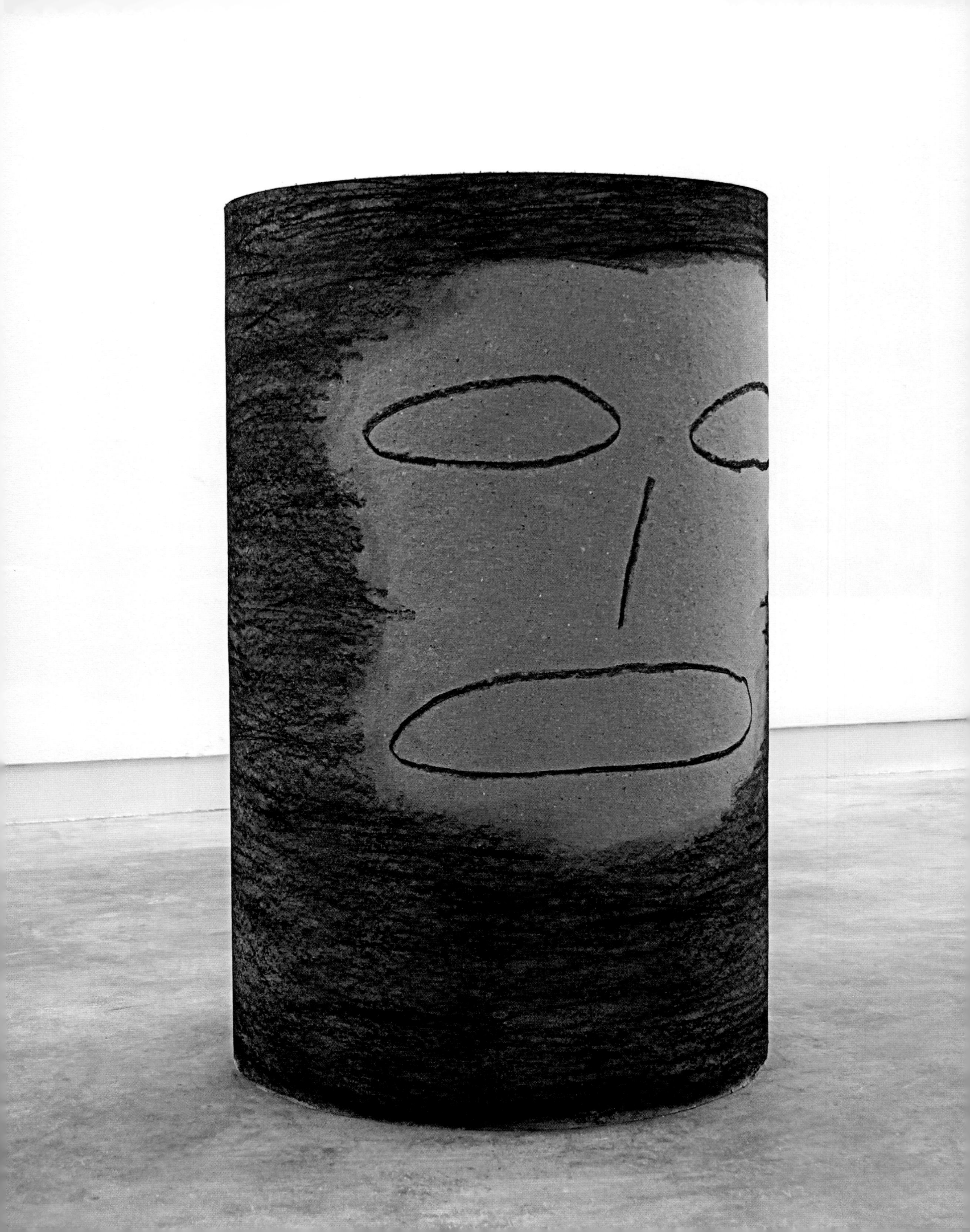

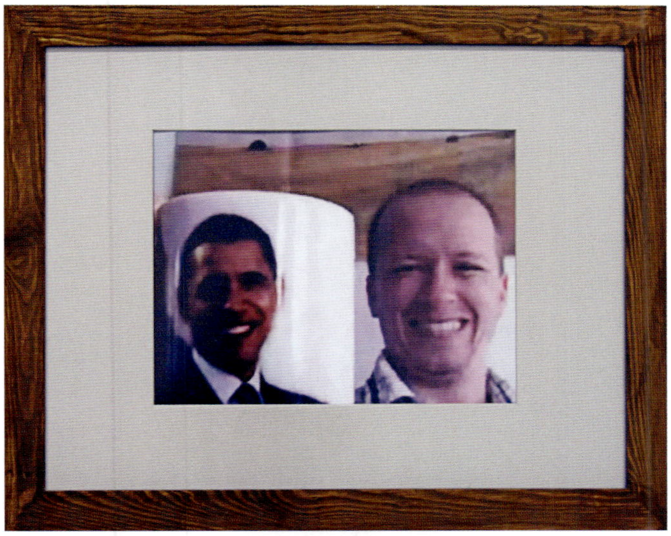

2

Shown by
Leto Gallery F12

Biography
Born 1981
Lives in Poznan

Zamojski's curious assemblages were the subject of the solo shows "Monumental Statues" at KIM?, Riga, and "Me, Myself and I" at Leto Gallery, Warsaw, in 2011. In recent years he has exhibited extensively in Poland and the United States, including the solo exhibition "I see things" (2010) at Cleopatra's, New York. Recent group shows include "Makeshift" at Municipal Gallery Arsenal, Poznan, and "Views" (2011), at Zacheta National Gallery of Art, Warsaw (2011). He is co-founder of Starter Gallery, Poznan (2005–2010) and runs the publishing house MORAVA.

1
Human Tree
2011
Pencil drawing on cardboard
39⅜ × 27¾ × 27¾"
(100 × 63 × 63 cm)
Courtesy of Leto Gallery

2
Self-Portrait (movin' presidential like Barack Obama)
2010–11
Digital photograph, cardboard, and wooden frame
24⅜ × 31⅛"
(62 × 79 cm)
Courtesy of Leto Gallery

Focus
Honza Zamojski

A multiplicity of materials, forms, and means of presentation and distribution informs Honza Zamojski's playful, identity-tasking practice, which variously finds him working as an artist, curator, or publisher. His 2011 book-ridden exhibition "Rhymes Like Dimes." at the Zachęta National Gallery of Art, Warsaw, takes its title from an MF Doom rap. The central book's 36 chambers (shades of Wu-Tang Clan) offer an elliptical meditation on language as self-portrait, aligning both hip-hop history and the artist's Czech identity. Sculptural works likewise turn a mirror on the artist: see *Self-Portrait* (2010), in which a tall cardboard tube sits on a found image like a pedestal, while a cactus emerges from the top like strange plumage—a decidedly prickly homage to the self. QL

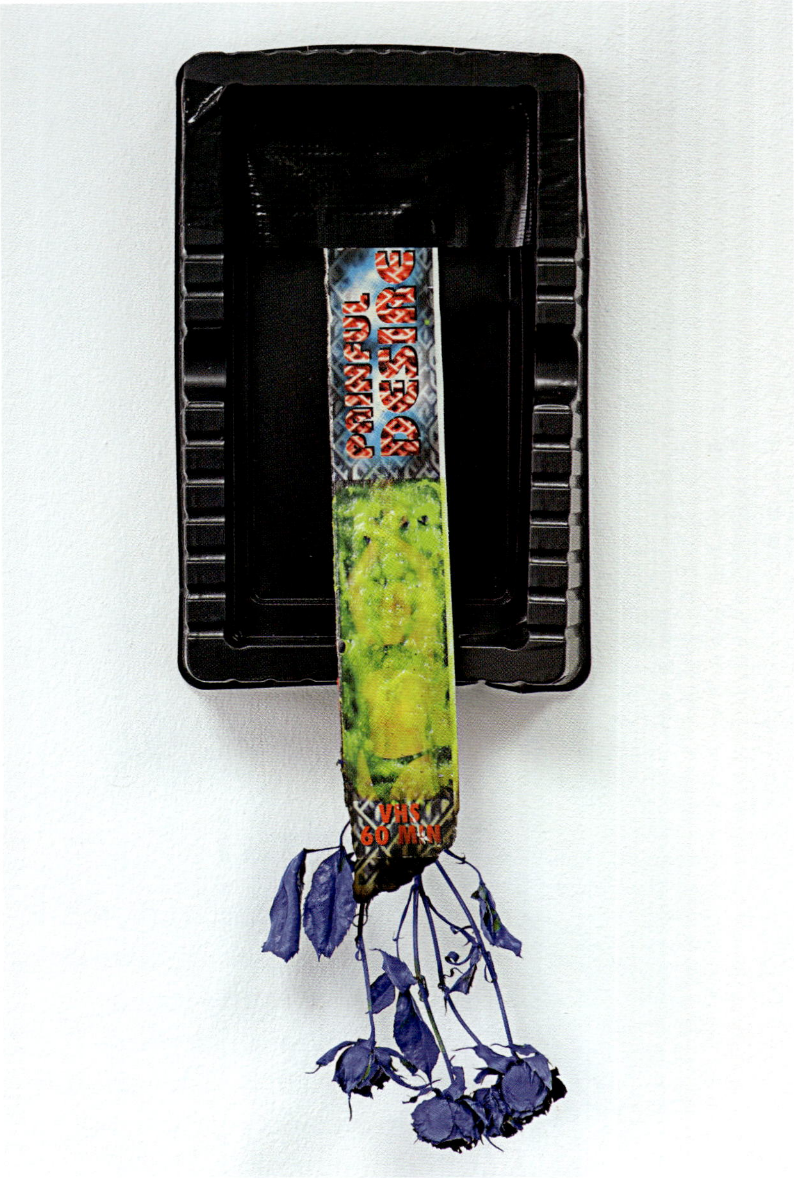

1

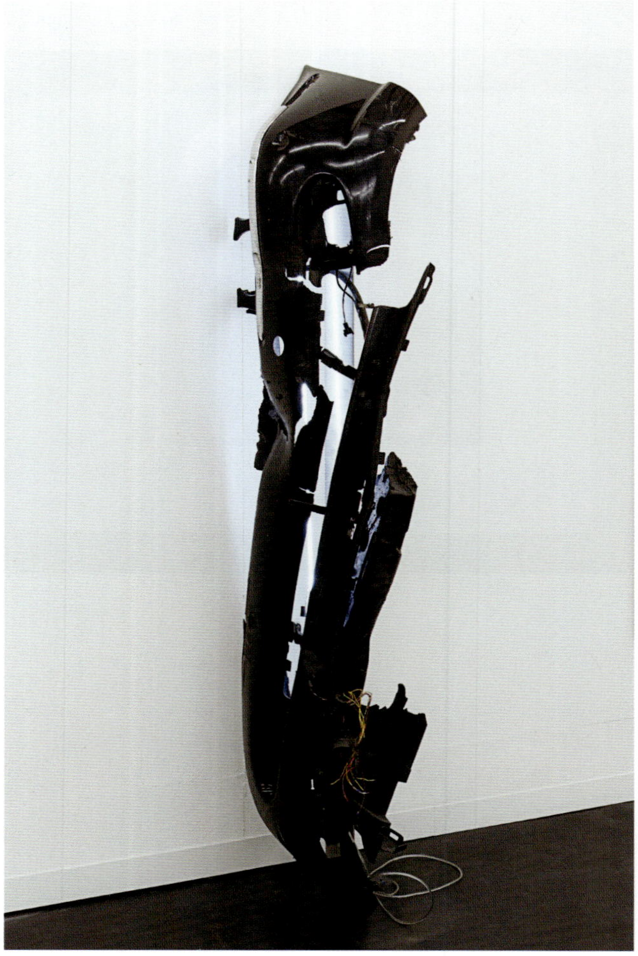

2

Shown by
Mary Mary F3
Micky Schubert F8

Biography
Born 1983
Lives in Berlin

German sculptor Zentz Zlomovitz has exhibited widely in Europe in the last decade. In 2011, he had a self-titled solo show at Mary Mary, Glasgow, and in 2010 a self-titled solo show at Karma International, Zurich, and "Flesh to flesh" at Galerie Micky Schubert, Berlin. He has participated in numerous group shows including "Bigminis" (2010), at CAPC, Bordeaux; "Out of Joint" (2010) at Galerie Kamm, Berlin; and "The Berlin Box" (2010) at CCA Andratx, Mallorca.

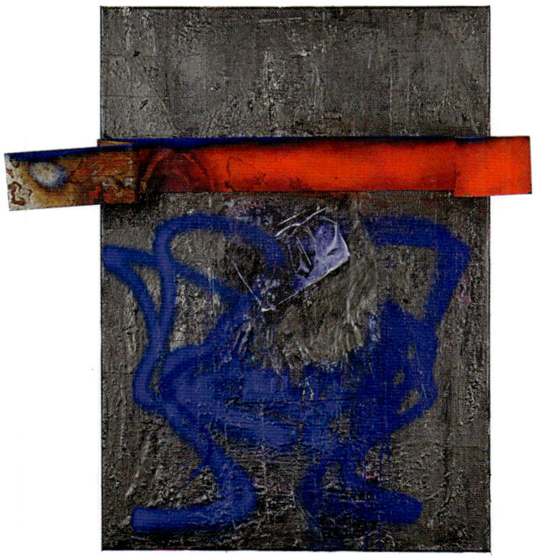

3

1
Pleasure
2011
Mixed media
16⅛ × 6 × 2"
(41 × 15 × 5 cm)
Courtesy of Mary Mary

2
Sotsass Death
2011
Plastic bumper, fluorescent tube, and stainless steel
78¾ × 15¾ × 23⅝"
(200 × 40 × 60 cm)
Courtesy of Galerie Micky Schubert

3
Asylum
2011
Metal, spraypaint, acrylic paint, epoxy, and inkjet print on canvas
27½ × 24⅞ × 17⅜"
(70 × 63 × 19 cm)
Courtesy of Mary Mary

4
Untitled
2010
Metal and spraypaint
74⅞ × 27½"
(190 × 70 cm)
Courtesy of Mary Mary

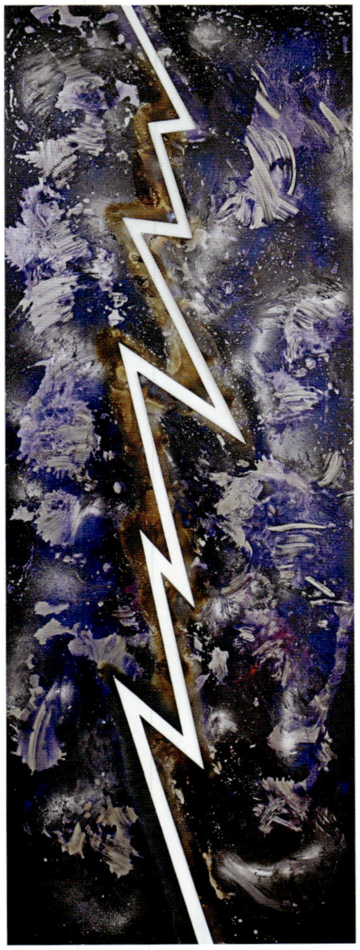

4

Focus
Maximilian Zentz Zlomovitz

In the 1980s, machines, although perhaps capable of turning against humanity, were still perceived as an extension of the human form's natural capacities. As a result, the cinematic imagination adhered to a post-apocalyptic aesthetic that was more mechanical than nano, more psychic than biochemical. Maximilian Zentz Zlomovitz revivifies these spooked relationships in sculptural installations such as *Relaxx* (2008), where everyday objects set up narratives of recent abandonment. Materials that sit uncomfortably with the body, such as brushed steel and Styrofoam, generate atmospheres in the installation *Flesh to Flesh* (2010), suggesting hidden spaces and unmentionable deeds in the underbelly of industrial urban culture. SOR

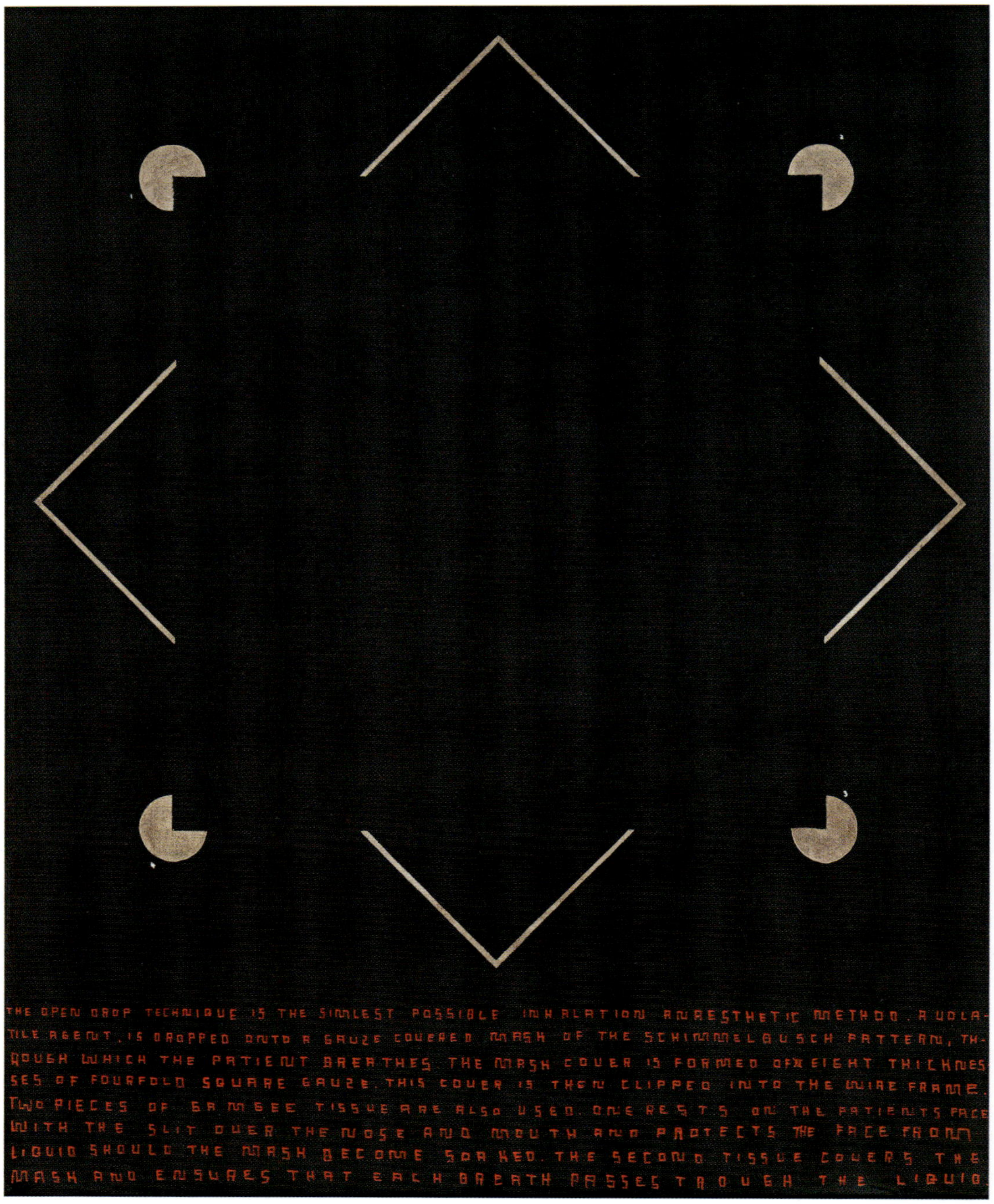
THE OPEN DROP TECHNIQUE IS THE SIMLEST POSSIBLE INHALATION ANAESTHETIC METHOD. A VOLA-
TILE AGENT, IS DROPPED ONTO A GAUZE COVERED MASK OF THE SCHIMMELBUSCH PATTERN, TH-
ROUGH WHICH THE PATIENT BREATHES THE MASK COVER IS FORMED OF EIGHT THICKNES-
SES OF FOURFOLD SQUARE GAUZE. THIS COVER IS THEN CLIPPED INTO THE WIRE FRAME.
TWO PIECES OF GAMGEE TISSUE ARE ALSO USED. ONE RESTS ON THE PATIENTS FACE
WITH THE SLIT OVER THE NOSE AND MOUTH AND PROTECTS THE FACE FROM
LIQUID SHOULD THE MASK BECOME SOAKED. THE SECOND TISSUE COVERS THE
MASK AND ENSURES THAT EACH BREATH PASSES TROUGH THE LIQUID.

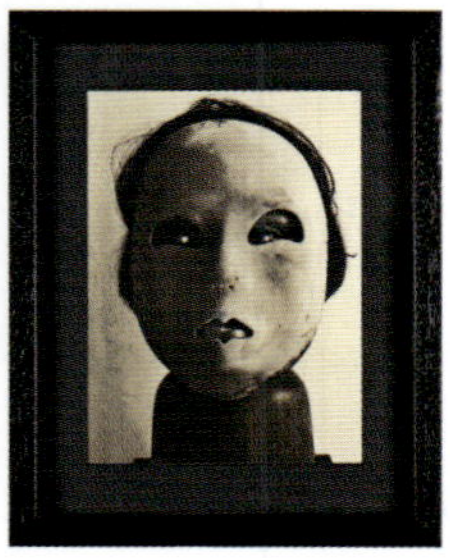

1

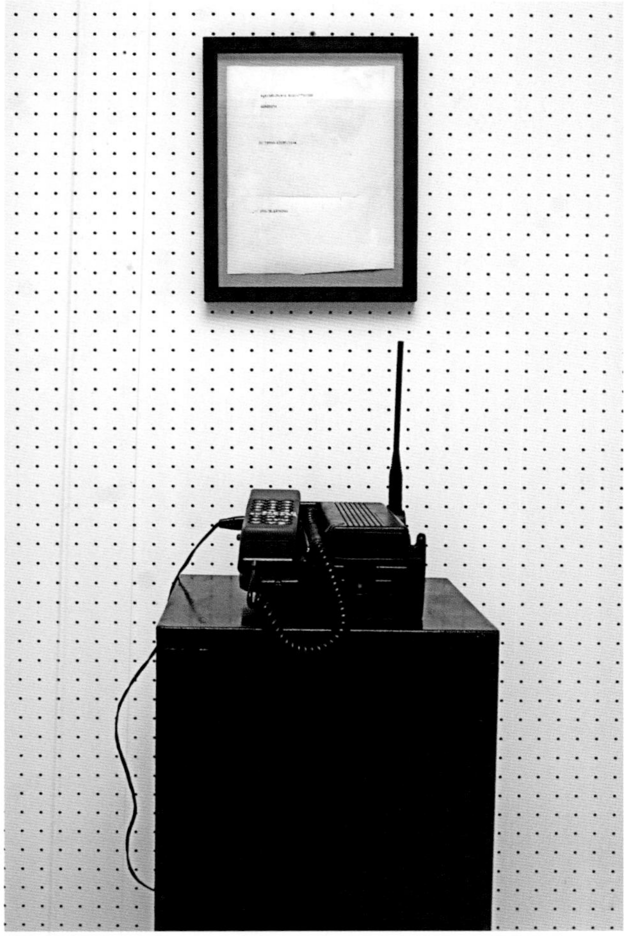

2

Shown by
Galerie Guido W. Baudach C30
Harris Lieberman B9
Alison Jacques Gallery A25
kaufmann repetto A23
Galerie Krinzinger B24
Galerie Rüdiger Schöttle D3
Sommer Contemporary Art C37

Biography
Born 1966
Lives in Berlin

German artist Zipp's paintings and installations question social and political norms. Recent exhibitions include "Achtung!: solarized deterritorialization. insanity against protestantism (England attacked by the Americas)" (2011), at Ausstellungsraum Céline und Heiner Bastian, Berlin; "The World's most complete Congress of RITATIN Treatments" (2011), at Kunstraum Innsbruck; and "(WHITE REFORMATION CO-OP) MENS SANA IN CORPORE SANO" (2010), at Kunsthalle Fridericianum, Kassel.

1
A.B.: OPEN PATTEX
2011
Acrylic and oil on canvas / mixed media on paper, 2 parts
70⅞ × 59" / 13 × 10⅝"
(180 × 150 cm / 33 × 27 cm)
Courtesy of Galerie Guido W. Baudach

2
A.B.: kike
2011
Mixed media, 2 parts
Dimensions variable
Courtesy of Galerie Guido W. Baudach

Thomas Zipp

Given its subdued and melancholy palette, its frequently sinister figural forms and countercultural allusions (including *H.K.A.*, 2009 and *A.B.O.*, 2010), it would be easy to align the work of Thomas Zipp with a general reanimation of the Gothic in the last decade or so. But such is Zipp's range of historical reference, so wryly eloquent his *noir* take on the styles and the sources of the 20th century avant-gardes, that his work is at once unmistakable and remarkably varied. *White Dada* (2008) is an installation in two parts, juxtaposing the institutional Modernism of a coolly apportioned lecture theatre with the dingy backroom of that movement's more emotionally, sexually, and pharmacologically adventurous milieu. BD

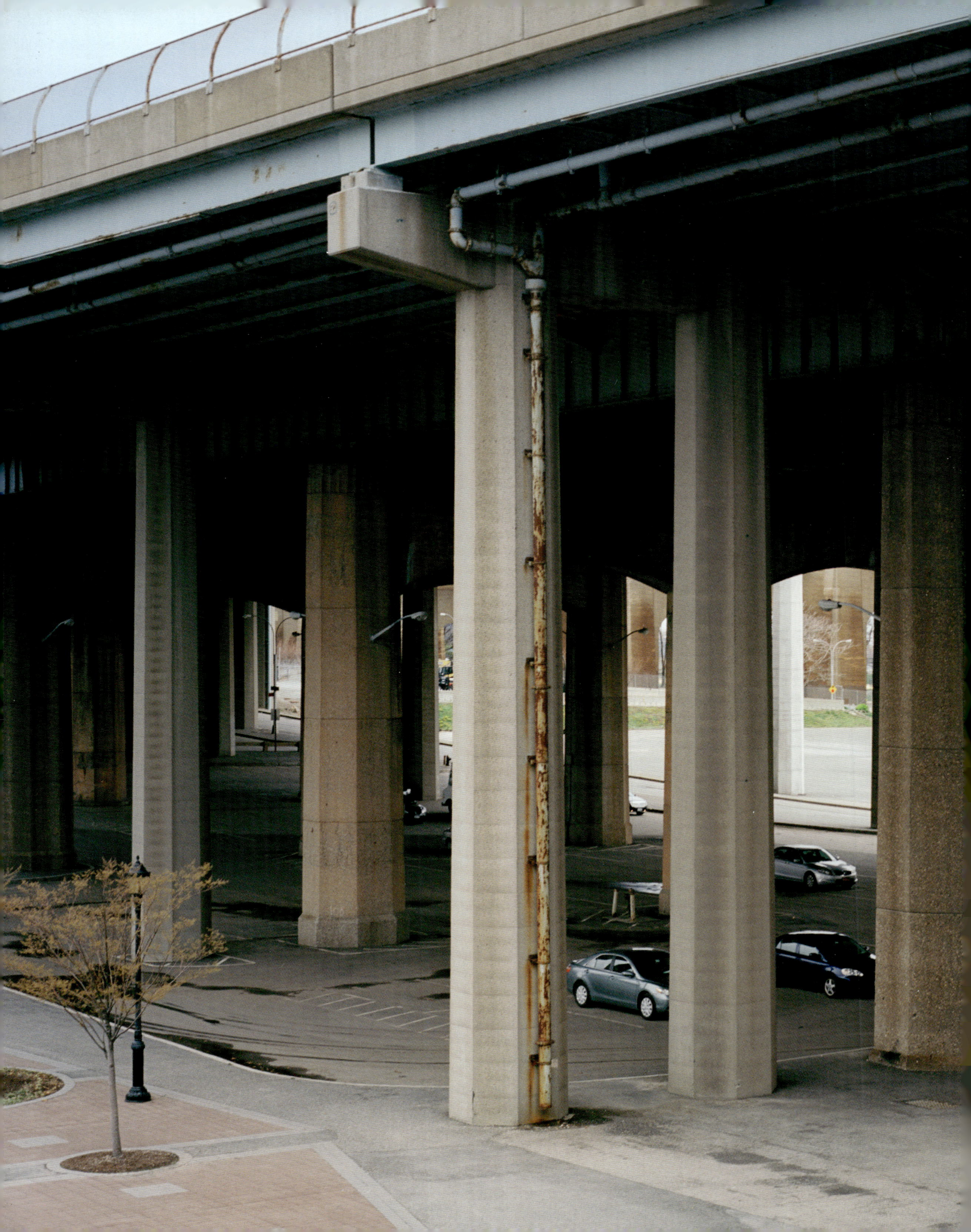

Frame Artists

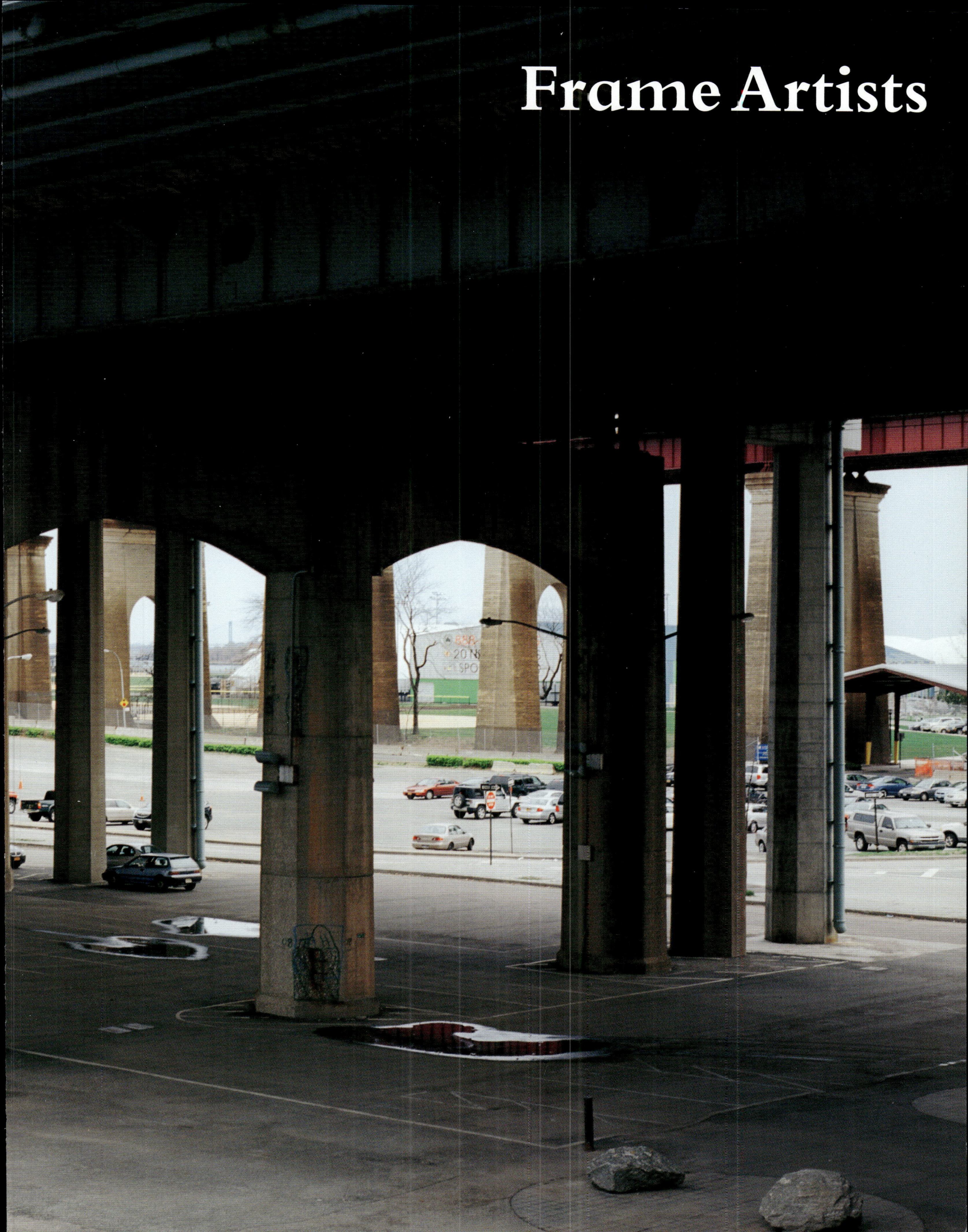

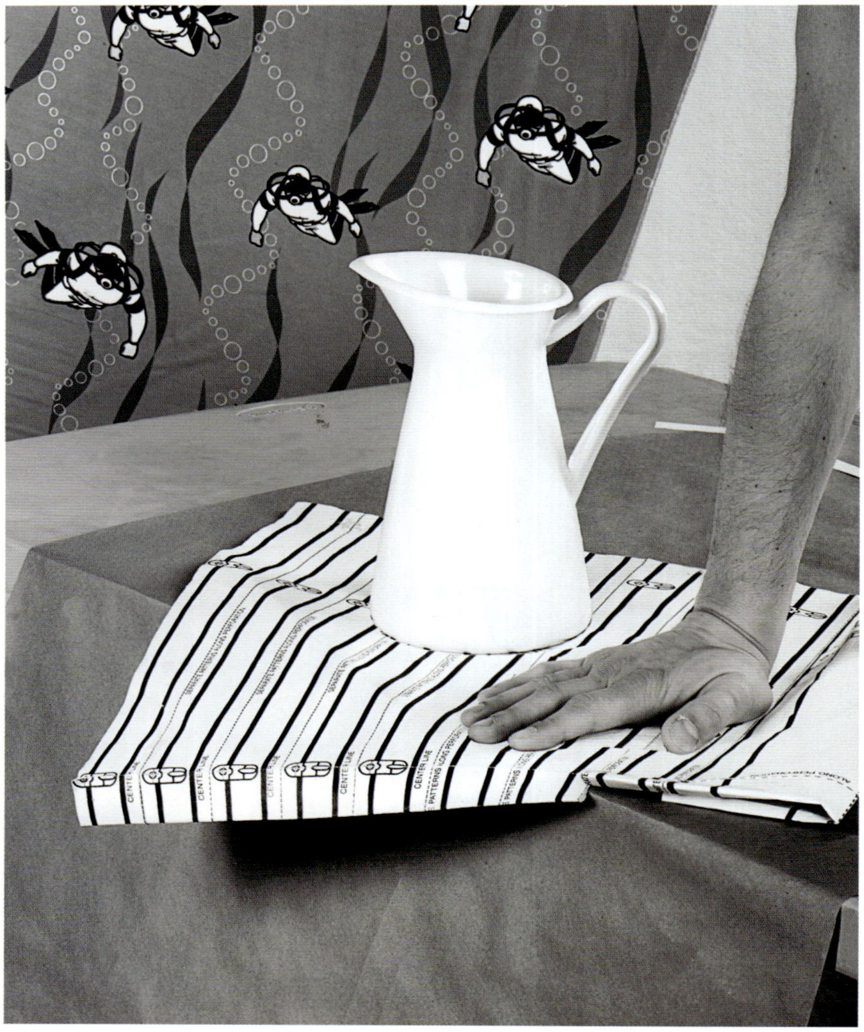

1

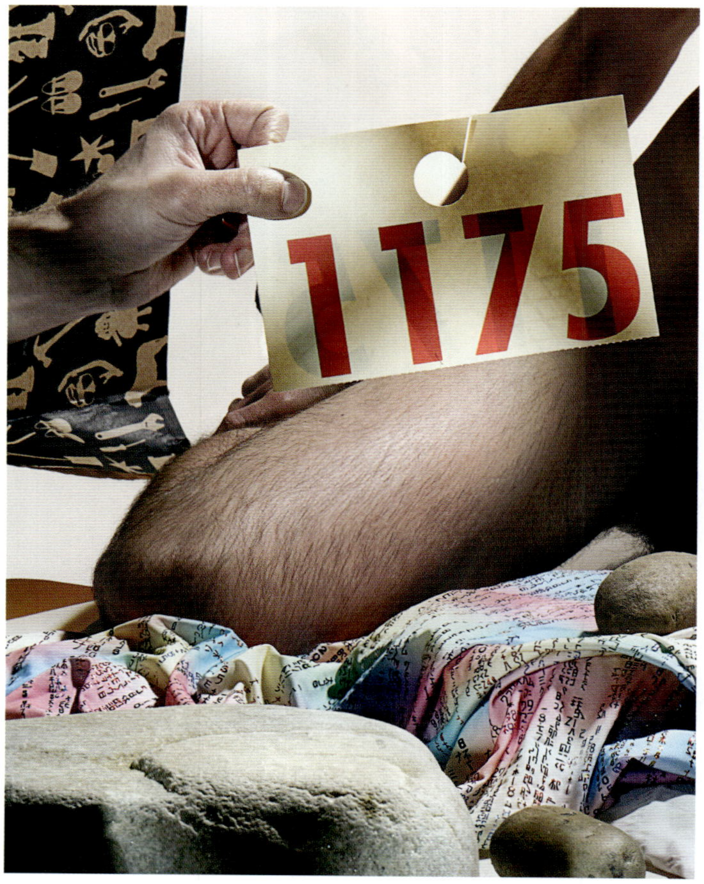

2

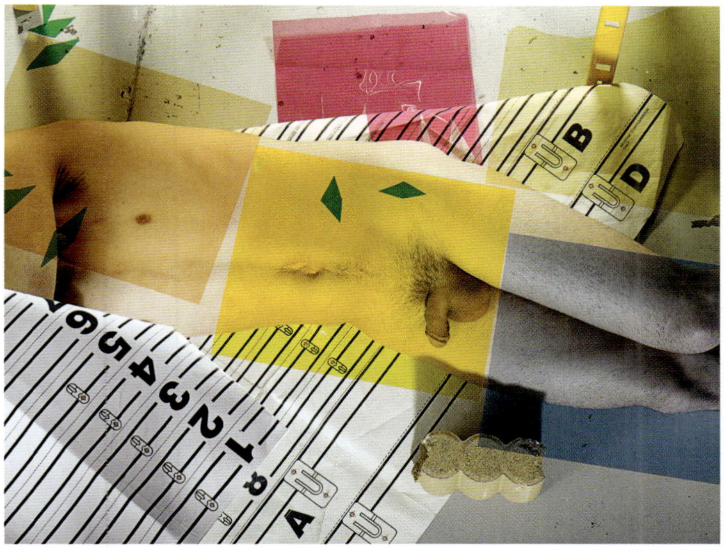

3

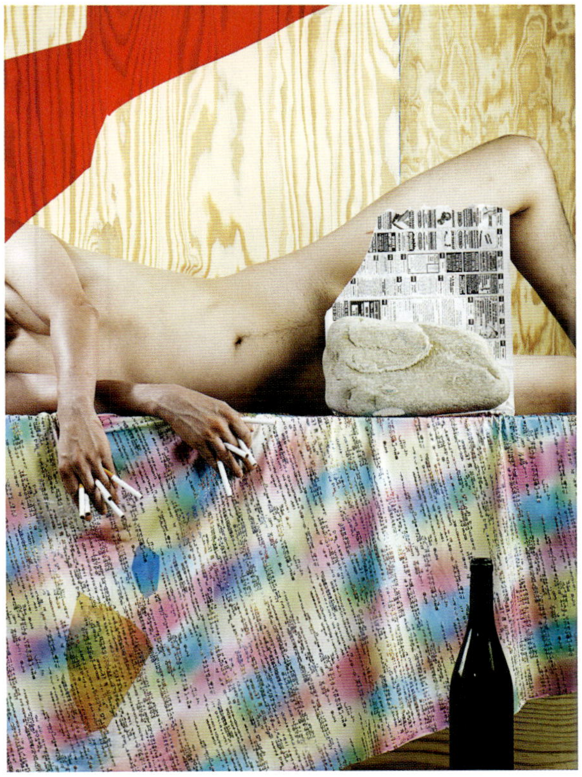

4

Frame
Michele Abeles

Shown by
47 Canal R15

Biography
Born 1977
Lives in New York

American artist Abeles received an MFA from Yale University, New Haven, in 2007, and a BA from Washington University, St. Louis, in 1999. Her first solo show "Re:Re:Re:Re:Re:" took place at 47 Canal, New York, in spring 2011. She participated in ReMap3, Athens (2011), and recent group shows include "Vide Poche" (2011), at SculptureCenter, Long Island City; and "Looking Back" (2011), at White Columns, New York, in collaboration with Amy Yao and Margaret Lee.

1
Pitcher, Paper, Arm, Scuba, Lycra
2011
Archival pigment print
31 × 26"
(78.5 × 66 cm)
Courtesy of 47 Canal

2
Number, Lycra, Man, Hand, Rock, M.L., Cardboard
2009
Archival pigment print
22½ × 18"
(57 × 45.5 cm)
Courtesy of 47 Canal

3
Fuchsia, Yellow, Green, Blue, Numbers, Man, Cement, Paper
2010
Archival pigment print
33 × 44"
(84 × 112 cm)
Courtesy of 47 Canal

4
Red, Rock, Cigarettes, Newspaper, Body, Wood, Lycra, Bottle
2011
Archival pigment print
40 × 30"
(101.5 × 76 cm)
Courtesy of 47 Canal

The title of Michele Abeles' first solo show, "Re:Re:Re:Re:Re:" (2011), implied an email exchange without a subject—a canny allusion to the artist's ongoing interest in digital exchange and uprooted images. Glossy and clinical, the photographs that Abeles produces are suggestive of stock photography, while their composition often resembles collage. She herself cuts an elusive figure, in the portrait *Sunglasses, Lips, Head, Reflection* (2009), a model is wearing reflective sunglasses, but in the reflection neither photographer nor camera are anywhere to be seen—while the artist's hand may not always be evident, her unique compositions remain personal and provocative. ST

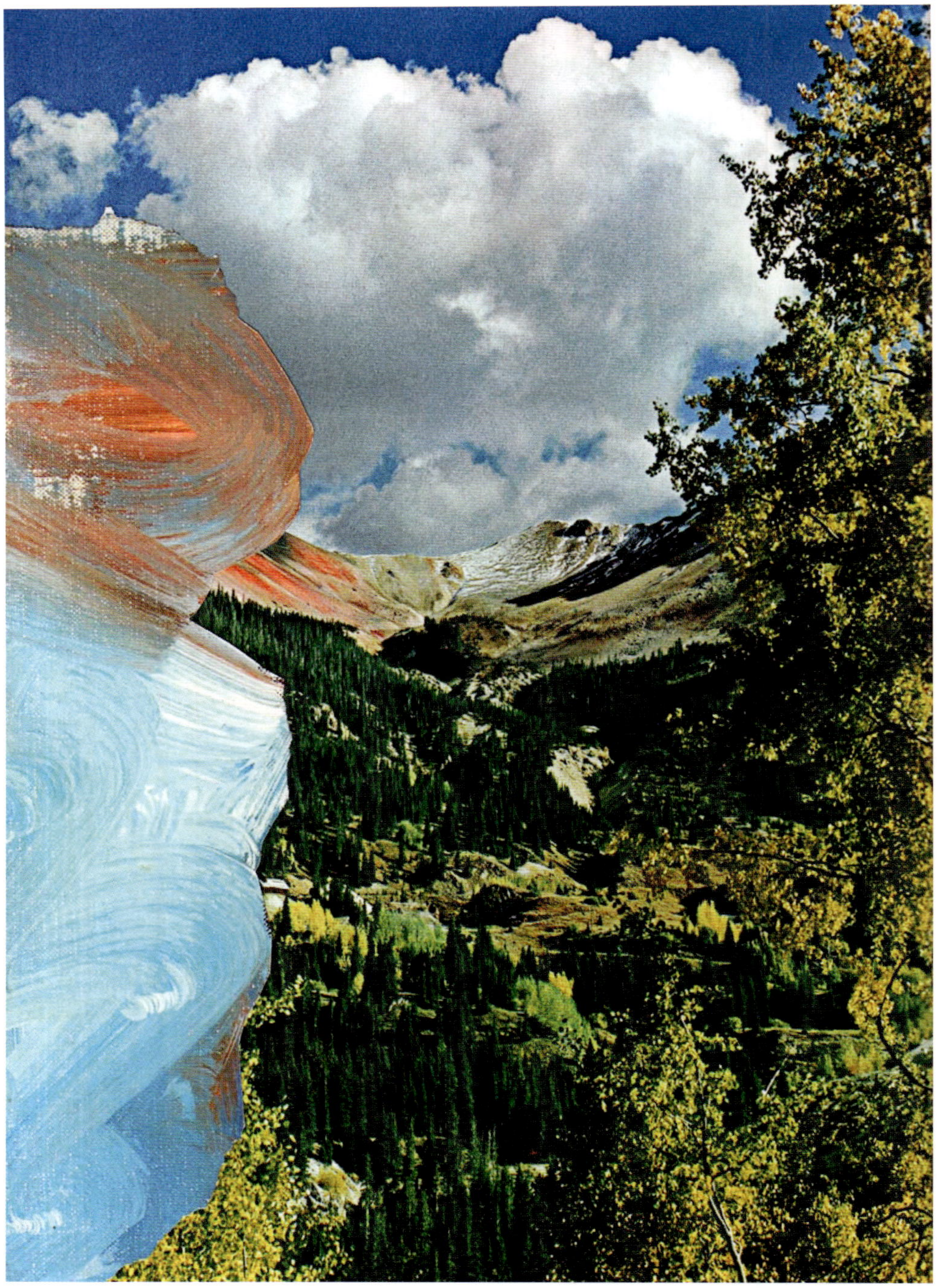

1

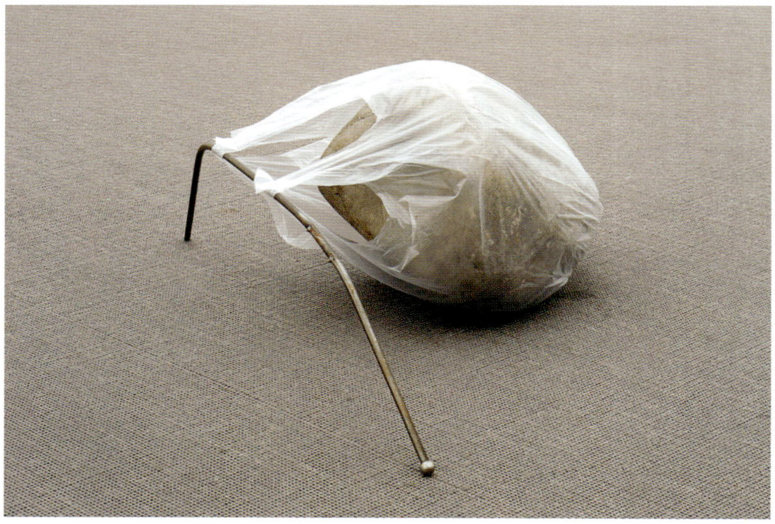

2

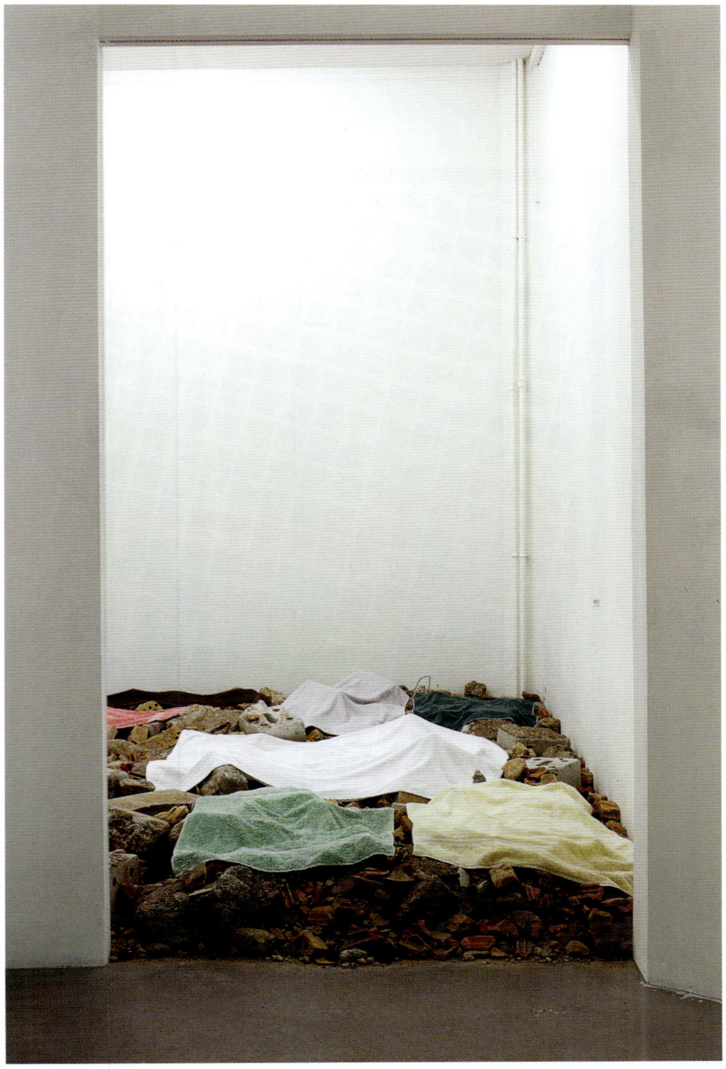

3

Shown by
BolteLang R16
Limoncello F19

Biography
Born 1978
Lives in Zurich and London

Swiss-born Billy's sculptural work has been exhibited extensively since she graduated from Chelsea College of Art, London, in 2001. The exhibition "Three times a day" (2011), at Kunsthalle Baselland, Basel, was her first institutional solo show in Switzerland. Other recent solo shows include "Natural means something like vegetables" (2011) at Christina Wilson, Copenhagen; "Who Shapes What" (2010) at Limoncello, London; and "Surfaces for the mind to rest or sink into" (2010) at The Photographers' Gallery Project Space, London.

1
Start here, go anywhere
2011
Collage
12½ × 10"
(32 × 25.5 cm)
Courtesy of BolteLang

2
To the shore
2011
Stone, plastic bag and steel
33⅜ × 20 × 11⅞"
(85 × 51 × 30 cm)
Courtesy of BolteLang

3
Making do
2011
Rubble and bath towels
Dimensions variable
Courtesy of BolteLang

Frame
Vanessa Billy

Vanessa Billy's collages and minimalist sculptural assemblages spot far-flung equivalences, bringing together forms and materials as different as ceramics, carpet, soil, and rags. *Wait, Sit, Converse* (2009), for example, reads like an update of Joseph Kosuth's ontological experiments of the 1960s: a similarly sized trio of objects—a rock, a lump of clay, and a sealed bag of water—sit obediently in line, like long-separated triplets. Elsewhere, in *Broken Fountain IV* (2011), a curving steel rod is held in place at the bottom by a lump of clay and at the top by a towel against the wall. Teasing out unsuspected rhythms and relationships between things and bodies, Billy confounds material difference with formal and conceptual rhymes. ST

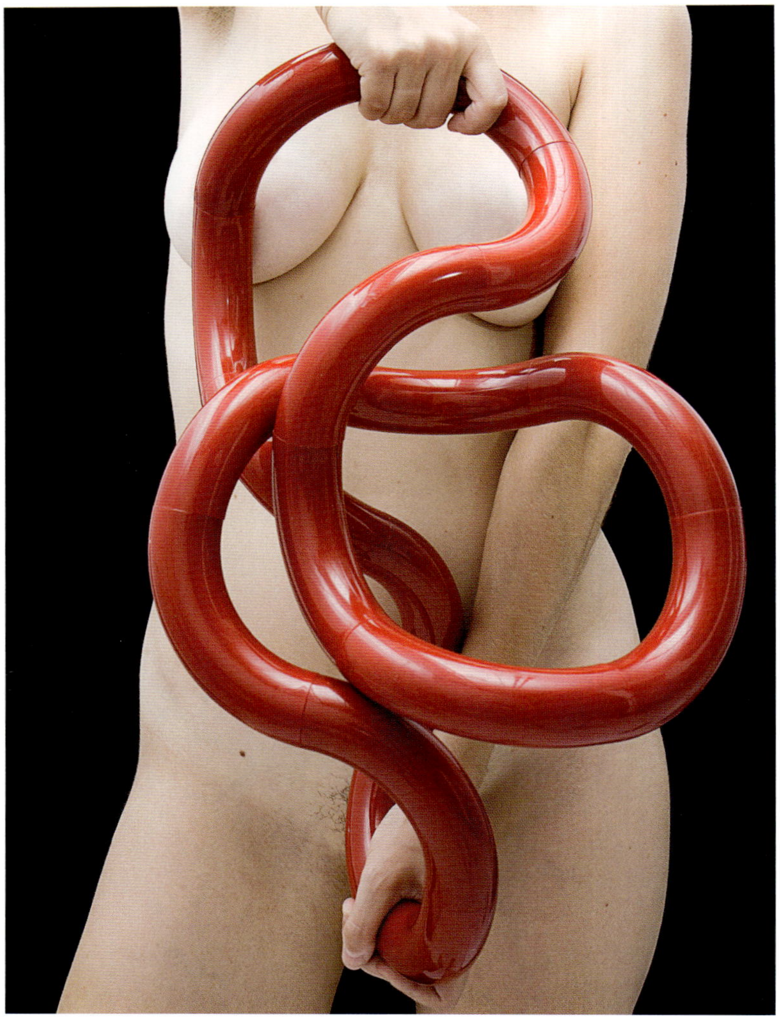
1

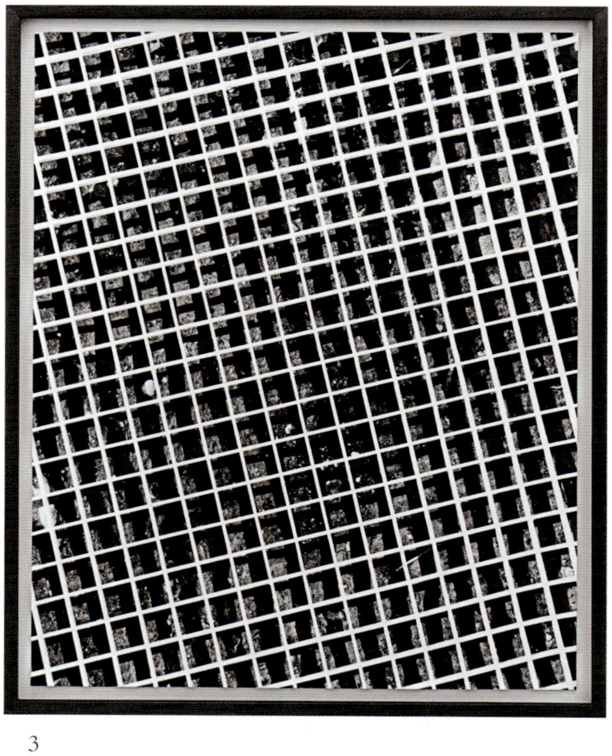
3

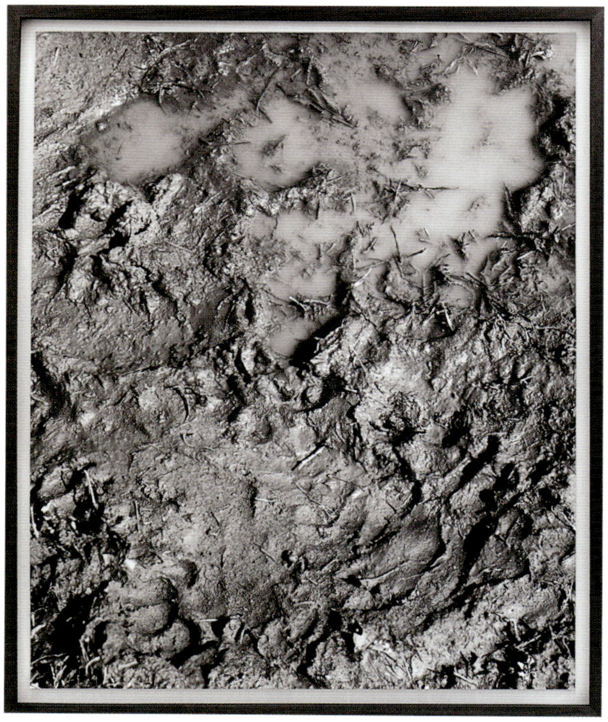
2

Frame
Talia Chetrit

Talia Chetrit's still-life photographs of objects often give the impression of carefully managed illusions. However, though these carefully lit pictures seem to be collaged or digitally manipulated, they are overwhelmingly involved with traditional analog photography. Her figurative subject matter is often at odds with manmade materials, *Modular Nude* (2011) for example features a Mobius plastic toy that domineers the frame, while another her sculptural arrangements—which owe something to both Bauhaus-era experimentation and to the clinical cool of 1980s' fashion photography—often feel somehow unreal. In a studio photograph such as *Handstand* (2011), a naked body seems to become almost sculptural, while elsewhere—such as in *Drip Vases* (2011)—the objects she focuses on come to feel pliable and bodily. Quiet confusion reigns. ST

Shown by
Renwick Gallery R6
Sies + Höke B15

Biography
Born 1982
Lives in New York

In recent years American photographer Chetrit has exhibited extensively in the United States. In early 2012, she participated in the group show "Object Fictions" at James Cohan Gallery, New York. Recent solo shows include "Ringer" (2011) at Michael Benevento, Los Angeles; "Marking" (2011) at Kaufmann Repetto, Milan; and a self-titled solo show at Renwick, New York (2011). Other group shows include "The light, the shape and the body" (2011), at Galerie Reinhard Hauff, Stuttgart, and "Cloud" (2011), at Foxy Production, New York.

1
Modular Nude
2011
Digital C-type print
26 × 20"
(66 × 51 cm)
Courtesy of Renwick Gallery

2
Mud
2011
Silver gelatin print
24 × 20"
(61 × 51 cm)
Courtesy of Renwick Gallery

3
Dirt/Grid
2011
Silver gelatin print
9⅜ × 7⅞"
(24 × 20 cm)
Courtesy of Renwick Gallery

4
Triangle/Tube
2011
Silver gelatin print
7⅞ × 6¼"
(20 × 16 cm)
Courtesy of Renwick Gallery

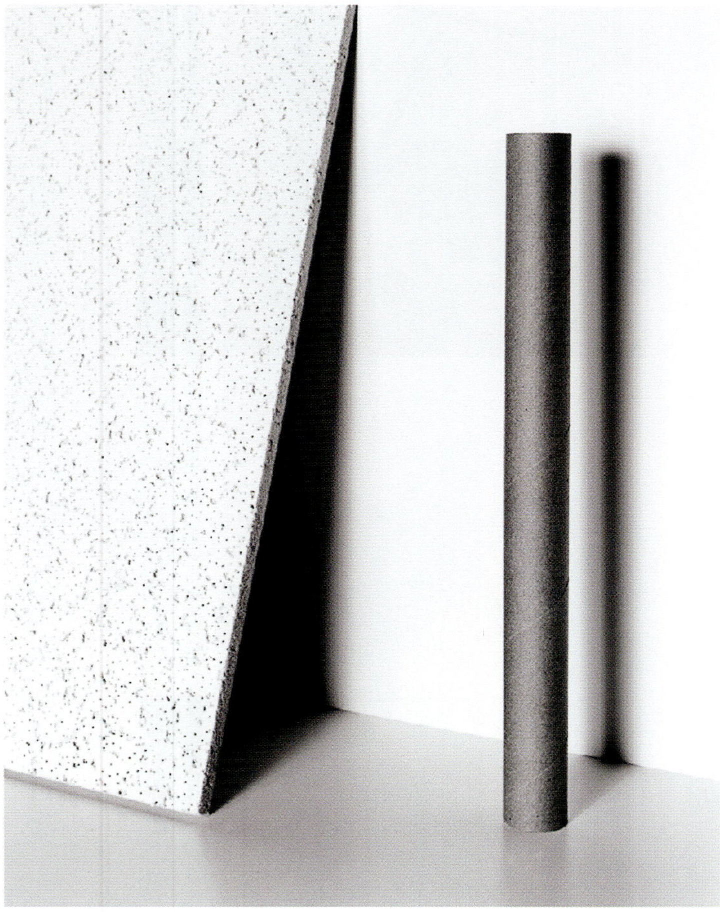

4

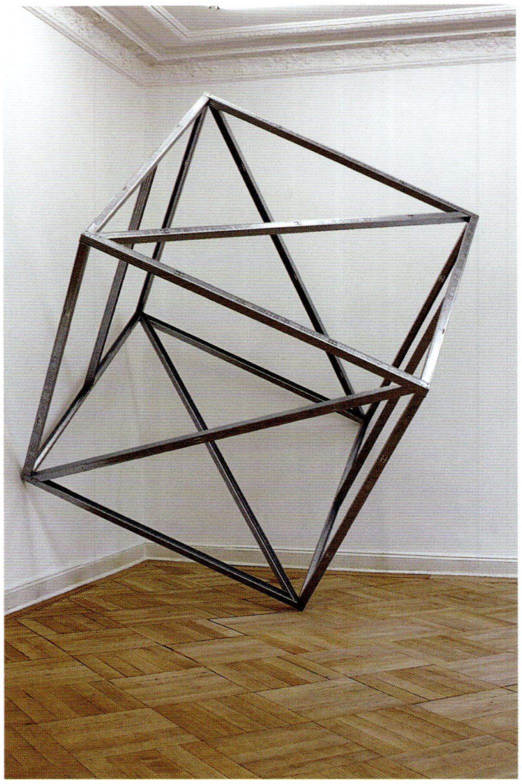

2

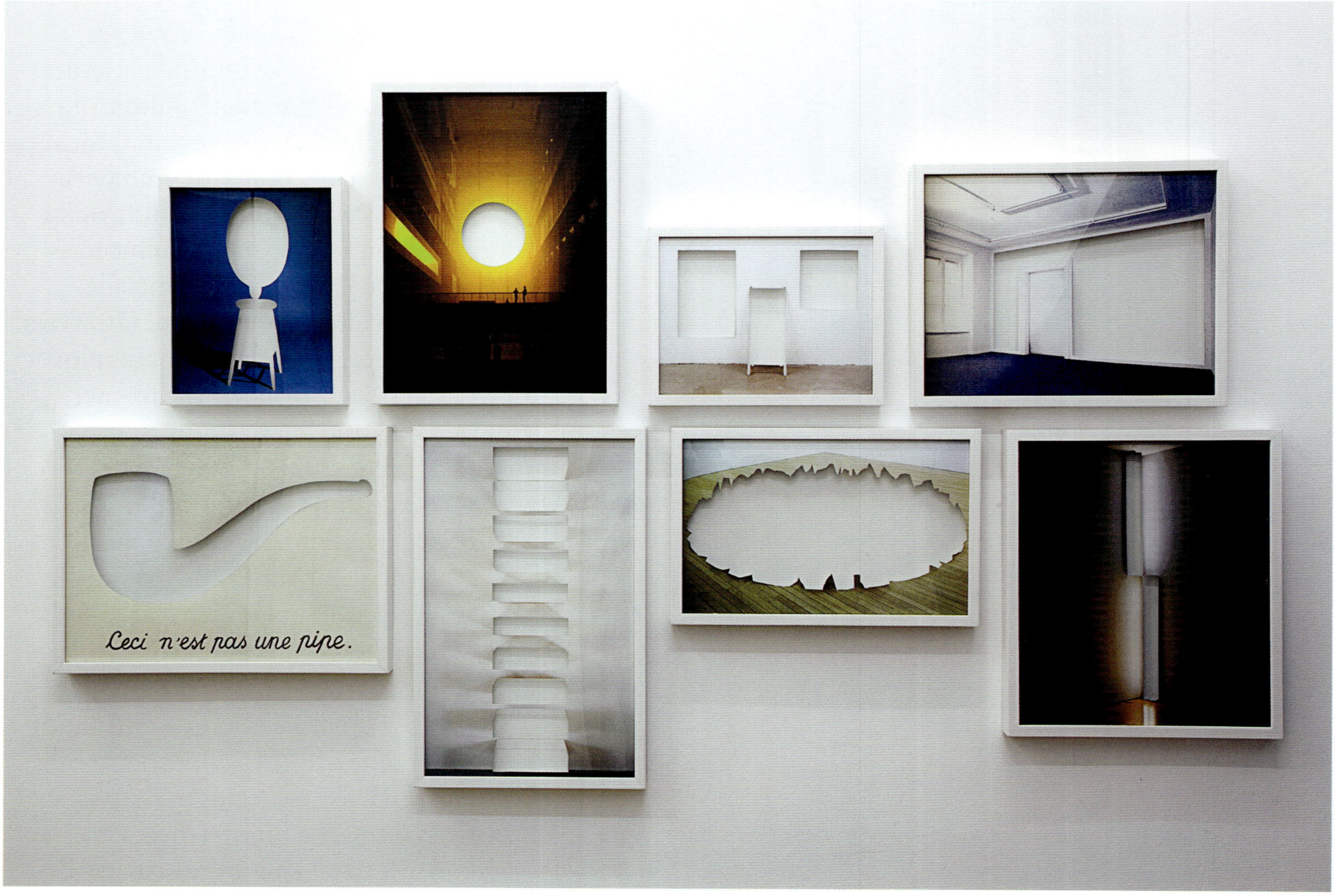

1

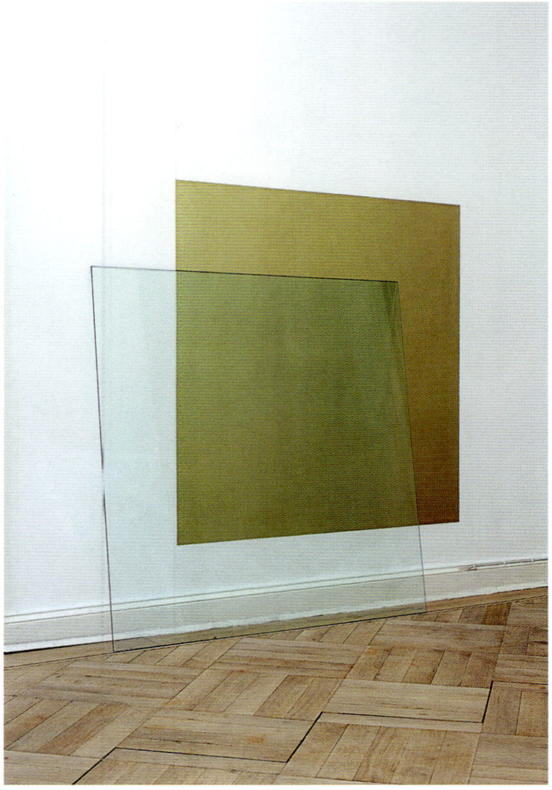

3

Shown by
Figge von Rosen
Galerie R8

Biography
Born 1974
Lives in Guadelajara

Mexican artist Dávila's photographs and sculptures have been exhibited internationally since the mid-1990s. In 2011 he had the solo shows "Nowhere Can Be Now Here" at Figge von Rosen Galerie, Berlin, and "Only the shadow knows" at Gentili Gallery, Florence. Recent group shows include "Rotary Connection" (2012), at Casey Kaplan, New York; "Everything must go" (2011), also Casey Kaplan, New York; and "Wir sind alle Astronauten" (We are all Astraunauts, 2011), at Marta Herford, Herford. His work is included in numerous public collections including MUDAM, Luxembourg, and the Jumex Collection, México City.

1
Iconic Topologies
2011
Offset print, handcut and framed
Dimensions variable
Courtesy of Figge von Rosen Galerie

2
Imbalance of Perfection
2011
Aluminum frames
119⅝ × 99⅝ × 121¼"
(304 × 253 × 308 cm)
Courtesy of Figge von Rosen Galerie

3
Double Message
2011
Glass and acrylic paint
68½ × 68½ × 7⅞"
(174 × 174 × 20 cm)
Courtesy of Figge von Rosen Galerie

Frame
Jose Dávila

The possibilities of how we construct our surroundings form a constantly unsettled question in the work of Jose Dávila. Taking on the inherited bulk of Modernist architecture, he responds with a range of informal and imaginary constructions in the form of drawings, sculptures, and installations. His recent exhibition at Hotel Demetria, Guadalajara, featured *Untitled* (2011), where several low brick walls were echoed by ghostly white neon light outlines, alongside the giant leaning aluminum frame of *Imbalance of Perfection* (2011), a cube resting three sharp corners on the gallery's walls and floor. For Dávila, the ideal space is a temporary, improvised inversion of everyday reality. CFW

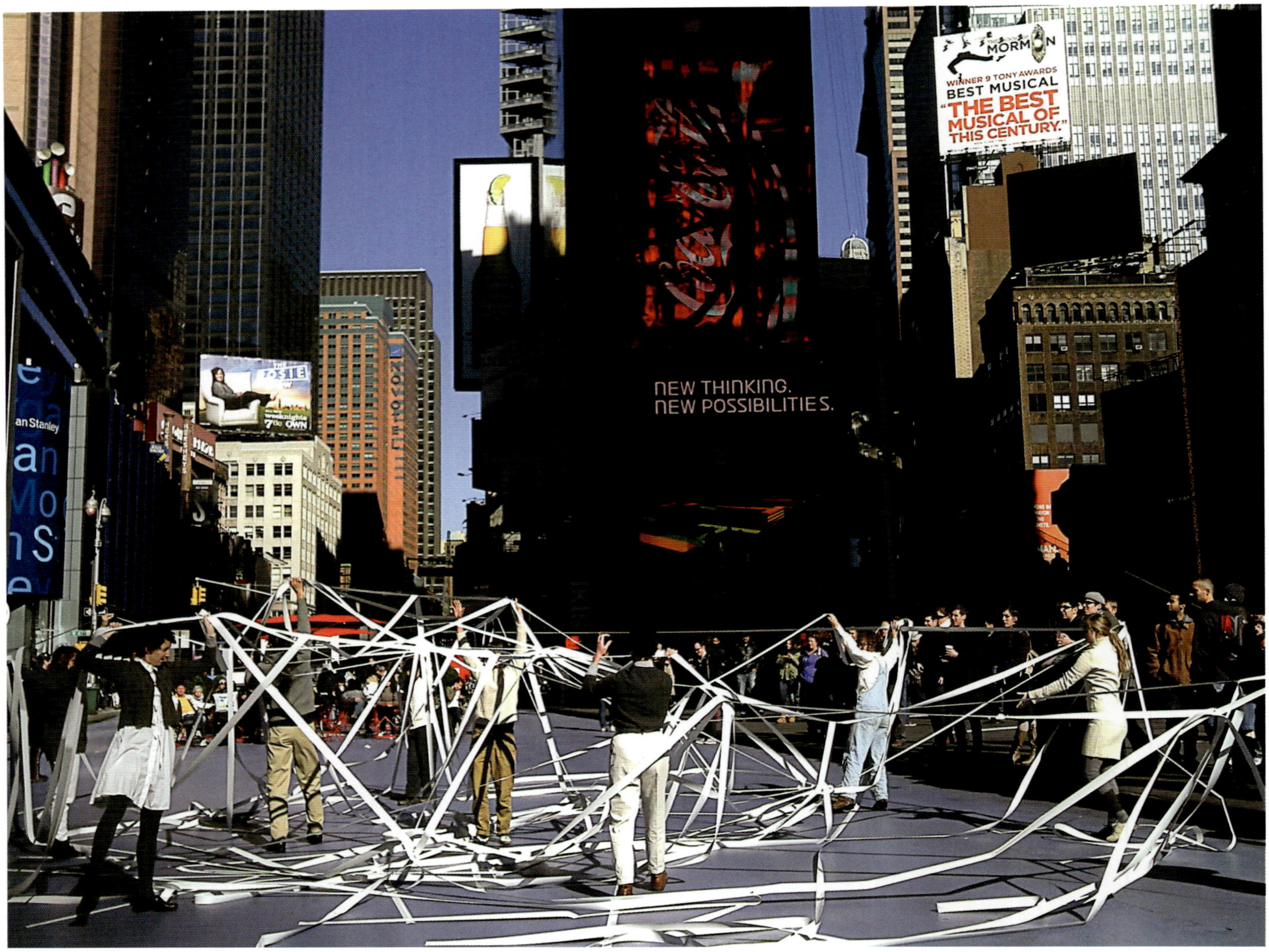
MORMON
WINNER 9 TONY AWARDS
BEST MUSICAL
"THE BEST MUSICAL OF THIS CENTURY."
NEW THINKING.
NEW POSSIBILITIES.

1

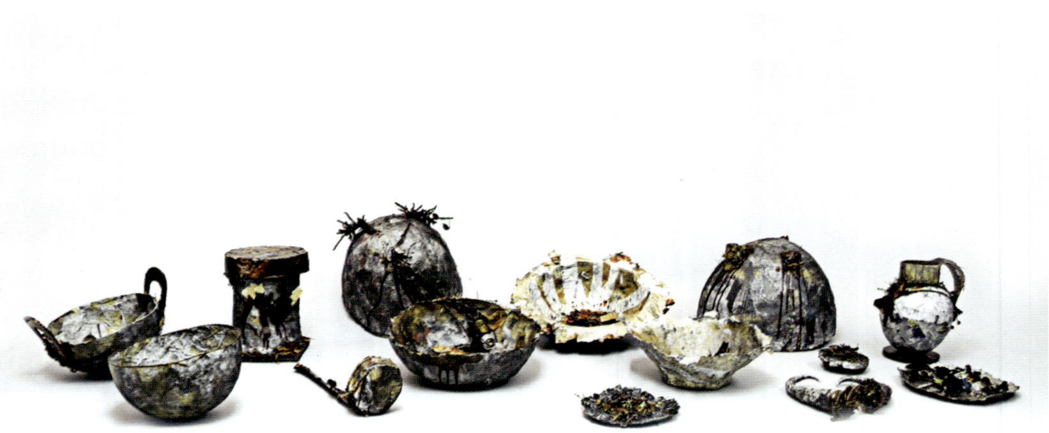

2

Frame
Liz Glynn

Liz Glynn's practice reactivates history through the process of fabricating handmade pseudo-relics, replicas, and models. In 2009, Glynn attracted significant attention with her *24 Hour Roman Reconstruction Project, or, Building Rome in a Day*, in which the artist and a team of collaborators built a model of the Italian capital in the lobby of New York's New Museum and then destroyed it. Glynn's replicas and surrogates are often assembled in rudimentary fashion, and using craft materials such as cardboard and tinfoil; the lopsided ancient-Greek drinking cup *Attic Red-Figured Kylix – 83. AE. 287* was fashioned and then photographed for the series of images entitled "California Surrogates for the Getty" (2010). SL

Shown by
Redling Fine Art R7

Biography
Born 1981
Lives in Los Angeles

American artist Glynn received an MFA from the California Institute of the Arts, Valencia, in 2008, and a BA from Harvard College, Cambridge, in 2003. In recent years she has exhibited her large-scale installations and performances in numerous exhibitions in the United States. She was commissioned by the Getty Research Institute and LA><ART to create "Black Box" for the Pacific Standard Time Performance and Public Art Festival, Los Angeles (2012). Her performance *Utopia or Oblivion* (2011) was included in Performa 11 (2011), New York, and *Loving you is like _______ the dead.* premiered at the Museum of Contemporary Art, Los Angeles, in fall 2011.

1
Utopia or Oblivion
2011
Times Square, New York. Part 2 of 3
Dimensions variable
Courtesy of Redling Fine Art

2
Hellenistic Silver Collection, 3rd Century B.C. (1981.11.15–22; 1982.11.7–13; 1984.11.3), from the series Surrogate Objects for the Metropolitan
2011
Trash, wax, and yard waste with silver leaf and *faux* patina
60 × 24 × 18"
(154.5 × 61 × 46 cm)
Courtesy of Redling Fine Art

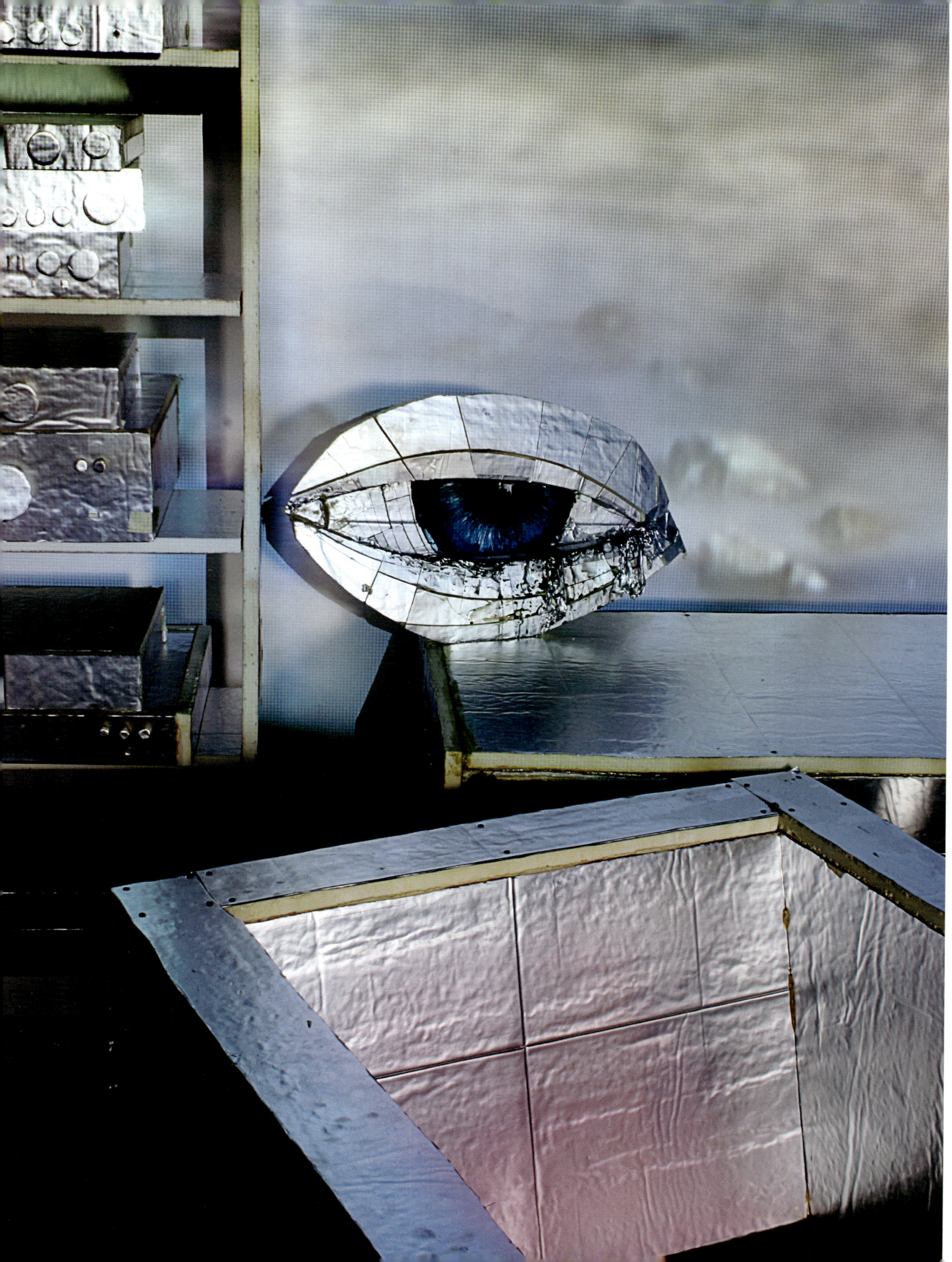

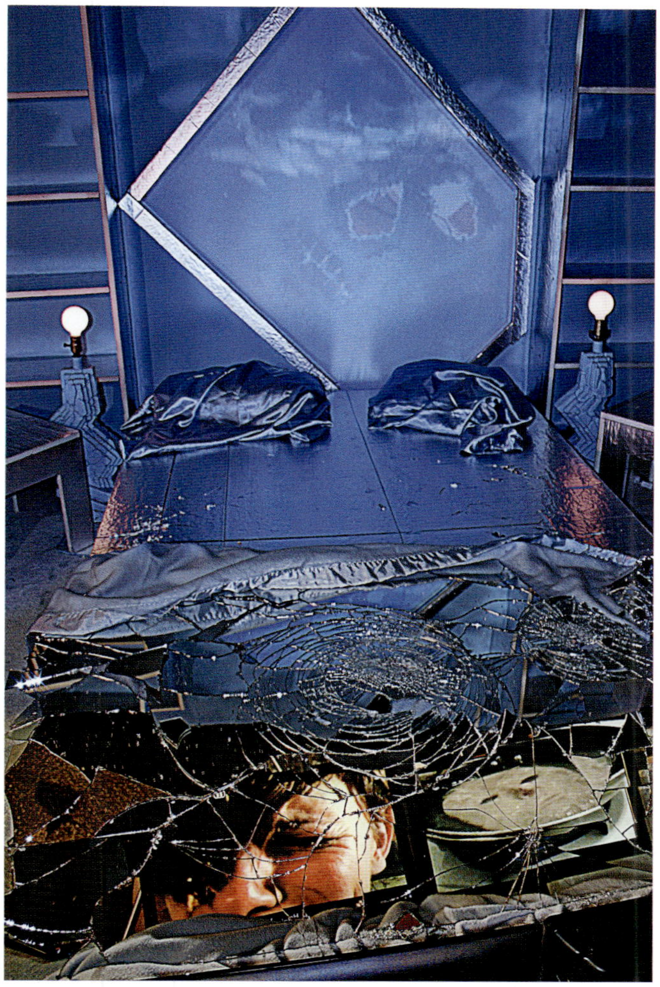

2

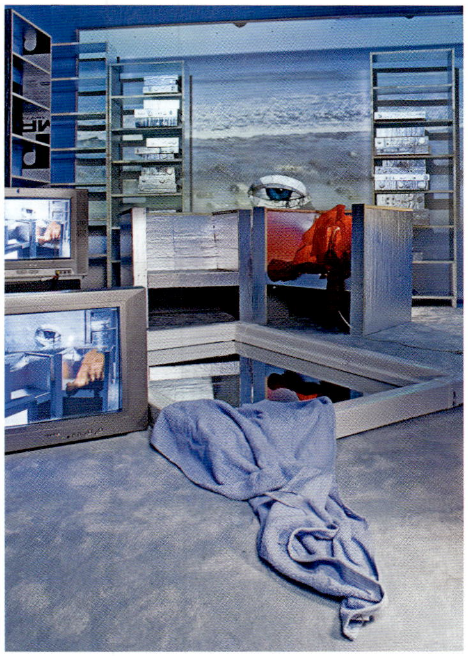

3

Shown by
Night Gallery R5

Biography
Born 1973
Lives in Los Angeles

American installation artist Golden received an MFA from Columbia University, New York, in 2009, and a BA from Minneapolis College of Art and Design in 1995. In recent years she has had significant solo shows in the United States and Europe, including "Busts: My Personal Winter" (2011) at Workspace, Los Angeles; "There's more but its invisible" (2010) at Marvelli Gallery, New York; and "Penumbra II" (2010) at Ferenbalm-Gurbrü Station, Karlsruhe. In 2011 she also participated in the three-person show "Fancy Finger," at Night Gallery, Los Angeles.

1
Rape of The Mirror. Bedroom Installation (detail)
2011
Mixed media
Dimensions variable
Courtesy of Night Gallery

2, 3
Rape of The Mirror: Beachside Installation
2011
Mixed media
Dimensions variable
Courtesy of Night Gallery

Frame
Samara Golden

Samara Golden creates walk-in installations where mirrors, cameras, and video displays draw the viewer into cluttered, immersive environments. Golden works with "found objects" culled from the Internet, reified as foamboard cut-outs—a practice she developed as a sort of therapeutic shopping substitute when too impoverished to actually make purchases. Laptops, televisions, and other miscellaneous items are cut and pasted in a method that Golden calls "physical Photoshop," as in *Yes No Party* (2009). Forcing us to physically occupy the kitschy realm of online commerce, she gives new tangibility to the way we consume online today, as the Internet develops increasingly sophisticated means to tell us what we "actually" want before we even know it. SNS

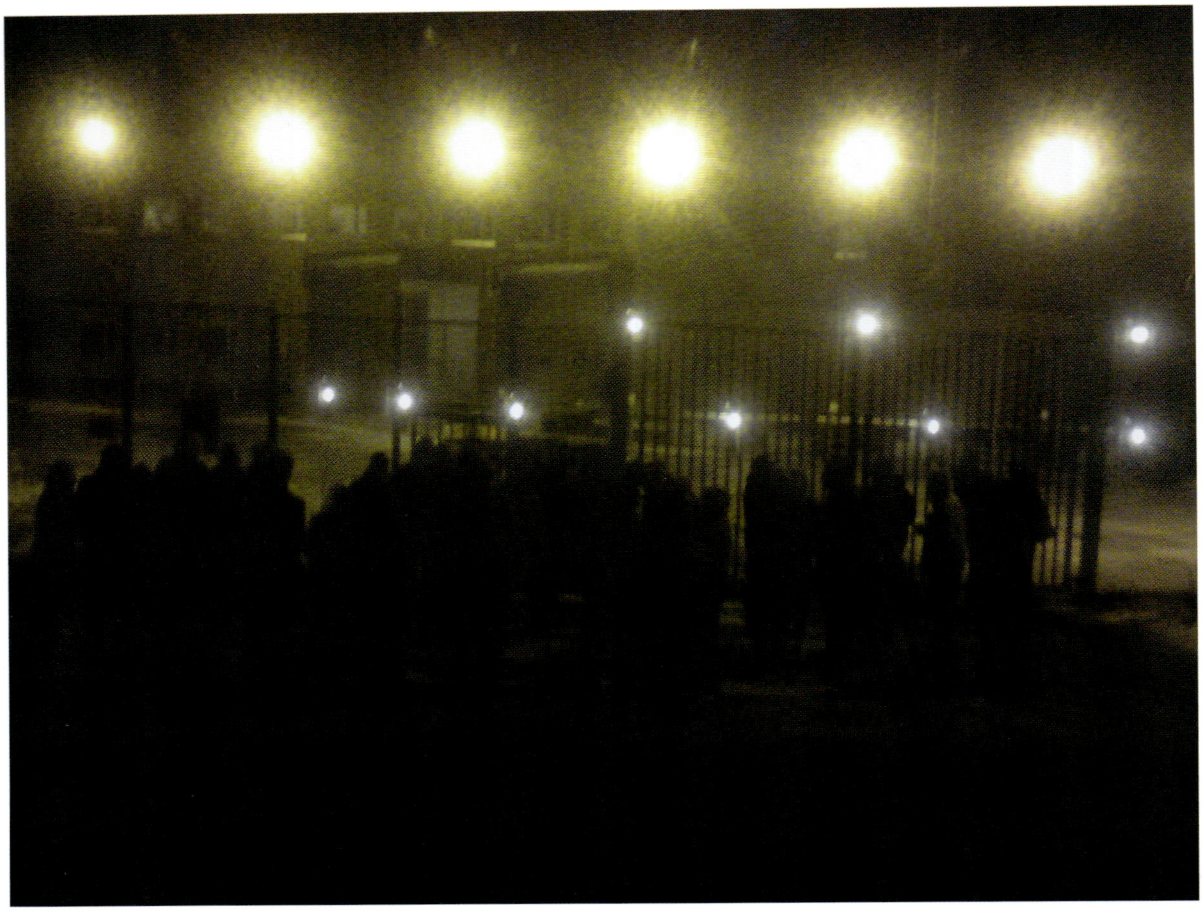

1

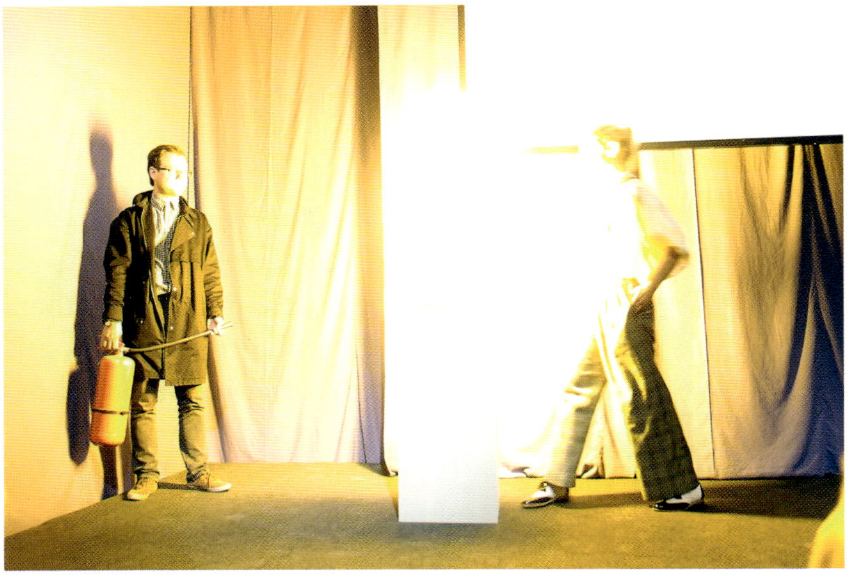

2

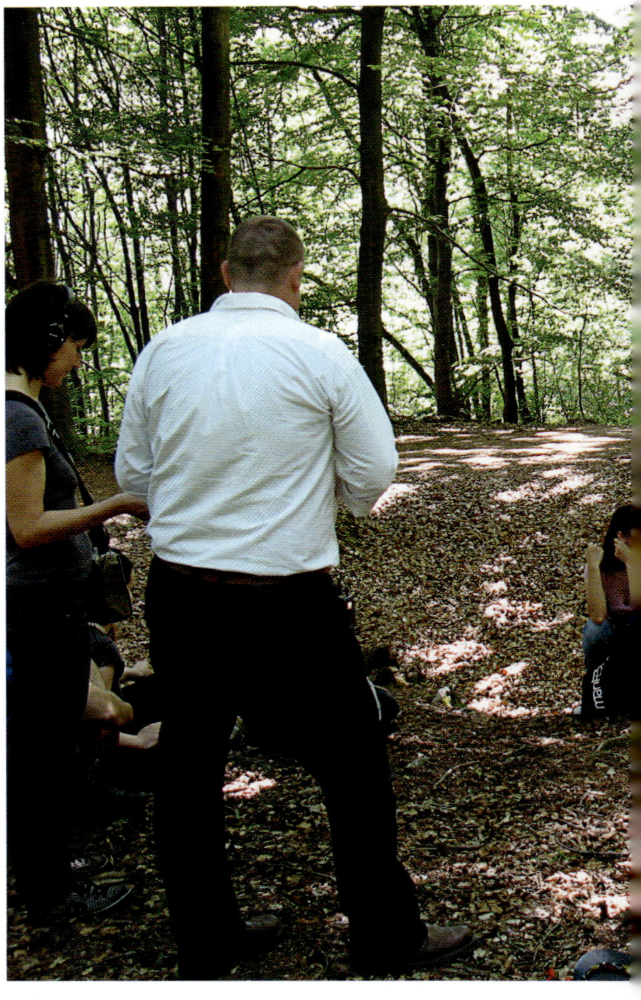

3

Shown by
Crystal R10

Biography
Live in Stockholm

Swedish collaborators Goldin+Senneby have worked together since 2004. Their comprehensive solo show "Standard Length of a Miracle" at CAC, Vilnius, surveyed they concept driven practice. In 2010, they had the solo shows "The Nordenskiöld Model", at Konsthall C, Hökarängen, and "The Decapitation of Money" at Kadist Art Foundation, Paris. They participated in the survey shows Göteborg International Biennial, Gothenburg (2011); Bucharest Biennale 4 (2010); and 28th Bienal de São Paulo (2008).

1
The Nordenskiöld Model, Act 1, Scene 2: A Story of Micro-Second Trading in Twenty Minutes
2010
Performance
Dimensions variable
Courtesy of Crystal

2
Standard Length of a Miracle
2011
Performance
Dimensions variable
Courtesy of Crystal

3
The Decapitation of Money
2010
Performance
Dimensions variable
Courtesy of Crystal

Frame
Goldin+ Senneby

Since 2007—thus just in time for the spectacular global collapse of markets and economies—Simon Goldin and Jakob Senneby have been engaged on *Headless*, a quasi-fictional project that purports to investigate the shady world of offshore banking and related financial practices. The project takes its title from Georges Bataille's enigmatic and secretive Acéphale group, and even—that is, in the fictional world of the novel *Looking for Headless* that Goldin+Senneby published in 2010—appears to flirt with some of their extreme sacrificial tendencies. The veils, ironies, and ruses of the project are seemingly endless, but the whole is, among other things, a pointed critique of the dematerialization of capital. BD

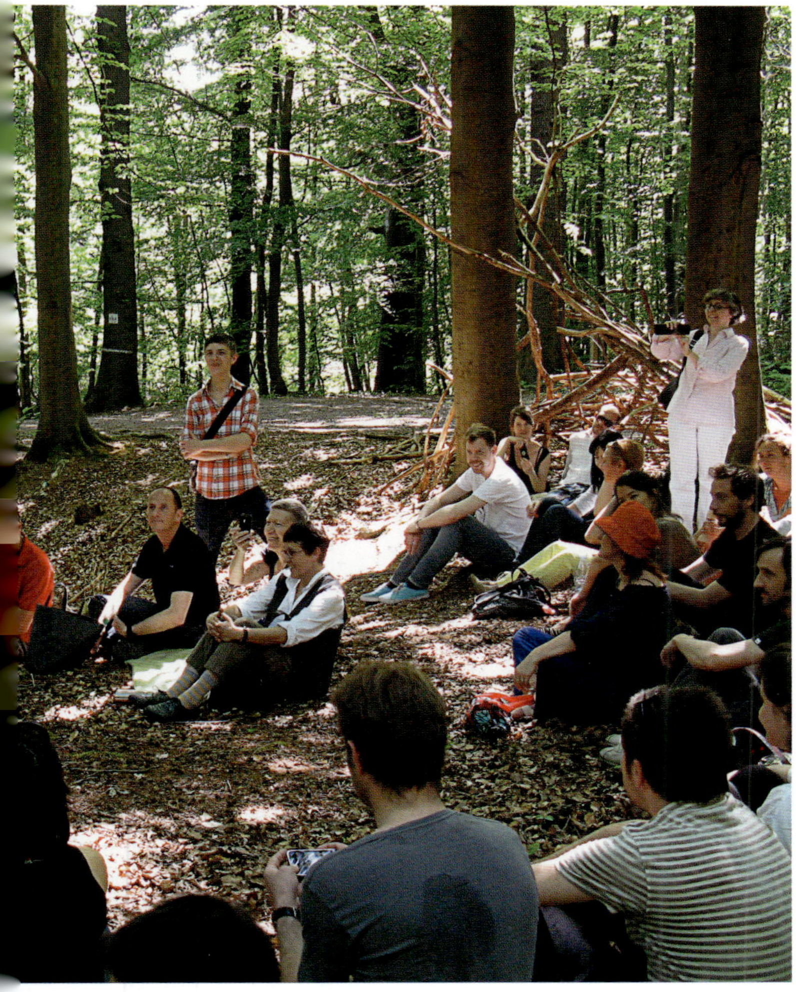

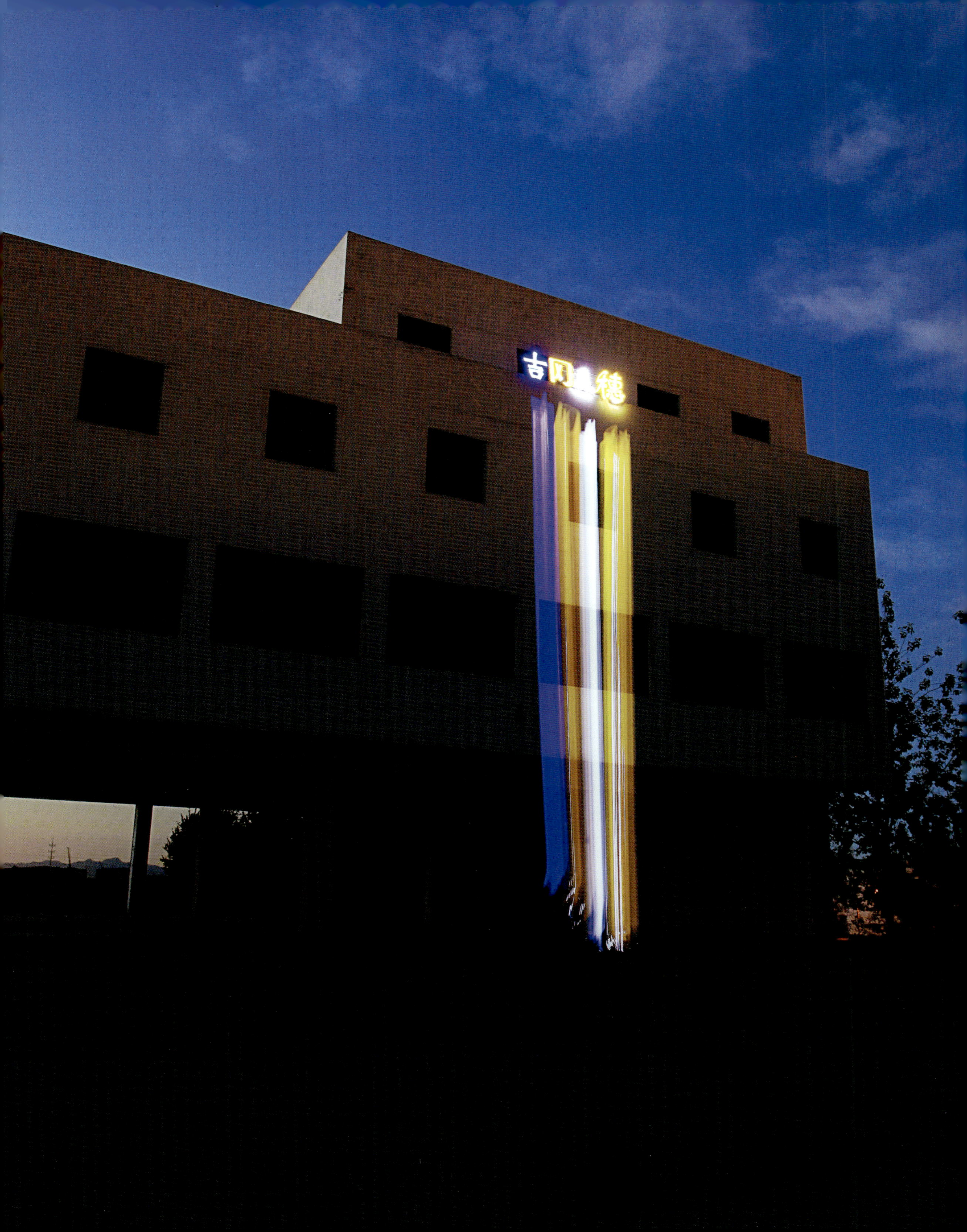

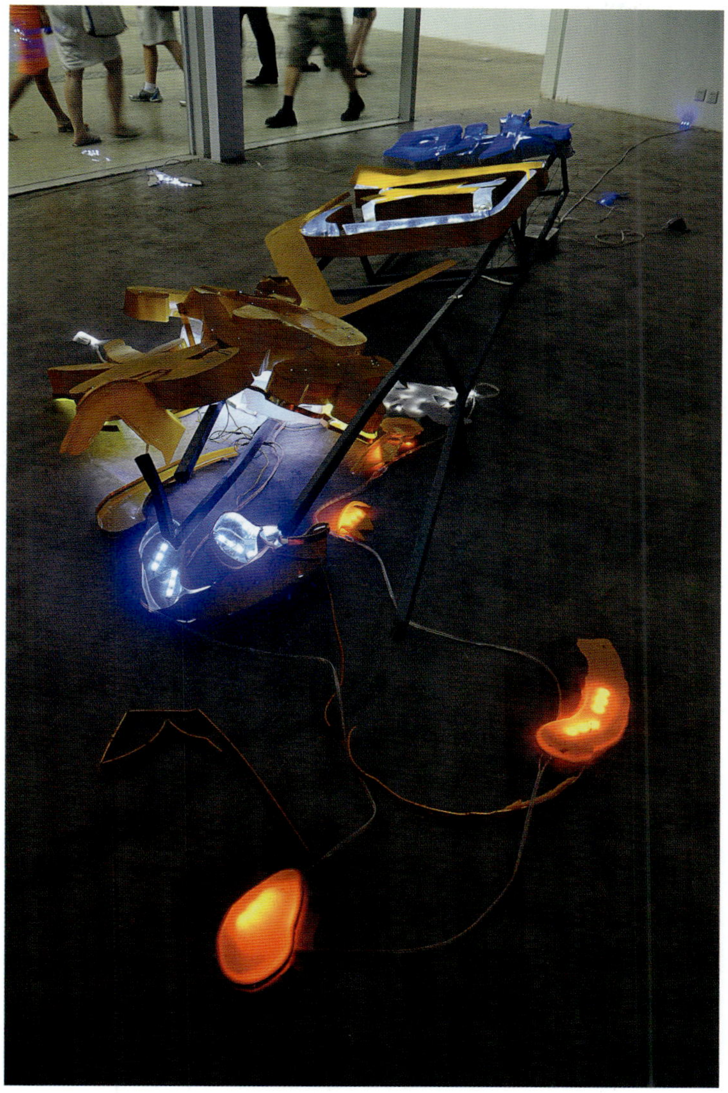

2

Shown by
Tang Contemporary Art R4

Biography
Born 1971
Lives in Beijing

Chinese artist He has exhibited his neon works in galleries and public locations for the past ten years. Recent solo shows include "I am Curious Yellow, I am Curious Blue" (2011) at Tang Contemporary, Beijing; a self-titled show at Galerie Daniel Templon, Paris (2011); and "What Makes Me Understand What I Know?" (2009) at UCCA, Beijing. Group shows include "Great Performances" (2010), Pace Beijing, and "Rendez-Vous" (2008), Mac-Lyon, Lyon. In 2011 he was recipient of the "Credit Suisse Today Art Award," Today Art Museum, Beijing.

1
I am Curious Yellow, I am Curious Blue (Light Box Image)
2011
Photographic light box, metal structure, acrylic neon letter signage
Dimensions variable
Courtesy of Tang Contemporary Art

2
I am Curious Yellow, I am Curious Blue
2011
Photographic light box, metal structure, acrylic neon letter signage
Dimensions variable
Courtesy of Tang Contemporary Art

Frame
He An

Probing the emotive power of signage, He An's light sculptures and urban interventions play with the intersection between public expression and loneliness, desire and death. *Miho Yoshioka* (2011) spells out the name of his favorite sexy Japanese actress in salvaged neon and LED characters. In *Miss You, Please Contact Me* (2000), He wrote his phone number in a red light-box. And in *Wind Light as a Thief* (2011), he bent a streetlamp to partially fit inside a storefront, but left the light itself and a switch—which also controlled a light in a nearby shop and another streetlamp—accessible to passers-by, allowing strangers to adjust the atmosphere of a dark street, as if in their own homes. KMJ

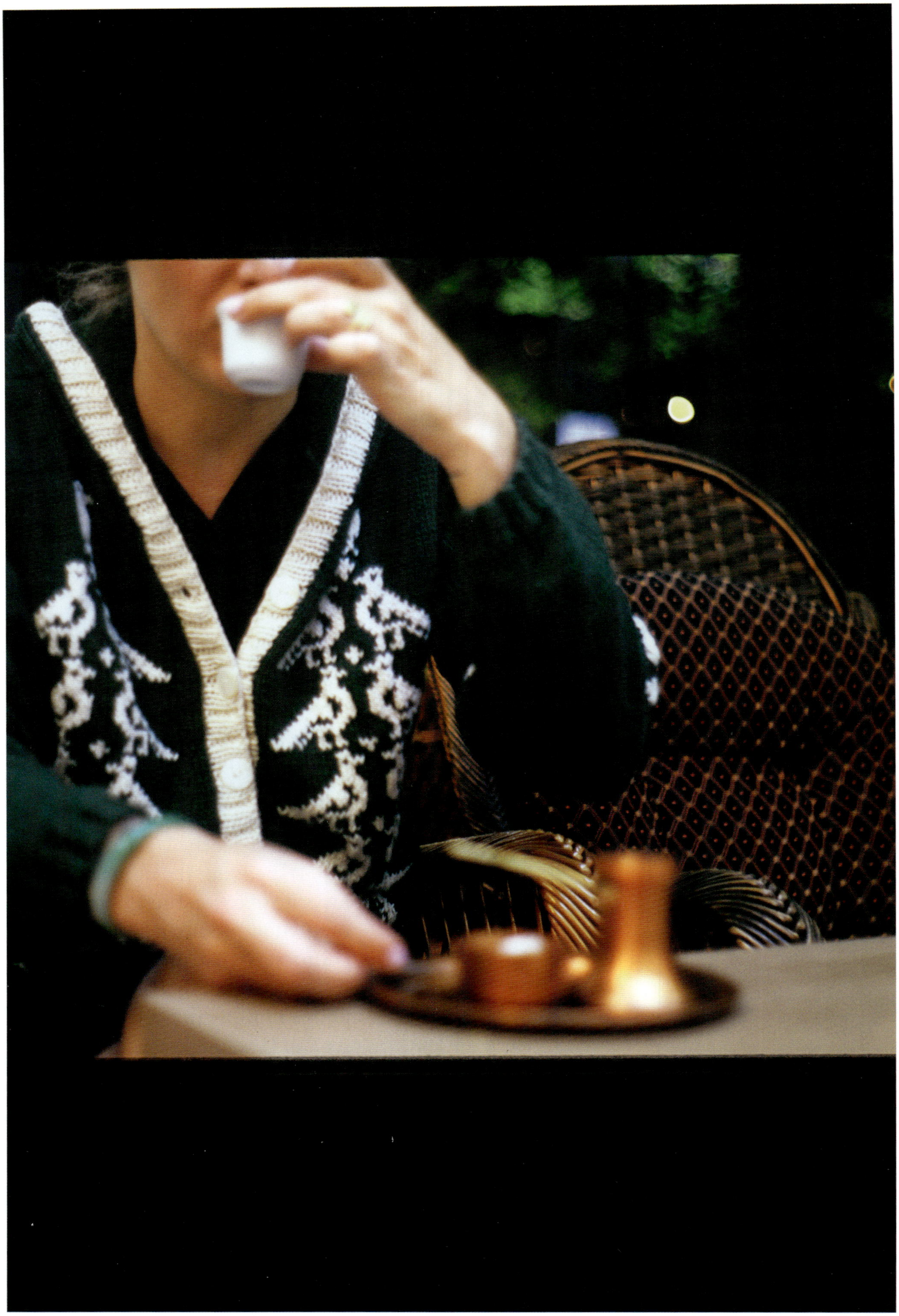

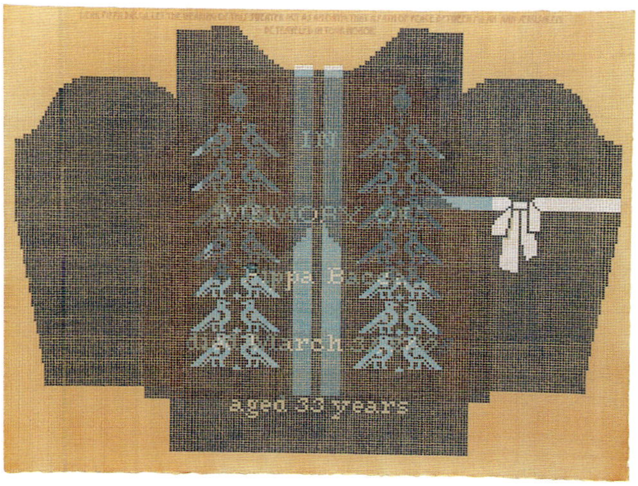

2

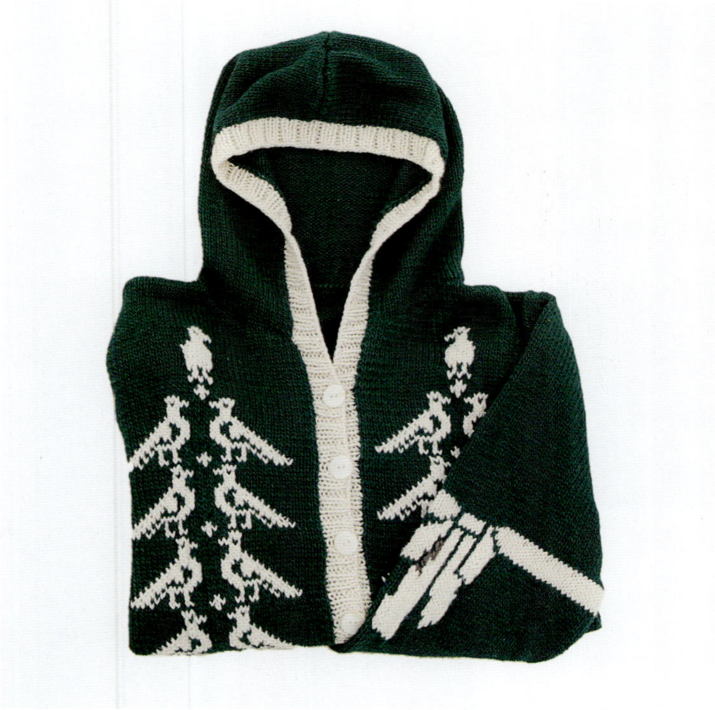

3

Frame
Ellen Lesperance

Can clothing embody ideology? Ellen Lesperance's austerely elegiac work, which resurrects hand-knitted sweaters worn by women engaged in direct action campaigns, suggests that it can. In works including *The Women of the Heresies Collective Meet on a Saturday Morning in 1977 Manhattan to Redress History* (2010), she draws on archival footage and photographs to create patterns in gouache and graphite on tea-stained paper, calculating the yarn gauges and sometimes reconstructing a complete design from a fragmentary image. Whether memorializing protesters who are still living or others who gave their lives, the works at once evoke shrouds and recall the need for warmth and a sense of community. The designs, which anyone can knit, can even be viewed as poetic matrixes for political action and solidarity. KMJ

Shown by
Ambach & Rice R20

Biography
Born 1971
Lives in Portland

American artist Lesperance's drawings and paintings have featured in numerous exhibitions in recent years. The solo show "The Strong, Star-Bright Companions" took place at Ambach & Rice, Seattle, in 2011, and featured a number of recent gouache and knitted works. Other solo shows include a self-titled exhibition at the Seattle Art Museum (2010), and "Off the Grid" at Monya Rowe Gallery, New York.

1
Untitled (Sarajevo)
2011
35mm slide
Dimensions variable
Courtesy of Ambach & Rice

2
Dear Pippa Bacca, Let the Wearing of This Sweater Act as an Oath: That a Path of Peace Between Milan and Jerusalem be Traveled in Your Honor
2011
Gouache and graphite on tea stained paper
22 × 29⅜"
(56 × 75 cm)
Courtesy of Ambach & Rice

3
Dear Pippa Bacca, Let the Wearing of This Sweater Act as an Oath: That a Path of Peace Between Milan and Jerusalem be Traveled in Your Honor.
2011
Wool sweater hand knited by the artist
Dimensions variable
Courtesy of Ambach & Rice

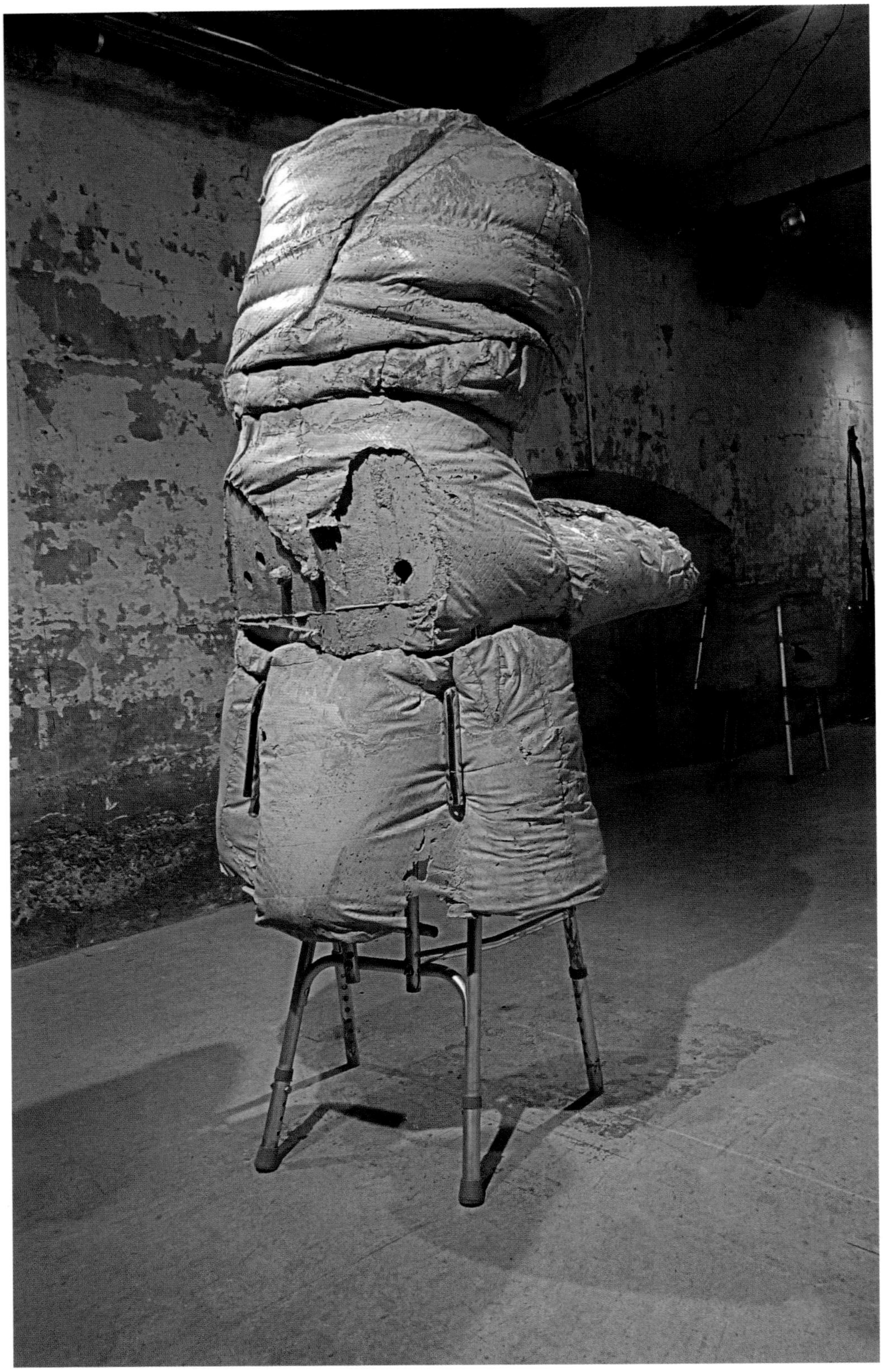

1

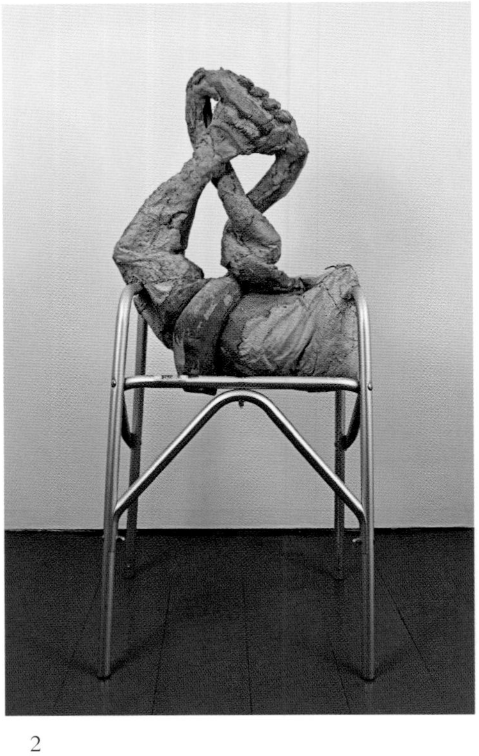

2

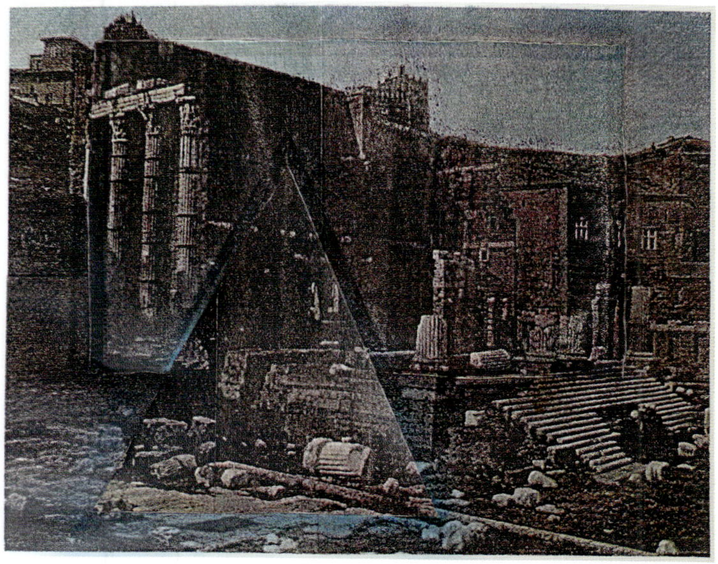

3

Shown by
Bureau R11

Biography
Born 1972
Lives in New York

American artist Matherly received an MFA from Hunter College, New York, in 2007, and a BFA from University of Pennsylvania, Philadelphia, in 2002. His anthropomorphic sculptures were the subject of the recent solo show "Readjusting my commitment to a greater legibility, or substance thinking and substance extended" (2011), at Bureau, New York. In 2010 he had a solo exhibition at Marginal Utility, Philadelphia, and contributed a sculptural project at FIAC, Paris.

1
The degenerated instinct which turns against life with subterranean vengefulness; See you again in your muck of tomorrow
2010
Concrete, ambulatory equipment
76 × 29⅛ × 39"
(193 × 74 × 99 cm)
Courtesy of Bureau

2
Fixed immovably into blank types of placid reverie; the eye is wide and without pupil
2011
Glass reinforced concrete, ambulatory equipment
48 × 22½ × 19"
(122 × 57 × 48 cm)
Courtesy of Bureau

3
Aestheticism is the garbage of intuitive feeling
2011
Inkjet monoprint transfer, spray paint
20⅞ × 26¾"
(53 × 68 cm)
Courtesy of Bureau

Frame

Justin Matherly

Justin Matherly has described his working process as "additive and subtractive," not only does he accrue a mass of reference material before beginning one of his sculptures, but his method of casting (in concrete, from foam and rubber or in heavy-duty bags) also involves both the building up and the "unearthing" of material. But the abiding thought is of something missing. Whether in the amputated bodies of Classical statues such as the Belvedere Torso, the subject of Matherly's *knowing, even the grass We must tear up so it will stay green* (2010–11), or the crutches and walking frames that support these concrete forms, his work is plagued by loss and sickness, and a melancholy sense of its own inadequacy. JG

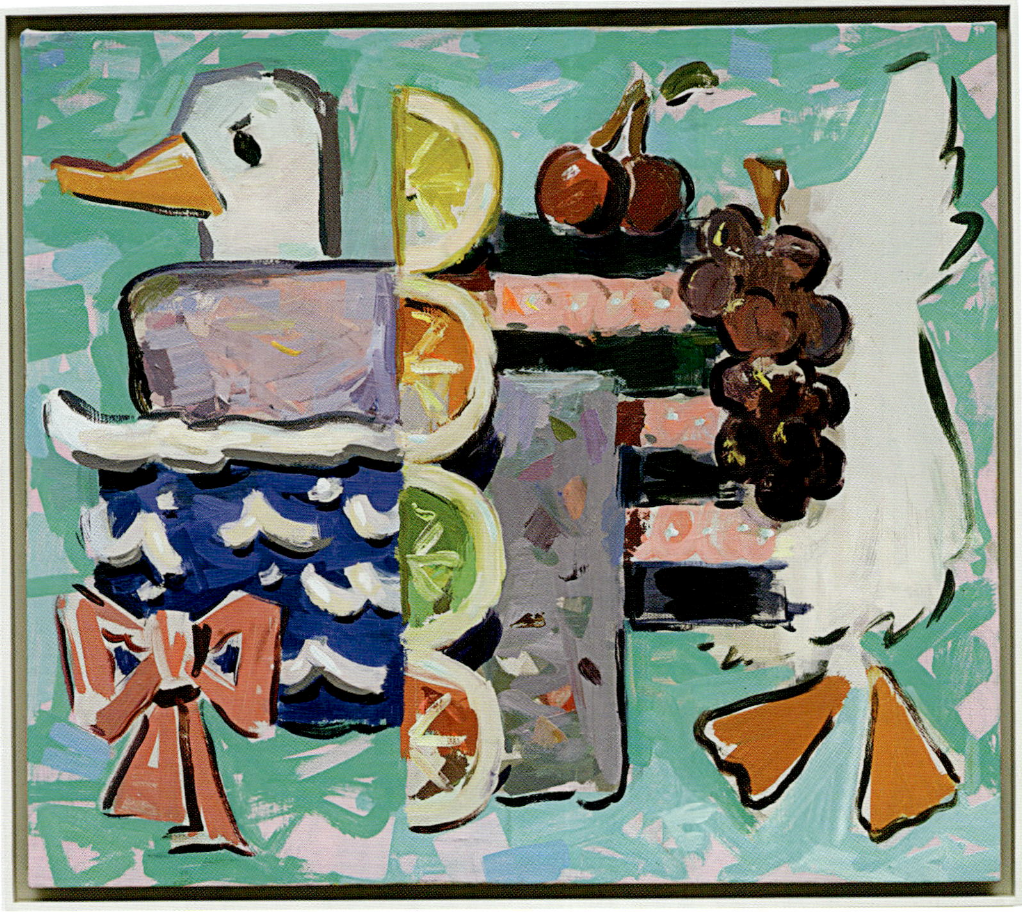

1

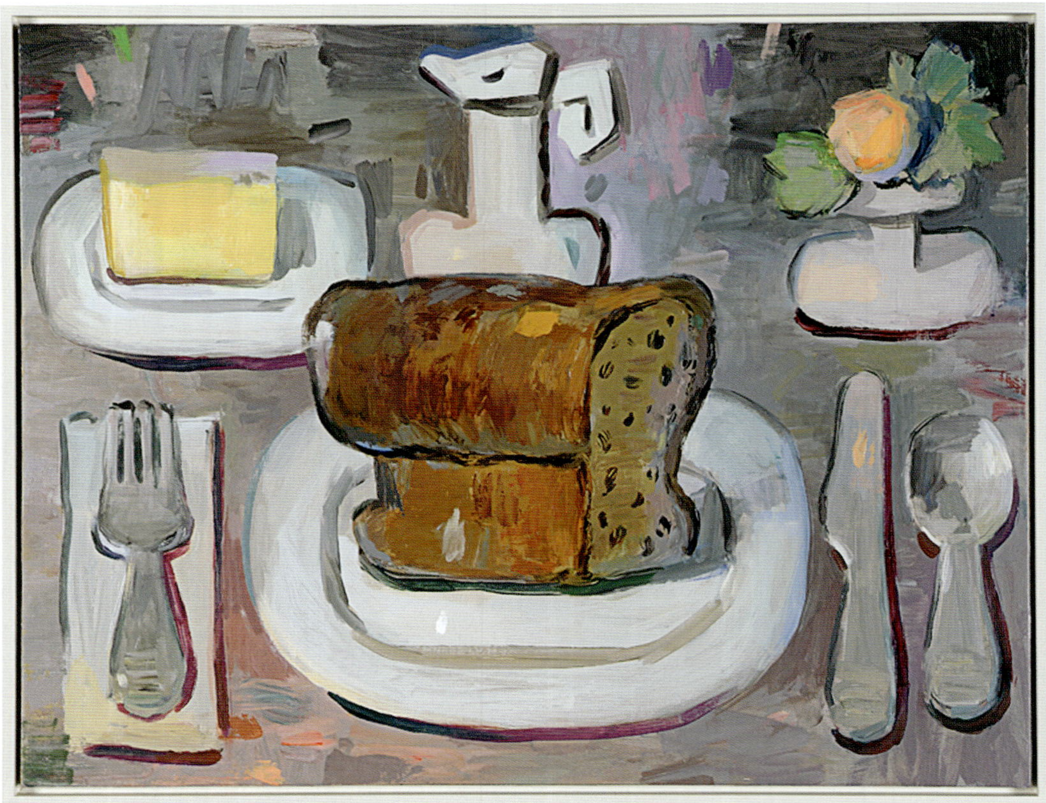

2

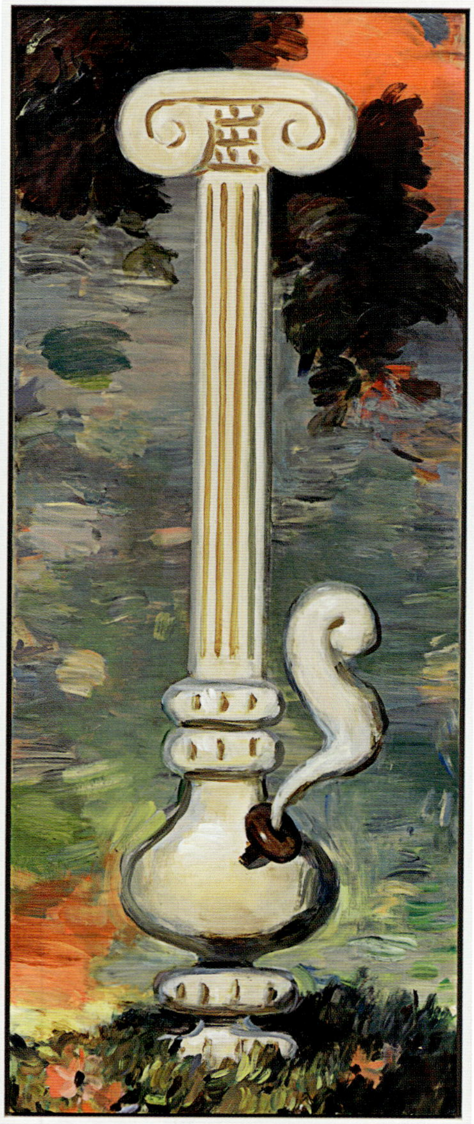

3

Shown by
Lüttgenmeijer R9

Biography
Born 1980
Lives in Berlin

American painter McLaughlin was included in the expansive survey exhibition "Based in Berlin" (2011). In recent years he has exhibited his work in the solo shows "Farley" (2010), at Timothy Taylor Gallery, London; "Bunsen" (2010) at The Two Jonnys, London; and "Nottle" (2009) Lüttgenmeijer, Berlin. In 2012 he will return to Lüttgenmeijer, Berlin, for a second solo show at the gallery.

1
Sour Duck Collage
2010
Oil on linen on board, frame
19⅝ × 22⅜"
(50 × 57 cm)
Courtesy of Lüttgenmeijer

2
Dinner Date (Brot)
2010
Oil on linen on board, frame
19⅝ × 26⅜"
(50 × 67 cm)
Courtesy of Lüttgenmeijer

3
The Classic
2009
Oil on linen on board, frame
38½ × 15¾"
(98 × 40 cm)
Courtesy of Lüttgenmeijer

Frame
Ryan McLaughlin

The objects and characters in the paintings of Ryan McLaughlin are always caught in the act of becoming—whether a pastry chef on the run in *The Jogging Croissantier* (2009) or his series of painted, mashed-up, still lifes that includes the aptly titled *Monti's Collage* (2010). McLaughlin's small paintings carry a quick, cartoon-like freedom with them, as in his "Dinner Date" series (2010), which in each rendition features a table set for dinner, a different item plonked down on the plate in each—a whole loaf of bread, a bunch of grapes, things that are *just* out of place enough to be unnerving. In McLaughlin's world of bristling possibilities, absurd narratives hover just beyond reality. CFW

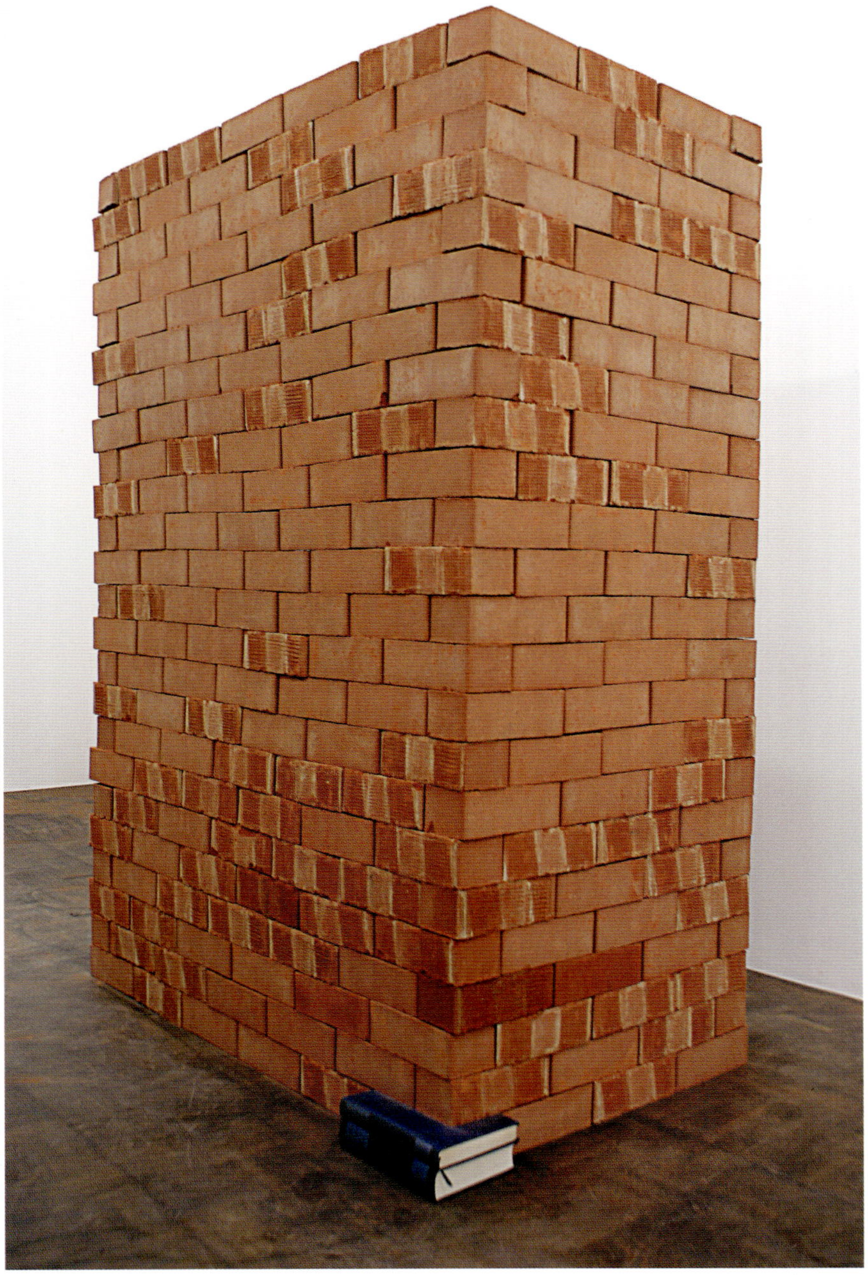

2

2

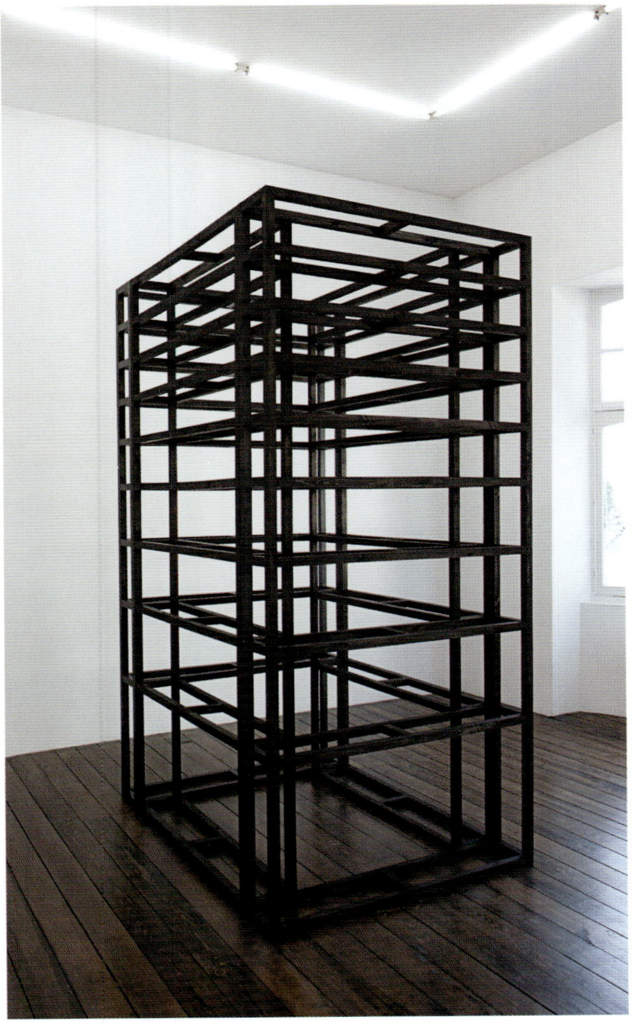

3

Shown by
Meessen De Clercq
R18

Biography
Born 1974
Lives in Guadalajara

Mexican artist Méndez Blake's literary influenced sculptures and installations have been exhibited prolifically in South America, Europe, and the United States, in the last decade. In 2012 he will have solo shows at OMR Galeria, Mexico City, and 1301PE, Los Angeles. Recent solo exhibitions include "Biblioteca Mallarmé" (Mallarmé Library, 2011), Travesia Cuatro, Madrid; "Empty Bookshelf" (2011) at Meessen De Clercq, Brussels; and "The Marquise Went Out at Five" (2010), Museo Rufino Tamayo, Mexico City.

1
The Capital and the Wall
2009
Medium
64⅛ × 46⅞ × 29½"
(163 × 119 × 75 cm)
Courtesy of Meessen De Clercq and OMR

2
Black Drawing
2011
Pencil on paper
59 × 59"
(150 × 120 cm)
Courtesy of Meessen De Clercq and OMR

3
Bookshelf Structure I
2011
Tainted wood
99¼ × 64½ × 47¼"
(252 × 164 × 120 cm)
Courtesy of Meessen De Clercq and OMR

Frame

Jorge Méndez Blake

Libraries are repositories of knowledge and potent symbols of civic identity. Jorge Méndez Blake's projects take off from multi-dimensionality to encompass audio, installation, architectural models, video, and performance. Often originating from literary sources—Conan Doyle, Kafka, Neruda—his interventions are driven by a concern with the fate of the library in what he calls the "age of iPads and Kindles." In *There Is No Easy Way From the Earth to the Stars* (2010), a model of Rem Koolhaas' iconic Seattle Public Library floats in a pool—a herald of a future when libraries have become so obsolete that they are simply pushed out to sea. SNS

Shown by
MISAKO & ROSEN
R19

Biography
Born 1972
Lives in Tokyo

Japanese painter Minamikawa has exhibited extensively in Japan in recent years. His solo show "Ghost, New Paintings, Tokyo, etc." at MISAKO & ROSEN, Tokyo, took place in 2011. Other recent solo shows include "And, ABC, Then," at Roppongi Hills A/D Gallery, Tokyo, and "Meguro Addresses—Artists in Urban Life," Meguro Museum of Art, Tokyo (2012). His work was included in the group shows "Selection" (2012), at the National Museum of Art, Osaka. He will have a solo show at 47 Canal, New York, in late 2012.

white / purple
2011
Acrylic on canvas
28¾ × 49⅝",
6¼" diameter
(73 × 126cm,
16cm diameter)
Courtesy of MISAKO & ROSEN

Frame
Shimon Minamikawa

Shimon Minamikawa finds a place for painting that thrives and relies on the quick-flip generation, making images and assemblages that feel like they've been suspended temporarily in stasis. Wallpaper patterns and geometric shapes contrast with flowers and floating heads—small canvases adjoin larger ones like footnotes or afterthoughts. In *Ghost (up up down up)* (2011), the profile of a blond-haired girl is repeated four times, faded underneath broad strokes of white paint that give the image the feel of a grainy photocopy. For Minamikawa, paintings are a spectral presence, visible fleetingly through the haze of the urban technology that surrounds us. CFW

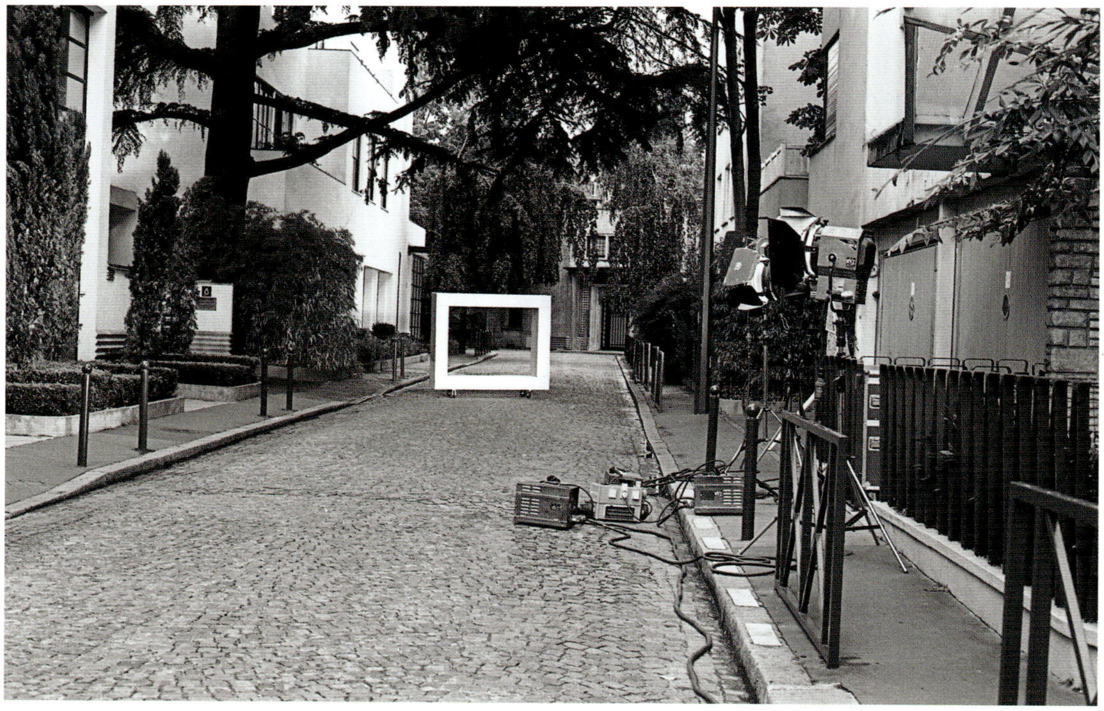

1

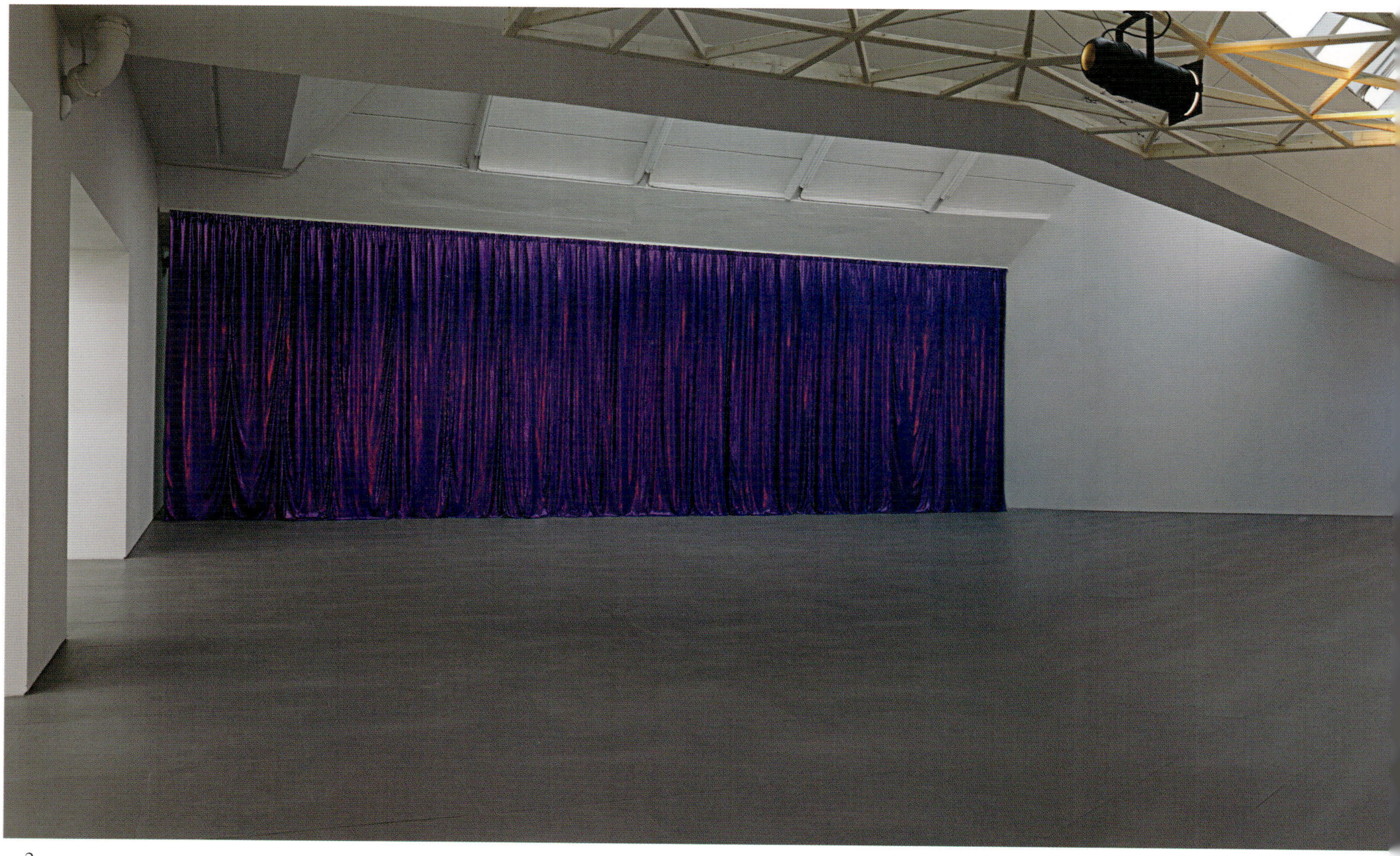

2

Shown by
Marcelle Alix R2

Biography
Born 1978
Lives in Paris

Moth's photographs and installations have been shown in numerous solo exhibitions in Europe and the United States in 2011. She had self-titled solo shows at Serralves Foundation, Porto, and Pied-à-Terre, San Francisco, while here fascination with language was encapsulated in the exhibitions; "Displacements" at carlier | gebauer, Berlin, and "Noting Thoughts" at Musée départemental d'art contemporain de Rochechouart. In 2010 Halle für Kunst, Lüneburg, staged "The Absent Forms"—another significant exhibition of her work.

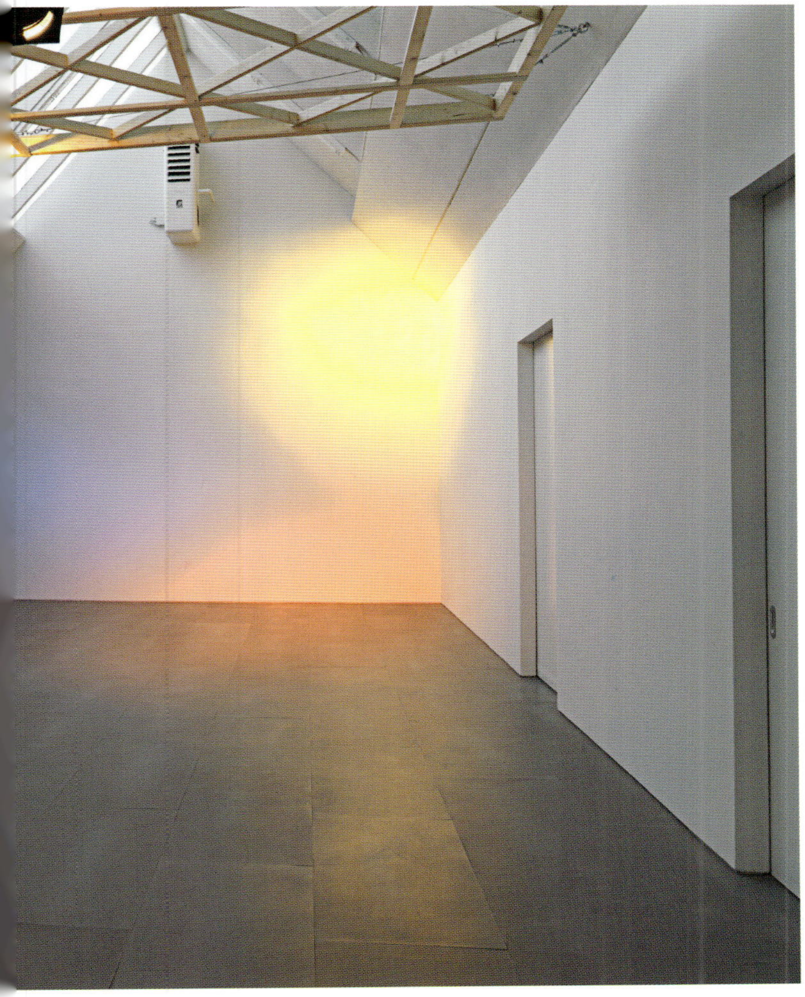

1
The Protagonists (1)
2010
Black and white analogue photograph, framed
12 × 16", 17⅜ × 22⅜" (30.5 × 40.5 cm, 44 × 57 cm) with frame
Courtesy of Marcelle Alix

2
LHS-Behind every surface there is a mystery: a hand that might emerge, an image that might be kindled, or a structure that might reveal its image (version 6)
2011
Installation of a sequined curtain
Made to measure
RHS-Wooden suspended lighting structure (version 2)
2011
Individually colored spot lights, wooden structure
163¾ x 203½" (416 x 517cm)
Installation view, carlier | gebauer
Courtesy of Marcelle Alix

Frame
Charlotte Moth

Since 1999, Charlotte Moth has worked on her *Travelogue*, composed from an ever-expanding collection of photographs shot in locales including Paris, Marseille, London, Los Angeles, Kyoto, Hamburg, Maastricht, and Brussels. She explains, "An image can later function as an aid to memory, it becomes a hybrid, and something perhaps better described as an 'image-memory'." This view, common in her photographs, sculptures, and films, is revealed in presentations of her work including her solo show at Bloomberg Space, London (2010), in which a slide show was concealed behind a glittering green curtain, and her recent exhibition "Noting Thoughts" (2011), inspired by photographs taken by Dadaist Raoul Hausmann in Ibiza in the 1930s. SL

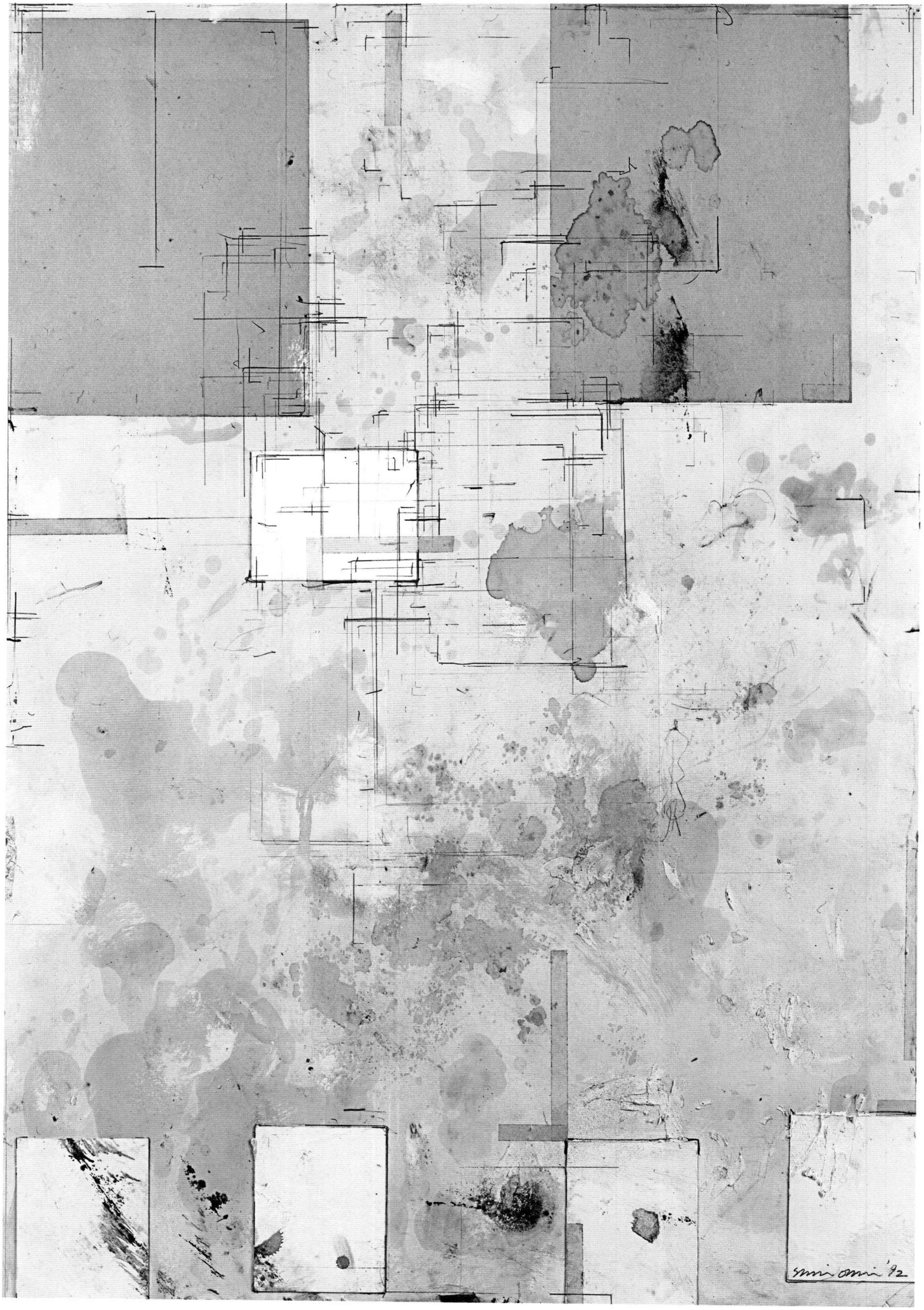

Frame
Shinro Ohtake

Shown by
Take Ninagawa R14

Biography
Born 1955
Lives in Uwajima

Japanese painter, sculptor, and musician Ohtake has exhibited internationally since the early 1980s. A retrospective exhibition of his work "New Universe on the Road," took place in 2007, at Fukuoka Art Museum, before touring to Hiroshima City Museum of Contemporary Art (2007). Forthcoming solo shows will take place at ArtSonje Center, Seoul (2012); Takamatsu City Museum of Art (2013); and 2nd Setouchi International Art Festival (2013). His work is in a number of prominent public collections including the Museum of Contemporary Art, Tokyo.

Retina Strobo
1992
Paper-mâché, tape, oil, and pencil on paper
39⅜ × 27½"
(100 × 70 cm)
Courtesy of Take Ninagawa

In 1977, when Japanese artmaking was dominated by Conceptualism and Minimalism, the 22-year-old Shinro Ohtake traveled from Tokyo to London, where he met Pop artists David Hockney and Russell Mills. Since then, his art has been ravenously accumulative, incorporating, he says, "whatever's in front of me." To date, that has included both Western and Japanese found imagery and text, which he pastes into elaborate scrapbooks, such as the 29 kilo *Scrapbook #65* (2005–10), onto paintings and collages (though he resists that term's Western, Modernist associations), and into messy, mystical sculptural assemblages such as *Zeroscape* (1991–9). Density—of time, and thus of memory—is central to his omnivorous work: what he has called "a delicate sense of thickness." JG

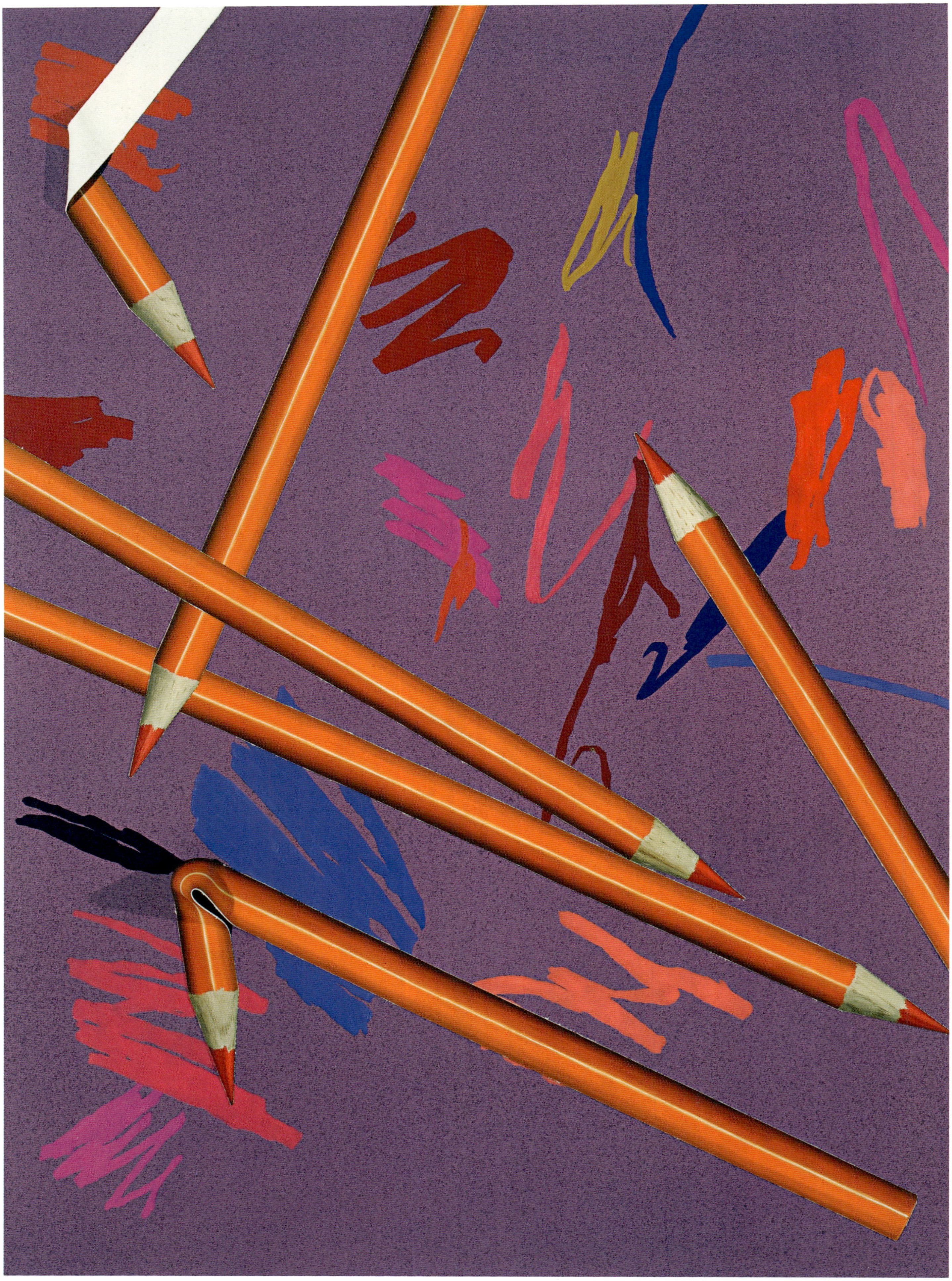

1

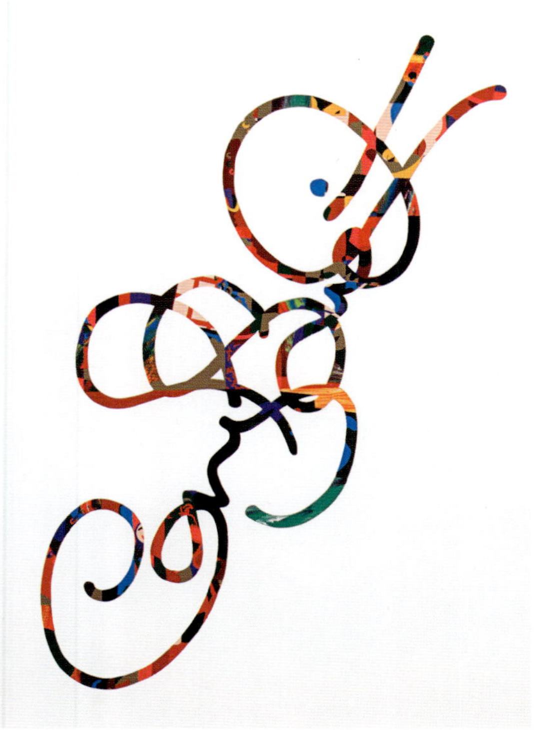

2

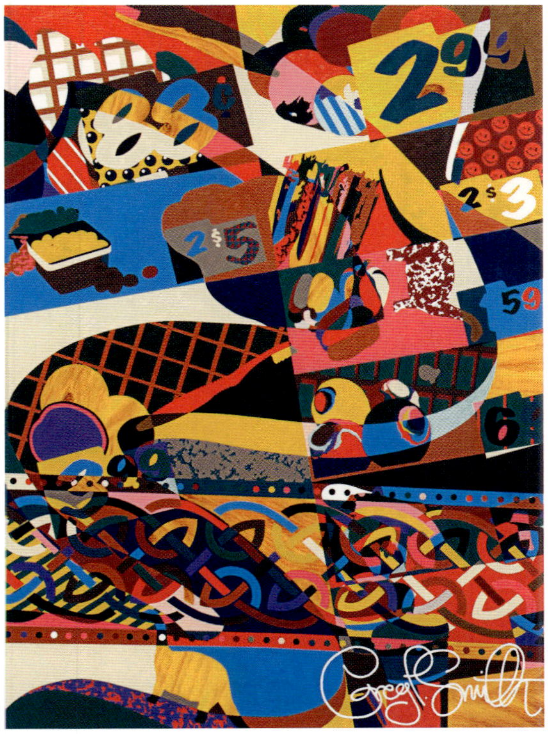

3

Shown by
BaliceHertling R12

Biography
Born 1983
Lives in New York

American painter Parma Smith received an MFA from Columbia University, New York, in 2007. Recent solo shows include "Life Drawings, Poseurs and 'thirteen paintings on canvas'" (2012), at Balice Hertling & Lewis; "Early Work" (2009) at Khastoo Gallery, Los Angeles; and "Adult Learning" (2008) at Swiss Institute, New York. Group shows include "Dick Blick meets Herr Boesner" (2011) at Everest/Fondation Gutzwiller, Zurich; "The Panel Discussion, The Tennis Match, and A Bodegón" (2011) at Andrew Roth Gallery, New York; and "Greg Parma Smith & Zin Taylor" (2010) at Front Room, Contemporary Art Musuem St. Louis.

1
Colored Pencil Techniques 4
2010
Oil on canvas collaged onto oil and acrylic on canvas
32 × 24"
(81.5 × 61 cm)
Courtesy of BaliceHertling

2
Early Work 2
2009
Oil on gessoed canvas
32 × 24"
(81.5 × 61 cm)
Courtesy of BaliceHertling

3
Early Work 3
2009
Oil on canvas
32 × 24"
(81.5 × 61 cm)
Courtesy of BaliceHertling

Frame

Greg Parma Smith

Combining formal examinations of surface with post-Pop styling, Greg Parma Smith's meticulous oil paintings feel freighted with psychological unease. Often depicting mass-produced mark-making tools familiar from the schoolroom (wax crayons, colored pencils), they explore the link between childhood art education and adult art practice while asking pointed questions about the nature of representation and the rewards of adhering to, or deviating from, certain models of competence. Notably, in his canvas *Early Work 1* (2009), an eyeless mask in the shape of a crescent moon appears to haunt an image of a packet of Crayola oil pastels. This, perhaps, is the cold face of sophistication. Comely, yes, but also expressionless and blind. TM

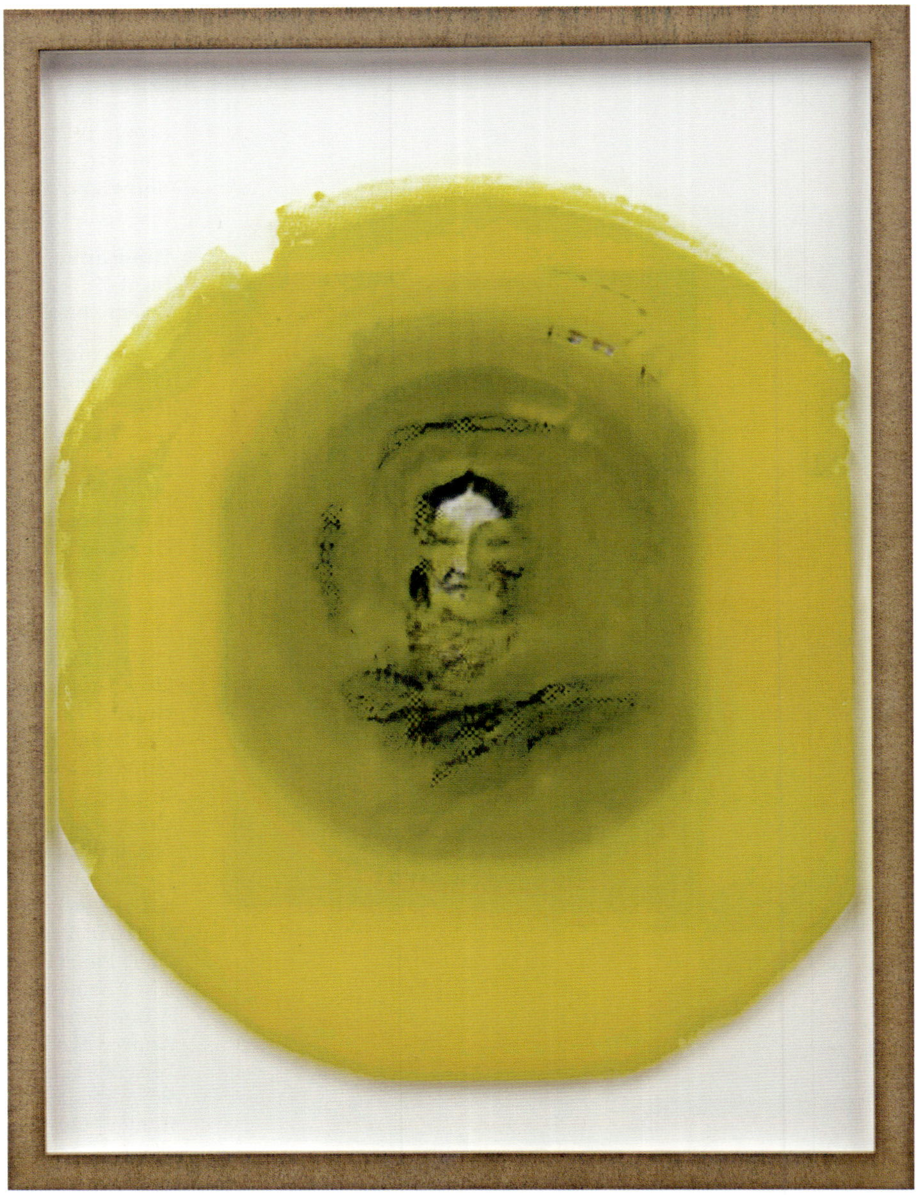

2

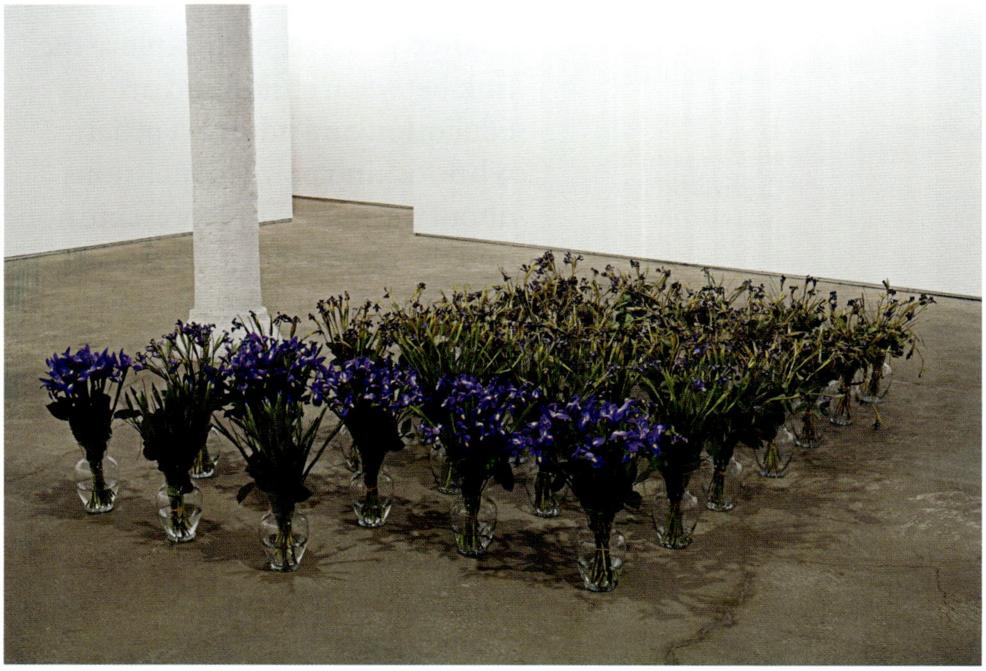

1

Frame

Matt Sheridan Smith

Matt Sheridan Smith likes to employ symbols in the sure knowledge that they never quite do what they should. *Soft Futures (price has no memory)* (2010), for instance, consisted of four large inflatable forms representing grain, coffee, wool, and canola. The icons are slippery not only semiotically—canola, for instance, was mystifyingly represented by a sphere—but also temporally, in that they refer to commodities traded speculatively on the futures market. The exhibition "Tell Me the Truth—Am I Still in the Game?" (2011) sketched the outlines of four characters, including the British World War II pilot Douglas Bader and a woman known only as "Katie,"with poised arrangements of prints and objects, such as a silk scarf or a banana, composed in unusual combinations: maddeningly abbreviated memorials to four unknowable lives. JG

Shown by
kaufmann repetto A23
mother's tankstation R1

Biography
Born 1980
Lives in New York

American sculptor and installation artist Sheridan Smith was recipient of the Lower Manhatten Cultural Council's Paris Residency in 2010. His installations have been the subject of the recent solo exhibitions "Tell me the truth—am I still in the game?" (2011) at Forde, Geneva and Kaufmann Repetto, Milan (2011). Group shows include "Flotsam/Jetsam" (2010), Western Bridge, Seattle, and a two-person show at Front Room, Contemporary Art Museum St. Louis (2011). He has a forthcoming show with mother's tankstation, Dublin in fall 2012.

1
Untitled (congratulations)
2007
Glass vases, irises delivered daily for the duration of an exhibition, shown here: Day 38
Dimensions variable
Collection of Ruth and William True

2
Double expiration portrait (widow)
2011
Enamel screenprint on plexiglas, and mounted digital photo print
21 × 16"
(53.5 × 40.6 cm)
Courtesy of mother's tankstation

3
Untitled
2010
Silver-plated bread
Two Pieces:
5 × 3 × 3"
(12.5 × 7.5 × 7.5 cm each)
Courtesy of mother's tankstation

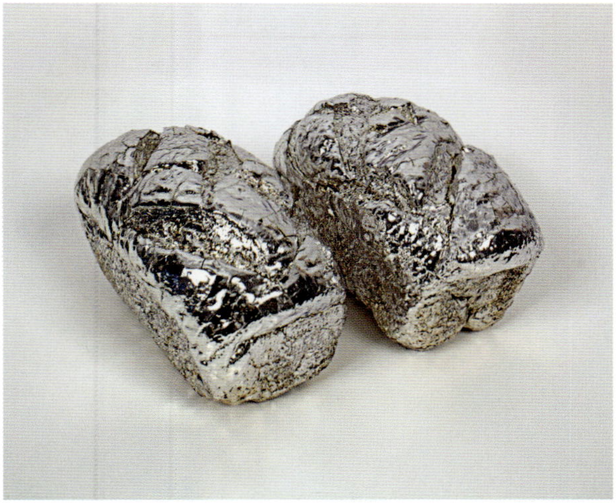

3

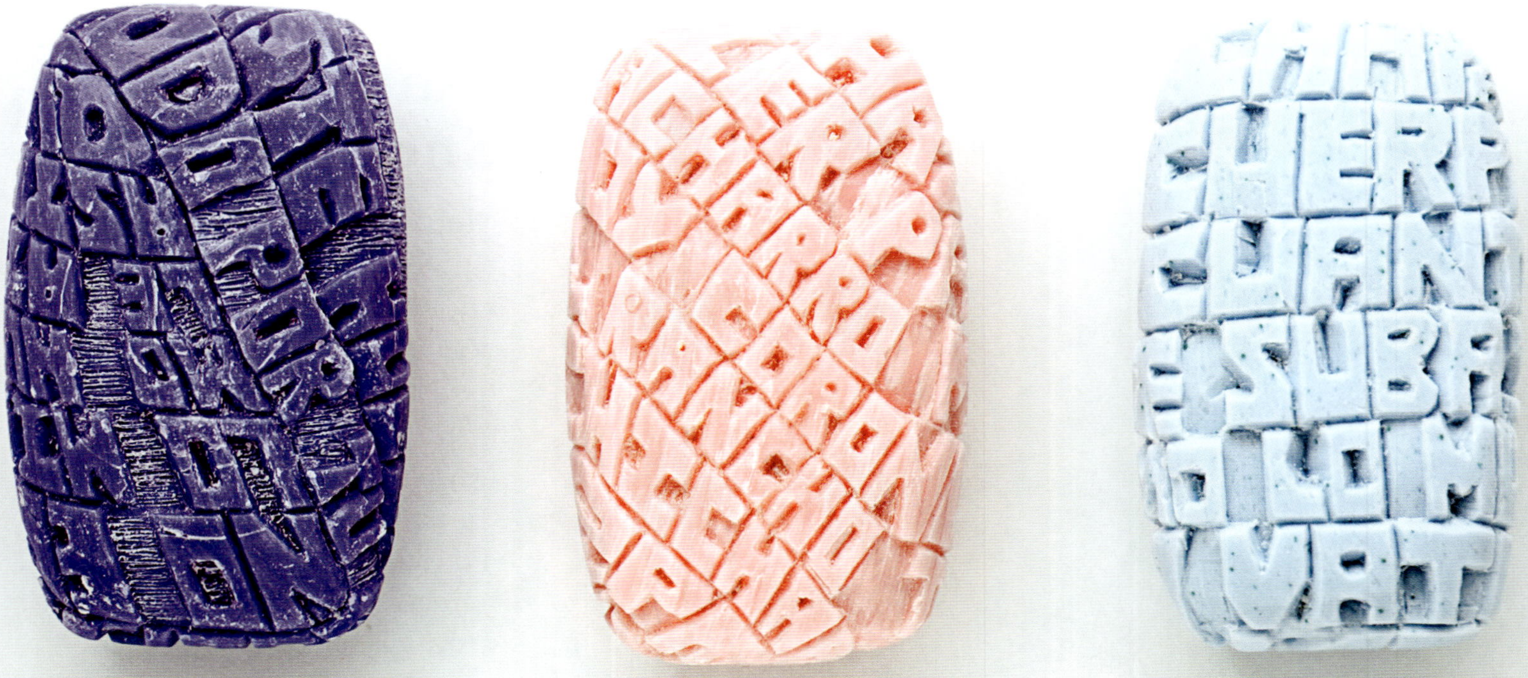
CUERP
CUANT
SUBR
LOM
VAT

Frame
Antonio Vega Macotela

Antonio Vega Macotela upends dominant models of capitalist exchange by creating his own resistant mini-economies. In 2011, for the "Visionary Trading Project," he collaborated with Alfadir Luna to purchase Londoners' house dust by weight at the market value of sterling silver—they later stored it in a bank box. In *Time Exchange* (2006–10), Vega Macotela collaborated with prison inmates, each completing a task for the other: he located a girlfriend or attended a family event on the "outside," while the inmate catalogued their pulse or mapped their steps, continuing to push the symbolic value of money, objects, and services into overdrive, chipping away at the standards of the mainstream market. SNS

Shown by
Steve Turner Contemporary R13

Biography
Born 1980
Lives in Mexico City and Amsterdam

Mexican artist Vega Macotela studied at the National School of Fine Arts, Mexico City, the Multimedia Seminary, Mexico City, and will graduate from the Rijksakademie van Beeldende Kunsten, Amsterdam, in 2012. In early 2012, the solo exhibition "Whispering" took place at Steve Turner Contemporary, Los Angeles. His concept-driven work is included in the survey exhibition "The Ungovernables" (2012), New Museum, New York, and he participated in the 29th São Paulo Biennial (2010).

1
Time Exchanges 346, 347, 348
2007
Three bars of soap: In exchange for the artist's attempts to return El Gochi's paralyzed face to its normal state, El Gochi carved three bars of soap using three forms of prison jargon
3½ × 2⅜ × 2" each
(9 × 5 × 5 cm each)
Courtesy of Steve Turner Contemporary

2
Time Exchange 108
2007
Photograph: In exchange for videotaping Carlos playing basketball, the artist had him write his autobiography on his arms so that it would appear in the recording.
14⅛ × 10⅝"
(36 × 27 cm)
Courtesy of Steve Turner Contemporary

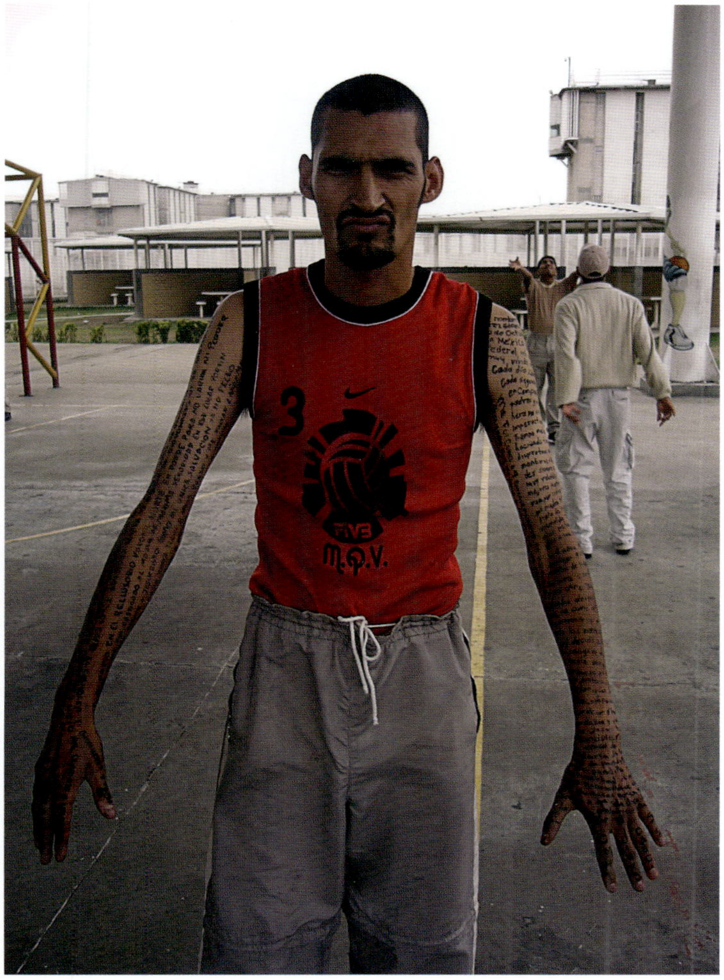

2

1

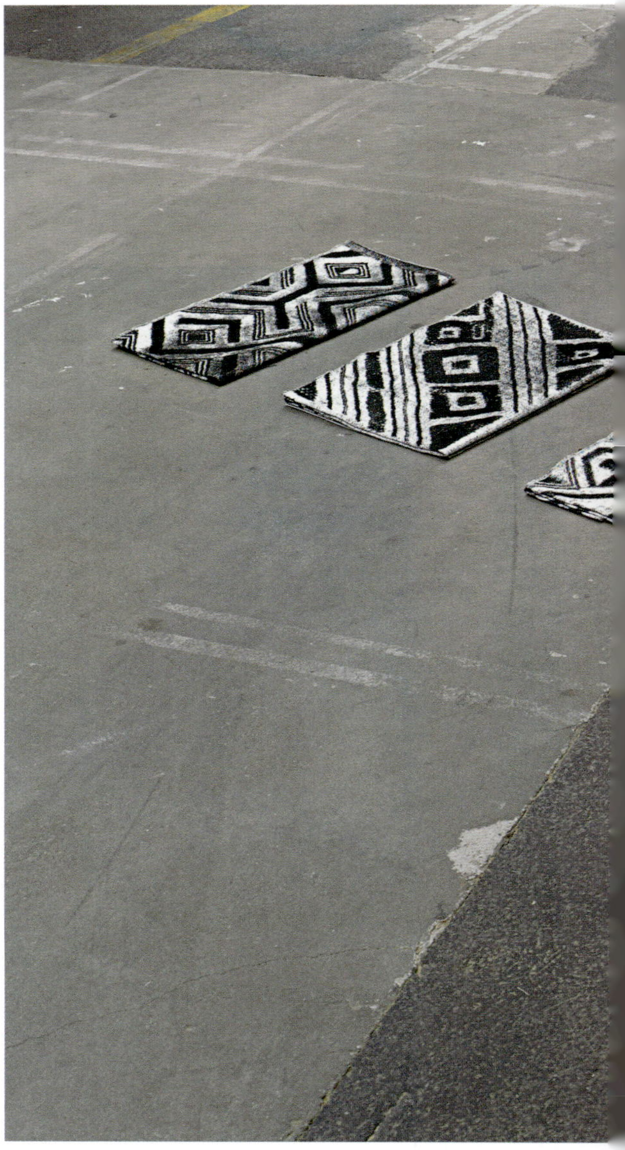

2

Frame
Vincent Vulsma

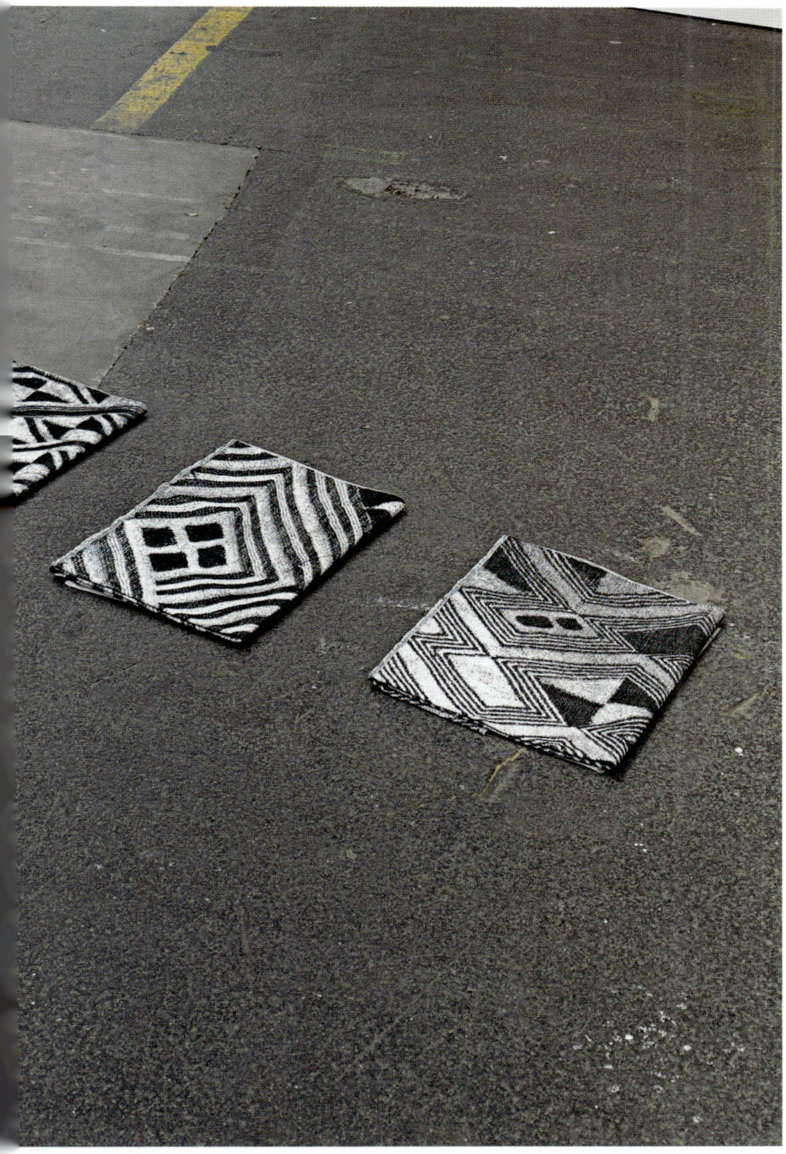

Shown by
Galerie Cinzia Friedlaender R3

Biography
Born 1982
Lives in Amsterdam

Dutch artist Vulsma's work has come to international prominence in recent years. In 2011, he had his second solo exhibition with Galerie Cinzia Friedlaender, Berlin. That year he also had the solo show "A Sign of Autumn" at Stedelijk Museum, SMBA Project, Amsterdam. His paintings have been included in numerous group shows including "A Text Is A Thing" Vistamare, Pescara; "Prix de Rome 2011" Smart Project Space, Amsterdam; and the 6th Berlin Biennial (2010).

1
ARS NOVA E5305-B #7
2009
Spray paint on shrink film over prefabricated cotton canvas
3 × 39⅜"
(80 × 100 cm)
Courtesy of Galerie Cinzia Friedlaender

2
Foreign Exchange
2011
Floor piece (5 parts): Tufted Cloths (S1016) jacquard fabric, black cotton yarn and raw white rayon raffia fibre
15 × 22", 14⅛ × 24", 13¾ × 26¾", 17⅜ × 25⅛", 13¾ × 27⅛"
(38 × 56 cm, 35 × 61 cm, 35 × 68 cm, 44 × 64 cm, 35 × 69 cm)
Courtesy of Galerie Cinzia Friedlaender

In 1935, during the exhibit "African Negro Art" at the Museum of Modern Art in New York, Walker Evans photographed most of the artifacts collected in the show. Among them were examples of Kuba textiles from the Congo, six of which Vincent Vulsma had replicated for the "WE455" (2011) series. The fabrics—made on a punchcard Jacquard loom, the mechanical precursor to early computers—are part of a constellation of works that juxtapose the objects of colonial inquiry (be it aesthetic or anthropological) with the forms and motivations of Western Modernism. For the show "A Sign of Autumn" (2011), Vulsma brought together walnut stools by Ray Eames and African stools from Belgium's notorious Royal Museum of Central Africa to produce ambiguous "unreadymades." BD

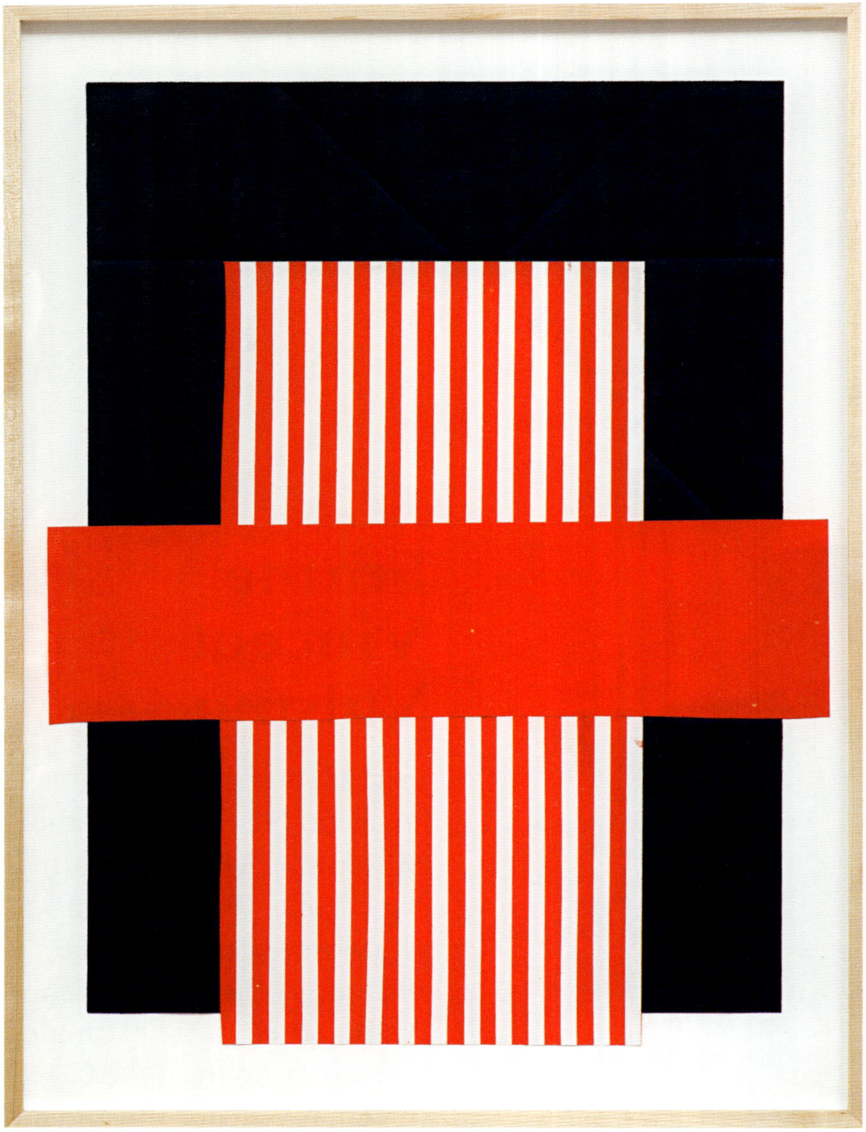

1

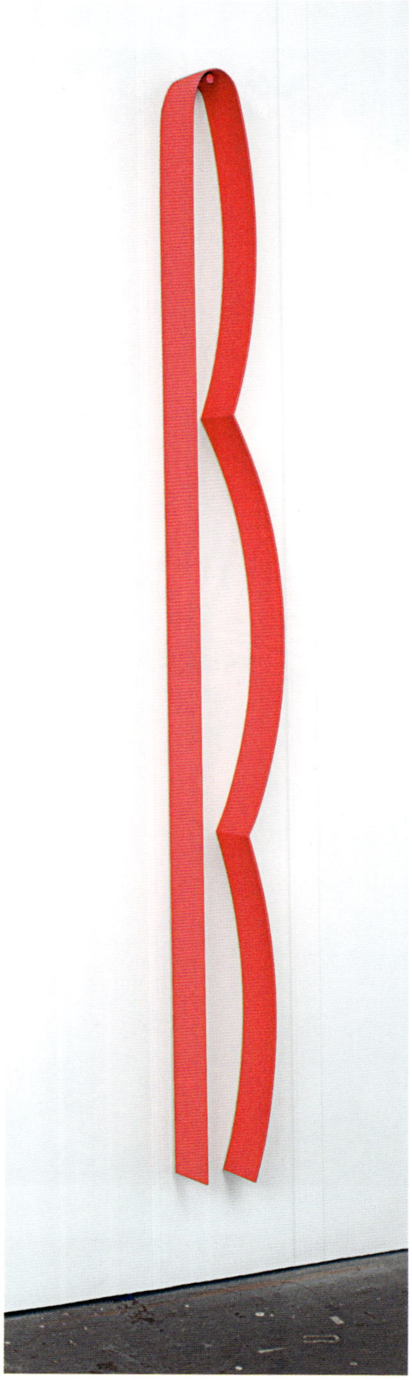

2

Frame
Lisa Williamson

The mordant wit of Lisa Williamson's colorful painted sculptures often derives from the failure of wood and other stiff materials to drape, as in *Untitled (Sag)* (2008), which looks like a striped towel hanging from a peg but is actually a stiff facsimile, rendered with acrylic and enamel paint on canvas. Her recent works have mapped the discrepancies between soft and hard materials on surreal considerations of the body: for example, *Flat Pants!* (2011), a pair of carved wooden trousers folded at right angles over a bench, or *Club Foot and The Towel* (2011), a wall-mounted frame hung with a "towel" of stiff pink canvas, supported by a solitary wooden leg with an amputated brick-shaped foot. SL

Shown by
Shane Campbell Gallery R17

Biography
Born 1977
Lives in Los Angeles

American artist Williamson received an MFA from University of Southern California, Los Angeles, in 2008. Her delicate works were the subject of the recent exhibition "Thinking Objects" (2011) at Shane Campbell Gallery, Chicago; and in 2010 "The Reader in the Garden" at Unosunove Arte Contemporanea, Rome. In 2011 she participated in group shows on both sides of the Atlantic with "Weird Walks into a Room (Comma)" at The Box, Los Angeles, and "Americans and Apricots" at Hilary Crisp, London.

1
Red, White and Blue, Folded and Pressed
2011
Acrylic on paper
29½ × 21⅝"
(75 × 55 cm)
Courtesy of Shane Campbell Gallery

2
Bump
2011
Acrylic on steel
78¾ × 7⅜ × 4"
(200 × 19 × 10 cm)
Courtesy of Shane Campbell Gallery

3
The Study
2011
Acrylic and linen on paper
30¾ × 21¼"
(78 × 54 cm)
Courtesy of Shane Campbell Gallery

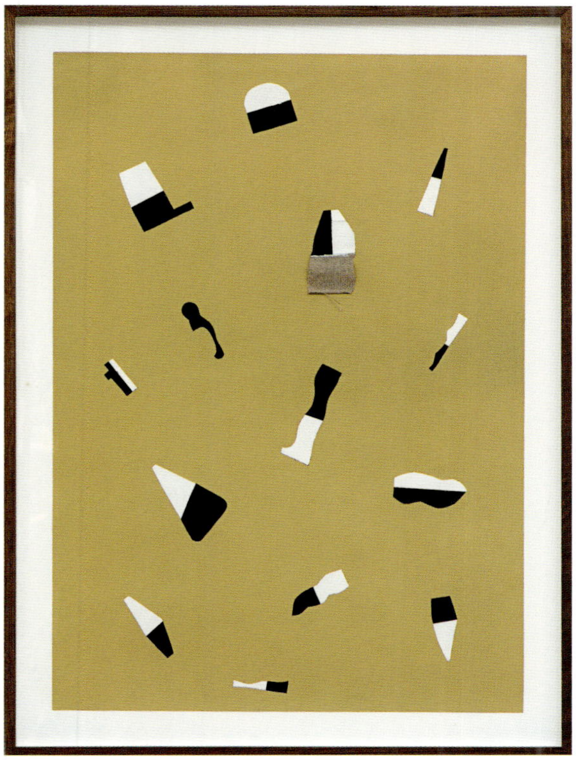

3

Contributors

(MA) Max Andrews is the co-founder and co-director of Latitudes, Barcelona, and is a regular contributor to *frieze.*

(AB) Andrew Bonacina is a curator and writer based in London.

(SC) Steven Cairns is a writer based in London.

(BD) Brian Dillon is a regular contributor to *frieze* and UK editor of *Cabinet.*

(CFW) Chris Fite-Wassilak is a writer and curator based in London. He is a regular contributor to *frieze, Art Review*, *Art Monthly*, and *Art Papers.*

(JG) Jonathan Griffin is a writer based in Los Angeles. He contributes to magazines including *frieze*, *Art Review*, *Texte zur Kunst*, *Mousse,* and *Flash Art.*

(KJ) Kristin M. Jones is a writer based in New York. She is a regular contributor to *frieze*, *Film Comment* and *The Wall Street Journal.*

(KK) Katie Kitamura is a critic and novelist based in New York.

(QL) Quinn Latimer is an American poet and critic based in Basel. She is a regular contributor to *frieze, Artforum*, and various artist monographs and anthologies.

(SL) Sarah Lowndes is a writer and curator based in Glasgow, where she is also a lecturer at Glasgow School of Art.

(SOR) Sally O'Reilly is a writer based in London.

(TM) Tom Morton is a writer, curator, and contributing editor for *frieze*, and is based in London

(SNS) Sarah-Neel Smith is a writer based in Los Angeles. She writes regularly for *frieze.*

(PT) Paul Teasdale is assistant editor of *frieze* and is based in London.

(ST) Sam Thorne is associate editor of *frieze* and is based in London. He is also a visiting lecturer at the Royal College of Art, London.

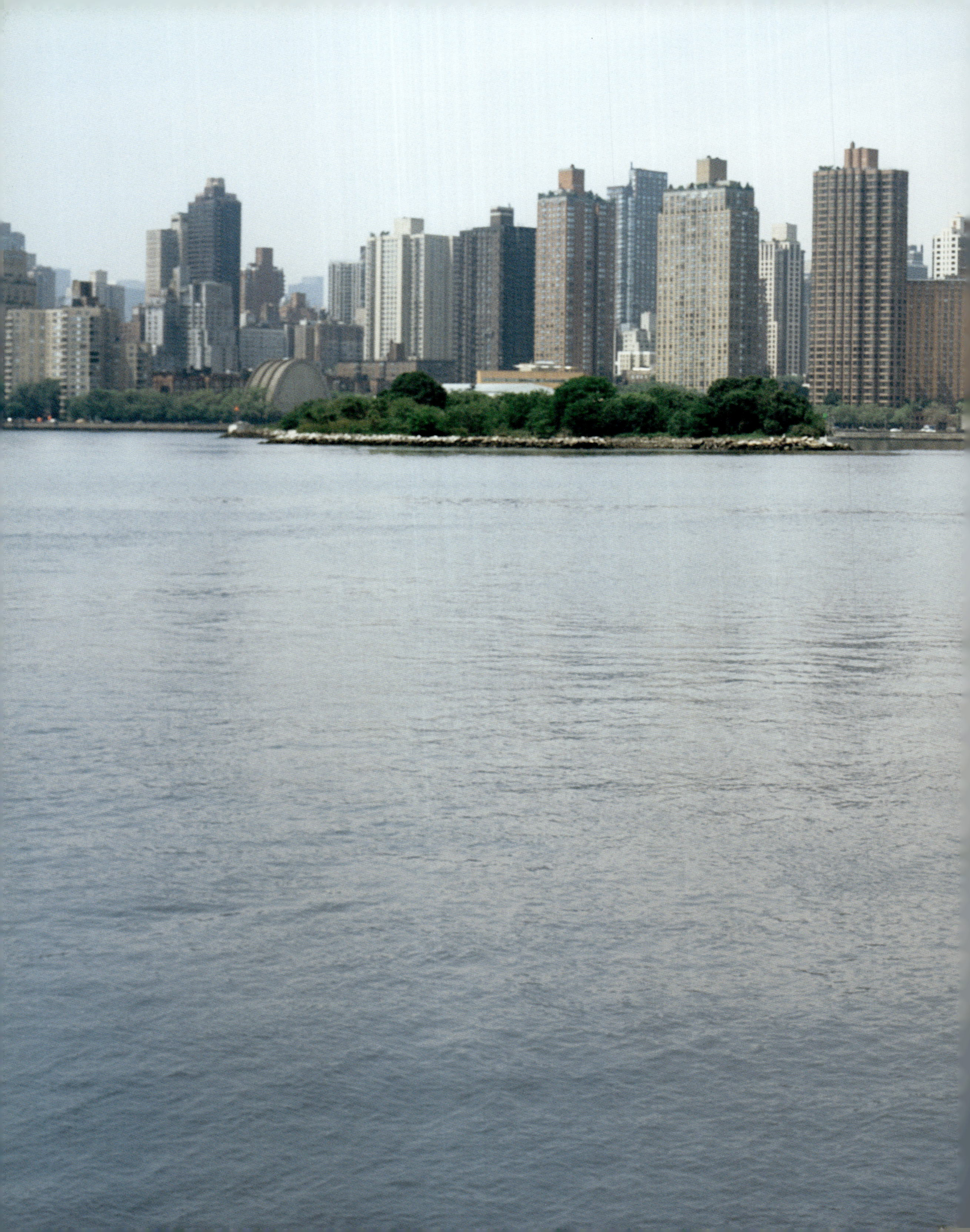

Advertisements

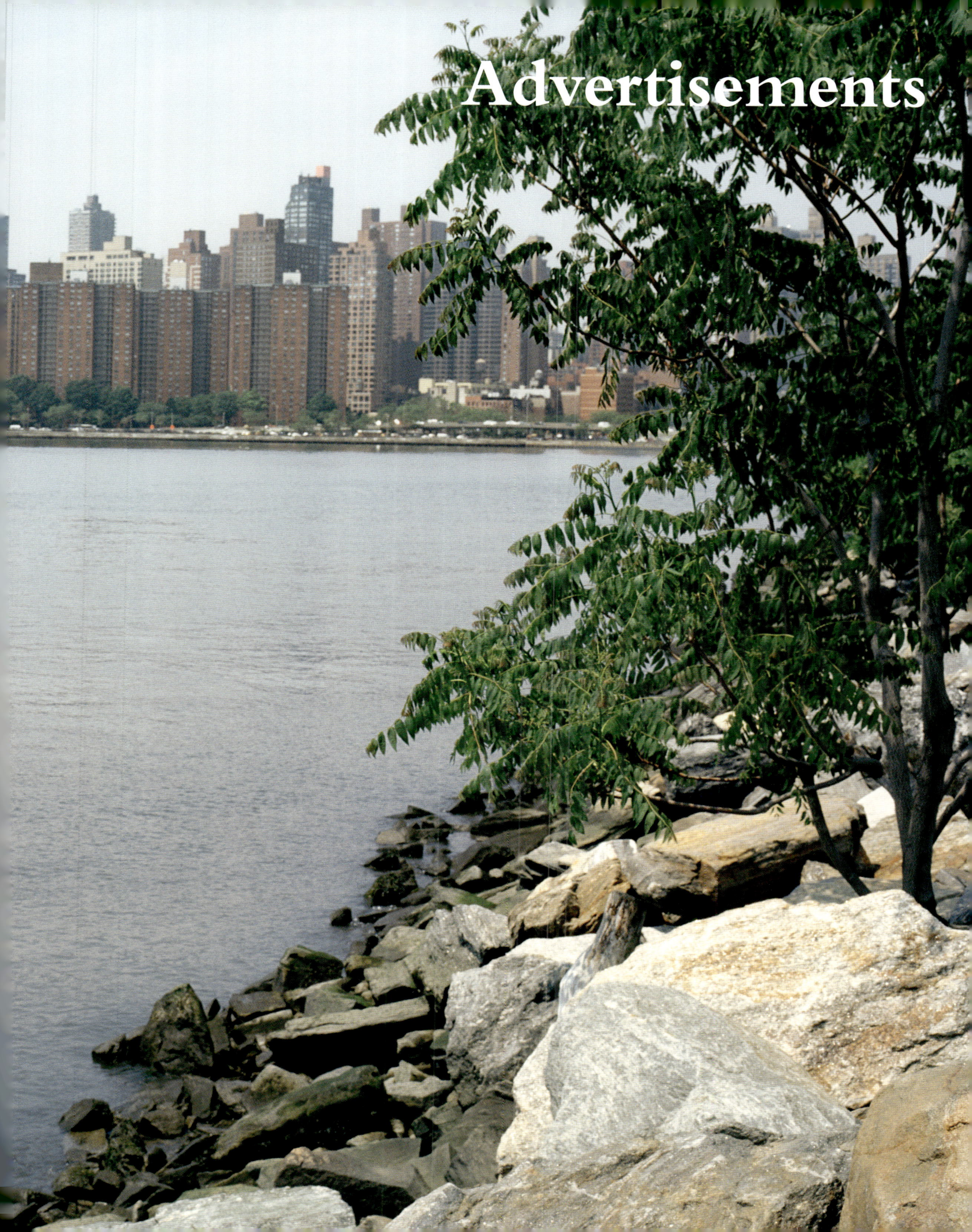

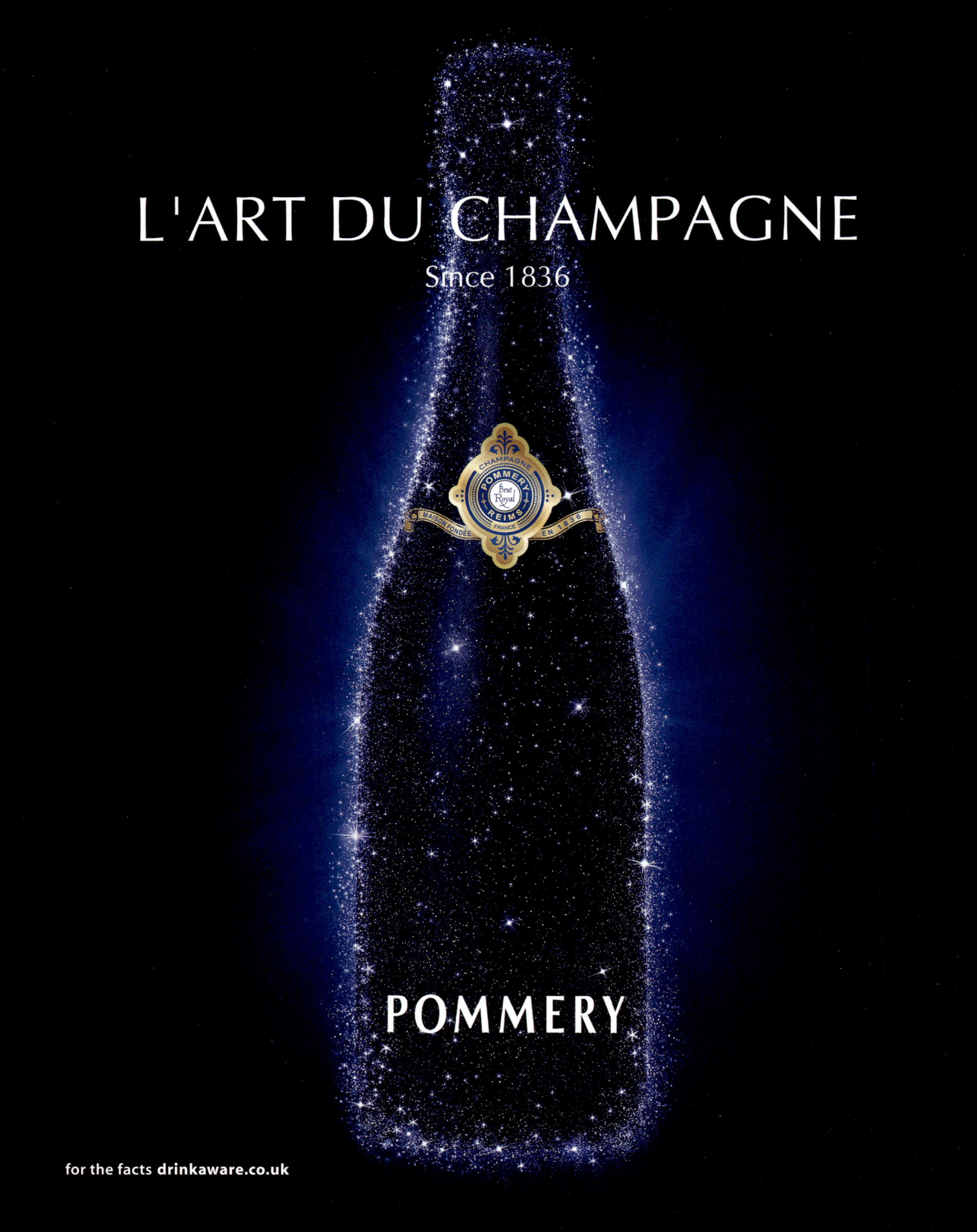
L'ART DU CHAMPAGNE
Since 1836
CHAMPAGNE
POMMERY
Brut Royal
REIMS
FRANCE
MAISON FONDÉE EN 1836
POMMERY
for the facts drinkaware.co.uk

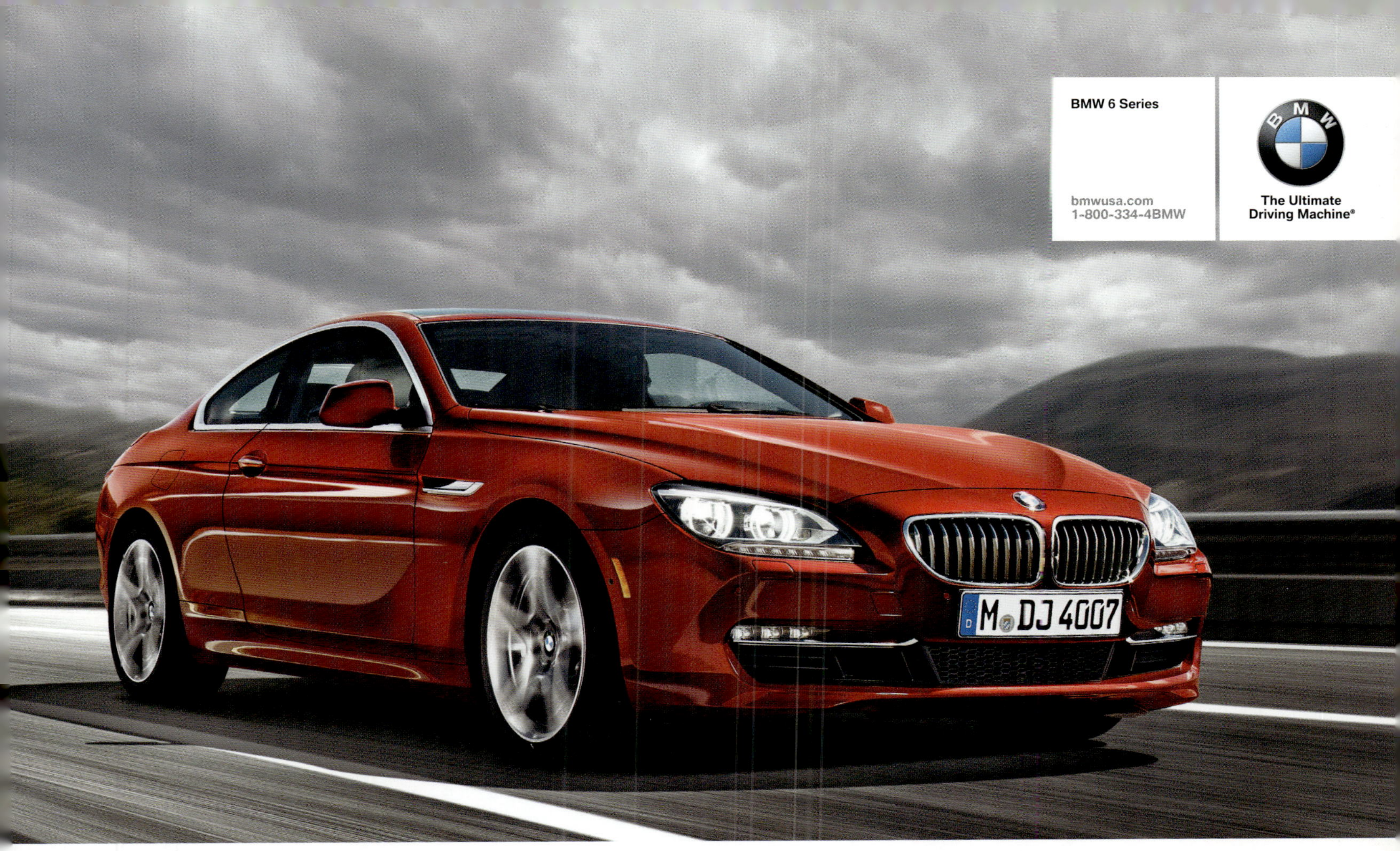

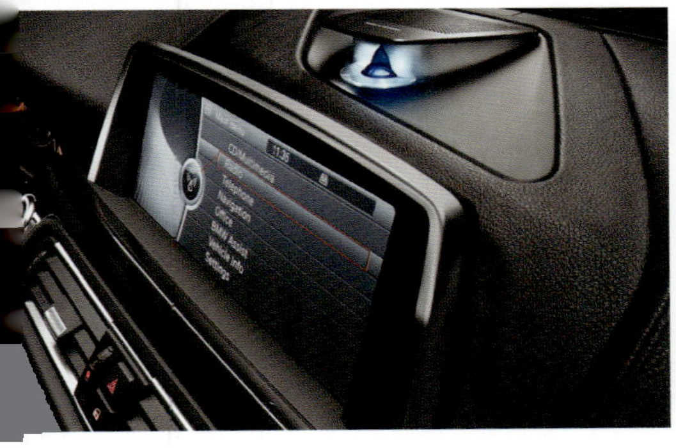

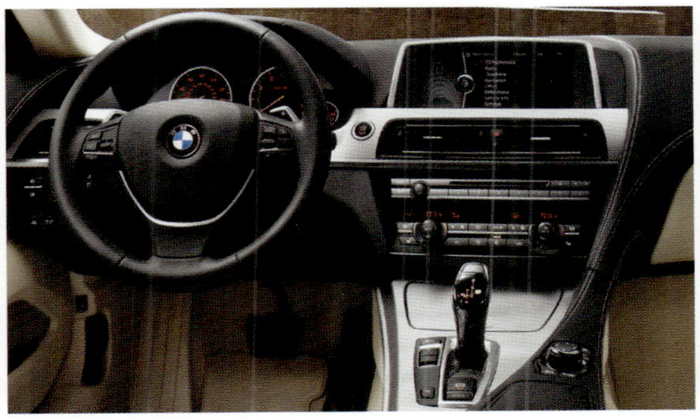

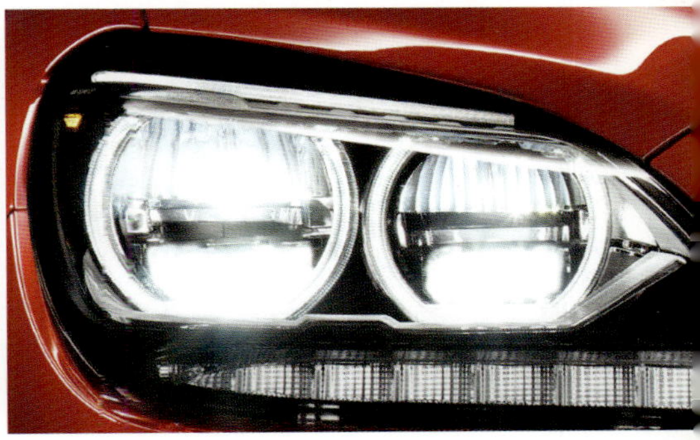

REMEMBER TO BREATHE.

It can be overwhelming. The moment — taken with beauty, fixated on performance. When visual allure is matched only by remarkable athleticism. But there's no need to catch your breath quite yet. Because elegance like this speaks for itself.
bmwusa.com/6coupe

THE BMW 6 SERIES COUPE. NOW WITH xDRIVE.

USA

Proud Partner

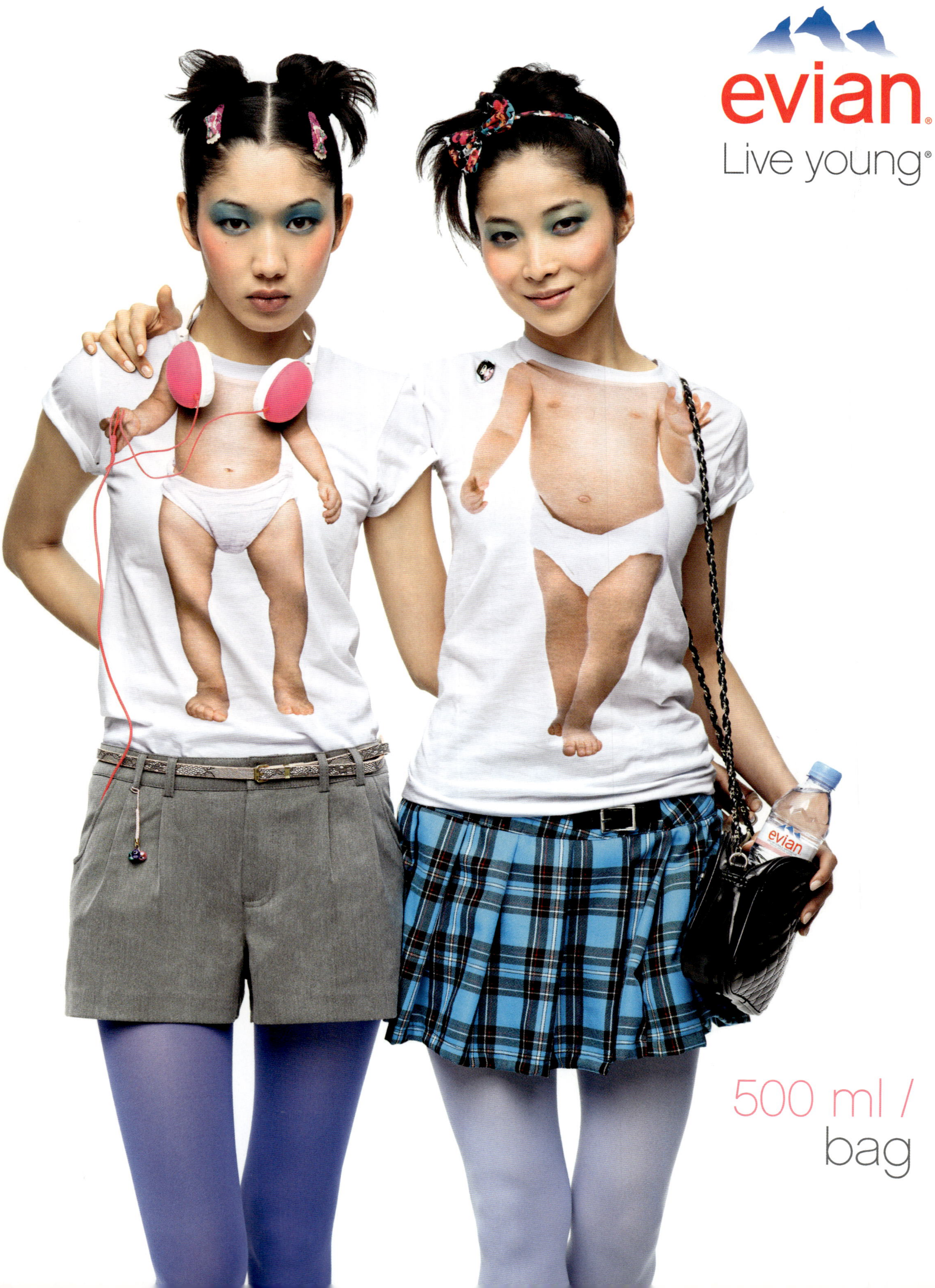
evian®
Live young®
evian
500 ml /
bag

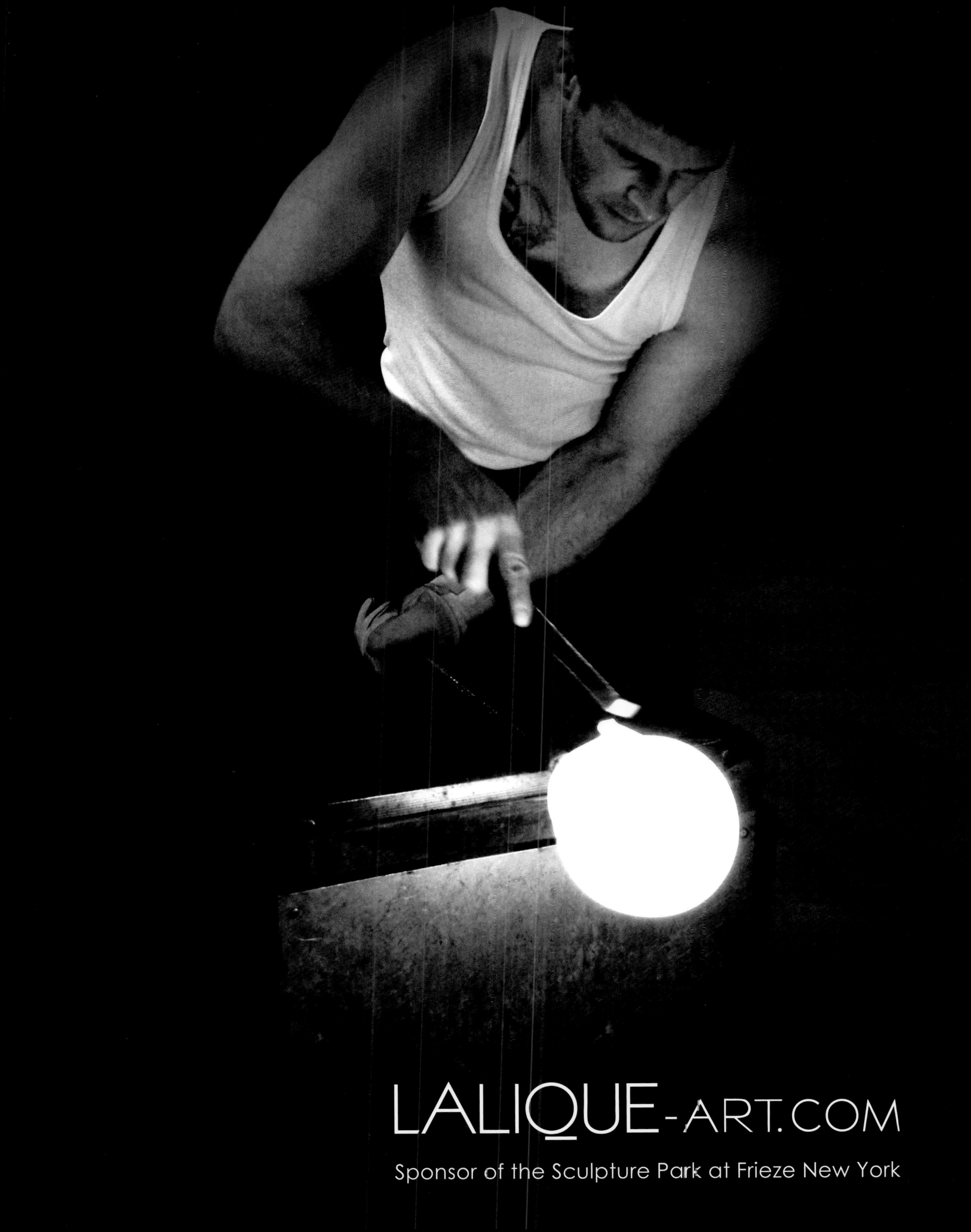
LALIQUE-ART.COM
Sponsor of the Sculpture Park at Frieze New York

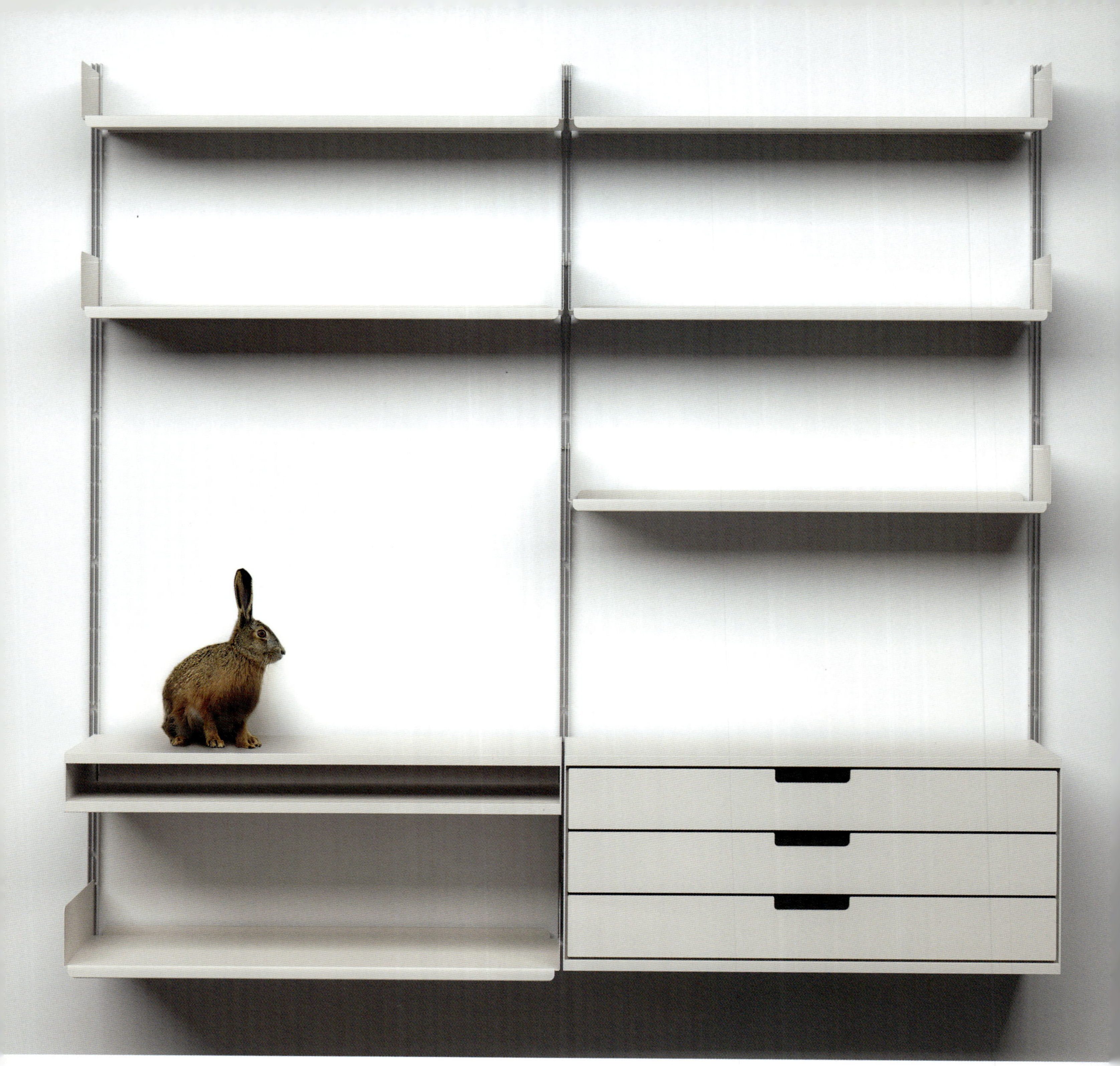

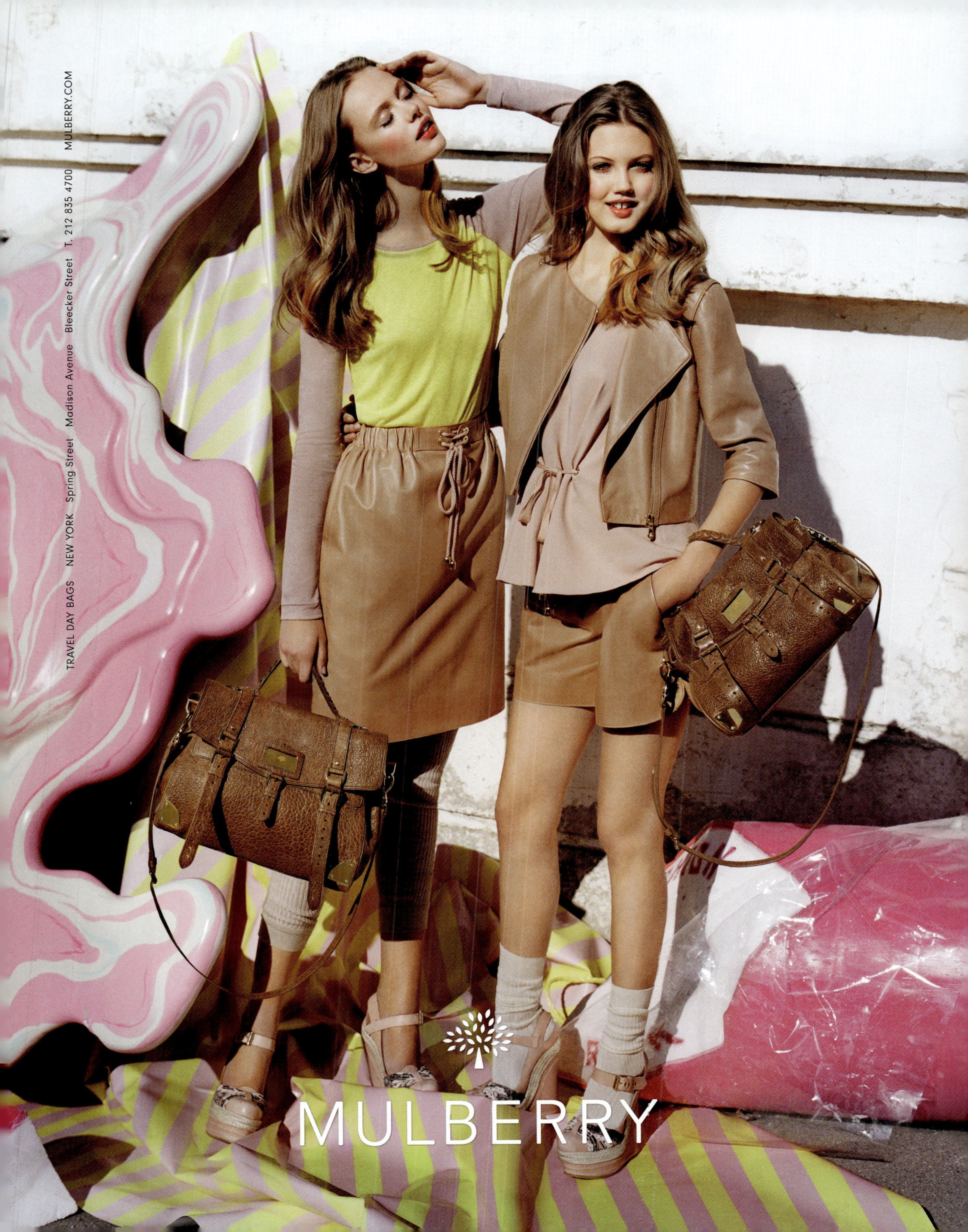

TRAVEL DAY BAGS NEW YORK Spring Street Madison Avenue Bleecker Street T. 212 835 4700 MULBERRY.COM
MULBERRY

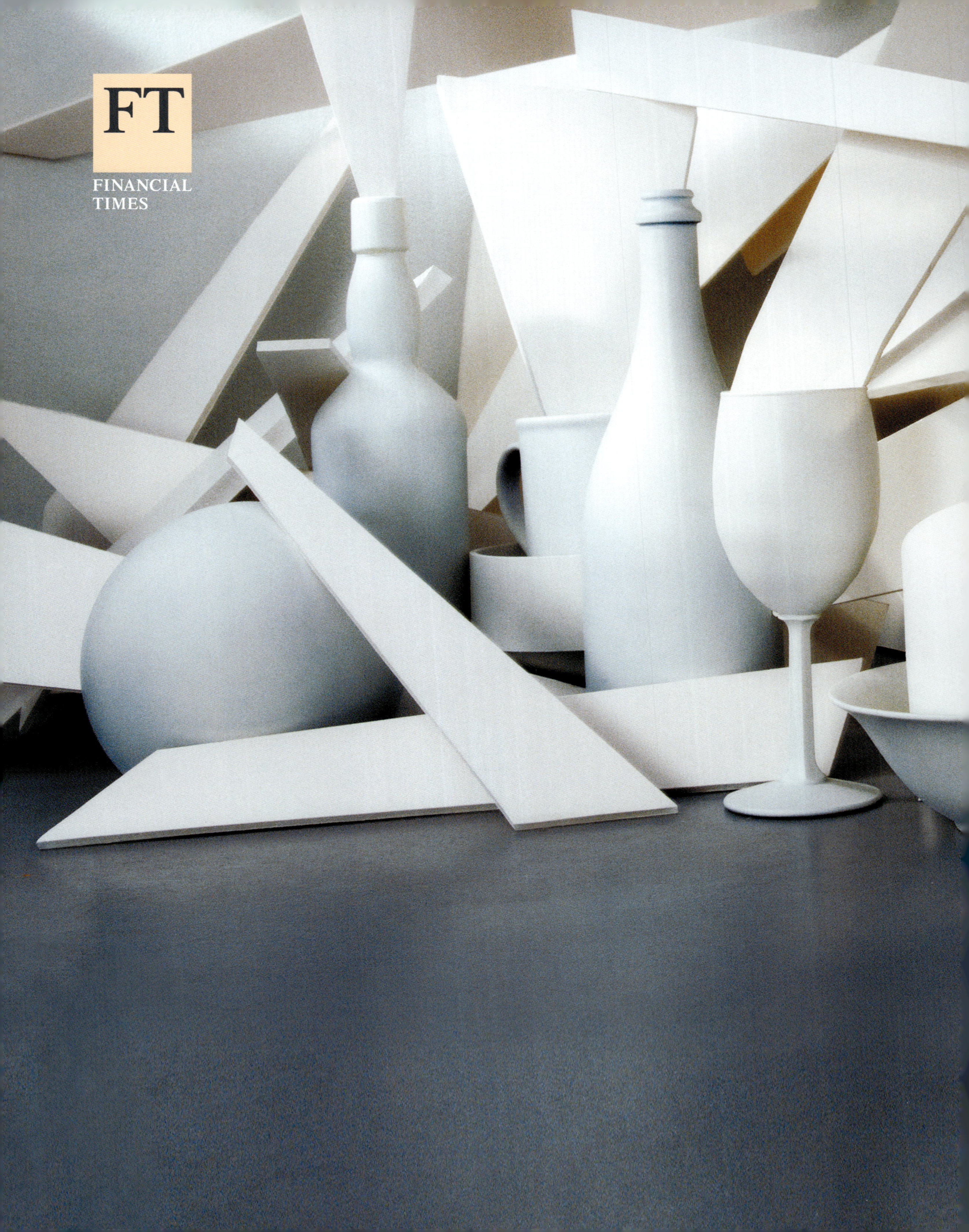
FT
FINANCIAL
TIMES

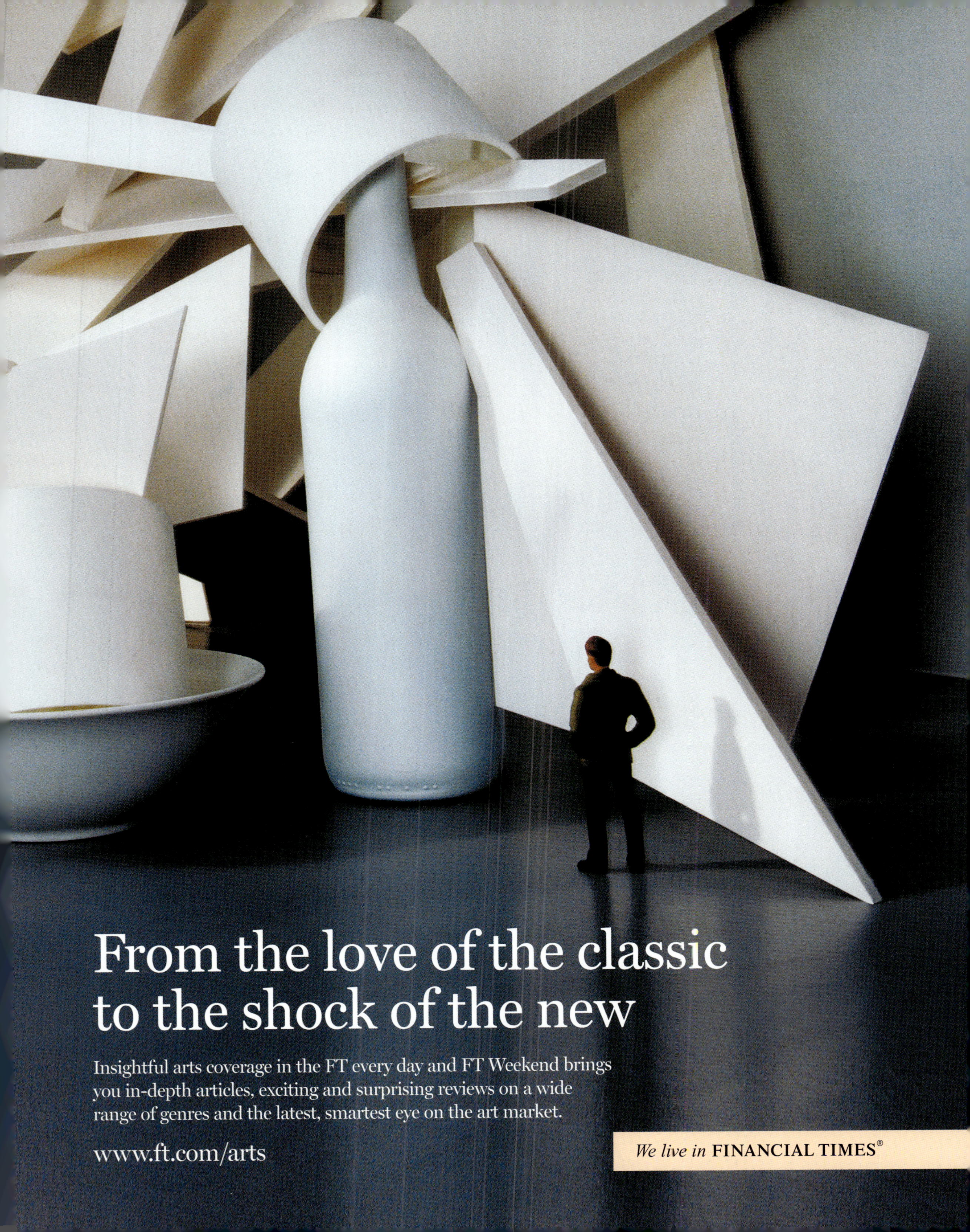
From the love of the classic
to the shock of the new
Insightful arts coverage in the FT every day and FT Weekend brings
you in-depth articles, exciting and surprising reviews on a wide
range of genres and the latest, smartest eye on the art market.
www.ft.com/arts
We live in FINANCIAL TIMES®

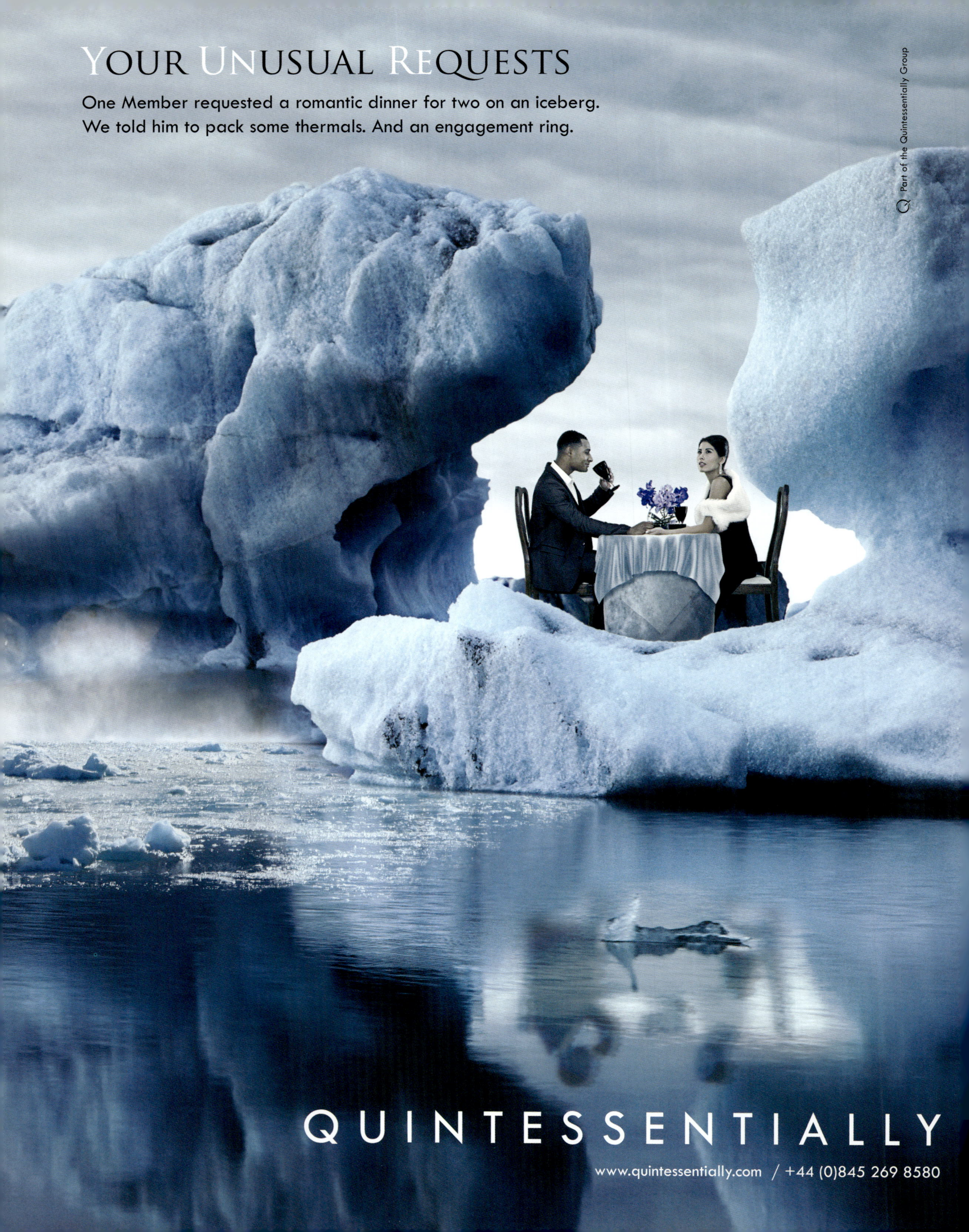
YOUR UNUSUAL REQUESTS
One Member requested a romantic dinner for two on an iceberg.
We told him to pack some thermals. And an engagement ring.
Part of the Quintessentially Group
QUINTESSENTIALLY
www.quintessentially.com / +44 (0)845 269 8580

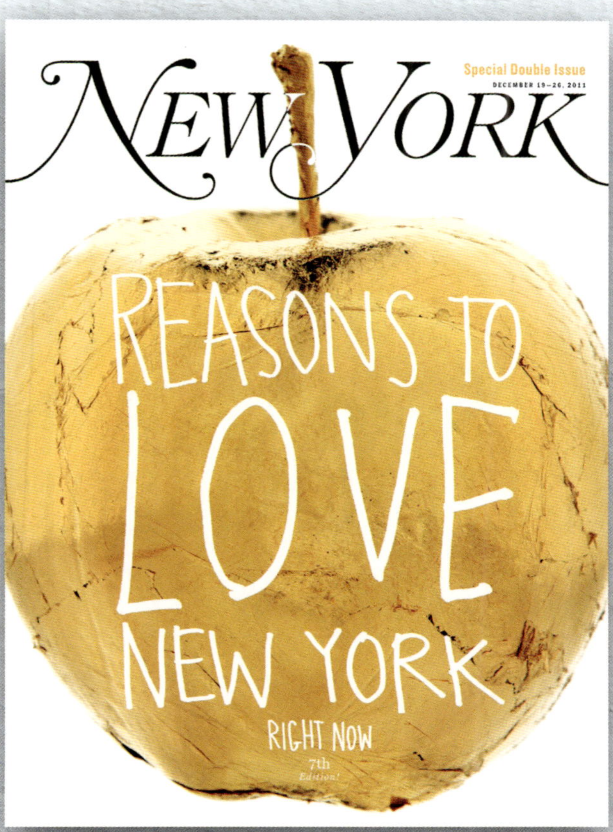
Special Double Issue
NEW YORK
DECEMBER 19–26, 2011
REASONS TO
LOVE
NEW YORK
RIGHT NOW
7th
Edition!

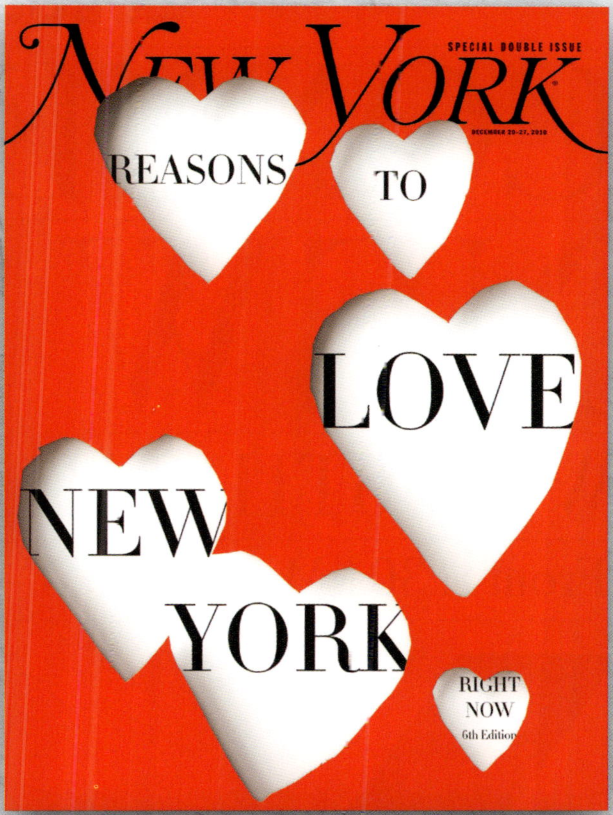
SPECIAL DOUBLE ISSUE
NEW YORK
DECEMBER 20–27, 2010
REASONS
TO
LOVE
NEW
YORK
RIGHT
NOW
6th Edition

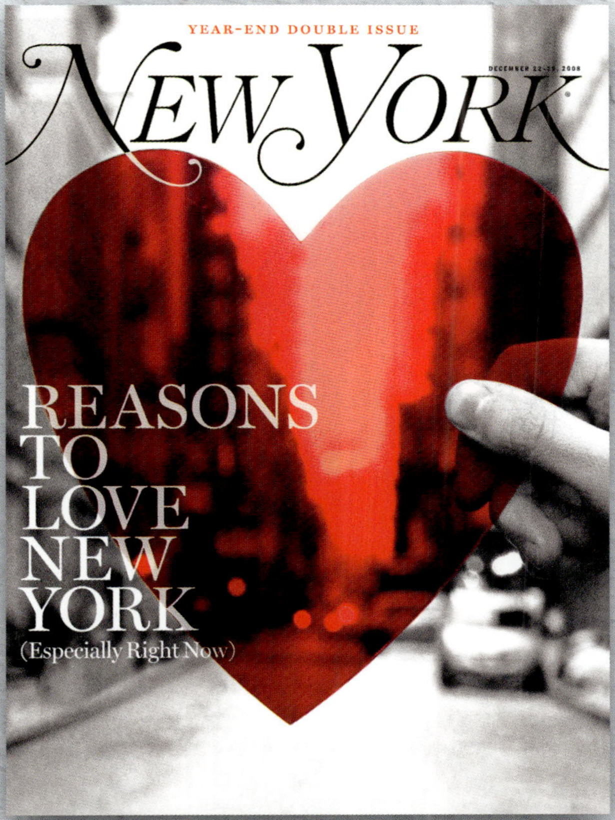
YEAR-END DOUBLE ISSUE
NEW YORK
REASONS
TO
LOVE
NEW
YORK
(Especially Right Now)

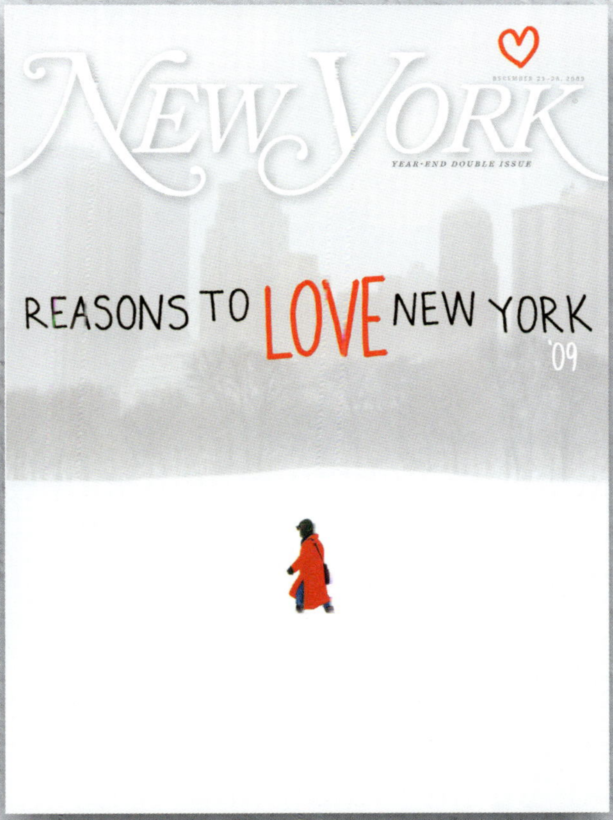
NEW YORK
YEAR-END DOUBLE ISSUE
REASONS TO LOVE NEW YORK
'09

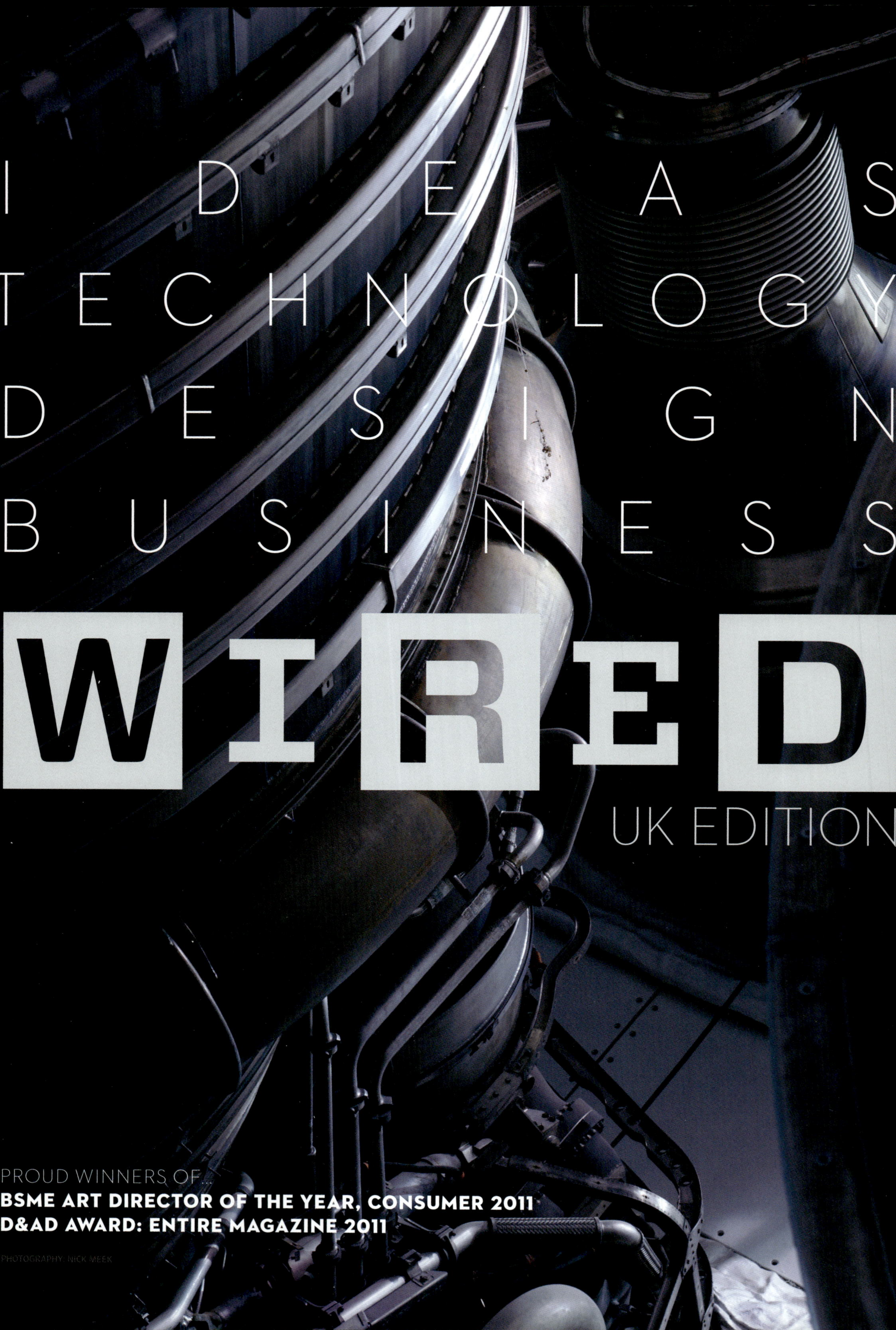
IDEAS
TECHNOLOGY
DESIGN
BUSINESS
WIRED
UK EDITION
PROUD WINNERS OF...
BSME ART DIRECTOR OF THE YEAR, CONSUMER 2011
D&AD AWARD: ENTIRE MAGAZINE 2011
PHOTOGRAPHY: NICK MEEK

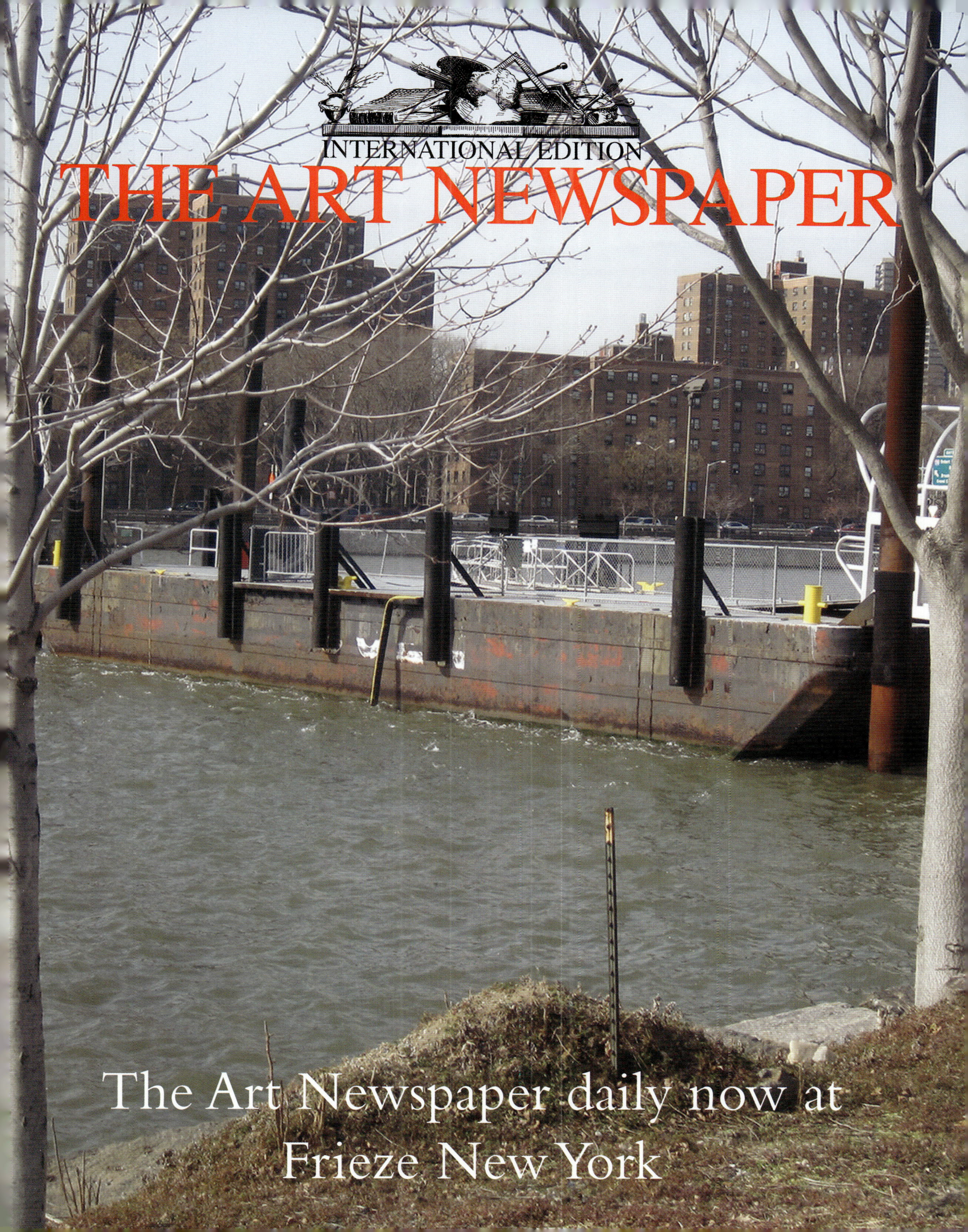
INTERNATIONAL EDITION
THE ART NEWSPAPER
The Art Newspaper daily now at
Frieze New York

Draw it with your eyes closed: the art of the art assignment

EDITED BY
PAPER MONUMENT

CONTRIBUTIONS FROM:

KAMROOZ ARAM AND
LANE ARTHUR
COLLEEN ASPER
JULIE AULT
JOHN BALDESSARI
JUDITH BARRY
JAY BATLLE
MARTIN BECK
JAMES BENNING
ANDREW BERARDINI
MARY WALLING BLACKBURN
JESSE BRANSFORD
THOMAS BRAUER
JACKIE BROOKNER
PETER BROWN
GRAHAM CAMPBELL
NATHAN CARTER
ANTOINE CATALA
ANNA CRAYCROFT
SEAN DOWNEY
ANGELA DUFRESNE
BRAD FARWELL
IRA FAY
ROCHELLE FEINSTEIN
RACHEL FOULLON
RACHEL FRANK
LAURA FRANTZ
KENJI FUJITA
MUNRO GALLOWAY
FIONA GARDNER
JACKIE GENDEL AND
TOM MCGRATH
LIAM GILLICK
ALFREDO GISHOLT
WAYNE GONZALES
MICHELLE GRABNER
HEATHER HART
CORIN HEWITT
CHRISTINE HILL
DANA HOEY
SHIRLEY IRONS
RYAN JOHNSON
DAVID KEARNS
BILL KOMODORE
CHRIS KRAUS
JULIAN KREIMER
FABIENNE LASSERRE
MARGARET LEE
DAVID LEVINE
MIRANDA LICHTENSTEIN
JUSTIN LIEBERMAN
PAM LINS
CAMERON MARTIN
JILLIAN MAYER
JOHN MENICK
HELEN MIRRA
CARRIE MOYER
JULIAN MYERS AND
DOMINIC WILLSDON
BOB NICKAS
SOFÍA OLASCOAGA
DEMETRIUS OLIVER
MATT PHILLIPS
WILLIAM POPE.L
JESSICA POWERS
JON PYLYPCHUCK
SARA GREENBERGER RAFFERTY
KURT RALSKE
DAVID ROBBINS
HARRY ROSEMAN
AURA ROSENBERG
MARINA ROSENFELD
GEORGE RUSH
MIRA SCHOR
AMIE SIEGEL
JEREMY SIGLER
AMY SILLMAN
MICHAEL SMITH
MOLLY SMITH
JO-EY TANG
PAUL THEK
MAMIE TINKLER
DAN TOROP
PATRICIA TREIB
DAVID TRUE
WILLIAM VILLALONGO
OLIVER WASOW
RICHARD WENTWORTH
TOMMY WHITE
KEVIN ZUCKER

WWW.PAPERMONUMENT.COM/DRAWIT

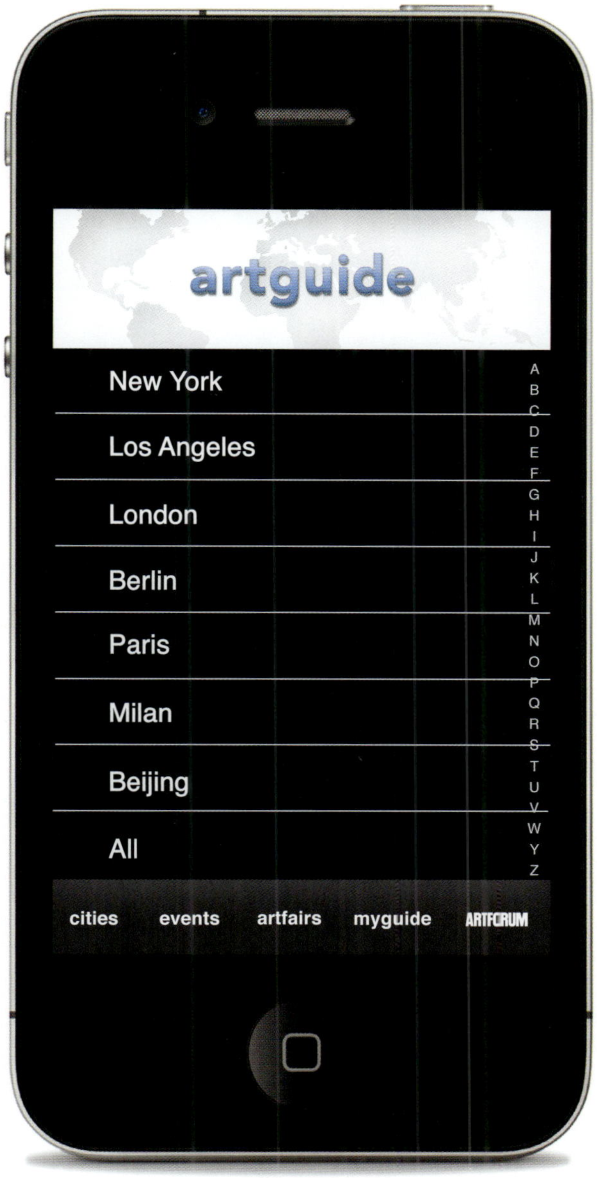
artguide
New York
Los Angeles
London
Berlin
Paris
Milan
Beijing
All
A B C D E F G H I J K L M N O P Q R S T U V W Y Z
cities
events
artfairs
myguide
ARTFORUM

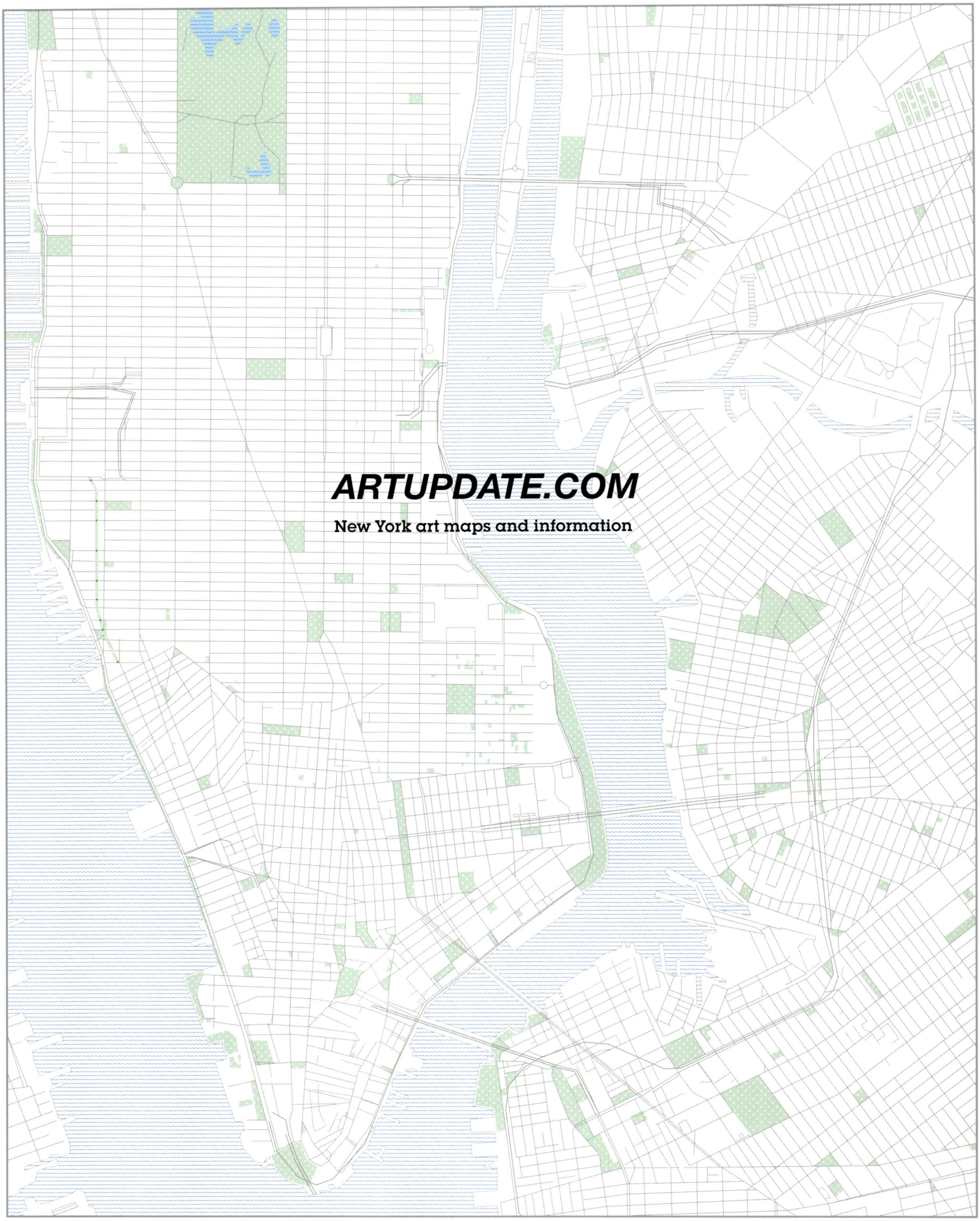
ARTUPDATE.COM
New York art maps and information

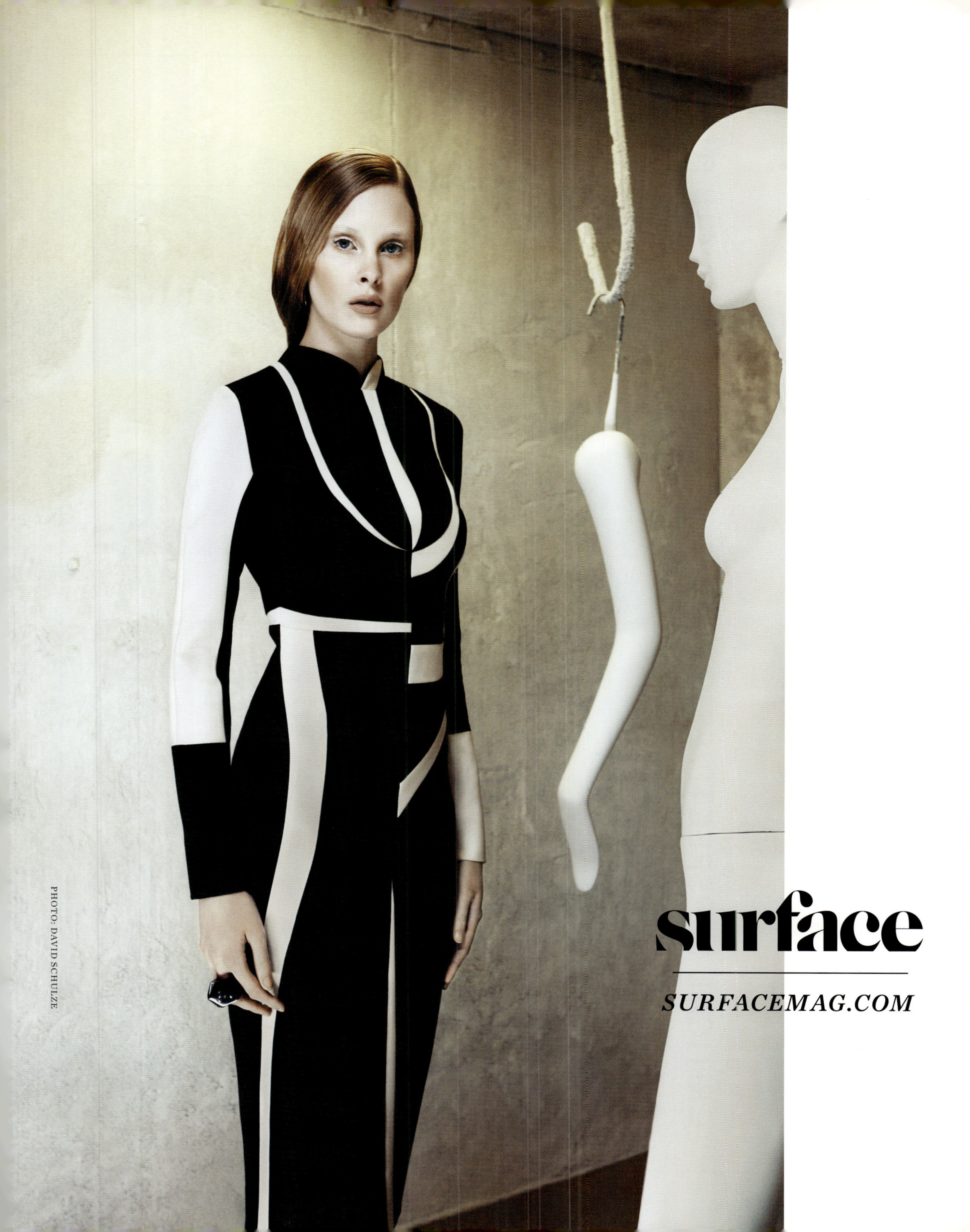
PHOTO: DAVID SCHULZE
surface
SURFACEMAG.COM

Camera Austria International

117

What Can Art Do For Real Politics?

Guest-editors:
Artur Żmijewski
Joanna Warsza

Column:
Jan Verwoert
Forum

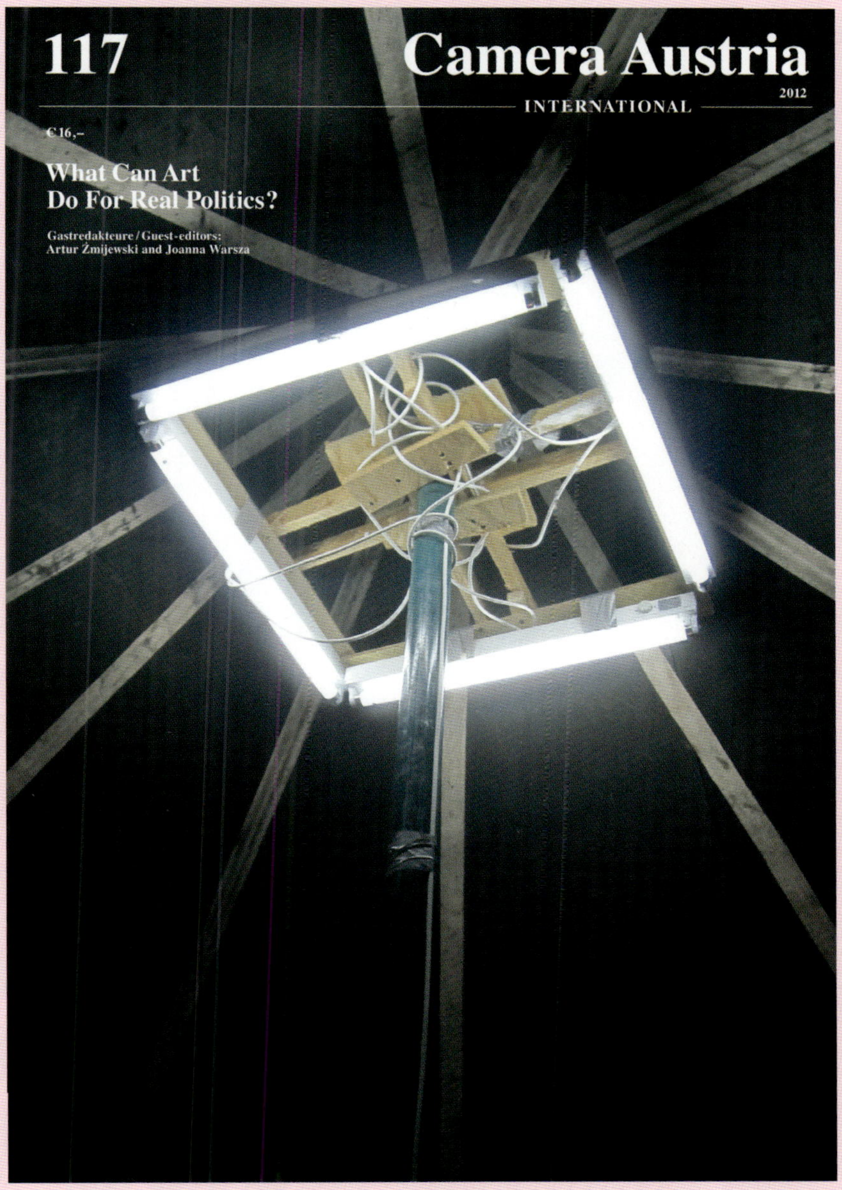

TEXTE ZUR KUNST

March 2012, No. 85

ART
HISTORY
REVISITED

WWW.TEXTEZURKUNST.DE

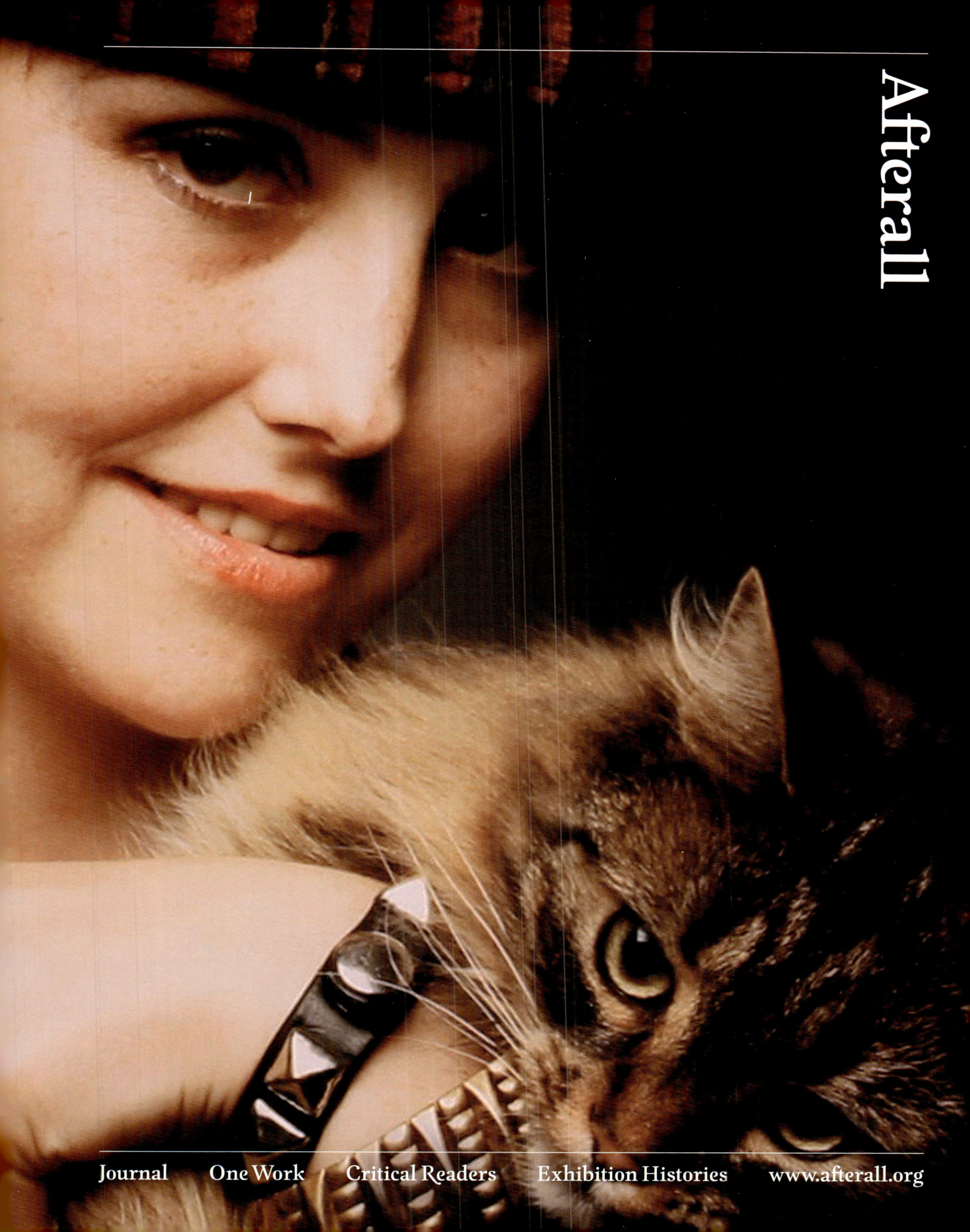
Afterall
Journal
One Work
Critical Readers
Exhibition Histories
www.afterall.org

PASCAL GRANDMAISON
HALF OF THE DARKNESS
MAY 3 – JULY 21, 2012

OPENING RECEPTION AND RELEASE PARTY FOR *PREFIX PHOTO* 25: THURSDAY, MAY 3 FROM 7 TO 10 PM THIS EXHIBITION IS CURATED BY SCOTT McLEOD AND ACCOMPANIED BY AN ESSAY BY ANJA BOCK.

Prefix gratefully acknowledges the assistance of the Toronto Arts Council, the Ontario Arts Council, the Canada Periodical Fund and the Canada Council for the Arts.

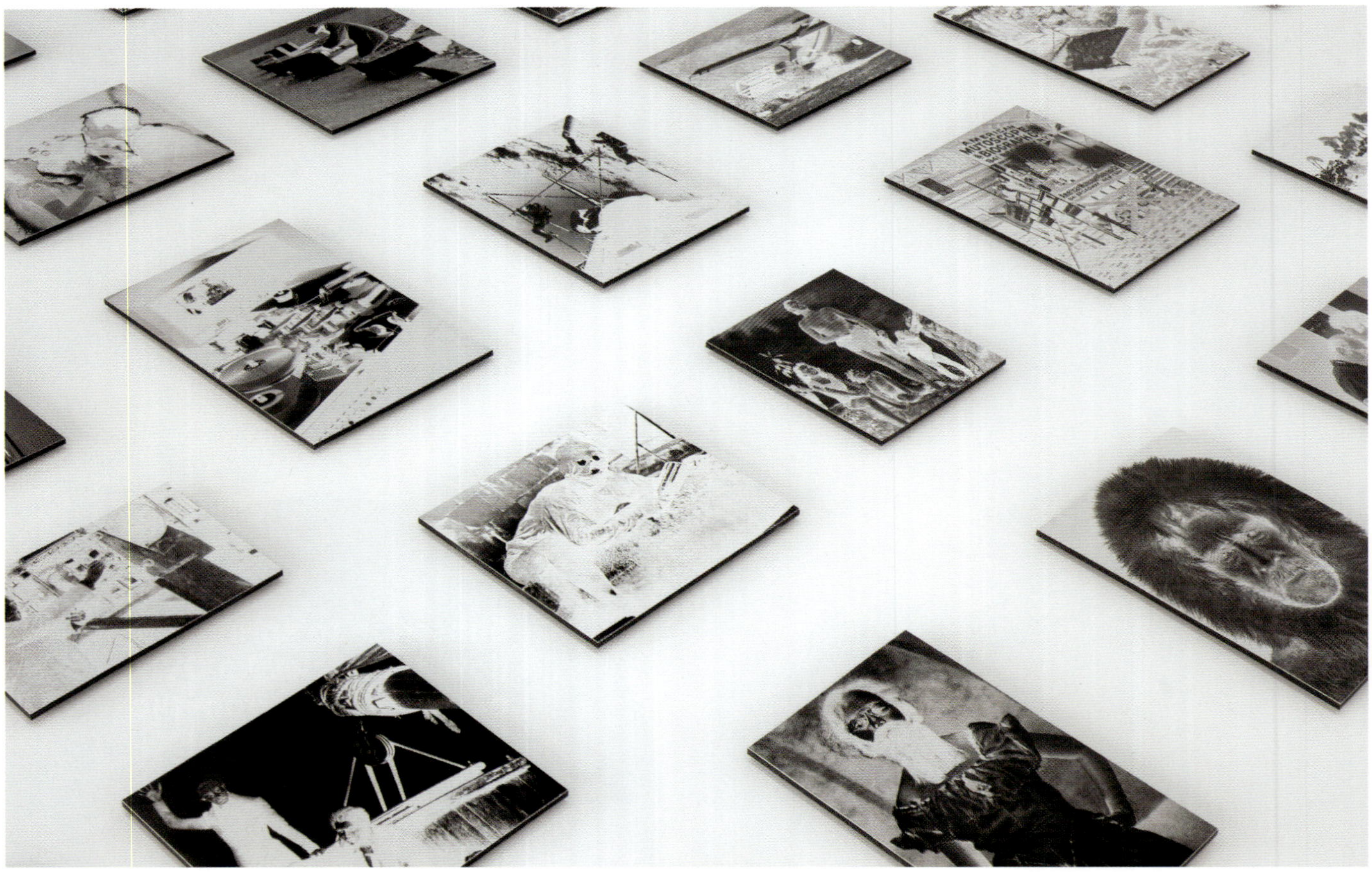

PASCAL GRANDMAISON, INSTALLATION VIEW OF *HALF OF THE DARKNESS*, 2010
COURTESY THE ARTIST AND THE MUSÉE D'ART CONTEMPORAIN DE MONTRÉAL
PHOTO: PASCAL GRANDMAISON

SUBSCRIBE TO
***PREFIX PHOTO* MAGAZINE**

Prefix Institute of Contemporary Art
Suite 124, Box 124
401 Richmond Street West
Toronto, Ontario, Canada M5V 3A8
T 416.591.0357 F 416.591.0358
info@prefix.ca www.prefix.ca
Photo Magazine. Visual, Audio and Surround Art Galleries.
Reference Library. Small Press. Travelling Shows.

PREFIX.

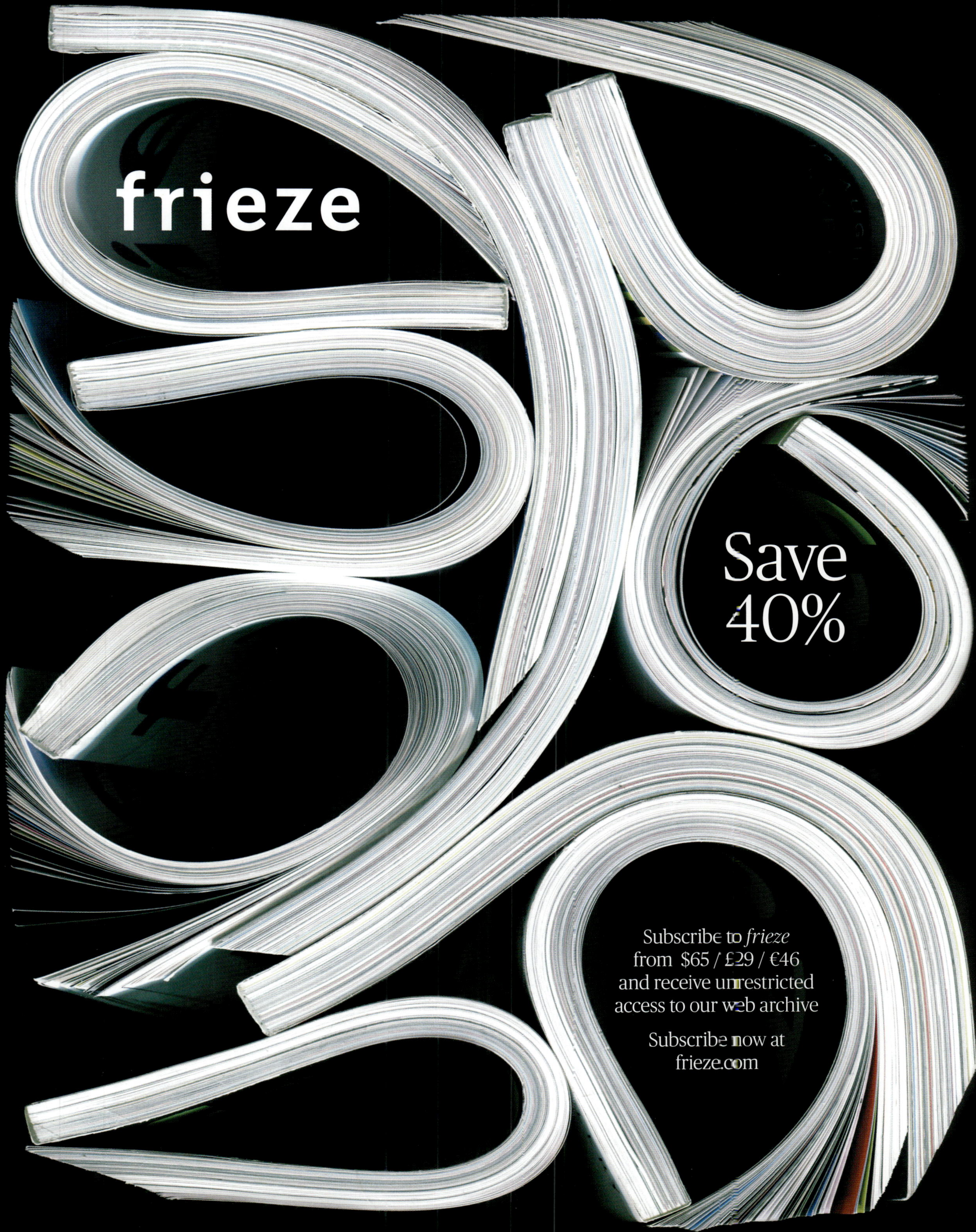
frieze
Save
40%
Subscribe to *frieze*
from $65 / £29 / €46
and receive unrestricted
access to our web archive
Subscribe now at
frieze.com

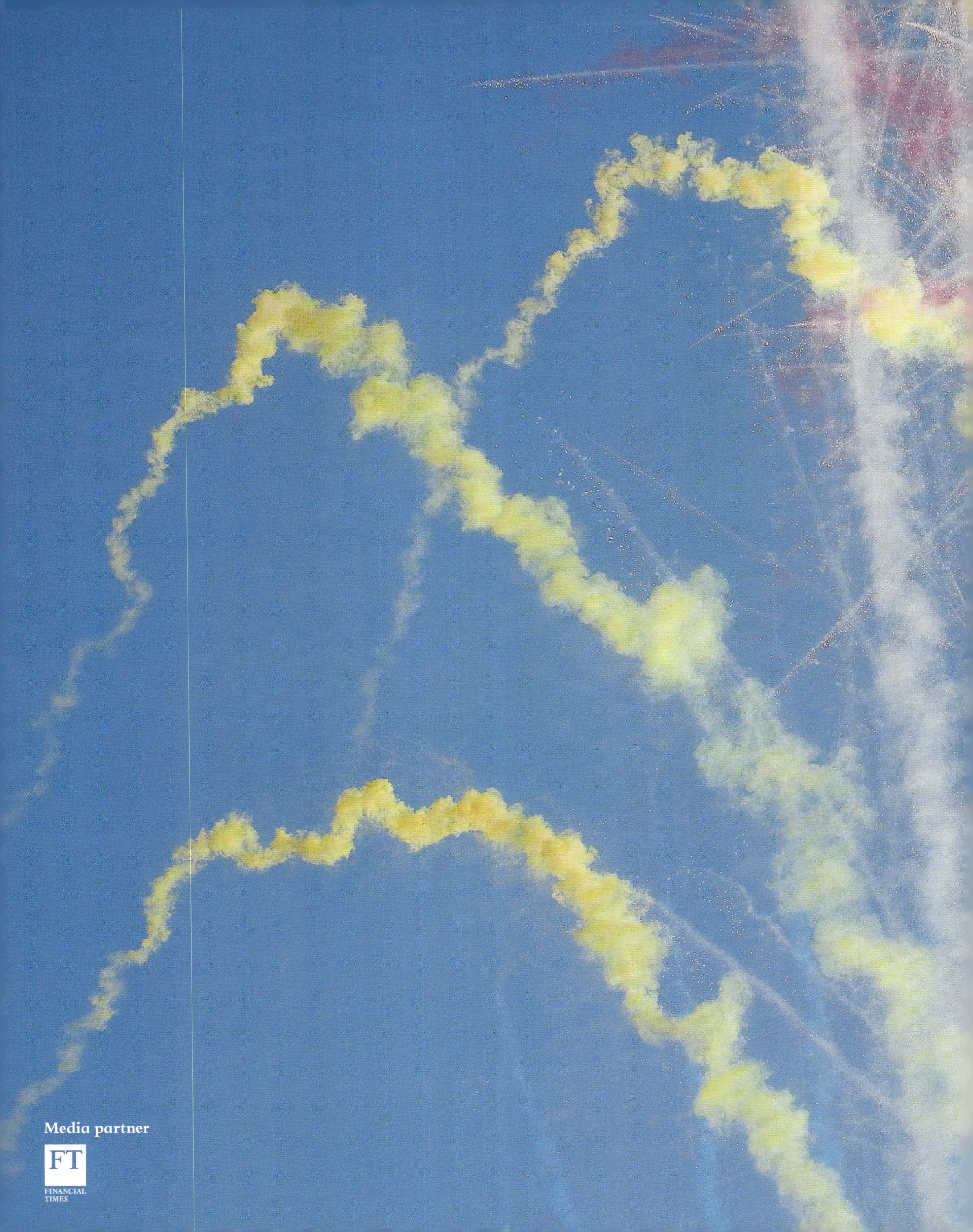

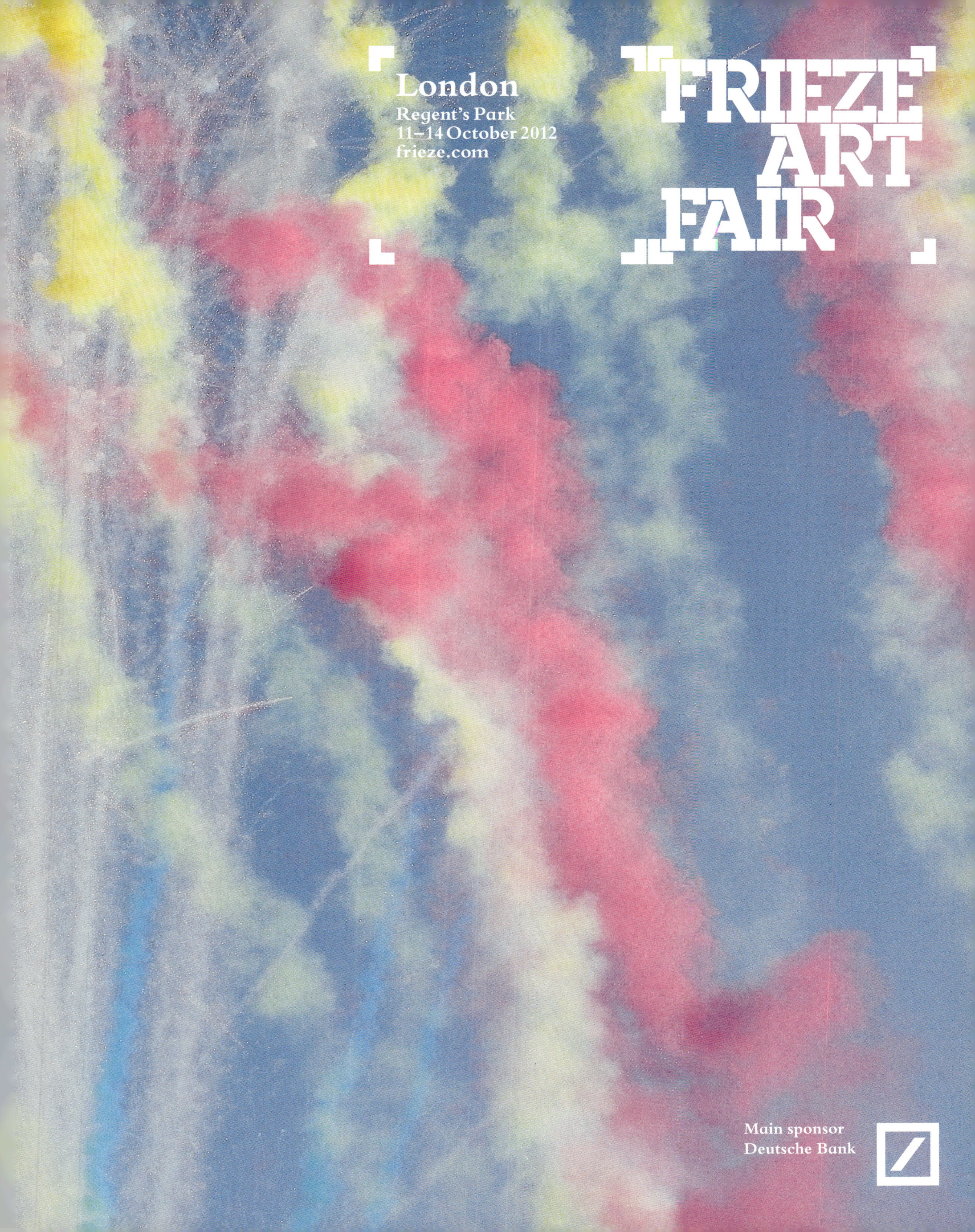

FRIEZE ART FAIR

London
Regent's Park
11–14 October 2012
frieze.com

Main sponsor
Deutsche Bank

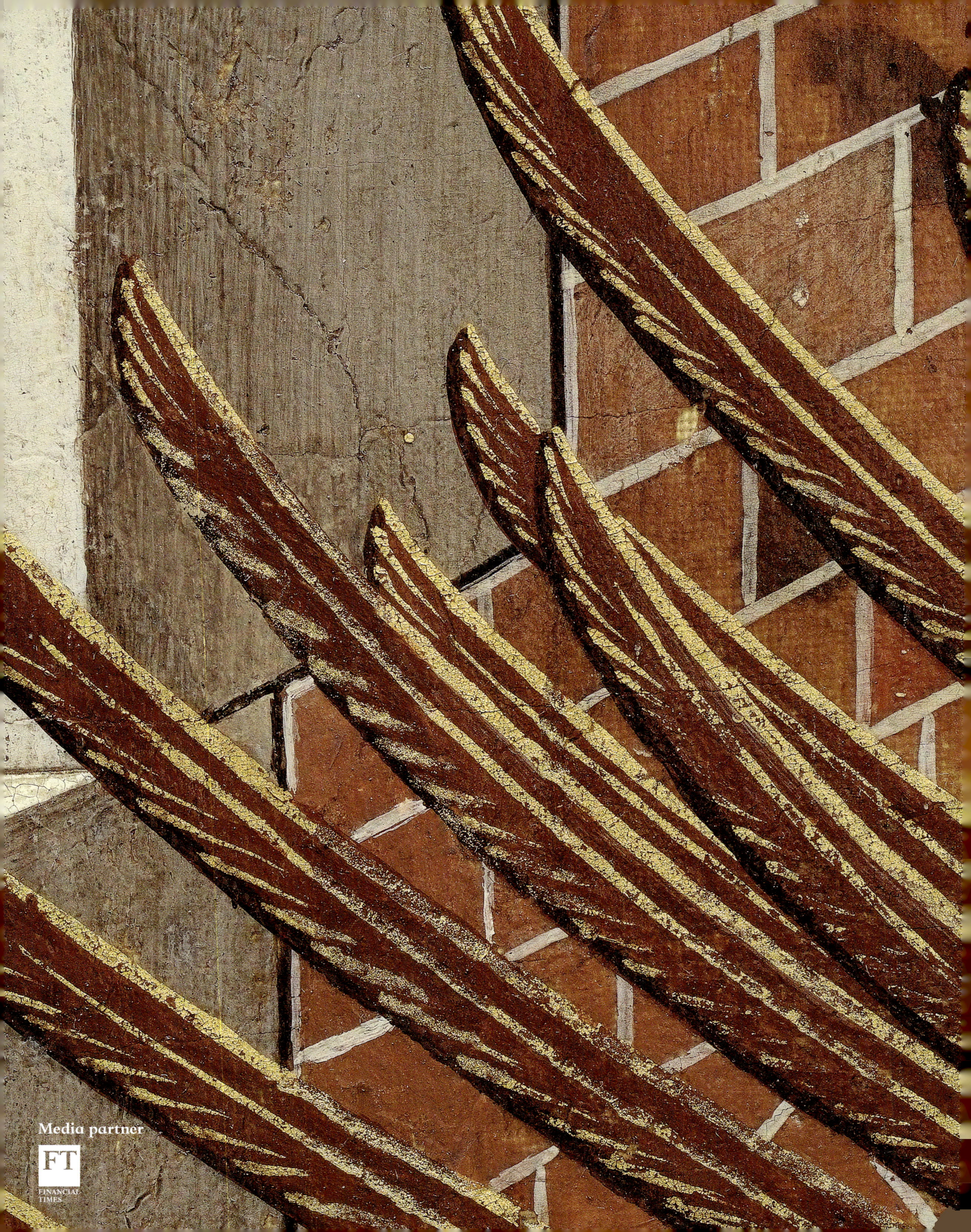

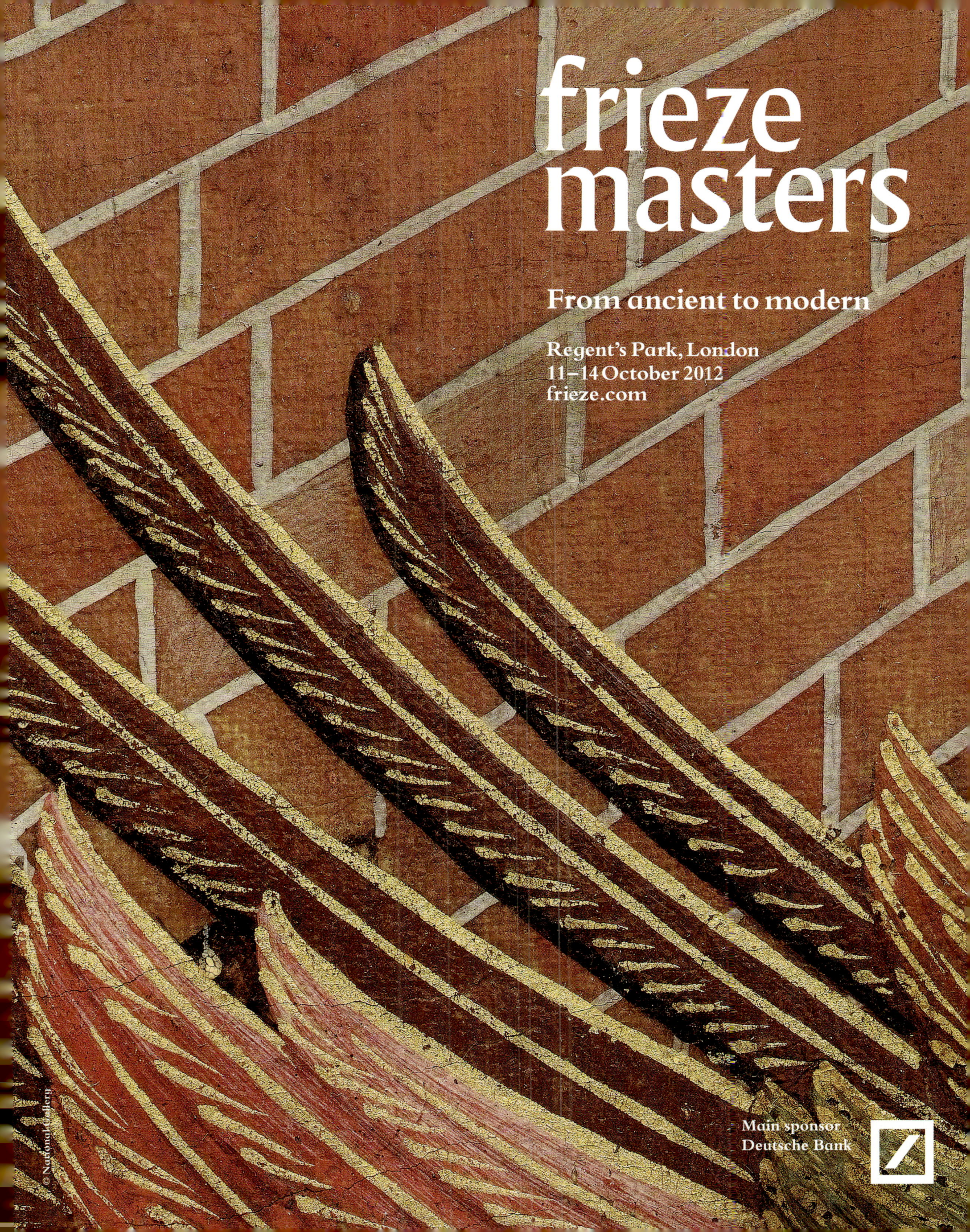
frieze
masters
From ancient to modern
Regent's Park, London
11–14 October 2012
frieze.com
Main sponsor
Deutsche Bank
© National Gallery

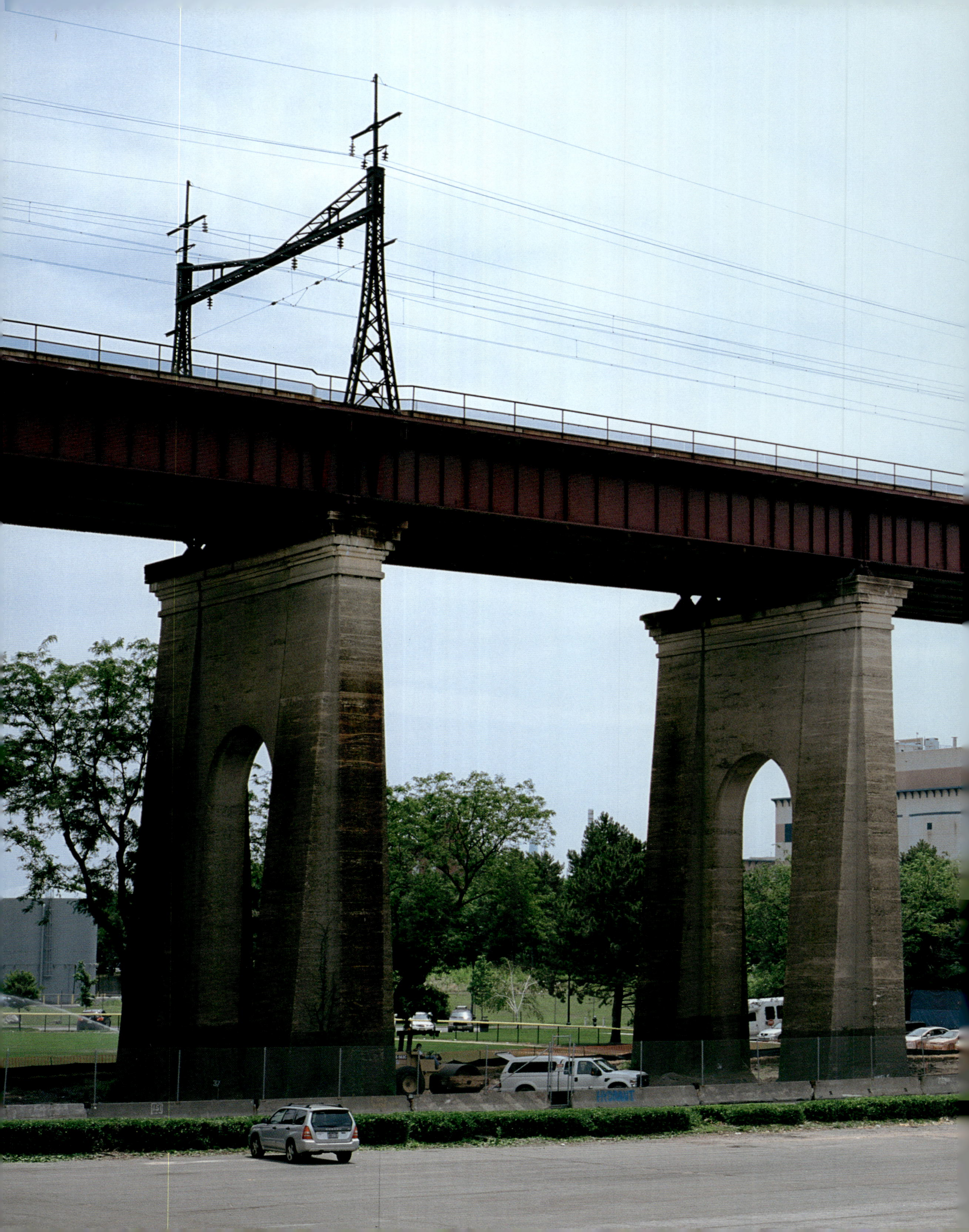

Index

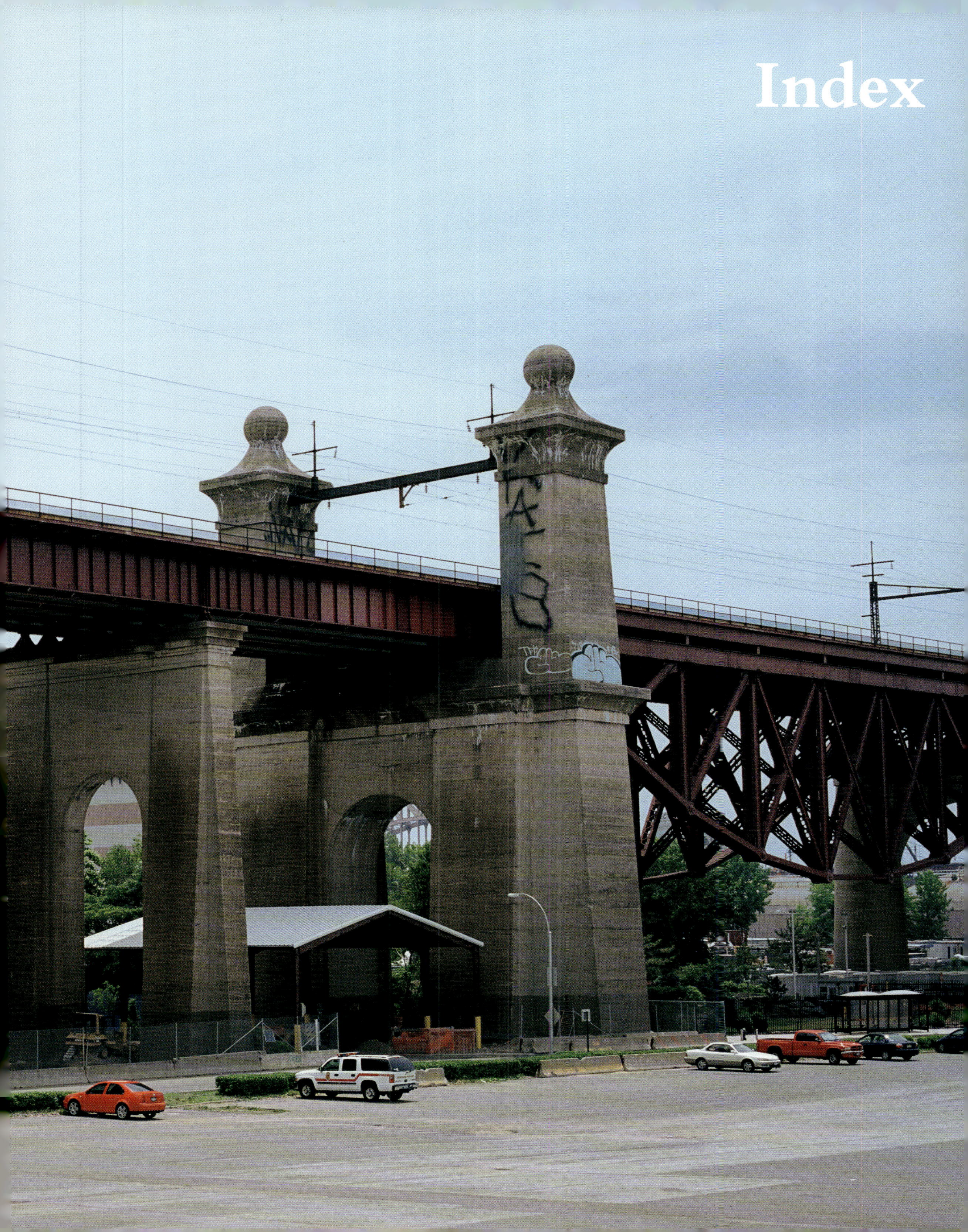

Gallery Index

303 Gallery

Stand B39
Tel +1 212-255-1121

547 West 21st Street
New York, NY 10011
United States
Tel +1 212-255-1121
Fax +1 212-255-5563
info@303gallery.com
www.303gallery.com

Contact
Lisa Spellman
Cristian Alexa
Mari Spirito
Barbara Corti

Artists
Doug Aitken
Valentin Carron
Anne Chu
Hans-Peter Feldmann
Ceal Floyer
Karel Funk
Maureen Gallace
Tim Gardner
Dominique Gonzalez-Foerster
Rodney Graham
Mary Heilmann
Jeppe Hein
Larry Johnson
Matt Johnson
Karen Kilimnik
Florian Maier-Aichen
Nick Mauss
Mike Nelson
Kristin Oppenheim
Eva Rothschild
Collier Schorr
Stephen Shore
Sue Williams
Jane & Louise Wilson

47 Canal

Stand R15
Tel +1 646-415-7712

47 Canal Street
2nd Floor
New York, NY 10002
United States
Tel +1 646-415-7712
info@47canalstreet.com
www.47canalstreet.com

Contact
Margaret Lee
Oliver Newton

Artists
Michele Abeles
Alisa Baremboym
Antoine Catala
Gregory Edwards
Josh Kline
Amy Lien & Enzo Camacho
Trevor Shimizu
Nolan Simon
Stewart Uoo
Anicka Yi

Miguel Abreu Gallery

Stand C14
Tel +1 212-995-1774

36 Orchard Street
New York, NY 10002
United States
Tel +1 212-995-1774
Fax +1 646-688-2302
post@miguelabreugallery.com
www.miguelabreugallery.com

Contact
Miguel Abreu
Andrea Neustein

Artists
Hans Bellmer
Liz Deschenes
Gareth James
Sam Lewitt
Scott Lyall
R. H. Quaytman
Eileen Quinlan
Raha Raissnia
Jimmy Raskin
Blake Rayne
Pamela Rosenkranz
Pieter Schoolwerth

Air de Paris

Stand C11
Tel +33 6-31-76-39-83

32 rue Louise Weiss
Paris 75013
France
Tel +33 1-44-23-02-77
Fax +33 1-53-61-22-84
fan@airdeparis.com
www.airdeparis.com

Contact
Florence Bonnefous
Edouard Merino

Artists
Leonor Antunes
Thomas Bayrle
Guy de Cointet
François Curlet
Stéphane Dafflon
Brice Dellsperger
Trisha Donnelly
Claire Fontaine
Liam Gillick
Joseph Grigely
Guyton\Walker
Carsten Höller
Dorothy Iannone
Aaron Flint Jamison
Ann Veronica Janssens
Pierre Joseph
Ben Kinmont
Adriana Lara
Ingrid Luche
M/M Paris
Monica Majoli
Sarah Morris
Mrzyk & Moriceau
Philippe Parreno
Rob Pruitt
Torbjørn Rødland
Allen Ruppersberg
Bruno Serralongue
Shimabuku
Josh Smith
Lily van der Stokker
Sturtevant
Jean-Luc Verna

Altman Siegel

Stand F5
Tel +1 917-674-4239

49 Geary Street, 4th Floor
San Francisco CA, 94108
United States
Tel +1 415-576-9300
Fax +1 415-373-4471
info@altmansiegel.com
www.altmansiegel.com

Contact
Claudia Altman-Siegel
David Berezin
Daelyn Farnham

Artists
Nate Boyce
Shannon Ebner
Liam Everett
Fran Herndon
Chris Johanson
Matt Keegan
Shinpei Kusanagi
Devin Leonardi
Trevor Paglen
Will Rogan
Sara VanDerBeek
Emily Wardill
Garth Weiser

Ambach & Rice

Stand R20
Tel +1 206-465-2333

6148 Wilshire Boulevard
Los Angeles CA 90048
United States
Tel +1 323-965-5500
Fax +1 323-965-5509
info@ambachandrice.com
www.ambachandrice.com

Contact
Charles Kitchings

Artists
Grant Barnhart
Ron van der Ende
Ellen Lesperance
Alon Levin
Roy McMakin
Jeffry Mitchell
Pablo Pijnappel
Abigail Reynolds
Karen Sargsyan
Martina Sauter
Eric Yahnker

The Approach

Stand B11
Tel +44 20-8983-3878

1st Floor, 47 Approach Road
London E2 9LY
United Kingdom
Tel +44 20-8983-3878
Fax +44 20-8983-3878
info@theapproach.co.uk
www.theapproach.co.uk

Contact
Jake Miller
Emma Robertson

Artists
Phillip Allen
Helene Appel
Cris Brodahl
Alice Channer
Stuart Cumberland
Peter Davies
Patrick Hill
Evan Holloway
Germaine Kruip
Rezi van Lankveld
Edward Lipski
Dave Muller
Lisa Oppenheim
Magali Reus
Amanda Ross-Ho
John Stezaker
Evren Tekinoktay
Sara VanDerBeek
Gary Webb
Martin Westwood
Sam Windett

art: concept

Stand A2
Tel +33 1-53-60-90-30

13 rue des Arquebusiers
Paris 75003
France
Tel +33 1-53-60-90-30
Fax +33 1-53-60-90-31
info@galerieartconcept.com
www.galerieartconcept.com

Contact
Olivier Antoine
Caroline Maestrali

Artists
Martine Aballéa
Pierre-Olivier Arnaud
Julien Audebert
Francis Baudevin
Whitney Bedford
Jean-Luc Blanc
Michel Blazy
Ulla von Brandenburg
Jeremy Deller
Richard Fauguet
Vidya Gastaldon
Geert Goiris
Lothar Hempel
Nathan Hylden
Jacob Kassay
Andrew Lewis
Adam McEwen
Philippe Perrot
Pietro Roccasalva
Gedi Sibony
Roman Signer
Alexandre Singh

Alfonso Artiaco

Stand C31
Tel +1 646-346-2835

Piazza dei Martiri 58
Naples 80121
Italy
Tel +39 081-497-6072
Fax +39 081-1936-0164
info@alfonsoartiaco.com
www.alfonsoartiaco.com

Contact
Alfonso Artiaco
Simona Di Sciullo

Artists
Darren Almond
Carl Andre
Giovanni Anselmo
Robert Barry
Botto & Bruno
Alan Charlton
Gilbert & George
Gioberto Noro
Laurent Grasso
Thomas Hirschhorn
Craigie Horsfield
Ann Veronica Janssens
Jannis Kounellis
Melissa Kretschmer
Wolfgang Laib
Sol LeWitt
Lello Lopez
Raffaele Luongo
Vera Lutter
Rita McBride
Gerhard Merz
Davide Minuti
Marco Neri
Albert Oehlen
Giulio Paolini
Giuseppe Penone
Perino & Vele
Anne & Patrick Poirier
Sergio Prego
Glen Rubsamen
Ulrich Rückriem
Anri Sala
Niele Toroni
David Tremlett
Lawrence Weiner

BaliceHertling

Stand R12
Tel +33 1-40-33-47-26

47 rue Ramponeau
Paris 75020
France
Tel +33 1-40-33-47-26
Fax +33 1-40-33-47-36
gallery@balicehertling.com
www.balicehertling.com

Contact
Daniele Balice
Alexander Hertling
Giulia Ruberti

Artists
Neïl Beloufa
Kerstin Brätsch
Isabelle Cornaro
Luca Frei
Nikolas Gambaroff
K8 Hardy
Alexander May
Greg Parma Smith
Falke Pisano
Reto Pulfer
Samuel Richardot
Oscar Tuazon
Stephen Willats

Laura Bartlett Gallery

Stand C26
Tel +44 7771-803606

10 Northington Street
London WC1N 2JG
United Kingdom
Tel +44 20-7404-9251
Fax +44 20-7430-1731
mail@laurabartlettgallery.com
www.laurabartlettgallery.com

Contact
Laura Bartlett
Madeleine Martin

Artists
Becky Beasley
Nina Beier
John Divola
Simon Dybbroe Møller
Harrell Fletcher
Cyprien Gaillard
Lydia Gifford
Ian Law
Marie Lund
Elizabeth McAlpine
Alex Olson
Martin Skauen

Galerie Guido W. Baudach

Stand C30
Tel +49 30-2804-7727

Oudenarder Strasse 16–20
Berlin 13347
Germany
Tel +49 30-2804-7727
Fax +49 30-4502-4481

Carmerstrasse 11
Berlin 10623
Germany
Tel +49 30-319-981-01
Fax +49 30-319-981-03
galerie@guidowbaudach.com
www.guidowbaudach.com

Contact
Guido W. Baudach
Berit Homburg
Sophie Prager

Artists
André Butzer
Björn Dahlem
Thilo Heinzmann
Thomas Helbig
Andy Hope 1930
Rashid Johnson
Jürgen Klauke
Erwin Kneihsl
Erik van Lieshout
Bjarne Melgaard
Aïda Ruilova
Markus Selg
Thomas Zipp

Johan Berggren Gallery

Stand F15
Tel +46 706-116-034

Ehrensvärdsgatan 8
21213 Malmö
Sweden
Tel +46 706-116-034
jb@johanberggren.com
www.johanberggren.com

Contact
Johan Berggren

Artists
Nicolas Ceccaldi
Julia Feyrer
Yngve Holen
Allison Katz
Andrei Koschmieder
Veit Laurent Kurz
Asher Penn
Fredrik Værslev

Boers-Li Gallery

Stand C18
Tel +86 10-6432-2620

1-706 Hou Jie, 798 Art
District, No.2 Yuan,
Jiuxianqiao Lu,
Chaoyang District
Beijing 100015
China
Tel +86 10-6432-2620
Fax +86 10-6432-2621
info@boersligallery.com
www.boersligallery.com

Contact
Waling Boers

Artists
Angela Bulloch
Chen Shaoxiong
Chen Yujun
Gade
Gong Jian
Guan Fengdong
Hou Yong
Ji Lei
Lei Benben
Liao Guohe
Liu Chang
Lu Yang
Qui Anxiong
Qui Xiaofei
Song Kun
Wang Wei
Wang Yuyang
Xie Zhengli
Xue Feng
Yang Xinguang
Zan Jbai
Zeng Hong
Zhan Rui
Zhang Peili
Zhang Wei

Marianne Boesky Gallery

Stand A26
Tel +1 212-680-9889

509 West 24th Street
New York, NY 10011
United States
Tel +1 212-680-9889
Fax +1 212-680-9897

118 East 64th Street
New York 10065
United States
info@marianneboeskygallery.com
www.marianneboeskygallery.com

Contact
Marianne Boesky
Adrian Turner

Artists
Diana Al-Hadid
Anisheh Avini
Pier Paolo Calzolari
Jesse Chapman
Hannah van Bart
Sue de Beer
Robert Elfgen
Rachel Feinstein
Barnaby Furnas
Melissa Gordon
Jay Heikes
Adam Helms
Yuichi Higashionna
Donald Moffett
William O'Brien
Jacco Olivier
Hans Op de Beeck
Anthony Pearson
Salvatore Scarpitta
Mindy Shapero
Kon Trubkovich
John Waters
Claudia Wieser

BolteLang

Stand R16
Tel +41 78-859-5635

Limmatstrasse 214
Zurich 8005
Switzerland
Tel +41 44-273-0010
Fax +41 44-273-0012
info@boltelang.com
www.boltelang.com

Contact
Anna Bolte
Chaja Lang

Artists
Vanessa Billy
Bianca Brunner
Daniel Gustav Cramer
Dagmar Heppner
Swantje Hielscher
Jill Spector

Tanya Bonakdar Gallery

Stand C6
Tel +1 212-414-4144

521 West 21st Street
New York, NY 10011
United States
Tel +1 212-414-4144
Fax +1 212-414-1535
mail@tanyabonakdargallery.com
www.tanyabonakdargallery.com

Contact
Tanya Bonakdar
Ethan Sklar

Artists
Atelier van Lieshout
Uta Barth
Martin Boyce
Sandra Cinto
Phil Collins
Mat Collishaw
Mark Dion
Olafur Eliasson
Siobhán Hapaska
Sabine Hornig
Teresa Hubbard/Alexander Birchler
Ian Kiaer
Carla Klein
Liz Larner
Charles Long
Rita Lundqvist
Mark Manders
Jason Meadows
Ernesto Neto
Rivane Neuenschwander
Susan Philipsz
Peggy Preheim
Analia Saban
Tomas Saraceno
Thomas Scheibitz
Hannah Starkey
Haim Steinbach
Dirk Stewen
Jack Strange
Sarah Sze
Neal Tait
Jeffrey Vallance
Gillian Wearing
Nicole Wermers

Bortolami

Stand A9
Tel +1 646-522-3978
520 West 20th Street
New York, NY 10011
United States
Tel +1 212-727-2050
Fax +1 212-727-2060
info@bortolamigallery.com
www.bortolamigallery.com

Contact
Stefania Bortolami
Christine Messineo

Artists
Richard Aldrich
Avner Ben-Gal
Daniel Buren
Tom Burr
Shane Campbell
Morgan Fisher
Michel François
Piero Golia
Thilo Heinzmann
Patrick Hill
Piotr Janas
Scott King
Jutta Koether
Jonathan Meese
Luigi Ontani
Anna Ostoya
Ben Schumacher
Gary Webb
Eric Wesley
Aaron Young

Galerie Isabella Bortolozzi

Stand F18
Tel +49 30-2639-4985

Schöneberger Ufer 61
Berlin 10785
Germany
Tel +49 30-2639-4985
Fax +49 30-2639-6539
info@bortolozzi.com
www.bortolozzi.com

Contact
Isabella Bortolozzi
Marta Lusena

Artists
Leonor Antunes
Ibon Aranberri
Ed Atkins
Juliette Blightman
Jay Chung & Q Takeki Maeda
Christian Frosi
Jos de Gruyter & Harald Thys
Maria Lai
Danny McDonald
Susan Philipsz
Seth Price
Carol Rama
Stephen G. Rhodes
Yorgos Sapountzis
Nora Schultz
Danh Vo

The Breeder

Stand C22
Tel +30 697-744-2712

Iasonos 45
Athens 10436
Greece
Tel +30 21-0331-7527
Fax +30 21-0331-7527
gallery@thebreedersystem.com
www.thebreedersystem.com

Contact
George Vamvakidis
Stathis Panagoulis
Nadia Gerazouni

Artists
Markus Amm
Marc Bijl
Vlassis Caniaris
Matt Connors
Antonis Donef
Iris van Dongen
Stef Driesen
Stelios Faitakis
Uwe Henneken
HOPE
Kalup Linzy
Andreas Lolis
Ryan McGinley
Irini Miga
Scott Myles
Angelos Papadimitriou
Ilias Papailiakis
Jennifer Rubell
Shirana Shahbazi
Mindy Shapero
Daniel Sinsel
Gert & Uwe Tobias
Scott Treleaven
Alexandros Tzannis
Jannis Varelas
Vangelis Vlahos
Gabriel Vormstein
Tao Xue

Broadway 1602

Stand C9
Tel +1 212-481-0362

1181 Broadway, Floor 3
New York, NY 10001
United States
Tel +1 212-481-0362
Fax +1 212-481-1699
gallery@broadway1602.com
www.broadway1602.com

Contact
Anke Kempkes

Artists
Evelyne Axell
Edwin Burdis
Anders Clausen
Margarete Jakschik
Devin Leonardi
Babette Mangolte
Anna Molska
Shana Moulton
Xanti Schawinsky
Penny Slinger
Lucy Stein
Marjorie Strider
Alina Szapocznikow

Gavin Brown's enterprise

Stand B18
Tel +1 917-477-9554

620 Greenwich Street
New York, NY 10014
United States
Tel +1 212-627-5258
gallery@gavinbrown.biz
www.gavinbrown.biz

Contact
Gavin Brown
Lucy Chadwick

Artists
Franz Ackermann
James Angus
Uri Aran
Thomas Bayrle
Dirk Bell
Jennifer Bornstein
Joe Bradley
Kerstin Braetsch
Martin Creed
Verne Dawson
Jeremy Deller
Peter Doig
Urs Fischer
Dara Friedman
Mark Handforth
Jonathan Horowitz
Alex Katz
Christopher Knowles
Udomsak Krisanamis
Mark Leckey
Silke Otto-Knapp
Laura Owens
Oliver Payne
Elizabeth Peyton
Steven Pippin
Rob Pruitt
Nick Relph
Steven Shearer
Frances Stark
Katja Strunz
Sturtevant
Spencer Sweeney
Rirkrit Tiravanija

Galerie Buchholz

Stand B35
Tel +49 170-430-0153

Fasanenstrasse 30
Berlin 10719
Germany
Tel +49 30-8862-4056
Fax +49 30-8862-4057

Neven-DuMont-Strasse 17
Cologne 50667
Germany
Tel +49 22-1257-4946
Fax +49 22-1253-351
post@galeriebuchholz.de
www.galeriebuchholz.de

Contact
Daniel Buchholz
Christopher Müller

Artists
Tomma Abts
Nairy Baghramian
Cosima von Bonin
Tony Conrad
Simon Denny
Lukas Duwenhögger
Thomas Eggerer
Cerith Wyn Evans
Vincent Fecteau
Morgan Fisher
Isa Genzken
Jack Goldstein
Julian Göthe
Richard Hawkins
Jochen Klein
Jutta Koether
Michael Krebber
Mark Leckey
Sam Lewitt
Lucy McKenzie
Henrik Olesen
Paulina Olowska
Silke Otto-Knapp
Mathias Poledna
Florian Pumhösl
R.H. Quaytman
de Rijke & de Rooij
Willem de Rooij
Frances Stark
Josef Strau
Stefan Thater
Cheyney Thompson
Wolfgang Tillmans
Danh Vo
Martin Wong
Katharina Wulff

Bureau

Stand R11
Tel +1 917-861-9300

127 Henry Street
New York, NY 10002
United States
Tel +1 212 227 2783
office@bureau-inc.com
www.bureau-inc.com

Contact
Gabrielle Giattino

Artists
Erica Baum
Ellie Ga
Tom Holmes
Matt Hoyt
Viktor Kopp
Justin Matherly
Lionel Maunz

Cabinet

Stand C7
Tel +44 7950-920126

Apartment 6
49-59 Old Street
London EC1V 9HX
United Kingdom
Tel +44 20-7251-6114
Fax +44 20-7608-2414
art@cabinetltd.demon.co.uk
www.cabinet.uk.com

Contact
Martin McGeown
Andrew Wheatley

Artists
Tariq Alvi
Atelier
Ed Atkins
Lutz Bacher
Bonnie Camplin
Gillian Carnegie
Marc Camille Chaimowicz
Jay Chung & Q Takeki Maeda
Lukas Duwenhögger
Cosey Fanni Tutti
Julian Göthe
Mark Leckey
Lucy McKenzie
Lily van der Stokker
Simon Thompson
Tris Vonna-Michell
J.D. Williams

Shane Campbell Gallery

Stand R17
Tel +1 312-226-2223

673 North Milwaukee Avenue
Chicago, IL 60642
United States
Tel +1 312-226-2223
shane@shanecampbellgallery.com
www.shanecampbellgallery.com

125 North Harvey Avenue
Oak Park 60302
United States
Tel +1 312-226-2223

Contact
Shane Campbell

Artists
Chris Bradley
Jesse Chapman
Ann Craven
Kim Fisher
Michelle Grabner
Joanne Greenbaum
Mark Grotjahn
Jay Heikes
Patrick Hill
Shio Kusaka
Suzanne McClelland
Jason Meadows
William J. O'Brien
Alex Olson
Anthony Pearson
Adam Pendleton
Jon Pestoni
Zak Prekop
Amanda Ross-Ho
Lisa Williamson
Jonas Wood

Canada

Stand F30
Tel +1 212-925-4631

55 Chrystie Street
New York, NY 10002
United States
Tel +1 212-925-4631
gallery@canadanewyork.com
www.canadanewyork.com

Contact

Sarah Braman
Suzanne Butler
Phil Grauer
Wallace Whitney

Artists
David Askevold
Katherine Bernhardt
Joe Bradley
Sarah Braman
Matt Connors
Xylor Jane
Lily Ludlow
Michael Mahalchick
Joanna Malinowska
Carrie Moyer
Luke Murphy
Elena Pankova
Robin Peck
Anke Weyer
Wallace Whitney
Michael Williams

Galerie Gisela Capitain

Stand B19
Tel +49 221-355-7010

St. Apern Strasse 26
Cologne 50667
Germany
Tel +49 221-355-7010
Fax +49 221-355-70129
info@galeriecapitain.de
www.galeriecapitain.de

Contact
Gisela Capitain
Regina Fiorito

Artists
Karla Black
Barbara Bloom
Maria Brunner
Gillian Carnegie
Günther Förg
Luke Fowler
Anna Gaskell
Wade Guyton
Uwe Henneken
Charline von Heyl
Margarete Jakschik
Rachel Khedoori
Martin Kippenberger
Zoe Leonard
Meuser
Marcel Odenbach
Albert Oehlen
Laura Owens
Jorge Pardo
Ascan Pinckernelle
Seth Price
Stephen Prina
Sam Samore
Elfie Semotan
Monika Sosnowska
John Stezaker
Kelley Walker
Franz West
Christopher Williams
Johannes Wohnseifer
Christopher Wool

carlier | gebauer

Stand C23
Tel +49 30-2400-8630

Markgrafenstrasse 67
Berlin 10969
Germany
Tel +49 30-2400-8630
Fax +49 30-2400-86333
mail@carliergebauer.com
www.carliergebauer.com

Contact
Marie-Blanche Carlier
Ulrich Gebaue
Sarah Miltenberger

Artists
Rosa Barba
Ernesto Caivano
Sebastian Diaz Morales
A K Dolven
Michel François
Paul Graham
Asta Gröting
Dor Guez
Tomasz Kowalski
Marcellvs L.
Marko Lehanka
Przemek Matecki
Julie Mehretu
Aernout Mik
Kirsi Mikkola
Jean-Luc Moulène
Paul Pfeiffer
Jessica Rankin
Erik Schmidt
Thomas Schütte
Peter Stauss
Fred Tomaselli
Janaina Tschäpe
Mark Wallinger
Kailiang Yang

Cheim & Read

Stand C36
Tel +1 646-221-6848

547 West 25th Street
New York, NY 10001
United States
Tel +1 212-242-7727
Fax +1 212-242-7737
gallery@cheimread.com
www.cheimread.com

Contact
John Cheim
Howard Read
Mary Gail Parr
Adam Sheffer
Maria Bueno
Daniel Lechner

Artists
Ghada Amer
Don Bachardy
Donald Baechler
Lynda Benglis
Louise Bourgeois
William Eggleston
Louise Fishman
Adam Fuss
Hans Hartung
Jenny Holzer
Bill Jensen
Chantal Joffe
Jannis Kounellis
Jonathan Lasker
McDermott & McGough
Barry McGee
Joan Mitchell
Paul Morrison
Jack Pierson
Tal R
Milton Resnick
John Sonsini
Pat Steir
Juan Uslé
Otto Zitko

Mehdi Chouakri

Stand C24
Tel +49 151-157-72-149

Invalidenstrasse 117
Entrance Schlegelstrasse 26
Berlin 10115
Germany
Tel +49 30-2839-1153
Fax +49 30-2839-1154
galerie@mehdi-chouakri.com
www.mehdi-chouakri.com

Contact
Mehdi Chouakri
Alexandra Alexopoulou
Saehee Hwang
Judith Schmerberg

Artists
Saâdane Afif
John M Armleder
Claude Closky
Phillipe Decrauzat
Hans-Peter Feldmann
Sylvie Fleury
Isabell Heimerdinger
Mathieu Mercier
Gerold Miller
Charlotte Posenenske
Gerwald Rockenschaub
Peter Roehr
Gitte Schäfer
Vincent Szarek
Luca Trevisani

James Cohan Gallery

Stand B30
Tel +1 212-714-9500

533 West 26th Street
New York, NY 10001
United States
Tel +1 212-714-9500
Fax +1 212-714-9510

1/F Building 1 No.1 Lane
170 Yue Yang Road
Shanghai 200031, PRC
China
Tel +86 21-5466-0825
Fax +86 21-5466-0823
info@jamescohan.com
www.jamescohan.com

Contact
James Cohan
Elyse Goldberg
Chrissie Shearman
Sean Anderson
Laurie Harrison

Artists
Ingrid Calame
Simon Evans
Trenton Doyle Hancock
Yun-Fei Ji
Folkert de Jong
Jesper Just
Byron Kim
Richard Long
Beatriz Milhazes
Ruben Ochoa
Bill Owens
Roxy Paine
Katie Paterson
Hiraki Sawa
Yinka Shonibare MBE
Shinique Smith
Estate of Robert Smithson
Erick Swenson
Tabaimo
Alison Elizabeth Taylor
Fred Tomaselli
Bill Viola
Wim Wenders
Xu Zhen (MadeIn)

Sadie Coles HQ

Stand C15
Tel +44 20-7493-8611

69 South Audley Street
London W1K 2QZ
United Kingdom
Tel +44 20-7493-8611
Fax +44 20-7499-4878

4 New Burlington Place
London W1S 2HS
United Kingdom
Tel +44 20-7493-8611
Fax +44 20-7499-4878
info@sadiecoles.com
www.sadiecoles.com

Contact
Sadie Coles
Pauline Daly

Artists
Carl Andre
Matthew Barney
Dirk Bell
Avner Ben Gal
Frank Benson
John Bock
Don Brown
Spartacus Chetwynd
Steven Claydon
John Currin
Sam Durant
Angus Fairhurst
Urs Fischer
Florian Hecker
Georg Herold
Jonathan Horowitz
David Korty
Gabriel Kuri
Jim Lambie
Hilary Lloyd
Sarah Lucas
Victoria Morton
JP Munro
Laura Owens
Simon Periton
Raymond Pettibon
Elizabeth Peyton
Richard Prince
Ugo Rondinone
Wilhelm Sasnal
Gregor Schneider
Daniel Sinsel
Andreas Slominski
Christiana Soulou
Rudolf Stingel
Nicola Tyson
Paloma Varga Weisz
T.J. Wilcox
Andrea Zittel

Contemporary Fine Arts

Stand C39
Tel +49 30-288-7870

Am Kupfergraben 10
Berlin 10117
Germany
Tel +49 30-288-7870
Fax +49 30-288-78726
gallery@cfa-berlin.de
www.cfa-berlin.de

Contact
Bruno Brunnet
Nicole Hackert
Philipp Haverkampf

Artists
Georg Baselitz
Peter Böhnisch
Marc Brandenburg
Cecily Brown
Christa Dichgans
Peter Doig
Zhivago Duncan
Marcel Eichner
Max Frisinger
Georg Herold
Thomas Kiesewetter
Michael Kunze
Jonathan Meese
Chris Ofili
Raymond Pettibon
Tal R
Anselm Reyle
Daniel Richter
Julian Schnabel
Dana Schutz
Norbert Schwontowski
Dash Snow
Katja Strunz
Gert & Uwe Tobias
Ralf Ziervogel

Galleria Continua

Stand C40
Tel +39 05-77-94-31-34

Via del Castello 11
San Gimignano 53037
Italy
Tel +39 05-77-94-31-34
Fax +39 05-77-94-04-84
info@galleriacontinua.com
www.galleriacontinua.com

Dashanzi Art District
798 #8503, 2 - Jiuxianqiao
Road, Chaoyang Dst
Beijing 100015
China
Tel +89 10-5978-9505

Contact
Mario Cristiani
Lorenzo Fiaschi
Maurizio Rigillo
Rossella Bracali

Artists
Ai Weiwei
Kader Attia
Berlinde de Bruyckere
Daniel Buren
Loris Cecchini
Estate of Chen Zhen
Leandro Erlich
Meschac Gaba
Carlos Garaicoa
Kendell Geers
Antony Gormley
Gu Dexin
Shilpa Gupta
Subodh Gupta
Mona Hatoum
Ilya & Emilia Kabakov
Kan Xuan
Anish Kapoor
Kimsooja
Jorge Macchi
Sabrina Mezzaqui
Moataz Nasr
Hans Op de Beeck
Giovanni Ozzola
Luca Pancrazzi
Michelangelo Pistoletto
Arcangelo Sassolino
Serse
Nedko Solakov
Sun Yuan & Peng Yu
Pascale Marthine Tayou
Nari Ward
Sophie Whettnall

Galleria Raffaella Cortese

Stand C17
Tel +39 02-20-43-55-55

Via A. Stradella 1 & 7
Milano 20129
Italy
Tel +39 02-20-43-55-55
Fax +39 02-29-53-390
rcortgal@tiscali.it
www.
galleriaraffaellacortese.com

Contact
Raffaella Cortese
Chiara Tiberio
Floriana Biundo

Artists
Miroslaw Balka
Yael Bartana
Barbara Bloom
Keren Cytter
Michael Fliri
Jitka Hanzlovà
Roni Horn
Joan Jonas
William E. Jones
Kimsooja
Zoe Leonard
Anna Maria Maiolino
Marcello Maloberti
Daria Martin
Ana Mendieta
Mathilde Rosier
Martha Rosler
Kiki Smith
Jana Sterbak
Jessica Stockholder
James Welling
T.J. Wilcox

Corvi-Mora

Stand A16
Tel +44 20-7840-9111

1A Kempsford Road
London SE11 4NU
United Kingdom
Tel +44 20-7840-9111
Fax +44 20-7840-9112
tcm@corvi-mora.com
www.corvi-mora.com

Contact
Tommaso Corvi-Mora
Tabitha Langton-Lockton

Artists
Richard Aldrich
Abel Auer
Brian Calvin
Pierpaolo Campanini
Anne Collier
Andy Collins
Rachel Feinstein
Dee Ferris
Dominique Gonzalez-Foerster
Richard Hawkins
Roger Hiorns
Jim Isermann
Colter Jacobsen
Dorota Jurczak
Aisha Khalid
Armin Krämer
David Lieske
Eva Marisaldi
Jason Meadows
Monique Prieto
Imran Qureshi
Andrea Salvino
Glenn Sorensen
Tomoaki Suzuki
Naoyuki Tsuji
Lynette Yiadom-Boakye

Galerie Chantal Crousel

Stand B28
Tel +33 6-80-65-24-42

10 rue Charlot
Paris 75003
France
Tel +33 1-42-77-38-87
Fax +33 1-42-77-59-00

La Douane
11F rue Léon Jouhaux
Paris 75003
France
Tel +33 1-42-01-64-97
Fax +33 1-42-77-59-00
galerie@crousel.com
www.crousel.com

Contact
Chantal Crousel
Niklas Svennung

Artists
Jennifer Allora & Guillermo Calzadilla
Fikret Atay
Abraham Cruzvillegas
Claire Fontaine
Isa Genzken
Wade Guyton
Fabrice Gygi
Mona Hatoum
Thomas Hirschhorn
Hassan Khan
Michael Krebber
Jean-Luc Moulène
Moshe Ninio
Melik Ohanian
Gabriel Orozco
Seth Price
Clément Rodzielski
Willem de Rooij
Anri Sala
Alain Séchas
José Maria Sicilia
Sean Snyder
Reena Spaulings
Wolfgang Tillmans
Rirkrit Tiravanija
Danh Vo
Wang Bing
Haegue Yang
Heimo Zobernig

Crystal

Stand R10
Tel +46 7-372-32258

Hudiksvallsgatan 4b
Stockholm 113 30
Sweden
Tel +46 8-322-850
info@
crystalcontemporaryart.se
www.
crystalcontemporaryart.se

Contact
Katarina Sjögren
Jun-Hi Wennergren
Nordling

Artists
Daniel Andersson
Fia Backström
Johanna Billing
Lina Bjerneld
Ditte Ejlerskov
Goldin+Senneby
Jenny Källman
Tracy Nakayama
Julia Peirone
Bella Rune

Massimo De Carlo

Stand B1
Tel +39 02-27-00-39-87

Via Giovanni Ventura 5
Milan 20134
Italy
Tel +39 02-27-00-39-87
Fax +39 02-74-92-135

6 Heddon Street
W1B 4BT
London
United Kingdom
Tel +44 20-7287-2005
Fax +44 20-7287-2005
info@massimodecarlo.it
www.massimodecarlo.it

Contact
Massimo De Carlo
Ludovica Barbieri
Roberto Moiraghi

Artists
John M Armleder
Massimo Bartolini
Maurizio Cattelan
Spartacus Chetwynd
Steven Claydon
Dan Colen
George Condo
Roberto Cuoghi
Elmgreen & Dragset
Roland Flexner
gelitin
Thomas Grünfeld
Carsten Höller
Christian Holstad
Rashid Johnson
Elad Lassry
Sol LeWitt
Nate Lowman
Matthew Monahan
Olivier Mosset
Matt Mullican
Steven Parrino
Yan Pei-Ming
Diego Perrone
Paola Pivi
Rob Pruitt
Jim Shaw
Josh Smith
Rudolf Stingel
Piotr Uklański
Kaari Upson
Kelley Walker
Aaron Young
Andrea Zittell

Elizabeth Dee

Stand D1
Tel +1 212-924-7545

545 West 20th Street
New York, NY 10011
United States
Tel +1 212-924-7545
Fax +1 212-924-7671
info@elizabethdee.com
www.elizabethdee.com

Contact
Elizabeth Dee
Jayne Drost
Lane La Colla
Kevin Tobin
Raoul Anchondo

Artists
Alex Bag
Mark Barrow
Eric Baudelaire
Miriam Cahn
Philippe Decrauzat
Harry Dodge & Stanya Kahn
Jeff Keen
Miranda Lichtenstein
Virgil Marti
Ryan McNamara
Josephine Meckseper
Carl Ostendarp
Adrian Piper
Renaud Regnery
Meredyth Sparks
Ryan Trecartin

Galerie Eigen + Art

Stand C33
Tel +49 34-1960-7886

Spinnereistrasse 7 Halle 5
Leipzig 04179
Germany
Tel +49 34-1960-7886
Fax +49 341-2254-214

Auguststrasse 26
Berlin 10117
Germany
Tel +49 30-2806-605
Fax +49 30-2806-616
berlin@eigen-art.com
www.eigen-art.com

Contact
Gerd Harry Lybke

Artists
Akos Birkas
Birgit Brenner
Martin Eder
Tim Eitel
Nina Fischer & Maroan el Sani
Stella Hamberg
Jörg Herold
Christine Hill
Uwe Kowski
Rémy Markowitsch
Maix Mayer
Ryan Mosley
Carsten Nicolai
Olaf Nicolai
Neo Rauch
Ricarda Roggan
Yehudit Sasportas
David Schnell
Annelies Strba
Matthias Weischer

galerie frank elbaz

Stand D6
Tel +33 6-03-33-85-85

7 rue Saint Claude
Paris 75003
France
Tel +33 1-48-87-50-04
info@galeriefrankelbaz.com
www.galeriefrankelbaz.com

Contact
Frank Elbaz
Daphné Kossmann
Estelle Gerberon

Artists
Davide Balula
Jesus Alberto Benitez
Wallace Berman
Susan Collis
Julije Knifer
Justine Kurland
Rainier Lericolais
Ari Marcopoulos
Audrey Nervi
Kaz Oshiro
Gyan Panchal
Bernard Piffaretti
Meredyth Sparks
Blair Thurman
Josip Vanista

Experimenter

Stand F23
Tel +91 33-2463-0465

2/1 Hindusthan Road
Kolkata 700029
India
Tel +91 33-2463-0465
info@experimenter.in
www.experimenter.in

Contact
Prateek Raja
Priyanka Raja

Artists
Bani Abidi
Rathin Barman
Adip Dutta
Sanchayan Ghosh
Naeem Mohaiemen
Mehreen Murtaza
The Otolith Group
Raqs Media Collective

Figge von Rosen Galerie

Stand R8
Tel +49 221-2705-6840

Aachener Strasse 65
Cologne 50674
Germany
Tel +49 221-2705-6840
Fax +49 221-2705-6849
info@figgevonrosen.com
www.figgevonrosen.com

Potsdamer Strasse 98
10785 Berlin
Germany
Tel +49 30-2639-2971
Fax +49 30-2639-2972

Contact
Philipp Figge
Philipp von Rosen

Artists
Shoja Azari
Koen van den Broek
Jose Dávila
Haïdée Henry
Nic Hess
Fränze Hoppe
Anna K.E.
Anna Malagrida
David Ostrowski
Javier Téllez
Rebecca Ann Tess
Ignacio Uriarte
Judi Werthein
Bas de Wit

Foksal Gallery Foundation

Stand B40
Tel +48 50-426-8910

Gorskiego 1A
Warsaw 00-033
Poland
Tel +48 22-826-5081
Fax +48 22-826-5081
mail@fgf.com.pl
www.fgf.com.pl

Contact
Andrzej Przywara

Artists
Pawel Althamer
Cezary Bodzianowski
Piotr Janas
Katarzyna Jozefowicz
Edward Krasinski
Robert Kusmirowski
Anna Molska
Anna Niesterowicz
Paulina Olowska
Wilhlem Sasnal
Monika Sosnowska
Jakub Julian Ziolkowski
Artur Zmijewski

Galeria Fortes Vilaça

Stand C48
Tel +55 11-3032-7066

Rua Fradique Coutinho, 1500
São Paulo 05416-001
Brazil
Tel +55 11-3032-7066
Fax +55 11-3097-0384

Rua James Holland, 71
São Paulo 01138-000
Brazil
+55 11-3392-3942
+55 11-3392-5969
galeria@fortesvilaca.com.
www.fortesvilaca.com.br

Contact
Marcia Fortes
Alessandra D'Aloia
Alexandre Gabriel

Artists
Franz Ackermann
Efrain Almeida
Barrão Barrão
Carlos Bevilacqua
Tiago Carneiro da Cunha
Los Carpinteros
Leda Catunda
José Damasceno
Iran do Espírito Santo
Simon Evans
Tamar Guimarães
Marine Hugonnier
Alejandra Icaza
Sergej Jensen
Jac Leirner
Rodrigo Matheus
Beatriz Milhazes
Gerben Mulder
Vik Muniz
Paulo Nenflidio
Ernesto Neto
Rivane Neuenschwander
Damián Ortega
osgemeos
Mauro Piva
Sara Ramo
Nuno Ramos
Mauro Restiffe
Marina Rheingantz
Michael Sailstorfer
Julião Sarmento
Valeska Soares
Hiroshi Sugito
Janaina Tschäpe
Adriana Varejão
Erika Verzutti
Cerith Wyn Evans
Luiz Zerbini

Marc Foxx

Stand C32
Tel +1 323-857-5571

6150 Wilshire Boulevard
Los Angeles, CA 90048
United States
Tel +1 323-857-5571
gallery@marcfoxx.com
www.marcfoxx.com

Contact
Marc Foxx
Rodney Hill
Lia Trinka-Browner
Vanesa Zendejas

Artists
Leonor Antunes
Cris Brodahl
Anne Collier
Andy Collins
William Daniels
Stef Driesen
Brian Fahlstrom
Sophie von Hellermann
Roger Hiorns
Sanya Kantarovsky
Annette Kelm
Makiko Kudo
Luisa Lambri
Kris Martin
Jason Meadows
Carter Mull
David Musgrave
Michael van Ofen
Alessandro Pessoli
Amalia Pica
Richard Rezac
Matthew Ronay
Maaike Schoorel
Frances Stark
Hiroshi Sugito
Ricky Swallow
Mateo Tannatt
Guido van der Werve
Jennifer West
Sam Windett

Carl Freedman Gallery

Stand C35
Tel +44 7714-087343

44A Charlotte Road
London EC2A 3PD
United Kingdom
Tel +44 20-7684-8890
Fax +44 20-7684-8889
info@carlfreedman.com
www.carlfreedman.com

Contact
Carl Freedman
Robert Diament

Artists
Armando Andrade Tudela
Jess Flood-Paddock
Michael Fullerton
Thilo Heinzmann
Ivan Seal
David Brian Smith
Fergal Stapleton
Catherine Story
Pieter Vermeersch

Galerie Cinzia Friedlaender

Stand R3
Tel +49 30-2639-3956

Potsdamer Strasse 105
Berlin 10785
Germany
Tel +49 30-2639-3956
Fax +49 30-2639-3958
mail@galeriefriedlaender.de
www.galeriefriedlaender.de

Contact
Cinzia Friedlaender

Artists
Bonnie Camplin
Sunah Choi
Justus Köhncke
Dirk von Lowtzow
Anna Möller
Jutta Pohlmann
Claus Rasmussen
Sabine Reitmaier
Susanne Riedel
Matthias Schaufler
Maria Volk
Jeronimo Voss
Vincent Vulsma
JD Williams

Stephen Friedman Gallery

Stand B10
Tel +1 646-346-2836

25–28 Old Burlington Street
London W1S 3AN
United Kingdom
Tel +44 20-7494-1434
Fax +44 20-7494-1431
info@stephenfriedman.com
www.stephenfriedman.com

Contact
Stephen Friedman
David Hubbard
Tobias Wagner

Artists
Mamma Andersson
Tonico Lemos Auad
Stephan Balkenhol
Claire Barclay
Huma Bhabha
Robert Buck
Tara Donovan
Tom Friedman
Kendell Geers
Wayne Gonzales
Daniel Guzmán
Thomas Hirschhorn
Jim Hodges
Li Tianbing
Paul McDevitt
Beatriz Milhazes
Yoshitomo Nara
Rivane Neuenschwander
Thomas Nozkowski
Catherine Opie
Cornelius Quabeck
Ged Quinn
Jennifer Rubell
Lucas Samaras
Mira Schendel
Yinka Shonibare MBE
David Shrigley
Anne Truitt

Frith Street Gallery

Stand C42
Tel +44 20-7494-1550

17–18 Golden Square
London W1F 9JJ
United Kingdom
Tel +44 20-7494-1550
info@frithstreetgallery.com
www.frithstreetgallery.com

Contact
Jane Hamlyn
Niru Ratnam

Artists
Chantal Akerman
Polly Apfelbaum
Fiona Banner
Anna Barriball
Massimo Bartolini
Ingrid Calame
Dorothy Cross
Tacita Dean
Marlene Dumas
Callum Innes
Jaki Irvine
Cornelia Parker
Raqs Media Collective
John Riddy
Thomas Schütte
Dayanita Singh
Bridget Smith
Annelies Strba
Fiona Tan
Juan Uslé
Daphne Wright

James Fuentes

Stand F24
Tel +1 212-577-1201

55 Delancey Street
New York, NY 10002
United States
Tel +1 212-577-1201
Fax +1 212-577-1202
info@jamesfuentes.com
www.jamesfuentes.com

Contact
James Fuentes
Adrianne Rubenstein

Artists
Joshua Abelow
Jonathan Allmaier
Lizzi Bougatsos
Brian DeGraw
Jessica Dickinson
John McAllister
Jonas Mekas
Noam Rappaport

Gagosian Gallery

Stand D4
Tel +1 212-744-2313

980 Madison Avenue
New York, NY 10075
United States
Tel + 1 212-744-2313
Fax + 1 212-710-3825
newyork@gagosian.com
www.gagosian.com

555 West 24th Street
New York 10011
United States
Tel +1 212-741-1111
Fax + 1 212-741-9611

522 West 21st Street
New York, NY 10011
United States
Tel +212 741 1717
Fax +212 741 0006

Contact
Larry Gagosian

Artists
Diane Arbus
Richard Artschwager
Richard Avedon
Francis Bacon
Georg Baselitz
Jean-Michel Basquiat
Cecily Brown
Glenn Brown
Chris Burden
Alexander Calder
John Chamberlain
Dan Colen
Michael Craig-Martin
Gregory Crewdson
John Currin
Dexter Dalwood
Walter De Maria
Alberto Di Fabio
William Eggleston
Roe Ethridge
Urs Fischer
Ellen Gallagher
Alberto Giacometti
Piero Golia
Douglas Gordon
Arshile Gorky
Mark Grotjahn
Andreas Gursky
Richard Hamilton
Damien Hirst
Howard Hodgkin
Carsten Höller
Neil Jenney
Y.Z. Kami
Mike Kelley
Anselm Kiefer
Jeff Koons
Yayoi Kusama
Roy Lichtenstein
Vera Lutter
Florian Maier-Aichen
Sally Mann
Piero Manzoni
Adam McEwen
Joel Morrison
Takashi Murakami
Marc Newson
Paul Noble
Albert Oehlen
Steven Parrino
Richard Phillips
Pablo Picasso
Richard Prince
Robert Rauschenberg
Anselm Reyle
Nancy Rubins
Thomas Ruff
Ed Ruscha
Jenny Saville
Richard Serra
Elisa Sighicelli
Taryn Simon
David Smith
Rudolf Stingel
Philip Taaffe
Mark Tansey
Robert Therrien
Tatiana Trouvé
James Turrell
Cy Twombly
Piotr Uklański
Francesco Vezzoli
Andy Warhol
Franz West
Rachel Whiteread
Christopher Wool
Richard Wright
Aaron Young
Zeng Fanzhi

gb agency

Stand F33
Tel +33 6-11-13-48-62

18 rue des 4 Fils
Paris 75003
France
Tel +33 1-44-78-00-60
gb@gbagency.fr
www.gbagency.fr

Contact
Solène Guillier
Nathalie Boutin

Artists
Mac Adams
Robert Breer
Elina Brotherus
Omer Fast
Ryan Gander
Mark Geffriaud
Július Koller
Jiří Kovanda
Deimantas Narkevičius
Roman Ondák
Dominique Petitgand
Pratchaya Phinthong
Pia Rönicke
Yann Sérandour

Annet Gelink Gallery

Stand A10
Tel +31 20-330-2066

Laurierstraat 187–189
Amsterdam 1016 PL
Netherlands
Tel +31 20-330-2066
Fax +31 20-330-2065
info@annetgelink.com
www.annetgelink.com

Contact
Floor Wullems
Carolien Sijberden
Macarena Dupouy
Alex Farrar

Artists
Carlos Amorales
Yael Bartana
Ed van der Elsken
Alicia Framis
Anya Gallaccio
Ryan Gander
Roger Hiorns
Carla Klein
Meiro Koizumi
Kiki Lamers
David Maljkovic
Dan McCarthy
Bradley Pitts
Wilfredo Prieto
Muzi Quawson
Sarah van Sonsbeeck
Glenn Sorensen
Barbara Visser
Marijke van Warmerdam
Erik Wesselo

A Gentil Carioca

Stand C27
Tel +55 21-2222-1651

Rua Gonçalves Lêdo 17
sobrado, Centro
Rio de Janeiro 20060-020
Brazil
Tel +55 21-2222-1651
Fax +55-21-2222-1651
correio@agentilcarioca.
com.br
www.agentilcarioca.com.br

Avenida Epitássio Pessoa,
1674/401, Lagoa
Rio de Janeiro 22411–071
Brazil
Tel +55 21-2523-1157

Contact
Marcio Botner
Laura Lima
Ernesto Neto
Tatiana Bührnheim
Cecilia Tanure
Fabiola Neves

Artists
Ricardo Basbaum
José Bento
Botner & Pedro
Cabelo
Carlos Contente
Guga Ferraz
Fabiano Gonper
Maria Laet
Laura Lima
Jarbas Lopes
Renata Lucas
Simone Michelin
João Modé
Paulo Nenflidio
Maria Nepomuceno
Bernardo Ramalho
Thiago Rocha Pitta
Rodrigo Torres
Pedro Varela
Alexandre Vogler

François Ghebaly Gallery

Stand F32
Tel +1 323-691-9133

2600 South La Cienega
Boulevard
Los Angeles, CA 90034
United States
Tel +1 310-280-0777
info@ghebaly.com
www.ghebaly.com

Contact
François Ghebaly
Karisa Morante

Artists
Dan Bayles
Neïl Beloufa
Marius Bercea
Channa Horwitz
Patrick Jackson
Joel Kyack
Anthony Lepore
David Levine
Candice Lin
Michael Müller
Gina Osterloh
Robert Russell

Alexander Gray Associates

Stand F21
Tel +1 212-399-2636

508 West 26th Street
No. 215
New York, NY 10001
United States
Tel +1 212-399-2636
Fax +1 212-399-2684
info@alexandergray.com
www.alexandergray.com

Contact
Alexander Gray
David Cabrera

Artists
Luis Camnitzer
Melvin Edwards
Coco Fusco
Jeremy Gilbert-Rolfe
Lorraine O'Grady
Dawit L. Petros
Paul Ramírez Jonas
Joan Semmel
Hassan Sharif
Regina Silveira
Estate of Hugh Steers
Jack Whitten
Bruce Yonemoto

Greene Naftali

Stand C44
Tel +1 212-463-7770

508 West 26th Street
New York, NY 10001
United States
Tel +1 212-463-7770
Fax +1 212-463-0890
info@greenenaftaligallery.com
www.greenenaftaligallery.com

Contact
Carol Greene
Alex Tuttle
Vera Alemani
Jeffrey Rowledge

Artists
Trisha Baga
Julie Becker
Bernadette Corporation
Paul Chan
Tony Conrad
Guy de Cointet
Jim Drain
Ida Ekblad
Harun Farocki
Günther Förg
Michael Fullerton
gelitin
Daan van Golden
Lucy Gunning
Guyton\Walker
Rachel Harrison
Richard Hawkins
Sophie von Hellerman
Jacqueline Humphries
John Knight
Joachim Koester
Michael Krebber
William Leavitt
Michaela Meise
Bjarne Melgaard
Daniel Pflumm
Daniela Rossell
Allen Ruppersberg
Paul Sharits
Gedi Sibony
Josef Strau
Katharina Wulff
Amelie von Wulffen
Haegue Yang

greengrassi

Stand A11
Tel +44 20-7840-9101

1A Kempsford Road
London SE11 4NU
United Kingdom
Tel +44 20-7840-9101
Fax +44 20-7840-9102
info@greengrassi.com
www.greengrassi.com

Contact
Cornelia Grassi
Charlaine Brandy
Edwige Cochois
Davide Minuti

Artists
Tomma Abts
Stefano Arienti
Jennifer Bornstein
Moyra Davey
Roe Ethridge
Gretchen Faust
Vincent Fecteau
Giuseppe Gabellone
Joanne Greenbaum
Ellen Gronemeyer
Janice Kerbel
Shio Kusaka
Sean Landers
Simon Ling
Margherita Manzelli
David Musgrave
Kristen Oppenheim
Silke Otto-Knapp
Jennifer Pastor
Alessandro Pessoli
Karin Ruggaber
Allen Ruppersberg
Anne Ryan
Frances Stark
Jennifer Steinkamp
Pae White
Lisa Yuskavage

Galerie Karin Guenther

Stand F20
Tel +49 17-0556-6994

Admiralitätstrassse 71
Hamburg 20459
Germany
Tel +49 17-0556-6994
info@galerie-karin-guenther.de
www.galerie-karin-guenther.de

Contact
Karin Guenther
Harald Popp

Artists
Markus Amm
Michael Bauch
Henning Bohl
Wolfgang Breuer
Friederike Clever
Edith Dekyndt
Jeanne Faust
Berta Fischer
Ellen Gronemeyer
Michael Hakimi
Alexander Heim
Kerstin Kartscher
Janice Kerbel
Stefan Kern
Nina Könnemann
Michaela Melián
Claudia and Julia Müller
Silke Otto-Knapp
Gunter Reski
Allen Ruppersberg
Dirk Stewen
Stefan Thater

Jack Hanley Gallery

Stand A1
Tel +1 646-918-5824

136 Watts Street
New York, NY 10013
United States
Tel +1 646-918-5824
mail@jackhanley.com
www.jackhanley.com

Contact
Jack Hanley
Kara Kazanoff

Artists
Ajit Chauhan
Bjorn Copeland
Bernhard Fuchs
Folke Koebberling & Martin Kaltwasser
Margaret Lee
Marie Lorenz
Alicia McCarthy
Eleanor Moreton
Emily Prince
Maeghan Reid
Andrei Roiter
Leslie Shows
Kal Spelletich
Erwin Wurm
Amy Yao

Harris Lieberman

Stand B9
Tel +1 212-206-1290

508 West 26th Street
New York, NY 10001
United States
Tel +1 212-206-1290
gallery@harrislieberman.com
www.harrislieberman.com

Contact
Jessie Washburne-Harris
Michael Lieberman
Kris Latocha

Artists
Armin Boehm
Matthias Dornfeld
Stef Driesen
Simon Dybbroe Møller
Daniel Guzmán
Karl Haendel
Julian Hoeber
Evan Holloway
Alicja Kwade
Ohad Meromi
Rebecca Morris
Lisa Oppenheim
Zak Prekop
Bernd Ribbeck
Matt Saunders
Tommy White
Thomas Zipp

Hauser & Wirth

Stand B6
Tel +1 212-794-4970

32 East 69th Street
New York, NY 10021
United States
Tel +1 212-794-4970
Fax +1 212-794-4971
newyork@hauserwirth.com
www.hauserwirth.com

196A Piccadilly
London W1J 9DY
Phone +44 207 287 2300
Fax +44 20-7287-6600
london@hauserwirth.com

23 Savile Row
London W1S 2ET
United Kingdom
Tel +44 20-7287-2300
Fax +44 20-7287-6600
london@hauserwirth.com

Hauser & Wirth
Albisriederstrasse 199A
8047 Zürich
Switzerland
Tel +41 44-446-8050
zurich@hauserwirth.com

Artists
Ida Applebroog
Phyllida Barlow
Louise Bourgeois
Berlinde de Bruyckere
Christoph Büchel
David Claerbout
Martin Creed
Martin Eder
Zhang Enli
Ellen Gallagher
Isa Genzken
Dan Graham
Rodney Graham
Subodh Gupta
Mary Heilmann
Eva Hesse
Andy Hope 1930
Roni Horn
Thomas Houseago
Matthew Day Jackson
Richard Jackson
Rashid Johnson
Hans Josephsohn
Allan Kaprow
Rachel Khedoori
Bharti Kher
Guillermo Kutica
Maria Lassnig
Lee Lozano
Paul McCarthy
John McCracken
Joan Mitchell
Henry Moore
Ron Mueck
Caro Niederer
Christopher Orr
Djordje Ozbolt
Michael Raedecker
Jason Rhoades
Pipilotti Rist
Dieter Roth
Anri Sala
Wilhelm Sasnal
Christoph Schlingensief
Roman Signer
Anj Smith
Monika Sosnowska
Diana Thater
André Thomkins
Ian Wallace
David Zink Yi
Jakub Julian Ziolkowski

Herald St

Stand A30
Tel +44 20-7168-2566

2 Herald Street
London E2 6JT
United Kingdom
Tel +44 20-7168-2566
Fax +44 20-7613-0009
mail@heraldst.com
www.heraldst.com

Contact
Nicky Verber
Ash L'ange
Samara Aster

Artists
Markus Amm
Alexandra Bircken
Josh Brand
Pablo Bronstein
Peter Coffin
Matthew Darbyshire
Michael Dean
Ida Ekblad
Annette Kelm
Scott King
Cary Kwok
Christina Mackie
Djordje Ozbolt
Oliver Payne
Amalia Pica
Nick Relph
Tony Swain
Donald Urquhart
Klaus Weber
Nicole Wermers

Hollybush Gardens

Stand F9
Tel +44 7977-264582

Unit 2, B.J. House
10-14 Hollybush Gardens
London E2 9QP
United Kingdom
Tel +44 20-7739-9651
office@hollybushgardens.co.uk
www.hollybushgardens.co.uk

Contact
Lisa Panting
Malin Stahl

Artists
Johanna Billing
Andrea Büttner
Knut Henrik Henriksen
Karl Holmqvist
Claire Hooper
Kirschner & Panos
Benoît Maire
Eline McGeorge
Bruno Pacheco
Falke Pisano
Ruth Proctor

Hotel

Stand F31
Tel +44 20-7729-3122

4 Herald Street
London E2 6JT
United Kingdom
Tel +44 20-7729-3122
email@generalhotel.org
www.generalhotel.org

Contact
Darren Flook
Christabel Stewart

Artists
Mike Bouchet
Carol Bove
Wolfgang Breuer
Agnieszka Brzezanska
Duncan Campbell
Anders Clausen
Keith Farquhar
Alistair Frost
Judith Hopf
Richard Kern
Alan Michael
Joyce Pensato
Peter Saville
Torsten Slama
Alexis Marguerite Teplin
Stefan Thater
Mark van Yetter

Xavier Hufkens

Stand B23
Tel +32 2-639-67-30

6–8 Rue Saint Georges
Brussels 1050
Belgium
Tel +32 2-639-67-30
Fax +32 2-639-67-38
info@xavierhufkens.com
www.xavierhufkens.com

Contact
Xavier Hufkens

Artists
Saâdane Afif
Philip Allen
David Altmejd
Richard Artschwager
Louise Bourgeois
Cris Brodahl
Daniel Buren
Jean-Marc Bustamante
John Chamberlain
George Condo
Thierry de Cordier
William Eggleston
Michel François
Adam Fuss
Antony Gormley
Evan Holloway
Roni Horn
Thomas Houseago
Pierre Huyghe
Jacob Kassay
Willem de Kooning
Bertrand Lavier
José Lerma
Martin Maloney
Robert Mapplethorpe
Malcolm Morley
David Noonan
Hans Op de Beeck
Alessandro Pessoli
Jack Pierson
Michelangelo Pistoletto
Ken Price
Tim Rollins and K.O.S.
Sterling Ruby
Robert Ryman
Padraig Timoney
Lesley Vance
Jan Vercruysse
Erwin Wurm

Gallery Hyundai

Stand C20
Tel +82 2-2287-3500

80 Sagan-dong
Jongno-gu
Seoul 110-190
Korea
Tel +82 2-2287-3500
Fax +82 2-2287-3580
mail@galleryhyundai.com
www.galleryhyundai.com

Art Tower 640-6
Sinsa-dong, Gangnam-gu
Seoul 135-896
Korea
Tel +82 2519-0800
Fax +82 2519-0880

Contact
Hyung-Teh Do

Artists
Ai Weiwei
Choe U-ram
Chun Kwang Young
Robert Indiana
Joonho Jeon
Ik Joong Kang
Kyungwon Moon
François Morellet
Sarah Morris
Nam June Paik
Hyun-Ki Park
Junebum Park
Thomas Struth
Sookyung Yee
Tschang-Yeul Kim
Lee Ufan
Young-Hae Chang
Heavy Industries
Zeng Fanzhi

Taka Ishii Gallery

Stand B13
Tel +81 35-646-6050

1–3–2 5F Kiyosumi
Koto-ku
Tokyo 135–0024
Japan
Tel +81 35-646-6050
Fax +81 03-3642-3067
tig@takaishiigallery.com
www.takaishiigallery.com

6–6–9 Ropponyi Minako-Ku 2F
Tokyo 106–0032
Japan
Tel +81 36-447-1035
Fax +81 36-447-1036

483 Nishigawa-cho
Shimogyo-ku
Kyoto 600 –8325
Japan
Tel +81 75-353-9807
Fax +81 75-353-9808

Contact
Taka Ishii
Jeffrey Ian Rosen
Elisa Uematsu
Nahoko Yamaguchi
Junko Yasumaru

Artists
Amy Adler
Ei Arakawa
Nobuyoshi Araki
Thomas Demand
Elmgreen & Dragset
Mario Garcia Torres
Tomoo Gokita
Dan Graham
Naoya Hatakeyama
Nobuya Hoki
Takashi Ishida
Zon Ito
Naoto Kawahara
Annette Kelm
Yuki Kimura
Sean Landers
Lisa Lapinski
Yukinori Maeda
Helen Mirra
Daido Moriyama
Kyoko Murase
Silke Otto-Knapp
Sterling Ruby
Hiroe Saeki
Kei Takemura
Miroslav Tichy
Marijke van Warmerdam
Christopher Wool
Cerith Wyn Evans

Alison Jacques Gallery

Stand A25
Tel +44 7917-194938

16–18 Berners Street
London W1T 3LN
United Kingdom
Tel +44 20-7631-4720
Fax +44 20-7631-4750
info@alisonjacquesgallery.com.
www.alisonjacquesgallery.com

Contact
Alison Jacques
Roger Tatley
Rory Mitchell

Artists
Haluk Akakçe
Michael Bauer
Lygia Clark
Tomory Dodge
Dan Fischer
Saul Fletcher
Matt Johnson
Ian Kiaer
Klara Kristalova
Graham Little
Robert Mapplethorpe
Ryan McGinley
Ana Mendieta
Paul Morrison
Ryan Mosley
Michael van Ofen
Hélio Oiticica
Alessandro Raho
Bernd Ribbeck
Mathew Weir
Hannah Wilke
Catherine Yass
Thomas Zipp

Galerie Martin Janda

Stand A28
Tel +43 664 233 5429

Eschenbachgasse 11
Vienna 1010
Austria
Tel +43 1-585-7371
Fax +43 1-585-7372
galerie@martinjanda.at
www.martinjanda.at

Contact
Martin Janda
Elisabeth Konrath

Artists
Martin Arnold
Alessandro Balteo Yazbeck
Benjamin Butler
Adriana Czernin
Svenja Deininger
Milena Dragicevic
Werner Feiersinger
Giuseppe Gabellone
Christine & Irene Hohenbüchler
Christian Hutzinger
Raoul de Keyser
Jakob Kolding
Július Koller
Jan Merta
Roman Ondák
Peter Pommerer
Allen Ruppersberg
Joe Scanlan
Ene-Liis Semper
Gabriel Sierra
Roman Signer
Adrien Tirtiaux
Johannes Vogl
Maja Vukoje
Corinne Wasmuht
Donelle Woolford
Sharon Ya'ari
Jun Yang
Jakub Julian Ziolkowski

Catriona Jeffries

Stand A17
Tel +1 604-736-1554

274 East 1st Avenue
Vancouver BC
V5T 1A6
Canada
Tel +1 604-736-1554
Fax +1 604-736-1054
gallery@catrionajeffries.com
www.catrionajeffries.com

Contact
Catriona Jeffries
Anne Low

Artists
Arabella Campbell
Christos Dikeakos
Sam Durant
Geoffrey Farmer
Julia Feyrer
Brian Jungen
Janice Kerbel
Germaine Koh
Christina Mackie
Myfanwy MacLeod
Liz Magor
Gareth Moore
Damian Moppett
Alex Morrison
Isabelle Pauwels
Jerry Pethick
Judy Radul
Kevin Schmidt
Ron Terada
Ian Wallace
Jin-me Yoon

Casey Kaplan

Stand A6
Tel +1 212-645-7335

525 West 21st Street
New York, NY 10011
United States
Tel +1 212-645-7335
Fax +1 212-645-7835
info@caseykaplangallery.com
www.caseykaplangallery.com

Contact
Casey Kaplan
Loring Randolph
Alice Conconi

Artists
Henning Bohl
Matthew Brannon
Jeff Burton
Nathan Carter
Miles Coolidge
Jason Dodge
Trisha Donnelly
Geoffrey Farmer
Liam Gillick
Giorgio Griffa
Annika von Hausswolff
Brian Jungen
Jonathan Monk
Marlo Pascual
Diego Perrone
Julia Schmidt
Simon Starling
David Thorpe
Gabriel Vormstein
Garth Weiser
Johannes Wohnseifer

Karma International

Stand F10
Tel +41 76-327-2278

Dufourstrasse 48
Zurich 8008
Switzerland
Tel +41 43-535-8591
info@karmainternational.org
wwwkarmainternational.org

Contact
Marina Leuenberger
Karolina Dankow

Artists
Kim Seob Boninsegni
Agnieszka Brzezanska
Ida Ekblad
David Hominal
Thomas Julier
Tobias Madison
Carissa Rodriguez
Pamela Rosenkranz
Emanuel Rossetti
Thomas Sauter
Martin Soto Climent

kaufmann repetto

Stand A23
Tel +39 02-72-09-43-31

Via di Porta Tenaglia 7
Milan 20121
Italy
Tel +39 02-72-09-43-31
Fax +39 02-72-09-68-73
info@kaufmannrepetto.com
www.kaufmannrepetto.com

Contact
Francesca Kaufmann
Chiara Repetto
Beatrice Girelli
Paolo Ripamonti

Artists
Candice Breitz
Pierpaolo Campanini
Gianni Caravaggio
Maggie Cardelus
Talia Chetrit
Thea Djordjadze
Shannon Ebner
Latifa Echakhch
Edi Hila
Judith Hopf
Carlo Mollino
Yoshua Okon
Adrian Paci
Eva Rothshild
Aida Ruilova
Matt Sheridan Smith
Billy Sullivan
Lily van der Stokker
Pae White
Thomas Zipp

Sean Kelly Gallery

Stand B25
Tel +1 212-239-1181

528 West 29th Street
New York, NY 10001
United States
Tel +1 212-239-1181
Fax +1 212-239-2467
info@skny.com
www.skny.com

Contact
Sean Kelly
Cecile Panzieri
Janine Cirincione
Maureen Bray

Artists
Marina Abramović
Los Carpinteros
James Casebere
Leandro Erlich
Iran do Espírito Santo
Antony Gormley
Laurent Grasso
Johan Grimonprez
Rebecca Horn
Tehching Hsieh
Callum Innes
Idris Khan
Joseph Kosuth
Wolfgang Laib
Peter Liversidge
Robert Mapplethorpe
Anthony McCall
Juliao Sarmento
Alec Soth
Frank Thiel
Kehinde Wiley

Kerlin Gallery

Stand A19
Tel +35 31-670-9093

Anne's Lane, South Anne Street
Dublin D2
Ireland
Tel +35 31-670-9093
Fax +35 31-670-9096
gallery@kerlin.ie
www.kerlin.ie

Contact
David Fitzgerald
Darragh Hogan
John Kennedy

Artists
Philip Allen
Phil Collins
Dorothy Cross
Willie Doherty
Mark Francis
Maureen Gallace
Mark Garry
Liam Gillick
David Godbold
Siobhán Hapaska
Callum Innes
Jaki Irvine
Merlin James
Sam Keogh
Elizabeth Magill
Eoin McHugh
Stephen McKenna
William McKeown
Isabel Nolan
Kathy Prendergast
Norbert Schwontkowski
Sean Scully
Paul Seawright
Seán Shanahan
Paul Winstanley

Anton Kern Gallery

Stand C2
Tel +1 212-367-9663

532 West 20th Street
New York, NY 10011
United States
Tel +1 212-367-9663
Fax +1 212-367-8135
info@antonkerngallery.com
www.antonkerngallery.com

Contact
Anton Kern
Christoph Gerozissis
Courtney Treut

Artists
Nobuyoshi Araki
Ellen Berkenblit
John Bock
Brian Calvin
Anne Collier
Saul Fletcher
Mark Grotjahn
Bendix Harms
Eberhard Havekost
Lothar Hempel
Richard Hughes
Sergej Jensen
Sarah Jones
Michael Joo
Edward Krasinski
Shio Kusaka
Jim Lambie
Marepe
Dan McCarthy
Matthew Monahan
Marcel Odenbach
Manfred Pernice
Alessandro Pessoli
Wilhelm Sasnal
Lara Schnitger
David Shrigley
Andy Warhol
Jonas Wood

Galerie Peter Kilchmann

Stand A24
Tel +1 646-785-2606

Zahnradstrasse 21
Zurich 8005
Switzerland
Tel +41 44-278-1010
Fax +41 44-278-1011
info@peterkilchmann.com
www.peterkilchmann.com

Contact
Peter Kilchmann
Annemarie Reichen

Artists
Francis Alÿs
Maja Bajević
Hernan Bas
Michael Bauer
Armin Boehm
Los Carpinteros
Willie Doherty
Valérie Favre
Bruno Jakob
Raffi Kalenderian
Zilla Leutenegger
Jorge Macchi
Teresa Margolles
Fabian Marti
Claudia & Julia Müller
Adrian Paci
Bernd Ribbeck
Melanie Smith
Javier Téllez
Tercerunquinto
Artur Zmijewski

Tina Kim Gallery

Stand B36
Tel +1 646-465-1009

545 West 25th Street
New York, NY 10001
United States
Tel +1 212-716-1100
Fax +1 212-716-1250
info@tinakimgallery.com
www.tinakimgallery.com

Contact
Tina Kim
Rany Moore
Eliza Coleman

Artists
Ghada Amer & Reza Farkhondeh
Gimhongsok
Kyung Jeon
Yeondoo Jung
Eemyun Kang
Marc André Robinson
Joanna M. Wezyk

Kimmerich

Stand F26
Tel +1 212-226-0070

50 White Street
New York, NY 10013
United States
Tel +1 212-226-0070
Fax +1 212-226-0079
info@kimmerich.com
www.kimmerich.com

Contact
Dennis Kimmerich

Artists
Alexandra Bircken
Steven Claydon
Ellen Gronemeyer
David Korty
Margherita Manzelli
Ivan Morley
Torsten Slama

Nicole Klagsbrun Gallery

Stand A21
Tel +1 212-243-3335

534 West 24th Street
New York, NY 10011
United States
Tel +1 212-243-3335
Fax +1 646-219-7338
gallery@nicoleklagsbrun.com
www.nicoleklagsbrun.com

Contact
Nicole Klagsbrun
Taylor Trabulus
Amanda Friedman

Artists
Sean Bluechel
Beth Campbell
Nancy Davenport
Ben Durham
John Giorno
Amy Granat
Patrick Jackson
Barney Kulok
Cameron Parsons
John Pilson
Elaine Reichek
Mika Rottenberg
Xaviera Simmons
Hiroshi Sugito
Billy Sullivan

Johann König

Stand A14
Tel +49 30-2610-3080

Dessauer Strasse 6–7
Berlin 10963
Germany
Tel +49 30-2610-3080
Fax +49 30-2610-30811
info@johannkoenig.de
www.johannkoenig.de

Contact
Johann König
Erika Weiss

Artists
Micol Assaël
Henning Bohl
Manuel Graf
Tue Greenfort
Katharina Grosse
Jeppe Hein
Nathan Hylden
Annette Kelm
Manfred Kuttner
Alicja Kwade
Lisa Lapinski
Helen Marten
Kris Martin
Michaela Meise
Natascha Sadr Haghighian
Michael Sailstorfer
Tatiana Trouvé
Johannes Wohnseifer
Jordan Wolfson
David Zink Yi
Andreas Zybach

David Kordansky Gallery

Stand C1
Tel +1 917-859-7747

3143 South La Cienega
Boulevard, Unit A
Los Angeles, CA 90016
United States
Tel +1 310-558-3030
Fax +1 310-558-3060
info@davidkordanskygallery.com
www.davidkordanskygallery.com

Contact
David Kordansky
Mike Homer
Stuart Krimko

Artists
Markus Amm
Kathryn Andrews
Amy Bessone
Matthew Brannon
Valentin Carron
Steven Claydon
Heather Cook
Aaron Curry
Mark Flores
Will Fowler
Patrick Hill
Richard Jackson
Larry Johnson
Rashid Johnson
William E. Jones
Elad Lassry
Thomas Lawson
Alan Michael
Ruby Neri
David Noonan
Anthony Pearson
Mai-Thu Perret
Jon Pestoni
Pietro Roccasalva
Lesley Vance
Jonas Wood

Tomio Koyama Gallery

Stand B8
Tel +81 3-3642-4090

1–3–2–7F Kiyosumi
Koto-ku, Tokyo 135–0024
Japan
Tel +81 3-3642-4090
Fax +81 3-3642-4091
info@tomiokoyamagallery.com
www.tomiokoyamagallery.com

483 Nishigawa-cho,
Shimogyo-ku
Kyoto 600-8325
Japan
Tel +81 75-353-9992
Fax +81 75-353-9993
kyoto@tomiokoyamagallery.com

Contact
Tomio Koyama
Yuko Nagase
Daisuke Watanabe

Artists
Franz Ackermann
Masako Ando
Ryota Aoki
Naomi Ashida
Stephan Balkenhol
Benjamin Butler
Varda Caivano
Jeremy Dickinson
Tom Friedman
Atsushi Fukui
Nobuhiro Fukui
Daisuke Fukunaga
Nana Funo
gelitin
Rieko Hidaka
Satoshi Hirose
Tamami Hitsuda
Dennis Hollingsworth
Aya Ito
Yuka Kashihara
Mika Kato
Hideaki Kawashima
Naoki Koide
Makiko Kudo
Masahiko Kuwahara
Toru Kuwakubo
Takuro Kuwata
Yoshino Masui
Shintaro Miyake
Satoko Nachi
Tomoko Nagai
Yoshitomo Nara
Ernesto Neto
Mika Ninagawa
Tam Ochiai
Satoshi Ohno
Yuko Okazaki
Rieko Otake
Jonathan Pylypchuk
Tal R
David Ratcliff
Mark Ryden
Tom Sachs
Makoto Saito
Adam Silverman
Laurie Simmons
Diego Singh
Yuko Someya
Kishio Suga
Hiroshi Sugito
Vibeke Tandberg
Jason Teraoka
Gert & Uwe Tobias
Kumie Tsuda
Naoyuki Tsuji
Mamoru Tsukada
Richard Tuttle
Yutaka Watanabe
Terry Winters
Erwin Wurm
Keisuke Yamamoto
Masaya Yoshimura

Andrew Kreps Gallery

Stand B14
Tel +1 212-741-8849

525 West 22nd Street
New York, NY 10011
United States
Tel +1 212-741-8849
Fax +1 212-741-5163
contact@andrewkreps.com
www.andrewkreps.com

Contact
Andrew Kreps
Liz Mulholland
Timo Kappeller

Artists
Ricci Albenda
Darren Bader
Martin Barré
Frank Benson
Andrea Bowers
Daniel Bozhkov
Roe Ethridge
Uwe Henneken
Jamie Isenstein
Annette Kelm
Goshka Macuga
Ján Mančuška
Robert Melee
Robert Overby
Peter Piller
Ruth Root
Cheyney Thompson
Padraig Timoney
Hayley Tompkins
Klaus Weber

Galerie Krinzinger

Stand B24
Tel +43 6-7632-48379

Seilerstätte 16
Vienna 1010
Austria
Tel +43 1-5133-00621
Fax +43 1-5133-00633
galeriekrinzinger@chello.at
www.galerie-krinzinger.at

Contact
Ursula Krinzinger

Artists
Marina Abramović
Vito Acconci
Nader Ahriman
Atelier van Lieshout
Kader Attia
Günter Brus
Chris Burden
Angela de la Cruz
Vladimir Dubossarsky &
Alexander Vinogradov
Valie Export
Terry Fox
Sakshi Gupta
Jonathan Hernández
Secundino Hernández
Zenita Komad
Valerie Koshlyakov
Angelika Krinzinger
Oleg Kulik
Ulrike Lienbacher
Erik van Lieshout
Jonathan Meese
Bjarne Melgaard
Shintaro Miyake
Otto Muehl
Hermann Nitsch
Hans Op de Beeck
Meret Oppenheim
Gina Pane
Werner Reiterer
Eva Schlegel
Erik Schmidt
Rudolf Schwarzkogler
Christian Schwarzwald
Sudarshan Shetty
Eliezer Sonnenschein
Daniel Spoerri
Frank Thiel
Gavin Turk
Jannis Varelas
Martin Walde
Mark Wallinger
Ding Zhang
Thomas Zipp

Kukje Gallery

Stand B36
Tel +1 646-455-1009

54 Samcheong-ro
Jongno-gu
Seoul 110–200
Korea
Tel +82 27-35-84-49
Fax +82 27-33-48-79
kukje@kukjegallery.com
www.kukjegallery.com

Contact
Hyun-Sook Lee
Tina Kim
Suzie Kim
Charles Kim

Artists
Ghada Amer
Joseph Beuys
Louise Bourgeois
Alexander Calder
Anthony Caro
Gimhongsok
Haegue Yang
Kyung-ah Ham
Hein-Kuhn Oh
Eva Hesse
Hideaki Kawashima
Candida Hofer
Jenny Holzer
Hong-Joo Kim
Roni Horn
Jae-Eun Choi
Kyung Jeon
Michael Joo
Eemyun Kang
Anish Kapoor
Anselm Kiefer
Kira Kim
Sora Kim
Kimsooja
Bohnchang Koo
Hye-Rim Lee
Kwang-Ho Lee
Lin Tianmiao
Richard Long
Meekyoung Shin
MeeNa Park
Joan Mitchell
David Nash
Julian Opie
Kibong Rhee
Choong-Hyun Roh
SaSa [44]
Sen Chung
Seo-Bo Park
Sungsic Moon
U Sunok
Lee Ufan
Bill Viola
Andy Warhol
Joanna M. Wezyk
Yeondoo Jung

kurimanzutto

Stand B16
Tel +521 55-34-33-33-44

Gobernador Rafael
Rebollar 94
Mexico City 11850
Mexico
Tel +52 55-52-56-24-08
Fax +52 55-52-56-24-08
info@kurimanzutto.com
www.kurimanzutto.com

Contact
Jose Kuri
Monica Manzutto

Artists
Eduardo Abaroa
Allora & Calzadilla
Carlos Amorales
Miguel Calderón
Abraham Cruzvillegas
Minerva Cuevas
Jimmie Durham
Daniel Guzmán
Jonathan Hernández
Gabriel Kuri
Dr. Lakra
Roman Ondák
Gabriel Orozco
Damián Ortega
Fernando Ortega
Anri Sala
Monika Sosnowska
Sofía Táboas
Rirkrit Tiravanija
Adrián Villar Rojas
Apichatpong Weerasethakul

Yvon Lambert

Stand C34
Tel +33 1-42-71-09-33

108 rue Vieille du Temple
Paris 75003
France
Tel +33 1-42-71-09-33
Fax +33 1-42-71-87-47
yvon@yvon-lambert.com
www.yvon-lambert.com

Contact
Yvon Lambert
Olivier Belot
Nicholas Nahab
Mélanie Meffer- Rondeau

Artists
Carlos Amorales
Carl Andre
Robert Barry
Stefan Brüggemann
Mircea Cantor
Carter
David Claerbout
Jason Dodge
Gardar Eide Einarsson
Spencer Finch
Vincent Ganivet
Anna Gaskell
Kendell Geers
Nan Goldin
Douglas Gordon
Loris Gréaud
Shilpa Gupta
Karl Haendel
Candida Höfer
Jenny Holzer
Koo Jeong-A
Joan Jonas
On Kawara
Zilvinas Kempinas
Idris Khan
Anselm Kiefer
Barbara Kruger
Bertrand Lavier
Louise Lawler
Sol LeWitt
Jill Magid
Jonathan Monk
Roman Opalka
Giulio Paolini
Diogo Pimentao
Charles Sandison
Markus Schinwald
Ariel Schlesinger
Andres Serrano
David Shrigley
Shinique Smith
Mario Testino
Niele Toroni
Salla Tykkä
Francesco Vezzoli
Ian Wallace
Lawrence Weiner
Nick van Woert
Cerith Wyn Evans

Simon Lee Gallery

Stand A5
Tel +44 20-7491-0100

12 Berkeley Street
London W1J 8DT
United Kingdom
Tel +44 20-7491-0100
Fax +44 20-7491-0200
info@simonleegallery.com
www.simonleegallery.com

Contact
Simon Lee
Lindsay Ramsay
Claudia Milic
Katharine Burton

Artists
John M. Armleder
Alighiero e Boetti
Angela Bulloch
Merlin Carpenter
Larry Clark
James Coleman
George Condo
Matias Faldbakken
Hans-Peter Feldmann
Bernard Frize
Alex Hubbard
Donald Judd
Sherrie Levine
Paulina Olowska
Claudio Parmiggiani
Joao Penalva
Michelangelo Pistoletto
Josephine Pryde
Jim Shaw
Gary Simmons
Robert Therrien
Marnie Weber
Christopher Wool
Toby Ziegler
Heimo Zobernig

Lehmann Maupin

Stand C10
Tel +1 212-255-2923

540 West 26th Street
New York, NY 10001
United States
Tel +1 212-255-2923
Fax +1 212-255-2924
info@lehmannmaupin.com
www.lehmannmaupin.com

201 Chrystie Street
New York, NY 10002
United States
Tel +1 212-254-0054
Fax +1 212-254-0055

Contact
Rachel Lehmann
David Maupin
Carla Camacho
Jessica Kreps
Stephanie Smith
Courtney Plummer

Artists
Stefano Arienti
Hernan Bas
Ashley Bickerton
Ross Bleckner
Lee Bul
Billy Childish
Mary Corse
Tracey Emin
Teresita Fernández
Anya Gallaccio
Gilbert & George
Shirazeh Houshiary
Klara Kristalova
Mr.
Jun Nguyen-Hatsushiba
Angel Otero
Tony Oursler
Tim Rollins and K.O.S.
Rei Sato
Jennifer Steinkamp
Do Ho Suh
Juergen Teller
Mickalene Thomas
Adriana Varejão
Suling Wang
Nari Ward
Erwin Wurm
Mario Ybarra, Jr

Tanya Leighton Gallery

Stand F16
Tel +49 30-2216-07770

Kurfürstenstrasse 156
Berlin 10785
Germany
Tel +49 30-2216-07770
Fax +49 30-2216-07770
info@tanyaleighton.com
www.tanyaleighton.com

Contact
Tanya Leighton
Robert O. Fitzpatrick

Artists
Ayreen Anastas &
Rene Gabri
Pavel Büchler
Alejandro Cesarco
David Diao
Aleksandra Domanović
Sean Edwards
Aurélien Gamboni
Sharon Hayes
Gregor Hylla
Oliver Laric
Enzo Mari
Bruce McLean
Lucas Ospina
Dan Rees
John Smith

Galerie Lelong

Stand B12
Tel +1 212-315-0470

528 West 26th Street
New York, NY 10001
United States
Tel +1 212-315-0470
Fax +1 212-262-0624
art@galerielelong.com
www.galerielelong.com

Contact
Mary Sabbatino
Lindsay Danckwerth
Dan Burns

Artists
Petah Coyne
Angelo Filomeno
Andy Goldsworthy
Jane Hammond
Alfredo Jaar
Rosemary Laing
Catherine Lee
Nalini Malani
Cildo Meireles
Ana Mendieta
Hélio Oiticica
Yoko Ono
Emilio Perez
Jaume Plensa
Ursula von Rydingsvard
Sean Scully
Kate Shepherd
Nancy Spero
Krzysztof Wodiczko
Catherine Yass

Leto Gallery

Stand F12
Tel +48 50-169-6440

Ulica Minska 25 [Soho Factory]
Warsaw 03-808
Poland
Tel +48 22-499-5916
Fax +48 22-784-7300
galeria@leto.pl
www.leto.pl

Contact
Marta Kolakowska

Artists
Maurycy Gomulicki
Wojciech Puś
Bianka Rolando
Iwo Rutkiewicz
Konrad Smoleński
Radek Szlaga
Aleksandra Urban
Aleksandra Waliszewska
Honza Zamojski

Lisson Gallery

Stand C5
Tel +1-646-346-2837

29 & 52–54 Bell Street
London NW1 5DA
United Kingdom
Tel +44 20-7535-7350
Fax +44 20-7724-7124
contact@lissongallery.com
www.lissongallery.com

241 Eldridge Street
New York, NY 10002
United States
Tel +1 212-505-6431

Via Zenale, 3
20123 Milan
Italy
Tel +39 02-89-05-06-08

Contact
Nicholas Logsdail
Alex Logsdail
Sam Chatterton Dickson
Greg Hilty
Annette Hofmann

Artists
Marina Abramović
Ai Weiwei
Allora & Calzadilla
Cory Arcangel
Art & Language
Daniel Buren
Gerard Byrne
James Casebere
Tony Cragg
Angela de la Cruz
Richard Deacon
Spencer Finch
Ceal Floyer
Ryan Gander
Dan Graham
Rodney Graham
Carmen Herrera
Shirazeh Houshiary
Christian Jankowski
Peter Joseph
Anish Kapoor
John Latham
Tim Lee
Sol LeWitt
Robert Mangold
Jason Martin
Haroon Mirza
Tatsuo Miyajima
Jonathan Monk
Julian Opie
Tony Oursler
Giulio Paolini
Florian Pumhösl
Rashid Rana
Santiago Sierra
Sean Snyder
Lee Ufan
Lawrence Weiner
Richard Wentworth

Limoncello

Stand F19
Tel +44 78-3511-2114

15A Cremer Street
London E2 8HD
United Kingdom
Tel +44 20-7739-2363
limoncello@
limoncellogallery.co.uk
www.limoncellogallery.
co.uk

Contact
Rebecca May Marston
Rosa Tyhurst

Artists
Vanessa Billy
Alice Browne
Lucy Clout
Sean Edwards
Matt Golden
The Hut Project
Matthew Richardson
Matthew Smith
Jack Strange
Santo Tolone
Yonatan Vinitsky

Long March Space

Stand C13
Tel +86 10-5978-9768

798 Art Zone
4 Jiuxianqiao Road
Chaoyang District
Beijing 100015
China
Tel +86 10-5978-9768
Fax +86 10-5978-9764
lm@longmarchspace.com
www.longmarchspace.com

Contact
Lu Jie
David Tung
Li Danqing

Artists
Chen Chieh-Jen
Guo Fengyi
Ran Huang
Li Tianbing
Liu Wei
MadeIn Company
Wang Jianwei
Wu Shanzhuan
Wu Shanzhuan & Inga
Svala Thorsdottir
Xu Zhen
Yang Shaobin
Yu Hong
Zhan Wang
Zhang Hui
Zhou Xiaohu
Zhu Yu

Lüttgenmeijer

Stand R9
Tel +49 30-2804-5805

Bartningallee 2-4
Berlin 10557
Germany
Tel +49 30-2804-5805
Fax +49 30-2804-5806
mail@luettgenmeijer.com
www.luettgenmeijer.com

Contact
Markus Lüttgen
Robert Meijer

Artists
Erica Baum
James Beckett
Matt Connors
Jason Dodge
Chris Evans
Stefan Hablützel
David Jablonowski
George Henry Longly
Ryan McLaughlin
Gareth Moore
Matthew Ronay
Matthew Smith
Matt Stokes
Susanne M. Winterling

Maccarone

Stand D5
Tel +1 212-431-4977

630 Greenwich Street
New York, NY 10014
United States
Tel +1 212-431-4977
Fax +1 347-394-0043
kitchen@maccarone.net
www.maccarone.net

Contact
Michele Maccarone
Ellen Langan
Victoria Cherasia

Artists
Edgar Arceneaux
Carol Bove
Christoph Büchel
Chivas Clem
Ann Craven
Roberto Cuoghi
Felix Gmelin
Eli Hansen
Alex Hubbard
David Lamelas
Paul Lee
Hanna Liden
Nate Lowman
Corey McCorkle
Rodney McMillian
Otto Muehl
Claudia + Julia Mueller
Daniel Roth
Ryan Sullivan
Oscar Tuazon

Kate MacGarry

Stand F13
Tel +44 20-7613-0515

27 Old Nichol Street
London E2 7HR
United Kingdom
Tel +44 20-7613-0515
mail@katemacgarry.com
www.katemacgarry.com

Contact
Kate MacGarry

Artists
Josh Blackwell
Matt Bryans
Tiago Carneiro da Cunha
Chicks on Speed
Marcus Coates
Dr Lakra
Iain Forsyth & Jane Pollard
Goshka Macuga
Peter McDonald
Florian Meisenberg
Ben Rivers
Luke Rudolf
Renee So
Francis Upritchard

Marcelle Alix

Stand R2
Tel +33 6 3245 8047

4 rue Jouye-Rouve
Paris 75020
France
Tel +33 9-50-04-16-80
Fax +33 9-55-04-16-80
demain@marcellealix.com
www.marcellealix.com

Contact
Isabelle Alfonsi
Cécilia Becanovic

Artists
Mathieu K. Abonnenc
Marie Cool & Fabio Balducci
Pauline Boudry / Renate Lorenz
Aurélien Froment
Louise Hervé & Chloé Maillet
Charlotte Moth
Ernesto Sartori
Marie Voignier

Giò Marconi

Stand A3
Tel +39 335-24-58-05

Via Tadino 15
Milan 20124
Italy
Tel +39 02-29-40-43-73
Fax +39 02-29-40-55-73
info@giomarconi.com
www.giomarconi.com

Contact
Giò Marconi
Esther Quiroga
Teresa Bovi

Artists
Franz Ackermann
Atelier Van Lieshout
Enrico Baj
Rosa Barba
Will Benedict
John Bock
Kerstin Braetsch
Matthew Brannon
André Butzer
Gianni Colombo
Nathalie Djurberg
Simon Fujiwara
Nikolas Gambaroff
Wade Guyton
Richard Hamilton
Lothar Hempel
Christian Jankowski
Annette Kelm
Sharon Lockhart
Maurizio Mochetti
Louise Nevelson
David Noonan
Giulio Paolini
Jorge Pardo
Tobias Rehberger
Markus Schinwald
Dasha Shishkin
Elisa Sighicelli
Catherine Sullivan
Vibeke Tandberg
Grazia Toderi
Luca Trevisani
Francesco Vezzoli

Mary Mary

Stand F3
Tel +44 7730-681415

Suite 2/1, 6 Dixon Street
Glasgow G1 4AX
United Kingdom
Tel +44 141-226-2257
Fax +44 141-226-2257
info@marymarygallery.co.uk
www.marymarygallery.co.uk

Contact
Hannah Robinson

Artists
Sara Barker
Ernst Caramelle
Aleana Egan
Nick Evans
Lotte Gertz
Torsten Lauschmann
Lorna Macintyre
Alan Reid
Lili Reynaud-Dewar
Gerda Scheepers
Alexis Marguerite Teplin
Maximilian Zentz Zlomovitz

Meessen De Clercq

Stand R18
Tel +32 2-644-34-54

Abdijstraat
2A Rue de l'Abbaye
Brussels B–1000
Belgium
Tel +32 2-644-34-54
info@meessendeclercq.be
www.meessendeclercq.com

Contact
Olivier Meessen
Jan De Clercq
Stéphanie Roisin
Valérie Delfosse

Artists
Ignasi Aballí
Sarah Bostwick
Jordi Colomer
Lieven De Boeck
Hreinn Fridfinnsson
Ellen Harvey
Jorge Méndez Blake
Claudio Parmiggiani
Bruno Perramant
Sarah Pickering
Evariste Richer
Fabrice Samyn
José María Sicilia
Maarten Vanden Eynde

Metro Pictures

Stand C16
Tel +1 212-206-7100

519 West 24th Street
New York, NY 10011
United States
Tel +1 212-206-7100
Fax +1 212-337-0070
gallery@metropictures.com
www.metropictures.com

Contact
Janelle Reiring
Helene Winer
Tom Heman
Allison Card
Manuela Mozo

Artists
Olaf Breuning
André Butzer
Claire Fontaine
Andy Hope 1930
Isaac Julien
Louise Lawler
Robert Longo
David Maljkovic
Yuri Masnyj
John Miller
Paulina Olowska
Tony Oursler
Trevor Paglen
Stephen G. Rhodes
Jim Shaw
Cindy Sherman
Gary Simmons
Andreas Slominski
Catherine Sullivan
Sara VanDerBeek
Tris Vonna-Michell
T. J. Wilcox

Galerie Meyer Kainer

Stand B27
Tel +43 676 51 73 116

Eschenbachgasse 9
Vienna 1010
Austria
Tel +43 1-585-7277
Fax +43 1-585-7277-88
contact@meyerkainer.com
www.meyerkainer.com

Contact
Christian Meyer
Renate Kainer

Artists
Will Benedict
Bernadette Corporation
John Bock
Wolfgang Breuer
Olaf Breuning
Verena Dengler
Peter Friedl
gelitin
Liam Gillick
Dan Graham
Rachel Harrison
Mary Heilmann
Siggi Hofer
Christian Jankowski
Elke Silvia Krystufek
Anita Leisz
Marcin Maciejowski
Sarah Morris
Yoshitomo Nara
Jorge Pardo
Raymond Pettibon
Mathias Poledna
Stefan Sander
Isa Schmidlehner
Reena Spaulings
Lucie Stahl
Martina Steckholzer
Franz West
T. J. Wilcox
Heimo Zobernig

Meyer Riegger

Stand B21
Tel +49 72-182-1292

Klauprechtstrasse 22
Karlsruhe 76137
Germany
Tel +49 72-182-1292
Fax +49 72-1982-2141
info@meyer-riegger.de
www.meyer-riegger.de

Contact
Jochen Meyer
Thomas Riegger

Artists
Franz Ackermann
Katinka Bock
Armin Boehm
Björn Braun
Miriam Cahn
Henrik Håkansson
Uwe Henneken
Anna Lea Hucht
Jamie Isenstein
Korpys / Löffler
Eva Kotatkova
Ján Mancuška
Meuser
John Miller
Helen Mirra
Jonathan Monk
Melvin Moti
Scott Myles
Daniel Roth
Silke Schatz
Julia Schmidt
David Thorpe
Gabriel Vormstein
Waldemar Zimbelmann

Galerie Mezzanin

Stand F29
Tel +43 1-526-4356

Getreidemarkt 14
Eschenbachgasse
Vienna 1010
Austria
Tel +43 1-526-4356
Fax +43 4-5269-187
office@galeriemezzanin.com
www.galeriemezzanin.com

Contact
Karin Handlbauer

Artists
Thomas Bayrle
Geta Brătescu
Bernhard Fruehwirth
Manuel Gorkiewicz
Michael Hakimi
Peter Kogler
Lisa Lapinski
Christian Mayer
Marzena Nowak
Michelangelo Pistoletto
Katrin Plavcak
Stephen Prina
Mandla Reuter
Sturtevant
Santos R. Vasquez
Alexander Wolff
Christina Zurfluh

Andreiana Mihail Gallery

Stand F28
Tel +40 72-265-0221

Strada Vasile Alecsandri 16,
Storck Museum
Bucharest 010639
Romania
Tel +40 72-265-0221
info@andreianamihail.com
www.andreianamihail.com

Contact
Andreiana Mihail

Artists
Matei Bejenaru
Razvan Botis
Pavel Braila
Tom Chamberlain
Eduard Constantin
Alexandra Croitoru
Katerina Drzkova
Ion Grigorescu
Mihai Iepure-Gorski
Ciprian Muresan
Cristi Pogacean
Kerim Seiler
Mona Vatamanu & Florin Tudor

Massimo Minini

Stand B22
Tel +39 030-38-30-34

Via Apollonio 68
Brescia 25128
Italy B–1000
Tel +39 030-38-30-34
Fax +39 030-39-24-46
info@galleriaminini.it
www.galleriaminini.it

Contact
Massimo Minini
Daniella Betta
Valentina Costa
Barbara Crespigni
Nicola Mafessoni

Artists
Carla Accardi
Ghada Amer
Stefano Arienti
Roger Ballen
Robert Barry
Gabriele Basilico
Vanessa Beecroft
Alighiero e Boetti
Daniel Buren
Jota Castro
Paolo Chiasera
Jan De Cock
Hans-Peter Feldmann
Ian Hamilton Finlay
Yona Friedman
Luigi Ghirri
Paolo Gioli
Dan Graham
Peter Halley
Paolo Icaro
Anish Kapoor
Sol LeWitt
David Maljkovic
Eva Marisaldi
Ryan Mendoza
Mathieu Mercier
Sabrina Mezzaqui
Paul P.
Giulio Paolini
Nedko Solakov
Ettore Spalletti
Paul Thorel
Ian Wilson
Betty Woodman

Victoria Miro

Stand C47
Tel +44 20-7336-8109

16 Wharf Road
London N1 7RW
United Kingdom
Tel +44 20-7336-8109
Fax +44 20-7251-5596
info@victoria-miro.com
www.victoria-miro.com

Contact
Victoria Miro
W.P. Miro
Glenn Scott Wright
Oliver Miro
Fabian Lang
Elke Seebauer
Jelena Seng

Artists
Doug Aitken
Hernan Bas
Varda Caivano
Phil Collins
Verne Dawson
Peter Doig
Stan Douglas
William Eggleston
Elmgreen & Dragset
Inka Essenhigh
Ian Hamilton Finlay
David Harrison
N.S. Harsha
Alex Hartley
Christian Holstad
Chantal Joffe
Isaac Julien
Idris Khan
John Kørner
Udomsak Krisanamis
Yayoi Kusama
Wangechi Mutu
Alice Neel
Maria Nepomuceno
Chris Ofili
Jacco Olivier
Grayson Perry
Tal R
Conrad Shawcross
Sarah Sze
Adriana Varejão
Suling Wang
Stephen Willats
Francesca Woodman

MISAKO & ROSEN

Stand R19
Tel +81 36-276-1452

3–27–6 1F, Kita-otsuka
Toshima-ku
Tokyo 170–0004
Japan
Tel +81 36-276-1452
Fax +81 03-6276-1453
gallery@misakoandrosen.com
www.misakoandrosen.com

Contact
Misako
Jeffrey Ian Rosen

Artists
Richard Aldrich
Kaoru Arima
Josh Brand
Fergus Feehily
Maya Hewitt
Naotaka Hiro
Nathan Hylden
Shimon Minamikawa
Miki Mochizuka
Ayako Mogi
Mie Morimoto
Yuki Okumura
Stephen G. Rhodes
Will Rogan
Kazuyuki Takezaki
Erika Verzutti
Takashi Yasumura

Mitchell-Innes & Nash

Stand B20
Tel +1 212-744-7400

534 West 26th Street
New York 10001
United States
Tel +1 212-744-7400
Fax +1 212-744-7401
info@miandn.com
www.miandn.com

1018 Madison Avenue
New York, NY 10075
United States

Contact
Lucy Mitchell-Innes
David Nash
Jay Gorney
Robert Grosman
Nicole Russo
Mamie Tinkler

Artists
Sarah Braman
Anthony Caro
Allan D'Arcangelo
Chris Johanson
Martin Kersels
Leon Kossoff
Justine Kurland
Daniel Lefcourt
Alexander Liberman
Roy Lichtenstein
Chris Martin
Christopher Miner
Kenneth Noland
Catherine Opie
Virginia Overton
William Pope.L
Martha Rosler
Amanda Ross-Ho
Norbert Schwontkowski
Jessica Stockholder
Jack Tworkov
Paul Winstanley

Stuart Shave/ Modern Art

Stand C43
Tel +44 20-7299-7950

23–25 Eastcastle Street
London W1W 8DF
United Kingdom
Tel +44 20-7299-7950
Fax +44 20-7299-7951
info@modernart.net
www.modernart.net

Contact
Stuart Shave
Jimi Lee
Ryan Moore
Kirk McInroy

Artists
David Altmejd
Karla Black
Tom Burr
Nigel Cooke
Tim Gardner
Lothar Hempel
Jacqueline Humphries
Ansel Krut
Phillip Lai
Paul Lee
Linder
Barry McGee
Jonathan Meese
Matthew Monahan
Katy Moran
Oscar Murillo
David Noonan
Eva Rothschild
Bojan Sarcevic
Lara Schnitger
Collier Schorr
Steven Shearer
Ricky Swallow
Richard Tuttle
Clare Woods

The Modern Institute

Stand C29
Tel +44 141-248-3711

14–20 Osborne Street
Glasgow G1 5QN
United Kingdom
Tel +44 141-248-3711
Fax +44 141-552-5988
mail@themoderninstitute.com
www.themoderninstitute.com

Contact
Toby Webster
Andrew Hamilton

Artists
Dirk Bell
Martin Boyce
Jeremy Deller
Alex Dordoy
Urs Fischer
Kim Fisher
Luke Fowler
Henrik Håkansson
Mark Handforth
Thomas Houseago
Richard Hughes
Chris Johanson
Andrew Kerr
Jim Lambie
Victoria Morton
Scott Myles
Nicolas Party
Toby Paterson
Simon Periton
Manfred Pernice
Mary Redmond
Anselm Reyle
Eva Rothschild
Monika Sosnowska
Simon Starling
Katja Strunz
Tony Swain
Spencer Sweeney
Joanne Tatham & Tom O'Sullivan
Pádraig Timoney
Hayley Tompkins
Sue Tompkins
Cathy Wilkes
Michael Wilkinson
Gregor Wright
Richard Wright

mother's tankstation

Stand R1
Tel +353 1-6717654

41–43 Watling Street
Dublin 8
Ireland
Tel +353 1-6717654
gallery@motherstankstation.com
www.motherstankstation.com

Contact
Finola Jones
Emma Dwyer
David Godbold
Anne Lynott

Artists
Uri Aran
Ian Burns
Nina Canell
Kevin Cosgrove
Brendan Earley
Atsushi Kaga
Locky Morris
Mairead O'hEocha
Garrett Phelan
Matt Sheridan Smith
David Sherry

Taro Nasu

Stand C25
Tel +81 3-5856-5713

1–2–11 Higashi-Kanda
Chiyoda-ku
Tokyo 101–0031
Japan
Tel +81 3-5856-5713
Fax +81 3-5856-5714
info@taronasugallery.com
www.taronasugallery.com

Contact
Taro Nasu
Masako Hosoi
Kei Kanomata
Ayako Nagata

Artists
Futo Akiyoshi
Simon Fujiwara
Ryan Gander
Maiko Haruki
Anton Henning
Taka Izumi
Hirofumi Katayama
Tatsuo Majima
Taiji Matsue
Ryuji Miyamoto
Takeharu Ogai
Djordje Ozbolt
Peter Pommerer
Akira Rachi
Alessandro Raho
Cozue Takagi
Yuki Tawada
Satoshi Watanabe
Chie Yasuda
Kumazou Yoshimura

Galerie Neu

Stand C49
Tel +49 172-413-03-73

Mehringdamm 72
Berlin 10961
Germany
Tel +49 30-2857-550
Fax +49 30-281-0085
mail@galerieneu.com
www.galerieneu.com

Contact
Thilo Wermke
Alexander Schröder

Artists
Kai Althoff
Cosima von Bonin
Tom Burr
Bernadette Corporation
Keith Farquhar
Christian Flamm
Saul Fletcher
Claire Fontaine
Florian Hecker
Ull Hohn
Sergej Jensen
Kitty Kraus
Klara Liden
Hilary Lloyd
Nick Mauss
Birgit Megerle
Manfred Pernice
Daniel Pflumm
Josephine Pryde
Gedi Sibony
Andreas Slominski
Sean Snyder
Francesco Vezzoli
Katharina Wulff
Cerith Wyn Evans

Night Gallery

Stand R5
Tel +1 650-384-5448

204 South Avenue 19
Los Angeles, LA 90031
United States
Tel +1 650-384-5448
nightgalleryla@gmail.com
www.nightgallery.ca

Contact
Davida Nemeroff
Mieke Marple

Artists
Alika Cooper
Mira Dancy
Samara Golden
Paul Heyer
Anna Rosen
Paul Waddell

Take Ninagawa

Stand R14
Tel +81-90-9870-5594

2–12–4 Higashi Azabu
Minatoku Tokyo 1060044
Japan
Tel +81 35-571-5844
Fax +81 3-5571-5844
info@takeninagawa.com
www.takeninagawa.com

Contact
Atsuko Ninagawa

Artists
Ryoko Aoki
Dale Berning
Aki Goto
Misaki Kawai
Yoriko Kita
Chikara Matsumoto
Yuuki Matsumura
Shinro Ohtake
Aki Sasamoto
Yukiko Suto
Soju Tao

Galleria Franco Noero

Stand C50
Tel +39 01-18-82-208

Via Giulia di Barolo 16D
Torino 10124
Italy
Tel +39 01-18-82-208
Fax+39 01-11-98-37408
info@franconoero.com
www.franconoero.com

Contact
Franco Noero
Pierpaolo Falone
Matteo Consonni

Artists
Pablo Bronstein
Tom Burr
Jeff Burton
Neil Campbell
Andrew Dadson
Jason Dodge
Lara Favaretto
Martino Gamper
Henrik Håkansson
Arturo Herrera
Gabriel Kuri
Phillip Lai
Jim Lambie
Mike Nelson
Henrik Olesen
João Onofre
Rob Pruitt
Steven Shearer
Simon Starling
Costa Vece
Francesco Vezzoli

Nogueras Blanchard

Stand F27
Tel +34 63-77-77-257

C/ Xuclà 7
Barcelona 08001
Spain
Tel +34 93-342-57-21
Fax +34 93-342-57-22
info@noguerasblanchard.com
www.noguerasblanchard.com

Contact
Rebeca Blanchard
Alex Nogueras

Artists
Anne-Lise Coste
Leandro Erlich
Rafel G. Bianchi
Rubén Grilo
Marine Hugonnier
Michael Lin
Juan López
David Maljkovic
Fran Meana
Ester Partegàs
Wilfredo Prieto
Shimabuku
Ignacio Uriarte

David Nolan Gallery

Stand A29
Tel +1 212-925 6190

527 West 29th Street
New York, NY 10001
United States
Tel +1 212-925 6190
Fax +1 212-334-9139
info@davidnolangallery.com
www.davidnolangallery.com

Contact
David Nolan
Katherine Chan
Susannah Palmer

Artists
Richard Artschwager
Steve DiBenedetto
Estate of Ian Hamilton Finlay
Neil Gall
Victoria Gitman
Estate of George Grosz
Mel Kendrick
Barry Le Va
Alice Maher
Ciprian Muresan
Jim Nutt
Alexander Ross
Serban Savu
Sandra Vásquez de la Horra
Jorinde Voigt

Overduin and Kite

Stand F4
Tel +1 323 350-7374

6693 Sunset Boulevard
Los Angeles, CA 90028
United States
Tel +1 323-464-3600
info@overduinandkite.com
www.overduinandkite.com

Contact
Lisa Overduin
Kristina Kite

Artists
Frank Benson
Merlin Carpenter
Marc Camille Chaimowicz
Maureen Gallace
Barry Johnston
Dianna Molzan
Scott Olson
Silke Otto-Knapp
Eileen Quinlan
Nick Relph
Stephen G. Rhodes
Haim Steinbach
Cheyney Thompson
Kaari Upson
Erika Vogt
Tris Vonna-Michell

Maureen Paley

Stand B34
Tel +44 20-7729-4112

21 Herald Street
London E2 6JT
United Kingdom
Tel +44 20-7729-4112
Fax +44 20-7729-4113
info@maureenpaley.com
www.maureenpaley.com

Contact
Maureen Paley
Oliver Evans
Susanna Chisholm
Tom Morris

Artists
Estate of Keith Arnatt
Kaye Donachie
Graham Durward
Thomas Eggerer
Hamish Fulton
Maureen Gallace
Liam Gillick
Andrew Grassie
Anne Hardy
Sarah Jones
Michael Krebber
Lars Laumann
Daria Martin
Muntean/Rosenblum
Saskia Olde Wolbers
Paul P.
Seb Patane
Stephen Prina
James Pyman
David Ratcliff
Ruth Root
David Salle
Maaike Schoorel
Hannah Starkey
Dirk Stewen
David Thorpe
Wolfgang Tillmans
Gert & Uwe Tobias
Donald Urquhart
Banks Violette
Rebecca Warren
Gillian Wearing
James Welling
Eric Wesley

Galerie Perrotin

Stand C41
Tel +33 1-42-16-79-79

76 rue de Turenne
Paris 75003
France
Tel +33 1-42-16-79-79
Fax +33 1-42-16-79-74
info@perrotin.com
www.perrotin.com

17F, 50 Connaught Road
Central
Hong Kong
info@perrotin.com

Contact
Emmanuel Perrotin
Peggy Leboeuf
Emmanuelle Orenga de Gaffory
Philippe Joppin
Julie Morhange

Artists
Chiho Aoshima
Ivan Argote
Daniel Arsham
Hernan Bas
Sophie Calle
Maurizio Cattelan
Johan Creten
Wim Delvoye
Elmgreen & Dragset
Lionel Estève
Daniel Firman
Bernard Frize
Giuseppe Gabellone
gelitin
Duane Hanson
JR
Jesper Just
Kaws
Bharti Kher
Kolkoz
Klara Kristalova
Guy Limone
Jin Meyerson
Farhad Moshiri
Mr.
Takashi Murakami
Jean-Michel Othoniel
Paola Pivi
Claude Rutault
Michael Sailstorfer
Aya Takano
Tatiana Trouvé
Piotr Uklanski
Xavier Veilhan
Peter Zimmermann

Friedrich Petzel Gallery

Stand B4
Tel +1 212-680-9467

535 & 537 West 22nd Street
New York, NY 10011
United States
Tel +1 212-680-9467
Fax +1 212-680-9473
info@petzel.com
www.petzel.com

Contact
Friedrich Petzel
Sam Tsao
Andrea Teschke
Jason Murison
Kat Parker

Artists
Cosima von Bonin
Troy Brauntuch
Simon Denny
Keith Edmier
Thomas Eggerer
Andrea Fraser
Wade Guyton
Robert Heinecken
Georg Herold
Charline von Heyl
Dana Hoey
Christian Jankowski
Sean Landers
Rezi van Lankveld
Maria Lassnig
Allan McCollum
Sarah Morris
Jorge Pardo
Philippe Parreno
Joyce Pensato
Seth Price
Stephen Prina
Jon Pylypchuk
Willem de Rooij
Dana Schutz
Dirk Skreber
John Stezaker
Nicola Tyson
Corinne Wasmuht
Heimo Zobernig

Galerie Francesca Pia

Stand A15
Tel +41 44-271-2444

Limmatstrasse 275
Zurich 8005
Switzerland
Tel +41 44-271-2444
Fax +41 44-271-2445
info@francescapia.com
www.francescapia.com

Contact
Francesca Pia
Murielle Henchoz

Artists
Thomas Bayrle
Stéphane Dafflon
Philippe Decrauzat
Hans-Peter Feldmann
Vidya Gastaldon
Aloïs Godinat
Joseph Grigely
Wade Guyton
Fabrice Gygi
Jutta Koether
Elad Lassry
Kaspar Müller
Joanne O'Sullivan & Tom Tatham
Mai-Thu Perret
Marta Riniker-Radich
Bruno Serralongue
David Shrigley
Josef Strau
John Tremblay

Galeria Plan B

Stand F7
Tel +40 74-065-8555

Strada Henri Barbusse
59–61
Cluj 400616
Romania
Tel +40 74-065-8555
contact@plan-b.ro
www.plan-b.ro

Heidestrasse 50
Berlin 10557
Germany
Tel +49 1723-21-0711

Contact
Mihai Pop
Mihaela Lutea

Artists
Alexandra Croitoru
Adrian Ghenie
Istvan Laszlo
Victor Man
Ciprian Muresan
Navid Nuur
Miklos Onucsan
Cristi Pogacean
Cristian Rusu
Şerban Savu
Gabriela Vanga

Galerija Gregor Podnar

Stand A4
Tel +49 178-908-984

Lindenstrasse 35
Berlin 10969
Germany
Tel +49 30-2593-4651
Fax+49 30-2593-4652
berlin@gregorpodnar.com
www.gregorpodnar.com

Kolodvorska 6
Ljubljana 1000
Slovenia
Tel +386 1-430-49-29
Fax +386 1-430-49-28

Contact
Gregor Podnar
Marie Graftieaux

Artists
Attila Csörgő
Vadim Fiškin
Ion Grigorescu
Alexander Gutke
Irwin
Yuri Leiderman
Marzena Nowak
Dan Perjovschi
Goran Petercol
Tobias Putrih
Ariel Schlesinger
Goran Trbuljak
B. Wurtz

Galerie Praz-Delavallade

Stand A18
Tel ++33 623-43-18-16

5 rue des Haudriettes
Paris 75003
France
Tel +33 1-45-86-20-00
Fax +33 1-45-86-20-10
info@praz-delavallade.com
www.praz-delavallade.com

Contact
Bruno Delavallade
Rene-Julien Praz
Silvia Ammon
Flavie Loizon

Artists
Edgar Arceneaux
Amy Bessone
Andrea Bowers
Philippe Decrauzat
Sam Durant
Thomas Fougeirol
Julian Hoeber
Jim Isermann
Nathan Mabry
Fabien Merelle
John Miller
Adi Nes
Robyn O'Neil
Amy O'Neill
Mai-Thu Perret
Dario Robleto
Brett Cody Rogers
Analia Saban
Erik Schmidt
Jim Shaw
Marnie Weber
Johannes Wohnseifer

Galerie Eva Presenhuber

Stand B29
Tel +41 43-444-7050

Diagonal Building, Maag
Areal, Zahnradstrasse 21
Zurich 8005
Switzerland
Tel +41 43-444-7050
Fax +41 43-444-7060
info@presenhuber.com
www.presenhuber.com

Contact
Eva Presenhuber
Markus Rischgasser

Artists
Doug Aitken
Emmanuelle Antille
Martin Boyce
Joe Bradley
Angela Bulloch
Valentin Carron
Verne Dawson
Trisha Donnelly
Maria Eichhorn
Matias Faldbakken
Urs Fischer
Peter Fischli & David Weiss
Sylvie Fleury
Liam Gillick
Douglas Gordon
Amy Granat
Mark Handforth
Candida Höfer
Alex Hubbard
Karen Kilimnik
Andrew Lord
Richard Prince
Gerwald Rockenschaub
Tim Rollins and K.O.S.
Ugo Rondinone
Dieter Roth
Eva Rothschild
Jean-Frédéric Schnyder
Steven Shearer
Josh Smith
Beat Streuli
Oscar Tuazon
Franz West
Sue Williams

Simon Preston Gallery

Stand F22
Tel +1 212-431-1105

301 Broome Street
New York, NY 10002
United States
Tel +1 212-431-1105
office@
simonprestongallery.com
www.simonprestongallery.
com

Contact
Simon Preston
Paula Naughton

Artists
Carlos Bevilacqua
John Gerrard
Nick Goss
Michelle Lopez
Daniel Joseph Martinez
Jessica Mein
Marco Rios
Hans Schabus
Kara Tanaka
Caragh Thuring
Josh Tonsfeldt

Rampa

Stand B31
Tel +90 212-327-0800

Sair Nedim Caddesi
21A Akaretler Besiktas
Istanbul 34357
Turkey
Tel +90 212-327-0800
Fax +90 212-327-0801
info@rampaistanbul.com
www.rampaistanbul.com

Contact
Leyla Tara Suyabatmaz
Özkan Cangüuen

Artists
Nevin Aladağ
Hüseyin Bahri Alptekin
Vahap Avşar
Ergin Cavusoğlu
Cengiz Çekil
Ayşe Erkmen
Leyla Gediz
Nilbar Güreş
Ahmet Oran
Güçlü Öztekin
Erinç Seymen

Almine Rech Gallery

Stand B7
Tel +32 2-648-5684

Abdijstraat 20
Brussel 1050
Belgium
Tel +32 2-648-5684
Fax +32 2-648-4484
www.alminerech.com

19 rue Saintonge
Paris 75003
France
Tel +33 1-4583-7190
Fax +33 1-4570-9130

Contact
Almine Rech
Anna Fisher
Jason Cori
Carlos Cardenas
Amelie Reisinger

Artists
Ziad Antar
Nobuyosh Araki
Matthias Bitzer
Joe Bradley
Don Brown
Tom Burr
Beatrice Caracciolo
Johan Creten
Philip-Lorca diCorcia
Teresita Fernández
Sylvie Fleury
John Giorno
Mark Hagen
Mark Handforth
Uwe Henneken
Sophie von Hellerman
Gregor Hildebrandt
Patrick Hill
Alex Israel
Xylor Jane
Isaac Julien
Barbara Kasten
Thomas Kiesewetter
Jeff Koons
Joseph Kosuth
Ange Leccia
Daniel Lergon
Curtis Mann
JohnMcCracken
Andrei Molodkin
Joel Morrison
Peter Peri
Richard Prince
Anselm Reyle
Zbigniew Rogalski
Ugo Rondinone
Matthieu Ronsse
Taryn Simon
Hedi Slimane
Yeesookyung
Katja Strunz
Tatiana Trouvé
Gavin Turk
James Turrell
Ida Tursic & Wilfried Mille
Not Vital
Gabriel Vormstein
Liu Wei
Franz West
Johannes Wohnseifer
Tsuruko Yamazaki
Aaron Young

Redling Fine Art

Stand R7
Tel +1 323-230-7415

6757 Santa Monica
Boulevard
Los Angeles, CA 90038
United States
Tel +1 323-230-7415
Fax +1 323-924-5560
office@redlingfineart.com
www.redlingfineart.com

Contact
Erica Redling
Lucy Campana

Artists
Mario Correa
Liz Glynn
Jeff Kopp
Jason Kraus
Erlea Maneros Zabala
Brian O'Connell
Laura Riboli

Regen Projects

Stand B17
Tel +1 310-276-5424

633 North Almont Drive
Los Angeles, CA 90069
United States
Tel +1 310-276-5424
Fax +1 310-276-7430
office@regenprojects.com
www.regenprojects.com

Contact
Shaun Caley Regen
Jennifer Loh
Heather Harmon

Artists
Doug Aitken
Matthew Barney
Walead Beshty
John Bock
Dan Graham
Rachel Harrison
Elliott Hundley
Anish Kapoor
Toba Khedoori
Liz Larner
Glenn Ligon
Scott McFarland
Marilyn Minter
Catherine Opie
Manfred Pernice
Raymond Pettibon
Elizabeth Peyton
Jack Pierson
Lari Pittman
Daniel Richter
Wolfgang Tillmans
Gillian Wearing
Lawrence Weiner
James Welling
Sue Williams
Andrea Zittel

Regina Gallery

Stand B33
Tel +44 20-7636-7768

22 Eastcastle Street
London W1W 8DE
United Kingdom
Tel +44 20-7636-7768
london@reginagallery.com
www.reginagallery.com

1, 4th Syromyatnichesky
Pereulok
Moscow 105120
Russia
Tel +7 495-228-1330
moscow@reginagallery.
com

Contact
Vladimir Ovcharenko
Mike Ovcharenko
Nadia Totskaya
Romilly Eveleigh

Artists
Victor Alimpiev
Evgeny Antufiev
Nikolay Bakharev
Sergey Bratkov
Ivan Chuikov
Semyon Faibisovich
Claire Fontaine
Oleg Golosiy
Inspection Medical
Hermeneutics
Tigran Khachatryan
Egor Koshelev
Oleg Kulik
Vlad Kulkov
Vladimir Logutov
Jonathan Meese
Slava Mogutin
Andrei Monastyrski
Pavel Pepperstein
Jack Pierson
Kerim Ragimov
Daniel Richter
Andrei Roiter
Maria Serebriakova
Natasha Struchkova
Jorinde Voigt
Stas Volyazlovsky
Rose Wylie
Erwin Wurm
Rose Wylie
Sergey Zarva
Arseniy Zhilyaev

Renwick Gallery

Stand R6
Tel +1 646-209-0303

45 Renwick Street
New York, CA 10013
United States
Tel +1 212-609-3535
info@renwickgallery.com
www.renwickgallery.com

Contact
Leslie Fritz

Artists
Talia Chetrit
Meredith Danluck
Drew Heitzler

Anthony Reynolds Gallery

Stand C3
Tel +44 7798-606343

60 Great Marlborough
Street
London W1F 7BG
United Kingdom
Tel +44 20-7439-2201
Fax +44 20-7439-1869
info@anthonyreynolds.com
www.anthonyreynolds.com

Contact
Anthony Reynolds

Artists
The Atlas Group
David Austen
Richard Billingham
Ian Breakwell
Erik Dietman
Leon Golub
Paul Graham
Lucy Harvey
Emily Jacir
Kai Kaljo
Andrew Mansfield
Asier Mendizabal
Lucia Nogueira
Walid Raad
Georgia Sagri
Nancy Spero
Sturtevant
Jon Thompson
Amikam Toren
Nobuko Tsuchiya
Mark Wallinger

Rodeo

Stand F25
Tel +90 212-293-5800

Tütün Deposu / Lüleci
Hendek Cad No12
Istanbul 34425
Turkey
Tel +90 212-293-5800
info@rodeo-gallery.com
www.rodeo-gallery.com

Contact
Sylvia Kouvali

Artists
Mark Aerial Waller
Anna Boghiguian
Banu Cennetoğlu
Haris Epaminonda
Apostlos Georğiou
Emre Hüner
Iman Issa
Gülsün Karamustafa
Ian Law
Shahryar Nashat
Christodoulos Panayiotou
Eftihis Patsourakis
James Richards

Galerie Thaddaeus Ropac

Stand C12
Tel +33 1-42-72-99-00

7 rue Debelleyme
Paris 75003
France
Tel +33 1-42-72-99-00
Fax +33 1-42-72-61-66
galerie@ropac.net
www.ropac.net

Mirabellplatz 2
Salzberg 5020
Austria
Tel +43 662-881-393
Fax +43 662-881-3939

Contact
Thaddaeus Ropac
Jill Silverman van
Coenegrachts Victoire de
Pourtalès
Bénédicte Burrus

Artists
Cory Arcangel
Art & Language
Donald Baechler
Mahmoud Bakhshi
Jules de Balincourt
Stephan Balkenhol
Ali Banisadr
Georg Baselitz
Philippe Bradshaw
Marc Brandenburg
Lee Bul
Jean-Marc Bustamante
Francesco Clemente
Tony Cragg
Matali Crasset
Richard Deacon
Elger Esser
Harun Farocki
Sylvie Fleury
Gilbert & George
Antony Gormley
Peter Halley
Lori Hersberger
Ilya & Emilia Kabakov
Alex Katz
Anselm Kiefer
Imi Knoebel
Terence Koh
Wolfgang Laib
Jonathan Lasker
Robert Longo
Liza Lou
Marcin Maciejowski
Robert Mapplethorpe
Bernhard Martin
Jason Martin
Farhad Moshiri

Jack Pierson
Rona Pondick
Marc Quinn
Arnulf Rainer
Gerwald Rockenschaub
Tom Sachs
David Salle
Hubert Scheibl
Raqib Shaw
Andreas Slominski
Sturtevant
Philip Taaffe
Lee Ufan
Sandra Vásquez de la Horra
Banks Violette
Not Vital
Andy Warhol
Lawrence Weiner
Erwin Wurm

Andrea Rosen Gallery

Stand C28
Tel +1 646 528-3044

525 West 24th Street
New York, NY 10011
United States
Tel +1 212-627-6000
Fax +1 212-627-5450
andrea@rosengallery.com
www.andrearosengallery.com

Contact
Andrea Rosen
Branwen Jones
Andrea Cashman
Cory Nomura
Samantha Sheiness

Artists
David Altmejd
Gillian Carnegie
Nigel Cooke
Walker Evans
Felix Gonzalez-Torres
Al Hansen
Elliott Hundley
Tetsumi Kudo
Friedrich Kunath
José Lerma
Josiah McElheny
Josephine Meckseper
László Moholy-Nagy
Katy Moran
Dan Peterman
Michael Raedecker
Matthew Ritchie
Matthew Ronay
Mika Rottenberg
Wolfgang Tillmans
Andrea Zittel

Salon 94

Stand C38
Tel +1 212-979-0001

243 Bowery
New York, NY 10002
United States
Tel +1 212-979-0001
Fax +1 212-979-0004
info@salon94.com
www.salon94.com

12 East 94th Street
New York 10128
United States
Tel +1 646-672-9212
Fax +1 646-672-9217

1 Freeman Alley
New York, NY 10002
United States
Tel. +1 212-529-7400
Fax. +1 212-529-7401

Contact
Jeanne Greenberg Rohatyn
Sarah Walzer
Alissa Friedman
Fabienne Stephan
Victoria Keddie

Artists
Jules de Balincourt
Amy Bessone
Huma Bhabha
Iona Rozeal Brown
Carter
Liz Cohen
Gerald Davis
Francesca DiMattio
Dzine
Katy Grannan
Kara Hamilton
Jon Kessler
Laleh Khorramian
Marilyn Minter
Carlo Mollino
Takeshi Murata
Aida Ruilova
David Benjamin Sherry
Laurie Simmons
Lorna Simpson
Francis Upritchard
Betty Woodman

Esther Schipper

Stand B2
Tel +49 162 208 9920

Schöneberger Ufer 65
Berlin 10785
Germany
Tel +49 30-3744-33133
Fax +49 30-3744-33134
office@estherschipper.com
www.estherschipper.com

Contact
Esther Schipper
Stefanie Bücker
Christophe Wiesner
Florian Lüde

Artists
Matti Braun
AA Bronson
Angela Bulloch
Nathan Carter
Thomas Demand
Ceal Floyer
Estate of General Idea
Liam Gillick
Dominique Gonzalez-Foerster
Grönlund-Nisunen
Pierre Huyghe
Ann Veronica Janssens
Christoph Keller
Gabriel Kuri
Isa Melsheimer
Philippe Parreno
Ugo Rondinone
Christopher Roth
Karin Sander
Julia Scher

Galerie Rüdiger Schöttle

Stand D3
Tel +49 89-333-686

Amalienstrasse 41
Munich 80799
Germany
Tel +49 89-333-686
Fax +49 89-342-296
info@galerie-schoettle.de
www.galerie-ruediger-schoettle.de

Contact
Rüdiger Schöttle
Dr. Sabine Heuser-Hauck
Sarah Gilder

Artists
Janis Avotins
Stephan Balkenhol
Maria Bartuszova
Armin Boehm
David Claerbout
Steven Claydon
Martin Creed
Slawomir Elsner
Elger Esser
Liam Gillick
Dan Graham
Rodney Graham
Thomas Helbig
Candida Höfer
John Knight
Bela Kolarova
Goshka Macuga
Jan Merta
Alex Mirutziu
Djordje Ozbolt
Thomas Ruff
Anri Sala
Thomas Schütte
Agathe Snow
Thomas Struth
Florian Süssmayr
Jeff Wall
Thomas Zipp

Micky Schubert

Stand F8
Tel +49 30-49 80-8487

Bartningallee 2–4
Berlin D–10557
Germany
Tel +49 30-49 80-8487
info@mickyschubert.de
www.mickyschubert.de

Contact
Micky Schubert

Artists
Marieta Chirulescu
Thea Djordjadze
Graham Fagen
Manuela Leinhoß
Carolin Leszczinski
Barry Macgregor Johnston
Alan Michael
Gerda Scheepers
Daniel Sinsel
Stephen Sutcliffe
Sue Tompkins
Mark van Yetter
Maximilian Zentz
Zlomovitz

Seventeen

Stand F11
Tel +44 7972-229395

17 Kingsland Road
London E2 8AA
United Kingdom
Tel +44 20-7729-5777
Fax +44 20-7729-4083
info@seventeengallery.com
www.seventeengallery.com

Contact
Dave Hoyland
Nick Letchford
Tim Steer

Artists
David Blandy
Susan Collis
David Raymond Conroy
Paul B. Davis
Graham Dolphin
Oliver Laric
Kate Owens
Abigail Reynolds

Sfeir-Semler

Stand A8
Tel +1 347 458 1248

Tannous Building
4th Floor
Street 56
Jisr Sector 77
Quarantine 2077 7209
Beirut
Lebanon
Tel +961 1-566-550
beirut@sfeir-semler.com
www.sfeir-semler.com

Admiralitätstrasse 71
Hamburg 20459
Germany
Tel +49 40-3751-9940
Fax +49 40-3751-9637
galerie@sfeir-semler.com

Contact
Andree Sfeir-Semler
Melina Younes
Rana Nasser Eddin
Claudia Lewis

Artists
Etel Adnan
Mounira Al Solh
The Atlas Group / Walid Raad
Yto Barrada
Robert Barry
Taysir Batniji
Balthasar Burkhard
Elger Esser
Ian Hamilton Finlay
Hans Haacke
Günter Haese
MARWAN
Hiroyuki Masuyama
Rabih Mroué
Timo Nasseri
Khalil Rabah
Marwan Rechmaoui
Hassan Sharif
Wael Shawky
Christine Streuli
Rayyane Tabet
Hoda Tawakol
Akram Zaatari

Sies + Höke

Stand B15
Tel +49 177-773-0289

Poststrasse 2 + 3
Dusseldorf 40213
Germany
Tel +49 211-301-4360
Fax +49 211-301-43629
post@sieshoeke.com
www.sieshoeke.com

Contact
Nina Höke
Alexander Sies

Artists
Abel Auer
Uta Barth
Gianni Caravaggio
Etienne Chambaud
Björn Dahlem
Hansjörg Dobliar
Marcel Dzama
João Maria Gusmão & Pedro Paiva
Federico Herrero
Dorota Jurczak
Thomas Kiesewetter
Kris Martin
Michael van Ofen
Fabrice Samyn
Florian Slotawa
Neal Tait
Markus Vater
Claudia Wieser
Sam Windett

Sikkema Jenkins & Co.

Stand C45
Tel +1 212-929-2262

530 West 22nd Street
New York, NY 10011
United States
Tel +1 212-929-2262
Fax +1 212-929-2340
gallery@sikkemajenkinsco.com
www.sikkemajenkinsco.com

Contact
Brent Sikkema
Michael Jenkins
Meg Malloy
Katie Rashid

Artists
Burt Barr
Mark Bradford
Trisha Brown
William Cordova
Leonardo Drew
Mitch Epstein
Josephine Halvorson
Marc Handelman
Jan Henle
Arturo Herrera
Sheila Hicks
Merlin James
Nikki S. Lee
Marlene McCarty
Vik Muniz
Elizabeth Neel
Jorge Queiroz
Kay Rosen
Shahzia Sikander
Amy Sillman
Janaina Tschäpe
Kara Walker

Sommer Contemporary Art

Stand C37
Tel +972 3-516-6400

13 Rothschild Boulevard
Tel Aviv 66881
Israel
Tel +972 3-516-6400
Fax +972 52-631-6004
info@sommergallery.com
www.sommergallery.com

Contact
Irit Fine-Sommer
Tamar Zagursky

Artists
Darren Almond
Yael Bartana
Boyan
Tom Burr
Rineke Dijkstra
Ofir Dor
Haim Elmoznino
Karl Haendel
Alona Harpaz
Tamar Harpaz
Michal Helfman
Gregor Hildebrandt
Itzik Livneh
Muntean & Rosenblum
Adi Nes
Ugo Rondinone
Christoph Ruckhaeberle
Wilhelm Sasnal
Yehudit Sasportas
Netally Schlosser
Efrat Shvily
Doron Solomons
Eliezer Sonnenschein
Tal R
Wolfgang Tillmans
Paloma Varga Weisz
Sharon Ya'ari
Rona Yefman
Guy Zagursky
Thomas Zipp

Reena Spaulings Fine Art

Stand F17
Tel +1 646-346-4152

165 East Broadway, 2nd Floor
New York, NY 10002
United States
Tel +1 212-477-5006
Fax +1 212-477-5006
reena@reenaspaulings.com
www.reenaspaulings.com

Contact
John Kelsey
Carissa Rodriguez
Emily Sundblad

Artists
Ei Arakawa
Merlin Carpenter
Stephan Dillemuth
Michaela Eichwald
Matias Faldbakken
Claire Fontaine
Kim Gordon
K8 Hardy
Alex Israel
Klara Liden
Hernrik Oleson
Jutta Koether
Seth Price
Josephine Pryde
Nora Schultz
Lee Williams
Shadi Habib Allah
Stephen Willats

Sprüth Magers Berlin London

Stand B37
Tel +44 7714-629084

Oranienburger Strasse 18
Berlin 10178
Germany
Tel +49 30-2888-4030
Fax +49 30-2888-40352
info@spruethmagers.com
www.spruethmagers.com

7A Grafton Street
London W1S 4EJ
United Kingdom
Tel +44 20-7408-1613
Fax +44 20-7499-4531

Contact
Monika Sprüth
Philomene Magers
Andreas Gegner
Franziska von Hasselbach
Patricia Pratas
Iris Scheffler
Andrew Silewicz

Artists
Siegfried Anzinger
Richard Artschwager
John Baldessari
Alighiero e Boetti
George Condo
Walter Dahn
Thomas Demand
Philip-Lorca diCorcia
Thea Djordjadze
Robert Elfgen
Peter Fischli & David Weiss
Sylvie Fleury
Cyprien Gaillard
Andreas Gursky
Jenny Holzer
Gary Hume
Donald Judd
Axel Kasseböhmer
Karen Kilimnik
Astrid Klein
Joseph Kosuth
Kraftwerk
Barbara Kruger
David Lamelas
Louise Lawler
David Maljkovic
Anthony McCall
Robert Morris
Jean-Luc Mylayne
Michail Pirgelis
Nina Pohl
Richard Prince
Sterling Ruby
Ed Ruscha
Gerda Scheepers
Thomas Scheibitz
Frances Scholz
Andreas Schulze
Cindy Sherman
Stephen Shore
Alexandre Singh
Robert Therrien
Rosemarie Trockel
Marcel van Eeden
Andrea Zittel

STANDARD (Oslo)

Stand B41
Tel +47 917-07-429

Hegdehaugsveien 3
Oslo N–0352
Norway
Tel +47 22-601-310
Fax +47 22-601 311
info@standardoslo.no
www.standardoslo.no

Contact
Eivind Furnesvik

Artists
Tauba Auerbach
Nina Beier
Johanna Billing
Ann Cathrin November Høibo
Simon Denny
Gardar Eide Einarsson
Marius Engh
Matias Faldbakken
Ane Graff
Kim Hiorthøy
Alex Hubbard
Michaela Meise
Anders Nordby
Chadwick Rantanen
Nick Relph
Torbjørn Rødland
Josh Smith
Oscar Tuazon
Fredrik Værslev
Emily Wardill

Stevenson

Stand B32
Tel +27 72-361-1362

Buchanan Building,
160 Sir Lowry Road,
Woodstock
Cape Town 7925
South Africa
Tel +27 21-462-1500
Fax +27 21-462-1501
info@stevenson.info
www.stevenson.info

62 Juta Street, Braamfontein
Johannesburg 2001
South Africa
Tel +27 11-326-0034
Fax +27 86-245-1918

Contact
Federica Angelucci
Joost Bosland
David Brodie
Andrew da Conceicao
Sophie Perryer
Michael Stevenson

Artists
Zander Blom
Dineo Seshee Bopape
Conrad Botes
Wim Botha
Steven Cohen
Paul Edmunds
Ângela Ferreira
Frohawk Two Feathers
Meschac Gaba
Simon Gush
Nicholas Hlobo
Pieter Hugo
Anton Kannemeyer
Michael MacGarry
Sabelo Mlangeni
Nandipha Mntambo
Estate of Billy Monk
Zanele Muholi
Daniel Naudé
Serge Alain Nitegeka
Odili Donald Odita
Deborah Poynton
Jo Ractliffe
Viviane Sassen
Claudette Schreuders
Berni Searle
Lerato Shadi
Penny Siopis
Guy Tillim

Diana Stigter

Stand F14
Tel +31 65-371-8596

Elandsstraat 90
Amsterdam 1016 SH
Netherlands
Tel +31 20-624-2361
Fax +31 20-624-2362
mail@dianastigter.nl
www.dianastigter.nl

Contact
Diana Stigter
David van Doesburg
Sjoerd Kloosterhuis
Elisa Sjelvgren

Artists
Tariq Alvi
Tjebbe Beekman
Semâ Bekirovic
Mark Boulos
Martha Colburn
Amie Dicke
Elspeth Diederix
Iris van Dongen
Irene Fortuyn
Tom Gidley
Sara van der Heide
Thomas Helbig
Aukje Koks
Nathaniel Mellors
Saskia Olde Wolbers
Amalia Pica
Jimmy Robert
Maaike Schoorel
Pilvi Takala
Sue Tompkins
Helen Verhoeven

T293

Stand F6
Tel +39 347-083-6509

Via Tribunali 293
Naples 80138
Italy
Tel +39 81-29-58-82
Fax +39 081-21-42-210
info@t293.it
www.t293.it

Via dei Leutari 32
Rome 00186
Italy
Tel +39 06-83-76-32-42

Contact
Paola Guadagnino
Marco Altavilla
Antoine Levi

Artists
Sonia Almeida
Pennacchio Argentato
James Beckett
Simon Denny
Patrizio Di Massimo
Gregory Fong
Claire Fontaine
John Henderson
Keller/Kosmas (Aids-3d)
Helen Marten
Dan Rees
Martin Soto Climent
Alberto Tadiello
Tris Vonna-Michell
Jordan Wolfson

Tang Contemporary Art

Stand R4
Tel +86 10-5978-9610

798 Art District,
JiuXianQiao Rd. No.2,
ChaoYang District
Beijing 100015
China
Tel +86 10-5978-9610
Fax +86 10-5978-9379
info@tangcontemporary.com
www.tangcontemporary.com

B-28, Silom Galleria Plaza,
919 / 1 Silom 19 Road
Bangkok 10500
Thailand
Tel +66 2-630-1114
Fax +66 2-630-3264

Contact
Zheng Lin
Josef Ng
Yang Sheng Nien
Zhao Ting Ting

Artists
Haritorn Akarapat
Chieh-Jen Chen
Wenbo Chen
Wei Guo
An He
Zhi Jiang
Sakarin Krue-on
Kamin Lertchaiprasert
Michael Lin
Yilin Lin
Jian Ling
Xiaodong Liu
Ken Lum
Yu Peng
Navin Rawanchaikul
Sun Yuan & Peng Yu
Rirkrit Tiravanija
Du Wang
Tawan Wattuya
Fen Weng
Jing Xiang
Lei Yan
Jiechang Yang
Yong Yang
Zhaoyang Yin
Guogu Zheng

Timothy Taylor Gallery

Stand C8
Tel +44 20-7409-3344

15 Carlos Place
London W1K 2EX
United Kingdom
Tel +44 20-7409-3344
Fax +44 20-7409-1316
mail@timothytaylorgallery.com
www.timothytaylorgallery.com

Contact
Timothy Taylor
Laurence Tuhey
Andreas Leventis
Emma Dexter

Artists
Craigie Aitchison
Ron Arad
Diane Arbus
Jean-Marc Bustamante
Armen Eloyan
Lee Friedlander
Adam Fuss
Ewan Gibbs
Philip Guston
Hans Hartung
Susan Hiller
Volker Hueller
Jessica Jackson Hutchins
Alex Katz
Jonathan Lasker
Agnes Martin
Josephine Meckseper
Richard Patterson
Mai-Thu Perret
Fiona Rae
Bridget Riley
Sean Scully
Kiki Smith
Andy Warhol
Lucy Williams

Team Gallery

Stand C4
Tel +1 212-279-9219

83 Grand Street
New York, NY 10013
United States
Tel +1 212-279-9219
Fax +1 212-279-9220
office@teamgal.com
www.teamgal.com

47 Wooster Street
New York, NY 10013
United States

Contact
José Freire
Miriam Katzeff

Artists
Cory Arcangel
Alex Bag
Pierre Bismuth
Slater Bradley
Vlassis Caniaris
Brice Dellsperger
Maria Eichhorn
Gardar Eide Einarsson
Massimo Grimaldi
Marc Hundley
Ross Knight
Jakob Kolding
Ryan McGinley
Dawn Mellor
Tam Ochiai
David Ratcliff
Davis Rhodes
Cristina Lei Rodriguez
Muntean /Rosenblum
Jon Routson
Sam Samore
Andreas Schulze
Santiago Sierra
Gert & Uwe Tobias
Chris Vasell
Banks Violette
Stanley Whitney

Richard Telles

Stand A20
Tel + 1 323-868-0300

7380 Beverly Boulevard
Los Angeles, CA 90036
United States
Tel +1 323-965-5578
Fax +1 323-965-5579
tellesfineart@earthlink.net
www.tellesfineart.com

Contact
Richard Telles
Max Maslansky

Artists
Tom Allen
Roy Arden
Monika Baer
Ginny Bishton
Eduardo Consuegra
Lecia Dole-Recio
Thomas Eggerer
Dan Finsel
Richard Hawkins
Nathan Hylden
Jim Isermann
Michael Krebber
Lisa Lapinski
John McAllister
Michaela Meise
Ivan Morley
Karthik Pandian
Mathias Poledna
Josephine Pryde
Ryan Sluggett
John Stezaker
Catherine Sullivan
B. Wurtz

The Third Line

Stand C19
Tel +971 4-341-1367

Al Quoz 3
Dubai 72036
United Arab Emirates
Tel +971 4-341-1367
Fax +971 04-341-1369
art@thethirdline.com
www.thethirdline.com

Contact
Claudia Cellini
Sunny Rahbar

Artists
Ebtisam Abdulaziz
Abbas Akhavan
Tarek Al-Ghoussein
Shirin Aliabadi
Rana Begum
Ala Ebtekar
Fouad Elkoury
Amir H. Fallah
Monir Shahroudy Farmanfarmaian
Golnaz Fathi
Lamya Gargash
Babak Golkar
Sherin Guirguis
Joana Hadjithomas & Khalil Joreige
Hassan Hajjaj
Susan Hefuna
Pouran Jinchi
Hayv Kahraman
Laleh Khorramian
Huda Lutfi
Farhad Moshiri
Youssef Nabil
Slavs & Tatars

Triple Canopy

Stand A13
Tel +1 347-529-5182

155 Freeman Street
Brooklyn
New York, NY 11222
United States
Tel +1 347-529-5182

Contact
Alexander Provan
Peter J. Russo
Hannah Whitaker
Christine Smallwood

Artists
Rachel Harrison
David Horvitz
Gareth Long
Matt Mullican
Boru O'Brien O'Connell

Steve Turner Contemporary

Stand R13
Tel +1 310-994-4613

6026 Wilshire Boulevard
Los Angeles, CA 90036
United States
Tel +1 323-931-3721
Fax +1 323-931-3751
info@steveturnercontemporary.com
www.steveturnercontemporary.com

Contact
Steve Turner
Lucy Chinen
Mélanie Badalato

Artists
Joshua Callaghan
Michael Decker
James Gobel
Deborah Grant
Camilo Ontiveros
Edgar Orlaineta
Pablo Rasgado
Antonio Vega Macotela
Rowan Wood
Jemima Wyman

Vermelho

Stand B26
Tel +55 11-3138-1520

Rua Minas Gerais 350
São Paulo 01244–010
Brazil
Tel +55 11-3138-1520
Fax +55 11-3138-1529
info@galeriavermelho.com.br
www.galeriavermelho.com.br

Contact
Eliana Finkelstein
Eduardo Brandao
Akio Aoki
Jan Erik Fjeld

Artists
Gabriela Albergaria
Jonathas de Andrade
Claudia Andujar
Rafael Assef
Chiara Banfi
Rodrigo Braga
Leya Mira Brander
Cadu
Lia Chaia
Marcelo Cidade
Marilá Dardot
Detanico & Lain
Dias & Riedweg
Chelpa Ferro
Cia. de Foto
Gisela Motta & Leandro Lima
Carmela Gross
Maurício Ianês
André Komatsu
Dora Longo Bahia
João Loureiro
Cinthia Marcelle
Odires Mlázsho
Fabio Morais
Guilherme Peters
Rosângela Rennó
Nicolás Robbio
Marco Paulo Rolla
Daniel Senise
Ana Maria Tavares
Carla Zaccagnini
Marcelo Zocchio

Susanne Vielmetter Los Angeles Projects

Stand C21
Tel +1 626-622-6757

6006 Washington Boulevard
Culver City, CA 90232
United States
Tel +1 310-837-2117
Fax +1 310-837-2148
info@vielmetter.com
www.vielmetter.com

Contact
Susanne Vielmetter
Kevin Scholl
Jacqueline Tarquinio
Mike Schuh
Tobias Vielmetter

Artists
Edgar Arceneaux
Andrea Bowers
Whitney Bedford
Jedediah Caesar
Sean Duffy
Nicole Eisenman
Charles Gaines
Karl Haendel
Stanya Kahn
Mary Reid Kelley
Jutta Koether
Olga Koumoundouros
Shana Lutker
Rodney McMillian
Martin McMurray
Yunhee Min
Wangechi Mutu
Ruben Ochoa
Steve Roden
Amy Sillman
Joel Tauber
Mickalene Thomas
Tam Van Tran
Patrick Wilson

Vilma Gold

Stand A22
Tel +44 7816-543380

6 Minerva Street
London E2 9EH
United Kingdom
Tel +44 20-7729-9888
mail@vilmagold.com
www.vilmagold.com

Contact
Rachel Williams
Laura Lord
Martin Rasmussen

Artists
Charles Atlas
Trisha Baga
KP Brehmer
Nicholas Byrne
William Daniels
Vladimir Dubossarsky & Alexander Vinogradov
Michaela Eichwald
Felix Gmelin
Brian Griffiths
Thomas Helbig
Sophie von Hellerman
Hobbypopmuseum
Thomas Hylander
Andrew Mania
Karthik Pandian
R.H. Quaytman
Stephen G. Rhodes
Hannah Sawtell
Markus Selg
Michael Stevenson
Josef Strau
Mark Titchner
Julia Wachtel
Jennifer West

Galleri Nicolai Wallner

Stand A7
Tel +45 51-28-19-89

Ny Carlsberg Vej 68 OG
Copenhagen 1760
Denmark
Tel +45 32-57-09-70
Fax +45 32-57-09-71
nw@nicolaiwallner.com
www.nicolaiwallner.com

Contact
Nicolai Wallner
Gitte Skjødt Madsen
Marie Gellert Jensen

Artists
Daniel Buren
Elmgreen & Dragset
Dan Graham
Jeppe Hein
Chris Johanson
Jesper Just
Joachim Koester
Jakob Kolding
Peter Land
Jonathan Monk
Claire Rojas
Christoph Ruckhäberle
Christian Schmidt-Rasmussen
David Shrigley
Glenn Sorensen
Alexander Tovborg
Richard Tuttle
Gitte Villesen

Wallspace

Stand D7
Tel +1 212-594-9478

619 West 27th Street
New York, NY 10001
United States
Tel +1 212-594-9478
Fax +1 212-594-9805
info@wallspacegallery.com
www.wallspacegallery.com

Contact
Janine Foeller
Jane Hait
Nichole Caruso

Artists
Ron Amstutz
Walead Beshty
Kate Costello
John Divola
Shannon Ebner
Martha Friedman
Gaylen Gerber
Daniel Gordon
Jiří Kovanda
Brad Phillips
Laura Riboli
Helen Verhoeven
Donelle Woolford
Mark Wyse

Galerie Barbara Weiss

Stand A27
Tel +49 160-742-2507

Kohlfurter Strasse 41–43
Berlin 10999
Germany
Tel +49 30-262-4284
Fax +49 30-265-1652
mail@galeriebarbaraweiss.de
www.galeriebarbaraweiss.de

Contact
Barbara Weiss

Artists
Monika Baer
Heike Baranowsky
Thomas Bayrle
Geta Brătescu
Janet Cardiff & George Bures Miller
Maria Eichhorn
Nicole Eisenman
Ayşe Erkmen
Harun Farocki
Friederike Feldmann
Mary Heilmann
Christine & Irene Hohenbüchler
Laura Horelli
Jonathan Horowitz
Raoul De Keyser
Boris Mikhailov
John Miller
Rebecca Morris
Deimantas Narkevičius
Susanne Paesler
Mai-Thu Perret
Collier Schorr
Andreas Siekmann
Roman Signer
Niele Toroni
Suse Weber

Michael Werner

Stand B5
Tel +1 212-988-1623

4 East 77 Street
New York, NY 10075
United States
Tel +1 212-988-1623
Fax +1 212-988-1774
info@michaelwerner.com
www.michaelwerner.com

Contact
Gordon VeneKlasen
Justine Birbil
Birte Kleemann
Kadee Robbins
Harry Scrymgeour

Artists
Hurvin Anderson
Georg Baselitz
Marcel Broodthaers
James Lee Byars
Aaron Curry
Enrico David
Peter Doig
Thomas Houseago
Jörg Immendorff
Per Kirkeby
Eugène Leroy
Markus Lüpertz
Ernst Wilhelm Nay
A.R. Penck
Sigmar Polke
Don Van Vliet

White Columns

Stand A12
Tel +1 917-514-3595

320 West 13th Street
New York, NY 10014
United States
Tel +1 1 212-924-4212
info@whitecolumns.org
www.whitecolumns.org

Contact
Matthew Higgs
Amie Scally
Carolyn Lockhart
Jeff Eaton

Artists
Joe Bradley
Kim Gordon
John Hiltunen
Klara Liden
Nate Lowman
Adam McEwen
Dan Miller
Judith Scott
Aurie Ramirez
Nick Relph

White Cube

Stand B38
Tel +44 20-7930-5373

48 Hoxton Square
London N1 6PB
United Kingdom
Tel +44 20-7930-5373
Fax +44 20-7749-7480
enquiries@whitecube.com
www.whitecube.com

144 – 152 Bermondsey Street
London SE1 3TQ
United Kingdom

25-26 Mason's Yard
London SW1Y 6BU
United Kingdom

50 Connaught Road
Central
Hong Kong

Contact
Jay Jopling
Daniela Gareh
Susan May
Tim Marlow

Artists
Franz Ackermann
Darren Almond
Ellen Altfest
Miroslaw Balka
Georg Baselitz
Ashley Bickerton
Mark Bradford
Candice Breitz
Ernesto Caivano
Jake & Dinos Chapman
Chuck Close
Gregory Crewdson
Tracey Emin
Katharina Fritsch
Theaster Gates
Gilbert & George
Antony Gormley
Andreas Gursky
Marcus Harvey
Mona Hatoum
Eberhard Havekost
Damien Hirst
Gary Hume
Robert Irwin
Runa Islam
Sergej Jensen
Anselm Kiefer
Rachel Kneebone
Friedrich Kunath
Elad Lassry
Liza Lou
Christian Marclay
Kris Martin
Josiah McElheny
Julie Mehretu
Harland Miller
Sarah Morris
Gabriel Orozco
Damián Ortega
Richard Phillips
Marc Quinn
Jessica Rankin
Robin Rhode
Doris Salcedo
Raqib Shaw
Neal Tait
Sam Taylor-Wood
Fred Tomaselli
Jeff Wall
Cerith Wyn Evans
Zhang Huan

Wilkinson

Stand D2
Tel +44 7980-892851

50–58 Vyner Street
London E2 9DQ
United Kingdom
Tel +44 20-8980-2662
info@wilkinsongallery.com
www.wilkinsongallery.com

Contact
Amanda Wilkinson
Anthony Wilkinson

Artists
Mark Alexander
Kevin Appel
Tilo Baumgärtel
Dara Birnbaum
Matt Calderwood
Clegg & Guttmann
Estate of Jimmy De Sana
A. K. Dolven
Harm van den Dorpel
Matthew Higgs
Joan Jonas
Jacob Dahl Jürgensen
Tillman Kaiser
Sung Hwan Kim
Thoralf Knobloch
Makiko Kudo
Marcin Maciejowski
Elizabeth Magill
Renzo Martens
Ciprian Muresan
Robert Orchardson
Anna Parkina
Barbara Probst
Silke Schatz
George Shaw
Shimabuku
Laurie Simmons
Martina Steckholzer
Phoebe Unwin
Olav Westphalen

Galerie Jocelyn Wolff

Stand F1
Tel +33 673-89-90-28

78 rue Julien-Lacroix
Paris 75020
France
Tel +33 1-42-03-05-65
Fax +33 1-42-03-05-46
info@galeriewolff.com
www.galeriewolff.com

Contact
Jocelyn Wolff
Sandrine Djerouet
Sarah Aguilar
Markus Lichti

Artists
Katinka Bock
Miriam Cahn
Valérie Favre
Guillaume Leblon
Isa Melsheimer
Frédéric Moser & Philippe Schwinger
Ulrich Polster
Prinz Gholam
Hans Schabus
Elodie Seguin
Franz Erhard Walther
Christoph Weber
Clemens von Wedemeyer

Alex Zachary Peter Currie

Stand F2
Tel +1 21-2-628-0189

16 East 77th Street
New York, NY 10075
United States
Tel +1 21-2-628-0189
front@azpcgallery.com
www.azpcgallery.com

Contact
Alex Zachary
Peter Currie

Artists
Lutz Bacher
Judith Bernstein
Rainer Ganahl
Karl Holmqvist
Judith Hopf
David Lieske
Ken Okiishi
Lily van der Stokker
Jordan Wolfson
Mark van Yetter

Zeno X Gallery

Stand B3
Tel +32 485 950 477

Leopold De Waelplaats 16
Antwerp 2000
Belgium
Tel +32 3-216-38-88
Fax +32 3-216-09-92
info@zeno-x.com
www.zeno-x.com

Appelstraat 37 Borgerhout
Antwerp 2140
Belgium

Contact
Frank Demaegd
Jelle Breynaert
Koen Van den Brande
Benedicte Goesaert

Artists
Michaël Borremans
Dirk Braeckman
Patrick van Caeckenbergh
Stan Douglas
Marlene Dumas
Kees Goudzwaard
Noritoshi Hirakawa
Yun-Fei Ji
Kim Jones
Johannes Kahrs
Naoto Kawahara
Anne-Mie van Kerckhoven
Raoul De Keyser
John Körmeling
Jan de Maesschalck
Mark Manders
Jockum Nordström
Jenny Scobel
Maria Serebriakova
Bart Stolle
Luc Tuymans
Jack Whitten
Cristof Yvoré

David Zwirner

Stand C46
Tel +1 212-727-2070

525 West 19th Street
New York, NY 10011
United States
Tel +1 212-727-2070
Fax +1 212-727-2072
information@davidzwirner.com
www.davidzwirner.com

Contact
David Zwirner
Kristine Bell
Angela Choon
Justine Durrett
Bellatrix Hubert
Greg Lulay
Ales Ortuzar
Hanna Schouwink

Artists
Adel Abdessemed
Tomma Abts
Francis Alÿs
Mamma Andersson
Michaël Borremans
Carol Bove
R. Crumb
Philip-Lorca diCorcia
Stan Douglas
Marlene Dumas
Marcel Dzama
Dan Flavin
Suzan Frecon
Isa Genzken
Donald Judd
On Kawara
Raoul De Keyser
Toba Khedoori
Gordon Matta-Clark
John McCracken
Alice Neel
Jockum Nordström
Chris Ofili
Raymond Pettibon
Neo Rauch
Jason Rhoades
Daniel Richter
Michael Riedel
Thomas Ruff
Fred Sandback
Katy Schimert
Yutaka Sone
Al Taylor
Diana Thater
Luc Tuymans
James Welling
Doug Wheeler
Christopher Williams
Yan Pei-Ming
Lisa Yuskavage

Magazine Index

Afterall

Stand M11
Central St Martins College of Arts and Design
University of the Arts London
Granary Building
1 Granary Square
London N1C 4AA
United Kingdom
Tel +44 20-7514-8173
contact@afterall.org
www.afterall.org

ArtAsiaPacific

Stand M8
GPO Box 10084
Hong Kong
Tel +852 2553-5586
Fax +852 2553-1199
info@aapmag.com
www.artasiapacific.com

Artforum International

Stand M23
19th Floor
350 Seventh Avenue
New York, NY 10001
United States
Tel +1 212-475-4000
Fax +1 212-529-1257
generalinfo@artforum.com
www.artforum.com

ArtNexus

Stand M13
2nd Floor
12500 NE 8th Avenue
North Miami, FL 33161
United States
Tel +1 305-891-7270
Fax +1 305-891-6408
zroca@artnexus.com
www.artnexus.com

ArtReview

Stand M19
1 Sekforde Street
London EC1R 0BE
United Kingdom
Tel +44 20-7107-2760
Fax +44 20-7107-2761
office@artreview.com
www.artreview.com

ART+ AUCTION

Stand M5
Suite 410
601 West 26th Street
New York, NY 10001
United States
Tel +1 212-447-9555
Fax +1 212-627-4165
artandauctionmag@artinfo.com
www.artinfo.com

Art in America

Stand M18
5th Floor
575 Broadway
New York, NY 10012
United States
Tel +1 212-941-2800
Fax +1 212-941-2870
info@brantpub.com
www.artinamericamagazine.com

The Art Newspaper

Stand M3
70 South Lambeth Road
London SW8 1RL
United Kingdom
Tel +44 20-7735-3331
Fax +44 20-7735-3332
subscribe@theartnewspaper.com
www.theartnewspaper.com

Bidoun Projects

Stand M16
Ground Floor
47 Orchard Street
New York, NY 10002
United States
Tel +1 212-475-0123
info@bidoun.com
www.bidoun.com

Cabinet

Stand M10
181 Wyckoff Street
Brooklyn, NY 11217
United States
Tel +1 718-222-8434
Fax +1 718-222-3700
info@cabinetmagazine.org
www.cabinetmagazine.org

Flash Art International/ Art Diary

Stand M7
Giancarlo Politi Editore
68 Via Carlo Farini
Milan 20159
Italy
Tel +39 02-688-7341
Fax +39 02-6680-1290
info@flashartonline.com
www.flashartonline.com

frieze

Stand M1
1 Montclare Street
London E2 7EU
United Kingdom
Tel +44 20-3372-6111
Fax +44 20-3372-6115
info@frieze.com
www.frieze.com

frieze d/e

Stand M1
Zehdenicker Strasse 28
Berlin 10119
Germany
Tel +49 30-2362-6506
Fax +49 30-2362-6505
berlin@frieze.de
www.frieze-magazin.de

Le Journal des Arts

Stand M15
8 rue Borromée
Paris 75015
France
Tel +33 1-48-42-90-00
Fax +33 1-48-42-90-01
contact@artclair.com
www.LeJournaldesArts.fr

Kaleidoscope

Stand M17
Galleria Buenos Aires 10
Milan 20124
Italy
Tel +39 02-3653-5563
magazine@kaleidoscope-press.com
www.kaleidoscope-press.com

LEAP

Stand M14
5F, Tower 1, China View
No. A2, Gongti East Road
Chaoyang District
Beijing 100027
China
Tel +86 10-6561-5550
Fax +86 10-6561-0819
leap@modernmedia.com.cn
www.leapleapleap.com

Modern Painters

Stand M5
Suite 410
601 West 26th Street
New York, NY 10001
United States
Tel +1 212-447-9555
Fax +1 212-627-4165
modernpaintersmag@artinfo.com
www.artinfo.com

Mousse

Stand M9
Via De Amicis 53
Milan 20123
Italy
Tel +39 02-835-6631
Fax +39 02-8320-0036
info@moussemagazine.it
www.moussemagazine.it

n+1

Stand M12
68 Jay Street, No. 405
Brooklyn, NY 11201
United States
Tel +1 718-797-0750
editors@nplusonemag.com
www.nplusonemag.com

New York Magazine

Stand M4
New York Media
75 Varick Street, 4th Floor
New York, NY 10013
Tel +1 212-508-0700
events@nymag.com
www.nymag.com

Paper Monument

Stand M12
c/o n+1 foundation
68 Jay Sreet, No. 405
Brooklyn, NY 11201
United States
info@papermonument.com
www.papermonument.com

Parkett

Stand M21
Quellenstrasse 27
Zurich 8031
Switzerland
Tel +41 44-271-8140
Fax +41 44-272-4301

Parkett Publishers
145 Avenue of the Americas
New York, NY 10013
United States
Tel +1 212-673-2660
Fax +1 212-271-0704
info@parkettart.com
www.parkettart.com

springerin

Stand M20
Museumplatz 1
Vienna 1070
Austria
Tel +43 15-229-124
Fax +43 15-229-125
springerin@springerin.at
www.springerin.at

Texte zur Kunst

Stand M22
Strausberger Platz 19
Berlin 10243
Germany
Tel +49 30-301-045-345
Fax +49 30-301-045-344
verlag@textezurkunst.de
www.textezurkunst.de

Artist Index

Askevold, David
Canada F30
Assaël, Micol
Johann König A14
Assef, Rafael
Vermelho B26
Atay, Fikret
Galerie Chantal Crousel B28
Atelier
Cabinet C7
Atelier van Lieshout
Tanya Bonakdar Gallery C6
Atkins, Ed
Galerie Isabella Bortolozzi F18
Cabinet C7
Atlas, Charles
Vilma Gold A22
The Atlas Group
Anthony Reynolds Gallery C3
Sfeir-Semler A8
Attia, Kader
Galleria Continua C40
Galerie Krinzinger B24
Auad, Tonico Lemos
Stephen Friedman Gallery B10
Audebert, Julien
art: concept A2
Auer, Abel
Corvi-Mora A16
Sies + Höke B15
Auerbach, Tauba
STANDARD (Oslo) B41
Austen, David
Anthony Reynolds Gallery C3
Avini, Anisheh
Marianne Boesky Gallery A26
Avedon, Richard
Gagosian Gallery D4
Avotins, Janis
Galerie Rüdiger Schöttle D3
Avşar, Vahap
Rampa B31
Axell, Evelyne
Broadway 1602 C9
Azari, Shoja
Figge von Rosen Galerie R8
Bachardy, Don
Cheim & Read C36
Bacher, Lutz
Cabinet C7
Alex Zachary Peter Currie F2
Backström, Fia
Crystal R10
Bacon, Francis
Gagosian Gallery D4
Bader, Darren
Andrew Kreps Gallery B14
Baechler, Donald
Cheim & Read C36
Galerie Thaddaeus Ropac C12
Baer, Monika
Richard Telles A20
Galerie Barbara Weiss A27
Bag, Alex
Elizabeth Dee D1
Team Gallery C4
Baga, Trisha
Greene Naftali C44
Vilma Gold A22
Baghramian, Nairy
Galerie Buchholz B35
Baj, Enrico
Giò Marconi A3
Bajević, Maja
Galerie Peter Kilchmann A24
Bakharev, Nikolay
Regina Gallery B33
Bakhshi, Mahmoud
Galerie Thaddaeus Ropac C12
Baldessari, John
Sprüth Magers Berlin London B37
de Balincourt, Jules
Galerie Thaddaeus Ropac C12
Salon 94 C38
Balka, Miroslaw
Galleria Raffaella Cortese C17
White Cube B38
Balkenhol, Stephan
Stephen Friedman Gallery B10
Tomio Koyama Gallery B8
Galerie Thaddaeus Ropac C12
Galerie Rüdiger Schöttle D3
Ballen, Roger
Massimo Minini B22
Balteo Yazbeck, Alessandro
Galerie Martin Janda A28
Balula, Davide
galerie frank elbaz D6
Banfi, Chiara
Vermelho B26
Banisadr, Ali
Galerie Thaddaeus Ropac C12
Banner, Fiona
Frith Street Gallery C42
Baranowsky, Heike
Galerie Barbara Weiss A27
Barba, Rosa
carlier | gebauer C23
Giò Marconi A3
Barclay, Claire
Stephen Friedman Gallery B10
Barembоym, Alisa
47 Canal R15
Barker, Sara
Mary Mary F3
Barlow, Phyllida
Hauser & Wirth B6
Barman, Rathin
Experimenter F23
Barney, Matthew
Sadie Coles HQ C15
Regen Projects B17
Barnhart, Grant
Ambach & Rice R20
Barr, Burt
Sikkema Jenkins & Co. C45
Barrada, Yto
Sfeir-Semler A8
Barrão, Barrão
Galeria Fortes Vilaça C48
Barré, Martin
Andrew Kreps Gallery B14
Barriball, Anna
Frith Street Gallery C42
Barrow, Mark
Elizabeth Dee D1
Barry, Robert
Alfonso Artiaco C31
Yvon Lambert C34
Sfeir-Semler A8
Massimo Minini B22
van Bart, Hannah
Marianne Boesky Gallery A26
Bartana, Yael
Galleria Raffaella Cortese C17
Annet Gelink Gallery A10
Sommer Contemporary Art C37
Barth, Uta
Tanya Bonakdar Gallery C6
Sies + Höke B15
Bartolini, Massimo
Massimo De Carlo B1
Frith Street Gallery C42
Bartuszova, Maria
Galerie Rüdiger Schöttle D3
Bas, Hernan
Galerie Peter Kilchmann A24
Lehmann Maupin C10
Victoria Miro C47
Galerie Perrotin C41
Basbaum, Ricardo
A Gentil Carioca C27
Baselitz, Georg
Contemporary Fine Arts C39
Gagosian Gallery D4
Galerie Thaddaeus Ropac C12
Michael Werner B5
White Cube B38
Basilico, Gabriele
Massimo Minini B22
Basquiat, Jean-Michel
Gagosian Gallery D4
Batniji, Taysir
Sfeir-Semler A8
Bauch, Michael
Galerie Karin Guenther F20
Baudelaire, Eric
Elizabeth Dee D1
Baudevin, Francis
art: concept A2
Bauer, Michael
Alison Jacques Gallery A25
Galerie Peter Kilchmann A24
Baum, Erica
Bureau R11
Lüttgenmeijer R9
Baumgärtel, Tilo
Wilkinson D2
Bayles, Dan
François Ghebaly Gallery F32
Bayrle, Thomas
Air de Paris C11
Gavin Brown's enterprise B18
Galerie Mezzanin F29
Galerie Francesca Pia A15
Galerie Barbara Weiss A27
Beasley, Becky
Laura Bartlett Gallery C26
Becker, Julie
Greene Naftali C44
Beckett, James
Lüttgenmeijer R9
T293 F6
Bedford, Whitney
art: concept A2
Susanne Vielmetter Los Angeles Projects C21
Beecroft, Vanessa
Massimo Minini B22
Beekman, Tjebbe
Diana Stigter F14
de Beer, Sue
Marianne Boesky Gallery A26
Begum, Rana
The Third Line C19
Beier, Nina
Laura Bartlett Gallery C26
STANDARD (Oslo) B41
Bejenaru, Matei
Andreiana Mihail Gallery F28
Bekirovicm, Semâ
Diana Stigter F14
Bell, Dirk
Gavin Brown's enterprise B18
Sadie Coles HQ C15
The Modern Institute C29
Bellmer, Hans
Miguel Abreu Gallery C14
Beloufa, Neïl
BaliceHertling R12
François Ghebaly Gallery F32
Ben-Gal, Avner
Bortolami A9
Sadie Coles HQ C15
Benedict, Will
Galerie Meyer Kainer B27
Giò Marconi A3
Benglis, Lynda
Cheim & Read C36
Benitez, Jesus Alberto
galerie frank elbaz D6
Benson, Frank
Sadie Coles HQ C15
Andrew Kreps Gallery B14
Overduin and Kite F4
Bento, José
A Gentil Carioca C27
Bercea, Marius
François Ghebaly Gallery F32
Berkenblit, Ellen
Anton Kern Gallery C2
Berman, Wallace
galerie frank elbaz D6
Bernhardt, Katherine
Canada F30
Berning, Dale
Take Ninagawa R14
Bernstein, Judith
Alex Zachary Peter Currie F2
Beshty, Walead

Artist Index

Yvon Lambert C34
Brunner, Bianca
BolteLang R16
Brunner, Maria
Galerie Gisela Capitain B19
Brus, Günter
Galerie Krinzinger B24
Bryans, Matt
Kate MacGarry F13
Brzezanska, Agnieszka
Hotel F31
Karma International F10
Büchel, Christoph
Hauser & Wirth B6
Maccarone D5
Büchler, Pavel
Tanya Leighton Gallery F16
Buck, Robert
Stephen Friedman Gallery B10
Bul, Lee
Lehmann Maupin C10
Galerie Thaddaeus Ropac C12
Bulloch, Angela
Boers-Li Gallery C18
Simon Lee Gallery A5
Galerie Eva Presenhuber B29
Esther Schipper B2
Burden, Chris
Gagosian Gallery D4
Galerie Krinzinger B24
Burdis, Edwin
Broadway 1602 C9
Buren, Daniel
Bortolami A9
Galleria Continua C40
Xavier Hufkens B23
Lisson Gallery C5
Massimo Minini B22
Galleri Nicolai Wallner A7
Burkhard, Balthasar
Sfeir-Semler A8
Burns, Ian
mother's tankstation R1
Burr, Tom
Bortolami A9
Stuart Shave/Modern Art C43
Galerie Neu C49
Galleria Franco Noero C50
Almine Rech Gallery B7
Sommer Contemporary Art C37
Burton, Jeff
Casey Kaplan A6
Galleria Franco Noero C50
Bustamante, Jean-Marc
Xavier Hufkens B23
Galerie Thaddaeus Ropac C12
Timothy Taylor Gallery C8
Butler, Benjamin
Galerie Martin Janda A28
Tomio Koyama Gallery B8
Büttner, Andrea
Hollybush Gardens F9
Butzer, André
Galerie Guido W. Baudach C30
Giò Marconi A3
Metro Pictures C16
Byars, James Lee
Michael Werner B5
Byrne, Gerard
Lisson Gallery C5
Byrne, Nicholas
Vilma Gold A22
Cabelo
A Gentil Carioca C27
Cadu
Vermelho B26
van Caeckenbergh, Patrick
Zeno X Gallery B3
Caesar, Jedediah
Susanne Vielmetter Los Angeles Projects C21
Cahn, Miriam
Elizabeth Dee D1
Meyer Riegger B21
Galerie Jocelyn Wolff F1
Caivano, Ernesto
carlier | gebauer C23
White Cube B38
Caivano, Varda
Tomio Koyama Gallery B8
Victoria Miro C47
Calame, Ingrid
James Cohan Gallery B30
Frith Street Gallery C42
Calder, Alexander
Gagosian Gallery D4
Kukje Gallery B36
Calderón, Miguel
kurimanzutto B16
Calderwood, Matt
Wilkinson D2
Callaghan, Joshua
Steve Turner Contemporary R13
Calle, Sophie
Galerie Perrotin C41
Calvin, Brian
Corvi-Mora A16
Anton Kern Gallery C2
Calzolari, Pier Paolo
Marianne Boesky Gallery A26
Cameron Parsons Foundation
Nicole Klagsbrun Gallery A21
Camnitzer, Luis
Alexander Gray Associates F21
Campanini, Pierpaolo
Corvi-Mora A16
kaufmann repetto A23
Campbell, Arabella
Catriona Jeffries A17
Campbell, Beth
Nicole Klagsbrun Gallery A21
Campbell, Duncan
Hotel F31
Campbell, Neil
Galleria Franco Noero C50
Campbell, Shane
Bortolami A9
Camplin, Bonnie
Cabinet C7
Galerie Cinzia Friedlaender R3
Canell, Nina
mother's tankstation R1
Caniaris, Vlassis
The Breeder C22
Team Gallery C4
Cantor, Mircea
Yvon Lambert C34
Caracciolo, Beatrice
Almine Rech Gallery B7
Caramelle, Ernst
Mary Mary F3
Caravaggio, Gianni
kaufmann repetto A23
Sies + Höke B15
Cardelus, Maggie
kaufmann repetto A23
Cardiff & Miller
Galerie Barbara Weiss A27
Carnegie, Gillian
Cabinet C7
Galerie Gisela Capitain B19
Andrea Rosen Gallery C28
Carneiro da Cunha, Tiago
Galeria Fortes Vilaça C48
Kate MacGarry F13
Caro, Anthony
Kukje Gallery B36
Mitchell-Innes & Nash B20
Carpenter, Merlin
Simon Lee Gallery A5
Overduin and Kite F4
Reena Spaulings Fine Art F17
Los Carpinteros
Galeria Fortes Vilaça C48
Sean Kelly Gallery B25
Galerie Peter Kilchmann A24
Carron, Valentin
303 Gallery B39
David Kordansky Gallery C1
Galerie Eva Presenhuber B29
Carter
Yvon Lambert C34
Salon 94 C38
Carter, Nathan
Casey Kaplan A6
Esther Schipper B2
Casebere, James
Sean Kelly Gallery B25
Lisson Gallery C5
Castro, Jota
Massimo Minini B22
Catala, Antoine
47 Canal R15
Cattelan, Maurizio
Massimo De Carlo B1
Galerie Perrotin C41
Catunda, Leda
Galeria Fortes Vilaça C48
Cavusoğlu, Ergin
Rampa B31
Ceccaldi, Nicolas
Johan Berggren Gallery F15
Cecchini, Loris
Galleria Continua C40
Çekil, Cengiz
Rampa B31
Cennetoğlu, Banu
Rodeo F25
Cesarco, Alejandro
Tanya Leighton Gallery F16
Chaia, Lia
Vermelho B26
Chaimowicz, Marc Camille
Cabinet C7
Overduin and Kite F4
Chambaud, Etienne
Sies + Höke B15
Chamberlain, John
Gagosian Gallery D4
Xavier Hufkens B23
Chamberlain, Tom
Andreiana Mihail Gallery F28
Chan, Paul
Greene Naftali C44
Channer, Alice
The Approach B11
Chapman, Jake & Dinos
White Cube B38
Chapman, Jesse
Marianne Boesky Gallery A26
Shane Campbell Gallery R17
Charlton, Alan
Alfonso Artiaco C31
Chauhan, Ajit
Jack Hanley Gallery A1
Chen, Shaoxiong
Boers-Li Gallery C18
Chen, Wenbo
Tang Contemporary Art R4
Chen, Yujun
Boers-Li Gallery C18
Chen, Zhen (estate of)
Galleria Continua C40
Chetrit, Talia
kaufmann repetto A23
Renwick Gallery R6
Sies + Höke B15
Chetwynd, Spartacus
Sadie Coles HQ C15
Massimo De Carlo B1
Chiasera, Paolo
Massimo Minini B22
Chicks on Speed
Kate MacGarry F13
Chieh-Jen Chen
Long March Space C13
Tang Contemporary Art R4
Childish, Billy
Lehmann Maupin C10
Chirulescu, Marieta
Micky Schubert F8
Choe, U-Ram
Gallery Hyundai C20
Choi, Sunah
Galerie Cinzia Friedlaender R3
Chu, Anne
303 Gallery B39
Chuikov, Ivan
Regina Gallery B33
Chun, Kwang Youhng

Artist Index

Artist Index

Artist Index

Artist Index

Kassay Jacob
art: concept A2
Xavier Hufkens B23
Kasseböhmer, Axel
Sprüth Magers Berlin London B37
Kasten, Barbara
Almine Rech Gallery B7
Katayama, Hirofumi
Taro Nasu C25
Kato, Mika
Tomio Koyama Gallery B8
Katz, Alex
Galerie Thaddaeus Ropac C12
Gavin Brown's enterprise B18
Timothy Taylor Gallery C8
Katz, Allison
Johan Berggren Gallery F15
Kawahara, Naoto
Taka Ishii Gallery B13
Zeno X Gallery B3
Kawai, Misaki
Take Ninagawa R14
Kawara, On
David Zwirner C46
Yvon Lambert C34
Kawashima, Hideaki
Kukje Gallery B36
Tomio Koyama Gallery B8
Kaws
Galerie Perrotin C41
Keegan, Matt
Altman Siegel F5
Keen, Jeff
Elizabeth Dee D1
Keller, Christoph
Esther Schipper B2
Keller/Kosmas (Aids-3d)
T293 F6
Kelley, Mary Reid
Susanne Vielmetter Los Angeles Projects C21
Kelley, Mike
Gagosian Gallery D4
Kelm, Annette
Marc Foxx C32
Herald St A30
Taka Ishii Gallery B13
Johann König A14
Andrew Kreps Gallery B14
Giò Marconi A3
Kempinas, Zilvinas
Yvon Lambert C34
Kendrick, Mel
David Nolan Gallery A29
Keogh, Sam
Kerlin Gallery A19
Kerbel, Janice
greengrassi A11
Galerie Karin Guenther F20
Catriona Jeffries A17\
van Kerckhoven, Anne-Mie
Zeno X Gallery B3
Kern, Richard
Hotel F31
Kern, Stefan
Galerie Karin Guenther F20
Kerr, Andrew
The Modern Institute C29
Kersels, Martin
Mitchell-Innes & Nash B20
Kessler, Jon
Salon 94 C38
De Keyser, Raoul
Galerie Martin Janda A28
Galerie Barbara Weiss A27
Zeno X Gallery B3
David Zwirner C46
Khachatryan, Tigran
Regina Gallery B33
Khalid, Aisha
Corvi-Mora A16
Khan, Hassan
Galerie Chantal Crousel B28
Khan, Idris
Sean Kelly Gallery B25
Yvon Lambert C34
Victoria Miro C47
Khedoori, Rachel
Galerie Gisela Capitain B19
Hauser & Wirth B6
Khedoori, Toba
Regen Projects B17
David Zwirner C46
Kher, Bharti
Galerie Perrotin C41
Hauser & Wirth B6
Khorramian, Laleh
Salon 94 C38
The Third Line C19
Kiaer, Ian
Alison Jacques Gallery A25
Tanya Bonakdar Gallery C6
Kiefer, Anselm
Gagosian Gallery D4
Galerie Thaddaeus Ropac C12
Kukje Gallery B36
White Cube B38
Yvon Lambert C34
Kiesewetter, Thomas
Contemporary Fine Arts C39
Almine Rech Gallery B7
Sies + Höke B15
Kilimnik, Karen
303 Gallery B39
Galerie Eva Presenhuber B29
Sprüth Magers Berlin London B37
Kim, Byron
James Cohan Gallery B30
Kim, Kira
Kukje Gallery B36
Kimsooja
Galleria Continua C40
Galleria Raffaella Cortese C17
Kukje Gallery B36
Kim, Sora
Kukje Gallery B36
Kim, Sung Hwan
Wilkinson D2
Kimura, Yuki
Taka Ishii Gallery B13
King, Scott
Bortolami A9
Herald St A30
Kinmont, Ben
Air de Paris C11
Kippenberger, Martin
Galerie Gisela Capitain B19
Kirkeby, Per
Michael Werner B5
Kirschner & Panos
Hollybush Gardens F9
Kita, Yoriko
Take Ninagawa R14
Klauke, Jürgen
Galerie Guido W. Baudach C30
Klein, Astrid
Sprüth Magers Berlin London B37
Klein, Carla
Tanya Bonakdar Gallery C6
Annet Gelink Gallery A10
Klein, Jochen
Galerie Buchholz B35
Kline, Josh
47 Canal R15
Kneebone, Rachel
White Cube B38
Kneihsl, Erwin
Galerie Guido W. Baudach C30
Knifer, Julije
galerie frank elbaz D6
Knight, John
Greene Naftali C44
Galerie Rüdiger Schöttle D3
Knight, Ross
Team Gallery C4
Knobloch, Thoralf
Wilkinson D2
Knoebel, Imi
Galerie Thaddaeus Ropac C12
Knowles, Christopher
Gavin Brown's enterprise B18
Kobberling & Kaltwasser
Jack Hanley Gallery A1
Koester, Joachim
Greene Naftali C44
Galleri Nicolai Wallner A7
Koether, Jutta
Bortolami A9
Galerie Buchholz B35
Galerie Francesca Pia A15
Reena Spaulings Fine Art F17
Susanne Vielmetter Los Angeles Projects C21
Kogler, Peter
Galerie Mezzanin F29
Koh, Germaine
Catriona Jeffries A17
Koh, Terence
Galerie Thaddaeus Ropac C12
Köhncke, Justus
Galerie Cinzia Friedlaender R3
Koide, Naoki
Tomio Koyama Gallery B8
Koizumi, Meiro
Annet Gelink Gallery A10
Koks, Aukje
Diana Stigter F14
Kolarova, Bela
Galerie Rüdiger Schöttle D3
Kolding, Jakob
Galerie Martin Janda A28
Galleri Nicolai Wallner A7
Team Gallery C4
Kolkoz
Galerie Perrotin C41
Koller, Július
gb agency F33
Galerie Martin Janda A28
Komad, Zenita
Galerie Krinzinger B24
Regina Gallery B33
Komatsu, André
Vermelho B26
Könnemann, Nina
Galerie Karin Guenther F20
Koo, Bohnchang
Kukje Gallery B36
de Kooning, Willem
Xavier Hufkens B23
Koons, Jeff
Gagosian Gallery D4
Almine Rech Gallery B7
Kopp, Jeff
Redling Fine Art R7
Kopp, Viktor
Bureau R11
Körmeling, John
Zeno X Gallery B3
Kørner, John
Victoria Miro C47
Korpys / Löffler
Meyer Riegger B21
Korty, David
Sadie Coles HQ C15
Kimmerich F26
Koschmieder, Andrei
Johan Berggren Gallery F15
Koshelev, Egor
Regina Gallery B33
Koshlyakov, Valerie
Galerie Krinzinger B24
Kossoff, Leon
Mitchell-Innes & Nash B20
Kosuth, Joseph
Sean Kelly Gallery B25
Almine Rech Gallery B7
Sprüth Magers Berlin London B37
Kotatkova, Eva
Meyer Riegger B21
Koumoundouros, Olga
Susanne Vielmetter Los Angeles Projects C21
Kounellis, Jannis
Alfonso Artiaco C31
Cheim & Read C36
Kovanda, Jiří
gb agency F33
Wallspace D7
Kowalski, Tomasz
carlier | gebauer C23

Artist Index

Artist Index

White Cube B38
Miller, John
Metro Pictures C16
Meyer Riegger B21
Galerie Praz-Delavallade A18
Galerie Barbara Weiss A27
Min, Yunhee
Susanne Vielmetter Los Angeles Projects C21
Minamikawa, Shimon
MISAKO & ROSEN R19
Miner, Christopher
Mitchell-Innes & Nash B20
Minter, Marilyn
Regen Projects B17
Salon 94 C38
Minuti, Davide
Alfonso Artiaco C31
Mirra, Helen
Taka Ishii Gallery B13
Meyer Riegger B21
Mirutziu, Alex
Galerie Rüdiger Schöttle D3
Mirza, Haroon
Lisson Gallery C5
Mitchell, Dane
A Gentil Carioca C27
Mitchell, Jeffry
Ambach & Rice R20
Mitchell, Joan
Cheim & Read C36
Hauser & Wirth B6
Kukje Gallery B36
Miyajima, Tatsuo
Lisson Gallery C5
Miyake, Shintaro
Tomio Koyama Gallery B8
Galerie Krinzinger B24
Miyamoto, Ryuji
Taro Nasu C25
Mlangeni, Sabelo
Stevenson B32
Mlázsho, Odires
Vermelho B26
Mntambo, Nandipha
Stevenson B32
Mochetti, Maurizio
Giò Marconi A3
Mochizuka, Miki
MISAKO & ROSEN R19
Modé, João
A Gentil Carioca C27
Moffett, Donald
Marianne Boesky Gallery A26
Mogi, Ayako
MISAKO & ROSEN R19
Mogutin, Slava
Regina Gallery B33
Mohaiemen, Naeem
Experimenter F23
Moholy-Nagy, László
Andrea Rosen Gallery C28
Möller, Anna
Galerie Cinzia Friedlaender R3
Møller, Simon Dybbroe
Harris Lieberman B9
Mollino, Carlo
kaufmann repetto A23
Salon 94 C38
Molodkin, Andrei
Almine Rech Gallery B7
Molska, Anna
Broadway 1602 C9
Foksal Gallery Foundation B40
Molzan, Dianna
Overduin and Kite F4
Monahan, Matthew
Massimo De Carlo B1
Anton Kern Gallery C2
Stuart Shave/Modern Art C43
Monastyrski, Andrei
Regina Gallery B33
Monk, Billy (estate of)
Stevenson B32
Monk, Jonathan
Casey Kaplan A6
Yvon Lambert C34
Lisson Gallery C5
Meyer Riegger B21
Galleri Nicolai Wallner A7
Moon, Kyungwon
Gallery Hyundai C20
Moore, Gareth
Catriona Jeffries A17
Lüttgenmeijer R9
Moore, Henry
Hauser & Wirth B6
Moppett Damian
Catriona Jeffries A17
Morais, Fabio
Vermelho B26
Moran, Katy
Stuart Shave/Modern Art C43
Andrea Rosen Gallery C28
Morellet, François
Gallery Hyundai C20
Moreton, Eleanor
Jack Hanley Gallery A1
Morimoto, Mie
MISAKO & ROSEN R19
Moriyama, Daido
Taka Ishii Gallery B13
Morley, Ivan
Kimmerich F26
Richard Telles A20
Morley, Malcolm
Xavier Hufkens B23
Morris, Locky
mother's tankstation R1
Morris, Rebecca
Harris Lieberman B9
Galerie Barbara Weiss A27
Morris, Robert
Sprüth Magers Berlin London B37
Morris, Sarah
Air de Paris C11
Gallery Hyundai C20
Galerie Meyer Kainer B27
Friedrich Petzel Gallery B4
White Cube B38
Morrison, Alex
Catriona Jeffries A17
Morrison, Joel
Gagosian Gallery D4
Almine Rech Gallery B7
Morrison, Paul
Cheim & Read C36
Alison Jacques Gallery A25
Morton, Victoria
Sadie Coles HQ C15
The Modern Institute C29
Mosely, Ryan
Galerie Eigen + Art C33
Alison Jacques Gallery A25
Regina Gallery B33
Moser & Schwinger
Galerie Jocelyn Wolff F1
Moshiri, Farhad
Galerie Perrotin C41
Galerie Thaddaeus Ropac C12
The Third Line C19
Mosset, Olivier
Massimo De Carlo B1
Moth, Charlotte
Marcelle Alix R2
Moti, Melvin
Meyer Riegger B21
Motta & Lima
Vermelho B26
Moulène, Jean-Luc
carlier | gebauer C23
Galerie Chantal Crousel B28
Moulton, Shana
Broadway 1602 C9
Moyer, Carrie
Canada F30
M.R.
Lehmann Maupin C10
Galerie Perrotin C41
Mroué, Rabih
Sfeir-Semler A8
Mrzyk & Moriceau
Air de Paris C11
Mueck, Ron
Hauser & Wirth B6
Muehl, Otto
Galerie Krinzinger B24
Maccarone D5
Muholi, Zanele
Stevenson B32
Mulder, Gerben
Galeria Fortes Vilaça C48
Mull, Carter
Marc Foxx C32
Muller, Dave
The Approach B11
Müller, Claudia & Julia
Galerie Karin Guenther F20
Galerie Peter Kilchmann A24
Maccarone D5
Müller, Kaspar
Galerie Francesca Pia A15
Müller, Michael
François Ghebaly Gallery F32
Mullican, Matt
Massimo De Carlo B1
Triple Canopy A13
Muniz, Vik
Galeria Fortes Vilaça C48
Sikkema Jenkins & Co. C45
Munro, JP
Sadie Coles HQ C15
Muntean/Rosenblum
Maureen Paley B34
Sommer Contemporary Art C37
Team Gallery C4
Murakami, Takashi
Gagosian Gallery D4
Galerie Perrotin C41
Murase, Kyoko
Taka Ishii Gallery B13
Murata, Takeshi
Salon 94 C38
Muresan, Ciprian
Andreiana Mihail Gallery F28
David Nolan Gallery A29
Galeria Plan B F7
Wilkinson D2
Murillo, Oscar
Stuart Shave/Modern Art C43
Murphy, Luke
Canada F30
Murtaza, Mehreen
Experimenter F23
Musgrave, David
Marc Foxx C32
greengrassi A11
Mutu, Wangechi
Victoria Miro C47
Susanne Vielmetter Los Angeles Projects C21
Mylayne, Jean-Luc
Sprüth Magers Berlin London B37
Myles, Scott
The Breeder C22
Meyer Riegger B21
The Modern Institute C29
Nabil, Youssef
The Third Line C19
Nachi, Satoko
Tomio Koyama Gallery B8
Nagai, Tomoko
Tomio Koyama Gallery B8
Nakayama, Tracy
Crystal R10
Nara, Yoshitomo
Stephen Friedman Gallery B10
Tomio Koyama Gallery B8
Galerie Meyer Kainer B27
Narkevičius Deimantas
gb agency F33
Galerie Barbara Weiss A27
Nash, David
Kukje Gallery B36
Nashat, Shahryar
Rodeo F25
Nasr, Moataz
Galleria Continua C40
Nasseri, Timo
Sfeir-Semler A8

Artist Index

Artist Index

Ribbeck, Bernd
Harris Lieberman B9
Alison Jacques Gallery A25
Galerie Peter Kilchmann A24
Riboli, Laura
Redling Fine Art R7
Wallspace D7
Rice, Amalia
Herald St A30
Richardot, Samuel
BaliceHertling R12
Richards, James
Rodeo F25
Richardson, Matthew
Limoncello F19
Richer, Evariste
Meessen De Clercq R18
Richter, Daniel
Contemporary Fine Arts C39
Regen Projects B17
Regina Gallery B33
David Zwirner C46
Riddy, John
Frith Street Gallery C42
Riedel, Michael
David Zwirner C46
Riedel, Susanne
Galerie Cinzia Friedlaender R3
de Rijke & de Rooij
Galerie Buchholz B35
Riley, Bridget
Timothy Taylor Gallery C8
Riniker-Radich, Marta
Galerie Francesca Pia A15
Rios, Marco
Simon Preston Gallery F22
Rist, Pipilotti
Hauser & Wirth B6
Ritchie, Matthew
Andrea Rosen Gallery C28
Rivers, Ben
Kate MacGarry F13
Robbio, Nicolás
Vermelho B26
Robert, Jimmy
Diana Stigter F14
Robinson, Marc André
Tina Kim Gallery B36
Robleto, Dario
Galerie Praz-Delavallade A18
Roccasalva, Pietro
art: concept A2
David Kordansky Gallery C1
Rocha Pitta, Thiago
A Gentil Carioca C27
Rockenschaub, Gerwald
Mehdi Chouakri C24
Galerie Eva Presenhuber B29
Galerie Thaddaeus Ropac C12
Roden, Steve
Susanne Vielmetter Los Angeles Projects C21
Rødland, Torbjørn
Air de Paris C11
STANDARD (Oslo) B41
Rodriguez, Carissa
Karma International F10
Rodriguez, Cristina Lei
Team Gallery C4
Rodzielski, Clément
Galerie Chantal Crousel B28
Roehr, Peter
Mehdi Chouakri C24
Rogalski, Zbigniew
Almine Rech Gallery B7
Rogan, Will
Altman Siegel F5
MISAKO & ROSEN R19
Rogers, Brett Cody
Galerie Praz-Delavallade A18
Roggan, Ricarda
Galerie Eigen + Art C33
Roh, Choong-Hyun
Kukje Gallery B36
Roiter, Andrei
Jack Hanley Gallery A1
Regina Gallery B33
Rojas, Claire
Galleri Nicolai Wallner A7
Rolando, Bianka
Leto Gallery F12
Rolla, Marco Paulo
Vermelho B26
Rollins, Tim and K.O.S.
Xavier Hufkens B23
Lehmann Maupin C10
Galerie Eva Presenhuber B29
Ronay, Matthew
Marc Foxx C32
Lüttgenmeijer R9
Andrea Rosen Gallery C28
Rondinone, Ugo
Sadie Coles HQ C15
Galerie Eva Presenhuber B29
Almine Rech Gallery B7
Esther Schipper B2
Sommer Contemporary Art C37
Rönicke, Pia
gb agency F33
Ronsse, Matthieu
Almine Rech Gallery B7
de Rooij, Willem
Galerie Buchholz B35
Galerie Chantal Crousel B28
Friedrich Petzel Gallery B4
Root, Ruth
Andrew Kreps Gallery B14
Maureen Paley B34
Rosen, Anna
Night Gallery R5
Rosen, Kay
Sikkema Jenkins & Co. C45
Muntean & Rosenblum
Team Gallery C4
Rosenkranz, Pamela
Miguel Abreu Gallery C14
Karma International F10
Rosier, Mathilde
Galleria Raffaella Cortese C17
Rosler, Martha
Galleria Raffaella Cortese C17
Mitchell-Innes & Nash B20
Ross, Alexander
David Nolan Gallery A29
Ross-Ho, Amanda
The Approach B11
Shane Campbell Gallery R17
Mitchell-Innes & Nash B20
Rossell, Daniela
Greene Naftali C44
Rossetti, Emanuel
Karma International F10
Roth, Christopher
Esther Schipper B2
Roth, Daniel
Maccarone D5
Meyer Riegger B21
Roth, Dieter
Hauser & Wirth B6
Galerie Eva Presenhuber B29
Rothschild, Eva
303 Gallery B39
kaufmann repetto A23
Stuart Shave/Modern Art C43
The Modern Institute C29
Galerie Eva Presenhuber B29
Rottenberg, Mika
Nicole Klagsbrun Gallery A21
Andrea Rosen Gallery C28
Routson, Jon
Team Gallery C4
Rubell, Jennifer
The Breeder C22
Stephen Friedman Gallery B10
Rubins, Nancy
Gagosian D4
Rubsamen, Glen
Alfonso Artiaco C31
Ruby, Sterling
Xavier Hufkens B23
Taka Ishii Gallery B13
Sprüth Magers Berlin London B37
Ruckhäberle, Christoph
Sommer Contemporary Art C37
Galleri Nicolai Wallner A7
Rückriem, Ulrich
Alfonso Artiaco C31
Rudolf, Luke
Kate MacGarry F13
Ruff, Thomas
Gagosian Gallery D4
Galerie Rüdiger Schöttle D3
David Zwirner C46
Ruggaber, Karin
greengrassi A11
Ruilova, Aida
Galerie Guido W. Baudach C30
kaufmann repetto A23
Salon 94 C38
Rune, Bella
Crystal R10
Ruppersberg, Allen
Air de Paris C11
Greene Naftali C44
greengrassi A11
Galerie Karin Guenther F20
Galerie Martin Janda A28
Ruscha, Ed
Gagosian Gallery D4
Sprüth Magers Berlin London B37
Russell, Robert
François Ghebaly Gallery F32
Rusu, Cristian
Galeria Plan B F7
Rutault, Claude
Galerie Perrotin C41
Rutkiewicz, Iwo
Leto Gallery F12
Ryan, Anne
greengrassi A11
Ryden, Mark
Tomio Koyama Gallery B8
von Rydingsvard, Ursula
Galerie Lelong B12
Ryman, Robert
Xavier Hufkens B23
Saban, Analia
Tanya Bonakdar Gallery C6
Galerie Praz-Delavallade A18
Sachs, Tom
Tomio Koyama Gallery B8
Galerie Thaddaeus Ropac C12
Sadr, Haghighian Natascha
Johann König A14
Saeki, Hiroe
Taka Ishii Gallery B13
Sagri, Georgia
Anthony Reynolds Gallery C3
Sailstorfer, Michael
Galeria Fortes Vilaça C48
Johann König A14
Galerie Perrotin C41
Saito, Makoto
Tomio Koyama Gallery B8
Sala, Anri
Alfonso Artiaco C31
Galerie Chantal Crousel B28
Hauser & Wirth B6
kurimanzutto B16
Galerie Rüdiger Schöttle D3
Salcedo, Doris
White Cube B38
Salle, David
Maureen Paley B34
Galerie Thaddaeus Ropac C12
Salvino, Andrea
Corvi-Mora A16
Samaras, Lucas
Stephen Friedman Gallery B10
Samore, Sam
Galerie Gisela Capitain B19
Team Gallery C4
Samyn, Fabrice
Meessen De Clercq R18
Sies + Höke B15
Sandback, Fred
David Zwirner C46
Sander, Karin
Esther Schipper B2
Sander, Stefan

Artist Index

Artist Index

Artist Index

Published in 2012 by Frieze
41 Union Square West
Suite 1001
New York, NY 10003
United States
Tel +1 212-463-7461
Email info@friezeartfair.com
www.friezeartfair.com

Frieze is an imprint of Frieze Events Inc.
Federal Tax ID: 38-3837850

Frieze New York Catalogue 2012

ISBN 978-0-9553201-8-7

Publisher: Anna Starling
Editor: Steven Cairns
Catalogue Co-ordinator: Madeleine Hodge
Copy-editor: Matthew Taylor
Catalogue Assistant: Amy Sherlock
Advertising Sales: Mareike Dittmer, Melissa Goldberg and Adair Lentini
Advertising Production: Sarah Hillier

Art Direction and Design: Graphic Thought Facility, London
Layout: Asuka Sawa
Cover and Divider Page Photography: Niv Rozenberg, New York
Printed by: Graphicom, Vicenza, Italy

Distributed in North America by
DAP
155 Sixth Avenue, 2nd Floor
New York, NY 10013
USA
Tel +1 212-627-1999
Fax +1 212-627-9484

Distributed outside North America by
Thames & Hudson Distributors Ltd
181a High Holborn
London WC1V 7QX
UK
Tel +44 20-7845-5000
Fax +44 20-7845-5050
Email customerservices@thameshudson.co.uk